Routledge Dictionary of
Language and Linguistics

Routledge Dictionary of Language and Linguistics

Hadumod Bussmann

translated and edited by
Gregory Trauth and Kerstin Kazzazi

London and New York

The dictionary is based on:

Hadumod Bussmann
Lexikon der Sprachwissenschaft
2nd, completely revised edition
in co-operation with and with contributions by colleagues
Kröner Verlag, Stuttgart 1990.
(Kröners Taschenausgabe, Vol. 452)
ISBN 3-520-45202-2

Contributors to the German edition
Gregorz Dogil, Bernd Gregor, Christopher Habel, Theo Ickler, Manfred Krifka, Hartmut Lauffer,
Katrin Lindner, Peter R. Lutzeier, Susan Olsen, Beatrice Primus, Hannes Scheutz, Wolfgang Sternefeld,
Wolf Thümmel, Hans Uszkoreit, Heinz Vater, Ulrich Wandruszka, Dietmar Zaefferer

Translation and adaptation
Lee Forester, Kerstin Kazzazi, Stephen Newton, Erin Thompson, Gregory Trauth

First published 1996
by Routledge
11 New Fetter Lane, London EC4P 4EE
29 West 35th Street, New York, NY 10001

Routledge is an International Thomson Publishing company

© 1996 Routledge

Typeset in Times by Solidus (Bristol) Ltd, Bristol
Printed and bound in Great Britain by
TJ Press (Padstow) Ltd, Padstow, Cornwall

British Library Cataloguing in Publication Data
A catalogue record for this book is available from the British Library

Library of Congress Cataloging in Publication Data
A catalogue record for this book is available on request

ISBN 0-415-02225-8

346356 94

Contents

Preface

Twenty-five years ago, when the idea for this dictionary was first conceived, researchers of linguistics had virtually no terminological reference works that could provide them with an introduction to this fast-growing international science or with source material for conducting their own linguistic research. This situation has changed greatly over the years, especially in the English-speaking world, where David Crystal's *Cambridge Encyclopedia of Language* and Frederick J. Newmeyer's *Cambridge Survey of Linguistics* were published in 1987. They were followed, in 1992 and 1994 respectively, by two impressive encyclopedic works, namely W. Bright's four-volume *International Encyclopedia of Linguistics* (Oxford University Press) and R.E. Asher's ten-volume *Encyclopedia of Language and Linguistics* (Pergamon Press).

About the development of this dictionary

The present dictionary differs fundamentally from these monumental works. In its scope and format, it fills a gap which, in spite of David Crystal's *Dictionary of Linguistics and Phonetics* (Oxford 1985²), has existed up until now: in a handy one-volume format, this dictionary provides a thorough overview of all areas of linguistics. Not restricted to specific theories, it encompasses descriptive and historical, comparative and typological linguistics, as well as the applied subdisciplines. Along with the traditional core areas (phonology, morphology, syntax, semantics and pragmatics), interdisciplinary fields (such as sociolinguistics, psycholinguistics, neurolinguistics and ethnolinguistics), as well as stylistics, rhetoric and philosophy of language are represented. In addition, the dictionary includes basic terminology from logic, mathematical and computational linguistics as well as applied linguistics; finally, descriptions of individual languages and language families are provided. With this broad range of content and its succinctly written articles, this dictionary is meant for both students and professional scholars in linguistics and allied fields.

This book is the result of over twenty years of development, in which numerous scholars from Germany and other countries were involved. The first German edition appeared in 1983 as the result of this author's ten-year efforts. Owing to the rapid development of linguistics, a second, completely revised edition became necessary. Seventeen scholars revised, corrected and extended the texts of the first edition. Their work was based on dozens of peer reviews and, no less importantly, on their own research. This second German edition provided the foundation for the present English edition, which was developed further by a team of translators along with numerous contributors and advisers, who checked the translation, made additions to the texts and bibliographies, and, in some cases, contributed new articles. In adapting the German edition, the difference in terminological usage and methodological approaches of Continental European linguists and of their British and North American colleagues became apparent. The task of 'translating' became, therefore, not a linear word-for-word rendering of German linguistic concepts into English, but rather an adaptation, in which terminology specific to German linguistics was eliminated and articles dealing with terminology specific to English were added. This adaptation is most apparent in the linguistic examples that illustrate many of the concepts and that were provided by the translators, contributors, and editors alike.

Contributors

Initially a one-woman project, the present dictionary is the collective work of some seventy European and North American linguists. The authors of the second German edition in many cases undertook revisions of their own work for this English edition. Since even the best linguists can never hope to become experts in all of the subdisciplines of linguistics, the American translators enlisted the assistance of more than two dozen North American linguists to review the translations and adaptation of the entries for accuracy and readability. All well versed and highly competent in their respective fields, the contributors to this English edition helped to adapt the translations by verifying the content, providing English-language examples, and rounding out the entries with additional bibliographical references. During the final revision of the manuscript, which took place in Munich, a second group of competent advisers provided additional editorial help with texts, bibliographies and the co-ordination of cross-references. Some of these new contributors even wrote new articles to supplement the already existing articles in their areas of specialization. Because so many people had a hand in developing, writing and revising the entries, individual names are not listed at the end of the articles. The author and editors accept responsibility for any errors. We are thankful for any corrections, additions, and other suggestions with which careful readers care to provide us.

The co-ordination of these complex stages of work was for many years the exclusive domain of the translator and editor-in-chief, Gregory Trauth, who, in the face of numerous obstacles, pushed hard for the completion of the translation with unremitting patience and in constant close contact with the author. Over the years, both the author and the editor undertook many journeys across the Atlantic; indeed, the number of faxes dealing with the dictionary would probably reach across the ocean, too! Owing to professional obligations, Gregory Trauth could not, however, see the project to its end; the final version of the dictionary, therefore, was prepared in Munich by Kerstin Kazzazi. A native speaker of German and English, she undertook this task with competence and commitment in co-operation with the author, Hadumod Bussmann, and the Routledge editorial staff. Her job consisted of making the complete text uniform and consistent in style, revising content, translating a number of new articles, extending the system of cross-references, updating the bibliographies and researching all of the etymological notes from English sources.

Acknowledgements

The author and editors were the fortunate recipients of a great amount of support: financial, scholarly, technical and moral. Many thanks are due to the Deutsche Forschungsgemeinschaft, who for two years subsidized the preparation of the expanded German edition, and to Inter Nationes, who sponsored the translation.

To mention the names of all the people who contributed to this book would exceed the scope of this preface. Therefore, a list of participants and their contributions is appended to the preface. I wish to thank specifically

all the German co-authors who checked, corrected and amended the adaptation of their special areas of specialization (list 1);

the translators, critical readers and advisers, who, in different ways, contributed to the task of bringing the text, which was originally addressed to a German-speaking readership, into a form that meets Anglo-American expectations (list 2);

the assistants in Munich, who, in the very last stages, made bibliographical emendations and/or gave (in some cases extensive) advice and made contributions in their areas of specialization (incorporated into list 3);

the Routledge editorial staff, especially Jonathan Price, Wendy Morris, Alex Clark, Sarah M. Hall, Samantha Parkinson, and Jenny Potts;

the editor-in-chief, Gregory Trauth, who over many years invested all of his spare time in the dictionary, and who, with competence, circumspection and organizational talent, co-ordinated the efforts of the translators and numerous contributors;

and, last but not least, the co-editor Kerstin Kazzazi, who set aside her own research for the dictionary, and without whose perseverance, co-operative patience and pleasure in the work the final goal of this book would never have been attained.

The motto of the German edition also applies to the present book:

> *Such a work is actually never finished, one must call it finished when, after time and circumstances, one has done what one can.*
>
> (J.W. Goethe, *Journey to Italy*,
> 16 March 1787)

Hadumod Bussmann
Munich, August 1995

Directory of participants

1 Contributors to the (second) German edition of the *Lexikon der Sprachwissenschaft*

Hadumod Bussmann
Dr. phil., Lecturer in Germanic Linguistics; University of Munich
Pertinent publications: *Lexikon der Sprachwissenschaft*, Stuttgart, 1983 (2nd revised and completely updated version Stuttgart, 1990). – *Das* Genus, *die* Grammatik und – *der* Mensch: Geschlechterdifferenz in der Sprachwissenschaft. In H. Bussmann and R. Hof (eds), *Genus: zur Geschlechterdifferenz in den Kulturwissenschaften*, Stuttgart, 1995. 114–60.
Areas: *basic terminology, grammar, linguistic schools, psycholinguistics, syntax.*

Grzegorz Dogil
Professor of Experimental Phonetics; Institute of Computational Linguistics, University of Stuttgart
Pertinent publication: *Autosegmental account of phonological emphasis*, Edmonton, 1979.
Area: *phonology.*

Bernd Gregor
Dr. phil., MBA, Vice President Interactive Services, Bertelsmann Distribution GmbH
Pertinent publication: *Computerfibel für Geisteswissenschaftler*, ed. B. Gregor and M. Krifka, Munich, 1986.
Area: *computational linguistics.*

Christopher Habel
Professor of Computer Science (Knowledge and Language Processing); University of Hamburg
Pertinent publications: *Prinzipien der Referentialität*, Berlin, 1986. – Stories: an artificial intelligence perspective. *Poetics* (1986), 15.111–25.
Area: *artificial intelligence.*

Theodor Ickler
Professor of German Linguistics and German as a Foreign Language; University of Erlangen-Nuremberg
Pertinent publications: *Deutsch als Fremdsprache: eine Einführung in das Studium*, Tübingen, 1984. – *Die Disziplinierung der Sprache*, Tübingen, 1996. Various articles on linguistics, language pedagogy, and language for special purposes.
Areas: *applied linguistics, second-language acquisition.* (Also worked on the English edition with revisions and additions.)

Manfred Krifka
Associate Professor of Linguistics; University of Texas, Austin
Pertinent publications: *Zur semantischen und pragmatischen Motivation syntaktischer Regularitäten: eine Studie zu Wortstellung und Wortstellungsveränderung im Swahili,*

Munich, 1983. – Thematic relations as links between nominal reference and temporal constitution. In I. Sag and A. Szábolcsi (eds), *Lexical Matters*, Chicago, 1992.
Areas: *non-European languages, typology of languages.*

Hartmut Lauffer
Dr. phil., Lecturer in Germanic Linguistics; University of Munich
Areas: *rhetoric, stylistics, text linguistics.* (Also worked on the English edition with revisions, and additions.)

Katrin Lindner
Dr. phil., Lecturer in German Linguistics; University of Munich
Pertinent publications: *Sprachliches Handeln bei Vorschulkindern*, Tübingen, 1983. – Various articles about German-learning children with specific language impairment.
Areas: *conversational analysis, discourse analysis, neurolinguistics, psycholinguistics.* (Also worked on the English edition with translations, revisions, and additions.)

Peter Rolf Lutzeier
Chair in German; University of Surrey, Guildford, UK
Pertinent publications: *Modelltheorie für Linguisten*, Tübingen, 1973. – *Wort und Feld*, Tübingen, 1981. – *Linguistische Semantik*, Stuttgart, 1985. – *Major pillars of German syntax*, Tübingen, 1991 (ed.) – *Studies in Lexical Field Theory*, Tübingen, 1993. – *Lexikologie.* Tübingen, 1995.
Areas: *semantics, logic.* (Also worked on the English edition with revisions and additions.)

Susan Olsen
Professor of German Linguistics; University of Stuttgart
Pertinent publications: *Wortbildung im Deutschen*, Stuttgart, 1986. – Various articles on word formation.
Areas: *morphology, word formation.* (Also worked on the English edition with revisions and additions.)

Beatrice Primus
Dr. habil., Lecturer in German and Theoretical Linguistics; University of Munich
Pertinent publications: *Grammatische Hierarchien*, München, 1987. – Syntactic relations. In J. Jacobs *et al.* (eds), *Syntax: an international handbook*, Berlin, 1993. 686–705. Word order and information structure. In J. Jacobs *et al.* (eds), 880–96.
Area: *syntax (particularly, articles on aspect, diatheses, case, syntactic functions, grammar models, markedness theory, relational typology, theme vs. rheme, word order).* (Also worked on the English edition with revisions and additions.)

Hannes Scheutz
Dr. phil., Lecturer in German Linguistics; University of Salzburg
Pertinent publication: *Strukturen der Lautveränderung*, Vienna, 1985.
Areas: *dialectology, language change, sociolinguistics.* (Also worked on the English edition with revisions and additions.)

Wolfgang Sternefeld
Associate Professor of Linguistics; University of Tübingen
Pertinent publications: (In co-operation with A. von Stechow): *Bausteine syntaktischen Wissens: ein Lehrbuch der generativen Grammatik*, Opladen, 1988. – *Syntaktische Grenzen: Chomskys Barrierentheorie und ihre Weiterentwicklungen.* Opladen, 1991. – (In co-operation with G. Müller): Improper movement and unambiguous binding. *Linguistic Inquiry* 24 (1993), 461–507.
Area: *generative/transformational grammar.* (Also worked on the English edition with revisions and additions.)

Wolf Thümmel
Professor of Linguistics; University of Osnabrück
Areas: *phonetics, graphemics, Slavic languages.* (Also worked on the English edition with revisions and additions.)

Hans Uszkoreit
Professor of Computational Linguistics; University of Saarbrücken
Pertinent publications: *Word Order and Constituent Structure in German.* (CSLI Lecture Notes 8.) Stanford, CA. 1986. – From feature bundles to abstract data types: new directions in the representation and processing of linguistic knowledge. In A. Blaser (ed.), *Natural Language on the Computer*, Berlin, 1988.
Area: *Unification Grammar.*

Heinz Vater
Professor of Germanic Linguistics; University of Cologne
Pertinent publications: *Das System der Artikelformen im gegenwärtigen Deutsch*, 2nd edn, Tübingen, 1979. – *Dänische Subjekt- und Objektsätze*, Tübingen, 1973. – *Einführung in die Raumlinguistik*, 2nd edn, Hürth, 1991. – *Einführung in die Zeitlinguistik*, 3rd edn, Hürth, 1994. – *Einführung in die Textlinguistik*, 2nd edn, Munich, 1994.
Area: *reference semantics.* (Also worked on the English edition with revisions and additions.)

Ulrich Wandruszka
Professor of Romance Linguistics; University of Klagenfurt
Pertinent publications: *Probleme der neufranzösischen Wortbildung*, Tübingen, 1976. Studien zur italienischen Wortstellung, Tübingen, 1982. – (With O. Gsell.) *Der romanische Konjunktiv*, Tübingen, 1986. – "Klassemisch" versus "Lexemisch": zwei Grundtypen sprachlicher Strukturbildung. *PzL* 41 (1989), 77–100. – Zur Suffixpräferenz: Prolegomena zu einer Theorie der morphologischen Abgeschlossenheit. *PzL* 46 (1992), 3–27.
Area: *Romance languages.* (Also worked on the English edition with revisions and additions.)

Dietmar Zaefferer
Associate Professor of German and Theoretical Linguistics; University of Munich
Pertinent publications: The semantics of non/declaratives: investigating German exclamatories. In R. Bäuerle *et al.* (eds), *Meaning, Use, and Interpretation of Language*, Berlin, 1983. 466–80. – *Frageausdrücke und Fragen im Deutschen: zu ihrer Syntax, Semantik und Pragmatik*, Munich, 1984. – On the coding of sentential modality. In J. Bechert *et al.* (eds), *Toward a Typology of European Languages*, Berlin, 1990. 215–37.
Areas: *pragmatics, discourse semantics.* (Also worked on the English edition with revisions and additions.)

2 Editors, contributors, translators, critical readers and advisers of the English text

Hersilia Alvarez-Ruf, Ph.D.
Professor of Spanish Languages; Hope College, Holland, MI
Critical reader of *Romance languages*

Helga Bister-Broosen, Ph.D.
Professor of German; University of North Carolina
Consultant for *sociolinguistics*

Mary Bosker
Bibliographical research

William A. Corsaro, Ph.D.
Professor of Sociology; Indiana University, Bloomington
Critical reader and adviser for *conversational analysis*

Lee Forester, Ph.D.
Professor of German; Hope College, Holland, MI
Translator: *basic terminology, grammar, languages, syntax, typology of languages*

Judith R. Johnston, Ph.D.
Professor and Director: School of Audiology and Speech Sciences, University of Columbia, Vancouver, BC, Canada
Critical reader and adviser for *neurolinguistics*

Kerstin Kazzazi, MA
Indo-European Studies, English; Munich
Editor, translator, contributor of articles, bibliographical research

Tracy Holloway King, Ph.D.
Visiting Research Associate
Linguistics Department, Indiana University, Bloomington
Critical reader and adviser for *generative/transformational grammar*

Paul Listen, MA
Bibliographical research

John Nerbonne
Professor of Computational Linguistics; Rijksuniversiteit Groningen
Critical reader, contributor and adviser for *mathematical and computational linguistics*

Stephen Newton, Ph.D.
Lecturer of German; University of California, Berkeley
Assistant editor and translator: *basic terminology, Bay Area Grammar, generative/ transformational grammar, rhetoric and stylistics, text linguistics, Unification Grammar*

Timothy Radzykewycz, MA
Critical reader and adviser for *phonetics*, *phonology*

Lyon Rathbun, Ph.D.
Critical reader and adviser for *rhetoric*, *stylistics*

William Reynolds, Ph.D.
Professor of English; Mesa State College, Grand Junction, CO
Consultant for *English*

Tom Shannon, Ph.D.
Professor of Germanic Linguistics; University of California, Berkeley
Critical reader and adviser for *grammar, syntax*

H. Jay Siskin, Ph.D.
Lecturer of French; Brandeis University
Critical reader and adviser for *applied linguistics, psycholinguistics*

Tiffany Stephens
Bibliographical research

Talbot J. Taylor, Ph.D.
Professor of Linguistics; College of William and Mary, Williamsburg, VA
Critical reader for *linguistic schools*

Erin Thompson, BA
Translator: *linguistic schools, phonetics, phonology*

Michael Toolan, Ph.D.
Professor of English; University of Washington, Seattle
Critical reader for *pragmatics*

Gregory Trauth, Ph.D.
Editor-in-chief and translator: *applied linguistics, artificial intelligence, computational linguistics, conversational analysis, discourse analysis, graphemics, language change, logic, morphology, neurolinguistics, phonetics, phonology, pragmatics, psycholinguistics, second-language acquisition, semantics, sociolinguistics*

Erwin Tschirner, Ph.D.
Professor of German; University of Iowa
Consultant for *applied linguistics, second language acquisition*

Ann Von Pohl, Ph.D.
Editorial assistant

Roland Willemyns
Universitet Brugge
Consultant for *sociolinguistics*

Adger Williams, Ph.D.
Critical reader for *Slavic languages*

Kirsten Windfuhr
Editorial assistant, bibliographical research

3 Colleagues who at different times and stages of the project and to a different extent assisted and contributed to the German and/or English edition

Karin Böhme-Dürr, Penny Boyes Braem, Vit Bubenik, Paola Cotticelli-Kurras, Rita Fejér, Helene Feulner, Winfried Fiedler, Hans Fromm, Monica Genesin, J. Th.M. Giesen, Heike Gläser, Wolfgang Hock, Joachim Jacobs, Corinna Jäger, MirKamaleddin Kazzazi, Suzanne Kemmer, Reinhard Köhler, Christoph Lehner, Stefan Liedtke, Godehard Link, Ulrich J. Lüders, Imke Mendoza, Peter-Arnold Mumm, Jochen Range, Marga Reis, Elke Ronneberger-Sibold, Wolfgang Schulze, Ariane von Seefranz, Klaus Strunk, Renate Syed, H.G. Wallbott, Stefan Weninger, Nora Wiedenmann.

User instructions

Basic structure of the entries

The individual entries are based on the following structure:

The square brackets immediately after the bold headword contain the following information:

(a) Abbreviations used in linguistics for the respective term, e.g. IPA for International Phonetic Alphabet
(b) Etymological remarks on loanwords. These are not to be understood as exact philological derivations; rather, they are meant to aid intuitive understanding of the formation of the respective term and are of mnemotechnical value. If several headwords are based on the same loanword, only the first receives the etymological remarks, e.g. Greek *hómos* 'same' for **homogenetic**, **homography**, **homonymy**, **homophony**, etc.

Defining/explanatory text: different usages of a term are designated by 1, 2, 3; different aspects of description or structure of a certain usage are marked by (a), (b), (c) or (i), (ii), (iii); see e.g. **transformational grammar** and **language change**.

Bibliographical material

All references within the text of the entries are cited below the entry. In order to avoid too much repetition, some entries do not have any references, but instead a cross-reference to more general entries with comprehensive bibliographies.

The bibliographies of central entries are structured into sections for general texts, bibliographies, and journals; in some, language articles, grammars, and dictionaries are also listed separately.

Within the individual groups, the titles are listed in alphabetical order.

The date in parentheses after the name is usually the date of first publication, with later editions following at the end of the reference.

Abbreviations and symbols

All rarely used abbreviations that are to be found in the text or in linguistic literature are listed on p. xxi.

The list of symbols (p. xvii) – structured according to the areas linguistics, logic, and set theory – provides an overview of all symbols used in the text, as well as alternative symbolic conventions, examples and cross-references to the respective entries in which these symbols are explained or used.

The abbreviations for journals used in the bibliographies are based mainly on the practice of the *Bibliographie linguistique*.

Phonetic transcription

The phonetic–phonological transcriptions of the examples are generally based on the International Phonetic Alphabet (IPA), as given on p. xix. Depending on the context, a 'narrower' or 'broader' transcription is used ($\Rightarrow$ **phonetic transcription**). Historical examples are usually – if a more exact phonetic–phonological differentiation is not required – given in the (quasi-orthographical) way commonly used in historical grammars (e.g. **Old High German consonant shift**).

List of symbols used in the book

Linguistics

‹…› pointed brackets for orthographical representation, e.g. ‹top›

[…] square brackets for:
    1 ⟹ **phonetic transcription**, e.g. [tɔp′].
    2 ⟹ **features**, e.g. [+nasal]
    3 ⟹ **domination (relation)**, e.g. [art + NP]$_{NP}$ 'NP dominates Art + N' (⟹ **tree diagram**)
    4 philological remarks on the headword

/…/ slashes for phonological transcription

{…} curly brackets for:
    1 ⟹ **morphemes**, e.g. {s} for the plural in nouns
    2 alternative rule application (⟹ **bracketing**)
    3 gathering of elements of a set, e.g. S = {singular, plural, dual}

(…) parentheses for optional elements, e.g. NP → ART + (ADJ) + N

/ alternative expressions: *come here / soon / again*

+ plus sign for:
    1 word formation or morpheme boundaries, e.g. *bed + room*
    2 sign for concatenation of elements, e.g. S → NP + VP
    3 positive specifications in features, e.g. [+nasal]

: colon for:
    1 length in vowels, e.g. [aː]
    2 designation of oppositions, e.g. [voiced] : [voiceless]

* asterisk for:
    1 an ungrammatical, inacceptable expression, e.g. **she sleep*
    2 a reconstructed, undocumented form, e.g. IE **g^{h}ab^h*-, IE root of Eng. *give*.

→ simple arrow:
    1 'expression is decomposed into …' (⟹ **phrase structure rules**)
    2 'implies' (⟹ **implication**)

⟹ double arrow:
    1 'expression is transformed into …' (⟹ **transformation**)
    2 cross-reference to other entry in the dictionary, e.g. ⟹ **linguistics**

> pointed bracket to the right:
    1 'becomes', e.g. West Gmc **drankjan* > Eng. *drench* (⟹ **umlaut**)
    2 'greater than'

< pointed bracket to the left:
    1 'comes from', e.g. Eng. *drench* < West Gmc **drankjan* (⟹ **umlaut**)
    2 'smaller than'

\# boundary symbol, e.g. # sentence #

Logic

Sign	Alternative sign notation	Designation	To be read as	Explanation under
∧	&	conjunction	'and'	**conjunction** (3)
∨	⋍, ⩵	disjunction	'or'	**disjunction**
→	⇒, ⊃, —<	material implication	'if, then'	**implication** (a)
↔	⇔, ≡	equivalence	'exactly if, then'	**equivalence**
¬	~, −	negation	'not'	**negation** (1)
⊦	⊧	logical/strict implication	'from … follows'	**implication** (b), (c)
⋁	∃, (E …)	existential operator	'there is at least one element x, for which it is the case …'	**operator** (a)
⋀	∀ (…)	universal operator	'for all x it is the case that'	**operator** (b)
ι	i	iota operator	'that element x, for which it is the case that'	**operator** (c)
λ		lambda operator	'those xs, for which it is the case that'	**operator** (d)
□	N	necessity operator	'it is necessary that'	**implication** (c)
◇	P	possibility operator	'it is possible that'	**modal logic**

Set theory

Sign	Designation	To be read as	Explanation under
{a₁,a₂}	combination of the elements a₁, a₂ to a set S		⇒ **set**
∅	empty set	'empty set'	⇒ **set**
ε	element relation	'is an element of'	⇒ **set** (b)
∉		'is not an element of'	
∩	intersection set	'intersects with'	⇒ **set** (h)
\	difference set	'minus'	⇒ **set** (i)
⊂	subset	'is contained in'	⇒ **set** (j)
C	complement set	'is complement of'	⇒ **set** (k)
∪	union set	'united with'	⇒ **set** (g)
P	power set	'set of all subsets'	⇒ **set** (l)
X	Cartesian product	'set of all ordered pairs'	⇒ **set** (n)
Card	cardinal number	'number of elements in a set'	⇒ **cardinal number**

The International Phonetic Alphabet

(revised to 1989)

	Bilabial	Labiodental	Dental	Alveolar	Postalveolar	Retroflex	Palatal	Velar	Uvular	Pharyngeal	Glottal
Plosive	p b			t d		ʈ ɖ	c ɟ	k g	q ɢ		ʔ
Nasal	m	ɱ		n		ɳ	ɲ	ŋ	N		
Trill	ʙ			r					R		
Tap or Flap				ɾ		ɽ					
Fricative	ɸ β	f v	θ ð	s z	ʃ ʒ	ʂ ʐ	ç ʝ	x ɣ	χ ʁ	ħ ʕ	h ɦ
Lateral fricative				ɬ ɮ							
Approximant		ʋ		ɹ		ɻ	j	ɰ			
Lateral approximant				l		ɭ	ʎ	ʟ			
Ejective stop	p’			t’		ʈ’	c’	k’	q’		
Implosive	ƥ ɓ			ƭ ɗ			ƈ ʄ	ƙ ɠ	ʠ ʛ		

DIACRITICS

◌̥ Voiceless	n̥ d̥	◌̹ More rounded	ɔ̹	◌ʷ Labialized	tʷ dʷ	◌̃ Nasalized	ẽ
◌̌ Voiced	s̬ t̬	◌̜ Less rounded	ɔ̜	◌ʲ Palatalized	tʲ dʲ	◌ⁿ Nasal release	dⁿ
◌ʰ Aspirated	tʰ dʰ	◌̟ Advanced	u̟	◌ˠ Velarized	tˠ dˠ	◌ˡ Lateral release	dˡ
◌̈ Breathy-voiced	b̤ a̤	◌̠ Retracted	i̠	◌ˤ Pharyngealized	tˤ dˤ	◌̚ No audible release	d̚
◌̰ Creaky voiced	b̰ a̰	◌̈ Centralized	ë	◌̴ Velarized or pharyngealized	ɫ	
◌̼ Linguo-labial	t̼ d̼	◌̽ Mid centralized	ĕ	◌̝ Raised	e̝ (ɹ̝ = voiced alveolar fricative)
◌̪ Dental	t̪ d̪	◌̩ Syllabic	ɹ̩	◌̞ Lowered	e̞ (β̞ = voiced bilabial approximant)
◌̺ Apical	t̺ d̺	◌̯ Non-syllabic	e̯	◌̘ + ATR	e̘
◌̻ Laminal	t̻ d̻	◌˞ Rhoticity	ɚ	◌̙ – ATR	e̙

VOWELS

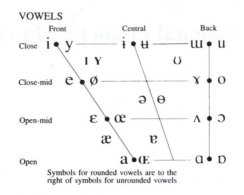

Symbols for rounded vowels are to the
right of symbols for unrounded vowels

OTHER SYMBOLS

ʍ	Voiceless labial-velar fricative	ʘ	Bilabial click
w	Voiced labial-velar approximant	ǀ	Dental click
ɥ	Voiced labial-palatal approximant	ǃ	(Post)-alveolar click
ʜ	Voiceless epiglottal fricative	ǂ	Palatoalveolar click
ʢ	Voiced epiglottal fricative	ǁ	Alveolar lateral click
ʡ	Voiced epiglottal plosive	ɺ	Alveolar lateral flap
ɕ ʑ	Alveolo-palatal fricatives	ɧ	Simultaneous ʃ and X

Affricates and double articulations can
be represented by two symbols joined   k͡p   t͡s
by a ligature/tie bar if necessary.

SUPRASEGMENTALS   TONES

ˈ	Primary stress ˌfoʊnəˈtɪʃən		
ˌ	Secondary stress	e̋ or ˥	Extra-high
ː	Long eː	é ˦	High
ˑ	Half-long eˑ	ē ˧	Mid
˘	Extra-short ĕ	è ˨	Low
.	Syllable break ɹi.ækt	ȅ ˩	Extra-low
ǀ	Minor (foot) group	↓	Downstep
‖	Major (intonation) group	↑	Upstep
‿	Linking (absence of a break)		
↗	Rising intonation		
↘	Falling intonation		

Contour tones may be symbolized
by two or more tone symbols

List of abbreviations in the text

AD	after Christ (*Anno Domini*)	1. pers.	1st person
BC	before Christ	2. pers.	2nd person
ca	circa	3. pers.	3rd person
cf.	1. compare	abl.	ablative
	2. see (Author name + year)	acc.	accusative
e.g.	for example	Adj.	adjective
etc.	etcetera	Adv.	adverb
i.e.	that is	approx.	approximately
mil.	million	Aux.	auxiliary
vs.	versus	C	consonant
		dat.	dative
Amer.	American	DO	direct object
Brit.	British	fem.	feminine
Bulg.	Bulgarian	fut.	future
Dan.	Danish	gen.	genitive
Eng.	English	indic.	indicative
Fr.	French	ins.	instrumental
Ger.	German	IO	indirect object
Gmc.	Germanic	irreg.	irregular
Grk	Greek	loc.	locative
Heb.	Hebrew	masc.	masculine
IE	Indo-European	N, NP	noun, noun phrase
Ital.	Italian	neut.	neuter
Lat.	Latin	nom.	nominative
ME	Middle English	O	object
MFr.	Middle French	Part.	participle
MHG	Middle High German	perf.	perfect
OCSlav	Old Church Slavic	pl.	plural
OE	Old English	Prep., PP	preposition, prepositional phrase
OFr.	Old French	pres.	present
OHG	Old High German	reg.	regular
OInd.	Old Indic	S	1. sentence
PGmc.	Proto-Germanic		2. subject
PIE	Proto-Indo-European	sg.	singular
Rum.	Rumanian	st.	strong
Russ.	Russian	subj.	subjunctive
Serb.	Serbo-Croatian	V	vowel
Skt	Sanskrit	V, VP	verb, verb phrase
Slav.	Slavic	vcd.	voiced
Span.	Spanish	vcls.	voiceless
Swed.	Swedish	voc.	vocative
		wk.	weak

List of abbreviations in the bibliographies

AA	American Anthropologist	DAI	Dissertation Abstracts International
ACiL	Amsterdam Studies in the Theory and History of Linguistic Science	DPr	Discourse Processes
		DRLAV	Documentation et Recherche en Linguistique Allemande Contemporaine Vincennes
AfL	Afroasiatic Linguistics		
AI	Artificial Intelligence	DSp	Deutsche Sprache
AJCL	American Journal of Computational Linguistics	ELT	English Literature in Transition
		ES	English Studies
ALASH	Acta Linguistica Academiae Scientiarum Hungaricae	FL	Foundations of Language
		FolH	Folia Linguistica Historia
ALLC	Bulletin of the Association for Literary and Linguistic Computing	FoLi	Folia Linguistica
		GAGL	Groninger Arbeiten zur Germanistischen Linguistik
AmP	American Psychologist		
AnL	Anthropological Linguistics	GJP	German Journal of Psychology
APhF	Acta Philosophica Fennica	GQ	German Quarterly
AppLing	Applied Linguistics	GRM	Germanisch-Romanische Monatsschrift
APsy	Applied Psycholinguistics		
ARAL	Annual Review of Applied Linguistics	GURT	Georgetown University Roundtable on Language and Linguistics
ArchL	Archivum Linguisticum		
AS	American Speech	HS	Historische Sprachforschung/Historical Linguistics (formerly ZVS)
ASNS	Archiv für das Studium der neueren Sprachen und Literaturen		
AÜ	Afrika und Übersee	IC	Information and Control
B&L	Brain and Language	IF	Indogermanische Forschungen
BSci	Behavioral Science	IJAL	International Journal of American Linguistics
BSLP	Bulletin de la Société de Linguistique de Paris		
		IJDL	International Journal of Dravidian Linguistics
CCrit	Comparative Criticism		
CD	Child Development	IJSL	International Journal of the Sociology of Language
CdL	Cahiers de Lexicologie		
CJL	Canadian Journal of Linguistics	IndLing	Indian Linguistics
CL	Computational Linguistics	IRAL	International Review of Applied Linguistics
ClassQ	The Classical Quarterly		
CLS	Chicago Linguistics Society	IULC	Indiana University Linguistics Club
CLTT	Child Language Teaching and Therapy		
		JanL	Janua linguarum
CMLR	Canadian Modern Language Review	JIdS	Jahrbuch des Instituts für Deutsche Sprache
COLING	Proceedings of the International Conference on Computational Linguistics	JC	Journal of Communications
		JChL	Journal of Child Language
		JEngL	Journal of English Linguistics
CPsy	Cognitive Psychology	JeP	Journal of Experimental Psychology
CSc	Cognitive Science		
CTL	Current Trends in Linguistics	JL	Journal of Linguistics
DaF	Deutsch als Fremdsprache	JLS	Journal of Literary Semantics

JLSP	*Journal of Language and Social Psychology*	PBLS	*Proceedings of the Annual Meeting of the Berkeley Linguistics Society*
JMemL	*Journal of Memory and Language*		
JP	*Journal of Philosophy*	PCLS	*Papers from the Regional Meeting of the Chicago Linguistics Society*
JPhon	*Journal of Phonetics*		
JPL	*Journal of Philosophical Logic*		
JPrag	*Journal of Pragmatics*	PhQ	*The Philosophical Quarterly*
JPSP	*Journal of Personality and Social Psychology*	PhR	*Philosophical Review*
		PhS	*Philosophical Studies*
JPsyR	*Journal of Psycholinguistic Research*	PICHOLS	*Proceedings of the International Conference on the History of the Language Sciences*
JSem	*Journal of Semantics*		
JSHD	*Journal of Speech and Hearing Disorders*	PICHL	*Proceedings from the International Congress on Historical Linguistics*
JSL	*Journal of Symbolic Logic*		
JVLVB	*Journal of Verbal Learning and Verbal Behavior*	PICL	*Proceedings of the International Congress of Linguists*
LALIES	*Actes des Sessions de Linguistiques et de Littérature*	PIL	*Papers in Linguistics*
		PJL	*Philippine Journal of Linguistics*
L&P	*Literature and Psychology*	PL	*Pacific Linguistics*
L&S	*Language and Speech*	PMS	*Perceptual and Motor Skills*
LangR	*Language Research*	PPR	*Philosophy and Phenomenological Research*
LangS	*Language Sciences*		
LB	*Leuvense Bijdragen*	PSCL	*Papers and Studies in Contrastive Linguistics*
LDDS	*Linguistic Data on Diskette Service (Lincom Europa, Munich)*		
		PsyB	*Psychological Bulletin*
LeS	*Lingua e Stile*	PsychologR	*Psychological Review*
Lg	*Language*	PY	*Phonology Yearbook*
LI	*Lettere Italiane*	PzL	*Papiere zur Linguistik*
Ling	*Linguistica*	RLiR	*Revue de Linguistique Romane*
Ling&P	*Linguistics and Philosophy*	S&S	*Syntax and Semantics*
LingA	*Linguistic Analysis*	SAL	*Studies in African Linguistics*
LingB	*Linguistische Berichte*	SAQ	*South African Quarterly*
LingI	*Linguistic Inquiry*	SBL	*Salzburger Beiträge zur Linguistik*
LIS	*Linguisticae Investigationes*		
LRev	*The Linguistic Review*	SFQ	*Southern Folklore Quarterly*
LSoc	*Language in Society*	SiL	*Studies in Linguistics*
LSt	*Linguistische Studien*	SLang	*Studies in Language*
MLJ	*The Modern Language Journal*	SLSc	*Studies in the Linguistic Sciences*
MPh	*Modern Philology*	SPh	*Studia Phonetica*
MRCD	*Monographs of the Society for the Research in Child Development*	Sprache	*Die Sprache*
		Sprachwiss	*Sprachwissenschaft*
MSS	*Münchener Studien zur Sprachwissenschaft*	Stgr	*Studia Grammatica*
		StL	*Studium Linguistik*
Nku	*Naamkunde*	TCLC	*Travaux du Cercle Linguistique de Copenhague*
NL&LT	*Natural Language & Linguistic Theory*		
		TCLP	*Travaux du Cercle Linguistique de Prague*
NLH	*New Literary History*		
NLing	*Notes on Linguistics*	TL	*Theoretical Linguistics*
NRun	*Nyttom runer*	TLP	*Travaux Linguistiques de Prague (Continuation of TCLP)*
OcL	*Oceanic Linguistics*		
PAPS	*Proceedings of the American Philosophical Society*	TPS	*Transactions of the Philological Society*
PBB (H)	*Beiträge zur Geschichte der deutschen Sprache und Literatur (Halle)*	UCCPh.	*University of California Publications in Philosophy*
		UCPL	*University of California Papers in Linguistics*
PBB (T)	*Beiträge zur Geschichte der deutschen Sprache und Literatur (Tübingen)*	WZUG	*Wissenschaftliche Zeitschrift der*

	Ernst Moritz Arndt-Universität		philosophische Kritik
	Greifswald	*ZPSK*	*Zeitschrift für Phonetik,*
ZFSL	*Zeitschrift für französische*		*Sprachwissenschaft und*
	Sprache und Literatur		*Kommunikationsforschung*
ZG	*Zeitschrift für Germanistik*	*ZS*	*Zeitschrift für Sprachwissenschaft*
ZGL	*Zeitschrift für Germanistische*	*ZSem*	*Zeitschrift für Semiotik*
	Linguistik	*ZVS*	*Zeitschrift für Vergleichende*
ZM	*Zeitschrift für (Hoch)deutsche*		*Sprachwissenschaft (now: HS =*
	Mundarten		*Historische Sprachforschung/*
ZMF	*Zeitschrift für Mundartforschung*		*Historical Linguistics)*
ZPhK	*Zeitschrift für Philosophie und*		

A

Abaza ⇒ **North-West Caucasian**

abbreviation [Lat. *brevis* 'short']

1 (*also* acronym) In the broad sense of the word, the process and result of **word formation** in which the first letters or syllables of word groups are written and pronounced as words. Abbreviations can be categorized as follows: (a) those pronounced as individual letters, for example *USA* ('U – S – A'), *VW* ('V – W'), *e.g.* ('E – G'); (b) those pronounced as syllable groups, for example, *NATO* ('NA – TO' = *North Atlantic Treaty Organization*), *ENIAC* ('EN – I – AC' = *electronic numerical integrator and computer*), *ASCII* ('AS – CII' = *American standard code for information interchange*); and (c) those whose initials virtually create a new word, for example, *AIDS* (= *acquired immune deficiency syndrome*), *RAM* (= *random access memory*). Abbreviations are a very productive source of new vocabulary (⇒ **neologism, nonce word**), as seen almost daily in the media by the coining of new words, for example, *dink* (= *double income/no kids*) and *nimby* (= *not in my backyard*); some abbreviations are themselves based in part on already existing abbreviations, for example, *ACT-UP* (= *AIDS coalition to unleash power*); *yuppie* (= *young urban professional*) > *buppie* (= *black urban professional*) and > *guppie* (= *gay urban professional*).

2 In the narrow sense of the word, a short form which may or may not become lexicalized (e.g. *prof < professor, telly < television*). (⇒ *also* **clipping**)

References
Geisler, H. 1994. 'Che fine fanno i BOT?' Anmerkungen zur Akronymenbildung im Italienischen. In A. Sabban and C. Schmitt (eds), *Sprachlicher Alltag: Linguistik–Rhetorik–Literaturwissenschaft. Festschrift für Wolf-Dieter Stempel*. Tübingen. 97–120.
Jung, U.O.H. 1987. 'Nemini parcetur'. Morphological aspects of acronyms in English and German: a contrastive analysis. In *Perspectives on language performance: studies in linguistics, literary criticism and language teaching and learning. To honour W. Hüllen on the occasion of his sixtieth birthday*. Tübingen. 148–58.
Kilani-Schoch, M. 1995. Syllable and foot in French clipping. In B. Hurch and R. Rhodes (eds), *Natural phonology: the state of the art*. Berlin. 135–52.
Kobler-Trill, R. 1994. *Das Kurzwort im Deutschen*. Tübingen.

Marchand, H. 1960. The categories and types of present-day English word-formation. Munich. (2nd edn 1969.)
McCully, C.B. and M. Holmes. 1988. Some notes on the structure of acronyms. *Lingua* 4.27–43.
Menzel, H.B. 1983. *Abkürzungen im heutigen Französisch*. Rheinfelden.
Ronneberger-Sibold, E. 1995. Preferred sound shape of new roots: on some phonotactic and prosodic properties of shortenings in German and French. In B. Hurch and R. Rhodes (eds), *Natural phonology: the state of the art*. Berlin. 261–92.
Ungerer, F. 1991. Acronyms, trade names and motivation. *Arbeiten aus Anglistik und Amerikanistik* 16.131–58.

Dictionary
The Oxford dictionary of abbreviations. 1992. Oxford.
⇒ **word formation**

Abkhaz ⇒ **North-West Caucasian**

Abkhazi-Adyge ⇒ **North-West Caucasian**

ablative [Lat. *ablatus* 'carried away,' (past part. of) *ferre* 'to carry']

Morphological **case** in certain languages (e.g. **Latin, Hungarian**) which indicates various types of adverbial relations, such as manner (Lat. *pedibusīre* 'to go on foot'), separation (Hung. *levéltól* 'away from the letter'), and time (Lat. *hieme* 'in the winter').

References
⇒ **case**

ablative absolute

Syntactic construction in **Latin** for abbreviating subordinate clauses. The ablative absolute is not **valence**-bound (and is thus 'absolute') and consists of a noun in the **ablative** case as well as an attributive participle, noun or adjective which is dependent on it: *Tarquinio regnante* 'when Tarquinius was king' or 'during the reign of Tarquinius'; *trānquillo mari* 'during calm at sea.' (⇒ *also* **case**)

References
⇒ **case**

ablaut (*also* apophony, vowel gradation)

German term for a systematic morphophonemic alternation (⇒ **morphophonemics**) of certain vowels in etymologically related words in **Indo-European** languages. The term has been used in this sense since Grimm (1819). Prior to that, it had been used pejoratively for any kind of vowel irregularity. (The Greek term 'apophony,' used in some languages, is a loan translation of Grimm's term: *apó* 'away from,' *phōnḗ* 'tone.') Originally, ablaut was purely phonetic–phonological; it was later morphologized (⇒ **morphologization**), especially in **Germanic**, where ablaut indicates **tense** differences in the inflection of strong verbs (⇒ **strong vs weak verb**), e.g. *sing – sang – sung* or other processes of word formation, e.g. *song*. Depending on the type of vowel alternation, one can distinguish between the following: (a) Qualitative ablaut (also 'Abtönung'), in which there is a change from *e* (in a few cases also from *a*) to *o*, cf. **Greek** *phér-ō* 'I bear, carry' : *phor-éō* 'I carry repeatedly' (⇒ **iterative**): *am(phi)-phor-eús* 'vessel with two handles for carrying,' which all go back to a common IE root **bʰer-* 'to bear, carry.' (b) Quantitative ablaut (also 'Abstufung'), in which an alternation of the short vowels mentioned (full grade) with the respective long vowels (lengthened grade) or an elimination of the short vowels (zero grade) occurs; cf. Grk *phṓr* 'thief,' lit. 'one who carries something off' (lengthened grade), **Sanskrit** *bhr-tí* 'bearing, carrying' (zero grade). It is hypothesized that this system is the descendant of a previous system of different rules of **stress**², in force at different times. It is assumed that qualitative ablaut results from a musical stress, quantitative ablaut from a dynamic stress.

The order of the different types of ablaut into ablaut classes that is to be found in historical grammars of the Germanic languages is based not on phonological, but rather on morphological regularities that can be explained from the different consonantal environments of the vowels undergoing ablaut; they can be observed most clearly in the conjugational classes of the Germanic strong verbs. As a rule, the ablaut classes are indicated by the stem forms of the strong verb (infinitive, preterite singular and plural, past participle). The order and number of the ablaut classes depends on which consonant or resonant follows the vowel undergoing ablaut. On details of the different historical stages ⇒ **historical grammars**.

References
Coetsem, F. van. 1990. *Ablaut and reduplication in the Germanic verb*. Heidelberg.
Fulk, R.D. 1986. *The origins of Indo-European quantitative ablaut*. Innsbruck.
Grimm, J. 1819–37. *Deutsche Grammatik*, 4 parts. Göttingen. (Facsimile printing of the 2nd edn of Berlin 1870–8. Hildesheim 1967.)

Lindeman, F.O. 1988. *Introduction to the 'Laryngeal theory.'* Oxford.
⇒ **Indo-European, laryngeal theory**

abrupt onset of voicing ⇒ glottalization

abruptive ⇒ ejective

absolute

Valence-independent occurrence of a case that is not integrated into the sentence structure, for example, **ablative absolute** in Latin, the accusative absolute in French (*La nuit tombée, elle chercha un hôtel* 'When night had fallen, she looked for a hotel') or the **absolute nominative**.

References
⇒ **case**

absolute antonymy

Good vs *bad*, in contrast to *excellent* vs *bad*, are absolute antonyms since they are more or less equidistant from the midpoint on a scale of **antonymy**.

Reference
Lehrer, A. and K. Lehrer. 1982. Antonymy. *Ling&P* 5.483–501.

absolute nominative

Term from **stylistics** for a special form of **prolepsis**. The absolute nominative is a nominal expression in the nominative case which occurs initially in a sentence and is referred to in the main clause by a pronoun or pronominal adverbial (e.g. *All those lost years, she didn't want to think about them*). The absolute nominative is a special case of left dislocation. (⇒ *also* **dislocation, left vs right dislocation**)

References
⇒ **stylistics**

absolute vs relative verbs

This distinction refers to the property of **verbs** to be used either with (= relative) or without (= absolute) complements (*to give, to love* vs *to sleep, to bloom*). In the absolute use of relative verbs the object is either understood from the context or is considered obvious due to the collocation (e.g. *to deal* [*cards*]). (⇒ *also* **government, valence**)

absolute superlative ⇒ degree

absolutive

Morphological **case** in **ergative languages** for indicating the subject of intransitive verbs and the object of transitive verbs. The absolutive can be considered the primary syntactic function of this language type. Like the **nominative** case in **nominative languages**, this case usually has a zero form.

References
⇒ **case**, **ergative language**

absolutive language ⇒ ergative language

abstract noun [Lat. *abstractus* 'dragged away, separated from']

In contrast to **concrete nouns**, abstracts form a semantically defined class of nouns that denote concepts (*psyche*), characteristics (*laziness*), relationships (*kinship*), institutions (*marriage*), etc., but not persons, objects, substances, or the like.

abstractness controversy

In generative **phonology**, the question of how far removed from the surface form (= the actually realized form), i.e. how abstract, the **underlying form** should be.

References
Fujimura, O. (ed.) 1973. *Three dimensions of linguistic theory*. Tokyo. 5–56.
Gussmann, E. 1980. *Studies in abstract phonology*. Cambridge, MA.
Kiparsky, P. 1968. *How abstract is phonology?* Bloomington, IN.
Sommerstein, A.H. 1977. *Modern phonology*. London. 211–25.

Abstufung ⇒ ablaut

Abtönung ⇒ ablaut

accent [Lat. *accentus*, from *ad-cantus* 'that which is sung (together with)']

1 ⇒ **stress**[2]

2 **Diacritic** marking stress, **tone**, or other phonetic modifications e.g. **acute** ‹ ´ ›, **grave** ‹ ` ›, **circumflex** ‹ ˜ › or ‹ ˆ ›.

3 Idiosyncratic pronunciation of a foreign language, especially due to the articulatory or phonotactic characteristics of one's native language. (⇒ *also* **applied linguistics**, **articulatory phonetics**, **phonotactics**)

References
⇒ **phonetics**, **phonology**

acceptability

A term from Chomsky (1965) for the acceptability of expressions in natural languages reflecting the view of the participant in communication, not the grammarian (⇒ **grammaticality**). The question of acceptability concerns

performance whereas grammaticality is an issue of competence (⇒ **competence vs performance**). Acceptability is a relative term, i.e. an expression is deemed more or less acceptable according to the context. There are various criteria for determining non-acceptability: (a) ungrammaticality; (b) complex sentence structure involving repeated encapsulating or self-embedding constructions; (c) semantic contradiction; (d) untruth in an expression as it relates to a situation; (e) an expression that cannot be interpreted because of missing reference or a differing knowledge of the world; (f) stylistic incompatibility. Since acceptability depends heavily on the limits of short-term memory, acceptability can be tested psycholinguistically.

References
Bever, I.G., J.J. Katz, and D.T. Langendoen (eds) 1976. *An integrated theory of linguistic ability*.
Chomsky, N. 1965. *Aspects of the theory of syntax*. Cambridge, MA.
Greenbaum, S. 1977. *Acceptability in language*. The Hague.
Quirk, R. and J. Svartvik 1966. *Investigating linguistic acceptability*. London and The Hague.
⇒ **grammaticality**

accessibility hierarchy ⇒ hierarchy universal

accidence

Property of linguistic expressions (based on Aristotelian categories) whose 'essential' fundamental forms can appear in different 'accidental' inflectional forms. Nouns are subject to **case** and **number**, verbs to **tense**, **mood**, and **voice**. (⇒ *also* **inflection**)

accomplishment ⇒ resultative

accusative [Lat. *accusare* 'to blame'; faulty translation of Grk (*ptōsis*) *aitiatikḗ* '(case) of that caused'] (*also objective*)

Morphological **case** in **nominative languages** such as **German** or **Latin**. Noun phrases in the accusative case generally function syntactically as a **direct object** (Ger. *Er liest ein Buch* 'He is reading a book'). The accusative case can also serve to indicate adverbial functions and/or relations (Ger. *den ganzen Tag lachen* 'to laugh all day'), or predicative complements (Ger. *Sie schimpft ihn einen Dummkopf* 'She calls him an idiot'). In addition, the accusative also occurs after certain prepositions (Ger. *gegen* 'against,' Lat. *ante* 'before'). There can also be cognate accusatives (⇒ **cognate object**) in which the semantic content of the verb is repeated by a nominal element in the accusative case (e.g. *to dream a dream*).

References
Moravcsik, E.A. 1978. Case marking of objects. In J.H. Greenberg (ed.), *Universals of human language*. Stanford, CA. Vol. 4, 250–89.
⇒ **case**, **direct object**

accusative language ⇒ nominative language

accusative plus infinitive construction
(*also* subject to object raising)

Syntactic construction consisting of an accusative object and a verb in the infinitive which occurs with verbs of saying and perception (*I heard him sing*) as well as **causatives** (e.g. *to have*: *The judge had the defendant come forward*; *to let*: *The policeman let him go*). This type of construction is often analyzed as two underlying sentences with the accusative functioning both as the underlying subject of the infinitive as well as the object of the dominant verb. In the framework of **transformational grammar** this analysis is called **raising**. Causative constructions are handled in a similar way, for example, in **Japanese**.

References
Bech, G. 1955–7. *Studien über das deutsche Verbum infinitum*, 2 vols. Copenhagen. (Repr. Tübingen 1983.)
Harbert, W. 1977. Clause union and the German accusative plus infinitive constructions. In P. Cole and J.M. Sadock (eds), *Grammatical relations*. New York. 121–50.
McKay, T. 1985. *Infinitival complements in German: lassen, scheinen and the verbs of perception*. Cambridge.

accusativization

Valence change occurring in many languages in which an object in another **case** (**dative**, **genitive**) or a prepositional object alternates with an accusative or a direct object: Ger. *Er kocht ihr/ für sie* 'He cooks for her' (dative/prepositional phrase) vs *Er bekocht sie* 'He cooks for her' (accusative). (⇒ also **applicative**)

References
Chung, S. 1976. An object-creating rule in Bahasa Indonesia. *LingI* 7.41–89.
Comrie, B. 1985. Causative verb formation and other verb-deriving morphology. In T. Shopen (ed.), *Language typology and syntactic description*. Cambridge, Vol. 3, 309–48.
Moravcsik, E.A. 1978. Case marking of objects. In J.H. Greenberg (ed.), *Universals of human language*. Stanford, CA. Vol. 4, 250–89.
Plank, F. (ed.) 1984. *Objects: towards a theory of grammatical relations*. London.

Achi ⇒ Mayan languages

achievement ⇒ punctual resultative

achievement test ⇒ language test

acoustic agnosia ⇒ agnosia

acoustic allesthesia ⇒ agnosia

acoustic analysis

Generally, the analysis of acoustic characteristics (such as amplitude, **quantity**, and frequency) by means of electronic instruments. ⇒ **acoustic phonetics**

acoustic cue

Any of the linguistically redundant components of acoustic features used to aid the perception of spoken language. Their characteristics and structure are studied with regard to the development of techniques for **speech recognition** and **speech synthesis**. (⇒ *also* **distinctive feature**)

Reference
Delattre, P. 1968. From acoustic cues to distinctive features. *Phonetica* 18.198–230.

acoustic image (*also* sound image)

In de Saussure's linguistic framework, a psychologically motivated aspect of the linguistic sign consisting of a sound and an associated concept. In Noreen's linguistic framework, the acoustic image corresponds to the concept of **morpheme** (⇒ **signifier vs signified**).

References
Noreen, A. 1903– . *Vårt språk. Nysvensk grammatik i utförlig framställning*. Lund.
⇒ **sign**

acoustic phonetics

Branch of general **phonetics** that investigates the physical properties of the acoustic structure of **speech sounds** according to frequency (**pitch**), **quantity** (duration), and intensity (spectrum). After 1930, acoustic phonetics advanced (a) through the use of electric, then later electronic, machines of great precision that could produce, intensify, transfer, store, and reproduce speech sounds and (b) through the expanded utility of **speech synthesis** (**speech recognition**) especially in **computational linguistics**. Signal phonetics is a branch of acoustic phonetics that predominantly investigates the phonetic signal. Many recent phonological investigations make extensive use of the concepts and terminology of acoustic phonetics.

References
Jakobson, R., G.G.M. Fant and M. Halle. 1952. *Preliminaries to speech analysis: the distinctive features and their correlates.* Cambridge, MA.
Ladefoged, P. 1962. *Elements of acoustic phonetics.* Chicago.
—— 1975. *A course in phonetics.* New York. 3rd edn 1993.
Lieberman, P. and S.E. Blumstein. 1988. *Speech physiology, speech perception, and acoustic phonetics.* Cambridge.
O'Shaughnessy, D. 1990. *Speech communication, human and machine.* Reading, MA.
⇒ **phonetics**

acquired dyslexia ⇒ **alexia**

acquired language disorder ⇒ **language disorder**

acquisition/learning hypothesis ⇒ **natural approach**

acrolect

Term introduced by Bickerton (1975) to designate the local variety of standard English found in creole societies. An acrolect is distinguished from the basilect, i.e. the pure creole language, and from the mesolect, a transitional variety of language between the two. (⇒ *also* **pidgin, creole**)

Reference
Bickerton, D. 1975 *The dynamics of a creole system.* Cambridge.

acronym ⇒ **abbreviation**[1]

acrophone (*also* phonetic acronym)

Abbreviations that are pronounced as words rather than as a series of letters. For example, in Eng. *AIDS* [eidz] for *acquired immune deficiency syndrome*. Acrophones are commonly found in many other European languages: cf. Span. and Fr. *SIDA* [sida] ('AIDS').

References
⇒ **abbreviation**

acrophony

Process of inventing and naming alphabetical writing systems from syllabic pictographs (⇒ **pictography**); the alphabetic symbols for sounds refer to the phonetic value of the first syllable of the original word to which the pictogram refers. (⇒ *also* **graphemics**)

References
⇒ **graphemics, writing**

actant ⇒ **dependency grammar**

ACTFL proficiency guidelines ⇒ **proficiency**

action-denoting verb ⇒ **verb of action**

active

1 ⇒ **active voice**
2 as an aspect category ⇒ **stative vs dynamic**

active articulator ⇒ **articulator**

active language

Language type according to **relational typology** which contrasts with **nominative languages** and **ergative languages**. Assuming that in simple sentences the categories transitive and intransitive (⇒ **transitivity**) and the semantic roles **agent** and **patient** are the most important, this language type can be described as follows: the agent of an intransitive verb is expressed in the same way as the agent of a transitive verb, and differently from the patient of an intransitive or transitive verb. The patient is also expressed in the same way in both intransitive and transitive clauses. This yields a split in the coding of intransitive clauses in active languages that has been described as split intransitivity (Dixon 1979; Merlan 1985). This situation can be represented as follows:

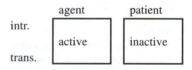

In contrast to this, the following distribution is found in nominative languages:

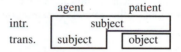

An example from Eastern Pomo: *há ce.xelka* 'I'm slipping (unintentionally)' vs *wí ce.xelka* 'I'm slipping/sliding (intentionally).' The semantic distinction underlying active coding differs somewhat from language to language: volitional vs non-volitional participant, active vs stative verb (see Van Valin 1990; Mithun 1991; Primus 1994). Some North American Indian languages (e.g. Dakota), as well as Lhasa-Tibetan and **Guaraní** are active languages. The tendency to encode the sole argument of intransitive verbs differently is marginally present in other languages, as in German, where with some intransitive statal verbs the entity experiencing the state is in the accusative or dative case: *Mich friert* 'It freezes me (acc.),' i.e. 'It's cold,' or *Mir ist angst* '(To) me (dat.) is fear,' i.e. 'I'm afraid.' In intransitive action verbs, however, the agent is in the nominative (*Ich arbeite* 'I'm working'). In contrast to German, the opposition active–inactive is dominant in active languages.

References
Delancey, S. 1985. On active typology and the nature of agentivity. In F. Plank (ed.), *Relational typology*. Berlin, 47–60.
Dixon, R.M.W. 1979. Ergativity. *Lg* 55.59–138.
Klimov, G.A. 1974. On the character of active languages. *Linguistics* 131.11–23.
———— 1977. *Typoplogija jazykov aktivnogo stroja*. Moscow.
Lazard, G. 1986. Le type linguistique dit 'actif': reflexions sur une typologie globale. *FoLi* 20.87–108.
Merlan, F. 1985. Split intransitivity: functional oppositions in intransitive inflection. In J. Nichols and A.C. Woodbury (eds), *Grammar inside and outside the clause*. Cambridge. 324–62.
Mithun, M. 1991. Active/agentive case marking and its motivations. *Lg* 67.510–46.
Nichols, J. 1990. Some preconditions and typical traits of stative–active language type. In W.P. Lehmann (ed.), *Language typology 1987. Systematic balance in language*. Amsterdam. 95–114.
Primus, B. 1994. Relational typology. In J. Jacobs *et al.* (eds), *Syntax: an international handbook of contemporary research*. Berlin. Vol. 2 1076–109.
Van Valin, R.D. 1990. Semantic parameters of split intransitivity. *Lg* 66. 221–60.

active voice

Verbal **voice** which contrasts with **passive** and **middle voice** in **nominative languages**. The active voice generally expresses the **agent** as the subject of a sentence and is considered the unmarked form, since it generally has no restrictions, appears with all verbs, and is morphologically the simplest construction.

References
⇒ voice

actor–action–model

Term in Bloomfield's sentence analysis used to indicate the most common basic type of complete sentence found in most Indo-European languages whose minimal form consists of the constituent denoting the performer of the action (actor, **agent**) and the constituent denoting the action carried out by the actor: *Louise* (agent) *plays the flute* (action).

Reference
Bloomfield, L. 1933. *Language*. New York.

acute accent [Lat. *acer* 'sharp']

1 Superscript **diacritic** serving several pur-
poses. It indicates length in **Czech**, **Hungarian**, and Old **Icelandic** (e.g. *á* for [aː]). In modern **Icelandic** it is used as a transcription of the sounds corresponding to the old long vowels, e.g. *á* for [ɑʊ]. In **French** a distinction is drawn between *é* for [e] and *è* for [ɛ]. In **Spanish** the acute accent is used to mark syllable stress as, for example, in *filosófico* ('philosophic') and to distinguish graphemically between homonyms, cf. *qué* ('what') vs *que* ('that'); similarly, some **Russian** texts use the acute accent for marking syllable stress. The acute accent is also used to mark tones as, for example, the long rising tone in **Serbo-Croatian** and rising tone in the Latinized Pīnyīn writing system of **Chinese**. Examples of other uses: in **Polish**: ń, ś, ź for [ɲ], [ş], and [ʐ] respectively; in **Dutch** for word stress *x staat vóór y* ('x comes before y'); in Greenlandic spelling, acute accent on a vowel indicates that the following consonant is long. (⇒ *also* **graphemics**, **writing**)

2 ⇒ **accent**[2]

3 In **comparative linguistics**, term for a stress of two morae (⇒ **mora, law of three morae**).

4 ⇒ **grave vs acute**

5 As a distinctive feature ⇒ **grave vs acute**[1]

Adamawa-Eastern ⇒ Adamawa-Ubangi

Adamawa-Ubangi (*also* Adamawa-Eastern)

Language branch of the **Niger-Congo** family with approximately 160 languages concentrated near the center of the African continent. These languages are generally divided into two main groups, Adamawa and Ubangian (Eastern). They have not yet been closely studied. The most important member of this family is Sango, which functions as a trade language for the central African republic.

References
Samarin, W.J. 1971. Adamawa-Eastern. In T.A. Sebeok (ed.), *Current Trends in Linguistics*, The Hague. Vol. 7, 213–44.
Schimizu, K. 1983. *The Zing dialect of Mumuye*. Hamburg.

adessive [Lat. *adesse* 'at' + 'to be']

Morphological **case** in some languages (e.g. **Finnish**) which expresses the location of an object. The adessive is often used to express ownership or instrumental use.

adhortative [Lat. *adhortativus* 'encouraging, urging on']

Subcategory of verbal **mood**, especially of the **subjunctive**. The adhortative designates a first person plural imperative of joint action. In most Indo-European languages, the adhortative does not have a special paradigm, but is expressed by the first person plural subjunctive, cf. *Let's go*; Fr. *Soyons amis* 'Let's be friends.'

References
Cole, P. 1975. The synchronic and diachronic status of conversational implicature. In P. Cole and J.L. Morgan (eds), *Syntax and semantics*, vol. 3: *Speech acts*, New York. 257–88.
⇒ **modality**

adjacency pair [Lat. *adiacens* 'lying beside, neighboring']

Coined by Sacks and Schegloff, the term refers to a particular instantiation of the turn-by-turn organization of conversations (⇒ **sequential organization, turn**). It is the affiliation of two utterance types into a pair type, where, upon production of the first pair part by the current speaker, the production of the second pair part by the addressee is relevant or expectable (⇒ **conditional relevance**). Such adjacency pairs are, for example, greeting – greeting or question – answer. First pair parts have identifiable, conventional properties, such as syntactic devices and sequential positioning (cf. Schegloff 1984). The second pair part can be identified primarily by its position, which is implied sequentially by the occurrence of the first pair part, that is, the second pair part is understood in regard to how it relates to the first pair part. Deviations offer evidence for this 'normative requirement' (Heritage 1984: 262f.). If a second pair part fails to occur, its absence will be noticed: (a) the first pair part will be repeated until the second is provided; or (b) the absence of the second will be accounted for (e.g. *'I don't know'*) preserving the normative framework of the adjacency-pair format; or (c) the delay of the second will be accounted for, for example, where another adjacency pair is inserted to supply the necessary information for the production of the second pair part:
Q1 S: What color do you think you want?
Q2 C: Do they just come in one solid color?
A2 S: No. They're black, blue, red, orange, light blue, dark blue, gray, green, tan [pause], black.
A1 C: Well, gimme a dark blue one, I guess.
(Merritt 1976: 333)
Additional evidence is provided by adjacency pairs with preferred second parts (⇒ **preference**). (⇒ also **discourse analysis**)

References
Heritage, J. 1984. *Garfinkel and ethnomethodology*. Cambridge.
Levinson, S. 1983. *Pragmatics*. Cambridge.
Merritt, M. 1976. On questions following answers in service encounters. *LSoc* 5.315–57.
Schegloff, E. 1968. Sequencing in conversational openings. *AA* 70.1075–95. (Repr. in J.J. Gumperz and D. Hymes (eds), *Directions in sociolinguistics*. New York. 346–80.)
——— 1984. On some questions and ambiguities. In J.M. Atkinson and J. Heritage (eds), *Structures of social action*. Cambridge. 28–52.
Schegloff, E. and H. Sacks. 1973. Opening and closing. *Semiotica* 8.289–327.
⇒ **conversation analysis**

adjectival adverb

Adjective used adverbially (e.g. *Caroline reads fast* vs *the fast reader*). Adjectival adverbs have comparative and superlative forms like adjectives (e.g. *Caroline reads the fastest of all*), while pure adverbs do not (e.g. *here, today*).

adjective [Lat. trans. of Grk *epítheton* 'that which is added']

Grammatical category (**part of speech**) that is used attributively with nouns (*a white fence*) or is governed by a **copular verb** (*The fence is white*). In some languages, adjectives may also exhibit **valence** (e.g. Ger. *sicher sein* + gen. 'to be sure of [something]'), be subject to **agreement** (**gender**, **number**, **case**), and/or have comparative and superlative forms (**degree**). In **German** and other **Germanic** languages, such as Old English, there is a distinction between strong (also: pronominal) and weak (also: nominal) inflection of adjectives. The use of the different types of inflection corresponds to the principle of 'mono-inflectional co-operation,' that is, the strong (determining) form is used whenever the syntactic form of the noun phrase that is modified by the adjective is not marked by any other (pronominal) elements, such as the article, or by gender: Ger. *grüner Apfel* 'green apple' vs *der grüne Apfel* 'the green apple'; OE *ʒōd cyninʒ* 'good king' vs *se ʒōda eorl* 'the good earl.' Syntactically speaking, they can be used predicatively or attributively, but not all adjectives can necessarily fulfill both of these latter functions: There are adjectives which can be used (a) attributively as well as predicatively (*red, big, new*), but are not gradable (*dead, single*) or (b) only attributively (*the former president* vs **The president is former*). There is a certain semantic similarity between adjectives and adverbs (e.g. *to write legibly: a legible hand*); both parts of speech modify the element they are connected to (noun, verb) with respect to particular characteristics. If this characterization is implicitly or explicitly based on a certain norm (as in *big, small, thick*), one speaks of relative or relational adjectives. For numeric adjectives, ⇒ **numerals**. For hierarchies between various adjectives, cf. Posner (1980).

References
Bartsch, R. and T. Vennemann. 1972. *Semantic structures: a study in the relation between semantics and syntax*. Frankfurt. (2nd edn 1973).
Bhat, D.N.S. 1994. *The adjectival category*. Amsterdam and Philadelphia.
Bierwisch, M. 1967. Some semantic universals of German adjectivals. *FL* 3.1–36.
Bierwisch, M. and E. Lang (eds). 1989. *Dimensional adjectives: grammatical structure and conceptual interpretation*. Berlin.
Bolinger, D.L. 1967. Adjectives in English. *Lingua* 18.1–34.
Ferris, C. 1993. *The meaning of syntax: a study in the adjectives of English*. London.
Hellan, L. 1981. *Towards an integrated analysis of comparatives*. Tübingen.
Posner, R. 1980. Ikonismus in der Syntax: zur natürlichen Stellung der Attribute. *ZSem* 2.57–82.
Rusiecki, J. 1985. *Adjectives and comparison in English*. London.
Schachter, P. 1985. Parts-of-speech systems. In T. Shopen (ed.), *Language typology and syntactic description*. Cambridge. Vol. 1, 3–63.
Vendler, Z. 1968. *Adjectives and nominalizations*. The Hague.
Warren, B. 1994. *Classifying adjectives*. Göteborg.

adjective phrase

Syntactic category (⇒ **phrase**) which has an **adjective** as its **head** and which can be modified by an **adverb** of degree (*really small, fairly bright, very beautiful*) or a **complement** (*tired of war, proud of an achievement*).

References
⇒ **adjective**

adjunct [Lat. *adiungere* 'to connect, to add']

Linguistic expression used attributively which semantically specifies either a preceding or a following element. This can be either restrictive through the use of an **article, pronoun, relative clause**, and the like (*that/my book; the book that he is reading right now*) or qualitative (*an unusual book; that book over there*). In contrast to **complements**, adjuncts are not grammatically required, that is, they are **free adjuncts**. (⇒ also **attribute**)

adjunction

1 In **transformational grammar**, an elementary syntactic operation through which **constituents**, after having been removed from their position in the **deep structure**, are inserted into a different position in the **surface structure**; they are linked to the **tree diagram** of the surface structure by an additional branch. (⇒ *also* **transformation**, ⇒ **Chomsky-adjunction**)

2 A synonym for **disjunction** in **formal logic**.

adsentential ⇒ sentence adverbial

adstratum [Lat. *stratum* 'layer']

A type of **interference** in which two languages come in contact or mix with each other. Adstratum refers to the mutual influence of two neighboring languages on each other over a period of time. The contact of **Flemish** and **French** in Belgium represents such a situation. (⇒ *also* **substratum, superstratum**)

References
⇒ **language contact**

adverb [Lat. *ad-verbum* 'belonging to the verb']

Grammatical category (**part of speech**) that serves to modify **verbs, adjectives,** other adverbs, and whole **clauses** semantically. Adverbs cannot be declined (⇒ **declension**) and thus are often grouped with prepositions and conjunctions as a subgroup of **particles**. Adverbs form a very heterogeneous group, containing numerous overlappings with other **parts of speech**, which is why they can be classified grammatically in a variety of ways. The following divisions can be made according to the particular classification of an adverb. (a) Syntactically, a distinction is made between adverbs which occur freely (*evenings, downhill, gladly*) and so-called 'pronominal adverbs' (*whereof, wherein, hereby*), which appear as pro-forms of prepositional phrases or adverbials. With regard to use, a distinction is usually drawn between adverbs which can be used both adverbially and attributively (*The book is here* vs *this book here*) and those which can be used only adverbially (*They work quickly*). Sentence adverbs (such as *hopefully, maybe, probably*) form a special class which can be used adsententially (⇒ **sentence adverbial**), that is, which constitute speaker judgments about the whole statement. (b) Semantically, there are groups with temporal (*now, afterwards, yesterday*), spatial (*here, inside, there*), modal (*gladly, reluctantly*), and causal (*correspondingly, regardless, notwithstanding*) meaning, or which show degree (*very, somewhat*). (c) Morphologically, adverbs can be classified as pure adverbs (*soon, now*), compound adverbs (*forthwith, henceforth*), and derived adverbs (*skyward, completely*).

References
⇒ **adverbial**

adverbial

Collective term for several syntactic functions with various semantic realizations: an adverbial characterizes a verbal action, process, or state of affairs with respect to time, place, kind, manner, etc. These semantic functions correspond to the classification in **school grammar** of temporal, spatial, modal, causal, conditional, and consecutive adverbs. In English, there are three major classifications: (a) valence-dependent adverbials which certain verbs require, e.g. *to inhabit* + spatial adverbial, *to feel* + modal adverbial, *to go* + directional adverbial; (b) valence-independent adverbials, such as modal adverbials that can occur with verbs of motion (*Louise runs/drives/swims pretty fast*); (c) valence-independent adverbials which do not impose any selectional restrictions (*Philip is working/relaxing/singing/ meditating in the backyard*). Adverbials from groups (a) and (b) are **complements**, while those in group (c) are **free adjuncts**. All these adverbials are dominated by the VP, while **sentence adverbials** (*Hopefully/Most likely/ Luckily he will come today*) have the sentence as their **scope**.

Various grammatical categories (**parts of speech**) can serve as adverbials: **adverbs** (*today, there*), **adjectives** (*beautiful, new*), pronominal adverbs (*therein, hereafter*), **prepositional phrases** (*on the table*), **noun phrases** (*one morning*), as well as adverbial clauses (*He followed her wherever she went*).

References
Cresswell, M.J. 1985. *Adverbial modification*. Dordrecht.
Rappaport, G.C. 1984. *Grammatical function and syntactic structure*. Columbus, OH.
Thompson, S.A. and R.E. Longacre. 1985. Adverbial clauses. In T. Shopen (ed.), *Language typology and syntactic description*. Cambridge. Vol. 2, 171–234.

Bibliographies
Sabourin, C. 1977. *Adverbs and comparatives: an analytical bibliography*. Amsterdam.
Siegrist, L. 1976. *Bibliographie zu Studien über das deutsche und englische Adverbial*. Tübingen.
⇒ **grammatical category**, **parts of speech**, **sentence adverbial**, **syntactic function**

advertising language

A **persuasive** use of language aimed at influencing people's behavior in politics, business, and especially in consumption. Pragmatic features of advertising language include its persuasive intention, its communicative distance to various addressees, and its distinctive use of certain expressions such as elliptical comparatives (*25 percent less car* – than what?), complex comparatives (*More car for less money*), and adjectivizations (*meaty taste*). Owing to its characteristic register, advertising language is readily recognizable as such by con-

sumers. Advertising language is innovative (e.g. in the formation of new words) on the one hand and functions as a means of language distribution between different language groups (technical language becoming standard language). On the other hand, it confirms and reinforces existing social norms and social stereotypes (⇒ **topos**). The extent to which it is effective in its persuasive goals is the subject of investigation in **semiotics** (e.g. visual advertising, sociology, and psychology).

References
Cook, G. 1992. *The discourse of advertising*. London.
Cumberbatch, G. *et al.* 1989. *A measure of uncertainty: the effects of the mass media*. London.
Geis, M. 1982. *The language of television advertising*. New York.
Tanaka, K. 1994. *Advertising language: A pragmatic approach to advertisements in Britain and Japan*. London.
Vestergaard, T. and K. Schrøder. 1985. *The language of advertising*. Oxford.
Vianello, R. 1988. *The rhetoric of the 'spot': the textual analysis of the American television commercial*. Ann Arbor, MI.
⇒ **mass communication**

Adyge ⇒ **North-West Caucasian**

affected object

Semantic relation (⇒ **thematic relation**) referring to an entity that exists independently from the action or process denoted by the verb, but yet affected by it, e.g. *Caroline corrects the letter*, as opposed to an **effected object**, e.g. *Caroline writes the letter*. Affected objects are typically expressed as direct objects in **nominative languages**.

affective filter hypothesis ⇒ **natural approach**

affective meaning ⇒ **connotation**[1]

affiliation [MLat. *affiliare* 'to adopt as a son,' from Lat. *ad* + *filius* 'son']
Relationship between languages which derive from a common language or **proto-language**. (⇒ *also* **classification of languages**)

affix [Lat. *afficere* 'to attach']
Collective term for bound formatives or word-forming elements that constitute subcategories of word classes. Affixes are classified according to their placement on the **stem**: **prefixes** precede the stem (Eng. *re* + *write*, Fr. *co* + *président*, Ger. *Un* + *tat*), **suffixes** follow the stem (Eng. *sister* + *hood*, Fr. *jeun* + *esse*, Ger. *taten* + *los*), while **infixes** are inserted into the

stem (e.g. *-m-* in Lat. *rumpo* 'I break' vs *ruptum* 'broken'). Affixes are frequently associated with a particular word class, cf. *happy + ness* vs **happy + able*, **mother + ness* vs *mother + hood*. The order of affix placement is rule-governed according to the underlying word class, cf. *standard + ize + able* vs **standard + able + ize*. Viewed synchronically, affixes are bound **morphemes** whose meanings have become abstract but whose origins as free morphemes with a clearly discernible lexical meaning can be reconstructed in many cases, cf. the Eng. suffix *-hood* used to form abstracts, which goes back to an independent noun with the meaning 'quality, characteristic,' as in Got. *haidus* and OHG *heit*. Besides semantic shift, the fact that some morphemes form semantic classes unto themselves indicates a transition from free morpheme status to affix status, cf. *-works* in *fire + works*, *water + works*, *road + works*. Such transitional affix-like elements are also called affixoids. (⇒ *also* **semi-prefix, semi-suffix**)

References
⇒ **derivation, word formation**

affixation

Process of **word formation** in which the **stem** is expanded by the addition of an **affix**. With regard to placement of the word-forming elements on the stem, a distinction is drawn between **prefixation** (= attachment of the affix before the stem: *happy* vs *unhappy*) and **suffixation** (= attachment of the affix after the stem: *happy* vs *happiness*). Infixation (⇒ **infix**) is found in some languages (e.g. Latin and Greek), though not in English.

References
⇒ **word formation**

affixoid ⇒ affix

affricate [Lat. *affricare* 'to rub']

Oral consonant (⇒ **consonant, oral**) in which the initial stop closure is followed by a small release, so that frication occurs. If the frication occurs at the same **place of articulation** as the **stop**, it is said to be **homorganic**, e.g. [pf, ts, dz, kx, bβ]. Otherwise it is **heterorganic**, as [t͡ʃ, p͡x]. While English affricates use only the pulmonic **airstream mechanism**, Georgian has **ejective** affricates, and Xhosa (⇒ **Bantu**) has a **click** affricate [!Xū]. According to theoretical criteria, an affricate can be analyzed as either a single (or 'unit') **phoneme** or a combination of two phonemes. (⇒ *also* **articulatory phonetics**)

References
⇒ **phonetics**

affrication

Sound change by which **affricates** are created from original **stops**, as for example OE [k] > Mod. Eng. [t͡ʃ] in *church* or [p, t, k,] > [p͡f, t͡s, k͡x] in the **Old High German consonant shift**. In this process, an intermediate stage with strongly aspirated stops is conceivable.

References
⇒ **sound change**

African languages

The languages of the African continent can be divided into four major groups according to the generally accepted division of J.H. Greenberg (1963): **Afro-Asiatic, Niger-Kordofanian, Nilo-Saharan** and **Khoisan**. The reconstruction of Afro-Asiatic (and especially of **Semitic**) has a long tradition, while the other three groups, especially Nilo-Saharan, have reconstructions that are still somewhat speculative.

References
Dihoff, I.R. *et al.* (eds) 1983. *Current approaches to African linguistics*. 2 vols. Dordrecht.
Greenberg, J.H. 1963. *The languages of Africa*. Bloomington, IN. (2nd edn 1966.)
Gregersen, E. 1977. *Language in Africa: an introductory survey*. New York.
Heine, B. 1976. *A typology of African languages*. Berlin.
Heine, B. *et al.* (eds) 1981. *Die Sprachen Afrikas*. Hamburg.
Mann, M. and D. Dalby (eds) 1987. *A thesaurus of African languages: a classified and annotated inventory of the spoken languages of Africa, with an appendix on their orthographic representation*. Munich.
Sebeok, T.A. (ed.) 1971. *Current trends in linguistics*, vol. 7: *Linguistics in Sub-Saharan Africa*. The Hague.
Tucker, A.N. and M.A. Bryan 1956. *Linguistic analyses: the non-Bantu languages of North Eastern Africa*. (*Handbook of African Languages* 5). Oxford
Welmers, W.E. 1973. *African language structures*. Berkeley, CA.

Bibliography
Meier, W. (ed.) 1984. *Bibliography of African languages*. Wiesbaden.

Journals
Afrika und Übersee
Journal of African Languages and Linguistics
Studies in African Languages

Afrikaans

Language of the Boers in South Africa which derived from **Dutch** dialects of the seventeenth century and has been used as a written language since 1875. Afrikaans is the only **creole** that has been elevated to an official language (1926 – along with **English**, in the Republic of South Africa and in Namibia); approx. 5 million speakers. The vocabulary and orthography of Afrikaans were determined by colloquial Dutch at the time of South Africa's colonization. Structurally, Afrikaans demonstrates even more morphological simplicity than Dutch (e.g. loss of endings in conjugation and declension, cf. Afrk. *sy loop* vs Du. *zij lopen* 'they run').

References

Breyne, M.R. 1936. *Afrikaans: eine Einführung in die Laut-, Formen- und Satzlehre mit Literaturproben*. Leipzig.

Donaldson, B.C. 1993. *A grammar of Afrikaans*. New York.

Kloeke, G.G. 1950. *Herkomst en groei van het Afrikaans*. Leiden.

Le Roux, J.J. 1923. *Oor die afrikaanse sintaksis*. Amsterdam.

Raidt, R. 1983. *Einführung in Geschichte und Struktur des Afrikaans*. Darmstadt.

Van Schoor, J.L. 1983. *Die grammatika van standard-Afrikaans*. Cape Town.

Afro-Asiatic (*also* Hamito-Semitic, Erythraic)

Language branch consisting of approx. 250 languages with about 175 million speakers in North Africa and southwest Asia which can be grouped into five or possibly six language families (**Egyptian, Berber, Cushitic, Semitic, Chadic,** and possibly **Omotic**). The first written attestations (Egyptian, **Akkadian**) date from the early third millennium BC.

Historically most of the research done on this group has focused on the reconstruction of Semitic. In the nineteenth century scholars realized that the languages of northern Africa were related to Semitic; these languages were called 'Hamitic' (after Ham, the son of Noah) and were contrasted with Semitic (Lepsius 1855). Later the term 'Hamitic' was used for all inflectional languages with masculine/feminine gender in northern Africa, which were considered to be languages of more culturally advanced peoples (Meinhof 1912). Today the current opinion is that the Semitic languages contrast with several language families instead of with a unified Hamitic group and that languages such as **Fula**, Massai, and Nama belong to other language groups.

Characteristics: **gender** system (masculine/feminine, with feminine marker *t*), verbal personal prefixes and free personal pronouns, separate conjugation for stative verbs, simple **case** system (nominative, accusative, objective, genitive) with indications of an underlying **ergative** system, verbal voice (causative, passive, middle, etc.), a rich number system (frequently dual-forms and a collective-singular distinction). Phonologically three types of articulation for obstruents (voiced, voiceless, and 'emphatic,' realized typically as pharyngeal, ejective, or similar sounds).

References

Diakonoff, I.M. 1965. *Semito-Hamitic languages*. Moscow.

Hodge, C.T. (ed.) 1968. *Afroasiatic: a survey*. The Hague.

Lepsius, R. 1855. *Standard alphabet for reducing unwritten languages and foreign graphic systems to a uniform orthography in European letters*. London. (2nd edn 1863.)

Meinhof, C. 1912. *Die Sprache der Hamiten*. Hamburg.

Sasse, H.J. 1981. Afroasiatisch. In B. Heine *et al.* (eds), *Die Sprachen Afrikas*. Hamburg, 129–48.

Etymological dictionary

Orel, V.E. and O.V. Stolbova. 1995. *Hamito-Semitic etymological dictionary: materials for reconstruction*. Leiden.

Journals

Comptes Rendus du Groupe Linguistique d'Etudes Chamito-Sémitiques
Journal of Afroasiatic Languages
⇒ **African languages**

agent [Lat. *agere* 'to do, to perform'] (*also* agentive, actor)

Semantic role (⇒ **thematic relation**) of the volitional initiator or causer of an action, which is usually expressed in **nominative languages** like English as the subject of the sentence: *He ate the apple*. In **passive** sentences the agent is expressed in an oblique case as, for example, in **Latin** or **Russian**, or by a **prepositional phrase**: *The apple was eaten by him*.

References
⇒ **case grammar, ergative, subject, voice**

agglutinating language [Lat. *agglutinare* 'to glue together']

Classification type postulated by von Humboldt (1836) from a morphological point of view for languages that exhibit a tendency toward **agglutination** in word formation, as, for example, **Turkish, Japanese, Finnish**. In contrast ⇒ **analytic language** (⇒ *also* **isolating language**), **inflectional language**. *also* ⇒ **language typology**

Reference

Von Humboldt, W. 1836. *Über die Verschiedenheit des menschlichen Sprachbaus*. Berlin. (Repr. in W. Von Humboldt, *Werke*, ed. A. Flitner and K. Gields. Darmstadt, 1963. Vol. 3, 144–367.)

agglutination [Lat. *agglutinare* 'to glue together']

Morphological process (⇒ **morphology**) of word formation in which individual **morphemes** have a single semantic meaning (⇒ **monosemy**) and are juxtaposed (⇒ **juxtaposition**), that is, each morpheme corresponds to a single meaning and the morphemes are simply connected linearly, cf. **Turkish:** *ev* 'house,' *-im* 'my,' *-ler* 'plural,' *-in* 'genitive' in *evlerimin* 'my houses'. (⇒ *also* **agglutinating language**)

References
⇒ **morphology**

agnosia [Grk *agnōsía* 'ignorance']

In **neuropsychology**, term referring to partial or complete inability, whether it be congenital or acquired, to recognize objects or persons despite the absence of any sensory loss in the respective organ. Thus, a noise (e.g. the rattling of keys) may be perceived, but its source cannot be identified (auditory imperception) or the distance and direction of a sound or noise may not be identified (acoustic allesthesia); or the minimal acoustic contrast between phonemes may not be recognized (partial weakness in differentiation, acoustic agnosia) or linguistic sound sequences may not be differentiated ('word deafness' or verbal agnosia). Similarly, in visual and tactile agnosia, objects may not be identified despite normal vision or sense of touch.

References
Brown, J. 1972. *Aphasia, apraxia and agnosia.* Springfield, IL.
Farah, M.J. 1990. *Visual agnosia: disorders of object recognition and what they tell us about normal vision.* Cambridge, MA.
Hecaen, H. and M. Albert. 1978. *Human neuropsychology.* New York.
Luria, A.R. 1966. *Higher cortical functions in man.* New York.
———— 1973. *The working brain: an introduction to neuropsychology.* New York.
⇒ **neuropsychology**

agrammatism [Grk *agrámmatos* 'illiterate']

In **neurolinguistics**, term referring to an acquired impairment or disorder of oral and written expression. A typical characteristic of this condition is the occurrence of fragmentary sentences in which function words and inflections are missing (so-called 'telegraphic style'). These morphological and syntactic features often co-occur with semantic and phonological impairments as well as with overall problems in language comprehension. This condition is often observed in cases of **Broca's aphasia**; and often 'agrammatism' is used synonymously

with the syndrome 'Broca's aphasia.' Recent studies show that there are language-specific characteristics of agrammatism (see Bates *et al.* 1987) and emphasize, moreover, that the distinction between agrammatism and **paragrammatism** – and thus between Broca's and **Wernicke's aphasia** – is not as clear-cut as has been assumed. Sometimes agrammatism is also used for disorders in the development of grammatical abilities in children.
(⇒ **dysgrammatism**)

References
Bates, E. *et al.* 1987. Grammatical morphology in aphasia: evidence from three languages. *Cortex* 23.545–74.
Caplan, D. 1987. *Neurolinguistics and linguistic aphasiology.* Cambridge.
Jakobson, R. 1971. Two aspects of language and two types of aphasic disturbance. In R. Jakobson and M. Halle (eds) *Fundamentals of language.* The Hague. 155–82. (Orig. 1956.)
Johnston, J.R. 1988. Specific language disorders in the child. In N. Lass *et al.* (eds), *Handbook of speech–language pathology and audiology.* Philadelphia. 685–715.
Kean, M. (ed.) 1985. *Agrammatism.* Orlando, FL.
Kolk, H. and C. Heeschen. 1992. Agrammatism, paragrammatism and the management of language. *Language and Cognitive Processes* 7.89–129.
Luria, A.R. 1966. *Higher cortical functions in man.* New York.
———— 1970. *Traumatic aphasia.* The Hague.
Menn, L. and L.K. Obler. 1989. *Agrammatism: a cross-linguistic narrative sourcebook.* Amsterdam.
Obler, L.K. and L. Menn. 1988. Agrammatism: the current issues. *Journal of Neurolinguistics* 3.63–76.
⇒ **aphasia, language disorder**

agraphia [Grk *gráphein* 'to write']

In **neurolinguistics**, term referring to an acquired impairment in, or loss of, the ability to write. Pure agraphia is, however, an exception, in that oral expression and reading are usually impaired as well. On the various types and classifications, see Hecaen and Albert (1978).
(⇒ *also* **alexia**, **aphasia**)

References
Benson, D.F. 1979. *Aphasia, alexia, agraphia.* New York.
Hecaen, H. and M. Albert. 1978. *Human neuropsychology.* New York.
Roeltgen, D.R. and S.Z. Rapcsak. 1993. Acquired disorders of writing and spelling. In G. Blanken *et al.* (eds), *Linguistic disorders and pathologies: an international handbook.* Berlin and New York. 262–78.
⇒ **aphasia**

agreement (*also* concord)

Correspondence between two or more sentence elements in respect to their morphosyntactic categories (**case**, **person**, **number**, **gender**). (a) Grammatical agreement occurs within a sentence or its constituents, such as in the noun phrase in German: *des jungen Baumes* 'of the young tree,' where all the elements agree in case (**genitive**), number (**singular**), and gender (**masculine**). Agreement can mark syntactic relations, such as two **constituents** belonging to the same complex constituent, as well as **syntactic functions**, such as **subject** and **attribute**. Grammatical agreement has three important domains: (i) in many languages the inflected verb phrase agrees with the subject with regard to person and number (*I sing* vs *she sings* vs *they sing*) and sometimes gender (cf. **Bantu**). There are also some languages with object–verb agreement, such as **Swahili**, Kinyarwanda (Rwanda), and other Bantu languages; Abkhaz, Laz and other **Caucasian languages**; and **Basque**, among others. Verbal agreement is determined primarily by the syntactic function (**subject**, **object**, **adverbial**) accompanying the verb. In object–verb agreement, animacy (⇒ **animate vs inanimate**), **definiteness**, and/or the **thematic relation** of the verb complement also play a role (see Givón 1976). (ii) Nominal agreement affects elements accompanying the noun, such as **determiners**, adjectival attributes, and **appositions**, which agree with their **antecedent** in case and other categories: cf. Ger. *Sie sucht einen Jungen, ihren kleinsten Sohn* 'She is looking for a boy, her youngest son,' where *Jungen* 'boy' and *Sohn* 'son' are both accusative masculine. (iii) In predicative agreement, the subject and predicate agree in gender, number, or case: *He is an actor* vs *She is an actress*. (b) Anaphoric agreement extends beyond the sentence boundary and indicates, for example, the coreference between a pronoun and its andecedent: *A young woman entered the room. She was carrying a large briefcase.* There may be a historical connection between anaphoric and grammatical agreement; in many languages, grammatical markers for agreement developed from pronouns (see Givón 1976).

References
Barlow, M. and C.A. Ferguson (eds) 1988. *Agreement in natural language*. Stanford, CA.
Bosch, P. 1983. *Agreement and anaphora*. London.
Bresnan, J. and S. Mchombo. 1986. Grammatical and anaphoric agreement. *CLS* 22.278–97.
Corbett, G.G. 1983. *Hierarchies, targets and controllers: agreement patterns in Slavic*. London.
Gazdar, G. *et al.* (eds) 1983. *Order, concord and constituency*. Dordrecht.
Givón, T. 1976. Topic, pronoun and grammatical agreement. In C.N. Li (ed.), *Subject and topic*. New York. 149–88.
Lehmann, C. 1982. Universal and typological aspects of agreement. In H. Seiler and J. Stachowiak (eds), *Apprehension: das sprachliche Erfassen von Gegenständen*. Tübingen. Part 2, 201–67.
Lyons, J. 1968. *Introduction to theoretical linguistics*. Cambridge.
Moravcsik, E.A. 1978. Agreement. In J.H. Greenberg (ed.), *Universals of human language*. Stanford, CA. Vol. 4, 352–74.
Steele, S. 1989. Subject values. *Lg* 65.537–78.
⇒ **gender**

AI ⇒ artificial intelligence

Ainu

Language with approx. 16,000 speakers on the northern Japanese island of Hokkaido, Sakhalin, and in the Kurile Islands. Its genetic affiliation has not yet been satisfactorily determined.

References
Dettmer, H. 1989. *Ainu-Grammatik*. Wiesbaden.
Patrie, J. 1982. *The genetic relationship of the Ainu language*. Honolulu, HI.
Shíbatani, M.Y. 1990. *The languages of Japan*. Cambridge.

airstream mechanism

Articulatory process involved in the formation of **speech sounds** in which air is forced from the lungs (pulmonic airstream mechanism), through the **glottis** (glottalic airstream mechanism), or between the **dorsum** and **velum** (velaric airstream mechanism). In English, all sounds are formed with the pulmonic airstream mechanism. **Implosives** and **ejectives** are formed with the glottalic airstream mechanism, and **clicks** with velaric airstream mechanism. (⇒ *also* **articulatory phonetics**)

References
⇒ **phonetics**

Akan ⇒ Kwa

Akkadian

Oldest attested **Semitic** language (app. 3200 BC to around the turn from BC to AD), the language of the Assyrian and Babylonian empires. After the second century BC Akkadian split into two dialects (Assyrian, Babylonian), written in **cuneiform** borrowed from **Sumerian**.

References
Caplice, R. 1980. *Introduction to Akkadian*. Rome.
Gelb, I.J. 1961. *Old Akkadian writing and grammar*, 2nd edn. Chicago.

——— 1969. *Sequential reconstruction of Proto-Akkadian*. Chicago.

Groneberg, B.R.M. 1987. *Syntax, Morphologie und Stil der jungbabylonischen 'hymnischen' Literatur*, 2 vols. Wiesbaden.

Hecker, K. 1968. *Grammatik der Kültepe-Texte*. Rome.

Huehnergard, J. 1988. *The Akkadian of Ugarit*. Cambridge, MA.

Lipin, L.A. 1973. *The Akkadian language*. Moscow.

Reiner, E. 1966. *A linguistic analysis of Akkadian*. The Hague.

Von Soden, W. 1952. *Grundriß der Akkadischen Grammatik*. Rome.

——— 1969. *Ergänzungsheft zum Grundriß der akkadischen Grammatik*. Rome.

Dictionaries
Assyrian dictionary of the Oriental Institute of the University of Chicago. 1956– . Vol. 17, 1989. Chicago, IL.

Von Soden, W. 1965–81. *Akkadisches Handwörterbuch*. Wiesbaden.

Journals
Akkadica
Orientalia
Zeitschrift für Assyriologie

Aktionsart (*also* manner of action)

German term meaning 'manner of action'; it is used by some linguists (especially German and Slavonic) to denote the lexicalization of semantic distinctions in verbal meaning, as opposed to **aspect**, which is then used to denote the systematic grammaticalization of such distinctions. Usage differs as to whether the term 'Aktionsart' covers all lexicalized semantic distinctions, i.e. those inherent in the meaning of the verb as well as those created by derivational morphology, e.g. suffixes denoting iterativity etc., or only the latter.

Most English-speaking linguists do not use the term 'Aktionsart', but subsume the distinctions described above under aspect.

References
⇒ **aspect**

Albanian

Branch of **Indo-European** consisting of one language which is the official language of Albania and spoken as well in parts of the former Yugoslavia, Greece, and Italy (approx. 5 million speakers). There are two main dialects: Gheg, in the north, and Tosk, in the south.

Characteristics: in addition to the usual categories of Indo-European languages, **definiteness** and indefiniteness are expressed in the noun by inflection (cf. *bukë* 'bread,' *buka* 'the loaf of bread'). Relatively complicated morphology, especially in the verbal system (highly complex tense, mood, and aspect system).

Development of object agreement by proclitic pronouns. Word order usually SVO, adjectives placed after the noun. Numerous lexical borrowings from **Latin** and some from other Balkan languages, mostly **Greek**, **Slavic**, and also **Turkish**. First written documents dating from the fifteenth century.

References
Bevington, G.L. 1974. *Albanian phonology*. Wiesbaden.

Buchholz, O. and W. Fiedler. 1987. *Albanische Grammatik*. Leipzig.

Çabej, E. 1975–7. *Studime Gjuhësore*, 5 vols. Prishtinë.

Camaj, M. 1984. *Albanian grammar*, collaborated on and trans. L. Fox. Wiesbaden.

Hamp, E.P. 1972. Albanian. In T.A. Sebeck (ed.), *Current trends in linguistics*. The Hague. Vol. 9, 1626–92.

——— 1991. Albanian. In J. Gvozdanović (ed.), *Indo-European numerals*. Berlin and New York. 835–922.

Huld, M.E. 1983. *Basic Albanian etymologies*. Columbus, OH.

Newmark, L., P. Hubbard, and P. Prifti. 1982. *Standard Albanian: a reference grammar for students*. Stanford, CA.

Historical grammars
Demiraj, S. 1986. *Gramatikë historike e gjuhës shqipe*. Tirana.

Mann, S. 1977. *An Albanian historical grammar*. Hamburg.

Dictionary
Fjalori i gjuhës së sotme shquipe. 1980. *Akademia e Shkencave e RPS të Shqipërisë*, ed. A. Kostallari. Tirana.

Journals
Gjurmime Albanologjike
Lidhja
Linguistique Balkanique
Studia Albanica
Studime filologjike
Zeitschrift für Balkanologie
Zjarri

Aleut ⇒ Eskimo-Aleut

alexia [Grk *léxis* 'speech wordly'] (*also* acquired dyslexia)

In **neurolinguistics**, term referring to an acquired impairment in the ability to read despite intact vision. Often associated with aphasia, alexia may be observed when patients attempt to say individual letters ('literal alexia'), read individual words or simple sentences ('verbal alexia' or 'word blindness'). For details on further classification, see Kay (1993). Of particular interest are investigations of patients' behavior in languages with different writing systems, for instance **Japanese** with one logographic and two phonological systems (see Paradis 1987). Alexia is generally differentiated from **developmental dyslexia**.

References
Benton, A.L. and R.J. Joynt. 1960. Early descriptions of aphasias. *Archives of Neurology* 3.205–21.
Brown, J.W. 1972. *Aphasia, apraxia and agnosia.* Springfield, IL.
Coltheart, M., K. Patterson, and J.C. Marshall (eds) 1987. *Deep dyslexia*, 2nd edn. London.
Kay, J. 1993. Acquired disorders of reading. In G. Blanken *et al.* (eds), *Linguistic disorders and pathologies: an international handbook.* Berlin and New York. 251–62.
Luria, A.R. 1966. *Higher cortical functions in man.* New York.
Marshall, J.C. 1987. Routes and representations in the processing of written language. In E. Keller and M. Gopnik (eds), *Motor and sensory processes of language.* Hillsdale, NJ. 237–56.
Paradis, M. 1987. The neurofunctional modularity of cognitive skills: evidence from Japanese alexia and polyglot aphasia. In E. Keller and M. Gopnik (eds), *Motor and sensory processes of language.* Hillsdale, NJ. 277–89.
⇒ **aphasia**

algebraic linguistics ⇒ **formal language, mathematical linguistics**

Algic ⇒ **Algonquian**

Algonquian

Language family in North America with approx. twenty languages located in the central and eastern parts of the continent; the largest languages are Cree (approx. 70,000 speakers) and Ojibwa (approx. 40,000 speakers). Bloomfield (1962) has done the most detailed analysis of a language from this family (Menomini). Algonquian and Ritwan (the languages Yurok and Wiyot of northern California) form the Algic language family.

Characteristics: very simple consonant and vowel systems; two genders derived from an **animate/inanimate** distinction; rich person system including indefinite ('one'), **inclusive/exclusive** and **proximate/obviative**; distinction between **alienable and inalienable** possession. The distinction noun/verb occurs only weakly: possessive verb conjugation (cf. *ne-suːmiyanəm* 'my money,' *ne-poːsem* 'I embark' = 'my embarkation'). Transitive verbs are marked; when the agent in the person hierarchy (second before first before third person) occurs before the patient, the verb is in a voice similar to passive.

The related language Yurok deviates strongly due to the areal influence of neighboring languages (rich sound system, numeral classification).

References
Bloomfield, L. 1962. *The Menomini language.* New Haven, CT.
Goddard, I. 1979. Comparative Algonkian. In L. Campbell and M. Mithun (eds), *The languages of native America: historical and comparative assessment.* Austin, TX. 70–132.
———1975. Algonquian, Wiyot and Yurok: providing a distant genetic relationship. In M.D. Kincade et al., *Linguistics and anthropology in honour of C.F. Voegelin*, Lisse. 249–62.
Robins, R.H. 1958. *The Yorok language.* Berkeley, CA.
Teeter, K. 1973. Algonquian. In T.A. Sebeok (ed.), *Current trends in linguistics.* The Hague. Vol. 10, 1143–63.

Bibliography
Pentland, D.H. *et al.* 1982. *Bibliography of Algonquian linguistics.* Winnipeg.

Dictionary
Aubin, G.F. 1976. *A Proto-Algonquian dictionary.* Ottawa.

Journal
Algonquian and Iroquoian Linguistics Newsletter

algorithm

Derived from the name of the Arabian mathematician Al Chwarism (approx. AD 825), the term denotes a mathematical process established through explicit rules designed to solve a class of problems automatically. An algorithm consists of an ordered system of basic operations and conditions of application that guarantee that, in a finite series of steps, given arbitrary input data from one domain, the corresponding output data (solutions) will be generated. (Cf. the mathematical rules for multiplication, algebraic simplification, and other operations.) For example, we may specify an algorithm to check whether a given natural n is prime. Simple check, for each i, $2 \Leftarrow i \Leftarrow n/2$, whether n is evenly divisible by i. This mechanical procedure is guaranteed to provide a correct answer to the question posed in a definite amount of time (in this example somewhat inefficiently). ($\Rightarrow$ *also* **automaton, formal language, Turing machine**)

References
⇒ **formal logic**

alienable vs inalienable possession [Lat. *alienus* 'belonging to others, not one's own']

Semantic subcategory which expresses possession in reference to whether or not the possessed object is easily removed, transferable, temporary or permanent, or essential. It is realized differently in various languages, cf. Eng. *own*: *I own a house/*a father/*a heart.* In

Swahili, inalienable possession is marked morphologically, while alienable possession is marked syntactically: *baba-ngu* 'my father,' *nyumba yangu* 'my house.' In Chickasaw (⇒ **Muskogean**), there are different morphological forms, e.g. *sa-holba* 'a picture of me' (in which I am depicted, = inalienable) vs *a-holba* 'my picture' (that I own, = alienable). Recent investigations show that the ability of the object to be transferred is not as important as whether or not the possessor noun is a **relational expression** or not.

all-quantifier

Synonym for the universal quantifier (⇒ **operator**).

allative [Lat. *allatus*, past part. of *afferre* 'to be moved (in the direction of)']

Morphological **case** of location in some languages (e.g. **Finnish**) which expresses the fact that an object is moving towards a location.

allegation [Lat. *allegare* 'to send on an errand, to cite'] (*also* necessitation)

Term introduced by Sgall (Sgall *et al.* 1973: 108–11) for a special type of implicational relations, which he defines as: from *S* follows *A*, but from *not S*, neither *A* nor *not A* follows. Along these lines, the concept of allegation lies between that of **assertion**, whose meaning is reversed through negation, and that of **presupposition** which remains constant under negation. The relation of allegation corresponds to the '*if*-verbs' in Karttunen (1971). Applications for relations of this sort are found primarily in **text linguistics**.

References
Karttunen, L. 1971. *The logic of English predicate complement constructions*. Bloomington, IN.
Sgall, P. *et al.* 1973. *Topic, focus and generative semantics*. Kronberg.

allegory

Extending a metaphor through an entire speech or passage, or representing abstract concepts through the image of an acting person ('personification'). Allegory is also referred to as an extended metaphor: for example, *Reverie ... a musical young girl, unpredictable, tender, enigmatic, provocative, from whom I never seek an explanation of her escapades* (André Breton, *Farouche à quatre feuilles*, p. 13). The allegory is sometimes called 'pure' when every main term in the passage has a double significance, 'mixed' when one or more terms do not.

References
Bloomfield, M.W. 1962–3. A grammatical approach

to personification allegory. *MPh* 60.161–71.
Fletcher, A. 1964. *Allegory: the theory of a symbolic mode*. Ithaca, NY.
Frye, N. 1957. *Anatomy of criticism: four essays*. Princeton, NJ.
MacQueen, J. 1976. *Allegory*. London.
Quilligan, M. 1979. *The language of allegory: defining the genre*. Ithaca, NY.
⇒ **trope**

alliteration [Lat. *ad* 'to,' *littera* 'letter (of the alphabet)']

Repetition of homophonous accented, syllable-initial phonemes, as in *house and home, cash and carry, tea for two*, usually for stylistic or poetic effect. Alliteration can be useful in the reconstruction of historical linguistic features; in Germanic alliterative verse (e.g. the 'Edda') all vowels were alliterative since the **glottal stop** before vowels was realized as a consonant. Moreover, the combinations *sp, st, sk* were considered phonetic–phonological units, since they – like all consonants – alliterated only with themselves.

allo- [Grk *állos* 'another, different']

A designation for morphological elements distinguishing variations of linguistic units on the level of parole (⇒ **langue US parole**). Allo-forms (e.g. **allophone, allomorph**) represent variation of fundamental linguistic units such as **phonemes, morphemes**, on all levels of description.

alloflex

The concrete realization of a grammatical morpheme signaling inflection. (⇒ *also* **flexive**)

allograph [Grk *gráphein* 'to write']

Graphic variant of the transcription of a non-graphic object where a distinction is drawn between the following: (a) The allograph of a phone: in the IPA (see chart, p. xix), [ɪ] and [ɪ], [ω] and [ʊ] are allographs denoting the same phone; ‹g› and ‹g› are, as a rule, allographs in writing systems based on Latin. (b) The allograph of a phonemic complex: in English *center* and *centre* are in an allographic relation. (c) Conceptual allographs are found in logographic writing systems (⇒ **logography**) like that of **Chinese**. Whether two written signs are allographs depends on the given system: for example, in contrast with English, German, and French orthography, ‹ɑ› and ‹a› do not represent allographs in the IPA. With regard to a phonological description of English, however, ‹a›, ‹ɑ›, ‹*a*›, ‹A›, and ‹*A*› can all be viewed as allographs; however, this view must be excluded when talking about upper vs lower case, or cursive vs Roman typeface as belonging to different systems. (⇒ *also* **graphemics**)

References
⇒ **writing**

allomorph [Grk *morphḗ* 'form, shape']

Concretely realized variant of a **morpheme**. The classification of **morphs** as allomorphs or as the tokens of a particular morpheme is based on (a) similarity of meaning and (b) **complementary distribution**: for example, [s], [z], and [tz] are considered allomorphs of the plural morpheme.

If the phonetic form of the allomorph is determined by the phonetic environment then it is a phonologically conditioned allomorph, e.g. in English the past tense marker *-ed* is realized as [d] (*said*) and [t] (*wished*). If, however, there are no phonetic conditions for allomorphic variation, then the allomorphs are morphologically conditioned, e.g. [swɪm] (*swim*) vs [swæm] (*swam*). (⇒ *also* **allophone**)

References
⇒ **morphology**

allophone [Grk *phōnḗ* 'sound, voice'] (*also* phonemic variant)

Concretely realized variants of a **phoneme**. The classification of **phones** as allophones of a phoneme is based on (a) their **distribution** and (b) their phonetic similarity. In final position, aspirated (⇒ **aspiration**) [pʰ] and unreleased [p'] (as in [tapʰ] vs [tap'] (*top*) are allophones in **free variation**. Most allophones, however, are in **complementary distribution**, as [pʰ] in [pʰaut] *pout* and [p] in [spaut] *spout*. (⇒ *also* **phonotactics**)

References
⇒ **phonology**

alloseme [Grk *sēma* 'sign']

An element of meaning of a **sememe** in the terminology of Nida. Semantic context is the important factor in determining the meaning: for example, the dictionary entry for *foot* [part of x, x = +living] also exhibits an alloseme that is realized as [–living] in the context of *foot of the mountain*.

Reference
Nida, E. 1946. *Morphology*, 2nd edn. Ann Arbor, MI.

allotagm [Grk *tágma* 'order, arrangement']

A concretely realized variation of a **tagmeme**, the smallest grammatical meaning-bearing unit.

Reference
Bloomfield, L. 1933. *Language*. New York.

allotax [Grk *táxis* 'arrangement']

An umbrella term for the smallest, concrete variant of a **taxeme** or **allophone** that does not carry any meaning.

alpha privativum [Lat. *privativus* 'negative,' from *privare* 'to deprive']

Term for the Greek **prefix** *a-/an-* derived from Indo-European **n̥-* (Lat. *in-*, Eng. *un-*) that is used to negate the expression it precedes, e.g. *a+thiest* (< Grk *átheos* 'godless'), *a+nonymous* (< Grk *anṓnymos* 'without a name').

References
⇒ **word formation**

alphabet [Grk *álpha* (α) + *bēta* (β), names of the first two letters of the Greek alphabet]

1 Inventory of written signs of an **alphabetic writing system** in a standardized order. The inventory and order of Latin-based alphabetic signs (= **letters**) is roughly the same from language to language, though alphabets for individual languages may have additional characters. Thus, the Spanish alphabet contains thirty characters and has the following additional letter (ñ); *k* occurs only in foreign loan words. Similarly, German shares a basic twenty-six character alphabet with English, though *ä*, *ö*, *ü*, and *ß* (**ligatures** for *ae*, *oe*, *ue*, and *sz* respectively) are generally considered to be additional characters in the German alphabet.

References
⇒ **alphabetic writing system**, **writing**

2 (*also* vocabulary) Finite set of symbols or basic signs upon which the description of formal (artificial) languages is based. For example, the Morse alphabet consists of two elements, namely short and long tones (dots and dashes), whose various strings constitute the Morse code. In **transformational grammar** a distinction is drawn between non-terminal symbols (*S*, *NP*, *VP*, etc.) and terminal symbols taken from the lexicon.

alphabetic writing system

System of writing based on phonetic and phonological criteria, i.e. a system in which graphic signs represent individual sounds or sound segments. Alphabetic writing systems are differentiated by this 'phonographic' principle from writing systems that use (a) picture-like signs to represent linguistic or non-linguistic phenomena (**pictograph**), (b) concepts (**ideograph**), (c) morphological units – morphemes or words – (**logograph**), or (d) syllables. In contrast to ideographic (and syllabographic) systems, which developed independently at different times with different peoples, all alphabetic writing systems can be traced back to a single system invented in the Semitic (Old Phoenician) linguistic area. The Greeks adapted this originally consonantal alphabetic writing system by adding vowels and writing out words in a linear series of consonants and vowels. The universal development and spread of alphabetic writing systems is based on the particularly favorable relationship between the simplicity and the learnability of the system as well as the economy of its use. While the modern Chinese (logographic) writing system (⇒ **Chinese script**) requires some 6,000–8,000 signs to accommodate colloquial communication and nearly ten times as many for scientific texts, alphabetic writing systems have an average of thirty characters: English has twenty-six, German thirty, French thirty-one, and Russian thirty-three. The transmission of the Latin alphabet to other European languages brought about various difficulties in adapting the alphabet, depending on the phonological structure of the language, as well as certain orthographic irregularities concerning the relation of sound to sign (and vice versa). Such problem cases, which were frequently intensified through historical changes or by chance, are especially due to unsystematically ascribing signs/graphemes to sounds/phonemes. Individual European languages are affected by the following complications to varying degrees: (a) one sign stands for several sounds (e.g. ‹c› stands for [k] in *cat*, [s] in *cell*, and [ts] in *cats*); (b) several signs denote the same sound (‹f, ph› stand for [f] in *file*, *philosophy*); (c) simple signs are used for complex sounds (‹j› stands for [dʒ] in *juice*); or (d) complex signs stand for individual sounds (‹sh› for [ʃ] in *shine*).

References

Cohen, M. 1958. *La Grande Invention de l'écriture et son évolution.* Paris.

Diringer, D. 1962. *Writing.* London.

Földes-Padd, K. 1966. *Vom Felsenbild zum Alphabet: die Geschichte der Schrift von ihren frühesten Vorstufen bis zur lateinischen Schreibschrift.* Stuttgart.

Friedrich, J. 1966. *Geschichte der Schrift unter besonderer Berücksichtigung ihrer geistigen Entwicklung.* Heidelberg.

Gelb, I.J. 1952. *A study of writing: the foundation of grammatology.* London.

Lüdtke, H. 1969. Die Alphabetschrift und das Problem der Lautsegmentierung. *Phonetica* 20. 147–76.

Naveh, J. 1982. *Early history of the alphabet: an introduction to West Semitic epigraphy and paleography.* Leiden.

Powell, B.B. 1991. *Homer and the origin of the Greek alphabet.* Cambridge.

Raible, W. 1991. *Zur Entwicklung von Alphabetschrift-Systemen.* Heidelberg.

⇒ **writing**

Alsea ⇒ Penutian

Altaic

Language group in central and northern Asia with approximately sixty languages and 250 million speakers, divided into the **Turkic, Mongolian**, and **Tungusic** families. The inclusion of **Korean, Japanese**, and **Ainu** into this group, as well as its possible relationship to the **Uralic** and **Eskimo-Aleut** language groups is debated. The first classification goes back to Strahlenberg (1730).

Characteristics: relatively uniform in its typology; simple phonemic system, simple syllable structure, **vowel harmony**; morphological **agglutination**, primarily suffixal; rich case system, subject–verb agreement. Word order SOV, strictly prespecifying; numerous participial forms (converbs) for conjunction and subordination of clauses.

References

Comrie, B. 1981. *The languages of the Soviet Union.* Cambridge.

Fortescue, M. 1981. Endoactive-exoactive markers in Eskimo-Aleut, Tungus and Japanese: an investigation into common origins. In L.J. Dorais (ed.), *The language of the Inuit: historical, phonological and grammatical issues*, Quebec. 5–41.

Poppe, N. 1960. *Vergleichende Grammatik der altaischen Sprachen.* Wiesbaden.

alternant

In Bloomfield's terms, the alternation of the elements of emic units (such as **phoneme** and **morpheme**), namely of **allophones** and **allomorphs** (*also* ⇒ **etic vs emic analysis**).

Reference

Bloomfield, L. 1933. *Language.* New York.

alternation

Regular synchronic **sound alternation** in etymologically related words. (a) In automatic (or 'complementary') alternation the sound change is conditioned through the phonetic context, cf. the alternation of [aɪ] ~ [ɪ] in *divine* ~ *divinity, crime* ~ *criminal*, conditioned through change in syllable stress. (b) Morphophonemic alternation differentiates words grammatically, such as through **ablaut** in tense formation (*sing* – *sang* – *sung*) and **word formation** (*bind* – *band* – *bound*), and **umlaut** in plural formation (*woman* – *women*). (⇒ *also* allomorph, morphophoneme)

References
⇒ **phonology**

alternative principle ⇒ **binary opposition**

alveolar [Lat. *alveolus* 'bowl, basin']

Speech sound classified according to its **place of articulation** (**alveolar ridge**), e.g. [t, d, n, s, z]. (⇒ *also* **articulator, phonetic transcription**)

References
⇒ **phonetics**

alveolar ridge (*also* alveolus)

alveolo-palatal ⇒ **lamino-palatal**

Bony ridge behind the upper teeth, in front of the **palate**. (⇒ *also* **articulator, phonetics, place of articulation**)

alveolus ⇒ **alveolar ridge**

amalgam ⇒ **blend**

amalgamation [mixture of a metal with mercury, orig. from Grk *málagma* 'emollient,' through Syrian *mālaĝmā* and Arab. *al-malgàm*]

1 In Katz and Fodor's semantic theory (1963), a step-by-step process employing **projection rules** that combines the meaning of individual constituents to arrive at **sentence meaning**. The process of amalgamation depends upon the syntactic relations of the **constituents** in the **deep structure**. (⇒ *also* **interpretive semantics, principle of compositionality**)

References
Katz, J.J. and J.A. Fodor. 1963. The structure of a semantic theory. *Lg* 39.170–210.

2 In **morphology**, a **back-formation**.

References
⇒ **back formation, word formation**

ambiguity

In natural languages, property of expressions that can be interpreted in several ways, or, rather, that can be multiply specified in linguistic description from lexical, semantic, syntactic, and other aspects. In this sense, ambiguity is different from the complementary term **vagueness** as a designation for pragmatic ambiguousness or indeterminacy, which cannot be systematically described. Ambiguity can be resolved or represented (a) by the competent speaker, who can clarify the different readings with the help of paraphrases, (b) by grammatical analysis, for instance, within the framework of generative syntax models, which accord each possible interpretation of ambiguous surface structures different underlying structures (⇒ **disambiguation**). Depending on whether ambiguity results from the use of specific lexemes or from the syntactic structure of complex expressions, a distinction is drawn between (a) lexical ambiguity (also **polysemy, homonymy**) and (b) syntactic ambiguity (also polysyntacticity, constructional homonymy). The representation and resolution of ambiguity by multiple interpretation is considered to be the most important criterion for the evaluation of the efficacy of grammars, especially as the occurrence of ambiguity plays a decisive part in numerous linguistic problems of description, as, for example, in **quantifiers, negation**, pronominalization (⇒ **personal pronoun**), as well as in **word formation**. In everyday communication, ambiguity is a rather marginal problem, as context, intonation, situation, etc. usually sift out the adequate reading.

References
Gorfein, D.S. (ed.) 1989. *Resolving semantic ambiguity.* Berlin
Kempson, R.M. 1977. *Semantic theory.* Cambridge. 123–138.
Kooij, J. 1971. *Ambiguity in natural language.* Amsterdam.
Su, S.P. 1994. *Lexical ambiguity in poetry.* London.
Zwicky, A. and J. Saddock. 1975. Ambiguity tests and how to fail them. In J. Kimball (ed.) *Syntax and semantics.* vol. 4 New York. 1–36.

Bibliography
Fries, N. 1980. *Ambiguität und Vagheit.* Tübingen.

ambisyllabic

A segment occurring on the boundary of two **syllables**, e.g. [r] in *Arab.*

American English ⇒ **English**

American Sign Language (*abbrev.* ASL) ⇒ **sign language**

American structuralism (*also* post-Bloomfieldian linguistics)

General term for variously developed branches of **structuralism** pioneered above all by E. Sapir (1884–1939) and L. Bloomfield (1887–1949). Although the various schools cannot be clearly distinguished from one another, a distinction is made between two general phases: the so-called 'Bloomfield Era,' and **distributionalism**, with Z. Harris as chief representative. Common to all branches are certain scientific prerequisites which decisively influenced the specific methodological orientation of American structuralism. At first, an interest in dying Native American languages brought about interdisciplinary research in linguistics and anthropology. The occupation with culturally distant and as yet completely unresearched languages, which existed only orally, was a significant catalyst for the parole-oriented, purely descriptive methods of American structuralism (⟹ **langue vs parole**). The works of E. Sapir and F. Boas are significant (⟹ *also* **field work**). The theoretical and methodological format came to be determined in large part by the principles of behaviorist psychology (⟹ **behaviorism**). Following the natural sciences, this direction of research reduces the object of its investigation to sensorally perceptible data and draws on observations made in animal experiments to explain human behavior. This restriction to an exact analysis of objectively experienced data meant that the problem of meaning was deemed an extralinguistic phenomenon, whereas **phonology** and **grammar** were subject to a strictly formal analysis, based on the **discovery procedures** of **segmentation** and **classification**. Methodologically, American structuralism is characterized by empirical (⟹ **empiricism**) and inductive procedures, in which only the identification and arrangement of linguistic elements are relevant for grammatical description. (⟹ *also* **antimentalism, descriptive linguistics, item-and–arrangement grammar**)

References
Bloch, B. 1942. *Outline of linguistic analysis*. Baltimore, MD.
Bloomfield, L. 1926. A set of postulates for the science of language. *Lg* 2. 153–64.
——— 1933. *Language*. New York.
Boas, F. (ed.) 1911. *Handbook of American Indian languages*. 3 vols. New York. (Repr. 1938.)
Fries, C.C. 1927. *The structure of English*. New York.
Gleason, H.A. 1955. *An introduction to descriptive linguistics*. New York.
Harris, Z.S. 1951. *Methods in structural linguistics*. Chicago, IL.
Hockett, C.F. 1958. *A course in modern linguistics*. New York.
Jespersen, O. 1937. *Analytic syntax*. Copenhagen.
Joos, M. (ed.) 1966. *Readings in linguistics*, vol. 1: *The development of descriptive linguistics in America 1925–1956*. Chicago, IL. (Orig. 1957.)
Newmeyer, F.J. 1984. *Linguistic theory in America*. Orlando, FL.
Postal, P.M. 1964. *Constituent structure: a study of contemporary models of syntactic description*. Bloomington, IN.
Sampson, G. 1980. *Schools of Linguistics*. Stanford, CA.
Sapir, E. 1921. *Language*. New York.
⟹ **distributionalism, linguistics (history)**

Amerindian

Language group postulated by Greenberg (1987) which comprises all language families of the Americas with the exception of the **Eskimo-Aleut** and **Na-Dene** languages. The hypothesis of a comprehensive Amerindian language group was highly controversial when first proposed.

References
Greenberg, J.H. 1987. *Language in the Americas*. Stanford, CA.
Ruhlen, M. 1987. *A guide to the world's languages*, vol. 1. Stanford, CA.
⟹ **classification of languages, North and Central American languages**

Amharic

Largest **Semitic** language of Ethiopia with approx. 16 million speakers, official language of Ethiopia.
Characteristics: Amharic is syntactically interesting because of the historically attested structure change from VSO to SOV word order. Unique syllabary (thirty-three consonant signs, each with seven diacritic vowel signs) developed from **Ge'ez**.

References
Hartmann, J. 1980. *Amharische Grammatik*. Wiesbaden.
Leslau, W. 1967. *Amharic textbook*. Wiesbaden.
Richter, R. 1987. *Lehrbuch der amharischen Sprache*. Leipzig.
Schramm, G.M. 1954. *A practical course in the Amharic language*. Washington, DC.

Dictionaries
Kane, T.L. 1990. *An Amharic–English dictionary*, 2 vols. Wiesbaden.
Leslau, W. 1976. *Concise Amharic dictionary*, 2 vols. Wiesbaden.

Bibliography
Leslau, W. 1965. *An annotated bibliography of the Semitic languages of Ethiopia*. The Hague.

amnesia [Grk *amnēsía* 'forgetfulness']

In psychiatry and **neuropsychology**, term referring to loss of memory. In **neurolinguistics**, this term may refer specifically to loss of memory for words.

References
⟹ **aphasia**

anacoluthon [Grk *anakoloúthon* 'inconsistent']

Sudden change of an originally planned sentence construction to an alternative, inconsistent one during sentence production due to unplanned speech. Anacoluthon is considered to be the result of self-correction during speech or also the blend of two different constructions, e.g. *Take mercy on me* (blend of *Have mercy on me* and *Take pity on me*). The 'permissible' ($\Rightarrow$ **left vs right dislocation**) forms of anacoluthon include **prolepsis** (*also* left dislocation), where an element which has been syntactically fronted is represented by a pronoun later in the sentence (*Sardines, I can't stand them*), as well as the so-called **absolute nominative**, where the pronominal antecedent of a fronted nominative does not correspond to this in case: *The memory* (= subject) *of Crete, her stay* (= subject) *in Venice, she became increasingly sad the more she thought about them* (= prepositional object).

References
$\Rightarrow$ **stylistics**

anagram [Grk *anagrammatízein* 'to transpose the letters of one word so as to form another']
A meaningful expression (word, word group, or sentence) rendered from another by scrambling or rearranging the letters, e.g. *dame – made*. Words and expressions which read the same backwards and forwards are called **palindromes**.

Analogists vs Anomalists

Opposing factions of Greek grammarians at the turn of the first millennium from BC to AD whose differences concerned the extent of regularity in grammatical systems. While the Analogists assumed that language is fundamentally logical, and therefore regular and classifiable into systematic patterns (i.e. **paradigms**), the Anomalists were oriented towards language use and held that no regular correspondence exists between language and reality. This is evidenced by the inconsistencies of **gender** in nouns or the problems of **synonymy** and **homonymy**. The position of the Anomalists was ultimately a result of their speculative interest in etymological research, while the Analogists were more engaged in literary criticism, i.e. with the analysis of inadequately transmitted historical texts. The hypothesis of regularity in grammar offered a firm basis for the reconstruction of these texts.

References
Colson, F.J. 1919. The analogist and anomalist controversy. *ClassQ* 13.24–36.
$\Rightarrow$ **linguistics (history)**

analogue communication

Term coined by Watzlawick *et al.* (1967) on the model of analogue calculators (which, like slide rules in contrast to digital calculators, operate with actual quantities) for non-verbal communication that operates mainly with **body language** and **sign language** and is based on a relationship of similarity between the **signal** and the **referent**. Analogue communication is used primarily for the representation of human relations; its semantics is complex, but situation-specific, and is often ambiguous (e.g. laughing, crying). As analogue communication possesses no morphological elements for marking syntactic relations (negation, conjunction), and no temporal differentiation, its translatability into **digital communication** is problematic.

Reference
Watzlawick, P., J.H. Beavin, and D.D. Jackson. 1967. *Pragmatics of human communication: a study of interactional patterns, pathologies and paradoxes.* New York.

analogy

Synchronic or diachronic ($\Rightarrow$ **synchrony vs diachrony**) process by which conceptually related linguistic units are made similar (or identical) in form, especially where previous phonetic change had created a variety of forms. Analogy is often regarded as the result of the move towards economy of form or as a way to facilitate the acquisition of the morphological forms of a language.

The main types of analogy are as follows (see Hock 1986: 167–237). (a) Analogical leveling (also 'paradigmatic leveling'), or the reduction or elimination of morphophonemic alternation within a morphological paradigm ($\Rightarrow$ **morphology, morphophoneme, paradigmatic vs syntagmatic relationship**), especially if there is no semantic differentiation involved (e.g. OE *cēosan – cēas – curon – (ge)coren* vs Mod. Eng. *choose – chose – chose – chosen*, where both the vowel and the consonant alternates have been leveled). (b) Proportional analogy, in which a regularity is carried over to irregular forms according to the formula $A:A' = B:X$ (e.g. the replacement of the original plural form *kine* by the analogized form *cows* according to the pattern *stone:stone-s = cow:X* (= *cow-s*)). Proportional analogy can affect (i) **morphology**, as in the above example; (ii) **orthography** (e.g. ME ‹wolde›, ‹coude›, becoming Mod. Eng. ‹would›, ‹could›, respectively); (iii) **word formation** (in the creation of **neologisms**), e.g. *xeroxing*. Proportional analogy can work in combination with morphological reanalysis in word formation as well (e.g. *Hamburger* with the original meaning 'from Hamburg,' reanalyzed as *ham+burger* and yielding analogized forms such as *cheeseburger, turkeyburger*).

Analogy is also an important factor in **sound change**. When a sound *A* becomes *A'* in word *X*, then it will usually undergo the same change in other words, given the same phonological conditioning (⇒ **phonologically conditioned**). Such inductive rules can become too 'potent,' especially under extralinguistic motivation, creating incorrect forms through overgeneralization (⇒ **hypercorrection**), for example forms found in children's speech, such as **foots* for *feet* or **goed* for *went*.

The concept of analogy goes back to classical times, but was then understood differently from today (⇒ **Analogists vs Anomalists**). Central to the modern notion is the **Neogrammarian** view of **sound laws**, where analogy was set forth as the 'psychological counterpart of physiologically motivated sound laws' (see Boretzky 1977: 131) in order to 'explain away exceptions to supposedly exceptionless sound laws as form associations and thereby justify the autonomy of the sound level' (cf. Sturtevant 1961). The transformational grammarians ⇒ (**transformational grammar**) interpret analogy as an instance of the universal process of simplification. In the case of analogy, a complex group of rules is simplified by a single rule that takes on the function of several others, which are then eliminated.

References
Andersen, H. 1973. Abductive and deductive change. *Lg* 49.765–93.
Anttila, R. 1977. *Analogy.* The Hague.
Becker, T. 1990. *Analogie und morphologische Theorie.* Munich.
Best, K.H. 1973. *Probleme der Analogieforschung.* Munich.
Boretzky, N. 1977. *Einführung in die historische Linguistik.* Reinbek.
Chene, B. de 1975. The treatment of analogy in a formal grammar. *PCLS* 11.152–64.
Hermann, E. 1931. *Lautgesetze und Analogie.* Berlin.
Hock, H.H. 1986. *Principles of historical linguistics.* Berlin. (2nd edn 1991).
Kuryłowicz, J. 1949. La nature des procès dits 'analogiques.' *ALH* 5.15–37.
Lehmann, W.P. 1962. *Historical linguistics: an introduction.* New York. (3rd edn London, 1994.)
Mańczak, W. 1958. Tendences générales des changements analogiques. *Lingua* 7.298–325 and 387–420.
——— 1980. Laws of analogy. In J. Fisiak (ed.), *Historical morphology.* The Hague. 283–8.
Meyerthaler, W. 1979. Aspekte der Analogietheorie. In H. Lüdtke (ed.), *Grundlagen des Sprachwandels.* Berlin. 80–130.
Paul, H. 1880. *Prinzipien der Sprachgeschichte.* Halle. (9th edn. Tübingen, 1975.). Ch. 5.
Rogge, C. 1925. Die Analogie im Sprachleben. *Archiv für die ges. Psychologie* 52.441–68.
Ross, J.F. 1982. *Portraying analogy.* Cambridge.
Sapir, E. 1921. *Language.* New York.
Saussure, F. de. 1916. *Cours de linguistique gén-*

érale, ed. C. Bally and A. Sechehaye. Paris. (*Course in general linguistics,* trans. R. Harris. London, 1983.)
Skousen, R. 1989. *Analogical modeling of language.* Dordrecht.
Sturtevant, E.H. 1961. *Linguistic change.* Chicago, IL. (Orig. 1907.)
Vennemann, T. 1972. Phonetic analogy and conceptual analogy. In T. Vennemann and T. Wilbur (eds), *Schuchardt, the Neogrammarians, and the transformational theory of phonological change.* Frankfurt. 181–204.

Bibliography
Anttila, R. and W.A. Brewer. 1977. A basic bibliography. Amsterdam.

analphabetic ⇒ phonetic transcription

analytic language

A type of classification postulated by Schlegel (1818) under morphological aspects for languages that have the tendency to mark the syntactic relations in the sentence word-externally with the help of function words (⇒ **synsemantic word**), such as prepositions or auxiliary verbs, e.g. Fr. *la maison du père* vs Ger. *Vaters Haus* 'father's house,' Eng. *more beautiful* vs Ger. *schöner.* In contrast see **synthetic language**. The tendency towards analyticity is to be found in most modern languages, the genuine type (e.g. **Chinese, Vietnamese**) is also termed **isolating**.

References
⇒ **language typology**

analytic vs synthetic sentence

In philosophy, a distinction is traditionally drawn between analytic and synthetic statements or sentences. (a) Analytic sentences in the narrow sense (also logically true sentences) are statements that necessarily, i.e. in all possible worlds, are true solely on the basis of their logical form and whose truth can be determined without empirically checking it; cf. *Either it's raining, or it's not raining.* Analytic sentences in the broader sense are those whose truth depends on their syntactic structure and on the meaning of their linguistic elements. They are based on semantic relations such as semantic similarity (i.e. **synonymy**) and semantic inclusion (i.e. **hyponymy**); cf. the statement *Siblings are related to one another.* (b) Synthetic sentences, on the other hand, are those statements about relationships of facts whose truth depends not only on their syntactic or semantic structure, but on extralinguistic factors and experience and thus can be empirically checked; cf. *Bill Clinton is the 42nd president of the United States.* That is, while analytic sentences are necessarily true, synthetic sentences are true or false depending on the composition of the world described by them. See Quine (1951) on the difficulties in distinguishing the two types. ($\Rightarrow$ *also* **formal logic**)

References

Kripke, S. 1972. Naming and necessity. In D. Davidson and G. Harmann (eds), Semantics of natural language. Dordrecht. 253–355 and 763–9 (addendum).

Quine, W.V. 1951. Two dogmas of empiricism. *PhR* 60.20–43.

Bibliographies

Hall, R. 1966. Analytic–Synthetic: a bibliography. *PhQ* 60.178–81.

Petöfi, J.S. (ed.) 1978. *Logic and the formal theory of natural language: selective bibliography.* Hamburg.
$\Rightarrow$ **formal logic**

anaphora [Grk *anaphor-á* 'carrying back; reference'] (*also* anaphoric element, coreference, **pro-form**)

1 Linguistic element which refers back to another linguistic element ($\Rightarrow$ **antecedent**) in the coreferential relationship, i.e. the **reference** of an anaphora can only be ascertained by interpreting its antecedent (see Wasow 1979; Thrane 1980). In this sense, anaphora is contrasted with **cataphora**, where the words refer forward. However, the term 'anaphora' may also be found subsuming both forward and backward reference. If the anaphoric element has the same reference as the antecedent, it is termed coreferent. The occurrence of anaphoras is considered to be a characteristic property of texts; it produces textual coherence ($\Rightarrow$ **textuality**; cf. **text linguistics**). The most common anaphoric elements are **pronouns** (*Philip read a novel. He liked it a lot*); in addition, certain forms of ellipsis can be evaluated as cases of anaphora (*Philip [bought a book], Caroline [0] too*). In **Government and Binding theory**, the traditional term *anaphora* takes a more restrictive sense, referring only to reflexive and reciprocal pronouns (*They hit themselves/each other*). Cf. **binding theory**.

References

Aoun, J. 1985. *A grammar of anaphora.* Cambridge, MA.

Bosch, P. 1983. *Agreement and anaphora.* London.

Fiengo, R. and R. May. 1994. *Indices and identity.* Cambridge, MA.

Fox, B.A. 1993. *Discourse structure and anaphora.* Cambridge.

Graeme, H. 1981. *Anaphora in natural language understanding: a survey.* New York.

Hintikka, J. and J. Kulas. 1987. *Anaphora and definite descriptions.* Dordrecht.

Huang, Y. 1994. *The syntax and pragmatics of anaphora: a study with special reference to Chinese.* Cambridge.

Koster, H. and E. Reuland (eds) 1991. *Long-distance anaphora.* Cambridge.

Kreimann, J. and A.E. Ojeda (eds) 1980. *Pronouns and anaphora.* Chicago, IL.

Kuno, S. 1987. *Functional syntax: anaphora, discourse and empathy.* Chicago, IL.

Reinhart, T. 1983. *Anaphora and semantic interpretation.* Chicago, IL. (Rev. repr. London, 1984.)

Sternefeld, W. 1993. Anaphoric reference. In J. Jacobs *et al.* (eds), *Syntax: an international handbook of contemporary research.* Berlin and New York. 940–65.

Thrane, T. 1980. *Referential–semantic analysis.* Cambridge.

Wasow, T. 1979. *Anaphora in generative grammar.* Ghent.

Weber, B.L. 1979. *A formal approach to discourse anaphora.* New York.

Westergaard, M.R. 1986. *Definite NP anaphora.* Oslo.

Wiese, B. 1983. Anaphora by pronouns. *Linguistics* 21.373–417.
$\Rightarrow$ **binding theory, deictic expression, deixis, discourse representation theory. Government and Binding theory, personal pronoun, reflexive pronoun, text linguistics, trace theory**

2 Stylistic device of ancient **rhetoric** which serves to increase rhetorical force by repeating words or syntactic structures at the beginning of two consecutive sentences or verses ($\Rightarrow$ **epiphora**).

References
$\Rightarrow$ **figure of speech**

anaphoric element $\Rightarrow$ **anaphora**

anaphoric island

A term from Postal (1969) related to the problems of **deixis**. Anaphoric island refers to a relational expression (e.g. *orphan*) which has an implicit, but not overtly expressed, semantic component (e.g. 'child without parents') that cannot be referred to by anaphoric elements. For example, one can say, *Philip's parents are dead; he misses them very much*, but not, *Philip is an orphan; he misses them very much*, despite the fact that the word *orphan* refers to a child without parents.

References

Postal, P.M. 1969. Anaphoric islands. *ChLS* 5.205–37.

——— 1972. Some further limitations of interpretative theories of anaphora. *LingI* 3.349–72.
$\Rightarrow$ **anaphora**

anaptyxis [Grk 'opening, unfolding'] (*also* **epenthesis**, parasite vowel, **svarabhakti**)

Change in **syllable** structure through the insertion of a **vowel** between two **consonants** (one or both of which are usually **sonorants**) for added ease of pronunciation, e.g. [æθəlit] *athlete* or [tʃiminiː] *chimney*. (⇒ *also* **epenthesis, language change, sound change**)

anarthria [Grk *an-* negation, *arthroūn* 'to utter distinctly']

Term used in neurology, **clinical phonology**, and **speech–language pathology** to denote the inability to perform any kind of oral expression or articulation. Anarthria is the severest type of **dysarthria**.

anastrophe [Grk *anastrophé* 'turning upside down']

A **figure of speech** that departs from normal word order, by placing the adjective after the noun, e.g. *three bags full*. Other examples can be found in **topicalization**, e.g. *To my mother, I leave my house* in the writing of a will, and **exbraciation**. Special cases of anastrophe are **hypallage** and hysteron proteron.

References
⇒ **figure of speech**

Anatolian (*also* Hittito-Luvian)

Extinct branch of **Indo-European** consisting of **Hittite**, Lŭvīan Hieroglyphic (Luvian), Palaic, Lydian, and Lycian in Asia Minor, of which Hittite is by far the best known.

References
Baiŭn, D.S. 1987. *Nadpisi i jazyki drevnej Maloi Azii, Kipra, i antichnogo Severnogo prichernomoria.* Moscow.
Friedrich, J. *et al.* 1969. *Altkleinasiatische Sprachen.* Leiden.
Gusmani, R. 1964–86. *Lydisches Wörterbuch*, 2 vols. Heidelberg.
Hawkins, J.D., A. Morpurgo-Davis, and G. Neumann. 1974. *Hittite hieroglyphs and Luwian: new evidence for the connection.* Göttingen.
Heubeck, A. 1969. Lykisch. In J. Friedrich *et al.* (eds), *Altkleinasiatische sprachen: Handbuch der Orientalistik 2, 1, 2.* Leiden. 397–425.
Marazzi, M. 1990. *Il geroglifico anatolico. Problemi di analisi e prospettive di ricerca.* Rome.
Melchert, H.C. 1993. *Cuneiform Luvian lexicon.* Chapel Hill, NC.
——— 1993. *Lycian lexicon.* Chapel Hill, NC.
——— 1994. *Anatolian historical phonology.* Amsterdam/Atlanta.
Neumann, G. 1969. Lykisch. In J. Friedrich *et al* (eds), *Altkleinasiatische Sprachen: Handbuch der Orientalistik 2, 1, 2.* Leiden. 358–96.
Rosenkranz, B. 1978. *Vergleichende Untersuchungen der altanotolischen Sprachen.* The Hague.

Journals
Anatolian Studies
Newsletters for Anatolian Studies
Orientalia
Zeitschrift für Assyriologie

Andean

Alleged language family in South America with approx. twenty languages, considered by Greenberg (1960) to be part of an (even more controversial) Andean-Equatorial language group. The most important language branch of Andean is Quechumaran with the languages **Quechua** (approx. 7 million speakers) and Aymara (approx. 2.5 million speakers) in Peru and Bolivia; in addition, Araucian (also called Mapuche) in Chile also belongs to this group (approx. 0.7 million speakers).

References
Greenberg, J.H. 1960, The general classification of Central and South American languages. In A. Wallace (ed.), *Selected Papers of the Fifth International Congress of Anthropological and Ethnological Sciences.* Philadelphia, PA, 791–4.
⇒ **South American languages**

animal communication (*also* animal language, primate communication (language))

Species-specific systems of communication whose investigation can be carried out only through interdisciplinary effort by (behavioral) psychologists, anthropologists, biologists, linguists, and others. Differences and similarities between animal and human systems of communication provide the basis for hypotheses and theories about the origin and development of human language from earlier forms of communication in the animal kingdom. To be sure, the results of such comparative investigations and their interpretation are largely dependent on the given fundamental definition of language. If natural language is defined as a system of phonetic signs, through the production of which the speaker can express objects, states of affairs (including those that are not spatially or temporally present), and conceptual generalizations in symbols, then the 'language' of animals can be distinguished from human languages accordingly: (a) Natural languages are characterized by the feature of **double articulation**, i.e. complex linguistic expressions are composed of meaningful elements, **monemes** or **morphemes**, which in turn can be described as combinations of the smallest meaningful phonetic elements, **phonemes**. The signals of animal communication, however, can only be analyzed on the first level of articulation for form and meaning, but not as the combination of smaller, more formal elements. (b) Utterances in animal communication are generally reflexes of external signals, i.e. they are connected with released stimuli and thus are not produced intentionally. (c) The meaning of the species-specific signals is apparently known largely by instinct (indeed, in many animals such signals are completely instinctive), and thus do not have to be learned. (d) It is not possible to combine elements of a given communication system to fit new situations, though more recent investigations seem to indicate that chimpanzees may possess latent, though unexploited, combinatory abilities (see Marler 1965). (e) In contrast to natural languages, animal communication cannot express conceptual generalizations with symbols. (f) Furthermore, animals cannot communicate about language by using language, i.e. they cannot formulate metalinguistic statements.

References
Altmann, S.A. 1968. Primates' communication in selected groups. In T.A. Sebeok (ed.) *Animal communication: techniques of study and results of research*. Bloomington, IN. 466–522.
Demers, R.A. 1988. Linguistics and animal communication. In F. Newmeyer (ed.), *Linguistics: The Cambridge survey*. Cambridge. Vol. 3, 314–35.
Gardner, R.A. and B.T. Gardner. 1969. Teaching sign language to a chimpanzee. *Science* 165.664–72.
Hockett, C.F. 1960. The origin of speech. *Scientific American* 203.88–96.
Linden, E. 1974. *Apes, men, language*. London.
Marler, P. 1965. Communication in monkeys and apes. In I. de Vore (ed.), *Primate behavior*. New York. 544–84.
Premack, D. 1971. Language in Chimpanzee? *Science* 172.808–22.
—— 1976. *Intelligence in ape and man*. Hillsdale, NJ.
—— 1990. Words: What are they, and do animals have them? *Cognition* 3.197–212.
Sebeok, T.A. (ed.) 1968. *Animal communication: techniques of study and results of research*. Bloomington, IN.
—— 1972. *Perspectives in zoosemiotics*. The Hague.
Smith, W.J. 1974. Zoosemiotics: ethology and the theory of signs. In T.A. Sebeok (ed.), *Current trends in linguistics*. The Hague. Vol. 12, 561–628.
⇒ **zoosemiotics**

animal language ⇒ **animal communication**

animate vs inanimate

Nominal subcategories referring to the distinction between 'living' creatures (humans, animals) and 'non-living' things. This distinction, which is significant in many languages, is of importance in English in the use of the interrogative/relative pronouns *who* and *which*, in the **Slavic** languages in inflection, in **Bantu** languages in the ordering of nouns into different classes (⇒ **noun class**) and in many languages with split ergativity (⇒ **ergative language**) in the choice of syntactic construc-

tion (see Silverstein 1976).

References
Silverstein, M. 1976. Hierarchy of features and ergativity. In R.M.W. Dixon (ed.), *Grammatical categories in Australian languages*. Canberra. 112–71.
⇒ **hierarchy universal**

Annamese ⇒ **Vietnamese**

Anomalists ⇒ **Analogists vs Anomalists**

anomia ⇒ **aphasia**

answer

A contextually specified type of statement: namely, the desired type of response to a **question**. A distinction is drawn between syntactically independent (*What time is it? – It's four o'clock*) and dependent answers, and syntactically dependent (or grammatically incomplete) ones. The latter are further divided into elliptic (*Four o'clock*) and anaphoric (*Both*, in response to the question *Do you take milk or sugar?*) answers. **Particles** used as answers belong to this last category. Dependent answers are more common than independent ones.

A further distinction must be made between semantically suitable answers, which give exactly the required information, neither less (underinformative answers) nor more (overinformative answers), and pragmatically appropriate answers: the utterance *In Paris* is a semantically suitable (and true) answer to the question *Where is the Eiffel Tower located?*, but if this question is posed, for example, by a tourist in Paris, it is probably a pragmatically inappropriate response, due to a wrong choice of **granularity**.

References
Goffman, E. 1976. Replies and responses. *LSoc* 5.257–313.
Grewendorf, G. 1983. What answers can be given? In F. Kiefer (ed.), *Questions and answers*. Dordrecht. 45–84.
Groenendijk, J. and M. Stokhof. 1984. The semantics of questions and the pragmatics of answers. In F. Landman and F. Veltman (eds), *Varieties of formal semantics: proceedings of the fourth Amsterdam Colloquium, September 1982*. Dordrecht. 143–70.

antecedent

1 In **formal logic**, the first statement (premise) in an argument, e.g. *I can't go to bed yet* in *I can't go to bed yet, because the TV show isn't over* (⇒ **implication**).
2 In linguistics, a linguistic expression to which an anaphoric expression (such as a **pronoun**) refers: *Caroline, who saw the stranger first, ...* (*Caroline* is the antecedent of *who*).

anterior vs non-anterior

Binary phonological **opposition** in articulatory **distinctive feature** analysis (⇒ **articulatory phonetics**, **phonology**). Sounds with the feature [+anterior] (**labials**, **dentals**, and **alveolars**) are made by a constriction at the front of the mouth (in front of the **palate**), while [–anterior] sounds (**palatals**, **velars**, and **vowels**) are constricted at or behind the palate. This distinction describes the opposition of [p, t] vs [ç, k] among others. (⇒ *also* **place of articulation**)

anthroponymy [Grk *ánthrōpos* 'human being,' *ónyma* (= *ónoma*) 'name']

Subdiscipline of **onomastics** concerned with the development, origin, and distribution of personal names.

anthroposemiotics

Subdiscipline of general **semiotics**. Anthroposemiotics studies all systems of human communication, including all natural languages (as primary systems), acoustic and visual forms of communication, **body language**, gesture, and other forms of **non-verbal communication**, whistling and drumming languages, as well as all other substitutes for linguistic communication (e.g. Morse code). More broadly, anthroposemiotics encompasses all secondary systems of representation such as the global representations of art, science, literature, religion, and politics. (⇒ *also* **zoosemiotics**)

References
⇒ **semiotics**

anticipatory assimilation ⇒ **assimilation**

antimentalism [Grk *antí-* 'against'; Lat. *mens* 'mind']

Derogatory designation for L. Bloomfield's behavioristic (⇒ **behaviorism**) approach to research which was based on the detachment of linguistics from psychology and the simultaneous turn towards the exact methods of the natural sciences. The rejection of any form of introspection, the exclusive confinement to observable linguistic data, i.e. surface phenomena (⇒ **empiricism**), and the reduction of the problem of **meaning** to **stimulus–response** mechanisms are recognized as the fundamentals of **taxonomic analysis**. N. Chomsky's mentalistic approach is an opposing view in modern linguistics (⇒ **mentalism**).

References
⇒ **behaviorism**

antipassive

Voice category in **ergative languages**. In the basic construction in ergative languages the patient is regularly treated as a subject, i.e. it is in the zero-marked case, the **absolutive**, and the agent is regularly treated as an object, i.e. it is in the **ergative**. In the antipassive, the patient is marked by an oblique case or an adposition, and the agent is in the absolutive. Additionally, the predicate takes a special antipassive form. The non-basic status of the antipassive is evident from this additional marking of the predicate, different restrictions of use, and a low text frequency.

References
Givón, T. (ed.) 1994. *Voice and inversion*. Amsterdam.
Heath, J. 1976. Antipassivization: a functional typology. *BLS* 2.202–11.
Shibatani, M. (ed.) 1988. *Passive and voice*. Amsterdam.
Van Valin, R.D. 1980. On the distribution of passive and antipassive constructions in universal grammar. *Lingua* 50.303–27.

References
⇒ **ergative language**

antithesis [Grk 'opposition']

Also known as 'contrapositio' and 'oppositio,' antithesis conjoins contrasting ideas, e.g. *steal from the rich and give to the poor*. Antithesis is a favored rhetorical device of **persuasive** speech in politics and advertising.

References
⇒ **advertising language, chiasm, oxymoron, parallelism**

antonomasia [Grk *antonomázein* 'to name instead']

The replacement of a **proper noun** by a reworded appellative (⇒ **common noun**) or a **periphrasis**: *the Almighty* (= *God*), *The eternal city* (= *Rome*). This also works the other way around for the appellative use of a **proper noun**, e.g. *an Odyssey*, or *the Paris of the West* (= *San Francisco*). Antonomasia led to a change in name in the case of the French word *renard*, which became the popular name for a fox, *Reynard*.

antonymy [Grk *antí-* 'against,' *ónyma* (= *ónoma*) 'name']

Relation of semantic opposition. In contrast to the general relation of **incompatibility**, antonymy is restricted to gradable expressions that usually correlate with opposite members of a scale: e.g. *good* vs *bad*. The various positions on the scale cannot be determined absolutely, but rather depend upon the context, e.g. *A large mouse is smaller than a small elephant.* (⇒ *also* **absolute antonymy**, **complementarity**, **gradable complementaries**, **polarity**, **semantic relation**).

References
Cruse, D.A. 1976. Three classes of antonyms in English. *Lingua* 38.281–92.
Hale, K. 1971. A note on a Walbiri tradition of antonymy. In D.D. Steinberg and L.A. Jakobovits (eds), *Semantics: an interdisciplinary reader in philosophy, linguistics, and psychology.* Cambridge, 472–82.
Katz, J.J. 1964. Analyticity and contradiction in natural language. In J.A. Fodor and J.J. Katz (eds), *The structure of language: readings in the philosophy of language.* Englewood Cliffs, NJ. 519–43.
Lehrer, A. and K. Lehrer. 1982. Antonymy. *Ling&P* 5.483–501.
⇒ **lexicology**

aorist [Grk *aóristos* 'indefinite']

Greek term for the perfective **aspect**. In **Greek** and Old Indic (⇒ **Sanskrit**), the aorist was used as a tense form for a succession of actions, especially in literary texts. In its use, it corresponds to the Latin perfect or to the historical perfect (*passé simple*) in French.

References
⇒ **aspect, tense**

A-over-A principle

A universal constraint on the use of **transformations** suggested by N. Chomsky in the **aspects model**. If a transformation refers to a node of category 'A,' and 'A' dominates a node of the same category 'A,' then the transformation can only operate on the dominating node. In particular, this constraint applies to transformations which move or delete noun phrases embedded in the noun phrase: for example, in the noun phrase *the boy walking to the railway station*, the embedded NP *the boy* cannot undergo a transformation alone and be taken out of the noun phrase. Criticism of this principle in later developments of **transformational grammar** can be found in Ross (1967). (⇒ **trace theory**)

References
Ross, J.R. 1967. Constraints on variables in syntax. Dissertation, Cambridge, MA.
⇒ **constraints**

Apache ⇒ **Na-Dene**

apex [Lat. 'tip, point']
The tip of the tongue, primary **articulator** of

apical sounds. (⇒ *also* **articulatory phonetics**)

aphaeresis ⇒ **aphesis**

aphasia [Grk 'speechlessness']

In **neurolinguistics**, cover term referring to a number of acquired **language disorders** due to cerebral lesions (caused by vascular problems, a tumor, or an accident, etc.). In this condition, comprehension and production in the oral and written modalities may be afflicted to varying degrees, thus leading to the differentiation of various aphasic syndromes. Aphasias often co-occur with articulatory disorders such as verbal **apraxia** or **dysarthria**. Excluded from aphasia are language impairments due to sensory deficits (e.g. hearing problems), dementia, or psychological–emotional problems. The classifications of aphasias and their symptoms associated with these syndromes are under debate. The traditional notions and classifications are based on the location of the lesion and the criteria of 'receptive vs expressive' disorder and 'fluent vs non-fluent' speech. The following distinctions have been drawn: (a) motor or **Broca's aphasia** (also expressive or non-fluent aphasia); (b) sensory or **Wernicke's aphasia** (also receptive or fluent aphasia); (c) global aphasia with the most severe impairments in all modalities; (d) anomia or **amnesia** (also nominal aphasia) characterized by difficulties in finding words, semantic **paraphasia**, and occasional minor problems in syntax and comprehension; (e) conduction aphasia with phonemic paraphasia and the inability to repeat what was just said; and (f) transcortical aphasia with possible impairments in the sensory or motor areas associated with no difficulties in the ability to repeat what was just said. For an overview see Benson (1979).

References
Benson, D.F. 1979. *Aphasia, agraphia, alexia.* New York.
Blanken, G. *et al.* (eds) 1993. *Linguistic disorders and pathologies: an international handbook.* Berlin and New York.
Brown, J. 1972. *Aphasia, apraxia, agnosia.* Springfield, IL.
Caplan, D. 1987. *Neurolinguistics and linguistic aphasiology.* Cambridge.
Caplan, D. and N. Hildebrandt. 1987. *Disorders of syntactic comprehension.* Cambridge, MA.
Eling, P. (ed.) 1994. *Reader in the history of aphasia: from Franz Gall to Norman Geschwind.* Amsterdam and Philadelphia.
Gitterman, M. and L.F. Sils. 1990. Aphasia in bilinguals and ASL-signers: implications for a theoretical model of neurolinguistic processing based on a review and synthesis of the literature. *Aphasiology* 4.233–9.

Grodzinsky, Y. 1990. *Theoretical perspectives on language deficits*. Cambridge, MA.
—— (ed.) 1993. *Grammatical investigation of aphasia*. Special issue of *Brain and Language*, Vol. 45(3).
Hecaen, H. and M. Albert. 1978. *Human neuropsychology*. New York.
Howard, D. and S. Franklin. 1988. *Missing the meaning? A cognitive neuropsychological study of the processing of words by an aphasic patient*. Cambridge, MA.
Lesser, R. and L. Milroy. 1993. *Linguistics and aphasia: psycholinguistic and pragmatic aspects of intervention*. London.
Luria, A.R. 1976. *Basic problems of neurolinguistics*. The Hague.
—— 1977. *Neurolinguistics*, vol. 6: *Neuropsychological studies in aphasia*. Amsterdam.
Martins, I.P. *et al.* 1991. *Acquired aphasia in children*. Dordrecht.
Packard, J.L. 1993. *A linguistic investigation of aphasic Chinese speech*. Dordrecht.
Paradis, M. 1987. *The assessment of bilingual aphasia*. Hillsdale, NJ.
Ryalls, J. 1984. Where does the term 'aphasia' come from? *B&L* 21.358–63.
Schnitzer, M.L. 1989. *The pragmatic basis of aphasia: a neurolinguistic study of morphosyntax among bilinguals*. Hillsdale, NJ.
Tyler, L.K. 1992. *Spoken language comprehension: an experimental approach to disordered and normal processing*. Cambridge, MA.
Wulfeck, B. *et al.* 1986. Sentence interpretation in healthy aphasic bilingual adults. In J. Vaid (ed.), *Language processing in bilinguals: psycholinguistic and neuropsychological perspectives*. Hillsdale, NJ. 199–219.

Journals
Aphasiology
Brain and Language
⇒ **neurolinguistics**, **psycholinguistics**

aphemia [Grk *phãnai* 'to speak']

Now obsolete term, used by P. Broca, to refer to **aphasia**.

Reference
Ryalls, J. 1984. Where does the term 'aphasia' come from? *B&L* 21.358–63.

aphesis [Grk 'release, dismissal'] (*also* aphaeresis, deglutination, **procope**, prosiopesis)

The loss of initial **vowel**, **consonant**, or **syllable**, as in *opossum* ~ *possum*, or the loss of initial [k] before [n] in *knee, knight*. (⇒ *also* **apocope**, **syncope**)

References
⇒ **language change**, **sound change**

aphonia [Grk *phōné* 'sound, voice']

In **speech–language pathology**, term referring to an impairment of phonation (the most severe degree of **dysphonia**) due to organic causes (e.g. infection or trauma) or psychogenic causes.

References
Scholefield, J.A. 1987. Aetiologies of aphonia following closed head injury. *British Journal of Disorders of Communication* 22.167–72.
⇒ **voice disorder**

apical

Having the **apex**, or tip, of the tongue as the primary **articulator**. In English, [t, d, n] are apical sounds. (⇒ *also* **articulatory phonetics**, **place of articulation**, **retroflex**)

References
⇒ **phonetics**

apico-alveolar

Speech sound classified according to its (primary) **articulator** (apex = tip of the tongue) and its (primary) **place of articulation** (alveolar ridge). In English, [t, d] are apico-alveolar sounds. (⇒ *also* **articulatory phonetics**)

apico-dental

Speech sound classified according to its primary **articulator** (apex = tip of the tongue) and its **place of articulation** (upper teeth). In English, the 'clear *l*' in *leave* [liːv] is apico-dental. (⇒ *also* **articulatory phonetics**)

apico-labial

Speech sound classified according to its primary **articulator** (apex = tip of the tongue) and its **place of articulation** (lips). Such sounds are found in some **Caucasian languages**, e.g. in Abkhaz. (⇒ *also* **articulatory phonetics**)

apico-post-alveolar ⇒ retroflex

apocopation ⇒ apocope

apocope [Grk 'cutting off']

Loss (synchronic or diachronic) of a final vowel, consonant, or syllable, as in *comb* [koːm] (< [koːmb]) or *come* [kʌm] (< [kome]). (⇒ *also* **aphesis**, **language change**, **sound change**, **syncope**)

apodosis ⇒ protasis vs apodosis

apokoinu [Grk *apó koinoū* 'from what is in common']

Syntactic construction in which two sentences share a common element that can be either in the second sentence or on the border between the two sentences. Apokoinu refers to both sentences grammatically and syntactically, cf. *This is the sword killed him*. It is debatable whether or not so-called contact clauses such as *There is a man below wants to speak to you* are instances of apokoinu or not (see Jespersen 1927).

Reference
Jespersen, O. 1927. *A modern English grammar on historical principles.* Heidelberg. Vol. III 2.132–5. (Repr. London, 1954.)

apophony ⇒ **ablaut**

aposiopesis [Grk 'becoming silent']
A **figure of speech** that shortens a sentence with an unexpected break to express (feigned) politeness, alarm, or concern. The idea, although unexpressed, is clearly perceived: *You can go to h——!* Synonyms: reticence, reserve.

References
⇒ **figure of speech**

apostrophe [Grk 'a turning away']
The turning away from an audience and addressing a second audience of present or absent persons: *Soul of the age! The wonder of our stage! The applause! Delight! May Shakespeare rise!* (Ben Jonson)
⇒ **figure of speech**

appellative function of language (*also* vocative function of language)
The appellative function of language constitutes one of the three subfunctions of the linguistic sign in K. Bühler's **organon model of language**. It refers to the relation between the linguistic sign and the 'receiver,' whose behavior is influenced by the linguistic sign. (⇒ *also* **axiomatics of linguistics**, **expressive function of language**, **representational function of language**)

References
⇒ **organon model of language**

appellative ⇒ **common noun**

application
Term adopted from H.B. Curry is mathematical logic that basically denotes 'linking' and represents the basis of Šaumjan's language theory (⇒ **applicational generative model**).

Applications are formal operations for generating symbols that represent linguistic expression. Through applications linguistic entities are connected to other linguistic entities to form new entities, that is, expressed formally: if X and Y are entities of the most general type *Ob(ject)*, then the combination of X and Y is also an entity of the type *Ob*. Every application can be interpreted as a **function**, but pre-supposes a subclassification of expressions for a meaningful application. Every type of **categorial grammar** is based on application.

References
Curry, H.B. and R. Feys. 1958. *Combinatory logic.* Amsterdam.
Šaumjan, S. 1965. Outline of the applicational generative model for the description of language. *FL* 1.189–222.

applicational generative model
Grammatical model developed by the Russian linguist Šaumjan, who was influenced by the mathematical logic of K. Ajdukiewicz and H.B. Curry. The term 'applicational' refers to the formal operation known as an **application**, i.e. the combination of linguistic units into new linguistic units, which is the foundation for the 'generative' objective of Šaumjan's grammatical theory. Šaumjan begins with a two-level model and differentiates between an abstract genotypical (⇒ **genotype**) language level, which as an ideal, universal semiotic system (⇒ **semiotics**) is the basis for all natural languages, and a phenotypical (⇒ **phenotype**) level, which represents the realization of logical constructs applied to the genotypical level in individual languages. On the genotypical level, there are no spatial relations between linguistic objects; only in the phenotypical level are these produced in a linear order. Unlike N. Chomsky's generative **transformational grammar**, which generates **surface structures**, Šaumjan's generative apparatus serves primarily to generate linguistic **universals**, i.e. highly abstract linguistic objects. A further significant difference from transformational grammar lies in the fact that Šaumjan does not restrict himself to the description of sentence structures, but rather integrates an equivalent process of **word formation** into his model. Therefore, Šaumjan introduces two types of production rules, the 'phrase generator' and the 'word class generator.' The fundamental operation in the formation of complex linguistic units on the basis of elementary units is the application, which largely corresponds to category formation on the basis of the operator–operand relation in **categorial grammar**. The applicational generative model is based on a foundation of very complex mathematics and **formal logic** and, up to now, has been exemplified only in Russian.

References
Ajdukiewicz, K. 1935. Die syntaktische Konnexität. *SPh* 1.1–27.
Curry, H.B. and R. Feys, 1958. *Combinatory logic.* Amsterdam.

Šaumjan, S. 1965. Outline of the applicational generative model for the description of language. *FL* 1.189–222.

applicative

Verbal **voice** which makes a non-subject (⇒ **benefactive**) a direct object, cf. **Swahili** *Mama alipika chakula kwa watoto* 'The mother cooked the food for the children' vs *Mama aliwapikia watoto chakula* 'The mother cooked the children food,' where *pika* is the basic form for 'cook' and *pikia* 'cooked for.'

applied linguistics

Term covering several linguistic subdisciplines as well as certain interdisciplinary areas that use linguistic methods: **language pedagogy, psycholinguistics, language acquisition, second language acquisition, translation, contrastive analysis, language planning, lexicography, computational linguistics, ethnolinguistics, sociolinguistics,** and others. Applied linguistics differs from theoretical linguistics in that the latter is concerned with the formal structure of language as an autonomous system of signs. The term 'applied linguistics' is in some cases misleading, since in many of the subdisciplines language is studied from both a theoretical and practical (i.e. applied) perspective. Moreover, some areas should be considered 'applications' of linguistics. Applied linguistics has become a field of growing linguistic interest, as evidenced by the many journals devoted to these allied studies which have been launched since the 1960s.

References

Allen, P.B. and S.P. Corder (eds.) 1973–7. The *Edinburgh course in applied linguistics*. 4 vols. London.
Corder, S.P. 1973. *Introducing applied linguistics*. Harmondsworth.
Jung, U. 1988. *Computers in applied linguistics and language teaching: ACALL handbook*. Frankfurt.
Kaplan, R.B. (ed.) 1979–. *Annual review of applied linguistics* (Vols 1, 5, 10: *A broad survey of the entire field of applied linguistics*). Cambridge.
Tomic, O.M. and R.W. Shuy (eds) 1987. *The relation of theoretical and applied linguistics*. New York.

Dictionary
Richards, J., J. Platt, and H. Weber. 1985. *Longman dictionary of applied linguistics*. London.

Journals
AILA Review
Annual Review of Applied Linguistics
Applied Linguistics
Bulletin CILA: Organe de la Commission interuniversitaire suisse de linguistique appliquée Neuchâtel
Cahiers de Linguistique Théorique et Appliqué
Gal-Bulletin
Glottodidactica: an International Journal of Applied Linguistics
IRAL: International Review of Applied Linguistics in Language Teaching
Issues in Applied Linguistics
⇒ **computational linguistics**

apposition

Optional **constituent** of a **noun phrase** which agrees syntactically and usually referentially with the nominal **head**. Appositions can be either closely or loosely connected with the nominal head, and preposed or postposed: *Aunt Nelly, Mr Smith, President Jones; Philip, my best friend*. Appositions are typically noun phrases, but are not absolutely limited to this category. Words and phrases in all syntactic categories (nouns, adjectives, adjective phrases, prepositional phrases, clauses, etc.) can occur as appositions, and even non-linguistic units as well: *the film 'One flew over the Cuckoo's nest,' the word 'and,' the symbol $, the musical note A♯*. There are also appositions which are major constituents of the sentence, e.g. *Young people, of course, don't want to hear anything about it.*

References

Burton-Roberts, N. 1975. Nominal apposition. *FL* 13.391–420.
Meyer, C.F. 1992. *Apposition in contemporary English*. Cambridge.
Schindler, W. 1990. *Untersuchungen zur Grammatik appositionsverdächtiger Einheiten im Deutschen*. Tübingen.
Seiler, H. 1960. *Relativsatz, Attribut, und Apposition*. Wiesbaden.

approximant

Manner of articulation in which the primary constriction is more open than for a **stop** or **fricative**. In English, [r, l, j, w, h] are approximants, [l] being **lateral**, the others being central (⇒ **compact vs diffuse**). (⇒ *also* **articulatory phonetics, place of articulation, semivowel**)

approximative system ⇒ interlanguage

apraxia [Grk 'non-action']

Neuropsychological term (⇒ **neuropsychology**) referring to an impairment of the ability to execute movements willfully (i.e. on demand) in spite of the ability to move the respective body parts. In this condition, involuntary movements remain intact. Symptoms of this syndrome are found, for example, in articulation (verbal apraxia or apraxia of speech), in writing of letters of the alphabet (e.g. apraxic **agraphia**) or in gestures and mimicry (bucco-facial apraxia). Minor disturbances are often called dyspraxia. Apraxia, characterized by inconsistent errors and variable substitutions, is distinguished from **dysarthria**. When occurring in childhood and interfering with **language acquisition**, apraxia may be called 'developmental apraxia.' ($\Rightarrow$ *also* **articulation disorder**)

References
Brown, J.W. 1972. *Aphasia, apraxia and agnosia.* Springfield, IL.
Darley, F., A. Aronson, and J.R. Brown. 1975. *Motor speech disorders.* Philadelphia.
Hecaen, H. and M. Albert. 1978. *Human neuropsychology.* New York.
Ryalls, J. (ed.) 1987. *Phonetic approaches to speech production in aphasia and related disorders.* Boston.
$\Rightarrow$ **aphasia, language disorder**

apraxic agraphia $\Rightarrow$ **apraxia**

Arabic

Largest **Semitic** language, spoken in North Africa, the Arabian Peninsula, and in the Middle East (approx. 150 million speakers); the cult language of Islam. A panregional form of Arabic exists which is broadly similar to the language of the Koran (Classical Arabic), as well as various regional dialects (main dialects: Egypt, West North Africa, Syria, Iraq, Arabian Peninsula; Maltese is strongly influenced by Italian). The term 'Old South Arabian' is used for the old independent languages in the southern part of the Arabian Peninsula. A unique alphabet developed from **Aramaic** (consonantal writing system with restricted ability to mark vowels) in two versions: the block letter Kūfī writing and the cursive form Nashī more often used.

Characteristics: rich consonant system (including uvular, pharyngeal and laryngeal sounds) contrasting with a simple vowel system. For its morphology $\Rightarrow$ **Semitic**. Word order VSO; in the dialects often SVO.

References
Bloch, A.A. 1991. *Studies in Arabic syntax and semantics,* 2nd rev. printing. Wiesbaden.
Eid, M. *et al.* (eds) 1990–4. *Perspectives on Arabic linguistics,* 6 vols. hitherto. Amsterdam and Philadelphia, PA.
Fischer, W. and H. Gätje (eds) 1982. *Grundriss der arabischen Philologie,* vol. I: *Sprachwissenschaft.* Wiesbaden.

Classical Arabic
Fischer, W. 1987. *Grammatik des Klassischen Arabisch,* 2nd edn. Wiesbaden.
Wright, W. 1955. *A grammar of the Arabic language,* 3rd edn, 2 vols. Cambridge.

Modern Standard Arabic
Cantarino, V. 1974–5. *Syntax of Modern Arabic prose.* Bloomington, IN and London.
Holes, C. 1994. *Modern Arabic.* London.

Stetkevych, J. 1970. *The Modern Arabic literary language: lexical and stylistic developments.* Chicago and London.

Individual dialects
Ahmed, M. 1992. *Lehrbuch des Ägyptisch-Arabischen,* 3rd rev. and enlarged edn. Wiesbaden.
Aquilina, J. 1973. *The structure of Maltese: A study in mixed grammar and vocabulary.* Msida.
Behnstedt, P. and M. Woidich. 1985–8. *Die ägyptisch-arabischen Dialekte,* 3 vols. Wiesbaden.
Blau, J. 1988. *Studies in Middle Arabic and its Judaeo-Arabic variety.* Leiden.
Cowell, M.W. 1964. *A short reference grammar of Syrian Arabic.* Washington, DC.
Erwin, W.M. 1963. *A short reference grammar of Iraqi Arabic.* Washington, DC.
Fischer, W. and O. Jastrow. 1980. *Handbuch der arabischen Dialekte.* Wiesbaden.
Harrell, R.S. 1962. *A short reference grammar of Moroccan Arabic.* Washington, DC.
Holes, C. 1989. *Gulf Arabic.* London.
Mitchell, T.F. 1956. *An introduction to colloquial Egyptian Arabic.* London.
Owens, J. 1984. *A short reference grammar of Eastern Libyan Arabic.* Wiesbaden.
——— 1993. *A grammar of Nigerian Arabic.* Wiesbaden.
Prochazka, T. 1988. *Saudi Arabian dialects.* London and New York.
Qafisheh, D.A. 1977. *A short reference grammar of Gulf Arabic.* Tucson, AZ.
Rice, F.A. and F.A. Majed. 1979. *Eastern Arabic: an introduction to the Arabic spoken by Palestinian, Syrian, and Lebanese Arabs,* re-issue. Washington.
Talmoudi, F. 1984. *The diglossic situation in North Africa: a study of Classical Arabic/dialectal Arabic diglossia with sample text in 'Mixed Arabic.'* Göteborg.
Tapiero, N. 1979. *Manuel d'arabe algérien moderne.* Paris.

Dictionaries
Deboo, J. 1989. *Jemenitisches Wörterbuch: Arabisch–Deutsch–Englisch.* Wiesbaden.
Piamenta, M. 1990–1. *A dictionary of post-classical Yemeni Arabic,* 2 vols. Amsterdam and Philadelphia.
Ullmann, M. *et al.* 1970–. *Wörterbuch der Klassischen Arabischen Sprache.* Wiesbaden.
Wehr, H. 1979. *A dictionary of Modern written Arabic: Arabic–English,* ed. J.M. Cowan, 4th edn. Wiesbaden.

Bibliographies
Bakalla, M.H. 1983. *Arabic linguistics: an introduction and bibliography.* London.
Woidich, M. 1989. *Bibliographie zum Ägyptisch-Arabischen.* Amsterdam.

Journals
Al-ʿArabiyya: Journal of the American Association of Teachers of Arabic.
Zeitschrift für Arabische Linguistik.

Aramaic

Group of **Semitic** dialects attested since the
tenth century BC, widespread throughout the
Near East from approx. 300 BC to AD 600.
Aramaic was used in the Assyrian, Babylonian,
and Persian Empires and is spoken today in
small enclaves in Syria, Turkey, and Iraq.

References
Arayathinal, T. 1957–9. *Aramaic grammar: method
    Gaspey–Otto–Sauer*. Mannanam.
Beyer, K. 1986. *The Aramaic language: its distribu-
    tion and subdivisions*, trans. J.F. Healey, Göttin-
    gen.
Kutscher, E.Y. 1977. Aramaic. In Ben-Ḥayyim, Z.
    (ed.), *Hebrew and Aramaic Studies*. Jerusalem.
    90–155.
Macuch, R. 1965. *Handbook of classical and modern
    Mandaic*. Berlin.
Marcus, D. 1981. *A manual of Babylonian Jewish
    Aramaic*. Washington, DC.
Noeldeke, T. 1904. *Compendious Syriac grammar*,
    trans. from the 2nd German edn by J. Crichton.
    London.
Rosenthal, F. 1961. *A grammar of Biblical Aramaic*.
    Wiesbaden.
———— (ed.) 1967. *An Aramaic handbook*, 2 parts.
    Wiesbaden.

Bibliographies
Fitzmeyer, J.A. *et al.* 1992–. *An Aramaic bibliogra-
    phy*. Baltimore, MD.
Krotkoff, G. 1990. An annotated bibliography of
    Neo-Aramaic. In W. Heinrichs (ed.), *Studies in
    Neo-Aramaic*. Atlanta, GA. 3–26.

Araucian ⇒ Andean

Arawakan (*also* Maipuran)

Language family in Central and South America
with approx. 80 languages, originally spread
throughout the Caribbean up to Florida. Greenberg (1956, 1987) considered it a member,
together with **Tupi**, of the Andean-Equatorial
language group (**Andean**). Gilij (1780–4) was
one of the first to suspect that several Arawakan
languages were related. Largest language: Goajiro in northern Columbia (approx. 60,000
speakers).

Characteristics: typologically very diverse;
original word order probably SOV with postpositions, under Caribbean influence also OVS;
case markings occur seldom (either **ergative** or
accusative); gender and classifying systems are
common.

References
Derbyshire, D.C. 1986. Comparative survey of mor-
    phology and syntax in Brazilian Arawakan. In
    D.C. Derbyshire and G. Pullum (eds), *Handbook
    of Amazonean languages*. Berlin. 469–566.
Greenberg, J. 1960. The general classification of
    Central and South American languages. In A.
    Wallace (ed.), *Selected Papers of the Fifth Inter-
    national Congress of Anthropological and Ethno-
    logical Sciences*. 791–4. Philadelphia.
———— 1987. *Languages in the Americas*. Stanford,
    CA.
Matteson, E. 1972. Proto-Arawakan. In E. Matteson
    (ed.), *Comparative studies in Amerindian lan-
    guages*. The Hague. 160–242.
Noble, G.K. 1965. Proto-Arawakan and its descen-
    dants. *IJAL* 31.3.2.
⇒ **South American languages**

arbitrariness

Basic property of linguistic **signs**, meaning that
between the signifier (= sound shape, shape of
the sign) and the signified (⇒ **signifier vs
signified**) there is an arbitrary, rather than a
natural, i.e. iconical, relationship. Depending
on the theoretical standpoint, this arbitrariness
refers either to the relationship between linguistic signs and the extralinguistic reality or to the
relationship between a linguistic sign and its
meaning. De Saussure (1916) uses arbitrariness for the relationship between the sound
shape (*image acoustique*) and the *concept*. As
proof for this assumption of arbitrariness, he
adduces the fact that the same object in reality
has different names in different languages.
Arbitrariness does not mean that the individual
speaker can proceed quite freely in the choice
of linguistic constructions: from the standpoint
of **language acquisition** and communication,
the speaker experiences the connection between
sign and meaning as customary and obligatory.
The arbitrariness of the linguistic sign corresponds its 'non-motivatedness' (⇒ **motivation**), which is, however, relativized in **word
formation**, e.g. in compounds such as *living
room*, or in onomatopoeic expressions such as
miaow and *crash* (⇒ **onomatopoeia**). In this
connection, one speaks of 'secondary motivation.' For another view see Wright (1976).

References
Saussure, F. de. 1916. *Cours de linguistique gén-
    érale*, ed. C. Bally and A. Sechehaye. Paris.
    (*Course in general linguistics*, trans. R. Harris.
    London, 1983.)
Taylor, T.J. 1990. Free will versus arbitrariness in the
    history of the linguistic sign. *PICHoLS* 4/1.
    79–88.
Wright, E.L. 1976. Arbitrariness and motivation: a
    new theory. *FL* 14.505–23.
⇒ **sign**

archaism [Grk *archaîos* 'old-fashioned, anti-
quated']

The effective use of outdated expressions for
poetic, ironic, or elevated **connotation**. Scott
and Tennyson, in using archaisms to give color
to conversation in historical romance, rendered
themselves guilty of what Robert Louis

Stevenson called 'tushery': *Knight / Slay me not: My three brothers bod me do it* (Tennyson, 'Gareth and Lynette,' in *Idylls of the King*).

archilexeme [Grk *archí* – 'main, chief,' *léxis* 'word']

Introduced by B. Pottier, the term (coined in analogy to **archiphoneme**) refers to a word whose meaning can be identified in relation to the collective meaning of the **lexical field**. The archilexeme of *birch*, *ash*, *maple*, etc. is *tree*, whose meaning is identical to the meaning of all the elements of the semantic field taken together. An archilexeme does not necessarily have to be the same **part of speech** as the other words in the particular lexical field. In other cases, a lexical field, such as the adjectives of temperature in English, may be lacking an archilexeme. (⇒ *also* **hyperonymy**)

Reference
Pottier, B. 1963. *Recherches sur l'analyse sémantique en linguistique et en traduction mécanique*. Paris.

archiphoneme [Grk *phoné* 'sound, voice']

Prague School term for the complete group of **distinctive features** which are common to two **phonemes** in binary **opposition**. Through **neutralization**, the removal of the differentiating feature can ensue in certain positions, e.g. the loss of the **voiced vs voiceless** opposition in medial position in Amer. Eng. *latter* vs *ladder* [(lærər], so that the archiphoneme of /t/ and /d/ is a non-nasal **alveolar stop**.

References
Davidsen-Nielsen, N. 1978. *Neutralization and the archiphoneme: two phonological concepts and their history*. Copenhagen.
⇒ **phonology**

Arc Pair Grammar ⇒ **relational grammar**

areal linguistics ⇒ **dialect geography**

argot

A **secret language**, roughly corresponding to **cant**, used by beggars and thieves in medieval France. More broadly, argot may refer to any specialized vocabulary or set of expressions (⇒ **jargon**) used by a particular group or class and not widely understood by mainstream society, e.g. the argot of gamblers or the argot of the underworld. (⇒ *also* **slang**)

argument

1 In **formal logic**, term that denotes the **empty slot** of a **predicate** or of a **function**[1]. Depending on how many arguments a predicate requires, it is called either a one-, two-, or three-place predicate. One-place predicates like *x is round* (notation: *round (x)*) assign a property to the argument; in this case the argument/predicate relation corresponds to the subject/predicate distinction in traditional grammar. Multi-place predicates, on the other hand, represent **relations** between arguments: *x is younger than y* (notation: *younger (x, y)*) or *x hands y a z* (notation: *hand (x, y, z)*), whereby the elements are ordered (and therefore not arbitrarily substitutable). The empty positions of the predicate correspond in other terminology to its syntactic **valence**.

2 In **Government and Binding theory** a referential expression which corresponds to a thematic role (⇒ **theta criterion**) in **logical form**. Chomsky characterizes the **deep structure** as a representational level in which every position occupied by an argument is assigned a thematic role and vice versa. The terms 'theta-marked position' and 'argument' are not synonymous in Government and Binding theory, because at s-structure an argument may no longer be in the position which defines the logical argument of the predicate in **surface structure** if a transformation affects that argument. The empty position left by the transformation is theta-marked, but is not an argument. Other empty categories, however, like PRO, are necessarily arguments because they fulfill the function of referential pronouns.

References
Comrie, B. 1993. Argument structure. In: J. Jacobs *et al.* (eds), *Syntax: an international handbook of contemporary research*. Berlin and New York. 905–13.
Grimshaw, J. 1990. *Argument structure*. Cambridge, MA.
⇒ **Government and Binding theory, theta criterion**

3 The distinction introduced by Williams (1981) between 'external vs internal' argument refers to the argument positions of a logical predicate and their realization in the syntax: an argument position of a predicate is syntactically external, if its thematic role appears or has to be assumed outside of the maximal projection (⇒ **X-bar theory**) of the predicate. Thus, subjects, as a rule, are external arguments, for they appear outside of the verb phrase (e.g. *Philip* in *Philip battles against untidiness*), whereas objects stand within the verb phrase and so are internal. arguments. Thus, *Philip* in *Philip's battle against untidiness* is the internal argument of *battle*, for the 'subject' of the noun *battle* appears within the noun phrase.

Williams (1981) uses the terms 'argument' and 'thematic role' synonymously; however, it would be more precise to distinguish between internal vs external thematic roles.

References
Williams, E. 1981. Argument structure and morphology. *LRev* 1.81–114.
———— 1993. *Thematic structure in syntax*. Cambridge, MA.

argument linking

In Lieber's (1983) **word formation**, assumed process in which a **thematic relation** is attributed by a verb or a preposition within the **word structure** to a word-internal or -external argument, e.g. *drawbridge* and *handpaint the picture*, respectively. (⇒ *also* **composition, verbal vs root compound, word syntax**)

Reference
Lieber, R. 1983. Argument linking and compounds in English. *LingI* 14.251–85.

argument position

N. Chomsky's term in **Government and Binding theory** for positions in the **tree diagram** that can be assigned a theta role (⇒ **theta criterion**) independently of any particular lexical item. Therefore, subject and object positions are argument positions, but the **COMP position** is not. The difference between argument positions and non-argument positions is especially important in **binding theory**, where there is an important distinction between **anaphora** and so-called variables. Anaphoras have a local antecedent in an argument position, whereas variables have a local antecedent in a non-argument position. Correspondingly, one differentiates between A-binding and A-bar-binding.

argumentation

Complexly structured linguistic act to explain a state of affairs or to justify an act. The foundation of argumentation is the Aristotelian **syllogism**, in which the truth of the conclusion necessarily arises from the linguistic form and the choice of **arguments** (premise). The so-called 'rhetorical argument' of everyday language (*entymon*), is much more complicated than such 'analytic conclusions,' which form the topics of **formal logic**. The persuasive power of 'rhetorical arguments' depends as much on their linguistic construction as on the credible substantiation of their claims. Arguments can take the form of dialogues, can be embedded in scientific discourse, and are found in all kinds of commercial advertising (⇒ **advertising language**). Argument theory, developed by S.A. Toulmin, C. Perelman, and others, is central to modern rhetoric and modern

text linguistics. It is an inherently interdisciplinary field of study.

References
Benoit, W.L., D. Hample, and P.J. Benoit (eds) 1992. *Readings in argumentation*. Berlin and New York.
Cox, R.J. and C.A. Willard (eds) 1982. *Advances in argumentation: theory and research*. Carbondale, IL.
Freeman, J.B. 1991. *Dialectics and the macrostructure of arguments*. Berlin and New York.
Govier, T. 1985. *A practical study of argument*. Belmont.
Hirsch, R. 1989. *Argumentation, information, and interaction*. Göteborg.
Hirschberg, S. 1990. *Strategies of argument*. New York.
Johnstone, H.W. 1968. Theory of argumentation. In R. Klibansky (ed.), *La Philosophie contemporaine*. Florence. Vol. I, 177–84.
Perelman, C. *et al.* 1969. *The new rhetoric: a treatise on argumentation*. London.
———— 1977. *L'Empire rhétorique: rhétorique et argumentation*. Paris.
Rescher, N. 1966. *The logic of commands*. London.
Richards, T.J. 1978. *The language of reason*. Oxford.
Scriven, M. 1976. *Reasoning*. New York.
Toulmin, S. 1958. *The uses of argument*. Cambridge.
———— *et al.* 1979. *An introduction to reasoning*. New York.
Van Eemeren, F. *et al.* (eds) 1987. *Argumentation: proceedings of the first international conference on argumentation*, 3 vols. Dordrecht.
———— *et al.* (eds) 1987. *Handbook of argumentation theory: critical survey of classical backgrounds and modern studies*. Dordrecht.

Bibliography
Nye, R.A. 1973. *Argument and debate: an annotated bibliography*. New York.

Journal
Argumentation: an International Journal of Reasoning

Armenian

Branch of **Indo-European** consisting of only one language with numerous dialects and approx. 5.5 million speakers located in the former Soviet Union, Turkey, Iran, and in numerous other countries. Written documents date from the fifth century AD. Armenian has its own alphabet which continues to be used today and according to tradition was developed by bishop Mesrop in AD 406, based on **Aramaic** and **Greek**. Armenian contains numerous loan words, particularly from **Persian**.

Characteristics: articulatory contrast of voiceless/voiceless aspirated/voiced; rich case system (seven cases); loss of Indo-European gender system; word order: SVO.

References
Bardakjian, K.B. and R.W. Thomson, 1977. *A textbook of modern western Armenian*. Delmar, NY.

Diakonoff, I.M. 1984. *The pre-history of the Armenian people*. Delmar, NY.

Godel, R. 1975. *An introduction to the study of Classical Armenian*. Wiesbaden.

Greppin, J.A.C. and A.A. Khachaturian. 1986. *A handbook of Armenian dialectology*. Delmar, NY.

Leroy, M. and F. Mawet. 1986. *La place de l'arménien dans les langues indo-européennes*. Leuven.

Solta, G. 1964. Die armenische Sprache. In B. Spuler (ed.), *Handbuch der Orientalistik I*, vol. 7: *Armenisch und kaukasische Sprachen*. Leiden. 80–128.

Thomson, R.W. 1975. *An introduction to Classical Armenian*. Delmar, NY.

Grammars

Hübschmann, H. 1897. *Armenische Grammatik*. Leipzig. (3rd repr. Hildesheim and New York 1972.)

Kogian, S.L. 1949. *Armenian grammar (west dialect)*. Vienna.

Meillet, A. 1913. *Altarmenisches Elementarbuch*. Heidelberg. (Repr. New York, 1981.)

—— 1936. *Esquisse d'une grammaire comparée de l'arménien classique*, 2nd edn. Vienna.

Minassian, M. 1980. *Grammaire d'Arménien oriental*. Delmar, NY.

Schmitt, R. 1981. *Grammatik des Klassisch-Armenischen mit sprachvergleichenden Erläuterungen*. Innsbruck.

Dictionary

Bedrossian, M. 1879. *New dictionary Armenian–English*. Beirut.

Journals

Annual of Armenian Linguistics
Revue des Études Arméniennes

arrow

1 In **comparative linguistics**, the arrow, as well as the '>,' is used to indicate historical developmental processes and should be read 'becomes' or 'changes to.'

2 In **formal logic**, the arrow is a symbol for **logical connectives** of **implication**: $p \rightarrow q$ reads 'p implies q' or 'if p, then q.'

3 In generative **transformational grammar**, the arrow is a symbol for replacement processes (also: expansion symbol): $S \rightarrow NP + VP$ means 'replace the symbol S with the symbols NP and VP.' The double arrow symbolizes the application of a **transformation**: $A + B \Rightarrow B + A$ means 'transform the symbols A and B into the symbol chain B and A.' ($\Rightarrow$ *also* **permutation**)

article [Lat. *articulus* 'joint']

Term from traditional and structural grammar for a **grammatical category** with two elements: definite articles (*the*) and indefinite articles (*a, an*). These elements are now grouped with **determiners** and, in the case of *a/an*, **quantifiers**. There are no articles in **Latin** or in most **Slavic languages**. In English,

French, and **German**, an article occurs before the noun and can only be moved in the sentence together with the noun. However, it can also come after the noun (= postposed) or, as in **Danish** and **Bulgarian**, appear in the form of a suffix. In English, articles are defined either as definite (e.g., *the*, which is a reflex of an original **demonstrative pronoun**) or as indefinite (*a, an*, stemming from the original **indefinite pronoun** and **numeral**, which were identical).

References
$\Rightarrow$ **determiner**

articulation

1 In the broader sense, intentional movement of the primary **articulators** for the creation of speech sounds, including those organs involved in the **airstream mechanism** and **phonation**. ($\Rightarrow$ *also* **articulatory phonetics**)

2 In the narrower sense, the restriction of the airstream by the tongue or lips. Because of their physiological preconditions, the tongue and the lips (especially the lower lips) contribute most effectively to the acoustically or auditively perceivable change of the airstream in that they constrict the airstream to a greater or lesser degree. A distinction is drawn between primary and **secondary articulation** if the airstream must overcome two obstructions. The parts of the lower lip and tongue that are actively used in the changes to the airstream are called primary **articulators**. They give their names to the sounds they form (following in parentheses): lower lip (**labial**[1]); tip of the tongue (**apical**); rim of the tongue (coronal $\Rightarrow$ **coronal vs non-coronal**); blade, or lamina, of the tongue (**laminal**); back, or dorsum, of the tongue (**dorsal**); root, or radix, of the tongue (**radical**). Those parts of the upper and back of the oral cavity and **pharynx** which can be reached completely or partly by the articulators are called **places of articulation** which give their names to the sounds they form (following in parentheses): upper lip (**labial**[2]); upper teeth (**dental**); alveolus (**alveolar**); hard palate (**palatal**); **velum** (**velar**); uvula (**uvular**); pharynx (**pharyngeal**). Since not every articulator can reach every place of articulation, the places of articulation can be simplified and classified (according to the IPA, see the table on p. xix) as the following speech sounds (the detailed terms are given in parentheses): (a) **bilabial** (bilabial); (b) **labio-dental** (labio-dental); (c) **dental** (**apico-dental**, lamino-dental); (d) **alveolar** (**apico-alveolar**, lamino-alveolar); (e) **retroflex** (apico-post-alveolar); (f) **palato-alveolar** (**lamino-post-alveolar**); (g) alveolo-palatal

(**lamino-palatal**); (h) **palatal** (pre-dorso-palatal); (i) **velar** (medio-dorso-palatal); (j) **uvular** (post-dorso-uvular); (k) **pharyngeal** (radico-pharyngeal).

In the articulation of **nasals** the velum is lowered, while in the articulation of **orals** it is raised.

In classifying vowels, instead of pre-dorso-palatal, medio-dorso-velar and post-dorso-velar, the terms 'front,' 'middle,' and 'back' are used to describe those vowels formed by using the front, middle, or back of the tongue (for further differentiation, ⇒ **vowel**).

Depending on the manner in which the airstream is constructed in the oral cavity or pharynx during articulation, a distinction is drawn between: (a) a **stop** with oral closure; (b) a **fricative** (also **spirant**) with friction; (c) an **approximant** with neither oral closure nor oral friction. A further distinction is drawn depending on the manner in which the obstruction of the airstream is bypassed in the pharynx or oral cavity: (d) a **median** with a grooved central opening; (e) a **lateral** with openings to the sides; (f) a **flap** or **tap** with a striking or tapping motion; (g) a **vibrant** (also 'trill') with vibration. Median stops, in which the closure is orally released, are called **plosives**[1]; those that

are formed with **expiration** are called **egressives** or **explosives**. **Affricates** are formed when friction occurs as the closure opens.

References
⇒ **phonetics**

articulation base

1 Group of articulatory characteristics common to all speakers in a **speech community**.

2 Starting position (= resting position) of the **articulators** in the **articulation** of a **speech sound**. (⇒ *also* **articulatory phonetics**)

References
⇒ **phonetics**

articulation disorder

A general term referring to impairments in the execution of **speech sounds**. Such a disorder may arise from a congenital problem (e.g. cleft palate) or a change in the peripheral organs of speech (⇒ **dysglossia**), from an inability to execute articulatory movements voluntarily (⇒ **apraxia**), or from an impairment of the neural mechanisms involved in speaking (⇒ **dysarthria**). It may also involve a faulty temporal and/or spatial co-ordination of movements of the speech organs. Recently, in

Articulation

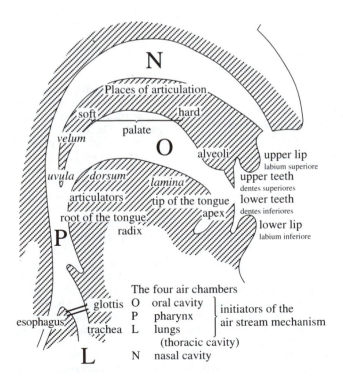

The air chambers during articulation

a: click   **b**: ejective
c: nasal vowel   **d**: oral vowel
e: nasal consonant   **f**: explosive

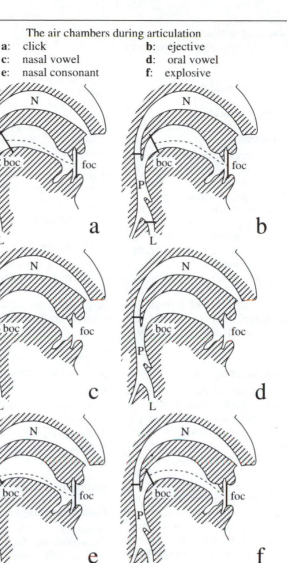

foc	front oral cavity	P	pharynx	——	stop
moc	mid oral cavity	L	lungs	⊢--⊣	area in which a
boc	back oral cavity	N	nasal cavity		stop is formed

speech-language pathology and **clinical lin-guistics**, this term has been distinguished from **phonological disorder**, which refers to the difficulty in acquiring the underlying categories of speech sounds though not in executing them. In Europe, the term may also refer to speech disorders that depend on the situation or relate to fluency, such as stuttering (⇒ **dysfluency**).

References
Benthal, J. and N.W. Bankson. 1988. *Articulation and phonological disorders*, 2nd rev. edn. Engle-wood Cliffs, NJ.
Ryalls, J. (ed.) 1987. *Phonetic approaches to speech*

production in aphasia and related disorders. Boston.

articulator (*also* articulatory organ)

1 In the narrow sense (*also* active articulator), the (relatively) mobile organs used for **articulation**, especially the lips, lower jaw, and the various parts of the tongue. The primary active articulator is the single most relevant active articulator.

2 In the broader sense, all organs involved in **articulation**, i.e. the movable organs as well as

the stationary **places of articulation**, the **glottis**, lungs, and so on. (⇒ *also* **articulatory phonetics**)

articulatory canal ⇒ **vocal tract**

articulatory organ ⇒ **articulator**

articulatory phonetics

Subdiscipline of general **phonetics** which describes the physiological processes occurring in the **vocal tract** during speech. From a physical standpoint, **speech sounds** are resonances, the production of which involves four factors: (1) **airstream mechanism**, the initiation of an actual or potential flow of air; (2) **phonation**, the activity of the **larynx** (other than for initiation or **articulation**); (3) the position of the **velum**, yielding **nasal** or nasalized sounds on the one hand and **oral** sounds on the other; and (4) the **place of articulation** and **manner of articulation**. (1) and (4) are factors in all speech sounds, (2) and (3) only in **pulmonic** sounds.

artificial intelligence (*abbrev.* AI)

Subdiscipline of computer science that attempts to simulate and understand human intelligence and cognitive abilities by using machines (i.e. computers). Two important currents can be seen in artificial intelligence: (a) an orientation towards cognition whose goal is to describe and explain cognitive processes; and (b) an orientation towards applied theory which has focused on constructing working computer systems. Every type of interaction between humans and machines is based on concepts of artificial intelligence. Its areas of application include theorem proving, knowledge-based **expert systems**, machine learning programs, **machine-aided translation**, and comprehending and generating spoken language, among many others.

References
Barr, A. and E.A. Feigenbaum, (eds) 1981–2. *The handbook of artificial intelligence*, 3 vols. Los Altos, CA.
———, P. Cohen and E.A. Feigenbaum (eds) 1989. *The handbook of artificial intelligence*. vol. 4. Los Altos, CA.
Broadbent, D. (ed.) 1992. *The simulation of human intelligence*. Oxford.
Charniak, E. 1994. *Statistical language learning*. Cambridge, MA.
Johnson-Laird, P. 1988. *The computer and the mind*. Cambridge, MA.
Krause, P. and D. Clark, 1993. *Representing uncertain knowledge: an artificial intelligence approach*. Dordrecht.
Paris, C.L., *et al.* 1991. *Natural language generation in artificial intelligence and computational linguistics*. Dordrecht.
Partridge, D. and Y. Wilks 1990. *The foundation of artificial intelligence*. Cambridge.
Rich, E. 1983. *Artificial intelligence*. London.
Shapiro, S. (ed.) 1987. *Encyclopedia of artificial intelligence*. New York.
Vollnhals, O. 1992. *Multilingual dictionary of artificial intelligence*. London.
Way, E.C. 1991. *Knowledge representation and metaphor*. Dordrecht.

Journal
Artificial Intelligence

artificial language

1 In contrast to a **natural language**, an artificially created language system (a) for purposes of international understanding (⇒ **planned language**), (b) as a logical sign system for explicit description (for eliminating ambiguities) of scientific systems (⇒ **formal language**), (c) as a symbolic language for computer programs (⇒ **computational linguistics, programming language**).

Reference
Garner, M. 1987. *Artificial languages: a critical history*. London.

2 An imitation of natural language through electro-acoustic processes. (⇒ *also* **synthetic speech**)

Arumanian ⇒ Rumanian

Asiatic languages

Genuinely Asiatic language groups are **Altaic, Sino-Tibetan, Dravidian**, and **Austro-Thai** and possibly some isolated language (groups) such as **Paleo-Siberian, Burushashki**, and Ket as well. It is uncertain whether or not **Japanese** or **Korean** belong to this group. Many of these languages belong to language groups spanning a number of continents (**Indo-European, Caucasian languages, Uralic, Afro-Asiatic**, Austronesian ⇒ **Malayo-Polynesian**).

The genetic distribution of the Asian languages was already understood fairly well by the eighteenth century, and a number of the individual languages had been studied even earlier.

References
Comrie, B. 1981. *The languages of the Soviet Union*. Cambridge.
Shapiro, M.C. and H.F. Schiffman (eds) 1983. *Language and society in South Asia*. Dordrecht.

ASL (American Sign Language) ⇒ **sign language**

aspect

Aspect refers to the internal temporal structure of a verb or sentence meaning. The most important aspectual distinctions are the following: (a) **stative vs active**, by which situations are classified into states, which do not involve a change in time (e.g. *own, know, like*), and processes, activities, or actions, which refer to an active situation (e.g. *blossom, hit*). (b) **perfective vs imperfective, durative vs non-durative, progressive vs non-progressive**. Imperfective, durative, or progressive aspect refers to situations which are viewed as temporally not delimited (e.g. *work, read, be burning*). Perfective, non-durative, non-progressive, or **punctual** aspect implies a temporal boundary of the situation denoted by a verb or sentence (e.g. *burn down, have read a novel*). (c) Repetition or frequency with **habituals** (*used to drink*) and **iteratives** (*flutter*). (d) Reference to causality is sometimes also related to aspect. Causality distinguishes an action which is caused by an agent (e.g. *hit, read*) from a state or process (*know, blossom*); ⇒ **process vs action**. With **causative verbs** (*fell, drench*) the causative component is added by morphological derivation (cf. *fall, drink*).

There is considerable disagreement in the treatment and description of aspect categories. This is partly due to the diverse grammatical and lexical means of expressing aspectual notions. The interaction of lexical meaning of verbs, the morphological form of the verb, the type of argument noun phrases (singular vs plural, **mass noun** vs **count noun**), adverbials, auxiliaries, tenses, etc. may contribute to the aspectual character of a sentence.

In English, most verbs have a simple and a progressive form (*I sing* vs *I am singing*) and the selection of the progressive is restricted, in general, to verbs whose lexical meaning is not stative (**I am knowing*). In **Russian**, the durative verb lexemes (e.g. *spat* 'to sleep,' *zit* 'to live, to dwell,' *sidet* 'to sit') have, in general, only imperfective forms, whereas non-durative verb lexemes may have both an imperfective and a perfective form, e.g. *probuzdat'sja* (imperf.) *probudit'sja* (perf.), 'to wake up,' *naxodit/najti* 'to find,' *umirat/umeret* 'to die'. The type of argument noun phrases influences aspect categorization: *he ate apples* (durative, imperfective) vs *he ate an apple* (non-durative, perfective). In **Finnish**, the case of the object noun phrase is relevant for the aspect of the sentence: *luen kirjaa* (partitive) 'I read some of the book' (durative, imperfective) vs *luen kir-*

jan (acc.) 'I read the book' (non-durative, perfective). The choice of adverbials denoting the duration of the event is also restricted by aspect: *she worked in Texas for two years* (durative, imperfective) vs *she wrote a novel in two years* (non-durative, perfective). There are also aspect-indicating verbs or auxiliaries: *she started working* (non-durative, inchoative), *she finished working* (non-durative, completive). Closely related to **Aktionsart**.

References
Bache, C. 1982. Aspect and Aktionsart: towards a semantic distinction. *JL* 18.57–72.
Bybee, J., R. Perkins, and W. Pagliuca. 1994. *The evolution of grammar: tense, aspect and modality in the languages of the world.* Chicago, IL.
Comrie, B. 1976. *Aspect: an introduction to the study of verbal aspect and related problems.* Cambridge.
Dahl, Ö. 1985. *Tense and aspect systems.* Cambridge.
Forsyth, J. 1970. *A grammar of aspect: usage and meaning in the Russian verb.* Cambridge.
Groot, C. de and H. Tommola (eds) 1984. *Aspect bound: a voyage into the realm of Germanic, Slavonic and Finno-Ugrian aspectology.* Dordrecht.
Hoepelmann, J. 1981. *Verb classification and the Russian verbal aspect: a formal analysis.* Tübingen.
Nedjalkou, V.P. (ed.) 1988. *Typology of resultative constructions.* Amsterdam.
Rohrer, C. (ed.) 1978. *Papers on tense, aspect and verb classification.* Tübingen.
Saurer, W. 1984. *A formal semantics of tense, aspects and Aktionsart.* Bloomington, IN.
Steinitz, R. 1981. Zum Status der Kategorie 'Aktionsart' in der Grammatik (oder: Gibt es Aktionsart im Deutschen?). *LSt* 76.1–122.
Tedeschi, P.J. and A. Zaenen (eds). 1981. *Tense and aspect.* New York.
Thelin, N.B. (ed.) 1990. *Verbal aspect in discourse: contributions to the semantics of time and temporal perspective in Slavic and non-Slavic languages.* Amsterdam and Philadelphia.
Tobin, Y. 1993. *Aspect in the English verb.* London.
Vendler, Z. 1967. *Linguistics in philosophy.* Ithaca, NY.
Verkuyl, H.J. 1972. *On the compositional nature of the aspects.* Dordrecht.
—— 1989. Aspectual classes and aspectual composition. *Ling&P* 12.39–94.
—— 1993. *A theory of aspectuality. Cambridge.*
⇒ **tense**

aspects model (*also* aspects theory, standard theory)

An abbreviated name for the model proposed in Chomsky's (1965) book *Aspects of the Theory of Syntax*, in which he revised his suggested model for **transformational grammar** published in *Syntactic Structures* in 1957. The most important changes and extensions of the aspects model are: (a) the differentiation between the terms competence and performance (⇒ **competence vs performance**), **grammaticality** and **acceptability**, **surface structure** and **deep structure**; (b) instead of generalized transformations, **recursiveness** is part of the **base components** of the grammar; (c) the lexicon is added to the grammar as a base component and the level of **semantics** is treated as an interpretive component. ⇒ **transformational grammar** for the extensions of the aspects model.

References
⇒ **transformational grammar**

aspects theory ⇒ aspects model

aspirate [Lat. *aspirare* 'to breathe']

1 (Usually voiceless) aspirated **plosive** (⇒ **voiced vs voiceless**, **aspiration**), as [tʰ] in Eng. [tʰi] *tea*.

2 One of the posited series of voiced aspirates in Proto-**Indo-European** and its etymological equivalent in the **daughter languages**. (⇒ *also* **historical linguistics**, **laryngeal theory**)

References
⇒ **phonetics**

aspiration

Voiceless breath (⇒ **voiced vs voiceless**) before (= preaspiration) or after (= postaspiration) the formation of a (usually voiceless) **stop** or **fricative**, due to the preceding (or succeeding) opening of the **glottis**, especially after (or before) the formation of a voiced **vowel**, e.g. [ʰp], [ʰk] in **Icelandic** [ˈhɛʰpːɪn] 'happy,' [ˈlYʰkːa] 'luck'; [ʰk'] in **Georgian** [ʰk'idia] '(he/she/it) hangs'; or Eng. [pʰ], [tʰ], [kʰ] in [pʰæn] *pan*, [tʰæn] *tan*, [kʰæn] *can*. The degree of air pressure determines the strength of aspiration. (⇒ *also* **articulatory phonetics**, **fortis vs lenis**, **phonotactics**)

References
⇒ **phonetics**

Assamese ⇒ Indo-Aryan

assertion ⇒ allegation, statement

assibilation

1 Formation of an epenthetic (⇒ **epenthesis**) **sibilant** through **palatalization** between a dorsal stop (⇒ **dorsal**, **stop**) and a following front **vowel** [i, e], e.g. the [s] in German *Nation* [natsion].

2 Change of [g] and [k] to sibilants before palatal sounds, e.g. OE *cirice* > Mod. Eng.

church; or Lat. *centum* (with initial [k]) > Fr. *cent* (with initial [s]). (⇒ *also* **assimilation**, **sound change**)

assimilation [Lat. *assimilare* 'to make like (to)']

Articulatory adaptation of one sound to a nearby sound with regard to one or more **features** (⇒ **articulation**). Assimilation has numerous aspects. (a) Assimilation can be a matter of (i) the **place of articulation**, e.g. the n in *incomplete* pronounced as [ŋ]; (ii) the **manner of articulation**, e.g. /in/ > [ir] in *irregular*); or (iii) the glottal state, e.g. the pronunciation of the plural **morpheme** {-s} in *dogs* [dɔgz] and *cats* [kæts]. (This is also called 'voicing assimilation.') (b) Depending on the direction of influence in a sound sequence, a distinction is drawn between progressive (or perseverative) assimilation, in which a following sound adapts itself to a preceding one (as in **vowel harmony**), and regressive (or anticipatory) assimilation, in which a preceding sound takes on a feature or features of a following sound (as in **umlaut**). (c) A distinction is also made between complete and partial assimilation. Complete assimilation describes the leveling of two sounds (as in *irregular*, above), which is always the case if the sounds are differentiated by only one feature. Partial assimilation refers to the change of only one of several features (as in *incomplete*, above). (d) Assimilation can also be reciprocal (also called 'bi-directional' or 'fusional'), when a mutual adaptation occurs, and a third sound replaces the two original sounds: [ti] > [ʃ] in *nation* [ˈneiʃən]. (e) If the process involves adjacent sounds, it is a case of contact assimilation. Otherwise it is called distant assimilation. (⇒ *also* **coarticulation**, **labialization**, **monophthongization**, **palatalization**)

References
Vennemann, T. 1972. Phonetic detail in assimilation. Problems in Germanic phonology. *Lg* 48.863–92.
⇒ **phonetics**, **sound change**

association

In psychology, process of conscious association of two or more aspects of the imagination. This simultaneous occurrence of several experiential units is triggered by specific associative rules such as temporal and spatial contiguity as well as similarity and contrast between the experienced content. Associations play a central role in the investigation and fostering of fantasy, thinking, **memory**, and in all learning processes. In **psycholinguistics**, associations (in connection with the neobehaviorist psychology) are defined as a connection between stimulus and response (or stimulus and reaction) and are used for **language tests**, especially to explain meaning (⇒ **stimulus–response**). Here a distinction is drawn between immediate associations (strings of words that are triggered by a particular stimulus word) and mediating associations that are assumed to function as not directly observable mediators in stimulus–response processes.

References
Anderson, J.R. and G.H. Bowers. 1973. *Human associate memory*. Washington, DC.
⇒ **mediation**, **memory**, **psycholinguistics**

associative meaning ⇒ **connotation**[1]

Assyrian ⇒ **Akkadian**

asterisk [Grk *asterískokos* 'little star']
Typographical symbol used in linguistics in two ways: (a) to mark an unattested protoform (⇒ **proto**) which has been hypothesized using comparative **reconstruction** or internal reconstruction, e.g. Proto-**Indo European** **ek̯uos* 'horse'; or (b) to characterize an ungrammatical utterance, e.g. **Eve eated the apple*. The asterisk has been used in this second fashion since Høysgaard in the mid-eighteenth century.

References
Høysgaard, J.P. 1751. *Methodisk Forsøg til en Fulstaendig Dansk Syntax*. Copenhagen.
Koerner, E.F.K. 1975. Zu Ursprung und Geschichte der Besternung in der historischen Sprachwissenschaft. *ZUS* 89.185–90.

asyndetic sentence construction ⇒ **asyndeton**

asyndeton [Grk 'unconnected']
Omission of conjunctions between words, phrases or clauses. Caesar used asyndeton in his famous expression *Veni, vidi, vici* 'I came, I saw, I conquered.' The opposite of asyndeton is **polysyndeton**. (⇒ *also* **syndesis**)

atelic ⇒ **durative vs non-durative, telic vs atelic**

aterminative vs terminative ⇒ **durative vs non-durative**

Athabaskan ⇒ **Na-Dene**

athematic verb ⇒ **stem vowel**

ATN grammar ⇒ **augmented transition network grammar**

atomic concept ⇒ **semantic primitive**

atomic sentence
In **propositional logic** (⇒ **formal logic**), an elementary sentence of a language that does not itself contain any sentence in this language (and thus also no **logical connectives**). Thus, *Philip is tall* is an atomic sentence, but not *Philip is tall and stocky*, since this expression consists of two sentences that are connected by the logical connective *and*: *Philip is tall and Philip is stocky*.

attenuative ⇒ **diminutive**

attribute
Dependent expression which modifies a nominal **head**. The term is not used uniformly everywhere; originally, it related only to attributive adjectives in English and Romance and some German linguistic literature, whereas in more recent grammars it is used as a designation for complements to any syntactic category in the sentence (with the exception of the verb). Attributes characterize or identify persons or states of affairs with respect to certain features; their semantic function is usually **predication**. Formally, attributes can be represented by different categorial fillings, e.g., as attributive **adjective**: *(the) new (book)*, genitive attribute: *Salomé's dance*, prepositional attribute: *the day at the sea*, adverbial attribute: *(this weather) today*, infinitive group: *the right to vote*, restrictive clause: *(the book) that interests us the most*, **apposition**: *(this book), a real masterpiece*.

References
Burton-Roberts, N. 1975. *Nominal apposition*. FL 13. 391–419
Huddleston, R. 1971. *The sentence in written English*. London.
Quirk, R., S. Greenbaum, G. Leech, and J. Svartvik 1985. *A comprehensive grammar of the English language*. London.
Seiler, H. 1960. *Relativsatz, Attribut und Apposition*. Wiesbaden.

attributive vs referential reading (*also* de dicto/intensional vs de re/extensional reading)
Term introduced by Donnellan (1966) to distinguish between various readings of definite **noun phrases**. The sentence *Caroline wants to see the play that is being presented at the theater tonight* is ambiguous. Either the speaker means a particular play, e.g. *Hamlet*, which he/she assumes will be presented tonight – though that may not necessarily be the case – (referential reading), or he/she means whatever play for which the noun phrase could be true, no matter what play that might be (attributive or non-referential reading). In the case of the

attributive reading, the form of the expression is essential for determining meaning. This is not so for the referential reading, i.e. any form is possible as long as the identity of the referent is clear.

References

Bartsch, R. 1976. The role of categorial syntax in grammatical theory. In A. Kasher (ed.), *Language in focus*. Dordrecht. 503–39.

Donnellan, K. 1966. Reference and definite descriptions. *Philosophische Rundschau* 75.281–304.

Kripke, S.A. 1977. Speaker's reference and semantic reference. *Midwest Studies in Philosophy* 2.225–76.

Lieb, H.H. 1979. Principles of semantics. In F. Henry and H. Schnelle (eds), *Syntax and semantics*, vol. 10: *Selections from the third Groningen round table*. New York. 353–78.

Montague, R. 1973. The proper treatment of quantification in ordinary English. In K.J.J. Hintikka *et al.* (eds), *Approaches to natural languages*. Dordrecht. 221–42.

Partee, B.H. 1970. Opacity, reference and pronouns. *Synthese* 21.359–85. (Repr. in D. Davidson and G. Harman (eds), *Semantics of natural language*. Dordrecht, 1972. 415–41.)

Searle, J.R. 1979. Referential and attributive. *The Monist* 13.190–208. (Repr. in *Expression and meaning*. Cambridge, 1979. 137–61.)

audio-lingual method [Lat. *audire* 'to hear,' *lingua* 'tongue'] (*also* audio-lingualism)

Method of foreign-language instruction based on structuralist (⇒ **structuralism**) principles and drawing on **stimulus-response** theory. The audio-lingual method became predominant in the United States in the late 1950s and throughout the 1960s, as the US government expanded its efforts to increase the number of people learning and teaching foreign languages. Its proponents believed that language learning is primarily a matter of developing proper mechanical habits, through positive reinforcement of correct utterances; that **target language**[2] forms should be presented in spoken form before introducing their written representation; that analogy is a more effective mode of language learning than analysis, and that linguistic forms should be presented in context rather than as isolated items. Characteristic of audio-lingualism is the extensive use of **pattern practice** in instruction. (⇒ *also* **language pedagogy, second language acquisition**)

References

Brooks, N. 1964. *Language and language learning: theory and practice*. 2nd ed. New York.

Brown, H.D. 1987. *Principles of language learning and teaching*. Englewood Cliffs, NJ.

Chastain, K. 1969. The audio-lingual habit theory versus the cognitive code-learning theory: some theoretical considerations. *IRAL* 7: 79–106.

Chastain, K. 1971. *The development of modern language skills: theory to practice*. Chicago.

Chomsky, N. 1959. A review of B.F. Skinner's *Verbal behavior*. *Lg* 355.1: 26–58.

Moulton, W. 1966. *A linguistic guide to language learning*. New York.

Richards, J.C. and Rodgers, T.S. 1986. *Approaches and methods in language teaching*. Cambridge.

Rivers, W.M. 1964. *The psychologist and the foreign language teacher*. Chicago, IL.

Skinner, B.F. 1957. *Verbal behavior*. New York.

audio-lingualism ⇒ audio-lingual method

auditory phonetics

Branch of **phonetics** which studies the anatomical and neurophysiological processes involved in the perception and decoding of spoken linguistic signals. In a comprehensive study of how language is comprehended, situational, psychological, and other such components are studied in auditory phonetics alongside of the capacity to perceive and differentiate speech sounds.

augment

The augment is a word-forming element preserved in some older **Indo-European** languages (**Greek, Indo-Iranian, Armenian,** and Phrygian) for the designation of the past. Originally probably an adverb **é* with the meaning 'then, in the past,' it later became a verbal prefix in the indicative mood of the **imperfect, aorist** and past perfect (e.g., Grk *éphere* : Skt *ábharat* : Arm. *eber*, all 'carried').

References
⇒ **Greek, Indo-European**

augmentative

1 In the narrow sense, **denominal** or **deadjectival** derivations by means of particular suffixes (especially in the southern Romance languages), that denote an enlargement of the designated object, cf. Ital. *naso* vs *nasone* ('big nose'), Span. *hombre* vs *hombrote* ('large man').

2 In a broader sense, any type of intensification of the basic meaning of a word by the addition of prefixes or prefixoids such as *arch-*, *extra-*, *macro-*, *mega-*, *super-*, and the like.

References
⇒ **word formation**

augmented transition network (ATN) grammar

Formalism used in **computational linguistics**[1]

for analyzing (and generating) sentences, which was developed around 1970 as an alternative model to **transformational grammar** that could be easily implemented on computers. Instead of **phrase structure rules** (PS rules), augmented transition network grammar uses an equivalent set of finite state automata ($\Rightarrow$ **finite state automaton**, **formal language**) that are called up recursively. Corresponding to the expansions of PS rules are permissible transitions between automata states; the working of **transformations** (e.g. in word order, congruence, active–passive–converse, **control**, etc.) is modeled by checking and modifying the register contents of the computer (through auxiliary functions). The latter represent augmentations to the simpler (recursive) network grammars that are equivalent to **context-free** (PS) **grammars**. Moreover, it is possible to associate any kind of actions – for example, ones which form **tree diagrams**, semantic representations, etc. – with the transitions between states. In this way, the augmented transition network grammar is not only a recognizing automaton, but also a transducer. Since the use of registers is, in principle, not subject to any limitations and all the possibilities of a conventional programming language can be used, the augmented transition network grammar is as powerful as the universal **Turing machine**. For the application of augmented transition network grammars to **psycholinguistics**, see Halle, Bresnan, and Miller (1978).

References
Bates, M. 1978. The theory and practice of augmented transition network grammars. In L. Bolc (ed.), *Natural language communication with computers*. Berlin. 191–259.
Bobrow, D. and B. Fraser. 1969. An augmented state transition network analysis procedure. *Proceedings of the IJCAI* 69.557–67.
Halle, M., J. Bresnan, and G. Miller (eds) 1978. *Linguistic theory and psychological reality*. Cambridge, MA.
Kaplan, R. 1972. Augmented transition networks as psychological models of sentence comprehension. *AI* 3.77–100.
Rumelhart, D. 1977. *Introduction to human information processing*. New York.
Thorne, J. *et al.* 1968. The syntactic analysis of English by machine. In D. Mitchie (ed.), *Machine intelligence*. New York.
Wanner, E. and M. Maratsos. 1978. An ATN approach to comprehension. In M. Halle, J. Bresnan, and G. Miller (eds), *Linguistic theory and psychological reality*. Cambridge, MA. 119–61.
Woods, W.A. 1970. Transition network grammars for natural language analysis. *Communications of the ACM* 13.591–606.
$\Rightarrow$ **formal language**

a-umlaut $\Rightarrow$ breaking

Australian languages

Group of languages which includes all the languages of Australia, numbering approx. 170 languages, many nearly extinct, with about 30,000 speakers. The largest language family, Pama-Nyungan, covers nearly the whole continent; twenty-eight smaller and typologically divergent languages are concentrated on the northern coast. The most important language, Pitjantjatjara (Western Desert), is the trade language of West Australia.

The main research on the Australian languages, with a few exceptions (e.g. the work of the Australian farmer E.M. Curr (1886), the Austrian priest W. Schmidt (1919) and the Australian A. Capell (1956)), did not start until 1960. Today numerous grammars as well as broader investigations are available on the individual languages. Languages such as Dyirbal or Warlpiri play an important role in current linguistic discussions.

Characteristics: numerous common Australian words due to intercultural contact; this, as well as the tabooization and coining of words, makes reconstruction difficult.

Characteristics of the Pama-Nyungan languages: simple phonetic system (only three vowels, no fricatives, no voice contrast, but a partially higher number of articulation oppositions). Complex words (suffixes), complex verb formation (tense, mood, government), **noun classes** with **agreement**; complex number categories (with dual), which often contrast with a very simple number system. They are primarily **ergative languages**, some languages (e.g. Dyirbal) showing clear syntactic ergativity. Extremely free word order. Complex locative **deixis**, including affixation on the verb. The non-Pama-Nyunga languages deviate strongly from this model: complex consonant systems, case prefixes, pronominal prefixes with the verb.

References
Blake, B.J. 1986. *Australian aboriginal grammar*. London.
Capell, A. 1956. *A new approach to Australian linguistics*. Sydney.
Curr, E.M. 1886–7. *The Australian race: its origins, languages, customs, places of landing in Australia, and the routes by which it spread itself over the continent*, 4 vols. Melbourne.
Dixon, R.M.W. 1980. *The languages of Australia*, Cambridge.
Dixon, R.M.W. and J. Blake. 1979–91. *Handbook of Australian languages*, 4 vols. Amsterdam. Vol. 4 Oxford.
Schmidt, W. 1919. *Die Gliederung der australischen Sprachen*. Vienna.

Wurm, S.A. 1972. *Languages of Australia and Tasmania*. The Hague.

Yallop, C. 1982. *Australian aboriginal languages*. London.

Austroasian ⇒ Austro-Asiatic

Austro-Asiatic

Language group of South and South-East Asia with approx. 150 languages and 56 million speakers. The most important branches are the **Munda** and **Mon-Khmer** languages. Schmidt (1906) was the first to suggest combining the Austroasian languages with the Austronesian languages (⇒ **Malayo-Polynesian**), a hypothesis which is still debated.

The larger languages were often influenced by other language families, such that the original characteristics of this language group are preserved only in the smaller languages occurring in more isolated areas. The affinity of this language group to **Vietnamese** was not recognized until fairly recently.

Characteristics: original features include: high number of vowel phonemes (up to forty, occasionally with creaky or breathy voice as distinctive feature), implosive consonants, in part **tonal languages**. Morphology usually prefixal or infixal; word order SVO.

References
Schmidt, W. 1906. *Die Mon-Khmer-Völker: ein Bindeglied zwischen Völkern Zentralasiens und Austronesiens*. Braunschweig.

Zide, N.H. 1969. Munda and Non-Munda Austroasiatic languages. In T.A. Sebeok (ed.), *Current Trends in Linguistics*. The Hague. Vol. 5, 411–30.

Austronesian ⇒ Malayo-Polynesian

Austro-Thai

Language group of South-East Asia which includes Austronesian (⇒ **Malayo-Polynesian**), Kam, **Thai**, and possibly **Miao-Yao**. A possible relationship to the **Austro-Asiatic** languages has been suggested.

Reference
Benedict, P.K. 1975. *Austro-Thai: language and culture*. New Haven, CT.

autism [Grk *autós* 'self,' 'by oneself, alone']

Term in child and adolescent psychiatry for a syndrome characterized by severe disorders in social behavior, abnormal development of communicative abilities, pronounced rituals and stereotypic behavior, and abnormal reactions to sensory stimuli. Believed to have various causes, autism starts in early childhood before the thirtieth month. With regard to their linguistic skills, autistic persons may manifest the following symptoms: **echolalia**, abnormal **prosody**, almost exclusively literal understanding of words or phrases, and pragmatic difficulties (e.g. topic violations, low responsivity, inappropriate register, deictic confusion, restricted range of function). (⇒ *also* **developmental language disorder**)

References
Baltaxe, C.A.M. and J.Q. Simmons, 1985. Prosodic development in normal and autistic children. In E. Schopler and G.B. Mesibov (eds), *Communication problems in autism*. New York. 95–120.

Cohen, D.J. *et al.* 1987. *Handbook of autism and pervasive developmental disorders*. New York.

Demyer, M.K. *et al.* 1981. Infantile autism reviewed: a decade of research. *Schizophrenia Bulletin* 7:3.3–451.

Eales, M.J. 1993. Pragmatic impairments in adults with childhood diagnoses of autism or developmental receptive language disorder. *Journal of Autism and Developmental Disorders.* 23.593–617.

Fay, W.H. and A. Schuler. 1980. *Emerging language in autistic children*. London.

Frith, U. 1989. A new look at language and communication in autism. *British Journal of Disorders of Communication* 24.123–50.

Kanner, L. 1973. Autistic disturbances of affective contact. *The Nervous Child* 2.217–50.

——— (ed.) 1973. *Childhood psychosis*. Washington, DC.

Rutter, M. and E. Schopler (eds) 1978. *Autism*. New York.

Schopler, E. and G.B. Mesibov. 1986. *Social behavior in autism*. New York.

——— 1988. *Diagnosis and assessment in autism*. New York.

Schreibman, L. 1988. *Autism*. Newsbury Park.

Tager-Flusberg, H. and M. Andersen. 1991. The development of contingent discourse ability in autistic children. *Journal of Child Psychology, Psychiatry and Allied Disciplines* 32.1123–34.

Wing, L. 1988. *Aspects of autism: biological research*. London.

Journal
Journal of Autism and Developmental Disorder

automata theory ⇒ automaton

automatic translation ⇒ machine-aided translation

automaton [Grk *autómatos* 'self-acting']

In the broad sense, any concrete machine that can perform independently, e.g. telephones or vending machines. In the narrow sense of automata theory, a mathematical model of concrete machines as information-processing systems which store and process input and provide output. All automata are defined as sets of automata states and transitions between these. More complex automata include a last-in-first-out memory (stack automata) or random access memory (**Turing machines**). In more recent linguistic research automata play an important role as processing models of language. Thus, regular grammars correspond to the **finite state automata** and context-free grammars correspond to the 'push-down automata' or stack automata, and unrestricted grammars (including, for example, all known transformational grammars) correspond to **Turing machines** (named after the mathematician A.M. Turing).

Reference

Hopcroft, J. and J. Ullmann, 1979. *Introduction to automata theory, languages and computation.* Reading, MA.

autonomy

In **glossematics**, a form of **constellation**. The paradigmatic relation between two free elements which may be joined and whose common appearance is independent from each other, as opposed to **determination** and **interdependence**.

autosegmental phonology

Proposed by J. Goldsmith, a representation of generative **phonology** which allows certain **features** to be described as belonging to one or more **segments**. This hypothesis has proven useful in the description of **tonal languages** and **vowel harmony**. Autosegmental phonology is one theory of **non-linear phonology**. (⇒ *also* **prosody**)

References

Clements, G.V. 1977. The autosegmental treatment of vowel harmony. In W.U. Dressler and O.E. Pfeiffer (eds), *Phonologica 1976.* Innsbruck. 111–19.
Goldsmith, J.A. 1976. *Autosegmental phonology.* Bloomington, IN.
——— 1989. *Autosegmental and metrical phonology: an introduction.* Oxford.
Van der Hulst, M. and N. Smith. 1985. *Advances in non-linear phonology.* Dordrecht.

autosemantic word [Grk *autós* 'self,' *sḗma* 'sign'] (*also* content word, open-class word)

In distinction to **synsemantic words**, autosemantic words have a meaning that is self-contained and independent of **context**. They are mainly **nouns**, **verbs**, and **adjectives**. The distinction between autosemantic and synse-

mantic words is not tenable in the strictest sense.

AUX ⇒ auxiliary

auxiliary [Lat. *auxiliaris* 'giving aid'] (*also* AUX, helping verb)

Subcategory of verbs which can be distinguished from **main verbs** by semantic and syntactic criteria. Auxiliaries have a reduced lexical meaning (cf. *have, will, be*). Their **valence** is different from main verbs, since they do not select nominal arguments but rather main verbs as their argument. Auxiliaries typically occur as exponents of morphological categories such as **tense**, **mood**, **voice**, **number**, and **person**. In English, auxiliaries allow the so-called subject–auxiliary inversion in certain constructions, e.g. *Caroline has eaten* vs *Has Caroline eaten?* It is a matter of debate whether these differences from main verbs are sufficient to treat auxiliaries as separate categories. Within earlier versions of **transformational grammar**, auxiliaries were treated as verbs with the feature AUX. In more recent generative grammar models the exponent of verbal inflection is a separate node called INFL (⇒ **INFL node**). Occasionally modal verbs and **copular verbs** are subsumed under the category auxiliary (⇒ **modal auxiliary**).

References

Chomsky, N. 1965. *Aspects of the theory of syntax.* Cambridge, MA.
Edmondson, J.A. and F. Plank. 1976. Auxiliaries and main verbs reconsidered. *Lingua* 38.109–23.
Gazdar, G. *et al.* 1982. Auxiliaries and related phenomena in a restrictive theory of grammar. *Lg* 58.591–638.
Harris, M. and P. Ramat (eds) 1987. *The historical development of auxiliaries.* Berlin.
Heine, B. 1994. *Auxiliaries: cognitive forces and gramaticalization.* Oxford.
Heny, F. and B. Richards (eds). 1983. *Grammatical categories: auxiliaries and related puzzles.* Dordrecht.
Ross, J.R. 1969. Auxiliaries as main verbs. In W. Todo (ed.), *Studies in philosophical linguistics.* Evanston, IL.
Steele, S. 1978. The category AUX as a language universal. In J.H. Greenberg (ed.), *Universals of human language*, vol. 3: *Word structure.* Stanford, CA. 7–45.
———. 1981. An encyclopedia of AUX. A study of cross-linguistic equivalence. Cambridge, MA.
Verharr, J.W.N. (ed.) 1957–9. *The word 'be' and its synonyms: philosophical and grammatical studies*, 4 parts. Dordrecht.
Warner, A.R. 1992. *English auxiliaries: structure and history.* Cambridge.

Avar ⇒ **North-East Caucasian**

Avestan ⇒ **Iranian**

Avaro-Andi ⇒ **North-East-Caucasian**

axiom [Grk *axíoma* 'worth, value']
In the framework of scientific theory a fundamental principle that forms the basis of a
scientific system from which all other theorems
can be logically derived. In the ancient logic of
Aristotle and Euclid, axioms were considered to
be incontestable, intuitively obvious principles
and the statements derived from them to be true
assertions. The development of axiomatic
geometry by Hilbert (1899) brought about a
new interpretation of the concept 'axiom'
according to which the truth of axioms is not
intuitively presupposed but rather that axioms
are arbitrarily determined. For the correctness
of logical axioms it is, however, necessary that
the axiom be proven true. The introduction of
axiomatic theory in language description plays
an important role in numerous more recent
descriptive models such as **transformational
grammar**, **categorial grammar**, integrative
linguistics and others.

References
Bühler, K. 1933. Die Axiomatik der Sprachwis-
    senschaften. *Kantstudien* 38.19–90. (2nd edn
    Frankfurt, 1969.)
Hilbert, D. 1899. *Grundlagen der Geometrie*. Stutt-
    gart. (Repr. 1977.)
Lieb, H.-H. 1975–6. Grammars as theories: the case

for axiomatic grammar. *TL* 1.39–115 and 3.1–98.
⇒ **formal logic, formalization**

axiomatics of linguistics
Basic principle of linguistic communication,
postulated by K. Bühler with reference to
mathematics and **logic**, from which allegedly
all linguistic factors can be deductively derived
and explained: (a) the basic functions of language are representation, expression and appel-
lation (⇒ **organon model of language**);
(b) language is a system of signs which are
used according to the **principle of abstractive
relevance**; (c) language is to be studied under
the subject-related phenomena *Sprachwerk*
'language work' and *Sprachgebilde* 'language
form' (four-field schema); (d) language is constituted by the two interrelated levels of semantics and syntax.

References
Bühler, K. 1934. *Sprachtheorie*. Jena. (Repr. Stutt-
    gart, 1965.)
Mulder, J.W.F. 1989. *Foundations of axiomatic lin-
    guistics*. Berlin.
Ortner, H. 1986. Bühlers Vierfelderschema (das
    dritte Axiom in der 'Sprachtheorie'): Grund-
    gedanken und Rezeption. *Kodikas* 9.211–26.
⇒ **Axiom**

Aymara ⇒ **Andean, Quechua**

Azerbaijani ⇒ **Turkic**

Aztecan ⇒ **Uto-Aztecan**

Azteco-Tanoan ⇒ **Uto-Aztecan**

B

Babylonian ⇒ **Akkadian**

Bach-Peters   paradox ⇒ **problominalization**

back channel

Verbal expressions, such as *uh, yes*, and their non-verbal equivalents, like nodding, are normally expressed during the speaker's turn and are used by the listener to demonstrate that he/she is paying attention to the speaker. Not considered conversational **turns** *per se*, such signals are said to occur 'in the back channel.' The term was first used by Yngve (1970). The status of these signals as turns is under debate (see Duncan 1974; Duncan and Fiske 1977; Schegloff 1982, 1988). (⇒ *also* **discourse analysis**)

References
Duncan, S. 1974. On the structure of speaker–audience–auditor interaction during speaking turns. *Language in Society* 3.161–86.
Duncan, S. and D.W. Fiske. 1977. *Face-to-face interaction: research, methods, and theory*. Hillsdale, NJ.
Goffman, E. 1978. Response cries. *Lg* 54.787–815.
Schegloff, E.A. 1982. Discourse as an interactional achievement: some uses of 'uh huh' and other things that come between sentences. In D. Tannen (ed.), *Analyzing discourse: text and talk*. GURT Washington, DC. 71–93.
———— 1988. Discourse as an interactional achievement II: An exercise in conversation analysis. In D. Tannen (ed.) *Linguistics in context: Connecting observation and understanding*. Norwood, NJ. 135–58.
Yngve, V. 1970. On getting a word in edgewise. *CLS* 6.567–77.
⇒ **conversation analysis**)

back formation

In **word formation**, a term denoting the process and result, by means of which an originally older and more complex expression gives rise to the formation of a new stem. The original expression is then analyzed synchronically as a derivation on the basis of the new stem and a productive suffix, e.g. *edit < editor, stagemanage < stagemanager* or *spoonfeed < spoonfed*. Nominal back formations derived from verbs (e.g. *walk < (to) walk*) are termed 'nomina post verbalia' by historical grammarians. Grammatical back formations occur when singular forms are derived from original plural forms, e.g. *pea < peas*.

References
Marchand, H. 1960. *The categories and types of present-day English word-formation*. Munich. (2nd edn 1969.)
———— 1963. On content as a criterion of derivational relationship with backderived words. *IF* 68.170–5.

back vowel ⇒ **vowel**

backing ⇒ **velarization**

bahuvrihi (*also* exocentric compound, possessive compound)

Term coined from the **Sanskrit** word which literally means 'having much rice.' A subgroup of determinative compounds, bahuvrihis are compounds whose first member modifies the second, while the whole compound refers exocentrically only to a part of its referent, that is, to one who is characterized by a certain trait: *longlegs*. Bahuvrihis are often strongly idiomatic: *dimwit, knucklehead, bignose*.

References
⇒ **composition**

Baltic

Branch of **Indo-European**. Baltic is closely related to **Slavic**, and some believe that there was a common Balto-Slavic language group in prehistorical times. The Baltic languages include **Old Prussian** (now extinct), **Lithuanian**, and **Latvian**.

References
Endzelīns, J. 1948. *Baltu valodu skaņas un formas. Riga.* (Transl. as Janis Endzelīns' comparative phonology and morphology of the Baltic languages, by W.R. Schmalstieg and B. Jēgers. The Hague and Paris 1971.)
Gimbutas, M. 1963. *The Balts*. New York and Washington.
Magener, T.F. and W.R. Schmalstieg (eds) 1970. *Baltic linguistics*. University Park, PA and London.
Stang, C.S. 1966. *Vergleichende Grammatik der baltischen Sprachen*. Oslo and Bergen.

Bibliography
Kubicka, W. 1967–77. *Języki bałtyckie. Bibliografia*, 4 vols. Lodz.

Journals
Baltistica.
Linguistica Baltica.

Balto-Finnish ⇒ Finno-Ugric

Bambara ⇒ Mande

Bantoid ⇒ Benue-Congo

Bantu

Largest language group of **Benue-Congo** languages with over 500 closely related languages forming a dialect continuum; the most significant languages are Congo, Zulu (approx. 6 million speakers), Rwanda, Xhosa, Luba, Shona (approx. 5 million speakers), and **Swahili**, which is widely used in East Africa as a trade language. Internal divisions: Rain Forest Bantu in the west, Savannah Bantu in the east and south. The high degree of similarity between these languages points to a relatively recent immigration of the Bantu-speaking peoples from the Benue area (Nigeria).

The unity of the Bantu languages was recognized relatively early (e.g. Bleek, 1856); in 1899, Meinhof succeeded in reconstructing the sound system of Proto-Bantu (⇒ **proto-language, reconstruction**). Guthrie (1967–71) collected comprehensive data for the reconstruction of 'Common Bantu,' creating the commonly used (if somewhat arbitrary) reference system of fifteen zones for Bantu languages and dialects.

Characteristics: usually **tonal** (two tones), tendency towards bisyllabic roots and reduced vowel system (seven or five vowels). Well-developed **noun class** system: each noun belongs to a separate class (one of usually about ten to twenty) with a specific prefix, where a certain plural class often corresponds to a singular class (cf. Swahili *ki-ti* 'chair,' *vi-ti* 'chairs'); the division into classes is often semantically motivated (animate, object, fluid, and other classes). Complex verb morphology (agreement prefixes, tense/mood/polarity prefixes, voice-marking suffixes). Word order SVO.

References
Bleek, W.H.I. 1856. *The languages of Mozambique: vocabularies of the dialects of Lourenço Marques.* London.
Byarushengo, E.A. *et al.* 1977. *Haya grammatical structure.* Los Angeles, CA.
Clements, G.N. and J.A. Goldsmith. 1984. *Autosegmental studies in Bantu tone.* Dordrecht.
Cole, D.T. 1955. *An introduction to Tswana grammar.* Cape Town.
Guthrie, M. 1967–71. *Comparative Bantu: an introduction to the comparative linguistics and pre-*

history of the Bantu languages. Farnborough.
Hinnebusch, T.H., D. Nurse and M. Mould. 1981. *Studies in the classification of Eastern Bantu languages.* Hamburg.
Kimenyi, A. 1980. *A relational grammar of Kinyarwanda.* Berkeley, CA.
Mchombo, S. 1994. *Theoretical aspects of Bantu grammar,* vol. 1. Chicago, IL.
Meinhof, C. 1899. *Grundriß einer Lautlehre der Bantusprachen nebst einer Anleitung zur Aufnahme von Bantusprachen.* Leipzig. (Repr. 1966.)
Möhlig, W.L.G. 1981. Die Bantusprachen im engeren Sinn. In B. Heine *et al.* (eds), *Die Sprachen Afrikas.* Hamburg. 77–116.

barbarism [Grk *bárbaros* 'non-Greek, foreign']

A term in classical **rhetoric** for the improper use of a word. Originally coined for the unusual use of foreign words, barbarism was later used for mistakes in orthography, pronunciation, and agreement. A barbarism violates the rhetorical style of correct speech (⇒ **solecism**). John Steinbeck illustrates its literary usefulness in writing: *'Awright,' she said contemptuously. 'Awright, cover 'im up if ya want ta. Whatta I care? ... I tell ya I could of went with shows. Not jus' one, neither. An' a guy tol' me he could put me in pitchers'* (*Of Mice and Men,* p. 86).

References
⇒ **rhetoric**

barriers

A term from Chomsky's (1986) book *Barriers* for the further development of **Government and Binding theory**. This theory strives for the unification of the theory of government with **subjacency** principle. This attempted unification is the result of the hypothesis that barriers are the basis for the local domains of government as well as the bounding nodes for subjacency. Modifications include: (a) the application of **X-bar theory** to the sentential categories S and S-bar, where S-bar is a projection of the **COMP position** and S is the **maximal projection** of the INFL-position (⇒ **INFL-node**); (b) the resulting modification of the term 'government,' so that only maximal projections can be barriers, and case is assigned to the subject position of IP.

References
Chomsky, N. 1986. *Barriers.* Cambridge, MA.
Johnson, K. 1988. Clausal gerunds, the ECP, and government. *LingI* 19.583–610.

Bartholomae's Law

A **sound change** in **Indo-Iranian** in consonant clusters consisting of aspirated voiced stops and non-aspirated voiceless stops. The root-final voiced aspirated stop is deaspirated; it gives voice and transfers aspiration to the following stop, cf. IE. *b^hud^hto-* > Indo-Iranian *bhuddha-*. It is debated whether Bartholomae's Law might not also have left some traces in Germanic.

References
Bartholomae. C. 1883. *Handbuch der iranischen Dialekte*. Leipzig. (Repr. Wiesbaden, 1968.)
Collinge, N.E. 1985. *The laws of Indo-European*. Amsterdam and Philadelphia. 7–11.

base ⇒ head²

base component

In **generative grammar** a level of grammatical description which is composed of **phrase structure rules**, **subcategorization** rules, and the **lexicon**, and which generates the structural description of simple sentences. The syntactically based **deep structure** is generated in the base component and can be illustrated by a **tree diagram**.

base (morpheme)

Forming the largest subset of a language's inventory of morphemes, base morphemes are free morphemes – as opposed to bound (inflectional and word-forming) morphemes (⇒ **affix**) – and are, as a rule, stressed elements. Occasionally, the term 'base' is used to refer to multimorphemic lexical constructions.

The inventory of bases is changed through direct **borrowing** from foreign languages (e.g. *atom*) or through **neologisms** created artificially with foreign elements (*product + ion*), as well as through the effects of **language change** as, for example, when constituents of earlier compounds lose their former motivation (*cupboard*) or through an obscuring of the original meaning, as in *lord*, from OE **hlāfweard* 'keeper of the bread.'

References
⇒ **word formation**

BASIC English

C.K. Ogden and I.E. Richards introduced BASIC ('British, American, Scientific, International, Commercial') English as a simplified form of English which consists of a **basic vocabulary** of 850 words (with eighteen verbs) and a greatly simplified grammar. BASIC English can supposedly be learned in about sixty hours, though it requires additional vocabulary lists for specialized jargons. Its value as a versatile means of international communication is disputed.

References
Ogden, C.K. 1930. *Basic English*. London.
——— 1942. *Basic for science*. London.

basic vocabulary (*also* core vocabulary)

The minimum number of lexical items in a language usually chosen for pedagogical purposes (e.g. the minimum vocabulary for second language learners or the spelling vocabulary for native-speaking pupils at a certain educational level). Beside the degree of utility, the most important criterion for determining the basic vocabulary is the frequency of use.

References
Carter, R. 1987. Is there a core vocabulary? Some implications for language teaching. *AppLing*, 8:2.178–93.
⇒ **frequency dictionary**, **lexicostatistics**

basic word order ⇒ word order

basilect ⇒ acrolect

basis ⇒ antecedent

Basque

Language isolate with approx. 1 million speakers in northern Spain and south-western France, divided into a number of strongly deviating dialects. Basque is possibly related to the Iberian language, which is attested solely in inscriptions. The first substantial written documents date from the sixteenth century.

Characteristics: phonologically, Basque resembles **Spanish**. Rich morphology (suffixal); syntactically an **ergative language**: the subject in transitive sentences is in the ergative, marked by *-ek* (e.g. *Martin ethorri-da* 'Martin came,' *Martin-ek haurra igorri-du* 'Martin sent the child,' in which *-ek* marks the ergative). Rich agreement system (with subject, direct and indirect object), agreement markers are typically fusional. Word order: SOV. Numerous lexical borrowings from **Latin**.

References
Hualde, J.I. 1991. *Basque phonology*. London.
——— and J. Oritz de Urbina (eds) 1993. *Generative studies in Basque linguistics*. Amsterdam and Philadelphia.
King, A.R. 1994. *The Basque language*. Reno, CA.
Lafitte, P. 1962. *Grammaire basque*. Bayonne.
Lüders, U.J. 1993. *The Souletin verbal complex: new approaches to Basque morphophonology*. Munich and Newcastle.
Saltarelli, M. 1988. *Basque*. London.

Dictionaries
Aulestia, G. 1989. *Basque–English dictionary*. Reno, CA.

—— and L. White. 1990. *English–Basque diction-ary*. Reno, CA.

Etymological dictionary
Löpelmann, M. 1968. *Etymologisches Wörterbuch der baskischen Sprache*. Berlin and New York.

battarism ⇒ cluttering

beech argument

Hypothesis for determining the original home of the **Indo-European** tribes as well as the Slavs based on the occurrence of words derived from IE *$b^h ag(u)gos$ 'beech.' West of the line Königsberg–Crimea this term is widely attested (cf. all the **Germanic** languages, Lat. *fagus*), while to the east of this line the word is used for various kinds of trees, cf. Grk *phēgós* 'oak,' Russ. *buz* 'elder,' and Kurdish *buz* 'elm.' The distribution of the reflexes of this Indo-European word suggests that after the break-up and spread of the Indo-European tribes the word came to be used for other trees in areas where there were no beeches.

References
Krogmann, W. 1955. Das Buchen-Argument. *ZVS* 73.1–25.
Lane, G.S. 1967. The beech argument. *ZVS* 81.197–202.
Wissmann, W. 1952. *Der Name der Buche*. Berlin.

Behaghel's laws

Basic principles of word order formulated by Otto Behaghel (1854–1936). (a) Behaghel's first law maintains that elements which are semantically closely connected to one another are placed close together. (b) A second law is that whatever is more important is placed after whatever is less important. (c) A third law is that the specifying element (= specifier) pre-cedes the specified element. And (d) the shorter constituent tends to precede the longer (⇒ **weight principle**). In addition, there is a tendency for constituents with stronger stress to alternate with constituents with weaker stress. (⇒ *also* **word order**)

References
Behaghel, O.P. 1932. *Deutsche Syntax*. Heidelberg. Vol. 4.
Collinge. N.E. 1985. *The laws of Indo-European*. Amsterdam and Philadelphia. 242.

behaviorism

Direction of psychological research founded by J.B. Watson (1878–1959) and modeled after natural science that takes aim at the methods of self-observation (introspection) as well as the description of the consciousness (such as feel-ings, thoughts, impulsive behavior). Behavior-ism investigates objectively observable behav-iors as a reaction to changes in environmental circumstances. The **stimulus–response** model (developed through experiments on animals) as well as the fundamental categories of 'con-ditioned reflexes' and **conditioning** provide the point of departure for behaviorist research. According to these theories, behavior is ana-lyzed as a reaction to particular environmen-tally conditioned external or internal stimuli and is thereby predictable based on the exact characterization of the corresponding instance of stimulus. Behaviorism has become partic-ularly significant in educational psychology. Its principle of the learning process as a condition-ing process, which was further developed in educational psychology, was also applied to the process of **language acquisition**. In contrast to the mentalist (⇒ *mentalism*) understanding of language acquisition as a maturation process that runs according to an innate plan derived from an inborn internal mechanism ('device'), behaviorism assumes that one can only pre-suppose the command of certain procedures or strategies for the acquisition of cognitive and, thus, also linguistic knowledge as an innate psychological ability, but that the learning process itself is carried out through continual experience. As Skinner presents in detail in his (to a great degree speculative) book *Verbal Behavior* (1957), language is explained as a learned behavior, as the sum of individual language habits developed and acquired through conditioning, reinforcement and gen-eralization, as a circumstantial network of asso-ciative connections of linguistic expressions. The conception of behaviorism is most clearly expressed in Bloomfield's antimentalist con-cept of language, especially in his taxonomic method of description which is itself geared towards those methods used in the natural sciences (cf. **antimentalism, distributional-ism**). For a critique of this approach from a linguistic point of view, see Chomsky (1959).

References
Bloomfield, L. 1933. *Language*. New York.
Chomsky, N. 1959. Verbal behavior (a discussion of B.F. Skinner, 1957). *Lg* 35.26–38.
Hull, C.L. 1930. Knowledge and purpose as habit mechanism. *PsycholR* 37.511–25.
—— 1977. *A behavior's system*. Westport, CT.
Mead, G.H. 1934. *Mind, self and society from the standpoint of a social behaviorist*. Chicago, IL.
Skinner, B.F. 1957. *Verbal behavior*. London.
—— 1978. *Reflections on behaviorism and soci-ety*. Englewood Cliffs, NJ.
Tolman, E.C. 1932. *Purposive behavior in animals and men*. New York.
Watson, J.B. 1919. *Psychology from the standpoint of a behaviorist*. Philadelphia, PA.
—— 1930. *Behaviorism*. New York.

Zuriff, G.E. 1985. *Behaviorism: a conceptual recon-struction*. New York.

Belochi ⇒ Iranian, Kurdish

Belorussian

East **Slavic** language with approx. 7 million speakers, primarily in Belorussia, but also in other former Soviet republics and in Poland. The first uses of Belorussian as a literary language date from the mid nineteenth century, before which **Old Church Slavic** was used with Belorussian editing. Belorussian has been developing as a modern literary language since 1918. Belorussian uses the **Cyrillic** alphabet with the additional letter ⟨ў⟩; in contrast to **Ukrainian** and **Russian**, the letters ⟨и⟩ and ⟨щ⟩ are not used. Differences from Russian include [dz] and [c] instead of [d] and [t] (so-called 'dzekanie' and 'cekanie').

Characteristics: nominative plural instead of genitive singular after the numerals *2*, *3*, and *4*.

References
Atraxovič, K.K. and M.H. Bulaxaŭ (eds) 1962. *Hramatyka belaruskaj movy*, vol. 1: Marfalohija. Minsk.
——— and P.P. Šuba (eds) 1966. Hramatyka belaruskaj movy, vol. 2: *Sintaksis*. Minsk.
Biryla, M.V. and P.P. Šuba. 1985–6. *Belaruskaja hramatyka*, 2 vols. Minsk.
Blinava, E. 1980. *Belaruskaja Dyjalektalohija*, 2nd edn. Minsk.
Jankoŭski, F.M. 1980. *Sučasnaja belaruskaja lit-eraturnaja mova. Marfalohija*, 2nd edn. Minsk.
Mayo, P.J. 1976. *A grammar of Byelorussian*. Sheffield.
Wexler, P. 1977. *A historical phonology of the Belorussian language*. Heidelberg.

Historical grammar
Jankoŭski, F.M. 1989. *Histaryčnaja hramatyka belaruskaj movy*, 3rd edn. Minsk.

Dictionaries
Martynaŭ, V.U. 1978–90. *Ètimalahičny sloŭnik belaruskaj movy*, 6 vols. Minsk.
Suša, T.M. and A.K. Ščuka. 1989. *Angla–belaruska-ruski sloŭnik*. Minsk.
Žuraŭski, A.I. 1982–90. *Histaryčny sloŭnik belaruskaj movy*, 10 vols. Minsk.

Journals
Belaruskaja Linhvistyka
Belaruskaja Mova

benefactive

Semantic (or **thematic**) **relation** for the benefi-ciary of the action expressed by the verb, for example, *her* and *himself* in: *He bought a record for her and a book for himself*. Cf. **case grammar**, **thematic relation**.

Bengali

Indo-Aryan language with approx. 150 million speakers in India and Bangladesh.

Characteristics: relatively simply noun morphology (loss of gender, four cases), rich verb morphology. Subject–verb agreement in person and status (polite, neutral, disparaging). Word order SOV.

References
Bender, E. and T. Riccardi, Jr. 1978. *An advanced course in Bengali*. Philadelphia, PA.
Chatterji, S.K. 1926. *The origin and development of the Bengali language*, 3 vols. Calcutta. (Repr. London.)
Hilali, M.R. 1990. *Learning Bengali*. London.
Ray, P.S. and L. Ray. 1966. *Bengali language handbook*. Washington, DC.
Sen, D.C. 1986. *History of Bengali language and literature*. London.

Dictionary
Biswas, S. 1987–8. *Samsad Bengali–English/English–Bengali dictionary*, 2 vols, 10th/5th edn. Calcutta.

Benue-Congo

Largest linguistic group of **Niger-Congo** (approx. 600 languages, spoken from Nigeria to South Africa). Divided into four groups: the largest, Bantoid (including the **Bantu** lan-guages), as well as three smaller groups (Plateau, Cross–River, Jukunoid) in Nigeria.

References
Gebhardt, L. 1983. *Beiträge zur Kenntnis der Spra-chen des nigerianischen Plateaus*. Glückstadt.
Shimizu, K. 1980. *A Jukun grammar*. Vienna.
Williamson, K. 1971. The Benue-Congo languages and Ijo. In T.A. Sebeok (ed.), *Current trends in linguistics*. The Hague. Vol. 7, 245–306.

Benue-Kwa ⇒ Niger-Congo

Berber

Language family of the **Afro-Asiatic** group in North Africa containing numerous languages and dialects (e.g. Tamashek (Tuareg), Shliḥ, Zenaga). Approx. 10 million speakers, primari-ly in isolated areas. Strong influence from **Arabic**. Tamashek has its own written system (borrowed from the Phoenicians).

Characteristics: word order VSO in verbal clauses; nominal clauses have no verbal ele-ment. Direct object and topicalized NP are in the citation form ('status liber'), while the subject, genitive, and indirect object are marked ('status annexus'). Complex consonant system with a tendency towards consonant harmony.

References
Applegate, J.R. 1970. The Berber languages. In T.A.

Sebeok (ed.), *Current trends in linguistics*. The Hague. Vol. 6, 586–664.

Chaker, S. 1984. *Textes en linguistique berbère: introduction au domaine berbère*. Paris.

Sadiqi, F. 1986. *Studies in Berber syntax: the complex sentence*. Würzburg.

Wolff, E. 1981. Die Berbersprachen. In B. Heine *et al.* (eds), *Die Sprachen Afrikas*, Hamburg. 171–85.

Berlitz method

Variation on the **direct method** used by M. Berlitz in his commercial language schools. Berlitz emphasized the acquisition of everyday vocabulary and sentences through presentation exclusively in the target language and making extensive use of demonstration and visuals. Follow-up practice consisted of teacher-directed question and answer exchanges. Grammar was presented though an inductive approach with an emphasis on formal accuracy.

References
Berlitz, M.D. 1887. *Méthode Berlitz*. New York.
Titone, R. 1968. *Teaching foreign languages: an historical sketch*. Washington, DC.

biconditional ⇒ equivalence

bidirectional assimilation ⇒ assimilation

Bihari ⇒ Indo-Aryan

bilabial

Speech sound classified according to its **place of articulation** (lower lip) and its primary **articulator** (upper lip), e.g. the [b], [m], and [p] in *bump*. (⇒ *also* **articulatory phonetics**)

bilateral implication ⇒ equivalence, implication

bilateral opposition ⇒ opposition

bilingualism [Lat. 'two', 'tongue, language']

1 A speaker's competence in two or more languages and their use in everyday communication (Cf. *also* ⇒ **multilingualism**). Depending on the kind and extent of the competence in both languages, a distinction can be made between: (a) the mastery of different, but only partially differentiated dialects or varieties vs distinct languages; (b) the acquisition of bilingual competence within a family (e.g. in mixed marriages) vs the acquisition in school or at work; (c) the (simultaneous or successive) acquisition of two languages in child- or adulthood; (d) directed vs non-directed language acquisition; (e) different competence in both languages (dominance of

one language) vs 'genuine' bilingualism (which is less common), where passive as well as active competence in both languages is actually equal ('coordinate bilingualism' according to Weinreich 1953).

2 Apart from these questions of individual bilingual competence (individual bilingualism), the existence of two or more languages within a society (societal bilingualism) and their communicative functions are also of interest (⇒ **diglossia**).

References
Alatis, J.E. and J.J. Staczek (eds) 1985. *Perspectives on bilingualism and bilingual education*. Washington, DC.

Beardsmore, H.B. 1982. *Bilingualism: basic principles*. Clevedon.

Bialystok, E. (ed.) 1991. *Language processing in bilingual children*. Cambridge.

Döpke, S. 1992. *One parent – one language. An interactional approach*. Amsterdam and Philadelphia.

Ervin, S. and C.E. Osgood. 1954. Second language learning and bilingualism. *JASP* 49 (suppl.). 134–46.

Hamers, J.F. and M. Blanc. 1988. *Bilinguality and bilingualism*. Cambridge.

Hoffmann, C. 1991. *An introduction to bilingualism*. London.

Houwer, A. de. 1990. *The acquisition of two languages from birth: a case study*. Cambridge.

Hyltenstam, K. and L. K. Obler. 1989. *Bilingualism across the lifespan: aspects of acquisition, maturity and loss*. Cambridge.

Mackey, W.F. 1987. Bilingualism and multilingualism. In U. Ammon *et al.* (eds), *Sociolinguistics: an international handbook on the science of language and society*. Berlin and New York. 799–813.

Meisel, J. (ed.) 1990. *Two first languages: early grammatical development in bilingual children.*. Dordrecht.

Schreuder, R. and B. Weltenss (eds) 1993. *The bilingual lexicon*. Amsterdam and Philadelphia.

Seliger, H.F. and R.M. Vago (eds) 1991. *First language attrition*. Cambridge.

Weinreich, U. 1953. *Languages in contact: findings and problems*. New York. (Repr. 1966.)

Williams J. and G. Snipper. 1990. *Literacy and bilingualism*. London.

Journal
Literacy and Bilingualism
⇒ **aphasia**, **language acquisition**, **language contact**, **literacy**, **psycholinguistics**

binary

The property of descriptive terms which are predicated upon the **opposition** of two units, e.g. upon the presence or absence of certain features. (⇒ *also* **binary opposition, distinctive feature**)

binary digit ⇒ bit

binary opposition

Classificatory and descriptive method used in many disciplines (e.g. biology, **information theory**, logic, mathematics) which is based on two values. A basic principle of this system is the fact that essentially all – even the most complex – states of affairs and occurrences can be reduced to a finite set of elementary *yes/no*-decisions: for example, the 64 squares of a chess board can be determined by six *yes/no*-questions, since $2^6 = 64$. Binary opposition goes back to classical logical principles and can be interpreted as a function in **propositional logic** in the sense of 'X is true or is not true' (⇒ **formal logic**). Primarily, binary decisions can be simulated in practice with simple technical devices, such as by an electrical switch with on/off positions or by punch cards with hole/non-hole markings. It is on this principle that the analytical workings of a calculator are based. In linguistics, especially in **phonology**, Jakobson and Halle (1956) introduced the method of binary segmentation by proposing a universal inventory of twelve binary phonetic features to describe all languages in the world (⇒ **distinctive feature**). Moreover, the concept of binary opposition has been adapted to **morphology, syntax²** (⇒ **phrase structure**), and **semantics** (⇒ **componential analysis**), even though some doubts remain as to the general validity of the process of binary segmentation for natural languages (see Henrici 1975). (⇒ **markedness**)

References
Halle, M. 1957. In defense of number two. In E. Pulgram (ed.), *Studies presented to J. Whatmough*. The Hague. 65–72.
Henrici, G. 1975. *Die Binarismus. Problematik in der neueren Linguistik*. Tübingen.
Jakobson, R., G. Fant, and M. Halle. 1951. *Preliminaries to speech analysis: the distinctive features and their correlates*. Cambridge, MA. (7th edn 1967.)
Jakobson, R. and M. Halle, 1956. *Fundamentals of language*. The Hague. (2nd revised edn 1975.)

binding

In Chomsky's **Government and Binding theory**, a syntactic representation of particular anaphoric relations, described by **binding theory**. A node *A* binds a node *B* when *A* c-commands *B*, and *A* and *B* are co-indexed. If binding occurs and *B* is not a trace (⇒ **trace theory**), then *A* and *B* are interpreted as coreferential, i.e. the expressions *A* and *B* relate semantically to the same object. In this case the binding theory describes whether the coreference between *A* and *B* is syntactically permissible. If *B* is a trace, then the binding theory formulates **constraints** on whether *B* can be the trace of *A*, i.e. whether the movement of material in position *B* into position *A* is syntactically permissible.

References
⇒ **binding theory**

binding theory

A subtheory of **transformational grammar** which governs the relationship between **anaphoras**, pronouns, referential expressions and traces and their potential antecedents. An antecedent binds the **noun phrase** (NP) coreferentially with it if the antecedent **c-commands** the NP. Binding restrictions operate as a **filter**, which restricts the formally possible coreference relations between NPs as well as between NPs and their traces, so that only well-formed structures meet the binding constraints. Chomsky (1981) distinguishes three types of NP: (a) **anaphors**, i.e. reciprocal and reflexive NPs, whose reference is bound by a preceding NP in the same clause, e.g. *Philip bought himself a new suit*, where *himself* refers to *Philip*, or *The cat washes herself*, where *herself* refers to the *cat*. (b) Personal pronouns which can be interpreted anaphorically (proximately) or deictically (obviately), e.g. *Caroline still thinks she was right* where *she* can refer either to *Caroline* or another person not mentioned in the sentence. (c) All NPs which do not fall into (a) or (b), e.g. proper nouns, labels, traces of *wh*-movement.

According to **binding theory**, anaphors (a) are bound within a specific syntactic domain, their **governing category**; that is, they have an antecedent which c-commands them within their governing category. Personal pronouns (b) are not bound within their governing categories; they can be bound only by elements outside of the governing category. All other NPs (c) are always free. Violations of these conditions can be found in the following sentences: **Philip Philip thinks that Jacob₁ is buying himself a picture*, where there is intended coreference between *Philip* and *himself*; **He₁ thinks that Jacob Jacob is buying Philip a picture*, where there is coreference between *he* and *Jacob*. (⇒ **constraints, pronominalization, reflexivization, transformational grammar**)

References
Aoun, J. 1985. *A grammar of anaphora*. Cambridge, MA.
—— 1986. *Generalized binding: the syntax and logical form of wh-interrogatives*. Dordrecht.

Chomsky, N. 1980. On binding. *LingI* 11.1–46.
──── 1981. *Lectures on government and binding.* Dordrecht.
──── 1986. *Knowledge of language: its nature, origin and use.* New York.
Everaert, M. 1986. *The syntax of reflexivization.* Dordrecht.
Kayne, R. 1980. Extensions of binding and case-marking. *LingI* 11.75–96.
Lasnik. H. 1988. *Essays on anaphora.* Dordrecht.
Lust, B. (ed.) 1986. *Studies in the acquisition of anaphora,* 2 vols. Dordrecht.
Manzini, R. 1992. *Locality.* Cambridge, MA.
Radford, A. 1981. *Transformational syntax: a student's guide to Chomsky's Extended Standard Theory.* Cambridge.
Reinhart, T. 1983. *Anaphora and semantic interpretation.* London.
Williams, E. 1987. Implicit arguments, the binding theory, and control *NL&LT* 5.151–80.
Yang, D.W. 1983. The extending binding theory of anaphors. *LangR* 19.169–92.

biphonemic classification ⇒ **polyphonemic classification**

bisegmentalization

Phonetically motivated **sound change** in which a complex **segment** is split into two simple segments, e.g. medial **gemination** in the OHG *Old High German consonant shift*: $\varepsilon't^han$ > *$\varepsilon't^3an$ > *$\varepsilon t'ʒan$ > $\varepsilon ʒʒan$ = NHG *essen* 'eat,' or Eng. *cop-per* (loan from Lat. *cuprum*) as well as Eng. *ham-mer* < OE *ha-mor*. The original **affricate** [ts] is bisegmentalized to /t+s/, and thereby assigned to different **syllables**; the **assimilation** of the **stop** to the following **fricative** [ts] > [ss] yields the gemination. (⇒ *also* **articulatory phonetics**)

Reference
⇒ **phonology**

bisemy [Grk *sēma* 'sign']

The simplest type of **ambiguity**. A word is bisemic, if it has two meanings which are frequently, though not necessarily, opposed to each other, e.g. Fr. *sacré*: 'holy' and 'damned.' (⇒ *also* **homonymy**, **polysemy**)

bit

Contraction of 'binary digit,' the smallest unit of measure for the informational content of binary decisions. Every unit contains one bit of information since it is equivalent to a single *yes/no*-decision (⇒ **binary opposition**). Thus, in the case of a coin, there are two possibilities as to which side is up; the corresponding information amounts to one bit. The information about which side of a die is up requires three bits since $3 = \log_2^6$. (⇒ *also* **information theory**)

biuniqueness [Lat. *unicus* 'the only']

A term coined by Chomsky in 1964. Biuniqueness is a principle associated with the so-called taxonomic **structuralism** by which a one-to-one relationship exists between phonetic and phonemic representations in a phonological analysis. That is, if two words are pronounced identically, then they are phonologically equivalent. This ensures that one and the same phone is not assigned to different phonemes as in *paws* and *pause*. (⇒ *also* **distributionalism**)

References
Chomsky, N. 1964. *Current issues in linguistic theory.* The Hague.
⇒ **phonology**

black box analysis

A metaphorical term for the investigation of systems in which only the input and output can be observed. The inner structure of the data and their relationships to each other cannot be observed; so the properties of the structure in the 'box' are inferred from the input and output data. This view, taken from cybernetics (⇒ **information theory**), is in keeping with the investigation of natural languages, whereby the system of grammatical rules can be equated with the internal structure of linguistic production. This is similar to the 'black box' of the human brain, whose neurophysiological processes during speech are not accessible to empirical observation and can only be hypothesized. (⇒ *also* **transformational grammar**)

Black English (*also* Black English vernacular)

Umbrella term used to denote a number of non-standard American English sociolects (⇒ **English**, **sociolect**) spoken by North Americans of African descent. The origin of Black English is believed to have possibly developed from a **creole** spoken by the first African slaves. It differs from standard English predominantly in its lexicon, morphology, and syntax: e.g. lack of verb–subject agreement, as in *he walk*; presence of an idiosyncratic grammatical form to express the habituative, as in *They be walkin' around here.* Originally considered by many linguists to be a deficient form of English (⇒ **code theory**), Black English has come to be understood since the 1960s, in the wake of seminal studies by Labov, Wolfram, and others, as a full-fledged variety of American English.

References
Bailey, G., N. Maynor, and P. Cukor-Avila (eds) 1991. *The emergence of Black English.* Amsterdam and Philadelphia, PA.

Bennett, J. 1908. Gullah: a Negro patois. *SAQ* 7.332–47.

Fasold, R.W. 1972. *Tense marking in Black English: a linguistic and social analysis*. Washington, DC.

Labov, W. *et al.* 1968. *A study of the non-standard English of Negro and Puerto Rican speakers in New York City*. Cooperative research project no. 3288. Washington, DC.

—— 1972. *Language in the inner city: studies in the Black English vernacular*. Philadelphia, PA.

Luelsdorff, P. 1975. *A segmental phonology of Black English*. Berlin and New York.

McDavid, R.I. and L.M. Davis. 1972. The speech of Negro Americans. In M.E. Smith (ed.), *Studies in linguistics in honor of George L. Trager*. The Hague. 303–12.

—— and V.G. McDavid. 1951. The relationship of the speech of American Negroes to the speech of whites. *AS* 26.3–17.

Millard, J.L. 1972. *Black English: its history and usage in the United States*. New York.

Stewart, W.A. 1967. Sociolinguistic factors in the history of American Negro dialects. *Florida FE Reporter* 5:2.11–26. (Repr. in W.A. Wolfram and N.H. Clarke (eds), *Black–white speech relationships*. Washington, DC. 74–89.)

—— 1968. Continuity and change in American Negro dialects. *Florida FL Reporter* 6:1.3–4, 14–16, 18.

Wolfram, W.A. and N.H. Clarke (eds) 1971. *Black–white speech relationships*. Washington, DC.

—— 1974. The relationship of white southern speech to vernacular black English. *Lg* 50.498–527.

⇒ **creole**

Black English vernacular ⇒ **Black English**

blend (*also* amalgam, fusion, hybrid, telescoped word)

In **word formation**, synchronic or diachronic crossing or combining of two expressions into a single new one. Blends may develop from an unconscious or unintentional misspeaking (⇒ **speech error**), e.g. in the blend of *innuendo* and *insinuation* to *insinuendo*, or through stylistic intent. In the latter case, a distinction may be drawn between (a) haplological blends (⇒ **hapology**) in which the last part of the first word and the first part of the second word are identical (*networkhorse, californicate*) or in which sound and syllable elements overlap (*tragicomic, guestimate*); (b) **neologisms** involving word splitting (= true blends) (*motel, eurocrat, telethon*); (c) analogous formations in which a base word is replaced by a similar sounding lexeme (*vidiot* < *video* + *idiot*); (d) orthographic variants that are recognized as blends only from their spelling (*Ronald Raygun*). Blends, in comparison with more usual **compounds**, tend to be formed spontaneously through the close association of two words and

do not themselves usually serve as models for further compounds. Because most blends can only usually be understood in context, only a very few of them (e.g. the linguistic term **Franglais**), are adopted into everyday language. On syntactic blends, see Paul (1880) and Bolinger (1961).

References

Bolinger, D. 1961. Syntactic blends and other matters. *Lg* 37.366–81.

Paul, H. 1880. *Prinzipien der Sprachgeschichte*. Tübingen. 121–6. (9th edn 1975.)

body language

Designation for instinctive, conscious and/or conventional expressive movements of the body. (⇒ *also* **non-verbal communication**) ⇒ **word formation**

Bokmål ⇒ **Norwegian**

Boolean function

In the mathematical logic developed by the English mathematician G. Boole (1815–69), function whose arguments and values can accept only the values 'true' or 'false' (or 1 or 0). Important examples are the truth functions of the operations of **conjunction**, **disjunction**, **implication**, and **negation** in **propositional logic** (⇒ **logical connective**).

References

Boole, G. 1847. *The mathematical analysis of logic*. London.

⇒ **formal logic**, **truth value**

border signal ⇒ **boundary marker**

borrowed meaning

Meaning that a word takes on owing to the influence of a foreign word or concept, whereby the original meaning is reinterpreted or is expanded in view of its original meaning, e.g. *write* (originally 'to scratch') and *read* (originally 'to advise') took on new meanings when reading and writing were introduced to the English by the Christians.

References

⇒ **borrowing**

borrowing

Adoption of a linguistic expression from one language into another language, usually when no term exists for the new object, concept, or state of affairs. Among the causes of such cross-linguistic influence (⇒ **language contact**) may be various political, cultural, social, or economic developments (importation of new products, prestige, local flavor, internationalization of specialized languages and jargons, among others). Throughout its history, English has been subjected to influences from foreign cultures and languages, for example, through expansion of the Roman Empire, the migrations of the Scandinavians, Christianization, the development and growth of science and the humanities, French borrowings on and off since the Norman conquest, and more recent borrowings from dozens of languages in modern times, especially through the growth of telecommunications and universal travel. (⇒ *also* **foreign word**, **loan word**, **semantic change**, **word formation**)

References
Gneuss, H. 1955. *Lehnbildungen und Lehnbedeutunger im Altenglischen*. Berlin.
Haugen, E. 1950. The analysis of linguistic borrowing. *Lg* 26.210–31.
Lokotsch, K. 1927. *Wörterbuch der europäischen (germanischen, romanischen und slawischen) Wörter orientalischen Ursprungs*. Heidelberg. (2nd edn 1975.)
Meillet, A. 1921. *Linguistique historique et linguistique générale*. Paris.
Weinreich, U. 1953. *Languages in contact*, 2nd rev. edn. The Hague.

Bibliography
Benjamin, S.M. and L. von Schneidemesser. 1979. German loan words in American English: a bibliography of studies, 1878–1978. *AS* 54.210–15.

bottom up vs top down

Hypothesis about analytical strategies in **language processing**. In the bottom-up process, language comprehension commences with the identification of individual words (as stimuli) that are analyzed according to possible meanings and syntactic functions and categories and are used as the basis for the construction of possible underlying **propositions**. The top-down process attempts to circumvent problems that arise particularly in polysemic expressions: here, the analysis is based on pre-expectations of the hearer/receiver regarding the grammatical function of an expression dependent on its immediate context; thus, in SOV languages (⇒ **word order**) a verb is expected after a noun phrase at the beginning of a sentence. Provided the corresponding expression occurs as a verb in the lexicon, all other possible readings are thereby simultaneously excluded. In **computational linguistics**, it has been shown in **parsing** that both strategies must be implemented for speech recognition. The same thing appears to be the case for human language processing. (⇒ *also* **psycholinguistics**)

Reference
Just, M.A. and P.A. Carpenter (eds) 1977. *Cognitive process in comprehension*. Hillsdale, NJ.

boundary marker (*also* border signal, demarcative feature)

Sound phenomenon that occurs only at the beginning or end of a linguistic unit (**morpheme**, **syllable**, **word**), e.g. the consonant cluster /ts/ which occurs only in word-medial or word-final position in English: *It's a pizza*.

References
Maddieson, I. 1985. Phonetic cues to syllabification. In: V. Fromkin (ed.), *Phonetic linguistics*. New York. 203–20.
Mayerthaler, W. 1971. Zur Theorie der Grenzsymbole. In A. von Stechow (ed.), *Beiträge zur generativen Grammatik*. Brunswick. 162–71.
Trubetzkoy, N. 1939. *Grundzüge der Phonologie*. Göttingen. (4th edn 1967.)

bounded vs non-bounded ⇒ telic vs atelic

bounding theory

A term introduced in the Revised Extended Standard Theory (REST) of **transformational grammar**. Bounding theory deals with constraints on the locality conditions for particular **transformations** (⇒ **subjacency**) and stops an NP from being moved over more than one S or NP node which dominates it.

References
⇒ **constraints**, **transformational grammar**

box diagram

In **immediate constituent analysis**, a box

Box diagram

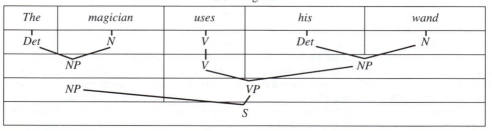

diagram is a form of representation used for illustrating the hierarchical structures of sentences. If the symbols of the **grammatical categories** are connected by **branches**, the result is a tree diagram turned upside down. The different levels of the box diagram correspond to the individual steps of division in immediate constituents. Box diagrams are equivalent to the corresponding **tree diagram**, **phrase structure rules** and **labeled bracketing**, cf. the diagram under **tree diagram**.

brace construction

Basic principle of German and Dutch word order that refers to a positional separation of the different parts of predication and/or of other elements of the sentence. The formation of the brace construction varies according to sentence and brace type. (a) The verbal brace construction is formed, among others, by (i) the separable parts of a morphologically complex verb: *Sie **lernte** gestern den Sachverhalt endlich genauer **kennen*** 'Yesterday she finally got to know the matter better'; (ii) finite auxiliary or modal verb and infinite main verb or predicate part: *Sie **wird**/**muß** den Sachverhalt **kennenlernen*** 'She will/must get to know the matter'; (iii) finite predicate part and certain verb complements or other information that in basic word order (⇒ **word order**) generally comes after the sentence negation (this itself is regarded as a brace-closing element in some of the pertinent literature): *Sie **bekam** den Fall nicht **unter Kontrolle***; *Sie **fühlte** sich nicht **überarbeitet*** 'She did not come to grips with the case'; 'She did not feel overworked.' The verbal brace construction divides verb-second sentences into three **positional fields** (termed *Vorfeld*, 'prefield' or 'front field,' *Mittelfeld* 'inner field' and *Nachfeld* 'final field,' 'post-field,' or 'end field'); the first stretches from the beginning of the sentence to the finite verb, the second from the finite verb to the closing element of the brace; the third only exists in sentences with **exbraciation**, i.e. if some part of the sentence is placed after the brace-closing element: *Er **schickte** mich ins Haus **hinein** zu seinem Vater* 'He sent me into the house to his father.' (Verb-initial sentences lack a prefield.) (b) The brace construction in a verb-final (usually subordinate) clause is formed by the clause-initiating elements (conjunctions etc.) and the verbal parts: ..., *weil er durstig **war*** '... because he was thirsty.' (c) The nominal brace construction is created by the distance position of article or preposition and head noun: *ein nicht mehr zu überbietendes großartiges Ereignis* 'a wonderful event which cannot be surpassed.'

References
Admoni, W. 1982. *Der deutsche Sprachbau*, 4th edn. Munich.
Kromann, H.P. 1974. Satz, Satzklammer und Ausklammerung. *Kopenhagener Beiträge zur Germanistischen Linguistik* 4.7–82.
Presch, G. 1974. *Die Satzklammer im Deutschen: syntaktische Beschreibung, Dekodierungsstrategien*. Konstanz.
Ronneberger-Sibold, E. 1993. 'Typological conservatism' and framing constructions in German morphosyntax. In J. Van Marle (ed.), *Historical linguistics 1991: papers from the tenth international conference on historical linguistics*. Amsterdam and Philadelphia. 295–314.
Thurmair, M. 1991. Warten auf das Verb. Die Gedächtnisrelevanz der Verbklammer im Deutschen. *Jahrbuch Deutsch als Fremdsprache* 17.174–202.
Vennemann, T. 1983. Verb second, verb late, and the brace construction in Germanic. In J. Fisiak (ed.), *Historical syntax*. The Hague. 627–36.
⇒ **constraint, German, transformational grammar, word order**

brachylogy [Grk *brachýs* 'short', *lógos* 'word'] (*also* brachylogia)

An intentional omission of essential thoughts. In its broadest sense, the term for expressing something in the most concise way possible: *The corps goeth before, we follow after, we come to the grave, she is put into the fire, a lamentation is made* (Peacham).

References
⇒ **figure of speech**

bracketing

An economical writing convention used in **rewrite rules** and **phrase structure rules**. Optional rules are written in parentheses and alternative rules in curly brackets. As a result of this notational convention, the following four phrase structure rules (a)–(d) can be combined in (e).

(a) $NP \rightarrow N$,
(b) $NP \rightarrow Art + N$,
(c) $NP \rightarrow Art + Adj + N$,
(d) $NP \rightarrow Pronoun$

$$(e)\ NP \rightarrow \left\{ \begin{array}{c} (Art) + (Adj) + N \\ Pronoun \end{array} \right\}$$

bracketing paradox

In **word formation**, a paradox found in several classes of complex words, in which a single constituent grouping cannot satisfy the phonological conditions of language while functioning as the basis of semantic interpretation. The comparative **suffix** in English, for example, can combine only with single-syllable **bases** or two-syllable bases with weak secondary stress on the last syllable (e.g. *nicer, cleverer, crueler, gentler, luckier*). In words with bases of two or more syllables, the comparative is formed analytically (*more direct*). According to this rule-governed system, the negated adjective *unluckier* would have the following bracketed structures: (a) [$_A$ un [$_A$ lucky + er]] or (b) [$_A$[$_A$ un + lucky] + er]. Yet, the structure (a) cannot be the basis of the semantic interpretation because *unluckier*, in accordance with the bracketed structure (b), is (*more (unlucky)*) and not, as in (a), (*not (more lucky)*); cf. also [*Gödel number+*]*ing*, [*atomic scient+*]*ist*. Different solutions to this problem, each tied to a specific theory, have been suggested in more recent literature.

References
Kiparsky, P. 1983. Word formation and the lexicon. In F. Ingman (ed.), *Proceedings of the 1982 Mid-American linguistics conference*, Lawrence, KS.
Pesetsky, D. 1985. Morphology and logical form. *LingI* 16.193–246.
Sproat, R. 1985. On deriving the lexicon. MIT Diss.
———— 1988. Bracketing paradoxes, cliticization and other topics: the mapping between syntactic and phonological structure. In M. Everaert *et al.* (eds), *Morphology and modularity*, Dordrecht. 339–60.
Williams, E. 1981. Argument structure and morphology. *LRev* 1.81–114.

Brāhmi ⇒ **Sanskrit**

Brahui ⇒ **Dravidian**

branch

In the representation of the syntactic structure of sentences in the form of a **tree diagram**, branches are the connecting lines between two **nodes**, the branching-off points.

branching diagram ⇒ **tree diagram**

breaking (*also a*-umlaut, lowering, voice mutation)

Term in traditional **comparative linguistics** used originally by J. Grimm to refer to a number of different assimilatory **vowel** changes (⇒ **assimilation**) in Germanic languages. Some examples include the lowering in **Gothic** of [i, u] to [e, o] before a following [r] or [h]. The **diphthongization** in Old Norse of [e] to [ia] before [a], or to [io] before [u] in the following **syllable**, the assimilatory lowering of high vowels before non-high vowels in the following syllable in Old High **German**, the diphthongization of [e], [i] to [eo], [io] before [u], and of [æ] to [ea] before [r], [l], [h] + consonant and simple [h]: *eahta* 'eight', *heard*

'hard', *feallan* 'fall.' These diphthongs were later leveled out again. Today, only the diphthongizations are referred to as breaking.

References
Grimm, J. 1848. *Geschichte der deutschen Sprache*. Leipzig.
Howell, R. 1991. *Old English breaking and its Germanic counterparts*. Tübingen.
Morgenroth, W. 1959–60. Brechung, Umlaut, Vokalharmonie: eine Begriffsklärung. *WZUG* 9.201–16.
⇒ **English, historical grammars, sound change, umlaut**

breathy voice ⇒ **murmuring**

Breton

Celtic language spoken in Brittany (France) with approx. 1.2 million speakers. Breton has been well attested since the eighth century, but the oldest documents are no earlier than the sixteenth century. It belongs to the p-Celtic group (along with Cornish, **Welsh**, and the extinct Gaulish), and was brought to Brittany by immigrants from the British isles.

References
Fleuriot, L. 1964. *Le Vieux Breton: éléments d'une grammaire*. Paris.
Le Gléau, R. 1973. *Syntaxe du breton moderne (1710–1972)*. La Baule.
McKenna, M. 1988. *A handbook of modern spoken Breton*. Tübingen.
Press, I.J. 1986. *A grammar of modern Breton*. Berlin.
Trépos, P. 1968. *Grammaire bretonne*. Rennes.
⇒ **Celtic**

bridge verb

A term introduced by N. Erteschik in 1973 for verbs which allow extractions from finite complements. For example, *Who do you think met Byron?* vs **Who do you regret/whisper met Byron?*

References
Erteschik, N. 1977. *On the nature of island constraints*. Bloomington, IN.
Koster, J. 1987. *Domains and dynasties: the radical autonomy of syntax*. Dordrecht.
[⇒ **constraints, island, transformational grammar**]

British contextualism ⇒ **London School**

British English

Umbrella term used to denote a number of **dialects** spoken in the British Isles that vary primarily according to the regional and socio-economic background of their speakers.

(⇒ *also* **Cockney English**)

References

Hughes, A. and P. Trudgill. 1979. *English accents and dialects: an introduction to social and regional varieties of British English.* London.

McIntosh, A. 1952. *Introduction to a survey of Scottish dialects.* Edinburgh.

Orton, H. 1960. An English dialect survey: Linguistic Atlas of England. *Orbis* 9.331–48. (Repr. in H.B. Allen and G.N. Underwood (eds), *Readings in American dialectology.* New York, 1971. 230–44.)

Trudgill, P. (ed.) 1978. *Sociolinguistic patterns in British English.* London.

Wakelin, M.F. 1972. *English dialects: an introduction.* London.

Broca's aphasia (*also* expressive aphasia, motor aphasia, non-fluent aphasia)

Named after the French surgeon Paul Broca (1824–80), Broca's aphasia is an acquired **language disorder** characterized by fragmentary sentences consisting mainly of content words and simplified, or absent, morphological marking (⇒ **agrammatism**), by phonemic **paraphasias**, by **dysprosody**, and by a non-fluent style of speaking. The extent of the impairment in understanding oral or written language, and in writing, varies from patient to patient. (⇒ *also* **language and brain**)

References

Bates, E. *et al.* 1987. Grammatical morphology in aphasia. *Cortex* 23.545–74.

——— 1988. On the preservation of word order in aphasia: cross-linguistic evidence. *B&L* 33.323–64.

Daffner, K.R. *et al.* 1991. Broca's aphasia following damage to Wernicke's area: for or against traditional aphasiology. *Archives of Neurology* 48.766–8.

Kean. M.L. (ed.) 1985. *Agrammatism.* Orlando, FL.

Kolk, H. and C. Heeschen. 1992. Agrammatism, paragrammatism and the management of language. *Language and Cognitive Processes* 7.89–129.

Zurif, E. *et al.* 1993. An on-line analysis of syntactic processing in Broca's and Wernicke's aphasia. *B&L* 45 (special issue, ed. Y. Grodinsky). 448–64.

Broca's area

Named after its discoverer, the French surgeon Paul Broca (1824–80), this term denotes a cortical area associated with speech motor functions that is located at the base of the third gyrus in the left hemisphere of the brain. Broca believed that one's ability to speak could be traced to this area and early views attributed **Broca's aphasia** to a lesion in this area. (⇒ *also* **language and brain**, **language area**)

Brythonic ⇒ **Celtic**

bucco-facial apraxie ⇒ **apraxia**

Bulgarian

South **Slavic** language with approx. 7.5 million speakers (mostly in Bulgaria), which developed from a dialect of Thessalonica.

Characteristics: multiple occurrence of the negative particle in simple negations; postclitic definite article (⇒ **clitícization**) with limited inflection (gender, number, nominative vs objective); no indefinite article; rich verbal inflection, but loss of nominal case inflection; complex tense and **aspect** system with a narrative form: *Nìàmalo da izléze níšto ot tová* 'Nothing (it is said) will come of that' vs *Niáma da izléze níšto ot tová* 'Nothing will come of that'; as in **Macedonian**, no verbal infinitive. The letter ‹ъ› is used to represent [ə] between consonants; before 1945, the letter ‹ѣ› was also used.

References

Andrejčin L.D. 1977. *Gramatika na bălgarskija ezik.* Sofia.

Conev, B.N. 1984. *Istorija na bălgarskija ezik.* Sofia.

Feuillet, J. 1994. *Bulgare.* Munich.

Georgieva, E. and N. Todorova. 1981. *Bălgarskata knižovna reč.* Sofia.

Gramatika na săvremennija bălgarski knižoven ezik. 1982–3. 2 vols. Sofia.

Khubenova, M.G. and A. Dzhumadanova. 1983. *A course in modern Bulgarian.* Columbus, OH.

Părvev, X. 1987. *Săzdateli i tvorci na bălgarskoto ezikoznanie.* Sofia.

Popov, K.P. 1985. *Iz istorijata na bălgarskija knižoven ezik.* Sofia.

Rusinov, R.C. 1985. *Bălgarskijat knižoven ezik sled osvoboždenieto: 1878–1944.* Veliko Tărnovo.

Scatton, E.A. 1984. *A reference grammar of Modern Bulgarian.* Columbus, OH.

Historical grammar

Mirčev, K. 1963. *Istoričeska gramatika na bălgarskija ezik*, 2nd edn. Sofia.

Dictionaries

Bălgarski etimologičen rečnik. 1971– . Sofia.

Čolakova, K. (ed.) 1977– . *Rečnik na bălgarskija ezik*, vol. 6. 1990. Sofia.

Journal

Bălgarski Ezik
⇒ **Slavic**

Burgundian ⇒ **Germanic**

Burmese

Sino-Tibetan language, official language of Burma (approx. 22 million speakers). Long writing tradition (since the twelfth century) in a script borrowed from India; strong lexical borrowing from Pali.

Characteristics: **tonal language**, voice qualities such as creaky voice also utilized. No inflection, but derivation and prefixization are used; word order: topic–comment; verb generally sentence-final. The ordering of **thematic relations** to specific elements of a sentence is often governed by **selection restrictions** or must be deduced from the context or general speaker knowledge.

References
Burling, R. 1967. *Proto Lolo-Burmese*. Bloomington, IN. (= *IJAL* 33:1, pub. 43.)
Okell, J. 1969. *A reference grammar of colloquial Burmese*, 2 vols. London.

Roop, D.H. 1972. *An introduction to the Burmese writing system*. New Haven, CT.

Burushaski

Language isolate in Kashmir with approx. 30,000 speakers (at least two dialects: Xunza, Yasin).

Characteristics: four **noun classes**, two numbers, rich morphology, **ergative language** (split ergativity), word order: SOV.

References
Berger, H. 1974. *Das Yasin-Burushaski (Werchikwar): Grammatik, Texte, Wörterbuch*. Wiesbaden.
—— 1992. *Das Burushaski: Schicksale einer zentralasiatischen Restsprache*. Heidelberg.
Lorimer, D. 1935. *The Burushaski Language*, 3 vols. Oslo.

C

cacophony [Grk *kakophōnía* 'ill sound']

Linguistic or musical discord resulting from a disagreeable combination of sounds. The antonym is **euphonism**.

cacuminal ⇒ **retroflex**

Caddoan

Language family in North America with four languages, each with fewer than 200 speakers. Chafe (1979) considers Caddoan to be a member, along with **Siouan** and **Iroquoian**, of the Macro-Siouan language group, while Greenberg (1987) adds Keresan to the group and designates it Keresiouan.

References
Chafe, W.L. 1979. Caddoan. In L. Campbell & M. Mithun (eds), *The languages of Native America: historical and comparative assessment*. Austin, TX, 213–35.
Greenberg, J.H. 1987. *Language in the Americas*. Stanford, CA.
⇒ **North and Central American languages**

calculus

Deductive system of basic signs and rules that guarantees that mathematical or logical operations are carried out in a controlled, non-contradictory, mechanical fashion. Such basic signs may be letters, natural numbers, words, **logical connectives**, **truth values**, among others. Rules are, for example, arithmetical operations such as multiplication, addition, syntactic rules, rules for logical connections. The concept of calculus plays a basic role in the formalization of grammatical theories about natural languages to the degree that the models of generative language descriptions can be construed as calculus (or as **algorithms** instead of rules, if commands are operative). A generative grammar (e.g. **transformational grammar**) contains a finite set of objects (all words in a language) and rules (constituent structure rules, transformational rules (⇒ **transformation**, **recursive rules**) by means of which an infinite set of sentences can be generated. The language of calculus is the **formal language** or **artificial language** of **formal logic**. (⇒ *also* **formalization, mathematical linguistics**)

References
Carnap, R. 1937. *Logical syntax of language*. London.

Curry, H.B. 1963. *Foundations of mathematical logic*. New York.
Whitehead, A.N. and B. Russell. 1910–13. *Principia mathematica*, 3 vols. Cambridge.

calque

A French term for a new word modeled after a word in another language. While, in the case of **borrowing**, a **foreign word** and its meaning are adopted wholesale into the other language as a **loan word**, a calque emerges when the language is adapted to new concepts. This can happen in several ways: (a) by way of a borrowed meaning through change and expansion of the meaning of native words – *write* (originally 'to scratch') influenced by Lat. *scribere*; (b) through **neologisms** loosely based on a foreign concept – Ger. *Sinnbild* for *symbol*; (c) through word-for-word **loan translation** – *crispbread* from Ger. *Knäckebrot*, *accomplished fact* from Fr. *fait accompli*, Span. *rascacielos* for *skyscraper*; (d) through a loose loan translation – *brotherhood* for Lat. *fraternitas*.

References
⇒ **borrowing**

Cambodian ⇒ **Mon-Khmer**

Campidanese ⇒ **Sardinian**

Cam-Thai

Branch of **Austro-Thai** in South-East Asia with approx. 60 million speakers. The most important languages are **Thai** (30 million) and Laotian (17 million).

Reference
Benedict, P.K. 1975. *Austro-Thai: language and culture*. New Haven, CT.

cant

The **jargon** or **secret language** of a socially isolated and often "asocial" group that deviates from the standard language especially in its specific vocabulary. Cants are intentionally meant to be unintelligible to those who have no command of them. Thus, whenever cant vocabulary is adopted into the standard language newly coined secret words become necessary. The typical process involves either changing the meanings of words in the common language through metaphor (e.g. *snow* for *cocaine*) or borrowing words from a foreign language. Various words of **Yiddish** origin have been taken over into colloquial English in this way: *shyster* 'swindler,' *meshuggener* 'crazy person,' etc. (⇒ *also* **argot**, **slang**)

Cantonese ⇒ Chinese

capital vs small (*also* upper case vs lower case)

Capital and small letters double the inventory of many **alphabetic writing systems** in that, as a rule, each capital letter has a corresponding small letter. Capital and small letters are found in all writing systems that are based on the Latin, Greek, or Cyrillic **alphabets**, as well as in the Armenian Khutsuri script (biblical script). Capital letters are used in proper names (in Greenlandic only in proper names), sentence-initially (not in Greenlandic), and in particular expressions (the first person singular pronoun ‹I› and all words in titles except particles, in English; all nouns in German and – prior to 1947 – in Danish).

References
⇒ **writing**

captation

Pragmatic **figure of speech**. An appeal to the goodwill of the reader or the listener, e.g. through stressed modesty. Captation is used as a **topos** (called 'ad captandum appeal') especially in introductory speech.

References
⇒ **figure of speech**

cardinal number [Lat. *cardinalis* 'that serves as a pivot']

1 In **set theory** the cardinal number of a (finite) set A is the number of elements of A. For example: $A = \{$red, orange, yellow, green, blue, indigo, violet$\}$, Card $(A) = 7$.

2 Subset of the **numerals**: the basic numbers *one*, *two*, *three*, etc.

cardinal vowel

Vowel reference system developed by the English phonetician D. Jones (1881–1967). The system was developed first as a two-, then as a three-dimensional reference system for abstract 'normal vowels' and offered a standardized phonetic description of vowels for all languages.

References
⇒ **phonetics**

Carib

Language family containing approx. 50 lan-guages in northern South America and the Antilles; today only approx. 25,000 speakers. Established by Gilij (1780–4), Carib is considered by Greenberg (1987) to belong to the Macro-Carib language family. Word order often OVS.

References
Derbyshire, D.C. 1979. *Hixkaryana*. Amsterdam.
Durbin, M. 1977. A survey of the Carib language family. In E.B. Grasso (ed.), *Carib speaking Indians*. Tucson, AZ.
Gilij, F.S. 1780–4. *Saggio di storia americana o sia storia naturale, civile e sacra, de' regni e delle provincie spagnuole de terra ferma nell' America Meridionale*, 4 vols. Rome.
Greenberg, J.H. 1987. *Language in the Americas*. Stanford, CA.
Hoff, B.J. 1968. *The Carib language*. The Hague.
Koehn, E. and S. Koehn. 1986. Apalai. In D.C. Derbyshire and G. Pullum (eds), *Handbook of Amazonean languages*. Berlin. 33–127.
Rodriguez, A.D. 1985. Evidence for Tupi–Carib relationships. In H.E. Klein and L. Stark (eds), *South American Indian languages*. Austin, TX.
⇒ **South American Languages**

Cartesian linguistics

Term introduced by N. Chomsky for all rationalistic linguistic approaches based on the approach of the French philosopher R. Descartes (1598–1650), the school of the **Port Royal grammar**, J.G. Herder and W. von Humboldt (⇒ **rationalism**). In assuming that 'innate ideas' exist prior to the cognitive (especially linguistic) development of humans, Cartesian linguistics contrasts with empirical approaches to language (⇒ **empiricism**) which postulate sensory perception (thus success and learning) as the source of all knowledge. (⇒ *also* **mentalism**)

Reference
Chomsky, N. 1966. *Cartesian linguistics: a chapter in the history of rationalist thought*. New York.

Cartesian product ⇒ set

case [Lat. *casus* 'a fall,' trans. of Grk *ptōsis* 'a fall']

Grammatical category of inflected words which serves to indicate their syntactic function in a sentence and, depending on the function, involves **government** and **agreement**. Case systems may vary from language to language and undergo continuous change. The cases of **nominative languages** are generally named after the reconstructed cases of **Indo-European**: **nominative**, **genitive**, **dative**, **accusative**, **ablative**, **locative**, **instrumental**, **vocative**. In other languages, there are often other cases: in **ergative languages ergative** and **absolutive** are used instead of nominative and accusative; in **Finno-Ugric** languages, the terms **partitive**, **elative**, **illative**, **inessive**, among others, occur. In modern Indo-European languages, many of the original eight cases have disappeared, with original locatives, ablatives, instrumentals, and some genitives being replaced by the dative case or prepositional phrases. The merger of various cases due to sound change is termed **syncretism**. In inflectional languages, case is marked by grammatical morphemes which often have a variety of functions, such as marking **gender** and **number**. Adpositions, as in *give to Caroline* are occasionally referred to as case. In non-inflectional languages, where syntactic functions are primarily encoded by word order or sentence structure (e.g. English and French), attempts have been made to associate cases with specific syntactic positions. (⇒ **case theory, Government and Binding theory**).

A general distinction can be made between (a) **casus rectus** (nominative) and **oblique cases** (genitive, dative, accusative, etc.), and (b) syntactic and semantic cases. The syntactic cases such as nominative and accusative encode primary syntactic functions such as subject and object and do not have any specific semantic function. On the other hand, cases like ablative, instrumental, and locative generally represent adverbials which have a more specific semantic content. In some languages (e.g. **Turkish, Finnish, Russian**) the use of cases is also sensitive to the definiteness and/or animacy of their constituents. Despite numerous attempts dating back to antiquity, there are as yet no satisfactory semantic classifications of individual cases.

References

Allen, C.L. 1995. *Case marking and reanalysis. Grammatical relations from Old to Early Modern English*. Oxford.

Blake, B.J. 1994. *Case*. Cambridge.

Brecht, R. and J. Levine (eds) 1987. *Case in Slavic*. Columbus, OH.

Comrie, B. 1991. Form and function in identifying cases. In F. Plank (ed.), *Paradigms: the economy of inflection*. Berlin. 41–56.

Gil, D. 1982. Case marking, phonological size and linear order. In J.P. Hopper and S.A. Thompson (eds), *Studies in transitivity*. New York.

Hjelmslev, L. 1935. *La catégorie des Cas: étude de grammaire générale*. Aarhus.

Jakobson, R. 1936. Beiträge zur allgemeinen Kasuslehre. *TCLP* 6. 240–88.

Kuryłowicz, J. 1964. *The inflectional categories of Indo-European*. Heidelberg.

Moravcsik, E.A. 1978. Case marking of objects. In J.H. Greenberg (ed.), *Universals of human language*. Stanford, CA. Vol. 4, 250–89.

Shibatani, M. 1983. Towards an understanding of the typology and function of case-marking. In S. Hattori and K. Inoue (eds), *Proceedings of the thirteenth International Congress of Linguistics, Tokyo 1982*. Tokyo. 45–58.

Van Kemenade, A. 1987. *Syntactic case and morphological case in the history of English*. Dordrecht.

Wierzbicka, A. 1980. *The case for surface case*. Ann Arbor, MI.

Yip, M., J. Maling, and R. Jackendoff. 1987. Case in tiers. *Lg* 63.217–50.

Bibliography

Campe, P. 1994. *Case, semantic roles, and grammatical relations: a comprehensive bibliography*. Amsterdam.

2 Term for semantic role (⇒ **thematic relation**), or 'deep case.' (⇒ *also* **case grammar**)

case grammar (*also* case theory, **functional grammar**)

General term for linguistic theories which employ the concept of 'deep case' (semantic roles or **thematic relations**) as the central means of explaining both the syntactic structure as well as the meaning of sentences. Deep cases name the various semantic roles of the various 'participants' in the situation described by the verb. The number and types of cases are a matter of continuous debate in the literature. Two main approaches to semantic roles can be distinguished.

(a) The case grammar introduced by Fillmore (1968, 1977), taken up and modified by Dik (1978, 1980) as **functional grammar** and by Starosta (1978) as the 'Lexicase Model.' The most important cases in the Fillmore model are the following: (i) **agent**, the relation of the animate volitional causer of an action: *Philip* in *Philip opened the door*; (ii) **instrumental**, the relation of the inanimate causer of an action (*The wind blew the door open*) or the object with which an action is accomplished (*Philip opened the door with his key*); (iii) objective (in earlier works, the most neutral case, later termed **patient** or goal), the role of the inanimate participant directly affected by an action (*the door* in (i)); (iv) dative (also: **recipient**, **benefactive**, experiencer), the role of the animate participant who is less directly affected by the action or state described by the verb (in contrast to the **patient**): *Philip opened the door for Caroline*); (v) locative for the location of the action.

More recent approaches to case grammar have proposed a classification of semantic roles on the basis of the **aspect** of the verb (see Dik 1978, 1983; Dowty 1991). Thus the agent of an action (⇒ **process US action**) is set in contrast to the experiencer of a state (*Philip* in *Philip is* *afraid*) (⇒ **stative vs active**), which is no longer equated with the recipient as in Fillmore's system.

(b) The so-called 'localistic theory' (see Gruber 1967; Anderson 1971, 1977; Jackendoff 1972, 1987; Lutzeier 1991) takes as its point of departure a very limited number of general locative roles which can be found in verbs of motion and position, and applies them to more 'abstract' events, especially to verbs of possession and change of possession. Jackendoff (1972) establishes the following roles he calls **thematic relations**: cause, goal, theme, source, and locative. In this relation system the agent is grouped with cause, while the patient, the experiencer, and the first argument of verbs of position (*The door is over there*) are grouped under theme. The goal corresponds to recipients (*Caroline* in *Philip promised Caroline that he would quit smoking*), as well as to the goal or direction of verbs of motion as in *The plane departed for Los Angeles*).

Semantic role theories determine not only the semantic roles, but also their function in grammar, i.e. how role structure, semantic structure, and syntactic structure interplay. According to Fillmore (1977), each verb selects a certain number of deep cases which form its case frame. Thus, a case frame describes important aspects of semantic **valence**, both of verbs and of other elements with valence (adjectives and nouns). Syntactic rules are determined by semantic role structures which are themselves determined by the case frame of the verb in question. Case frames are subject to certain restrictions, such as that a deep case can occur only once per sentence. **Syntactic functions** are assigned on the basis of thematic relations. The strongest hypothesis of case grammar is that syntactic functions can be defined in terms of deep cases. Fillmore (1968) takes the following hierarchy for his universal subject selection rule: Agent < Instrumental < Objective. If the case frame of a predicate contains an agent, it is realized as the subject of an active sentence; otherwise, the role following the agent in the hierarchy (i.e. Instrumental) is selected as the subject. The general rule is the following: if the roles X, Y, or Z occur in a sentence, then the element highest in the hierarchy is realized as the subject in the basic voice of the language. Jackendoff (1972) and Dik (1980) formulate other **hierarchy universals**, based on a slightly modified hierarchy, which apply for various universal phenomena such as object selection, verbal agreement, passive, reflexivization, etc. Case grammar stands out from other recent linguistic theories by the assumption that (1) syntactic functions are concepts of universal grammar derived from deep cases and (2) deep cases can explain phenomena that are handled in other theories by syntactic notions. The influence of case grammar on more recent research can be seen in the fact that numerous linguistic theories incorporate thematic relations, cf. **theta criterion** in **transformational grammar**, **relational grammar**, **functional grammar**.

References

Abraham, W. (ed.) 1978. *Valence, semantic case and grammatical relations.* Amsterdam.

Anderson, J.M. 1971. *The grammar of case: towards a localistic theory.* Cambridge.

——— 1977. *On case grammar: prolegomena to a theory of grammatical relations.* London.

——— 1990. Case grammar contrasts. In J. Fisiak (ed.), *Further insights into contrastive analysis.* Amsterdam. 23–8.

Dik, S.C. 1978. *Functional grammar.* Amsterdam.

——— 1980. *Studies in functional grammar.* London/New York.

——— (ed.) 1983. *Advances in functional grammar.* Dordrecht.

Dirven, R. and G. Radden (eds) 1987. *Concepts of case.* Tübingen.

——— 1987. *Fillmore's case grammar: a reader.* Heidelberg.

Dowty, D.R. 1991. Thematic proto-roles and argument selection. *Lg* 67.547–619.

Fillmore, C.J. 1968. The case for case. In E. Bach and R.T. Harms (eds), *Universals in linguistic theory.* New York. 1–88.

——— 1977. The case for case reopened. In P. Cole and J.M. Sadock (eds), *Syntax and semantics*, vol. 8: *Grammatical relations.* New York. 59–82.

Finke, P. 1974. *Theoretische Probleme der Kasusgrammatik.* Kronberg.

Gruber, J.S. 1967. *Studies in lexical relations.* Bloomington, IN. (Also in *Lexical structures in syntax and semantics.* Amsterdam, 1976.)

Halliday, M.L. 1967–8. Notes on transitivity and theme in English. *JL* part I, 1967, 37–81; part II, 1967, 177–274; part III, 1968, 153–308.

Huddlestone, R. 1970. Some remarks on case-grammar. *LingI* 1.501–11.

Jackendoff, R.S. 1972. *Semantic interpretation in generative grammar.* Cambridge, MA.

——— 1987. The status of thematic relations in linguistic theory. *LingI* 18.369–411.

——— 1991. *Semantic structures.* Cambridge, MA.

Lutzeier, P. 1991. *Major pillars of German syntax.* Tübingen.

Roca, I.M. (ed.) 1992. *Thematic structure: its role in grammar.* Berlin and New York.

Schwarze, C. (ed.) 1978. *Kasusgrammatik und Sprachvergleich: kontrastive Analysen zum Italienischen und Deutschen.* Tübingen.

Starosta, S. 1978. The one per cent solution. In W. Abraham (ed.), *Valence, semantic case and grammatical relations.* Amsterdam. 459–577.

Bibliographies
Rubattel, C. 1977. Eine Bibliographie zur Kasus-grammatik. *LingB* 51.88–106.
Wotjak, G. 1979. Bibliographie zur Kasusgrammatik. *DaF* 16.184–91.

case theory

1 A basic theory of the **Government and Binding theory** whereby certain lexical categories can assign **case**. The following distinctions are made in case theory: (1) case dependent on lexical items, e.g. the German verb *helfen* 'to help' governs the **dative** case; (2) case dependent on semantic roles (⇒ **thematic relation**); (3) case dependent on the grammatical functions of lexical items, e.g. *Philip's book* where *Philip* is in the **genitive** case. This theory is more elaborate in 'case languages' such as German and Latin than in English.

References
Chomsky, N. 1981. *Lectures on government and binding*. Dordrecht.
Ostler, N. 1980. *A theory of case linking and agreement*. Bloomington, IN.
Schlesinger, I.M. 1995. *Cognitive space and linguistic case*. Cambridge.

2 ⇒ **case grammar**

Cassubian ⇒ Kashubian

Castillian ⇒ Spanish

casus rectus [Lat. *rectus* 'straight']

Nominative case, as opposed to all other cases, which are grouped together as **oblique cases**. The image implied by 'casus rectus' refers to an upright rod or pole which is declined (inflected) to various degrees (⇒ **inflection**)

References
⇒ **case**

catachresis [Grk *katáchrēsis* 'analytical application']

The use of a rhetorical **trope** to name something that otherwise has no name, (in contrast to **metaphor**): e.g. (*table*) *leg*. Quintilian called catachresis a 'necessary misuse.' Catachresis is often used to name products that are the result of new technology. In Brit. Eng. the crossing-point of several highways is called *spaghetti junction*. Catachresis is common in advertising slogans such as *Spalding, the longest ball*, or *Molson's dry beer*. Many terms now considered proper are catachresis in origin: *a leaf* (*of paper*), *the foot* (*of a mountain*), *balkanization*.

References
⇒ **figure of speech**

Catalan

Romance language spoken by approx. 7 million speakers in the eastern and northeastern part of the Iberian peninsula, on the Balearic Islands, in French Roussillon, in the Sardinian city of Alghero, the official language of Andorra. The dialect of Barcelona, long suppressed by Franco and now enjoying a limited resurgence, forms the basis for the written language. The status of Catalan as an independent language can be seen at the phonological level in the palatalization of initial [l] (Lat. *luna > lluna* 'moon'). Catalan dialects break into east and west variants, with Valencian belonging to the latter. Whether Catalan belongs to Ibero-Romance (⇒ **Spanish**) or Gallo-Romance (⇒ **Occitan**) is still debated; in many ways the area where it is spoken can be seen as a transition zone between the two.

References
Badía Margarit, A.M. 1962. *Gramática catalana*, 2 vols. Madrid.
——— 1981. *Gramática histórica catalana*. Valencia.
Berquist, M.F. 1981. *Ibero-Romance: comparative phonology and morphology*. Washington, DC.
Blasco Ferrer, E. 1985. *Gramatica storica del Catalano e dei suoi dialetti con speciale riguardo all'Algherese*. Tübingen.
Bonet, S. and J. Solá. 1986. *Sintaxi generativa catalana*. Barcelona.
Fabra, P. 1981. *Gramática catalana*, 10th edn. Barcelona.
Gili, J. 1967. *Introductory Catalan grammar: with a brief outline of the language and literature*, 3rd edn. Oxford.
Griera, A. 1966. *Tresor de la llengua*, 14 vols. Barcelona.
Holtus, G.M. Metzeltin, and C. Schmitt (eds), 1989. *Lexikon der romanistischen Linguistik*, vol. 5. Tübingen.
Hualde, J.I. 1992. *Catalan*. London.
Kremnitz, G. 1979. *Sprachen im Konflikt: Theorie und Praxis der katalanischen Soziolinguisten*. Tübingen.
Lüdtke, J. 1984. *Katalanisch: ein einführende Sprachbeschreibung*. Munich.

Dictionaries
Catalan dictionary. 1994. London.
Coromines, J. 1980. *Diccionari etimològici complementari de la llengua catalana* (to date, 7 vols to 'SOF'). Barcelona.

cataphor ⇒ cataphora

cataphora [Grk *kataphorá* 'bringing down, downward motion']

Term coined by K. Bühler (1934) in analogy to **anaphora** indicating a linguistic element which points to information immediately following the utterance. Such cataphoric elements of speech (**deixis**) include **determiners**, personal **pronouns**, possessive pronouns, and interrogative pronouns in questions, e.g. *He who* in *He who laughs last laughs longest.*

References
Bühler, K. 1934. *Sprachtheorie.* Jena. (2nd edn Stuttgart, 1965.)
Halliday, M.A.K. and R. Hasan. 1976. *Cohesion in English.* London.
Reinhart, T. 1983. *Anaphora and semantic interpretation.* London. (Rev. repr. 1984.)
Wiese, B. 1983. Anaphora by pronouns. *Linguistics* 21.373–417.

catastrophe theory [Grk *katastréphein* 'to overturn']

General mathematical theory of planes in *n*-dimensional spaces. Singularities (i.e. 'catastrophes') frequently arise for the descriptive functions in sections of such planes. With some imagination one can interpret such sections as dynamic processes. Wildgen (1982) tries to make this potentially useful for linguistics; so far, it has been applied to morphology and semantics.

References
Wildgen, W. 1982. *Catastrophe theoretic semantics: an elaboration and application of René Thom's theory.* Amsterdam.
—— 1989. Catastrophe theory as a basic tool in theoretical linguistics. *TL* 14.259–94.

catchword

1 A much-used word that implicitly interprets or evaluates a complex state of affairs. A catchword has the effect of bringing solidarity to groups in society. Because catchwords have a **persuasive**–agitative function, they are often the cause of public controversy, e.g. *traditional values*, *equal opportunity*, *discrimination*. A catchword can be understood as a condensed, linguistically fixed form of a **topos**.

2 ⇒ **lemma**

categorematic expression

In **Montague grammar**, categorematic expressions are understood to be expressions without any (lexical) meaning of their own. To the extent that this is the case, they do not appear in the lexicon, but are only introduced via syntactic rules. The corresponding semantic (interpretation) rules encompass the semantic effect of the categorematic expressions in more extensive syntagms. Examples of categorematic expressions are conjunctions, articles and quantifiers.

Reference
Montague, R. 1974. *Formal philosophy: selected papers of Richard Montague.* New Haven, CT.

categorial grammar

Grammatical model developed by Polish logicians (Ajdukiewicz 1935) as an algorithm for checking the wellformedness of sentences. Its application to natural language was worked out primarily by J. Lambek, Y. Bar-Hillel, D. Lewis, and R. Montague. New developments of categorial grammar are represented by generalized categorial grammar and **categorial unification grammar**. All variants of categorial grammar are characterized by a specific category concept as well as by the parallel treatment of syntax and semantics. The names of categories in categorial grammar encode the combinatorial properties of linguistic expressions and as a consequence important aspects of their distribution and syntactic function. For instance, the category S/N expresses the fact that an expression of this category can be combined with an expression of category N to form an expression of category S. (This corresponds to the traditional statement that a noun and a verb form a sentence.) The category 'verb' in contrast to S/N does not explicitly reflect this fact. Complex categories such as S/N are derived from a limited number of basic categories: N for nominal expressions (*Philip, he, the book*) and S for sentences (*Philip is reading the book*). From these, any number of complex categories can be derived, such as S/N (for *sleep, work*), (S/N)/N for *greet, shave*, (S/N)/(S/N) for *eagerly, secretly*, etc. The complex categories are analyzed as mathematical functions and named functor categories. Thus S/N names a function (operation) which has N as an argument and S as a value. Correspondingly, expressions are classified into functor (or operator) and argument (or operand) expressions. This categorial system has many advantages:

(a) There is no need to indicate all the various syntactic combinatory rules; instead, the following rule schema is sufficient: an expression of category A/B is combined with an expression of category B to form an expression of category A. This rule schema corresponds mathematically to a functional application: a functor expression of category A/B is applied to an 'appropriate' argument of category B, yielding a value of category A. According to this schema, an intransitive verb of the category S/N can be combined with a nominal expression of category N to yield a sentence S. If, however, one tries to combine an S/N expression with a transitive verb of the category (S/N)/N, the functional application will fail since the argument is of the wrong category. In order to see whether *Philip works well* is a well-formed sentence, each expression must first be assigned a category, and then the functional application schema is applied successively to all categories. If the result is S, then the sentence is well formed. The following diagram illustrates the successive functional applications:

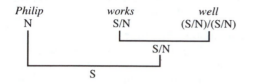

(b) Syntactic representations reconstruct both the constituent structure of complex expressions as well as their function–argument structure. Thus the successive functional applications above represent the analysis of the sentence into constituents: the sentence is composed of the immediate constituents *Philip* and *works well*. The latter in turn is a complex expression consisting of *works* and *well*. In addition, the sentence is also analyzed in terms of dependency relations between sister constituents. Two sister constituents are not of the same rank, but rather are distinguished from one another as functor and argument. Thus *well* is the functor of *works* and the complex expression *works well* is the functor of *Philip*. This functional hierarchy is important for the semantic interpretation of sentences. It can also be used for the reconstruction of **dependency** in general and **valence** in particular, or for making more precise the concept 'head of a construction' (Vennemann 1977).

(c) The mathematical representation simplifies the verification of the grammar and its application, such as in **computational linguistics**.

The syntactic system of categories as well as the syntactic combination of expressions into sentences runs parallel to the semantic system of categories and to the semantic combination of the meanings of simple expressions into sentence meaning. The relation between syntax and semantics is compositional, with syntactic categories and semantic types standing in the closest possible relation, the former merely encoding the latter. Thus categorial grammars have a semantically motivated formal syntax. For approaches to categorial grammar in morphology, see Šaumjan (1971), Reichl (1982), Hoeksema (1985), Hoeksema and Janda (1987), Moortgat (1987); in phonology, Wheeler (1987); in pragmatics Zaefferer (1979).

'Classical' categorial grammar is not adequate for the complete and adequate description of a language, since it cannot handle discontinuous constituents, word order permutations, as well as morphological markings and relationships such as **agreement** and **government**. Extensions of the 'classical' model include the introduction of **transformations** (Lewis 1970; Partee 1975), syntactic features (Bach 1983, in the framework of generalized categorial grammar and categorial unification grammar), as well as rules which are not functional applications according to rule schema in (a) mentioned above, see Lambek (1958), Geach (1972), and Oehrle *et al.* (1987). ($\Rightarrow$ *also* **intensional logic, Montague grammar**)

References

Ajdukiewicz, K. 1935. Die syntaktische Konnexität. *Studia Philosophica* 1.1–27. (Trans. in S. McCall (ed.), *Polish logic*. Oxford, 1967. 207–31.)

Bach, E. 1983. On the relationship between word-grammar and phrase-grammar. *NL&LT* 1.65–89.

Bar-Hillel, Y. 1954. Logical syntax and semantics. *Lg* 30.230–7.

——— 1964. *Language and information*. Reading, MA.

Bartsch, R. and T. Vennemann. 1972. *Semantic structures: a study in the relation between semantics and syntax*. Frankfurt. (2nd edn 1973.)

Buszkowski, W., W. Marciszewski, and J. van Benthem (eds) 1988. *Categorial grammar*. Amsterdam.

Cresswell, M.J. 1973. *Logics and languages*. London.

Dowty, D.R. 1982. Grammatical relations and Montague grammar. In P.T. Jacobson and G.K. Pullum (eds), *The nature of syntactic representation*. Dordrecht. 79–130.

Geach, P. 1972. A program for syntax. In D. Davidson and G. Harman (eds), *Semantics of natural language*. Dordrecht. 483–97.

Hoeksma, J. 1985. *Categorial morphology*. New York.

——— and R.D. Janda. 1987. Implications of process-morphology for categorial grammar. In R. Oehrle, E. Bach, and D. Wheeler (eds), *Categorial grammars and natural language*. Dordrecht. 199–248.

Lambek, J. 1958. The mathematics of sentence structure. *American Mathematical Monthly* 65.154–70.

Lewis, D. 1970. General semantics. *Synthese* 22.18–67.

Montague, R. 1974. *Formal philosophy: selected papers of R. Montague*, ed. R.H. Thomason. New Haven, CT.

Moortgat, M. 1987. Mixed composition and discontinuous dependencies. In R. Oehrle, E. Bach, and D. Wheeler (eds), *Categorial grammars and natural language*. Dordrecht. 319–48.

——— 1989. *Categorial investigations*. Dordrecht.

Oehrle, R., E. Bach, and D. Wheeler (eds) 1987. *Categorial grammars and natural language*. Dordrecht.

Partee, B. 1975. Montague grammar and transformational grammar. *LingI* 6.203–300.

Reichl, K. 1982. *Categorial grammar and word-formation: the de-adjectival abstract noun in English*. Tübingen.

Šaumjan, S. 1971. *Strukturelle Linguistik*. Munich.

Steedman, M. 1993a. Categorial grammar. *Lingua* 90.221–58.

—— 1993b. Categorial grammar. In J. Jacobs *et al.* (eds), *Syntax: an international handbook of contemporary research*. Berlin and New York. 395–412.

Vennemann, T. 1977. Konstituenz und Dependenz in einigen neueren Grammatiktheorien. *Sprachwissenschaft* 2. 259–301.

Von Stechow, A. 1990. Categorial grammar and linguistic theory. *SLang* 14.433–78.

Wheeler, D. 1987. Consequences of some categorially motivated phonological assumptions. In R. Oehrle, E. Bach, and D. Wheeler (eds), *Categorial grammars and natural language*. Dordrecht. 467–88.

Wood, M.M. 1993. *Categorial grammars*. London.

Zaefferer, D. 1979. Sprechakttypen in einer Montague-Grammatik. In G. Grewendorf (ed), *Sprechakttheorie und Semantik*. Frankfurt. 386–417.

categorial unification grammar (*abbrev.* CUG)

An umbrella term for grammatical models in which the syntactic theory of **categorial grammar** is realized using the methods of **unification grammar**. The simple and derived syntactic categories of categorial grammar and the combination rules can be encoded as feature structures. The application of combination rules takes place with the help of feature unification. Calder, Klein, and Zeevat (1988) developed a version of CUG called unification categorial grammar which combines a categorial syntax with a compositional semantics based on **discourse representation theory**. Another version was suggested by Karttunen (1986) and used to describe word order variations in **Finnish**. CUG formalisms are used for the implementation of several experimental **computational linguistics** program systems.

References

Calder, J., E. Klein, and H. Zeevat. 1988. Unification Categorial Grammar: a concise, extendible grammar for natural language processing. *COLING* 88.83–6.

Karttunen, L. 1986. *Radical lexicalism*. CSLI Report 86–68. Stanford, CA.

Uškzoreit, H. 1986. Categorial Unification Grammar. *COLING* 86.187–94.

category feature

A subgroup of semantic–syntactic features in **transformational grammar** described by N. Chomsky in 1965. Category features identify linguistic units as belonging to specific gram-matical categories such as noun or verb.

category symbol

In **transformational grammar**, an abbreviation for classes of grammatical (syntactic) categories such as *NP, VP, V* as well as for individual elements from these classes. (⇒ *also* **grammatical categories**)

Caucasian languages

Geographical term for the languages which are spoken in the linguistically diverse Caucasus region. In addition to a number of **Indo-European** and **Turkic** languages, the term includes especially the languages of three local language families, **North-West Caucasian**, **North-East Caucasian**, and **South Caucasian**. Genetic affinity among the three groups has hitherto not been proved. Other attempts at relating the Caucasian languages to languages outside of the Caucasus, e.g. **Basque**, are equally dubious. (⇒ *also* **classification of languages**)

References

Catford, J.C. 1977. Mountain of tongues: the languages of the Caucasus. *Annual Review of Anthropology* 6.283–314.

Comrie, B. 1981. *The languages of the Soviet Union*. Cambridge. Chap. 5.

Deeters, G. 1963. Die kaukasischen Sprachen. In B. Spuler (ed.), *Handbuch der Orientalistik*, vol. I, 7: *Armenisch und kaukasische Sprachen*. Leiden. 1–79.

Dirr, A. 1928. *Einführung in das Studium der kaukasischen Sprachen*. Leipzig.

Geiger, B. *et al.* 1959. *Peoples and languages of the Caucasus*. The Hague.

Hewitt, G. 1992. *Caucasian perspectives*. Munich.

Klimov, G.A. 1994. *Einführung in die kaukasische Sprachwissenschaft*, trans. J. Gippert. Hamburg.

Vinogradov, V.V. *et al.* (eds) 1966–8. *Jazyki narodov SSSR*, 5 vols. Moscow.

Journal
Studia Caucasica

causal clause

Semantically defined clause which usually functions as an adverbial modifier describing the cause of the state of affairs expressed in the main clause: *He was tired because he had been hiking all day*.

causative (*also* factitive verb)

Semantically defined class of verbs and verb phrases which describe a caused action. Formally the following subgroups can be distinguished. (a) morphological causatives: certain derived regular (= weak) verbs which can be paraphrased as 'to cause that': *to set = to make sit, to lay = to make lie, to fell = to make fall*. Historically, these verbs in English were formed by suffixing the causative element *-jan* to certain strong verbs which caused **umlaut** in the root vowel: cf. Goth. *dōmjan*, OE *dēman* 'to judge, to deem.' Another type of causative verb is formed from adjectives with the suffix *-en*: *black – blacken, red – redden, fat – fatten*. (b) Ergative verbs (⇒ **unaccusative**) used both transitively and intransitively where the transitive use expresses causation, cf. *The sun is melting the ice* vs *The ice is melting*. There are also corresponding verb pairs that are not etymologically related: *to die – to kill*. (c) **Auxiliaries** with causative meaning such as *to make, to have*, cf. *Have him brought in*; *You can't make me do that*. (⇒ *also* **recessive**)

References

Cole, P. 1983. The grammatical role of the cause in universal grammar. *IJAL* 49.115–83.
Comrie, B. 1985. Causative verb formation and other verb-deriving morphology. In T. Shopen (ed.), *Language typology and syntactic description*. Cambridge. Vol. 3, 309–48.
Comrie, B. and M. Polinsky (eds) 1993. *Causatives and transitivity*. Amsterdam and Philadelphia, PA.
Dubinsky, S., M.-R. Lloret, and P. Newman. 1988. Lexical and syntactic causatives in Oromo. *Lg* 64.485–500.
Kastovsky, D. 1973. Causatives. *FL* 10.255–315.
Shibatani, M. (ed.) 1976. *Syntax and semantics*, vol. 6: *The grammar of causative constructions*. New York.
Syeed, S.M. 1985. *Morphological causatives and the problem of the transformational approach*. Bloomington, IN.
⇒ **generative semantics**

c-command

An abbreviation for 'constituent command'. C-command is one of the most important universal structure-related terms in generative grammar (⇒ **transformational grammar**) along with **domination** and **maximal projection**. A constituent X c-commands Y (a constituent which is different from X) if and only if the first branching node dominating X also dominates Y and when neither X nor Y dominates the other. In the **prepositional phrase** (PP) *in the book* (=[prep + NP]$_{PP}$), the preposition *in* c-commands the following noun phrase *the book*; *the* c-commands *book*, but not *in*. C-command plays a central role in the various modules of the theory and thus defines **binding**, **government**, and the **scope** of **quantifiers**.

References

Aoun, J. and D. Sportiche. 1983. On the formal theory of government. *LRev* 2.211–36.
Chomsky, N. 1981. *Lectures on government and binding*. Dordrecht.
Radford, A. *Transformational syntax: a student's guide to Chomsky's Extended Standard Theory*. Cambridge. Chs 10 and 11.
Reinhart, T. 1976. The syntactic domain of anaphora. Dissertation, MIT, Cambridge, MA.
―――― 1983. *Anaphora and semantic interpretation*. London.

Cebuano ⇒ Malayo-Polynesian

cedilla

Derived from Span. *zedilla* 'little z,' the cedilla is a comma-shaped **diacritic** that originally comes from Greek ζ (zēta) and functions variously as a subscript beneath Roman letters: when placed below the letter *c*, it corresponds in **French** to [s] or /s/ before the dark vowels *a, o, u* (e.g. *garçon* 'boy'); in **Rumanian**, the cedilla differentiates between ţ [ts], ş [ʃ] and *t* [t], *s* [s]; in **Latvian** it denotes **palatalization**.

Celtiberian ⇒ Celtic

Celtic

Branch of **Indo-European**, formerly spread over large parts of Europe and Asia Minor, but today found only in northwestern Europe. Geographically, Celtic falls into two groups. (a) Continental Celtic, which is extinct today and attested only in inscriptions, borrowings and place-names; to this group belong Celtiberian (or Hispano-Celtic), Gaulish, Lepontic (sometimes subsumed under Gaulish), and Galatian. In the last two decades, there have been some important finds of longer texts, such as the tablets in Botorrita (Celtiberian) and Larzac (Gaulish). (b) Insular Celtic, under which fall the two groups **Gaelic** (or Goidelic), with the subdivisions Irish (approx. 500,000 speakers), Scots-Gaelic (approx. 90,000 speakers) and the recently extinct Manx (on the Isle of Man), on the one hand, and Brythonic, with the branches **Welsh** (approx. 400,000 speakers, attested since the eighth century), **Breton** (approx. 1.2 million speakers in the French province of Brittany, where speakers emigrated to from Britain some 1,400 years ago), and Cornish (extinct since the eighteenth century, but currently experiencing a revival), on the other hand. It is still under debate whether the division into Continental and Insular Celtic also constitutes a genetic grouping. For there is a further division that exists between the Celtic languages which does not coincide with the former grouping, i.e. that into the so-called p- and q-Celtic languages depending on the fate of IE *k^w, which in the q-Celtic languages remained a velar sound (Celtiberian, Irish, and some Gaulish dialects), whereas in the p-Celtic languages it became *p* (the Brythonic languages and Gaulish along with Lepontic). The exact genetic relationship between these groups remains controversial to date.

Other characteristics: the whole of the Celtic branch of languages lost IE *p, which is the most significant feature. Furthermore, there is no infinitive and no verb 'have.' Features characteristic of all the Insular Celtic languages include initial consonantal mutations, originally a **sandhi** phenomenon caused by a preceding vowel, but later heavily grammaticalized, and pronominal forms affixed to the verb. Its orthography leaves it unclear whether Continental Celtic had any kind of mutation. Word order in Insular Celtic is VSO, which deviates from other IE languages.

References
Ball, M. (ed.) 1993. *The Celtic languages*. London and New York.
Gregor, D.B. 1980. *Celtic: a comparative survey.* Cambridge.
Hendrick, R. (ed.) 1990. *Syntax and semantics*, vol. 23: *The syntax of the modern Celtic languages.* New York.
Jackson, K. 1953. *Language and history in Early Britain*. Edinburgh.
Macauley, D. (ed.) 1992. *The Celtic languages.* Cambridge.
McCone, K.R. 1992. Relative Chronologie: Keltisch. In R. Beekes *et al.* (eds), *Rekonstruktion und relative Chronologie: Akten der VIII. Fachtagung der Indogermanischen Gesellschaft.* Innsbruck. 11–39.
Pedersen, H. 1909/13. *Vergleichende Grammatik der keltischen Sprachen.* 2 vols. Göttingen. (Repr. Zürich 1976.) Abbrev. English version: H. Lewis and H. Pedersen. 1937. *A concise comparative Celtic grammar.* Göttingen.)
Schmidt, K.H. (ed.) 1977. *Indogermanisch und Keltisch.* Wiesbaden.

Journals
Bulletin of the Board of Celtic Studies.
Celtica.
Eriu.
Etudes Celtiques.
Revue Celtique.
Zeitschrift für Celtische Philologie.

center ⇒ **antecedent**

Central Sudan languages ⇒ **Chari-Nile languages**

central vs peripheral ⇒ **compact vs diffuse**

centralization

Replacement of a less central vowel with a more central vowel. For example, centralization in English takes place in virtually all unstressed vowels and is represented by **schwa** [ə], cf. ['tɛlə‾græf] ‹telegraph›.

centrifugal vs centripetal [Lat. *fugare* 'to drive away'; *petere* 'to aim at']

Terms borrowed from physics which indicate the properties of forces which proceed either from or towards a center.

1 L. Tesnière uses these two terms in his **dependency grammar** for the relationship between the dependency of elements on each other and their syntactic order relative to one another. The linear order: governing expression (= center)/dependent expression he terms 'centrifugal' (cf. Fr. *cheval blanc*), the reverse order, 'centripetal' (cf. *white horse*). His concept of language typology is based on this distinction, which in another terminology is called postspecifying vs prespecifying (⇒ **word order**).

References
Greenberg, J.H. 1966. *Language universals: with specific reference to feature hierarchies.* The Hague.
Lehmann, W.P. (ed.) 1978. *Syntactic typology: studies in the phenomenology of language.* Austin, TX.
Tesnière, L. 1959. *Elements de syntaxe structurale.* Paris.
Vennemann, T. and R. Harlow, 1977. Categorial grammar and consistent basic VX serialization. *TL* 4.227–54.

2 B.A. Abramov among others uses these terms in Russian linguistics to distinguish various syntactic 'potencies' (= the ability to fulfill certain syntactic functions). 'Centrifugal potency' expresses the ability of linguistic expressions to dominate other expressions: this term corresponds largely with **valence**. 'Centripetal potency' on the other hand refers to the syntactic property of being able to function as a dependent element.

Reference
Abramov, B.A. 1967. Zum Begriff der zentripetalen und zentrifugalen Potenzen. *DaF* 3.155–68.

centum vs satem languages [Lat. *centum*, Skt *śatám* 'one hundred']

In **historical linguistics**, a division set up according to the reconstruction of the **Indo-European** languages into a Western and an Eastern group that are named after their respective term for the numeral '100.' The original (now not uncontroversial) thesis maintained the following: The Indo-European proto-language had three series of guttural sounds, i.e. velars [k, g, gʰ], palatals [k', g', gʰ'] and labio-velars [kᵘ, gᵘ, gᵘʰ]. These three rows were developed differently in the individual daughter languages: in the so-called centum languages (= **Germanic**, **Celtic**, **Italic**, etc.) the palatals merged with the velars, the labio-velars remaining separate; in the so-called satem languages (= Indic (⇒ **Indo-Aryan**), **Iranian**, **Slavic**, etc.) the velars merged with the labio-velars, while the palatals here remained separate and subsequently developed further into spirants. Consequently, the originally palatal **stop** corresponds to [k] in centum languages (in Germanic to [h] due to subsequent **Grimm's law**) and to some kind of sibilant in the satem languages. Several criticisms of a phonological kind have been leveled against this hypothesis; but especially the more recent discoveries of **Tocharian** (1904) and **Hittite** (1906), two centum languages located in the east, have proved this classification into two geographically and phonologically distinguished language branches to be not unproblematic; also, the development within the individual languages is not as unequivocal as was formerly believed.

References
⇒ **classification of languages, historical linguistics, Indo-European**

Cercle Linguistique de Copenhague ⇒ **glossematics**

Cezian ⇒ **North-East Caucasian**

Chadic

Language family of **Afro-Asiatic** south of Lake Chad with more than 125 languages; by far the largest is **Hausa** with over 25 million speakers.
   Characteristics: **tonal languages** (high, low, occasionally falling), glottalized consonants; three-member gender system (masculine, feminine, plural) with complex plural formation; rich system of voices (including directional meaning components). Verbal groups consist of a complex of auxiliary (marking aspect, mood, person) and a verbal noun; word order SVO.

References
Newman, P. 1977. Chadic classification and reconstructions. *AfL* 5. 42.
——— 1980. *The classification of Chadic within Afroasiatic*. Leiden.
Wolff, E. 1981. Die tschadischen Sprachen. In B. Heine *et al.* (eds), *Die Sprachen Afrikas*, Hamburg. 239–62.

chain

A technical term from **Government and Binding theory** which formally represents the steps of a (possibly repeated) **movement transformation** as a sequence of positions in s-structure. The positions affected by a movement are joined in a chain in such a way that the first member of the chain is the end point of the movement, the last member of the chain is the point of departure and all points in between are intermediate landing sites of the movement. Chains serve to define the so-called **theta criterion**, which requires an unambiguous correspondence between **arguments** and thematic roles (⇒ **thematic relation**): as a result of the theta criterion, a chain must possess only one theta-marked position if it contains an argument, and correspondingly, every chain must contain exactly one argument, if it is assigned a theta role.

References
McClosky, J. and P. Sells. 1988. Control and A-chains in modern Irish. *NL&LT* 6.143–90.
Rizzi, L. 1986. On chain formation. In H. Borer (ed.), *Syntax and semantics*, vol. 19: *The syntax of pronominal clitics*. Orlando, FL. 65–95.
——— 1986. Relativized minimality. Cambridge, MA.

characteristic function

Special type of **function**[1]: let there be two sets A and B, where B is a subset of A. The characteristic function of B assigns, from a third set C (that contains only the elements 'true' and 'false,' or 1 and 0) to every element x of A exactly the value 'true' (or 1), if x is an element of B. Cf. as set A the set of all **phonemes** in English, as set B the set of all vowels in English. The characteristic function indicates which phonemes from A are vowels in English. In **categorial grammar** or **model-theoretic semantics**, the characteristic function corresponds to the **extension** of the **predicate**.

References
⇒ **categorial grammar, formal logic**

Chari-Nile languages

Language family in Africa, considered by Greenberg (1963) to be a branch of the **Nilo-Saharan** languages. The following subgroupings can be made: the East Sudan languages (with nine branches, including Nubian and Nilotic), the Central Sudan languages, and a number of individual languages. The most widely spoken languages include Dinka (approx. 2.7 million speakers) and Nubian (approx. 2 million speakers) in Sudan, Luo (approx. 2.2 million speakers) and Kalenjin (approx. 2 million speakers) in Kenya, Turkana (approx 1.5 million speakers) in Uganda and Kenya. Historically there have been a number of debates regarding these languages, since researchers such as Müller (1877) and Meinhof (1912) considered some languages to be 'Hamitic,' based on cultural and anthropological considerations (⇒ **Afro-Asiatic**).

Important contributions were made by Lepsius (1880), Westermann (1935), Köhler (1955) and Tucker and Bryan (1956).

Characteristics of these fairly diverse languages: lack of noun classes which are common to the neighboring **Bantu** languages; isolated development of a gender system (e.g. in Massai, masculine and feminine); a distinction between singular and plural in the noun is widely made. Old written attestations exist of Nubian (eighth century).

References
Dimmendaal, G.W. 1983. *The Turkana language.* Dordrecht.
Greenberg, J.H. 1963. *The languages of Africa.* Bloomington, IN. (2nd edn 1966.)
Köhler, O. 1955. *Geschichte der Erforschung der nilotischen Sprachen.* Berlin.
Lepsius, R. 1880. *Nubische Grammatik mit einer Einleitung über die Völker und Sprachen Afrikas.* Berlin.
Meinhof, C. 1912. *Die Sprache der Hamiten.* Hamburg.
Müller, F. 1877. *Die Sprachen Basa, Grebo und Kru im westlichen Afrika.* Vienna.
Tucker, A.N. and M.S. Bryan. 1956. *The non-Bantu languages of North-Eastern Africa.* (Handbook of African languages 3). Oxford.
Vossen, R. 1982. *The Eastern Nilotes, linguistic and historical reconstructions.* Berlin.
Westermann, D. 1935. Charakter und Einteilung der Sudansprachen. *Africa* 8.129–48.

chart

In **parsing**, a schematic way to show, economically and without redundancy, the syntactic representations of all possible well-formed substrings of a sentence. Since sentences of natural language frequently contain structurally ambiguous strings of words, as well as clearly definable constituents, it is often not possible to decide which of the possible structures of a string of words are appropriate for interpretation (⇒ **ambiguity**). In order not to recompute all the parts of each new analysis (i.e. backtrack) in ambiguous structures, all pieces of accumulated knowledge are put into the chart, where they can be consulted as often as necessary and in any possible combination. One can picture a chart simply as a collection of all the possible tree diagrams of all the substrings of a sentence, in which the same parts of different tree diagrams are always represented only once.

References
Kaplan, R. 1970. *The mind system. A grammar rule language.* Santa Monica, CA.
Kay, M. 1967. Experiments with a powerful parser. *AJCL.* Microfiche 43.
———— 1980. *Algorithmic schemata and data struc-*

tures in syntactic processing. Stockholm.
Varile, G.B. 1983. Charts: a data structure for parsing. In M. King (ed.), *Parsing natural language.* London. 73–87.
(⇒ *also* **computational linguistics**)

Chechen ⇒ North-East Caucasian

checked syllable ⇒ closed vs open

checked vs unchecked

Binary phonological **opposition** in **distinctive feature** analysis, based on acoustically analyzed and spectrally defined criteria (⇒ **acoustic phonetics**, **spectral analysis**). Acoustic characteristic: strong energy release over a short period vs lower energy release over a longer period. Articulatory characteristic (⇒ **articulation**): closing vs opening of the glottis.

Reference
Jakobson, R. *et al.* 1951. *Preliminaries to speech analysis.* Cambridge, MA. (6th edn 1965.)

Cheremis ⇒ Finno-Ugric

Cherokee ⇒ Iroquoian

chiasmus [Grk *chiasmós* 'diagonal arrangement' (after the Greek letter χ 'chi')] (*also* chiasm)

The inversion of the second of two parallel phrases or clauses, e.g. *The French live to eat, the English eat to live.* Chiasm is often used as a syntactic form of **anthithesis**, and has long been popular in **advertising language** (*The question isn't whether grape nuts are good enough for you, it's whether you are good enough for grape nuts*).

References
⇒ **figure of speech**

Chibchan ⇒ Chibchan-Paezan

Chibchan-Paezan

Language group consisting of about forty languages located in Central America and in northwestern South America with approx. 400,000 speakers. Greenberg (1960, 1987) combined the Chibchan languages in the more restricted sense with the Paezan languages into a common language family, 'Chibchan-Paezan'; this grouping is still debated. The largest languages are Guaymi in Panama (approx. 65,000 speakers) and Paez in Columbia (approx. 60,000 speakers).

Characteristics: relatively simple sound system; tendency towards **polysynthesis** and descriptivity. Occasional numeral classification, **noun classes**, and verb classification (⇒

classifying verb) in the southern language Itonama. One unusual syntactic trait: the subject of past tense sentences is marked with the genitive. Word order usually SVO.

References
Craig, C. 1985. Indigenous languages of Nicaragua of Chibchan affiliation. In E.M. Peña (ed.), Estudios de lingüística Chibcha. San José. 47–55.
Greenberg, J.H. 1956. The general classification of Central and South American languages. Repr. in A.F.C. Wallace (ed.), Men and cultures. Philadelphia, PA, 1960.
—— 1960. The general classification of Central and South American languages. In: A. Wallace (ed.), Selected Papers of the Fifth International Congress of Anthropological and Ethnological Sciences. 791–4. Philadelphia.
—— 1987. Languages in the Americas. Stanford, CA.
Lopez-Garcia, A. 1995. Gramática muisca. Munich.

Dictionary
Holmer, N.M. 1952. Ethno-linguistic Cuna dictionary. Göteborg.
⇒ South American languages

Chicksaw ⇒ Muskogen

childhood dysphasia ⇒ developmental aphasia, specific language impairment

Chinese

Largest **Sino-Tibetan** language, which is actually a group of at least six languages: Mandarin (in the form Putenghua the official language of the People's Republic of China, in the form Guoyu the official language of Taiwan; with 613 million speakers the most widely spoken language in the world), Wu (on the Yangtze, 84 million), Yue (in South China, along with Cantonese, 54 million), Min (Taiwan and off-shore coast, 77 million), Kan-Hakka (South China, 67 million), and Hsiang (Hunan, 49 million). The beginnings of the ideographic writing system date back 4,000 years; today it is the oldest writing system in use.

Characteristics: all are **tonal languages** (Mandarin: four tones: high, rising, falling–rising, falling; Cantonese: nine tones) with somewhat complex tone–sandhi rules (combinations of tones). Simple syllable structure. Morphology: no inflection, but frequent derivations and compounds; in contrast to Classical Chinese, modern Chinese is not a strictly **isolating language**. Example of compounding: *fù-mǔ* 'father-mother' = 'parents'; *zhěn-tóu* 'rest-head' = 'pillow' (⇒ **classifying language**). Word order: topic–comment; the placement of the object depends on, among other things, definiteness. **Serial verb constructions** are frequent, where certain verbs take on the function of prepositions.

References
Baxter, W.H. 1992. A handbook of Old Chinese phonology. Berlin and New York.
Chao, Y.-R. 1968. A grammar of spoken Chinese. Berkeley, CA.
Henne, H. et al. 1977. A handbook of Chinese language structure. Oslo.
Killingley, S.-Y. 1994. Cantonese. Munich.
Kratochvil, P. 1968. The Chinese language today. London.
Li, C.N. and S. Thompson. 1981. Mandarin Chinese: a functional reference grammar. Berkeley, CA.
Matthews, S. and V. Yip. 1994. Cantonese: a comprehensive grammar. London.
Norman, J. 1988. Chinese. Cambridge.

Dictionaries
Chi, W. 1977. Chinese–English dictionary of contemporary usage. Berkeley, CA.
A classified and illustrated Chinese–English dictionary. 1981. By the compiling group, Guangzhou Institute of Foreign languages. Hong Kong.
Hornby, A.S. 1989. Oxford advanced learner's English–Chinese dictionary, 3rd edn. Hong Kong.

Chinese writing

Logographic script dating back to the early second century BC and still used for **Chinese** (and partly for **Japanese**). Typically, a sign consists of two parts, one so-called 'radical' indicating a semantic area, and the rest which contains indications as to the phonetic realization. The 214 radicals also serve for the lexicographical classification of the signs. Altogether, there are over 40,000 signs; however, fewer than 10,000 are sufficient for nearly all purposes.

References
Schmidt, W.G.A. 1990. Einführung in die chinesische Schrift- und Zeichenkunde. Hamburg.
⇒ **Chinese, writing**

Chinookan ⇒ Penutian

Chocktaw ⇒ Muskogean

Chomsky adjunction

A special case of **adjunction** in which a constituent B is the sister of A and daughter of another node A which immediately dominates the sisters A and B, i.e. the adjoined constituent is simultaneously the sister and daughter of an A constituent which is copied to create two segments.

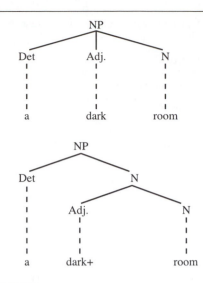

References
⇒ **transformational grammar**

Chomsky hierarchy ⇒ generative capacity

Chukchi ⇒ Paleo-Siberian

Chukotko-Kamchatkan ⇒ Paleo-Siberian

chunk(ing)
Term introduced by Miller and Selfridge (1950), and again by Miller (1956), in **memory** research to denote the (individually differing) segmentation and bundling of information units. Based on such a schematization of knowledge, which depends on personal experience or expert knowledge, it is quite plausible that the capacity to remember information is variable: a professional chess player will be able to recall the positions of a particular move (that was just played out before one's eyes) much more completely than a novice player, since the professional chess player can engage his/her command of the rules for chunking (to structure the information of the playing board).

References
Miller, G.A. 1956. The magical number seven, plus or minus two: some limits on our capacity for processing information. *PsychologR* 63.81–97.
Miller, G.A. and J.A. Selfridge. 1950. Verbal context and the recall of meaningful material. *American Journal of Psychology* 63.176–85.
⇒ **comprehensibility**

circonstant ⇒ dependency grammar

circumflex [Lat. *circumflexus* 'in rounded form']
1 **Diacritic** mark, in the shape of a hat ‹^› and placed above Latin letters or in the shape of a

snake (⇒ **tilde**) and placed above a Greek letter (⇒ **accent**[2]). In ancient Greek, the circumflex denotes a particular tone for the given vowel. In Romance languages, the circumflex has various uses: in **French** in combination with *e* to denote the open vowel [ɛ] (e.g. *forêt*) and in combination with *o* to denote the closed vowel [o] (e.g. *rôle*); in **Rumanian** to distinguish between ‹i› for [i] and ‹î› for [ɨ]; in Greenlandic to denote vowel length.

2 In **Indo-European** studies, a designation for overlong syllables (those of three morae). (⇒ *also* **mora**, **law of three morae**)

class
A whole set of (linguistic) elements that are characterized by at least one common property. For example, the words *book*, *back*, and *bathe* belong to the class of expressions in English that begin with the letter *b*, while *aunt*, *sister*, and *daughter* belong to the class of female kinship terms. In this use, 'class' is synonymous with **set**. Classes determined in this way can be in various relations to one another, a distinction being drawn primarily between hierarchical (organized according to the schema of *genus proximum – differentia specifica*) classifications and cross-classifications (⇒ **definition**). Examples of a hierarchical classification are speech act classes (⇒ **speech act theory**) as well as morphological classes (⇒ **morphology**); the systematization in **phonology** by means of **distinctive features** is based on a cross-classification. In taxonomic **structuralism** the form classes, characterized by their different realizations, are the basis of language description (⇒ **distribution**).

class noun ⇒ common noun

classical Arabic ⇒ Arabic

classical Greek ⇒ Greek

classical Latin ⇒ Latin

classification
An elementary method of analysis of taxonomic **structuralism** that after the **segmentation** of the linguistic continuum into basic units (**phone**, **morph**), attributes the units arrived at in this way to certain classes of elements with the same characteristics by comparing these units with one another. After a linguistic continuum has been divided into such basic units, these units are co-ordinated. Such paradigms can be found at all levels of description and the phonological, morphological, syntactic, and semantic analysis of languages is based on this.

References
⇒ **operational procedures**

classification of languages

The process and result of grouping several languages together based on certain criteria. (a) Areal (geographical) classification, based on linguistic similarities which have arisen from cultural contact between linguistic communities as well as geographical proximity through **borrowing** of words and grammatical constructions. Languages which share essential characteristics due to borrowings are termed **linguistic areas**; examples include the Balkan languages or the influence of **Chinese** on **Vietnamese**. (b) Genealogical (genetic) classification, based on linguistic similarities that result from being descendants of a common **proto-language**. Languages that derive from a common proto-language are called language families, e.g. the **Indo-European** languages. Genealogical classification is based primarily on words and grammatical forms preserved in common (Voegelin and Voegelin 1977; Ruhlen 1987). (c) Typological classification, based on structural similarities that are independent of geographical influence and/or genealogical affiliation, e.g. **isolating/analytic** vs **synthetic languages**, **ergative** vs **nominative languages**, languages with various **word orders**.

Typological similarities can be explained either functionally, i.e. as performing functions which are common to all human languages, or as resulting from a common biological capacity for language present in all human beings (⇒ **universals**). In specific cases, it is often very difficult to discern between areal, genealogical, and typological factors: for example, there are cases where genealogically related languages are still in geographical contact after their development into separate languages.

References
Campbell, G.L. 1991. *Compendium of the world's languages*, 2 vols. London and New York.
Comrie, B. (ed.), 1987. *The world's major languages*. London. (2nd edn 1991).
—— (ed.) 1990. *The major languages of East and South-East Asia*. London.
—— (ed.) 1990. *The major languages of South Asia, the Middle East and Africa*. London.
—— (ed.) 1990. *The major languages of Eastern Europe*. London.
—— (ed.) 1990. *The major languages of Western Europe*. London.
Haarman, H. 1976. *Aspekte der Arealtypologie*. Tübingen.
Haas, M.R. 1966. Historical linguistics and the genetic relationship of languages. In T.A. Sebeok (ed.), *Current trends in linguistics*. The Hague. Vol. 3, 113–54.
Hymes, D.H. 1959. Genetic classification: retrospect and prospect. *AnL* 1.50–66.
Katzner, K. 1986. *The languages of the world*. London. (2nd rev. edn 1994.)
Lyovin, A.V. 1966. *An introduction to the languages of the world*. Oxford.
Parlett, D.S. 1967. *A short dictionary of languages*. London.
Robins, R.H. 1973. The history of language classification. In T.A. Sebeok (ed.), *Current trends in linguistics*. The Hague. Vol. 11, 3–44.
Ruhlen, M. 1987. *A guide to the world's languages*, vol. I: *Classification*. London.
Voegelin, C.F. and F.M. Voegelin. 1977. *Classification and index of the world's languages*. Bloomington, IN.

Bibliography
Troike, R.C. 1990. *A bibliography of bibliographies of the languages of the world*, 2 vols. Amsterdam.
⇒ **historical linguistics**, **language typology**, **universals**

classifier

Particle used to combine a numeral and a mass noun, e.g. *head* in *five head of cattle*. Classifiers refer to something countable in the denotation of the noun, and thus must be distinguished from expressions which refer to a certain measuring standard, such as *pound* in *five pounds of beef*. In many languages (especially in East Asia), classifier constructions are very common, because a noun cannot be directly connected to a numeral, cf. **Chinese** *san ge ren*, lit. 'three piece people,' i.e. 'three people.' In these **classifying languages**, there are numerous classifiers which are used for nouns belonging to certain semantic domains (e.g. for nouns which indicate flat, round, or edible objects). (⇒ *also* **gender**, **noun class**)

Reference
Hundius, H. and U. Kölver. 1983. Syntax and semantics of numeral classifiers in Thai. *SLang* 7.165–214.

classifying language

Classification type for languages that have the tendency to relate all expressions to certain logical mental categories (such as person, object, characteristics, etc.) through the affixation of **noun class**-forming prefixes. These prefixes also serve for syntactic structuring, as all word groups belonging together are characterized by the same prefix. There are classifying languages, for instance, among South African native dialects.

References
⇒ **language typology**

classifying verb

A phenomenon which became known primarily

through Apache (⇒ **Na-Dene**) languages such as **Navajo**. With different types of objects, action verbs have varying morphological forms which are characteristic for their corresponding objects, cf. Navajo *-ʔál-tìn / -ká* 'to carry a small object / long object / container with its contents'; *-ʔààh / -tììh / -kààh* 'to place a small object / long object / container with its contents.'

References
Sapir, E. and H. Hoijer. 1967. *The phonology and morphology of the Navaho language*. Berkeley and Los Angeles, CA.
Seiler, H. 1986. *Apprehension: language, object and order*, part III: *The universal dimension of apprehension*. Tübingen. Chapter 4.
Langacker, R. 1969. Pronominalization and the chain of command. In D.A. Reibel and S.A. Schane (eds), *Modern studies in English*, Englewood Cliffs, NJ.

clause

Neutral term for both **dependent** (⇒ **subordinate clause**) and independent (⇒ clauses **main clause**).

clause-mate condition

A restriction on **transformations**, so that a transformation may only relate an element to other elements within the same clause. These clause-mate conditions appear in the early versions of **generative grammar**, e.g. with respect to reflexivization. (⇒ *also* **constraints, transformational grammar**)

Reference
Klima, E.S. 1964. Negation in English. In J.A. Fodor and J.J. Katz (eds), *The structure of language*, Englewood Cliifs, NJ. 246–323.

cleft sentence (*also* clefting)

Syntactic construction where a single clause has been divided into two clauses. The term 'clefting' refers to the transformation in generative **transformational grammar** which derives the cleft sentence from basic sentences: *Caroline found the dog – It was Caroline who found the dog*. The paraphrase *What Caroline found was the dog* is termed pseudo-clefting. In this case, the clefted constituent is moved to the right and transformed into a predicate noun, leaving behind an **interrogative pronoun** as a pronominal copy. Cleft sentences serve to mark the **constituents** that are the **focus** of the sentence and are especially used to indicate contrast. (⇒ *also* **theme vs rheme, topic vs comment**)

References
Akmajian, A. 1970. On deriving cleft sentences from pseudo-cleft sentences. *Ling* I. 1.149–68.

Collins, P.C. 1991. *Cleft and pseudo-cleft constructions in English*. London.
Cullicover, P.W. 1977. Some observations concerning pseudoclefts. *Ling&P* 1.347–75.
Halvorsen, P.-K. 1978. *The syntax and semantics of cleft constructions*. Austin, TX.
Higgins, F.R. 1979. *The pseudo-cleft construction in English*. New York.
Jenkins, L. 1974. Cleft reduction. In C. Rohrer and N. Ruwet (eds), *Actes du Colloque Franco-Allemand de grammaire transformationnelle*. Tübingen. Vol. 1, 182–91.

clefting ⇒ cleft sentence

cliché

Pejorative term taken from printers' language, generally used to refer to a commonly occurring utterance that is used schematically. 'Cliché' is also used as a more neutral synonym for **stereotype, idiom**, or **formula**.

Reference
Partridge, E. 1978. *A dictionary of clichés*. London.
Redfern, W. 1989. *Clichés and coinages*. Oxford.

click

1 **Speech sound** caused by the sudden opening of an oral air chamber which causes the surrounding air to rush into that chamber. The chamber is formed by a truncated closure at the velum and, for **stops**, by a further closure – possible for stops – in the front of the oral cavity. Clicks are found in several languages of southern Africa, e.g. in the **Khoisan** language Nama as well as in the **Bantu** languages of Zulu and Xhosan. In African language studies and in the International Phonetic Alphabet (1989) the following notations are customary: ⊙, ǀ, ǁ, ! (these correspond to the following symbols in the International Phonetic Alphabet (1979): [⊙], [ʇ], [ʗ], [ʖ]). The sound that occurs, for example in a kiss, is a labial click: [⊙].

References
⇒ **phonetics**

2 Acoustic signal used in psycholinguistic tests on **speech recognition** and **language production** to determine the psychological reality of grammatical units. In several investigations subjects were exposed simultaneously to linguistic utterances in one ear and click signals in the other ear. In these tests, clicks are remembered exactly at constituent boundaries, while clicks within constituents were displaced in their memories to constituent boundaries ('click displacement'). By changing the click position in this way the hypothesis could be confirmed that constituents play a more decisive role in speech recognition than other grammatical units (syllables, words) since they immediately

serve the formation of **propositions**.

References
Bever, T.G. 1970. The cognitive basis for linguistic structures. In J.R. Hayes (ed.), *Cognition and the development of language*. 279–352.
Kimball, J.P. 1973. Seven principles of surface structure parsing in natural language. *Cognition* 2.15–47.
Levelt, W.J.M. 1974. *Formal grammars in linguistics and psycholinguistics*, vol. 3: *Psycholinguistic applications*. The Hague.
[⇒ **psycholinguistics**]

climax

Mounting by degrees through linked words or phrases with related meaning of increasing intensity, e.g. *Veni, vidi, vici* (Caesar).

References
⇒ **figure of speech**

clinical linguistics

A subdiscipline of **applied linguistics** that makes use of linguistic theories, methodology, and research findings for the explanation, diagnosis, and treatment of organic and/or psychological disturbances in communication and language acquisition. While clinical linguistics *applies* linguistic theories, **neurolinguistics** *develops* linguistic theories. In Britain, clinical linguistics is viewed as a link between linguistics and **speech-language pathology**.

References
Crystal, D. 1984. *Linguistic encounters with language handicaps*. Oxford.
———— 1987. *Clinical linguistics*. London.

Journal
Clinical Linguistics and Phonetics

clinical phonology

Term referring to a subdiscipline of **clinical linguistics**.

clipping

Short variant of a complex word. (a) In 'head words,' the first part is used: *ad*(*vertisement*), *math*(*ematics*). (b) In 'end words,' the beginning of a word is dropped: (*tele*)*phone*, (*air*)*plane*). (c) Occasionally, the middle part of a word is dropped to create an 'elliptical word': *news*(*paper*)*boy*. (⇒ *also* **word formation**)

Reference
Marchand, H. 1960. *The categories and types of present-day English word-formation*. Munich. (2nd edn 1969.)

cliticization

General term for the process of adding **proclitics** and **enclitics**.

Reference
Uhlenbeck, E.M. 1990. Clitics, morphemes and words: their structural differences. *PICL* 14.637–41.

closed-class word ⇒ synsematic word

closed set

Characteristic of a **set** whose number of elements is closed, e.g. the rules of phoneme combinations in a given language.

closed vs open

1 Characteristic of **vowels**. The opposition refers to the degree to which the resonance chamber is open during the formation of vowels.

2 Characteristic of **syllables**. Syllables are 'open' when they end in a vowel, 'closed' when they end in one or more consonants. English has both open (e.g. [piː] in ['piːkak] *peacock*) and closed (e.g. [piːk] *peak*) syllables. Closed syllables are not found at all in the Austronesian language (⇒ **Malayo-Polynesian**) of Tahiti nor in **Old Church Slavic**.

cluster

In Weinreich's semantic theory, an unordered set of semantic features. For example, *daughter* has among other features [+feminine] and [+offspring]. The order of the features is arbitrary. In contrast ⇒ **concatenation**[2]. (⇒ *also* **interpretive semantics**)

Reference
Weinreich, U. 1966. Explorations in semantic theory. In T.A. Sebeok (ed.), *Current trends in linguistics*. The Hague. Vol. 3, 395–477.

cluttering (*also* battarism, tachysphemia)

Term used in neurology, **speech–language pathology**, and psychopathology for one type of fluency disorder and/or its associated thought processes. Characteristics include an accelerated rate of speech in long sentences or those with polysyllabic words, the omission or repetition of syllables, a distortion of sounds as well as a reduction of consonant clusters (⇒ **anaptyxis**, **assimilation**, **blend**, **metathesis**). Cluttering is associated with impulsive behavior and sudden vasomotor reactions such as blushing. As a symptom, it represents a distortion of temporal structure; as a syndrome it may be associated with **specific language impairment** and **developmental dyslexia**. In contrast to stutterers (⇒ **dysfluency**), clutterers are able to control their behavior in situations where 'good speaking' is required. This phenomenon is not widely accepted as a clinical entity in North America.

References
Daly, D.A. 1986. The clutterer. In K. St Louis (ed.), *The atypical stutterer*. Orlando, FL.
Silverman, F. 1992. *Stuttering and other fluency disorders*. Englewood Cliffs, NJ.

coalescence [Lat. *coalescere* 'to grow together']

Sound change that brings about a simplification in the syllable structure of a word, e.g. a CV–VC sequence lacking an initial consonantal syllable after a preceding syllable with an empty **coda** is to be avoided. Both syllables coalesce, the combination of which brings about either a long vowel or a diphthong as a new syllable **nucleus**[2].

References
⇒ **syllable**

co-articulation

In **phonetics**, term for anticipatory articulation. Contrasting with the orthographic representation of individual letters, the occurrences of sounds that correspond to speech sounds are not discrete units. Speech production occurs through the continuous movement of the articulators without natural pauses. Not all **articulators** are always equally involved: for example, English vowels are regularly nasalized before nasal consonants, cf. *bag* [bæg] vs *bang* [bæ̃ŋ]. Co-articulation can bring about all types of **assimilation**.

References
⇒ **phonetics, sound change**

Cockney

Dialectal variant of **British English** spoken in the inner city of London. The name, derived from ME **cokenay** ('cock's egg'), was used originally as a nickname to refer to effeminate townspeople in London.

References
Chambers, R.W. and M. Daunt. 1931. *A book of London English*. London.
MacKenzie, B.A. 1928. *The early London dialect*. Oxford.
Matthews, W. 1938. *Cockney: past and present*. London.
Sivertsen, E. 1960. *Cockney phonology*. Oslo.

co-constituent

Constituents which are immediately dominated by the same **node** (⇒ **domination**). In the tree diagram of *The Chairwoman held a lecture*, the NP *the chairwoman* and the VP *held a lecture* are co-constituents, but also *the* and *chairwoman*, as well as *a* and *lecture* are co-constituents; not, however, *held* and *a*, because they are not dominated by a common node.

References
⇒ (*also* **immediate constituent analysis**).

coda [Lat. *coda* 'the extreme, end part of something']

Final segment of a **syllable** between the **nucleus**[2] and the head of the following syllable, e.g. [t] in *bitter*, [d] in *head*.

References
Kaye, J. 1990. 'Coda' licensing. *Phonology* 7.301–30.
⇒ **syllable**

code [Lat. *codex* 'notebook (orig. made of wooden tablets)']

1 In **information theory**, the rule for the coordination of two different repertoires of signs, which can represent the same information. For example, the binary code is based on the values 1 and 0 (i.e. yes and no). The numbers *1, 2, 3, 4* can be indicated by the codes 00, 01, 10, 11, whereby both systems are semantically equivalent. Morse code is based upon a similar system. The development of rational codes is indispensable for electronic data processing.

2 In linguistics, code is used in the sense of 1 above for linguistic signs and the syntactic rules which bind them together. Martinet used the term 'code' for *langue* (language system) as opposed to 'message' for *parole* (language use) (⇒ **langue vs parole**).

Reference
Martinet, A. 1960. *Eléments de linguistique générale*. Paris.

3 A term used in computational analysis. (⇒ **compiler**).

4 A term in **sociolinguistics** for class-specific language variations, especially for the different strategies of verbal planning (⇒ **code theory**).

code-switching

Depending on the demands of a particular communicative situation, bilingual or multilingual speakers (⇒ **bilingualism** ⇒ **multilingualism**) will switch between language varieties. A distinction must be made between 'situative' code-switching, in which the functional distribution of varieties that are evaluated differently in society is subject to normative rules (e.g. standard language on high-status occasions, dialect on more familiar, low-status occasions; ⇒ **diglossia**), and 'conversational' code-switching, which is not linked to a change of external factors of the speech constellation, but occurs within an externally invariant speech situation, within a turn or even intrasententially. Conversational code-switching serves to create various contexts (⇒ **contextualization**). For example, 'informality' in a formal situation, the different types of relationships between individual participants in a conversation, irony vs seriousness, and background information vs the 'actual' message can all be contextualized by means of code-switching.

References
Berk-Seligson, S. 1986. Linguistic constraints on intrasentential code-switching: a study of Spanish/ Hebrew bilingualism. *LSoc* 15.313–48.
Blom, J.-P. and J.J. Gumperz. 1972. Social meaning in linguistic structure: code-switching in Norway. In J.J. Gumperz and D. Hymes (eds), *Directions in sociolinguistics: the ethnography of communication.* New York. 407–34.
Clyne, M. 1987. Constraints on code-switching: how universal are they? *Linguistics* 25.739–64.
Gumperz, J.J. 1976. The sociolinguistic significance of conversational code-switching. In J.J. Gumperz and J. Cook-Gumperz (eds), *Papers on language and context.* Berkeley, CA.
—— 1978. Dialect and conversational inference in urban communication. *LSoc* 7.393–409.
—— 1982. *Discourse strategies.* Cambridge.
Hudson, R.A. 1980. *Sociolinguistics.* Cambridge.
Milroy, L. and P. Muysken (ed.). 1995. *One speaker, two languages. Cross-disciplinary perspective on code-switching.* Cambridge.
Myers-Scotton, C. 1993a. *Social motivations for codeswitching: evidence from Africa.* Oxford.
—— 1993b. *Duelling languages: grammatical structure in codeswitching.* Oxford.
⇒ **sociolinguistics**

code theory

Sociolinguistic theory developed by Bernstein (1958) that is based on the premise that different classes within a society are marked by different types of social relations. From such relations different 'codes' arise which, through a process of linguistic socialization, have a stabilizing effect upon the social structure. Corresponding to the class divisions of society is the linguistic dichotomy of an 'elaborated' (middle-class) code and a 'restricted' (lower-class) code; the degree of elaborateness or restrictedness is measured by the complexity of sentences and by the extent of grammatical and lexical alternatives. Based on its relative paucity of variants, the restricted code is considered more predictable, more redundant, less complex, and, measured against the norm-setting standards of the middle class, 'deficient' (deficit hypothesis).

The mixed reception of Bernstein's code theory gave strong impetus to the development of **sociolinguistics** and social dialectology in the 1960s, at which time dialects, in the sense of non-standard social or regional varieties, were considered by many to be restricted codes. This theory had an explosive effect on the politics of mass education by prompting a number of empirical studies and a more intensified demand for 'compensatory language instruction' which would reduce the linguistic deficit and the inequality of social opportunity associated with it.

Criticism of these assumptions came above all from Labov in his **variational linguistics**. In his studies of **Black English** vernacular in the United States, he emphasized the unique character and value of this form of language, namely that it is not deficient, but rather only a variety distinct from standard English with its own regularities and turns of expression ('difference hypothesis').

References
Bernstein, B. 1958. Some sociological developments of perception. *British Journal of Sociology* 9.159–74.
—— 1971. *Class, codes and control*, vol. 1: *Theoretical studies towards a sociology of language.* London.
—— (ed.) 1973. *Class, codes and control*, vol. 2: *Empirical studies.* London.
—— 1987. Social class, codes and communication. In U. Ammon *et al.* (eds), *Sociolinguistics: an international handbook of the science of language and society.* Berlin. 563–78.
Dittmar, N. 1976. *Sociolinguistics: a critical survey of theory and application.* London.
Edwards, A.D. 1976. *Language in culture and class.* London.
Labov, W. 1972. *Language in the inner city: studies in the Black English vernacular.* Philadelphia, PA.

cognate object [Lat. *cognatus* 'related by birth']

Object that is etymologically or semantically related to the verb on which it is dependent, e.g. *to sleep the sleep of the simple, to die a cruel death.* Cognate objects cannot normally be passivized: **A cruel death was died by him.*

Reference
Baron, N.S. 1971. On defining 'cognate object.' *Glossa* 51.71–98.

cognitive grammar [Lat. *cognitio* 'acquaintance; comprehension']

Cognitive grammar attempts to describe language by what is known about cognitive processes. In this view, grammar is no longer an autonomous system, but rather serves to structure and symbolize conceptual content. Lexical, morphological, and syntactic units are altogether symbolic units and can only be assigned to different components in a relatively arbitrary manner. Meaning is equated with conceptual-ization, in which semantic structures are characterized only according to elementary cognitive realms, such as the experience of time or space. In particular, it is the task of the linguist to investigate the possibilities of alternative linguistic structures for a perceptual or conceptual situation.

References
Langacker, R.W. 1986. An introduction to cognitive grammar. *CSc* 10.1–40.
——— 1987–99. *Foundations of cognitive grammar*, 2 vols. Stanford, CA.
——— 1990. *Concept, image and symbol: the cognitive basis of grammar*. Berlin and New York.
Lange, K.-P. 1985. *Language and cognition: an essay on cognitive grammar*. Tübingen.

cognitive linguistics (*also* cognitive psychology)

Interdisciplinary direction of research developed at the end of the 1950s in the United States that is concerned with the investigation of mental processes in the acquisition and use of knowledge and language. In contrast with **behaviorism** that concentrates on observable behavior and **stimulus-response** processes, behavior in cognitive linguistics plays only a mediating role inasmuch as it supports insights into cognitive processes. The object of investigation is research into cognitive or mental structure and organization by analyzing cognitive strategies used by humans in thinking, storing information, comprehending, and producing language.

References
Bever, T.G. *et al.* (eds) 1985. *The study of language in cognitive sciences*. Cambridge, MA.
Carston, R. 1988. Language and cognition. In F. Newmeyer (ed.), *Linguistics: the Cambridge survey*. Cambridge. Vol. 3, 28–68.
Deane, P.D. 1992. *Grammar in mind and brain. Explorations in cognitive syntax*. Berlin and New York.
Dressler, W.U. 1990. The cognitive perspective of 'naturalist' linguistic models. *Cognitive Linguistics* 1.75–98.
Estes, W.K. 1978. *Handbook of learning and cognitive processes*, vol. 6: *Linguistic functions in cognitive theory*. Hillsdale, NJ.
Howard, D.V. 1983. *Cognitive psychology: memory, language, and thought*. New York.
Jackendoff, R. 1992. *Languages of the mind: essays on mental representation*. Cambridge, MA.
Lakoff, G. 1987. *Women, fire and dangerous things. What categories reveal about the mind*. Chicago and London.
Reuland, E. and Abraham, W. (eds) 1992. *Knowledge and language*, 2 vols. Dordrecht.
Rudzka-Ostyn, B. (ed.) 1988. *Topics in cognitive linguistics*. Amsterdam.

Schwarz, M. (ed.) 1994. *Kognitive Semantik/ Cognitive semantics: Ergebnisse, Probleme, Perspektiven*. Tübingen.
Von Geert, P. 1981. *The development of perception, cognition, and language*. London.

Journals
Cognition
Cognitive Linguistics

cognitive psychology ⇒ cognitive linguistics

coherence [Lat. *cohaerere* 'to stick together']

A term from **text linguistics**.

1 In general, the grammatical and semantic interconnectedness between sentences that form a text (⇒ **discourse grammar**). It is the semantic structure, not its formal meaning, which create coherence.

2 In a narrower sense, coherence is separate from grammatical **cohesion** and specifically signifies the semantic meaning and the cohesion of the basic interconnection of the meanings of the text, its content/semantic and cognitive structure. Semantic coherence can be represented as a sequence of **propositions** (⇒ **thematic development**, **macrostructure**) that form a constellation of abstract concepts and connected relations. When a series of sentences seems incoherent, the listener can use **inference** to understand the text.

References
Charolles, M., J.S. Petöfi, and E. Sözer (eds) 1986. *Research in text connexity and text coherence*. Hamburg.
Gernsbacher, M.A. and T. Givón (eds) 1995. *Coherence in spontaneous text*. Amsterdam and Philadelphia.
Halliday, M.A.K. and R. Hasan. 1976. *Cohesion in English*. London.
Hartveldt, R. 1987. *Pragmatic aspects of coherence in discourse*. Groningen.
Heydrich, W. *et al.* (eds) 1989. *Connexity and coherence: analysis of text and discourse*. New York.
Neubauer, F. (ed.) 1983. *Coherence in natural-language texts*. Hamburg.
Norgard-Sørensen, J. 1992. *Coherence theory: the case of Russian*. Berlin and New York.
Petöfi, J.S. and E. Sözer (eds) 1988. *Micro and macro connexity of texts*. Hamburg.
Sözer, E. (ed.) 1985. *Text connexity, text coherence*. Hamburg.
Tannen, D. (ed.) 1984. *Coherence in written and spoken discourse*. Norwood, NJ.
Tomlin, R.S. (ed.) 1987. *Coherence and grounding in discourse*. Amsterdam.
Werth, P. 1984. *Focus, coherence and emphasis*. London.

Bibliographies
Lohmann, P. 1988. Connectedness of texts: a biblio-

graphical survey, Part 1. In J.S. Petöfi (ed.), *Text and discourse constitution.* Berlin. 478–501.

—— 1989. Connectedness of texts: a bibliographical survey, Part 2. In W. Heydrich *et al.* (eds), *Connexity and coherence: analysis of text and discourse.* New York.

cohesion

Cohesion refers to the various linguistic means (grammatical, lexical, phonological) by which sentences 'stick together' and are linked into larger units of paragraphs, or stanzas, or chapters. Cohesion is produced by (a) the repetition of elements of the text, e.g. **recurrence, textphoric, paraphrase, parallelism**; (b) the compacting of text through the use of devices such as **ellipsis**; (c) the use of morphological and syntactic devices to express different kinds of relationships such as **connection, tense, aspect, deixis**, or theme–rheme relationships (⇒ **theme vs rheme**) (⇒ *also* **coherence**).

References
Barthes, R. 1970. *S/Z.* Paris.
Halliday, M.A.K. and R. Hasan. 1976. *Cohesion in English.* London.
Stoddard, S. 1991. *Text and texture: patterns of cohesion.* Norwood, NJ.

cohortative [Lat. *cohortatio* 'encouragement']

Mood of admonition, encouragement, or recommendation, which can be part of either verbal mood or sentential mood. (⇒ *also* **imperative, jussive, modality**)

References
⇒ **modality**

coining

In contrast to **word formation** by means of **derivation** and **composition** using already present linguistic elements, coining is the first-time creation of an unmotivated (⇒ **motivation**), i.e. non-complex and completely arbitrary (⇒ **arbitrariness**) connection between expression and content. It is generally believed that the basic elements of a language's vocabulary were created by coining in its earliest stages of development.

References
⇒ **word formation**

collective noun

Semantically defined class of nouns that express a group or set of several members in terms of a single unit: *cattle, herd, furniture, people, government.* Some languages can form collective nouns with the help of affixes (e.g. **German** *Berg* 'mountain': *Gebirge* 'mountain range').

References
⇒ **word formation**

colligation [Lat. *colligatio* 'bond']

Morphologically and syntactically motivated conditions for the ability of linguistic elements to be combined. These conditions, as expressed in **government** or **valence**, can lead to differences in meaning: *The car stopped* vs *The car stopped honking.* On semantically motivated factors of combinability, ⇒ **collocation**.

collocation [Lat. *collocatio* 'arrangement, ordering'] (*also* concomitance, selection)

1 Term introduced by J.R. Firth in his semantic theory to designate characteristic word combinations which have developed an idiomatic semantic relation based on their frequent co-occurrence. Collocations are, therefore, primarily semantically (not grammatically) based, e.g. *dog : bark, dark : night.* This concept of collocation touches on W. Porzig's '**inherent semantic relation**' as well as on E. Coseriu's '**lexical solidarities**.' (⇒ *also* **co-occurrence, compatibility, distribution**)

References
Coseriu, E. 1967. Lexikalische Solidaritäten. *Poetica* 1.293–303.
Firth, J.R. 1957. Modes of meaning. In his *Papers in linguistics 1934–1951.* London. 190–215.
Kastovsky, D. 1981. Selectional restrictions and lexical solidarities. In D. Kastovsky (ed.), *Perspektiven der lexikalischen Semantik.* Tübingen. 70–98.
Porzig, W. 1934. Wesenhafte Bedeutungsbeziehungen. *PBB* 58.70–97.

2 In the wider sense, a term referring to the conditions of syntactic–semantic grammaticality.

collocation test

A method to describe semantic differences based on their conditions of occurrence. For example, in the distinct collocations of *green* with *tree, vegetable,* and *person,* each of the various semantic components of *green* is realized. This test was developed in analogy to a method used by M. Joos and A. Neubert in phonology.

References
Joos, M. 1958. Semology: a linguistic theory of meaning. *SiL* 13.53–70.
—— 1964. *The English verb: form and meanings.* Madison, WI. (2nd edn 1968.)
Leisi, E. 1952. *Der Wortinhalt: seine Struktur im Deutschen und Englischen.* Heidelberg. (5th edn 1975.)

collogation ⇒ juxtaposition

colloquial expression ⇒ idiom

colloquial speech

1 As 'everyday language,' colloquial speech refers to the total set of utterances in a familiar, informal context such as at home or at the workplace.

2 Product of panregional leveling between social and regional spoken language variants.

References
⇒ **dialect, spoken language**

colloquialism ⇒ idiom

colon [Grk *kōlon* 'limb, member']

1 Linguistic unit in classical **rhetoric** which occurs between two breath pauses, contains seven to sixteen syllables, forms a unit of meaning, and is made up of several dependent subunits (⇒ **comma**[1]).

2 Punctuation mark ‹:› used to direct attention to following sentence elements. (⇒ *also* **punctuation**)

color terms

Color terms belong to the **basic vocabulary** of all natural languages. Owing to their shared perceptive abilities, speakers of different languages view the color spectrum in the same way; yet the color terms in their languages may correspond to a different breakdown of the color spectrum. In their study of ninety-eight languages, Berlin *et al.* (1969) ascertained a number of universal color terms: for example, they found eleven elementary color categories which correspond to the English **prototypes** of black, white, red, orange, yellow, brown, green, blue, crimson, pink, and gray. For languages that linguistically express fewer than these eleven categories, the relationships can be expressed in the form of absolute **universals**, e.g. 'All languages have color terms for white and black,' or in the form of implicative universals, e.g. 'If a language has three color terms, then one of them will necessarily be a color term for red.' Interestingly, a high percentage of color terms have restrictions on their uses. Note the following English examples: *white wine* vs *yellow wine or *black coffee* vs *brown coffee.

References
Berlin, B., E.A. Berlin, and P. Kay. 1969. *Basic color terms: their universality and evolution*. Berkeley, CA.
Davies, I. and G. Corbett. 1994. The basic color terms of Russian. *Linguistics* 32.65–89.

Heider, E.R. 1972. Universals in color naming and memory. *JeP* 93.10–20.
Kay, P. 1975. Synchronic variability and diachronic change in basic color terms. *LSoc* 4.257–70.
Kay, P. and C.K. McDaniel. 1978. The linguistic significance of the meanings of basic color terms. *Lg* 54.610–46.
Sahlins, M. 1976. Colors and cultures. *Semiotica* 16.1–22.
Witkowski, S.R. and C.H. Brown. 1977. An explanation of color nomenclature universals. *AA* 70.50–7.

combination

In **glossematics**, a form of **constellation**: a syntagmatic (*as well as*) relation that exists between two elements that are syntacto-semantically compatible, i.e. can follow upon each other in the same context, but also occur independently of each other, as in Latin the preposition *ab* and the **ablative**, which can be present together, but also separately (see Hjelmslev 1943).

References
Hjelmslev, L. 1943. *Omkring sprogteoriens grund-laeggelse*. Copenhagen. (*Prolegomena to a theory of language*, trans. F.J. Whitfield. Baltimore, MD, 1953.)
⇒ **glossematics**

comitative [Lat. *comitatus* 'escort, company']

1 Verbal **aspect** which characterizes an action as accompanying another action.

2 Case in the **Finno-Ugric** languages which serves to mark the accompaniment of a person or thing.

comma [Grk *kómma* 'that which is cut off, piece']

1 In classical **rhetoric**, dependent subunit of larger units of meaning consisting of approximately two to six syllables. (⇒ *also* **colon**)

2 **Punctuation** ‹,› mark for indicating syntactic ordering, such as separating introductory clauses from the main clause.

comment (*also* **focus**, rheme)

The term 'comment' refers semantically to the part of an utterance that contains new information. Syntactically, in unmarked word order the comment refers to the predicate, while the subject is usually the **topic**, containing information which is contextually bound or already mentioned. The comment can also be identified by means of the question test, where the **scope** of the question refers to the focus of the corresponding natural (unmarked) **answer**, i.e. to the new information requested by the question; e.g. *What did Philip buy himself? – A new* *car* (*he bought himself*).

References
⇒ **theme vs rheme**, **topic vs comment**

commissive

Speech act meant to commit a speaker to some future course of action, expressed in the propositional content (**proposition**) of the act. Commissives are, for example, promises, oaths, commitments, etc. (⇒ *also* **speech act classification**)

References
Levinson, S.C. 1983. *Pragmatics*. Cambridge.
Searle, J.R. 1975. A taxonomy of illocutionary acts. In K. Gunderson (ed.), *Language, mind and knowledge*. Minneapolis, MN. (Repr. in *Expression and meaning*. Cambridge, 1979 1–29.)

common noun (*also* class noun, generic noun, (nomen) appellativum)

Semantically defined class of nouns which denotes objects or states of affairs or individual representatives thereof, e.g. *animal*(*s*) or *human*(*s*), as opposed to **proper nouns**, which serve to identify particular individual objects. The transition from common to proper nouns (and vice versa) is fluid.

References
Carlson, G. 1991. Natural kinds and common nouns. In A. von Stechow and D. Wunderlich (eds), *Semantik/Semantics: an international handbook of contemporary research*. Berlin. 370–98.
Chur, J. 1993. *Generische Nominalphrasen im Deutschen: eine Untersuchung zu Referenz und Semantik*. Tübingen.
Krifka, M. 1991. Massennomina. In A. von Stechow and D. Wunderlich (eds), *Semantik/Semantics: an international handbook of contemporary research*. Berlin. 399–417.
Werner, O. 1974. Appellativa – Nomina Propria. Wie kann man mit einem begrenzten Vokabular über unbegrenzt viele Gegenstände sprechen? In L. Heilmann (ed.), *Proceedings of the eleventh International Congress of Linguists*. Bologna. Vol. 2, 171–87.

commonsense knowledge ⇒ commonsense reasoning

commonsense reasoning (*also* commonsense knowledge)

In **artificial intelligence** (AI) and **computational linguistics** the representation of common knowledge plays an important role. Linguistic data processing in AI rests on the assumption that knowledge about the world is a necessary prerequisite for understanding and producing natural-language texts. The particular problems of reconstructing 'natural reasoning' arise in developing models for basic concepts, such as time, space, causality, and the like, in a form that takes common knowledge about these aspects into account. For this reason, it is not enough to consider only theories proposed in the natural sciences about the nature of space and time. In **user modeling**, one attempts to account for common concepts of these areas.

Reference
Hobbs, J. and R. Moore (eds) 1985. *Formal theories of the commonsense world*. Norwood, NJ.

communication [Lat. *communicatio* 'the action of imparting']

In its broadest sense, this term refers to every kind of mutual transmission of information using signs or symbols between living beings (humans, animals), between people and data-processing machines. For information on the technical and cybernetic use of communication, ⇒ **information theory**.

In its narrower, linguistic sense, communication is the understanding which occurs between humans through linguistic and non-linguistic means like gestures, mimicry and voice (⇒ **non-verbal communication**). The basic components of communication are shown in communication models. Research into its qualities and mutual co-operation is the concern mainly of pragmatically and sociolinguistically oriented linguistics and general communication science. (⇒ *also* **animal communication**, **communication model**, **communication science**, **non-verbal communication**, **semiotics**, **sociolinguistics**)

References
Mellor, D.H. (ed.) 1990. *Ways of communication*. Cambridge.

Journal
European Journal of Communication

communication model

The schematic (usually graphic) representation of the conditions, the structure, and the path of communicative processes based on the following formula: '*Who* is saying *what* by *what means* to *whom* with *what effect*?' (Lasswell 1948). Most communication models are based on one designed in 1949 by Shannon and Weaver for news transmission. The basic components of a communication model, which may be differentiated according to one's focus, are (a) sender and receiver (speaker/hearer), (b) channel or medium of the transmission of information (acoustic, optical, tactile), (c) code (inventory of signs and combination rules), (d) news, (e) disruptions (white noise), (f) pragmatic meaning, (g) feedback. The most well-known communication models are those of K.

Bühler (⇒ **organon model of language**) and R. Jakobson.

References
Bühler, K. 1934. *Sprachtheorie*. Jena. (Repr. Stuttgart, 1965.)
Hymes, D. 1968. The ethnography of speaking. In J.A. Fishman (ed.), *Readings in the sociology of language*. The Hague. 99–138.
Jakobson, R. 1960. Linguistics and poetics. In T.A. Sebeok (ed.), *Style in language*. London. 350–77.
Lasswell, H.D. 1948. *The analysis of political behaviour*. London.
Shannon, C.E. and W. Weaver. 1949. *The mathematical theory of communication*. Urbana, IL.

communication science

Study of the conditions, structure, and course of the exchange of information on the basis of sign systems. In this sense, communication comprises sociologically oriented directions of research which deal with processes of communication from psychological, sociological, ethnological, political, or linguistic aspects, as well as disciplines on information processing with the help of data-processing machines.

In the narrow sense, communication science is considered a cover term for all studies on the conditions, structure and course of interhuman communication that have a close connection with psychology, sociology, anthropology, linguistics, etc. and are concerned especially with research on (a) means of communication, (b) motivation and behavior of communication participants as well as (c) the sociocultural conditions of communication.

References
Gumperz, J.J. and D. Hymes (eds) 1972. *Directions in sociolinguistics: the ethnography of communication*. New York.
Halliday, M.A.K. 1973. *Explorations in the function of language*. London.
Watzlawick, P., J.H. Beavin, and D.D. Jackson. 1967. *Pragmatics of human communication: a study of interactional patterns, pathologies and paradoxes*. New York.

communicative competence

Coined by D. Hymes in his ethnography of communication (⇒ **ethnography of speaking**), this term is a critical expansion of N. Chomsky's concept of competence (⇒ **competence vs performance**) (which concerns only the linguistic capabilities of the ideal speaker–hearer, so that the social function of language remains unaddressed). Communicative competence is the fundamental concept of a pragmalinguistic model of linguistic communication: it refers to the repertoire of know-how that individuals must develop if they are to be able to communicate with one another appropriately in the changing situations and conditions. In this model, speaking is understood as the action of transmitting symbols (i.e. interaction). Communicative competence is the descriptive goal of various social-psychological disciplines.

References
Habermas, J. 1971. Vorbereitende Bemerkungen zu einer Theorie der kommunikativen Kompetenz. In J. Habermas and N. Luhmann (eds), *Theorie der Gesellschaft oder Sozialtechnologie*. Frankfurt. 101–41.
Hymes, D. 1968. The ethnography of speaking. In J.A. Fishman (ed.), *Readings in the sociology of language*. The Hague. 99–138.
Kochan, D.C. (ed.) 1973. *Sprache und kommunikative Kompetenz*. Stuttgart.
Russell, J. 1981. *Communicative competence in a minority group: a sociolinguistic study of the Swahili-speaking community in the Old Town, Mombasa*. Amsterdam and Philadelphia.

commutation ⇒ **substitution**

commutation test [Lat. *commutatio* 'exchange']

Experimental analytical procedure used in **structuralism** to discover syntactic regularities. Single syntactic elements are rearranged in a sentence, so that the new sentence is grammatical, and the syntactic effects are noted. As a result of this test, constituents are shown to be commutable sentence units. Sentences can be analyzed as declarative, interrogative, and imperative, depending on the position of the verb, and rules of word order can describe and resolve structural ambiguities: *Caesar loved fat men and women* ⇒ *Caesar loved women and fat men*. (⇒ also **operational procedures**)

References
⇒ **glossematics**

COMP position

The term for a position in the **tree diagram** which can contain the **complementizer** or other sentence-initial elements. It was shown in the Revised Extended Standard Theory (⇒ **transformational grammar**, **trace theory**) that COMP serves as an *escape hatch* for **movement transformations** which move an element into the COMP of an **embedded sentence** and then into the COMP of the matrix sentence. This splitting up of a long movement into shorter movements makes it possible to circumvent locality constraints: for example, in *Who* [$_S$*do you think* [t [$_S$*Philip loves* t]] the object moves in two steps (indicated by the first trace t in COMP) so that subjacency is met at each step.

References
⇒ **complementizer**, **subjacency**

compact vs diffuse (*also* central vs peripheral)

Binary phonological **opposition** in **distinctive feature** analysis, based on acoustically analyzed and spectrally defined criteria (⇒ **acoustic phonetics**, **spectral analysis**). Acoustic characteristic: greater (more compact) vs lesser (more diffuse) concentration of energy in a relatively narrow area of the spectrum, for compact vowels, broader **formants**. Articulatory characteristic (⇒ **articulation**): constriction farther to the back vs to the front of the **vocal tract** with broader vs narrower lip-opening. The distinction characterizes the opposition between [ŋ, k, g] vs [m, p, b].

References
Jakobson, R. *et al.* 1951. Preliminaries to speech analysis. Cambridge, MA. 27–9. (6th edn 1965.)
⇒ **distinctive feature**

comparative ⇒ **degree**

comparative clause

Semantically specified modal clause which functions as an adverbial modifier to express a comparison to the state of affairs described in the main clause. They are introduced by such conjunctions as *like*, *as*, *as if*, *like when*: *He acted like he understood everything.*

comparative linguistics

Developed in the nineteenth century as an independent linguistic discipline with the goal of reconstructing the origins, developmental history, and relationships of and between individual languages on the basis of comparative studies (⇒ **reconstruction**). It can be stated that comparative linguistics was born in Germany during the 'Romantic period,' in which both the study of the history of the Europeans as well as of **Sanskrit** were pursued. This period is associated primarily with the names of F.V. Schlegel, F. Bopp, R. Rask, J. Grimm, and A. Schleicher, each of whom studied the genetic relationships between the Germanic languages and other **Indo-European** languages throughout their recorded history. Based on a thorough description of the most important Indo-European languages, as undertaken by Bopp and Grimm, Schleicher attempted to derive all such languages from a reconstructed Indo-European **proto-language**; the genetic relationships that were uncovered were represented in the form of a genetic 'family tree' (⇒ **genetic tree theory**). Through the so-called **Neogrammarians** the

historical view of language became the primary, indeed for a while almost exclusive, direction of linguistic studies (see Paul 1880, and the overviews in Brugmann and Delbrück 1886–1900; Hirt 1921–37; Meillet 1903; and others).

References
Anttila, R. 1989. *Historical and comparative linguistics*, 2nd rev. edn. Amsterdam and Philadelphia.
Baldi, P. (ed.) 1990. *Linguistic change and reconstruction methodology*. Berlin and New York.
Bopp, F. 1816. *Über das Conjugationssystem der Sanskritsprache in Vergleichung mit jenem der griechischen, lateinischen, persischen und germanischen Sprache*. Frankfurt.
Brugmann, K. and B. Delbrück. 1886–1900. *Grundriß der vergleichenden Grammatik der indogermanischen Sprachen*, 5 vols. Strassburg. (Unabr. repr. 1970.)
Durie, M. (ed.) 1996. *The comparative method reviewed*. Oxford.
Grimm, J. 1819–37. *Deutsche Grammatik*, 4 parts. Göttingen. (Facsimile edn of the 2nd edn of Berlin 1870–8. Hildesheim, 1967.)
Hirt, H. 1921–37. *Indogermanische Grammatik*. Heidelberg.
Hock, H.H. 1986. *Principles of historical linguistics*. (2nd edn, rev. and updated 1991.) Berlin and New York.
Katičić, R. 1970. *A contribution to the general theory of comparative linguistics*. The Hague.
Mauro, T. de *et al.* 1990. *Leibniz, Humboldt and the origins of comparativism*. Amsterdam.
Meillet, A. 1903. *Introduction à l'étude comparative des langues indo-européenens*. Paris.
Paul, H. 1880. *Prinzipien der Sprachgeschichte*. Tübingen. (9th edn 1975.)
Rask, R. 1932. *Ausgewählte Abhandlungen*, ed. L. Hjelmslev. Copenhagen.
Schlegel, F. 1808. Die Sprache und Weisheit der Indier. (In *Sämtliche Werke*, vol. 7. Vienna, 1846.)
Schleicher, A. 1861–2. *Compendium der vergleichended Grammatik der indogermanischen Sprachen*. Weimar.
Von Humboldt, W. 1836. *Über die Verschiedenheit des menschlichen Sprachbaues*. Berlin. (Repr. 1963.)
——— 1963. *Schriften zur Sprachphilosophie*. Darmstadt.
⇒ **linguistics (history)**

comparative method ⇒ **comparative linguistics**, **reconstruction**

comparison ⇒ **degree**

compatibility

Compatibility refers to the conditions of grammaticality that depend on specific semantic-syntactic features between linguistic expressions found in particular syntactic positions. (⇒ *also* **collocation**, **incompatibility**, **inherent** semantic relation, lexical solidarities, selection restriction)

compensatory lengthening (*also* loss with compensatory lengthening)

Diachronic (⇒ **synchrony vs diachrony**) phonological process (⇒ **phonology**) by which the loss of a segment results in the lengthening of a neighboring syllabic segment, e.g., PIE **nizdó-* > Lat. *nīdus* 'nest', or *hard* pronounced as [haːd] in '*r*-less' dialects of English. In such cases, the original quantitative relations are retained.

References
Clements, G.N. 1982. *Compensatory lengthening.* Bloomington, IN.
Lehiste, I. 1972. Temporal compensation in a quantitative language. In *Proceedings of the third International Congress of Phonetic Sciences.* 929–37.
Wetzels, L. and E. Sezer (eds), 1986. *Studies in compensatory lengthening.* Dordrecht.

competence vs performance

Chomsky's postulated dichotomy between general linguistic ability and individual language use, which is connected to de Saussure's distinction **langue vs parole.** Competence is that knowledge about the native language which is acquired along with the language used by an **ideal speaker/listener** of a homogeneous **speech community** (i.e. free from dialectal and sociolectal variations). Due to an infinite inventory of elements (sounds, words) and syntactic rules, the speaker can theoretically produce and understand an infinite number of utterances. Performance refers not only to this, but also to the ability of the speaker to pass judgment on the **grammaticality** of sentences, on ambiguity, and paraphrases. The goal of **transformational grammar** is to formulate a grammar that illustrates as truly as possible the ability of a speaker's competence, and at the same time to offer a hypothesis about **language acquisition.** Linguistic theories based on the notion of competence have been reproached for being too idealistic, which has led to a broadening of the original concept to mean **communicative competence.** Whereas the terms 'performance' (Chomsky) and 'parole' (de Saussure) can be used almost interchangeably, their counterparts 'competence' and 'langue' are quite different from each other. 'Langue' is a static system of signs, whereas competence is understood as a dynamic concept, as a mechanism that will generate language endlessly.

References
Chomsky, N. 1965. *Aspects of the theory of syntax.* Cambridge, MA.
Newmeyer, F.J. 1990. Competence vs performance: theoretical vs applied; the development and interplay of two dichotomies in modern linguistics. *Historiographia Linguistica*, 17.167–81.
Putnam, H. 1967. The 'innateness hypothesis' and explanatory models in linguistics. *Synthese* 17.
Saussure, F. de. 1916. *Cours de linguistique générale*, ed. C. Bally and A. Sechehaye. Paris. (*Course in general linguistics*, trans. R. Harris. London, 1983.)

compiler

Computer program that translates a higher-level **programming language** (e.g. FORTRAN, LISP or PROLOG) from a (problem-oriented) notation into an equivalent machine-oriented notation. The higher-level language is called the 'source code,' the generated machine language the 'object code.' While **interpreters** immediately execute the program in the process of translation, a compiler first translates an entire source code program, before individual operations are carried out.

References
Aho, A.V., R. Sethi and J.D. Ulllman. 1985. *Compilers.* Reading, MA.
⇒ **computational linguistics**

complement (*also* argument of a verb or predicate)

A constituent X is a complement of a constituent Y, if X is valence-dependent on Y (⇒ **valence**). Thus, *flowers* is a complement of the verb in *I am picking flowers in the garden*, whereas *in the garden* is a **modifier** of the verb. In some usage, the terms complement and **complementation** are limited to relations in which the complement is a clause (*He said he enjoyed wine*). Within **Government and Binding theory**, subjects are not considered to be complements, since they are not valence-dependent on the predicate in English (i.e. every predicate or sentence requires a subject). Complements are distinguished from modifiers by the fact that the former may be governed by the verb, whereas the latter are never governed (⇒ **government**). In addition, complements may be obligatory, as in the examples above, or optional (*He was eating an apple*), whereas modifiers are always optional.

complement clause

Subordinate clause which functions syntactically either as a subject (*It became clear that he had no intention of coming*) or an object (*She asked herself if she had said the right thing*). Complement clauses for the most part have the same distributional patterns as nominals, which is expressed in generative **transformational grammar** by a **phrase structure rule** deriving complement clauses from noun phrases (NP ⇒ S).

References
Grosu, A. and S. Thompson. 1977. Constraints on the distribution of NP clauses. *Lg* 53.104–51.
Koster, J. 1978. Why subject sentences don't exist. In S.J. Keyser (ed.), *Recent transformational studies in European languages*. Cambridge, MA. 53–64.
Noonan, M. 1985. Complementation. In T. Shopen (ed.), *Language typology and syntactic description*. Cambridge. Vol. 2, 42–140.

complementarity

Semantic relation of opposition. Two expressions are in a relation of complementarity when both expressions split their semantic range into disjunct parts. A heuristic test for complementarity can be performed by cross-substituting the given lexemes l_1 and l_2 in suitable sentences $S(\ldots)$. If $S(l_1)$ and $S(l_2)$ are strongly contradictory (⇒ **contradiction**), then the two lexemes are said to be complementaries, in the sense that from $S(l_1)$ the **negation** of $S(l_2)$ follows, from $S(l_2)$ the negation of $S(l_1)$ follows, from the negation of $S(l_1)$ $S(l_2)$ follows, and from the negation of $S(l_2)$ $S(l_1)$ follows. Contradictory expressions like *married* vs *unmarried* and *dead* vs *alive* are frequently neither gradable (**to be somewhat dead*), nor have comparative forms (**X is more married than Y*). Complementarity is a special type of **incompatibility**. (⇒ *also* **gradable complementaries**)

References
⇒ **semantic relation, semantics**

complementary distribution

Concept introduced by N. Trubetzkoy (1939), term for the **distribution** of two **allophones** of the same **phoneme** which never occur in the same phonetic environment. (⇒ *also* **free variation**)

References
Trubetzkoy, N. 1939. *Grundzüge der Phonologie*. Göttingen. (4th edn 1967.)
⇒ **phonology**

complementation

1 In transformational grammar, the generation of **complements**, such as obligatory verb complements that are immediate parts of the verb phrase. The generation of complements with sentential value that in the deep structure are embedded as constituent clauses are regarded as a special case of this general concept of complementation. Their partly obligatory, partly optional realization as *that/whether/if*-sentences or as **infinitive constructions** in the surface structure is verb-dependent. (⇒ *also* **complementizer, equi-NP-deletion, raising**)

References
Bresnan, J.W. 1970. On complementizers: toward a syntactic theory of complement types. *FL* 6.297–321.
Burt, M.K. 1971. *From deep to surface structure: an introduction to transformational syntax*. New York.
Esau, H. 1973. *Nominalization and complementation in modern German*. Amsterdam.
Geest, W. de and Y. Putseys (eds) 1984. *Sentential complementation*. Dordrecht.
Jacobs, R.A. and P.S. Rosenbaum. 1968. *English transformational grammar*. Waltham, MA.
Karttunen, L. 1971. *The logic of English predicate complement constructions*. Bloomington, IN.
Kiparsky, P. and C. Kiparsky. 1970. Fact. In M. Bierwisch and K.E. Heidolph (eds), *Progress in linguistics*. The Hague. 243–73.
Olsen, S. 1981. *Problems of* seem/scheinen *constructions and their implications for the theory of predicate sentential complementation*. Tübingen.
Rosenbaum, P.S. 1967. *The grammar of English predicate complement constructions*. Cambridge, MA.
Stockwell, R.P. *et al.* 1973. *The major syntactic structures of English*. New York.
⇒ **subcategorization**

2 ⇒ **complementation and modification**

complementation and modification (*also* **dependency**, **determination**, operator–operand relation)

Complementation and modification are dependency relations within phrases. Complementation includes the dependency both of nouns on prepositions (*the sky* in *in the sky*) and of nouns and other complements on predicators (e.g. *the lawn* in *mows the lawn*).

Another such relationship is modification. Thus, an attributive adjective is described as modifying the **head** noun (*twinkling* in *the twinkling stars*); so too, a prepositional phrase relative to a modifying verb (e.g. *shine in the sky*). In the modification structure *the twinkling stars*, *twinkling* can be dropped without changing the function of *the stars* in the larger construction. But in the complementation *in the sky* neither *in* or *the sky* can in general be deleted.

Terminological variants include: **endocentric construction** (modification) vs **exocentric construction** (complementation) (Bloomfield). Subtypes of complementation are also called **predication**, or function–argument structure. Subtypes of modifiers are **attributes**, satellites (⇒ **nucleus vs satellite**) and **adjuncts** (⇒ *also* **nexus, valence**)

References
Bloomfield, L. 1933. *Language*. New York.
Matthews, P.H. 1981. *Syntax*. Cambridge.

complementizer (*also* subordinator)

A term introduced by Rosenbaum in 1967 to describe a small group of grammatical elements like subordinating conjunctions (e.g. *that, whether, because*) which indicate the specific function of embedded sentential structures. The abbreviation COMP indicates a node in the tree structure which determines the position of lexical insertion of the complementizer (⇒ **COMP position**).

References

Bayer, J. 1984. COMP in Bavarian syntax. *LRev* 3.209–74.

Bresnan, J.W. 1970. On complementizers: toward a syntactic theory of complement types. *FL* 6.297–321.

Chomsky, N. 1970. Remarks on nominalization. In R.A. Jacobs and P.S. Rosenbaum (eds), *Readings in English transformational grammar*. Waltham, MA. 170–221.

Haider, H. 1986. V-second in German. In H. Haider and M. Prinzhorn (eds), *Verb second phenomena in Germanic languages*. Dordrecht. 49–76.

Reinhart, T. 1979. A second COMP position. In A. Belletti, L. Brandi, and L. Rizzi (eds), *The theory of markedness in generative grammar*. Pisa. 517–57.

Rosenbaum, P.S. 1967. *The grammar of English predicate complement constructions*. Cambridge, MA.

⇒ **complementation**, **transformational grammar**

complete ⇒ **durative vs non-durative**

complex sentence

1 More narrowly defined, a sentence that is composed of a main clause and one or more dependent clauses introduced by a subordinating conjunction (*because, since, although*).

2 More broadly defined, a sentence that contains two or more clauses joined either by subordination, as in sense 1 above, or by co-ordination, that is, by a co-ordinating conjunction (*and, or*). (⇒ *also* **compound sentence**)

3 In **transformational grammar**, a sentence that consists of a **matrix sentence** as well as one or more embedded **constituent clauses**. (⇒ *also* **embedding**)

complex symbol

1 In general, a group of features which completely describes a linguistic unit. For example in **phonology**, all **distinctive features** which fully describe a **phoneme** form a complex symbol, thus [+stop, +bilabial, +voiced] is the description for /b/.

2 In **transformational grammar**, the context-free and context-sensitive features associated with a **category symbol** by the **phrase struc-**

ture rules and **subcategorization** rules. These specify the corresponding category syntactically as well as semantically: for example, the noun *people* is categorized as [+plural] syntactically and [+living, +human, …] semantically.

3 In **X-bar theory**, a characterization of category symbols as a group of primary features, e.g. N = [–verbal, +nominal], V = [+verbal, –nominal], A = [+verbal, +nominal], P = [–verbal, –nominal]. The analysis of categories as complex symbols allows reference to **natural classes** for syntactic processes. As in **phonology**, the notation N, V, P, A, etc. as complex symbols represent abbreviations for **feature bundles**. (⇒ **Generalized Phrase Structure Grammar**, **selectional features**, **subcategorization**)

Reference

Gazdar, G., E. Klein, G. Pullum, and I. Sag. 1985. *Generalized phrase structure grammar*. Oxford.

complexity (*also* computational complexity)

Analysis of **algorithms** in terms of the time and memory resources they demand. Because algorithms apply to classes of input problems, their complexity is expressed as a function of input size: for example, one can search an ordered list (e.g. a dictionary) in time proportional to a (base 2) logarithm of list size. Because the time and memory used by concrete algorithms vary by a constant factor for irrelevant reasons (e.g. owing to the machine or **compiler** used), complexity is expressed in abstraction from constant factors. Thus, searching an ordered list of length n is $O(log\ n)$, i.e. of the order logarithmic. (⇒ *also* **tractable**)

References

Barton, G., R. Berwick, and E. Ristad. 1987. *Computational complexity and natural language*. Cambridge.

Garey, M. and D. Johnson, 1979. *Computers and intractability: a guide to the theory of NP completeness*. New York.

component

1 In **semantics**, a synonym for **semantic feature**.

2 In **transformational grammar**, a level of description of a grammatical model which consists of a syntactic, semantic, and phonological component.

componential analysis (*also* **semantic feature** analysis)

Description of the meaning of lexemes as well as of the inner structure of the lexicon through (structured) sets of semantic features. Phonological methods of investigation, principally

Componential analysis of kinship terms

features:	relative	parent	father	mother	siblings	brother	sister	child	son	daughter	uncle	aunt	cousin m.	cousin f.	nephew	niece
animate	+	+	+	+	+	+	+	+	+	+	+	+	+	+	+	+
human	+	+	+	+	+	+	+	+	+	+	+	+	+	+	+	+
related	+	+	+	+	+	+	+	+	+	+	+	+	+	+	+	+
directly rel.	(−)	+	+	+	+	+	+	+	+	+	−	−	−	−	−	−
same generation	0	−	−	−	+	+	+	−	−	−	−	−	+	+	−	−
older	0	+	+	+	0	0	0	+	−	−	+	+	0	0	−	−
male	0	0	+	−	0	+	−	0	+	−	+	−	+	−	+	−
female	0	0	−	+	0	−	+	0	−	+	−	+	−	+	−	+
plural	0	+	0	0	+	0	0	0	0	0	0	0	0	0	0	0

+ = applies
− = does not apply
0 = indifferent with reference to feature

After: Manfred Bierwisch. 1969. 'Strukturelle Semantik'. *DaF* 6. 67.

those of the **Prague School**, Hjelmslev's analysis of meaning levels in figures, and especially the ethnolinguistic investigations of Goodenough and Lounsbury gave impetus to componential analysis and provided a source for a model that parses whole meanings into their smallest elements. Corresponding to the phonological model, componential analysis operates on the assumption that it is possible, even in semantics, to describe the whole lexicon of a language with a limited inventory of universally valid features. The descriptions of categories already subjected to such analyses (**color terms**, **kinship terms**, dimensions, military ranks, verbs of motion, among others) are not yet comprehensive enough to confirm this assumption. Above all, the discovery procedures for **semantic features** are not objectifiable enough and remain problematic since the analysis of semantic units into smaller elements of meaning presupposes an intuitive knowledge of semantic relationships, which are, however, at the same time the empirical aim of the semantic analysis. Further difficulties arise through the fact that only a part of the vocabulary can be described through unstructured bundles of semantic features (as is the case for kinship relationships of ego); yet more complex ways of describing must be developed to account for transitive verbs like *kill*, for example, which express relations between two arguments (*X kills Y*). (Generative semantics has suggested and developed such a model.) In this latter type of analysis, the types of combinations can no longer be restricted to the mere conjunction of features. Furthermore, the theoretical status of the semantic features has also been debated. Such features are first indicated by object-language expressions like *male*, *concrete*, *vertical*, to which then a metalinguistic nature is ascribed: [+/−male], [+/−concrete], [+/−vertical]. The semantic features do not correspond directly to physical properties of the real world; rather, they are abstract (theoretical) constructs which represent the cognitive and social conditions according to which the surrounding world is categorized by humans. They may possibly correspond to the basic character of the cognitive and perceptive structure of the human organism. To this extent, the universal claim of componential analysis is justified: every individual language makes use of a universal inventory of features in a manner specifically required by its given historical conditions. The semantic description of componential analysis can be improved by distinguishing different types of semantic features (see Lipka 1979, 1985). Furthermore, componential analysis can even be of use in a holistic conception of meaning by using it to describe **stereotypes** (see Lutzeier 1981, 1985). Componential analysis as a process of semantic description has been the basis for various models in **generative semantics**, **interpretive semantics**, **lexical field theory**, and **transformational grammar**.

References
Bendix, E.H. 1966. *Componential analysis of general vocabulary: the semantic structure of a set of verbs in English, Hindi, and Japanese*. The Hague.
Fillmore, J.C. 1975. An alternative to checklist theories of meaning. In C. Cosen *et al.* (eds),

Proceedings of the first annual meeting of the Berkeley Linguistic Society. Berkeley, CA. 123–31.

Goodenough, W. 1956. Componential analysis and the study of meaning. *Lg* 32.195–216.

—— 1965. Yankee kinship terminology: a problem in componential analysis. *AA* 67.129–287.

Katz, J.J. 1964. Semantic theory and the meaning of 'good.' *JP* 61.739–66.

—— 1966. *The philosophy of language.* New York.

—— 1967. Recent issues in semantic theory. *FL* 3.124–94.

Lipka, L. 1979. Semantic components of English nouns and verbs and their justification. *Angol Filológiai Tanulmángok* 12.187–203.

—— 1985. A meeting place for synchrony and diachrony: inferential features in English. In M. Pfister (ed.), *Anglistentag 1984 Passau.* Giessen. 144–58.

Lounsbury, F.G. 1956. Semantic analysis of the Pawnee kinship usage. *Lg* 32.158–94.

—— 1963. The structural analysis of kinship semantics. In H. Lunt (ed.), *Proceedings of the Ninth International Congress of Linguists.* The Hague. 1073–93.

Lutzeier, P. 1981. *Wort und Feld. Wortsemantische Fragestellen mit besonderer Berücksichtigung des Wortfeldbegriffs.* Tübingen.

—— 1985. *Linguistische Semantik.* Stuttgart.

Lyons, J. 1977. *Semantics,* vol. 1. Cambridge.

McNamara, T.P. and R.J. Sternberg. 1983. Mental models of word meaning. *JVLVB* 22.449–74.

Nida, E. 1975a. *Componential analysis of meaning: an introduction to semantic structures.* The Hague.

—— 1975b. *Exploring semantic structures.* Munich.

Osgood, C.E. 1976. *Focus on meaning,* vol. 1: *Explorations in semantic space.* The Hague.

Putnam, H. 1975. Is semantics possible? In *Mind, language, and reality: philosophical papers.* Cambridge. Vol. 2, 139–52.

Rommetveit, R. 1968. *Words, meanings, and messages: theory and experiments in psycholinguistics.* New York.

Van Eynde, F. 1981. Some deficiencies of semantic feature analysis: a farewell to bachelorhood of lexical semantics. In G. Hindelang and W. Zillig (eds) *Sprache: Verstehen und Handeln. Akten des 15. Linguistischen Kolloquiums Münster 1980.* Tübingen. Vol. 2, 3–13.

⇒ **lexicology**

composition (*also* compounding)

Next to **derivation**, the most important process of **word formation** is composition, i.e. combining two or more otherwise free **morphemes** or series of morphemes (= words) to form a **compound** in which, as a rule, the last element determines the word class (⇒ **juxtaposition** for exceptions like *good-for-nothing, speakeasy*). The productivity of composition varies from language to language (cf. the decreasing order of productivity in **German**, English, **Spanish**, **French**; while, in **Latin**, composition hardly occurs) and is influenced by the category of first and final element. Compositions of two nominal elements (so-called 'N + N compositions,' e.g. *beer can*), are particularly productive; less frequent are compositions of adjective + noun (*darkroom*); and even rarer those of verb + verb (*step turn*). The following types of compositions are distinguished:

(a) Synchronically, according to semantic interpretation. (i) **Determinative compounds** like *coffeepot, living room,* in which the syntactically dependent, content-specifying element (the determining word) precedes the base word. They are often called 'endocentric.' (ii) Possessive compositions (⇒ **bahuvrihi**) as a subgroup of determinative compounds, in which the first element again specifies the second semantically, but the compound as a whole refers only to a prominent characteristic of the referent, e.g. *redhead, loudmouth, hatchback.* Possessive compositions are often called 'exocentric,' since they allow for paraphrases, e.g. 'someone who has a loud mouth.' (iii) Copulative compositions (or 'dvandva' forms) like *author–editor, sweetsour* in which the individual elements are of semantically equal weight and, as a composition, denote a new concept.

(b) Historically and genetically: (i) **juxtaposition**, i.e. the attaching of individual stems to each other without inflection. Since such formations (e.g. OHG *tagaliocht* 'daylight') are seen as older forms of composition, Grimm (1826) called them 'actual' or 'real' compositions, in contrast with (ii) so-called 'case' compositions, which can be traced back to inflectional endings (e.g. Ger. *Tageslicht* 'daylight'; and English compositions containing the possessive case **linking morpheme**, e.g. *women's liberation, children's literature*). Grimm called the latter 'artificial' compositions. (iii) Opaque compositions whose origins cannot be reconstructed synchronically owing to sound changes that have rendered the original form of the individual elements unrecognizable or because the etymological transparency has been lost, as in *world* (OE *weorold* < Gmc **weraldh-* 'age of man').

The transition from composition to derivation (prefix vs suffix formation) is continuous both synchronically and diachronically, cf. *-work* in *artwork* vs *bookwork*; similarly the transition of fully motivated formation to lexicalized formations: *table board, cupboard, blackboard.* (⇒ **lexicalization**)

References

Allen, M. 1978. Morphological investigations. Dissertation, University of Connecticut.

Bauer, L. 1983. *English word formation*. London.

Brekle, H.E. 1978. Reflections on the conditions for the coining, use and understanding of nominal compounds. In W. Dressler and W. Meid (eds), *Proceedings of the twelfth International Congress of Linguistics*. Innsbruck. 68–77.

Di Sciullo, A.M. and E. Williams. 1987. *On the definition of words*. Cambridge, MA.

Downing, P. 1977. On the creation and use of English compound nouns. *Lg* 53.810–42.

Fabb, N. 1984. Syntactic affixation. Dissertation, MIT.

Grimm, J. 1826. *Deutsche Grammatik*, vol. 2. Göttingen.

Meyer, R. 1993. *Compound comprehension in isolation and in context*. Tübingen.

Roeper, T. and M. Siegel. 1978. A lexical transformation for verbal compounds. *LingI* 9.199–260.

Selkirk, E. 1982. *The syntax of words*. Cambridge.

Sproat, R. 1985. On deriving the lexicon. Dissertation, MIT.

⇒ **word formation**

compositionality of meaning ⇒ principle of compositionality

compound

Result of the process of word formation of **composition**, a linguistic expression that consists of at least two free **morphemes** or morpheme constructions: *bath+room*, *refrigeration* (+) *mechanic*. The normal pattern of intonation in English is primary stress followed by secondary stress (as opposed to main stress and zero stress in multi-elemental 'simple' compounds: *youngster*. In **determinative compounds** with a subordinate relation between the **constituents** (determining word, base word), the order cannot be changed without changing the meaning (*dance step* vs *step dance*). In principle, the relation of co-ordination between constituents of a copulative composition allows free word order (*owner-operator*, *operator-owner*), though some forms quickly become lexicalized (⇒ **lexicalization**) in one order or another: *child prodigy* vs **prodigy child* or *chief editor* vs **editor chief*, in which the first elements have become virtually adjectival. Compounding is syntactically and semantically differentiated from simple word groupings: often, though not necessarily, written as a single word, generally with the primary stress on the first constituent, e.g. *bookworm*; set order, e.g. *child psychology* vs *the psychology of children*; inflection only on the base word, e.g. *textbook* (pl. *textbooks*), openness of the semantic relation between the individual elements, e.g. *paper trail* ('trail on which paper moves,' 'trail of paper') and the lexicalized idiom, e.g. *paper trail* ('documental evidence'). The junction between the two immediate constituents may be characterized by a special **linking morpheme**. To the extent that its occurrence is rule-governed, they are dependent on the type of first element, where at least for a number of first constituents, completely different formations may occur, cf. *doghouse*, *dog's-ear*, or Ger. *Rindfleisch* ('beef'), *Rindsfilet* ('fillet of beef'), *Rinderbraten* ('roast beef').

References
⇒ **word formation**

compound bilingualism ⇒ bilingualism

compound sentence

A sentence that contains at least two **main clauses**. Compound sentences differ from **complex sentences** in that they are asyndetic (⇒ **asyndeton**), i.e. joined without means of a conjunction, or are conjoined by means of either **co-ordinating conjunctions** or **sentence adverbials** (*thus*, *however*). Complex sentences, on the other hand, are connected by means of **subordinating conjunctions** (*because*, *since*, *although*), **relative pronouns**, etc. Compound sentences can be either copulative (= co-ordinating) when connected by *and* or disjunctive when connected by *but* or *or* (⇒ **co-ordination**).

compounding ⇒ composition, compound

comprehensibility

Collective term for characteristics of text composition that influence the process of comprehending and memorizing a text. 'Readability formulas' oriented towards practical demands are based on countable lexical and syntactic features, such as word length, word frequency, or sentence length. Other concepts also take into consideration complex text dimensions comprising semantic and cognitive features such as simplicity, structure, conciseness, stimulance or stylistic simplicity, semantic redundancy, cognitive structuring, conceptual conflict. In the framework of a model of **text processing**, comprehensibility is not conceived of as a text-immanent property, but as an alternating interaction between text properties and reader characteristics (e.g. pre-knowledge, motivation).

computational complexity ⇒ complexity

computational linguistics

1 Discipline straddling linguistics and (applied) computer science that is concerned with the computer processing of natural languages (on all levels of linguistic description).

Particular areas of interest are (a) the development of formalisms for precisely representing linguistic knowledge or models that can be interpreted by computers (⇒ **definite clause grammar**, **knowledge representation**); (b) the development of processes and algorithms for analyzing and generating natural-language texts (⇒ **parsing**, **machine-aided translation**, **text generation**); (c) models for simulating linguistic behavior (e.g. for dialogue strategies or question–answer systems); (d) work benches for grammar models, and the like, that make the testing of rules and rule-based systems possible; and (e) programs for collecting and statistically evaluating large amounts of language data, e.g. for automatic lemmatization (attributing word forms to a particular lexeme), for producing word frequency lists, for automatically indexing according to specific key words, for producing concordances (word lists with contexts). For information regarding the state of education in computational linguistics, see Cohen (1986) and Evans (1986).

2 A more general view of computational linguistics than that above includes the area of speech processing.

References
Alshawi, H. (ed.) 1992. *The core language engine*. Cambridge, MA.
Bates, M. and R.M. Weischedel (eds) 1992. *Challenges in natural language processing*. Cambridge.
Bátori, S.I., W. Lenders and W. Putschke (eds) 1989. *Computational linguistics: an international handbook on computer oriented language research and applications*. Berlin and New York.
Bird, S. 1995. *Computational phonology. A constraint-based approach*. Cambridge.
Bridge, P. and S. Harlow. 1995. *An introduction to computational linguistics*. Oxford.
Briscoe, T. and B. Boguraev. 1988. *Computational lexicography for natural language processing*. London.
Butler, C.S. 1985. *Computers in linguistics*. Oxford.
Carberry, S. 1990. *Plan recognition in natural language dialogue*. Cambridge, MA.
Cawsey, A. 1993. *Explanation and interaction: the computer generation of explanatory dialogues*. Cambridge, MA.
Cohen, R. 1986. Survey of computational linguistics courses. *CL* 12 (Course Survey Supplement).
Evans, M. 1986. Directory of graduate programs in computational linguistics, 2nd edn. *CL* 12 (Graduate Directory Supplement).
Gazdar, G. (ed.) 1985. Computational tools for doing linguistics. *Linguistics* 23.185–7.
Gazdar, G. and C.S. Mellish. 1989. *Natural language processing in PROLOG*. Reading, MA.
Grosz, B., K. Sparck-Jones, and B.L. Webber (eds) 1986. *Readings in natural language processing*. Los Altos, CA.
Halvorsen, P.-K. 1988. Computer application of linguistic theory. In F. Newmeyer (ed.), *Linguistics: the Cambridge survey*. Cambridge. Vol. 1, 187–219.
Kronfeld, A. 1990. *Reference and computation*. Cambridge.
Krulee, G.K. 1991. *Computer processing of natural language*. Englewood Cliffs, NJ.
Moore, J.D. 1993. *Participating in explanatory dialogues*. Cambridge, MA.
Paris, C.L., W.R. Swartout and W.C. Mann. 1991. *Natural language generation in artificial intelligence and computational linguistics*. Dordrecht.
Pennington, M.C. and V. Stevens (eds) 1991. *Computers in applied linguistics: an international perspective*. Clevedon.
Pustejovsky, J. (ed.) 1993. *Semantics and the lexicon*. Dordrecht.
Ristad, E.S. 1993. *The complexity of human language*. Cambridge, MA.
Rosner, M. and R. Johnson. 1992. *Computational linguistics and formal semantics*. Cambridge.
Saint-Dizier, P. and E. Viegas. 1995. *Computational lexical semantics*. Cambridge.
Salton, G. and M.J. McGill. 1983. *Introduction to modern information retrieval*. New York.
Smith, G.W. 1991. *Computers and human language*. Oxford.
Sproat, R. 1992. *Morphology and computation*. Cambridge, MA.
Winograd, T. 1983. *Language as a cognitive process*, vol. 1: *Syntax*. Reading, MA.

Journals
Computational Linguistics
Journal of Logic, Language and Information

computer translation ⇒ **machine-aided translation**

conative

Semantic aspect of the **imperfect** tense found, for example, in *Latin*, which describes an action as an unsuccessful attempt: Lat. *Explicabat hanc sententiam* 'She/he tried to explain the sentence.'

concatenation [Lat. *catena* 'chain']

1 Process and product of the rule-ordered, linear placement of linguistic elements or linguistic categories. As a rule (though not necessarily), concatenation is notated by the symbols of connection '+' or '⌢'. Concatenations connect at least two elements (e.g. NP + VP), whose order is determined by the given concatenational operation. In **transformational grammar**, concatenations are produced through rules of substitution in the basis part.

2 In Weinreich's (1966) semantic theory, concatenation refers to a semantic process that results in the formation of subcategorized sets (⇒ **cluster**) of semantic features, the origin of the features no longer being reconstructible in

reference to the individual constituents (in contrast, ⇒ **nesting**). According to Weinreich, concatenating constructions are (a) nouns functioning as subjects with main verbs, (b) nouns functioning as subjects with predicate nouns and predicate adjectives, (c) main verbs and adverbials of manner, and (d) descriptive adverbs and adjectives.

Reference
Weinreich, U. 1966. Explorations in semantic theory. In T.A. Sebeok (ed.), *Current trends in linguistics*. The Hague. Vol. 3, 395–477.

concept ⇒ **notion**

concession [Lat. *concedere* 'to give way'] (*also* concessio)
Figure of speech used in **argumentation** to concede a point, either to hurt the adversary directly or to prepare for a more important argument: *I like disorder, but not a mess.*

concessive clause
Semantically defined subordinate clause functioning syntactically as an adverbial complement (⇒ **adverbial**) which indicates conditions that, even if they are fulfilled, still will not result in the state of affairs expressed in the main clause (*Even if he apologized in person, she still wouldn't forgive him*). They can also indicate a situation whose expected consequence fails to occur (*Even though she responded quickly, she still couldn't reach him*). Concessive clauses are usually introduced by subordinating conjunctions such as *although, even though, in spite of the fact that, however much, regardless.*

conclusion
Inference whose truth follows logically from the truth of particular premises; for example, from the premises (a) *All humans are mortal* and (b) *Socrates is human*, one arrives at the conclusion (c) *Socrates is mortal.*

References
⇒ **formal logic**

conclusive ⇒ **resultative**

concomitance ⇒ **collocation**

concord
1 In languages with **noun class** systems, the **agreement** of adnominals and verbs with the noun according to the noun's class: e.g. **Swahili** *vi-su vi-wili vi-natosha* 'Two knives are enough,' *wa-tu wa-wili wa-natosha* 'Two people are enough,' *ma-tunda ma-wili ya-natosha* 'Two pieces of fruit are enough.'

2 ⇒ **agreement**

concrete noun [Lat. *concretus* 'solid, dense']
Concretes form a class of nouns that contrasts semantically with **abstract nouns**; they are divided into proper names (⇒ **proper nouns**, e.g. *Philip, Chomsky*), **common** (or generic) nouns (e.g. *human, linguist*), materials (e.g. *ink, iron*) and groups (⇒ **collective noun**), (e.g. *family, cattle*).

conditional
1 Subcategory of verbal **mood** which characterizes a state of affairs as 'conditional.' While the conditional mood has a developed morphological system in French (the **preterite** of the **future tense**), it is expressed in English by *would* + infinitive: *If my boss said something like that to me, I would tell him a thing or two.*

References
Closs-Traugott, E. (ed.) 1986. *On conditionals*. Cambridge.
⇒ **modality**

2 ⇒ **implication**

conditional clause
Semantically defined subordinate clause functioning as an adverbial modifier which indicates the condition on which the action in the **main clause** is contingent. They are normally introduced by such conjunctions as *if, in case, in as far as*: *If it rains tomorrow, we'll have to cancel our trip.*

References
Haiman, J. 1993. Conditionals. In J. Jacobs *et al.* (eds), *Syntax: an international handbook of contemporary research*. Berlin and New York. 923–9.
Jackson, F. 1987. *Conditionals*. Oxford.

conditional implication ⇒ **implication**

conditional relevance
In **conversation analysis**, the term (introduced by Schegloff) characterizes participants' expectations with regard to the **sequential organization** of **turns** in conversations. The production of a token of an utterance type *A* establishes the expectation (or relevance) of a token of a particular type *B* by the next speaker. If *B* fails to occur, its absence will be noticed; for example, *A* may be repeated until *B* is provided. *A* and *B* may be parts of an **adjacency pair** or may be sequences as in mutual greetings (*A*) and the first topic (*B*).

References
Goffman, E. 1976. Replies and responses. *LSoc* 5.257–313.
Grice, H. 1975. Logic and conversation. In P. Cole

and J. Morgan (eds), *Syntax and semantics*, vol. 3: *Speech acts*. New York. 41–58.

Merritt, M. 1976. On questions following answers in service encounters. *LSoc* 5.315–57.

Schegloff, E. 1968. Sequencing in conversational openings. *AA* 70.1075–95. (Repr. in J.J. Gumperz and D. Hymes (eds), *Directions in sociolinguistics*. New York, 1972. 346–80.)

Schegloff, E. and H. Sacks. 1973. Opening up closings. *Semiotica* 8.289–327.

conditioning

Theory of learning investigated and developed by the Russian physiologist J.P. Pavlov (1849–1936). A spontaneous (conditioned) reaction, triggered by a particular stimulus can in turn be triggered by another stimulus if this other stimulus is repeatedly combined with the original stimulus; after training, the reaction will occur in response to the second stimulus even if it is given without the original stimulus (⇒ **stimulus-response**). This form of conditioning was used, influenced by the behaviorist school (⇒ **behaviorism**; see Skinner 1957), to explain **language acquisition**. Thus, meanings are purportedly learned by pointing to (unconditioned stimulus) and naming (second stimulus) the given object until such time as merely uttering the word produces reference to the object. Producing such reactions can be accelerated and stabilized or intensified by an appropriate reward. Such cases are known as 'instrumental' or 'operant' conditioning (in contrast to the 'classical' conditioning by Pavlov 1929).

References
Pavlov, J.P. 1929. *Lectures on reflexes*. London.
Skinner, B.F. 1957. *Verbal behavior*. London.
⇒ **behaviorism**, **language acquisition**

conduction aphasia ⇒ aphasia

configuration

In Weinreich's semantic theory (1966), a relation between semantic features. In contrast to the subcategorized set of features in a **cluster**, a configuration consists of an ordered set of **semantic features**. The features of *chair*, [furniture] and [sitting], form a configuration: [furniture for sitting on], since they stand in a modified relationship to each other and are not merely added together ([furniture] plus [for sitting]). Compare *daughter*, to which the features [feminine] as well as [offspring] apply.

Reference
Weinreich, U. 1966. Explorations in semantic theory. In T.A. Sebeok (ed.), *Current trends in linguistics*. The Hague. Vol. 3, 395–477.

Congo ⇒ Bantu

congruence ⇒ agreement

conjugation [Lat. *coniugatio* 'connection']

Morphological marking of the verb stem with regard to the verbal grammatical categories of **person**, **number**, **tense**, **mood**, **voice**, and (to the extent it is grammaticalized) **aspect**. Conjugational patterns differ from language to language. The formal distinction between regular and irregular verbs is a fundamental one in the English conjugational system. (⇒ *also* **inflection**, **strong vs weak verb**)

References
⇒ **morphology**

conjunct [Lat. *coniungere* 'to join']

Partial sentence in a sentence with co-ordinating **conjunction**.

conjunction

Class of words whose function is to connect words, phrases, or sentences syntactically, while characterizing semantic relations between those elements. With regard to their syntactic function a distinction is drawn between co-ordinating and subordinating conjunctions: because co-ordinating conjunctions connect elements that are equally ordered with each other, they generally cannot be used sentence-initially (e.g. *For Philip was sick, he didn't go to work*); on the other hand, subordinating conjunctions introduce dependent clauses and can occur sentence initially (e.g. *Because Philip was sick, he didn't go to work*). The following semantic relations can be expressed with co-ordinating conjunctions: (a) copulative: *and, as well as, neither … nor, namely*; (b) disjunctive: *or, either … or*; (c) adversative: *but, however, on the contrary*; (d) causal: *for*. Subordinating conjunctions introduce adverbial clauses and characterize causal (*since, because*), modal (*by*) and temporal (*when, before*) relations.

References
⇒ **co-ordination**

2 ⇒ **co-ordination**.

3 In **formal logic**, connection of two elementary propositions p and q by the logical particle (⇒ **logical connective**) *and*, the resulting proposition of which is true only if both parts of the proposition (= conjuncts) p and q are true. The compound proposition *Tokyo is the capital of Japan, and Tokyo is a European city* has a false truth value because the second half of the proposition is false. The following (two-value)

truth table represents a definition of conjunction:

p	q		p ∧ q
t	t		t
t	f		f
f	t		f
f	f		f

In everyday language *and* is realized as a conjunction by *also, as well as, besides, in addition, not only ... but also, both ... and*. In contrast with everyday use, however, the logical conjunction *and* does not distinguish between *and* and *but* nor temporally between the propositions (cf. *The horse stumbled and fell down* in contrast to *The horse fell down and stumbled*, that is, $p \wedge q$ is equally logical as $q \wedge p$). Nor do both parts of the proposition necessarily have to be semantically related, that is, be in a communicatively relevant relation. The term 'conjunction' refers both to the function of the two-place sentence operator *and* as well as to the resulting proposition defined by it. With the aid of set theory, conjunction can be characterized semantically as the intersection set of both model sets that make the connected propositions true (⇒ **set**).

4 Synonym for **logical connective** (⇒ *also* **formal logic**)

conjunctive ⇒ co-ordination

conjunctive adverb

Adverb which occurs as an independent constituent before the finite verb and which has a co-ordinating function, e.g. *so* in *It was raining, so we stayed at home*. Conjunctive adverbs can have other semantic and syntactic functions besides co-ordination, such as **particles** or **adverbials**.

connecting vowel ⇒ linking vowel

connection

1 In the syntactic model of L. Tesnière's **dependency grammar**, a syntactic relation that denotes the abstract dependency relation between syntactic elements regardless of their linear surface order. The set of all connections constitutes the sentence. Thus, *Figaro swears* not only consists of the sum of the elements (a) *Figaro* and (b) *swears*, but also of (c) the abstract connection that relates the two to each other. In the framework of Tesnière's model, connection is the basic structural relationship between the elements of a sentence, which are represented in a **tree diagram** by directed branches. Additional semantic connections are marked by dotted lines: *Philip loses his magic wand*.

References
⇒ **dependency grammar**

2 The joining of **propositions** or **illocutions** by causal, temporal, disjunctive, or other relationships. The relationship can be expressed by a **connective** or by another asyndetic (⇒ **asyndeton**) expression. Connection is an important means of **cohesion** and **coherence** of texts.

References
Charolles, M. *et al.* (eds) 1986. *Research in text connexity and text coherence: a survey*. Hamburg.
Conte, M.E., J.S. Petöfi, and E. Sözer (eds) 1989. *Text and discourse connectedness: proceedings of the conference on 'Text Connexity and Coherence' (Urbino 1984)*. Amsterdam.
Haiman, J. (ed.) 1988. *Clause combining in grammar and discourse*. Amsterdam.
Halliday, M.A.K. and R. Hasan. 1976. *Cohesion in English*. London.
Petöfi, J.S. and E. Sözer (eds) 1983. *Micro and macro connexity of texts*. Hamburg.
Rudolph, E. 1988. Connective relations – connective expressions – connective structures. In J.S. Petöfi (ed.), *Text and discourse constitution*. Berlin. 97–133.
Van Dijk, T.A. 1977a. Connectives in text grammar and text logic. In T.S. van Dijk and J.S. Petöfi (eds), *Grammars and descriptions*. Berlin. 11–63.
——— 1977b. *Text and context*. London.
——— 1981. *Studies in the pragmatics of discourse*. The Hague.

Bibliographies
Lohmann, P. 1988. Connectedness of texts: a bibliographical survey. In J.S. Petöfi (ed.), *Text and discourse constitution*. Berlin. 478–501.
——— 1988–9. Connectedness of texts: A bibliographical survey. Part 1 in: *Text and discourse constitution*, ed. by J.S. Petöfi. Berlin. 478–501: Part 2 in: *Connexity and coherence*, ed. by W. Heydrich *et al*. New York.

connectionism

Paradigm of research in **artificial intelligence** that is oriented towards neurology. In contrast to the symbolic processing method of traditional artificial intelligence that uses sequential, globally directed processes, in connectionism processing takes place through numerous local and highly parallel processes. Recent debate between adherents of connectionism and its challengers has centered on whether connectionist approaches represent an alternative to or

a complement of symbolic information processing, which is based on the fundamental concepts of **rule** and representations, eschewed in
connectionism.

References.
Elman, J.L. 1993. Learning and development in
neural networks: the importance of starting small.
Cognition 48.71–99.
Mikkulainen, R. 1993. *Subsymbolic natural language processes.* Cambridge, MA.
Pinker, S. and J. Mehler (eds) 1988. *Cognition*
28:1–2 (special issue).
Plunkett, K. and V. Marchman. 1991. U-shaped
learning and frequency effects in a multi-layered
perceptron: Implications for child language acquisition. *Cognition* 38.43–102.
——— 1993. From rote learning to system building:
acquiring verb morphology in children and connectionist nets. *Cognition* 48.21–69.
Rumelhart, D. and E.J. McClelland. 1986. *Parallel
distributed processing*, 2 vols. Cambridge, MA.

connective

1 Linguistic expression with the function of
joining sentences (⇒ **connection**). **Conjunctions** and **conjunctive adverbs** belong to the
class of connectives. They join either **propositions** or states of affairs (semantic connectives)
or **illocutions** (pragmatic connectives): for
example, *He is happy, because it is raining*
(joining of states of affairs) vs *He is happy, for
it is raining* (reason for a proposition).

References
⇒ **connection**

2 Logical particle. (⇒ **logical connective**)

connexity ⇒ connex relation

connex relation (*also* connexity)

Property of a two-place relation *R* in a set *A* that
is exactly true if it is the case for any two non-
identical elements *x* and *y* of *A* that: *R(x, y)* or
R(y, x), in everyday language: either *x* is in a
relation *R* to *y* or *y* is in a relation *R* to *x*. This
is the case, for example, for the relation 'smaller than' in natural numbers, since for two
arbitrary numbers *x, y* it is the case that: either
x is smaller than *y*, or *y* is smaller than *x*.

References
⇒ **formal logic**, **set theory**

connotation [Lat. *con-* 'with,' *notatio* 'defini-tion']

1 (*also* affective, associative or occasional
meaning). The emotive or affective component
of a linguistic expression (such as style, idiolect, dialect, and emotional charge), which is
superimposed upon its basic meaning and
which – in contrast to the static conceptual

meaning – is difficult to describe generally and
context-independently. Consider, for example,
the emotional charge of Ger. *Führer* ('leader').
In contrast, the cognitive, referential aspect of
meaning is called **denotation**.

References
⇒ **meaning, semantics**

2 (*also* significative meaning) In logic, the
conceptual content or **sense**, in contrast to
denotation which is the **reference** to extralinguistic reality. (⇒ *also* **extension**, **intension**,
intensional logic)

References
⇒ **formal logic, meaning**

consecutive interpreting ⇒ interpreting

consequence clause

Semantically defined dependent clause functioning as an adverbial modifier to describe the
consequences of the action expressed in the
main clause. They are generally introduced by
such conjunctions as *that, so that*: *She was so
hoarse that she had to call off her recital.*

consequent

In **formal logic**, the second part of a complex
proposition in a propositional connection (cf.
antecedent).

consociation

Property of linguistic expressions which always
occur in the same combination: *year-in, year-
out, (sitting on) pins and needles.*

consonant [Lat. *consonare* 'to sound toge-ther']

Phonetically, a **speech sound** that is not an
approximant and, therefore, is either a **stop** or
a **fricative**. Consonants are initiated with (a)
pulmonic (as a rule, expiratory), (b) **pharyngeal**, or (c) **oral** air. A corresponding distinction is drawn between (a) expiratory sounds, (b)
ejectives and **implosives**, and (c) **clicks**. While
some approximants are formed with the pul-
monic **airstream mechanism** (**vowels** and
semivowels), no approximants are formed with
pharyngeal or oral air. Ejectives are found, for
example, in **Georgian** and in Kera, spoken in
Chad, and **clicks** in, for example, the **Khoisan**
language Nama. In European languages consonants are, as a rule, voiced or voiceless (⇒
voiced vs voiceless). Murmured consonants are
found in Miao of Weining (⇒ **Miao-Yao**), and
laryngeal consonants in Lango (language spoken in Nigeria). Consonants are divided into
subclasses according to their **manner of**

Consonant chart

places of articulation → ↓ manner of articulation		labials	labials	teeth (dentes)	teeth (dentes)	alveolar ridge (alveolus)	hard palate (palatum)	hard palate (palatum)	soft palate (velum)	uvula (uvula)	larynx (larynx)
		bilabials	labiodentals	interdentals	—	apico-alveolars	palato-alveolars	palato-dorsals	velars-dorsals	uvulars	laryngeals
fricatives	voiceless (fortis)		f	θ		s	ʃ				h
	voiced (lenis)		v	ð		z	ʒ				
plosives	voiceless (fortis)	p				t			k		
	voiced (lenis)	b				d			g		
affricates											
nasals		m				n		ŋ			
laterals						l					
approximants						ɹ	j	w			

Notes on chart structure:

- articulatory organs: upper lip / lower lip (labium); tip of the tongue (apex); blade of the tongue (corona); root of the tongue (dorsum)
- classification of consonants: obstruents (fricatives, plosives, affricates) and sonorants (nasals, liquids — laterals, approximants)
- manner of articulation by points of articulation:
  - constriction
  - formation of stop • with a following oral release
  - • with release and a following constriction
  - • with a lowered palate
  - • with lateral constriction

articulation (stop, fricative, approximant, **median**, **lateral**, **flap**, **tap**, **vibrant**), their **place of articulation**, and any **secondary articulation**. In order to resolve some of the ambiguity surrounding the term 'consonant,' Pike introduced the term 'contoid' (⇒ **contoid vs vocoid**) for these phonetic entities.

References
⇒ **phonetics**

consonantal vs non-consonantal

Binary phonological **opposition** in **distinctive feature** analysis, based on acoustically analyzed and spectrally defined criteria (⇒ **acoustic phonetics**, **spectral analysis**). Acoustic characteristic: decrease vs increase of the total intensity on the spectrum. Articulatory characteristic: presence vs absence of an occlusion of the **vocal tract**.

References
Jakobson, R. *et al.* 1951. *Preliminaries to speech analysis*. Cambridge, MA. 19–20. (6th edn 1965.)
⇒ **distinctive feature**

constant ⇒ variability

constant opposition ⇒ opposition

constative utterance [Lat. *constare* 'to be manifest; to be an established fact']

In the early stages of J.L. Austin's philosophy of language, including the first part of his 1958 lectures (see Austin 1963) on **speech act theory**, this term denoted utterances that describe or depict facts or states of affairs and so (in contrast to performatives (⇒ **performative utterance**) may be either true or false. In this sense, 'constative' corresponds to the philosophical term 'statement.' In the latter half of his lectures, Austin virtually abandoned his performative-constative distinction, concluding that constatives also have a performative aspect (the actual uttering of a statement) and, as such, should be considered illocutionary acts (⇒ **illocution**).

Reference
Austin, J.L. 1963. Performative – constative. In C.E. Caton (ed.), *Philosophy and ordinary language*. Urbana, IL. 22–54.

constellation [Lat. *constellatio* 'position of the stars']

In **glossematics**, the relation between two linguistic elements that have some sort of connection with each other, but are not, as in the case of **interdependence** and **determination**, in any way dependent on each other, as, for example, *away* in *carry away*, as *away* can also occur in other contexts. Syntagmatic constellation is

termed **combination**, paradigmatic constellation is called **autonomy**.

References
⇒ **glossematics**

constituency [Lat. *constituere* 'to make up (of)']

Basic syntactic relation in the description of the hierarchical structure of sentences: between two elements *A* and *B* occurring in a linear fashion there holds the relation of constituency, if and only if they are both dominated by a common element *C* (⇒ **domination**). Constituent structure grammar is based on this relation. (⇒ **dependency**)

References
⇒ **immediate constituent analysis, phrase structure grammar, transformational grammar**

constituent

A term used in structural sentence analysis for every linguistic unit, which is part of a larger linguistic unit. Several constituents together form a construction: for example, in the sentence, *Money doesn't grow on trees*, each word is a constituent, as is the prepositional phrase *on trees*. Constituents can be joined together with other constituents to form larger units. If two constituents, *A* and *B*, are joined to form a hierarchically higher constituent *C*, then *A* and *B* are said to be immediate constituents of *C*. (⇒ **phrase structure rule**, **rewrite rule**)

References
⇒ **immediate constituent analysis**

constituent clause

Term introduced by R.B. Lees for partial sentences which are embedded in **matrix sentences**. Constituent clauses are expanded **constituents** which are dominated in the **tree diagram** by an S-node which is not identical with the initial S-node (**embedding**). The term 'constituent clause' corresponds to the traditional notion of **dependent** or **subordinate clause**.

Reference
Lees, R.B. 1963. *The grammar of English nominalizations*. Bloomington, IN. (5th edn 1968.)

constitutive rule

A rule that, by identifying certain manners of behavior as foundational of a definite type of activity, constitutes or creates that activity. For example, kicking a ball around does not constitute a game of soccer until at least the basic rules of the game are followed. One of the constitutive rules of soccer is that kicking the ball through the opposing team's goalposts counts as a goal. The same principle applies to the movement of chess pieces on the chess board. **Regulative rules**, in contrast, are those rules that contingently constrain or delimit an antecedently constituted activity. In the case of goal scoring in soccer, a couple of regulative rules are that the ball must be 'in play' and that one's team-mate is not permitted to pin down the opposing goalkeeper. Thus, formulations of constitutive rules are analytical statements since they only explicate something that is already contained in the concept of the type of behavior concerned. According to Searle, speech acts are performed in accordance with constitutive rules: an **utterance** of a particular form is a promise only under certain conditions. (⇒ *also* **speech act theory**)

References
Searle, J.R. 1969. *Speech acts: an essay in the philosophy of language*. Cambridge.
⇒ **speech act theory**

constraints

General conditions for the use and formation of rules which universally restrict the very general **phrase structure rules** and transformational rules (⇒ **transformation**) so that they only generate the structures of natural languages. In N. Chomsky's revisions of his concepts of **transformational grammar**, constraints make empirical declarations about rules which are in principle possible in the grammars of human languages. Such general declarations about the structure of human languages should also correspond to certain properties of the human capabilities for language. They are interpreted as part of the prestructured, biologically asserted expectations, which can plausibly explain the rapid process of language acquisition in early childhood. Constraints for transformational rules relate above all to the description of structure. Since Ross (1967), an abundance of different, but partly overlapping, suggestions has been formulated in this area, for instance, the **A-over-A-principle**, the **principle of cyclic rule application**, the **propositional island constraint**, the **sentential-subject constraint**, the **specified subject condition**, the **subjacency** condition, as well as the **structure-preserving constraint**. In their broadest sense, **trace theory**, **binding theory**, **X-bar theory**, and constraints on rule filters are also constraints, since they determine the conditions for wellformedness for various levels of the description of language.

References
Bresnan, J.W. 1976. On the form and functioning of transformations. *LingI* 7.3–40.
Chomsky, N. 1973. Conditions on transformations. In S.R. Anderson and P. Kiparsky (eds), *Festschrift for Morris Halle*. New York. 232–86.
———— 1975. *Reflections on language*. New York.
———— 1976. Conditions on rules of grammar. *LingA* 2.303–51.
———— 1977a. *Essays on form and interpretation*. New York.
———— 1977b. On wh-movement. In P.W. Culticover, T. Wasow, and A. Akmajian (eds), *Formal syntax*. New York. 71–132.
———— 1981. *Lectures on government and binding*. Dordrecht.
Emonds, J.E. 1976. *A transformational approach to English syntax*. New York.
Freidin, R. 1978. Cyclicity and the theory of grammar. *LingI* 9.519–49.
Koster, J. 1978. *Locality principles in syntax*. Dordrecht.
Perlmutter, D.M. 1970. Surface structure constraints in syntax. *LingI* 1.182–255.
Postal, P.M. 1971. *Cross-over phenomena: a study in the grammar of coreference*. New York.
Ross, J.R. 1967. Constraints on variables in syntax. Dissertation, MIT. (Repr. as *Infinite syntax!* Norwood, NJ, 1986.)
Soames, S. and D.M. Perlmutter. 1979. *Syntactic argumentation and the structure of English*. Berkeley, CA.
Van Riemsdijk, H. and E. Williams. 1986. *Introduction to the theory of grammar*. Cambridge, MA.

constrictive ⇒ **fricative**

contact assimilation ⇒ **assimilation**

contact test (*also* exclusion)

Experimental analytical procedure in structural linguistics (⇒ **structuralism**) for determining syntactic and semantic regularities. Depending on whether the insertion of a linguistic element into a given context yields grammatical or ungrammatical expressions, conclusions can be drawn as to the grammatical properties of the elements brought into contact with each other by this test. For example, the contact test can show whether two linguistic units determined by the **substitution test** are elements of the same or different constituent classes: thus, *for two years* and *linguistics* are substitutable for one another: *he studied for two years* and *he studied linguistics*; however, the contact test demonstrates that they are also combinable: *he studied linguistics for two years*, i.e. that they belong to different constituent classes and functions (**object** and **adverbial**, respectively). (⇒ *also* **adjunction**)

References
⇒ **operational procedures**

content

Term used in various ways for the designation of the meaning of the linguistic **sign**, in contrast to its material realization, the **expression**[2]. Depending on the theoretical concept, content refers to (a) the signified in the extralinguistic reality (⇒ **referent**, ⇒ **signifier vs signified**), (b) the conceptual side of the sign (⇒ **meaning**), or (c) the linguistic interworld of super-individual views, which are constituted by language.

References
⇒ **meaning**

content analysis

Empirical approach developed by Lasswell (1938) and others for the objective, systematic, and quantifiable analysis of communicative content found in all types of texts (newspaper articles, radio copy, literary texts, etc.). On the basis of a predetermined framework of quantifiable data such as key words, syntactic combinations and the like, different levels of content can be analyzed: pure information, commentary, the speaker's subjective viewpoint towards this information, and the hearer's ability to apprehend how all the information interrelates based on his/her knowledge of the context. In this analysis, linguistic data realized in the surface structure play a primary role in that they are classified and analyzed statistically according to predetermined categories. Mahl (1959) pointed out that the communicative context, that is, the specific situation in which the text is produced, can in certain circumstances be more important for the interpretation of its content than the literal meaning of a statement. Content analysis gained attention during World War II, when attempts were made to use it as a tool to determine enemy objectives and plans based solely on remarks made by the enemy. Content analysis has been used with success in journalism, literary arts, culture studies, psychology, and elsewhere. And, with computers, great progress in the level of accuracy and the degree of effectiveness has been made.

References
Carley, K. and M. Palmquist. 1992. Extracting, representing and analyzing mental models. *Social Forces* 70. 601–36.
Gerbner, G. *et al.* (eds) 1969. *The analysis of communication content*. New York.
Krippendorff, K. 1980. *Content analysis: an introduction to its methodology*. Beverly Hills, CA.
Lasswell, H.D. 1938. A provisional classification of symbol data. *Psychiatry* 1.197–204.

———— *et al.* 1952. *The comparative study of symbols*. Stanford, CA.
Mahl, G.F. 1959. Exploring emotional states by content analysis. In I. De Sola Pool (ed.), *Trends in content analysis*. Urbana, IL.
Neuman, W.R. 1989. Parallel content analysis: Old paradigms and new proposals. *Public communication and Behavior* 2. 205–89.
Roberts, C.W. 1989. Other than counting words: a linguistic approach to content analysis. *Social Forces* 68. 147–77.
Weber, R. 1984. Computer-aided content analysis: A short primer. *Qualitative Sociology* 7. 126–47.

content-based instruction

The incorporation of materials drawn from content areas such as social sciences, literature, the arts, and so forth into language instruction. Proponents criticize other approaches for over-emphasizing skills acquisition in a narrow here-and-now context and claim that such other approaches have led to a marginalization of foreign language instruction in the curriculum. Content-based instruction, as well as cross-disciplinary programs such as FLAC (Foreign Language Across the Curriculum), seek to realign foreign language instruction with the humanistic and intellectual missions of the academic curriculum.

References
Brinton, D.M., M.A. Snow, and M.B. Wesche. 1989. *Content-based second language instruction*. Boston, MA.
Krueger, M. and F. Ryan (eds) 1993. *Language and context: discipline- and content-based approaches to language study*. Lexington, MA.

content clause

Term for dependent *that*-clauses which express important meaning relative to the whole utterance: *Caroline suspected (that), that the weather would change.* The subordinate clause expresses the content of an element of the main clause which can be conceived of as a referential pronoun *that*.

References
⇒ **subordinate clause**

content plane ⇒ expression plane vs content plane

content word ⇒ autosemantic word

context [Lat. *contextus* 'an ordered scheme; the state of being joined']

As a comprehensive concept in communication theory, 'context' refers to all elements of a communicative situation: the verbal and non-verbal context, the context of the given speech situation and the social context of the relationship between the speaker and hearer, their knowledge, and their attitudes. Catford distinguishes between linguistic context and situational **co-text**.

References
Catford, J.C. 1965. *A linguistic theory of translation.* London.
Duranti, A. and C. Goodwin (eds) 1992. *Rethinking context.* Cambridge.
Firbas, J. 1964. On defining the theme in functional sentence analysis. *TLP* 1.267–80.
Schiffrin, D. 1987. Discovering the context of an utterance. *Linguistics* 25.11–32.
⇒ **cohesion**

context-free grammar

A **phrase structure grammar** which consists of rules for which no context requirements exist. (⇒ *also* **generative grammar**)

context-free rule

A **phrase structure rule** which is formulated without any regard for context. (⇒ *also* **generative grammar**, **phrase structure rule**, **transformational grammar**)

context-restricted grammar ⇒ **context-sensitive grammar**

context-restricted rule ⇒ **context-sensitive rule**

context-sensitive grammar

A **phrase structure grammar** which comprises rules in which the semantic and syntactic environments are important for rule application. (⇒ *also* **generative grammar**)

context-sensitive rule

A **phrase structure rule** in which formulation of the context (syntactic-semantic environment) affects its application. (⇒ *also* **generative grammar**, **phrase structure grammar**)

contextual implication ⇒ **implication**

contextualism ⇒ **Firthian linguistics**

contextualization

Introduced by Gumperz and Cook-Gumperz (1976), 'contextualization' refers to the shared construction of contexts (i.e. contexts are not a given) by the participants in the course of their interaction. Contextualization consists of a set of procedures that relate contextualization cues to background knowledge. Such cues can be prosodic (⇒ **prosody**), proxemic (⇒ **proxemics**), or kinetic (⇒ **kinesics**); they may consist of choosing a particular lexical item, syntactic construction, or formulaic expression, or in **code-switching**, etc. Background knowledge is organized in overlapping and interrelated **frames** that constrain the interpretation of a cue. The meaning of cues is derived from the co-occurrence of other cues related to the same or different frames: for instance, with regard to the frame of 'turn-taking' (⇒ **turn**), a decrease in loudness and a change in body posture may indicate that the current speaker intends to end his/her turn. The co-occurrence of cues leads to redundancy, which allows one to interpret the behavior of one's co-participant(s), even if not all cues were clearly understood. Because frames are culturally determined, misunderstandings may result in cross-cultural interactions (see Gumperz 1982).

References
Goffman, E. 1974. *Frame analysis.* Cambridge, MA.
Gumperz, J.J. 1982. *Discourse strategies.* Cambridge.
Gumperz, J.J. and J. Cook-Gumperz. 1976. Context in children's speech. In J.J. Gumperz and J. Cook-Gumperz (eds), *Papers on language and context.* Berkeley, CA.
Tannen, D. 1986. *That's not what I meant.* New York.

contiguity [Lat. *contiguus* 'adjacent']

1 ⇒ **constituency**

2 In semantics, a relation between **lexemes** that belong to the same semantic, logical, cultural, or situational sphere. Such relations of contiguity constitute the semantic structure of a text. Consider, for example, meteorological expressions in a weather report as contrasted with an arbitrary series of lexemes from various contexts.

3 In psycholinguistics, ⇒ **association**

Continental Celtic ⇒ **Celtic**

contingent proposition

In **formal logic**, proposition whose **truth value** is not determined by its logical form. Contingent propositions can have different truth values in different **possible worlds** or situations (⇒ **situation semantics**), in contrast with **tautologies**, which are true in every (classical) possible world or (normal) situation, and in contrast with **contradictions**, which are false in all (classical) possible worlds or (normal) situations.

continuant

1 ⇒ **interrupted vs continuant**

2 **Speech sound** having an incomplete closure

of the oral cavity. If there is friction, the sound is a **fricative**; without friction it is an **approximant**.

continuative

1 Subcategory of **aspect** synonymous with durative (⇒ **durative vs non-durative**)

2 ⇒ **progressive**

continuous ⇒ progressive

contoid vs vocoid [hybrid formation, from Lat. *consonare* 'to sound together,' and *vocalis* 'sounding,' with Grk *eīdos* 'form']

Terms introduced by K. Pike to differentiate between the various usages of '**consonant**' and '**vowel**.' 'Contoid' and 'vocoid' refer to the phonetically defined speech sounds and 'consonant' and 'vowel' to their phonological aspects. Thus the [r] in Czech [strt͡ʃ prst skrz krk] 'stick the finger in the throat' is phonetically contoid, but phonologically a vowel, since it functions as the **nucleus**[2] of the **syllable**.

References
⇒ **phonetics**

contraction

Process and result of the **coalescence** of two consecutive vowels into a single long vowel: Gmc **maisōn* > OE *māra* > Mod. Eng. *more* (⇒ **synaeresis**). Also generally, every form of lexical shortening, e.g. Eng. *don't* for *do not*, Fr. *au* for **à le*.

contradictio in adjecto

A term from **rhetoric** to indicate a contradiction between a noun and its attributes. It is a special kind of **oxymoron**, e.g. *an old child*. Often used as a figure of argumentation, contradictio in adjecto couples opposite ideas with **persuasive** intent, e.g. *creeping inflation*.

contradiction

In **formal logic** a sentence that is false on the basis of its logical form, i.e. in all (classical) **possible worlds**. For example, *p and (simultaneously) not p*: *It's raining, and it's not raining*. Contradictions are analytically and logically false propositions. In contrast, ⇒ **tautology**.

contrast

1 Where 'contrast' and 'opposition' are not synonymous, 'contrast' is the differentiation of elements in a syntagmatic relation, 'opposition' the differentiation of elements in a paradigmatic relation. Thus, in /pæt/ vs /mæt/, /p/, /æ/, /t/ are in contrast, /p/ and /m/ are in opposition.

2 In American linguistics, synonym for **opposition** as a semantically significant counterpart for **contrast**[1] on the paradigmatic level.

References
(⇒ *also* **distributionalism**)

3 **Stress**[2], in the sense of contrastive accent.

contrastive analysis (*also* contrastive linguistics)

Linguistic subdiscipline concerned with the synchronic, comparative study of two or more languages or language varieties (e.g. dialects). Generally, both differences and similarities in the languages are studied, although the emphasis is usually placed on differences thought to lead to **interference** (i.e. negative transfer, the faulty application of structures from one's native language to the second language). Here the role of theoretical linguistics consists primarily in developing suitable grammar models that make it possible to compare languages systematically, especially in view of interference. Contrastive analysis emphasized the study of phonology and morphology. It did not address communicative contexts, i.e. contrasting socio-pragmatic conditions that influence linguistic production. Recent work in error analysis has emphasized errors as a source of knowledge of a learner's interlanguage and linguistic hypotheses. (⇒ *also* **error analysis, foreign-language pedagogy, language typology**)

References
Alatis, J.E. (ed.) 1968. *Contrastive linguistics and its pedagogical implications*. Washington, DC.
Fisiak, J. (ed.) 1990. *Further insights into contrastive analysis*. Amsterdam.
James, C. 1980. *Contrastive analysis*. London.
Krzeszowski, T.P. 1990. *Contrasting languages: the scope of contrastive linguistics*. Berlin.
Lado, R. 1957. *Linguistics across culture*. Ann Arbor, MI.
Nehls, D. 1979. *Studies in contrastive linguistics and error analysis: studies in contrastive linguistics*, vol. 2. Heidelberg.

Bibliographies
Gottwald, K. 1970. *Auswahlbibliographie zur kontrastiven Linguistik*. Cologne.
Hammer, J.H. and F.A. Rice. 1965. *A bibliography of contrastive linguistics*. Washington, DC.

Journal
Papers and Studies in Contrastive Linguistics

contrastive distribution ⇒ distribution

contrastive linguistics ⇒ contrastive analysis

control

Relationship governing the interpretation of 'phonetically missing subject expressions' or of the corresponding **PRO element** in infinitive constructions. In complement clauses after a verb like *try*, the PRO of the underlying infinitive construction is controlled by the subject of the **matrix sentence**. In sentences with verbs like *convince*, the subject of the infinitive complement is coreferential with the object of the matrix clause. Compare, for example, *She tried to fly to London* vs *She convinced him to fly to London*. In the Revised Extended Standard Theory of **transformational grammar**, **binding theory** includes a theory of control which governs the reference of the abstract pronominal element PRO, according to the structural configuration and on intrinsic verbal properties.

References
Abraham, W. 1983. The control relation in German. In W. Abraham (ed.), *On the formal syntax of the Westgermania*. Amsterdam. 217–42.
Bouchard, D. 1984. *On the content of empty categories*. Dordrecht.
Iwakura, K. 1985. The binding theory and PRO. *LingA* 15.29–55.
Jackendoff, R. 1987. The status of thematic relations in linguistic theory. *LingI* 18.369–412.
Koster, J. 1984. On binding and control. *LingI* 15.417–59.
Manzini, M.R. 1983. On control and control theory. *LingI* 14.421–46.
McClosky, J. and P. Sells. 1988. Control and A-chains in modern Irish. *NL&LT* 6.143–90.
Růžička, R. 1983. Remarks on control. *LingI* 14.309–24.
Williams, E. 1987. Implicit arguments, the binding theory, and control. *NL&LT* 5.151–80.

Control Agreement Principle ⇒ Generalized Phrase Structure Grammar

convention [Lat. *conventio* 'agreement']

A regularity in the behavior of members of a given group who repeatedly find themselves confronted by a problem of co-ordination (i.e. in a situation dependent upon co-ordinated behavior), who solve this problem in one of several possible ways, and in return expect the same response by others in the group (see Lewis 1969). Part of the convention-oriented approach to solving such problems of co-ordination is the fact that members of a given group will prefer another solution, if other members of the group act similarly: for example, drivers in North America who are heading towards each other on a one-lane road will automatically veer to the right. If all other drivers were to veer to the left, then everybody would adopt and adhere to this alternative regulation. Similarly, if one understands linguistic communication as a problem of co-ordination, then the fundamental behavioral regularities in the use of language and the conventions of a specific language are a solution to the problem of co-ordination, and the conventions of other languages can all be viewed as answers to the same problem. The **arbitrariness** of the linguistic **sign** thus arises from the conventionality of language. In their social rootedness, conventions are often contrasted with explanations of linguistic or non-linguistic behavior which claim a natural or genetic basis.

References
Lewis, D. 1969. *Convention: a philosophical study*. Cambridge, MA.
Quine, W.V. 1936. Truth by convention. In O.H. Lee (ed.), *Philosophical essays for A.N. Whitehead*. New York, 90–124.
Searle, J.R. 1969. *Speech acts: an essay in the philosophy of language*. Cambridge.
Shwayder, D. 1965. *The stratification of behavior*. New York.
Strawson, P.F. 1964. Intention and convention in speech acts. *PhR*. 73.439–60.
⇒ **speech act theory**

convergence area ⇒ transitional area

conversation analysis (*also* ethnomethodological conversation analysis)

An area of empirical research developed from **ethnomethodology**, conversation analysis is represented primarily in the studies of H. Sacks, E. Schegloff, and G. Jefferson. Sacks' earlier studies emphasized the properties of practical reasoning (see Garfinkel and Sacks 1970), i.e. devices and techniques used by participants in producing and interpreting social events like telling a story or a joke (see Sacks 1972, 1978; Sacks *et al.* 1974). Later studies concerned with reconstructing the 'orderliness' of conversations as participants' accomplishments have been most influential on **discourse analysis**. Of interest are recurring patterns and their structural properties in the overall organization of conversations. The most dominant and effective device in organizing interaction is seen in the local, turn-by-turn management (⇒ **sequential organization**) of **turn-taking** which reflects the participation of all parties in structuring the interaction. In the way they handle turn-taking and turns, participants display their understanding of the evolving activities: their interpretation of the preceding turn and their expectations for the following turn(s) (⇒ **adjacency pair, conditional relevance, preference, recipient design**). Thus, conversations are considered to be products of participants' work over time. This basic assumption constitutes one of the main differences between conversation analysis and other approaches in **discourse analysis**, in particular that of **discourse grammar** and **speech act theory** (see Streeck 1980; Levinson 1983).

References
Atkinson, J.M. and J. Heritage (eds) 1984. *The structure of social actions*. Cambridge.
Drew, P. and J. Heritage (eds) 1993. *Talk at work: interaction in institutional settings*. Cambridge.
Garfinkel, H. and H. Sacks. 1970. On formal structures of practical actions. In J.C. McKinney and E.A. Tiryakian (eds), *Theoretical sociology*. New York. 337–66.
Goodwin, C. and M.H. Goodwin. 1991. Interstitial argument. In A. Grimshaw (ed.), *Conflict talk*. Cambridge. 85–117.
Goodwin, C. and J. Heritage. 1990. Conversation analysis. *Annual Review of Anthropology* 19.283–307.
Levinson, S. 1983. *Pragmatics*. Cambridge.
Maynard, D. and S. Clayman. 1991. The diversity of ethnomethodology. *Annual Review of Anthropology* 17.285–418.
McLaughlin, M.L. 1984. *Conversation: how talk is organized*. London.
Nofsinger, R.E. 1991. *The conduct of everyday conversation*. London.
Sacks, H. 1972. On the analyzability of stories by children. In J.J. Gumperz and D. Hymes (eds), *Directions in sociolinguistics*. New York. 325–45.
——— 1978. An analysis of the course of a joke's telling in conversation. In J. Bauman and J. Sherzer (eds), *Explorations in the ethnography of speaking*. London. 249–69.
——— 1992. *Lectures on conversation*. 2 vols. Oxford.
Sacks, H., E. Schegloff, and G. Jefferson. 1974. A simplest systematics for the organization of turn-taking in conversations. *Lg* 50.696–735.
Schegloff, E. 1968. Sequencing in conversational openings. *AA* 70.1075–95. (Repr. in J.J. Gumperz and D. Hymes (eds), *Directions in sociolinguistics*. New York, 1972. 346–80.)
——— 1992. Repair after next turn. *American Journal of Sociology* 97.1295–345.
——— and H. Sacks. 1973. Opening up closings. *Semiotica* 8.289–327.
Schenkein, J. (ed.) 1978. *Studies in the organization of interaction*. New York.
Stenström, A.-B. 1994. *An introduction to spoken interaction*. London.
Streeck, J. 1980. Speech acts in interaction: a critique of Searle. *DPr* 3.133–54.
Sudnow, D. (ed.) 1972. *Studies in interaction*. New York.
⇒ **ethnomethodology**

conversational implicature ⇒ **implicature**

conversational maxim ⇒ **maxim of conversation**

converse relation

1 ⇒ **conversion**
2 In L. Tesnière's **dependency grammar**, a special type of semantic relation of dependency (⇒ **connection**) between linguistic elements, for which there is no underlying corresponding syntactic relation, such as the semantic relationship between *Philip* and *his* in *Philip is looking for his magic wand*.

converseness ⇒ **converse relation**

conversion

1 Relation of semantic opposition that denotes the polarity between two-place predicates and is defined as an **equivalence** relation: *If Philip is older than Caroline, then Caroline is younger than Philip* (and vice versa). Such converse expressions usually take the form of polar adjectives, of verbs that describe relations of exchanging (*give : receive, buy : sell,* and the like) and of **kinship terms** (*father : son,* etc.).

2 Process of **word formation** brought about by a change in lexical category of a **base** (*to drive > a drive*) and also of compound **stems** (*to sandpaper*), but also exceptionally those with a **prefix** or **suffix**. In contemporary English, denominal verbs are particularly productive (⇒ **productivity**): (*to*) *bicycle,* (*to*) *stamp*; similarly, deverbal nouns: *hit, buy*; and deadjectival verbs: *to tidy*. Instead of a process of transferring one stem category into the other, Marchand (1960) understands conversion as derivation with the aid of a **zero morpheme**.

References
Lieber, R. 1981. Morphological conversion within a restricted theory of the lexicon. In M. Moortgat *et al.* (eds), *The scope of lexical rules*. Dordrecht. 161–200.
Marchand, H. 1960. *The categories and types of present-day English word-formation*. Munich. (2nd edn 1969.)
Meyers, S. 1984. Zero-derivation and inflection. In M. Speas and R. Sproat (eds), *MIT Working papers in linguistics*, vol. 7, Cambridge, MA. 53–69.
Neeleman, A. and J. Schipper. 1993. Verbal prefixation in Dutch: thematic evidence for conversion. In G. Booij and J. van Marle (eds), *Yearbook of*

morphology 1992. Dordrecht. 57–92.

co-occurrence

A basic syntactic relation in structuralist taxonomy which signifies the simultaneous incidence of linguistic elements of different classes in sentences. Co-occurrence or distribution of an element is the sum of all syntactic environments in which it can occur. Thus Z.S. Harris defined his **transformations** as the formal relationship between structures which have the same number of individual co-occurrences.

References
⇒ **distributionalism**

co-ordinate bilingualism ⇒ bilingualism

co-ordinating conjunction ⇒ conjunction

co-ordination (*also* conjunction, **juncture**)

1 Syntactic structure which consists of two or more **conjuncts** (= words, phrases, or clauses). Co-ordination can occur as an asyndetic (⇒ **asyndeton**) construction, where the individual elements are not connected with conjunctions, or as a syndetic construction where the individual elements are connected by a co-ordinating **conjunction** (*and*, *or*, *but*). The 'connection' established by conjunctions refers to morphological and syntactic as well as to semantic and pragmatic aspects. The syntactic description of co-ordination in the framework of **transformational grammar** focuses mainly on the typology of co-ordinating constructions as well as on the assumed deletion procedures and conditions involved (= conjunction reduction, ⇒ **gapping**). On co-ordination in **formal logic**, ⇒ **conjunction**[3].

References
Dik, S. 1968. *Co-ordination*. Amsterdam.
Dougherty, R.C. 1970–1. A grammar of coordinate conjoined structures. *Lg* 46.850–98; 47.298–339.
Sanders, G.A. 1977. A functional typology of elliptical coordinations. In F.R. Eckmann (ed.), *Current themes in linguistics*. Washington, DC. 241–70.
Schmerling, S.F. 1975. Asymmetric conjunction and rules of conversation. In P. Cole and J.L. Morgan (eds), *Syntax and semantics*, vol. 3: *Speech acts*. New York.
Van Oisouw, R. 1987. *The syntax of coordination*. London.

Bibliography
Wiese, B. 1980. Bibliographie zur Koordination. *Linguistische Arbeiten und Berichte* 14.182–228.
⇒ **connection**

2 Synonym for **parataxis**.

Coosan ⇒ Penutian

Copenhagen Linguistic Circle ⇒ glossematics

Coptic ⇒ Egyptian

copular verb

Subset of verbs that, in contrast to **main verbs**, have a mainly grammatical function in that they serve to create the relation between **subject** and **predicate**: *She is a dancer/unmarried/21 years of age, He has become very handsome.* The term 'copula' is used only for the verb *be*, whereas 'copular verb' comprises all verbs (*be*, *become*, *seem*, *get*, and some others) that function in a similar way to *be*.

References
Quirk, R. *et al.* 1985. *A comprehensive grammar of the English language*. London and New York.
⇒ **auxiliary**

copulative composition ⇒ composition

core grammar

A central theme of linguistic description in Chomsky's Revised Extended Standard Theory (1975) (⇒ **transformational grammar**). Core grammar includes those universal linguistic facts and principles which tend to appear as unmarked grammatical phenomena in all natural languages. They form at the same time the core of individual competence (⇒ **competence vs performance**) which comprises the regularities among individual languages of differing natures. The mastery of language-specific irregularities, which belong to the periphery as marked occurrences, also belongs to the field of competence. They complement core grammar and the parameters of individual languages which are available as possible options from universal grammar (⇒ **markedness** for an explanation of 'marked' vs 'unmarked'). The theory of markedness and the concept of core grammar are motivated by hypotheses about corresponding phenomena in language acquisition. Core grammar and specifically unmarked linguistic phenomena are understood as 'genetic learning aids' in language acquisition and do not have to be learned as such. Marked (language-specific) occurrences must be learned gradually.

References
Chomsky, N. 1975. *Reflections on language*. New York.
———— 1981. *Lectures on government and binding*. Dordrecht. (7th edn Berlin and New York, 1993.)
⇒ **transformational grammar**

core vocabulary ⇒ basic vocabulary

coreference ⇒ anaphora

coreferentiality

In **generative grammar**, coreferentiality is present when different noun phrases have the same extralinguistic reference. Coreferentiality is formalized by numbers or small Roman letters: *Philip₁ discovered his friend₂ and greeted him₂ heartily. He₁ was glad to have this jovial fellow₂ finally nearby.* Presumably, the coreferential identity of different noun phrases must be indexed exactly in order to describe transformational processes like pronominalization (⇒ **personal pronoun**) and reflexivization (⇒ **reflexive pronoun**). The limitations of coreferentiality are discussed in Wiese (1983).

References
Comrie, B. 1992. *Coreference in grammar and discourse.* Oxford.
Hintikka, J. and G. Sandu. 1991. *On the methodology of linguistics: a case study.* Oxford.
Wiese, B. 1983. Anaphora by pronouns. *Linguistics* 21.373–417.

Cornish ⇒ Celtic

coronal vs non-coronal

Binary phonological **opposition** in **distinctive feature** analysis. In the **articulation** of coronal sounds, the tip of the tongue moves from its neutral position against the hard palate. The distinction describes the opposition between **dental** or **apical** vs **labial** or **velar** consonants, thus [t] vs [p, k]. (⇒ *also* **phonetics**)

corpus [Lat. 'body; collection of facts']

A finite set of concrete linguistic utterances that serves as an empirical basis for linguistic research. The value and quality of the corpus depend largely upon the specific approach and methodology of the theoretical framework of the given study. Note, for example, the different value placed on empirical data in **structuralism** and in **generative grammar**.

References
Greenbaum, S. and R. Quirk. 1970. *Elicitation experiments in English: linguistic studies in use and attitude.* London.
Kempson, R.M. and R. Quirk. 1971. Controlled activation of latent contrast. *Lg* 47. 548–72.
Kytö, M. *et al.* (eds) 1994. *Corpora across the centuries: proceedings of the first International Colloquium on English Diachronic Corpora.* Amsterdam.
Labov, W. 1971. Methodology. In W. Dingwall (ed.), *A survey of linguistic science.* College Park, MD. 412–97.

Leech, G. 1970. On the theory and practice of semantic testing. *Lingua* 24.343–64.
Pilch, H. 1976. *Empirical linguistics.* Bern.
Quirk, R. and J. Svartvik. 1966. *Investigating linguistic acceptability.* The Hague.
Svartvik, J. (ed.) 1992. *Directions in corpus linguistics.* Berlin and New York.
⇒ **field work**

correlate ⇒ dummy symbol

correlation

Prague School term designating the relationships between pairs or series of **phonemes** which are distinguished from one another through the same **distinctive feature**, e.g. /b, d, g/ vs /p, t, k/ are related to one another through a voicing correlation (⇒ **opposition**).

References
⇒ **phonetics, phonology**

correlational bundle

Tie between two or more phonological **correlations**. For example, the **phonemes** /p, t, k/ vs /b, d, g/ vs /m, n/ form a correlational bundle that is distinguished by the features [voiceless] vs [voiced] and [nasal] vs [oral].

References
⇒ **phonetics, phonology**

Costanoan ⇒ Penutian

co-text

Term coined by Catford (1965) and used to denote the 'situational context' of an utterance in contrast to its linguistic **context**.

References
Catford, J.C. 1965. *A linguistic theory of translation.* London.

count noun

Noun which can be directly combined with a numeral (e.g. *apple*) as opposed to **mass nouns** which cannot (e.g. *gold*). In some cases, nouns can belong to both classes (e.g. *fish*).

counterfactual sentence

Conditional sentence with a subjunctive form in the opening clause (e.g. *If I were hungry, I would eat something*) whose closing clause would be true if the opening clause were true. Counterfactual sentences play an important role with regard to **possible worlds** in semantic descriptions.

References
⇒ **possible world**

covered vs non-covered

Binary phonological **opposition** in **distinctive**

feature analysis based on **articulation. Speech sounds** with the feature [+covered] are produced by narrowing and tensing the **pharynx** and raising the **larynx**.

References
⇒ **distinctive feature, phonetics**

covert category

Term introduced by B.L. Whorf. A covert category is a conceptual category for which the language in question furnishes either no formal elements at all or elements only for specific situations. For example, in English intransitivity (⇒ **transitivity**) is a covert category of the first type, since intransitive verbs can be characterized only by their absence from particular syntactic constructions (such as **passive**), while **gender** is a covert category of the second type, since personal pronouns of the third person singular constitute formal elements for particular situations. The structure of the lexicon of a particular language can reveal covert categories. Thus, in English there is no adjective that serves as a superordinate term (⇒ **hyperonymy**) for all adjectives of temperature.

References
Cruse, D.A. 1986. *Lexical semantics*. Cambridge.
Whorf, B.L. 1956. Grammatical category. In J.B. Carroll (ed.), *Language, thought and reality: selected writings of Benjamin Lee Whorf*. New York. 87–101.

cranberry morph ⇒ hapax legomenon, pseudomorpheme, semi-morpheme

crasis [Grk *krãsis* 'mixing, blending']

The diachronic collapsing of two vowels into a long vowel, the first of which is in final position, the second of which is in the initial position of the following item, e.g. Lat. *cō-agō* > *cōgō* 'I force' (⇒ **hiatus**).

creativity

Essential trait of all natural languages whose functioning is based on the speaker being able to produce and interpret – by means of a finite set of (a) linguistic expressions and (b) combinatory rules – an infinite set of utterances. This ability to command a complex rule apparatus has long intrigued and motivated researchers just as much as its apparent quick learnability in **language acquisition**. Since Chomsky, creativity is a central notion of **transformational grammar**, the objective of which is to describe this infinite use of finite resources in a technically appropriate form. Chomsky distinguishes between 'rule-governed' and 'rule-changing' creativity. While rule-governed creativity is limited by the pre-given possibilities in the linguistic system, rule-changing creativity affects this system.

References
Chomsky, N. 1964. *Current issues in linguistic theory*. The Hague.
——— 1965. *Aspects of the theory of syntax*. Cambridge, MA.
——— 1966. *Topics in the theory of generative grammar*. The Hague.

Cree ⇒ Algonquian

creole ['European born in the West Indies,' from Span. *criollo* 'native']

Creoles are former **pidgins** whose functional and grammatical limitations and simplification have been eliminated and which now function as full-fledged, standardized native languages. Creoles originated primarily in regions of colonialization where the indigenous people were either enslaved or otherwise made to be highly dependent upon their white masters. The social pressures of assimilation lead originally from **bilingualism** (indigenous language and pidginized European language) to pidgin **monolingualism** and eventually to a complete loss of the original native language replaced by the creole. Creoles are characterized by a considerably expanded and altered grammar and vocabulary. According to Bickerton (1981, 1984), this can be traced to the innate linguistic capacities of humans that impose grammatical structure upon the relatively unstructured pidgins. This would explain why creoles have a generally similar grammatical structure, an observation made as early as 1850 by H. Schuchardt. The classification of a creole is based upon its main source of vocabulary, viz. French Creole (Louisiana, French Guyana, Haiti, Mauritius), English Creole (Hawaii), Dutch Creole (Georgetown).

References
Alleyne, M.C. 1980. *Comparative Afro-American: an historical–comparative study of English-based Afro-American dialects of the New World*. Ann Arbor, MI.
Andersen, R. (ed.) 1983. *Pidginization and creolization as language acquisition*. Rowley, MA.
Arends, J. (ed.) 1994. *The early stages of creolization*. Amsterdam and Philadelphia.
Arends, J., P. Muysken, and N. Smith (eds) 1995. *Pidgins and creoles: an introduction*. Amsterdam and Philadelphia.
Bickerton, D. 1973. The nature of the creole continuum. *Lg* 49.640–69.
——— 1975. *Dynamics of a creole system*. London.
——— 1981. *Roots of language*. Ann Arbor, MI.
——— 1984. The language biprogram hypothesis. *Behavioral and Brain Sciences* 7.173–221.
Bollée, A. 1977. *Le Créole français des Seychelles:*

esquisse d'une grammaire. Tübingen.

Decamp, D. and I.F. Hancock (eds) 1974. *Pidgins and creoles: current trends and prospects*. Washington, DC.

Foley, W. 1988. Language birth: the processes of pidginization and creolization. In F.J. Newmeyer (ed.), *Linguistics: the Cambridge survey*, vol. 4: *Language: the socio-cultural context*. Cambridge. 162–83.

Hall, R.A. 1966. *Pidgin and creole languages*. Ithaca, NY.

Hancock, I. 1987. History of research on pidgins and creoles. In U. Ammon *et al.* (eds), *Sociolinguistics: an international handbook on the science of language and society*. Berlin. 459–69.

Holm, J. 1988–9. *Pidgins and creoles*, 2 vols. London.

Hymes, D. (ed.) 1971. *Pidginization and creolization of languages*. Cambridge.

Lepage, R.B. and A. Tabourer-Keller. 1985. *Acts of identity*. Cambridge.

Ludwig, R. (ed.) 1989. *Les Créoles français entre l'oral et l'écrit*. Tübingen.

Meisel, J. (ed.) 1977. *Langues en contact: pidgins/ creoles; languages in contact*. Tübingen.

Mühlhäusler, P. 1986. *Pidgin and creole linguistics*. Oxford.

Muysken, P. and N. Smith (eds) 1986. *Substrata versus universals in creole genesis: papers from the Amsterdam Creole Workshop, 1985*. Amsterdam.

Reinecke, J.E. 1971. Tay Bói: notes on the Pidgin French spoken in Vietnam. In D. Hymes (ed.), *Pidginization and creolization of languages*. Cambridge. 43–56.

Rickford, J.R. 1987. *Dimensions of a creole continuum: history, texts, and linguistic analysis of Guyanese Creole*. Stanford, CA.

Romaine, S. 1988. *Pidgin and creole languages*. London.

Schuchardt, H. 1882–91. *Kreolische Studien*, 9 vols. Vienna.

Stewart, W.A. 1962. Creole languages in the Caribbean. In F.A. Rice (ed.), *Study of the role of second languages in Asia, Africa and Latin America*. Washington, DC. 34–53.

Sutcliffe, D. and Figueroa, J. 1992. *System in black language*. Clevedon.

Thomason, S.G. and T.S. Kaufmann. 1988. *Language contact, creolization, and genetic linguistics*. Berkeley, CA.

Todd, L. 1975. *Pidgins and creoles*. London. (2nd edn 1990.)

Valdman, A. (ed.) 1977. *Pidgin and creole linguistics*. Bloomington, IN.

Valdman, A. and A. Highfield (eds) 1980. *Theoretical orientations in creole studies*. New York.

Versteegh, K. 1984. *Pidginization and creolization: the case of Arabic*. Amsterdam.

Whinnom, K. 1965. The origin of European-based pidgins and creoles. *Orbis* 14.509–27.

—— 1971. Linguistic hybridization and the special case of pidgins and creoles. In D. Hymes (ed.), *Pidginization and creolization of languages*. Cambridge. 91–115.

Bibliography

Reinecke, J.E. *et al.* 1975. *A bibliography of pidgin and creole languages*. Honolulu, HI.

⇒ **Black English, classification of languages, pidgin, variational linguistics**

creolization ⇒ **creole**

crest ⇒ **nucleus**^{2}

Croatian ⇒ **Serbo-Croatian**

cross-over principle

A **constraint** on transformational rules (⇒ **transformation**) for the situation in which coreferential constituents would be crossed over. This could occur, for example, in the movement of a *wh*-element in **COMP position** over a co-indexed pronoun. In accordance with the current grading of ungrammaticality, one can distinguish between weak cross-over and strong cross-over. Thus *Who$_i$ does his$_i$ mother love* t$_i$ (weak cross-over) is clearly more acceptable than *Who$_i$ did he$_i$ love* t$_i$ or *Who$_i$ did he$_i$ say Caroline kissed* t$_i$ (strong cross-over). The cross-over principle has been the center of interest for many in **generative grammar** since the early 1970s. In **Government and Binding theory**, it is simply a descriptive term and relevant cases must be explained by general principles and parameters of the syntactic theory. An example of this would be the assimilation of the empty category (⇒ **empty category principle**) left by *wh*-movement to independently referential expressions where principle C of the **binding theory** would be relevant; as a result the strong cross-over phenomena would be excluded from the grammar, since the pronoun would be excluded from binding the empty category.

References

Aoun, J. 1986. *Generalized binding: the syntax and logical form of wh-interrogatives*. Dordrecht.

Chomsky, N. 1981. *Lectures on government and binding*. Dordrecht.

Farmer, A., K. Hale, and N. Tsujimura. 1988. A note on weak crossover in Japanese. *NL&LT* 4.33–42.

Freidin, R. and H. Lasnik. 1981. Disjoint reference and wh-trace. *LingI* 12.39–53.

Koopman, H. and D. Sportiche. 1982. Variables and the bijection principle. *LRev* 2.139–61.

Koster, J. 1987. *Domains and dynasties: the radical autonomy of syntax*. Dordrecht.

May, R. 1985. *Logical form: its structure and derivation*. Cambridge, MA.

Postal, P.M. 1971. *Cross-over phenomena: a study in the grammar of coreference*. New York.

Van Riemsdijk, H. and E. Williams. 1981. NP-structure. *LRev* 1.171–217.

Wasow, T. 1972. Anaphoric relations in English. Dissertation, MIT.

—— 1975. *Anaphora in generative grammar.* Ghent.

cross-reference ⇒ anaphora

Cross-River ⇒ Benue-Congo languages

crytotpe [Grk *kryptḗ* 'crypt, vault,' *krýptein* 'to hide, to cover']

A term coined by B.L. Whorf to describe hidden but available grammatical properties of linguistic expressions. Such class-forming properties have no formal correspondence at the surface: cf., for example, the grammatical genders in **German** or **French**.

Reference
Whorf, B.L. 1956. Language, thought and reality. In *Selected writings of B.L. Whorf*, ed. J.B. Carroll. Cambridge, MA.

CUG ⇒ categorial unification grammar

cuneiform [Lat. *cuneus* 'wedge']

Writing system of the Sumerians and Babylonians (dating back to about 2900 BC). Its name is derived from the wedge-shaped impressions scratched into clay tablets with styluses.

References
Edzard, D.O. 1976–80. Keilschrift. In D.O. Edzard *et al.* (eds), *Reallexikon der Assyriologie*. Berlin. Vol. 5, 544–68.
Jaritz, K. 1967. *Schriftarchäologie der altmesopotamischen Kultur*. Graz.
Meissner, B. and K. Oberhuber. 1967. *Die Keilschrift*. (3rd, completely rev. edn.) Berlin.
⇒ **writing**

cursive ⇒ durative vs non-durative, imperfective vs perfective

cursive writing [Lat. *cursiva* (*littera*) 'running script']

A form of writing that connects one character with the following one. In scripts written from left to right (e.g. Latin, Greek, Armenian, Cyrillic), a form of **writing** that leans towards the right. Cursive characters are used in linguistic texts to denote expressions in the object language (⇒ **object language vs meta language**) as, for example, in this dictionary. In **Chinese**, cursive denotes a quick writing style, in which individual marks – depending on personal style and writing speed – are consolidated into a cursive writing.

References
⇒ **writing**

Cushitic

Named after Cush, the son of Ham, subgroup of the **Afro-Asiatic** languages in East Africa with thirty languages and approx. 30 million speakers divided into four main groups (East, Central, North and South Cushitic); the so-called 'West Cushitic' is possibly a separate language family (**Omotic**). The most important languages are Oromo (formerly called Galla, with approx. 15 million speakers) and Somali (national language of Somalia, with approx. 6 million speakers).

Characteristics: **tonal languages** (two or three tones); tones serve as grammatical markers (gender, number, case, mood). **Vowel harmony**. Often extremely complex verb conjugation (separate paradigms for perfective, imperfective; various clause forms). Word order SOV, marked subject case (often identical with genitive), morphological focus marking.

References
Bell, C.R.V. 1953. *The Somali language*. London (Repr. 1969.)
Ehret, C. 1980. *The historical reconstruction of Southern Cushitic phonology and vocabulary*. Berlin.
Hayward, D. 1983. *The Arbore language*. Hamburg.
Lamberti, M. 1986. *Somali language and literature*. Hamburg.
Owens, J. 1985. *A grammar of Harar Oromo (Northeastern Ethiopia)*. Hamburg.
Palmer, F.R. 1970. Cushitic. In T.A. Sebeok (ed.), *Current trends in linguistics*, vol. 6: *Linguistics in South West Asia and North Africa*. The Hague. 571–85.
Sasse, H.J. 1981. Die kuschitischen Sprachen. In B. Heine *et al.* (eds), *Die Sprachen Afrikas*. Hamburg. 187–215.
Stroomer, H. 1987. *A comparative study of three Southern Oromo dialects in Kenya: phonology, morphology and vocabulary*. Hamburg.
Stroomer, H.A. 1995. *A grammar of Boraana Oromo*. Cologne.
Zaborski, A. 1976. Cushitic overview. In M.L. Bender (ed.), *The non-Semitic languages of Ethiopia*. East Lansing, MI. 67–84.

Dictionaries
Abraham, R.C. 1962. *Somali–English dictionary*. London.
Gragg, G. 1982. *Oromo dictionary*. East Lansing, MI.
Hudson, G. 1989. *Highland East Cushitic dictionary*. Hamburg.
Sasse, H.-J. 1982. *An etymological dictionary of Burji*. Hamburg.

cybernetics ⇒ information theory

cyclic nodes [Grk *kýklos* 'circle']

Categories within morphology, syntax, and phonology that represent a domain for the application of cyclic rules. They are probably language-specific. The application of cyclic rules follows the **principle of cyclic rule application**.

Cyrillic script

Writing system based on Greek **uncial script**, developed by the Greek-Orthodox Slavs, and incorrectly attributed to the Greek missionary to the Slavs, Kyrillos (ninth century) (⇒ **Glagolitic script**). Under Peter the Great, the Cyrillic script was simplified and adapted to approximate Latin script. Today the Cyrillic script is the basis for the following Slavic orthographic systems (**Russian**, **Belorussian**, **Ukrainian**, **Serbian**, **Bulgarian**, **Macedonian**); for a number of non-Slavic Indo-European languages (Moldavian, **Kurdish**, Ossete (**Iranian**), Tajikich (⇒ **Persian**)); as well as a number of non-Indo-European languages of the former Soviet Union (e.g. Bashkirish, Tartar, Turkmenian, Usbeki (⇒ **Turkic**) Uiguric).

References
⇒ **writing**

Czech

West **Slavic** language with approx. 9 million speakers, primarily in Czechia. The oldest texts date from the eleventh century, with secular texts beginning to appear from the fourteenth century (Alexander tales, Catherine legends). The orthography is based on the Latin alphabet. Jan Hus, in his *Orthographia Bohemica* (1406) introduced numerous diacritics which can be used to distinguish Czech from other Slavic languages: ‹á›, ‹č›, ‹d'›, ‹é›, ‹ě›, ‹í›, ‹ď›, ‹ň›, ‹ó›, ‹ř›, ‹š›, ‹t'›, ‹ů›, ‹ú›, ‹ý›, ‹ž›. The written language was suppressed by the Hapsburgs after the Thirty Years' War. Resuscitated two centuries later by Dobrovský on the basis of the old Bible translation, it is quite disjoint from the normal spoken language of today.

Specific characteristics: initial word stress which recedes to prepositions; short and long vowels in both stressed and unstressed syllables; syllabic *r*: *strč prst skrz krk* 'stick the finger in the throat'; alveolar voiced fricative trill [r] as in *Dvořák*); distinctive vocative case; in the masculine, distinction between [±animate].

References
Havránek, B. and A. Jedlička. 1960. *Česká mluvnice*. Prague. (4th edn 1981.)
Heim, M. 1982. *Contemporary Czech*. Columbus, OH.
Kavka, S. 1988. *An outline of Modern Czech grammar*. Uppsala.
Kučera, H. 1961. *The phonology of Czech*. The Hague.
Mazon, A. 1952. *Grammaire de la langue tchèque*, 3rd edn. Paris.
Mluvnice češtiny. 1986–7. 3 vols. Prague.
Townsend, C. 1990. *A description of spoken Prague Czech*. Columbus, OH.

Dictionaries
Machek, V. 1957. *Etymologický slovník jazyka českého*. Prague. (2nd edn 1968.)
Slovník spisovného jazyka českého. 1958–71. 4 vols. Prague.
⇒ **Slavic**

D

Daco-Rumanian ⇒ Rumanian

Dagestanian ⇒ North-East Caucasian

Danish

North **Germanic** (**Scandinavian**) language with approx. 5 million speakers, primarily in Denmark. Danish began to develop independently as a written language around AD 1500. It was the written language in Norway from the Reformation (1536) until the mid-nineteenth century. A spelling reform was conducted in 1948: nouns, except for proper nouns, are no longer capitalized (unlike **German**, which continues to capitalize all nouns).

References
Diderichsen, P. 1957. *Elementær dansk grammatik.* Copenhagen.
Holmes, P., R. Allan and T. Lundskaer-Nielsen. 1995. *Danish. A Comprehensive Grammar.* London.

Dictionary
Danish dictionary. 1994. London.
⇒ **Scandinavian**

Dardic

Group of about fifteen **Indo-Iranian** languages in northwestern India; the most significant language is Kashmiri (approx. 3 million speakers). It is still unclear whether the Dardic languages belong to the **Indo-Aryan** or to the **Iranian** languages.

References
Bhat, R. 1987. *A descriptive study of Kashmiri.* Delhi.
Edelman, D.I. 1983. *The Dardic and Nuristani languages.* Moscow.
Fussman, G. 1972. *Atlas linguistique des parlers dardes et kafir,* 2 vols. Paris.
Kachru, B.B. 1969a. Kashmiri and other Dardic languages. In T. Sebeok (ed.), *Current trends in linguistics,* vol. 5: *Linguistics in South Asia.* The Hague and Paris. 284–306.
—— 1969b. *A reference grammar of Kashmiri.* Urbana, IL.
Koul, M.K. 1986. *A sociolinguistic study of Kashmiri.* Patiala.
Morgenstierne, G. 1973. *Irano-Dardica.* Wiesbaden.

Dictionary
Grierson, G.A. 1916–32. *A dictionary of the Kashmiri language,* 4 vols. (Repr. 1985.) Calcutta.

Bibliography
Schmidt, R.L. and O.N. Koul. 1981. *Kohistani to Kashmiri: an annotated bibliography of Dardic languages.* Patiala.
⇒ **Indo-Aryan, Indo-Iranian**

Dari ⇒ Persian

data vs facts

A terminological distinction made by N. Chomsky which is the forerunner of the distinction **competence vs performance**. Data are linguistic utterances which form the basis for linguistic investigation. Facts, on the other hand, are inner regularities that one observes from the performance data which form the competence of the **ideal speaker/listener**. (⇒ *also* **transformational grammar**)

dative [Lat. *datum* 'given'; trans. of Grk *dōtikḗ ptōsis* 'case relating to the act of giving']

1 Morphological **case** which generally serves to indicate **indirect objects**. Depending on whether or not a verb requires the dative case, one can distinguish between obligatory datives in the function of indirect objects in the narrower sense, whose deletion can be analyzed as **ellipsis** (*Who's treating [us to lunch]?*), and the so-called free datives. The free datives can be differentiated as follows: (a) ethical dative, which expresses a personal point of view: Ger. *Das war mir zu viel* 'That was too much for me'; (b) possessive dative, which expresses a relationship of possession: Ger. *Ihm schmerzen die Beine*, lit. 'him are hurting the legs,' where English uses a possessive pronoun; (c) dative of interest (dativus commodi/incommodi), which designates a person or thing to whose benefit or detriment the action expressed by the verb is carried out: *She knitted him a sweater*; (d) dativus iudicantis, which indicates the person or thing from whose point of view the statement is expressed: Ger. *Er ist mir zu intelligent* 'He is too smart for me.' The dative can also be required by certain adjectives, such as Ger. *Sie ist ihm treu* 'She is faithful to him,' and occasionally functions as an adnominal (e.g. Ger. *der Mutter ihr Haus*, lit. '(to) the mother her house,' i.e. 'the mother's house'). In languages like English, which do not have a dative case, the term 'dative' refers to the function

expressed by the dative in case-inflecting languages.

References
Abraham, W. 1973. The ethic dative in German. In F. Kiefer and N. Ruwet (eds), *Generative grammar in Europe*. Dordrecht. 1–19.
Barnes, B.K. 1980. The notion of 'dative' in linguistic theory and the grammar of French. *LIS* 4.245–92.
Wegener, H. 1985. *Der Dativ im heutigen Deutsch.* Tübingen.

2 Term in **case grammar** for the **semantic role** of animate objects that are affected by a state of affairs or an action, generally to a lesser degree than a **patient**.
⇒ **case**

dative movement ⇒ dative shift

dative shift (*also* dative movement, dativization)

Alternation by which an object in another oblique case or a prepositional object is changed into a dative or indirect object: *He gave the book to Caroline* : *He gave Caroline the book.*

References
Dowty, D. 1979. Dative 'movement' and Thomason's extensions of Montague Grammar. In S. Davis and M. Mithun (eds), *Linguistics, philosophy and Montague Grammar*. Austin, TX. 153–222.
Dryer, M. 1986. Primary objects, secondary objects and antidative. *Language* 62.808–45.
Fillmore, C. 1965. *Indirect object constructions in English and the ordering of transformations*. The Hague.
Green, G. 1974. *Semantics and syntactic regularity.* Bloomington, IN.
Marchand, H. 1951. The syntactical change from inflectional to word order system and some effects of this change on the relation 'verb/object' in English: a diachronic–synchronic interpretation. *Anglia* 70. 70–89.
Oehrle, R. 1986. *The English 'dative' construction, grammatical form and interpretation*. Dordrecht.

dativization ⇒ dative shift

daughter dependency grammar ⇒ dependency grammar, surface syntax

daughter languages

Languages which derive from a common language or **proto-language** and which are at the same developmental stage. For example, **French**, **Italian**, and **Spanish** are daughter languages of (Vulgar) **Latin**.

DCG ⇒ definite clause grammar

de dicto reading ⇒ attributive vs referential reading

de re reading ⇒ attributive vs referential reading

deadjectival

Words derived from adjective **stems** such as (*to*) *harden* (< *hard*), *stupidity* (< *stupid*), *happily* (< *happy*).

Reference
⇒ **word formation**

debitive [Lat. *debere* 'to be obliged to']

Mood that expresses objective necessity to carry out the action denoted by the verb. It is found, for example, in **Latvian**, where it is encoded by prefixing the particle *ja-* to the third person indicative of the verb in a construction with the appropriate tense of the copula (optional in non-negative sentences) and the dative of the corresponding agent expression: *man* (*ir*) *ja-dzied* (I dat. sg. (COP) deb. 3rd sg. indic.) 'I have to sing.' A possible theme is in the nominative or accusative. Asher (1982) hypothesizes a debitive also for **Tamil**.

References
Asher, R.E. 1982. *Tamil*. Amsterdam.
Palmer, F.R. 1986. *Mood and modality*. Cambridge.

declaration

A speech act which, if successfully performed, results in the realization of the propositional content (⇒ **proposition**) of the uttered sentence as a conventional consequence of its merely having been uttered (e.g. *The meeting is now in session*, said at the appropriate time by the chairperson). According to Searle, as opposed to Bach and Harnish (1992), explicitly **performative utterances** like *I hereby declare this building open to the public* are special types of declarations.

References
Bach, K. and R.M. Harnish. 1992. How performatives really work: a reply to Searle. *Ling&P* 15.93–110.
Searle, J.R. 1989. How performatives work. *Ling&P* 12.535–58.
Searle, J.R. and D. Vanderveken. 1985. *Foundations of illocutionary logic*. Cambridge.

declarative sentence

Sentence type whose primary purpose is to give information, as opposed to questions or imperatives. Declarative sentences can be assumed to have an underlying structure containing such verbs as *say, assert, maintain*: the sentence

Prices are rising would be derived from *I say to you that prices are rising*. This sort of derivation is termed **performative analysis**. Basic **word order** in a language is generally determined from the word order of the unmarked declarative sentence. (⇒ *also* **imperative, interrogative, mood**)

Reference
Ross, J.R. 1968. On declarative sentences. In R.A. Jacobs and P.S. Rosenbaum (eds), *Readings in English transformational grammar*, Waltham, MA, 1970. 222–72.

declension [Lat. *declinare* 'to change the direction of, to bend']

Type of **inflection** of nouns, articles, adjectives, numerals, and pronouns that varies according to **case**, **gender**, and **number**. The corresponding inflectional forms of a word constitute the declensional **paradigms** that are subsumed in declensional classes according to regularities and predictability or practicability. English has largely lost its declensional system, with vestiges apparent only in plural formation (e.g. *books*), the possessive case (e.g. *Caroline's*), and object pronouns (e.g. *him, her*). Modern languages such as **German** and **Russian** have retained more complete declensional systems. (⇒ *also* **paradigm morphology**)

decoding (*also* **language comprehension, speech recognition**)

Complementary process to **encoding** in which the hearer 'deciphers' the message encoded by the speaker and correspondingly assigns (conventionalized) meanings to the linguistic signs. Decoding, like encoding, occurs on all descriptive levels of language.

decompositum

Term introduced by J. Grimm to denote compounds of more than two elements: *bedroom windowsill*. Such compounds are becoming more and more common in English, especially in the **sublanguage** of law, e.g. *fire insurance litigation proceedings, emergency management administration*.

Reference
Grimm, J. 1826. *Deutsche Grammatik*, vol. 3: *Von der Wortbildung*. Göttingen. (2nd edn. 1878; facsimile printing Hildesheim, 1967.)
⇒ **word formation**

deep case ⇒ **case grammar, thematic relation**

deep hypothesis

Psycholinguistic hypothesis put forth by Yngve (1960) according to which the development and structure of natural language depends on the limited storage capacity of the short-term **memory**, which can store only a maximum of seven independent units of information (e.g. names, numbers) at once. On the basis of Yngve's calculations it turns out that **left-branching constructions** and **self-embedding constructions** burden the memory more than **right-branching constructions**.

Reference
Yngve, V.H. 1960. A model and an hypothesis for language structures. *PAPS* 104.444–66.

deep structure (*also* underlying structure)

A term from **transformational grammar**, developed by N. Chomsky, to describe the underlying structure of a linguistic utterance. Deep structure specifies the grammatical relations and functions of the syntactic elements, as well as the linguistic meaning of the elements of a sentence which contain the lexemes, the information important for the execution of **transformations**. The idea of a difference between two levels of structure in language (deep structure vs **surface structure**) has a long and complex history and can be found in the writings of the Indian grammarian Pāṇini (fourth century BC), in the seventeenth-century grammar of **Port Royal**, and in the writings of Humboldt, Wittgenstein, and Hockett. In transformational grammar both structural levels can be represented by **tree diagrams**. In Chomsky's (1965) **aspects model**, meaning-neutral transformations mediate between the basic tree structure of the deep structure and the derived tree structure of the surface structure, so that the syntactic structure can be interpreted phonetically. This syntactically motivated concept began a great debate between the supporters of Chomsky and the advocates of **generative semantics**, who regarded the basic structure as semantic. In the various revisions of the standard theory, the level relevant for semantic interpretation was also changed, the structural information of the deep structure being encoded into the surface structure (now S-structure). In this way, the semantic information remains at S-structure, which has been the input for the semantic interpretation since the Revised Extended Standard Theory. (⇒ *also* **logical form**)

References
Chomsky, N. 1965. *Aspects of the theory of syntax*. Cambridge, MA.
—— 1968. *Language and mind*. New York.
—— 1971. Deep structure, surface structure, and semantic interpretation. In D.D. Steinberg and L.A. Jakobovits (eds), *Semantics*. London. 183–216.

—— 1992. *A minimalist program for linguistic theory.* Cambridge, MA.

Hockett, C.F. 1958. *A course in modern linguistics.* New York.

Lakoff, G. and J.R. Ross. 1968. *Is deep structure necessary?* Bloomington, IN.

Postal, P.M. 1964. *Constituent structure: a study of contemporary models of syntactic description.* Bloomington, IN.

⇒ **transformational grammar**

default knowledge ⇒ default reasoning

default reasoning (*also* default knowledge)

In the framework of **artificial intelligence**, reasoning based on standard assumptions, especially knowledge about typical objects and situations (⇒ **frame, script**). Default reasoning is an essential element of everyday knowledge (⇒ **commonsense reasoning**). Among other purposes, default reasoning serves to make a cognitive system functional, by closing gaps in knowledge with the aid of such normality assumptions (⇒ **non-monotonic logic**). Such knowledge can be applied, for example, to resolve anaphoric or temporal relations in text comprehension.

References

Hunt, R. and J. Shelley. 1983. *Computers and common sense.* London.

Reiter, R. 1980. A logic for default reasoning. *AI* 13.81–132.

defective

Term referring to an element which in comparison to other representatives of its class is more limited in its grammatical use or distribution, e.g. certain adjectives which can only be used attributively, such as *mere*: *The mere fact that ...* vs **The fact is mere.* Apart from words, paradigms and distribution patterns that show 'gaps' can be termed as defective.

deficit theory ⇒ code theory

definiendum ⇒ definition

definiens ⇒ definition

definite clause ⇒ definite clause grammar

definite clause grammar (*abbrev.* DCG)

Formalism used in **computational linguistics** that arose around 1980, as a development of logic programming, used to analyze (and also generate) sentences. Definite clause grammar, abbreviated DCG, is based on the **metamorphosis grammar** of A. Colmerauer, and is as powerful as the universal **Turing machine**. For the notation of grammatical regularities definite clause grammar uses a formalism similar to

first-order **predicate logic**: the so-called 'definite clauses.' Declaratively interpreted, a set of definite clauses (just like a set of **phrase structure rules**) produces a description in the given language, while a procedural interpretation can be used to analyze the wellformedness of sentences. In this, the procedure to recognize whether an input sentence is grammatical corresponds to the proof of a theorem in predicate logic, whereby a PROLOG translator (⇒ **interpreter**) functions as a theorem prover. Definite clause grammars are executable PROLOG programs. The major significance of definite clause grammar is attributed to 'unification' (⇒ **unification grammar**), which makes various things possible, such as checking congruences and constructing representations of syntactic and semantic structure. In this, definite clause grammars are not only recognizing automata, but also so-called transducers. (⇒ *also* **extraposition grammar**)

References

Kowalski, R. 1974. Predicate logic as a programming language. *Information Processing* 74.569–74.

McCord, M.C. 1982. Using slots and modifiers in logic grammars for natural language. *AI* 18.327–67.

Pereira, F.C.N. and D.H.D. Warren. 1980. Definite clause grammars for language analysis. *AI* 13.231–78.

Ramsay, A. 1989. Computer and syntactic description of language systems. In S. Bátorí *et al.* (eds), *Computerlinguistik/Computational linguistics.* Berlin and New York. 204–18.

(definite) description

Term used in **formal logic** that goes back to Frege (1892) and Russell (1905) and denotes expressions that describe certain objects with the aid of the definite article *the* and a **predicate** that applies to exactly one entity. For example, the property designated by the propositional form *father(x, W.A. Mozart)* applies exactly to only one person, namely to Leopold Mozart, who is designated by the definite description of *the father of W.A. Mozart.* Such definite descriptions, which are used to identify particular entities, are introduced in formal logic by means of the so-called iota operator (⇒ **operator[2c]**).

References

Donnellan, K. 1966. Reference and definite description. *PhR* 75.281–304.

—— 1970. Proper names and identifying descriptions. *Synthese* 21.335–58.

Frege, G. 1892. Über Sinn und Bedeutung. *ZPhK* (new series) 100.25–50. (Repr. in *Kleine Schriften,* ed. I. Angelelli. Darmstadt, 1967. 143–62.)

Karttunen, L. 1971. Definite descriptions with crossing coreference: a study of the Bach–Peters Paradox. *FL* 7.157–82.

Kripke, S. 1972. Naming and necessity. In D. Davidson and G. Harman (eds), *Semantics of natural language*. Dordrecht. 253–355.

Russell, B. 1905. On denoting. *Mind* 14.479–93.

Strawson, P.F. 1950. On referring. *Mind* 59.320–44.

definiteness

In logic, a definite description designates an individual with a property that only he/she has. In more recent linguistic studies definiteness (through the influence of logic) is seen as the localization of a **referent** in a set of referents which is conveyed to the hearer by the situation (⇒ **deixis**) as having been previously mentioned in the text or as previous knowledge (see Hawkins 1978). The definiteness of a **noun phrase** is denoted above all by **determiners**. Proper names are inherently definite, since they do not require further description by determiners; the definite article (e.g. in *The Hague*, *the Thames*) does not indicate any definiteness in proper names since *Hague* or *Thames* are never without it. (⇒ **proper noun**)

References

Chesterman, A. 1991. *On definiteness: a study with special reference to English and Finnish.* Cambridge.

Diesling, M. 1992. *Indefinites.* Cambridge, MA.

Donnellan, K. 1966. Reference and definite description. *PhR* 75.281–304.

Fodor, J.D. and I. Sag. 1982. Referential and quantificational indefinites. *Ling&P* 5.355–98.

Givón, T. 1978. Definiteness and referentiality. In J.H. Greenberg (ed.), *Universals of human language*. Stanford, CA. Vol. 4, 291–330.

Hauenschild, C. 1993. Definitheit. In J. Jacobs *et al.* (eds), *Syntax: an international handbook of contemporary research*. Berlin and New York. 988–97.

Hawkins, J. 1978. *Definiteness and indefiniteness.* London.

Heim, I. 1982. *The semantics of definite and indefinite noun phrases.* Constance.

——— 1991. Artikel und Definitheit. In D. Wunderlich *et al.* (eds), *Semantik/Semantics: an international handbook of contemporary research*. Berlin. 487–534.

Kramsky, J. 1972. *The article and the concept of definiteness in language.* The Hague and Paris.

Kripke, S. 1972. Naming and necessity. In D. Davidson and G. Harman (eds), *Semantics of natural language*. Dordrecht. 253–355.

Löbner, S. 1985. Definites. *JoS* 4.279–326.

Milsark, G. 1974. Existential sentences in English. Dissertation, MIT.

Reichenbach, H. 1947. *Elements of symbolic logic.* New York.

Reuland, E.J. and G.B. ter Meulen (eds) 1987. *The representation of (in)definiteness. (Fifth Groningen Round Table.)* London and Cambridge, MA.

Russell, B. 1905. On denoting. *Mind* 14.479–93.

Safir, K. 1982. Syntactic chains and the Definiteness Effect. Dissertation, MIT.

Vater, H. 1984. Determinantien und Quantoren im Deutschen. *ZS* 3.19–42.

Wright, S. and T. Givón. 1987. The pragmatics of indefinite reference: quantified text-based studies. *SLang* 11.1–13.

definition

A statement about the content of a linguistic expression (ideally based on rules of **formal logic**). Viewed formally, every scientific definition is a relation of **equivalence** that consists of an unknown entity to be defined (= *definiendum*) and a known entity that is used to define (= *definiens*). The following types of definition and their respective rules of formation are relevant for linguistic and scientific descriptive methods. (a) Real definitions: the definition of an object or of a concrete concept by indicating the genus *G* (= *genus proximum*) and the specifying type trait *T* (= *differentia specifica*), e.g. *A plosive is a consonant that is formed by stopping and releasing two articulators.* In traditional logic general rules must be taken into consideration: a definition must encompass the essence of the concept being defined; it may be neither negative nor circular; the defining concepts *G* and *T* must be sufficiently clear and sharply delineated. (b) Operational (or genetic) definitions are a special type of real definition that indicate on the basis of which method a concept 'emerges' or is verifiable, e.g. the definition *Constituents are syntactic units that can be permutated within a sentence* (⇒ **operational procedures**). (c) Nominal definitions: in contrast to a real definitions, which have to do with objects and concrete characteristics, nominal definitions involve designating objects and abstract characteristics, i.e. names, concepts, or linguistic expressions. They are statements that represent a relation of **synonymy** between the definiens and the (initially meaningless) definiendum. A necessary condition for a concrete nominal definition is that the definiens and the definiendum are expressions of the same category. In particular, variables not found in the definiendum must not be found in the definiens. Explicit definitions are those definitions in which the definiendum next to the sign being defined only contains variables but not already defined logical symbols and the like. Such explicit definitions have the character of abbreviations, i.e. a complex state of affairs is denoted by an abbreviation. With this, the demand for the eliminability of the defined expressions is simultaneously taken into account, i.e. the reducibility of all statements to the basic concept and the axioms. (d) Inductive definitions serve to characterize a class that, as a rule, has an infinite number of objects, by means of a set *B* of basic elements and a number of linking rules or operations. In grammar theory the set of well-formed (= grammatical) expressions of a language *L* is typically defined inductively. So, for example, the inductive definition of a well-formed expression (abbreviated 'WFE') in **propositional logic** *L* reads: (i) every propositional variable *A* is a WFE of *L*; (ii) if *E* is an expression of language *L*, then *not-E* is an expression of *L*; (iii) if E_1 and E_2 are expressions of *L*, then $E_1 \wedge E_2, E_1 \vee E_2, E_1 \rightarrow E_2, E_1 \leftrightarrow E_2$ are also expressions of *L*; (iv) no expression in *L* is a WFE, unless it is generated by (i), (ii), or (iii); (v) recursive definitions ($\Rightarrow$ **recursive rules**); (vi) for extensional vs intensional definitions $\Rightarrow$ **extension**, **intension**.

References
Bierwisch, M. and M. Kiefer, 1969. Remarks on definition in natural language. In F. Kiefer (ed.), *Studies in syntax and semantics*. Dordrecht. 55–79.
Borsodi, R. 1967. *The definition of definition: a new linguistic approach to the integration of knowledge*. Boston, MA.
Haas, W. 1955. On defining linguistic units. *TPS* 1954. 54–84.
Kutschera, F.V. and A. Breitkopf. 1971. *Einführung in die moderne Logik*. Freiburg.
Robinson, R. 1954. *Definition*. Oxford.
Schnelle, H. 1973. *Sprachphilosophie und Linguistik: Prinzipien der Sprachanalyse a priori und a posteriori*. Reinbek.

Bibliography
Petöfi, J.S. (ed.) 1978. *Logic and the formal theory of natural language: selective bibliography*. Hamburg.

deglutination $\Rightarrow$ **aphesis**

degree (*also* comparison, **gradation**)

All constructions which express a comparison properly fall under the category of degree; it generally refers to a morphological category of adjectives and adverbs that indicates a comparative degree or comparison to some quantity. There are three levels of degree: (a) positive, or basic level of degree: *The hamburgers tasted good*; (b) comparative, which marks an inequality of two states of affairs relative to a certain characteristic: *The steaks were better than the hamburgers*; (c) **superlative**, which marks the highest degree of some quantity: *The potato salad was the best of all*; (d) cf. **elative** (absolute superlative), which marks a very high degree of some property without comparison to some other state of affairs: *The performance was most impressive* ($\Rightarrow$ **equative**).

Degree is not grammaticalized in all languages through the use of systematic morphological changes; where such formal means are not present, lexical paraphrases are used to mark **gradation**. In modern Indo-European languages, degree is expressed either (a) synthetically by means of **suffixation** (*new*: *newer*: (*the*) *newest*); (b) analytically by means of particles (*anxious*: *more/most anxious*); or (c) through suppletion ($\Rightarrow$ **suppletivism**), i.e. the use of different word stems: *good : better : (the) best*.

References
Hellan, L. 1981. *Towards an integrated analysis of comparatives*. Tübingen.
Klein, E. 1980. A semantics for positive and comparative adjectives. *Ling&P* 4.1–45.
Pinkham, C. 1982. The formation of comparative classes. Dissertation, Bloomington, IN.
Stassen, L. 1985. *Comparison and universal grammar*. Oxford.
Von Stechow, A. 1984. Comparing semantic theories of comparison. *JoS* 3.1–77.

deictic expression [Grk *deiknýnai* 'to show'] (*also* indexical expression)

Term adopted by C.S. Peirce from **formal logic** for linguistic expressions that refer to the personal, temporal, or spatial aspect of any given **utterance act** and whose designation is therefore dependent on the context of the speech situation. Among the many different kinds of deictic expressions are the personal pronouns (*I*, *you*, etc.), adverbial expressions (*here*, *there*, etc.), and the demonstrative pronouns (*this*, *that*, etc.). In contrast to proper names ($\Rightarrow$ **proper nouns**) and **definite descriptions**, which refer to real objects and states of affairs independent of their context, deictic expressions denote other linguistic signs in a given text or extralinguistic elements in a given speech situation. Among several near-synonymous terms are Russell's (1940) 'egocentric particular,' Bar-Hillel's (1954) 'indexical expression,' Jespersen's (1923) 'shifter,' and Reichenbach's (1947) 'token reflexive word.'

References
Bar-Hillel, Y. 1954. Indexical expressions. *Mind*. 63.359–76.
Jespersen, O. 1923. *Language: its nature, development and origin*. New York.
Reichenbach, H. 1947. *Elements of symbolic logic*. New York.
Russell, B. 1940. *An inquiry into meaning and truth*. London.
$\Rightarrow$ **deixis**, **pragmatics**

deixis

1 Act of pointing out or indicating elements of a situation by gesture or linguistic expressions. ($\Rightarrow$ *also* **anaphora**)

2 Characteristic function of linguistic expressions that relate to the personal, spatial, and temporal aspect of utterances depending upon the given utterance situation (⇒ **deictic expression**). In this regard, one speaks of personal deixis, spatial deixis, and temporal deixis. Deictic expressions may also refer to other linguistic signs within a given text (⇒ **anaphora, quotative, textual reference**). Putnam (1975) has shown that natural languages possess a deictic component. Deixis acts as a link between **semantics** and **pragmatics** to the extent that deictic expressions can only be determined within the context of the actual speech situation. Thus, the statements *I am hungry*, *It's muggy here*, *There's a full moon today* cannot be assigned **truth value** out of context, since their interpretation will always depend upon by whom, when, and where they were uttered. The study of deixis in linguistic expressions, which can be traced back to ancient times, has been of major interest to Indo-European linguistics, especially as it concerns the question of the origin of language (see Brugmann 1904). Pragmatics has shown a renewed interest in Bühler's (1934) statements on the so-called 'indexical field' (⇒ **index field of language**). According to Lyons (1977), deixis is a central linguistic concept (⇒ **localist hypothesis**). In more recent models of grammar, the description of deixis is a matter of either semantics or pragmatics, depending on the theory in question.

References
Brugmann, K. 1904. Die Demonstrativpronomina der indogermanischen Sprachen, eine bedeutungsgeschichtliche Untersuchung. *Sächsische Abhandlungen* 22:6.
Bühler, K. 1934. *Sprachtheorie*. Jena. (Repr. Stuttgart, 1965.)
Innis, R.E. (trans.) 1982. Karl Bühler: semiotic foundations of language theory. In T.A. Sebeok and J. Umiker-Sebeok (eds), *Topics in contemporary semiotics*. New York.
Jarvella, R. and W. Klein (eds) 1982. *Speech, place, and action*. Chichester.
Kleiber, G. 1981. *Problèmes de référence: descriptions définies et noms propres*. Paris.
Lyons, J. 1975. Deixis as the source of reference. In E. Keenan (ed.), *Formal semantics of natural language*. Cambridge. 61–83.
—— 1977. *Semantics*, 2 vols. Cambridge.
Perkins, R.D. 1992. *Deixis, grammar and culture*. Amsterdam and Philadelphia, PA.
Putnam, H. 1975. The meaning of meaning. In K. Gunderson (ed.), *Language, mind, and knowledge*. Minneapolis, MN. 131–93.
Rauh, G. (ed.) 1983. *Essays on deixis*. Tübingen.
Schwarz, M. and J. Chur. 1993. *Semantik: ein Arbeitsbuch*. Tübingen.
Weissenborn, J. and W. Klein (eds) 1982. *Here and there: cross-linguistic studies on deixis and demonstration*. Amsterdam.
Wunderlich, D. 1971. Pragmatik, Sprechsituation und Deixis. *Zeitschrift für Literaturwissenschaft und Linguistik* 1.153–90.
⇒ **anaphora, deictic expression, pragmatics, reference, topology**

delabialization ⇒ unrounding

deletion

An elementary syntactic operation in **transformational grammar**. Certain elements are deleted from a phrase or sentence on the way from **deep structure** to **surface structure**. The basic condition for the use of deletion **transformations** is **recoverability** of the deleted elements. For example, recoverability is guaranteed in **gapping**, where the deletion occurs under specific conditions of identity with the retained categorical element: for example, *Philip plays the flute, and Caroline plays the piano* ⇒ *Philip plays the flute and Caroline the piano*. In the Revised Extended Standard Theory (⇒ **transformational grammar**), deletion rules operate according to transformational rules (⇒ **transformation**).

References
⇒ **constraints, operational procedures, transformational grammar**

delimitative ⇒ resultative

delimitative function ⇒ boundary marker

demarcative feature ⇒ boundary marker

demonstrative pronoun

Syntactic category, subgroup of **determiners** with the semantic function of referring to things either in the speech situation (**deixis**) or previously mentioned (**anaphora**). In most **Indo-European** languages there are two parallel series for indicating distant vs proximate (i.e. 'near' vs 'far'), e.g. Eng. *this* : *that*, Ger. *dieser* : *jener*, Fr. *celui-ci* : *celui-là*, Lat. *hic* : *ille*.

References
Kleiber, G. 1984. Sur la sémantique des descriptions démonstratives. *LIS* 8.63–85.
⇒ **definiteness, deictic expression, deixis**

Demotic ⇒ Egyptian, Greek

denominal

Words derived from nouns, e.g. (*to*) *hammer* (< *hammer*).

References
⇒ **word formation**

denotation [Lat. *denotare* 'to mark, to indicate, to mean']

1 Denotation vs **connotation**: denotation
refers to the constant, abstract, and basic meaning of a linguistic expression independent of
context and situation, as opposed to the connotative, i.e. subjectively variable, emotive
components of meaning. Thus, the denotation
of *night* can be described as the 'period of time
from sunset to the following sunrise,' while the
connotation may include such components as
'scary,' 'lonely,' or 'romantic.'

2 Denotation as **reference** (*also* **designation**):
when a lexeme 'denotes' a particular object or
state of affairs, it does so in the sense of an
extensional reference (⇒ **extension**). Intensional meaning (⇒ **intension**), which refers to
characteristics, traits, or features, is distinguished from extensional meaning.

3 Denotation vs **designation**: following the
second definition above, denotation refers to
individual elements (e.g. *bluegill, pike, trout*),
whereas by designation, one understands the
reference to classes of elements (e.g. *freshwater
fish*). In unique objects (e.g. *sun, God*) the
distinction is more or less moot, since the
identity of element and set is one and the same.

References
⇒ **meaning, semantics**

denotatum

1 Generally, any object in reality that is denoted by a sign.

2 Denotatum vs designatum: the denotatum of
a linguistic expression (e.g. *poets*) denotes the
single elements of the **class**, e.g. *Shakespeare,
Goethe*, etc., whereas 'designatum' refers to the
class as such (⇒ **extension**).

References
⇒ **meaning, semantics**

dental [Lat. *dens* 'tooth']

Speech sound having the upper incisors as the
place of articulation, in the broader sense
including **labio-dental** and **interdental** sounds.
In many languages, dental **consonants** would
include [n̪, t̪, d̪, s̪, z̪, l̪]; in most varieties of
English, however, the corresponding sounds are
alveolar [n, t, d, s, z, l]. (⇒ *also* **articulator,
articulatory phonetics, phonetic transcription**)

References
⇒ **phonetics**

deontic logic [Grk *déon* 'that which is need-
ful, right']

Special type of a philosophical logic that, in
addition to logical expressions such as logical
particles (⇒ **logical connective**) (*and, or*, and
others) and **operators** in **formal logic**, also
introduces operators into the semantic analysis
for expressions such as 'obligation,' 'permission,' and 'prohibition.'

References
Hilpinen, R. (ed.) 1971. *Deontic logic: introductory
and systematic readings*. Dordrecht.
Hintikka, J. 1969. Deontic logic and its philosophical
morals. In *Models for modalities*. Dordrecht.
184–214.
Meyer, J.-J. Ch. 1989. Using programming concepts
in deontic reasoning. In R. Bartsch *et al.* (eds),
Semantics and contextual expression. Dordrecht.
117–45.
Rescher, N. (ed.) 1965. *The logic of decision and
action*. Pittsburgh, PA.
Wright, G.H.V. 1963. *Norm and action*. London

Bibliography
Petöfi, J.S. (ed.) 1978. *Logic and the formal theory of
natural language: selective bibliography*. Hamburg.

deontics ⇒ **deontic logic**

depalatalization ⇒ **palatalization**

dependency

Syntactic relation of dependence between an
element *A* and an element *B*, where *B* can occur
without *A*, but *A* (the dependent element) cannot
occur without *B*. Thus dependency can be
defined as a directional case of concomitance (⇒
collocation). In English some examples of
dependency include dependency between adjective and noun ((*loud*) *applause*) and between
adjective and adverb ((*very*) *loud applause*).
Dependency as a grammatical relation forms the
basis of Tesnière's **dependency grammar**. For
contrast, see the basic relation of **constituency**
(**domination**) in constituent grammar.

References
⇒ **dependency grammar**

dependency grammar

Syntactic model of natural languages developed
by Tesnière (1953, 1959), based on structuralism. Important contributions to this theory were
made by Gaifman (1961), Hays (1964). For
another direction of dependency grammar, cf.
'daughter dependency grammar' (Hudson
1976; Schachter 1980) and 'word grammar'
(Hudson 1984). The main concern of dependency grammar is the description of **dependency** structures of sentences, i.e. the structure
of dependency relations between the elements
of a sentence. In this it is assumed that in a
syntactic connection between two elements one
is the governing and the other the dependent

element. When a governing element is dependent on another governing element, a complex hierarchical dependency order results. Dependency grammar represents these structures with **tree diagrams** whose central node represents the absolute governer of a linguistic structure (in sentences this is the verb). The dependency relationship to an immediately dependent element is shown by a line to a lower node. The dependency structure of the sentence *The goat likes the hay very much* is represented by the structure below.

The lines symbolize the categorization of linguistic expressions. In this analysis the verb governs two nominal elements and one adverbial element; each noun governs an article; the adverb *much* governs the adverb *very*. In addition to the **connection**, the dependency relation between two elements, the relationship of **junction** and of **translation**, is considered as well. Conjunction includes co-ordination as in *Philip and Caroline study linguistics*; translations describe the case where some **particles** (translatives) change the syntactic category of an expression and thus allow its connection to the next higher governer: for example, the noun *glory* in *days of glory* can become an attribute only with the help of the **translative** *of*, when it can be governed by *days*.

Dependency grammar contributed greatly to the development of **valence** theory. The valence of a verb (its property of requiring certain elements in a sentence) determines the structure of the sentence it occurs in. Tesnière distinguishes between actants, which are required by the valence of the verb, and circonstants which are optional. In the sentence given above, *The goat likes the hay very much*, *the goat* and *the hay* are two actants and *very much* is a circonstant of the verb *like*. Diagrams give no indications of the constituent structure of a sentence. Thus, for example, it cannot be gleaned from the diagram below that *the goat* or *likes the hay very much* have been joined into more complex units (subject and complex predicate). Although the relationship between dependency structure and serialization (⇒ **word order**) was already investigated by Tesnière (⇒ **centrifugal vs centripetal**), the diagrams do not take the linear order of the sentence elements into account. More recent investigations attempt to

explain the constituency (Hudson 1976) as well as the serialization of sentences (Heringer *et al.* 1980) by introducing additional descriptive tools. The descriptive capacity of dependency grammar can also be enhanced by the addition of transformations (Robinson 1970). Although dependency grammar, in the spirit of structuralism, defends the autonomy of syntax, sentence-semantic considerations are also included in its framework. Tesnière assumes that each syntactic connection corresponds to a semantic relation, and in this context he introduces the term **nucleus**.

References
Gaifman, H. 1961. *Dependency systems and phrase structure systems*. Santa Monica, CA.
Hays, D.G. 1964. Dependency theory: a formalism and some observations. *Lg* 40.511–25.
Heringer, H.J. *et al.* 1980. *Syntax: Fragen – Lösungen – Alternativen*. Munich.
Hudson, R. 1976. *Arguments for a non-transformational grammar*. Chicago, IL.
—— 1990. *English word grammar*. Oxford.
Mel'čuk, J.A. 1988. *Dependency syntax: Theory and practice*. Albany, NY.
Robinson, J.J. 1970. Dependency structures and transformational rules. *Lg* 46.259–85.
Schachter, P. 1980. Daughter-dependency grammar. In E. Moravcsik and J.R. Wirth (eds), *Syntax and semantics*, vol. 13: *Current approaches to syntax*. New York. 267–99.
Tarvainen, K. 1981. *Einführung in die Dependenzgrammatik*. Tübingen.
Tesnière, L. 1953. *Esquisse d'une syntaxe structurale*. Paris.
—— 1959. *Eléments de syntaxe structurale*. Paris.
Vennemann, T. 1977. Konstituenz und Dependenz in einigen neueren Grammatiktheorien. *Sprachwissenschaft* 1.259–301.

Bibliographies
Hays, D.G. 1965. *An annotated bibliography of publications on dependency theory*. Santa Monica, CA.
Schumacher, H. and N. Trautz. 1976. Bibliographie zur Valenz und Dependenz. In H. Schumacher (ed.), *Untersuchungen zur Verbvalenz*. Tübingen. 317–43.

dependency phonology

A phonological (⇒ **phonology**) model developed by J. Anderson which derives the entire phonological description from the **dependency** relationships between phonological units. (⇒

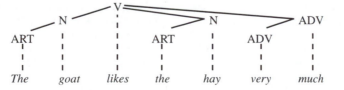

also **accent**, **distinctive feature**, **syllable**)

References
Anderson, J.M. and C.J. Ewen. 1987a. *Principles of dependency phonology*. Cambridge.
—— (eds) 1987b. *Explorations in dependency phonology*. Dordrecht.
Anderson, J.M. and C. Jones. 1974. Three theses concerning phonological representations. *JL* 10.1–26.
Durand, J. 1986. *Dependency and non-linear phonology*. London.
Ewen, C.J. 1977. Aitkin's Law and the phonatory gesture in dependency phonology. *Lingua* 41.307–29.
—— 1980. Aspects of phonological structure, with particular reference to English and Dutch. Dissertation, University of Edinburgh.

dependent clause ⇒ **subordinate clause**

deponent verb [Lat. *deponere* 'to put down, abandon']

Group of verbs in **Latin** which only occur in the **passive** form but have 'given up' (lit. 'deposed') their passive meaning and have only active meaning: *hortari* 'exhort,' *loqui* 'talk,' *pati* 'suffer.' Deponent verbs are remnants of the **middle voice**, which is preserved in **Greek**.

derivation

1 In **transformational grammar**, the process and result of deriving sentences through the use of successive **transformations** or **phrase structure rules**.

2 In **historical linguistics**, the reconstruction of etymological relationships that exist, for example, between Eng. *father* and Lat. *pater*. (⇒ *also* **etymology**, **language change**)

3 Process and result of **word formation** in which new words are created from already existing words through various processes. Derivation is generally distinguished from **inflection**, which encompasses changes in a word according to its relation to other words in an utterance and consists of **declension** and **conjugation**. Derivation covers various processes of word formation, such as the creation of adjectives from nouns (*professional* < *profession*), nouns from verbs (*computer* < *compute*), adjectives from verbs (*conceivable* < *conceive*), and verbs from nouns (*eulogize* < *eulogy*). A distinction is drawn between explicit derivation, in which new words are created through the addition of **prefixes** (⇒ **prefixation**) and **suffixes** (⇒ **suffixation**) to word roots, e.g. *common* > *uncommon*, *stupid* > *stupidity* or through (diachronic) sound changes (also: inner derivation), *sing* vs *song*, and implicit derivation, in which new words are

created either as **back formations** (*televise* < *television*) or as **conversion**[2] into another lexical category ((*to*) *calm* < *calm*). Depending on the word class, one speaks of **deverbatives** (*teacher* < *teach*), **denominals** (*fruity* < *fruit*), or **deadjectivals** (*wetness* < *wet*). Similarly, particular suffixes form semantic classes; for example, *-ness*, *-ship*, and *-dom* generally form **abstract nouns**, *-er* **nomen agentis**, *-let* and *-y* **diminutives**, and *-ess* feminine nouns (⇒ *also* **composition**).

References
Alsina, A. and S. Mchombo. 1990. The syntax of applicatives in Chichewa: problems for a theta theoretic asymmetry. *NL&LT* 6.493–506.
Aronoff, M. 1976. *Word formation in generative grammar*. Cambridge, MA.
Baker, M. 1998a. *Incorporation: a theory of grammatical functional changing*. Chicago.
—— 1988b. Theta theory and the syntax of applicatives in Chichewa. *NL&LT* 6.353–89.
Bierwisch, M. 1989. Event nominalizations. In W. Motsch (ed.), *Wortstruktur und Satzstruktur*. Berlin. 1–73.
Di Sciullo, A.M. and E. Williams. 1987. *On the definition of word*. Cambridge, MA.
Selkirk, E. 1982. *Syntax of words*. Cambridge, MA.
⇒ **word formation**

derivational history

In **transformational grammar**, the group of all derivational paths of a sentence which arise through the successive application of **phrase structure rules** and **transformations**, and which bring a sentence from **deep structure** to **surface structure**. The levels of the derivational history can be illustrated by listing the derived chains or by reconstructing the corresponding **tree diagrams** for each derivational path.

References
⇒ **transformational grammar**

description ⇒ **set**

descriptive adequacy ⇒ **levels of adequacy**

descriptive grammar ⇒ **descriptive linguistics**

descriptive linguistics

1 In its narrower sense, a term for the approaches in **American structuralism** represented by L. Bloomfield, Z.S. Harris, H.A. Gleason, and others, in which the label 'descriptive' accentuates various aspects: (a) synchronic (⇒ **synchrony vs diachrony**) linguistics in the sense of de Saussure (1916), i.e. without reference to historical contexts; (b)

description of individual languages through generalization from corpus analysis (e.g. F. Boas' procedures in the investigation of Native American languages), as opposed to the construction of **universal grammars**; (c) empirical, positivistic procedures (⇒ **empiricism**), i.e. observationally based objective inventory with distributional analysis (⇒ **distributionalism**). (⇒ *also* **structuralism**)

References
Saussure, F. de. 1916. *Cours de linguistique générale*, ed. C. Bally and A. Sechehaye. Paris. (*Course in general linguistics*, trans. R. Harris. London, 1983.)
⇒ **linguistics (history)**

2 (*also* descriptive grammar. In its broader sense, any type of non-prescriptive or non-normative description of different linguistic **varieties**, which codifies regularities according to use. (⇒ **prescriptive grammar**)

descriptivity

Tendency in some languages, especially in polysynthetic languages (⇒ **polysynthesis**) of the Americas, to use highly descriptive terms for names or objects, cf. **Iroquoian** (Oneida) *skahnaks* 'fox,' literally 'the one who is bad in reference to his fur.' (⇒ *also* **incorporating language**)

designation [Lat. *designare* 'to mark, to indicate']

1 ⇒ **denotation**[2]

2 ⇒ **extension**

3 In **glossematics**, the relation between (linguistic) **form** and the (extralinguistic) **substance** on the semantic level.

designator

In C.W. Morris' theory of signs (**semiotics**), **signs** which refer to observable characteristics of objects in the real world. If the receiver of a sign is convinced that the intended state of affairs actually possesses the characteristics ascribed to it by the designator, then – even if this is actually not the case – informative adequacy has been attained.

Reference
Morris, C.W. 1946. *Sign, language and behavior*. New York.

designatum ⇒ denotatum[2], referent

determination

1 The syntactic–semantic relation between two linguistic elements whereby one element modifies the other, as does *scientific* in *scientific book*. (⇒ **complementation modification**)

2 In **glossematics**, a term for **dependency**, i.e. unilateral dependency between two linguistic elements such that one element is a prerequisite for the other, but not vice versa. For example, the relationship between adjectives and adverbs.

determinative compound (*also* endocentric compound)

The most frequent type of noun compound in which the second element (the base word) is semantically determined by the first element: *coffeehouse, dance hall*. The grammatical relations between the individual elements within the compound are largely dissolved, the order of the elements alone determines the interpretation: *piano player* is a player, but a *player piano* is a piano. In the interpretation of (potentially ambiguous) semantic relations between first and second elements, perceptual categories like appearance, size, function, make-up, among others have a determinative function, cf. *Gold Coast* (place), *gold sand* (element), *gold chain* (composition), *gold scale* (function), *gold finch* (comparison). In more recent studies on **composition** these semantic relations are described on the basis of **stereotypes**[2].

References
⇒ **composition, stereotype**[2]**, word formation**

determiner

Category of words that specify a noun more closely. In English these include **articles**, **demonstrative pronouns**, and other words which previously were grouped with **pronouns**. The precise definition of this class of words is still somewhat problematic (see Vater 1986). While determiners were previously seen as **constituents** of a **noun phrase** (i.e. co-constituents of N), in **binding theory** they are now seen as realizations of a functional category D which has a **determiner phrase** (DP) as a maximal projection and is the bearer of the grammatical features of the DP (person, case, gender, number). Determiners specify the accompanying N semantically and restrict its **reference**. Thus the determiner makes the N explicit, that is, it makes it 'known' through the context, hearer knowledge, or reference to the speech situation (see Hawkins 1978). The word *this* functions in a similar fashion, but it is limited to **deixis** (reference to speech situations) and **anaphora** (reference to something already mentioned in the speech context), and cannot refer to knowledge of the world. Thus it can replace *the* in *I see a village. The/this village is picturesque* but not *the* in *I see a village. The/*this church is very picturesque*.

References
Bisle-Müller, H. 1991. *Artikelwörter im Deutschen: semantische und pragmatische Aspekte ihrer Verwendung.* Tübingen.
Hawkins, J.A. 1978. *Definiteness and indefiniteness: a study in reference and grammaticality prediction.* London.
Heim, I. 1982. *The semantics of definite and indefinite noun phrases.* Constance.
—— 1991. Artikel und Definitheit. In D. Wunderlich *et al.* (eds), *Semantik/Semantics: an international handbook of contemporary research.* Berlin. 487–534.
Kasher, A. and D.M. Gabbay. 1976. On the semantics and pragmatics of specific and nonspecific indefinite expression. *TL* 3.245–90.
Kolde, G. 1989. *Der Artikel in deutschen Sachverhaltsnominalen.* Tübingen.
Kramsky, J. 1968. Some ways of expressing the category of determinedness. *TLP* 3.241–53.
Löbner, S. Definites. *JoS* 4.279–326.
Van der Auwera, J. 1980. *The semantics of determiners.* London.
Vater, H. 1984. Determiners and quantifiers. *Kwartalnik neofilologiczny* 31.305–22.
—— 1986. *Zur Syntax der Determinantien.* Tübingen.
—— 1994. Determination and quantification. In V. Koseka and D. Rytel-Kuc (eds), *Semantics and confrontation of languages.* Warsaw.

determiner phrase (*abbrev.* DP)

Grammatical category (or **phrase**) which in recent **Government and Binding theory** is defined as the **maximal projection** of a functional category D under which the agreement features AGR of the DP (**case**, **gender**, **number**, **person**) are positioned. A **noun phrase** (NP) is, in this interpretation, a **complement** of D, the AGR features of D being passed on to the complement NP by percolation (⇒ **percolate**). AGR can be realized as a **determiner** ending, but also as an adjective ending. For example, the word *the* in *the big tree* forms the core of the DP, with *big tree* as its complement. The D-position can be realized lexically by a determiner or can contain the feature [POSS] (according to Olsen 1991), which gives the specifier-position of the DP the **genitive** case. Pronouns are Pro-DPs (i.e. intransitive D-elements), since they compose an entire DP. (⇒ *also* **definiteness**)

References
Abney, S.P. 1987. The English noun phrase and its sentential aspect. Dissertation, MIT.
Felix, S. 1988. The structure of functional categories. Ms, University of Passau.
Olsen, S. 1991. Die deutsche Nominalphrase als 'Determinansphrase'. In S. Olsen and G. Fanselow (eds), *DET, COMP und INFL: zur Syntax funktionaler Kategorien und grammatischer Funktionen.* Tübingen. 35–56.

determinism ⇒ **linguistic determinism**

Devanāgarī ⇒ **Hindi-Urdu**, **Panjabi**, **Sanskrit**

developmental aphasia (*also* childhood aphasia, dysphasia)

In **neurolinguistics** and **speech-language pathology**, term used in the 1950s and 1960s for **specific language impairment** in children, contrasting 'developmental aphasia,' a congenital disorder, with **aphasia**, an acquired disorder. (⇒ *also* **developmental dysphasia**)

References
Eisensen, J. 1968. Developmental aphasia (dyslogia): a postulation of a unitary concept of the disorder. *Cortex* 4.184–200.
Mykleburst, H.R. 1957. Childhood aphasia: an evolving concept. In L. Travis (ed.), *Handbook of speech pathology and audiology.* New York. 1181–202. (2nd edn 1971).
⇒ **specific language impairment**

developmental apraxia ⇒ **apraxia**

developmental dyslexia (*also* dyslexia)

A subclass of learning disabilities, this term denotes reading and writing disorders in children of at least average intelligence. Debates over causal factors began in the 1960s and still continue, with researchers variously emphasizing (a) perceptual impairments, (b) linguistic impairments, or (c) cognitive disorders in, for example, attention and memory. Developmental dyslexia is often associated with behavior problems which may further impede learning. While sociocultural circumstances may hinder **literacy**, such difficulties are not generally considered dyslexia. (⇒ *also* **developmental language disorder**)

References
Bakker, D. *et al.* (eds) 1987. *Developmental dyslexia and learning disorders.* Basle.
Firth, U. (ed.) 1980. *Cognitive processes in spelling.* London.
Grimm, H. and H. Skowronek. 1993. *Language acquisition problems and reading disorders: aspects of diagnosis and intervention.* Berlin and New York.
Hume, C. and M. Snowling. 1993. Developmental dyslexia and cognitive processes. In G. Blanken *et al.* (eds), *Linguistic disorders and pathologies: an international handbook.* Berlin and New York. 733–41.
Kavanagh, J.F. and R.L. Venetzky (eds) 1980. *Orthography, reading and dyslexia.* Baltimore, MD.
Pavlidis, G. and D. Fisher. 1986. *Dyslexia: its neuropsychology and treatment.* Chichester.
Perlin, P. 1982. Spelling strategies in good and poor readers. *APsy* 3.1–14.

Snowling, M. 1987. *Dyslexia: a cognitive developmental perspective*. London.

—— 1991. Developmental reading disorders. *Journal of Child Psychology and Psychiatry* 32.49–77.

Snowling, M. and C. Hume. 1993. Developmental dyslexia and language disorders. In G. Blanken *et al.* (eds), *Linguistic disorders and pathologies: an international handbook*. Berlin and New York. 724–33.

Thomson, M.E. 1984. *Developmental dyslexia: its nature, assessment and remediation*. London.

Vellutino, F.R. 1979. *Dyslexia: theory and research*. Cambridge.

Wimmer, H. 1993. Characteristics of developmental dyslexia in a regular writing system. *APsy* 14.1–33.

developmental dysphasia

An older term for **specific language impairment**, developmental dysphasia refers to the selective impairment of children's ability to acquire language.

References
⇒ *also* **developmental language disorder, specific language impairment**.

developmental language disorder

Refers broadly to any pattern of delay or impairment in a child's first language acquisition and may be caused by neural or emotional trauma during the language acquisition period, but more usually implies a causal agent present before language learning begins. Significant **language disorders** are found in children with mental retardation, **specific language impairment**, or **autism**, as well as in children with impaired hearing or vision. Such disorders entail the delayed onset of speech and certain characteristic patterns of atypical language development and use, which may persist throughout life. When the disorder occurs after the onset of language, there may be virtual recovery due to neural plasticity during the childhood years. The extent of recovery depends upon the nature and severity of the trauma and the degree to which language specialization (⇒ **lateralization**) has already occurred. Developmental language disorders may affect the ability to understand spoken or written language just as much as the ability to speak or write (⇒ **developmental dyslexia**), and are frequently associated with articulatory impairments (⇒ **phonological disorder, dyslalia**) and/or impairments in speech rhythm (⇒ **cluttering**). Research in developmental language disorders is pursued within the disciplines of psychiatry, neurology, **psycholinguistics**, developmental psychology, and **neurolinguistics**, often with the intent of illu-

minating normal acquisition processes by studying the dissociations which mark these clinical syndromes. Professionals within **speech-language pathology, clinical linguistics**, and **neuropsychology** are concerned with the diagnosis and treatment of developmental language disorders and with research on these topics.

References

Aram, D. and J. Nation. 1982. *Child language disorders*. St Louis, MO.

Ball, M.J. 1988. *Theoretical linguistics and disordered language*. London.

Beitchman, J.H. and A. Inglis. 1991. The continuum of linguistic dysfunction from pervasive developmental disorders to dyslexia. *Psychiatric Clinics of North America* 14.95–111.

Benthal, J. and N.W. Bankson. 1988. *Articulation and phonological disorders*, 2nd rev. edn. Englewood Cliffs, NJ.

Bishop, D. and K. Mogford (eds) 1988. *Language development in exceptional circumstances*. Edinburgh.

Cantwell, D.P. and L. Baker. 1988. *Developmental speech and language disorders*. Hillside, NJ.

Grunwell, P. 1987. *Clinical phonology*. London.

Johnston, J.R. 1993. Definition and diagnosis of language developmental disorders. In G. Blanken *et al* (eds), *Linguistic disorders and pathologies: an international handbook*. Berlin and New York. 574–84.

Lahey, M. 1988. *Language disorders and language development*. New York.

Landau, B. and L. Gleitman. 1985. *Language and experience*. Cambridge, MA.

Mills, A. (ed.) 1983. *Language acquisition in the blind child*. London.

Nelson, N. 1993. *Childhood language disorders in context: infancy through adulthood*. New York.

Nicolosi, L. *et al.* 1983. *Terminology of communication disorder*, 2nd edn. Baltimore, MD.

Obler, L. and L. Menn (eds) 1982. *Linguistics and exceptional language*. New York.

Rosenberg, S. (ed.) 1987. *Advances in applied psycholinguistics: disorders of first-language development*. Cambridge.

Journals

British Journal of Disorders of Communication.
Journal of Communication Duisorders.
Journal of Speech and Hearing Disorders.
Journal of Speech and Hearing Research.
Topics in Language Disorders.
Topics in Learning and Learning Disabilities.

deverbative

Words derived from verbs, such as *equipment* (< *equip*) and *readable* (< *read*). (⇒ *also* **word formation**)

References
⇒ **word formation**

deviance ⇒ deviation

deviation (*also* deviance)

Property of expressions in a natural language which do not agree either explicitly or implicitly with compatible linguistic agreements (⇒ **linguistic norms**) or with linguistic descriptions (⇒ **rule**). Deviation can be manifested at the phonetic, phonological, morphological, syntactic, or semantic level. Syntactic–semantic deviations can vary in type, and may be a violation of: (a) the combination of syntactic categories: *Philip can wall*; (b) strict subcategorization: *Caroline snores the owl*; (c) **selection restrictions**: *The rock looms over the mountain*. The term is also frequently used to describe semantic and pragmatic discrepancies, e.g. *the American monarchy*. ⇒ **metaphor** for forms of deviation with a poetic and stylistic function.

References
⇒ **acceptability, grammaticality, linguistic norms**

dia-

Prefix derived from Grk *diá-* ('through; apart; between; one with another'). Used in linguistic terminology, *dia-* often denotes the idea of variety or heterogeneity as in *diaphasic, diasituative, diastratic, diatopic*, which are terms for linguistic conditions differentiated by time, situation, social class, and space, respectively. As a further example, while **sociolects** are diastratic varieties of language, **dialects** are diatopical varieties. (⇒ *also* **diachrony, diasystem**)

diachronic linguistics [Grk *chrónos* 'time']

Systematic description and elucidation of all linguistic changes through time (internal historical linguistics) with regard to external facts such as political history, cultural influences, social change, territorial changes, language contact (external historical linguistics) among others (⇒ **language change**) (⇒ *also* **historical linguistics**).

References
⇒ **comparative linguistics, historical grammars, historical linguistics, language change, synchrony vs diachrony**

diachrony

A term introduced by F. de Saussure for the type of **historical linguistics** conducted nearly exclusively by the **Neogrammarians** in the nineteenth century, whose atomistic procedure (e.g. study of the development of single sounds or forms without regard to the systemic character of language) was vigorously attacked by de

Saussure. In the dichotomy **synchrony vs diachrony**, diachrony is accorded a subordinate function; at the most it is regarded as complementary to synchronic study. The generally ahistorical, purely descriptive linguistics carried out by the structuralist stream of research largely adopted this view. It is only since the 1960s that problems of **language change** have moved into the general focus of research again.

References
⇒ **historical linguistics, language change, synchrony vs diachrony**

diacritic [Grk *diakritikós* 'separative, distinguishing']

A graphemic addition to a written symbol used to create a new symbol from a pre-existing symbol. Economically, diacritics help keep the inventory of basic phonetic signs as small and as comprehensive as possible: for example, in German the diaeresis is used to distinguish between *ä, ö, ü* for [ɛ], [ø], and [y] vs *a, o, u* for [a], [o], and [u]. In the IPA (⇒ **phonetic transcription**), a little circle set below or above a letter distinguishes between voiceless and voiced consonants (e.g. voiceless /b/, /d/, /g/ as [b̥], [d̥], [g̥] vs voiced /b/, /d/, /g/ as [b], [d], [g]). In syllabic **writing**, where there are basic signs with standardized voicing, diacritics can be used to indicate the rest of the voicings (e.g. *o* in Siamese, *a* in **Hindu** writings). Here are some examples with the Roman alphabet as the basis for new symbols: *ā* for [aː] in Latvian; *ă* for [ə] in **Rumanian**; *å* for [o] in **Swedish**; *á* for [au] in **Icelandic**; *ñ, Ñ* for [ɲ] in **Spanish**, *ø* for [ø] in **Norwegian**; *è* for [ɛ] in **French**; *ń* and *ọ* for [ŋ] or [ɔ], respectively, in **Igbo**. Up to 1976, modern **Greek** writing was oriented towards ancient Greek such that there were numerous (and virtually superfluous) diacritics. There are also various diacritics in **Hebrew** as well as in the different orthographies of the **Semitic** languages. In **Indonesian** a superscript 2 can indicate **reduplication**: *orang²* for *orang-orang* ('persons') vs *orang* ('person'). Diacritics are also used to indicate that the symbol refers to a number as opposed to a sound, e.g. Grk ɛ' for *5* vs ɛ for /e/. (⇒ *also* **acute accent, cedilla, circumflex, diaeresis, grave accent, tilde**)

References
⇒ **writing**

diaeresis

1 Separation of two adjacent **vowels** (⇒ **hiatus**), dividing one **syllable** into two, e.g. Eng. *i.de.al* or Fr. *ou.vri.er*. This is often accomplished through insertion of a **glottal stop** or

glide. (⇒ also **epenthesis**, **language change**, **phonology**)

2 (*also* trema). A diacritic ‹¨› used over a Latin, Greek, or **Cyrillic** letter (a) to indicate the second of two adjacent vowels belonging to distinct syllables (e.g. French *naïve* 'naive' or Greek *ὄϊσ* [ois] 'sheep'), (b) to indicate vowel mutation (⇒ **umlaut**) (e.g. Ger. *schön* 'pretty'), (c) to indicate alternate pronunciations of syllables (e.g. Spanish *-güi-* [gwi] in *lingüística* vs *-gui-* [gi] in *guitarra*); (d) in **Russian** to distinguish a regressively palatalized stressed ['o] vs a palatal [e̦] (usually unmarked in writing), i.e. *ё* vs *e*.

diahyponymy [Grk *hypó-* 'under,' *ónyma* 'name']

Paradigmatic **semantic relation** and special type of **hyponymy**: two linguistic expressions are in a relation of diahyponymy if they can be distinguished as hyponyms (⇒ **hyponymy**) from other subordinate terms by a common feature. Thus, in the semantic field of 'kinship relationships' (⇒ **kinship term**) the expressions *mother*, *daughter*, and *sister* are differentiated by the feature [direct relationship] from the expressions *aunt* and *niece* or by the feature [female] from *father*, *son*, and *brother*.

References
⇒ **hyponymy**, **semantic relation**

dialect [Grk *diálektos* 'common language']

A linguistic system (in the sense of langue (⇒ **langue vs parole**)) that (a) shows a high degree of similarity to other systems so that at least partial mutual intelligibility is possible; (b) is tied to a specific region in such a way that the regional distribution of the system does not overlap with an area covered by another such system; (c) does not have a written or standardized form, i.e. does not have officially standardized orthographic and grammatical rules. Apart from this narrow definition which describes, for example, the situation in Britain, the term 'dialect' is used by linguists in various other senses. Note, for example, the broader use of 'dialects' to refer to the various languages that stem from a single ancestral language, such as the 'Romance dialects' from Latin.

In the investigation of the conditions and the origin of the dialectal structure (⇒ **dialectology**), dialects must be defined as individual languages in which extralinguistic aspects like topography (mountains and rivers as natural borders), trade routes, and political and religious centers are taken into account alongside strictly linguistic criteria. Seen from a genetic and historical perspective, dialects must be considered older than standardized languages and can, therefore, in their modern form, be seen as a reflex of a historical development. Since dialects – owing to their oral tradition and lack of standardization – are 'more natural' than standardized languages, they are particularly suited for testing linguistic hypotheses about historical processes, as is evident in both neogrammarian (⇒ **Neogrammarians**) and structuralist (⇒ **structuralism**) investigations. More recent investigations of dialect have been increasingly influenced by the sociolinguistic approach. These focus above all on the different uses of dialect and standard language, the greater private use of dialect as well as possible correlations between dialect and social class. (⇒ *also* **sociolinguistics**)

References
Milroy, J. and L. Milroy (eds) 1993. *Real English: the grammar of English dialects in the British Isles*. London.
Noble, C.A.M. 1983. *Modern German dialects*. New York.
Orton, H. 1962. *Survey of English dialects: an introduction*. Leeds.
Orton H. *et al.* 1962–71. *Survey of English dialects: basic material*, 4 vols. Leeds.
Russ, C.V.J. 1990. *The dialects of modern German*. London.
Trudgill, P. 1983. *On dialect: social and geographical perspectives*. New York.
———— 1994. *Dialects*. London.
——and J.K. Chambers (eds) 1991. *English dialects: studies in grammatical variation*. London.
⇒ **dialectology**

dialect dictionary

The codification of regional linguistic variants from a synchronic and/or diachronic perspective. There are three principal types of dialect dictionaries: (a) comprehensive, multiregional dialect dictionaries that comprise the vocabulary of several regional dialectal variants; (b) regional dictionaries that comprise the complete dialect of a specific area (town, village, region, and so on); (c) those limited to a specific city or local dialect (⇒ **idioticon**). (⇒ **British English, English**)

References
Adams, R. 1968. *Western words: a dictionary of the American West*, 2nd edn. Norman, OK.
Bailey, R.W. (ed.) 1987. *Dictionaries of English: prospects for the record of our language*. Ann Arbor, MI.
Bickerton, A. 1970. *American–English, English–American: a two-way glossary of words in daily use on both sides of the Atlantic*. Bristol.
Craigie, W. and J.R. Hulbert *et al.* (eds) 1938–44. *A dictionary of American English on historical principles*. Chicago, IL.
Everhart, J. 1968. *The illustrated Texas dictionary of*

the English language, 2 vols. Lincoln, NE.
Grant, W. and D. Murison (eds) 1931. *The Scottish national dictionary*. Edinburgh.
Herman, L.H. and M.S. Herman. 1947. *Manual of American dialects for radio, stage, screen and television*. Chicago, IL.
Schur, N.W. 1987. *British English: A to Z*. New York.
Wentworth, H. (ed.) 1944. *American dialect dictionary*. New York.
Wright, J. 1898–1905. *English dialect dictionary*, 6 vols. Oxford. (Repr. New York 1963.)
⇒ **dialectology**

dialect geography (*also* areal linguistics, linguistic geography)

Subdiscipline of dialectology (sometimes equated with it) concerned with the investigation of the geographic distribution of linguistic phenomena. In dialect geography, phonetic, phonological, morphological, and lexical approaches are primarily employed. The comprehensive collection of materials in written records (the mailing of questionnaires), oral data recorded phonetically, on the spot, by the interviewer in a 'question book,' and the collection of freely spoken texts form the basis of linguistic geographic analysis. The recorded data are then presented in the form of linguistic maps (⇒ **dialect mapping, linguistic atlas**) which facilitate the interpretation of the specific geographic distribution and the structure of individual features from a historical, cultural, social (extralinguistic), and language-internal (intralinguistic) point of view.

References

Davis, A.L. 1949. A word atlas of the Great Lakes region. Dissertation, Ann Arbor, MI.
Kirk, J.M. *et al.* (eds) 1985. *Studies in linguistic geography: the dialects of English in Britain and Ireland*. London.
Kurath, H. 1939–43. *Linguistic atlas of New England*, 3 vols. Providence, RI.
——— 1949. *A word geography of the eastern United States*. Ann Arbor, MI.
——— 1972. *Studies in area linguistics*. Bloomington, IN.
Kurath, H. and B. Bloch. 1939. *Handbook of linguistic geography of New England*. Providence, RI.
Lehmann, W. 1962. Broadening of language materials: dialect geography. In *Historical linguistics: an introduction*. New York.
McDavid, R.I. 1957. Tape recording in dialect geography: a cautionary note. *Journal of the Canadian Linguistic Association* 3.3–8.
Moulton, W.G. 1972. Geographical linguistics. In T.A. Sebeok (ed.), *Current trends in linguistics*. The Hague. Vol. 9, 186–222.
Orton, H. and N. Wright. 1974. *A word geography of England*. London.
Pickford, G.R. 1956. American linguistic geography: a sociological appraisal. *Word* 12.211–33.
Trubetzkoy, N. 1949. Phonologie et géographie linguistique. In *Principes de phonologie*. Paris.
Trudgill, P. 1974. Linguistic change and diffusion: description and explanation in sociolinguistic dialect geography. *LSoc* 3.215–46.
——— 1975. Linguistic geography and geographical linguistics. In C. Board *et al.* (eds), *Progress in geography*, vol. 3. London.
Wood, G.R. 1971. *Vocabulary change: a study of variation in regional words in eight of the southern states*. Carbondale, IL.

dialect mapping

The documentation of dialectal conditions and developments in the form of a geographic map on which the results of linguistic-geographic analyses are presented either as a non-keyed text (e.g. individual words in their regional distribution) or in the form of symbols. Currently, the basic methods of representing linguistic data on maps are to key the pertinent linguistic data to each locality of occurrence with dots or to draw boundary lines around areas with the same linguistic features. Maps may be drawn to show individual linguistic levels (e.g. phonetic or phonological, morphological, lexical, or syntactic dialect maps) or to show a combination of features that give a cumulative overview of the dialectal geographic distribution. A **linguistic atlas** is a comprehensive representation of dialectal features for a whole region or a whole linguistic area. (⇒ *also* **dialect geography**)

dialectic [Grk *dialektikḗ* (*technḗ*) 'discussion by question and answer']

Originally the study of correct argumentation of debatable points involving a method of dialogue developed by Aristotle and Plato for discovering the truth. Part of the linguistic trivium in the middle ages, a logical academic discipline alongside grammar and **rhetoric**, especially broadened as a method of cognition. Modern rhetoric (see Perelman 1977) defines dialectic according to the classical model as the science of controversy.

Reference

Perelman, C. 1977. *L'Empire rhétorique: rhétorique et argumentation*. Paris.

dialectology

Linguistic subdiscipline concerned with **dialects**. The origin of dialectology – apart from a few early glossaries and **dialect dictionaries** – can be traced back to the beginnings of nineteenth-century **historical** and **comparative linguistics**. During the Romantic era the 'dialects of the common people,' which were up to then held in low esteem, were elevated to the position of 'more original' linguistic forms; the comparative method was also used to reconstruct the earlier stages of a language from its dialects. In the investigation of general historical linguistic principles by the **Neogrammarians**, the dialects were even seen as being superior to the written language, since it was here that 'consistencies in sound formation' were genuinely apparent. There have been numerous historical phonetic studies conducted on dialects and many synchronic descriptions of local dialects in which the relationship of the present state of the language to the historical stages of linguistic development is demonstrated. The geographic diffusion of differing forms and varieties and the search for specific dialectal regions represent areas of interest pursued by **dialect geography** (often understood and used as a synonym for 'dialectology' (⇒ **dialect mapping** and **linguistic atlas** on methods used in compiling dialect data). Contrary to original assumptions, collected dialect data have shown a definite lack of 'homogeneity' inasmuch as the uniform distribution of **isoglosses** is concerned. Instead one finds a multitude of intersecting and opposite linguistic boundaries. 'Extralinguistic' analyses of such isoglosses have discovered the relevance of topographical, political, and sociocultural preconditions, i.e. many of the isogloss boundaries correspond to historical trade routes, state and church borders, etc. Sociolinguistic influences (⇒ **sociolinguistics**) have led to an increased consideration of sociological methods and the development of a sociodialectological approach with various focuses: (a) class-specific distribution of dialect and standard language, e.g. dialect as a 'restricted code' (⇒ **code theory**) and 'speech barriers'; (b) covariation of linguistic, macrosocial, and situative categories (⇒ **diglossia**), social conditions for language variation and language change (see Labov 1975, 1978); (c) communicative function of the conversational use of the different language varieties (cf. **contextualization**) (see Gumperz 1978).

References
Allen, H.B. and G.N. Underwood (eds) 1971. *Readings in American dialectology*. New York.
Besch, W. *et al.* (eds) 1982–3. *Dialektologie: ein Handbuch zur deutschen und allgemeinen Dialektforschung*, 2 vols. Berlin and New York.
Chambers, J.K. and P. Trudgill. 1980. *Dialectology*. Cambridge.
Davis, L. 1983. *English dialectology: an introduction*. Birmingham, AL.
Elert, C. *et al.* (eds) 1977. *Dialectology and sociolinguistics*. Umeå.
Fisiak, J. (ed.) 1988. *Historical dialectology: region-*

al and social. Berlin and New York.
Francis, W.N. 1984. *Dialectology: an introduction*. London.
Moulton, W.G. 1968. Structural dialectology. *Lg* 44.451–66.
Petyt, K. 1980. *The study of dialect: an introduction to dialectology*. Boulder, CO.
Trudgill, P. 1983. *On dialect: social and geographical perspectives*. New York.
—— 1986. *Dialects in contact*. Oxford.
Walters, K. 1988. Dialectology. In F. Newmeyer (ed.), *Linguistics: the Cambridge Survey*. Cambridge. Vol. 4, 119–39.
Weinreich, U. 1954. Is a structural dialectology possible? *Word* 10.388–400. (Repr. in H.B. Allen and G.N. Underwood (eds), *Readings in American dialectology*. New York, 1971. 300–13.)
Wejnen, A. 1978. *Outlines for an interlingual European dialectology*. Assen.

Journals
Dialectologia et Geolinguistica.
Zeitschrift für Dialektologie und Linguistik.
⇒ **sociolinguistics**, **spoken language**

dialogue system

In natural language processing, a system which carries out a dialogue with a human user, normally for the purpose of allowing the user access to a software system such as a database or **expert system**. Dialogue systems have been the focus of especially intense development because they provide the user with a familiar and efficient interface and thus obviate the usual need for training. (⇒ *also* **computational linguistics, user modeling**)

Reference
Allen, J. 1987. *Natural language understanding*. Menlo Park, CA.

diasystem

Term coined by U. Weinreich for a 'system of systems.' Two or more linguistic systems with partial similarities are subsumed under a diasystem which reflects the structural similarities or overlappings and differences between them. This concept was applied above all to the description of overlapping phonological systems in multi(dia)lectal linguistic situations, as for example in different, though neighboring and coexisting, regional and social varieties within a **speech community**.

References
Cochrane, G.R. 1959. The Australian English vowels as a diasystem. *Word* 15.69–88.
Weinreich, U. 1954. Is a structural dialectology possible? *Word* 10.388–400. (Repr. in H.B. Allen and G.N. Underwood (eds), *Readings in American dialectology*. New York, 1971, 300–13.)

diathesis [Grk *diáthesis* 'state, condition']
(*also* **voice**)

Term from **Greek** for voice (**active, passive, middle**) as well as for other regular valence shifts such as **applicative, accusativization,** and **dative shift**.

dichotomy [Grk *dichotomía* 'division into two parts']

A bipartite, complementary opposition, such as **langue vs parole, synchronic vs diachronic** linguistics, **competence vs performance**.

Reference
Markey, T.L. 1976. *Studies in European linguistic theory: the dichotomy precept*. Grossen-Linden.

difference ⇒ **set**

difference hypothesis ⇒ **code theory**

differentia specifica ⇒ **definition**

diffuse ⇒ **compact vs diffuse**

digital [Lat. *digitus* 'finger']

'Digital' is a term used in information processing to refer to a way of representing a definite set of signs (digits) through a code that is applied to the information being processed, such as when fingers are applied to numbers in counting from 1 to 10. Analogue representations are the counterpart of digital representations.

digital communication

A borrowing from the notion of digital calculators which, unlike analogue calculators, function on the basis of *yes/no* oppositions and on the representation of information as numbers. This designation of verbal communication based on a conventional verbal sign language was developed by Watzlawick *et al.* (1967). In contrast to **analogue communication**, the signs, or 'names,' bear no similarity to the facts which they represent (an exception is **onomatopoeia**). Digital communication serves to transmit knowledge. It employs a logical syntax to produce complex syntactic relations, but lacks sufficiently differentiated semantics for the communication of human relations.

Reference
Watzlawick, P., J.H. Beavin, and D.D. Jackson. 1967. *Pragmatics of human communication: a study of interactional patterns, pathologies and paradoxes*. New York.

diglossia [Grk prefix *dí-* 'two-, bi-'; *glōssá* 'language']

Term used originally by Grecist scholars for describing the linguistic situation in Greece, with its two (functionally different) varieties Katharévousa and Dhimotiki (⇒ **Greek**). It was later taken up again by Ferguson (1959). It now describes any stable linguistic situation, in which there exists a strict functional differentiation between a (socially) 'L(ow)-variety' and a distinct 'H(igh)-variety.' The H-variety is differentiated from the L-variety mostly through a greater degree of grammatical complexity. It is a strictly standardized and codified language whose transmission does not occur in the context of primary socialization, but rather secondarily in schools. It is not used in everyday conversation, but instead in formal speech situations and for written communication.

Apart from Greece, characteristic examples of such situations can be found in German-speaking Switzerland (standard High **German** vs Schwyzerdütsch (⇒ **German**), in Arabia (classical vs modern **Arabic**), in Haiti (**French** vs **creole**), etc. Gumperz (1964) extends this definition to linguistic societies in which functionally distinct varieties are found, though without being considered 'bilingual'; Fishman (1967) sees every linguistic society with two functionally distinct varieties as diglossic and also relates the sociolinguistically oriented concept of diglossia to the psycholinguistic concept of **bilingualism**. For a useful summary of the European perspective, specifically with regard to Romance linguistics, see Kremnitz (1987). For a detailed overview on the change in meaning and use of the term diglossia see Willemyns and Bister (1989).

References
Ferguson, C. 1959. Diglossia. *Word* 15.325–40.
Fishman, J.A. 1967. Bilingualism with and without diglossia; diglossia with and without bilingualism. *Journal of Social Issues* 23.29–38.
——— 1968. Sociolinguistic perspectives on the study of bilingualism. *Linguistics* 39.21–49.
Gumperz, J.J. 1964. Linguistic and social interaction in two communities. *AA* 66.137–53.
Hymes, D. (ed.) 1964. *Language in culture and society: a reader in linguistics and anthropology*. New York.
Kremnitz, G. 1987. Diglossie/Polyglossie. In U. Ammon *et al.* (eds), *Sociolinguistics: an international handbook on the science of language and society*. Berlin. 208–18.
Labov, W. 1966. *The social stratification of English in New York City*. Washington, DC.
Weinreich, U. 1953. *Languages in contact: findings and problems*. New York.
Willemyns, R. and H. Bister. 1989. The language continuum as a pluridimensional concept. In U. Ammon (ed.), *Status and function of languages and language varieties*. Berlin and New York. 541–51.

Bibliography
Fernandez, M. 1993. *Diglossia: a comprehensive bibliography, 1960–1990 and supplements.* Amsterdam and Philadelphia.

digraphy [Grk *gráphein* 'to write']

The representation of a single phoneme with two graphic signs, e.g. Eng. ‹sh› for [ʃ]. (⇒ *also* **graphemics**)

diminutive [Lat. *deminuere* 'to lessen'] (*also* attenuative)

1 Nouns derived by means of certain **suffixes** like *-et*(*te*) (*cigarette*), *-let* (*booklet*), and *-ie/-y* (*Billie, kitty*) or a **prefix** like *mini-* (*mini-vac*) that as a rule modify (⇒ **modification**) the meaning of the stem to 'little,' but which can also signal an emotional attitude of the speaker (*What a cute kitty!*, which can be said of a cat of any size). The latter are often called **hypocoristics**. The opposite derivations are **augmentatives**, which are not present in all languages. (⇒ *also* **sound symbolism**)

References
⇒ **word formation**

2 A type of verbal **aspect** which is a subgroup of duratives (⇒ **durative vs non-durative**). In German, the suffix *-ln* is used with verbs to indicate a lower intensity of the action: *hüsteln* 'cough a little' from *husten* 'to cough,' *spötteln* 'to scorn somewhat' from *spotten* 'to scorn.'

Dinka ⇒ **Chari-Nile languages**

diphthong [Grk *díphthongos* 'with two sounds']

Vowel in the **articulation** of which the **articulators** move enough so that two separate phonological phases can be distinguished, e.g. [ay], [aʊ] in *high, how.* According to different theoretical criteria, a diphthong can be considered a single ('unit') **phoneme** or a combination of two phonemes. The terms 'rising' and 'falling' are used to describe diphthongs in two different ways. (a) If the first phase is more open (⇒ **closed vs open**) than the second, it is a rising diphthong, as in the examples above. If the first phase is more closed, it is falling, e.g. [oa] in Fr. *bois* 'woods.' (b) In a different terminology, a diphthong is said to be rising if the first element carries less **stress**[1] than the second, as in Span. *país* 'country'; it is falling if the first element carries greater stress, as in the English examples above. There is much debate about whether diphthongs in English consist of two vowels, or of one vowel and one **glide**. Numerous orthographic conventions prevail, e.g. [aʊ] [aᵘ], [āʊw]. (⇒ *also* **diaeresis**, **syllable**)

References
⇒ **phonetics**

diphthongization

Sound change by which simple (long) **vowels** turn into variable vowels (**diphthongs**), due to a shift in **articulation** or to phonological or phonotactic pressures (⇒ **phonology**), e.g. in the **Great Vowel Shift** OE *īs* [iːs] > Mod. Eng. *ice* [ays], OE *hūs* [huːs] Mod. Eng. *house* [haʊs]. (⇒ *also* **push chain vs drag chain**)

References
Andersen, H. 1972. Diphthongization. *Lg.* 48.11–50.
Hayes, B. 1990. Dipthongization and coindexing. *Phonology* 7.31–71.
Rauch, I. 1967. *The Old High German diphthongization: a description of a phonemic change.* The Hague.
Vennemann, T. 1972. Phonetic detail in assimilation: problems in Germanic phonology. *Lg* 48.863–92.
⇒ **historical linguistics, language change, sound change**

direct method (*also* natural method)

Language-teaching method developed as an outgrowth of the natural method attributed to L. Sauveau (1826–1907) in the 1860s. The direct method, according to which instruction is to take place exclusively in the target language, became established in France and Germany around the turn of the century. Other goals and strategies that characterize this methodology include: the presentation of vocabulary through the use of pantomime, realia and visuals, thus avoiding translation; an inductive approach to grammar; the primacy of the spoken language and the emphasis on correct pronunciation; a reliance on question-answer exercise formats. It was only cautiously and marginally embraced in Britain and North America outside of commercial schools. Recent communicative approaches to language teaching have questioned the theoretical basis and techniques of the direct method, including its teacher-centered strategies, its disregard for process strategies, its lack of emphasis on sociopragmatic competency, etc. (⇒ *also* **language pedagogy, second language acquisition**)

References
Gouin, F. 1882. *The art of teaching and studying languages.* Trans. by H. Swan and V. Betts. London.
Krause, C.A. 1916. *The direct method in modern languages.* New York.
Richards, J.C. and T.S. Rodgers. 1986. *Approaches and methods in language teaching.* Cambridge.
Sauzé, E.B. de 1929. *The Cleveland plan for the teaching of modern languages with special reference to French.* (Rev. edn 1959.) Philadelphia, PA.

direct object

Syntactic function in **nominative languages** which, depending on the language, can be expressed morphologically, positionally, or structurally. The most common morphological marker is the **accusative**, although **dative** and **genitive** objects are sometimes treated as direct objects, due to their behavior. A characteristic of direct objects is that they become the subject in passive sentences: *Philip is eating the apple* ⇒ *The apple is being eaten.* In addition, the distinction between transitive (e.g. *to see, to love, to meet*) and intransitive verbs (e.g. *to sleep, to work*) depends on whether or not the verb selects a direct object. A direct object can usually be identified positionally by its unmarked position after the subject and in SVO languages (⇒ **word order**) immediately after the finite verb as well. In the constituent structure of a sentence the direct object is immediately dominated by the verbal or predicate phrase, in contrast to the subject which is immediately dominated by the sentence node. The term 'direct object' refers to its usual semantic function of denoting the thing that is directly affected by the action of the verb (**patient**).

References
Dryer, M. 1986. Primary objects, secondary objects and antidative. *Lg.* 62.808–45.
Moravcsik, E.A. 1978. Case marking of objects. In J.H. Greenberg (ed.), *Universals of human language.* Stanford, CA. Vol. 4, 250–89.
Plank, F. (ed.) 1984. *Objects: towards a theory of grammatical relations.* London.
⇒ **syntactic function**

direct speech ⇒ direct vs indirect discourse

direct vs indirect discourse

Form of recounting speech (statements, questions, as well as thoughts or wishes) either through direct quoting or through paraphrase. Indirect discourse is dependent on a previous utterance (either exactly known or reconstructable): *She said she wouldn't be here until tomorrow.* The change of direct into indirect discourse is often accompanied with a change in the deictic elements (pronouns, adverbs) and in some languages **mood** or **tense**: *She said, 'I will come tomorrow'* vs *(Yesterday) she said she would come today.*

References
Banfield, A. 1973. Narrative style and the grammar of direct and indirect speech. *FL* 10.1–39.
Bertolet, R. 1988. *What is said: a theory of indirect speech reports.* Dordrecht.
Coulmas, F. (ed.) 1986. *Direct and indirect speech:*

reported speech across languages. Berlin.

directive

1 A speech act whose main purpose consists in causing the person addressed to undertake a particular activity. Directives (e.g. requests, commands, and prohibitions) are performed not only by uttering **imperatives**[2], but also with the aid of **declarative sentences** (*You will come here this instant!*), gerund phrases (*No smoking*), elliptical expressions (*Quiet!, A cappuccino!, Over here!*), the impersonal passive (*Hard hats are to be worn on site*), non-embedded **complements** (*Just so you don't forget the milk*), and through modal expressions (*You ought to come right now!*).

Reference
Searle, J.R. 1975. A taxonomy of illocutionary acts. In K. Gunderson (ed.), *Language, mind and knowledge.* Minneapolis, MN. (Repr. in *Expression and meaning.* Cambridge, 1979. 1–29.)

2 Accusative of direction or goal accompanying verbs of motion (e.g. Lat. *domum ire* 'to go home').

disambiguation

Process and result of clarifying lexical or structural **ambiguity** (or **vagueness**) of linguistic expressions by the linguistic or extralinguistic context. (a) Linguistic disambiguation on the lexical level (⇒ **polysemy, homonymy**) is carried out as a rule by excluding semantically incompatible lexeme combinations: for example, the ambiguity of *The chicken is ready to eat* can be cleared up by following it with *so please serve it* or *so please feed it*, thus disambiguating *chicken₁* (= meat) from *chicken₂* (= live animal). (b) Disambiguation of structural ambiguity is carried out by explicit reformulation of the underlying **deep structure**. Thus, the two readings of the sentence *The investigation of the politician was applauded* can be disambiguated by the paraphrases P_1 *That the politician was being investigated was applauded* or P_2 *That the politician undertook the investigation was applauded.* Disambiguation through extralinguistic context depends on the particular situation, on prior knowledge, attitudes, expectations of the speaker/hearer as well as on non-verbal cues (gesture (⇒ **body language**), mimicry). Disambiguated **formal languages** are often used to describe meaning.

References
⇒ **ambiguity**

discontinuous elements

Linguistic elements which belong together, but whose linear concatenation is broken by another element, e.g. *a-whole-nother* where *another* is split by the insertion of *whole*. The description of discontinuous elements presents difficulties for the **phrase structure rules**, since according to these rules only adjacent constituents can comprise one constituent. In the drawing of discontinuous elements in a **tree diagram**, there is a crossing of branches which is formally excluded.

References
⇒ **transformational grammar**

discourse

Generic term for various types of **text**[2]. The term has been used with various differences in meaning: connected speech (Harris 1952); the product of an interactive process in a socio-cultural context (Pike 1954); performance (vs 'text' as a representation of the formal grammatical structure of discourse) (van Dijk 1974); talk (vs written prose, or 'text') (Cicourel 1975); conversational interaction (Coulthard 1977); 'language in context across all forms and modes' (Tannen 1981); and process (vs product, or 'text') (Brown and Yule 1983). (⇒ *also* **ethnography of speaking, functional grammar**)

References
Brown, G. and G. Yule. 1983. *Discourse analysis*. Cambridge.
Coulthard, M. 1977. *An introduction to discourse analysis*. London.
Coupland, N. (ed.) 1988. *Styles of discourse*. London.
Erdmann, P. 1990. *Discourse and grammar: focussing and defocussing in English*. Tübingen.
Fleischmann, S. and L.R. Waugh. 1991. *Discourse pragmatics and the verb: the evidence from Romance*. London.
Harris, Z. 1952. Discourse analysis. *Lg* 28.1–30.
Longacre, R.E. 1983. *The grammar of discourse*. New York.
McCarthy, M. and R. Carter. 1993. *Language as discourse*. London.
Pike, K.L. 1954. *Language in relation to a unified theory of the structure of human behavior*. The Hague. (2nd edn 1967).
Schriffin, D. 1993. *Approaches to discourse*. Oxford.
Tannen, D. 1979. What's in a frame? Surface evidence for underlying expectations. In R. Freedle (ed.), *New directions in discourse processing*. Norwood, NJ. 137–81.
Tannen, D. (ed.) 1981. Analyzing discourses. Gurt.
Van Dijk, T. 1974. *Philosophy of action and theory of narrative*. Amsterdam.

Journal
Discourse and Society.
⇒ **anaphora, conversation analysis, discourse analysis, pragmatics, tense**

discourse analysis

Cover term for various analyses of **discourse**. Motivated by linguistic terminology and theory (⇒ **formal logic, structuralism, transformational grammar**) it is used synonymously with **text analysis**, with a particular interest in wellformedness (⇒ **coherence, cohesion**) and deductive rules (e.g. rules for **speech acts**). While in this strand of research, texts are mainly taken to be static products (**discourse grammar, text linguistics**), there is another strand influenced by **functional grammar, psycholinguistics**, and approaches to cognitive science that emphasizes the dynamic character of discourse as construction and interpretation processes by the speaker/writer and the listener/reader (see Brown and Yule 1983). According to Van Dijk (1985), discourse analysis has become a new cross-disciplinary field of analysis since the early 1970s. It is of interest to disciplines such as anthropology and sociolinguistics (**ethnography of speaking**), **artificial intelligence**, cognitive science, philosophy of language (**speech act theory**), **psycholinguistics**, sociology of language (**conversation analysis**), **rhetoric (style)**, and text linguistics. For an overview see van Dijk (1985).

References
Brown, G. and G. Yule. 1983. *Discourse analysis*. Cambridge.
Coulthard, M. 1977. *An introduction to discourse analysis*. London.
—— (ed.) 1992. *Advances in spoken discourse analysis*. London.
Givón, T. (ed.) 1979. *Syntax and semantics*, vol. 12: *Discourse and syntax*. New York.
Labov, W. and D. Fanshel. 1977. *Therapeutic discourse*. New York.
Levinson, S. 1983. *Pragmatics*. Cambridge.
Mann, W.C. and S.A. Thompson (eds) 1992. *Discourse description: diverse linguistic analyses of a fund-raising text*. Amsterdam.
Myhill, J. 1992. *Typological discourse analysis*. Oxford.
Petöfi, J. (ed.) 1987. *Text and discourse constitution: empirical aspects, theoretical approaches*. Berlin.
Potter, J. and M. Wetherell. 1987. *Discourse and social psychology: beyond attitudes and behaviour*. London.
Salkie, R. 1995. *Text and discourse analysis*. London.
Steiner, E.E. and R. Veltmann (eds) 1988. *Pragmatics, discourse and text: some systematically inspired approaches*. London.
Stubbs, M. 1983. *Discourse analysis*. Oxford.
Stutterheim, C. v. and W. Klein. 1989. Referential movement in descriptive and narrative discourse. In R. Dietrich and C. Graumann (eds), *Language processing in social contexts*. Amsterdam. 39–76.
Van Dijk, T. (ed.) 1985. *Handbook of discourse analysis*, 4 vols. London.

Journals
Discourse and Society.
Discourse Processes.
⇒ **discourse grammar, text linguistics**

discourse grammar

An area of investigation within **text linguistics**, discourse grammar involves the analysis and presentation of grammatical regularities that overlap sentences in texts. In contrast to the pragmatically oriented direction of text linguistics, discourse grammar departs from a grammatical concept of text that is analogous to 'sentence'. The object of investigation is primarily the phenomenon of **cohesion**, thus the syntactic-morphological connecting of texts by **textphoric, recurrence**, and **connective**.

References
Greimas, A.J. 1966. *Sémantique structurale.* Paris.
Longacre, R.E. 1983. *The grammar of discourse.* New York.
Petöfi, J.S. and H. Rieser (eds) 1973. *Studies in text grammar.* Dordrecht.
Rieser, H. 1978. On the development of text grammar. In W. Dressler (ed.), *Current trends in textlinguistics.* Berlin. 6–20.
Van Dijk, T.A. 1972. *Some aspects of text grammars: a study in theoretical linguistics and poetics.* The Hague.

Bibliography
Lohmann, P. 1988. Connectedness of texts: a bibliographical survey. In J.S. Petöfi (ed.), *Text and discourse constitution.* Berlin. 478–501. Part 2 in W. Heydrich *et al.* (eds), *Connexity and coherence.* New York.

discourse marker (*also* discourse particle)

Linguistic devices that help structure **discourse**. Among such markers are expressions that are equivalent to sentences such as *uh* (⇒ **interjection**), syntactic constructions such as left dislocation (⇒ **left vs right dislocation**) and syntactically integrated expressions such as **adjuncts** or **conjunctions**. Discourse markers have many functions, some of which overlap. In (a) **turn-taking**, they help structure the **turn** (e.g. *well* in first position and *you know* in final position), indicate the end of a turn (e.g. *uh*) (⇒ **back channel**), or order the next speaker's turn (e.g. when the current speaker uses a tag question like *right?*). In (b) topic management, discourse markers foreground a topic (e.g. with syntagms like *concerning X* or left dislocation) or indicate that the current speaker is digressing from the current topic (e.g. with displacement markers like *by the way*). Discourse markers also (c) indicate the speaker's attitude (e.g. with attitudinal disjuncts (⇒ **disjunction**), or (d) help organize the overall discourse structure, e.g. by indicating the beginning or end of paragraphs or sequences (e.g. with *first, then, finally, and then*). (⇒ *also* **discourse analysis**)

References
Abraham, W. (ed.) 1990. *Discourse particles.* Amsterdam.
—— (ed.) 1991a. *Discourse particles: descriptive and theoretical investigations on the logical, syntactic and pragmatic properties of discourse particles in German and English.* Amsterdam.
—— (ed.) 1991b. *Discourse particles across languages.* Berlin and New York.
Ameka, F. (ed.) 1992. *Interjections* (special issue of *Journal of Pragmatics*) 18.101–301.
Fraser, B. 1990. An approach to discourse marker. *JPrag* 14.383–95.
Labov, W. and D. Fanshel. 1977. *Therapeutic discourse.* New York.
Maynard, S.K. 1986. On back-channel behavior in Japanese and English casual conversation. *Linguistics* 24.1079–108.
Redeker, G. 1990. Ideational and pragmatic markers of discourse structure. *JPrag* 14.367–81.
Sacks, H. and E. Schegloff. 1973. Opening up closings. *Semiotica* 8.289–327.
Sacks, H., E. Schegloff, and G. Jefferson. 1974. A simplest systematics for the organization of turn-taking in conversations. *Lg* 50.696–735.
Schiffrin, D. 1987. *Discourse markers.* Cambridge.
Wierzbicka, A. (ed.) 1992. *Journal of Pragmatics*, special issue on particles. 10.519–645.
⇒ **back channel, conversation analysis, discourse analysis, particle**

discourse particle ⇒ discourse marker

discourse representation structure ⇒ discourse representation theory

discourse representation theory

Variant of **discourse semantics** developed by H. Kamp which first assigns so-called discourse representation structures (DRS) to simple discourse (namely sequences of **declarative sentences**) and then assigns truth conditions to them. Often abbreviated as DRT, its central notion is that of 'discourse referents,' a type of place-holders for objects to which the various text predications – even those in different sentences (text **anaphora**) – refer and which are, in the default case, treated as existence-quantifying variables in truth conditions. The **scope** of a discourse referent is depicted graphically by a box. While Kamp was formulating his theory, I. Heim independently developed a similar type of discourse semantics in her 'file change semantics.'

References
Asher, N. 1986. Belief in discourse representation theory. *JPL* 5.127–89.
Heim, I. 1982. The semantics of definite and indefinite noun phrases. Dissertation, Amherst, MA.
Kamp, H. 1981. A theory of truth and semantic

representation. In J. Groenendijk *et al.* (eds), *Formal methods in the study of language*. Amsterdam. 277–322.

Kamp, H. and U. Reyle. 1993. *From discourse to logic*. Dordrecht.
Oakhill, J. and A. Garnham. 1992. *Discourse representation and text processing* (Special issue of *Language and Cognitive Processes*). Hove.
Stirling, L. 1993. *Switch reference and discourse representation*. Cambridge.
⇒ **model-theoretic semantics**

discourse semantics

A type of semantics that focuses on the semantic relations of sentences within a **text**. Central concepts include **anaphora** and **cataphora**, which extend beyond sentential boundaries, and phenomena such as **model subordination**. (⇒ *also* **discourse representation theory**)

Reference
Seuren, P.A.M. 1985. *Discourse semantics*. Oxford.

discovery procedure

In general, a procedure used to elicit linguistic regularities (⇒ **operational procedure**). In particular, methods and operations employed in structural linguistics which seek to 'reveal' by means of segmentation and classification the relevant fundamental categories, and their relation to one another, of a given language on the basis of a finite number of sentences.

References
⇒ **operational procedures**

discreteness [Lat. *discretus* 'separate']

Fundamental characteristic of linguistically relevant units. Definable boundaries are a prerequisite for linguistic analysis by means of **segmentation** and **substitution**. The discrete elements obtained by such procedures have the function of either distinguishing between meanings (= **phonemes**) or carrying meaning (= **morphemes**).

disjoint reference

Reading of pronominal expressions in complex sentences whose reference does not correspond to nouns or denotations present in the sentence. In the ambiguous expression *Tanya proudly showed the picture she drew*, *Tanya* and *she* denote by disjoint reference two different people, e.g. that someone other than Tanya drew the picture that Tanya is showing. On the **set theory** definition of disjoint reference, ⇒ **coreferentiality**, **set**.

References
⇒ **personal pronoun**

disjunction [Lat. *disiunctio* 'separation']

1 In **formal logic** the conjunction of two elementary propositions p and q by the logical **particle** or_1 which is true if and only if at least one of the elementary propositions is true. Or_1 corresponds to Lat. *vel* ('or also') which can be paraphrased by 'one or the other, or both.' This inclusive (i.e. non-exclusive) *or*, which is basic to disjunction, must be differentiated from the exclusive or_2 (Lat. *aut ... aut ...*) which means 'either one or the other, but not both'), compare or_1 (*Louise is either sad or tired, (or perhaps both)*) with or_2 (*Louise is either older or younger than her friend, (but in no case both)*). In everyday usage the exclusive or_2 is more common (expressed by *either/or* or *otherwise*), since the inclusive reading is usually barred by the pragmatic context. This relation is represented as follows in the (two-place) **truth table**:

p	q	$p \vee q^1$	$p \vee q^2$
t	t	t	f
t	f	t	t
f	t	t	t
f	f	f	f

The term 'disjunction' refers to the operation of the two-place sentence operator *or* as well as to the propositional connective defined by it. The propositions connected by *or* are not necessarily semantically cohesive. For that reason the connection *Socrates is a philosopher or Aristotle is a unicorn* is 'true' (because the first part of the sentence is true), while it would have to be rejected as an utterance in an actual speech situation as an unsuccessful speech act (⇒ **speech act theory**). With the aid of **set theory**, disjunction can be semantically characterized as the union of both model sets that make the propositions connected with each other true.

References
Pelletier, J.F. 1977. Or. *TL* 4.61–74.
⇒ **formal logic**

2 In **unification grammar** the dual of the operation of unification, used, for example, in **Functional Unification Grammar** (FUG), lexical **Unification Grammar** (LUG), and **Head-driven Phrase Structure Grammar** (HPSG). The disjunction of two feature structures indicates the unification bundle of the denotata of their two disjuncts. The disjunctive feature structure (in curly brackets) in the following example stands for the group of all verbs, which are in the plural or in the first or second person singular:

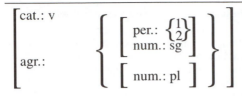

Equivalent notations for disjunction:

$$\left\{ \begin{matrix} 1 \\ 2 \end{matrix} \right\} = 1 \vee 2 = 1 \cap 2$$

For discussion of the necessity of disjunction in unification grammar, see Karttunen (1984), for algorithms for the implementation of disjunctive unification grammars, see Kasper (1987) and Eisele and Dörre (1988).

References
Eisele, A. and J. Dörre. 1988. Unification of disjunctive feature descriptions. In *ACL Proceedings*. New York. 26.286–94.
Karttunen, L. 1984. Features and values. In *Coling 84*. Stanford, CA. 28–33.
Kasper, R.T. 1987. A unification method for disjunctive feature descriptions. In *ACL Proceedings*. Stanford, CA. 25.235–42.

disjunctive question

Interrogative sentence in the form of two *yes/ no*-questions joined by *or* (*Is Caroline coming today or tomorrow?*) which cannot be answered by *yes* or *no*. Disjunctive questions are mostly ambiguous but can at the same time be interpreted as **yes/no-questions** (e.g. *Is Caroline coming today?* or *Is Caroline coming tomorrow?* vs *Is Caroline coming today or tomorrow?*).

dislocation

Term for syntactic constructions in which sentence elements appear at or outside the sentence boundary. In a broad classification there exist left and right dislocation (⇒ **left vs right dislocation**). Related constructions are **hanging topic, extraposition, exbraciation, apposition**. An unambiguous classification of each type is not always possible; criteria for identification include morphological and intonational characteristics, typical introductory phrases, pronominal (copies) and theme-rheme (⇒ **theme vs rheme**) considerations.

References
Altmann, H. 1981. *Formen der 'Herausstellung' im Deutschen*. Tübingen.
⇒ **exbraciation, extraposition, word order**

dissimilation [Lat. *dissimilis* 'unlike']

Process and result of differentiation of two similar sounds with a view to greater clarity, e.g. Eng. *pilgrim* < Lat. *peregrīnus*, where the

first *r* has dissimilated into *l*. The opposite process is known as **assimilation**.

References
Dressler, W.U. 1977. Phono-morphological dissimilation. *Phonologica* 1976.41–8.
⇒ **phonetics, sound change**

dissimilation of aspirates ⇒ Grassmann's law

distant assimilation ⇒ assimilation

distinctive [Lat. *distinguere* 'to mark off as separate']

Characteristics of (phonological) features that function to distinguish meaning. (⇒ *also* **distinctive feature, phonology**)

References
⇒ **distinctive feature**

distinctive feature

Class of phonetically defined components of phonemes that function to distinguish meaning. In contrast to redundant features, distinctive features constitute relevant phonological features. In the structuralist framework, phonemes are described as 'bundles' of distinctive features, e.g. /p/ as [+consonant, –voiced, +bilabial, –nasal], with the differentiation from /b/ resting alone on the distinctive feature of [+voiced]. The number of distinctive features is smaller than the number of phonemes, for example Jakobson and Halle (1956) have suggested a universal **binary** system (⇒ **binary opposition**) of twelve distinctive features believed to be sufficient to describe all languages of the world. The differentiation of distinctive features is based on spectrally defined and acoustically analyzed criteria such as the position of the **formants**. **Distinctive feature theory**, based on the premise that all humans are psychologically and physically the same, is a fundamental concept of structural and generative phonology. It has further applications in other levels of linguistic description, such as **semantic primitives, componential analysis**, and **lexical decomposition** in semantics.

References
Chomsky, N. and M. Halle. 1968. *The sound pattern of English*. New York.
Clements, G.N. 1985. The geometry of phonological features. *PY* 2.225–52.
Jakobson, R. and M. Halle. 1956. *Fundamentals of language*. The Hague. (2nd rev. edn. 1975.)
Jakobson, R., G. Faist, and M. Halle. 1951. *Preliminaries to speech analysis: the distinctive features and their correlates*. Cambridge, MA. (7th edn 1967.)

Stevens, K.N., S.J. Keyser, and H. Kawasaki. 1986. Towards a phonetic and phonological theory of redundant features. In J. Perkell and D.H. Klatt (eds), *Invariance and variability of speech processes*. Hillsdale, NJ. 426–49.
⇒ **phonetics**, **phonology**

distinctive feature theory

In **phonology**, a system developed to describe the elemental structure of language sounds that are based on articulatory and/or acoustic characteristics or productive mechanisms. (⇒ *also* **distinctive feature**, **markedness**)

References
Chomsky, N. and M. Halle. 1968. *The sound pattern of English*. New York.
Halle, M. 1983. On distinctive features and their articulatory implementation. *NL&LT* 1:1.91–105.
Hyman, L.M. 1975. *Phonology: theory and analysis*. New York.
Jakobson, R., G. Fant and M. Halle. 1951. *Preliminaries to speech analysis*. Cambridge, MA. (7th edn 1967).
Jakobson, R. and M. Halle. 1956. *Fundamentals of language*. The Hague. (2nd rev. edn 1975.)
Ladefoged, P. 1971. *Preliminaries to linguistic phonetics*. Chicago, IL.

distinguisher

In Katz and Fodor's (1963) **interpretive semantics**, a distinguisher is a subgroup of meaning features that denote the specific reading of an expression. In contrast to systematically occurring **semantic features** such as sex opposition (which systematically denotes the semantic difference in word pairs like *man : woman, bride : groom, rooster : hen*), distinguishers occur only as non-systematic, idiosyncratic features, i.e. they are linguistically irrelevant. Thus, the various readings of *ball* can be rendered by the distinguishers [+ for the purpose of dancing] and [+spherical].

Reference
Katz, J.J. and J.A. Fodor. 1963. The structure of a semantic theory. *Lg* 39.170–210.

distribution (*also* co-occurrence)

The collective environments of all established features. In American **distributionalism** (see Harris 1954), distribution is the primary criterion for determining and classifying linguistic units. On the basis of **propositional logic** and **set theory** the following types of distribution can be distinguished. (a) Equivalent distribution: two elements occur in the same environment either in (i) **free variation** (= free alternation or **correlation**) without distinguishing meaning, e.g. in the alternation of [iː] and [ay] in *either*; or in (ii) contrastive distribution, i.e. functioning as distinguishers of meaning, e.g.

initial /g/, /k/, /t/ *game, came, tame* (⇒ **minimal pair**). (b) Partially equivalent distribution: two elements occur largely, but not exclusively, in the same environment, in which either (i) the distribution of the one element includes that of the other, e.g. the distribution of the velar plosives /k/ and /g/ includes that of the velar nasal /ŋ/ since the first two occur word-medially and word-finally, while the last one does not occur word-initially; or (ii) the distribution of two elements overlaps (also: partially complementary), /h/ and /ŋ/, both of which occur word-medially (*inherent, angle*), while only /h/ occurs word-initially (*heart*) and only /ŋ/ occurs word-finally (*song*). (c) **Complementary distribution**: two elements never occur in the same environment, e.g. [t] and [tʰ] are said to be in a relation of complementary distribution since the latter does not occur after word-initial /s/. Distribution is used to determine and define different basic linguistic elements: equivalent distribution uncovers **phonemes** functioning as distinguishers of meaning, while complementary distribution uncovers **allophones** and **allomorphs**, among others.

References
Harris, Z. 1954. Distributional structure. *Word* 10.146–62.
⇒ **distributionalism**

distribution class

A class of linguistic elements, such as **phonemes** or **morphemes**, constituted by means of distribution analysis, i.e. classified and segmented on the basis of occurrence in identical environments.

References
⇒ **distributionalism**

distributionalism (*also* taxonomic analysis, taxonomic structuralism)

Branch of **American structuralism** in the 1940s and 1950s characterized by the works of Harris, Bloch, Trager, Joos, and others, which superseded the Bloomfield era. Harris' *Methods in Structural Linguistics* (1951) is viewed as the standard work of this phase. The goal of distributionalism is an experimentally verifiable, objective description of the relations inherent in the systems of individual languages, exclusive of all subjective and semantic factors (**semantics**). These relations are the result of the **distribution** of the individual elements among the various hierarchical linguistic levels (**phonology**, **morphology**, **syntax**), i.e. the derivation and classification of linguistic elements results from their occurrence in the sentence. The structure of each individual language can be described by means of experimental methods, the so-called **discovery procedures**, in which essentially two analytical steps are applied: (a) **segmentation** of the material through **substitution**, i.e. through paradigmatic interchangeability of elements having the same function (⇒ **paradigm**); and (b) **classification** of elements as **phonemes**, **morphemes**, among others, on the basis of their distribution and environment in the sentence. These analytical methods derive largely from research into Native American languages, which explains the asemantic character of the procedure: since the linguistic analysis had to be carried out without knowledge of the given language (especially its **meaning**), the purely physical description of distribution was elevated to the highest principle, and meaning was likewise regarded as a function of distribution. Fundamental criticism, revision, and extension, especially with regard to transformational aspects, are found in Postal (1964a).

References
Bloch, B. 1942. *Outline of linguistic analysis*. Baltimore, MD.
———— 1948. A set of postulates for phonetic analysis. *Lg* 24.2–46.
Chomsky, N. 1964. *Current issues in linguistic theory*. The Hague.
Fries, C.C. 1961. The Bloomfield 'school.' In C. Mohrmann *et al.* (eds), *Trends in European and American linguistics 1930–1960*. Utrecht. 196–224.
Harris, Z.S. 1946. From morpheme to utterance. *Lg* 22.161–83.
———— 1951. *Methods in structural linguistics*. Chicago, IL.
———— 1954. Distributional structure. *Word* 10.146–62.
Nida, E. 1946. *Morphology: the descriptive analysis of words*. Ann Arbor, MI. (Repr. 1949.)
Postal, P.M. 1964a. *Constituent structure: a study of contemporary models of syntactic description*. Bloomington, IN.
———— 1964b. Limitations of phrase structure grammars. In J.A. Fodor and J.J. Katz (eds), *The structure of language: readings in the philosophy of language*. Englewood Cliffs, NJ. 137–54.
Wells, R.S. 1947. Immediate constituents. *Lg* 23.71–117.
⇒ **American structuralism, linguistics, structuralism, transformational grammar**

distributive

Subgroup of **numerals** formed by words or phrases such as *apiece, each, per person*, where the units in question are distributed to some or all members of a group individually: *They will receive six books each.*

distributive reading ⇒ **distributive vs non-distributive reading**

distributive vs non-distributive reading

In nouns denoting sets, reference to the given set may relate to its individual elements ('distributive') or to the set as a whole ('non-distributive'). In sentences, such reference causes ambiguity if the meanings of the other elements do not exclude a particular reading. Thus, the sentence *The team is responsible for the defeat* can be understood as both 'each player is responsible' and 'the team as a whole is responsible,' while the meaning of the verb *surround* in *The police are surrounding the demonstrators* is contradictory to the distributive reading. The use of determiners or quantifiers like *every* and *all* may disambiguate a sentence, as in *Every human dies, All humans die*.

Reference
Scha, R.J. 1981. Distributive, collective, and cumulative quantification. In J. Groenendijk, T. Janssen, and M. Stokhof (eds), *Formal methods in the study of language*. Amsterdam. 483–512.

dittography

Writing error in which a single letter or syllable is written as a double letter or syllable. The inverse is known as **haplography**.

dittology

Accidental or conventionalized repetition of a syllable, e.g. *dittolology* or *preventive* ~ *preventative*. The opposite process is known as **haplology**.

domain

1 *Function*
2 Term introduced into **sociolinguistics** by J. Fishman, denoting a bundle of social situations that are characterized by specific settings and role relationships between the interactants, as well as by typical themes (e.g. school, family, workplace, state administration, etc.). Thus, the domain 'family' comprises a number of different ('familiar') situations with generally accepted norms of behavior. One of these norms relates to the choice of an appropriate – informal – linguistic variety, for example, in the case of diglossic linguistic situations (⇒ **diglossia**) the choice of the 'lower,' non-standard (e.g. dialectal) variety.

References
Fishman, J. 1964. Language maintenance and language shift as a field of inquiry. *Linguistics* 9.32–70.
———— 1965. Who speaks what language to whom

and when? *La Linguistique* 2.67–88.

Mioni, A. 1987. Domain. In U. Ammon *et al.* (eds), *Sociolinguistics. An international handbook of the science of language and society.* Berlin and New York. 170–8.

domain extension

A concept developed by Koster (1986) in **Government and Binding theory**, whereby prototypical local domains can be extended on the basis of language-specific or lexical factors to less local domains. This makes possible grammatical relations outside the prototypical local domain. The so-called **bridge verbs** are domain-extending for **movement transformations**. For example, in *Who$_i$ do you think Philip saw t$_i$*, the object can be questioned out of the embedded clause.

Reference
Koster, J. 1987. *Domains and dynasties: the radical autonomy of syntax.* Dordrecht.

domination

A term from **phrase structure grammar**. In a **tree diagram** a constituent *A* dominates another constituent *B* if *B* is a constituent of *A*. In other words, *A* dominates *B* if *A* is on the path from *B* to the root of the tree diagram. That is, domination occurs in **phrase structure rules** of the form $A \to \ldots B \ldots$

References
⇒ **phrase structure grammar**

dorsal [Lat. *dorsum* 'back']

Speech sound classified according to its **articulator** (**dorsum** = tongue), e.g. [k], [ŋ], and [g] in *king*. A distinction is drawn between predorsal, mediodorsal, and postdorsal sounds, especially with regard to the description of the **articulation** of certain **vowels**. In such cases one usually speaks of 'front,' 'middle,' and 'back' vowels.

References
⇒ **phonetics**

dorsum

The back of the tongue. The **articulator** used to form **dorsal** sounds. (⇒ *also* **articulation**)

double articulation

Structural characteristic of natural languages which distinguishes them from other systems of communication. According to Martinet (1965), linguistic expressions can be broken down into two different levels: (a) the smallest meaning-bearing level (⇒ **morpheme**, or in Martinet's terminology **moneme**); this is the smallest segment consisting of form and meaning; and (b) the smallest units which distinguish or contrast meaning (⇒ **phoneme**); the latter units have form, but no meaning in themselves. The second structuring at the phonological level leads to the infinite productivity of natural language based on a few dozen different sounds (or phonemes) and corresponding combinatory rules. While bird calls, traffic signs, or groans (as an expression of pain) can only be broken down into meaning-bearing units at the first level, and not into any smaller contrasting units, linguistic expressions can be analyzed at both levels: *no pet/s allow/ed* consists of at least five meaning-bearing units, whereas the expression *pet* is composed of three phonemes. Thus double articulation is the basis for the economy and creativity of human language.

References
Martinet, A. 1965. *La Linguistique synchronique, études et recherches.* Paris.
——— 1966. *Elements of general linguistics; with a foreword by L.R. Palmer*, trans. by Elisabeth Palmer. Chicago, IL.
Martinet, A., J. Martinet, and H. Walter (eds) 1969. *La Linguistique: guide alphabétique. Sous la direction d'André Martinet.* Paris.
⇒ **animal communication**

double-bind theory

Term introduced by G. Bateson and P. Watzlawick in their research on schizophrenia for a pathological behavior pattern in which a speaker *A* simultaneously directs two contradictory messages to an emotionally dependent hearer *B*. Because of the asymmetrical relationship between *A* and *B* (e.g. parent–child), *B* is not in a position to criticize the paradoxical manner of behavior or to point out the absurdity of the expression. According to this theory, continued exposure to such contrary messages can lead to schizophrenic symptoms. The contradictory directions can be expressed through both verbal and non-verbal channels, e.g. words of approval combined with a look of rejection. A decisive factor in the double-bind theory is the impossibility of escape from the paradox.

References
Bateson, G., D.D. Jackson, J. Haley, and J. Weakland. 1956. Toward a theory of schizophrenia. *BSci* 1.251–64.
Bugental, D.F. *et al.* 1970. Perception and contradictory meanings, conveyed by verbal and non-verbal channels. *JPSP* 16.647–55.
Gunderson, J.G., J.H. Autry, and L.R. Mosher. 1974. Special report: schizophrenia 1973. *Schizophrenia Bulletin* 9.15–54.
Liem, J.H. 1974. Effects of verbal communications of parents and children: a comparison of normal and schizophrenic families. *Journal of Consulting and Clinical Psychology* 42.438–50.

Watzlawick, P., J.H. Beavin, and D.D. Jackson. 1967. *Pragmatics of human communication: a study of interactional patterns, pathologies, and paradoxes*. New York.

double consonant ⇒ geminate

downdrift

Property of **tonal languages** where the absolute pitch of the tones gradually sinks from the beginning of the sentence to the end even though the tones still maintain their value relative to one another.

References
⇒ tonology

downstep

In **tonal languages**, toneme (⇒ **tone**) which, after a certain number of syllables, causes the absolute pitch of the following tones to sink, their values relative to one another remaining unchanged. This phenomenon occurs in some West African languages.

References
⇒ tonology

DP ⇒ determiner phrase

drag chain ⇒ push chain vs drag chain

Dravidian

Language group of South-East Asia with about twenty-five languages and 175 million speakers, primarily in southern and eastern India and Sri Lanka, as well as in Pakistan (Brahui). These languages, probably originally extending over the whole Indian subcontinent, were displaced by the languages of the **Indo-Aryan** immigrants. The most important languages are Telugu (approx. 53 million speakers), **Tamil** (approx. 45 million speakers), Malayalam (approx. 28 million speakers), and Kannada (approx. 28 million speakers), and have writing systems with a literary tradition of more than 2,000 years.

Ellis (1816) demonstrated the relatedness of the major Dravidian languages; the later work of R.A. Caldwell also was foundational. The Dravidian languages are possibly related to Elamite, a dead language of Iran. They evince numerous lexical borrowings from Indo-Aryan, while Dravidian languages have in turn influenced the Indo-Aryan languages phonologically, morphologically, and syntactically.

Characteristics: strongly **agglutinating**, suffixal languages with many compound constructions. The gender system points to an original [± masculine] in the singular and [± human] in the plural. Word order SOV; rich case system.

The subject of stative verbs and verbs of sensation is frequently in the dative. No clause conjunction; instead, frequent participial constructions (converbs) for subordinating clauses. Complex system of auxiliaries with which the attitude of the speaker can be expressed (e.g. pejorative). The more widely spoken Dravidian languages are largely diglossic (⇒ **diglossia**), i.e. they distinguish between formal and informal registers.

References
Andorov, M.S. 1970. *Dravidian languages*. Moscow.
Bloch, J. 1946. *Structure grammaticale des langues dravidiennes*. Paris.
Emeneau, M.B. 1969. The non-literary Dravidian languages. In T.A. Sebeok (ed.), *Current trends in linguistics*. The Hague. Vol. 5, 334–42.
Krishnamurti, B. 1969. Comparative Dravidian studies. In T.A. Sebeok (ed.), *Current trends in linguistics*. The Hague. Vol. 5, 309–33.
McAlpin, D. 1981. *Proto-Elamo-Dravidian: the evidence and its implications*. Philadelphia, PA.
Zvelebil, K. 1977. *A sketch of comparative Dravidian morphology*. The Hague.
——— 1990. *Dravidian linguistics: an introduction*. Pondicherry.

Grammars
Agesthialingom, S. and N.R. Nair (eds) 1981. *Dravidian syntax*. Annamalainagar.
Bray, D.D.S. 1909–34. *The Brahui language*, 2 vols. Calcutta (Repr. 1986.)
Caldwell, R. 1856. *A comparative grammar of the Dravidian South-Indian family of languages*. (3rd rev. edn 1913 by J.L. Wyatt and T.R. Pillai. London. Repr. New Delhi 1974.)
Ellis, F.W. 1816. Note to the introduction. In *A grammar of the Teloogoo language*, by A.D. Campbell.
Frohnmeyer, L.J. 1913. *A progressive grammar of the Malayalam language*, 2nd rev. edn. (Repr. 1979.) Mangalore.
Krishnamurti, B. and J.P.L. Gwynn. 1985. *A grammar of modern Telugu*. Delhi.
Schiffman, H.F. 1979. *A reference grammar of spoken Kannada*. Seattle and London. (Repr. 1983.)
Sridhar, S.N. (ed.) 1990. *Kannada*. London.
Syamala, K. 1981. *An intensive course in Malayalam*. Mysore.

Dictionaries
Kittel, F. 1894. *A Kannada–English dictionary*. Mangalore and Leipzig.
Sankaranarayana, P. 1986. *Telugu–English dictionary*. 10th rev. and enlarged edn. New Delhi.
Malayalam lexicon. 1965–. Published by the University of Kerala. Trivandrum. Vol. 6 1988.

Etymological dictionary
Burrow, T. and M.B. Emeneau. 1960. *A Dravidian etymological dictionary*. (2nd edn 1984.) London.

Journal
International Journal of Dravidian Linguistics.

drift

Sapir's (1921) term for intralinguistic tendencies on the basis of which the direction of **language change** can be predicted. Sapir notes three interdependent grammatical trends in English: (a) loss of case marking; (b) stabilization of word order; and (c) invariability of word forms. These drifts, which are not only characteristic of English, are the result of the loss of final syllables in **Germanic** which, in turn, is seen as a consequence of Germanic stress relationships. More recent studies (see Vennemann 1975) have attempted to confirm drift as a **universal** characteristic of language change.

References
Lakoff, R. 1972. Another look at drift. In R. Stockwell and R. Macaulay (eds), *Historical linguistics and generative theory*. Bloomington, IN. 172–98.
Sapir, E. 1921. *Language*. New York.
Vennemann, T. 1975. An explanation of drift. In C.N. Li (ed.), *Word order and word order change*. Austin, TX. 269–305.

DRS (discourse representation structure) ⇒ **discourse representation theory**

DRT ⇒ **discourse representation theory**

d-structure ⇒ **deep structure**

dual [Lat. *dualis* 'relating to two persons or things']

Subcategory of **number** which indicates elements appearing in pairs as opposed to single elements (**singular**) or more than two elements (**plural**). Remnants of the dual, which was originally fully operative in **Indo-European**, can be found in **Greek**, **Indo-Iranian**, and **Gothic** in the personal pronouns (e.g. Goth. nominative *weis* 'we' vs *wit* 'we two'), as well as in some **Slavic** languages.

References
⇒ **number**

dummy element

Linguistic elements whose only function is to fill empty syntactic positions in certain syntactic structures where the **valence** of the verb requires that they be filled (e.g. *it* in *It is raining*). They are lexically and morphologically unspecified and often do not agree formally with other elements in the sentence. When paraphrased, they can usually be deleted: *it* in *It is impossible for him to come on time* vs *For him to come on time is impossible* (⇒ **extraposition**).

dummy symbol

Symbol used in generative **transformational grammar** which is lexically and morphologically unspecified and has the function of marking the syntactic position of categories.

durative vs non-durative (*also* aterminative/cursive vs terminative, immutative vs mutative, **imperfective vs perfective**, incomplete vs complete, **telic vs atelic**)

Fundamental subcategorization of **aspect**. Durative verbs describe processes which are temporally not delimited (*burn, work, read*), in contrast to non-durative verbs, whose lexical meaning implies temporal delimitation, an accomplishment, or a change in the process involved (*burn down, burn up*). This distinction determines the choice of temporal modifiers indicating the duration of the action. Durative verbs can be used with modifiers such as *for two hours* or *for a long time*, but not with modifiers such as *in an hour*: *The house has been burning for two hours/*in two hours*. Cf. the non-durative verb: *The house burnt down in two hours/*for two hours*.

In addition, non-durative verbs can be recognized as such because their imperfective variants (*She was eating an apple when I came in*) do not imply the perfective variant: *She ate an apple*. Durative verbs have numerous subcategories: (a) iterative verbs (⇒ **iterative vs semelfactive**), which indicate the repetition of a process (e.g. *breathe, flutter*); (b) **diminutive** verbs which indicate a low intensity of the action expressed by the verb. Non-durative verbs can be divided into the following categories: (a) **ingressive** verbs or **inchoative** verbs, which indicate the beginning of an action (*burst into flames, fall asleep*); (b) **resultative** or accomplishment verbs, which denote a process and its final result (*burn down, shatter*); (c) **transformative verbs**, which indicate a change from one state into another (*age, cool off*); and (d) **punctual** or achievement verbs, which imply a sudden change in the situation (*explode, find*). In the literature on aspect the distinction between durative and non-durative is often equated with that of **imperfective vs perfective**. In a narrower sense, durative vs non-durative is identified with non-punctual vs punctual.

References
⇒ **aspect**

Dutch

Germanic language which developed from West Low Franconian and has two historical dialect variants: **Flemish** (south) and Dutch (north). Dutch is the official language (approx. 20 million speakers) of the Netherlands and its overseas territories and is the second official language of Belgium next to French. **Afrikaans**, which developed from seventeenth-century dialects, is now an independent language. The oldest literary attestations (Middle Dutch) date from 1150 in the area of Limburg-Brabant (Henric van Feldeke). Since the seventeenth century the dialect of Amsterdam has been considered the written norm (e.g. the official Bible translation of the *Statenbijebel*, 1626–37), while Dutch is spoken in the south only as the dialect variant 'Flemish.' With the signing of the Nederlandse Taalunie (Netherlandic Language Union, 1980) century-long attempts at unifying the Netherlands and Belgium were officially recognized.

In its older forms, Dutch was not much farther removed from High German than Low German, and still today shows marked similarities to **German**, though it has preserved a number of archaic forms in its lexicon (cf. *oorlog* 'war' vs Ger. *Krieg, geheugen* 'memory' vs Ger. *Gedächtnis, eeuw* 'century' vs Ger. *Jahrhundert*). The nominal inflectional system of Dutch is much more reduced than that of German.

References
Booij, G. 1995. *The phonology of Dutch*. Oxford.
Brachin, P. 1987. *Die niederländische Sprache*. Hamburg.
Devleeschouwer, J. 1981. Het ontstaan der Nederlandse Franse taalgrens. *Naamkunde* 13.188–225.
Geerts, G. 1987. *Dutch reference grammar*, 3rd edn. Leiden.
Overdiep, G.S. 1949. *Stilistische Grammatica van het moderne Nederlands*, 2nd edn. Zwolle.
Shetter, W.Z. 1994. *Dutch: an essential grammar*. London.
Van Haeringen, C.B. 1960. *Netherlandic language research: men and works in the study of Dutch*, 2nd edn. Leiden.
Van Loey, A. 1970. *Schoenfeld's Historische Grammatica van het Nederlands*, 8th edn. Zutphen.

History
Donaldson, B.C. 1983. *Dutch: a linguistic history of Holland and Belgium*. Leiden.
Franck, J. 1910. *Mittelniederländische Grammatik*. Arnhem. (Repr. 1976.)
Van Kerckvoorde, C.M. 1993. *An introduction to Middle Dutch*. Berlin and New York.

Dictionaries
De Vries, J. 1971. *Nederlands etymologisch woordenboek*, 2 vols. Leiden. (Repr. 1992.)
Renier, F. 1982. *Dutch dictionary*. London.
Woordenboek der nederlandsche taal. 1882–. Vol. 27 1994. 's-Gravenhage and Leiden.

dvandva ⇒ composition

Dyirbal ⇒ Australian languages

dynamic ⇒ stative vs active

dynamic accent ⇒ stress accent

dynamic stress ⇒ stress²

dysarthria [Grk *dys-* 'un-, mis-'; *arthroūn* 'to utter distinctly']

Term denoting any number of speech-motor disorders in the central or peripheral nervous system in which articulation, phonation, or prosody are affected. In contrast with **apraxia**, in dysarthria consistently recurring errors or substitutions are typical. (⇒ *also* **specific language impairment**)

References
Darley, F. *et al.* 1975. *Motor speech disorders*. Philadelphia, PA.
⇒ aphasia, language disorder

dysfluency (*also* stammering, stuttering)

In **speech-language pathology**, widely used as a synonym for 'stuttering.' As such, it denotes a situation-specific speech production disorder in which fluency of speech is disrupted by a lack of motor co-ordination in the muscles involved in articulation, phonation, or respiration. Two symptoms are generally distinguished: (a) tonic dysfluency (stuttering), characterized by interruptions in articulatory movements due to a spasm in the articulatory muscles; and (b) clonic dysfluency (stammering) due to a quick sequence of contractions of the speech muscles that causes repetitions of sounds, syllables, or words. Both symptoms can occur isolated or combined. Stuttering is more common in male than in female speakers. In North America, stuttering and stammering are not sharply distinguished. The term 'dysfluency' can also be used more generally to refer to any sort of breakdown in speech fluency, such as **cluttering**.

References
Andrews, G. *et al.* 1982. Stuttering: a review of research findings and theories circa 1982. *JSHD* 48.226–46.
Bloodstein, O. 1987. *A handbook of stuttering*. New York.

dysglossia [Grk *glōssa* 'tongue; language']

Term referring to **articulation disorders** due to changes (e.g. paralysis or defect) in the peripheral speech organs. Dysglossia is classified anatomically according to the part of the speech organ involved, e.g. 'labial dysglossia.' Pharyngeal and laryngeal dysglossia are also classified as **voice disorders**. Dysglossia is distinguished from **dyslalia**, a condition in which articulation problems are unrelated to deficiencies in the peripheral mechanism. Neither term is currently used in North America.

dysgrammatism ⇒ **agrammatism**

dyslalia [Grk *lalía* 'talk, chat']

In the study of **developmental language disorders**, term referring to speech production disorders in children, such as syllable reduction, mispronunciation, or substitution of individual sounds (partial dyslalia) or of many sounds (multiple dyslalia) up to the point of unintelligibility (universal dyslalia). A particular kind of dyslalia is known as **paralalia**. Dyslalia is distinguished from **dysglossia**, a condition which results from structural defects, and from **dysarthria**, a condition due to acquired neural impairments. The term 'dyslalia' is not currently used in North America. (⇒ *also* **articulation disorder, phonological disorder**)

dyslexia [Grk *léxis* 'word, speech']

Term covering a number of reading disorders with different causes. As with **language disorder**, acquired dyslexia, often referred to as **alexia**, and **developmental dyslexia** are distinguished.

References
Coltheart, M., K. Patterson, and J.C. Marshall (eds) 1987. *Deep dyslexia*, 2nd edn. London.
Miles, T.R. 1985. Dyslexia: the current status of the term. *CLTT* 1:1.54–64.
Søvik, N., O. Arntzen, and R. Thygeson. Relation of spelling and writing in learning disabilities. *PMS* 64:1.219–36.

dysphasia ⇒ **developmental aphasia, developmental dysphasia**

dysphonia [Grk *dysphōnía* 'roughness of sound']

In **speech-language pathology**, term covering a number of **voice disorders** caused by deficient phonatory techniques, growths or infections in the larynx, or psychological factors, such as stress or depression. (⇒ *also* **aphonia**)

dyspraxia ⇒ **apraxia**

dysprosody [Grk *prosōidía* 'voice modulation']

In **neurolinguistics**, term referring to a grave impairment of **prosody**, such as a disturbance in the contour, intensity, or the temporal structure of the utterance. For instance, differences between main and secondary stress in syllables may be leveled so that all syllables are spoken with the same intensity. (⇒ *also* **language disorder, specific language impairment**)

References
Baltaxe, C. and J.Q. Simmons. 1985. Prosodic development in normal and autistic children. In E. Schoper and G.V. Mesibov (eds), *Communication problems in autism*. New York. 95–125.
Burton, A. 1981. Linguistic analysis of dysprosody: a case study. *UCLA Working Papers in Cognitive Linguistics* 3.189–98.
Von Benda, U. and H. Amorosa. 1987. Intonation as a potential diagnostic tool in developmental disorders of speech communication. In Academy of Sciences of the Estonian SSR (eds), *Proceedings of the 11th International Congress of Phonetic Sciences*. Tallinn. Vol. 5, 160–3.
⇒ **articulation disorder, language disorder**

E

East Germanic ⇒ Germanic

East Ladinian ⇒ Rhaeto-Romance

East Sudan languages ⇒ Chari-Nile languages

Eblaite ⇒ Semitic

echo question

Interrogative sentence which answers a question by reformulating and repeating it. For example, *Who are you looking for? – Who am I looking for?*, *What is an echo question? – What's an echo question?* In English, echo questions have the same form as the questions they are based on, but in discourse they have different **intonation**. (⇒ *also* **interrogative, question**)

References
⇒ **interrogative**

echolalia [Grk *ēchō* 'ringing sound'; *lalía* 'talk']

In **neurolinguistics** and psychology, term referring to the repetition of one's utterances or of those of others by autistic persons (⇒ **autism**), schizophrenic persons, mentally retarded people, and patients with aphasia, among others. The term connotes meaningless, rote repetition, but recent studies with autistic children have shown that 'echolalia' may actually have a range of communicative and non-communicative functions. Echolalia is distinguished from the more general term 'imitation,' which carries no connotation as to function.

References
Prizant, B.M.P. and J.F. Duchan. 1981. The functions of immediate echolalia in autistic children. *JSHD* 46.241–49.
Prizant, B.M.P. and J. Rydell. 1984. Analysis of functions of delayed echolalia in autistic children. *JSHR* 27.183–92.
Schuler, A.L. 1979. Echolalia: issues and clinical applications. *JSHD* 44.411–34.
⇒ **autism, developmental language disorder, language disorder**

ECM ⇒ exceptional case marking

ECP ⇒ empty category principle

ectosemantic sphere [Grk *ektós* 'outside'; *sēma* 'sign']

In **information theory**, all the features of a speech occurrence that are semantically irrelevant for the dissemination of information, such as the social, regional, emotional, stylistic, or gender-specific characteristics of the speaker.

editorial we ⇒ plural of modesty

educational language policy ⇒ language policy

effected object [Lat. *efficere* 'to cause, to bring about']

Semantic relation between a **transitive verb** and its object **noun phrase**. The thing denoted by the object is the result of the action denoted by the verb, e.g. *Philip writes a letter*. This contrasts with the **affected object**, which modifies the object. In semantics, such verbs are called 'existential causatives.' A semantic analysis must account for the connection of such verbs with their corresponding 'result-objects.'

References
⇒ **case, case grammar, semantic relation**

effective ⇒ egressive[2], resultative

EFL

Abbreviation, used primarily in Great Britain, for English as a Foreign Language. (⇒ *also* **foreign vs second language**)

egocentric language [Lat. *ego* 'I']

According to J. Piaget (1896–1980), an indication of the inability of children (aged about four to seven years) to change their perspective in order to recognize different aspects of an object or to recognize the difference between one's own perspective and that of another. Piaget's interest centered primarily on the development of logical thinking, which develops from autistic via egocentric thinking. Piaget's concept of egocentric language was challenged by Vygotskij (1934). According to Vygotskij language and thinking develop phylogenetically and ontogenetically from different roots. Language, social in its origin, develops into communicative and **internal language** (linguistic thinking in differentiation to instrumental thinking). Egocentric language is structurally different from communicative language and has the function of self-guidance in problem-solving. Cf. in this connection also the significance of conversations with oneself as a stimulus for the development of the identity of the self in Mead's (1934) theory.

References
Mead, G.H. 1934. *Mind, self and society from the standpoint of a social behaviorist*. Chicago, IL.
Piaget, J. 1923. *Le Langage et la pensée chez l'enfant*. Paris.
Rieber, R.W. and A.S. Carton (eds) 1987/1990. *The collected works of L.S. Vygotskij*. 2 vols. (transl. N. Minick). New York/London.
Vygotskij, L.S. 1934/1962. *Thought and language*. (Russ. 1934, transl. E. Hanfman and G. Vakar). Cambridge, MA.
—— 1978. *Mind in society*. Cambridge, MA.
⇒ **language acquisition**

egocentric particular ⇒ **deictic expression**

egressive [Lat. *egressus* 'the action of going out']

1 Outward direction of the **airstream mechanism** (⇒ **ingressive**). As a rule, only **pulmonic** and **glottalic** sounds are egressive.

References
⇒ **articulatory phonetics, phonetics**

2 (*also* finitive, effective, **resultative**) Verbal **aspect** which falls under the category of **durative vs non-durative** verbs. It refers variously to either resultatives or to **punctuals**.

Egyptian

Language branch of **Afro-Asiatic**, consisting of one language which is attested in various stages: Ancient Egyptian (Old Egyptian, 3000–2200 BC), Middle Egyptian and Neo-Egyptian (1300–660 BC), as well as Demotic up to AD 300 and Coptic up until the nineteenth century, still used today as a liturgical language in the Coptic church. Writing systems: **hieroglyphics** for Old Egyptian, out of which a cursive writing system developed (Hieratic, Demotic); Coptic was written with a modified **Greek** alphabet. For the older linguistic stages only the consonant values are known.
Characteristics: Generally similar to the **Semitic** type (root inflection, gender); independent form for non-stative sentences (suffixal conjugation with genitive subjects); evidence for **ergative** sentence constructions in older language stages (the ergative was encoded as the genitive).

References
Kees, H. (ed.) 1959. *Ägyptologie*. (Handbuch der Orientalistik, I, vol. 1, 1.) (Repr. 1973.) Leiden.

Grammars
Brunner, H. 1967. *Abriß der mittelägyptischen Grammatik*. Graz.
Edel, E. 1955. *Altägyptische Grammatik*. Rome. (2nd edn 1964.)

Gardiner, A. 1927. *Egyptian grammar*. Oxford. (3rd edn 1957.)
Störk, L. 1981. Ägyptisch. In B. Heine *et al.* (eds), *Die Sprachen Afrikas*. Hamburg. 149–70.
Vergote, J. 1973. *Grammaire copte*, 2 vols. Louvain.

Bibliography
Annual Egyptological Bibliography. Leiden.

Dictionary
Erman, A. and H. Grapow. 1926–31. *Wörterbuch der ägyptischen Sprache*. Leipzig.

Etymological dictionary
Vycichl, W. 1984. *Dictionnaire étymologique de la langue copte*. Louvain.

Journal
Journal of Egyptian Language and Archeology.

eidetic vs operative sense [Grk *eĩdos* 'idea']

Cognitive theoretical distinction made in **semiotics** (of linguistic signs). The eidetic sense of a sign derives from its semantic relations to objects and states of affairs in the real world (i.e. its semantic function) as well as to other signs; it is determined by the **semantics** of a language. In contrast, the operative sense derives from the rules of usage (i.e. operations) for linguistic signs, which are established on the level of **syntax**. This distinction is particularly relevant in the natural sciences, e.g. a scientist may perform operations using signs without a concrete eidetic sense (e.g. in mathematics with negative numbers). On the other hand, computers are only able to work with the operative sense of signs; completely new eidetic senses can be derived from the corresponding (syntactic) operations or at least narrowed down from them.

References
⇒ **semiotics**

ejective [Lat. *eicere* 'to throw out'] (*also* abruptive)

Egressive plosive made with a glottalic **airstream mechanism**. As a rule, the glottal and oral closures are released almost simultaneously. Delayed release of the glottal closure results in a postglottalized plosive (⇒ **glottalization**). Ejectives are found in **Caucasian languages** as well as in many Native American and African languages. (⇒ *also* **articulatory phonetics, phonetics**)

elaborated code ⇒ **code theory**

elaborative inference ⇒ **inference**[2]

Elamite ⇒ **Dravidian**

elative [Lat. *elatio* 'the act of lifting; elevation']

1 **Superlative** form of an **adjective** used to

indicate a high degree of some characteristic, which, in contrast to the relative superlative, has no comparative component; thus elatives are also called absolute superlatives (e.g. *It was the greatest!*). (⇒ *also* **degree**)

2 Morphological case in the **Finno-Ugric** languages used to indicate a direction of motion from inside to outside. (⇒ *also* **illative**)

elective mutism ⇒ mutism

element of style

Any linguistic element that determines the **stylistic features** of a text. In addition to particular stylistic devices like **figures of speech**, any linguistic phenomenon can have a stylistic function. There are phonetic elements of style, (**alliteration, phonostylistics**), lexical elements of style (**nominalization, archaism**), morphological elements of style (genitive ending *'s*), syntactic elements of style (sentence complexity, length of sentence), and textual and pragmatic elements of style (types of **cohesion, theme-rheme, thematic development**).

References
⇒ **stylistics**

elementary phonetics

Method of researching the structure of speech sounds, based exclusively on what the (trained) human ear is capable of distinguishing. This approach has been largely surpassed by the development of **experimental phonetics** and instrumental phonetics. (⇒ *also* **auditory phonetics**)

References
⇒ **phonetics**

elision [Lat. *elidere* 'to force out']

In **phonetics** and **phonology**, the loss of a **vowel**, **consonant**, or **syllable**. Elision commonly occurs in complex consonant clusters (e.g. *clothes* [kloːðz] ~ [kloːz]), in unstressed (⇒ **stress**) syllables (e.g. *probably* [prabli]) or syntactically (⇒ **syntax**) unstressed words (e.g. *you and me* → *you 'n' me*). (⇒ *also* **aphesis, apocope, haplology, syncope**)

References
⇒ **language change, phonetics, phonology, sound change**

ellipsis [Grk *élleipsis* 'omission']

Deletion of linguistic elements that are required because of either syntactical rules or lexical properties (e.g. verbal **valence**). There are various constructions that can be interpreted as ellipsis. (a) Co-ordinating reduction, where identical material is left out: *He had too much to drink but I didn't* (⇒ **gapping**). (b) Lexical ellipsis, which refers to complements required by valence, e.g. *It's your turn to deal* (*the cards*). Lexical ellipses are further divided into indefinite vs definite ellipses, e.g. *He's eating* (something) vs *Philip finally got up the nerve* (for something which must be known from the context). In English, definite ellipsis is rather rare, and the subject cannot normally be omitted (except in the so-called telegram style – *arriving tomorrow* – and other restricted situations, such as *Coming!* when answering the door, etc.). In other languages (⇒ **Romance languages, Japanese, Chinese**), however, the omission of a definite pronominal subject is quite usual: Ital. *lavoro* '(I) work.' (c) In questions and answers, previously mentioned material is often omitted: *Who's coming tomorrow? – Caroline* (*is coming tomorrow*). (d) Infinitive and participial constructions can also be analyzed as regular forms of ellipsis in that the subject must be omitted: *Louise stopped smoking* (⇒ **equi-NP deletion**). (e) In imperatives obligatory deletion of the subject occurs: *Go home!*

References

Kino, S. 1982. Principles of discourse deletion: case studies from English, Russian and Japanese. *JoS* 1.61–93.
Klein, W. 1981. Some rules of regular ellipsis in German. In W.K. Levelt and W. Levelt (eds), *Crossing the boundaries of linguistics*. Amsterdam. 51–78.
Lobeck, A. 1995. *Ellipsis. Functional heads, licensing and identification*. Oxford.
Mittwoch, A. 1982. On the difference between 'eating' and 'eating something': activities vs accomplishments. *LingI* 13.113–22.
Shopen, T. 1973. Ellipsis as grammatical indeterminacy. *FL* 10.65–77.
Thomas, A.L. 1979. Ellipsis: the interplay of sentence structure and context. *Lingua* 47.43–68.
Vennemann, T. 1975. Topics, sentence accent, ellipsis: a proposal for their formal treatment. In E.L. Keenan (ed.), *Formal semantics and natural language*. Cambridge. 313–28.
⇒ **rhetoric, spoken language**

elliptic form

In **word formation** an elliptic **determinative compound** in which the second element of a three-element compound is dropped, e.g. *shoe* (*repair*) *shop*. In contrast to fore-clippings and back-clippings (⇒ **clipping**), such elliptic forms can develop directly from determinative compounds.

-em

A Greek suffix used to indicate functional units on the level of langue (⇒ **langue vs parole**).

($\Rightarrow$ *also* **morpheme**, **phoneme**)

References
$\Rightarrow$ **etic vs emic analysis**

embedding

A syntactic relation in **transformational grammar** in which an independent sentence of **surface structure** becomes a dependent sentence in the **matrix sentence**, if the independent sentence is a constituent of the matrix sentence. It is then said to be embedded. Thus the traditional distinction between a main clause and a subordinate clause becomes the distinction between a matrix sentence and a constituent sentence.

References
$\Rightarrow$ **complementizer**, **transformational grammar**

emic $\Rightarrow$ etic vs emic analysis

empathetic deixis $\Rightarrow$ empathy

empathy [Grk *empátheia* 'affection']

The speaker's adoption or occupying of a perspective or standpoint other than his/her own. Normally speakers maintain and reflect their own point of view, but frequently they will shift the perspective (the origo of the **deixis**) from their own to that of another person or thing (Lyons called this 'empathetic deixis' (1977: 677). For example, in the pair *come:go*, *come* contains the component 'towards the speaker' and *go* the component 'away from the speaker'; but it is possible to say not only *Afterwards I'll go to the café*, but also *Afterwards I'll come to the café*, the latter, namely, when one takes the standpoint of the addressee who will be in the café afterwards. Empathy plays an important role in the interpretation of zero anaphora in **Japanese** in which each predicate selects one of its arguments as the place in which speaker empathy is localized (see Kuno and Kaburaki 1977).

References
Kuno, S. and E. Kaburaki. 1977. Empathy and syntax. *LingI* 8.627–72.
Lyons, J. 1977. *Semantics*, 2 vols. Cambridge.

emphasis [Grk *émphasis* 'exposition,' from *emphaínein* 'to exhibit; to indicate']

Also known as 'significatio,' emphasis means to imply more than is actually stated. This can be accomplished by choosing an exceptionally strong word or phrase: *Be a man!* Emphasis can also be achieved by saying less than you mean, implying more than you say: for example, *He has such charm* ... Various devices can create emphasis: **tautology**, **pleonasm**, **cliché**, simile,

litotes, interjection, and exclamation.

References
$\Rightarrow$ **figure of speech**

emphatic

Term commonly used in **Arabic** linguistics for pharyngealized ($\Rightarrow$ **pharyngeal**) or velarized ($\Rightarrow$ **velar**) **speech sounds**. ($\Rightarrow$ *also* **secondary articulation**)

empiricism [Grk *émpeiros* 'experienced']

In psychology an approach based on English positivism (Locke, Berkeley, Hume), which views experience as the foundation of all understanding. This contrasts with **nativism**, which sees innate ideas as the basis for all cognitive development. As a methodological principle, namely ensuring the verifiability of knowledge through observable experience, empiricism plays a decisive role in the behaviorist views of **language acquisition**. ($\Rightarrow$ *also* **antimentalism**, **behaviorism**, **stimulus-response**)

References
$\Rightarrow$ **behaviorism**, **language acquisition**, **stimulus-response**

empractical use of language

Term coined by K. Bühler, denoting communication by means of isolated, syntactically irregular or incomplete linguistic elements whose meaning is determined through 'practical' use in the given situation and which in turn is sympractically embedded, e.g. the customer to the café waiter: *Bill, please*; or the commuter at the ticket counter: *San Francisco and back*. ($\Rightarrow$ *also* **sympractical field of language**)

References
Bühler, K. 1934. *Sprachtheorie*. Jena. (Repr. Stuttgart, 1965.)
Innis, R.E. (trans.) 1982. *Karl Bühler: semiotic foundations of language theory*. New York.

empty category principle (*abbrev.* ECP)

A principle of **transformational grammar** by which traces ($\Rightarrow$ **trace theory**) must be visible, i.e. they must be identifiable as empty positions in the **surface structure**, similar to the principle of **reconstruction** for **deletion**. Thus an empty category is in a position subcategorized for by a verb. In **Government and Binding theory** this is known as proper government. Proper government occurs either if the **empty position** is governed by a lexical category (especially if it is not a subject) or if it is co-indexed with a maximal projection which governs it (antecedent government). The ECP has been revised many times and is now a central part of Government and Binding theory.

References
Chomsky, N. 1981. *Lectures on government and binding*. Dordrecht. (7th edn Berlin and New York, 1993).
———— 1986. *Barriers*. Cambridge, MA.
Kayne, R. 1984. *Connectedness and binary branching*. Dordrecht.
Lasnik, H. and M. Saito. 1984. On the nature of proper government. *LingI* 15.235–89.
Pesetsky, D.M. 1982. Paths and categories. Dissertation, MIT.
Rizzi, L. 1990. *Relativized minimality*. Cambridge, MA.
Sobin, N. 1987. The variable status of COMP–trace phenomena. *NL&LT* 5.33–60.
⇒ **noun phrase**

empty position

1 (*also* slot) In **formal logic**, the **arguments** required by **predicates**.

2 In linguistics: (a) a position in a sentence which the syntax dictates could be occupied by another element. Depending on the sentence, it may be obligatory or optional that the position be filled: for example, the empty position in *the . . . sky* may optionally be filled by an adjective. (b) A position determined by the valence of the verb. (⇒ *also* **dependency grammar**)

3 A syntactic category of the Revised Extended Standard Theory (⇒ **transformational grammar**) which may contain morphological and syntactic features, but no phonological features. These categories include traces of **trace theory**, the **PRO element** of **control** theory, and the pro-element of **pro-drop languages**. Empty positions are subclassified in various ways in **Government and Binding theory** and are subject to the **binding theory**, the **empty category principle**, and **theta criterion**.

References
⇒ **Government and Binding theory**

empty set ⇒ set

empty slot

1 In **phonology**, designation for presumed gaps in the phonemic inventory of a language in systems assumed to be phonologically symmetrical. An empty slot in the English phonological system would be the absence of the unrounded back vowel counterpart to /u/, namely /ɯ/.

References
⇒ **phonology**
2 ⇒ **empty position**

enallage ⇒ hypallage

enclave (*also* relic area, speech island)

1 **Speech community** that develops when small groups (e.g. farmers, manual laborers, miners, religious sects, etc.) settle in areas where other languages have already been established. The language of such groups is most usually characterized by its relative conservativeness in respect to the language spoken in the country of origin. For this reason, the investigation of the linguistic conditions surrounding enclaves is particularly suitable for the reconstruction of older stages of the language in question, above all for dating language change. The language of the Amish (a Mennonite sect) in the Midwestern United States, derived from **German**, and the language of the 'Hillbillies' in Appalachia show characteristics of older German and English forms, respectively. The linguistic classification and delineation of the probable area of origin as well as the study of interference between the language of the enclave and other contact languages have become important areas of research in **dialectology**.

2 In a more general sense, an enclave is every linguistic variety that can be delineated in terms of its geographic location, deviates from the form of the surrounding language, and shows characteristics related to the varieties on the other side of the linguistic border. The most frequent manifestation of such enclaves are, to be sure, the relic areas which, for whatever reasons, did not take part in the process of language change seen in other related dialects. But areas of innovation, which are found beyond the more conservative adjacent dialect areas and in which prestige forms from distant areas have been adopted, are also possible. Frequently such areas are found in the vicinity of cities.

References
Maher, J. 1986. Contact linguistics: the language enclave phenomenon. *DAI* 46:8.2282A.
Vasek, A. 1980. On the functioning of the developmental factors of an isolated language in contact and the way in which we come to know them. *Makadonski Jasik* 31.91–9.
Wiesinger, P. 1980. Deutsche Sprachinseln. In H. Althaus *et al.* (eds), *Lexikon der germanistischen Linguistik*. 2nd edn. Tübingen.

enclisis [Grk *énklisis* 'inclination']

Attachment of a weakly stressed or unstressed word (**enclitic**) onto the preceding word, generally with simultaneous phonetic weakening, e.g. *I'm* for *I am*. For attachment to the following word ⇒ **proclitic**. (⇒ *also* **cliticiza-tion**)

References
⇒ **phonetics**, **phonology**

enclitic

Weakly stressed or unstressed element which attaches itself to a preceding stressed word, e.g. *I am > I'm*. (⇒ *also* **enclisis**, **proclitic**)

encoding

1 In **information theory**, the process and result of the association of an inventory of signs with special information from other inventories of signs, through which the same information can be presented.

2 In linguistics, the transfer of thoughts and ideas into the linguistic sign system of the speaker, from which the hearer deciphers meaning by use of **decoding**. Encoding occurs simultaneously on the lexical, syntactic-morphological, and phonological levels and is guided by the pragmatics of the context.

References
⇒ **language production**

endocentric compound ⇒ determinative compound

endocentric construction [Grk *éndon* 'within']

Term introduced by Bloomfield (1933) referring to a syntactic construction which belongs to the same form class/category (i.e. shows the same distribution) as one or more of its **constituents**. Thus *fresh fruit* can be replaced by *fruit* because both can occur as *X* in the environment *He is buying X. Fruit* is considered the **nucleus** (or **head**, center) and the adjective *fresh* a satellite (⇒ **modifier**). On the difference between these terms, see **exocentric construction**. Bloomfield differentiates between co-ordinate and subordinate endocentric constructions: when two or more immediate constituents belong to the same form class as the entire expression, he speaks of co-ordinate (also: serial) endocentric constructions as in the co-ordination of *John and Mary*. If only one of several elements belongs to the same form class as the whole expression, then it is a subordinate (also: attributive) endocentric construction: *new books*. These distinctions also define important dependency relations, upon which **dependency grammar** and **categorial grammar** systematically build. (⇒ *also* **complementation and modification**).

References
Barri, N. 1975. Note terminologique: endocentrique–

exocentrique. *Linguistics* 13.5–18.
Bloomfield, L. 1933. *Language*. New York. 194–7.
Harris, Z.S. 1951. *Methods in structural linguistics*. Chicago, IL.
Hincha, G. 1961. Endocentric vs exocentric constructions. *Lingua* 10.267–74.
Hockett, C.F. 1958. *A course in modern linguistics*. New York. 183–98.
⇒ **categorial grammar**, **dependency grammar**

energeia [Grk *enérgeia* 'activity']

Concept traceable to Wilhelm von Humboldt (1767–1835) viewing language as 'action' or 'effective energy' rather than a static entity (⇒ **ergon**). Language is not a 'material lying there to be surveyed in its entirety,' but rather must be seen as a 'continuously self-generating' process (1903–36, vol. 8:58). Language, in this sense, makes 'infinite use of finite resources' (p. 99). Numerous linguistic theories appeal to this 'energetic' conception of language, including the generative **transformational grammar** of N. Chomsky, which is concerned with the creative aspect of the energeia concept. This is represented in the framework of his theory as a 'system of recursive processes.'

References
Harris, R. and T.J. Taylor. 1989. *Landmarks in linguistic thought*. London. Ch. 12.
Robins, R.H. 1967. *A short history of linguistics*. Bloomington, IN.
Manchester, M. 1986. *The philosophical foundations of Humboldt's linguistic doctrines*. Amsterdam.
Von Humboldt, W. 1836. *On language: the diversity of human language structure and its influence on the mental development of mankind*, trans. P. Heath. Cambridge. (Trans. 1988.)
—— 1903–36. *Gesammelte Schriften*, vol. I: *Werke*, ed. A. Leitzmann. 9 vols. Berlin. (Repr. 1968.)

energetic

Modal category of verbs used to express a categorial assertion. While **Arabic** has independent forms of the energetic, English and related languages realize it through paraphrases: *She does like him*.

References
⇒ **modality**

Enga ⇒ Papuan

English

West **Germanic** language which has approx. 325 million native speakers, in England (56 million), the United States (232 million), Canada (24 million), and Australia and New Zealand (17 million). It is the sole official language in more than two dozen countries (e.g. South Africa), and is used as a language of commerce in India and Pakistan. Today it is the most important language of commerce and the most widely learned second language. The name 'English' comes from the Angles, who together with other tribes (Saxons, Jutes) conquered Britain in the fifth century AD and forced the native Celts (⇒ **Celtic**) into remote areas (Scotland, Wales, Cornwall). Three main periods in the history of English can be distinguished. (a) Old English (fifth century to 1050), with the dialect of Wessex as the 'standard language.' (b) Middle English (1050–1500): during the Norman occupation of England (from the Battle of Hastings in 1066 to the mid fourteenth century England was bilingual English–French). The effects of Norman **French** are seen especially in the vocabulary, where distinctions between words with similar meanings often rest on coexisting Germanic and **Romance** roots: e.g. *freedom* (Gmc.) vs *liberty* (Rom.). While Old English was an **inflectional** language with grammatical **gender** for substantives (masculine, feminine, neuter), four cases, and strong and weak adjectival declension, this structure was simplified as the loss of final syllables increasingly led to the loss of grammatical gender, the simplification of plural formation, and the widespread loss of inflectional morphemes. (c) Modern English, as a result, is virtually without inflection; grammatical relations which were formerly marked morphologically are now expressed by firm **word order** rules (subject–verb–object). Current orthography of English, with its wide discrepancies between spelling and pronunciation, represents the sound inventory of the late Middle English period at the end of the fifteenth century (cf. the various pronunciations of ⟨ou⟩ in *through, thousand, thought, though, tough, cough, could*).

References

Baker, C.L. 1988. *English syntax*. Cambridge, MA.
Cheshire, J. (ed.) 1991. *English around the world: sociolinguistic perspectives*. Cambridge.
Crystal, D. 1988. *The English language*. London.
—— (ed.) 1995. *The Cambridge encyclopedia of the English language*. Cambridge.
Ghadessy, M. 1988. *Registers in written English*. London.
Gramley, S. and K.-M. Pätzold. 1992. *A survey of Modern English*. London.
Greenbaum, S. (ed.) 1985. *The English language today*. Oxford.
Harris, J. 1994. *English sound structure*. Oxford.
Jacobs, R.A. 1995. *English syntax*. Oxford.
McCawley, J.D. 1988. *The syntactic phenomena of English*, vol. 1. Chicago, IL.
McCrum, R., W. Cran, and R. MacNeil. 1986. *The story of English*. New York.
Oxford library of English usage. 1991. Oxford.

Pennycook. A. 1994. *The cultural politics of English as an international language*. London.
Pyles, T. and J. Algeo. 1993. *The origins and development of the English language*, 4th edn. New York.

History

Barber, C. 1993. *The English language: a historical introduction*. Cambridge.
Bauer, L. 1994. *Watching English change: an introduction to the study of linguistic change in standard Englishes in the twentieth century*. London.
Baugh, A.C. and T. Cable. 1993. *A history of the English language*, 4th edn. Englewood Cliffs, NJ. (1st edn. New York 1935.)
Brunner, K. 1950–1. *Die englische Sprache: ihre geschichtliche Entwicklung*, 2 vols. Halle (2nd edn 1960–2 Tübingen. Repr. 1984.)
Denison, D. 1993. *English historical syntax*. London.
Dillard, J.L. 1992. *A history of American English*. London.
Görlach, M. 1978. *Einführung in das Frühneuenglische*. Heidelberg. (Transl. as *Introduction to early modern English*. Cambridge.)
Graddol, D., J. Swann, and D. Leith. 1996. *English. History, diversity and change*. London.
Jones, C. 1989. *A history of English phonology*. London.
Kastovsky, D. (ed.) 1991. *Historical English syntax*. Berlin and New York.
Lass, R. 1994. *Old English: a historical linguistic companion*. Cambridge.
Milroy, J. 1992. *Linguistic variation and change: on the historical sociolinguistics of English*. Oxford.
Rissanen, M. *et al.* (eds) 1992. *History of Englishes: new methods and interpretations in historical linguistics*. Berlin and New York.
Robinson, O.W. 1994. *Old English and its closest relatives*. London.
Strang, B. 1970. *A history of English*. London.

Modern grammars

Greenbaum, S. 1994. *The Oxford English grammar*. Oxford.
Jespersen, O. 1909–49. *A modern English grammar on historical principles*, 7 vols. London.
Leech, G. 1975. *A communicative grammar of English*. London.
Matthews, P.H. 1981. *Syntax*. Cambridge.
Quirk, R. and S. Greenbaum. 1973. *A university grammar of English*. London.
Quirk, R. *et al.* 1972. *A grammar of contemporary English*. London.
—— 1985. *A comprehensive grammar of the English language*. London.
Young, D.J. 1981. *The structure of English clauses*. London.
Zandvoort, R. 1969. *A handbook of English grammar*, 5th edn. London.

Historical grammars

Brunner, K. 1942. *Altenglische Grammatik: nach der Angelsächsischen Grammatik von Eduard Sievers*. (3rd rev. edn 1965.) Tübingen.

Campbell, A. 1959. *Old English grammar*, 3rd edn. Oxford.

Hogg, R.M. 1992. *A grammar of Old English*, vol. I: *Phonology*. Oxford and Cambridge, MA.

Jespersen, O. 1905. *The growth and structure of the English language*. Leipzig. (10th edn Chicago, 1982.)

Mitchell, B. 1985. *Old English syntax*, 2 vols. Oxford.

Mossé, F. 1952. *A handbook of Middle English*. Baltimore, MD.

Mustanoja, T.F. 1960. *A Middle English syntax*. Helsinki.

History of English

Hogg, R.M. (gen. ed.) 1991– . *Cambridge history of the English language*, 6 vols. Cambridge.

Etymology

Bammesberger, A. 1984. *English etymology*. Heidelberg.

Varieties of English

Baumgardner, R.J. (ed.) 1994. *The English language in Pakistan*. Oxford.

Ferguson, C.A. and S.B. Heath. 1981. *Language in the USA*. Cambridge.

Graddol, D. and S. Goodman. 1996. *English in a postmodern world*. London.

Hammarström, G. 1980. *Australian English: its origin and status*. Hamburg.

Hughes, A. and P. Trudgill. 1987. *English accents and dialects: an introduction to social and regional varieties of British English*, 2nd edn. London.

Mencken, H.L. 1919. *The American language: an inquiry into the development of English in the United States*. New York. (7th rev. edn. 1986.)

O'Donnell, W.R. and L. Todd. 1980. *Variety in contemporary English*. London.

Schmied, J.J. 1991. *English in Africa*. London.

Todd, L. and I. Hancock (eds) 1990. *International English usage*. London.

Trudgill, P. 1994. *Dialects*. London.

Trudgill, P. and J. Hannah. 1982. *International English: a guide to varieties of standard English*. London. (2nd edn 1989.)

Upton, C., J. Widdowson, and D. Parry. 1994. *Survey of English dialects: the dictionary and grammar*. London.

Wilkes, G.A. 1991. *A dictionary of Australian colloquialisms*. Sydney.

Bibliographies

Glauser, B., E.W. Schneider, and M. Görlach. 1993. *A new bibliography of writings on varieties of English, 1984–1992/3*. Amsterdam and Philadelphia.

Fisiak, J. (ed.) 1987. *A bibliography of writings for the history of the English language*, 2nd edn. Berlin and New York. Reichl. K. 1993. *Englische Sprachwissenschaft: eine Bibliographie*. Bielefeld and Munich.

Viereck, W. 1984. *A bibliography of writings on varieties of English, 1965–1983*. Amsterdam and Philadelphia.

Vorlat, E. 1978. *Analytical bibliography of writings on Modern English morphology and syntax*.

Dictionaries

Branford, J. 1991. *A dictionary of South African English*. Oxford.

Cassidy, F.G. and J.H. Hall (eds) 1991. *Dictionary of American regional English*. vol. II: *D–H*. Cambridge, MA.

Lutz, W.D. (ed.) *The Cambridge thesaurus of American English*. Cambridge.

The Oxford English dictionary. 1933. 12 vols. Oxford. (2nd edn 1989.)

Ramson, W.S. (ed.) 1989. *The Australian national dictionary*. Random House unabridged dictionary. 1993. New York.

Webster's third new international dictionary of the English language. 1976. 3 vols. Chicago, IL.

Etymological dictionaries

The Oxford dictionary of English etymology. 1966. Oxford. (Repr. with corrections 1967.)

Historical dictionaries

Bosworth, J. and T. Toller. 1898. *The Anglo-Saxon dictionary*. London. (Exp. 1921, 1972.)

Campbell, A. 1972. *Enlarged Addenda and Corrigenda to the supplement by T.N. Toller*. Oxford.

Dictionary of Old English. 1986– (microfiche edn). Toronto.

Kurath, H. *et al.* (eds) 1956– . *Middle English dictionary*. Ann Arbor, MI. (Vol. Sm–Sz 1988.)

Toller, T.N. 1921. *An Anglo-Saxon dictionary: supplement*. Oxford.

Journals
Anglia.
English Studies.
English Today.
English World-Wide.
⇒ **dialect**

entailment ⇒ **implication**

enthymeme [Grk *enthymázein* 'to ponder']

An abridged **syllogism**, the major premise being omitted as understood. Aristotle, who introduced the term, used it to mean a syllogism in which the premises are only generally true, a rhetorical, or probable, syllogism. In contrast to the 'analytical' or 'apodictic' **syllogism**, the points of proof of the enthymeme can remain unexpressed, e.g. *Socrates is a man, and therefore mortal*. They must not necessarily be true, but simply plausible. The characteristic argument of an enthymeme is the **topos**.

References
Anderson, A.R. and N.P. Belnap. 1961. Enthymemes. *Journal of Philosophy* 58.712–22.

Burney, M.C. 1974. The place of the enthymeme in rhetorical theory. In K.V. Erickson (ed.), *Aristotle: the classical heritage of rhetoric*. Metuchen, NJ. 117–40.

⇒ **rhetoric**

English for Speakers of Other Languages
(*abbrev.* ESOL) ⇒ **ESL**

entropy [Grk *entropía* 'twist, turn']

In **information theory**, the mean informational content of a set of signs. The term is derived from thermodynamics and is frequently used as a synonym for **information**[2].

enumeration ⇒ **set**

epenthesis [Grk 'insertion']

Insertion of transitional sounds without etymological motivation, e.g. the ‹p› in *Thompson* or the **diphthongs** found before **palatals** and **velars** in some dialects: [bæig] *bag*. In generative **phonology**, epenthesis is formulated as a phonological insertion rule. For contrast, ⇒ **epithesis**. (⇒ *also* **anaptyxis**, **prothesis**, **sound change**)

References
⇒ **language change**, **sound change**

epic preterite

Temporal use of the preterite tense, which is the predominant form for epic narrative or narration in general. It constructs a fictitious present and thus can also be modified by adverbials referring to the future: *The following week she wrote him a letter.*

References
⇒ **tense**

epicene [Grk *epíkoinos* 'common']

Noun which can refer to both male and female entities without changing its grammatical **gender**, e.g. Ger. *die Ratte* 'the rat' (grammatical feminine), Span. *el pájaro* 'the bird' (grammatical masculine).

epiphora [Grk *epiphorá* 'bringing to; repetition']

Figure of speech: repetition of a word or expression at the end of a set of sentences or phrases (⇒ **anaphora**, **gemination**). Like its opposite, **anaphora**, epiphora can create an emphatic rhythm that acquires a special emotional change because the repeated word is used to conclude the sentence or passage: *I'll have my bond! Speak not against my bond! I have sworn an oath that I will have my bond!* (Shakespeare, *Merchant of Venice*, 3.3.4).

References
⇒ **figure of speech**

epistemic logic [Grk *epistḗmē* 'knowledge']

Special type of philosophical logic that, in addition to the logical expressions such as logical particles (⇒ **logical connective**) (*and*, *or*, and others) and **operators** in **formal logic**, also uses expressions of 'believing' and 'knowing' by introducing appropriate operators into the semantic analysis. Since contexts of believing and knowing that are expressed by 'epistemic expressions' like *X believes/knows that p*, are typical examples of opaque contexts (⇒ **opaque vs transparent contexts**), epistemic logic plays a decisive role within a logically oriented semantics of natural language, as founded primarily by Montague (1970).

References
Hintikka, J. 1962. *Knowledge and belief.* Ithaca, NY.
Montague, R. 1970. English as a formal language, I. In B. Visentini *et al.* (ed.), *Linguaggi nella società et nella tecnica.* Milan. 189–224. (Repr. in *Formal philosophy: selected papers of R. Montague*, ed. R.H. Thomason. New Haven CT, 1974. 188–221.)
Quine, W.V.O. 1960. *Word and object.* Cambridge, MA. (4th edn 1965.)
Rescher, N. (ed.) 1968. *Studies in logical theory.* Oxford.

Bibliography
Petöfi, J.S. (ed.) 1978. *Logic and the formal theory of natural language: selective bibliography.* Hamburg. 285–96.

epithesis [Grk 'laying on']

Attachment of an etymologically unmotivated sound to a word. For contrast, ⇒ **epenthesis**, **prothesis**. For example, ME *soun* > Mod. Eng. *sound* (from Lat. *sonus*). (⇒ **homonymy**)

References
⇒ **language change**, **sound change**

epithets [Grk *epítheton* 'that which is added']

A term in **rhetoric** for attributive adjectives and appositions. The term is used particularly in **figures of speech** of expansion, especially in unusual semantic collocations or in special characterizations like *William the Conqueror* or *Richard the Lionheart*. (⇒ **pleonasm**)

epizeuxis ⇒ **gemination**

equational sentence

Sentence of the form subject + copula + predicate nominal, e.g. *Philip is a busy student.*

equative [Lat. *aequare* 'to make even']

Form of comparison (⇒ **degree**) which expresses an equal degree of some property or characteristic, e.g. *Philip is just as tall as Caroline.*

Equatorial languages

Language group postulated by Greenberg (1987) with approx. 150 languages in South

America, the most important branches being **Arawakan** and **Tupi**.

References
Greenberg, J.H. 1987. *Language in the Americas.* Stanford, CA.
⇒ **North and Central American languages**, **South American languages**

equi-NP deletion

A deletional **transformation** in **transformational grammar** which deletes the subject **noun phrase** (NP) of an embedded sentence (⇒ **embedding**) if it is coreferential with an NP of the **matrix sentence**. Equi-NP deletion is used in the generation of infinitive constructions, e.g. *Philip asked Caroline to drive*, which can be generated from the two sentences *Philip asked Caroline* and *Caroline drives*. The second mention of *Caroline* is deleted and the form *drive* is changed to the infinitive. (⇒ *also* **control**)

Philip asked Caroline   -   *Caroline drives*

equi

delete

Philip asked Caroline to drive.

References
Chomsky, C. 1969. *The acquisition of syntax in children from 5 to 10*. Cambridge, MA.
Rosenbaum, P.S. 1970. A principle governing deletion in English sentential complementation. In P.S. Rosenbaum and R.A. Jacobs (eds), *Readings in English transformational grammar*. Waltham, MA. 220–9.
Soames, S. and D.M. Perlmutter. 1979. *Syntactic argumentation and the structure of English.* Berkeley, CA.
⇒ **transformational grammar**

equipollent opposition ⇒ opposition

equivalence (*also* biconditional, bilateral implication)

In **formal logic** the conjunction of two elementary propositions p and q that is true if and only if both parts of the sentence have the same truth value (notation: $p \equiv q$ or $p \leftrightarrow q$). This relation is represented in the (two-place) **truth table**:

p	q	$p \leftrightarrow q$
t	t	t
t	f	f
f	t	f
f	f	t

Equivalence refers to the two-place sentence operator *if p, then q* as well as the propositional connective defined by it. The equivalence corresponds to bilateral **implication**, i.e. both $p \rightarrow q$ and $q \rightarrow p$ are valid: *Ralph is Philip's father → Philip is Ralph's son* and vice versa. In everyday usage, equivalences correspond to paraphrases like *p, if and only if q* or *p is a necessary and sufficient condition for q*, in which case it frequently remains ambiguous as to whether it is a matter of equivalence or of implication. In the framework of lexical semantics (⇒ **meaning**, **semantics**) equivalence corresponds to the conventional truth-functional semantic relation of **synonymy**.

References
⇒ **formal logic**

equivalence grammars

A property of **generative grammars**. Two grammars are called 'weakly equivalent' if they **generate** the same set of sentences. They are called 'strongly equivalent' if they generate the same set of sentences and assign the same structural description to them.

References
⇒ **levels of adequacy**

equivalent distribution ⇒ distribution

equivocation

A form of lexical ambiguity in words of related etymology (e.g. *foot* (*of a human/of a mountain*)). Systematic equivocation arises when two meanings occur in various word forms in the vocabulary: take, for example, the meanings 'action' or 'process' vs 'result' in *work, drawing*, and *expression*. Equivocation is primarily a lexicological problem. (⇒ *also* **homonymy**, **lexicology**, **polysemy**)

References
⇒ **semantics**

ergative [Grk *ergátēs* 'doer (of an action)']

1 (*also* agentive, narrative) Morphological case in **ergative languages** which indicates the **agent** of transitive verbs in the basic **voice**. In contrast to the **nominative** in **nominative languages** (e.g. English), which generally also encodes the agent of transitive verbs, the ergative is not the basic (= unmarked) case in languages of this type. Thus the ergative does not usually have a zero form (⇒ **zero morpheme**) and is not used to mark the 'subject,' i.e. the primary syntactic function, which is in the **absolutive**; instead, it marks a syntactic function which is similar to the direct object in nominative languages. This means that ergative

arguments in ergative languages show the syntactic behavior of direct objects in nominative languages. For example, an argument in the ergative only agrees with the predicate in an ergative language if an argument in the absolutive also agrees with the predicate (⇒ **hierarchy universal**). In addition, the ergative case of an argument is changed into the absolutive in the derived, non-basic voice category of an ergative language, i.e. the **antipassive**.

2 In **case grammar**, a deep case for the agent of an action.

References
Anderson, J.M. 1968. Ergative and nominative in English. *JL* 4.1–32.
――――― 1971. *The grammar of case: towards a localistic theory*. Cambridge.
⇒ **ergative language**

ergative language (*also* absolute language)

Language type in **relational typology** which contrasts with **nominative languages** and **active languages**. Assuming that the most important **thematic relations** in basic transitive and intransitive sentences are those of agent and patient, ergative languages can be defined as follows: the basic (= unmarked) case in these languages, the **absolutive**, designates the **patient** of transitive verbs as well as the single argument of intransitive verbs regardless of its thematic relation. The marked case, the **ergative** serves to express the agent of transitive verbs. This situation can be depicted as follows:

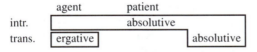

The following sentences from Basque serve as an illustration: *Mi-k* ('I' erg.) *gizona* ('man' abs.) *ikusi dut* ('have seen') 'I saw the man' vs *Gizona* ('man' abs.) *etorri da* ('has come') 'The man has come.' The patient of transitive verbs and the single argument of intransitive verbs are treated alike morphologically and, in a consistent ergative language, syntactically as well. In contrast, nominative languages such as English treat the agent of transitive verbs and the single argument of intransitive verbs in the same way:

	agent	patient
intr.	subject	
trans.	subject	object

Ergative languages are frequent among the **Caucasian** (**Georgian**, Ubykh), Austronesian (⇒ **Malayo-Polynesian**) (Tongan), **Australian** (Dyirbal), and **Mayan** (Tzeltal) languages. Sometimes ergative languages are split nominative–ergative. Thus in many Australian languages the pronominal system patterns as in a **nominative** language, while the nouns are case-marked according to the ergative system. In some Asian languages (e.g. in Hindi (⇒ **Hindi-Urdu**)) sentences in some tenses are ergative, but otherwise the language is nominative. Some authors claim that ergativity is also found in languages such as German and Italian; cf. ⇒ **unaccusative**).

References
Comrie, B. 1978. Ergativity. In W.P. Lehmann (ed.), *Syntactic typology: studies in the phenomenology of language*. Austin, TX. 329–94.
Dixon, R.M.W. 1979. Ergativity. *Lg* 55.59–138.
――――― (ed.) 1987. Studies in ergativity. *Lingua* 71 (special issue).
――――― 1994. *Ergativity*. Cambridge.
Mallinson, G. and B.J. Blake. 1981. *Language typology*. Amsterdam.
Moravcsik, A. 1978. On the distribution of ergative and accusative patterns. *Lingua* 45.233–79.
Plank, F. (ed.) 1979. *Ergativity: towards a theory of grammatical relations*. London.
――――― (ed.) 1985. *Relational typology*. Berlin and New York.
Primus, B. 1994. Relational typology. In J. Jacobs *et al.* (eds), *Syntax: an international handbook of contemporary research*, vol. 2. Berlin and New York. 1076–109.
Sapir, E. 1917. Review of C.C. Uhlenbeck, Het passieve karakter van het verbum transitivum van het verbum actionis in talen van Noord Amerika. *IJAL* 1.82–6.
Silverstein, M. 1976. Hierarchy of features and ergativity. In R.M.W. Dixon (ed.), *Grammatical categories in Australian languages*. Canberra. 112–71.
Van Valin, R. 1977. Ergativity and the universality of subjects. *CLS* 13.689–705.

Bibliography
Plank, F. 1979. Bibliography on ergativity. In F. Plank (ed.), *Ergativity: towards a theory of grammatical relations*. London. 511–54.

ergative verb ⇒ **recessive, unaccusative**

ergon [Grk *érgon* 'work']

Concept going back to Wilhelm von Humboldt (1767–1835) viewing language as the product of a completed action. Humboldt contrasts this concept of language as a (static) entity with his own view of language as **energeia**, as 'action' or 'effective energy'.

References
⇒ **energeia**

Eritreic ⇒ Afro-Asiatic

error analysis

1 In **second language acquisition**, error analysis studies the types and causes of linguistic errors. This sometimes includes the evaluation and correction of errors. Errors may be classified according to (a) modality (i.e. level of proficiency in speaking, listening comprehension, writing, and reading); (b) levels of linguistic description (e.g. phonetics/phonology, orthography, graphemics, morphology, syntax, lexicon, phraseology, or stylistics); (c) form (omission, insertion, substitution, contamination, etc.); (d) type (systematic errors vs occasional errors or errors in competence vs errors in performance); and (e) cause (e.g. interference, development-related errors, interlanguage). In the evaluation of errors, the level of error (norm error vs system error), the degree of communication breakdown, and the tendency towards fossilization play an equally important role.

2 In **speech-language pathology** error analysis has in part the same object of investigation as error analysis in language pedagogy. (⇒ *also* **language disorder**)

3 Error analysis also studies errors made by native speakers without speech disorders and investigates errors in normal speech. Note the intentional use of the term 'error' as opposed to 'mistake,' which is a prescriptive term. (⇒ *also* **speech error**)

4 Studies involving native speaker reactions to errors made by non-native speakers have identified those grammatical and socio-linguistic errors that stigmatize and should be the focus of correction, in contrast to those errors which produce a less negative reaction or no reaction at all.

References
Corder, S.P. 1981. *Error analysis and interlanguage.* Oxford.
Cutler, A. (ed.) 1982. *Slips of the tongue and language production.* Berlin.
Ensz, K. 1982. French attitudes toward speech errors. *MLJ* 66.133–9.
Fromkin, V. (ed.) 1973. *Speech errors as linguistic evidence.* The Hague.
Hendrickson, H.M. 1978. Error correction in foreign language teaching: recent theory, research, and practice. *MLJ* 62.387–98.
Politzer, R.L. 1978. Errors of English speakers of German as perceived and evaluated by German natives. *MLJ* 62.253–61.
Richards, J.C. (ed.) 1974. *Error analysis: perspectives on second language acquisition.* London.
Schairer, K.E. 1992. Native speaker reaction to non-native speech. *MLJ* 76.309–19.
Selinker, L. and J.T. Lamendella. 1979. The role of extrinsic feedback in interlanguage fossilization. *Language Learning* 29.363–75.
Svartvik, J. (ed.) 1973. *Errata: papers in error analysis.* Lund.

Bibliography
Spillner, B. 1991. *Error analysis: a comprehensive bibliography.* Amsterdam and Philadelphia.
⇒ **speech error**

Erythraic ⇒ Afro-Asiatic

Eskimo ⇒ Eskimo-Aleut

Eskimo-Aleut

Language group comprised of Aleut (spoken in the Aleutian islands in the Bering Sea, approx. 700 speakers) and Eskimo (with two branches, Yuit (Yupik) in east Siberia and southwest Alaska, and Inuit in north Alaska, northern Canada and Greenland, approx. 100,000), which themselves form dialect continua. The largest linguistic community is found in Greenland with approx. 43,000 speakers. There are possible relationships with **Altaic** and Yukagir (⇒ **Paleo-Siberian**).

Characteristics: simple sound system; complex morphology (suffixal). **Ergative languages**: the ergative is identical with the genitive (possessive sentence construction); hardly any indication of a noun–verb distinction. Word order SOV. The verb agrees with the subject and the object. Complex number system (with dual), very productive derivational mechanisms, tendency towards descriptivity. Complex system of spatial demonstrative pronouns.

References
Bok-Bennema, R. 1991. *Case and agreement in Inuit.* Berlin and New York.
Fortescue, M. 1988. The Eskimo-Aleut–Yukagir relationship: an alternative to the genetic/contact dichotomy. *Acta Linguistica Hafniensia* 21.21–50.
Fortescue, M. 1984. *West Greenlandic.* London.
Krauss, M.E. 1973. Eskimo-Aleut. In T.A. Sebeok (ed.), *Current trends in linguistics.* The Hague. Vol. 10, 796–902.
——— 1979. Na-Dené and Eskimo-Aleut. In L. Campbell and M. Mithun (eds), *The languages of native America.* Austin, TX. 803–901.
Reed, I. *et al.* 1977. *Yup'ik Eskimo grammar.* Fairbanks, AL.
⇒ **North and Central American languages**

ESL

Abbreviation, used primarily in North America, for 'English as a Second Language.' This term is gradually being replaced by 'ESOL' (English for Speakers of Other Languages). (⇒ *also* **foreign vs second language**)

ESOL ⇒ ESL

Esperanto

Artificial language invented by the Warsaw optometrist L.L. Zamenhof (pseudonym 'Esperanto' = 'he who hopes'). Thought to be the most successful **interlingua** of international understanding, Esperanto consists of a very simple phonetic-phonological, morphological, and syntactic structure. Its vocabulary is based on a mixture of **Romance** and **Germanic** word stems (originally numbering some 3,500) which can be combined with ten prefixes and twenty-seven suffixes (⇒ *also* **agglutinating language**). Its grammar consists of sixteen rules, which have no exceptions.

References
Courtinat, L. 1964–5. *Historio de Esperanto*, 3 vols. Agen.
Forster, P.G. 1981. *The Esperanto movement.* The Hague.
Zamenhof, L.L. 1929. Lingvo internacia. In J. Dietterle (ed.), *Originala verkaro de L.L. Zamenhof.* Leipzig. (Original 1887).

Bibliography
Tonkin, H. 1967. *A research bibliography on Esperanto and international language problems.* New York.

Estonian

Finno-Ugric language closely related to **Finnish**, spoken mainly in Estonia; approx. 1 million speakers.

References
Harms, R.T. 1962. *Estonian grammar.* The Hague.
Raun, A. and A. Saareste, 1965. *Introduction to Estonian linguistics.* Wiesbaden.
Tauli, V. 1983. *Standard Estonian grammar.* Uppsala.

Ethiopic ⇒ Ge'ez

Ethiosemitic ⇒ Semitic

ethnography of communication ⇒ ethnography of speaking

ethnography of speaking [Grk *éthnos* 'a people'] (*also* ethnography of communication)

This approach, introduced in the 1950s and early 1960s by D. Hymes and J.J. Gumperz (see also Pike 1954), is concerned with the analysis of language use (⇒ **usage vs use**) in its sociocultural setting. In contrast to the then popular linguistic theories of **structuralism** and **transformational grammar**, this approach is based on the premise that the meaning of an utterance can be understood only in relation to the 'speech event,' or 'communicative event,' in which it is embedded (see Hymes 1962). The character of such speech events (e.g. a sermon, a trial, or a telephone call) is culturally determined. It is believed that the rules governing language use can be established by systematic observation, analysis of spontaneous language, and interviews with native speakers (⇒ **field work**).

Ethnography of speaking led to the ethnographic approach to **discourse analysis**, in which conversational inferences play a key role: participants link the content of an utterance and other verbal, vocal, and non-vocal cues with background knowledge (⇒ **contextualization**) in order to come to an understanding about the specific interchange. For example, in a situation involving doctor and patient, **code-switching** (or even a change in loudness) may indicate whether the doctor is talking to the patient or the nurse. Furthermore, the way in which discourse proceeds may demonstrate how social identities are negotiated (see Erickson and Shultz 1982). The ethnographic approach is close to other current sociological approaches in its methodology and areas of research (see Goffman and Cicourel in discourse analysis; for an overview, see Corsaro 1981). (⇒ *also* **conversation analysis**)

References
Bauman, R. and J. Sherzer (eds) 1989. *Explorations in the ethnography of speaking,* 2nd edn. (1st edn 1978.) Cambridge.
Boden, D. and D. Zimmerman (eds) 1992. *Talk and social structure.* Cambridge.
Cicourel, A. 1975. Discourse and text: cognitive and linguistic processes in studies of social structures. *Versus* 12.33–84.
—— 1980. Three models of discourse analysis. *DPr* 3.102–32.
—— 1987. The interpretation of communicative contexts: examples from medical encounters. *Social Psychology Quarterly* 50.217–26.
Duranti, A. 1988. Ethnography of speaking: toward a linguistics of the praxis. In F. Newmeyer (ed.), *Linguistics: the Cambridge survey.* Cambridge. Vol. 4, 210–28.
Erickson, F. and J. Shultz. 1982. *The counselor as gate keeper.* New York.
Goffman, E. 1971. *Relations in public.* New York.
—— 1974. *Frame analysis.* New York.
—— 1981. *Forms of talk.* Philadelphia, PA.
Grimshaw, A. (ed.) 1991. *Conflict talk.* Cambridge.
Gumperz, J.J. 1982. *Discourse strategies.* Cambridge.
—— (ed.) 1982. *Language and social identity.* Cambridge.
Hymes, D. 1962. The ethnography of speaking. In T. Gladwin and W.C. Sturtevant (eds), *Anthropology and human behavior.* Washington, DC. 99–138.
—— 1972. Models of the interaction of language and social life. In J.J. Gumperz and D. Hymes

(eds), *Directions in sociolinguistics: the ethno-graphy of communication.* New York. 35–71.

Lindenfeld, J. 1990. *Speech and sociability at French urban marketplaces.* Amsterdam.

Pike, K.L. 1954. *Language in relation to a unified theory of the structure of human behavior.* The Hague. (2nd edn 1967.)

Saville-Troike, M. 1989. *The ethnography of communication*, 2nd edn. Oxford.

Tannen, D. (ed.) 1981. *Analyzing discourse.* Gurt.

────── 1984. *Conversational style.* Norwood, NJ.

────── (ed.) 1984. *Coherence in spoken and written discourse.* Norwood, NJ.

────── 1986. *That's not what I meant.* New York.

⇒ **contextualization, discourse analysis**

ethnolinguistics (*also* neo-Humboldtianism)

Collective term for anthropological and linguistic investigations into the connections between language and ethnically based, sociocultural aspects of the given linguistic community. Most work in ethnolinguistics can be traced to the linguistic philosophy of Wilhelm von Humboldt (1767–1835) (⇒ **energeia**).

References
Basilius, H. 1952. Neo-Humboldtian ethnolinguistics. *Word* 8.95–105.

Miller, R.L. 1968. *The linguistic relativity principle and Humboldtian ethnolinguistics: a history and appraisal.* The Hague.

⇒ **ethnography of speaking, Sapir–Whorf hypothesis**

ethnomethodological conversation analysis ⇒ conversation analysis

ethnomethodology

An area of research in interpretative sociology initiated by H. Garfinkel concerned with the analysis of formal properties of practical reasoning. It investigates the activities whereby members of a sociocultural community produce and manage settings for their everyday lives. These activities are considered to be identical to those which members use to make settings 'accountable' (i.e. observable, reportable, and interpretable for themselves and others). Ethnomethodology assumes that members make sense out of their actions by interpreting them against a background of underlying patterns, i.e. they take certain shared commonsense knowledge for granted. One way of finding out about such tacit knowledge that members rely on are 'quasi-experiments' designed to disrupt those patterns and induce a break in the subject's background expectancies. For instance, some students were asked to have an acquaintance explain the meaning of an utterance: Subject (waving cheerfully to experimenter): *How are you?* – Experimenter: *How am I with regard to what? My health, my finances, my*

school work, my peace of mind, my ... ? Subject (red in the face and suddenly out of control): *Look, I was just trying to be polite. Frankly, I don't give a damn how you are* (Garfinkel 1967). Following Schuetz (1961–2), Garfinkel proposes a number of strategies that members use to make sense out of their actions, such as the retrospective and prospective interpretation of activities (see also Cicourel 1973). For an interpretation of Garfinkel's approach, see Heritage (1984). One branch of research developed from ethnomethodology is **conversation analysis**.

References
Button, G. (ed.) 1991. *Ethnomethodology and the human sciences.* Cambridge.

Cicourel, A. 1973. *Cognitive sociology.* Harmondsworth.

Flynn, P.J. 1991. *The ethnomethodological movement: sociosemiotic interpretations.* Berlin and New York.

Garfinkel, H. 1967. *Studies in ethnomethodology.* Englewood Cliffs, NJ.

Heritage, J. 1984. *Garfinkel and ethnomethodology.* Cambridge.

Hill, R. and K. Stones Crittenden (eds) 1968. *Proceedings of the Purdue Symposium on Ethnomethodology.* Purdue, IN.

Maynard, D. and S. Clayman. 1991. The diversity of ethnomethodology. *Annual Review of Sociology* 17.385–418.

Psathas, G. (ed.) 1979. *Everyday language studies in ethnomethodology.* New York.

Schuetz, A. 1961–2. *Collected papers*, 2 vols. The Hague.

Turner, R. (ed.) 1974. *Ethnomethodology.* Harmondsworth.

Watson, G. and R.M. Seiler (eds) 1991. *Text in context: contributions in ethnomethodology.* New York.

etic vs emic analysis

Following the suffix formations of (*phon*)*etics* vs (*phon*)*emics*, this term was introduced into the social sciences by Swadesh (1934) and Pike (1967) to denote the distinction between the material and functional study of language: **phonetics** studies the acoustically measurable and articulatorily definable immediate sound utterances, whereas **phonemics** analyzes the specific selection each language makes from that universal catalogue from a functional (= distinctive) aspect.

References
Pike, K. 1967. *Language in relation to a unified theory of the structure of human behavior.* The Hague. (2nd edn 1971.)

Siertsma, B. 1959. 'Etic' and 'emic.' *ES* 50.586–8.

Swadesh, M. 1934. The phonemic principle. *Lg* 10.117–29.

Etruscan

Ancient language of northern Italy, known primarily from grave inscriptions; though recorded in a **Greek**-based alphabet, it is not well known and its genetic affiliation is uncertain.

References
Bonfante, G. and L. Bonfante. 1983. *The Etruscan language: an introduction.* Manchester and New York.
Rix, H. 1984 La scrittura e la lingua. In M. Cristofani (ed.), *Gli Etruschi, una nuova immagine.* Florence. 210–38.

Journal
Studi Etruschi.

etymology [Grk *étymos* 'true'; *lógos* 'word']

The study of the origin, basic meaning, and development of individual words as well as of their relationship to words in different languages of the same origin. In ancient times the search for the original semantic motivation of a word was essentially the search for the essence and origin of the thing denoted by the word, which was believed to be revealed in the original meaning of the word. Diachronic studies in **comparative linguistics** in the eighteenth and nineteenth centuries used the study of etymological relationships to reconstruct a common proto-**Indo-European** language or as evidence for the relationship of individual languages or words. The existence of lexeme correspondences in different languages was founded on **sound laws**, processes of word formation and conceptual relationships, historical and sociocultural facts as well as their systematic placement in the given vocabulary. Seebold (1981: 316–22) provides a useful list of reference works for individual languages. (⇒ *also* **borrowing, folk etymology, semantic change**)

References
Guiraud, P. 1964. *L'Etymologie.* Paris.
Malkiel, Y. 1993. *Etymology.* Cambridge.
Pisani, V. 1947. *L'etimologia.* Brescia.
Seebold, E. 1981. *Etymologie: eine Einführung am Beispiel der deutschen Sprache.* Munich.

Reference works
English
Holthausen, F. 1927. *Altenglisches etymologisches Wörterbuch.* Heidelberg. (Repr. 1963.)
Murray, J. 1898–1936. *A new English dictionary on historical principles.* Oxford.
Onions, C.T. *et al.* (eds) 1977. *The Oxford dictionary of English etymology.* Oxford.
Partridge, E. 1990. *Origins: an etymological dictionary of Modern English,* 4th edn. London.
Skeat, W.W. 1882. *A concise etymological dictionary of the English language.* Oxford. (Rev. edn 1976.)

French
Bloch, O. and W.V. Wartburg. 1960. *Dictionnaire étymologique de la langue française.* Paris. (5th edn 1968.)
Dauzat, A., J. Dubois, and H. Mitterand. 1971. *Nouveau dictionnaire étymologique et historique.* Paris.
Gamillscheg, E. 1928. *Etymologisches Wörterbuch der französischen Sprache.* Heidelberg. (2nd edn 1969.)
Wartburg, W.V. 1922–. *Französisches etymologisches Wörterbuch.* Bonn, Basle and Tübingen. (Vol. 25, 1992.)

German
Drosdowski, G. (ed.) 1989. *Duden: das Herkunftswörterbuch. Etymologie der deutschen Sprache.* Munich. (2nd rev. and exp. edn Mannheim.)
Grimm, J. and W. Grimm. 1854/1954. *Deutsches Wörterbuch,* 16 vols. Leipzig. (Repr. in 33 vols, Munich, 1984.)
Hirt, H. 1909. *Etymologie der neuhochdeutschen Sprache.* Munich. (2nd edn 1921.)
Kluge, F. 1883. *Etymologisches Wörterbuch der deutschen Sprache.* Berlin. (22nd rev. edn, ed. E. Seebold, Berlin, 1989.)
Pfeifer, W. (ed.) 1989. *Etymologisches Wörterbuch des Deutschen.* 3 vols. Berlin.

Gothic
Feist, S. 1939. *Vergleichendes Wörterbuch der gotischen Sprache,* 3rd edn. Leiden.
Lehman, W.P. 1986. *A Gothic etymological dictionary.* Leiden
Schulze, E. 1847. *Gotisches Glossar.* Magdeburg.

Greek
Chantraine, P. 1968–80. *Dictionnaire de la langue grecque: histoire des mots.* 4 vols. Paris.
Frisk, H. 1954–72. *Griechisches etymologisches Wörterbuch,* 3 vols. Heidelberg.

Indo-European
Buck, C.D. 1949. *A dictionary of selected synonyms in the principal Indo-European languages.* Chicago, IL.
Pokorny, J. 1948–59. *Indogermanisches etymologisches Wörterbuch,* 2 vols. Bern. (3rd edn Tübingen 1994.)

Italian
Cortelazzo, M. and P. Zolli. 1990. *Dizionario etimologico della lingua italiana.* Bologna.
Pfister, M. 1979–. *Lessico etimologico italiano.* Wiesbaden. (Vol. IV 1994.)

Latin
Alessio, G. 1976. *Lexicon etymologicum.* Neapel.
Ernout, A. and A. Meillet. 1959. *Dictionnaire étymologique de la langue latine,* 4th edn. Paris.
Thesaurus linguae latinae. 1900–58. Leipzig.
Walde, A. and J.B. Hofmann. 1959. *Lateinisches etymologisches Wörterbuch.* 4th edn. Heidelberg.

Russian
Vasmer, M. 1953–8. *Russisches etymologisches Wörterbuch.* Heidelberg.

etymon

The original meaning or form of a word (⇒ **etymology**).

euphemism [Grk *euphēmía* 'use of words of good omen']

Rhetorical **trope**: a pleasant replacement for an objectionable word that has pejorative **connotations**, e.g. *to pass on* for 'to die.' Euphemisms are common in political language: e.g. *a period of negative growth* for 'recession.' Like **hyperbole**, euphemisms often lose their semantic significance, so that a new euphemism has to take its place: e.g. *graveyard* became *cemetery* became *memorial garden*.

References
Allan, K. and K. Burridge. 1991. *Euphemism and dysphemism: language used as a shield and weapon*. Oxford.
Ayto, J. 1993. *Euphemisms: over 3,000 ways to avoid being rude or giving offence*. London.
Enright, D.J. (ed.) 1985. *Fair of speech: the uses of euphemism*. Oxford.
Holder, R.W. 1985. *A dictionary of American and British euphemisms: the language of evasion, hypocrisy, prudery and deceit*. Bath. (Rev. edn London 1989.)
Lawrence, J. 1973. *Unmentionable and other euphemisms*. London.
⇒ **figure of speech**, **slang**

euphonism [Grk *euphōnía* 'excellence of sounds']

An agreeable combination of sounds. Euphonism can lead to **assimilation**, **dissimilation**, **vowel harmony**, or **epenthesis** so that words are easier to pronounce. Broadly speaking, euphonism also helps account for assonance, **onomatopoeia**, and rhythm. The antonym is **cacophony**.

European languages

The European languages generally belong to the **Indo-European** language family. Exceptions are **Basque** in the west (a **language isolate**), **Hungarian** and **Finnish** (⇒ **Finno-Ugric**, **Uralic** languages), **Turkish** (an **Altaic** language), as well as Maltese in Malta, which is closely related to **Arabic** and thus belongs to the **Afro-Asiatic** language group.

References
Bechert, J., G. Bernini, and C. Buridant (eds) 1990. *Toward a typology of European languages*. Berlin and New York.
Decsy, G. 1973. *Die linguistische Struktur Europas: Vergangenheit, Gegenwart, Zukunft*. Wiesbaden.
Haarmann, H. 1975. *Soziologie und Politik der Sprachen Europas*. Munich.
Krantz, G.S. 1988. *Geographical development of European languages* (American university stud-
ies, series XI: Anthropology and sociology, vol. 26). New York.
Rundle, S. 1946. *Language as a social and political factor in Europe*. London.
Stephens, M. 1976. *Linguistic minorities in Western Europe*. Llandysul.
Stevenson, V. (ed.) 1983. *Words, the evolution of Western languages*. New York.

evaluation procedure

A technique for choosing the better of two linguistic descriptions on the basis of criteria like simplicity and elegance.

References
Chomsky, N. 1965. *Aspects of the theory of syntax*. Cambridge, MA.
⇒ **levels of adequacy**, **transformational grammar**

evidentiality

Structural dimension of grammar that codifies the source of information transmitted by a speaker with the aid of various types of constructions. One's personal observation is considered the primary source of information; other important sources of information are hearsay (**quotative**) and the deductive skills of the speaker (**inferential**). In English, evidentiality is expressed only peripherally as in the special use of **mood** in indirect discourse (⇒ **direct vs indirect discourse**) (e.g. the subjunctive of the past tense stem as a quotative: *The spokesman said that the president had signed the amendment*, derived from the direct quote '*The president (has) signed the amendment*') and with certain modal expressions (e.g. *supposedly* as a quotative marker for the subject or third person: *Michael is supposedly a descendant of William Shakespeare*, i.e. *Michael claims to be a descendant of William Shakespeare*; or *must* and *might* as a strong, respectively weak, inferential marker: *There must/might be a mistake*).

References
Chafe, W. and J. Nichols (eds) 1986. *Evidentiality: the linguistic coding of epistemology*. Norwood, NJ.
Willett, T. 1988. A cross-linguistic survey of the grammaticalization of evidentiality. *SLang* 12.51–97.
⇒ **modality**

exam question

Contrasted with 'genuine' questions, an exam question is used when the questioner typically already knows what the correct answer is and is instead interested in ascertaining whether the person being questioned knows that correct answer.

exbraciation

In **German**, the placement of one or several constituents outside the sentence frame (⇒ **brace construction**). The tendency towards exbraciation is especially strong in colloquial speech, but is also increasingly observed in the written standard language. In the following cases, exbraciation has become the norm: (a) accumulation of complex constituents that would result in an awkward brace construction: *Also zunächst einmal muß man unterscheiden bei der Reformpolitik zwischen solchen Reformen, die Geld kosten und solchen, die kein Geld kosten* 'Well, to start with, in reform politics one has to distinguish between reforms that cost money and those that don't' (instead of placing *unterscheiden* right at the end of the sentence); (b) subordinate clauses with conjunctions and infinitive constructions (⇒ **extraposition**); and especially (c) when certain constituents are meant to be emphasized.

References
Beneš, E. 1968. Die Ausklammerung im Deutschen als grammatische Norm und stilistischer Effekt. *Muttersprache* 78.289–98.
Engel, U. 1970. Studien zur Geschichte des Satzrahmens und seiner Durchbrechung. *Sprache der Gegenwart* 6.45–61.
Lambert, P.J. 1976. *Ausklammerung in Modern Standard German*. Hamburg.
Petrovic, V. 1978. Zur Satzmelodie der Ausrahmungsstrukturen. *ZPSK* 2.170–82.
Rath, R. 1965. Trennbare Verben und Ausklammerung: zur Syntax der deutschen Sprache der Gegenwart. *Wirkendes Wort* 15.217–32.
⇒ **brace construction, extraposition, word order**

exceptional case marking (*abbrev.* ECM)

The description of a type of construction in **Government and Binding theory** in which the logical subject of an embedded sentence appears in the objective case. In these constructions the verb of the matrix sentence is an exceptional case marker. So-called ECM verbs correspond to the traditional Latin **accusative plus infinitive construction**, and to verbs like *believe*: for example, *Philip believes him to be a liar*, where *him* is in the objective case.

References
⇒ **case theory**

exchange ⇒ interchange

exclamatory

Basic verbal **mood** which can formally be described as a statement, question, or command depending on the word order, and whose primary function is to express a strong emotional state in the speaker through intonation, **inter**jections, and/or modal **particles**: *You're stupid! Isn't it a shame? Help me!*

References
Elliott, D. 1974. Toward a grammar of exclamations. *FL* 11.231–46.
Oomen, U. 1980. Structural properties of English exclamatory sentences. *FoLi* 13.159–74.
Zaefferer, D. 1983. The semantics of non-declaratives: investigating German exclamatories. In R. Bäuerle *et al.* (eds), *Meaning, use, and interpretation of language*. Berlin. 466–90.
⇒ **modality**

exclusion ⇒ contact test

exclusive disjunction

In **formal logic** connection of two elementary propositions *p* and *q* by *or*, such that the propositional connection is true if and only if either *p* or *q* is true, but not if both are true (in contrast with inclusive *or*, ⇒ **disjunction**). This relation is represented in the (two-place) **truth table**:

p	q	$p \vee q$
t	t	f
t	f	t
f	t	t
f	f	f

This *or* (also: exclusive *or*), which corresponds to Lat. *aut ... aut ...* ('either this one or the other one, but not both of them') frequently occurs in everyday language.

exhortative [Lat. *exhortari* 'to encourage']

Sentence type with verb-initial placement in English and many **Indo-European** languages which expresses a request for joint action, often coded in the first person plural: *Let's meet tomorrow in the park!*

existential causative ⇒ effected object

existential operator ⇒ operator

existential presupposition ⇒ presupposition

existential proposition

Proposition about at least one element (individual, state of affairs, etc.) of a particular range in contrast with **universal propositions** that refer to all elements of a particular range. Existential propositions are represented in **formal logic** with the aid of the so-called existential quantifier (⇒ **operator**): $\bigvee x\,[A(x)]$, read as: 'There is at least one *x* for which it is true that *x* has the property *A*' (e.g. 'being a doctor').

References
⇒ **formal logic**

existential quantifier ⇒ **operator**

exocentric compound ⇒ **bahuvrihi**

exocentric construction [Grk *éxō* 'outside']
(*also* non-headed construction)

Term introduced by Bloomfield (1933) indicating a syntactic construction which, in contrast to the more common **endocentric construction**, neither belongs to the same form class or category as any of its constituents, nor shows the same **distribution**. Thus the exocentric construction *She sells fresh fish* as a total construction is neither a **noun phrase** (*she, fresh fish*) nor a **verb phrase** (*to sell fresh fish*). Other exocentric constructions are **prepositional phrases** (*at the marketplace*), constructions with **auxiliary** and **participle** (*has sold*) or copula (⇒ **copular verb**) and predicate noun (*is a salesperson*). The term 'exocentric' is regularly defined in contrast to endocentric, i.e. its literal translation ('to have a center outside of itself') is misleading.

Reference
Bloomfield, L. 1933. *Language*. New York.

exophoric pronoun [Grk *phérein* 'to carry']

Pronoun that does not refer to the immediately preceding or following **noun phrase**, but to a more distant one.

experiencer ⇒ **case grammar**

experimental phonetics

Phonetic analysis practiced since the end of the nineteenth century which, in contrast to **auditory phonetics** (which is based on subjective observations), works with electro-acoustic recording and storing machines (such as the oscillograph and **spectrograph**).

Reference
Ladefoged, P. 1967. *Three areas of experimental phonetics*. London.

expert system

In **artificial intelligence**, application-oriented knowledge-based system that is meant to solve special tasks in the same way and with the same level of achievement as human 'experts.' Currently, the principal areas of application are in medicine, finance, and technical fields. As well as problems faced in representation and reasoning, other general problems, primarily in the acquisition of expert knowledge, remain to be solved. Frequently, natural-language access systems are used to interact with expert systems.

References
Buchanan, B.G. and E.H. Shortliffe. 1984. *Rule-based expert systems*. Reading, MA.
Hayes-Roth, F., D.A. Waterman, and D.B. Lenat. 1983. *Building expert systems*. Reading, MA.
Jackson, P. 1986. *Introduction to expert systems*. Wockingham.

expiration [Lat. *exspirare* 'to breathe out']

Exhaling as a necessary condition for all **speech sounds** formed with the pulmonic **airstream mechanism**. (⇒ *also* **articulatory phonetics, phonetics**)

expiratory accent ⇒ **stress accent**

explanatory adequacy ⇒ **levels of adequacy**

explicit derivation ⇒ **derivation**

explosive [Lat. *explodere* 'to eject, to cast out']

Plosive with **oral**, medial release, e.g. the initial [tʰ] (as opposed to the final unreleased (t⁻]) in *tat* [tʰætʰ⁻]. (⇒ *also* **articulatory phonetics, aspiration**)

References
⇒ **phonetics**

expression

1 Unclassified linguistic unit of any length: words, phrases, sentences, paragraphs, etc. In contrast to **utterance**, which is part of parole, an expression belongs to langue (⇒ **langue vs parole**).

2 In **semiotics**, the material, perceivable aspect of the (linguistic) sign in contrast to its semantic content, e.g. sound waves, written characters, **pictographs**.

expression plane vs content plane

In L. Hjelmslev's **glossematics** and drawing on F. de Saussure's *Cours de linguistique générale*, the distinction between the two levels of analysis of the linguistic sign. The expression plane refers to the material aspect of the linguistic sign, the content plane to the semantic aspect, there not necessarily being a one-to-one correspondence between both aspects of the linguistic sign. In analogy to de Saussure's bilateral model of the sign, the two levels are again subdivided through the dichotomy of 'form vs substance.' Derived from the combination of the four levels are the linguistic subdisciplines of **phonetics** (i.e. the substance of the expression), **semantics** (the substance of the content), **phonology** (the form of the expression), and grammar (the form of the content). In Hjelmslev's autonomous linguistics only the langue-specific form-oriented domains of phonology and grammar are objects of linguistic study, while the substance domains of phonetics and semantics are extralinguistic aspects. (⇒ *also* **langue vs parole**)

References
Hjelmslev, L. 1943. *Omkring sprogteoriens grundlaeggelse*. Copenhagen. 1961. *Prolegomena to a theory of language*, trans. F.J. Whitfield. Madison, WI.
Saussure, F. de. 1916. *Cours de linguistique générale*, ed. C. Bally and A. Sechehaye. Paris. (*Course in general linguistics*, trans. R. Harris. London, 1983.)

expressive aphasia ⇒ **aphasia, Broca's aphasia**

expressive function of language

The expressive function of language constitutes one of the three subfunctions of the linguistic sign in K. Bühler's **organon model of language**. It refers to the relation between the linguistic sign and the 'sender,' whose intention is expressed as a 'symptom' by the linguistic sign. (⇒ *also* **appellative function of language**, **representational function of language**)

References
⇒ **organon model of language**

extension [Lat. *extensio* 'stretch, span'] (*also* denotation², designation, referent)

The extension of a linguistic expression is the class of elements that the expression denotes. Therefore, an extensional **definition** is based on counting all objects to which the expression applies, in contrast with **intension** ('sense'), which is determined according to the features by which the concept is defined. Two predicates have the same extension if they apply to the same class of elements, in this sense both expressions *evening star* and *morning star* are extensionally identical, since they both denote the planet Venus, even though they both have a different intensional content. In **formal logic** extension is defined depending on the different categories of expressions. The extension of a singular term (= individual constant) t is the individual to which t refers (e.g. the extension of *Mozart* is the 'composer of the "Magic Flute"'). The extension of a predicate p is the set of elements to which this predicate applies, e.g. the extension of *larger than* is the set of all pairs x, y for which it is true that x is larger than y. The extension of a sentence is its **truth**

value. The extension of a complex sentence can be conveyed truth-functionally, if the following is true: if in sentence S an element e is replaced by an element of the same extension as e, then the extension of S is unchanged (⇒ **principle of compositionality**).

References
⇒ **intension, semantics**

extensional [Lat. *extendere* 'to stretch']

In **formal logic**, property of propositional connections whose **truth value** alone is dependent on the truth values of the elementary propositions, but not on their actual semantic content. This extensional interpretation is fundamental to the logical connections of classical **propositional logic** and **predicate logic**, e.g. **adjunction, implication, operator**, among others.

Reference
Asher, N. 1985. The trouble with extensional semantics. *PhS* 47.1–14.

extensional definition ⇒ **extension**

extensional logic ⇒ **formal logic**

extensional reading ⇒ **attributive vs referential reading**

extraposition

Term coined by O. Jespersen indicating a word order variant which is similar in form to right dislocation (⇒ **left vs right dislocation**). Sentential elements (e.g. infinitive constructions, sentential subject, object and attribute clauses, adverbial clauses) can be shifted rightwards to the end of the sentence: *That she came made him glad* vs *It made him glad that she came*.

References
Bennis, H. 1986. *Gaps and dummies*. Dordrecht.
Emonds, J.E. 1970. *Root- and structure-preserving transformations*. Bloomington, IN.
Higgins, F.R. 1972. On J. Emond's analysis of extraposition. In J.P. Kimball (ed.), *Syntax and semantics*. New York. Vol. 2, 149–95.
Huck, G.J. and Y. Na. 1990. Extraposition and focus. *Lg* 66.51–77.
Jacobs, R.A. and P.S. Rosenbaum. 1968. *English transformational grammar*. Waltham, MA
Jespersen, O. 1937. *Analytic syntax*. Copenhagen.
Kohrt, M. 1976. *Extraposition in German: evidence for global rules*, *LingI* 7.729–32.
Mallinson, G. 1986. Languages with and without extraposition. *FoLi* 20.146–63.
Mallinson, G. and B.J. Blake. 1981. *Language typology*. Amsterdam. Section 5.2.4.
Ross, J.R. 1967. Constraints on variables in syntax. Dissertation, MIT.
Scherpenisse, W. 1985. The final field in German: extraposition and frozen positions. *GAGL* 26.
⇒ **exbraciation**

extraposition grammar

Grammatical formalism used in **computational linguistics** that is derived from **definite clause grammar** and **metamorphosis grammar** and that introduces a particular type of rule for treating 'left extraposition' (e.g. the unbounded movement found in interrogative sentences and in relative clauses in English and French, ⇒ **trace theory**). In extraposition grammar, the description of structure (i.e. a non-terminal ('motivated') category, followed by an arbitrary chain, followed by an empty non-terminal category ('trace') is placed on the left side of a rule that expands into a chain without a 'trace.' Thus, given the rule we may begin with: 'rel. marker ... trace ⇒ rel. pronoun.' *The mouse* rel. marker *the cat chased* trace *squeaks* to derive *The mouse* rel. pronoun *the cat chased squeaks* ('rel. marker' and 'trace' are non-terminal categories, ' ... ' stands for an arbitrary chain). In this way, on the one hand the structural relation between 'motivated' categories and 'traces' is made clear in a rule, on the other hand it is no longer necessary to expand a non-terminal category into an empty chain.

References
Pereira, F. 1981. Extraposition grammars. *AJCL* 7.243–56.
⇒ **computational linguistics**

extrasyllabic

In **metrical phonology**, a free-standing segment not incorporated into any **syllable**, e.g. /s/ in *speak*, /θs/ in *fifths*, final /s/ in *busts*.

Reference
Clements, G.N. and S.J. Keyser. 1983. *CV phonology: a generative theory of the syllable.* Cambridge, MA.

extrinsic vs intrinsic ordering of rules [Lat. *extrinsecus* 'from without'; *intrinsecus* 'from within']

The order in which several rules are put into operation can be determined by an 'outer,' extrinsic ordering, which is empirically based on linguistic facts, or an 'inner,' intrinsic order which necessarily follows from the formulation of the rules, i.e. the application of one rule depends on that of another. In the Revised Extended Standard Theory (⇒ **transformational grammar**), a specific ordering of rules is completely dispensed with (i.e. all rules operate optionally), since it can be shown that entire cases of seemingly extrinsic rule ordering can be derived from independently motivated, general principles (e.g. the **transformational cycle**). In contrast, an extrinsic ordering of rules for phonology appears to be indispensable. (⇒ **principle of cyclic rule application, phonology**)

References
Chomsky, N. 1965. *Aspects of the theory of syntax.* Cambridge, MA.
Chomsky, N. and M. Halle. 1968. *The sound pattern of English.* New York.
Koutsoudas, A. 1973. Extrinsic order and the complete NP constraint. *LingI* 4.69–81.
——— (ed.) 1976. *The application and ordering of grammatical rules.* The Hague.
Koutsoudas, A., G. Sanders, and C. Noll. 1974. The application of phonological rules. *Lg* 50.1–28.
Pelletier, F.J. 1980. The generative power of rule orderings in formal grammars. *Linguistics* 18.17–72.
Pullum, G. 1979. *Rule interaction and the organization of a grammar.* New York.
Ringen, C. 1972. The arguments for rule ordering. *FL* 8.266–73.

F

face ⇒ politeness

face-to-face interaction

Communicative behavior in speech situations where the speaker and listener make immediate contact. Research into face-to-face interaction considers linguistic features, but is primarily concerned with non-linguistic features like facial expression, eye contact, gestures, posture as well as paralinguistic features like manner of articulation (whispering, shouting). ⇒ **non-verbal communication**

References
Kendon, A., R.M. Harris, and M.R. Key (eds) 1975. *Organization of behaviour in face-to-face inter-action*. The Hague and Paris.
Laver, J. and S. Hutcheson (eds) 1972). *Face-to-face interaction*. Harmondsworth.
⇒ **non-verbal communication**

factitive [Lat. *facere* 'to make']

1 Verbal aspect of category of events that are caused by a participant. Factitives comprise verbs (usually morphologically derived forms) that express the idea of 'cause to,' such as the deverbal derivations *fell* 'cause to fall' and *drench* 'cause to drink', or the deadjectival derivations *redden* 'cause to become/make red', *strengthen* 'cause to become/make strong' (⇒ **causative**).

2 In Fillmore's early version of **case grammar** (1968), the semantic role (or deep case) of an entity that is the result of the process of state denoted by the verb (e.g. *make a suggestion*). Occasionally, factitive is still used as a general term for patient-like roles.

Reference
Fillmore, C. 1968. The case for case. In E. Bach and R.T. Harms (eds), *Linguistic theory*. New York. 1–88.

factitive verb ⇒ factitive

factive ⇒ factive predicate

factive predicate (*also* factive)

Type of predicate that produces a so-called 'factive **presupposition**,' that is, the speaker (usually) presupposes the truth of the clause depending on the factive predicate, e.g. *He is surprised that it is snowing again* presupposes *It is snowing again*. Examples of factive pre-

dicates are *regret, understand, know*, and *it is notable/curious/too bad that x*. The relation between a fact and its factive predicate is not always straightforward. This is amply evident in the following statement in which the suspect challenges the chief of police: *You know, of course, that I murdered him*. Contrasting with factive predicates are **implicative verbs**.

References
Karttunen, L. 1971. *The logic of English predicate complement constructions*. Bloomington, IN.
Kiparsky, P. and C. Kiparsky. 1970. Fact. In M. Bierwisch and K.E. Heidolph (eds), *Progress in linguistics*. The Hague. 143–73.
Norrick, N.R. 1978. *Factive adjectives and the theory of factivity*. Tübingen.
⇒ **presupposition**

factivity ⇒ factive predicate

factorization

In general, factorization refers to the division of large sequences into partial sequences. In **transformational grammar**, factorization refers to the division of the end nodes in a **tree diagram** with regard to the use of **transformational rules**. If the division can be undertaken so that there is an element corresponding to every term in the structural description of the rules, then the sentence has a proper analysis.

References
⇒ **transformational grammar**

facultative variation ⇒ free variation

falling diphthong ⇒ diphthong, intonation

falling vs rising ⇒ diphthong, intonation

family tree theory ⇒ genetic tree theory

Faroese

North **Germanic** language with approx. 40,000 speakers, one of the two standard written languages of the Faroe Islands (the other being **Danish**). (⇒ *also* **Scandinavian**)

References
Kuspert, K.C. 1988. *Vokalsysteme im Westnordi-schen. Isländisch, Faröisch, Westnorwegisch: Prinzipien der Differenzierung*. Tübingen.
Lockwood, W.B. 1955. *An introduction to modern Faroese*. Copenhagen.
⇒ **Scandinavian**

Farsi ⇒ **Persian**

faucal [Lat. *fauces* (p. 2.) 'throat']
Obsolete term for **pharyngeal**.

faux amis
Term (from French meaning 'false friends')
denoting word pairs from different languages
which, in spite of similarities in form, have
different meanings. Frequently such similarities
lead to **interference** errors in **second language
acquisition**, e.g. Eng. *figure* vs Fr. *figure*
('face') or Eng. *cold* vs Ital. *caldo* ('warm'), or
Span. *presidio* 'prison, imprisonment' and Ger.
Präsidium 'residence of a president; office of
chairman.' (⇒ *also* **error analysis**, **contrastive
analysis**)

Reference
Hayward, T. and A. Moulin. 1984. False friends
  invigorated. In R.K.K. Hartmann (ed.), *Lexeter
  '83 proceedings: papers from the International
  Conference on Lexicography at Exeter*. Tübingen
  190–8.

feature
Linguistically relevant properties of phonological, semantic, or syntactic units. Features
are conceptual representations for linguistically
important elements of description which relate
to facts of non-linguistic reality, but are not
identical to them. As a rule, features are binary,
i.e. used in the context of 'either–or.' For
example, a **phoneme** is either described as
[+nasal] or [–nasal]. In addition, there are
features which are graduated, especially phonetic or prosodic features. Graduated features
are used to specify different degrees of an
attribute. Linguistic description based on features was significantly advanced by structuralist
phonology (⇒ **structuralism**), which posited a
distinction between **distinctive features** and
redundant features (⇒ **redundancy**) in linguistic analysis at all levels of description. Likewise, a distinction is made between inherent
features and contextual features, by which
contextually independent features are delimited
from predictable, contextually dependent features. Chomsky based his hypothesis that there
is an unlimited universal inventory of features,
from which every language uses a specific
assortment and grouping, on the observations
of structural phonology. In the notation, features are signified by square brackets or by a
feature **matrix**. (⇒ *also* **componential analysis**)

References
⇒ **componential analysis**, **distinctive feature**

feature bundle (*also* feature complex)
A type of description developed in structural
phonology and semantic **componential analysis** for representing linguistic units on the basis
of sets of elementary characteristic components
through which such linguistic units are structured, e.g. the (articulatory) phonological
description of /p/ as [+stop, –voiced, +bilabial,
–nasal]. On the further development of the
concept, ⇒ **unification grammar**.

References
⇒ **phonology**

feature complex ⇒ **feature bundle**

feature structure
In **unification grammar**, a **feature bundle**
with complex values and indexes.

References
⇒ **unification grammar**

felicity conditions ⇒ **speech act theory**

feminine ⇒ **gender**

feminist linguistics
A research approach initiated by the New
Women's Liberation Movement, which was
established in the Anglo–American sphere in
the mid-seventies through publications by Key,
Lakoff and Thorne/Henley (all 1975). Whereas
the mainstream linguistics current then was
dominated by structuralist priorities such as
language system before language use, homogeneity before heterogeneity, synchrony before
diachrony (⇒ **synchrony vs diachrony**), linguistic competence of an ideal speaker/hearer
before language use of individual speakers (⇒
competence vs performance), feminist linguistics studies the gender-typical language use
and the gender-specific asymmetries (established through thousands of years of tradition)
in the language system and makes a connection
between linguistic and social discrimination. In
English, the ambiguity of *man* (for humans in
general or for male humans specifically), problems of pronominalization and of the vocabulary (specific terms for females are usually
derived from terms for males) are the critical
points for departure (see for a summary Baron
1986, Cameron 1985). In German and French,
the problems of linguistic inequality are
enhanced through the grammatical **gender** system and its connection with the extralinguistic
category of 'sex'. Particularly the ambiguity of
the masculine form, which can refer both to
male referents and to referents of both sexes
(generic use), has led to many suggestions for

change in the language of law and administration, which are by now already being practiced. Empirical studies of language use within the framework of **conversation analysis** deal mainly with gender-specific discourse behavior as well as with problems of the influence of the sex on linguistic socialization. In order to be able to use verifiable results (not merely uncertain tendencies) as the basis for the changes pursued, greater differentiation in the construction of hypotheses is necessary; especially, the isolation of the variable 'gender' must be given up in favor of its interplay with other variables, such as age, status, nationality etc. The comprehensive success of feminist language-political demands is astounding, as here a Europe-wide language change has been set in motion by a decentralized group without any political power.

References

Cameron, D. 1985. *Feminism and linguistic theory*. Basingstoke. (2nd edn 1992.)

Coates, J. 1986. *Women, men, and language: a sociolinguistic account of sex differences in language*. London. (2nd edn 1993.)

Coates, J. and D. Cameron (eds) (1989). *Women in their speech communities. New perspectives on language and sex*. London.

Crawford, M. 1995. *Talking difference. On gender and language*. London.

Frank, K. 1992. *Sprachgewalt. Die sprachliche Reproduktion der Geschlechterhierarchie. Elemente einer feministischen Linguistik im Kontext sozialwissenschaftlicher Frauenforschung*. Tübingen.

Jespersen, O. 1922. *Language. Its nature, development and origin*. New York.

Lakoff, R. 1975. *Language and women's place*. New York.

Mills, S. 1995. *Feminist stylistics*. London.

Philips, S.U., S. Steele, and C. Tanz. 1987. *Language, gender and sex in comparative perspective*. Cambridge.

Postl, G. 1991. *Weibliches Sprechen. Feministische Entwürfe zu Sprache und Geschlecht*. Vienna.

Pusch, L.F. 1984. *Das Deutsche als Männersprache*. Frankfurt.

Tannen, D. 1991. *You just don't understand: women and men in conversation*. London.

——— 1996. *Gender and discourse*. Oxford.

Thorne, B., C. Kramarae and N. Henley (eds) 1983. *Language, gender and society*. Rowley, MA.

Trömel-Plötz, S. 1982. *Frauensprache: Sprache der Veränderung*. Frankfurt.

State-of-the-art-reports

Baron, D. 1986. *Grammar and gender*. New Haven.

Bussmann, H. 1995. DAS Genus. DIE Grammatik und – DER Mensch: Geschlechterdifferenz in der Sprachwissenschatt. In: *Genus. Zur Geschlechterdifferenz iu den Kulturwissenschaften*, ed. by H. Bussmann and R. Hof, 114.–160. Stuttgart.

McConnell-Ginet, S. 1988. Language and gender. In:

Linguistics: The Cambridge survey, ed. by F.J. Newmeyer. Vol. 4: *Language: The socio-cultural context*. 75–99. Cambridge.

Samel, I. 1995. *Einführung in die feministische Sprachwissenschaft*. Berlin.

⇒ **gender**, ⇒ **agreement**

field work

Methodological process for the collection of linguistic data and texts (⇒ **corpus**) of spoken language or of a language which is only orally transmitted. The selection of data and the specific way in which the field work is carried out depends upon the particular objectives of the study concerned. The most important techniques comprise the recording of conversations in 'participatory observation' or in structured interviews with a subsequent **transcription**, the questioning of informants by the investigator where all the answers are recorded or transcribed during the process of the interview, linguistic tests, language attitude tests (⇒ **matched guise technique**), etc. It was primarily in sociolinguistic studies on linguistic varieties in a social context that several procedures were developed to evade the 'observer's paradox' (Labor): the informal, uninhibited everyday language that the linguist wants to study and observe is only used if the speakers do not feel under surveillance.

References

Labov, W. 1972. *Sociolinguistic patterns*. Philadelphia, PA.

——— 1973. *Language in the inner city: studies in the Black English vernacular*. Philadelphia, PA.

Samarin, W.J. 1967. *Field linguistics: a guide to linguistic field work*. New York.

Bibliography

Hymes, H.D. 1959. Field work in linguistics and anthropology: annotated bibliography. *SiL* 14.82–91.

⇒ **operational procedures**

figura etymologica

Figure of speech of repetition, a special case of **polyptoton**: a coupling of words that are etymologically related, e.g. *to give a gift, to dance a dance*.

References

⇒ **figure of speech**

figure of speech

A collective term in **rhetoric** for all kinds of striking or unusual configurations of words or phrases. The variation can affect all units of the linguistic system (graphic, phonological, morphological, syntactic, semantic, and pragmatic patterns) and occur through (a) repetition, e.g. **alliteration, polyptoton, parallelism**; (b) extension, e.g. **parenthesis**, **pleonasm**; (c) abbreviation, e.g. **apocope**, **ellipsis**, **zeugma**; (d) permutation/transposition, e.g. **palindrome**, **anastrophe**, **hyperbaton**. Certain types of substitution and replacement are also considered figures of speech today, e.g. **trope**, as well as various pragmatic figures such as the **rhetorical question** or **concession** or **prolepsis**.

References
Dixon, P. 1971. *Rhetoric*. London.
Fowler, G. 1986. *Linguistic criticism*. Oxford.
Lanham, R.A. 1968. *A handlist of rhetorical terms*. Berkeley, CA.
Leech, G. 1966. Linguistics and the figures of rhetoric. In R. Fowler (ed.), *Essays on style and language*. London.
Leech, N.G. 1969. *A linguistic guide to English poetry*. London.
Murphy, J.J. (ed.) 1983. *Renaissance eloquence*. Berkeley, CA.
Nash, W. 1989. *Rhetoric*. Oxford.
Nowottny, W. 1962. *The language poets use*. London.
Ortony, A. (ed.) 1979. *Metaphor and thought*. Cambridge.
Plett, H.F. 1985. Rhetoric. In T.A. van Dijk (ed.), *Discourse and literature*. Amsterdam.
Quinn, A. 1987. *Figures of speech: sixty ways to turn a phrase*. Salt Lake City, UT.
Vickers, B. 1988. *In defense of rhetoric*. Oxford.
Wine, J.D. 1993. *Figurative language in Cynewulf: defining aspects of a poetic style*. New York.
⇒ **rhetoric**

Fijian ⇒ **Malayo-Polynesian**

filter

A **constraint** in the Revised Extended Standard Theory (REST) of **transformational grammar** which prevents overgeneration by syntactic rules. Filters are language-specific constraints on wellformedness at the **surface structure**: for example, in Chomsky and Lasnik (1977), the ungrammatical sentence **Who did we want for to win?* is excluded by the *for–to* filter. In contrast to the filter formulated by Ross in 1967, the REST filters perform functions which correspond to dependency among the application of transformational rules (⇒ **transformation**) in the early stages of transformational grammar.

References
Brame, M. 1981. Lexicon vs filters. In T. Hoekstra, H. van der Hulst, and M. Moortgat (eds), *Lexical grammar*. Dordrecht. 73–95.
Chomsky, N. and H. Lasnik. 1977. Filters and control. *LingI* 8.425–504.
Heny, F. (ed.) 1981. *Binding and filtering*. London.
Perlmutter, D.M. 1971. *Deep and surface structure constraints in syntax*. New York.
Radford, A. 1981. *Transformational syntax: a stu-

dent's guide to Chomsky's Extended Standard Theory*. Cambridge.
Ross, J.R. 1967. Constraints on variables in syntax. Dissertation, MIT. (Repr. as *Infinite syntax!* Norwood, NJ, 1986.)
⇒ **constraints, finite state automaton, transformational grammar**

finite state automaton (*abbrev.* FSA; *also* finite automaton)

A kind of **automaton** consisting of a finite number of states connected by transitions. Some states are initial, some final, and the transitions are decorated by symbols (see figure). An automaton accepts a string of symbols whenever one can begin at an initial state and follow transitions designated in the string, arriving at a final state with no further elements to process. Generation is similar.

FSAs generate (or accept) exactly the regular, or type 3 languages, the simplest in the **Chomsky hierarchy** of **formal language theory**. Center-embedding constructions cannot, in general, be described in FSAs, which led Chomsky to reject them as syntax models. Computational linguists revived interest in **finite state transducers**, however, as models of morphophonemics.

Finite state automata whose transitions are further decorated with probabilities (indicating likelihood of transition) are Markov models (⇒ **Markov process**) or **hidden Markov models**.

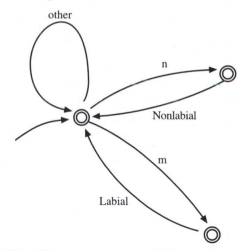

FSA A finite state automaton enforcing nasal assimilation

References
Chomsky, N. 1957. *Syntactic structures*. The Hague.
Hopcroft, J. and J. Ullman. 1979. *Introduction to automata theory, languages and computation*. Reading, MA.

finite state transducer (*abbrev.* FST)

Similar to a **finite state automaton**, except that its transitions are decorated with pairs of corresponding symbols. In operation, it reads one string and writes a second, always based on the correspondences of transitions. Johnson (1972) showed that the phonology derived from Chomsky and Halle's *Sound pattern of English* (1968) could be modeled by FSTs, and that these could operate reversibly – for generation or analysis.

References
Chomsky, N. and M. Halle. 1968. *The sound pattern of English*. New York.
Johnson, C. 1972. *Formal aspects of phonological description*. The Hague.
Kaplan, R. and M. Kay. 1994. Regular models of phonological rule systems. *CL.*

finite verb form [Lat. *finitus* 'bounded'] (*also* tensed form)

Conjugated verb form marked according to **tense**, **voice**, **person**, **number**, and **mood**: *She eats* vs the non-finite forms (*to*) *eat* (⇒ **infinitive**) and *eaten* (⇒ **participle**).

finitive ⇒ effective, egressive², resultative

Finnish

Finno-Ugric language (Fin. *Suomi*) with approx. 5 million speakers; official language of Finland. Literary documents since the sixteenth century.
Characteristics: relatively small consonant and large vowel inventory, including distinctive length. Complex morphology with numerous morphophonological changes. Comprehensive case system (fifteen cases), including the noticeably heavy use of the **partitive** case (partial objects, negation, incomplete actions, etc.); nine locative cases which are systematically related (inside : outside : general ; rest : motion towards : motion away). Subject–verb agreement. Four infinitive forms which denote various degrees of subordination. Word order SVO.

References
Atkinson, J. 1977. *A Finnish grammar*. Helsinki.
Fromm, H. 1982. *Finnische Grammatik*. Heidelberg.
Hakulinen, L. 1957. *Handbuch der finnischen Sprache*. Wiesbaden.
Karlsson, F. 1983. *Finnish grammar*. Juva.
Sulkala, H. and M. Karalainen. 1992. *Finnish*. London.
⇒ **Finno-Ugric**

Finno-Ugric

Largest branch of the **Uralic** language family, divided into (a) the Ugric languages (with

Hungarian, approx. 14 million speakers, and the Ob-Ugric languages Khanty (Ostyak) and Mansi (approx. 20,000 speakers) and (b) the Finnish languages. The latter consist of the Balto-Finnish languages (with **Finnish** (approx. 5 million speakers), **Estonian** (approx. 1 million speakers), Karelian (approx. 86,000 speakers), Veps, Ingrian, Liv, and Vot, the Volgaic languages with Mordva (approx. 1 million speakers) and Mari (Cheremis, approx. 600,000 speakers) and the Permic languages with Udmurt (approx. 900,000 speakers) and Komi (approx. 300,000 speakers) to the north. The **Lapp** languages in northern Scandinavia are usually considered to belong to the Finnish branch.

References
Collinder, B. 1960. *Comparative grammar of the Uralic languages*. Stockholm.
———— 1965. *An introduction to the Uralic languages*. Berkeley, CA.
———— 1969. Survey of the Uralic languages, 2nd edn, Stockholm.
Décsy, G. 1965. *Einführung in die finnisch-ugrische Sprachwissenschaft*. Wiesbaden.
Haarmann, H. 1974. *Die finnisch-ugrischen Sprachen*. Hamburg.
Hajdú, P. 1962. *Finnugor népek es nyelvek*. Budapest. (*Finno-Ugrian languages and peoples*, trans. G.F. Cushing. London, 1975.)
Stipa, G.J. 1990. *Finnisch-ugrische Sprachforschung: von der Renaissance bis zum Neupositivismus*. Helsinki.

Dictionary
Collinder, B. 1977. *Fenno-Ugric vocabulary: An etymological dictionary of the Uralic languages*. (Handbook 1.) 2nd, rev. edn. Hamburg.
⇒ **Uralic languages**

first-sister principle

In Roeper and Siegel's (1978) **word formation** theory, principle postulated for forming and interpreting verbal **compounds**. The first-sister principle controls the transformational incorporation of a noun into the immediately adjacent (= first sister) position to the verb in its **subcategorization** frame. Accordingly, *peacemaker*, but not **peace-thinker* can be derived as a possible compound. Selkirk (1982) assumes a similar principle in **word syntax** in the 'first-order projection principle.'

References
Roeper, T. and M. Siegel. 1978. A lexical transformation for verbal compounds. *LingI* 9.199–259.
Selkirk, E. 1982. *The syntax of words*. Cambridge.
⇒ **verbal vs root compound**, **word syntax**

Firthian linguistics (*also* contextualism, London School)

British variant of **structuralism**, which distinguishes itself from other branches above all through the following. (a) The object of investigation is not primarily the language system (langue) (⇒ **langue vs parole**), but rather language use (⇒ **usage vs use**) as part of a more extensive social process. (b) This social process takes place in situations, i.e. each linguistic expression is determined by its situational context as well as by its linguistic context (i.e. its **distribution**). (c) In contrast to mentalistic approaches (⇒ **mentalism**), **meaning** is understood to be a complex relation in the context of situations. Based on the research of the Polish anthropologist B. Malinowski (1884–1942) and developed primarily by J.R. Firth (1890–1960), Firthian linguistics has exerted significant influence on **language acquisition** theory, due to its orientation towards language use.

References
Firth, J.R. 1957a. *Papers in linguistics, 1934–1951.* London.
—— 1957b. A synopsis of linguistic theory 1930–1955. In Philosophical Society of London (ed.) *Studies in linguistic analysis.* (Special issue). Oxford, pp. 1–32.
—— 1968. *Selected papers.* London.
Kühlwein, W. (ed.) 1970. *Linguistics in Great Britain.* Tübingen.
Love, N. 1988. The linguistic thought of J.R. Firth. In R. Harris (ed.), *Linguistic thought in England, 1914–1945.* London.
Malinowski, B. 1935. *Coral gardens and their magic,* 2 vols. London.
Mitchell, T.F. 1975. *Principles of Firthian linguistics.* Oxford.
Robins, H.R. 1963. General linguistics in Great Britain 1930–1960. In C. Mohrmann *et al.* (eds), *Trends in modern linguistics.* Utrecht. 11–37.
Sampson, G. 1980. *Schools of linguistics.* Stanford, CA.
⇒ **collocation, linguistics (history), systemic linguistics**

fixed stress ⇒ **stress²**

FLAC ⇒ **content-based instruction**

flap
Speech sound so called because of its flapping motion as it bypasses its obstruction. In the formation of a flap, the tip of the tongue is bent backwards and upwards and moves with a continuous striking motion against its **place of articulation** (**alveolar ridge** or hard front palate) before returning to its resting position, e.g. [ɾ] in Amer. Eng. [bæɾər] *batter* (⇒ **tap**).

References
⇒ **phonetics**

Flemish
Belgian variant of **Dutch**.

flexive
A bound morpheme used to mark word forms grammatically, e.g. -(*e*)s in *does* or *works* or -(*e*)s in *notches* or *pens.*

References
⇒ **morphology**

fluent aphasia ⇒ **aphasia, Wernicke's aphasia**

focus [Lat. *focŭs* 'hearth, fireplace'] (*also* **comment**, psychological object, rheme)
Term for the informational content of a sentence which the speaker wishes to express. The main grammatical means used to indicate the focus of a sentence are word order (⇒ **topicalization**) and **intonation**. If the question test is applied to a sentence, the focus will be the **scope** of the most normal question posed. Thus in the sentence *We went to the movies yesterday*, the most natural question is *Who went to the movies yesterday?* With different intonation *We went to the móvies yesterday*, the natural question would be *Where did you go yesterday?* Because a speaker generally emphasizes new information in a sentence, the focus will usually correspond to the rheme or comment. (⇒ *also* **functional sentence perspective**)

References
Chomsky, N. 1969. Deep structure, surface structure and semantic interpretation. In D.D. Steinberg and L.A. Jakobovits (eds), *Semantics.* London and Cambridge. (Repr. in N. Chomsky, *Studies on semantics in generative grammar.* The Hague, 1972. 11–61.)
Jacobs, J. 1986. The syntax of focus and adverbials in German. In W. Abraham and S. de Meij (eds), *Topic, focus and configurationality.* Amsterdam. 103–27.
König, E. 1993. Focus particles. In J. Jacobs *et al.* (eds), *Syntax: an international handbook of contemporary research.* Berlin and New York. 978–88.
Lyons, J. 1977. *Semantics,* 2 vols. Cambridge.
Quirk, R. *et al.* 1985. *A comprehensive grammar of the English language.* New York.
Rochemont, M.S. 1986. *Focus in generative grammar.* Amsterdam.
Taglicht, J. 1984. *Message and emphasis: on focus and scope in English.* London.
—— 1993. Focus and background. In J. Jacobs *et al.* (eds), *Syntax: an international handbook of contemporary research.* Berlin and New York. 998–1005.
⇒ **theme vs rheme, topic vs comment**

folk etymology

Process of **word formation** based on a reinterpretation of meaning and a reformation of an archaic, foreign word modeled after a similar-sounding known word with a similar meaning. Through this diachronic linguistic process, incomprehensible words are (secondarily) motivated, i.e. their meanings are made transparent through a seemingly plausible interpretation. **Analogy** and **assimilation** play an important role in this process, and the original meaning is obscured, cf. Eng. *asparagus* as *sparrow-grass* and Fr. *choucroute* (lit. 'cabbage crust,' an assimilated **loan word** based on Ger. *Sauerkraut*), or **Arawakan** *hamaca* 'hammock' > Span. *hamaca* > Fr. *hamac* became Du. *hangmak, hangmat*, NHG *Hängematte* (*hängen* 'to hang,' *Matte* 'mat').

References
⇒ **etymology**

Foot Feature Principle ⇒ Generalized Phrase Structure Grammar

footing

Term introduced by Goffman (1981) to characterize a particular type of activity in which participants use framing devices (⇒ **frame**) that identify their position *vis-à-vis* themselves and others in the way they manage the production or reception of an utterance. **Code-switching**, a change in paralinguistic features (in pitch and voice quality) and/or in posture may indicate a new footing, leading to a change in the interpretation of the relationship between participants from a symmetric to an asymmetric relation. According to Goffman, changes in footing are a natural feature of spoken language.

References
Goffman, E. 1974. *Frame analysis*. New York.
────── 1981. *Forms of talk*. Philadelphia, PA.
Tannen, D. 1986. *That's not what I meant! How conversational style makes and breaks your relations with others*. New York.

Foreign Language Across the Curriculum ⇒ content-based instruction

foreign-language pedagogy

Most common designation for those areas in **applied linguistics** and **language pedagogy** that are concerned with the theory and practice of foreign-language instruction. Important areas of foreign-language pedagogy are (a) decisions about instructional goals (type and scope of desired proficiency); (b) studies on the requisites of language learning (motivation, talent, prior knowledge, age of the learner, the organization of language instruction, etc.); (c) research and compilation of instructional materials; and (d) diagnostic methods of evaluating proficiency (proficiency tests, testing procedures). (⇒ *also* **language test**, **second language acquisition**)

References
Hammerly, H. 1991. *Fluency and accuracy: toward balance in language teaching and learning*. Clevedon.
Kelly, L.G. 1969. *Twenty-five centuries of language teaching*. Rowley, MA.
Larsen-Freeman, D. 1986. *Techniques and principles of language teaching*. New York.
Omaggio-Hadley, A. 1993. *Teaching language in context*. Boston.
Richards, J.C. and T.S. Rodgers. 1986. *Approaches and methods in language teaching*. Cambridge.
Stevick, E.W. 1980. *Teaching languages: a way and ways*. Rowley, MA.
────── 1982. *Teaching and language learning*. Cambridge.
Stern, H.H. 1983. *Fundamental concepts of language teaching*. Oxford.
⇒ **applied linguistics**

foreign vs second language

A foreign language is any language that is not officially recognized in a given country or state. In this view, for example, the Spanish language in the United States would be considered a 'foreign language' even though it is spoken by approx. 19 million people. In contrast, a second language is an officially sanctioned language spoken by an identifiable population in a given country or state, such as French in Canada.

A theoretical distinction is often drawn between the concept of a 'foreign' vs a 'second' language. In calling a language a 'second' language, emphasis is placed equally on the mastery of receptive and productive skills with the goal of making the new language one's own and of becoming a productive, functioning member in the L_2 society. In contrast, 'foreign' languages are usually learned with more specific goals in mind, such as learning how to read specific types of written material, acquiring rudimentary listening skills, learning how to make oneself understood as a tourist in a foreign country, and so on. In the United States in recent years, the term foreign language has been rejected by many teachers for political and pragmatic reasons. Among suggested replacements is 'world languages', a term that emphasizes internationalism and inclusion rather than the distance and strangeness by the term 'foreign'.

References
⇒ **second language acquisition**

foreign word

The concept of 'foreign' words goes back to the middle of the seventeenth century, a foreign word being a linguistic expression adopted from one language into another (usually together with that which it denotes) and which, in contrast to a **loan word**, has not been phonetically, graphemically, or grammatically assimilated into the new language (e.g. *Gemütlichkeit*, *Sushi*). To be sure, the distinction between a foreign word and a loan word is often fuzzy (e.g. *independence*, *culture*, *lox*, *cocaine*), and foreign-word status is particularly questionable in lexicalized hybrids like *anti-aircraft*, *regretful*, *megabuck*. Criteria for distinguishing foreign words from loan words are (a) the presence of 'foreign' morphophonemic structure (e.g. *mahi-mahi*); (b) the frequency of occurrences or the familiarity of the speaker/hearer with the term and concept, with the 'life' of the foreign word being irrelevant: *influenza* (in use since the mid eighteenth century) would more likely be characterized as 'foreign' than *radio* or *diskette*, both in currency only in this century; (c) the orthographic representation (*bologna* vs *baloney*). The determination of foreign-word status varies; it depends a great deal on a society's attitude towards other languages and cultures and, hence, ranges from purist judgments (particularly by language associations in the seventeenth century) to prestige value (found particularly in scholarly language).

References
⇒ **borrowing**, **language contact**, **language maintenance**, **stylistics**

form

This term is used in various ways, depending on the terminological context:

1 In traditional grammar (⇒ **school grammar**), it is the designation for words of the same stem, but different inflection: in this sense *run*, *ran*, *runs* are different word forms of the word *run*.

2 Since antiquity (Aristotle), form has denoted the sensorily perceptible aspect of the linguistic **sign** (⇒ **signifier vs signified**), in contrast to **content/meaning** or function.

3 In **American structuralism**, form is an unclassified linguistic utterance to which a meaning is attributed. A distinction is drawn between (a) *free forms*, which can occur alone, such as the **word**, which is defined as the smallest free form, and (b) *bound forms*, such as inflectional or word formation suffixes, which can only occur together with other, i.e. free, forms.

Reference
Bloomfield, L. 1926. A set of postulates for the science of language. *Lg* 2.153–64.

4 In **glossematics**, form in the opposition 'form vs **substance**' denotes abstract characteristics (which are at the base of all possible substantial realizations of a linguistic expression). Substances represent material linguistic realizations at the level of parole, whereas forms represent units at the level of langue (⇒ **langue vs parole**). The distinction of form vs substance applies to all levels of description: thus, form on the content level refers to the abstract semantic relations of the lexicon, by which the meaning substance (= unstructured set of thoughts and concepts) is differently structured from language to language. For an impressive example cf. the designation of the basic colors in different languages: the substance (the chromatic spectrum) is structured language, specifically through different formal relations (⇒ **color terms**).

References
⇒ **glossematics**

form association ⇒ analogy

form class

A term introduced by Bloomfield for groups of linguistic expressions with identical format, phonological and morphological structure as well as syntactic properties. Criteria for membership of expressions in a form class are the ability to be substituted in certain contexts and the ability to occur in complex expressions. Similar concepts are proposed by other **structuralists** such as C. Fries, C. Hockett, and O. Jespersen.

References
Bloomfield, L. 1926. A set of postulates for the science of language. *Lg* 2.153–64.
⇒ **American structuralism**

formal language

In contrast with natural languages, a formal language is a linguistic system based on logic and/or mathematics that is distinguished by its clarity, explicitness, and simple verifiability. (⇒ *also* **formal logic**, **formalization**)

formal language theory

The mathematical study of the form of languages, i.e. divorced from properties such as meaning and use. The fundamental result of this theory is the **Chomsky hierarchy**: the division of language types into regular languages (⇒ **finite state automaton**), context-free (CF) languages (⇒ **context-free grammar**), context-sensitive (CS) languages (⇒ **context-sensitive grammar**), and unrestricted ones. These are often referred to as type 3 languages (regular) and type 0 languages.

A set is *closed* under an operation if applying the operation to appropriate arguments from the set yields an element in the set. Each of these language families is closed under union, concatenation and repetition. In addition, there are deep parallels between formal language theory and **automata theory**. The following table summarizes these:

Language type		Automata type
regular	→	finite-state
context-free	→	(push-down) stack
context-sensitive	→	linear bounded
unrestricted	→	Turing machines

In addition, correspondences have been demonstrated with programming theory and the theory of recursive functions. Thus, regular languages are exactly those characterized by finite memory programs, CF by recursive finite domain programs. CS languages are included in those characterized by recursive functions, and unrestricted languages are exactly those characterized by partially recursive functions (thus these languages are just the recursively enumerable sets).

Current research in linguistically oriented formal language theory focuses on **mildly context-sensitive languages**, a language family between CF and CS, which may include all human languages. See Hopcroft and Ullman (1979) for language/automata correspondences and recursive function theory; see Gurari (1989) for programming theory.

References
Guran. 1989. *An introduction to the theory of computation*. Rockville.
Hopcroft, J. and J. Ullman. 1979. *Introduction to automata theory, languages and computation*. Reading, MA.

formal logic (*also* extensional/mathematical/ symbolic logic, logistics)

As the study of correct and logical thought, logic is fundamental to all theoretical and empirical sciences in that it provides a method for arriving at valid conclusions and at necessarily true sentences required to propose and test scientific theories. To represent the logical form of sentences formal logic uses a formalized artificial language with a distinctive inventory of symbols (see p. xvii) that can represent certain phenomena of natural language, but dispenses with all stylistic variants as well as ambiguity and vagueness. The main focus of formal logic is on (a) the study of

logical connections of **propositions** and their **truth values** (⇒ **propositional logic**), (b) the study of the internal structure of propositions (⇒ **predicate logic**), (c) the theory of concluding and proving, and (d) the description of **inferences** (⇒ **presupposition**).

References
Allwood, J., L.-G. Andersson, and Ö. Dahl. 1977. *Logic in linguistics*. Cambridge.
Cresswell, M.J. 1973. *Logics and languages*. London.
Feys, R. and F. Fitch. 1969. *Dictionary of symbols of mathematical logic*. Amsterdam.
Gabbay, D.M. and F. Guenthner (eds) 1983–9. *Handbook of philosophical logic*, 4 vols. Dordrecht.
Guttenplan, S. 1986. *The languages of logic*. Oxford.
Hodges, W. 1983. Elementary logic. In D.M. Gabbay and F. Guenthner (eds), *Handbook of philosophical logic*. Dordrecht. Vol. 2, 1–131.
Marciszewski, W. (ed.) 1981. *Dictionary of logic as applied in the study of language: concepts, methods, theories*. The Hague.
McCawley, J.D. 1981. *Everything that linguists have always wanted to know about logic but were ashamed to ask*. Oxford.
Moore, R.C. 1993. *Logic and representation*. Chicago, IL.
Quine, W.V.O. 1950. *Methods of logic*. New York.
Reichenbach, H. 1947. *Elements of symbolic logic*. New York (5th edn 1956.)
Van Fraassen, B. 1971. *Formal semantics and logic*. New York.
Wall, R. 1972. *Introduction to mathematical linguistics*. Englewood Cliffs, NJ.
Zierer, E. 1972. *Formal logic and linguistics*. The Hague.

Bibliographies
Partee, B., S. Sabsay, and J. Soper. 1971. *Bibliography: logic and language*. Bloomington, IN.
Petöfi, J.S. (ed.) 1978. *Logic and the formal theory of natural language: selective bibliography*. Hamburg.

formal meaning ⇒ **lexical meaning vs grammatical meaning**

formal semantics ⇒ **logical semantics**

formalization

Use of formal languages of mathematics and **formal logic** to describe natural languages. The advantage of formalization as opposed to nonformalized descriptions is the greater explicitness of the vocabulary (= terminology), precision and economy, as well as simpler verification of argumentation.

References
Chomsky, N. and G.A. Miller. 1963. Introduction to the formal analysis of natural languages. In R.D. Luce *et al.* (eds), *Handbook of mathematical psychology*. New York. Vol. 2, 269–321.
Salomea, A. 1973. *Formal languages*. New York.

formant

Bundle of sound elements that together form the quality of a sound and are made visible through the frequency stripes of a **spectral analysis** (⇒ **spectrograph**). For every **vowel** four to five formants can be found, of which the first and the second are characteristic for the vowel coloring and the others for individual speech features. Formants are defined according to their frequency, amplitude, and width. In vowels, articulatory resonance characteristics of the **resonance chamber** correspond to formants.

References
⇒ **phonetics**

formative

1 In **word formation**, term for bound word-forming **morphemes** (⇒ **affix**).

2 In **generative grammar**, the smallest linear units with syntactic function, a distinction being drawn between **lexical formatives** (⇒ **lexical entry**) and grammatical formatives, e.g. *table, red* in contrast with 'present tense,' 'plural.'

formator

In Morris' theory of signs (1946) (⇒ **semiotics**), a sign which, in contrast to a **designator**, has no denotative function, and thus does not refer directly to an object or state of affairs in the real world, and which consequently does not have an independent semantic value (⇒ **function word**).

Weinreich (1963) distinguishes four different types of formators: (a) pragmatic formators, which express the function of an utterance as a command or question; (b) deictic formators (like *here, there, tomorrow, I, you,* and others), which refer to the spatial or temporal context of the utterance (⇒ **deixis**); (c) **logical constants** (like the conjunctions *and, or,* and others), which connect utterances and determine their **truth values** (⇒ **predicate logic**); (d) and **quantifiers** (like *several, all, some, only,* and others), which specify the quantity of sets (⇒ **quantification**). The problems encountered in the semantic description of formators in natural languages have played a central role in many recent grammatical theories.

References
Morris, C.W. 1946. *Sign, language and behavior.* New York.
Weinreich, U. 1963. On the semantic structure of language. In J.H. Greenberg (ed.), *Universals of language.* Cambridge, MA. 114–71.
⇒ **quantification, semiotics.**

formula

1 In **formal logic**, the result of a formalization process, through which a sentence of a natural language is translated into an appropriate formal-logical target language, e.g. the formula for the sentence *Caroline is Philip's sister*: (a) *is (Caroline, Philip's sister)*, (b) *is the sister of (Caroline, Philip)*.

2 A term from phraseology (⇒ **idiomatics**) for a lexically and syntactically unchangeable group of words that frequently has the value of a sentence and is thematized as a formula of politeness or greeting according to a pragmatic point of view: e.g. *good afternoon, to your health, good luck.* (⇒ **twin formula**)

fortis vs lenis [Lat. *fortis* 'strong'; *lenis* 'weak']

Articulatory feature of **stops** and **fricatives** that refers to differing degrees of muscle tension. In fortis sounds, the subglottalic air pressure behind the point of articulation is stronger than in lenis sounds. The partially synonymous terms **tenuis vs media** refer only to stops and denote that aspect of voicelessness vs voicedness (⇒ **voiced vs voiceless**) that correlates with the features [fortis] vs [lenis] in English. Moreover, the fortis/tenuis sounds [p, t, k] in English are aspirated (⇒ **aspiration**) to varying degrees depending on their position in the given word (e.g. word-initial, word-medial, word-final).

References
⇒ **phonetics**

fossilization [Lat. *fossilis* 'obtained by digging']

Permanent retention of linguistic habits which, when taken together, constitute a language-learner's **interlanguage** (e.g. French uvular /r/ in the English interlanguage of native speakers of French, American English retroflex /r/ in the French of native speakers of American English, German time–place word order in the English interlanguage of native speakers of German, etc.). Fossilization may occur despite optimal learning factors and corrective feedback; it may result, in particular, when a language learner perceives that his communicative strategies are effective and adequate.

References
Higgs, T. and R. Clifford. 1982. The push toward communication. In T.V. Higgs (ed.), *Curriculum, competence, and the foreign language teacher.* (The ACTFL Foreign Language Education Series, Vol. 13.) Lincolnwood, IL.
Selinker, L. 1979. Interlanguage. In D. Nehls (ed.),

Studies in descriptive linguistics. Heidelberg. Vol. 2, 55–77.

Selinker, L. and J.T. Lamendella. 1979. The role of extrinsic feedback in interlanguage fossilization. *Language Learning* 29.363–75.

⇒ **interlanguage**

four skills

In language instruction and acquisition, listening, speaking, reading, and writing constitute the 'four skills.' Developing proficiency in the four skills is one of the primary goals of current foreign-language instruction.

frame

1 Schema-based (⇒ **schema-based text comprehension**) approach of **artificial intelligence** for **knowledge representation** that is used particularly for objects, although it provides more general perspectives as well. Many knowledge representation approaches (e.g. KL-ONE) are based on the concept of frames, which, among other things, makes the **inheritance** of properties within frame hierarchies possible. Frames, which have a strong connection to case frames of Fillmore's **case grammar** (though in contrast to these can be seen as conceptual entities), have a number of 'slots' through which the elements or aspects of a concept are represented. (⇒ *also* **script**)

References
Brachman, R. and J. Schmolze. 1985. An overview of the KL-ONE knowledge representation system. *CSc* 9.171–216.
Flickinger, D., C. Pollard, and T. Wasow. 1985. Structure-sharing in lexical representation. *ACL Proceedings* 262–7.
Minsky, M. 1974. A framework for representing knowledge. In P. Winston (ed.), *The psychology of computer vision*. New York 211–77.

2 In sociological and sociolinguistic approaches to **discourse analysis**, a principle of organization which governs a participant's subjective involvement in social events (see Goffman 1974). A frame provides a tacit point of orientation for participants as they make sense of the ongoing interaction: for instance, pitch contour and/or facial expression may represent a frame for an utterance that is to be understood as serious or ironic (⇒ **contextualization**). Participants may change, break, or exploit frames (e.g. in advertisements (Tannen 1986)). Since frames are tacit, labeling one frame creates another higher-level frame. A particular type of a framing device is **footing**. (⇒ *also* **ethnography of speaking**)

References
Bateson, G. 1972. *Steps to an ecology of mind*. New York.

Goffman, E. 1974. *Frame analysis*. New York.
——— 1981. *Forms of talk*. Oxford.
Tannen, D. 1979. What's in a frame? Surface evidence for underlying expectations. In R.O. Freedle (ed.), *New directions in discourse processing*. Norwood, NJ. 137–81.
——— 1986. *That's not what I meant! How conversational style makes or breaks your relations with others*. New York.

frame construction ⇒ **brace construction**

Franco-Provençal ⇒ **Romance languages**

Franglais

A **blend** of the words *fr(ançais)* ('French') and *anglais* ('English') for the borrowings from English that are found in French, e.g. *un handicapé* or *le week-end*. Franglais can also refer to a comical mixture of French and English.

Reference
Etiemble, R. 1964. *Parlez-vous franglais?* Paris.

free adjunct [Lat. *adiungere* 'to connect, to add']

Syntactic element serving as a **modifier** which is not required by the **valence** of the verb, but which can be added freely to a sentence: (*He was reading a book*) *under a tree*. (⇒ *also* **complement**)

Reference
Kortmann, B. 1991. *Free adjuncts and absolutes in English: problems of control and interpretation*. London.

free alternation ⇒ **distribution**

free correlation ⇒ **distribution**

free stress ⇒ **stress**^{2}

free variation (*also* facultative variation)

Term introduced by N.S. Trubetzkoy to describe **allophones** which can occur in the same position without causing a change in meaning, e.g. the pronunciation of /p/ in the word *cap* in different Eng. dialects as kʰæpʰ / kʰæp°/kʰæp′/. In this example, free variation occurs at the phonetic level, but there is also free variation on the phonemic level, when a phonemic difference is suspended in certain cases, e.g. as /iː/ or /ay/ in the pronunciation of the initial vowel sound in *either*. (⇒ *also* **complementary distribution**, **distribution**)

References
Trubetzkoy, N.S. 1939. *Grundzüge der Phonologie*. Göttingen. (4th edn 1967.)

⇒ **phonology**

Fregean principle ⇒ principle of compositionality

Frege's principle of meaning ⇒ principle of compositionality

French

Language belonging to the **Romance language** family of **Indo-European**, native language of about 80 million speakers in France, Canada, Belgium, Luxemburg, Switzerland, and some countries formerly colonized by France. After **English**, French is one of the most important languages of education today. The term 'French' (from the Vulgar Lat. *franciscus*) refers particularly to the dialect of the Ile-de-France (the region around Paris), which is the basis for the literary language. Early on two separate linguistic regions developed: in the north the *langue d'oïl* and in the south the *langue d'oc* (⇒ **Occitan**); these terms are derived from the different words for 'yes': in the north the Old French *oïl* (from Lat. *hoc ille*), in the south *oc* (from Lat. *hoc*). French is the earliest and most richly attested descendant of Latin; the oldest attestation is the Strasburg Oath from the year 842. Usually three periodizations are undertaken: Old French (until approx. 1350), Middle French (until approx. 1600) and Modern French, whose sound inventory, morphology, and syntax diverge the most from Latin of all the Romance languages. (⇒ *also* **creole**)

References
Battye, A. and M.-A. Hintze. 1992. *The French language today*. London.
Ewert, A. 1943. *The French language*, 2nd edn. London.
Holtus, G., M. Metzeltin, and C. Schmitt (eds) 1991. *Lexikon der romanistischen Linguistik*, vol. 5, 1. Tübingen.
Sanders, C. (ed.) 1993. *French today: language in its social context*. Cambridge.

Atlas
Gillierón, J. and E. Edmont, 1902–10. *Atlas linguistique de France*. Paris.

Modern grammars
Byrne, L.S.R. and E.L. Churchill. 1986. *A comprehensive French grammar*, 3rd edn completely rev. by G. Price. Oxford. (Reprint with corrections 1987.)
Confais, J.P. 1978. *Grammaire explicative*. Munich.
Damourette, J. and E. Pichon. 1911–40. *Des mots à la pensée: essai de grammaire de la langue française*, 6 vols. Paris.
Grevisse, M. 1936. *Le bon usage*. Gembloux. (12th edn 1986.)
Judge, A. and F.G. Healey. 1985. *A reference grammar of modern French*. London.

Togeby, K. 1982–5. *Grammaire française*, 5 vols. Copenhagen.
Von Wartburg, W. and P. Zumthor. 1947. *Précis de syntaxe du français contemporain*. Bern. (3rd rev. edn 1973.)
Wagner, R.L. and J. Pinchon. 1962. *Grammaire du française classique et moderne*. Paris. (2nd edn 1974.)

Historical grammars
Einhorn, E. 1974. *Old French: a concise handbook*. Cambridge.
Foulet, L. 1919. *Petit syntaxe de l'ancien français*. Paris. (3rd rev. edn 1965.)
Harris, M. 1978. *The evolution of French syntax: a comparative approach*. London.
Rheinfelder, H. 1936. *Altfranzösische Grammatik*. Munich. 2 vols (2nd edn 1976.)

History
Brunot, F. 1913– . *Histoire de la langue française des origines à nos jours*. Paris.
Lodge, R.A. 1993. *French: from dialect to standard*. London.
Pope, M.K. 1952. *From Latin to Modern French, with especial consideration of Anglo-Norman*, 2nd edn. Manchester.
Price, G. 1971. *The French language: present and past*. London.
Rickard, P. 1993. *A history of the French language*, 2nd edn London.
Wartburg, W.V. 1934, *Evolution et structure de la langue française*. Leipzig. (10th edn Bern 1971.)

Dictionaries
Grand Larousse de la langue française. 1971–8. 6 vols. Paris.
Mel'čuk, I. *et al.* 1984–92. *Dictionnaire explicatif et combinatoire du français contemporain*, 3 vols. Amsterdam and Philadelphia.
Robert, P. 1951–70. *Le grand Robert de la langue française: dictionnaire alphabétique et analogique de la langue française*, 7 vols. Paris. (2nd edn 1985.)
Trésor de la langue française: dictionnaire de la langue du XIX et du XX siècle (1789–1960). 1971– . Paris.

Historical dictionaries
Bloch, O. and W. von Wartburg. 1968. *Dictionnaire étymologique de la langue française*, 5th rev. edn. Paris.
Dauzat, A., J. Dubois, and H. Mitterand. 1971. *Nouveau dictionnaire étymologique et historique*. Paris.
Godefroy, F. 1880–1902. *Dictionnaire de l'ancienne langue française*, 10 vols. Paris. (Repr. 1937–8.)
Greimas, A.J. and T.M. Keane. 1992. *Dictionnaire du moyen français*. Paris.
Huguet, E. 1925. *Dictionnaire de la langue française du seizième siècle*. Paris.
Tobler, A. and E. Lommatzsch. 1925–76. *Altfranzösisches Wörterbuch*, 10 vols. Berlin and Wiesbaden.
Wartburg, W. von. 1922– . *Französisches etymologisches Wörterbuch*. Bonn, Tübingen and Basle. (Vol. 25 1992, Basle.)

Bibliographies

Heckenbach, W. and F.G. Hirschmann. 1981. *Weltsprache Französisch: kommentierte Bibliographie zur Frankophonie (1945–1978)*. Tübingen.

Ineichen, G. 1974. *Bibliographische Einführung in die französische Sprachwissenschaft*. Berlin.

Martin, R. 1973. *Guide bibliographique de linguistique française*. Paris.

Romanische Bibliographie (= supplements for the *Zeitschrift für Romanische Philologie*). Tübingen.

Schutz, H. 1978. *Gesprochenes und geschriebenes Französisch: bibliographische Materialien (1964–1976)*. Tübingen.

Journal

Journal of French Language Studies.

frequency dictionary

Statistical register of the most frequently encountered words in a language which, on the basis of quantitative criteria, are selected as the words with the greatest degree of use. Such lexicographical investigations of frequency are based upon a wide variety of texts that are believed to be representative of the given language. Linguistic applications may be found in studies on **BASIC English**.

References

Brunet, E. 1981. *Le Vocabulaire française de 1789 à nos jours: d'après les données du trésor de la langue française*. Geneva.

Carroll, J.B. *et al.* 1971. *The American heritage word frequency book*. Boston.

Eaton, H.S. 1940. *A semantic frequency list for English, French, German and Spanish*. Chicago, IL.

Gougenheim, G. 1958. *Dictionnaire fondamental de la langue française*. Paris.

Hindmarsh, R. 1980. *Cambridge English lexicon*. Cambridge.

Jones, L.U. 1966. *A spoken word count*. Chicago, IL.

Josselson, H.H. 1953. *Russian word count*. Detroit, MI.

Juilland, A., D. Brodin, and C. Davidovitch. 1970. *Frequency dictionary of French words*. The Hague and Paris.

Kaeding, F.W. 1898. *Häufigkeitswörterbuch der deutschen Sprache*. Steglitz.

Kučera, H. and W.N. Francis. 1967. *Computational analysis of present-day American English*. Providence, RI.

Kühn, P. 1978. *Deutsche Wörterbücher: eine systematische Bibliographie*. Tübingen.

Meier, H. 1964. *Deutsche Sprachstatistik*. Hildesheim. (2nd edn 1967.)

Morgan, B.Q. 1928. *German frequency word book*. New York.

Roberts, A.H. 1965. *A statistical linguistic analysis of American English*. London.

Rosengren, I. 1972. *Ein Frequenzwörterbuch der deutschen Zeitungssprache: Die Welt, Süddeutsche Zeitung*. Lund.

Ruoff, A. 1981. *Häufigkeitswörterbuch gesprochener Sprache: gesondert nach Wortarten, alphabetisch,* *rückläufig alphabetisch und nach Häufigkeit geordnet*. Tübingen.

Steinfeldt, E. 1973. *Russian word count: 2,500 words most commonly used in modern literary Russian. Guide for teachers of Russian*, trans. V. Korotky. Moscow. (Orig. 1966.)

Thorndike, E.L. 1944. *The teacher's word book of 30,000 words*. New York.

Wängler, H.-H. 1963. *Rangwörterbuch hochdeutscher Umgangssprache*. Marburg.

West, M. 1953. *A general service list of English words*. London. (5th edn 1960.)

frequentative ⇒ **iterative vs semelfactive**

Freudian slip ⇒ **speech error**

fricative [Lat. *fricare* 'to rub'] (*also* **spirant**)

Speech sound classified according to its **manner of articulation**, namely with pulmonic or pharyngeal air (⇒ **ejective**), and in which at least in one position the oral cavity forms a narrow passage through which the expired air creates sound through friction. Subclasses of fricatives are formed by **labialization, palatalization**, velarization, pharyngealization (⇒ **secondary articulation**), **aspiration**, nasalization, **glottalization**. Further classificatory characteristics are **phonation**, the **articulator**, and **place of articulation** (⇒ **articulatory phonetics**). In English, all fricatives are formed with the pulmonic **airstream mechanism**. Ejective fricatives are found in **Amharic** and **Caucasian**. Unlike (non-nasal) **stops**, fricatives can function as syllables, e.g. in the **Sino-Tibetan** language of Hani. In English, syllabic fricatives occur only paralinguistically, as in [pst⌐].

References

⇒ **phonetics**

Frisian

West **Germanic** language with strong dialectal differences: West Frisian, official language along with **Dutch** of the Dutch province of Frisia (approx. 300,000 speakers); East Frisian, surviving only in the Lower Saxon Saterland with about 1,000 speakers; North Frisian, with various dialects along the west coast of Schleswig-Holstein, on the islands of Helgoland, Sylt, Amrum, Föhr and on the northern Halligs, altogether about 10,000 speakers. The oldest written attestations, dating from the thirteenth century (Old Frisian), show a close relationship to Old English. The vocabulary and idiomatic usage show a strong influence from the standard languages which have dominated since the end of the Middle Ages: Dutch, Low German, and, later, High **German**. Nevertheless, there are still a large number of similarities with **English** in respect to the vowel and consonant systems and loss of inflectional endings.

References
Markey, T.L. 1981. *Frisian*. The Hague.
Tiersma, P.L. 1985. *Frisian reference grammar.* Dordrecht.

Friulian ⇒ Rhaeto-Romance

front vowel ⇒ vowel

fronting ⇒ palatalization

FUG ⇒ Functional Unification Grammar

FSA ⇒ finite state automaton

Fula (*also* Fulani)
Largest **West Atlantic** language (approx. 11.5 million speakers) spoken by the nomadic Fulbe people between Senegal and Lake Chad.

References
Arnott, D.W. 1970. *The nominal and verbal systems of Fula*. Oxford.
Pelletier, C. and A. Sinner. 1979. *Adamawa Fulfulde*. Madison, WI.
Sylla, Y. 1982. *Grammaire moderne du pulaar*. Dakar.

Fulani ⇒ Fula

function (*also* mapping)
1 Basic term in **set theory** taken from geometry: assignment to each element x of a set A (= domain) exactly one element $y = f(x)$ of a set B (= range) (notation: f:A → B or A → B). In set theory, f represents a subset of the product set $A \times B$, namely the subset of the ordered pairs $\langle x, y \rangle$ with $x \varepsilon A$ and $y = f(x)$ εB. Types of functions are as follows: (a) Injection: a function f of A into B is injective (or unidirectional), if f is left-directional, that is if the equation $f(x) = f(y)$ consistently yields $x = y$.

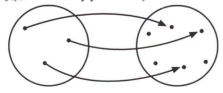

(b) Surjection (= mapping onto): a function f of A into B is surjective if every element in B is the value of at least one element x in A under f.

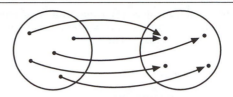

(c) Bijection: a function is bijective or unidirectional up if it is both injective and surjective.

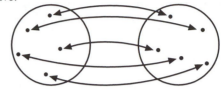

References
⇒ **formal logic**

2 Basic term taken from mathematics and logic for describing structures and systems. Widely used synonymously with **function**[1]. (⇒ *also* **formal logic**, **set theory**)

3 In Hjelmslev's (1943) **glossematics**, 'function' refers to the concept of **relation**. Hjelmslev uses 'function' 'in a meaning that lies intermediately between the logical–mathematical and the etymological' (p. 33), i.e. function relates both to the different forms of dependencies of various quantities amongst themselves (which he calls **interdependence**, **determination**, or **constellation**) as well as to the fact that these quantities 'function' in certain ways and occupy a certain role in the text.

References
Hjelmslev, L. 1943. *Omkring sprogteoriens grundlaeggelse*. Copenhagen. 1961. *Prolegomena to a theory of language*, trans. F.J. Whitfield. Madison, WI.
⇒ **glossematics**

4 ⇒ **syntactic function**

function verb

Subcategory of **verbs** (such as *bring, come, find, stand, take*) which in certain contexts have lost their lexical meaning as **main verbs**. In this usage, these verbs serve mainly a grammatical function in **nominal sentences** by connecting the subject and the prepositional object as well as by bearing syntactic and morphological features. (⇒ **functional verb structure**)

function word

1 Term for linguistic elements which carry primarily grammatical, rather than lexical, meaning and which fulfill mainly syntactic and

structural functions. Function words include **articles**, **pronouns**, **prepositions**, and **conjunctions**. (⇒ *also* **formator**)

2 ⇒ **particle**

3 ⇒ **synseman word**

functional composition

Mechanism of argument **inheritance** studied in **categorial grammar** and introduced by Moortgat (1981) into **word formation**. Starting with G. Frege's **principle of compositionality**, which says that the interpretation of a complex expression reflects the meaning of the component parts and their manner of composition, Moortgat developed a generalized version of functional composition, which was known in logic, in order to explain correspondence in the argument structure between simple verbs and adjectives and their **derivations** (cf Eng. *to rely on him*, *reliance on him*; *willing to go*, *willingness to go*). In **word syntax** the nominal affix (*-ance*, *-ness*) forms a constituent with the base verb or adjective. Semantically, however, it takes as its scope the verb or adjective together with its complement. The operation needed to represent this expanded semantic scope of the affix is, according to Moortgat, functional composition. It causes the derivation to take over the argument of the base category, while the base simultaneously fulfills the argument structure of the affix. Generalized functional composition, in other words, represents a complex function that combines two functions into a compound function, which in turn can be applied to the unsatisfied argument of one of the combined functions (= that of the base). Along with the principle of compositionality, this semantic operation guarantees that *on him* or *to go* are complements of the bases (and not derivations), although the derivation arises from the structural unit base + affix. This operation was further adapted to the theories of argument inheritance in Di Sciullo and Williams (1987) and Bierwisch (1989).

References
Bierwisch, M. 1989. Event nominalizations. In W. Motsch (ed.), *Wortstruktur und Satzstruktur*. Berlin. 1–73.
Di Sciullo, A.M. and E. Williams. 1987. *On the definition of word*. Cambridge, MA.
Moortgat, M. 1981. A Fregean restriction on metarules. In V. Burke and J. Pustejovsky (eds), NELS = Proceedings of the 17th annual meeting of the North Eastern Linguistic Society, ed. by J. McDonough and B. Plunkett. Amherst, MA 1986, pp. 306–25.
——— 1985. Functional composition and complement inheritance. In G.A.L. Hoppenbrouwers, P.A.M. Seuren, and A.J.M.M. Weijters (eds),
Meaning and the lexicon. Dordrecht. 39–48.
⇒ **word formation**

functional grammar

In the broader sense: theoretical approach to the description and explanation of linguistic phenomena based on their various functions. The following functions are generally investigated: **topic vs comment**, **theme vs rheme**, **definiteness** or animacy (animate vs inanimate) of a noun phrase, the semantic roles (⇒ **thematic relations**) or **syntactic functions** of the expressions in question. Semantic roles are the central means of description in **case grammar**. **Lexical Functional Grammar** and **relational grammar** are based on **syntactic functions**.

The basic assumption of functional grammar is that linguistic phenomena cannot be explained without examining their function. Thus functional grammar offers an alternative to (post-)structuralist attempts at describing linguistic phenomena formally (i.e. assuming the autonomy of syntax). These differing assumptions can be seen clearly in their descriptions of verbal agreement. In a nonfunctional approach this phenomenon is generally described at the level of form by means of morphosyntactic case. Thus the finite verb agrees with the nominative complement of the predicate. This description fits well for English. In a functional approach the influence of semantic roles, animacy, and/or definiteness of the noun phrase on verbal agreement is examined. This approach works better in some cases, e.g. in object–verb agreement in **Swahili** (see Givón 1984). In this language there is subject–verb agreement as well as object–verb agreement depending on whether the object is a human being or is definite. Functional descriptions are preferred in the empirically oriented research on **universals**, since the formal (i.e. morphological and topological) means of marking syntactic function vary across languages, while their functions are universal.

References
Bolkestein, A.M. and C. de Groot. 1990. Functional grammar: new trends and applications. *PICL* 14.302–10.
Bondarko, A.V. 1991. *Functional grammar: a field approach*. Amsterdam and Philadelphia, PA.
Connolly, J. 1991. *Constituent order in functional grammar: synchronic and diachronic perspectives*. Berlin and New York.
Connolly, J.H. and S.C. Dik. 1989. *Functional grammar and the computer*. Dordrecht.
Dik, S.C. 1989. *The theory of functional grammar, part 1*. Dordrecht.
——— 1990. Some developments in functional grammar: predicate formation. In F. Aarts and T.

van Els (eds), *Contemporary Dutch linguistics*. Washington. 58–79.

—— 1992. *Functional grammar in Prolog*. Berlin and New York.

—— 1993. Functional grammar. In J. Jacobs *et al.* (eds), *Syntax: an international handbook of contemporary research*. Berlin and New York. 368–94.

Dirven, R. and V. Fried. 1987. *Functionalism in linguistics*. Amsterdam.

Engberg-Pedersen, E. *et al.* (eds) 1994. *Function and expression in functional grammar*. Berlin and New York.

Givón, T. (ed.) 1979. *Syntax and semantics*, vol. 12: *Discourse and syntax*. New York.

—— 1984–90. *Syntax: a functional–typological introduction*, 2 vols. Amsterdam.

Grossmann, R.E. *et al.* (eds) 1975. *Papers from the parasession on functionalism*. Chicago, IL.

Halliday, M.A.K. 1985. *Introduction to functional grammar*. London.

Hengeveld, K. 1992. *Non-verbal predication: theory, typology, diachrony*. Berlin and New York.

Horn, G. 1988. *Essentials of functional grammar*. Berlin.

Keenan, E. 1974. The functional principles: generalizing the notion of 'subject of.' *CLS* 10.298–309.

Kuno, S. 1980. Functional syntax. In E. Moravcsik and J.R. Wirth (eds), *Syntax and semantics*, vol. 13: *Current approaches to syntax*. New York. 117–35.

—— 1987. *Functional syntax: anaphora, discourse and empathy*. Chicago, IL.

Levine, R. 1992. *Formal grammar: theory and implementation*. Oxford.

Nuyts, J. *et al.* (eds) 1990. *Layers and levels of representation in language theory: a functional view*. Amsterdam and Philadelphia, PA.

Siewierska, A. 1991. *Functional grammar*. London.

Van Gelderen, E. 1993. *The rise of functional categories*. Amsterdam and Philadelphia, PA.

Van Valin, R.D. Jr (ed.) 1993. *Advances in role and reference grammar*. Amsterdam and Philadelphia, PA.

Van Valin, R.D. and W.A. Foley. 1984. *Functional syntax and universal grammar*. Cambridge.

functional illiteracy

The inability to carry out survival-level tasks due to deficiencies in reading and/or writing skills.

functional linguistics ⇒ Prague School

functional meaning ⇒ lexical meaning vs grammatical meaning

functional phonetics ⇒ phonology

functional sentence perspective (*also* theme vs rheme, topic vs comment)

Prague School term introduced by Matthesius (1929) for denoting the analysis of a sentence in respect to its communicative function. The basis of the sentence is known information, called the theme (topic, given), while that which is said about the known information is considered to be the rheme (comment, new). This semantic classification, which has both semantic and contextual aspects, is reflected in **word order**, use of pronouns, articles, and **intonation**.

References
Brömser, B. 1982. *Funktionale Satzperspektive im Englischen*. Tübingen.

Dik, S.C. 1989. *Theory of functional grammar*, part 1. Dordrecht.

Firbas, J. 1992. *Functional sentence perspective in written and spoken communication*. Cambridge.

Grewendorf, G. 1980. Funktionale Satzperspektive und deutsche Wortstellung. *LingB* 66.28–40.

Jacobs, J. 1984. Funktionale Satzperspektive und Illokutionssemantik. *LingB* 91.25–58.

Lötscher, A. 1984. Satzgliedstellung und funktionale Satzperspektive. *JIdS* 1983.118–51.

Matthesius, V. 1929. Zur Satzperspektive im modernen Englisch. *ASNS* 84:202–10.

functional uncertainty

A term introduced by Kaplan and Zaenen (1989) as a formal means of description for feature structures in the treatment of non-local dependencies in **Lexical Functional Grammar** (LFG). In feature structures, the list of attributes from the root of the feature structure to an embedded value is called a 'path.' The concept of functional uncertainty is based on the use of regular expressions in path names: for example, if during topicalization in English the topicalized element has to be unified with an object position in the matrix sentence, then this can happen through the following feature equation: TOPIC = OBJ. The topicalized object can also be extracted from a multiply embedded complement: *Mary*₁ *John claimed that Bill said that Henry telephoned*₁. Therefore Kaplan and Zaenen suggest the following type of feature equation: TOPIC = COMP* OBJ. The Kleene-operator '*' at the COMP attribute reveals that any number of COMP attributes can be found in the path. Thus the equation stands for an infinite disjunction of feature structures. Functional uncertainty is also used for the treatment of other non-local dependencies. An algorithm for the implementation of functional uncertainty can be found in Kaplan and Maxwell (1988).

References
Kaplan, R. and J.T. Maxwell. 1988. An algorithm for functional uncertainty. In *COLING 88*. Budapest. Vol. 1, 297–302.

Kaplan, R. and A. Zaenen. 1988. Long distance dependencies, constituent structure, and functional uncertainty. In M. Baltin and A. Kroch (eds),

Alternative conceptions of phrase structure. Chicago, IL. 17–42.

Netter, K. 1988. Nonlocal-dependencies and infinitival constructions in German. In U. Reyle and C. Rohrer (eds), *Natural language parsing and linguistic theories.* Dordrecht. 356–410.

Functional Unification Grammar (*abbrev.* FUG)

A generative grammatical formalism developed by Kay (1979) within the family of unification grammars. In FUG, all grammatical representations take the form of **feature structures**. Feature structures of syntactic units, which represent the phrase structure, comprise two attributes. The value of the attribute CSET contains the immediate constituents; the value of the attribute PATTERN is a (partial) specification of the linear order of these constituents. The rules of FUG are also feature structures. The grammar is the disjunction of all grammar rules and of all lexical entries, which must be in a specific place with respect to the representation of every syntactic unit. FUG forms the basis for numerous experimental natural-language systems.

References
Appelt, D.E. 1985. *Planning English sentences.* Cambridge.

Kay, M. 1979. Functional grammar. *BLS* 5.142–58.

—— 1984. Functional Unification Grammar: a formalism for machine translation. *COLING* 84.75–8.

—— 1985. Parsing in Functional Unification Grammar. In D.R. Dowty, L. Karttunen, and A. Zwicky (eds), *Natural language parsing.* Cambridge. 251–78.

McKeown, K.R. and C.R. Paris. 1987. Functional Unification Grammar revisited. *ACL Proceedings* 25.97–103.

Ritchie, G.D. 1985. Simulating a Turing machine using Functional Unification Grammar. In T. O'Shea (ed.), *Advances in artificial intelligence.* Amsterdam. 285–94.

functional verb structure (*also* nominal construction)

Syntactic structure which consists of a prepositional object and a **function verb** (e.g. *to bring to completion*). Functional verb structures are formed in the following manner: the original verbal meaning of completion is realized by nominalization to an abstract noun and by adding a semantically weak verb functioning as an **auxiliary** which produces the grammatical connection between the subject and the prepositional object. The wide use of functional verb structures, especially in more technical language, is due both to a desire of greater precision and economy as well as to various semantic aspects of functional verb structures: (a) variation of **aspect**: *to flee, to be in flight* vs *to put to flight*; (b) replacement of a passive construction: *His proposals were approved by all the participants* vs *His proposals found approval with all the participants*; (c) modification of the theme–rheme (⇒ **theme vs rheme**) structure of the sentence by placing important meaning-carrying elements at the end of the sentence in order to have a better communicative position: *He consented wholeheartedly* vs *He gave his wholehearted consent.*

References
Esau, H. 1973. *Nominalization and complementation in modern German.* Amsterdam.
⇒ **nominal style**

functionalism ⇒ Prague School

functive

1 In **glossematics**, elements belonging to the **substance** of language that refer to each other by relations (Hjelmslev 1943, ch. 1 calls them 'functions'); cf. **function**.

2 In glossematics, the objects of study are not the functives themselves, but the system of dependency relations holding between them; cf. **interdependence**, **determination**, and **constellation**.

References
Hjelmslev, L. 1943. *Omkring sprogteoriens grundlaeggelse.* Copenhagen. (*Prolegomena to a theory of language*, trans. F.J. Whitfield. Baltimore, MD, 1953.)
⇒ **glossematics**

functor ⇒ logical connective

Fur ⇒ Nilo-Saharan

fusion

1 Sound change in morphemes when connected with other morphemes, e.g. **umlaut** in **German**: *blau* vs *bläulich* 'blue vs bluish.' (⇒ *also* **collocation**, **juxtaposition**)

References
Sapir, E. 1921. *Language.* New York.
⇒ **morphology**

2 ⇒ **blend**

fusional assimilation ⇒ assimilation

futhark

The name given to the Runic alphabet (⇒

rune). It stands for the names of the first six letters of the alphabet (*fuþark*).

future perfect

Verb **tense** which expresses anteriority relative to a future event. It is formed in English with *will have* + past participle: *By the time you come, he will have finished washing the car.* The future perfect owes its existence both to the influence of **Latin** as well as to the desire of many grammarians for a symmetrical analog to the correlation present vs present perfect and past vs past perfect to augment the normal future tense with a relative tense expressing temporal anteriority.

References
⇒ **tense**

future tense

Verb **tense** formed in English with *will* + infinitive: *She will come.* The future tense characterizes the state of affairs expressed by the utterance as lying temporally after the speech act. In English the present progressive often fulfills this function as well, usually supported by an adverbial element referring to the temporal context: *She will come tomorrow* vs *She is coming tomorrow.* The temporal aspect is almost always colored by shades of **modality**, especially when the future tense is used to express reassurance, command, or suspicion: *Everything will turn out fine, You WILL be home by seven, You'll be wanting the car tonight?*

References
⇒ **tense**

G

Gaelic (*also* Goidelic)

Branch of **Celtic** consisting of Irish (West Ireland, approx. 500,000 speakers, official language of the Republic of Ireland) and Scots-Gaelic (northern Scotland and the Hebrides, about 90,000, descendants of sixteenth-century Irish settlers). Attested since the eighth century. Belongs to the q-Celtic languages.

References
Elsie, R. 1986. *Dialect relationships in Goidelic: a study in Celtic dialectology.* Hamburg.
Lehmann, R.P.M. and W.P. Lehmann. 1975. *An introduction to Old Irish.* New York.
O Murchú, M. 1985. *The Irish language.* Dublin.
O'Siadhail, M. 1989. *Modern Irish: grammatical structure and dialectal variation.* Cambridge.
Ternes, E. 1973. *The phonemic analysis of Scottish Gaelic.* Hamburg.
Thurneysen, R. 1946. *A grammar of Old Irish.* Dublin. (rev. edn 1980).
Withers, C.W.J. 1984. *Gaelic in Scotland 1698–1981.* Edinburgh.

Dictionary
Quin, E. (ed.) 1983. *Dictionary of the Irish language.* Dublin.

Etymological dictionary
Vendryes, J. *et al.* 1959– . *Lexique étymologique de l'irlandais ancien.* Paris.

Journal
Ériu.
⇒ **Celtic**

Galatian ⇒ **Celtic**

Galician ⇒ **Portuguese, Spanish**

Galla ⇒ **Cushitic**

Gallego ⇒ **Portuguese**

Gallo-Romance ⇒ **Romance languages**

game-theoretical semantics

A theory of **semantics** that relates the coherences of an assertion to the postulation of a winning strategy in a semantic game for the proponent of the particular assertion. Expansions comprise utterances other than statements, e.g. questions and commands as moves in a well-defined linguistic game. The intellectual background has its foundation in Wittgenstein's concept of the **language game** which provided inspiration for the work of Stenius and Hintikka. Lorenzen's dialogic interpretation of effective logic can be seen as the precursor to Hintikka's semantic games and their generalization in Carlson's dialog games.

References
Carlson, L. 1983. *Dialogue games: an approach to discourse analysis.* Dordrecht.
Hintikka, J. 1973. *Logic, language games, and information.* Oxford.
Hintikka, J. and J. Kulas. 1983. *The game of language: studies in game-theoretical semantics and its applications.* Dordrecht.
Lorenzen, P. 1967. *Formale Logik.* Berlin.
—— 1969. *Normative logic and ethics.* Mannheim.
Saarinen, E. (ed.) 1979. *Game-theoretical semantics: essays on semantics by Hintikka, Carlson, Peacocke, Rantala and Saarinen.* Dordrecht.
Stenius, E. 1967. Mood and language game. *Synthese* 17.254–74.
Wittgenstein, L. 1953. *Philosophical investigations.* Oxford.

gapping

A term coined by Ross (1970) to describe a **transformation** which creates gaps in a sentence after a conjunction by deleting a verb which would otherwise reappear, e.g. *Caroline plays the flute and Louise (plays) the piano.* Gapping can work forwards, as above, or backwards as in the deletion of the first mention of the word. According to Ross the direction of gapping depends on the constituent branching in the **deep structure**, and provides insight into the underlying word order of a language, whether S(ubject)–V(erb)–O(bject) or SOV. (⇒ *also* **co-ordination, ellipsis**)

References
Hudson, R.A. 1976. Conjunction reduction, gapping, and right-node raising. *Lg* 52.535–62.
Maling, J.M. 1972. On gapping and the order of constituents. *LingI* 3.101–8.
Nijt, A. 1979. *Gapping.* Dordrecht.
Ross, J.R. 1970. Gapping and the order of constituents. In M. Bierwisch and K.E. Heidolph (eds), *Progress in linguistics.* The Hague. 249–59.
Stockwell, R.P., P. Schachter, and B. Hall Partee. 1973. *The major syntactic structures of English.* New York.
⇒ **co-ordination, ellipsis, transformational grammar**

Gascon ⇒ **Occitan**

Gaulish ⇒ **Celtic**

GB theory ⇒ **Government and Binding theory**

Ge'ez (*also* Ethiopic)

Extinct **Semitic** language attested from the fourth to the ninth centuries AD, precursor of Tigrinya, closely related to **Amharic**. Still used today as the liturgical language of the Ethiopian church. Independent writing system developed from early South **Arabic** script.

References
Dillmann, A. 1907. *Ethiopic grammar*, 2nd rev. edn, ed. C. Bezold, trans. by J.A. Crichton. London. (Repr. Amsterdam, 1974.)
Weninger, S. 1993. *Ge'ez (Classical Ethiopic)*. Munich.

Bibliography
Leslau, W. 1965. *An annotated bibliography of the Semitic languages of Ethiopia*. The Hague.

Dictionary
Leslau, W. 1987. *Comparative dictionary of Ge'ez (Classical Ethiopic): Ge'ez–English, English–Ge'ez, with an index of the Semitic roots*. Wiesbaden. (2nd printing 1991.)

geminate [Lat. *geminata* 'doubled'] (*also* double consonant, long consonant)

Consonant that is distinguished from another exclusively by its longer period of articulation (⇒ **quantity**). The difference between simple and long consonants is phonologically relevant in some languages, e.g. in Ital. *fato* ('fate') and *fatto* ('done'), but not in others, e.g. English, where double consonant characters/letters serve only orthographically to indicate a preceding short vowel: *redden*.

References
⇒ **phonetics**

gemination [Lat. *geminatio* 'doubling']

1 **Figure of speech** (*also* epizeuxis) featuring the immediate repetition of an expression or word, e.g. *sing softly, softly, softly*. Gemination can be used to express strong emotion or to emphasize a nuance, as Ortega y Gasset did in writing *Curiosity is almost, almost, the definition of frivolity*. (⇒ *also* **anaphora**, **epiphora**)

References
⇒ **figure of speech**

2 **Sound change** that brings about a doubling of consonants. Gemination is caused and favored primarily by (a) **assimilation**, cf. Old Indo-Iranian (**Sanskrit**) vs Middle Indo-Iranian (Pali): *bhartum* > *bhattum* 'carry,' *svapna-* > *soppa-* 'sleep,' *sahasra-* > *sahassa* 'thousand' (see Hock 1986: 65); (b) change in syllabic structure in intervocalic consonant clusters, especially before a following **semivowel** or **sonorant**; problems of syllabification that occur here are often solved with the aid of gemination in favor of (universally preferred) 'strong' **syllable** onset. An example of this is found in the West Germanic consonant gemination that occurs before *j, w, r, l, m, n*, cf. Proto-Gmc *sitjan > *sittjan > OE *sittan* 'sit.'

References
Hock, H.-H. 1986. *Principles of historical linguistics*. Berlin. (2nd rev. edn 1991.)
Murray, R.W. and T. Vennemann. 1983. Sound change and syllable structure in Germanic phonology. *Lg* 59.514–28.
⇒ **phonetics, sound change**

gender [Lat. *genus* 'kind, class'] (*also* grammatical gender)

Lexical-grammatical category, which in most languages of the world divides the nominal lexicon into formally and/or semantically motivated groups, the number of classes varying just as the kind of criteria for the division (Royen 1929; Corbett 1992). However, gender systems in the narrower sense are only those classifications which exhibit a limited number of closed classes (as a rule weak semantic transparency) as well as **agreement**. This definitorial demarcation of gender from **classifying languages** (which order nouns according to purely semantic qualities such as plant, animal, edible etc., cf. Mandarin Chinese) is based on the syntactic characteristic of the formal agreement of all elements in a noun group with the core noun; in German agreement exists with regard to the three categories gender, **number** (singular, plural) and **case** (nominative, genitive, dative, accusative), cf. the noun group in *In den meisten indogermanischen, semitischen und afrikanischen Sprachen*, 'In most Indo-European, Semitic and African languages'. The morphological characterization creates cohesion over complex structures and thereby makes possible – for stylistic purposes – a freer **word order** than is possible in languages without gender and agreement, such as English.

With regard to the principles of the classification, a distinction is made between (a) semantic systems (such as, e.g., **Tamil**, Zande, Dyirbal and some **Caucasian languages**, (b) formal systems, which are to be found in morphological respect in **Russian, Swahili** and other **Bantu** languages, and (c) phonologically predictable systems such as **French**. Eighty-five per cent of the nouns in the approx. 200

languages studied by Corbett (1992) can be attributed to a specific class through formal criteria; in case of doubt semantic aspects are decisive.

In the course of its history, English has lost all morphological signs of the original three-class gender system through the loss of final syllables, but 'covert' gender (semantic gender) is to be found in the selection of anaphorical pronouns, and this selection in return is mainly motivated by gender-related analogies (natural gender), cf. the common differentiation between natural gender (*mother – she*), social gender (*lorry-driver – he, nurse – she*), and psychological gender (*the baby – it; the ship – she*). In contrast to German, personal designations are usually gender-neutral (*teacher, student, lawyer*); a general derivational suffix comparable to German *–in* is also lacking (*–ess* is less generally applicable and in many cases already has a pejorative connotation as compared to its male counterpart, cf. *mister/mistress, governor/governess*). Where sexual specification is necessary, this takes place through adjectival (*female/male* citizen) or nominal (*woman writer*) modification (Baron 1986). On the connection between gender and sex under language-political aspects cf. **feminist linguistics**.

References
Baron, D. 1986. *Grammar and gender*. New Haven.
Brugmann, K. 1897. The nature and origin of the noun genders in the Indo-European languages. A lecture delivered on the occasion of the sesquicentennial celebration of Princeton University. *New Allgemeine Sprachwissenschaft* 9.100–9.
Bussmann, H. 1995. DAS Genus, DIE Grammatik und – DER Mensch: Geschlechterdifferenz in der Sprachwissenschaft. In H. Bussmann and R. Hof (eds), *Genus. Zur Geschlechterdifferenz iu den Kulturwissenschaften*. Stuttgart. 114–60.
Corbett, G.G. 1991. *Gender*. Cambridge.
Fodor, I. 1959. The origin of grammatical gender. *Lingua* 8.1–41, 186–214.
Greenberg, J.H. 1978. How does a language acquire gender markers? In *Universals of human language, III: Word structure*. Stanford. 47–82.
Ibrahim, I.M. 1973. *Grammatical gender. Its origin and development*. The Hague.
Jespersen, O. 1922. *Language. Its nature, development and origin*. New York.
Jones, C. 1988. *Grammatical gender in English*. London. 950–1250.
Köpke, K.-M. 1982. *Zum Genussystem der deutschen Gegenwartssprache*. Tübingen.
Royen, G. 1929. *Die nominalen Klassifikationssysteme in den Sprachen der Erde. Historisch-kritische Studie, mit besonderer Berücksichtigung des Indogermanischen*. Wien.
⇒ **agreement, feminist linguistics, government, noun class**

general grammar (*also* philosophical grammar, universal grammar)

The attempt to develop a general model of grammar, based on logical principles and from which the structures and regularities of all languages can be derived. (⇒ *also* **language acquisition device, universal grammar**)

References
Chomsky, N. 1966. *Cartesian linguistics: a chapter in the history of rationalist thought*. New York.
Harris, R. and T.J. Taylor. 1989. *Landmarks in linguistic thought*. London. Ch. 8.
Padley, G.A. 1985. *Grammatical theory in Western Europe, 1500–1700: trends in vernacular grammar*, vol. I. Cambridge. Ch. 4.

general reading ⇒ **generic reading**

general semantics

Founded by the Polish mathematician A. Korzybski in the United States, a semantic conceptualization of language, more ideological than linguistic. General semantics investigates the relationship between speaker, language, and reality, with the notion of freeing humans from the 'tyranny' of language (see Chase 1938). In contrast to the materialistically oriented **reflection theory**, general semantics assumes that, due to the present structure of language, human beings are not able to conceive of reality objectively, since the linguistic transmission of experience is always already determined by certain abstractions and symbolizations (⇒ **Sapir–Whorf hypothesis**). For pedagogical reasons, therefore, it is necessary to see through the manipulations and distortions of language, i.e. to unmask language as a deceptive likeness of reality.

References
Chase, S. 1938. *The tyranny of words*. London.
Hayakawa, S.I. 1941. *Language in thought and action*. New York.
Korzybski. A. 1933. *Science and sanity: an introduction to non-Aristotelian systems and General Semantics*. Lancaster, PA.

Generalized Phrase Structure Grammar (*abbrev.* GPSG)

A generative grammatical theory from the family of **unification grammars**. GPSG arose from the work of Gazdar as he attempted to oppose a formally limited grammatical model of the generative Revised Extended Standard Theory (⇒ **transformational grammar**). GPSG has just one level of representation and no transformations. The syntactic representation is a **tree diagram** whose non-terminal nodes are syntactic categories in the form of partially specified **feature structures**. The grammatical formalism of GPSG provides a complex system of rules and conditions which determine the wellformedness of the local trees in the representation of a sentence, and thereby the grammaticality of the sentence. The **phrase structure rules** of GPSG correspond to a version of **X-bar theory**. They are annotated with feature descriptions which allow the transmission of features. Many of the syntactic regularities described in transformational grammar by **transformations** are represented in GPSG by **metarules** which generate phrase structure rules from other phrase structure rules: for example, the rules for a passive construction can be derived from the rules for an active construction. Every category in the syntactic structure must satisfy the feature co-occurrence restrictions and the feature specification defaults, i.e. conditions which ensure wellformedness. The transmission of features is achieved through feature unification in the local tree and is guided by three global conditions: (a) the Head Feature Convention provides for the transmission of features like number and gender from the mother constituent to the head constituent; (b) the Foot Feature Principle guarantees the transmission of features which should pass to immediate constituents; (c) the Control Agreement Principle regulates the congruence of constituents on the basis of their semantic properties. GPSG uses the **ID/LP format**. In contrast to the traditional **phrase structure grammar**, immediate dominance and linear precedence are described by different types of rules. The lexicon of GPSG contains little information. Subcategorization involves a feature [subcat] whose numeric value selects the ID rule, which introduces the lexical element. Long-distance dependencies, such as those found in *wh*-questions and topicalization, are handled by the interaction of metarules and the transmission of features. Meanings are represented using formulae from intensional logic in the style of **Montague grammar**.

References
Gawron, J.M. *et al.* 1982. Processing English with a Generalized Phrase Structure Grammar. *ACL Proceedings* 20.74–81.
Gazdar, G. 1981. Unbounded dependencies and coordinate structure. *LingI* 12.155–84.
——— 1982. Phrase structure grammar. In P. Jacobson and G.K. Pullum (eds), *The nature of syntactic representation*. Dordrecht. 131–86.
Gazdar, G. and G.K. Pullum. 1981. Subcategorization, constituent order and the notion 'head.' In M. Moortgat, H.D.V. Hulst, and T. Hoekstra (eds), *The scope of lexical rules*. Dordrecht. 107–23.
Gazdar, G., G.K. Pullum, and I.A. Sag. 1982. Auxiliaries and related phenomena in a restrictive theory of grammar. *Lg* 58.591–638.
Gazdar, G., E. Klein, G.K. Pullum, and I.A. Sag. 1985. *Generalized Phrase Structure Grammar*. Cambridge, MA.
Gunji, T. 1986. *Japanese phrase structure grammar*. Dordrecht.
Kilbury, J. 1988. Parsing with category cooccurrence restrictions. *COLING 88* 1.324–7.
Phillips, J.D. and H.S. Thompson. 1985. GPSG: a parser for Generalized Phrase Structure Grammars. *Ling* 23:2.245–61.
Pollard, C. and I.A. Sag. 1988. *An information-based syntax and semantics*, vol. 1: *Fundamentals*. Stanford, CA.
Sells, P. 1985. *Lectures on contemporary syntactic theories*. Stanford, CA.
Shieber, S.M. 1986. A simple reconstruction of GPSG. *COLING* 86.211–15.
Stucky, S. 1986. *Order in Makua syntax*. New York.
Uszkoreit, H. 1986. *Word order and constituent structure in German*. Stanford, CA.
Verheijen, R. 1990. Generalized phrase structure grammar and contrastive analysis. In J. Fisiak (ed.), *Further insights into contrastive analysis*. Amsterdam. 67–84.

generate [Lat. *generare* 'to create']

A term coined by N. Chomsky in response to Humboldt's (1836) linguistic theory. Whereas Humboldt's term 'generate' refers to the historical development of language, Chomsky uses the term in a strictly mathematical-logical way for the listing of sentences on the basis of a recursive rule mechanism. (⇒ *also* **generative grammar, recursiveness**)

References
Chomsky, N. 1965. *Aspects of the theory of syntax*. Cambridge, MA.
Humboldt, W. von. 1836. *Über die Verschiedenheit des menschlichen Sprachbaues*. Berlin. (Repr. Berlin, 1963.)

generative capacity

The output of a **grammar**. If attention is restricted to strings, then one speaks of a *weak* generative capacity. If trees (or other structures) are included, then of a *strong* generative capacity. Grammars with the same generative capacity are thus weakly or (strongly) *equivalent*. (⇒ *also* **formal language theory**)

generative grammar

1 A blanket term for a grammar model that is based on **algorithm** and generates sentences.

2 A synonym for Chomsky's **transformational grammar**. All sentences of formal and natural languages can be produced by the application of the rules of generative grammar.

References
⇒ **transformational grammar**

generative phonology ⇒ **phonology**

generative semantics

The name for the counterposition taken by G. Lakoff, J. McCawley, and J. Ross among others in the late 1960s in response to Chomsky's conception of semantics in his 1965 'standard theory' (⇒ **aspects model**) of **transformational grammar**. Chomsky, Katz and Fodor (1963) argued that the syntactically motivated **deep structure** presents the only structure applicable to the semantic interpretive components of the grammar (⇒ **interpretive semantics**). In contrast, the proponents of generative semantics maintained that semantic structures are generated in a form of basic (universal) rules similar to those of **predicate logic**. The meaning of individual lexemes is described as a syntactically structured complex of basic semantic elements (⇒ **lexical decomposition**). For example, the verb *convince* (*x* convinces *y* to do *z*) is paraphrased by *x does that y wants that z*, where *do* and *want* are atomic predicates (⇒ **semantic primitives**) which form more complex predicates through transformations. In addition, the number of syntactic categories is reduced to three: S (= **proposition**), NP (= **argument**), and V (= **predicate**). Since the logical-semantic form of the sentence is now seen as the underlying (generative) structure, the otherwise strict division between syntax and semantics collapses, especially between lexical semantics, word formation and the semantics of propositions. Critics of generative semantics pointed out the *ad hoc* nature of the descriptive mechanism and the 'overpowerful' generative power of this model (cf. **global rule**), whose apparatus could generate more complex structures than are realized in human languages. Interesting counterperspectives are found in Chomsky (1971) and Katz (1970) (interpretive semantics), Bartsch and Vennemann (1972) (**categorial grammar**), and Seuren (1985) (generative semantics).

References
Bartsch, R. and T. Vennemann. 1972. *Semantic structures: a study in the relation between semantics and syntax*. Frankfurt. (2nd edn 1973.)
Chomsky, N. 1971. Deep structure, surface structure, and semantic interpretation. In D.D. Steinberg and L.A. Jakobovits (eds), *Semantics*. Cambridge. 183–216.
—— 1972. *Studies on semantics in generative grammar*. The Hague.
Katz, J.J. 1970. Interpretative semantics vs generative semantics. *FL* 6.220–59.
—— 1972. *Semantic theory*. New York.
Katz, J.J. and J.A. Fodor. 1963. The structure of semantic theory. *Lg* 39.170–210.

Lakoff, G. 1970. Linguistics and natural logic. *Synthese* 22.151–271.
—— 1971. On generative semantics. In D.D. Steinberg and L.A. Jakobovits (eds), *Semantics*. Cambridge. 232–96.
Seuren, P.A.M. 1985. *Discourse semantics*. Oxford.
⇒ **interpretive semantics**, **semantics**, **transformational grammar**

generic [Lat. *genus* 'class, stock, kind']

1 In **predicate logic**, property of a proposition which comes about through prefixation of the universal quantifier on a propositional function (i.e. a universal proposition); see Reichenbach (1947).

Reference
Reichenbach, H. 1947. *Elements of symbolic logic*. New York.

2 In **semantics**, (a) a reference of **noun phrases** to kinds instead of concrete objects, e.g. *In 1969 man landed on the moon* or *Every day at least one species of beetles becomes extinct.* (According to Burton-Roberts (1976) and Hawkins (1989), the distinction between definites and indefinites remains valid, however.) (b) The expression of regular or predictable states of affairs, e.g. *A Scot drinks whisky* or *Philip smokes pipes.* Both types can occur together, e.g. *The typical Scot drinks whisky.*

References
Burton-Roberts, N. 1976. On the generic indefinite article. *Lg* 52.427–48.
Carlson, G. 1990. *Reference to kinds in English*. New York.
Chur, J. 1993. *Generische Nominalphrasen im Deutschen: eine Untersuchung zu Referenz und Semantik*. Tübingen.
Dahl, Ö. 1975. On generics. In E. Keenan (ed.), *Formal semantics of natural language*. Cambridge. 99–111.
Gerster, C. and M. Krifka. 1993. Genericity. In J. Jacobs *et al.* (eds), *Syntax: an international handbook of contemporary research*. Berlin and New York. 966–78.
Hawkins, J. 1978. *Definiteness and indefiniteness*. London.
Heyer, G. 1987. *Generische Kennzeichnungen: zur Logik und Ontologie generischer Bedeutung*. Munich.
Krifka, M. (ed.) 1988. *Genericity in natural language*. Tübingen.

generic noun ⇒ **common noun**

generic reading (*also* general reading)

The meaning of linguistic expressions which, as generic concepts independent of context, refer to classes of individual elements, e.g. *books* in *Books are expensive*. In sentences of the type *A lion is a mammal*, the indefinite article (normally) has the generic reading. This contrasts with the indefinite article in *A lion is sitting in the cage*, which does not have the generic reading.

References
⇒ **determiner, feminist linguistics**

genericity ⇒ **generic**

genetic definition ⇒ **definition**

genetic phonetics ⇒ **articulatory phonetics**

genetic tree theory [Grk *génesis* 'race, descent'] (*also* family tree theory)
Conceptual model developed by Schleicher (1861–2) to describe the origin of individual languages which were believed to have 'branched off' from older languages. Influenced by Darwin's theory of evolution, Schleicher reconstructed the origin of the individual **Indo-European** languages from a hypothetical Indo-European '**proto-language**' in the form of a genetic tree whose branches are meant to correspond to the differentiation of individual languages caused by an interruption in their contact with other languages. Apart from its adoption of biological terminology ('genetic,' 'descendant') to describe the relationship between languages, which leads to faulty associations, the genetic tree model with its (abrupt) branching cannot depict possible mutual influences or parallel linguistic developments. The principal competing model is the **wave theory**.

References
Jankowsky, K.R. 1972. *The Neogrammarians: a re-evaluation of their place in the development of linguistic science.* The Hague and Paris.
Pedersen, H. 1931. *Linguistic science in the nineteenth century.* Cambridge, MA.
Pulgram, E. 1953. Family tree, wave theory, and dialectology. *Orbis* 2.67–72.
Schleicher, A. 1861–2. *Compendium der vergleichenden Grammatik der indogermanischen Sprachen.* Weimar.
———— 1873. *Die Darwinsche Theorie und die Sprachwissenschaft.* Weimar.
Schmidt, J. 1872. *Die Verwandtschaftsverhältnisse der indogermanischen Sprachen.* Weimar.
Strunk, K. 1981. Stammbaumtheorie und Selektion. In H. Geckeler *et al.* (ed.), *Studia linguistica in honorem Eugenio Coseriu.* Berlin and Madrid. Vol. 2, 159–70.

Geneva School

Direction of structuralist research (⇒ **structuralism**) based on the posthumously published writings of F. de Saussure (1857–1913) and represented above all by subsequent holders of his chair at the University of Geneva (Bally, Sechehaye, Karcevski, and Frei), as well as the editors of his work and the administrators of his will. In this framework, the 'Ferdinand de Saussure Circle' primarily attempts to interpret, defend, and define de Saussure's position, and publishes its findings in the *Cahiers F. de Saussure*.

References
Godel, R. 1969. *A Geneva school reader in linguistics.* Bloomington, IN.
———— 1970. L'école saussurienne de Genève. In C. Mohrmann *et al.* (eds), *Trends in European and American linguistics 1930–1960*, Utrecht. 294–9.
Sechehaye, A. 1927. L'école génévoise de linguistique générale. *IF* 44.217–41.
⇒ **linguistics (history), structuralism**

genitive

Morphological **case** found in many languages (e.g. **Latin, Russian, German**) whose primary function is to mark an **attribute** of a noun. The most usual type of attribute is one of possession, which is why the genitive is often called a possessive marker in the literature on universals. Other syntactic functions of noun phrases in the genitive case include the **oblique object** of a verb or an adjective (Ger. *Philip ist sich seines Fehlers bewusst* 'Philip is aware of his mistake'; for further uses, see Teubert 1979), (Ger. *eines Tages* 'one day'), or predicative (Ger. *des Teufels sein* 'to be of the devil'). Some prepositions in these languages can require the genitive as well (Ger. *wegen des Regens* 'because of the rain'). Genitive attributes are sometimes classified, following Latin grammars according to the semantic relation to the modified noun: (a) subject genitive: *the sleep of a child* (cf. the subject–predicate relationship in *A child sleeps*); (b) object genitive: the *distribution of goods* (cf. the object–predicate relationship: *Someone distributes goods*); (c) possessive genitive: *the senator's hat* (possessive relationship: *The senator has a hat*); (d) partitive genitive: Ger. *die Hälfte meines Kuchens* 'half of my cake'.

Historically the use of the genitive case in **Indo-European** languages has decreased significantly; while it is fully active in the **Slavic languages**, its use has been reduced in German, and in many **Romance languages** it has been completely lost. In Old English the genitive case was fully functional, while modern English preserves it mainly in the possessive marker -*s*: *Philip's book*. The term 'genitive' is also used for the function expressed by the genitive case, e.g. *book of Philip*.

References
Anttila, H. 1983. Zur geschichtlichen Entwicklung

des Genitivobjekts im Deutschen. *Linguistische Studien* 107.97–113.

Debrunner, A. 1940. *Aus der Krankheitsgeschichte des Genitivs.* Bern.

Michaelis, C. 1980. Formale Bestimmung und Interpretation einer syntaktischen Relation: das Genitivattribut im Deutschen. Doctoral dissertation, Berlin.

Teubert, W. 1979. *Valenz des Substantivs: attributive Ergänzungen und Angaben.* Düsseldorf.

Wellander, E. 1956. Zum Schwund des Genitivs. In Deutsche Akademie der Wissenschaften zu Berlin (ed.), *Fragen und Forschungen im Bereich der germanischen Philologie. Festgabe für Th. Frings*, Berlin. 156–72.

⇒ **case**.

genotype

A term in semiotics borrowed from genetics by Šaumjan to describe the sum of inherited properties. This contrasts with **phenotype**, which refers to the external and apparent image. According to Šaumjan, the genotype represents the abstract level of a language model which is a universal semiotic system fundamental to all languages. The genotype is bound to various phenotypes by correspondence rules. The primary goal of linguistic analysis is the description of the genotype, upon which a description of the phenotype can be based.

References
⇒ **applicational-generative model**

Georgian

Largest **South Caucasian** language with 3.5 million speakers and a literary tradition extending back to the fifth century AD. The Georgian writing system seems to be developed on the basis of **Aramaic**.

Characteristics: In comparison to other **Caucasian languages**, a relatively simple sound system (with glottalized consonants), but with complex consonant clusters. Rich inflectional morphology. **Ergative** case system when the verb is in the aorist; dative subjects with verbs of perception. Verb agreement with the subject, direct and indirect object. Numerous **aspects** can be expressed by verbal prefixes.

References
Aronson, H. 1982. *Georgian: a reading grammar.* Columbus, OH.

Fähnrich, H. 1986. *Kurze Grammatik der georgischen Sprache.* Leipzig.

——— 1994. *Grammatik der altgeorgischen Sprache.* Hamburg.

Harris, A.C. 1981. *Georgian syntax: a study in relational grammar.* Cambridge.

Hewitt, G. 1996. *Georgian. A learner's grammar.* London.

Tshenkéli, K. 1958. *Einführung in die georgische Sprache.* Zurich.

Vogt. H. 1971. *Grammaire de la langue géorgienne.* Oslo.
⇒ **South Caucasian**

German

Indo-European language belonging to the **Germanic** branch, spoken as a native language in various dialects by approx. 90 million speakers in Germany (approx. 77 million speakers), Austria (approx. 7 million speakers), Switzerland (approx. 4 million speakers), Liechtenstein, and elsewhere. It is also either the first or the second language of approx. 40 million people in France (Alsace), Italy (South Tyrol), Belgium, Rumania, Poland and Russia, as well as in non-European countries with German-speaking emigrees (United States, Argentina, Brazil, Canada). German differs from the other Germanic languages due in part to the results of the **Old High German consonant shift** (also second sound shift) in which the voiceless stops [p, t, k] became either fricatives or affricates, depending on their position, cf. Eng. *ship, foot, book* vs Ger. *Schiff, Fuß, Buch*; also Eng. *apple, sit,* vs Ger. *Apfel, sitzen*. The dialect distinctions between Low German (*ik* 'I,' *maken* 'make,' *dorp* 'village,' *dat* 'that,' *appel* 'apple'), Middle German (*ich, machen, dorf, das, appel*) and Upper German (*ich, machen, dorf, das, apfel*) are based on the regional distribution of this sound shift.

While the nature and duration of the historical stages of German are still debated, the following main periods can be distinguished. (a) Old High German (OHG) (from the beginning of written documentation until AD 1050): linguistically distinguished by the spread of the second sound shift and the beginning of vowel mutation (⇒ **umlaut**); lexically marked by strong influence from **Latin**. Written documents in various dialects stem mainly from monasteries in the form of Latin translations and poems in alliterative verse. (b) Middle High German (MHG) (from 1050 to 1350, divided into Early Middle High German (1050–1170/80), classical Middle High German (1170/80–1250), and late Middle High German (1250–1350): the transition from Old to Middle High German is linguistically marked by the weakening and loss of final syllables (OHG *scôno* > MHG *schône* > NHG *schon* 'already'), while Middle and New High German (NHG) differ through **monophthongization** (MHG *lieber müeder bruoder* > NHG *lieber müder Bruder* 'dear tired brother'), **diphthongization** (MHG *mîn níuwes hûs* > NHG *mein neues Haus* 'my new house') and lengthening (⇒ **lengthening vs shortening**) in open syllables

(MHG *wege* [vɛgə] > NHG *Wege* [veːgə]). The vocabulary of the court epic is strongly influenced by **French**. The literary tradition was largely maintained by knights. During this period, the German-speaking territory was greatly enlarged due to colonization of areas to the east. (c) Early New High German (1500–1650): this period is marked by Luther and the Reformation, the invention of the printing press, and the rise of the middle class. Several dialectal variants, such as Middle Low German of the Hanseatic league, the 'Common German' of the Hapsburg chancery in southern Germany, 'Meissen German' in the territory of Wettin competed against one another for supremacy. (d) New High German, arising in the course of the eighteenth century, based on East Middle German, and resulting from leveling processes between north and south. It occurs as a written standard with numerous variants (dialects, sociolects) and levels (idiomatic, technical, etc.) which show primarily phonetic and lexical differences.

Grammatical characteristics (compared to other Germanic languages): no voiced stops in the syllable coda (= word-final devoicing), relatively complex inflectional system and productive case system, set rules on the placement of the finite verb with otherwise relatively free word order. Special characters: *ß* (= *ss*), *ä*, *ö*, *ü*. (⇒ also **brace construction**, **positional fields**)

Modern grammars

Clément, D. and W. Thümmel. 1975. *Grundzüge einer Syntax der deutschen Standardsprache*. Frankfurt.

Duden. 1995. *Grammatik der deutschen Gegenwartssprache*, 5th rev. edn, ed. G. Drosdowski *et al.* Mannheim.

Eisenberg, P. 1994. *Grundriß der deutschen Grammatik*, 3rd edn. Stuttgart.

Engel, U. 1977. *Syntax der deutschen Gegenwartssprache*. Berlin. (3rd rev. edn Bielefeld and Munich, 1994.)

—— 1988. *Deutsche Grammatik*, 2nd rev. edn. 1991, Heidelberg.

Fox, A. 1990. *The structure of German*. Oxford.

Hammer, A.E. 1971. *German grammar and usage*. London. (2nd rev. edn by M. Durrell 1983.)

Heidolph, K.E. *et al.* 1981. *Grundzüge einer deutschen Grammatik*. Berlin. (2nd unrev. edn 1984.)

Helbig, G. and J. Buscha. 1974. *Deutsche Grammatik: ein Handbuch für den Ausländerunterricht*. Leipzig. (16th edn 1994, Munich).

Lohnes, W.F.W. and F.W. Strohmann. 1967. *German: a structural approach*. New York.

Russ, C.V. 1994. *The German language today*. London.

Weinrich, H. 1993. *Textgrammatik der deutschen Sprache*. Mannheim.

Wiese, R. 1995. *The phonology of German*. Oxford.

History and historical grammars

Bach, A. 1938. *Geschichte der deutschen Sprache*. Leipzig.

Bergmann, R., *et al.* (eds) 1987. *Althochdeutsch*, 2 vols. Heidelberg.

Besch, W., O. Reichmann and S. Sonderegger (eds) 1982–4. *Sprachgeschichte: ein Handbuch zur Geschichte der deutschen Sprache und ihrer Erforschung*, 2 vols. Berlin and New York.

Braune, W. 1987. *Althochdeutsche Grammatik*, 14th edn, rev. by H. Eggers. Tübingen.

Eggers, H. 1963. *Deutsche Sprachgeschlichte*. 4 vols. Reinbek.

Grimm, J. 1819–1837. *Deutsche Grammatik*. 4 parts. Göttingen (Facsimile printing of the 2nd edn of Berlin 1870/78. Hildesheim 1967).

—— 1848. *Geschichte der deutschen Sprache*. Leipzig.

Moser, M. 1950. *Deutsche Sprachgeschichte*. Stuttgart. (6th rev. edn Tübingen 1969).

Moser, H., H. Stopp, and W. Besch (eds) 1970– . *Grammatik des Frühneuhochdeutschen*. Heidelberg.

Paul, H. 1989. *Mittelhochdeutsche Grammatik*, 23rd. edn, rev. by S. Grosse and P. Wiehl. Tübingen.

Voyles, J.B. 1976. *The phonology of Old High German*. Göttingen.

⇒ **language history**

Dictionaries

Adelung, J.C. 1774–86. *Versuch eines vollständigen grammatisch-kirtiischen Wörterbuches der Hochdeutschen Mundart, mit beständiger Vergleichung der fübrigen Mundarten, besonders aber der oberdeutschen*, 5 vols. Leipzig. (Repr. Hildesheim, 1970.)

Duden. 1976–81. *Das große Wörterbuch der deutschen Sprace*, ed. G. Drosdowski, 6 vols. Mannheim.

Paul, H. 1897. *Deutsches Wörterbuch*. 9th rev. edn, ed. H. Heine *et al.* Tübingen, 1992.

Historical dictionaries

Goebel, U. and O. Reichmann (eds) 1989–. *Frühneuhochdeutsches Wörterbuch*. Berlin and New York. Vol. II.3 1993.

Grimm, J. and W. Grimm. 1854–60. *Deutsches Wörterbuch*, 16 vols. Leipzig. (Repr. Munich 1884; new rev. edn by the Deutsche Akademie der Wissenschaften Berlin and Göttingen. Leipzig 1965–.)

Lexer, M. 1872–8. *Mittelhochdeutsches Handwörterbuch*, 3 vols. Leipzig.

Splett, J. 1992. *Althochdeutsches Wörterbuch*, 3 vols. Berlin and New York.

Etymological dictionaries

Duden Etymologie. 1989. *Herkunftswörterbuch der deutschen Sprache*, ed. G. Drosdowski. 2nd rev. edn. Mannheim.

Kluge, F. 1883. *Etymologisches Wörterbuch des Deutschen*. (22nd. edn, rev. by E. Seebold. Berlin and New York, 1989.)

Pfeifer, W. *et al.* 1992. *Etymologisches Wörterbuch des Deutschen*, 2nd edn. Berlin.

Bibliographies

Germanistik. Internationales Referatenorgan mit bibliographischen Hinweisen. Tübingen.

Kühn, P. 1978. *Deutsche Wörterbücher: eine systematische Bibliographie.* Tübingen.

Lemmer, M. 1968. *Deutscher Wortschatz: Bibliographie zur deutschen Lexikologie.* Halle.

Piirainen, I.T. 1980. *Frühneuhochdeutsche Bibliographie: Literatur zur Sprache des 14.–17. Jahrhunderte.* Tübingen.

Ronneberger–Sibold, E. 1989. *Historische Phonologie und Morphologie des Deutschen: eine kommentierte Bibliographie zur strukturellen Forschung.* Tübingen.

Varieties of German

Ammon, U. 1995. *Die deutsche Sprache in Deutschland, Österreich und der Schweiz. Das Problem der nationalen Varietäten.* Berlin and New York.

Barbour, S. and P. Stevenson. 1990. *Variation in German. A critical approach to German sociolinguistics.* Cambridge.

Noble, C.A.M. 1983. *Modern German dialects.* New York.

Journals

Beiträge zur Geschichte der deutschen Sprache und Literatur.

Beiträge zur Namenforschung. Neue Folge.

Deutsch als Fremdsprache.

Deutsche Sprache.

Der Deutschunterricht.

English and American Studies in German.

The German Quarterly.

The German Review.

Germanistik.

Germanistische Linguistik.

LiLi. Zeitschrift für Literaturwissenschaft und Linguistik.

Linguistische Berichte.

Sprachwissenschaft.

Zeitschrift für deutsche Philologie.

Zeitschrift für deutsche Sprache.

Zeitschrift für deutsches Altertum und deutsche Literature.

Zeitschrift für Dialektologie und Linguistik.

Zeitschrift für Germanistische Linguistik.

Reference works

Althaus, H.P., H. Henne, and H.E. Wiegand (eds) 1973. *Lexikon der germanischen Linguistik.* Tübingen. (2nd rev. edn 1980.)

History

Bach, A. 1938. *Geschichte der deutschen Sprache.* Leipzig.

Eggers, H. 1963. *Deutsche Sprachgeschichte*, 4 vols. Reinbek.

Grimm, J. 1848. *Geschichte der deutschen Sprache.* Leipzig.

Keller, R.E. 1978. *The German language.* London.

Moser, M. 1950. *Deutsche Sprachgeschichte.* Stuttgart. (6th rev. edn Tübingen, 1969.)

German in Austria

Kranzmayer, E. 1956. *Historische Lautgeographie des gesamtbairischen Dialektraums.* Vienna.

Österreichisches Wörterbuch. 1979. (Hrg. im Auftrag des Bundesministeriums für Unterricht und Kultus.) 35th rev. edn. Vienna.

Schikola, H. 1954. *Schriftdeutsch und Wienerisch.* Vienna.

Wiesinger, P. (ed.) 1988. *Das österreichische Deutsch.* Berlin.

German in Switzerland

Hotzenköcherle, R. 1962– . *Sprachatlas der deutschen Schweiz.* Bern.

Stucki, K. 1921. *Schweizerdeutsch: Abriß einer Grammatik mit Laut- und Formenlehre.* Zurich.

Germanic

Member of the **Indo-European** language family which differs from the other Indo-European branches due to **Grimm's law**, the fixation of word accent in the first root syllable, reduction of the original variety of **cases** (from eight to four) and the three **number** categories to two (loss of the **dual**), simplification of the verbal morphology (loss of the **middle voice**, syncre-

Germanic Languages

North Germanic		East Germanic	West Germanic		
North West Germanic	East North Germanic	Burgundian Gothic	North Sea G. Ingvaeonic	Istvaeonic	Elbe Germanic (Hermionic)
Faroesc Icelandic Norwegian	Danish Swedish	Crimean Gothic East Gothic West Gothic	Anglo-Saxon (English) Frisian Dutch Afrikaans	Franconian etc. Middle G.	Alamannic Bavarian Langobardic Upper German

Low German   High German

German

tism of **subjunctive** and **optative**), differentiation between **strong vs weak verb** formation, as well as the development of strong and weak adjective endings. Vocabulary, inflection, and syntax have developed differently in the various Germanic languages. There have been several suggestions on the grouping of the Germanic languages, most of which do not overtly conflict with each other. Usually they are divided into three groups based on historical and geographical concerns (cf. van Coetsem and Kufner 1972; Hawkins 1987): (a) East Germanic: **Gothic** and Burgundian; (b) North Germanic: **Faroese, Icelandic,** and the **Scandinavian** languages **Danish, Norwegian,** and **Swedish;** (c) West Germanic: **German** (including **Yiddish), English** (including several related **creole** languages), **Frisian,** and **Dutch** (including **Afrikaans**). Based on the linguistic correspondences between all the individual Germanic languages, a common **proto-language** is assumed. The earliest attestations are Scandinavian runic inscriptions (third century) (⇒ **rune**) and Wulfila's Bible translation (Gothic, fourth century).

References

Abraham, W., W. Kosmeijer, and E. Reuland (eds) 1990. *Issues in Germanic syntax.* Berlin and New York.

Bammesberger, A. 1986. *Der Aufbau des germanischen Verbalsystems.* Heidelberg.

—— 1990. *Die Morphologie des urgermanischen Nomens.* Heidelberg.

Brogyányi, B. and T. Krömmelbein (eds) 1986. *Germanic dialects: linguistic and philological investigations.* Amsterdam.

Fullerton, G.L. 1977. *Historical Germanic verb morphology.* The Hague and Berlin.

Haugen, E. 1976. *The Scandinavian languages: an introduction to their history.* London.

—— 1982. *Scandinavian language structures: a comparative historical survey.* Tübingen.

Hawkins, J.A. 1987. Germanic languages. In B. Comrie (ed.), *The world's major languages.* London. 68–76.

Hutterer, C.J. 1975. *Die germanischen Sprachen: ihre Geschichte in Grundzügen.* Budapest. (3rd rev. edn 1990.)

König, E. and J. van der Auwera. 1994. *The Germanic languages.* London.

Lehmann, W.P. 1966. The grouping of the Germanic languages. In H. Birnbaum and J. Puhvel (eds), *Ancient Indo-European dialects.* Berkeley, CA. 13–27.

Rauch, I., G.F. Carr, and R. Keyes (eds) 1992. *On Germanic linguistics: issues and methods.* Berlin and New York.

Swan, T., E. Morck, and O.J. Westvik (eds) 1994. *Language change and language structure: older Germanic languages in a comparative perspective.* Berlin and New York.

Grammars

Krahe, H. and W. Meid. 1967–9. *Germanische Sprachwissenschaft,* 7th edn. Berlin.

Prokosch, E. 1939. *A comparative Germanic grammar.* Philadelphia, PA.

Streitberg, W. 1954. *Urgermanische Grammatik,* 4th edn. Heidelberg.

Voyles, J.B. 1992. *Early Germanic grammar: pre-, proto-, and post-Germanic languages.* San Diego, CA.

Dialectology

Markey, T.L. 1976. *Germanic dialect grouping and the position of Ingvaeonic.* Innsbruck.

Bibliography

Germanistik. Internationales Referatenorgan mit bibliographischen Hinweisen. Tübingen.

Markey, T.L., R.L. Keyes, and P.T. Roberge. 1978. *Germanic and its dialects: a grammar of Proto-Germanic,* vol. 3: *Bibliography and indices.* Amsterdam.

Journals

American Journal of Germanic Languages and Literature.

The Journal of English and Germanic Philology.

Zeitschrift für germanistische Linguistik.
⇒ **ablaut**

Germanic law of spirants

The **Indo-European** consonant clusters *bt, gt, gs, dt* occur in Proto-Germanic not – as to be expected from the Germanic sound shift (⇒ **Grimm's law**) – as *pt, kt, ks, tt,* but rather as [ft, χt, χs, s(s)]. Therefore, it may be assumed that in Indo-European the stem-final voiced stops assimilated (⇒ **assimilation**) to the voiceless stops of the following syllable, cf. e.g. Lat. *scrībere : scrīptum; regere : rēctus.* In the Germanic sound shift these voiceless stops regularly turned into their corresponding voiceless fricatives, cf. IE **skabt-, *reĝ-tos* : Proto-Gmc **skaft *reχt;* in the case of *dt* and *tt* there was an additional assimilatory fricativization of the stops, cf. IE **sedtos* > Lat. (*ob*)*sessus:* Proto-Gmc **sedˢtos* > **sestos* > **sessos.*

References

Prokosch, E. 1939. *A comparative Germanic grammar.* Baltimore, MD.

Wisniewski, R. 1963. Die Bildung des schwachen Präteritums und die primären Berührungseffekte. *PBB (T)* 85.1–17.
⇒ **sound change**

Germanic sound shift ⇒ Grimm's law

gerund [Lat. *gerere* 'to perform, to do']

1 Impersonally used verbal noun in **Latin** which replaces the lacking case inflection of the infinitive. Formally the gerund corresponds to a future passive participle; semantically it indicates the action in and of itself: *ars libros recte*

legendi 'the art of reading books correctly.' Grammatically the gerund functions as an attribute to the dominating element (*ars*) and at the same time its valence determines the form of the dependent elements (*libros*).

2 In English, a verb in the form of a present participle which is used as a noun: *Reading spy-novels was his favorite pastime.*

References
⇒ **nominalization**

gerundive (*also* verbal adjective)

Verbal adjective in **Latin** with passive meaning. It is similar in form to the **gerund**[1]; semantically it expresses purpose or necessity; *pacis faciendae causa* 'for the purpose of making peace' from the verb *facere* 'to make.' This corresponds in English to attributive constructions such as (*There remains*) *much to be done*. (⇒ *also* **supine**)

References
Hettrich, H. 1993. Nochmals zu Gerundium und Gerundivum. In G. Meiser (ed.), *Indogermanica et Italica: für Helmut Rix zum 65. Geburtstag.* Innsbruck. 190–208.
Risch, E. 1984. *Gerundium und Gerundivum: Gebrauch im klassischen und älteren Latein. Entstehung und Vorgeschichte.* Berlin.
Strunk, K. 1962. Über Gerundium und Gerundivum. *Gymnasium* 69.445–60.

Gheg ⇒ Albanian

Gilyak ⇒ language isolate, Paleo-Siberian

Glagolitic script

Alphabetic writing system devised by the Greek missionary to the Slavs, Kyrill, in the ninth century for recording texts in **Old Church Slavic**. The letters of the Glagolitic script show (virtually) no similarities to those in the **Cyrillic script** which replaced the Glagolitic script in the centuries that followed.

References
⇒ **writing**

glide

1 ⇒ **semivowel**

2 **Speech sound** without etymological basis that is inserted epenthetically, such as ‹s› in Ger. *Kunst* 'art' (< *können* 'to be able') and the epenthetical ‹l› in Russ. *tomlyú* 'I torture.' (⇒ *also* **epenthesis**)

References
⇒ **phonetics**

global aphasia ⇒ aphasia

global rules

Rules in **generative semantics** introduced by G. Lakoff. They ensure the wellformedness of derivations in that they relate not only to the adjacent **tree diagrams** in a **transformational history** but the whole derivation of the sentence.

References
Lakoff, G. 1970. Global rules. *Lg* 46.627–39.
⇒ **generative semantics**

gloss

Explications in old manuscripts of unintelligible passages in the text or their translation. Depending on the place of the explication, a distinction is made between interlinear glosses, marginal glosses and context glosses. The philological research into glosses, which are often written in a secret language, yields important insights into linguistic and cultural history and can be viewed as a stage prior to lexicology.

glossematics

Developed in Denmark by L. Hjelmslev (1899–1965) and others, glossematics is the structural linguistic theory of the so-called 'Copenhagen Linguistic Circle.' The term 'glossematics,' meaning 'combination of **glossemes**' was coined in 1936 by L. Hjelmslev and H.J. Uldall to delineate their theories from more traditional forms of structural linguistics, especially the **Prague School** (⇒ **structuralism**). The linguistic theory of glossematics is understood as a continuation of the fundamental structuralist principles set forth by de Saussure (1916) in his *Cours de linguistique générale*; however, Hjelmslev, influenced by the logical **empiricism** of A. Whitehead, B. Russell, R. Carnap, and others, aims to make the theory more axiomatic, which his complex terminological apparatus so aptly reveals. Glossematics is based on the hypothesis that language represents a system of internal relations whose structure can be described exclusively through language-internal criteria, autonomously from other disciplines. In strong accord with the methodological principles of de Saussure, glossematics assumes langue (⇒ **langue vs parole**) to be the object of linguistic research, investigated independently of parole.

Crucial to Hjelmslev's outline of a general theory of language is his attempt to construct a non-contradictory descriptive language by using abstraction and mathematical logic, which would eliminate the confusion between object language and metalanguage (⇒ **object** language vs **metalanguage**). Presumably, however, it is precisely this demanding terminological form which has hindered the broader effectiveness of glossematics.

Fundamental to the methodology of glossematics is the delineation of two research planes, expression and content (⇒ **expression plane vs content plane**), i.e. the distinction between the material aspect of the linguistic **sign** and its meaningful contents, postulated in accordance with de Saussure. Each plane is further divided by the dichotomy 'substance vs **form**,' resulting in four combinations: (a) **phonetics** or the (physical) substance of the expression; (b) **semantics** or the substance of the content (by which is meant the extralinguistic reality); (c) **phonology** or the form of the expression; and (d) **grammar** or the form of the content. In glossematics, the investigation of phonology and grammar is understood to be the only task of linguistics, while phonetics and semantics are excluded as being extralinguistic.

The goal of linguistic analysis is not primarily the classification of linguistic objects, but rather the description of the structural relations that exist between them. Hjelmslev calls these relations 'functions,' and differentiates, according to the type of relation, between (a) bilateral dependence (**interdependence**), (b) unilateral dependence (**determination**), and (c) free **constellation**. To describe these structural combinatory principles, Hjemslev again draws on de Saussure and distinguishes between **paradigmatic vs syntagmatic relations**. Here the paradigmatic level refers to the language system and the syntagmatic to the co-occurrence of elements in the text. The connection between the paradigmatic and syntagmatic relations is determined by the **commutation test**.

Glossematics influenced the development of formal linguistic description through its concept of the autonomy of language and through its drafting of an axiomatic-deductive linguistic theory which was to fulfill the demands of completeness, simplicity, and freedom from contradiction.

References
Hjelmslev, L. 1928. *Principles de grammaire générale*. Copenhagen.
———— 1943. *Omkring sprogteoriens grundlaeggelse*. Copenhagen. (*Prolegomena to a theory of language*, trans. F.J. Whitfield. Baltimore, MD, 1953.)
Saussure, F. de. 1916. *Cours de linguistique générale*, ed. C. Bally and A. Sechehaye. Paris. (*Course in general linguistics*, trans. R. Harris. London. 1983.)
Siertsema, B. 1955. *A study of glossematics*, part I: *General Theory* (TCLC 10). Copenhagen.

Spang-Hanssen, H. 1961. Glossematics. In C. Mohrmann *et al.* (eds), *Trends in European and American linguistics, 1930–1960*. Utrecht. 128–64.
⇒ **linguistics (history)**

glosseme

1 In L. Bloomfield's terminology, the smallest meaning-bearing unit. Glosseme functions as the cover term for the (grammatically interpreted) **tagmemes** and the (lexically interpreted) **morphemes**.

References
⇒ **etic vs emic analysis**

2 In **glossematics**, cover term for minimal linguistic units of langue (⇒ **langue vs parole**), which on the expression plane consist of phonological features (**kenemes**) and on the content plane of **semantic features (pleremes)** (⇒ *also* **expression plane vs content plane**).

References
⇒ **glossematics**

glossography

The collection, examination, and codification of **glosses**.

glottal [Grk. *glōttis* 'mouthpiece of a windpipe, larynx']

Speech sound formed with the pulmonic **airstream mechanism** in an on-glide or off-glide (⇒ **on-glide vs off-glide**). A distinction is drawn between voiceless on- or off-glide [h], voiced on- or off-glide [ɦ], laryngealized on- or off-glide [h̬], or a breathy on- or off-glide [h̤]. These characteristics are, as a rule, interpreted as independent speech sounds, especially when the pulmonic air is forced through the resonance chamber with great pressure. A glottal stop [ʔ]) is formed when the glottis is closed and opened again with a plosive. In preglottalized vowels (⇒ **glottalization**) there is abrupt onset of voice, in vowels with voiced on-glide there is delayed onset of voice (⇒ **articulatory phonetics**).

References
⇒ **phonetics**

glottal closure

Closure of the **glottis** in the formation of glottalized language sounds. Closing and opening of the glottis produces a glottal sound. Notation: [ʔ], e.g. [ʔʌʔo] *uh-oh*.

References
⇒ **phonetics**

glottal stop

Stop formed by closing and opening the **glottis**,

e.g. Eng. [ʔok] *oak*, Dan. [ˈvenʔdɐʁ] 'winter.'
(⇒ *also* **glottal closure**)

References
⇒ **phonetics**

glottalic

1 Of or referring to the **glottis**.

2 Sounds formed with the glottalic **airstream mechanism**.

glottalic airstream mechanism ⇒ **airstream mechanism**

glottalization

Glottal closure before (= preglottalization) or after (= postglottalization) a **speech sound**. Preglottalized consonants are closest to **implosives**, postglottalized are closest to **ejectives**. Preglottalized vowels can be found occasionally in English when, for example, a speaker attempts to avoid running words [nat+ʔætʔɔl] 'not at all' (see Moulton 1962); postglottalized vowels are found in the **Sino-Tibetan** language of Tsaiwa-Jingpo. In preglottalized vowels, one also speaks of abrupt onset of voicing, e.g. in [ʔa] in Ger. [bəˈʔaxtn] *beachten* 'regard' (in contrast to delayed onset of voicing, e.g. in Fr. [ˈaleː] *aller* 'to go'). Some English dialects, most notably **Cockney**, substitute a glottal stop for intervocalic consonants, e.g. [baʔl] *bottle*.

References
Moulton, W.G. 1962. *The sounds of English and German*. Chicago, IL.
⇒ **phonetics**

glottis

The gap between the vocal chords in the larynx of humans and other mammals. The action of the glottis determines **phonation**. (⇒ *also* **articulatory phonetics**)

References
⇒ **phonetics**

glottochronology [Grk *glȭtta* 'language']

Subdiscipline of **lexicostatistics** founded by M. Swadesh that investigates historically comparable vocabularies using statistical methods. The aim of glottochronology is to determine the degree of relatedness between languages as well as an approximate dating of their common origin and divergent development. This process was developed in analogy to the carbon-14 method, in which the age of organic substances can be determined based on the decay of the radio-active isotopes contained within them. Similarly, glottochronology is used to determine the 'life span' of words in their respective vocabularies. So it seems that after 1,000 years

from the time of its separation from a common proto-language about 81 percent of the original common basic vocabulary of a language remains intact, and then, after an additional 1,000 years, another 81 percent of the remaining original vocabulary remains intact. The methods and conflicting results of glottochronology have come under criticism.

References
Bergsland, K. and H. Vogt. 1962. On the validity of glottochronology. *Current Anthropology* 3.115–53.
Swadesh, M. 1952. Lexicostatistic dating of prehistoric ethnic contacts. *Proceedings of the American Philological Society* 96.452–63.
⇒ **lexicostatistics**

gnomic [Grk *gnōmḗ* 'judgment, (general) opinion']

Verbal **aspect** which expresses 'eternal' or 'timeless' truths (e.g. *Snow is white*) and forms a subgroup of iterative verbs (⇒ **iterative vs semelfactive**).

References
⇒ **generic**[2]

Goajiro ⇒ **Arawakan**

goal ⇒ **case grammar**

God's truth vs hocuspocus

Facetious term for the controversy within **distributionalism** over the status of system and structure in language. The hocuspocus position uses W.F. Twaddell's definition of the **phoneme** as a 'fictitious unit,' which the linguist distills from a body of data on the basis of particular rules and operations. The 'God's truth' linguists, however, maintain that system and structure really do occur in the data and are not merely obtained through sleight of hand. On the one hand, the rules criticized by the hocuspocus supporters are not arbitrary, but rather mechanically and scientifically verifiable; on the other hand, the system of the language is not itself the reality, but only an abstract model of reality. It would seem, therefore, that either position in its extreme form needs revision.

References
Burling, R. 1964. Cognition and componential analysis: God's truth or hocuspocus. *AA* 66.20–8.
Harris, Z.S. 1951. *Methods in structural linguistics*. Chicago, IL. (Reviewed by F. Householder. *IJAL* 18 (1952). 260–8.)
Joos, M. (ed.) 1966. *Readings in linguistics*, vol. 1: *The development of descriptive linguistics in America since 1925*. Chicago, IL. (Orig. 1957).
Twaddell, W.F. 1935. *On defining the phoneme*. (Language Monograph 16.) (Repr. in M. Joos (ed.), *Readings in linguistics*, vol. 1: *The develop-*

ment of descriptive linguistics in America since 1925. Chicago, IL, 1966. 55–80.)

Goidelic ⇒ Celtic, Gaelic

Gothic

East **Germanic** language spoken by the Goths, a group of southern Scandinavian tribes which spread out during the second to sixth centuries from the Black Sea over all of southern Europe to Spain. The most important written attestation (which is also the oldest Germanic text in existence) is Wulfila's (West, Gothic) Bible translation from Greek, dating from the fourth century.

References

Bennett, W.H. 1960. *An introduction to the Gothic language*. New York.
Braune, W. 1981. *Gotische Grammatik*, 19th edn, rev. E.A. Ebbinghaus. Tübingen.
Köbler, W. 1989. *Gotisches Wörterbuch*. Leiden.
Lehmann, W.P. 1986. *A Gothic etymological dictionary*. Leiden.
Mossé, F. and J.W. Marchand. 1950– . *Bibliographia Gotica*. (Medieval Studies 12.)
Wright, J. 1954. *Grammar of the Gothic language*, 2nd edn, ed. O.L. Sayce. Oxford.

governing category

A syntactic domain in **binding theory** within which a reflexive pronoun must have an antecedent. In Chomsky's **Government and Binding theory**, the governing category of a node X is defined as a first approximation by Y (= NP or S) is the governing category for X, if Y is the minimal category containing X, a governor of X, and a subject. A category is minimal with respect to *P*, if it contains *P* and does not dominate any other category that contains *P*.

References
⇒ **binding theory**

government

1 Lexeme-specific property of **verbs, adjectives, prepositions**, or **nouns** that determines the morphological realization (especially **case**) of dependent elements. Government can be subsumed under **valence** in so far as elements with valence govern the morphological form of their 'governed' (dependent) elements. The term 'government' is used especially with verbs whose differing valence is the primary criterion for distinguishing between transitive and intransitive verbs (⇒ **transitivity**). The **syntactic functions** of the elements accompanying the verb are based on the various governing cases. Case can also be determined by genitive or prepositional attributes (Ger. *Land des Glaubens* (genitive) 'land of faith,' *Hoffnung auf*

Frieden (accusative) 'hope for peace'), adjectives (Ger. *dem Vater ähnlich* (dative) 'like the father'), and prepositions (Russ. *c* (instrumental) 'with, by means of'). The term government is used in some studies to indicate the marking of object functions by means of prepositions rather than case marking: the verb *to think* governs the preposition *of*. (⇒ *also* **prepositional object**)

References

Barlow, M. and C.A. Ferguson (eds) 1988. *Agreement in natural language: approaches, theories, descriptions*. Chicago, IL.
Hjelmslev, L. 1939. La notion de rection. *Acta Linguistica* 1.10–23.
Lyons, J. 1968. *Introduction to theoretical linguistics*. Cambridge.
Van Valin, R.D. 1987. The role of government in the grammar of head-marking languages. *IJAL* 53.371–97.

2 In the framework of **transformational grammar** (⇒ **Government and Binding theory**), the term government has a more precise use: in order for government to be possible, in a local area in a **phrase structure** diagram there can be no **maximal projection**, in the sense of **X-bar theory**, between the governor and the governed, i.e. there can be no phrasal category which does not dominate both the governor as well as the governed. This local area plays a central role both in **case theory** as well as in various other theoretical areas, such as **governing category** and **empty category principle**. (⇒ *also* **binding theory**)

Government and Binding theory

A variation of **generative grammar** in Chomsky's (1981) *Lectures on Government and Binding*. The essential differences of this theory are the **modularity** of the syntax and constraints on syntactic processes, particularly the **binding theory**, the theory of **government** and the **empty category principle**.

References

Borsley, R.D. 1991. *Syntactic theory*. London.
Chomsky, N. 1981. *Lectures on government and binding*. Dordrecht. (7th edn Berlin and New York, 1993.)
Cinque, G. 1991. *Types of A'-dependencies*. Cambridge, MA.
Cowper, E.A. 1992. *A concise introduction to syntactic theory: the Government–Binding approach*. Chicago, IL.
Haegeman, L. 1991. *Introduction to government and binding theory*. Oxford.
————— 1992. *Theory and description in generative syntax*. Cambridge.
Lasnik, H. and J. Uriagereka. 1988. *A course in GB syntax*. Cambridge, MA.

Rizzi, L. 1990. *Relativized minimality*. Cambridge, MA.

Stabler, E.P. Jr. 1992. *The logical approach to syntax*. Cambridge, MA.

Webelhuth, G. (ed.). 1995. *Government and Binding Theory. A handbook*. Oxford.

⇒ **noun phrase, transformational grammar**

governor

In some grammatical theories (e.g. **dependency grammar**), 'governing' element on which other constituents are dependent.

References
⇒ **government**

GPSG ⇒ Generalized Phrase Structure Grammar

gradable complementaries

A class of complementary expressions (⇒ **complementarity**) so named by Cruse (1980) because they are both scalar and gradable, e.g. *clean* vs *dirty*. In contrast to antonymous expressions (⇒ **antonymy**), gradable complementaries divide the conceptual domain into two mutually exclusive segments. In order to understand gradable complementaries, one must generally make a value judgment about the degree to which a characteristic is undesirable, e.g. *safe* vs *dangerous* or *sober* vs *drunk*.

References
Cruse, D.A. 1980. Antonyms and gradable complementaries. In D. Kastovsky (ed.), *Perspektiven der lexikalischen Semantik*. Bonn. 14–25.
⇒ **semantic relations**

gradation

Semantic category which indicates various degrees (i.e. gradation) of a property or state of affairs. The most important means of gradation are the comparative and superlative **degrees** of adjectives and some (deadjectival) adverbs. In addition, varying degrees of some property can also be expressed lexically, e.g. *especially/ really quick*, *quick as lightning*, *quicker and quicker*.

gradual opposition ⇒ opposition

grammar [Grk *grámma* 'letter']

Originally, grammar designated the ancient study of the letters of the alphabet and in the middle ages of the entirety of Latin language, stylistics, and rhetoric. The term 'grammar' is presently used to refer to various areas of study.

1 Grammar as the knowledge and study of the morphological and syntactic regularities of a natural language. In this traditional sense, grammar caters to the formal aspects of language, excluding **phonetics**, **phonology** and **semantics** as specialized areas of linguistics.

2 Grammar as a system of structural rules (in the sense of de Saussure's langue (⇒ **langue vs parole**) fundamental to all processes of linguistic production and comprehension.

3 Grammar as language theory, and in **transformational grammar** as a model representing linguistic competence (⇒ **competence vs performance**).

4 Systematic description of the formal regularities of a natural language in the form of a reference work or textbook. Due to the numerous interpretations of the term grammar, scientific criteria for its classification overlap. The following aspects of grammar are relevant for the typological classification of the concept of grammar: (a) Object of study: depending on the particular focus of study, one can cite competence grammar, belonging to the notion of grammar as a language theory whereby a model provides an explanation of the sub- (or non-)conscious linguistic rule apparatus. This can be distinguished from a corpus grammar, which seeks a comprehensive description of observed regularities of a language or of a representative sample of that language. (b) Depending upon theoretical precepts, one can distinguish between grammatical descriptions of individual languages and those seeking to describe linguistic universals upon which individual language-specific properties are based. (c) According to methodological premises, one can distinguish between descriptive grammars which objectively elucidate synchronically observed properties of a language and normative grammars. The latter seek to teach 'proper' or standardized language (⇒ **descriptive linguistics, prescriptive grammar**). Distributional grammars serve to classify surface structure elements according to distributional criteria (⇒ **distributionalism**) whereas operational grammars concentrate on the process of devising rules (⇒ **operational procedures**). (d) Language view or philosophy: depending on linguistic theories expounded by researchers, other grammars exist, in part opposing one another, such as **general grammar, dependency grammar, functional grammar,** content-based grammar, **case grammar,** structural grammar (⇒ **structuralism**), generative **transformational grammar,** and **valence** grammar. (e) The distinction is made between scientific and pedagogical grammars in view of the various uses to which each is put, e.g. reference use by native speakers vs language learners (⇒ **contrastive analysis**). Grammars are currently evaluated on the basis of applica-

bility, simplicity, completeness, explicitness, coherence, and lack of contradiction. (⇒ *also* **levels of adequacy**)

References

Chomsky, N. 1965. *Aspects of the theory of syntax.* Cambridge, MA.

Covington, M.A. 1984. *Syntactic theory in the high middle ages.* Cambridge.

Droste, F.G. and J.E. Joseph (eds) 1991. *Linguistic theory and grammatical description: nine current approaches.* Amsterdam and Philadelphia.

Newmeyer, F.H. 1986. *Linguistic theory in America,* 2nd edn. Orlando, FL.

Padley, G.A. 1985. *Grammatical theory in Western Europe, 1500–1700.* Cambridge.

Riemsdijk, H. van and E. Williams. 1985. *Introduction to the theory of grammar.* Cambridge, MA.

Swiggers, P. 1984. *Les conceptions linguistiques des encyclopédistes.* Heidelberg.

grammar translation method

Traditional method of foreign language instruction based on techniques used for the study of Greek and Latin, whereby the foreign language is learned principally by studying its syntax and morphology and by translating from one's native language into the foreign language and vice versa. The emphasis is on the acquisition of reading and writing skills with the goal of reading literary texts. The grammar translation method, which dominated foreign language instruction for nearly a century until the 1940s, now plays only a limited role in current second language teaching approaches.

References

Coleman, A. 1929. *The teaching of modern foreign languages in the United States.* New York.

Howatt, A.P.R. 1984. *A history of English language teaching.* Oxford.

Kelly, L.G. 1969. *25 centuries of language teaching.* Rowley, MA.

Larsen-Freeman, D. 1986. *Techniques and principles in language teaching.* Oxford.

Richards, J.C. and T.S. Rodgers. 1986. *Approaches and methods in language teaching.* Cambridge.

Titone, R. 1968. *Teaching foreign languages: an historical sketch.* Washington, DC.

⇒ **language pedagogy**, **second language acquisition**

grammatical alternation

English equivalent of J. Grimm's term for the synchronic alternation between voiceless and voiced sounds (primarily fricatives) within etymologically related words of **Germanic**, cf. Eng. *freeze* vs Ger. *frieren* (⇒ **rhotacism**). The conditions of this sound change were formulated by K. Verner (⇒ **Verner's law**) as an exception to the Germanic sound shift (⇒ **Grimm's law**); according to this theory, the placement of word accent played a decisive role in the resulting shift of **Indo-European** intervocalic stops (voiceless vs voiced fricatives). Since Indo-European had free word accent (the present tense and preterite singular had root stress, and the preterite plural and past participle had final syllable stress), grammatical alternation plays an important role particularly in the inflection of strong verbs. However, this change has been extensively eliminated in modern dialects through **analogy**, cf. OE *cēosan* : *coren* vs Mod. Eng. *choose* : *chosen*.

References

H.-H. Hock. 1986. *Principles of historical linguistics.* Berlin. (2nd rev. edn 1991.)

⇒ **language change**, **sound change**, **Verner's law**

grammatical category [Grk *katēgoría* 'predication'] (*also* syntactic category)

Abstract class of linguistic units whose kind, scope, and number depend on the specific language, the level of description, and the grammatical theory being used. The following categories are generally used. (a) Morphological categories, which in traditional grammar include parts of speech and/or their grammatical aspects, i.e. **gender**, **case**, and **number** with **nouns**; **aspect**, **voice**, **mood**, **person**, and number with **verbs**. (b) Syntactic categories: class of linguistic elements/**constituents** with the same morphosyntactic properties. Such categories (abbreviated with category symbols) are both lexical (N(oun), V(erb), A(djective)) as well as phrasal: NP = Noun Phrase, VP = Verb Phrase. In the framework of **structuralism**, grammatical categories are linguistic expressions which can be freely substituted for one another in a specific context while preserving grammaticality (⇒ **acceptability**). In **transformational grammar**, it is a term for constituent classes, i.e. for classes of expressions which can occupy certain structural positions in a sentence (⇒ **syntactic function**). (c) Formal logical-semantic categories: in both **generative semantics** and **categorial grammar** the number of basic categories are kept to a finite number which correspond to the categories of **logic**, e.g. sentences, terms (ling. = nominal expressions, log. = arguments) and predicates (ling. = verbal expressions, log. = predicates).

References

Bloomfield, L. 1926. A set of postulates for the science of language. *Lg* 2.153–64.

Chomsky, N. 1965. *Aspects of the theory of syntax.* Cambridge, MA.

Edmonds, J.E. 1985. *A unified theory of syntactic categories.* Dordrecht.

Heine, B. and U. Claudi. 1986. *On the rise of grammatical categories.* Berlin.

Hopper, P. and S.A. Thompson. 1984. The discourse basis for lexical categories in universal grammar. *Lg* 60.702–52.

Kuryłowicz, J. 1964. *The inflectional categories of Indo-European.* Heidelberg.

Langacker, R.W. 1987. Nouns and verbs. *Lg* 63.53–94.

Sasse, H.-J. 1993. Syntactic categories and sub-categories. In J. Jacobs (ed.), *Syntax: an international handbook of contemporary research.* Berlin and New York. 646–86.

Schachter, P. 1985. Parts-of-speech systems. In T. Shopen (ed.), *Language typology and syntactic description*, vol. 1. Cambridge. 3–61.

⇒ **syntactic function**

grammatical function ⇒ **syntactic function**

grammatical gender ⇒ **gender**

grammatical meaning ⇒ **lexical meaning vs grammatical meaning**

grammatical relation ⇒ **syntactic function**

grammaticality

A term coined by Chomsky (1965) to indicate the wellformedness of expressions of natural languages. Grammaticality is used for two aspects of the same phenomenon.

1 The property of grammaticality refers to expressions that can be derived by the rules of a **generative grammar**. It concerns an (abstract) wellformedness with regard to a particular linguistic analysis (e.g. a grammar of standard English), semantic aspects not (necessarily) being taken into account. In this respect, grammaticality is not provable by direct observation or by statistical frequency.

2 'Grammaticality vs ungrammaticality' is also used as a measure by competent speakers of a language who can judge different expressions on the basis of intuitive knowledge of the rules of the language. Of course, regional and social variations (**idiolects**) provide areas of disagreement. Grammaticality, like **acceptability**, is a relative term, which corresponds to a scale of greater or lesser deviation of linguistic expressions from the underlying rules. (⇒ **error analysis**)

References

Chomsky, N. 1961. On the notion 'rule of grammar.' In R. Jakobson (ed.), *Proceedings of symposia on applied mathematics*, vol. 12: *The structure of language and its mathematical aspects*, Providence, RI. 255–7.

——— 1965. *Aspects of the theory of syntax.* Cambridge, MA.

Greenbaum, S. (ed.) 1977. *Acceptability in language.* The Hague.

Hudson, A. and A.H. Edwards. 1988. Syntactic, semantic, and pragmatic influences on judgements of grammaticality. *Texas Linguistic Forum* 30.137–41.

Kac, M. 1991. *Grammars and grammaticality.* Amsterdam and Philadelphia.

Quirk, R. and J. Svartvik, 1966. *Investigating linguistic acceptability.* The Hague.

Spencer, N.J. 1973. Differences between linguistics and nonlinguistics in intuitions of grammaticality-acceptability. *JPsyR* 12.83–98.

grammaticalization

Term coined by Meillet (1912) to indicate a process of linguistic change whereby an autonomous lexical unit gradually acquires the function of a dependent grammatical category, cf. Lat. *habere* 'to have, possess' > Fr. *avoir* 'PERFECT TENSE'; Lat. *passum* 'step' > Fr. *pas* 'NEGATION.' Semantically, this involves a development from autosemantic (lexical) meaning (⇒ **autosemantic word**) to synsemantic (grammatical) meaning (⇒ **synsemantic word**) (on this continuum and its poles, see Sapir 1921; Talmy 1988; Langacker 1989). Seen formally, a loss of syntactic independence and morphological distinctiveness from other elements of the same paradigm occurs (on the developmental steps, ⇒ **agglutination, cliticization, fusion**). In addition, the presence of the grammaticalized element becomes increasingly obligatory, with correspondingly increasing dependence on and phonological assimilation to another (autonomous) linguistic unit. This process is accompanied by a gradual disappearance of segmental and suprasegmental phonological features (⇒ **segmental feature, suprasegmental feature**); as a rule, its absolute conclusion is 'zero phonological content' (see Heine and Reh 1984; Lehmann 1985).

More recent investigations on grammaticalization have primarily addressed its semantic and pragmatic aspects with regard to the following questions. (a) Is the change of meaning that is inherent to grammaticalization a process of desemanticization (see Heine and Reh 1984), or is it rather a case (at least in the early stages of grammaticalization) of a semantic and pragmatic concentration (see Traugott 1989; Traugott and König 1991? (b) What productive parts do **metaphors** (see Sweetser 1984; Claudi and Heine 1986) and **metonyms** play in grammaticalization (Traugott and König 1991)? (c) What rôle does pragmatics play in grammaticalization? Givón (1979) and Hopper (1988) see grammaticalization as a process of **fossilization** of discourse-pragmatic strategies. Traugott and König (1991) propose conversational principles (specifically content, **relevance**) as the cause of changes of meaning in grammaticalization processes. (d) Are there any universal principles for the direction of grammaticalization, and, if so, what are they? Suggestions for such 'directed' principles include: (i) increasing schematicization (Talmy 1988); (ii) increasing generalization (Bybee and Pagliuca 1985); (iii) increasing speaker-related meaning (Traugott 1989); and (iv) increasing conceptual subjectivity (Langacker 1989).

So far, grammaticalization processes have been studied in reference to the following areas: **gender** marking (Greenberg 1978), pronouns (Givón 1976), **switch reference** (Frajzyngier 1986), **serial verb constructions** (Givón 1975; Lord 1976), modal and epistemic expressions (Shepherd 1982; Sweetser 1984; Traugott 1989), concessive and conditional conjunctions (König 1985, 1986; Traugott 1985), causal conjunctions (Traugott 1982), **conjunctions** (Traugott 1986; Batzeev Shyldkrot and Kemmer (1988), **middle voice** and **reflexivity** (Kemmer 1988), terms for parts of the body (Wilkins 1980).

References

Axmaker, S. *et al.* (eds) 1988. *Proceedings of the annual meeting of the Berkeley Linguistics Society*, vol. 14: *General session and parasession on grammaticalization*. Berkeley, CA.

Batzeev Shyldkrot, H. and S. Kemmer. 1988. Le développement sémantique des conjonctions en français: quelques concepts généraux. *RLiR* 23.9–20.

Bybee, J. and W. Pagliuca. 1985. Cross-linguistic comparison and the development of grammatical meanings. In J. Fisiak (ed.), *Historical semantics and historical word formation*. Berlin. 263–82.

Claudi, G. and B. Heine. 1986. On the metaphorical base of grammar. *SLang* 10.297–335.

Frajzyngier, Z. 1986. Grammaticalization through analysis: a case of switch reference. *Proceedings of the second annual meeting of the Pacific Linguistics Conference*. ed. by S. Delancey and R.S. Tomlin. Eugene, OR. 125–40.

Givón, T. 1975. Serial verbs and syntactic change: Niger-Congo. In C.N. Li (ed.), *Word order and word order change*. Austin, TX. 47–112.

—— 1976. Topic, pronoun and grammatical agreement. In C.N. Li (ed.), *Subject and topic*. New York. 151–88.

—— 1979. *On understanding grammar*. New York.

Greenberg, J.H. 1978. How does a language acquire gender markers? In J.H. Greenberg (ed.), *Universals of human language*. Stanford, CA. Vol. 3, 47–82.

Heine, B. and M. Reh. 1984. *Grammaticalization and reanalysis in African languages*. Hamburg.

Heine, B. and E.C. Traugott (eds) 1991. *Approaches to grammaticalization*, 2 vols. Amsterdam.

Heine, B., U. Claudi, and F. Hünnemeyer. 1991. *Grammaticalization: a conceptual framework*. Chicago, IL.

Hopper, P.J. 1988. Emergent grammar and the *a priori* grammar postulate. In D. Tannen (ed.), *Linguistics in context: connecting observation and understanding*. Norwood, NJ. 117–34.

Hopper, P.J. and E.C. Traugott, 1993. *Grammaticalization*. Cambridge.

Kemmer, S. 1993. The middle voice: a typological and diachronic study. Amsterdam and Philadelphia.

König, R. 1986. Conditionals, concessive conditionals, and concessive: areas of contrast, overlap and neutralization. In E.C. Traugott *et al.* (eds), *On conditionals*. Cambridge. 229–46.

Langacker, R. 1977. Syntactic reanalysis. In C.N. Li (ed.), *Mechanisms of syntactic change*. Austin, TX. 57–139.

—— 1989. *Subjectification*. San Diego, CA.

Lehmann, C. 1985. Grammaticalization: synchronic variation and diachronic change. *LeS* 20.303–18.

—— 1995. *Thoughts on grammaticalization*. Munich.

Lord, C. 1976. Evidence for syntactic reanalysis: from verb to complementizer in Kwa. In S.B. Steever *et al.* (eds), *Papers from the parassession on diachronic syntax*. Chicago, IL. 179–91.

Meillet, A. 1912. L'évolution des formes grammaticales. In *Linguistique historique et linguistique générale*. Paris. 130–48. (2nd edn 1921).

Pagliuca, W. (ed.) 1994. *Perspectives on grammaticalization*. Amsterdam and Philadelphia, PA.

Sapir, E. 1921. *Language: an introduction to the study of speech*. New York.

Shepherd, S. 1982. From deontic to epistemic: an analysis of modals in the history of English, creoles, and language acquisition. In A. Ahlqvist (ed.), *Papers from the fifth International Conference on Historical Linguistics*. Amsterdam. 316–23.

Sweetser, E. 1984. Semantic structure and semantic change: a cognitive linguistic study of modality, perception, speech acts, and logical relations. Dissertation, Berkeley, CA.

Talmy, L. 1988. The relation of grammar to cognition. In B. Rudzka-Ostyn (ed.). *Topics in cognitive linguistics*. Amsterdam. 165–205.

Traugott, E.C. 1982. From propositional to textual and expressive meanings: some semantic–pragmatic aspects of grammaticalization. In W.P. Lehmann and Y. Malkiel (eds), *Perspectives on historical linguistics*. Amsterdam. 245–71.

—— 1985. Condition markers. In J. Haiman (ed.), *Iconicity in syntax*. Amsterdam. 239–307.

—— 1986. On the origins of 'and' and 'but' connectives in English. *SLang* 10.137–50.

—— 1988. Pragmatic strengthening and grammaticalization. *BLS* 14.406–16.

—— 1989. On the rise of epistemic meanings in English: an example of subjectification in semantic change. *Lg* 65.31–55.

Traugott, E.C. and E. König. 1991. The semantics–pragmatics of grammaticalization revisited. In B. Heine and E.C. Traugott (eds), *Approaches to grammaticalization*. Amsterdam. Vol. 1.

Wilkins, D. 1980. Towards a theory of semantic change. Dissertation, Canberra.

granularity [Lat. *granum* 'seed']

Degree of coarseness or precision in the linguistic characterization of a state of affairs. It is preset by the given type of text, but can be raised, or made more precise (*in exact terms*), or lowered, or made less precise (*roughly*), with certain expressions. In ascertaining the truth value of a statement, one presupposes that the degree of granularity has already been determined. So, for example, a statement like *France is a hexagonal country* can be considered true with regard to a rough granularity, though false with regard to a fine granularity.

Reference
Austin, J.L. 1962. *How to do things with words.* Oxford.

graph [Grk *gráphein* 'to write']

1 Single letter realized in writing whose relation to a certain **grapheme** is not determined. Analogous to the **phone** as a variant of a **phoneme** on the sound level, the graph is a variant on the level of writing.

2 Geometric representation of a two-place **relation** defined by a **set** *S*, whereby the elements of *S* are designated as **nodes** and the connections between the nodes, which are determined by the relation, are designated as **branches**. A graph is 'directed,' once the direction of its branches is set. This is the case, for example, for a special type of graph, the **tree diagram** that represents phonological, morphological, or syntactic structures in linguistics. (⇒ *also* **formalization**)

3 In mathematics and logic the graph of a **function** *f* is the set of ordered pairs ⟨*x*,*f(x)*⟩ for all *x* in the definition sphere of *f*. Usually a function is identified with its graph. (⇒ *also* **formal logic**)

grapheme

Distinctive unit of a writing system. Variants of any given grapheme are called **allographs**. In general, graphemes are considered the smallest distinctive units of a writing system. In **alphabetic writing systems**, graphemes are a written approximation of phonemes; however, ⇒ **digraphy**, **ligature**. (⇒ *also* **graphemics**)

Reference
Henderson, L. 1985. On the use of the term 'grapheme.' *Language and Cognitive Processes* 1/2.135–48.

graphemics

Study of the distinctive units of a writing system or of the writing systems of a particular language (⇒ **grapheme**). The object of study is written texts in handwritten or typographic form. In **alphabetic writing systems**, graphemics largely makes use of the methods of analysis developed for **phonology** because of the close relationship between the spoken and the written language. Generally speaking, this is also the case for syllabic writing systems (⇒ **syllabary**). Graphemic studies primarily serve as a foundation for prescribed orthographic norms, the comparison between spoken and written language, the deciphering of historical texts, as well as the transfer of writing systems to computerized systems in **computational linguistics**.

References
⇒ **orthography**, **phonology**, **writing**

graphetics

Subdiscipline of **graphemics**. Analogous to the relationship between **phonetics** and **phonology**, graphetics is a prerequisite for graphemic investigations, to the degree that it studies different writing and transcription systems from individual, social, historical, or typographic aspects. Graphetics is used in palaeography (= deciphering historical writing systems), typography, instruction in reading and writing, as well as graphology (= the study of the relationship between handwriting and personal character traits) and **graphometry** (= the identification of handwriting in criminal cases).

References
⇒ **orthography**, **writing**

graphics

The particular manner in which a text or part of a text (e.g. a word) is written or printed. In general, all written characteristics of a text fall under the concept of 'graphics.'

graphometry

The measure of scripts for comparing and ascertaining the creator (or author) of particular writings, e.g. in criminal cases.

Grassmann's law (*also* dissimilation of aspirates)

Discovered by Grassmann (1863), **sound change** occurring independently in **Sanskrit** and **Greek** which consistently results in a dissimilation of aspirated stops. If at least two aspirated stops occur in a single word, then only the last stop retains its aspiration, all preceding aspirates are deaspirated; cf. IE *$b^heb^houd^he$ > Skt *bubodha* 'had awakened,' IE *$d^hid^he^hmi$ > Grk *títhēmi* 'I set, I put.' This law, which was discovered through internal **reconstruction**, turned a putative 'exception' to the Germanic sound shift (⇒ **Grimm's law**) into a law.

References
Anderson, S.R. 1970. On Grassmann's law in Sanskrit. *LingI* 1.387–96.
Collinge, N.E. 1985. *The laws of Indo-European.* Amsterdam and Philadelphia, PA. 47–61.
Grassmann, H. 1863. Über das ursprüngliche vorhandensein von wurzeln deren anlaut und auslaut eine aspriate enthielt. *ZVS* 12.110–38.
Vennemann, T. 1979. Grassmann's law, Bartholomae's law and linguistic methodology. In I. Rauch and G.F. Carr (eds), *Linguistic method: essays in Honor of Herbert Penzl*, The Hague. 557–84.

grave accent [Lat. *gravis* 'heavy']

1 Superscript **diacritic** serving several purposes. It indicates syllable stress in **Italian** and accentuated **Bulgarian** texts. In **French** a distinction is drawn between *è* for [ɛ] and *é* for [e]; graphemically, grave accent is issued to distinguish between homonyms, cf. *où* ('where') vs *ou* ('or'), and *à* ('to') vs *a* ('has'); similarly Ital. *è* ('is') vs *e* ('and'). Morphologically, a grave accent is used to indicate a short rising tone in **Serbo-Croatian** dictionaries and, in the Latinized Pīnyīn writing system for falling tone in **Chinese**.

2 ⇒ **accent**[2]

grave vs acute

1 Binary phonological **opposition** in **distinctive feature** analysis, based on acoustically analyzed and spectrally defined criteria (⇒ **acoustic phonetics**, **spectral analysis**). Acoustic characteristic: greater or lesser concentration of energy in the lower (grave) or upper (acute) spectral range. Articulatory characteristic (⇒ **articulation**): grave **phones** have a larger or less clearly divided resonance chamber than acute phones. The distinction characterizes the opposition between [m, p, b, f] vs [n, t, d, s], as well as between front and back **vowels**: [i, e] vs [u, o].

2 In the Pīnyīn transcription of Chinese, syllable accent with falling tone (grave) or rising tone (acute).

3 Diacritic mark ⟨`⟩ (grave) or ⟨´⟩ (acute) as a specification for accentuation or pronunciation.

Great Vowel Shift

Significant historical event in the development of the Modern **English** vowel system, beginning around the fifteenth century, in which the Middle English long low vowels were raised and the long high vowels were lowered, presumably through the effects of a push chain or drag chain (⇒ **push chain vs drag chain**). The development of the shift and its effects on the phonetic representation of English orthography can be illustrated as follows:

Middle English		Modern English	Examples
[iː]	>	[ay]	*ride*
[eː]	>	[iː]	*meet*
[ɛː]	>	[iː]	*meat*
[aː]	>	[eː]	*take*
[uː]	>	[aw]	*house*
[oː]	>	[uː]	*moon*
[ɔː]	>	[oː]	*foam*

While the exact causes of the Great Vowel Shift are unknown, it represents one of the most systematic attested sound changes. A thorough analysis of this sound shift can be found in Lass (1984).

Reference
Lass, R. 1984. *Phonology: an introduction to basic concepts.* Cambridge.
⇒ **English**

Grecism

An idiom of the **Greek** language, or an imitation in English of Greek idiom.

Greek (*also* Hellenic)

Branch of **Indo-European** consisting of a single language with numerous dialects and 10 million speakers. Greek has been well attested for a long period of time and is divided into the following periods: Mycenaean Greek (1500–1150 BC), the language discovered on Cretan tablets and deciphered by M. Ventris in 1952 (Linear B); Classical Greek (800–300 BC), with several dialects, the language of the Homeric epics and the rich classical literature in the Attic-Ionic dialect; Hellenistic or **Koinē** ('common') Greek (300 BC–AD 300), the language of the Alexandrian Empire and its successors, which was used as a **trade language** in the entire eastern Mediterranean area, as well as in the writings of the New Testament; Middle Greek, including Byzantine Greek (AD 300–1100) and Medieval Greek (AD 1100–1600); and finally Modern Greek. In addition to strong dialectal variation there are two standards: Demotic (*Dhímotīkī*), the common everyday language, and Katharévusa (lit. 'purifying'), a written language with archaic forms. The Greek alphabet, used since the Classical Greek period, was developed from the Phoenician writing system.

Characteristics: Ancient Greek (= Classical and Hellenistic) had a complex vowel system (distinctive length, diphthongs) and musical stress; in Modern Greek the vowel system is reduced and the musical stress has developed into dynamic stress. The case system has simplified from Mycenaean (seven cases) to Ancient Greek (five) to Modern Greek (four), just like the number system (Ancient Greek had a **dual**, Modern Greek only singular and plural). Relatively complex tense and aspect system; forms earlier marked synthetically are today to a large extent expressed analytically. The infinitive in Modern Greek, as in other Balkan languages, has been lost, while Ancient Greek still had rich possibilities of expressing clause subordination with infinite and finite verb forms.

General and history

Blass, F. and A. Debrunner. 1961. *Grammatik des neutestamentlichen Griechisch*, 9th–10th edns. Göttingen. (*A Greek grammar of the New Testament and other early Christian literature*. trans. and rev. R. Funk. Cambridge, 1981.)

Browning, R. 1982. *Medieval and modern Greek*. (2nd edn 1983.) Cambridge.

Costas, P.S. 1936. *An outline of the history of the Greek language, with particular emphasis on the Koiné and subsequent periods*. Chicago, IL.

Joseph, B. and I. Philippaki–Warburton. 1987. *Modern Greek*. London.

Palmer, L. 1980. *The Greek language*. Atlantic Heights, NJ.

Vilborg, E. 1960. A tentative grammar of Mycenaean Greek. Göteborg.

Mycenean Greek

Chadwick, J. and L. Baumbach. The Mycenean Greek vocabulary. *Glotta* 41.157–271.

Hooker, J.T. 1980. *Linear B: an introduction*. Bristol.

Classical Greek

Buck, C.D. 1955. *The Greek dialects*. (Repr. 1973.) Chicago and London.

Chantraine, P. 1973. *Grammaire homérique*, 5th rev. edn. Paris.

——— 1984. *Morphologie historique du grec*. Paris.

Lejeune, M. 1972. *Phonétique historique du mycénien et du grec*. Paris.

Schwyzer, E. and A. Debrunner. 1939/50. *Griechische Grammatik*. Munich.

Threatte, L. 1980. *The grammar of Attic inscriptions*. Berlin.

Hellenistic Greek

Brixhe, C. 1993. *La koiné grecque antique*: Vol. I: *une langue introuvable?* Nancy.

Gignac, F.T. 1976. *A grammar of the Greek papyri of the Roman and Byzantine periods*, vol. I: *Phonology*. Milan.

Thumb, A. 1901. *Die griechische Sprache im Zeitalter des Hellenismus*. Strasburg.

Middle Greek

Mirambel, A. 1963. Pour une grammaire historique du grec médiéval. *Actes du XIIe congrès inter-*

national des études byzantines, 2. Belgrad. 391–403.

Psaltes, S.B. 1913. *Grammatik der byzantinischen Chroniken*. Göttingen.

Modern Greek

Householder, F.W., K. Kazazis, and A. Koutsoudas. 1964. Reference grammar of literary Dhimotiki. *IJAL* 30:2, pub. 31.

Thumb, A. 1895. *Handbuch der neugriechischen Volkssprache: Grammatik, Texte, Glossar*. Strasburg. (Engl.: *A handbook of the Modern Greek language: grammar, texts, glossary*. Chicago, 1964.)

Historical grammar

Rix, H. 1976. *Historische Grammatik des Griechischen*. Darmstadt.

Dictionary

Liddell, H.G. and R. Scott. 1940. *A Greek–English lexicon*, 9th rev. edn, (reissue 1989.) Oxford.

Etymological dictionaries

Andriōtēs, N.P. 1983. *Etymologiko lexiko tēs koinēs Neoellēnikēs*, 3rd edn. Thessalonica.

Chantraine, P. 1968–80. *Dictionnaire étymologique de la langue grecque: histoire des mots*, 4 vols. Paris.

Frisk, H. 1954–72. *Griechisches etymologisches Wörterbuch*. 3 vols. Heidelberg.

Windekens, A.J. van. 1986. *Dictionnaire étymologique complémentaire de la langue grecque: nouvelles contributions à l'interprétation historique et comparée du vocabulaire*. Leuven.

Grimm's law (*also* Germanic sound shift)

Systematic changes in the **Indo-European** system of **obstruents** that led to the development of **Germanic** and its differentiation from the other Indo-European language families. Differences between Old Norse, **Greek**, and **Latin**, discovered by the Danish linguist R.K. Rask, based on language comparisons (⇒ **comparative linguistics, reconstruction**), were first represented in 1822 by J. Grimm as systematic **sound changes**. In his comparison, Grimm drew on Sanskrit as the (supposedly direct) successor to Indo-European.

Grimm's law deals primarily with three consonantal changes. (a) The voiceless stops [p, t, k] become voiceless **fricatives** [f, θ, χ] [IE *pǝtér, Lat. *pater*, Eng. *father*; IE *tréies, Lat. *tres*, Goth. *þreis*, Eng. *three*; IE *kṃtóm, Lat. *centum*, Eng. *hundred*]. Regular exceptions to these changes are: (i) the shift does not take effect after Indo-European obstruents (Grk *steícho*, OE *stīgan*; Lat. *spuo*, OE *spīwan*; Lat. *piscis*, OE *fisc*; Lat. *captus*; OE *hæft*); (ii) **Verner's law** supersedes Grimm's law; thus voiceless or voiced fricatives arise, depending on the placement of word accent; the latter collapse into the group of voiced fricatives that develop from the shift of aspirated stops (see (c) below). (b) The voiced stops [b, d, g] become voiceless stops [p, t, k] (Lat. *decem*, Eng. *ten*; Lat. *genu*, Eng. *knee*). (c) The aspirated stops [bʰ, dʰ, gʰ] become voiced fricatives [v, ð, ɣ], which in turn shift to the stops [b, d, g] (Old Indic *bharati*, Goth. *bairan* 'bear'; Old Indic *madhya*, Goth. *midjis* 'middle'; IE *g^hostis*, Eng. *guest*).

Much controversy surrounds the dating of the Germanic sound shift; in any case, it is plausible to posit its beginning around 1200–1000 BC and its completion, as evidenced by **Celtic** loan words, around 500–300 BC. Similarly controversial are hypotheses about the cause(s) and course of the sound shift; recently, the very existence of the Germanic sound shift, in the form described here, has been denied. Among other pieces of evidence adduced is the topological implausibility of the customary reconstruction of the Indo-European consonant system (voiceless tenues, voiced mediac, voiced aspirated mediae) which speaks against the prevailing conception of the sound shift. Gamkrelidze and Ivanov (1973) proposed a typologically more realistic reconstruction of Indo-European, according to which the changes occurring in Germanic are to be seen as relatively marginal; however, in this analysis those languages traditionally considered to have been affected by the sound shift would be more closely related to the Indo-European consonantism than those languages that were not so affected. (⇒ *also* **language change, sound change, tenuis vs media**)

References

Collinge, N.E. 1985. *The laws of Indo-European*. Amsterdam and Philadelphia. 63–71.

Fourquet, J. 1948. *Les mutations consonantiques du germanique*. Paris.

—— 1954. Die Nachwirkungen der ersten und zweiten Lautverschiebung. *ZM* 22.1–33.

Gamkrelidze, T. and V. Ivanov. 1973. Sprachtypologie und die Rekonstruktion der gemeinindogermanischen Verschlüsse. *Phonetica* 27.150–6.

Gamkrelidze, T.V. 1981. Language typology and language universals and their implications for the reconstruction of the Indo-European stop system. In Y. Arbeitman and A.R. Bomhard (eds), *Essays in historical linguistics in honor of J.A. Kerns*. Amsterdam. 571–609.

Grimm, J. 1819–37. *Deutsche Grammatik*, 4 parts. Göttingen. (Facsimile printing of the 2nd edn of Berlin 1870/8, Hildesheim, 1967.)

Hammerich, L.L. 1955. Die Germanische und die Hochdeutsche Lautverschiebung. *PBB (H)* 77.1–29 and 165–203.

Hopper, P. 1973. Glottalized and murmured occlusives in Indo-European. *Glossa* 7.141–66.

Rask, R.K. 1818. Untersuchung über den Ursprung der alten nordischen oder isländischen Sprache. (Repr. in L. Hjelmslev (ed.), *Ausgewählte Abhand-lungen*. Copenhagen, 1932.)

Schrodt, R. 1976. *Die germanische Lautverschiebung und ihre Stellung im Kreise der indogermanischen Sprachen*, 2nd edn. Vienna.

Vennemann, T. 1984. Hoch- und Niedergermanisch: die Verzweigungstheorie der germanisch-deutschen Lautverschiebungen. *PBB* 106.1–45.

Guaraní

Largest **Tupi** language with approx. 3 million speakers; official language of Paraguay (along with **Spanish**). Used as a **trade language** for South American Jesuit missions.

Characteristics: simple sound system. Syntactically an **active language**: there are two classes of verbs with distinctive conjugational patterns which are used for the verbal concepts of stative/non-agentive vs agentive. Occasionally a verb stem with a characteristic difference in meaning can be used in both classes (cf. *a-karú* 'I am eating' vs *s'e-karú* 'I am a glutton'). With transitive verbs the verb agrees with the highest ranking person in the hierarchy first- second- third person; the **thematic relation** is expressed by the choice of the agreement prefix (cf. *s'e-pete* '(you/he/she …) hit … me' vs *a-pete* 'I hit (him)'). Syntactic possessive (*s'e* is also possessive: 'my').

References

Gregores, E. and J.A. Suárez. 1967. *A description of colloquial Guaraní*. The Hague.
⇒ **South American languages**

Guaymi ⇒ Chibchan-Paezan

Gujarati ⇒ Indo-Aryan

Gulf languages

Language group of North America postulated by M. Haas (1951). The most important branch is **Muskogean** in the southeastern United States; in addition, other languages such as Yuki and Wappo in northern California are also included in a larger group, Yukic-Gulf. According to Greenberg (1987), the Gulf languages belong to the **Penutian** language group.

References

Greenberg, J.H. 1987. *Language in the Americas*. Stanford, CA.

Haas, M.R. 1951. The Proto-Gulf word for 'water' (with notes on Siouan-Yuchi). *IJAL* 17.71–9.
⇒ **North and Central American languages**

Guoyu ⇒ Chinese

Gur (*also* Voltaic)

Branch of the **Niger-Congo** group with approx. eighty languages in West Africa; the most significant language: Mossi (Burkina Faso, approx. 3.6 million speakers).

Characteristics: **tonal languages**, **noun classes** (marked by suffixes, occasionally together with prefixes) with verb agreement, **serial verb constructions**.

References

Bendor-Samuel, J.T. 1971. Niger-Kongo, Gur. In T.A. Sebeok (ed.), *Current trends in linguistics*. The Hague. Vol. 7, 141–78.
Manessy, G. 1979. *Contribution à la classification généalogique des langues voltaiques*. Paris.
⇒ **African languages**

Gurage ⇒ **Semitic**

Gurumukhi ⇒ **Panjabi**

guttural [Lat. *guttur* 'throat']

Outdated designation for **velar**, **uvular**, **laryngeal**, and **pharyngeal** (and occasionally also for **post-alveolar** and **palatal**) consonants.

References
⇒ **phonetics**

Gypsy ⇒ **Romany**

H

habitual

Verbal **aspect** which characterizes an action as happening habitually over a long period of time: e.g. *Caroline works in England.* (⇒ *also* **aspect**, **generic**, **iterative vs semelfactive**)

Haida ⇒ Na-Dene

Hamitic ⇒ Afro-Asiatic

Hamito-Semitic ⇒ Afro-Asiatic

hanging topic

Term introduced by Grosu (1975) indicating a type of word order in which an element appears to the left of the sentence, as in left dislocation (⇒ **left vs right dislocation**) and is copied in the following sentence by a coreferential pronoun, hyponym (⇒ **hyponymy**), **hyperonym**, or by an expression that has a loose associative relationship to the hanging topic, e.g. *As far as meat goes I prefer beef.* In contrast to left dislocation, with which a hanging topic is often identified in the literature, the pronominal copy is optional and does not agree with the elements dislocated. A further difference is that the hanging topic is also set apart from the sentence by **intonation**. (⇒ *also* **dislocation**)

References
Altmann, H. 1981. *Formen der 'Herausstellung' im Deutschen.* Tübingen.
Grosu, A. 1975. On the status of positionally-defined constraints in syntax. *TL*, 2.159–201.

Han'gul ⇒ Korean

hapax legomenon [Grk *hápax legómenon* 'said once']

Linguistic expression with only one attested occurrence and whose meaning is often, therefore, difficult to ascertain. Hapax legomena serve as a basis for defining the morphological notion of productivity in Baayer and Lieber (1991). (⇒ *also* **pseudomorpheme**, **semimorpheme**)

Reference
Baayer, H. and R. Lieber. 1991. Productivity and English derivation. *Linguistics* 29.801–3.

haplography [Grk *haplóos* 'single,' *gráphein* 'to write']

Writing error in which a double letter or syllable is written as a single letter or syllable. The inverse is known as **dittography**.

haplogy ⇒ haplology

haplology [Grk *lógos* 'word'] (*also* haplogy)

Special type of dissimilation in which a syllable within a word disappears before or after a phonetically similar or the same syllable, e.g. Lat. **nutrītrīx > nutrīx* 'wet nurse,' Eng. *haplogy* for *haplology*(!) or *preventive ~ preventative.* For the reverse process ⇒ **dittology**.

References
Cardona, G. 1968. *On haplology in Indo-European.* Philadelphia, PA.
Stemberger, J.P. 1981. Morphological haplology. *Lg* 57.791–817.
Wurzel, W.U. 1976. Zur Haplologie. *LingB* 41.50–7.

Harari ⇒ Semitic

Hatsa ⇒ Khoisan

Hausa

Largest **Chadic** language with approx. 25 million speakers in northern Nigeria and Niger; important trade language.

Characteristics: rich consonant system, simple syllable structure. Two alphabets (Arabic, Latin). Fairly complicated morphology, both with nouns (e.g. plural formation) as well as with verbs (voices). Word order SVO.

References
Abraham, R.C. 1959. *The language of the Hausa people.* London.
Kraft, C.H. and A.H.M. Kirk-Greene. 1973. *Hausa.* London.
Parsons, F.W. 1981. *Writings on Hausa grammar.* London.

Hawaiian ⇒ Polynesian

head

1 In **X-bar theory**, the part of a complex constituent *X* which is a lexical item of the same category type as *X*. Thus, the head of the **noun phrase** *the bridge to San Francisco* is the noun *bridge*. This lexical item is also known as the lexical head of the noun phrase. The lexical head is not necessarily an immediate constituent of the phrase which it heads.

2 (*also* nucleus, base) Linguistic element in a

complex syntactic structure which either (a) is in a morphologically marked relationship of coreference with the preceding or following coreferential elements or (b) is modified semantically by these coreferential elements as attributes (⇒ **predication**). In pronominalization (⇒ **personal pronoun**), the head and its pro-form are coreferential, as is the case with coreferential pro-forms in some **exbraciation** structures (e.g. in **left vs right dislocation**). Heads and attributes (⇒ **apposition**), however, are related to each other predicatively: *The book, fascinating as well as instructive, held her spellbound.* (⇒ *also* **coreferentiality**, **dislocation**, **textual**)

References
Corbett, G.G., N.M. Fraser, and S. McGlashan (eds) 1993. *Heads in grammatical theory.* Cambridge.
⇒ **X-bar theory**

3 ⇒ **syllable**

4 In **metrical phonology**, that part of the metrical foot which carries the stress.

References
⇒ **metrical phonology**, **syllable**

Head Feature Convention ⇒ Generalized Phrase Structure Grammar

head grammar

A mildly context-sensitive extension (⇒ **mildly context-sensitive languages**, **context-sensitive grammar**) of **context-free (CF) grammar** including operations which 'wrap' headed phrases around others. Developed further into **Head-driven Phrase Structure Grammar**.

In the figure below the 'right-wrap' operation inserts a second complement into a headed phrase.

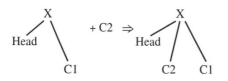

Reference
Pollard, C. 1984. Head grammars, generalized phrase structure grammars and natural languages. Dissertation, Stanford, CA.

Head-driven Phrase Structure Grammar (*abbrev.* HPSG)

A generative theory of grammar from the family of **unification grammars** which combines elements of **Generalized Phrase Structure Grammar** (GPSG), **Functional Unification Grammar** and PATR Formalism. HPSG uses a comprehensive inventory of descriptive tools from unification grammar. As in Functional Unification Grammar, in HPSG all linguistic units are represented by **feature structures**, which are called 'signs' by de Saussure. They contain features for the encoding of phonological, syntactic, and semantic information ([PHON], [SYN], [SEM]). The links between the values of these features determine the grammatical correspondence between sounds and meaning. The grammar is likewise represented in the form of feature structures, which are linguistic wellformedness constraints on the signs. In contrast to Generalized Phrase Structure Grammar, the grammar of HPSG is heavily lexicalized, i.e. the lexicon, which is structured hierarchically by the unification formalism, contains a large part of the syntactic information. There are only a few syntactic rules. **X-bar theory**, especially the parallels between verb phrases and noun phrases, is used in such a way that complement binding can be accomplished with just two rules, which connect the head category containing the external argument to the bound argument. Likewise, one rule accounts for adjunct modification. **Phrase structure rules** are free of redundancy due to the formulation of general (universal) principles which are also encoded as feature structures. Revised versions of some principles of GPSG can be found in HPSG. Subcategorization takes place through the feature [SUBCAT]. Long-distance dependencies are captured by the co-operation of feature transmission and grammatical principles. The organization of the grammar is borrowed from Functional Unification Grammar. The grammar is the disjunction of all rules and all lexical entries, in conjunction with the grammatical principles. Every well-formed sign must be compatible with the grammar. So far there are very few grammatical descriptions using HPSG; however, there are experimental computational linguistics systems which use it.

References
Nerbonne, J., C. Pollard, and K. Netter (eds) 1994. *German in Head-Driven Phrase Structure Grammar.* Chicago, IL.
Pollard, C. and I.A. Sag. 1988. *An information-based syntax and semantics*, vol. 1: *Fundamentals.* Stanford, CA.
—— 1993. *Head Driven Phrase Structure Grammar.* Chicago, IL.
Proudian, D. and C. Pollard. 1985. Parsing Head-Driven Phrase Structure Grammar. *ACL Proceedings* 23.167–71.

head-marking vs dependent-marking

Typological distinction introduced by J. Nichols which distinguishes languages depending on whether they code **syntactic functions** on the dependent constituents of a phrase or on the head of the phrase. At clausal level, consistent dependent-marking implies case or adpositional marking of the arguments of the predicate in the absence of predicate agreement, as in **Korean** and **Japanese**; consistent head-marking of the syntactic functions of the clause is expressed on the predicate in the absence of case or adpositional marking of the major arguments, as in Abkhaz (⇒ **North-West Caucasian**) and many American Indian languages, including Wishram, Kiowa (⇒ **Uto-Aztecan**), and Tzutujil. English and many other European languages have mixed head- and dependent-marking.

References
Nichols, J. 1986. Head-marking and dependent-marking grammar. *Language* 62.56–119.
—— 1992. *Linguistic diversity in space and time.* Chicago, IL.

Hebrew

Semitic language spoken until the third century BC in Palestine (Biblical Hebrew), written language of the Mishnaic texts ('Rabbinical Hebrew,' approx. 200 BC), Medieval Hebrew from the sixth century until the thirteenth, today the national language of Israel as Modern Hebrew (Ivrit), approx. 4 million speakers; liturgical language of the Jewish religion. Modern Hebrew was developed out of Medieval Hebrew, which was purely a written language, on the basis of the pronunciation of the Sephardic (Spanish-Portuguese) Jews. An independent writing system developed based on **Aramaic**, a consonant alphabet, which can be provided with vowel marks. Rich literary tradition in the Old Testament with texts from a period of over 1,000 years in various dialects.
Characteristics: ⇒ **Semitic**.

References
Berman, R. 1978. *Modern Hebrew structure.* Tel-Aviv.
Blau, J. 1976. *A grammar of Biblical Hebrew.* Wiesbaden. (2nd edn 1993.)
Gesenius, W. 1910. *Gesenius' Hebrew grammar.* Oxford. (Rev edn, ed. E. Kautsch. 2nd Eng. edn, ed. A.E. Cowley.)
Glinert, L. 1993. *Modern Hebrew: an essential grammar.* London.
Joüon, P. 1991. *A grammar of Biblical Hebrew,* trans. and rev. T Muraoka. Rome.
Lambert, M. 1931–8. *Traité de grammaire hébraïque.* Paris. (Repr. Hildesheim, 1972.)
Rosén, H.B. 1977. *Contemporary Hebrew.* Berlin.
Sáenz-Badillos, A. 1993. *A history of the Hebrew language,* trans. J. Elwolde. Cambridge.
Waldmann, M. 1989. *The recent study of Hebrew: a survey of the literature with selected bibliography.*

Cincinnati and Winona Lake.

Bibliography
Index of articles on Jewish studies.

Journals
Hebrew Computational Linguistics.
Hebrew Teaching and Applied Linguistics.
Lešŏnēnū (Hebrew with Engl. abstracts).
Zeitschrift für Althebraistik.
⇒ **Semitic**

hedge

Term introduced by Lakoff (1973). Hedges provide a means for indicating in what sense a member belongs to its particular category. The need for hedges is based on the fact that certain members are considered to be better or more typical examples of the category, depending on the given cultural background (⇒ **prototype**). For example, in the central European language area, sparrows are certainly more typical examples of birds than penguins. For that reason, of these two actually true sentences, *A sparrow is a bird* and *A penguin is a bird*, only the former can be modified by the hedge *typical* or *par excellence*, while the latter can be modified only by the hedges *in the strictest sense* or *technically speaking*.

References
Bolinger, D. 1972. *Degree words.* The Hague.
Lakoff, G. 1973. Hedges: a study in meaning criteria and the logic of fuzzy concepts. *JPL* 2.458–508.
⇒ **prototype**

Hellenic ⇒ **Greek**

helping verb ⇒ **auxiliary, modal auxiliary**

hendiadys [Grk *hèn dià dyoīn* 'one by two']

figure of speech of expansion.

1 The dissection of a compound into two co-ordinated but semantically unequal expressions, e.g. *language and shock* instead of *shocking language.*

2 In general, an intensifying combination of two terms that are related in meaning: for example, *furious sound* becomes *sound and fury, nicely warm* becomes *nice and warm*. The most common reason for using a hendiadys is emphasis. (⇒ *also* **twin formula**)

References
⇒ **figure of speech**

heteroclitic [Grk *heteróklitos* 'having different inflection']

Nouns with an irregular paradigm where either (a) the case and number forms follow at least two different declensional patterns, [e.g. Grk *hýdōr* (nom. sg.), *hýdatos* (gen. sg.) 'water'; or

(b) different stem forms are found in one paradigm (e.g. Eng. *to be*, *are*, *was* from three **Indo-European** roots). (⇒ *also* **suppletivism**)

heterography [Grk *héteros* 'different,' *gráphein* 'to write']

1 Use of the same written sign for different sounds, cf. Eng. <gh> in *through*, *enough*, *ghost*.

2 Different writing of words with the same pronunciation or meaning, cf. Amer. Eng. *center* vs Brit. Eng. *centre*, or colloquial Amer. Eng. *nite* for *night*.

3 Any manner of spelling that differs from the norm.

References
⇒ orthography

heteronymy [Grk *ónyma* (= *ónoma*) 'name']

1 **Semantic relation** in which expressions belong to the same semantic dimension (e.g. colors, days of the week, numbers) but have different lexical stems (e.g. *uncle* vs *aunt* as contrasted with Span. *tío* vs *tía*).

2 Synonym for the **semantic relation** of **incompatibility**.

References
⇒ semantic relation

heterorganic

Speech sounds that are not formed with the same articulatory organ (⇒ **homorganic**), e.g. the laminal [θ] and the apical [s] are heterorganic.

hiatus [Lat. 'an opening, crevice']

Auditorily perceivable distribution of two consecutive (heterosyllabic) monophthongs over two syllables. For example, the two heterosyllabic monophthongs in Ital. ['mjɛːi,] 'mine' vs the diphthong [ɛːĭ] in the competing [mjɛːĭ] or in Eng. [hay'ĕtəs] *hiatus*. Hiatus can also occur between words in a sentence (*the egg*). In English, the insertion of a **semivowel**[1] may be introduced to eliminate hiatus or, in some dialects the insertion of *r*: *Edna-r-interjected*. Hiatus bridging can also occur through **contraction**, **crasis**, **liaison**, and **synaeresis**.

References
⇒ phonetics

hidden Markov model (*abbrev.* HMM)

A further elaboration on **Markov process**, a **finite state automaton** in which not only transitions are probabilistic, but also output behavior. The symbols consumed (or produced) are not deterministic in a given state, but rather probabilistic. Thus the state itself is 'hidden.'

Currently the most successful speech recognition techniques are all based on HMMs.

Reference
Rabbiner, L. 1989. A tutorial on Hidden Markov models and selected applications in speech recognition. *Proceedings of the IEEE* 77. (Repr. in A. Waibel and K.-F. Lee (eds), *Readings in Speech recognition*, San Mateo, CA, 1990. 267–96).

hierarchy

The basic structural principle according to which elements of a set are ordered. The graphic representation of a hierarchy furnishes a tree diagram which branches downwards. Hierarchies may be specified as follows: a two-placed relation R is a hierarchy if and only if the following five conditions are met: (a) there is a point of origin; (b) all elements are connected to this point of origin; (c) there is no upward branching; (d) R is asymmetric (⇒ **symmetric relation**); (e) R is transitive (⇒ **transitive relation**). Hierarchies have a broad range of applications from taxonomic classifications of the human environment to dominance relations in society. In linguistics, hierarchies exist in syntax (⇒ **immediate constituent analysis**), in lexical semantics (⇒ **hyponymy**, **taxonomic anlaysis**), and in **markedness** theory.

References
⇒ lexicology

hierarchy universal

Hierarchy universals are universal, usually statistical restrictions which refer to hierarchies of **grammatical categories** or **syntactic functions**. Well known are the hierarchy universals formulated in the framework of **relational grammar** and by E.L. Keenan and B. Comrie and are based on the following hierarchy of syntactic functions: *subject* > *direct object* > *indirect object* > *oblique object*. One of the most important claims of such a hierarchy universal is the following implicational schema: if a syntactic function A ranks before a syntactic function B, and if B is accessible to a linguistic regularity R, then A is also accessible to R. In other words, if $A > B$ then A is more accessible to a linguistic regularity than B. With regard to verb agreement, for example, this law predicts that subjects are more accessible to verbal agreement than objects, i.e. there is no language in which verbs agree with objects but not with subjects. Hierarchy universals have also been formulated for relative clause constructions, passive, and reflexivization, as well as for hierarchies of other categories, e.g. **thematic relations** (⇒ **case grammar**), animacy, and topicality (⇒ **topic vs comment**).

References
Corbett, G.G. 1983. *Hierarchies, targets and controllers: agreement patterns in Slavic*. London.
Croft, W. 1990. *Typology and universals*. Cambridge.
Edmondson, J. 1978. Ergative languages, accessibility hierarchies, governing reflexives and questions of formal analysis. In W. Abraham (ed.), *Valence, semantic case and grammatical relations*. Amsterdam. 633–60.
Givón, T. 1976. Topic, pronoun and grammatical agreement. In C.N. Li (ed.), *Subject and topic*. New York. 149–78.
Johnson, D.E. 1977. On relational constraints on grammars. In P. Cole and J.M. Sadock (eds), *Grammatical relations*. New York. 151–78.
Keenan, E.L. and B. Comrie. 1977. Noun phrase accessibility and universal grammar. *LingI* 8. 63–99.
Moravcsik, E.A. 1978. Agreement. In J.H. Greenberg (ed.), *Universals of human language*. Stanford, CA. Vol. 4, 352–74.
Primus, B. 1987. *Grammatische Hierarchien*. Munich.
Silverstein, M. 1976. Hierarchy of features and ergativity. In R.M.W. Dixon (ed.), *Grammatical categories in Australian languages*. Canberra. 112–71.

Hieratic ⇒ Egyptian

Hieroglyphic (Luvian) ⇒ Anatolian

hieroglyphics

The term hieroglyphics comes from Grk *hieroglyphiká grámmata* ('the holy written signs'). In 1822, J.F. Champollion deciphered Egyptian writings dating from the fourth century BC to the fourth century AD. Hieroglyphics united the principle of the ideograph with the concept of **phonography** and thus developed into phonograms. A hieroglyph is basically a pictogram (⇒ **pictography**) or an abstract sign developed from a pictogram. In the broader sense, the term 'hieroglyphics' is used to refer to the writings of the Anatolians, Aztecs, and Maya (⇒ **Mayan writing**).

References
Davies, N.M. 1958. *Picture writing in ancient Egypt*. London.
Erman, A. 1912. *Die Hieroglyphen*. Berlin.
Laroche, E. 1960. *Les Hiéroglyphes Hittites*. Paris.
Sethe, K. 1939. *Vom Bilde zum Buchstaben*. Leipzig.
⇒ **writing**

High German

1 In the sociolinguistic sense, the (supraregionally valid, normed, codified) standard language, in contrast to the **colloquial language**, which differs regionally, or to the **dia**lects, which are restricted to smaller regions.

2 In the dialect-geographical sense (⇒ **dialect geography**), all dialects that underwent the second sound shift (⇒ **Old High German consonant shift**), in contrast to the Low German dialects, which did not take part in this sound shift. The border between High German and Low German (with High German–Low German interference especially in the West (Low Franconian) and East (the Brandenburg dialect, Upper Saxon) runs along the so-called '*maken/machen*' line (the 'Benrath line' between Düsseldorf and Cologne). Within High German, there is a further subdivision into Middle German and Upper German, depending on the intensity with which the sound shift occurred.

References
⇒ **dialectology**, **German**

high variety ⇒ high vs low variety

high vs low variety

Synonymous with **standard language**, high variety is used to refer to any prestige form of spoken or written language. One frequently speaks of a high vs low standard, the latter usually referring to the language of the lower socio-economic classes.

References
⇒ **variational linguistics**

Hindi ⇒ Hindi-Urdu

Hindi-Urdu

Indo-Aryan language with several dialects. Hindi, along with **English** the official language of India, has approx. 200 million speakers; Urdu, the official language of Pakistan, has approx. 30 million speakers. Hindi and Urdu can be seen as dialects of one language, whose differences seem largely a factor of the cultural differences of the speakers (Hindus vs Muslims) and of the use of different writing systems (Devanāgarī vs Persian-Arabic).

Characteristics: relatively complex sound system (forty consonants, ten vowels); no distinctive word accent. Two numbers, two genders (masculine, feminine), and three cases. Numerous causative and compound verbs (e.g. *kha lena* 'take to eat, eat up'). **Aspect** is expressed morphologically, tense by auxiliaries. Several classes of verbs must be distinguished (including volitional vs nonvolitional, affective vs non-affective), which require syntactically different constructions. Causatives often serve to derive volitional verbs from non-volitional ones. Participial forms are often used instead of subordinate clauses. Word order SOV.

References
Bahri, H. 1986. *Hindi semantics*. (New edn, rev. and enlarged.) New Delhi.
Beg, M.K.A. 1988. *Urdu grammar, history and structure*. New Delhi.
Bhatia, T.K. 1987. *A history of the Hindi grammatical tradition: Hindi–Hindustani grammar, grammarians, history and problems*. Leiden.
Kachru. Y. 1966. *An introduction to Hindi syntax*. Urbana, IL.
—— 1980. *Aspects of Hindi grammar*. New Delhi.
McGregor, R.S. 1972. *Outline of Hindi grammar*. Oxford. (3rd edn. Delhi, 1995.)
Neim, C.M. *et al.* 1975. *Introductory Urdu*, 2 vols. Chicago, IL.
Ohala, M. 1983. *Aspects of Hindi phonology*. Delhi.
Rai, A. 1984. *A house divided: the origin and development of Hindi/Hindavi*. Delhi.
Ucida, N. 1977. *Hindi phonology*. Calcutta.

Dictionaries
Abdul Haqim. 1985. *The Standard English–Urdu dictionary*, 4th edn. Karachi.
—— 1989. *Urdu–English dictionary*. Delhi.
Bahri, H. 1985. *Comprehensive English–Hindu dictionary*, 2 vols. (3rd rev. and enlarged edn.) Varanasi.
Chaturvedi, M. and B.N. Tiwari. 1980. *A practical Hindi–English dictionary*. New Delhi.
Fallon, S.W. 1879. *A new Hindustani–English dictionary*. Allahabad.
McGregor, R.S. (ed.) 1993. *The Oxford Hindi–English dictionary*. Oxford and Delhi.
Platts, I.T. 1930. *A dictionary of Urdu, Classical Hindi, and English*. (5th impr. Repr. 1968.) Oxford.

Bibliography
Aggarwal, N.K. 1978. *A bibliography of studies on Hindi language and linguistics*. Gurgaon (Haryana).
⇒ **Indo-Aryan**

Hiragana ⇒ **Japanese**

Hispano-Celtic ⇒ **Celtic**

historical grammars

Description of the individual historical stages of a language as well as the representation of the historical relationships between individual languages. The most comprehensive historical grammars of **Indo-European** and its **daughter languages** were compiled in the nineteenth century by the **Neogrammarians** as part of **comparative linguistics**.

References
Indo-European
Brugmann, K. and B. Delbrück. 1886–1900. *Grundriß der vergleichenden Grammatik der indo-*
germanischen Sprachen, 5 vols. Berlin. (Unabridged repr. 1970; English: K. Brugmann, 1888–95. Comparative grammar of the Indo-Germanic languages, trans. J. Wright, R.S. Conway and W.H.D. Rouse. 5 vols. Strasburg (Repr. 1972).)
Krahe, H. 1943. *Indogermanische Sprachwissenschaft*, 2 vols. Berlin. (5th edn 1966–9.)
Lehmann, W.P. 1974. *Proto-Indo-European syntax*. Austin, TX.

Proto-Germanic
Hirt, H. 1931–4. *Handbuch des Urgermanischen*, 3 vols. Heidelberg.
Krahe, H. 1942. *Germanische Sprachwissenschaft*, 2 vols. Berlin. (7th rev. edn, ed. W. Meid, 1969.)
Prokosch, E. 1939. *A comparative Germanic grammar*. Philadelphia, PA.
Streitberg, W. 1896. *Urgermanische Grammatik*. Heidelberg.

historical linguistics

Subdiscipline of general linguistics concerned with developing a theory of **language change** in general or of a specific language. This comprises, among others, the following subareas: (a) representation of the origins and development of individual languages and language groups (through internal and, where actual linguistic data are lacking, external **reconstruction**); (b) development of a typology of processes leading to language change (types of phonological, morphological, syntactic, semantic changes); (c) explanation of individual processes of change or universal types of change with special reference to **articulatory phonetics**, cognitive psychology (⇒ **cognitive linguistics**), **sociolinguistics**, and communication theory; and (d) study of the origin and the spread of language-internal and language-external changes. (⇒ *also* **comparative linguistics**)

References
Aertsen, H. and R.J. Jeffers (eds) 1989. *Historical linguistics: papers from the ninth International Conference on Historical Linguistics*. Amsterdam and Philadelphia, PA.
Andersen, H. and K. Koerner (eds) 1990. *Historical linguistics 1987*. Amsterdam and Philadelphia, PA.
Anttila, R. 1989. *Historical and comparative linguistics*, 2nd rev. edn. Amsterdam and Philadelphia, PA.
Bynon, T. 1977. *Historical linguistics*. Cambridge.
Crowley, T. 1992. *An introduction to historical linguistics*. Oxford.
Davis, G.W. and G. Iverson (eds) 1992. *Explanation in historical linguistics*. Amsterdam and Philadelphia, PA.
Fisiak, J. (ed.) 1990. *Historical linguistics and philology*. Berlin and New York.
Hock, H.H. 1986. *Principles of historical linguistics*.

(2nd edn, rev. and updated 1991.) Berlin and New York.

Jones, C. (ed.) 1993. *Historical linguistics: problems and perspectives*. London and New York.

Lehmann, W.P. 1993. *Historical linguistics*, 3rd edn. London.

Marle, J. van (ed.) 1993. *Historical linguistics 1991: papers from the tenth International Conference on Historical Linguistics*. Amsterdam and Philadelphia, PA.

Meillet, A. 1921. *Linguistique historique et linguistique générale*. Paris.

Journals
Diachronica: International Journal for Historical Linguistics.
Folia Linguistica Historica.
Historical Linguistics/Historische Sprachforschung.
⇒ **language change**, **linguistics (history)**

Hittite

Extinct **Indo-European** language belonging to the **Anatolian** branch, the language of the Hittite Empire in Asia Minor, dating to the second millennium BC. The language is recorded on **cuneiform** tablets, mostly from the region around what is today Boğazköy, excavated in 1905, and fairly quickly deciphered. Hrozný (1917) recognized that it was an Indo-European language. Hittite preserved several archaisms (⇒ e.g. **laryngeal theory**), but on the other hand is much more simply structured than other Indo-European languages of that time (only two **genders**, animate/non-animate; simple tense system). Hittite is the earliest-attested Indo-European language; Sturtevant (1933) saw Anatolian and Indo-European as independent branches of an Indo-Hittite language group.

References
Bayun, L. 1991. Hittito-Luvian historical phonology. *Journal of Ancient Civilization* 6.97–122.
Benveniste, E. 1962. *Hittite et indo-européenne*. Paris.
Friedrich, J. 1960. *Hethitisches Elementarbuch*. Heidelberg.
Held, W.H., W.R. Schmalstieg and J.E. Gertz. 1987. *Beginning Hittite*. Columbus, OH.
Hrozný, B. 1917. *Die Sprache der Hethiter*. Leipzig.
Kammenhuber, A. 1969. Hethitisch, Palaisch, Luwisch und Hieroglyphen-Luwisch. In J. Friedrich *et al.* (eds), *Altkleinasiatische Sprachen* (*Handbuch der Orientalistik*, vol. 2/12). Leiden. 119–57.
Kimball, S. 1995. *Historical phonology of Hittite*. Innsbruck.
Kronasser, H. 1956. *Vergleichende Laut- und Formenlehre des Hethitischen*. Heidelberg.
Oettinger, N. 1979. *Die Stammbildung des hethitischen Verbums*. Nürnberg.
Sturtevant, E.H. 1933. *A comparative grammar of the Hittite language*. New Haven, CT. (2nd edn 1951).

Dictionaries
Friedrich, J. and A. Kammenhuber. 1975– . *Hethitisches Wörterbuch* (vol. 3/12, 1994). Heidelberg.
Güterbock, H.G. and G.A. Hoffner. 1980– . *The Hittite dictionary*. Chicago, IL.
Hoffner, H.A. 1967. An English–Hittite glossary. *Revue Hittite Asianique* (Special issue).
Puhvel, J. 1984– . *Hittite etymological dictionary*, 3 vols. so far. Berlin and New York.

Journal
Hethitica.
⇒ **Indo-European**

Hittito-Luvian ⇒ Anatolian

Hokan

Language group of North and Central America postulated by Dixon and Kroeber (1919), whose reconstruction is questioned today. The Hokan languages include the Yuman languages (e.g. Mohave, approx. 2000 speakers in California), Tequistlatec, and Huamelultec (southern Mexico, approx. 5000 speakers each).

Characteristics: complex consonant system (with glottalized plosives and voiceless nasals); tendency towards ergativity (⇒ **ergative language**) (Washo).

References
Dixon, R.B. and A.L. Kroeber. 1913. New linguistic families in California. *American Anthropologist* 15. 647–55.
Gursky, K. 1974. Der Hoka-Sprachstamm: eine Bestandsaufnahme des lexikalischen Beweismaterials. *Orbis* 23.170–215.
——— 1988. *Der Hoka-Sprachstamm. Nachtrag I.* Nortorf.
Jacobsen, W. 1979. Hokan inter-branch comparison. In L. Campbell and M. Mithun (eds), *The languages of native America: historial and comparative assessment*. Austin, TX. 545–91.
Langdon, M. 1970. *A grammar of Diegueño*. Berkeley, CA.
Langdon, M. and S. Silver. 1976. *Hokan studies*. The Hague.
Munro, P. 1976. *Mohave syntax*. New York.
Sapir, E. 1917. The position of Yana in the Hokan stock. *University of California publications in American archeology and ethnology* 13.1–34.
Watahomigie, L.J. *et al.* 1982. *Hualapai reference grammar*. Los Angeles, CA.
Waterhouse, V.G. 1962. *The grammatical structure of Oaxaca Chontal*. Bloomington, IN (= *IJAL* 28:2, pub. 19).
⇒ **North and Central American languages**

holophrastic construction [Grk *hólos* 'whole'; *phrastikós* 'expressive,' from *phrázein* 'to express']

Syntactically non-structured or only partially structured expressions (one-word expressions) with a complex, often polysemic meaning, like *thanks*, *sorry*, *help*. In language acquisition, one-word expressions used in the first half of the second year of life that refer to more complex complete meanings as the lexical meaning of individual words in adult language. Holophrastic utterances have therefore been interpreted as 'implicit sentences' (McNeill 1970). Their lacking syntactic structure is replaced by direct reference to the immediate environment as well as by **intonation** and gesture.

References
Barrett, M.D. 1982. The holophrastic hypotheses: conceptual and empirical issues. *Cognition* 11.47–76.
Dore, J. 1975. Holophrases, speech acts, and language universals. *JChL* 2.21–40.
Greenfield, P.M. 1982. The role of perceived variability in the transition to language. *JChL* 9.1–12.
McNeill, D. 1970. *The acquisition of language: the study of developmental psycholinguistics.* New York.
⇒ **language acquisition**

homogenetic sound [Grk *homós* 'same,' *génos* 'kind']

Speech sound that is formed in the same **manner of articulation** as another speech sound, e.g. **fricatives** are homogenetic sounds, as well as all **stops** [p] and [Φ] are not homogenetic, but [f] and [Φ] are, and so are [p] and [b] (⇒ *also* **articulatory phonetics**).

References
⇒ **phonetics**

homography [Grk *gráphein* 'to write']
A form of lexical ambiguity and special type of **homonymy**. Two expressions are homographic if they are orthographically identical but have different meanings. Such expressions usually have different pronunciations, e.g. *bass* (fish) vs *bass* (tone) and are not normally etymologically related to one another (⇒ **polysemy**). Homographs, which are customarily listed as separate dictionary entries, may in some cases be etymologically related: e.g. *réfuse* vs *refúse*.

References
⇒ **homonymy, semantics**

homonym clash ⇒ **homonym conflict**

homonym conflict (*also* homonym clash)
Homonym conflict arises from the phonetic similarity, or **homophony**, of two or more homonyms and is frequently associated with at least one of the following features: (a) paradigmatic similarity, i.e. homonyms of the same word class are more likely to conflict, e.g. ME *heal* and *hele* ('to cover, hide'); (b) syntactic

confusion, i.e. 'homonyms' may be created through phonetic similarity brought about in certain syntactic environments, e.g. ME *ear* and *nere* ('kidney') conflicting in the syntactic environment of *an ear* vs *a nere*; (c) occurrence in the same **lexical field** or **domain**, e.g. OFr. **gat* ('cat' and 'cock'), both agricultural terms. Homonym conflict may be avoided by (a) differentiation of gender in some languages, e.g. Ger. *der/das Band* ('volume'/'ribbon'); (b) orthographic distinction, e.g. *plane* vs *plain* (⇒ **homography**); (c) lexical expansion, e.g. *light* (in weight) > *light-weight* vs *light* (in color) > *light-colored*; and (d) loss or replacement of one of the conflicting words, e.g. ME *quēn* ('queen') vs *quēne* ('harlot'). Apparent aversion to homonym conflict is offset by the fact that a language may at any given time have numerous instances of potentially conflicting homonyms, as illustrated by the English homophonic pairs *flower* : *flour* and *pray* : *prey*.

References
Malkiel, Y. 1979. Problems in the diachronic differentiation of near-homophones. *Lg* 55.1–36.
Menner, R.J. 1936. The conflict of homonyms in English. *Lg* 12.229–44.
Wartburg, W. von. 1943. *Einführung in die Problematik und Methodik der Sprachwissenschaft.* Halle. (3rd rev. edn Tübingen, 1970.)
Williams, E.R. 1944. *The conflict of homonyms in English.* New Haven, CT.
⇒ **homonymy, polysemy, semantics**

homonymy [Grk *ónyma* (= *ónoma*) 'name']
A type of lexical ambiguity involving two or more different words: Homonymous expressions are phonologically (⇒ **homophony**) and orthographically (⇒ **homography**) identical but have different meanings and often distinct etymological origins, e.g. *found* ('establish' or 'cast'), *kitty* ('fund' or 'cat'), *scour* ('polish' or 'search'). Occasionally, homonyms have a common etymological origin, e.g. *meter* ('unit of length' or 'instrument used to measure'). The etymological criterion is generally problematic, since the point of divergence from a common etymological origin is often unclear. Homonymy is traditionally distinguished from **polysemy** in that a polysemic expression has several closely related variations in its meaning, e.g. *green* ('fresh,' 'inexperienced,' and 'raw', among others), while the meanings of homonymous expressions have no apparent semantic relation to one another.

Diachronically, homonymy arises through 'coincidental' phonetic and semantic developments, through which (a) originally distinct expressions collapse into a single form (e.g.

*sound*₁ 'distinctive noise' < ME *sun, soun* < MFr. *son* < Lat. *sonus*; *sound*₂ 'healthy; secure' < ME *sund* < OE *gesund*; *sound*₃ 'channel of water' < ME *sound* < OE *sund*; and *sound*₄ 'probe, investigate' < ME *sounden* < OFr. *sonder*; or (b) a single original expression branches into two or more expressions retaining the original orthographic (and phonological) form, e.g. *snow*₁ 'solid precipitation' and *snow*₂ 'cocaine.' Synchronically, the etymological criterion does not apply in most cases, since the genetic relationships are not generally part of competence (⇒ **competence vs performance**) of a speaker.

Problems in homonymy are often language-specific. Consider morphosyntactic criteria, such as distinct **genders** in some languages (e.g. Ger. *der/das Band* ('volume,' 'ribbon') or different plural forms (e.g. Ger. *die Leiter/Leitern* ('leaders,' 'ladders')). Allan (1986) has established various causes for homonymy in English. Rhyming **slang** (*china*₁ 'plates' vs *china*₂ 'mate'), **euphemisms** (*bull*₁ 'male, bovine' vs *bull*₂ 'nonsense'), and dialectal differences or regionalisms (*braces* Brit. 'support straps for trousers') are among the many ways homonyms arise. The most essential, if not sufficiently exact, criterion between homonymy and polysemy is the distinctness of meaning between the expressions in question.

References
Allan, K. 1986. *Linguistic meaning*, 2 vols. London.
Lipka, L. 1990. *An outline of English lexicology*. Tübingen.
Lyons, J. 1977. *Semantics*. Cambridge.
⇒ **semantics**

homophony [Grk *phōnḗ* 'sound']

A type of lexical ambiguity in which two or more expressions have an identical pronunciation but different spellings and meanings, e.g. *pray* vs *prey* and *course* vs *coarse*. Even when homographic expressions (⇒ **homography**) are disambiguated by a change in spelling (e.g. *plain* and *plane*, both derived from Lat. *planus* 'flat'), homphony often remains. Homophony is a special type of **homonymy**.

References
⇒ **homonymy, polysemy, semantics**

homorganic

Speech sounds that are formed with the same articulatory organ, e.g. the **labials** [p] and [f] are homorganic.

References
⇒ **phonetics**

honorative ⇒ honorific

honorific [Lat. *honorificus* 'showing honor'] (*also* honorative)

Grammatical encoding of the social position and the level of intimacy between the speaker, the hearer, and others; more specifically, honorifics grammatically encode a higher social status. This can be seen in **Romance languages** such as **French** in the choice between *vous* and *tu*, **German** *Sie* vs *du*, as well as in English in the choice between first name or title + last name (*Bill* vs *President Clinton* vs *Mr President*). In many languages there are morphological paradigms for various subcategories, e.g. in **Japanese** with verb inflection. (⇒ *also* **pronominal form of address**)

References
Brown, P and S. Levinson. 1978. *Politeness: some universals in language usage*. Cambridge.
⇒ **politeness**

Hopi

Uto-Aztecan language in northern Arizona with approximately 7,000 speakers. Hopi is relatively well known because B.L. Whorf utilized data from it to support his theory of linguistic relativity (⇒ **Sapir–Whorf hypothesis**). Because Hopi (like many other languages) does not mark tense, a different concept of time for the Hopi culture was assumed. Whorf's grammar of Hopi is still incomplete, and the grammatical presentations which are available are not always reliable.

References
Kalectaca, M. 1978. *Lessons in Hopi*. Tucson, AZ.
Malotki, E. 1979. *Hopi-Raum*. Tübingen.
——— 1983. *Hopi time*. The Hague.

Dictionary
Albert, R.A. and D.L. Shaul. 1985. *A concise Hopi and English lexicon*. Amsterdam and Philadelphia, PA.
⇒ **North and Central American languages**

hortative ⇒ adhortative

HPSG ⇒ Head-driven Phrase Structure Grammar

Hsiang ⇒ Chinese

Huamelultec ⇒ Hokan

Huastec ⇒ Mayan

Hungarian (*also* Magyar)

Largest **Uralic** language with about 14 million speakers; official language of Hungary. Hungarian has lost many of its Uralic characteristics due to long contact with other unrelated languages. First written documents date from the thirteenth century. Heavy lexical borrowing from numerous **Turkic** and **European languages**. (⇒ **Finno-Ugric**)

Characteristics: free syntax, pragmatically oriented word order with a special position for focused constituents (before the finite verb). The verb agrees with the subject in person and number; in addition, the so-called object agreement – the relationship between the person of the subject and the person of the object – is marked. A rich system of verb prefixes serves to mark **aspect**. Complex case system, including ten spatial cases with oppositions such as at rest–moving, approaching–receding, inside–outside.

References
Bencédy, J. *et al.* 1968. *A mai magyar nyelv*. Budapest.
Benkö, L. and S. Imre (eds) 1972. *The Hungarian language*. The Hague.
Keresztes, L. 1992. *Praktische ungarische Grammatik. Debreceni Nyári Egyetem*. Debrecen.
Kiefer, F. and K.E. Kiss (eds) 1994. *Syntax and semantics*, vol. 27: *The syntactic structure of Hungarian*. New York.
Szent-Iváyi, B. 1964. *Der ungarische Sprachbau: eine kurze Darstellung mit Erläuterungen für die Praxis*. Leipzig.
Tompa, J. 1972. *Kleine ungarische Grammatik*. Budapest.

hybrid

1 In **morphology** a compound or derived word (⇒ **derivation**, **composition**) whose single elements come from different languages, e.g. *bureau* + *-cracy* (French, Greek) > *bureaucracy*; *tele-* + *vision* (Greek, Latin) > *television*; *re-* + *work* (Latin, English) > *rework*.

2 ⇒ **blend**

References
⇒ **word formation**

hybrid language ⇒ **pidgin**

hydronymy [Grk *hýdōr* 'water,' *ónyma* 'name']
Subdiscipline of **onomastics** concerned with the development, origin, and distribution of names of bodies of water.

hypallage
Figure of speech for transposition of words. Semantically differing reference of the adjectival attribute in a complex construction.

References
Bers, V. 1974. *Enallage and Greek style*. Leiden.

⇒ **figure of speech**

hyperbaton [Grk *hypérbatos* 'transposed inverted']
Any intended deviation from ordinary word order. Kant used hyperbaton in writing *From such crooked wood as that which man is made of, nothing straight can be fashioned*. Deviation from the expected word order can add emphasis or be used to create a rhetorical effect by violating the reader's expectations. Rabelais thus wrote *Few and signally blest are those whom Jupiter has destined to be cabbage planters*.

References
⇒ **figure of speech**

hyperbole [Grk *hyperbolē* 'overshouting, exaggeration, overstrained phrase']
Rhetorical **trope**. An exaggerated description intended to ellicit alienation, revaluation, or any kind of emotional reaction, e.g. *snail's pace, dead tired, heart of steel*. (⇒ *also* **litotes**)

References
⇒ **figure of speech**

hypercharacterization ⇒ **redundancy**

hypercorrection [Grk *hypér* 'over'] (*also* hyperurbanism)
Process and result of an exaggerated attempt on the part of a speaker to adopt or imitate linguistic forms or a linguistic variety that he/she considers to be particularly prestigious. Hypercorrection, which is frequently found in the behavior of social groups aspiring to raise their stature, tends even to exceed the ideal norms of speech of the higher social classes and therefore sounds 'unnatural.'

In principle, similar mechanisms can be found for every situation in language acquisition and language adoption, where speakers recognize regularities and systematic correspondences in the variety they wish to acquire, but when they cannot adequately apprehend the restrictions on or the exceptions to the rules. The rules that have been abstracted by them in such a manner are accordingly too general and correspondingly generate many ungrammatical forms; note the pronunciation of *potato* as [potaːto] following *tomato* [tomaːto].

References
Labov, W. 1966. Hypercorrection by the lower middle class as a factor in linguistic change. In W. Bright (ed.), *Sociolinguistics*. The Hague. 81–113.
⇒ **variational linguistics**

hyperonym ⇒ **hyperonymy**

hyperonymy [Grk *ónoma* 'name'] (*also* superordination)

Semantic relation of lexical superordination (i.e. the converse of lexical subordination, ⇒ **hyponymy**) which reflects a hierarchy-like distribution of the vocabulary or lexicon: *fruit* is a hyperonym, or superordinate, of *apple*, *pear*, and *plum*, because the transition from *apple* to *fruit*, for example, is accompanied by a generalization in meaning. A superordinate relation has some similarities to various logical and semantic relations: part–whole relations (*nose, head*), generals vs specifics (*living being* vs *human*), 'element-of' relations (*book* : *library*).

References
⇒ **hyponymy**, **semantic relation**, **semantics**

hyperphoneme

Term introduced by Pike (1967) as an umbrella term for all relevant segmental units of phonological structure within an individual language, such as **syllables**, **accent**, and **pauses**.

References
Pike, K.L. 1967. *Language in relation to a unified theory of the structure of human behavior*. The Hague. 364 ff. (2nd edn 1971.)
⇒ **phonology**

hypersentence

Sadock's (1968) term for explicitly performative matrix sentences, e.g. *I hereby assert that X.* Such explicit hypersentences show the pragmatic sense in which the embedded sentence is used (assertion, command, promise, etc.). In early generative semantics, Ross, Sadock and others assumed them to be in the deep structure of every sentence and blocked their surface appearance, where necessary, with a subsequent **deletion** transformation.

References
Sadock, J.M. 1968. Hypersentences. Dissertation, Urbana, IL.
——— 1969. Hypersentences. *Papers in Linguistics* 1:2.283–370.
——— 1974. *Toward a linguistic theory of speech acts*. New York.

hyperurbanism ⇒ **hypercorrection**

hypocoristic [Grk *hypokoristikón* 'pet name']

Expression with a **diminutive** semantic component that is formed by **suffixes** (*cigarette*), short forms (*Phil*), or syllable doubling (*choo-choo*), and so on. (⇒ *also* **euphemism**, **word formation**)

References
⇒ **word formation**

hyponymy [Grk *hypó* 'under,' *ónyma* (= *ónoma*), 'name'] (*also* **subordination**)

Term suggested by Lyons (1963) (in analogy to **synonymy**) for the **semantic relation** of subordination, i.e. the specification of semantic content. For example, *apple* is a hyponym of *fruit*, since *apple* has a more specific meaning than *fruit*. In expressions with **extensions**, the hyponymy can be viewed as the subset relation: l_1 (lexeme$_1$) is subordinate to l_2 only if the extension of l_1 is contained in the extension of l_2. Seen intensionally (⇒ **intension**) with a view to **componential analysis**, the relation is the inverse: l_1 is subordinate to l_2 only if l_1 contains at least all **semantic features** of l_2, but not vice versa. *Apple, pear, plum* are co-hyponyms relative to each other and hyponyms of the generic term *fruit* (⇒ **hyperonymy**). Every hyponym is distinguished from its hyperonym, or superordinate, by at least one feature that specifies it further. There are at least two heuristic tests for hyponymy: embedded lexemes in suitable contexts, e.g. l_1 is of the type l_2, or mutual substitution in suitable sentences $S(\ldots)$, whereby $S(l_1)$ implies $S(l_2)$ (**implication**). At closer look, it is necessary (a) to view a particular case of hyponymy relative to a given semantic perspective and (b) to test the hyponymy in terms of the actual use of the expressions (see Lutzeier 1981). Since 'upward branching' occurs in hyponymy (consider, for example, the relation of *mother*, *woman*, and *parent*), hyponymy does not constitute a true **hierarchy**.

References
Cruse, D.A. 1975. Hyponymy and lexical hierarchies. *ArchL* 6.26–31.
Lipka, L. 1990. *An outline of English lexicology*. Tübingen.
Lutzeier, P. 1981. *Wort und Feld. Wortsemantische Fragestellungen mit besonderer Berücksichtigung des Wortfeldbegriffs*. Tübingen.
Lyons, J. 1963. *Structural semantics: an analysis of part of the vocabulary of Plato*. Oxford.
⇒ **lexicology**, **semantics**

hypotaxis [Grk 'subjection, submission,' from *hypotássein* 'to arrange under, to subject'] (*also* **subordination**)

Syntactic relationship of subordination of clauses, as opposed to co-ordinating conjunction (⇒ **parataxis**). The structural dependency is formally marked by subordinating conjunctions (*because, although*), relative pronouns (*who*, *which*), and infinitive constructions. The subordinate clause can precede, follow, or be embedded in the main clause (⇒ **embedding**).

(⇒ *also* **relative clause**)

hysteron proteron ⇒ **anastrophe**

I

Iberian ⇒ **Basque**

Ibero-Romance ⇒ **Romance languages**

Icelandic

North **Germanic (Scandinavian)** language, since 1935 the official language of Iceland (approx. 250,000 speakers).

Characteristics: in contrast to **Norwegian**, good preservation of historical morphological characteristics; purifying tendencies (new words are introduced primarily by new word formations rather than loan words).

References
Einarsson, S. 1945. *Icelandic*. Baltimore, MD. (7th edn 1976.)
Gordon, E.V. 1927. *An introduction to Old Norse*. Oxford. (2nd rev. edn, ed. A.R. Taylor, 1957.)
Maling, J. and A. Zaenen (eds) 1990. *Syntax and semantics*, vol. 24: *Modern Icelandic syntax*. New York.
Noreen, A. 1970. *Altisländische und altnorwegische Grammatik*, 5th edn Tübingen.
Valfells, S. and J.E.Cathey. 1981. *Old Icelandic: an introductory course*. Oxford.

ICM ⇒ prototype

icon [Grk *eikōn* 'image, picture']

In the **semiotics** of C.S. Peirce, a class of visual or acoustic **signs** that stand in a directly perceivable relation to the object of reference, by illustratively imitating aspects of the real object and thereby revealing similarities to or features held in common with the object, e.g. charts, graphs, diagrams, traffic signs, maps, as well as the musical representation of sounds like **onomatopoeia**. (⇒ *also* **index**, **symbol**)

References
Eco, U. 1972. Introduction to a semiotics of iconic signs. *Versus* 2:1.1–15.
Wallis, M. 1973. On iconic signs. In J. Rey-Debove (ed.), *Recherches sur les systèmes significants*. The Hague. 481–98.
⇒ **iconicity, semiotics**

iconicity

1 Term coined by C.W. Morris that designates the measure of similarity between the **icon** and the object to which it refers.

2 Concept of text interpretations developed within the framework of **semiotics** that is based on a correspondence between the characteristics of a particular representation and the characteristics of that which it represents. Thus, under certain stylistic conditions, a report addressed to a hearer or reader is as complex as the event(s) being described in the report. Similarly, the linear structure of a report can be deduced from the natural sequence of the event(s). Iconic text interpretation is not restricted to verbal communication; its success depends primarily on the co-operative behavior of the speaker/hearer, as postulated in Grice's **maxims of conversation**. Iconicity plays a major role in **cognitive grammar** (see Haiman 1985; Givón 1990).

References
Givón, T. 1990. *Syntax: a functional–typological introduction*, vol. II. Amsterdam.
Grice, H.P. 1975. Logic and conversation. In P. Cole and J.L. Morgan (eds), *Syntax and semantics*, vol. 3: *Speech acts*. New York, 41–58. (Orig. 1968.)
Haiman, J. 1980. The iconicity of grammar. *Lg* 56.515–40.
—— 1983. Iconic and economic motivation. *Lg* 59.781–819.
—— (ed.) 1985. *Iconicity in syntax*. Amsterdam.
—— 1993. Iconicity. In J. Jacobs *et al.* (eds), *Syntax: an international handbook of contemporary research*. Berlin and New York. 896–904.
Simone, R. (ed.) 1994. *Iconicity in language*. Amsterdam and Philadelphia, PA.
Verhaar, J.W. 1985. On iconicity and hierarchy. *SiL* 9.21–76.
⇒ **maxim of conversation, semiotics**

ictus [Lat. 'struck; a blow']

The first stressed **syllable** of a meter.

ID rule ⇒ ID/LP format

ideal speaker/listener

A term from Chomsky (1965) in which the state of the research into language is idealized. 'Linguistic theory is concerned primarily with an ideal speaker/listener, in a completely homogeneous speech-community, who knows his language perfectly and is unaffected by such grammatically irrelevant conditions as memory limitations, distractions, shifts of attention and interest, and errors (random or characteristic) in applying his knowledge of the language in actual performance' (p. 3). The goal of the linguistic theory is to describe the competence (⇒ **competence vs performance**) of the ideal speaker/listener.

References
Chomsky, N. 1965. *Aspects of the theory of syntax.* Cambridge, MA.
⇒ **competence vs performance, transformational grammar**

idealized cognitive model ⇒ **prototype**

ideogram ⇒ **ideography**

ideograph [Grk *ideĩn* 'to see,' *gráphein* 'to write']

Type of transcription in which meanings are expressed by graphic signs (ideograms), whereby complex complete meanings are symbolized synthetically by a single conceptual sign. Such conventionalized ideograms (e.g. those found in traffic signs) are not restricted to use in individual languages, since they are not basically signs that express the meaning of linguistic expressions. A special type of ideogram is found in Frege's (1879) 'conceptual writing,' which is one of the first formalized languages for representing **predicate logic**. (⇒ *also* **pictography**)

References
Frege, G. 1879. *Begriffsschrift: eine der arithmetischen nachgebildete Formelsprache des reinen Denkens.* Halle. (Repr. ed. I. Angelelli, Darmstadt, 1964.)
⇒ **writing**

ideophone [Grk *phōnḗ* 'sound, voice']

Generally, an onomatopoetic (⇒ **onomatopoeia**) representation of a concept, often consisting of reduplicated syllables and not adhering to the phonotactic structure of the given language. Examples from Baule (a) sound concepts [kɛtɛkɛtɛkɛtɛ] 'a running elephant,' [foooooo] 'the laughter of an elephant'; (b) visual concepts [gudugudu] 'something large and round,' [mlãmlãlã] 'something large and fat.'

Reference
Timyan, J. 1976. A discourse-based grammar of Baule. Dissertation, New York. 254–61.

idiolect [Grk *ídios* 'one's own, personal,' *Léktos* 'chosen; expression word']

Language use characteristic of an individual speaker. This personal manner of expression is, to varying degrees, apparent in an individual's pronunciation, active vocabulary, and syntax. The first and most restrictive definition of idiolect was offered by Bloch (1948).

References
Bloch, B. 1948. A set of postulates for phonetic analysis. *Lg* 24.3–46.
⇒ **dialect, lect, sociolect**

idiom (*also* colloquial expression, colloquialism, idiomatic expression, set phrase)

1 A set, multi-elemental group of words, or lexical entity with the following characteristics: (a) the complete meaning cannot be derived from the meaning of the individual elements, e.g. *to have a crush on someone* ('to be in love with someone'); (b) the substitution of single elements does not bring about a systematic change of meaning (which is not true of non-idiomatic syntagms), e.g. **to have a smash on someone*; (c) a literal reading results in a homophonic non-idiomatic variant, to which conditions (a) and (b) no longer apply (⇒ **metaphor**). Frequently there is a diachronic connection between the literal reading and the idiomatic reading (⇒ **idiomatization**). In such cases, the treatment of the idiom as an unanalyzable lexical entity is insufficient. Depending upon the theoretical preconception, sayings, **figures of speech**, **nominal constructions**, and **twin formulas** are all subsumed under idioms.

References
⇒ **idiomatics**

2 The idiosyncratic features of an **idiolect**, a **dialect**, or a language.

idiomatic expression ⇒ **idiom**

idiomatics (*also* phraseology)

The compilation, description, and classification of the total corpus of **idioms**[1] in a language. Depending on the theoretical framework, various typologies (based on criteria such as grammatical structure, permutability of individual elements, stability of expressions, **distribution**, and semantic **motivation**) were developed, especially by Soviet linguists. Fernando and Flavell (1981) provide an overview with bibliographic references.

References
Chafe, W.L. 1968. Idiomaticity as anomaly in the Chomskyan paradigm. *FL* 4.109–27.
Fernando, C. and R. Flavell. 1981. *On idiom: critical views and perspectives.* Exeter.
Fraser, B. 1970. Idioms within a tranformational grammar. *FL* 6.22–42.
Makkai, A. 1972. *Idiom structure in English.* The Hague.

idiomaticity

Characteristic of natural languages to use set word combinations (⇒ **idiom**[1]) whose meaning cannot be described as the sum of their individual elements.

Reference
Makkai, A. 1978. Idiomaticity as a language universal. In J.H. Greenberg (ed.), *Universals in human language*. Stanford, CA. 401–48.

idiomatization (*also* lexicalization)

Historical process of semantic change in complex constructions whose complete meaning, originally motivated on the basis of the meaning of its individual components, can no longer be derived from the meaning of these components, cf. *cupboard*. Completely idiomatized phrases or expressions form a (new) semantic unit, and the original motivation of this unit can only be reconstructed through historical knowledge.

References
⇒ **idiomatics, word formation**

idiosyncratic feature [Grk *idiosynkrāsía* 'peculiar temperament or habit of body']

Phonological, morphological, syntactic, or semantic features of a word that cannot be predicted on the basis of general rules; consequently, they must be represented as separate lexicon entries. In **morphology**, one speaks of idiosyncratic features especially in regard to phenomena of demotivation (⇒ **lexicalization**), i.e. development of meaning through elements not based on the meaning of the individual elements. (⇒ *also* **lexicon**)

References
⇒ **word formation**

idioticon

Dictionary that contains specifically the vocabulary and idiomatic expressions (**idiotisms**) of a particular **dialect** or speech area. (In contrast, ⇒ **dialect dictionary**.)

idiotism

In **dialectology**, a regionally restricted word typical of a certain dialect. Idiotisms were used in dialectology as markers whose occurrence marked the geographic spread of a particular dialectal area, cf. *hulp* 'helped' as a marker for Appalachian English.

References
Falk, Y. 1983. Constituency, word order and phrase structure rules. *LingA* 11.331–60.
Gazdar, G. and G.K. Pullum. 1981. Subcategorization, constituent order and the notion 'head.' In M. Moortgat, H. van der Hulst, and T. Hoekstra (eds), *The scope of lexical rules*. Dordrecht. 107–23.
Kay, M. 1979. Functional grammars. *BLS* 5.142–58.
Pollard, C. and I.A. Sag. 1988. *An information-based*

syntax and semantics, vol. 1: *Fundamentals*. Stanford, CA.
Uszkoreit, H. 1986. Constraints on order. *Linguistics* 24.883–906.

ID/LP format ⇒ immediate dominance

IE ⇒ Indo-European

IFID (illocutionary force indicating device) ⇒ illocution

Igbo

Kwa language (approx. 16 million speakers) in southeastern Nigeria.

Characteristics: **tonal language** (with **downstep**), **vowel harmony**; **serial verb construction**, no inflection. Word order SVO.

References
Emenanjo, E.N. 1978. *Elements of modern Igbo grammar*. Ibadan.
Green, M.M. and G.E. Igwe. 1963. *A descriptive grammar of Igbo*. Berlin.
Meier, P. *et al.* 1975. *A grammar of Izi, an Igbo language*. Norman, OK.
Ogbalu, F.C. and E.N. Emananjo (eds) 1982. *Igbo language and culture*. Oxford.

Ịjọ ⇒ Kwa

illative (Lat. *illatus* 'brought in']

Morphological **case** in some languages (e.g. **Finnish**) which expresses the movement of an object into a location. (⇒ *also* **elative**)

illiteracy ⇒ literacy

illocution [Lat. *in* 'in' + *loqui* 'to talk, to speak,' i.e. 'what one does by speaking'] (*also* illocutionary act)

The fundamental aspect of a speech act in the **speech act theory** of J.L. Austin and J.R. Searle. According to Searle, a simple illocution consists of an illocutionary force and a propositional content and, thus, has the form $f(p)$, where f and p may vary – within certain limits – independently from one another. If one takes f as the forces of an assertion and a question and p as the proposition that it is cold and that the car will not start, then there are four different illocutions: (a) the assertion that it is cold; (b) the assertion that the car will not start; (c) the question of whether it is cold; and (d) the question of whether the car will not start. **Intonation**, **punctuation**, **interrogative pronouns**, interrogative adverbs, **modal auxiliary**, and indicators of verb **mood**, word and clausal order, modal particles, special **affixes**, special constructions like the A-not-A interrogative in Mandarin, as well as the form of explicit **performative utterances** all function as illocutionary force indicating devices (IFIDs). The latter types are used in disambiguating an illocution as, for example, in legal contexts (*I hereby make a final request that you pay your bill from the 29th of February of 1992*). According to Searle, the meaning of the illocutionary force indicating devices is based on the rules for their use (cf. **constitutive rules**, **regulative rules**, **speech act theory**, **meaning as use**). In every language, one indicator (or a combination of several) serves as a base indicator. An **indirect speech act** occurs whenever an illocution other than that indicated literally by the base indicator is performed with the utterance of a sentence.

References
⇒ **indirect speech act**, **sentence mood**, **speech act classification**, **speech act theory**

illocutionary act ⇒ **illocution**

illocutionary force ⇒ **illocution**

illocutionary force indicating device ⇒ **illocution**

imitation ⇒ **echolalia**

immediate constituent analysis

A model of sentence analysis developed by the American structuralists. The goal and consequence of immediate constituent analysis is to analyze a linguistic expression into a hierarchically defined series of **constituents**. This analysis (⇒ **segmentation**) is supported by various tests, above all the **commutation test** and the **substitution test**. If the complex expression to be analyzed is movable or can be replaced in the sentence by a simple expression belonging to the same grammatical category, then it counts as a constituent. Thus a sentence like *The professor gives a lecture* can be split into two parts, because *the professor* can be replaced by *she* (= noun phrase), and *gives a lecture* can be replaced by *teaches* (= verb phrase). This can be represented in a **tree diagram** as follows:

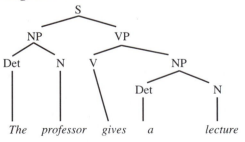

The elements produced in the first stage of the analysis are called immediate constituents: NP and VP are immediate constituents of S, Det and N of NP, and so on. Det, N, and V are irreducible constituents of S. The branching nodes are called constitutes and the relation between the branching nodes and their constituents is called constituency. The results of an immediate constituent analysis can be presented in various ways, using a **tree diagram**, **phrase structure rules**, or a **box diagram**. Immediate constituent analysis is the most basic syntactic organizational principle of **transformational grammar**. The tests to justify the constituents are only necessary, but not sufficient, for to justify a constituent structure it must be proven that it is necessary for the formulation of syntactic processes.

References
Bloomfield, L. 1933. *Language*. New York.
Harris, Z.S. 1962. *String analysis of sentence structure*. The Hague.
Hockett, C.F. 1958. *A course in modern linguistics*. New York.
Postal, P.M. 1964. *Constituent structure: a study of contemporary models of syntactic description*. Bloomington, IN.
Wells, R.S. 1947. Immediate constituents. *Lg* 23.71–117.

Immediate dominance/linear precedence format (*abbrev.* ID/LP format)

A grammatical format proposed by Gazdar and Pullum for **Generalized Phrase Structure Grammar**. This format contains separate types of rules to describe immediate dominance and linear precedence. (a) The hierarchical relationships in tree diagrams are determined by immediate dominance rules. Such ID rules are unordered **phrase structure rules** which express nothing about the order of the daughter constituents. In the notation of ID rules, the absence of linear ordering is indicated by commas between the categorial symbols on the right-hand side of the rule, e.g. *VP → V, NP, PP*. (b) The order of the sister constituents in a local tree is determined by linear precedence rules, which dictate a partial ordering for the categories of grammar. LP rules are ordered pairs of syntactic categories: for example, the LP rule *V < NP* states that in every local tree in which a verb and a noun phrase appear as sister nodes, *V* must precede *NP*. Immediate dominance allows for local variations in word order; an expansion of this by Uszkoreit (1986) allows for the representation of partially free word order. An extension of immediate dominance is also used by Pollard and Sag in **Head-driven Phrase Structure Grammar**. Other formats for the separation of immediate dominance and linear precedence can be found in **Functional Unification Grammar** by Kay (1979) and in Falk's (1983) suggestion for the extension of **Lexical-Functional Grammar**.

immersion

Approach in second language pedagogy (⇒ **second language acquisition, natural approach**), where academic subjects are taught exclusively in the target language.

References
Lyster, R. 1987. Speaking immersion. *CMLR* 43:4.701–17.
Singh, R. 1986. Immersion: problems and principles. *CMLR* 42:3.559–71.
Swain, M. and H. Barik. 1978. Bilingual education in Canada: French and English. In B. Spolsky and R. Cooper (eds), *Case studies in bilingual education.* Rowley, MA. 22–71.

immutative vs mutative ⇒ durative vs non-durative, imperfective vs perfective

imperative [Lat. *imperare* 'to order, to command']

Subcategory of verbal **mood** used primarily to express a request or command: *Come here!* However, it can also fulfill other functions, such as a conditional: *Lose my book and I'll make you buy me a new one.* On the other hand, requests can also be expressed in **declarative sentences** *You'll keep your mouth shut!* or in interrogatives *Why don't you keep your mouth shut?*, where **intonation** and modal **particles** contribute to the identification of the speech act in question.

While indicative and subjunctive generally have fully developed systems, the imperative has only second person singular and plural forms, the other persons usually being expressed by some other means (cf. *Let's go, Let them try*). Other tenses or passive forms cannot be formed from an imperative. Syntactic markers for imperatives for English include initial position of the verb (*Come here quick!*) and special intonation, as well as (generally) the omission of the subject. In many languages imperative forms are very simple morphologically (typically identical to the verb root); verbs that are often used as commands (*come, go*) can have **suppletive** forms. For first person plural imperative, ⇒ **adhortative**; on third person imperatives, ⇒ **jussive**.

Except for **modal auxiliaries**, all verbs that have an animate subject seem to be able to form an imperative. Since they are used primarily as commands to act, only action verbs generally appear as imperatives.

References
Davies, E. 1986. *The Engish imperatives*. London.
Hamblin, C. 1987. *Imperatives*. Oxford.
⇒ **modality**

imperative transformation

In **transformational grammar**, the derivation of an imperative sentence from a **deep structure** sentence. The **ellipsis** of the subject pronoun is described as a transformational deletion in the imperative transformation. For criticism, see work by Fries. In **generative semantics** and **speech act theory**, every sentence is embedded in a **matrix sentence** with a performative verb. In the case of the imperative, this performative matrix clause is *I command you*. For example, *I command you: you should be quiet*. Through the application of several transformations, the imperative *be quiet* is derived. ⇒ **performative analysis** for the difficulties of this approach.

References
⇒ **generative grammar, performative analysis**

imperfect [Lat. *imperfectus* 'unfinished, incomplete'] (*also* past tense, **preterite**)

Past **tense** for events which extend into the present in languages which distinguish between **aorist** (comparable to French passé simple as a historical perfect), **perfect** (= term for an action that is completed at a specific point in time), and imperfect. In contrast to **preterite**, the imperfect is marked in regard to **aspect**.

References
⇒ **tense**

imperfective vs perfective (*also* aterminative/cursive vs terminative, **durative vs non-durative**, immutative vs mutative, incomplete vs complete)

Basic subcategorization in terms of **aspect** which characterizes an event either as temporally unstructured (imperfective) or as having a beginning (⇒ **inchoative**) or end point (⇒ **resultative**). Because of this, some see the perfective as indicating an event as a whole while the imperfective describes the continuous part of it. In the literature the pair imperfective–perfective is often equated with **durative vs non-durative**. In the **Slavic languages** this distinction is marked morphologically, where entire classes of verbs have perfective and imperfective variants: Russ. *pisal* vs *napisal* 'write' vs 'finish writing,' *čital* vs *pročital* 'read' vs 'finish reading.' There are also perfective forms which describe an action as happening over a short period of time: Russ. *my tancevali* 'we danced' vs *my potancevali* 'we danced for a while.' English lacks a specific formal marker for the imperfective–perfective distinction. Instead, it is indicated by various linguistic features whose function is not primarily aspectual, such as tense, verb type, verbal constructions (e.g. *She works in Texas* (imperfective) vs *She swallowed the gum* (perfective)).

References

Dowty, D.R. 1977. Toward a semantic analysis of verb aspect and the English 'imperfective' progressive. *Ling&P* 1.45–77.
⇒ **aspect**

impersonal construction

Syntactic constructions in which the logical subject is not expressed as the grammatical subject, especially in sentences with impersonal verbs: *It so happens that . . . , it's raining.*

impersonal verb

Verb that can only be used in the third person singular, for which the **agent**, if one exists at all, cannot appear in the **nominative** (as the subject). In English, this empty position is generally filled with *it* or *there*. Impersonal verbs in English are generally used for weather phenomena (⇒ **weather verb**) (*it was raining, it snowed*).

implication [Lat. *implicatio* 'the action of weaving in; an intertwined system']

The term 'implication' is used in everyday language as well as in logic and semantics in different ways, though with much overlap. (a) Material implication (*also* conditional implication, logical implication, subjunction): quantifier in propositional logic that connects two elementary propositions p and q in a new single proposition that is false if and only if the first part of the proposition is true and the second part is false (notation: $p \rightarrow q$): *If London is on the Thames, then $3 \times 3 = 10$* (= f(alse)); but: *If $3 \times 3 = 10$, then London is on the Thames* (= t(rue)). The following (two-value) truth table represents a definition of this type of implication:

p	q	$p \rightarrow q$
t	t	t
t	f	f
f	t	t
f	f	t

The definition of implication in the truth table is based on the fact that implication is logically equivalent with the expression $\neg p \lor q$ which can be paraphrased as 'first part false or second part true,' and which are exactly the truth conditions for implication. Another property of material implication is that both the **rule of inference** and the **rule of negative inference** hold true for it (in contrast with **presupposition**). Material implication is the appropriate quantifier for formalizations of conditional existential propositions in predicate logic. This truth-functional interpretation of implication is purely an extensional one, therefore any presupposed semantic relation between the two parts of the proposition does not come into play in everyday language. The intensional relation between the two parts of the proposition that exists in natural language use is covered below in (d). (b) Logical implication (*also* entailment): metalinguistic relation between two propositions p and q: q logically follows from p (notation: $p \rightarrow q$), if every semantic interpretation of the language that makes p true automatically (i.e. based solely on the logical form of p and q) makes q true. For example, p = *All humans are mortal and Socrates is a human*, q = *Socrates is mortal*, then it holds true that $p \rightarrow q$. (c) Strict implication (*also* entailment): implicational relation in modal logic: 'p necessarily implies q' or 'It necessarily follows from q that p.' With the operator of necessitation $\Box$ this relation can be expressed as $\Box (p \rightarrow q)$ (⇒ **modal logic**). (d) Semantic implication (*also* (semantic) entailment, conditional): a narrower (intensional) interpretation of implication in regard to natural languages. In contrast with logical implication, the partial propositions of semantic implication are in a semantic relation and their validity is based on appropriate (lexical) **meaning postulates**. Cf. Austin's (1962) example: from *The cat is lying on the mat* it follows semantically that *The mat is underneath the cat*. In contrast with presupposition, q will remain true if p is negated: from *The cat is not on the mat* it does not follow that *The mat is underneath the cat*. This relation of implication can be checked with the *but*-test: if a speaker maintains that *The cat is on the mat, but the mat is not underneath the cat* his/her semantic competence is called into question. The concept of semantic implication plays a basic role in structural lexical semantics: (uni-lateral) implication corresponds largely to the semantic relation of **hyponymy**, bilateral implication (= **equivalence**) corresponds largely to **synonymy**. (e) Contextual implication: expansion of the concept of implication with pragmatic aspects. Contextual implications are conversational conditions that must be fulfilled so that an utterance can be seen as 'normal' under the given circumstances of a specific speech situation. Thus by uttering an assertion, one implies 'contextually' that this assertion is also really true, and the speaker must similarly be able to defend him-/herself if the hearer is doubtful. Cf. **allegation**, **implicature**, **invited inference** for other types of implication.

References
Austin, J.L. 1962. *How to do things with words.* Oxford.
⇒ **formal logic**

implicational analysis (*also* implicational hierarchy, accessibility hierarchy)

Approach developed within the 'qualitative paradigm' of **variational linguistics** for representing linguistic variability in the form of a model. The approach is based on the presumption that linguistic varieties are hierarchically structured and clearly distinguishable from one another. Individual linguistic features that define varieties are ordered in an implicational matrix in such a way that the presence of certain given features allows one to deduce the presence of certain other features, though not vice versa, as represented in the following matrix:

Varieties	Features			
V1	F1	F2	F3	F4
V2	F1	F2	F3	
V3	F1	F2		
V4	F1			

The matrix represents an implicational hierarchy and affords a schematic representation of the rule-ordered features among the related varieties.

References
Bailey, C.-J.N. 1973. *Variation and linguistic theory.* Arlington, VA.
Bickerton, D. 1973. Quantitative versus dynamic paradigms: the case of Montreal *que*. In C.-J.N. Bailey and R.W. Shuy (eds), *New ways of analyzing variation in English*. Washington, DC. 23–44.
Decamp, D. 1971. Implicational scales and sociolinguistic linearity. *Linguistics* 73.30–43.
Dittmar, N. and P. Schlobinski. 1988. Implikationsanalyse. In U. Ammon *et al.* (eds), *Sociolinguistics: an international handbook of the science of language and society*. Berlin and New York. 1014–26.

implicational hierarchy ⇒ implicational analysis

implicational universal ⇒ hierarchy universal, universal

implicative verb

Type of verb with an infinitive complement for which the following relation exists between the whole sentence M (= matrix sentence) and the complementary sentence C (= constituent sentence): M implies C and not-M implies not-C, e.g. *Philip took the trouble to fix his old car* implies that *Philip fixed his old car*; *Philip didn't take the trouble to fix his old car* implies *Philip didn't fix his old car*. Some other verbs in this class are *bring about, take the time*, and *lower oneself*; negative implicative verbs are *miss* and *neglect*. (⇒ *also* **factive predicate**)

References
Coleman, L. 1975. The case of the vanishing presupposition. *BLS* 1.78–89.
Karttunen, L. 1971a. Implicative verbs. *Lg* 47. 340–58.
—— 1971b. *The logic of English predicate complement constructions*. Bloomington, IN.
⇒ **presupposition**

implicature

Grice's (1968) term (see Grice 1975): in uttering a sentence S, a speaker implies that p is the case if, by having been uttered, S suggests as its conclusion p, without p having been literally said. If the conclusion rests exclusively on the conventional meaning of the words and grammatical constructions that occur in S, then the conclusion is called a 'conventional implicature.' Since Karttunen and Peters (1979) most **presuppositions** are interpreted as conventional implicatures. Conventional implicatures can be elicited by **factive predicates** like *forget* (*Philip forgot that today is Caroline's birthday*, with the conventional implicature being: 'Today is Caroline's birthday'), by certain particles like *only* and *even* (*Only Philip is going to London*, with the conventional implicature being: 'No one else is going to London'), and certain types of **aspect** such as a **resultative** (*The rosebush has wilted*, with the conventional implicature: 'The rosebush was previously thriving'). Conventional implicatures cannot be canceled, i.e. the speaker cannot debate their validity without contradicting or correcting him-/herself, but they can be detached, i.e. there is always a paraphrase that says the same thing without triggering the implicature.

Where an implicature rests not only on the conventional meaning of the uttered expression but also on the supposition that the speaker is following or is intentionally breaking certain **maxims of conversation** then that implicature is called a 'conversational implicature.' If it appears in all normal contexts, it is called a 'generalized conversational implicature'; and if it only appears in certain utterance contexts, it is called a 'particularized conversational implicature.' In contrast with conventional implicatures, conversational implicatures can be canceled, but cannot be detached. An indefinite article can trigger conversational implicature: in *Philip is meeting a woman this evening*, the generalized conversational implicature is that the woman is not Philip's wife. The reasoning is that speakers ordinarily, and in a co-operative spirit, observe such maxims of conversation as the quantity maxim, which enjoins speakers to supply a contextually appropriate amount of information; the addressee assumes the speaker would not misleadingly refer to Philip's wife as a 'woman' if reference to his wife were indeed intended; the addressee therefore 'conversationally implies' that the speaker intends the reference to be someone other than Philip's wife. Particularized conversational implicatures are not triggered by certain elements *in vacuo*, but rather by interaction of utterances and contexts: for example, *Mr Smith has an excellent command of his native tongue and attended my seminars regularly* (in the context of a letter of recommendation for a college graduate who has applied for a position), may have the (cancelable) particularized conversational implicature that Mr Smith has no other qualities that make him particularly suited for the position sought.

References
Grandy, R. 1990. On the foundations of conversational implicature, *PBLS* 16: *General session and parasession on the legacy of Grice*. Berkeley, CA. 405–10.
Grice, H.P. 1975. Logic and conversation. In P. Cole and J.L. Morgan (eds), *Syntax and semantics*, vol. 3: *Speech acts*. New York. 41–58. (Orig. 1968.)
Karttunen, L. and S. Peters. 1979. Conventional implicatures. In C. Oh and D. Dinneen (eds), *Syntax and semantics*. vol. 11: *Presuppositions*. New York. 1–56.
Kemmerling, A. 1991. Implikatur. In A. von Stechow and D. Wunderlich (eds), *Semantik: ein internationales Handbuch der zeitgenössischen Forschung (Semantics: an international handbook of contemporary research)*. Berlin. 319–33.
⇒ **conversation analysis**, **maxim of conversation**

implicit derivation ⇒ derivation

implosive [Lat. *in* 'in,' *plaudere* 'to make a clapping sound']

1 Non-nasal **stop** that is formed with the pharyngeal **airstream mechanism** by lowering the larynx when the glottis is almost closed. In this process, the air does not literally flow from the outside to the inside, rather the air pressure in the oral cavity is almost the same as on the outside of the oral cavity. For example, in [ɓ] and [ɗ] in the **Chadic** language Kera [ˉɓiˉgi] 'surrounded' vs [ˌbiˉgi] 'bury', [ˌgeˉɗe] 'to lose its time' vs [ˌgeˉde] 'to jump off.'

2 Non-nasal **stop** in which the stop is not released as in the contraction *tip'em* [tipm̩]. (⇒

also **articulatory phonetics**)

References
⇒ **phonetics**

inchoative

Aspect of a verb or verb phrase. Inchoatives belong to the non-duratives (⇒ **durative vs non-durative**) and indicate the inception or the coming into existence of a state or process, e.g. *to bloom, to wilt*. Occasionally the term inchoative is also used synonymously for **ingressive**, which denotes the sudden beginning of an action: *to burst into flames*.

References
Newmeyer, F. 1969. The underlying structure of the *begin*-class verbs. *CLS* 5.
⇒ **aspect**

inclusion

Logical relation between classes of **sets** of elements in which it is the case that every element of class *A* is also an element of class *B*: *All brothers* (= class *A*) *are male relatives* (= class *B*). In the semantic aspect of relations between meanings (⇒ **semantic relation**), inclusion often corresponds to **hyponymy**, and in **propositional logic** to **implication**. (⇒ *also* **formal logic**, **set theory**)

References
⇒ **formal logic**, **set theory**

inclusive vs exclusive

Distinction in the person system of many languages in which there are different forms for speaker + hearer (inclusive) vs speaker + third person (exclusive): Chinese women *lai le* 'we (you and I) came,' *zanmen lai le* 'we (he and I) came.'

incompatibility

1 The most common **semantic relation** of lexical opposition. Two expressions are incompatible if they are semantically similar yet differ in a single semantic feature. To this extent, cohyponyms (⇒ **hyponymy**) are incompatible: for example, *burgundy* and *chablis* are both hyponyms of *wine*, but differ according to the single semantic feature of 'color.' With incompatibility, it is particularly essential to relativize the terms against a common semantic background: thus, *burgundy* and *chablis*, against the background of 'suitable for drinking,' are not incompatible. Substitution of one expression l_1 and l_2 in suitable sentences $S(\ldots)$ is a useful heuristic test for incompatibility. In this test, a contradiction arises between $S(l_1)$ and $S(l_2)$, in that the negation of $S(l_2)$ follows from $S(l_1)$ while the negation of $S(l_1)$

follows from S(l₂). (⇒ **antonymy, complementarity, converse relation, reversivity**)

References
⇒ **semantic relations, semantics**

2 In the framework of N. Chomsky's theory of syntax, the violation of **selection restrictions** which exist between elements of certain syntactic positions. For example, the verb *think* is only compatible (i.e. grammatical) in literal uses with a subject having the feature [+ human]: *The man is thinking* vs **The stone is thinking*.

References
⇒ **selection restrictions**

incomplete ⇒ durative vs non-durative

incorporating language [from Late Lat. *incorporation*; *in* 'in,' *corpus* 'body']

Classificational category established by Humboldt (1836) which refers to languages that tend to express syntactic relations in a sentence by compounding lexical and grammatical elements into long complex words. Syntactic functions such as object and adverbial are 'incorporated' into the predicate (cf. Greenlandic, **Iroquoian**, and – occasionally – **German**, cf. *radfahren* 'to ride a bike.')

References
Humboldt, W. 1836. *Über die Verschiedenheit des menschlichen Sprachbaus*. Berlin. (Repr. 1963.)
⇒ **incorporation, language typology, polysynthesis**

incorporation

Compound consisting of a (usually nominal) word stem with a verb, forming a complex verb. The incorporated stem expresses a concept and does not refer to a specific entity. Incorporation is a widespread phenomenon among the languages of the world, e.g. the **Altaic** languages.

References
Baker, M. 1988. *Incorporation*. Chicago, IL.
Mithun, M. 1984. The evolution of noun incorporation. *Lg* 60.847–95.
Rosen, S.T. 1989. Two types of noun incorporation: a lexical analysis. *Lg* 65:294–317.
⇒ **word formation**

indefinite pronoun [Lat. *indefinitus* 'unlimited']

Subgroup of **pronouns** which serve to represent a person or thing without specifying gender (*one, everyone, someone*) and/or number (*everyone, some, no one*); their **reference**, however, may be definite (e.g. *everyone, no one*). *Everyone* and *someone* function only as noun phrases, while *something, all,* and *some* can occur alone or combined with nouns, e.g.

All were present vs *All gold glitters*. There is a fluid border between indefinite pronouns and indefinite **numerals** (*all, several, few*).

References
⇒ **determiner, quantification**

independent clause ⇒ main clause

index [Lat. 'something that shows, indicator']

In the **semiotics** of C.S. Peirce, a class of **signs** in which the relation between the sign and that which it designates does not rest on convention (⇒ **symbol**) or similarity (⇒ **icon**), but on a direct real (causal) relationship to the singular object actually present. An index may be thought of as a 'symptom' of the object it refers to. The comprehension of a sign as an index may be based on experience: a fever is an index for an underlying illness, while smoke is an index of fire.

References
⇒ **semiotics**

index field of language

In K. Bühler's **two-field theory**, the person–space–time structure of a particular situation with the **I–now–here origo** as the origin of the co-ordinates for subjective orientation, which can be realized by various deictic means (⇒ **deixis**): (a) within the perceptive situation of the speaker and hearer via 'demonstratio ad oculos' (visual presentation), such as by means of gesture or the demonstrative and personal pronouns; (b) in the context of speech through **anaphora**, i.e. through the contextual use of deictic particles; and (c) in the domain of memory and fantasy through the so-called 'deixis of the fantasm.'

References
⇒ **axiomatics of linguistics**

indexical expression ⇒ deictic expression

Indic ⇒ Indo-Aryan

indicative

Verbal **mood** which portrays the state of affairs described by the verb as 'real.' In contrast to **subjunctive** and **imperative**, the indicative is considered the most basic mood and is used to express neutral, objective statements. (⇒ *also* **modality**)

References
⇒ **modality**

indirect interrogative clause [Lat. *interrogare* 'to ask']

Relative clause introduced by an interrogative pronoun (*who, where, why*), as well as such words as *if*, *how*, etc., that is dependent on a main clause: *He wanted to know why she had called him*. In contrast to direct interrogatives, indirect interrogatives cannot occur independently.

indirect object

Syntactic function which can be expressed morphologically, positionally, and/or structurally, depending on the language type. The most common way to express the indirect object morphologically is through the **dative** case, although accusative and genitive complements (e.g. when they are treated as second objects) are sometimes treated as indirect objects. In some languages (e.g. English, the **Romance languages**) the function of the dative is taken over by a preposition (e.g. Fr. *à*, Span., Ital. *a*, Eng. *to*, e.g. *I gave it to him*). In contrast to a direct object, the indirect object in many languages (e.g. **German, French**) cannot occur as the subject in passive constructions: *Philip hilft ihm* 'Philip is helping him' vs *Er wurde geholfen* 'He was helped'. In languages where indirect objects are not marked by case or adposition, there are different opinions as to the structural position of indirect objects. Thus, for the sentence *John gave Mary the book*, one finds analyses where both *Mary* and *the book* are considered to be indirect objects (see Ziv and Sheintuch 1979).

Some typical semantic functions of indirect objects include the recipient with verbs of giving and taking, the **benefactive** ($\Rightarrow$ **dative**), or the experiencer of a state (*This occurred to me*). Since the formal and semantic criteria for indirect objects are more diverse and heterogeneous than those for subjects and direct objects, the usefulness of this term has been questioned, both in regard to a specific language (Ziv and Sheintuch 1979) as well as for universal grammar (Faltz 1978). ($\Rightarrow$ *also* **syntactic function**)

References
Dryer, M. 1986. Primary objects, secondary objects and antidative. *Lg* 62.808–45.
Faltz, L.M. 1978. On indirect objects in universal syntax. *CLS* 14.76–87.
Ziv, Y. and G. Sheintuch. 1979. Indirect objects reconsidered. *CLS* 15.390–403.
$\Rightarrow$ **syntactic function**

indirect speech $\Rightarrow$ direct vs indirect discourse

indirect speech act

Type of speech act, in which the **illocution** literally expressed by the sentence type (or additional base indicators) of the uttered expression differs from the illocution that was actually performed (i.e. from the 'primary'

illocution). Thus, the combination of features [main verb in the indicative; verb in second place; lack of question word in stressed position; independent clause; falling intonation] in the sentence *There is the door* indicates a declarative sentence whose content seems merely to establish a precondition for the performance of some speech act involving a door. Under certain circumstances, however, the utterance of the sentence can be meant and understood as an order for the addressee to leave the room. The command is indirectly performed through the assertion. The interpretation or reconstruction of the indirect speech act is based primarily on the **maxims of conversation** formulated by Grice (see Grice 1975) and on the mechanism of conversational **implicature**. ($\Rightarrow$ *also* **speech act theory**)

References
Grice, H.P. 1975. Logic and conversation. In P. Cole and H.L. Morgan (eds), *Syntax and semantics*, vol. 3: *Speech acts*, New York. 41–58. (Orig. 1968.)
Searle, J.R. 1975. Indirect speech acts. In P. Cole and J.L. Morgan (eds), *Syntax and semantics* vol. 3: *Speech acts*. New York. 344–69. (Orig. 1968.)
$\Rightarrow$ **maxims of conversation, speech act theory**

Indo-Aryan (*also* Indic)

Branch of **Indo-European** which belongs to the **Indo-Iranian** subgroup, with over thirty languages, some of which contain numerous dialects; in total about 650 million speakers. The most significant languages are **Hindi-Urdu** (over 220 million speakers, official language of India and Pakistan respectively), **Bengali** (approx. 150 million speakers, official language of Bangladesh), **Panjabi** (approx. 45 million speakers), **Marathi** (approx. 52 million speakers), Bihari (a group of languages, approx. 37 million speakers), Gujarati (approx. 33 million speakers), Rajasthani (approx. 25 million speakers), Assamese (approx. 12 million speakers), Sindhi (approx. 12 million speakers, Pakistan), Singhalese (approx. 11 million speakers, official language of Sri Lanka), Nepali (approx. 9.5 million speakers, official language of Nepal). The oldest known form of Indo-Aryan is **Sanskrit** (richly attested since about 1200 BC in its oldest stage, Vedic, the language of the religious hymns of the Vedas); the older Indo-Aryan languages have developed from the corresponding everyday language, Prakrit. 'Middle Indo-Aryan' is used to refer to the state of the language between the third century BC and the fourth century AD; the most important documents are the Buddhist writings in Pali, the Aśoka inscriptions.
Characteristics: unusual voiced aspirated

plosives such as [bʰ], as well as retroflexes in the sound system.

General

Bloch, J. 1965. *Indo-Aryan from the Vedas to modern times*, trans. by A. Master. Paris.

Gonda, J. 1971. *Old Indian (Handbuch der Orientalistik 2, vol. 1: Die indischen Sprachen, 1)*. Leiden.

Masica, C.P. 1991. *The Indo-Aryan languages*. Cambridge.

Sebeok, T. (ed.) 1969. *Current Trends in Linguistics*, vol. 5: *Linguistics in South Asia*: Part I: *Indo-Aryan languages*. The Hague and Paris. 3–306.

Old Indo-Aryan

MacDonell, A.A. 1910. *Vedic grammar*. Strasburg.

Middle Indo-Aryan

Elizarenkova, T.Y. and V.N. Toporov, 1976. *The Pali language*. Moscow.

Hinüber, O. von. 1986. *Das ältere Mittelindoarische im Überblick*. Vienna.

Mishra, M. 1986. *A comparative and historical Pali grammar*. New Delhi.

Pischel, R. 1900. *Grammatik der Prakrit-Sprachen*. (Trans. as: *A grammar of the Prakrit languages*, by S. Jha. (2nd rev. edn). Delhi, 1981.)

Sen, S. 1960. *A comparative grammar of Middle Indo-Aryan*. Poona.

Warder, A.K. 1991. *Introduction to Pali*, 3rd edn. London.

Woolner, A.C. 1928. *Introduction to Prakrit*, 2nd edn. (Repr. Delhi 1975.)

New Indo-Aryan

Bahl, K.C. 1972. *On the present state of Modern Rajashthani grammar*. Jodhpur.

Barua, P.N.D. 1980. *An intensive course in Assamese*. Mysore.

Beames, J. 1872–9. *Comparative grammar of the modern Aryan languages of India: Hindi, Panjabi, Sindhi, Gujarati, Marathi, Orija and Bangali*, 3 vols. London. (Repr. 1970.)

Cardona, G. 1965. *A Gujarati reference grammar*. Philadelphia, PA.

—— 1974. The Indo-Aryan languages. *Encyclopedia Britannica*, 15th edn, vol. 9, 439–50.

Chatterji, S.K. 1960. *Indo-Aryan and Hindi*. Calcutta.

Clark, T.W. 1977. *Introduction to Nepali*. Cambridge.

Gair, J.W. 1970. *Colloquial Sinhalese clause structures*. The Hague.

Garusinghe, D. 1962. *Sinhalese: the spoken idiom*. Munich.

Geiger, W. 1938. *A grammar of the Sinhalese language*. Colombo.

Grierson, G.A. 1883–6. *Seven grammars of the dialects and subdialects of the Bihari language*. Calcutta.

—— 1903–28. *Linguistic survey of India*, 11 vols. Calcutta. (Repr. Delhi 1968.)

Kavadi, N.B. and F.C. Southworth. 1968. *Spoken Marathi*. Philadelphia, PA.

Lambert, H.M. 1971. *Gujarati language course*. Cambridge.

Matthews, D. 1984. *A course in Nepali*. (2nd edn 1992.) London.

Nair, U. 1991. *An intensive course in Gujarati*. Mysore.

Reynolds, C.H.B. 1980. *Sinhalese: an introductory course*. London.

Srivastava, D. 1962. *Nepali language: its history and development*. Calcutta.

Trumpp, E. 1872. *Grammar of the Sindhi language*. (Repr. Osnabrück 1970.)

Dictionaries

Barua, H.C. 1965. *The Assamese–English dictionary*. Sibsagar.

Carter, C. 1924. *A Sinhalese–English dictionary*. Colombo.

Childers, R.C. 1875. *Dictionary of the Pali language*. London.

Critical Pali dictionary. 1924–. Begun by V. Trenckner. Vol. III, 1 1992. Copenhagen.

Deshpande, P.G. 1984. *Gujarati–English dictionary*, 3rd edn. Ahmedabad.

Moscrop, T. and T. Candy. 1899. A Sinhalese–English dictionary. (Repr. 1987.) Kallupitiya.

Rhys Davids, T.W. and W. Stede (eds) 1921. *The Pali Text Society's Pali–English dictionary*. (Repr. 1979.) London.

Turner, R.L. 1931. *A comparative and etymological dictionary of the Nepali language*. London. (Repr. New Delhi, 1980.)

Turner, R. and D. Rivers. 1966–71. *A comparative dictionary of Indo-Aryan languages*, 3 vols. London.

Etymological dictionaries

Mayrhofer, M. 1956–80. *Kurzgefaßtes etymologisches Wörterbuch des Altindischen/Concise etymological Sanskrit dictionary*, 4 vols. Heidelberg.

—— 1986– . *Etymologisches Wörterbuch des Altindoarischen*. Vol. II, 17, 1995. Heidelberg.

Journals

Bulletin of the Philological Society of Calcutta
Indian Linguistics
⇒ **Sanskrit**

Indo-European (*abbrev.* IE; *also* Indo-Germanic)

Today the most widespread language group in the world. The following branches make up Indo-European: **Indo-Iranian, Tocharian, Armenian, Anatolian, Albanian, Greek, Italic** (and its modern offshoots, the **Romance languages**), **Slavic, Baltic** (the latter possibly form a genetic unity Balto-Slavic), **Germanic**, and **Celtic**. Two of these, Anatolian and Tocharian, are now extinct. Numerous older languages are attested merely in fragments or through other languages (e.g. in names, glosses), e.g. Venetic, Messapic, Phrygian, etc., and their affiliation to the above-listed branches is not always clearly determinable due to their fragmentary documentation. The relative position of the branches to one another is still unclear; it has been suggested that they were spoken as dialects of a **proto-language**, the exact area and time of existence of which, however, still remains under debate (the area north of the Black Sea around 3000 BC has been suggested, but other regions and times equally have been discussed, cf. Lehmann 1990). As yet, it has not been possible to identify the Indo-Europeans for certain with any archeologically attested culture. Many older stages of the language groups are documented, and these form the main subject of Indo-European studies.

Characteristics: strongly **inflectional**, utilizing both affixes and word-internal mutation (**ablaut**). Eight **cases** can be reconstructed, as well as a **gender** system (it is still under debate whether with two or three genders; see also below) and three **numbers** (**singular**, **dual**, **plural**). **Agreement** of the noun with the adjective and of the subject with the verb. **Tense**, **mood**, and **aspect** are generally expressed in the verb by inflectional means. There are still some problems concerning the reconstruction of the category of aspect (see also below). Some modern Indo-European offshoots, e.g. English, have developed into very different types of language.

History of research: it had long been recognized that some European languages exhibit similarities, and some branches, such as the Romance languages, were accepted as genetic units early on. But the actual beginning of the systematic investigation of Indo-European can be traced back to the discovery of the relation of **Sanskrit** and **Persian** (⇒ **Indo-Iranian**) on the one hand and European languages on the other, by Jones in 1788. The nineteenth century witnessed the beginning of academic research, and in the process, the methodology of **historical linguistics** was developed, especially through attempts at describing systematic sound correspondences and the **reconstruction** of an Indo-European proto-language (⇒ *also* **comparative linguistics**). The most influential works were those of Schlegel (1808), Rask (1814–1818), and Bopp (1816), which systematically demonstrate the relatedness of those branches of Indo-European known at that time (based primarily on the consideration of the inflectional systems), as well as the work of Grimm (1819–22), in which systematic **sound laws** between important individual languages (Sanskrit, **Greek**, **Latin**) were postulated. Schleicher (1861–2) was the first to undertake the reconstruction of specific forms of the proto-language; he also did pioneer work on **Lithuanian** (a Baltic language), which in many ways is especially conservative. The succeed-

ing period was marked by differences between the **Neogrammarians** (K. Brugmann, B. Delbrück, H. Osthoff, A. Leskien, K. Verner, early F. de Saussure), on the one hand, who assumed **sound changes** occur without exceptions, i.e. to be inviolable **sound laws**, and attempted to explain apparent irregularities by **analogy**, and other scholars, such as H. Schuchardt, who contested this hypothesis. **Tocharian** was recognized as an Indo-European language in 1908; even though it was spoken far to the east, it shows some similarities to the western branches (⇒ **centum vs satem languages**). At about the same time, it became clear that **Hittite** (an Anatolian language) was also related to the Indo-European languages. E. Sturtevant's suggestion that Hittite occupies a position equal to the rest of the Indo-European languages ('Indo-Hittite hypothesis'), remains controversial; the crucial point is at what stage the separation of Hittite (or rather of Anatolian) from the rest of the Indo-European languages took place, and whether it lost or never possessed certain features of the common proto-language (e.g. a three-gender system or the verbal aspect distinction; see e.g., the contributions in Neu and Meid 1979); in this connection, a temporal stratification of Proto-Indo-European has been proposed by some scholars (see e.g., the contributions in Dunkel *et al.* 1994). Hittite also played an important role in the reconstruction of the Indo-European sound system (⇒ **laryngeal theory**).

In the first half of the twentieth century, research centered mainly on the phonology and morphology of the Indo-European languages. In more recent times, issues of the syntax of the proto-language have moved into the focus of attention again as well (e.g. Lehmann 1974; Hettrich 1988). But phonology and morphology remain important fields of research: a reconstruction of the plosive system that differs from the traditional system is discussed (see the suggestion of glottalized sounds by Gamkrelidze and Ivanov 1973 and Hopper 1973; see also Gamkrelidze and Ivanov 1984; for a bibliographical overview of this theory see Salmons 1993). According to this view, Old Indic would then be innovative and Germanic especially conservative (⇒ **Grimm's law**); however, this theory remains under debate. Also, the role of **stress** in morphology has been studied more thoroughly; one particular line of research was begun by Kuiper (1942) and terminologically developed by Hoffmann in his lectures (see Eichner 1973; see also, e.g., Narten 1968, Strunk 1985, Schindler 1975; for further bibliographical references see Szemerényi 1990: 171). Questions relating to the verbal system, e.g. the development of the moods (e.g. Hoffmann, 1967; Rix 1986) and of the aspect distinction have been investigated, the latter also in connnection with the position of Hittite (see e.g. Cowgill 1974, Strunk 1984). For detailed overviews see Szemerényi 1985, Szemerényi 1990 and Lehmann 1990, all with extensive bibliographies.

Pioneer works, general works and overviews
Bader, F. (ed.) 1994. *Langues indo-européennes.* Paris.
Baldi, P. 1983. *An Introduction to the Indo-European languages.* Carbondale, IL.
Beekes, R.S.P. 1995. *Comparative Indo-European linguistics. An introduction.* Amsterdam.
Bopp, F. 1816. *Über das Conjugationssystem der Sanskritsprache in Vergleichung mit jenem der griechischen, lateinischen, persischen und germanischen Sprache.* Frankfurt-am-Main. (Repr. Hildesheim and New York, 1975.) (English: F. Bopp. 1845-1853. *A Comparative grammar of the Sanscrit, Zend, Greek, Latin, Lithuanian, Gothic, German, and Sclavonic languages,* (trans. E.B. Eastwick; repr. 1985, London.))
Gamkrelidze, T. and V.V. Ivanov. 1984. *Indoevropejskij jazyk i indoevropejcy.* Tblisi. (*Indo-European and Indo-Europeans.* trans. J. Nichols, vol. I. Berlin and New York 1995.)
Giacolone, A. and P. Ramat. 1996. *The Indo-European languages.* London.
Grimm, J. 1819-37. *Deutsche Grammatik,* 4 parts. Göttingen (Facsimile printing of the 2nd edn of Berlin 1870/8. Hildesheim, 1967).
Lehmann, W.P. 1990. The current thrust of Indo-European Studies. *General Linguistics* 30.1-52. (German extended version: Die gegenwärtige Richtung der indogermanistischen Forschung. Transl. by K. Wöbking. Budapest 1992).
——— 1993. *Theoretical bases of Indo-European linguistics.* London.
Lockwood, W.B. 1972. *A panorama of Indo-European languages.* London.
Meillet, A. 1903. *Introduction à l'étude comparative des langues indo-européennes.* Paris. (8th edn 1937, repr. 1964.)
Rask, R.K. 1818. *Undersögelse om det gamle nordiske eller islandske sprogs oprindelse.* Copenhagen. (*A grammar of the Icelandic or Old Norse tongue,* trans. G.W. Dasent. Amsterdam, 1976.)
Schlegel, F. 1808. *Über die Sprache und Weisheit der Indier.* Heidelberg. (Repr. Amsterdam, 1977.)
Schleicher, A. 1861-2. *Compendium der vergleichenden Grammatik der indogermanischen Sprachen.* Weimar. (*A compendium of the comparative grammar of the Indo-European, Sanskrit, Greek and Latin languages,* trans. H. Bendall. London, 1874-7.)
Schmalstieg, W.R. 1980. *Indo-European linguistics: a new synthesis.* University Park, PA and London.
Szemerényi, O. 1990. *Einführung in die vergleichende Sprachwissenschaft,* 4th rev. edn. Darmstadt. (1st edn 1970.)
——— 1985. Recent developments in Indo-European linguistics. *TPS* 1-71.

Different research areas
Cowgill, W. 1974. More evidence for Indo-Hittite: the tense–aspect systems. In L. Heilmann, (ed.) Bologna. vol. 2, 557-70.
Dunkel, G.E. *et al.* (eds) 1994. *Früh-, Mittel-, Spätindogermanisch. Akten der IV. Fachtagung der Indogermanischen Gesellschaft, Zürich 1992.* Wiesbaden.
Eichner, H. 1973. Die Etymologie von heth. mehur. *MSS* 31.53-107.
Gamkrelidze, T. 1981. Language typology and language universals and their implications for the reconstruction of the Indo-European stop system. In Y. Arbeitman and A.R. Bomhard (eds), *Essays in historical linguistics in honor of J.A. Kerns.* Amsterdam. 571-609.
Gamkrelidze, T. and V. Ivanov. 1973. Sprachtypologie und die Rekonstruktion der geminindogermanischen Verschlüsse. *Phonetica* 27.150-6.
Hettrich, H. 1988. *Untersuchungen zur Hypotaxe im Vedischen.* Berlin and New York.
Hoffmann, K. 1967. *Der Injunktiv im Veda.* Heidelberg.
Hopper, P. 1973. Glottalized and murmured occlusives in Indo-European. *Glossa* 7.141-66.
Krahe, H. 1972. *Grundzüge der vergleichenden Syntax der indogermanischen Sprachen,* ed. W. Meid and H. Schmeja. Innsbruck.
Kiparsky, P. 1973. The inflectional accent in IE. *Lg* 49.794-849.
Kuiper, F.B.J. 1942. *Notes on Vedic noun inflection.* Amsterdam.
Lehmann, W.P. 1974. *Proto-Indo-European syntax.* Austin, TX.
Narten, J. 1964. *Die sigmatischen Aoriste im Veda.* Wiesbaden.
——— 1968. Zum 'proterodynamischen Wurzelpräsens'. In J.C. Heesterman *et al.* (eds), *Pratidānam: Indian, Iranian and Indo-European studies presented to F.B.J. Kuiper on his sixtieth birthday.* The Hague. 9-19.
Neu, E. and W. Meid (eds) 1979. *Hethitisch und Indogermanisch: vergleichende Studien zur historischen Grammatik und zur dialektgeographischen Stellung der indogermanischen Sprachgruppe Altkleinasiens.* Innsbruck.
Rix, H. 1986. *Zur Entstehung des urindogermanischen Modussystems.* Innsbruck.
Salmons, J.C. 1993. *The glottalic theory: survey and synthesis.* Mclean, VA.
Schindler, J. 1975. L'apophonie des thèmes indo-europeénnes en -n/n. *BSL* 70.1-10.
Strunk, K. 1984. Probleme der Sprachrekonstruktion und das Fehlen zweier Modi im Hethitischen. *Incontri Linguistici* 9.135-52.
——— 1985. Flexionskategorien mit akrostatischem Akzent und die sigmatischen Aoriste. In B. Schlerath and V. Rittner (eds), *Grammatische Kategorien: Funktion und Geschichte. Akten der VII. Fachtagung der Indogermanischen Gesellschaft, Berlin 1983.* Wiesbaden. 490-514.
Vennemann, T. (ed.) 1989. *The new sound of Indo-European: essays in phonological reconstruction.* Berlin.

Grammars

Brugmann, K. and B. Delbrück. 1886–1900. *Grundriß der vergleichenden Grammatik der indogermanischen Sprachen*, 5 vols (in several parts). Strasburg. (English: K. Brugmann, 1888–95. *Comparative grammar of the Indo-Germanic languages*, trans. J. Wright, R.S. Conway, and W.H.D. Rouse, 5 vols. Strassburg. (Repr. 1972.)

Hirt, H. 1921–37. *Indogermanische Grammatik*. Heidelberg.

Indogermanische Grammatik. 3 vols: vol. I: W. Cowgill, *Einleitung*, M. Mayrhofer, *Lautlehre*, 1986; vol. II: J. Kuryłowicz, *Akzent, Ablaut*, 1968; vol. III: C. Watkins, *Formenlehre*, part 1: *Geschichte der Verbalflexion*, 1969. Heidelberg.

Krahe, H. 1943. *Indogermanische Sprachwissenschaft*. Berlin. (3rd rev. ed. in 2 vols 1958 and 1959; 5th ed. Vol. I 1966).

Archeology, culture and history

Benveniste, E. 1969. *Le Vocabulaire des institutions Indo-Européennes*, 2 vols. Paris. (transl. as *Indo-European language and society*. Coral Gables, FL, 1973.)

Gimbutas, M. 1970. Proto-Indo-European culture: the Kurgan culture during the fifth, fourth, and third millennia BC. In G. Cardona *et al.* (eds), *Indo-European and Indo-Europeans*. Philadelphia, PA. 155–97.

Mallory, J.P. 1989. *In search of the Indo-Europeans: language, archaeology and myth*. London.

Polomé, E. (ed.) 1982. *The Indo-Europeans in the fourth and third millennium*. Ann Arbor, MI.

Polomé, E.C. and Winter, W. (eds) 1992. *Reconstructing languages and cultures*. Berlin and New York.

Renfrew, C. 1987. *Archeology and language: the puzzle of Indo-Eruopean origins*. London.

Scherer, A. (ed.) 1968. *Urheimat der Indogermanen*. Darmstadt.

Schlerath, B. 1973. *Die Indogermanen*. Innsbruck.

Thieme, P. 1953. *Die Heimat der indogermanischen Gemeinsprache*. Mainz.

Dictionaries

Buck, C.D. 1949. *A dictionary of selected synonyms in the principal Indo-European languages*. Chicago, IL.

Pokorny, J. 1948–59. *Indogermanisches etymologisches Wörterbuch*. Bern. (3rd edn Tübingen, 1994.)

Watkins, C. (ed.) 1985. *The American Heritage dictionary of Indo-European roots*. Boston, MA.

Bibliography

'Indogermanische Chronik' (Bibliography of Indo-European studies), in *Die Sprache*, since vol. 13, 1967.

Journals

Etudes Indo-Européennes
Bulletin de la Société de Linguistique de Paris
Münchener Studien zur Sprachwissenschaft
Indogermanische Forschungen (IF)
Die Sprache
Zeitschrift für Vergleichende Sprachforschung (now:

Historische Sprachwissenschaft/Historical Linguistics)
The Journal of Indo-European Studies

Indo-Germanic ⇒ Indo-European

Indo-Iranian

Branch of **Indo-European** consisting of two main branches, **Indo-Aryan** and **Iranian**, as well as **Dardic**.

Characteristics: merger of IE *e, o, a* to *a*, which led to the loss of qualitative **ablaut** and the heavy use of quantitative ablaut (e.g. Skt *sádas* 'seat,' *sādáyati* 'he/she sets') as well as numerous **glosses**, e.g. the name which the speakers of these languages used for themselves, *Árya* 'Aryan.'

References

Morgenstierne, G. 1929–56. *Indo-Iranian frontier languages*, 3 vols. Oslo.

Journal

Indo-Iranian Journal.
⇒ **Indo-Aryan, Indo-European, Iranian**

Indonesian

Official language of Indonesia, based on Malay (⇒ **Malayo-Polynesian**), with over 100 million speakers (mostly as a second language).

Characteristics: simple sound system, nominal classifiers (e.g. *se-ekor ayam* 'one tail hen'); optional expression of plurals by reduplication of the entire word (e.g. *potong* 'piece,' *potong-potong* 'pieces'); well-developed **honorific** markers by means of 'distinguishing articles'; developed voice system (marking of transitivity), various passive forms (for nouns vs pronouns, **statal passive**), no clear class differences between verbs and nouns. Word order SVO; strict postspecification in the noun phrase. Numerous loan words from **Sanskrit** and **Arabic**.

Reference

MacDonald, R.R. and S. Dardjowidjojo. 1967. *A student's reference grammar of modern formal Indonesian*. Washington, DC.

Indo-Pacific ⇒ Papuan

inductive definition ⇒ definition

inessive [formed from Lat. *in* 'in' + *esse* 'to be']

Morphological case in some languages (e.g. **Finnish**) which describes an object as being located 'in' a place (⇒ **adessive**).

inference

1 Cognitive process in **text processing** that involves filling in or expanding the semantic representation of a text (⇒ **text basis**) by using

its **implications** and **presuppositions**, i.e. by using content which, though unspoken, is necessary for comprehension (intended inference), and by using one's own speaker/hearer knowledge (which is stored in a **schema**) about the content of the text (elaborative inference). Textual content and knowledge about the text added inferentially coalesce in the memory and cannot be clearly distinguished when the text is reconstructed.

References
Balota, D.A. *et al.* (eds) 1990. *Comprehension processes in reading*. Hillsdale, NJ.
Garrod, S. *et al.* 1988. Thematic subjecthood and cognitive constraints on discourse structure. *JPrag* 12.519–34.
Nicholas, D.W. *et al.* 1981. Towards a taxonomy of inferences. In F. Wilkening *et al.* (eds) *Information integration by children*. Hillsdale, NJ.
Rickheit, G. and H. Kock. 1983. Inference processes in text comprehension. In G. Rickheit and M. Bock (eds), *Psycholinguistic studies in language processing*. Berlin. 182–206.
Sperber, S. and D. Wilson. 1986. *Relevance: communication and cognition*. Cambridge, MA.
Van de Velde, R.G. 1988. Inference as (de)compositional principles. In J.S. Petöfi (ed.), *Text and discourse constitution*. Berlin. 283–314.
Van Dijk, T.A. and W. Kintsch. 1983. *Strategies of discourse comprehension*. Orlando, FL.
⇒ **text processing**

2 ⇒ **inference rule**

inference rule

In **propositional logic** (⇒ **formal logic**), a rule that indicates which conclusion can be drawn from the given **propositions** (= premises). (⇒ *also* **rule of inference**, **rule of negative inference**)

References
⇒ **formal logic**

inferential

Type of construction that expresses a value for the grammatical parameter of **evidentiality** and marks the content of a statement as being inferred from various premises. In English, constructions with the modal verb *must* are sometimes used inferentially, e.g. in *That must be Philip*, when the doorbell rings and if no one other than Philip is expected. The so-called inferential in **Turkish** (meaning 'one says' or 'I presume') is actually both an inferential and a **quotative**.

References
⇒ **evidentiality**

inferential semantics

Collective term for all types of logical and intuitive deductions that can be deduced from a given statement and are the object of logical and/or semantic description. For example, from the sentence *Caroline is a woman* one may infer 'Caroline is female,' 'Caroline is an adult,' and 'Caroline is a human being.' (⇒ *also* **allegation**, **equivalence**, **implication**, **implicature**, **presupposition**)

References
Allan, K. 1986. *Linguistic meaning*, 2 vols. London.
⇒ **semantics**

infinitive [Lat. *infinitivus* 'having no limits,' 'not specified']

Nominal verb form which has functional and formal properties of both nouns and verbs: verbal properties are **government** (*the reading of the book*), **aspect** (*to read* vs *to have read*), **voice** (*to read* vs *to be read*); because of its nominal properties, the verbal categories **person** and **number** are lost. In addition, infinitives can be used as nouns, i.e. in the syntactic function of a noun phrase (e.g. *To eat is to live*). On other nominal forms of verbs, ⇒ **gerund**, **gerundive**, **participle**, **supine**.

infinitive construction

Syntactic construction which contains an infinitive, e.g. *Philip wants to go*. In older forms of **transformational grammar**, such sentences were formerly derived via **equi-NP deletion** from more complex structures which contain NPs with the same reference: *Philip wants/ Philip goes*. By deleting the subject of the object clause, the agreement transformation which links the person and number of the subject to the verb is blocked, and the verb of the embedded object clause is realized as an infinitive construction (⇒ **complementation**). In more recent forms of transformational grammar, the subject of an infinitive is analyzed as a phonetically empty pronoun (⇒ **control**). Infinitive constructions may function as constituents and thus can be realized as **subjects**, **objects**, predicate nominals, **adverbials**, or **attributes**. (⇒ *also* **equi-NP-deletion**, **raising**)

References
⇒ **transformational grammar**

infix [Lat. *infigere* 'to set firmly into']

Word formation morpheme that is inserted into the **stem**, e.g. *-n-* in Lat. *iungere* 'to tie' vs *iugum* ('yoke') or the *-t-* in the reflexive function between the first and second consonants of the root in the eighth binyan of classical Arabic, cf. *ftarag* 'to separate,' *ftarad* 'to place before oneself.' **Ablaut** and **umlaut**

are often considered infixes. (⇒ *also* **affix**)

References
Matthews, P.H. 1972. *Inflectional morphology.* Cambridge.
McCarthy, J. 1981. A prosodic theory of non-concatenative morphology. *LingI* 12.373–418.
⇒ **word formation**

INFL node

An abbreviation for 'inflection,' this is an abstract representation of the morphological features of the subject via agreement and the predicate via tense as a syntactic category in a **tree diagram.** This category was introduced by N. Chomsky in **Government and Binding theory** and comprises features of agreement (in person and number, and gender for some languages) of the verb and tense. In earlier versions of **generative grammar** this was accomplished by the **auxiliary.** The **phrase structure rule** S → NP INFL VP (earlier versions required S → NP VP) makes it possible to regard the sentences as a projection of INFL, in agreement with **X-bar theory**, not of NP or VP. Since considering S to be a projection of NP or of VP led to internal theoretical problems, Chomsky postulated the analysis of the category S as a projection of the INFL node. That is to say, S is an element of the same category as INFL, but of greater complexity than INFL. The above-mentioned phrase structure rule is, according to Chomsky, therefore simply an abbreviation for the more explicit rule INFL¹ → NP INFL⁰ VP.

References
⇒ **transformational grammar**, **X-bar theory**

inflection [Lat. *inflexio* 'bending, modification'] (*also* accidence)

Word stems (⇒ **lexemes**) of particular **parts of speech** are realized in morphologically different **word forms** that regularly mark different syntactic and semantic functions: declination (nouns), conjugation (verbs), comparison (adjectives). The complete set of inflectional forms of a word constitute its inflectional **paradigm.** Such paradigms categorize inflectional classes according to parallels in and predictability of morphological forms. Inflection can occur in different morphological forms in English, such as through a change in the stem (*sing > sang*) or through the addition of particular endings (*worked, dreamt*). In some cases, inflectional endings may signal different **inflectional categories** (e.g. *-s* in *works* signals both present tense in the verb and plural in the noun). In other languages (e.g. Greek, Latin, Gothic), **reduplication** is used as a means for inflection (Goth. *haihait* 'was called'). Regardless of certain borderline cases (such as comparatives and participles) a distinction is generally drawn between inflection (= formation of word forms) and **word formation** (= formation of word stems) as separate areas of study in **morphology.** In more recent studies on **word syntax**, the distinctness in function of inflectional vs derivational affixes has been subject to doubt (⇒ **word structure**).

References
Anderson, S. 1982. Where's morphology? *LingI* 13.571–612.
Carstairs-McCarthy, A. 1987. *Allomorphy in inflection.* London.
Di Sciullo, A.M. and E. Williams. 1987. *On the definition of word.* Cambridge, MA.
Lapointe, S. 1984. The representation of inflectional morphology within the lexicon. *Proceedings of the Northeastern Linguistics Society* 14.190–204.
Plank, F. 1991. *Paradigms: the economy of inflection.* Berlin and New York.
⇒ **morphology**

inflectional category

Semantic syntactic functions that are characterized according to word class and rule-governed along with the realization of word stems, e.g. **gender, case, number, person, tense.** These inflectional categories are represented by lexical inflectional features, such as gender and inflectional class, on the one hand, and grammatical features such as number, case, and tense on the other. (⇒ *also* **morphology**)

inflectional language

Classificational category of languages established by von Humboldt (1836) based on morphological criteria. In inflectional languages, the morphemes tend formally towards fusion (i.e. they influence and are influenced by adjoining morphemes); functionally they tend towards **polysemy** (i.e. one morpheme corresponds to more than one meaning or semantic feature). In contrast to **agglutinating languages**, an exact segmentation of root and derivational morpheme is not always possible. Many **Indo-European** and **Semitic** languages are inflectional languages, e.g. **Lithuanian:** *draug-as* 'friend (nom. sg.),' *drarug-o* 'friend (gen. sg.),' *draũg-ui* 'friend (dat. sg.),' *draug-è* 'friend (loc. sg.),' *draug-aĩ* 'friend (nom. pl.),' *draug-ū* 'friend (gen. pl.),' *draug-áms* 'friend (dat. pl.),' *draug-uosè* 'friend (loc. pl.)'

References
Humboldt, W. von 1836. *Über die Verschiedenheit des menschlichen Sprachbaues.* Berlin. (Repr. 1963.)
⇒ **language typology**

information

1 In the qualitative sense, that which can be deduced from observing a carrier of information (i.e. from perceiving a symptom or sign) about the object of information. For example, a frosty window carries the information that it is freezing outside.

2 In the technically defined sense of **information theory**, a quantifiable dimension that correlates with the probability that a particular occurrence will take place: the smaller the probability that a particular occurrence will take place, the higher the information value of the occurrence (which is measured in **bits**). Contrasting with the colloquial use of 'information' in the sense of 'facts' or 'details,' the use of the term in communication technology is abstracted from the semantic content or meaning of the information. The tests and observations of **statistical linguistics** are based on the concept of information as a dimension of probability of occurrence.

References
⇒ **information theory**, **statistical linguistics**

information-based instruction ⇒ content-based instruction

information linguistics ⇒ computational linguistics, information theory

information theory (*also* cybernetics)

Mathematical theory that is concerned with the statistical regularities (formal structure and disruptive factors) in the transmission and processing of **information**[2] and which can be viewed as a discipline fundamental to various sciences (among them biology, psychology, theoretical linguistics). Numerous terms that play a role in the description of linguistic regularities are tied to knowledge about and definitions of information (⇒ **bit**, **code**, **data**, **entropy**, **communication**, **redundancy**, **sign**). The development of a theory of a qualitative concept of information is still in its infancy; it belongs to the investigational agenda of **situation semantics**. (⇒ *also* **computational linguistics**, **mathematical linguistics**)

References
Shannon, C.E. and W. Weaver. 1949. *The mathematical theory of communication.* Urbana, IL.

Bibliography
Stumpers, F.L. 1953. *A bibliography of information theory – communication theory – cybernetics.* Cambridge, MA.
⇒ **computational linguistics**, **mathematical linguistics**

ingressive [Lat. *ingredi* 'to go into,' 'to begin']

1 Verbal **aspect**, subcategory of non-duratives (⇒ **durative** vs **non-durative**), which indicates the sudden start of an action: *to burst into flames, to explode.* For the term denoting a gradual change of state, ⇒ **inchoative**.

References
⇒ **aspect**

2 **Speech sound** formed, in contrast with an **egressive**, when air flows into the initiating air chamber. As a rule, **clicks** are ingressive; **implosives** are by definition ingressive. If air flows into the lungs, then the ingressive is said to be an **inspiratory** sound. (⇒ *also* **phonetics**)

References
⇒ **phonetics**

Ingrian ⇒ Finno-Ugric

inherent semantic relation

Term coined by Porzig (1934) to denote the syntagmatic relationship of **compatibility** between pairs of linguistic expressions with a unidirectional semantic implication, such as *bark : dog, blond : hair.* This type of semantic relation plays an especially significant role in metaphorical transfer (e.g. *barking cough*). Inherent semantic relations are, in great part, dependent on **idiolect**. Paradigmatic semantic relations, such as those studied by J. Trier in his **lexical field theory**, must be distinguished from these contextually dependent semantic relations. (⇒ *also* **selection restriction**)

Reference
Porzig, W. 1934. Wesenhafte Bedeutungsbeziehungen. PBB 58.70–97.

inheritance

1 In **word formation**, process of transferring morphological and syntactic characteristics of the parts to the whole in a regular fashion. Also, the argument structure of an underlying verb is inherited by a new derivation, cf. *to develop pictures – the development of pictures.* Selkirk (1982) traces argument inheritance back to lexical operations defined in the lexical analysis of an affix, while Toman (1983) and Lieber (1991) assume the partial transfer of subcategorization features on the basis of the categorial information of the head by means of percolation. For Moortgat (1985) and, following him, Di Sciullo and Williams (1987) and Bierwisch (1989), the derived argument structure arises from the **functional composition** of the argument structure of an affix with that of its basic category. Fanselow (1988), on the

other hand, takes the position that the apparently formal inheritance of arguments really represents a process of the semantic interpretation ($\Rightarrow$ **possible word**).

References
Bierwisch, M. 1989. Event nominalizations. In W. Motsch (ed.), *Wortstruktur und Satzstruktur*. Berlin. 1–73.
Borer, H. 1991. The causative–inchoative alternation: a case study in parallel morphology. *The Linguistic Review* 8.119–58.
Di Sciullo, A.M. and E. Williams. 1987. *On the definition of word*. Cambridge, MA.
Fanselow, G. 1988. 'Word syntax' and semantic principles. In G. Booij and J. van Marle (eds), *Yearbook of morphology*. Dordrecht. 95–122.
Levin, B. and M.R. Hovav. 1991. Wiping the slate clean: a lexical semantic exploration. *Cognition* 41.123–51.
Lieber, R. 1991. *Deconstructing morphology*. Chicago, IL.
Moortgat, M. 1985. Functional composition and complement inheritance. In G.A.L. Hoppenbrouwers *et al.* (eds), *Meaning and the lexicon*. Dordrecht. 39–48.
Reis, M. 1988. Word structure and argument inheritance: how much is semantics? *LSt* (series A) 179.53–67.
Selkirk, E. 1982. *The syntax of words*. Cambridge, MA.
Toman, J. 1983. *Wortsyntax*. Tübingen.
Williams, E. 1981. Argument structure and morphology. *LRev* 1.81–114.

2 In **artificial intelligence**, the assumption of traits from a superordinate concept by a subconcept. This behavior, which was originally restricted to conceptual hierarchies in **semantic networks**, was later introduced into other formalisms for **knowledge representation**, e.g. that of the **frame**. The most essential problem is in determining if or when **default reasoning** must be used. Inheritance is an essential principle of **unification grammar**.

References
Brachman, M. and J. Schmolze. 1985. An overview of the KL-ONE knowledge representation system. *CSc* 9.171–216.
Daelmans, W. and G. Gazdar. 1992. Inheritance in natural language processing. *CL* 18.
Touretzky, D.S. 1986. *The mathematics of inheritance systems*. London.

initiation $\Rightarrow$ **airstream mechanism**

initive $\Rightarrow$ **ingressive**

injection $\Rightarrow$ **function**

injective [Lat. *inicere* 'to throw in']
Ingressive speech sound formed with the pharyngeal **airstream mechanism**. While the larynx is raised in an **ejective**, it is lowered in an injective. As in an ejective, the glottis is closed and the vocal chords are unable to vibrate. **Implosives** are similar to injectives. ($\Rightarrow$ *also* **articulatory phonetics, speech sound**)

References
$\Rightarrow$ **phonetics**

injunctive [Lat. *iniungere* 'to impose']
1 Collective term for all linguistic constructions which express a 'command' such as the **imperative**.

2 In **Indo-European** linguistics, verb forms which are not specified in respect to tense or mood, e.g. without an **augment**. It is used in the older Indo-European languages (e.g. in the earliest documents of **Indo-Iranian**) for the mere mention of an action, for example.

Reference
Hoffmann, K. 1967. *Der Injunktiv im Veda*. Heidelberg.

inner derivation $\Rightarrow$ **derivation**

I–now–here origo [Lat. *origo* 'starting-point, origin']
In Bühler's (1934) linguistic theory the origin of the co-ordinates of the personal, spatial, and time dimension of utterances in speech situations. In contrast to words of naming, which always denote the same referents, expressions of the I–now–here origo (*I, you, yesterday, tomorrow, there, here*) can denote different referents in different situations, e.g. *I* refers to the given user of the word in a given speech act. ($\Rightarrow$ *also* **axiomatics of linguistics, deixis, index field of language**)

References
Bühler, K. 1934. *Sprachtheorie*. Jena. (Repr. Stuttgart, 1965.)
Innis, R.E. (trans.) 1982. *Karl Bühler: Semiotic foundations of language theory*. New York.

input hypothesis $\Rightarrow$ **natural approach**

input model $\Rightarrow$ **natural approach**

inspiratory [Lat. *inspirare* 'to draw breath']
Speech sound formed by inhaling. Inspiratory sounds occur only paralinguistically ($\Rightarrow$ **paralinguistics, ingressive**).

instrumental
1 Morphological **case**, e.g. in some **Indo-European** languages, which identifies the means of accomplishing the action expressed in the verb. In languages which lack this case (e.g. **English, German, French**), this meaning is expressed by prepositional phrases (e.g. *work with a hammer*) or sometimes the **dative**.

2 thematic relation ⇒ case grammar

References
⇒ **case**

instrumental clause

Semantically defined clause functioning syntactically as a modal **adverbial**. Instrumental clauses describe the means by which the state of affairs expressed in the main clause is achieved, and are introduced by conjunctions such as *by*: *By carefully dissolving the paint, the original portrait could be restored.* (⇒ *also* **modal clause**)

instrumental noun

Designation for nouns (often derived from verbs) that denote the corresponding instrument: *cleanser, humidifier.* Frequently, there is an overlap between instrumental nouns and nominal agents (⇒ **nomen agentis**) such that one must posit a vague *-er* suffix, cf. (*record*) *player* vs (*football*) *player.*

References
⇒ **word formation**

instrumental phonetics ⇒ experimental phonetics, phonetics

instrumentative (*also* instrumentative verb)

Class of **denominal** verbs that (at least in their literal reading) designate the instrument expressed by the verbal action, e.g. (*to*) *hammer*, (*to*) *vacuum*, (*to*) *brush*. (⇒ *also* **lexical decomposition**)

References
⇒ **word formation**

instrumentative verb ⇒ instrumentative

Insular Celtic ⇒ Celtic

integrational linguistics

Linguistic theory developed by H.H. Lieb that is based on the following premises. (a) Integrative aspect: grammars of individual languages and the terms for their description (such as syntactic unit, syntactic structure, constituent structure, morphological marking categories, etc.) are to be defined as integrative elements of a general language theory. (b) The object of study in integrational linguistics are homogeneous idiolects as individual means of communication; sets of idiolects yield linguistic varieties such as dialects, sociolects, or individual languages such as English or German. (c) The syntacto-semantic interpretation begins with structures close to the surface (in contrast to **transformational grammar**); it is thus also termed **surface syntax**. (d) The syntactic description is based mainly on the traditional syntactic relations of the surface structure, such as **subject**, **object**, etc., as well as on the three most important syntactic means of relations of order, morphological marking and sentence intonation.

References
Lieb, H.H. 1977. *Outline of integrational linguistics.* Berlin
——— 1993. Integrational linguistics. In J. Jacobs *et al.* (eds), *Syntax: an international handbook of contemporary research.* Berlin and New York. 430–68.

intended inference ⇒ inference[2]

intensifier [Lat. *intendere* 'to make stronger']

Elements that are used with other expressions to indicate an intensification of the meaning denoted by the expression they modify; this can happen in various ways (as amplifiers, emphasizers, downtoners, etc.). Both adjectives and adverbs can be used in this function: *a clear victory, clearly wrong.* There are some intensifiers that can be used only in this function (e.g. the prefix *ultra-*). A striking fact is the large number of intensifiers in contemporary speech: *dead wrong, super elegant, ultramodern,* etc., where they are subject to an unusually high rate of wear and tear, which is due to the probably affective component of these elements.

References
Bolinger, D. 1972. *Degree words.* The Hague.
Quirk, R. *et al.,* 1985. *A comprehensive grammar of the English language.* London and New York.
⇒ **word formation**

intension [Lat. *intensio* 'a state of tension']

The intension of a concept (or of a **set**) is defined by indicating the properties or traits that characterize it; the intension corresponds to its content in contrast with its **extension**, which is defined by counting all the elements that fall under the concept. Two predicates are intensionally identical if they mean the same thing in regard to their content, i.e. if they have the same **semantic features** when subjected to **componential analysis**; e.g. *car*/*auto*; *X is the mother of Y* / *Y is the child of X.* They are extensionally identical if they refer to the same class of countable elements as, for example, *evening star*/*morning star*; both expressions refer to Venus, their intensional meaning, however, is different (⇒ **connotation**). The dichotomy of intensional vs extensional semantic analysis goes back to G. Frege's distinction between 'sense' and 'meaning.' It is the same basic distinction between extensional interpretations in **referential semantics** and intensional theories of meaning (cf. **logical semantics**), as they pertain to **categorial grammar** or **Montague grammar**, for example; there is, however, no agreement about the interpretation of intension or 'sense.'

References
Carnap, R. 1947. *Meaning and necessity*. Chicago, IL.
——— 1947. Meaning and synonymy in natural languages. *PhS* 6.33–47.
Cresswell, M.J. 1973. *Logics and languages*. London.
Frege, G. 1892. Über Sinn und Bedeutung. *ZPhK* (new series) 100.25–50. (Repr. in *Kleine Schriften*, ed. I. Angelelli. Darmstadt, 1967. 143–62.)
Lewis, D. 1970. General semantics. *Synthese* 22.18–67.
⇒ **categorial grammar**, **formal logic**, **intensional logic**, **Montague grammar**

intensional

In **formal logic**, property of propositional connections or contexts whose **truth value** depends not only on the truth values of the elementary propositions, but also on their non-logical, semantic content. In contrast to extensional (⇒ **extension**) propositional connections studied in **propositional logic**, such as **conjunction**[3], an intensional propositional connection like *p because q* is true only if both parts of the proposition are true: *It's dark out because there's a new moon* (true) vs *It's dark out, because 7 is a sacred number* (not true).

References
⇒ **formal logic**

intensional context

A context in which the free substitutability of expressions of the same **extension** cannot be carried out without exception. For example, both the sentences *Miss Marple is looking for the murderer in the garden* vs *Miss Marple is looking for Roberts in the garden* have different truth values if Miss Marple does not know that Roberts is in fact the murderer she is looking for. This is true even though the extension (⇒ **reference**, **denotation**) of *the murderer in the garden* and *Roberts* is identical in the context of the example and therefore the expressions are substitutable in extensional contexts *salva veritate* (i.e. without influence on the truth value of the given complete sentence). Intensional contexts are created in natural languages by modal expressions like *it is necessary*, by predicates that relate to propositional attitudes like *believe* and *know*, as well as by some transitive verbs as, e.g. *to seek*, and tense markers (⇒ **intensional verb**).

References
⇒ **intensional logic**

intensional definition ⇒ **intension**

intensional logic

Umbrella term for systems of philosophical logic which, in addition to the logical expressions such as logical particles (⇒ **logical connective**) (*and*, *or*, and others) and **operators** of **formal logic**, use other expressions (that are also important for natural-language semantic analysis) such as *it is necessary that*, and *X believes that*. In contrast with mathematical logical systems (like **propositional logic** and **predicate logic**), which are based on a purely extensional concept of meaning, intensional logic tries to interpret meaning along intensional lines, i.e. the **intension** of an expression is to be understood as the function that determines its **extension** depending on the different possible worlds. For more information on the various systems of intensional logic, ⇒ **deontic logic**, **epistemic logic**, **extension**, **modal logic**, **Montague grammar**, **temporal logic**.

References
Anderson, C.A. 1984. General intensional logic. In D. Gabbay and F. Guenthner (eds), *Handbook of philosophical logic*. Dordrecht. Vol. 2, 355–85.
Benthem, J.V. 1986. *Manual of intensional logic*. Chicago, IL.
Carnap, R. 1947. *Meaning and necessity*. Chicago, IL.
Gamut, L.T.F. 1991. *Logic, grammar and meaning*, vol. 2: *Intensional logic and logical grammar*. Chicago, IL.
Quine, W.V.O. 1953. Quantifiers and propositional attitudes. *JP* 53.177–87.
Thomason, R.H. (ed.) 1974. *Formal philosophy: selected papers of R. Montague*. New Haven, CT.
⇒ **modal logic**, **Montague grammar**

intensional reading ⇒ **attributive vs referential reading**

intensional semantics ⇒ **intensional logic**

intensional verb

Intensional verbs constitute a semantically defined subset of verbs (e.g. *assert*, *believe*, *seek*) with the following properties. (a) In their context, noun phrases are ambiguous, they can be read both attributively as well as referentially (⇒ **attributive vs referential reading**); for example, in *Caroline is looking for a cat with white paws*, *cat* can refer both to any cat with white paws as well as to a particular cat with white paws. (b) In **complement clauses**, noun phrases of the same **extension** (which refer to the same referent) cannot be substituted in all contexts without changing the **truth**

value of the superordinate sentence, cf. *Philip wants to know if Shakespeare is the author of 'Macbeth'* vs *Philip wants to know if Shakespeare is Shakespeare.*

References
⇒ **intensional logic**

intensive

Verbal **aspect** which indicates events characterized by a high degree of intensity: *scream, smash.*

References
⇒ **aspect**

intentionality

According to H.P. Grice and J. Searle a fundamental category of every theory of linguistic meaning; accordingly, linguistic exchanges are essentially acts determined by a definite communicative intention; they are successful to the degree that this intention is recognized.

References
Cohen, P.R., J. Morgan, and M.E. Pollack (eds) 1990. *Intentions in communication.* Cambridge, MA.
Grice, H.P. 1957. Meaning. *PhR* 66.377–88.
———— 1968. Utterer's meaning, sentence-meaning, and word-meaning. *FL* 4.1–18. (Repr. in J. Searle (ed.), *The Philosophy of language.* Oxford, 1971, 54–70.)
Searle, J.R. 1985. *Intentionality.* Cambridge.

interchange (*also* exchange)

In Goffman's terminology, a 'round' of at least two participants in which each makes a move. A move is a term from game theory (⇒ **game-theoretical semantics**) that refers to an action in a set of alternatives that leads to concrete advantages and disadvantages for the participants (cf. a move in a game of chess). A move is a unit that is to be identified neither with a speech act nor with a turn, though it may coincide with them. According to Goffman participants use their communicative abilities to stage appropriate selves. Such activities give rise to and are governed by two kinds of ritual constraints: supportive and remedial interchanges. While supportive interchanges (like *Thanks for your call*) serve to initiate or terminate an interaction, remedial interchanges (like excuses, or explanations) transform the meaning of an action that could be considered an offense or a violation of a constraint.

References
Corsaro, W.A. 1981. Communicative processes in studies of social organization: sociological approaches to discourse analysis. *Text* 1.5–63.
Goffman, E. 1967. *Interaction rituals.* New York.
———— 1971. *Relations in public.* London.
———— 1981. *Forms of talk.* Philadelphia, PA.

interdental [Lat. *inter* 'between,' *dens* 'tooth']

Speech sound classified according to its **articulator** (blade of the tongue = laminal) and its **place of articulation** (upper teeth = dental), e.g. [θ], [ð] in Icelandic [θåð] 'this.' (⇒ *also* **articulatory phonetics**)

References
⇒ **phonetics**

interdependence

In **glossematics**, relation between the mutual precondition of two elements A and B, the presence of A presupposing the presence of B and vice versa. Syntagmatic interdependence (as existing between *she* and *-s* in *she doe-s*) is called **solidarity**; paradigmatic interdependence (as it exists universally between the occurrence of vowels and consonants) is called complementarity (see Hjelmslev 1943: ch. 9).

References
⇒ **glossematics**

interference

The influence of one linguistic system on another in either (a) the individual speaker (⇒ **transfer**) or (b) the **speech community** (⇒ **borrowing, language contact**). In an individual, interference is seen as a source of errors (⇒ **error analysis, contrastive analysis**); in a speech community, as a cause of **language change**. For many linguists, the term 'interference' has come to include the concept of **analogy** (as in 'language-internal interference').

References
⇒ **borrowing, language contact**

interjection [Lat. *intericere* 'to throw between']

Group of words which express feelings, curses, and wishes or are used to initiate conversation (*Ouch!, Darn!, Hi!*). Their status as a grammatical category is debatable, as they behave strangely in respect to morphology, syntax, and semantics: they are formally indeclinable, stand outside the syntactic frame, and have no lexical meaning, strictly speaking. Interjections often have onomatopoeic (⇒ **onomatopoeia**) characteristics: *Brrrrr!, Whoops!, Pow!*

References
⇒ **discourse marker**

interlanguage (*also* approximative system, transitional competence)

The relatively systematic transition from initial knowledge of a language to (near-)native proficiency during the process of language acquisition. Often manifested as an unstable set of productive characteristics, interlanguage includes the rules of both the native language and the target language as well as a set of rules that belongs to neither, but rather manifests universal principles inherent in the language learner's competence.

References
Blum-Kulka, S. and G. Kasper (eds) 1993. *Interlanguage pragmatics*. Oxford.
Davies, A., C. Cripper, and A.P.R. Howatt (eds) 1984. *Interlanguage*, Edinburgh.
Dechert, H.W. and M. Raupach (eds) 1989. *Interlingual processes*. Tübingen.
Eisenstein, M.R. 1989. *The dynamic interlanguage: empirical studies in second language acquisition*. New York.
Nehls, D. (ed.) 1987. *Interlanguage studies*. Heidelberg.
Sato, C.J. 1990. *The syntax of conversation in interlanguage development*. Tübingen.
Selinker, L. 1972. Interlanguage. *IRAL* 10.209–31. (Repr. in D. Nehls (ed.), *Interlanguage studies*. Heidelberg.)
—— 1992. *Rediscovering interlanguage*. London.

Journal
Multilingua.
⇒ **second language acquisition**

interlinear version [MLat. *interlinearis*, from *inter* 'between,' *linearis* 'linear']
The word-for-word translation of a foreign-language text into another language in which the translation is written between the lines of the original text.

Reference
Lehmann, C. 1980. *Guidelines for interlinear morphemic translations: a proposal for standardization*. (Institut für Sprachwissenschaft Universität Köln. Arbeitspapier, 37.) Cologne.

interlingua [Lat. *lingua* 'tongue,' 'language'] (*also* planned language)
Either a completely freely ('*a priori*') invented language or (as in most attempts) a language derived from natural languages ('*a posteriori*') through simplification which is used for international communication. In the 'naturalistic' type of interlingua (e.g. **Esperanto**) the vocabulary is based extensively on words of Germanic and Romance languages, in the 'schematic' type (e.g. **Volapük**) the vocabulary is based upon a relatively small inventory of roots and a number of derivational elements. The learnability and the neutrality of an interlingua as compared to individual natural languages are factors which theoretically determine the acceptance (or non-acceptance) of interlinguas.

References
⇒ **interlinguistics**

interlinguistics
The theory and practice of constructing and evaluating 'artificial' international languages in the sense of **interlinguas**.

References
Aguchi, A. 1989. Towards a clarification of the function and status of international planned languages. In U. Ammon (ed.), *Status and function of languages and language varieties*. Berlin.
Laycock, D.C. and Mühlhäusler, P. 1990. Language engineering: special languages. In N.E. Collinge (ed.), *An encyclopedia of language*. London. 843–75.
Schubert, K. and D. Maxwell (eds) 1989. *Interlinguistics: aspects of the science of planned languages*. Berlin and New York.

Bibliography
Ejsmont, H. and T. Ejsmont. 1986. Enkonduka bibliografio al la problemo de internacia lingva komunikado. (Bibliography of interlinguistics). In T. Ejsmont (ed.), *Internacia lingva kominikado*. Lodž. 135–64.

Journal
Journal of Planned Languages.

interlude ⇒ **syllable**

internal inflection [Lat. *internus* 'within, inside']
Cover term for all forms of grammatical markings in which the **root** or word **stem** is changed, e.g. through **ablaut** (*sing* vs *sang*), **umlaut** (*man* vs *men*), consonant change (*think* vs *thought*), or vowel change (*drink* vs *drench*).

internal language (*also* private speech)
Language form that serves not as verbal communication but rather as a vehicle for thinking. There are different approaches for explaining the function, form, and development of internal language; a detailed discussion can be found in Vygotskij (1934). He characterizes internal language by the 'tendency for shortening and weakening the syntactic segmentation, and making it more dense' (p. 341). (⇒ *also* **egocentric language**, **language acquisition**)

References
Kohlberg, L., J. Yeager, and E. Hjertholm, 1968. Private speech: four studies and a review of theories. *CD* 39.691–736.
Piaget, J. 1923. *Le Langage et la pensée chez l'enfant*. Neuchâtel.
Vygotskij, L.S. 1934. *Denken und Sprechen*. Frankfurt. (5th edn 1974.) (English: *Thought and language*, trans. E. Hanfman and G. Vakar. Cambridge, MA, 1962.)

internal reconstruction ⇒ **reconstruction**

interpolation   [Lat. *interpolatio* 'touching upon, altering']

Changes made to a text by someone other than the original author. **Text criticism** is concerned, among other things, with the investigation and evaluation of interpolation.

References
⇒ **text criticism**

interpretant

In the **semiotics** of C.S. Peirce, a sign by which another sign is comprehended. Thus, *automobile*, *sedan*, *Mercedes Benz*, *convertible*, and others may be interpretants of *car*.

References
⇒ **semiotics**

interpreter

Computer program that translates a higher-level **programming language** (e.g. BASIC, **LISP**, **PROLOG**) from a (problem-oriented) notation into an equivalent lower-level (machine-oriented) notation. In contrast to a **compiler**, the interpreter reads the 'source code' and immediately executes the corresponding operations, which is advantageous for interactively testing parts of programs.

References
⇒ **programming language**

interpreting

The practice of (oral) translation of one language into another. Two types of interpreting are distinguished: (a) simultaneous interpreting, in which smaller semantic units are translated in synchrony with the actual production of the foreign language text; and (b) consecutive interpreting in which a large portion of closed text is translated. (⇒ *also* **translation**)

interpretive semantics

In the framework of **generative grammar**, position held by N. Chomsky, J.J. Katz, and others according to which syntax is considered an autonomous generative component, while the semantic component has a purely interpretive character in that it interprets the syntactically motivated abstract **deep structures** through semantic rules, i.e. gives them one or more readings. The aim of interpretive semantics is to describe the competence of the ideal speaker/hearer who 'can semantically interpret any sentence ... under any of its grammatical derivations. He can determine the number and content of the readings of a sentence, tell whether or not a sentence is semantically anomalous, and decide which sentences ... are paraphrases of each other' (Katz and Fodor 1963: 182). The semantic representation of interpretive semantics rests initially and above all upon three now widely debated hypotheses: (a) the meaning of linguistic expressions can be completely described on the basis of a limited inventory of semantic features of a largely universal nature; (b) the syntactically motivated deep structure supplies all the necessary semantic-syntactic information for the semantic interpretation; and (c) transformations between deep and surface structures are semantically neutral. The semantic theory of interpretive semantics consists of two components, the **lexicon**[3] and **projection rules**. The lexicon supplies both syntactic and semantic information. The semantic information is composed of (a) systematic semantic relationships between individual lexemes and the rest of the vocabulary of the language (⇒ **semantic feature**); (b) the idiosyncratic, non-systematic features (⇒ **distinguisher**); and (c) **selectional features**. The lexicon entries are placed in the syntactic deep structure, with polysemic lexemes (⇒ **polysemy**) having a corresponding number of readings. These potential readings are selected via projection rules on the basis of conditions of grammaticality, and the individual lexical elements are summarized with consideration of their grammatical relations (as depicted in their tree) to the whole meaning of the sentence, that is, they are 'amalgamated' (⇒ **amalgamation**). The concept of interpretive semantics has been criticized on various fronts: for example, D.L. Bolinger questions the status of the distinguisher, Y. Bar-Hillel the claim of universality, and U. Weinreich the whole concept. In addition, interpretive semantics has been vigorously challenged by the proponents of **generative semantics**. Interpretive semantics has been developed further within the **aspects model** of generative grammar.

References
Bierwisch, M. 1967. Some semantic universals of German adjectivals. *FL* 3.1–36.
Bolinger, D.L. 1965. The atomization of meaning. *Lg* 41.555–73.
Chomsky, N. 1965. *Aspects of the theory of syntax*. Cambridge, MA.
—— 1972. *Studies on semantics in generative grammar*. The Hague.
Fiengo, R. 1974. Semantic conditions on surface structure. Dissertation, Cambridge, MA.
Fillmore, C.J. 1969. Types of lexical information. In F. Kiefer (ed.), *Studies in syntax and semantics*. Dordrecht. 109–37.
Jackendoff, R.S. 1972. *Semantic interpretation in generative grammar*. New York.

Katz, J.J. 1966.*The Philosophy of language*. New York.
———— 1967. Recent issues in semantic theory. *FL* 3.124–94.
———— 1970. Interpretative semantics vs generative semantics. *FL* 6.220–59.
———— 1972. *Semantic theory*. New York.
Katz, J.J. and J.A. Fodor. 1963. The structure of a semantic theory. *Lg* 39.170–210.
Weinreich, U. 1966. Explorations in semantic theory. In T.A. Sebeok (ed.), *Current trends in linguistics*. The Hague. Vol. 3, 395–477.
⇒ **anaphora**, **generative semantics**, **semantics**, **transformational grammar**

interrogative ⇒ rhetorical question

interrogative pronoun (*also wh*-word)

Subgroup of **pronouns** whose members serve to introduce questions, e.g. *who?*, *what?*, *which one?*, *what kind?* (⇒ *also* **wh-question**)

interrogative sentence

Class of sentences in which the hearer is requested to give information about something. Interrogatives can usually be identified by one or more of the following syntactic characteristics: initial position of the verb, **interrogative pronoun**, question **intonation**, or modal **particle**. Interrogatives can be classified as either direct and indirect (dependent, **indirect interrogative clause**), depending on whether they occur independently or as clauses introduced by interrogative pronouns or interrogative adverbs (⇒ **adverb**, **interrogative**): *Is Philip coming today?* vs (*I don't know*) *if Philip is coming today*. Semantically there are four primary types of interrogative sentences, each of which is denoted by specific characteristics: (a) *yes/no* questions (in English, with verb-initial and question intonation): *Is Philip coming today?* or *Philip is coming today?*; (b) disjunctive question (*yes/no* questions connected by *or*): *Is Philip coming today or tomorrow?* In contrast to *yes/no* questions, these questions cannot be answered with *yes* or *no*; (c) *wh*-questions (introduced by interrogative pronouns or interrogative adverbs): *Who is coming today?*, *Where are you going?*; (d) **echo questions**, which take question types (a)–(c) and reiterate them into a counter-question to determine whether the first question was correctly understood: first question: *Is Philip coming today?* – echo question: (*Are you asking:*) *Is Philip coming today?*

With reference to pragmatics, the relationship between linguistic form and illocutive function is often discussed in the literature, as well as how much weight is to be put on institutional or situational factors as they become important in rhetorical questions or questions in tests. Numerous studies have also treated the relationship between non-interrogative utterances in the form of questions (*Are you ever going to listen to me?*), as well as between interrogative utterances which are not in the form of a question: *He's coming today?*

References
Chisholm, W.S. Jr (ed.) 1984. *Interrogativity*. Amsterdam.
Enghahl, E. 1986. *Constituent questions*. Dordrecht.
Ficht, H. 1978. Supplement to a bibliography on the theory of questions and answers. *LingB* 55.92.
Hiz, H. (ed.) 1978. *Questions*. Dordrecht.
Hudson, R.A. 1975. The meaning of questions. *Lg* 51.1–31.
Kubinski, T. 1978. *An outline of the logical theory of questions*. Berlin.
Meyer, M. (ed.) 1988. *Questions and questioning*. Berlin and New York.

Bibliographies
Belnap, N.D. and T.B.Steel, 1976. *The logic of questions and answers: bibliography on the theory of questions and answers by Urs Egli and Hubert Schleichert*. New Haven, CT.
Egli, U. and H. Schleichert. 1976. A bibliography on the theory of questions and answers. *LingB* 41.105–28.

interrupted vs continuant

Binary phonological **opposition** in **distinctive feature** analysis, based on acoustically analyzed and spectrally defined criteria (⇒ **acoustic phonetics**, **spectral analysis**). Acoustic characteristic: abrupt vs gradual onset as seen in a **spectrogram**. Articulatory characteristic: abrupt vs gradual onset of ·**phonation**. This opposition distinguishes between **stops** and **continuants**. (⇒ *also* **checked vs unchecked**)

References
⇒ **phonetics**

interruption

In **conversation analysis**, a violation of the smooth (no-gap) functioning of **turn-taking** due to (a) simultaneous speaking (see Zimmerman and West 1975), (b) short pauses between turns of the same or different speakers, (c) a longer period of silence (lapse) of all participants or (d) a delay in the turn of the designated next speaker (significant pause), which – if options are offered (⇒ **preference**) – may be interpreted as an indication of a non-preferred option (e.g. the decline of an invitation in the previous turn instead of its acceptance) (⇒ **pause**).

References
Bennett, A. 1978. Interruptions and the interpretation

of conversation. *BLS* 4.557–75.

Goodwin, C. 1981. *Conversatinal organization: interaction between speakers and hearers.* New York.

Jefferson, G. 1973. A case of precision timing in ordinary conversation: overlapped tag-positioned address terms in closing sequences. *Semiotica* 9.47–96.

Philips, S.U. 1976. Some sources of cultural variability in the regulation of talk. *LSoc* 5.81–95.

Polyani, L. 1978. False starts can be true. *BLS* 4.628–39.

Sacks, H., E. Schegloff, and G. Jefferson, 1974. A simplest systematics in turn-taking for conversation. *Lg* 50.696–735.

Tannen, D. and M. Saville-Troike. 1985. *Perspectives on silence.* Norwood, NJ.

Zimmerman, D. and C. West. 1975. Sex roles, interruptions and silences in conversation. In B. Thorne and N. Henley (eds), *Language and sex.* Rowley, MA. 105–29.
⇒ **conversation analysis**

intersection set ⇒ set

interview

Method of gathering and exchanging information in the form of a dialogue, for example, in journalism or in **dialectology**. As a **text type** of **mass communication**, the interview can be distinguished from other types of conversation by particularly pragmatic characteristics, among others, multiple addressing (interviewee and audience), degree of openness, and asymmetric directing of the dialogue by the interviewer.

References
Adelswärd, V. 1992. Interviewer styles: on interactive strategies in professional interviews. In A. Gridstead *et al.* (eds), *Communication for specific purposes.* Tübingen.

Komter, M. 1991. *Conflict and cooperation in job interviews: a study of talk, tasks, and ideas.* Amsterdam.
⇒ **conversation analysis**

intonation

1 In the broad sense, all prosodic characteristics of a linguistic utterance that are not tied to a single sound. Since intonational features are an overlay on the segmentable individual sounds, they are also called **suprasegmental** features. Three aspects are involved in the description of intonation phenomena: (a) **stress**[2] (= accent) through emphasis placed on a syllable (often accompanied by an increase in volume); (b) pitch; and (c) pausing which can be described only in relation to stress and pitch. Intonation can affect a particular syllable, a word, a phrase, or a sentence.

References
Bald, W.D. 1975. Englische Intonation in Forschung und Lehre: ein Überblick. In C. Gutsknecht (ed.) *Contributions to applied linguistics, I.* Bern. 139–63.

—— 1976. Contrastive studies in English and German intonation: a survey. *PSCL* 4.37–47.

Bolinger, D. 1978. Intonation across languages. In J.H. Greenberg (ed.), *Universals of human language.* Stanford, CA. 471–524.

—— 1989. *Intonation and its uses.* London.

Esser, J. 1975. *Intonationszeichen im Englischen.* Tübingen.

Halliday, M.A.K. 1967. *Intonation and grammar in British English.* The Hague.

't Hart, J., R. Collier, and A. Cohen. 1990. *A perceptual study of intonation: an experimental-phonetic approach to speech melody.* Cambridge.

Hirst, D.J. 1977. *Intonative features: a syntactic approach to English intonation.* The Hague.

Lieberman, P. 1967. *Intonation, perception, and language.* Cambridge, MA.

Schmerling, S.F. 1976. *Aspects of English sentence stress.* London.

Scufil, M. 1982. *Experiments in comparative intonation: a case-study of English and German.* Tübingen.

Bibliography
Meier, R. 1984. *Bibliographie zur Intonation.* Tübingen.

2 In the narrow sense (particularly in Slavic studies), the occurrence of pitch as it relates to morphologically defined segments (morphs, words) in **tonal languages**. The term '**tone**' is used to refer to distinctive levels of pitch in a language.

intonational phrase

Unit in an intonational system (⇒ **intonation**[2]) that establishes a domain for the operating of the **tonal pattern**. In every intonational phrase only one tonal pattern (e.g. rising, falling, steady) is selected. Often intonational phrases are separated by **pauses**.

Reference
Nespor, M. and I. Vogel. 1986. *Prosodic phonology.* Dordrecht. 187–221.

intralinguistic vs extralinguistic (Lat. *intra* 'inside', *extra* 'outside']

Intralinguistic are those linguistic aspects that are covered in the description of linguistic regularities, such as **distinctive features** of phonemes or **semantic features** in the analysis of meaning. Extralinguistic, on the other hand, are non-linguistic aspects of communication, such as gestures (⇒ **kinesics**), non-verbal phonetic sounds (⇒ **paralinguistics**) as well as sociocultural facts.

intransitivity ⇒ **transitivity**

Inuit ⇒ **Eskimo-Aleut**

inversion [Lat. *inversio* 'reversal of order']

1 Term for syntactic process whereby two types of constituents are permuted. Inversion in English is one means of forming a question, e.g. *That is true* vs *Is that true?* It can also be used in **topicalization**: *That film I haven't seen yet.*

2 Transformation in **relational grammar** which exchanges the syntactic functions of two arguments of a predicate. The most common type of inversion involves psychological predicates: *Pictures of himself are horrifying to Philip.* Because the surface object *to Philip* has properties that characterize both subjects (e.g. functions as an antecedent for the reflexive) and objects (e.g. lacks verb agreement) it is treated as an underlying subject and the surface subject *pictures of himself* is analyzed as an underlying object. The inversion exchanges the syntactic functions of the two arguments: the underlying subject turns into an object and the underlying object into a subject. In the framework of **transformational grammar** such a **transformation** is called a 'flip' or 'psych-movement.'

References

Anderson, S. 1984. On representation in morphology: case marking, agreement and inversion in Georgian. *NL&LT* 2.117–218.

Bresnan, J. and J.M. Kanerva. 1989. Locative inversion in Chicheŵa: a case study of factorization in grammar. *LI* 20.1–50.

Coopmans, P. 1989. Where stylistic and syntactic processes meet: locative inversion in English. *Lg* 65.728–51.

Givón, T. (ed.) 1994. *Voice and inversion.* Amsterdam.

Harris, A. 1981. *Georgian syntax.* Cambridge.

Legendre, G. 1989. Inversion with certain French experiencer verbs. *Lg* 65.752–82.

Perlmutter, D.M. 1979. Working 1s and inversion in Italian, Japanese and Quechua. *BLS* 5.277–324.

Postal, P.M. 1971. *Cross-over phenomena: a study in the grammar of coreference.* New York.

——— 1989. *Masked inversion in French.* Chicago, IL.

Rogers, A. 1972. Another look at flip perception verbs. *CLS* 8.303–15.

Sridhar, S.N. 1976. Dative subjects, rule government and relational grammar. *Studies in the Linguistic Sciences* 6:1.130–50.

invited inference

A subtype of conversational **implicature** described by M. Geis and A.M. Zwicky. The promise *If you mow my lawn, I'll give you five dollars,* generally speaking, 'invites' the unexpressed inference *If you don't mow my lawn, I won't give you five dollars.* Invited inferences, which have a pragmatic basis, must be distinguished from logical conclusions.

References

Zwicky, A.M. and M. Geis. 1971. On invited inferences. *LingI* 2.561–6.

⇒ **implication**, **maxims of conversation**, **presupposition**

iota operator ⇒ **operator**

iotacism [Grk *iōta* = name for the Greek letter ‹ι›]

Term taken from Greek phonetics for the raising of Ancient Greek *ēta* [eː] to [iː] or the collapsing of Ancient Greek [ei, oi, y] with *iōta* [i].

IPA (International Phonetic Alphabet) ⇒ **phonetic transcription**

Iranian

Branch of **Indo-Iranian** and thus of **Indo-European**, composed today of about forty languages with over 80 million speakers; main languages are **Persian** (Farsī), **Pashto, Kurdish**, Belochi (esp. in Pakistan), and Ossete in the Caucasus. The oldest known languages are Avestan, the language of the Avesta, a Zoroastrian collection of texts (approx. 1000 BC (Gāthās) – 500 BC (Young Avestan)) and Old Persian, recorded in cuneiform documents from the Persian Empire (approx. 500 BC). Middle Iranian is also well documented in several dialects, e.g. Parthian and Sogdian (300 BC – AD 900), which have been handed down in two different kinds of writing, Pahlavi and Manichean, both developed from **Aramaic** script.

Characteristics: While the older languages show typical Indo-European features, especially a strong similarity to **Sanskrit**, the modern Iranian languages have developed in new ways. Especially remarkable is the development of an **ergative** system in the preterite based on the **reanalysis** of a participial passive as an active verb. This ergative system is still maintained in Kurdish and Pashto, but has become an accusative system in modern Persian. Otherwise the development is marked by continuous simplification of the morphology (e.g. reduction of the case system), addition of analytic structures, and fixing of word order (SOV or SVO).

References

Abaev, V.I. 1964. *A grammatical sketch of Ossetic.* Bloomington, IN and The Hague (= *IJAL* 30:4, pub. 35).

Acta Iranica. 1975ff. Leiden and Teheran.

Beekes, R.S.P. 1988. *A grammar of Gatha-Avestan.* Leiden.

Brandenstein, W. and M. Mayrhofer, 1964. *Handbuch des Altpersischen*. Wiesbaden.

Dresden, M. 1983. Sogdian language and literature. In E. Yarshater (ed.), *The Cambridge history of Iran*. Vol. 3(1–2). Cambridge. 1216–29.

Encyclopaedia Iranica. 1982– . ed. E. Yarshater. Vol. I–IV 1989–1990 London. Since 1992 Costa Mesa, CA. Vol I–VII (Aa–Daylam).

Geiger, W. and E. Kuhn (eds) 1895–1901. Grundriß der iranischen Philologie, 2 vols. Strasburg.

Gershevitch, I. 1954. *A grammar of Manichean Sogdian*. Oxford.

Hoffmann, K. 1989. Avestan language. In *Encyclopaedia Iranica*, Vol. III.47–62.

Jackson, A.V.W. 1892. *An Avesta grammar*. Stuttgart.

Kellens, J. 1984. *Le Verbe avestique*. Wiesbaden.

Kent, R.G. 1953. *Old Persian: Grammar, texts, lexicon*, 2nd rev. edn. New Haven, CT.

Mackenzie, D.N. 1969. Iranian languages. In T.A. Sebeok (ed.), *Current trends in linguistics*. The Hague. Vol. 5, 450–77.

—— 1983. Khwarazmian language and literature. In E. Yarshater (ed.), *The Cambridge history of Iran*. Vol. 3(1–2). Cambridge. 1244–9.

Nyberg, H.S. 1964–74. *A manual of Pahlavi*. 2 vols. Wiesbaden.

Oranskij, I.O. 1977. *Les Langues iraniénnes*, (trans. J. Blau). Paris.

Payne, J.R. 1981. Iranian languages. In B. Comrie (ed.), *The languages of the Soviet Union*. Cambridge. 158–79.

Redard, G. 1970. Other Iranian languages. In T.A. Sebeok (ed.), *Current trends in linguistics*. The Hague. Vol. 6, 97–135.

Schmitt, R. (ed.) 1989. *Compendium linguarum iranicarum*. Wiesbaden.

Sebeok, T. (ed.) 1970. *Current Trends in Linguistics*, vol. 6: *Linguistics in Southeast Asia and North Africa: A. Iranian languages*. The Hague and Paris. 9–135.

Spuler, B. *et al.* (cds) 1958. *Iranistik* (Handbuch der Orientalistik I, Vol. 4.1). (Repr. 1967.) Leiden.

Dictionaries

Bailey, H.W. 1979. *Dictionary of Khotan Saka*. Cambridge.

Bartholomae, C. 1904. *Altiranisches Wörterbuch*. Strasburg.

Benzing, J. 1983. *Chwaresmischer Wortindex*. Wiesbaden.

Gharib, B. 1995. *Sogdian dictionary (Sogdian–Persian–English)*. Teheran.

Kanga, K.E. 1909. *An English–Avesta dictionary*. Bombay.

MacKenzie, D.N. 1971. *A concise Pahlavi dictionary*. London.

Miller, W. 1927–9. *Ossetisch-russisch-deutsches Wörterbuch*, 3 vols. Leningrad. (Repr. The Hague, 1972.)

Journal
Studia Iranica.
⇒ **Indo-Iranian**

Irish ⇒ **Celtic**, **Gaelic**

irony [Grk *eirōneía* 'dissimulation, i.e. ignorance purposely affected']

Rhetorical **trope**: the replacement of an expression that is meant by its opposite. Characteristic of ironical speech are ambiguous structures or structures that contain contradictory expressions, which implicitly point to the opposite by **polysemy**, **homonymy**, or **antonymy**, e.g. *You are charming = You are mean*, or by ambiguous illocution, e.g. *Just keep it up*. In order to make irony recognizable and therefore effective, the contrast between the spoken and the intended meaning should be as large as possible. Blatant contradictions often indicate irony, e.g. *What beautiful weather*, when it is pouring with rain. Various other linguistic signals can be used, e.g. **modal particles**, **hyperbole**, exclamative sentences, and **intonation**.

References

Booth, W.C. 1974. *A rhetoric of irony*. (6th ed. 1987.) Chicago, IL.

Grice, H.P. 1968. Logic and conversation. In P. Cole and J.L. Morgan (eds), *Syntax and semantics*, vol. 3: *Speech acts*. New York. 41–58.

Handwerk, G.J. 1986. *Irony and ethics in narrative: from Schlegel to Lacan*. New Haven, CT.

Muecke, D.C. 1982. *Irony and the ironic*. London.

Sperber, D. *et al.* 1981. Irony and the use-mention distinction. In P. Cole (ed.), *Radical pragmatics*. New York. 295–318.

Swearingen, C.J. 1991. *Rhetoric and irony: Western literacy and Western lies*. New York.
⇒ **figure of speech**

Iroquoian

Language group in eastern North America with eight languages. Greenberg (1987) assigns it, along with **Siouan** and **Caddoan**, to the Macro-Siouan languages; the largest language is Cherokee (approx. 20,000 speakers).

Characteristics: simple sound system, but complex morphophonemic changes. Strong tendency towards **polysynthesis**, **incorporation**, and descriptivity. No formal differences between nouns and verbs, the only tenable word class distinction is between main words and particles (e.g. the word for the animal 'bear' in Oneida, *o-hkwalí*, can be analyzed as the reference marker *o-* and the predicate *hkwalí*, literally 'it "bears" him,' where the predicate *hkwalí*, as in other polysynthetic languages, cannot occur alone). Complex verb morphology, including various voices, aspects, reflexive forms, spatial distinctions. Distinction between active and inactive verbs. Four genders (masculine, feminine, animal, neuter, with differences in the individual languages).

References
Chafe, W.L. 1970. *A semantically based sketch of Onondaga*. Baltimore, MD.
Greenberg, J.H. 1987. *Language in the Americas*. Stanford, CA.
Lounsbury, F.G. 1953. *Oneida verb morphology*. London.
Mithun, M. 1976. *A grammar of Tuscarora*. New York.
—— 1979. Iroquoian. In L. Campbell and M. Mithun (eds), *The languages of native America: historical and comparative assessment*. Austin, TX. 133–212.
Sasse, H.-J. 1988. Der irokesische Sprachtyp. *ZS* 7.173–213.

Journal
Algonquian and Iroquoian Linguistics Newsletter.
⇒ **North and Central American languages**

irregular verb

1 Type of verb present in all languages which has paradigms that deviate from regular patterns. In English (as a **Germanic** language), these include (a) historically 'strong' verbs which form the past tense by some other means than the suffix *-ed* (*eat : ate* vs *work : worked*); (b) suppletive verbs (⇒ **suppletivism**), which form the past tense and past participle by suppleting them with different roots (*to be, are, is, was, been*); (c) modals (*can, should, may*), many of which trace back to **preterite-presents**; (d) the **auxiliaries** *will, have*; (e) so-called **rückumlaut** verbs, which are historically weak but have vowel and consonant alternations in the past and participle (*bring–brought–brought, think–thought–thought*).

2 For English, any verb that does not form its past tense and past participle by adding *-d* or *-ed*.

island

A term in **transformational grammar** for syntactic structures which limit the scope of transformational rules (⇒ **transformation**) and interpretation rules so that they can only be used within certain domains. For example, (a) adnominal sentences, (b) sentential subjects, and (c) co-ordinated structures are islands. For certain rules, this term, coined by Ross in 1967, suggests that it is impossible to leave an island with a transformational movement.

References
Goodluck, H. and M. Rochemont, eds 1992. *Island constraints*. Dordrecht.
Grosu, A. 1981. *Approaches to island phenomena*. Amsterdam.
Ross, J.R. 1967. Constraints on variables in syntax. Dissertation, Cambridge, MA. (Repr. as *Infinite syntax!* Norwood, NJ, 1986.)

⇒ **constraints, subjacency, transformational grammar**

isogloss [Grk *ísos* 'same,' *glõssa* 'language']

In **dialectology**, boundary lines on language maps that show the geographical spread of a certain word. In contrast, cf. **isophones**, which refer to the sound inventory.

References
⇒ **linguistic atlas**

isolated opposition ⇒ opposition

isolating language (*also* analytic language, root-isolating language)

Classificational category established by Schlegel (1818) and Humboldt (1836) which refers to languages that do not use morphological means (i.e. **inflection**) to express syntactic relations, but rather independent grammatical units (**particles, words**) and/or **word order**. Isolating languages contrast with **synthetic languages**, which make use of inflection and other morphological means to express syntactic relations. Examples of isolating languages include Classical **Chinese** and **Vietnamese**.

References
Humboldt, W. von 1836. *Über die Verschiedenheit des menschlichen Sprachbaues*. Berlin. (Repr. 1963.)
Schlegel, A.W. von 1818. *Observations sur la langue et la littérature provençales*. Paris.
⇒ **language typology**

isolect [Grk *ísos* 'equal,' *léktos* 'chosen, picked out; expression, word']

Term used in dialectology to describe varieties that differ from each other by only one feature. An isolect may designate the speech of an individual or of many individuals using the same **style**. (⇒ *also* **lect, variety**)

isomorphism [Grk *morphé* 'form, shape']

1 In **set theory**, fundamental concept of a general structural theory that denotes structural **equivalence** in regard to certain relations between elements of two (or more) sets. Isomorphism can be comprehended with the help of bijective mapping (⇒ **function**) that maintains the structure: for example, the set of natural numbers $\{1,2,3,4, \ldots\}$ is isomorphic to the set of natural even numbers $\{2,4,6, \ldots\}$ with regard to the relation of 'greater than' (notation: $>$), since the function $f(n) = 2xn$ is a subjective function between the sets in question, and $n > m$ is equivalent to $f(n) > f(m)$.

References
⇒ **formal logic, set theory**

2 Concept introduced by J. Kuryłowicz (1949)

into linguistics that refers to the structural parallelism between different levels of description (phonology, morphology, etc.). The assumption of isomorphism is meant to justify the use of the same investigative or descriptive methods, a hypothesis that has been only partly confirmed in the transfer of phonological concepts (**distinctive features**) to semantic concepts (**componential analysis**).

References
Kuryłowicz, J. 1949. La notion de l'isomorphisme. *TCLC* 5.48–60.

isophone [Grk *phōnē* 'sound, voice']

In **dialectology**, border line on language maps that indicates the geographic range of a particular phonetic phenomenon. For contrast, ⇒ **isogloss**, which refers to the border line of lexical occurrence.

References
⇒ **linguistic atlas**

isotopy [Grk *ísos tópos* 'the same place']

A term used in **text linguistics** that was taken from chemistry. The repetition of words of the same area of meaning in a text, e.g. *doctor*, *fever*, *injection*, *fee*. Isotopy is based on the repetition of a **semantic feature** and is therefore a particular kind of **recurrence** and thus a text-forming tool of **cohesion** or **coherence**. The thematic complexity of a text is reflected in the number of levels of isotopy. In its broadest sense, isotopy also refers to the repetition of syntactic and phonological elements in a text.

References
Bellert, I. 1970. On the semantic interpretation of subject–predicate relations in the sentences of particular reference. In M. Bierwisch and K.E. Heidolph (eds), *Progress in linguistics*. The Hague. 9–26.
Greimas, A.J. 1966. *Sémantique structurale*. Paris.

issue

Thematic **proposition** for which no assumptions are made about its truth or falseness in a given discourse.

Istro-Rumanian ⇒ **Rumanian**

Italian

Language belonging to the **Romance language** family of the **Indo-European** language family, spoken as a native language by about 55 million speakers in Italy, Switzerland, Corsica, Istria, and Monaco. Its numerous dialects can be divided into three major groups: (a) the north Italian dialects in Piedmont, Lombardy, Emilia Romagna, Liguria, and Venice; (b) the south Italian dialects (south of Pescara–Rome); and

(c) the central Italian dialects (including Corsican and Toscan) whose rich literary tradition (Dante, Boccaccio, Petrarch) has formed the basis for the standard Italian written language since the sixteenth century. The issue of regional expressions of the standard language ('la questione della lingua') is still debated. In general, Italian varies little from Vulgar **Latin**, as can be seen in the well-preserved inflectional system, only slightly reduced by the loss of final syllables. The loss of final consonants (Lat. *dormis* > *dormi* 'you sleep') and the preservation of intervocalic voiceless stops (Lat./Ital. *vita* 'life') in standard Italian show it to belong to the eastern Romance languages.

References
Holtus, G., M. Metzeltin, and C. Schmitt (eds) 1988. *Lexikon der romanistischen Linguistik*. Tübingen. Vol. 4, 1–798.
Jaberg, K. and J. Jud. 1928–40. *Sprach- und Sachatlas Italiens und der Südschweiz*, 8 vols. Zofingen.
Lepschy, A.L. and G.C. Lepschy. 1977. *The Italian language today*. London. (2nd edn 1988.)

History and dialectology
Cortelazzo, M. 1969–72. *Avviamento critico allo studio della dialettologia italiana*, vols 1 and 3. Pisa.
Maiden, M. 1994. *A linguistic history of Italian*. London.
Migliorini, B. 1988. *Storia della lingua italiana*, 2 vols. Milan.
Migliorini, B. and T.G. Griffith. 1984. *The Italian language*, 2nd edn. London.
Rizzi, L. 1982. *Issues in Italian syntax*. Dordrecht.
Rohlfs, G. 1949–54. *Historische Grammatik der italienischen Sprache und ihrer Mundarten*, 3 vols. Bern. (*Grammatica storica della lingua italiana e dei suoi dialetti*. Turin, 1966–9.)
Tekavčić, P. 1972. *Grammatica storica della lingua italiana*, 3 vols. (2nd edn Bologna, 1980.)

Grammars
Dardano, M. and P. Trifone. 1985. *La lingua italiana*. Bologna.
———— 1990. *Grammatica italiana con nozioni di linguistica*, 2nd edn. Florence.
Regula, M. and J. Jernei. 1965. *Grammatica italiana descrittiva su basi storiche e psicologiche*, 2nd edn. Bern.
Renzi, L. and G. Salvi (eds) 1988–93. *Grande grammatica italiana di consultazione*, 3 vols. Bologna.
Serianni, L. and A. Castelvecchi. 1988. *Grammatica italiana: italiano commune e lingua letteraria*. Turin.

Dictionaries
Battaglia, S. 1961. *Grande dizionario della lingua italiana*. 3 vols. Turin.
Nuovissimo Dardano: dizionario della lingua italiana. 1986. Rome.
Vocabolario della lingua italiana. 1986. Istituto della enciclopedia italiana edn. Rome.

Etymological dictionaries
Battisti, C. and G. Alesso. 1950–7. *Dizionario etimologico italiano*, 5 vols. Florence.
Cortelazzo, M. and P. Zolli. 1990. *Dizionario etimologico della lingua italiana*. Bologna.
Pfister, M. 1979– . *Lessico etimologico italiano*. (Vol. V 1995.) Wiesbaden.

Bibliographies
Hall, R.A., Jr 1958–69. *Bibliografia della linguistica italiana*. Florence.
——— 1973. *Bibliografia essenziale della linguistica italiana e romanza*. Florence.

Italic

Language branch of the **Indo-European** family with numerous dialects on the Italian peninsula, all now extinct. The classification of the Italic languages poses numerous difficulties (such as Latin–Faliscan, and Oscan–Umbrian). Included in this group is **Latin**, the former dialect of Rome, whose various regional variants (e.g. Vulgar Latin) have developed into the modern **Romance languages**.

References
Buck, C.D. 1928. *A grammar of Oscan and Umbrian*. Boston, MA.
Pisani, V. 1964. *Le lingue dell'Italia antica oltre il latino*, 2nd edn. Turin.
Prosdocimi, A.L. (ed.) 1978. *Lingue e dialetti dell' Italia antica*. Rome.
Pulgram, E. 1958. *The tongues of Italy*. Cambridge, MA.

item-and-arrangement grammar

Term introduced by C.F. Hockett for the grammar concept of **American Structuralism**, especially that of Harris (⇒ **distributionalism**) which is conceived of as a static system of unambiguously delimited items, or more precisely, **morphemes**, and certain arrangements, which are to be understood as rules for the ordering of these elements. The limits of this approach are to be seen where no unambiguous allocation of morpheme and meaning is possible, e.g. in *drink* vs *drank*: in contrast to *link* vs *linked*, the morpheme 'preterite' in *drank* cannot be isolated from the meaning of the stem by **segmentation**. The interpretation suggested for *drank* as a **portmanteau morpheme** runs counter to the basic principle of the unambiguous segmentability of the items. For a critique of the item-and-arrangement concept as well as for a new approach by Hockett, see **item-and-process grammar**. (⇒ *also* **paradigm morphology**)

Reference
Hockett, C.F. 1954. Two models of grammatical description. *Word* 10.210–34.

item-and-process grammar (*abbrev.* IP)

Term coined by C.F. Hockett for a grammar concept that was later systematically developed in **transformational grammar** (as well as in **stratificational grammar**). In contrast to the static **item-and-arrangement grammar**, IP is founded on a dynamic principle. The basic elements are not the morphemes of **surface structure**, but underlying abstract forms that are transformed (⇒ **transformation**) into their actual form by processes of change: *drank* is thus the result of an abstract basic form 'drink' and a transformation that changes the stem vowel from /i/ to /a/.

Reference
Hockett, C.F. 1954. Two models of grammatical description. *Word* 10.210–34.

iterative vs semelfactive [Lat. *iterum* 'again, twice,' *semel* 'once'] (*also* frequentative, habitual)

Aspect distinction: iteratives describe durative (⇒ **durative vs non-durative**) events that occur repeatedly or regularly, while semelfactive verbs refer to one individual occurrence. Iteratives and **intensives** and **diminutives** overlap. Iteratives are also often equated with **habituals**; cf., however, *She kept hugging her cat* vs *She likes to hug her cat* (repetition vs habitual activity). An example of an iterative with habitual meaning is *She used to go to work by car.*

References
Mønnesland, S. 1984. The Slavonic frequentative habitual. In C. De Groot and H. Tommola (eds), *Aspect bound*, Dordrecht. 53–76.
⇒ **aspect**

Itonama ⇒ Chibchan-Paezan

Ivrit ⇒ Hebrew

J

Jacaltec ⇒ **Mayan languages**

Japanese

Official language of Japan, spoken by over 120 million speakers. Its genetic affinity is unclear; a relationship with **Korean** and the **Altaic** languages as well as with **Malayo-Polynesian** is often suggested. Ryukyu, the language of Okinawa, is closely related to Japanese. Japanese has many dialects; the standard is based on the dialect of Tokyo.

Written documents date from the eighth century. The writing system of modern Japanese is a combination of the Chinese logographic writing Kanji (for expressing lexical morphemes) and two independent syllabaries, Hiragana, originally a writing system for women, now used, among other things, for marking grammatical morphemes and functional words, and Katakana, now used, among other things, for foreign words. A normalized writing system in the Latin alphabet, Romaji, also exists. The syllabaries contain forty-six characters each; in everyday language about 2,000 Kanji characters are used.

Characteristics: relatively simple sound system and syllable structure, but numerous morphophonemic alternations (palatalization, affrication). Musical stress. Morphological type: **agglutinating**. Rich verbal inflection (tense, **aspect**, mood, voice, negation, **politeness**, but no agreement). No number distinction; in number constructions, **classifiers** are employed. Numerous 'cases' are indicated by postpositions. The **topic** is marked by the postposition -*wa* and does not have to be an argument of the verb; this led to the erroneously named 'double subject' sentences such as *sakana wa tai ga ii* 'fish-TOP red snapper-SUBJ good' (= 'As far as fish are concerned, red snappers taste good'). Nominal sentential elements can often be omitted if the reference is clear from the context (so-called 'zero anaphors'); one result of this is that pronouns are rarely used and can be derived from nouns, for which numerous forms are available for marking social position. Word order SOV; dependent clauses marked by participial forms of the verb.

References

Choi, S. 1993. *Japanese/Korean linguistics*, vol. 3. Chicago, IL.

Clancy, P. 1993. *Japanese/Korean linguistics*, vol. 2. Chicago, IL.
Hinds, J. 1986. *Japanese*. London.
Hoji, H. 1993. *Japanese/Korean linguistics*. Chicago, IL.
Kuno, S. 1973. *The structure of the Japanese language*. Cambridge, MA.
Lewin, B. *et al.* 1989. *Sprache und Schrift Japans*. (Handbuch der Orientalistik 5, vol. 1, 2.) Leiden.
Miller, R.A. 1967. *The Japanese language*. Chicago, IL.
—— 1980. *The origin of the Japanese language*. Washington, DC.
Shibatani, M. 1976. *Syntax and semantics*, vol. 5: *Japanese generative grammar*. New York, San Francisco, and London.
—— 1990. *The languages of Japan*. Cambridge.
Twine, N. 1991. *Language and the modern state: the reform of written Japanese*. London.
Wenck, G. 1966. *The phonemics of Japanese: questions and attempts*. Wiesbaden.

Dictionary

Hepburn, J.C. 1988. *A Japanese and English dictionary with an English and Japanese index*. Rutland.

jargon [French, prob. of imitative origin]

1 Language which is inaccessible to non-specialists. Jargon entails an extended and terminologically normalized vocabulary, and correspondingly different uses of morphological rules, e.g. **compounds**, special prefixed forms, **foreign words**, technical terms, **metaphor** are characteristic of jargon (⇒ **catachresis**). Jargon is often characterized by the **nominal style** and **impersonal constructions** in **syntax** as well as the explicit characteristic of structure and semantic **coherence** on the level of text, e.g. through **connectives**, **recurrence**, and other means of **cohesion**. General characteristics of modern jargon in technology, science, and government include its standardization over large regions, its exactness and economy in transmitting information and its introduction into the general language, for example into **slang** or **advertising language**.

References

Brennan, R.P. 1992. *Dictionary of scientific literacy*. New York.
Nash, W. 1993. *Jargon: its uses and abuses*. Oxford.

Bibliographies

Schröder, H. 1991. Linguistic and text-theoretical research on languages for special purposes: a thematic and bibliographical guide. In H. Schröder (ed.), *Subject-oriented texts: languages for special*

purposes and text theory. Berlin.
UNESCO (ed.) 1961. *Bibliography of interlingual scientific and technical dictionaries*, 4th edn. Paris.
⇒ **cliché, slang**

2 In **neurolinguistics**, term referring to fluent but unintelligible utterances, usually those associated with **Wernicke's aphasia**. One distinguishes between semantic and phonological jargon: utterances either consist of a meaningless sequence of words, **neologisms**, and stereotypic coinages ('semantic jargon'), or the sound sequences themselves, though following the phonotactic rules of the language, do not form conventional sequences ('phonological jargon').

References
⇒ **Wernicke's aphasia**

Javanese

Largest **Malayo-Polynesian** language spoken in central and eastern Java (approx. 66 million speakers). Javanese has a highly developed hierarchy of stylistic levels (**honorific**, derogatory, etc.). Written attestations since approx. AD 750 in an alphabet derived from **Sanskrit**.

References
Errington, J.J. 1988. *Structure and style in Javanese: a semiotic view of linguistic ettiquette*. Philadelphia.
Horne, E.M.C. 1961. *Beginning Javanese*. New Haven, CT.
—— 1963. *Intermediate Javanese*. New Haven, CT.
Suharo, I.A. 1982. *A descriptive study of Javanese*. Canberra.

Je

Language group in central Brazil with about twelve languages.

References
Davis, I. 1968. Some Macro-Je relationships. *IJAL* 34.42–7.
Popies, J. and J. Popies. 1986. Canela-Kraho. In D.C. Derbyshire and G. Pullum (eds), *Handbook of Amazonean languages*. Berlin. 128–99.
⇒ **South American languages**

journalistic language

Term for languages used specifically by journalists in newspapers or in news broadcasts. Journalistic language is not a uniform **variety** in the sense of a linguistic subsystem; rather, its features are conditioned by the structure of **mass communication** and depend individually on the intended audience (sensational newspapers, political magazines), frequency of publication (daily, weekly), circulation (regional, national, international), covered topics (sports, business), types of texts (commentaries, weath-

er reports), among other factors. Journalistic language has long been part of text-critical studies owing to its distinct stylistic features such as **nominalization** and the creation of **neologisms**. Today, journalistic language is seen as an important factor in **language change**, since it is often responsible for the introduction, maintenance, and changing of linguistic norms (such as the spread of neologisms and **jargon**). (⇒ *also* **sublanguage**)

References
Bell, A. 1991. *The language of news media*. Oxford.
Hicks, W. 1993. *English for journalists*. London.
Lüger, H.-H. 1983. *Pressesprache*. Tübingen.
Simon-Vandenbergen, A.M. (ed.) 1986. *Aspects of style in British newspapers*. Ghent.
Wandruszka, U. 1994. Zur Semiotik der Schlagzeile: Der Kommunikationsakt 'Meldung'. In A. Sabban and C. Schmitt (eds), *Der sprachliche Alltag. Festschrift für Wolf-Dieter Stempel*. Tübingen.
⇒ **advertising language, mass communication, stylistics**

Jukunoid ⇒ Benue-Congo languages

junction [Lat. *iungere* 'to connect']

1 In L. Tesnière's **dependency grammar**, junction is both a two-place syntactic relationship of subordination, as well as the process of explaining linguistic combinations that are possible when nodes of the same syntactic function are connected with co-ordinating conjunctions (*and*, *or*). Junction, together with the subordinating relationships of **connection** and **translation**, form the basis of dependential linguistic description, where translation and junction serve to form and describe complex sentence structures. (⇒ *also* **co-ordination**)
2 In O. Jespersen's terminology, a syntactic type of attributive concatenation (e.g. *the expensive book*), which Jespersen distinguishes from nexus (predicative concatenation).

References
Jespersen, O. 1937. *Analytic syntax*. Copenhagen.
⇒ **dependency grammar**

junctive

In L. Tesnière's **dependency grammar**, class of co-ordinating **conjunctions** (*and*, *or*, *but*). Junctives are 'empty words' (Fr. *mots vides*) with a purely syntactic function, which connect 'full words' (Fr. *mots pleins*) and/or their nodes with the same syntactic function (⇒ **junction**).

References
⇒ **dependency grammar**

juncture [Lat. *iunctura* 'joint, link']

In structural **phonology**, **suprasegmental**, and **distinctive feature**, frequently (but not necessarily) realized as a pause. Juncture (notation: +) refers to the boundary between two morphemes which, among other things, prevents regular application of phonetic processes which would otherwise occur between two neighboring sounds. With juncture, *Good day!* is pronounced [gʊd+dey], as opposed to [gʊdey]. A distinction is generally drawn between open (= realized) and closed juncture. (⇒ *also* **boundary marker**)

References
Moulton, W.G. 1947. Juncture in modern standard German. *Lg* 23.212–26.
⇒ **suprasegmental features**

Junggrammatiker ⇒ Neogrammarians

jussive [Lat. *iussum* 'a command, order']

1 Term introduced by O. Jespersen and used by J. Lyons to denote sentences functioning as 'mands,' i.e. commands and requests (*Will you keep quiet, (please)?*). In terms of grammatical **mood**, jussives are usually either **imperative**[1] or **interrogative**.

2 Verb **mood** occurring alongside the **imperative**[1] with a related but different meaning, for example in **Amharic**. Its precise function seems to vary from language to language.

References
Lyons, J. 1977. *Semantics*, 2 vols. Cambridge.
⇒ **modality**

juxtaposition [Lat. *iuxta* 'close by,' *ponere* 'to place, set']

1 Concatenation of morphemes without any phonetic changes, typical of **agglutinating languages**. (⇒ *also* **fusion**, **morphology**)

Reference
Sapir, E. 1921. *Language*. New York.

2 In general, the placement of individual elements in a row. Appositional constructions (⇒ **apposition**) like *King George* and *Ms Jones* are known as 'determinative juxtapositions.'

K

Kabard ⇒ North-West Caucasian

Kadugli ⇒ Niger-Kordofanian

Kakchiquel ⇒ Mayan languages

Kalenjin ⇒ Chari-Nile languages

Kam ⇒ Austro-Thai

Kan-Hakka ⇒ Chinese

Kanji ⇒ Japanese

Kannada ⇒ Dravidian, Marathi

Kanuri ⇒ Saharan

Karelian ⇒ Finno-Ugric

Kartvelian ⇒ South Caucasian

Kashmiri ⇒ Dardic

Kashubian (*also* Cassubian)

West **Slavic** language now spoken only by a few thousand speakers in the area around Gdansk, Poland. Often considered a dialect of **Polish**, although it no longer maintains any palatalization distinction.

References
Atlas językowy kaszubszczyzny i dialektów sąsiednich. 1964–78. 15 vols. Warsaw.
Lorentz, F. *et al.* 1935. *The Cassubian civilization.* London.
Popowska-Taborska, H. 1980. *Kaszubszczyzna: zarys dziejów.* Warsaw.
Sychta, B. 1967–76. *Słownik gwar kaszubskich,* 7 vols. Warsaw.
Topolinska, Z. 1974. *A historical phonology of the Kashubian dialects of Polish.* The Hague.

Dictionary
Lorentz, F. 1958–83. *Pomoranisches Wörterbuch,* 5 Vols. Berlin.

Katakana ⇒ Japanese

Katharévusa ⇒ Greek

Kekchi ⇒ Mayan languages

keneme [Grk *kenós* 'empty']

In **glossematics**, the smallest 'empty' units of the content plane (= phonological features) that together with the semantic features (⇒ **plereme**) are subsumed under the term **glosseme**.

References
⇒ **glossematics**

Keresan ⇒ Caddoan

Keresiouan ⇒ Caddoan

kernel sentence [OE *cyrnel*, diminutive of *corn*]

In the terminology of Z.S. Harris, a simple sentence that cannot be further reduced structurally or semantically. These minimal sentences form the syntactic nucleus of a language, and all other sentences can be derived from them using **transformations**. Thus kernel sentences form the basis for transformational derivations. In the early phases of **transformational grammar** (represented by Chomsky 1957), kernel sentences are **declarative sentences** that are generated by **rewrite rules** and obligatory transformations and from which **non-kernel sentences** can be derived using optional transformations. For example, kernel sentences are those simple, active positive statements from which passives or negative statements and questions can be derived using optional transformations. The difference between kernel sentences and non-kernel sentences is discussed in the revised versions of the **aspects model** and is replaced by the concept of **deep structure** and **surface structure**.

References
Chomsky, N. 1957. *Syntactic structures.* The Hague.
Harris, Z.S. 1957. Co-occurrence and transformation in linguistic structure. *Lg* 33.283–340.
⇒ **transformational grammar**

Ket ⇒ Asiatic languages, language isolate, Paleo-Siberian

Khanty ⇒ Finno-Ugric

Khmer ⇒ Mon-Khmer

Khoikhoin ⇒ Khoisan

Khoisan

Language group comprised of about thirty languages in southwestern Africa (with two isolates, Hatsa and Sandawe, in East Africa). The largest languages are Nama (approx. 120,000 speakers) and Sandawe (approx. 35,000 speakers); the other languages are generally dying out. The Khoisan languages have traditionally been divided on cultural-anthropological grounds into Khoikhoin (so-called 'Hottentots,' cattle herders) and San ('Bushmen,' hunter-gatherers); linguistic reconstructions, however, point to three branches (South, North, and Central Khoisan). Khoisan languages were previously spread over large parts of southern Africa and were driven into remote areas by Bantus and Cape Dutch.

Characteristics: **clicks**, borrowed into neighboring **Bantu** languages and otherwise not used as phonemes in any other language; exceptionally comprehensive sound systems (often over 100 phonemes). Gender or **noun class** systems, agreement, complex number formation (including **dual**). Word order mostly SOV.

References
Schapera, I. 1965. *The Khoisan peoples of South Africa*. London.
Stopa, R. 1972. *The structure of Bushman and its traces in Indo-European*. Warsaw.
Winter, J.C. 1981. Khoisan. In B. Heine *et al.* (eds), *Die Sprachen Afrikas*. Hamburg. 329–74.
Vossen, R. (ed.) 1988. *New perspectives on the study of Khoisan*. Hamburg.

kinemics ⇒ kinesics

kinesics [Grk *kinéma* 'movement'] (*also* kinemics)

In the area of **non-verbal communication**, the investigation of structure and function of non-phonetic means of communication like facial expressions, gestures, mimicry, body language, eye contact, and others. The observation of such signals of movement plays a role in the interpretation of meaning, insofar as, for example, knitting one's brow or a movement of the hand (can) decisively influence the interpretation of an utterance. (⇒ *also* **paralinguistics**)

References
Bates, B.L. and R.N. St Clair. 1981. *Developmental kinesics, the emerging paradigm*. Baltimore, MD.
Key, M.R. 1975. *Paralanguage and kinesics, with a bibliography*. Metuchen, NJ.
⇒ **face-to-face interaction, non-verbal communication, sign language, transcription**

kinship term

Kinship terms belong to the **basic vocabulary** of a language. Although kinship terms can be uniformly fixed in genealogical categories according to their relationship to an Ego, languages show great diachronic and synchronic differences in kinship terms. Objective differentiations (e.g. patrilineage vs matrilineage or older vs younger siblings) are normally reflected in the kinship terms of a language community only if they are relevant for the given community. The closest relatives (e.g. parents) also appear to be uniformly denoted with morphologically simple forms. The study of kinship terms is an interdisciplinary field, in which both anthropologists and sociologists are involved. (⇒ *also* **componential analysis**)

References
Benveniste, E. 1969. Le vocabulaire de la parenté. In *Le vocabulaire des institutions indo-européennes*, vol. 2.203–76. Paris.
Goodenough, W. 1956. Yankee kinship terminology: a problem in componential analysis. *AA* 67.129–287.
Heath, J. *et al.* (eds) 1978. *Languages of kinship in Australia*. Canberra.
Hettrich, H. 1985. Indo-European kinship terminology in linguistics and anthropology. *AnL* 27.453–80.
Jones, W.J. 1990. *German kinship terms (750–1500)*. Berlin.
Kay, P. 1977. Constants and variables of English kinship semantics. In R.W. Fasold and R.W. Shuy (eds), *Studies in language variation: semantics, syntax, phonology, pragmatics, social situations, ethnographic approaches*. Washington, DC. 294–311.
Lounsbury, F.G. 1956. The semantic analysis of Pawnee kinship usage. *Lg* 32.158–94.
—— 1963. The structural analysis of kinship semantics. In H. Lunt (ed.), *Proceedings of the ninth International Congress of Linguists*. The Hague. 1073–93.
Szemerényi, O. 1977. Studies in the kinship terminology of the Indo-European languages, with special reference to Indian, Iranian, Greek and Latin. *Acta Iranica* 16.1–240.
White, H.C. 1963. *An anatomy of kinship*. Englewood Cliffs, NJ.
⇒ **componential analysis**

Kinyarwanda ⇒ Bantu

Kiowa ⇒ Uto-Aztecan

Klamath ⇒ Penutian

knowledge representation

Area of **artificial intelligence** in which formal methods of representation and processing of knowledge – in particular everyday knowledge (⇒ **commonsense reasoning**), suitable for computer processing – are developed. For example, everyday knowledge may be employed to support inferences needed in language processing. Within artificial intelligence, knowledge representation and meaning representations are usually realized within the same descriptive system. (⇒ *also* **default reasoning, frame, non-monotonic logic, script, semantic network**)

References
Cercone, N. and G. McCalla (eds) 1987. *The knowledge frontier*. New York.
Mylopoulos, J. and H.J. Levesque. 1984. An overview of knowledge representation. In M.L. Brodie, J. Mylopulos, and J.W. Schmidt (eds), *On conceptual modelling*. New York.
⇒ **artificial intelligence, machine-aided translation**

koiné [Grk *koinós* 'common']

1 The common trade language of classical Greece. Developed from the dialect of Athens, it lost its specifically Attic features and consequently its strictly local flavor. Through this process, koiné became the accepted panregional variety, with various dialectal differences, in the other Greek city-states from about the fourth century BC on.

References
⇒ **Greek**

2 Term for every 'deregionalized' variety that develops from a group of several regionally related varieties of equal stature and becomes the generally accepted panregional 'standard' of those varieties. (⇒ *also* **standard language**)

Koman ⇒ Nilo-Saharan

Komi ⇒ Finno-Ugric

Kordofanian

Language group belonging to the **Niger-Kordofanian** family with about thirty languages in the Nuba Mountains area in Sudan. **Noun class** systems as in the **Niger-Congo** languages.

Reference
Schadeberg, T. 1981. *A survey of Kordofanian*, 2 vols. Hamburg.

Korean

Official language of Korea with approx. 60 million speakers. Its genetic affiliation is still unclear, though it is possibly related to the **Altaic** languages and/or **Japanese**. Continuous written documentation since 1446 in the Han'gul script, a syllabary developed from Chinese which, like Japanese writing, combines syllabic signs with Chinese logographic characters. Numerous lexical borrowings from **Chinese**.
Characteristics: relatively complex consonant system with three kinds of articulation for voiceless plosives (simple, aspirated, glottalized). Numerous morphophonemic changes with vowels and consonants, relatively complex syllable structure. Except for the phonology, Korean resembles Japanese fairly closely, which can probably be attributed to the long

contact these two languages have had.

References
Choi, S. 1993. *Japanese/Korean linguistics*, vol. 3. Chicago, IL.
Clancy, P. 1993. *Japanese/Korean linguistics*, vol. 2. Chicago, IL.
Hoji, H. 1993. *Japanese/Korean linguistics*. Chicago, IL.
Kim, C.-W. 1974. *The making of the Korean language*. Honolulu, HI.
Lee, H.H.B. 1989. *Korean grammar*. Oxford.
Lukoff, F. 1982. *An introductory course in Korean*. Seoul.
Martin, S. 1969. *Beginning Korean*. New Haven, CT.
O'Grady, W. 1991. *Categories and case: the sentence structure of Korean*. Amsterdam and Philadelphia, PA.
Ramstedt, G.J. 1949. *Studies in Korean etymology*. Helsinki.
Sohn, H. 1994. *Korean*. London.

Kru ⇒ Kwa

Kufi ⇒ Arabic

Kurdish

Iranian language with numerous dialects and approx. 10 million speakers in Iran, Iraq, Syria, Turkey, and the former Soviet Union. The closely related language Belochi (approx. 2 million speakers) is spoken over a wide area extending to Pakistan.

References
Bedir Khan, E.D. and R. Lescot. 1986. *Kurdische Grammatik* (Kurmanči-Dialekt). Bonn.
Blau, J. 1980. *Manuel de Kurde, dialecte Sorani*. Paris.
MacKenzie, D.N. 1951–62. *Kurdish dialect studies*. London.
Elfenbein, J.H. 1966. *The Baluchi language*. London.

Dictionary
Wahby, T. and C.J. Edmonds. 1966. *A Kurdish–English dictionary*. Oxford.
⇒ **Iranian**

Kwa

Branch of the **Niger-Congo** languages with about eighty languages, spoken in the West African coastal area; most important languages: **Yoruba** (approx. 19 million speakers) and **Igbo** (approx. 16 million speakers) in Nigeria, Akan (Twi-Fante, approx. 9 million speakers) in Ghana; an important subgroup includes the Kru languages in Liberia.
Characteristics: **tonal languages** (up to four tones, sometimes **downstep**); rich vowel system, vowel harmony; syntactically **isolating**, tendency towards monosyllables, **serial verb constructions**. Word order SVO with the exception of I jo in the Niger delta (SOV).

References
Koopman, H. 1984. The syntax of verbs: from verb movement in the Kru languages to universal grammar. Dordrecht.
Stewart, J.M. 1971. Niger-Kongo, Kwa. In T.A. Sebeok (ed.), *Current trends in linguisics*. The Hague. Vol. 7, 179–212.

Trutenau, H. (ed.) 1976. *Languages of the Akan area: papers in Western Kwa linguistics and on the linguistic geography of the area of ancient Begho.* Basel.
⇒ **creole**

Kwakiutl ⇒ **Wakashan**

L

L₁ vs L₂

L_1 is used in **applied linguistics, second language acquisition**, and **error analysis** to designate a speaker's 'first language,' 'native language,' or 'mother tongue.' In contrast, L_2 designates the second or **target language**.

labelled bracketing

Writing convention adopted by linguistics on the model of mathematical representations for illustrating syntactic structures. Labelled bracketing is equivalent to the representation in **tree diagrams** (see example there).

References
⇒ **glossematics**

labial [Lat. *labium* 'lip']

1 **Speech sound** classified according to its **articulator** (lower lip), in contrast to a **lingual**, e.g. [f], [m] in [frʌm].

2 **Speech sound** classified according to its **place of articulation** (upper lip) e.g. [b], [m], and [p] in [bʌmp].

3 **Speech sound** classified according to its **articulator** (lower lip) and its **place of articulation** (upper lips). A more exact classification distinguishes between bilabials [p, b, m], labio-dentals [f, v], and labio-velars [w], among others. (⇒ *also* **articulatory phonetics, phonetics**)

References
⇒ **phonetics**

labialization (*also* rounding)

1 **Articulation** with rounded lips, as in the vowels [u, o, y, ø], as opposed to the unrounded [i, e]. Labialization can also refer to a secondary articulation (⇒ **articulatory phonetics**), involving any noticeable lip-rounding, as in the initial [k] or [ʃ] in [ku] *coo* and [ʃu] *shoe*, as opposed to [k] and [ʃ] in [ki] *key*, [ʃi] *she*. There are also labialized consonants in some languages, in which the labialization of the consonant has phonemic status, such as the labio-velar k^w in **Indo-European**, as well as labialized consonants in many native languages of the northwest coast of America or in **Caucasian languages**.

References
⇒ **phonetics**

2 Diachronic (⇒ **synchrony vs diachrony**) **sound change** through which an originally unrounded sound is rounded in **assimilation** to a labial sound, e.g. MHG *leffel* > NHG *Löffel* 'spoon.' The opposite process is called delabialization. (⇒ **unrounding**)

References
⇒ **sound change**

labio-dental [Lat. *dens* 'tooth']

Speech sound classified according to its **articulator** (lips = labial) and its **place of articulation** (teeth = dental), e.g. [f], [ɱ] in Ital. ['niɱfa] 'nymph.' (⇒ *also* **phonetics**)

References
⇒ **phonetics**

LAD ⇒ language acquisition device

Ladinian ⇒ Rhaeto-Romance

Lakhota ⇒ Siouan

Lako-Dargwa ⇒ North-East Caucasian

lambda operator ⇒ operator

laminal [Lat. *lamina* 'a thin sheet']

Speech sound classified according to its **articulator** (blade of the tongue = lamina). (⇒ *also* **articulatory phonetics, phonetics**)

References
⇒ **phonetics**

lamino-alveolar ⇒ articulation

lamino-dental ⇒ interdental

lamino-palatal

Speech sound classified according to its **articulator** (blade of the tongue = lamina) and its **place of articulation** (**palate**), e.g. [ɕ] in Chinese [ɕyɛɕi] 'to learn.' Lamino-palatals are called alveolo-palatals in the IPA (see chart, p. xix). (⇒ *also* **articulatory phonetics**)

References
⇒ **phonetics**

lamino-post-alveolar

Speech sound classified according to its **articulator** (blade of the tongue = lamina) and its **place of articulation** (behind the alveolar ridge = post-alveolar), e.g. [ʒ] [mɛʒər] *measure*. Lamino-post-alveolars are called palato-alveolars in the IPA (see chart, p. xix). (⇒ *also* **articulatory phonetics, phonetics**)

References
⇒ **phonetics**

Landsmål ⇒ Norwegian

langage [Fr. 'language']

An umbrella term used by F. de Saussure for *langue* and *parole*. The 'faculté de langage' signifies general human linguistic and language ability, that is to say, the ability to communicate using a system of sounds and symbols. 'Taken as a whole, speech is many-sided and heterogeneous; straddling several areas simultaneously – physical, physiological, and psychological – it belongs both to the individual and to society' (Saussure 1916/1983: 11).

References
Saussure, F. de 1916. *Cours de linguistique générale*, ed. C. Bally and A. Sechehaye. Paris. (*Course in general linguistics*, trans. R. Harris. London, 1983.)
⇒ **langue vs parole**

language

Vehicle for the expression or exchanging of thoughts, concepts, knowledge, and information as well as the fixing and transmission of experience and knowledge. It is based on cognitive processes, subject to societal factors and subject to historical change and development. In this definition, language refers to a specific form of expression that is restricted to humans, and differs from all other possible languages, such as **animal communication** and **artificial languages** through **creativity**, the ability to make conceptional abstractions, and the possibility of metalinguistic reflection. (⇒ *also* **linguistic theory, origin of language, philosophy of language**)

1 In linguistics, the ambiguity of the term language (to be understood as 'language,' 'linguistic competence,' and 'individual language') is differentiated and clarified depending on the given theoretical concept and interest through abstraction and delimitation of subaspects. In this process the following concepts are distinguished (with varying terminology). (a) A specific system of signs and combinatory rules which are arbitrary but passed on as conventions. Such linguistic systems, which F. de Saussure calls langue (⇒ **langue vs parole**), are the object of structural investigations, while research oriented towards a generative understanding of language attempts to describe the underlying linguistic competence of a speaker

as well as the speaker's creative ability to produce a potentially infinite number of sentences, depending on his/her communicative needs. **Transformational grammar** is based on this kind of dynamic understanding of language. (b) Language as an individual activity, as a concrete speech act, undertaken on the basis of (a). In this sense one also speaks of 'parole' (de Saussure) or 'performance' (N. Chomsky). On the theoretical justification of these differentiations ⇒ **langue vs parole, competence vs performance**. To what extent single speech acts form the empirical basis for linguistic studies on the description of the underlying grammatical system depends on the respective theoretical conception or on the extent of idealization of the object of study.

For the differentiation of language under idiolectal, regional, social, and other aspects ⇒ **dialectology, sociolinguistics**, and **variational linguistics**.

References
⇒ **linguistics**

2 Genetically innate human capacity based on neurophysiological processes for directing cognitive and communicative processes (corresponding to de Saussure's 'faculté de langue'). This is the primary object of study of neurophysiology, psychology, and others. Linguistic investigations in this area (such as problems of language acquisition and aphasia) are perforce of an interdisciplinary nature, as can be seen in such terms as **psycholinguistics** and **neurolinguistics**.

References
⇒ **language acquisition, language disorder**

3 An individual national language, such as English, Russian, Japanese, etc.

References
⇒ **classification of languages, language change, language typology, universals**

4 In **semiotics** and **information theory**, a system of signs used for communication. This includes, in addition to natural languages, artificial languages such as **programming languages**, formal languages of logic and mathematics, semaphore, and animal languages.

References
⇒ **animal communication, information theory, planned language**

language acquisition

Umbrella term for (a) the natural acquisition of one's first language, (b) the natural acquisition of a second or multiple languages, (c) **second language acquisition** in a formal learning environment, and (d) the relearning of one's first language in therapy (⇒ **language disorder**). It is the basic concept of language which, in the approaches to (a)–(d), determines the individual hypotheses as to which linguistic skills are acquired, under what conditions, in which way, when the process begins, and how long it lasts. Research in this area has been strongly influenced by current linguistic, psycholinguistic, and sociological theories.

From 1950 to 1980 research brought forth four main hypotheses regarding first language acquisition: (i) the behavioristic hypothesis (⇒ **behaviorism**, **empiricism**) propounded by Skinner (1957), which traces language-learning processes back to experience, imitation, and selective conditioning; (ii) the nativistic hypothesis (⇒ **nativism**), arising from Chomsky's criticism of Skinner (see Chomsky 1959, 1975) and according to which language acquisition is considered to be a more or less autonomous process of maturation based on an inborn mechanism of language acquisition. This hypothesis places emphasis on the development of linguistic competence (⇒ **competence vs performance**) (⇒ also **transformational grammar**); (iii) the cognition hypothesis, which takes into account the relationship between the developing cognitive and intellectual abilities (see Rice and Kemper 1984, also Bowerman 1989); and (iv) the social constitution hypothesis, which gives priority to the importance of the child's socialization and interaction (Miller 1980). In this hypothesis, the child's desire for experience and communication with others provides the principal impetus for the development of linguistic abilities.

In the 1980s, research in language acquisition turned more strongly towards the acquisition of grammar. This is evidenced by the following two positions. The first, which was clearly influenced by more recent linguistic theories (e.g. **Government and Binding theory** and **Lexical-Functional Grammar**), can be seen as a further development of the nativistic hypothesis. It holds that there are specific inherent abilities and specific acquisition mechanisms, and discusses to what extent child grammars at any given time are true grammars in terms of a **universal grammar** (see Pinker 1984; Hyams 1986; Felix 1987; for an overview see Weissenborn and Schriefers 1987). The second position, which was strongly influenced by functional language models (**functional grammar**, **discourse analysis**), generally ascribes an important role to input and views language acquisition, among other things, as embedded in general cognitive processes. This position encompasses learning processes (see (i), and its further development, **connection-**

ism), cognitive abilities (see (iii)), as well as socialization and interactive experiences (see (iv)) (e.g. Maratsos and Chalkley 1980; Slobin 1985; McWhinney 1987). Issues currently under debate also between both positions are, for example, the acquisition of regular and irregular verb morphology (e.g. Rumelhart and McClelland 1986; Marcus *et al.* 1992; Plunkett and Marchman 1993). An essential test for all approaches are cross-linguistic studies (see Slobin 1985–93; Hyams 1986; McWhinney and Bates 1989), and possible explanations offered by individual learning styles or learning strategies (see Nelson 1981; Peters 1983). Here it is a matter of styles, such as the pronominal or holistic, in which children begin with memorized sentences that, for example, also contain pronouns, and the (hitherto more thoroughly researched) nominal or analytical style, in which children begin with individual words, especially nouns or noun combinations.

References

Bates, E. *et al.* 1988. *From first words to grammar.* Cambridge.

Berko-Gleason, J. 1989. *The development of language.* Columbus, OH.

Bloom, L. 1991. *Language development from two to three.* Cambridge.

Bloom, P. (ed.) 1994. *Language acquisition: core readings.* Cambridge, MA.

Bowerman, M. 1989. Learning a semantic system: what role do cognitive predispositions play? In M. Rice and R.L. Schiefelbusch (eds), *The teachability of language.* Baltimore, MD. 133–69.

Chapman, R.S. (ed.) 1992. *Child talk: processes in language acquisition and disorders.* Chicago, IL.

Chomsky, N. 1959. Verbal behaviour. (A discussion of B.F. Skinner, 1957). *Lg* 35.26–58.

—— 1965. *Aspects of the theory of syntax.* Cambridge, MA.

—— 1975. *Reflections on language.* New York.

Clark, E. 1993. *The lexicon in acquisition.* Cambridge.

Cromer, R. 1991. *Language and cognition in normal and handicapped children.* Oxford.

Donaldson, M. 1978. *Children's minds.* Glasgow.

Dromi, E. (ed.) 1992. *Language and cognition: a developmental perspective.* Hillsdale, NJ.

Ervin-Tripp, S.M. 1971. An overview of theories of grammatical development. In D. Slobin (ed.), *The ontogenesis of grammar: a theoretical symposium.* New York. 189–212.

Felix, S. 1987. *Cognition and language growth.* Dordrecht.

Fletcher, P. and M. Garman, 1986. *Language acquisition*, 2nd edn. Cambridge.

Fletcher, P. and B. McWhinney. 1994. *The handbook of child language.* Oxford.

Gallaway, C. and B.J. Richards. 1994. *Input and interaction in language acquisition.* Cambridge.

Gleitman, L.R. *et al.* 1984. The current status of the motherese hypothesis. *JChL* 11.43–79.

Goodluck, H. 1991. *Language acquisition: a linguistic introduction*. Oxford.

Harris, M. 1993. *Language experience and early language development: from input to uptake*. Hillsdale, NJ.

Hornstein, N. and D. Lightfoot. 1981. *Explanation in linguistics: the logical problem of language acquisition*. London.

Howe, C. 1993. *Language learning: a special case for developmental psychology?* Hillsdale, NJ.

Hyams, N.M. 1986. *Language acquisition and the theory of parameters*. Dordrecht.

Ingram, S. 1989. *First language acquisition*. Cambridge.

Jakobson, R. 1944. *Kindersprache, Aphasie und allgemeine Lautgesetze*. Uppsala. (English: *Child language, aphasia and phonological universals*, trans. by A. Keiler. The Hague and Paris 1968. (Repr. Berlin and New York, 1980.))

Karmiloff-Smith, A. 1979. *A functional approach to child language*. Cambridge.

—— 1992. *Beyond modularity: a developmental perspective on cognitive science*. Cambridge, MA.

Kessel, F. (ed.) 1988. *The development of language and language researchers: essays in honor of R. Brown*. Hillsdale, NJ.

Krasnegor, N. *et al.* (eds) 1991. *Biological and behavioral determinants of language development*. Hillsdale, NJ.

Levy, Y. *et al.* 1988. *Categories and processes in language acquisition*. Hillsdale, NJ.

Locke, J. 1993. *The child's path to spoken language*. Cambridge, MA.

McWhinney (ed.) 1987. *Mechanisms of language acquisition*. Hillsdale, NJ.

McWhinney, B. and E. Bates. 1989. Functionalism and the competition model. In B. McWhinney and E. Bates (eds), *The cross-linguistic study of sentence processing*. Cambridge. 3–73.

McWhinney, B. *et al.* 1989. Language learning: cues or rules? *JMemL* 28.255–77.

Malave, L.M. and G. Duquette (eds) 1991. *Language, culture and cognition: a collection of studies in first and second language acquisition*. Clevedon.

Maratsos, M. and A. Chalkley. 1980. The internal language of children's syntax: The ontogenesis and representation of syntactic categories. In K. Nelson (ed.), *Children's language*. New York. Vol. 2, 127–214.

Marcus, G. *et al.* 1992. *Overgeneralization in language acquisition*. (MRCD 57/4.) Chicago, IL.

McTear, M. 1985. *Children's conversation*. London.

Miller, M. 1980. Sprachliche Sozialisation. In K. Hurrelmann and D. Ulrich (eds), *Handbuch der Sozialisation*. Weinheim.

Muma, J.R. 1986. *Language acquisition: a functionalist perspective*. Austin, TX.

Nelson, K. 1981. Individual differences in language development: implications for development and language. *Developmental Psychology* 17.170–87.

Ochs, E. and B. Schiefelin (eds) 1979. *Developmental pragmatics*. New York.

Peters, A. 1983. *The units of language acquisition*. Cambridge.

Piatelli-Palmerini, M. (ed.) 1979. *Théories du langage, théories de l'aprentissage*. Paris. (English: *Language and learning: the debate between Jean Piaget and Noam Chomsky*. Cambridge, MA, 1980.)

—— 1989. Evolution, selection and cognition: from learning to parameter setting in biology and in the study of language. *Cognition* 31.1–44.

Pinker, S. 1984. *Language learnability and language development*. Cambridge, MA.

—— 1989. *Learnability and cognition: the acquisition of argument structure*. Cambridge, MA.

Plunkett, K. and V. Marchman. 1993. From rote learning to system building: acquiring verb morphology in children and connectionist nets. *Cognition* 48.21–69.

Rice, M. and S. Kemper. 1984. *Child language and cognition*. Baltimore, MD.

Rice, M. and R. Schiefelbusch (eds) 1989. *The teachability of language*. Baltimore, MD.

Richards, B. 1990. *Language development and individual differences: a study of auxiliary verb learning*. Cambridge.

Roeper, T. 1988. Grammatical principles of first language acquisition: theory and evidence. In F. Newmeyer (ed.), *Linguistics: the Cambridge survey*. Cambridge. Vol. 2, 35–52.

Rumelhart, D. and E.J. McClelland. 1986. *Parallel distributed processing*, 2 vols. Cambridge, MA.

Sinclair, A.W. and J.M. Levelt (eds) 1978. *The child's conception of language*. Berlin.

Skinner, B.F. 1957. *Verbal behavior*. London.

Slobin, D.I. 1985. Cross-linguistic evidence for the language making capacity. In D.I. Slobin (ed.), *The cross-linguistic evidence of language acquisition*. Hillsdale, NJ. Vol. 2, 1157–256.

—— 1985–93. *The cross-linguistic study of language acquisition*, 3 vols. Hillsdale, NJ.

Tracy, R. and E. Lattey (eds) 1994. *How tolerant is Universal Grammar? Essays on language learnability and language variation*. Tübingen.

Wannder, E. and L.R. Gleitman. 1982. *Language acquisition: the state of the art*. Cambridge.

Weissenborn, J. and J. Meisel (eds) 1986. Studies on morphological and syntactic development. *Linguistics* 24 (special issue).

Weissenborn, J. and H. Schriefers. 1987. Psycholinguistics. In U. Ammon *et al.* (eds), *Sociolinguistics: an international handbook of the science of language and society*. Berlin and New York, 470–87.

Bibliographies

Leopold, W.F. 1972. *Bibliography of child language*. Bloomington, IN.

Slobin, D.I. 1972. *Leopold's bibliography of child language*, revised and augmented. Bloomington, IN.

Journals

Child Development.

First Language.

Journal of Child Language.

⇒ **developmental language disorder, language acquisition device, language disorder, psycholinguistics, universal grammar**

on

language acquisition device (*abbrev.* LAD)

Specifically human mechanism postulated by N. Chomsky, in connection with the linguistic interpretation of **rationalism**, to explain the phenomenon that children – although the linguistic utterances of their environment represent only deficient and incomplete input – gain a command of the syntactic rules of their mother tongue in a relatively short time and can produce and understand an almost unlimited number of grammatical expressions. Every child is equipped with an innate schema for valid grammars (⇒ **universals**) and with a system of cognitive procedures for developing and checking hypotheses about the input. Thus, a child formulates hypotheses about the grammatical structure of the given sentences, makes predictions about them, and checks these predictions with new sentences. He/she eliminates those sentences that contradict the evidence and validates those that were not eliminated through the criterion of simplicity. This mechanism is engaged with the very first input. The child essentially forms a theory, comparable to that of a linguist who constructs a descriptively and explanatorily adequate theory of a language. This parallel, at the same time, justifies linguists in considering problems of language acquisition with linguistic methods of investigation. See Levelt's (1975) critique of the language acquisition device.

References
Chomsky, N. 1965. *Aspects of the theory of syntax.* Cambridge, MA.
—— 1975. *Reflections on language.* New York.
Katz, J.J. 1966. *The philosophy of language.* London.
Levelt, W.J.M. 1975. *What became of LAD?* The Hague.
McNeill, D. 1970. *The acquisition of language: the study of developmental psycholinguistics.* New York.
Piatelli-Palmarini, M. (ed.) 1980. *Language and learning.* London.
⇒ **language acquisition**, **mentalism**, **psycholinguistics**, **universals**

language and brain

Study of the relationships between components of language processing and regions of the brain. Evidence for such relationships is provided by studies of **lateralization** and of **language disorders** in **neurolinguistics**, neurology, **neuropsychology**, and psychology. The relationships have been conceptualized in two principal ways: The 'localistic' view holds that particular, narrowly defined regions of the brain are specialized for particular functions in language processing (⇒ **language area**). Classic representatives of this view are P. Broca, C. Wernicke, K. Kleise. The 'holistic' view, on the other hand, posits complex neural systems and a closer relationship between various processing components (e.g. hierarchical structures, or factors such as attention and motivation working in concert), and thus questions a one-to-one relationship. Classic representatives of this view are J.H. Jackson, H. Head, and K. Goldstein. Localistic and holistic views are integrated in Luria's (1973) approach. The discussions about the nature of language and brain relationships continue as models of language processing evolve. Improved methodologies (e.g. tomographic imagery and psychometric procedures) have recently made it possible to study such relationships more precisely: for example, some patients with global **Broca's aphasia** or **Wernicke's aphasia** have failed to demonstrate a unique relationship between linguistic symptom and location of lesion (see de Bleser 1988). Studies of the relationship between language and brain are of particular interest in current discussions of the modular make-up of cognitive systems and their biological foundations (see Chomsky 1980; Fodor 1983).

References
Bleser, R. de. 1987. From agrammatism to paragrammatism: German aphasiological traditions and grammatical disturbances. *Cognitive Neuropsychology* 4.187–256.
—— 1988. Localization of aphasia: science or fiction. In G. Denes, C. Semenza, and P. Bisiacchi (eds), *Perspectives on cognitive neuropsychology.* Hove and London. 161–85.
Caplan, D. 1987. *Neurolinguistics and linguistic aphasiology.* Cambridge.
Chomsky, N. 1980. *Rules and representations.* Oxford.
Cresson, B. 1985. Subcortical functions in language: a working model. *B&L* 25.257–92.
Dingwall, W.O. 1981. *Language and the brain: a bibliographical guide*, 2 vols. New York.
Fodor, J.A. 1983. *The modularity of mind.* Cambridge, MA.
Gibson, K.R. and A.C. Peterson (eds) 1991. *Brain maturation and cognitive development.* Berlin and New York.
Kean, M.L. 1988. Brain structures and linguistic capacity. In F. Newmeyer (ed.), *Linguistics: the Cambridge survey.* Cambridge. Vol. 2, 74–95.
Kertesz, A. (ed.) 1983. *Localization in neuropsychology.* New York.
Luria, A. 1966. *Higher cortical functions in man.* New York.
—— 1973. *The working brain.* New York.
Neville, H., D.L. Mills, and D.S. Lawson. 1992. Fractionating language: different neural subsystems with different sensitive periods. *Cerebral Cortex* 2.244–58.
Popper, K. and J. Eccles. 1977. *The self and its brain.* Berlin.

Posner, M. *et al.* 1988. Localization of cognitive operations in the human brain. *Science* 240.1627–31.

Sejnowski, T.J. and P.S. Churchland. 1989. Brain and cognition. In M.I. Posner (ed.), *Foundations of cognitive science*. Cambridge, MA and London. 301–56.

⇒ **connectionism, developmental language disorder, language acquisition, language disorder, language processing, lateralization, modularity**

language and cognition

Cognition is knowledge or understanding in its broadest sense. Therefore, studies in cognition concern all mental processes through which an organism becomes conscious of objects of thought or gains an understanding of its environment. Since the symbolic representation of a thing is an important means of understanding, language constitutes a principal object of investigation for cognitive approaches. In this respect, linguistics can also be construed as a cognitive science, which heretofore has been most clearly realized in **cognitive grammar**. The human brain is viewed, in analogy to the construction of a computer, as a structured system. As far as linguistic abilities are concerned, much controversy surrounds the question as to what degree a special module in the whole system should be hypothesized. Representing the one extreme is Chomsky who, in his theory of language, provides an autonomous module for language that interacts only loosely with other modules, while Langacker, in his cognitive grammar (which probably represents the other extreme), understands language only as one among many different expressions of a general abstract capacity. Interdisciplinary approaches will, no doubt, bring about further developments in this area. The relationship of language and cognition has been of particular interest for the cognition hypothesis in **language acquisition** as well as for studies in **language processing**.

References

Anderson, J.R. 1983. *The architecture of cognition.* Cambridge, MA.

Chomsky, N. 1980. *Rules and representations.* Oxford.

—— 1981. *Lectures on government and binding.* Dordrecht. (7th edn Berlin and New York 1993).

Fodor, J.A. 1983. *The modularity of mind.* Cambridge, MA.

Gentner, D. and A.L. Stevens. 1983. *The mind's new science: a history of the cognitive revolution.* New York.

Higginbotham, J. 1995. *Language and cognition.* Oxford.

Jackendoff, R. 1987. *Consciousness and the computational mind.* Cambridge, MA.

—— 1993. *Languages of the mind: essays on*

mental representation. Cambridge, MA and London.

Jorna, R. *et al.* 1992. *Semiotics of cognition and expert systems.* Berlin and New York.

Langacker, R.W. 1987. *Foundations of cognitive grammar,* vol. 1: *Theoretical perspectives.* Stanford, CA.

—— 1992. *Concept, image, and symbol: the cognitive basis of grammar.* Berlin and New York.

Lindsay, P.H. and D.M. Norman, 1972. *Human information processing: an introduction to psychology.* New York. (2nd edn 1977.)

Lycan, W.G. (ed.) 1990. *Mind and cognition.* Oxford.

Rudzka-Ostyn, B. (ed.) 1987. *Topics in cognitive linguistics.* Amsterdam.

Schank, R. 1980. Language and memory. *CSc* 4.243–84.

Stillings, N.A. *et al.* 1987. *Cognitive science: an introduction.* Cambridge, MA.

Journals
Cognitive Linguistics.
Language and Cognitive Processes.
⇒ **language acquisition, language processing**

language and gender ⇒ feminist linguistics, gender

language area (*also* language center)

Term denoting a specific region (or area) in the brain that has been ascribed a particular function or specialization in language processing. Our understanding of such areas is based on studies showing correlations between certain language disorders and specifically situated brain lesions. The most well-known areas are the motor area (or **Broca's area**) and the sensory area (or **Wernicke's area**). This 'localization' view of the relationship between language and brain, however, continues to be subject to debate.

References

Bleser, R. de. 1988. Localization of aphasia: science or fiction. In G. Denes, C. Semenza, and P. Bisiacchi (eds), *Perspectives on cognitive neuropsychology.* Hove and London, 181–85.

Caplan, D. 1987. *Neurolinguistics and linguistic aphasiology.* Cambridge.

Cresson, B. 1985. Subcortical functions in language: a working model. *B&L* 25.257–92.

Luria, A. 1973. *The working brain.* New York.

language center ⇒ language area

language change

In **historical linguistics**, the study of the diachronic process(es) of change in language elements and language systems (⇒ **diachronic linguistics**). Language change takes place on all levels of linguistic description: (a) in **phonology**, depending on conditioning factors, a distinction is drawn between phonetic and phonological change and changes motivated by **analogy** or by extralinguistic factors (⇒ **sound change**). (b) In **morphology**, a distinction is drawn between changes in the inflectional system and changes in **word formation**. (i) In inflectional morphology, such processes involve the occurrence and classification of morphological categories (e.g. in the development of the **Indo-European languages** several categories have disappeared: most frequently the **dual**, but also **case**, **gender**, **mood**, and **tense** differentiations); on the other hand, the realization of different categories has been retained, for example, by substituting inflected forms for periphrastic forms (⇒ **periphrasis**). (ii) In word formation, language change concerns above all the change from compositional to derivational regularities (⇒ **composition**, **derivation**) as well as the process of **back formation**. (c) In **syntax**, language change involves, among other things, regularities in word and phrase order (⇒ **word order**). In such cases, there is an interrelation between the changes on the individual levels (e.g. the phonological decay of case endings from Old English to Middle English which led to fundamental changes in English morphology and syntax; ⇒ **syncretism**) that results in an increase in stricter rules for word and phrase order. (d) In semantics, ⇒ **semantic change** and **borrowing**.

The causes of language change are sought primarily in internal or external conditions, depending on the theoretical viewpoint. Internal conditions for language change are motivated in general by economy, i.e. the tendency towards simplification of the language system. Studies of such linguistic changes refer either (a) to physiological conditions, i.e. to problems of articulatory-phonetic simplification like **assimilation**, or (b) to functional aspects, i.e. to problems of the functional load or balance of individual expressions in the system with regard to the differentiation of important contrasts or to structural conditions such as the tendency towards symmetric distribution of elements and characteristics in linguistic systems through which **empty slots** or double-occupied positions are leveled out. Among external conditions are interference from foreign (neighboring) languages or from different language varieties within a linguistic community (⇒ **bilingualism**, **language contact**, **substratum**, **superstratum**), historically conditioned changes in forms of communication, sociological changes, and others. (⇒ also **drift**, **reconstruction**, **synchrony vs diachrony**)

References

Aitchison, J. 1981. *Language change: progress or decay?* London. (2nd edn Cambridge, 1991.)

Andersen, H. 1973. Abductive and deductive change. *Lg* 49.765–93.

Anderson, S.R. 1988. Morphological change. In F. Newmeyer (ed.), *Linguistics: the Cambridge survey*. Cambridge. Vol. I, 324–62.

Antilla, R. 1972. *An introduction to historical and comparative linguistics*. New York.

Baldi, P. (ed.) 1990. *Linguistic change and reconstruction methodology*. Berlin and New York.

Bartsch, R. and T. Vennemann. 1982. *Grundzüge der Sprachtheorie*. Tübingen.

Breivik, L.E.. and E.H. Jahr (eds) 1989. *Language change: contributions to the study of its causes*. Berlin and New York.

Bynon, T. 1977. *Historical linguistics*. Cambridge.

Coseriu, E. 1958. *Synchronie, Diachronie und Geschichte*. Munich.

Crowley, T. 1992. *An introduction to historical linguistics*. Oxford.

Davis, G.W. and G. Iverson (eds) 1992. *Explanation in historical linguistics*, Amsterdam.

Faarlaund, J.T. 1990. *Syntactic change: toward a theory of historical syntax*. Berlin and New York.

Gerritsen, M. and D. Stein (eds) 1992. *Internal and external factors in syntactic change*. Berlin and New York.

Gvozdanovic, J. 1985. *Language system and its change*. Berlin and New York.

Hock, H.H. 1986. *Principles of historical linguistics*. Berlin. (2nd edn 1990).

Hoenigswald, H.N. 1965. *Language change and linguistic reconstruction*. Chicago, IL.

Jeffers, R.J. and I. Lehiste. 1979. *Principles and methods for historical linguistics*. Cambridge, MA.

Jones, C. (ed.) 1993. *Historical linguistics: problems and perspectives*. London and New York.

Keller, R. 1994. *On language change. The invisible hand in language*. Trans. B. Nerlich. London.

King, R. 1969. *Historical linguistics and generative grammar*. Englewood Cliffs, NJ.

Kiparsky, P. 1968. Linguistic universals and linguistic change. In E. Bach and R.T. Harms (eds), *Universals in linguistic theory*. New York. 170–202.

——— 1988. Phonological change. In F. Newmeyer (ed.), *Linguistics: the Cambridge survey*. Cambridge. Vol. I, 363–415.

Labov, W., M. Yaeger, and R. Steiner (eds) 1972. *A quantitative study of sound change in progress*. Philadelphia, PA.

Labov, W. 1994. *Principles of linguistic change*. Vol. 1: internal factors. Oxford.

Lass, R. 1980. *On explaining language change*. Cambridge.

Lehmann, W.P. 1962. *Historical linguistics: an introduction*. New York. (2nd edn 1973).

Lightfoot, D.W. 1979. *Principles of diachronic syntax*. Cambridge.

——— 1988. Syntactic change. In F. Newmeyer (ed.), *Linguistics: the Cambridge survey*. Cambridge. Vol. 1.303–23.

——— 1992. *How to set parameters: arguments from language change*. Cambridge

McMahon, A.M.S. 1994. *Understanding language change*. Cambridge.

Martinet, A. 1955. *Economie des changements phonétiques: traité de phonologie diachronique*. Bern.

McMahon, A,M.S. 1994. *Understanding language change*. Cambridge.

Meillet, A. 1925. *La méthode comparative en linguistique historique* . Oslo.

Milroy, J. 1992. *Linguistic variation and change: on the historical sociolinguistics of English*. Oxford.

Nerlich, B. 1990. *Change in language. Whitney, Bréal and Wegener*. London.

Paul, H. 1880. *Prinzipien der Sprachgeschichte*. Tübingen. (9th edn Tübingen 1975).

Polomé, E.C. (ed.) 1990. *Research guide on language change*. Berlin and New York.

Sturtevant, E.H. 1907. *Linguistic change*. Chicago, IL.

Trask, R.L. 1994. *Language change*. London.

Vennemann, T. 1983. Causality in language change: theories of linguistic preferences as a basis for linguistic explanations. *FolH* 6.5–26.

Weinreich, U., W. Labov, and W. Herzog, 1968. Empirical foundations for a theory of language change. In W.P. Lehmann and Y. Malkiel (eds), *Direction for historical linguistics*. Austin, TX. 95–188.

Collected papers

Ahlqvist, A. (ed.) 1982. *Papers from the fifth International Conference on Historical Linguistics*. Amsterdam

Anderson, J.M. and C. Jones (eds) 1974. *Historical linguistics*, 2 vols. Amsterdam.

Baldi, P. and R.N. Werth (eds) 1978. *Readings in historical phonology*. University Park, PA.

Blount, B. and G.M. Sanches (ed.) 1977. *Sociocultural dimensions of language change*. New York.

Cherubim, D. (ed.) 1975. *Sprachwandel: Reader zur diachronischen Sprachwissenschaft*. Berlin.

Fisiak, J. (ed.) 1978. *Recent developments in historical linguistics*. The Hague.

——— (ed.) 1980. *Historical morphology*. The Hague.

——— (ed.) 1984. *Historical syntax*. The Hague.

Keiler, A.R. (ed.) 1972. *A reader in historical and comparative linguistics*. New York.

Lehmann, W.P. and Y. Malkiel (eds) 1982. *Perspectives on historical linguistics*. Amsterdam.

Li, C.N. (ed.) 1975. *Word order and word order change*. Austin, TX.

——— (ed.) 1977. *Mechanisms of syntactic change*. Austin, TX.

Lüdtke, H. (ed.) 1980. *Kommunikationstheoretische Grundlagen des Sprachwandels*. Berlin.

Rauch, I. and G.F. Carr (eds) 1983. *Language change*. Bloomington, IN.

Stockwell, R. and R. MacAulay (eds) 1972. *Historical linguistics and generative theory*. Bloomington, IN.

Trask, R.L. 1994. *Language change*. London.

Traugott, E.C. *et al.* (eds) 1980. *Papers from the fourth International Conference on Historical Linguistics*. Amsterdam.

language comprehension (*also* language perception, speech comprehension)

Term referring to processes involved in understanding spoken (speech comprehension), signed (**sign language**) or written language (*also* ⇒ **reading**). Traditionally, speech perception and language perception or comprehension were two distinct fields, the former being interested in the perception of units such as phonemes and syllables, the latter interested in the perception of units such as phrases and sentences. However, both fields have come closer insofar as speech perception now also considers such units in connected speech, and language comprehension takes account of intonational and phonological information. In language comprehension, a number of complex processes on different levels are involved: the perception, segmentation and identification of sensory (acoustic or visual) information, word recognition, i.e. matching the sounds against probable words (lexical access and delimiting the various possibilities to one word on the level of the **mental lexicon**), processes such as the assignment of structure to the word sequences on the syntactic level (**parsing**), processes of integrating meaning on the level of propositional structure, inferences (conversational **implicature**, **inference**), and integrating the meaning of sentences into the meaning of the ongoing discourse. At the discourse level, cultural standards may come in (e.g. organized in terms of **scripts** or **frames**). At what level and in which way knowledge of the world comes in, is a matter of the various models.

How the various processes are organized is still under debate. Two major types of processing models (⇒ **language processing**) have been distinguished: autonomous and interactive models. The former assume that all relevant processes are applied in serial and hierarchical order ('bottom-up') with each subprocess working autonomously (⇒ **modularity**); the latter, in contrast, assume parallel and interactive processing at all different levels ('bottom-up' and 'top-down'; ⇒ **bottom-up vs top-down**, **connectionism**; see e.g. Marslen-Wilson 1984; see also MacWhinney and Bates 1989). Besides autonomous or interactive models, there are also models which combine autonomous and interactive processes, e.g. the Cohort model for word recognition by Marslen-Wilson (see Marslen-Wilson and Welsh 1978; see also Marslen-Wilson 1987). To capture language comprehension (e.g. word recognition), traditionally 'off-line' tasks were chosen, in which the subject reacts after listening or reading the relevant item. 'On-line' tasks, in which the subject reacts while listening or reading the sentence or word and where reaction-time is measured, now allow insights into the ongoing interaction of information from different levels as well as into real-time processing (see e.g.Tyler 1992). For an overview see Weissenborn and Schriefers (1987), Flores d'Arcais (1988), Tannenhaus (1988).

References

Altmann, G.T.M. (ed.) 1990. *Cognitive models of speech processing*. Cambridge, MA.
Bransford, J.D. 1979. *Human cognition: learning, understanding and remembering*. Belmont, CA.
Brown, G. and G. Yule. 1983. *Discourse analysis*. Cambridge.
Forster, K.I. 1981. Priming and the effects of sentence and lexical contexts in naming times. Evidence for autonomous lexical processing. *Quarterly Journal of Experimental Psychology* 33.465–95.
Frazier, L. 1988. Grammar and language processing. In F. Newmeyer (ed.), *Linguistics: the Cambridge survey*. Cambridge. Vol. 2, 15–34.
Flores D'Arcais, G. 1988. *Language perception*. In F. Newmeyer (ed.), *Linguistics: the Cambridge survey*. Cambridge. Vol. 3, 97–123.
Flores D'Arcais, G.B. and R.J. Jarvella (eds) 1983. *The process of language understanding*. Chichester.
Garfield, J. 1986. *Modularity in knowledge representation and natural language understanding*. London.
Gernsbacher, M.A. 1990. *Language comprehension as structure building*. Hillsdale, NJ.
McWhinney, B. and E. Bates. 1989. *Cross-linguistic study of sentence processing*. Cambridge.
Marslen-Wilson, W. 1984. Function and process in spoken word recognition: a tutorial. In H. Bouma and D.G. Bouwhuis (eds), *Attention and performance X*. 125–50.
—— 1987. Functional parallelism in spoken word recognition. *Cognition* 25.71–102.
Marslen-Wilson, W. and A. Welsh. 1978. Processing interactions and lexical access during word recognition in continuous speech. *Cognitive Psychology* 10.29–63.
Schank, R.C. and R.P. Abelson. 1977. *Scripts, plans, goals, and understanding*. Hillsdale, NJ.
Tannenhaus, M.K. 1988. Psycholinguistics: an overview. In F.J. Newmeyer (ed.), *Linguistics: the Cambridge survey*. Cambridge. Vol. 3, 1–37.
Tyler, L.K. 1992. *Spoken language comprehension: an experimental approach to disordered and normal processing*. Cambridge, MA.
Weissenborn, J. and H. Schriefers. 1987. Psycholinguistics. In U. Ammon *et al.* (eds), *Sociolinguistics: an international handbook of the science of language and society*. Berlin and New York. 470–87.
Winograd, T. 1977. A framework for understanding discourse. In M.A. Just and P.A. Carpenter (eds), *Cognitive processes in comprehension*. Hillsdale, NJ.

⇒ **language processing**, **psycholinguistics**

language contact

Situation in which two or more languages coexist within one state and where the speakers use these different languages alternately in specific situations. Contemporary examples are found in Belgium, Switzerland, China, India, Peru, and other countries. Such linguistic contacts can have a political, historical, geographic, or cultural-historical basis. The mutual influences can be shown on all levels of description. While linguistics in the past has been primarily concerned with the analysis and description of the processes of linguistic exchanges, it has meanwhile become more concerned with proposals on **language planning**, on the development and institution of panregional trade languages (see Rubin and Shuy 1973). Since such questions of **language policy** are dependent to such a high degree on political, national, economic and cultural factors, their solution can be found only through interdisciplinary efforts. (⇒ *also* **interference**, **loan word**, **substratum**, **superstratum**)

References

Appel, R. and P. Muysken. 1987. *Language contact and bilingualism*. London.
Fishman, J.A. *et al.* 1968. *Bilingualism in the barrio*. Washington, D.C.
Fisiak, J. (ed.) 1994. *Language contact and linguistic change*. Berlin and New York.
Haugen, E. 1956. *Bilingualism in the Americas*. Tuscaloosa, AL.
Hymes, D. (ed.) 1964. *Language in culture and society: a reader in linguistics and anthropology*. New York.
Jahr, E.H. (ed.) 1992. *Language contact: theoretical and empirical studies*. Berlin and New York.
Ivir, V. and Kalogjera, D. (eds) 1991. *Languages in contact and contrast*. Berlin and New York.
Lehiste, I. 1988. *Lectures on language contact*. Cambridge, MA.
Lüdi, G. (ed.) 1992. *The dynamics of languages in contact: linguistic, sociolinguistic and sociopolitical aspects*. Berlin and New York.
Moloney, C., H. Zobl, and W. Stölting (eds) 1977. *Deutsch im Kontakt mit anderen Sprachen. German in contact with other languages*. Kronberg.
Nelde, P.-H. (ed.) 1980. *Sprachkontakt und Sprachkonflikt*. Wiesbaden.
Nelde, P. *et al.* (eds) 1986. *Language contact in Europe: proceedings of the working groups 12 and 13 of the International Congress of Linguists*. Tübingen.
Pütz, M. (ed.) 1994. *Language contact and language conflict*. Amsterdam and Philadelphia, PA.
Rubin. J. and R. Shuy (eds) 1973. *Language planning: current issues and research*. Washington, DC.

Spolsky, B. and R.L. Cooper. 1991. *The languages of Jerusalem*. Oxford.

Tauli, V. 1968. *Introduction to a theory of language planning*. Uppsala.

Thomason, S.G. and T. Kaufman. 1988. *Language contact, creolization, and genetic linguistics*. Berkeley, Los Angeles and London.

Ureland, P.S. and G. Broderick (eds) 1991. *Language contact in the British Isles: proceedings of the eighth International Symposium on Language Contact in Europe*. Tübingen.

Van Coetsem, F. 1987. *Loan phonology and the two transfer types in language contact*. Dordrecht.

Weinreich, U. 1953. *Languages in contact: findings and problems*. New York.

language death (*also* language obsolescence)

The decline or extinction of a language in situations where languages come into contact with each other (⇒ **language contact**). Different causes and processes can be distinguished: the most common is a 'gradual' language death, i.e. a language that has become obsolete is used by fewer and fewer speakers in more and more restricted situations, until it is finally only used as an 'intimate code' in certain formulas and idioms (e.g. greetings, proverbs, songs, jokes) as the expression of social or regional membership in a group. A possible residue of a dying language is also to be found in ritualized (e.g. religious) contexts. All forms of 'radical' or 'sudden' language death are evoked by catastrophes of different kinds, ranging from the destruction and abandonment of a culture, massive political oppression and intimidation to the physical elimination of whole populations of speakers.

References

Brenzinger, M. (ed.) 1992. *Language death: factual and theoretical explorations with special reference to East Africa*. Berlin and New York.

Dorian, N.C. 1986. Making do with less: some surprises along the language death proficiency continuum. *APsy* 7:3.257–76.

—— (ed.) 1989. *Investigating obsolescence: studies in language contraction and death*. Cambridge.

Dressler, W.U. 1981. Language shift and language death: a protean challenge for the linguist. *FoLi* 15.5–28.

—— 1988. Language death. In F. Newmeyer (ed.), *Linguistics: the Cambridge survey*. Cambridge. Vol. 4, 184–92.

Hill, J.H. 1983. Language death in Uto-Aztecan. *IJAL* 49.258–76.

Mackey, W.F. 1985. La mortalité des langues et le bilinguisme des peuples. In U. Pieper and G. Stickel (eds), *Studia linguistica diachronica et synchronica Werner Winter sexagenario anno MCMLXXXIII gratis animis ab eius collegis, amicis discipulisque oblata*. Berlin. 537–61.

Pan, B.A. and J.B. Gleason, 1986. The study of language loss: models and hypotheses for an emerging discipline. *APsy* 7:3.193–206.

Robins, R.H. and E.M. Uhlenbeck (eds) 1991. *Endangered languages*. Oxford.

Taylor, A.R. 1992. Language obsolescence, shift, and death in several Native American Communities (*International Journal of the Sociology of Language*, special issue 93).

Van Ness, S. 1990. *Changes in an obsolescing language: Pennsylvania German in West Virginia*. Tübingen.

Bibliography

Weber, R.L. 1986. A partially annotated bibliography of language death. *NLing* 35.4–24.

⇒ **language maintenance**

language disorder (*also* acquired language disorder)

A language disorder may be either congenital, i.e. present from the time of birth (⇒ **developmental language disorder**) or acquired. Acquired disorders, affecting adolescents and adults, occur well after the acquisition of language and involve the loss, diminution, or disruption of previously intact language abilities. Congenital disorders, in contrast, involve the failure to acquire the language system in the normal time and/or patterns. Language disorders are generally viewed as 'central' disorders, i.e. as caused by central nervous system pathology, and are distinguished from 'peripheral' disorders, i.e. those caused by impairments of speech organs such as the larynx or palate, though the two types of disorder may co-occur. Language disorders may be manifest in speech or writing as well as in the comprehension of spoken or written texts (⇒ **agraphia**, **alexia**, **aphasia**). Associated deficits in the ability to perform simple mathematical calculations or in the ability to recognize sound sequences or words ('verbal' **agnosia**) may also occur. Language disorders are generally presumed to be caused by organic factors such as brain lesion, neural dysfunction, neural degeneration, sensory deficit, or to be the secondary symptoms of psycho-emotional disorders. However, some congenital language disorders may represent extremes in the normal distribution of language capacities rather than organic pathology or psychosis. The study of language disorders is of interest to many disciplines, among others, neurology, **neurolinguistics**, **neuropsychology** and psychology.

References

Bates, E. and B. Wulfeck. 1989. Cross-linguistic studies of aphasia. In B. MacWhinney and E. Bates (eds), *Cross-linguistic studies of sentence processing*. New York. 328–74.

Blanken, G. *et al.* 1993. *Linguistic disorders and*

pathologies: an international handbook. Berlin and New York.
Caplan, D. 1987. *Neurolinguistics and linguistic aphasiology.* Cambridge.
——— 1992. *Language structure, processing and disorders.* Cambridge, MA.
Crystal, D. 1980. *Introduction to language pathology.* London.
Grodinsky, Y. 1984. The syntactic characterization of agrammatism. *Cognition* 16.99–120.
——— 1990. *Theoretical perspectives on language deficits.* Cambridge, MA.
Joshi, R.M. 1991. *Written language disorders.* Dordrecht.
Leonard, L. 1991. Specific language impairment as a clinical category. *Language Speech and Hearing Services in Schools* 22.66–8.
Tyler, L.K. 1992. *Spoken language comprehension: an experimental approach to disordered and normal processing.* Cambridge, MA.
Weigl, E. and M. Bierwisch. 1970. Neuropsychology and linguistics. *FL* 6.1–18.
Winitz, H. (ed.) 1987/9. *Human communication and its disorders*, 2 vols. Hove.
Yavas, M.S. 1991. *Phonological disorders in children: theory, research and practice.* London.
⇒ **aphasia**

language economy

The reason for the tendency to strive for maximum linguistic effectiveness with minimal linguistic effort. This can be attained by various means, e.g. simplification by reduction, use of abbreviations, systematization and merging of inflectional forms or analogical leveling between related forms (⇒ **analogy**).

References
Jespersen, O. 1925. *The philosophy of grammar.* London.
Martinet, A. 1955. *Economie des changements phonétiques.* Bern.
⇒ **Zipf's law**

language family

Group of languages that are genetically related, i.e. can be traced to a common **proto-language**. The ordering of languages into a common language family is usually based on phonological, morphological, and lexical correspondences that stem from the proto-language. The use of the term 'language family' is not always the same; in its broader sense (*also* phylum), it refers to the largest spectrum of languages for which a genetic relationship can be demonstrated, e.g. the **Indo-European languages**; in its narrower sense (*also* branch), it refers to languages which are more closely related, e.g. the **Germanic** languages.

References
⇒ **classification of languages**

language game

L. Wittgenstein's term referring to complex units of communication that consist of linguistic and non-linguistic activities (e.g. the giving of and complying with commands in the course of collaborating on the building of a house). Signs, words, and sentences as 'tools of language' have in and of themselves no meaning; rather, meaning is derived only from the use of these items in particular contexts of language behavior. (⇒ *also* **meaning as use**, **speech act theory**)

References
Stenius, E. 1967. Mood and language game. *Synthese* 17.254–74.
Wittgenstein, L. 1953. *Philosophical investigations.* Oxford.

language history

1 Totality of all linguistic changes in time (internal language history) while also considering external factors such as political history, cultural influences, social changes, territorial changes, language contact, etc. (external language history).

2 Systematic description of **language change**.

References
English
Bammesberger, A. 1984. *English etymology.* Heidelberg.
Baugh, A.C. and T. Cable, 1993. *A history of the English language*, 4th edn. Englewood Cliffs, NJ. (1st edn New York, 1935.)
Brunner, K. 1942. *Altenglische Grammatik: nach der Angelsächsischen Grammatik von Eduard Sievers.* (3rd rev. edn 1965.) Tübingen.
——— 1950/1. *Die englische Sprache: ihre geschichtliche Entwicklung*, 2 vols. Halle. (2nd edn Tübingen, 1960/2. Repr. 1984.)
Cannon, G. 1987. *Historical change and English word-formation: recent vocabulary.* New York.
Hogg, R.M. (ed.) 1991. *Cambridge history of the English language*, 6 vols. Cambridge.
Luick, K. 1914ff. *Historische Grammatik der englischen Sprache.* Oxford and Stuttgart.
Pyles, T. and J. Algeo. 1982. *The origins and development of the English language.* London.

German
Besch, W., O. Reichmann, and S. Sonderegger (eds) 1984/5. *Sprachgeschichte: ein Handbuch zur Geschichte der deutschen Sprache und ihrer Erforschung*, 2 vols. Berlin.
Keller, R.E. 1978. *The German language.* London.
Ronneberger-Sibold, E. 1989. *Historische Phonologie und Morphologie des Deutschen: eine kommentierte Bibliographie zur strukturellen Forschung.* Tübingen.
Russ, C. 1978. *Historical German phonology and morphology.* Oxford.
Wells, C.J. 1987. *German: a linguistic history to 1945.* Oxford.

⇒ **English**, **German**, **historical grammars**, **language change**

language interference ⇒ interference

language isolate

Language which cannot be grouped in any **language family** on the basis of current evidence. Naturally, the linguistic criteria established for relatedness will determine which languages are considered to be isolates. Some languages generally considered to be isolates are **Basque** (Iberian peninsula), **Burushaski** (Karakorum mountains), Nahali (India), Ket (central Siberia), Gilyak (eastern Siberia), and **Sumerian** (Mesopotamia). The term 'isolate' is also often used for languages which are not closely related to other languages inside a specific genetic group, e.g. **Albanian** in **Indo-European**.

References
⇒ **language typology**

language manipulation

1 Derogatory term for **language regulation** as well as for the language of advertising and propaganda. Language manipulation, in contrast to language regulation, concerns the influences upon the receiver, but not the changes in language use. (⇒ *also* **rhetoric**)

2 In language planning and bilingual education, the practice of providing instruction in the minority language as well as the majority language throughout a child's schooling to promote ethnic diversity, reinforce cultural identity, and foster a sense of psychological well-being. Critics object that this approach results in divisiveness and limited social/economic opportunities.

language minimum

The selection of vocabulary and grammar of a language for instructional purposes. Selection criteria are: (a) the frequency (⇒ **lexico statistics**); (b) their use in reaching particular communicative goals, as in the linguistic mastery of certain situations and topics (e.g. those catalogued in the project of the European Council on Foreign Languages 'threshold level'). Most extensively worked out are hitherto basic lexical minimums (⇒ **basic vocabulary**).

language mixing ⇒ mixed language

language obsolescence ⇒ language death

language of gestures ⇒ body language, sign language

language pedagogy [Grk *paidagogia*

'instruction, training,'] (*also* language teaching)

Scientific and instructional discipline (subdiscipline of general pedagogy) concerned with the needs, goals, content, and methods of language instruction with a view to linguistic, socio-cultural, educational psychological, and pedagogical aspects. In language pedagogy, methods of language transmission are also developed, tested, and established. As a generic term, language pedagogy refers to either native or foreign language instruction or, in contrast to **foreign language pedagogy**, to instruction in the native language which encompasses the following three domains: (a) enhancement of linguistic competence; (b) transmission of knowledge about the structure of the language; and (c) reflections about language. Regarding the enhancement of competence (which is especially concerned with offsetting socially or personally caused differences), pedagogical decisions pertain to the basic concept of language (whether it be language as a system of signs or language as an emotional, cognitive, creative or persuasive means of communicative behavior). Though lagging somewhat behind the most current developments in linguistics, the form and method of language instruction more or less reflect the general direction of the linguistic sciences insofar as the concepts of **prescriptive grammar** are based on scientific insights and findings, e.g. **structuralism**, **functional grammar**, **transformational grammar**, **dependency grammar**, **behaviorism** and **pragmatics**.

References
Berns, M. 1990. *Contexts of competence: social and cultural considerations in communicative language teaching*. New York.
Bot, K. de *et al*. 1990. *Foreign language research in cross-cultural perspective*. Amsterdam.
Brown, H.D. 1987. *Principles of language learning and teaching*. Englewood Cliffs, NJ.
Halliday, M.A.K., A. McIntosh, and P. Strevens, 1964. *The linguistic sciences and language teaching*. London.
Omaggio-Hadley, A. 1993. *Teaching language in context*. Boston.

Journals
Applied Language Learning.
Foreign Language Annals.
Modern Language Journal.
⇒ **foreign language pedagogy**, **second language acquisition**, **school grammar**

language perception ⇒ language comprehension

language planning

1 Measures taken by organizations (usually

sanctioned and supported by the state) for the development and dissemination of panregional trade languages. Emphasis may be placed on (a) the **transcription** of previously unwritten languages; (b) the modernization of the language system (primarily by expanding the vocabulary with specialized terminology); and (c) the expansion of the regional use of a language. (⇒ *also* **language policy**)

References
Alisjahbana, S.T. 1976. *Language planning for modernization*. The Hague.
Altehenger-Smith, S. 1989. *Language change via language planning: some theoretical and empirical aspects with a focus on Singapore*. Hamburg.
Christian, D. 1988. *Language planning: the view from linguistics*. In F. Newmeyer (ed.), *Linguistics: the Cambridge survey*. Cambridge. Vol. IV, 193–209.
Cooper, R.L. 1990. *Language planning and social change*. Cambridge.
Cyffer, N. *et al.* (eds) 1991. *Language standardization in Africa*. Hamburg.
Davis, K.A. 1994. *Language planning in multilingual contexts*. Amsterdam and Philadelphia.
Dua, H.R. 1992. *Communication policy and language planning*. Mysore.
Fardon, R. and G. Furniss (eds) 1993. *African languages, development and the state*. London.
Fierman, W. 1991. *Language planning and national development: the Uzbek experience*. Berlin and New York.
Fishman, J.A., C.A. Ferguson, and J. Das Gupta (eds) 1968. *Language problems of developing nations*. New York.
Fodor, I. and C. Hagège (eds) 1983– . *Language reform; history and future*. Vol. 6 1994. Hamburg.
Jahr, E.G. (ed.) 1993. *Language conflict and language planning*. New York and Berlin.
Laitin, D.D. 1992. *Language repertoires and state construction in Africa*. Cambridge.
Marshall, D. (ed.) 1990. *Language planning*. Amsterdam and Philadelphia.
Rubin, S. and R. Shuy (eds) 1973. *Language planning: current issues and research*. Washington, DC.
Singh, U.N. 1992. *On language development and planning: a pluralistic paradigm*. New Delhi.
Tauli, V. 1968. *Introduction to a theory of language planning*. Uppsala.
⇒ **language policy**, **multilingualism**, **sociolinguistics**

2 ⇒ **interlinguistics**

language policy

1 Political measures aimed at introducing, implementing, and defining the regional use of languages, such as the use of individual languages in multilingual states (⇒ **language planning**), the acceptance of official languages and working languages in international organizations, and regulations and agreements about foreign-language instruction (education language policy).

References
Bangbose, A. 1991. *Language and the nation: the question of language in sub-Saharan Africa*. Edinburgh.
Coulmas, F. 1991. *A language policy for the European Community: prospects and quandaries*. Berlin and New York.
Schiffmann, H. 1995. *Linguistic culture and language policy*. London.
Tollefson, J.W. 1991. *Planning language, planning inequality: language policy in the community*. London.
Vilfan, S. (ed.) 1991. *Ethnic groups and language rights*. Dartmouth.
Weinstein, B. 1990. *Language policy and political development*. Hove.
Williams, C.H. (ed.) 1991. *Linguistic minorities, society and territory*. Clevedon.
⇒ **literacy**, **multilingualism**

2 Political **language regulation**.

References
⇒ **language planning**

language processing

Term sometimes used to refer to understanding language (⇒ **language comprehension**) or cover term denoting the processes involved in understanding as well as producing language (language comprehension and **language production**). The major issues are what types of knowledge are involved (grammatical knowledge, lexical knowledge, contextual knowledge, world knowledge) and how the mediating processes are organized. As for the latter: do these processes apply obligatorily or optionally, do they work in serial order and thus make use of the relevant information independently of other information (autonomous models, serial processing, ⇒ **modularity**) or do these processes use different kinds of information simultaneously and thus work interactively and possibly in parallel (interactive models, parallel distributed processing, ⇒ **connectionism**)? For an overview, see Weissenborn and Schriefers (1987), Frazier (1988), Tannenhaus (1988).

References
Allport, A. *et al.* 1987. *Language perception and production: relationships between listening, speaking, reading and writing*. New York.
Altmann, G.T.M. (ed.) 1990. *Cognitive models of speech processing*. Cambridge, MA.
Bates, E. *et al.* 1982. Functional constraints on sentence processing: a cross-linguistic study. *Cognition* 11.245–99.
Bialystok, E. (ed.) 1991. *Language processing in bilingual children*. Cambridge.
Bock, M. and G. Rickheit (eds) 1983. *Psycholinguistic studies in language processing*. Berlin.

Bouma, H. and D.G. Bouwhuis (eds) 1984. *Attention and performance*, vol. 10: *Control of language processes*. Hillsdale, NJ.

Cole, R.A. (ed.) 1980. *Perception and production of fluent speech*. Hillsdale, NJ.

Fodor, J.A. 1983. *The modularity of the mind*. Cambridge, MA.

Frazier, L. 1988. Grammar and language processing. In F. Newmeyer (ed.), *Linguistics: the Cambridge survey*. Cambridge. Vol. 1, 15–34.

Frazier, L. and J. de Villiers (eds) 1990. *Language processing and language acquisition*. Dordrecht.

Garfield, J. 1986. *Modularity in knowledge representation and natural language understanding*. London.

Harris, M. 1986. *Language processing in children and adults*. London.

Marslen-Wilson, W. (ed.) 1989. *Lexical representation and process*. Cambridge, MA.

Mikkulainen, R. 1993. *Subsymbolic natural language processing: an integrated model of scripts, lexicon, and memory*. Cambridge, MA.

Pereira, F. and B. Grosz (eds) 1994. *Natural language processing*. Cambridge, MA.

Sells, P., S.M. Shieber, and T. Wasow (eds) 1991. *Foundational issues in natural language processing*. Cambridge, MA.

Singer, M. 1990. *Psychology of language: an introduction to sentence and discourse processes*. Hove.

Tannenhaus, M. 1988. Psycholinguistics: an overview. In F.J. Newmeyer (ed.), *Linguistics: the Cambridge survey*. Cambridge. Vol. 3, 7–20.

Weissenborn, J. and H. Schriefers. 1987. Psycholinguistics. In U. Ammon *et al.* (eds), *Sociolinguistics: an international handbook of the science of language and society*. Berlin and New York. 470–87.

Bibliography

Gazdar, G. 1987. *Natural language processing in the 1980s: a bibliography*. Chicago, IL.

Dictionary

Aitchison, J. 1989. *Introducing language and mind*. London.

⇒ **language and brain**, **language comprehension**, **language production**, **parsing**, **psycholinguistics**, **text processing**

language production

Term referring to the processes involved in producing language, predominantly used in connection with the production of spoken language (⇒ *also* **sign language**). These processes include planning the utterance with regard to what to say, retrieving the words and integrating them into a sentence, articulating the sentence and monitoring the output. Evidence for such processes comes from hesitation phenomena, **pauses**, **speech errors**, **anakoluthons**, and furthermore self-**repair**. As with **language comprehension**, here also two basic types of processing models and their variants are under debate: serial/autonomous models

and parallel/interactive models. Interaction is often assumed with regard to difficulties with word retrieval, as evidenced by speech errors. The most comprehensive model of language production was developed by Levelt 1989.

References

Bever, T.G. 1971. The integrated study of language behaviour. In J. Morton (ed.), *Biological and social factors in psycholinguistics*. London. 158–209.

Carroll, W. 1986. *Psychology of language*. Monterey, CA.

Clark, H.H. and E.V. Clark. 1977. *Psychology and language*. San Diego, CA.

Frazier, L. 1988. Grammar and language processing. In F.J. Newmeyer (ed.), *Linguistics: the Cambridge survey*. Cambridge. Vol. 2, 15–34.

Fujimura, O. 1990. Methods and goals in speech production research. *L&S* 33.215–58.

Garrett, M.F. 1975. The analysis of sentence production. In G.H. Bower (ed.), *The psychology of learning and memory*. New York. Vol. 9, 133–77.

——— 1988. Processes in language production. In F.J. Newmeyer (ed.), *Linguistics: the Cambridge survey*. Cambridge. Vol. 3, 69–98.

Howard, D.V. 1983. *Cognitive psychology: memory, language and thought*. New York.

Kohn, S.A. *et al.* 1987. Lexical retrieval: the tip of the tongue phenomenon. *APsy* 8.245–66.

Lenneberg, H. and E. Lenneberg (eds) 1976. *Foundations of language development: a multidisciplinary approach*, vol. I. New York.

Levelt, W.J.M. 1989. *Speaking: from intention to articulation*. Cambridge, MA.

Lindsay, P.H. and D.A. Norman. 1977. *Human information processing*, 2nd edn. New York.

Martin, N., R.W. Weisberg, and E.M. Saffran. 1989. Variables influencing the occurrence of naming errors: implication for models of lexical retrieval. *JMemL* 28.462–85.

Osgood, C.E. 1957. A behaviorist analysis of perception and language as cognitive phenomena. In J.S. Bruner *et al.* (eds), *Contemporary approaches to cognition*. Cambridge, MA. 75–118.

Weissenborn, J. and H. Schriefers. 1987. Psycholinguistics; In U. Ammon *et al.* (eds), *Sociolinguistics: an international handbook of the science of language and society*. Berlin and New York. 470–87.

⇒ **language acquisition**, **language processing**, **neurolinguistics**, **psycholinguistics**, **speech error**

language regulation

1 In the narrow sense, involvement in the use of language (usually by the state) aimed at bringing about or suppressing certain conscious associations. (⇒ **language manipulation**, **language planning**, **language policy**)

2 In the broad sense, any kind of intentional control of language use, often (though not necessarily exclusively) with a view to affect-

ing the denotation and connotation of certain terms, by any group with a vested interest.

language structure

In mathematics and the natural sciences, the term 'structure' refers to the 'set of relations which connect the elements of a system, and all isomorphic relational constructions pertaining thereto' (Klaus 1969: 625). When used with language, this term refers to the system of grammatical rules in language which underlies language use, i.e. the set of paradigmatic and syntagmatic relations between the elements of the language system (**phonemes**, **morphemes**, **sentences**, etc.), as well as their reciprocal connections at all levels of description. Similar to the term 'system,' with which it is often used synonymously, structure is often set forth as a theoretical premise; it is also the goal of all structurally oriented linguistic research.

References
Greenberg, J.H. Structure and function in language. Repr. in J.H. Greenberg (ed.), *Essays in linguistics*. Chicago, IL. 75–85.
Haas, W. 1960. Linguistic structures. *Word* 16.251–76.
Klaus, G. 1969. *Wörterbuch der Kybernetik*, 2 vols. Frankfurt.
Parsons, T. 1960. *Structure and process in modern societies*. Glencoe.
⇒ **structuralism**

language synthesis [Grk *sýnthesis* 'putting together, combination']

In the broader sense, process of natural or artificial production of texts. Natural language synthesis occurs in every normal instance of speech of a competent speaker, artificial language synthesis takes place via machines (through primarily electronic means). Language synthesis in the narrower sense refers to the third phase of **machine-aided translation** (after the analysis and transfer phase), in which the text of the **target language** is produced in a morphologically and syntactically appropriate form.

References
⇒ **computational linguistics, information theory, text generation**

language system [Grk *sýstēma* 'a whole compounded of several parts']

In mathematics and the natural sciences, the term 'system' refers to 'a set of elements and a set of relations which exist between these elements' (Klaus 1969: 634). When used with language, this term refers to the internal ordering of linguistic elements (⇒ **phonemes, morphemes, sentences**, etc.) and their functional

relationships at all levels of the grammar and in relation to social, dialectal, and other subsystems. In a narrower sense, a language system is synonymous with the Saussurean term langue (⇒ **langue vs parole**), referring to language as a synchronic, static system of signs and their combinatory rules.

References
Klaus, G. 1969. *Wörterbuch der Kybernetik*, 2 vols. Frankfurt.
⇒ **language structure, langue vs parole, structuralism**

language teaching ⇒ language pedagogy

language test

The measurement of linguistic achievement (globally or according to different types of proficiency) through more or less standardized procedures which, if possible, should be sufficient for the usual qualitative criteria of the test, above all: objectivity (independence from the person acting as the tester), validity (characteristic of the procedure to measure only what is meant to be measured), reliability (consistent results whenever repeated), etc.

Achievement tests assess functional ability in a language and are unrelated to any course of study. Test items tend to be open-ended and meaningful. They are scored holistically and usually administered in summative or high stakes contexts, i.e., placement, to show fulfillment of requirements or qualification for employment. Achievement tests contain form-focused items and are curricular-driven exams. They ask a learner to show what he/she knows rather than what he/she can do and are scored using discrete-point formats. Prochievement tests attempt to incorporate aspects of both types of testing, a mix of open-ended and form-focused items, for example.

References
Alderson, J.C. and B. North (eds) 1991. *Language testing in the 1990s*. Basingstoke.
Bachman, L.F. 1990. *Fundamental considerations in language testing*. Oxford.
Baker, D. 1989. *Language testing: a critical perspective and practical guide*. London.
Bernhardt, E.B. and C.J. James. 1987. The teaching and testing of comprehension in foreign language learning. In D.W. Birckbichler (ed.), *Proficiency, policy, and professionalism in foreign language education*. (Report of the Central States Conference on the Teaching of Foreign Languages.) Lincolnwood, IL. 65–81.
Buck, K., H. Byrnes and I. Thompson (eds) 1989. *The ACTFL oral proficiency interview tester training manual*. Yonkers, NY.
Henning, G. 1987. *A guide to language testing:*

development evaluation, research. Cambridge, MA.

Hughes, A. 1989. *Testing for language teachers.* Cambridge.

Kohonen, V., H. von Essen, and C. Klein-Braley (eds) 1985. *Practice and problems in language testing.* Tampere.

Lantolf, J.P. and W. Frawley. 1985. Oral proficiency testing: a critical analysis. *MLJ* 69:337–45.

Oller, J.W. (ed.) 1983. *Issues in language testing research.* Rowley, MA.

Shohamy, E. 1991. Connecting testing and learning in the classroom and on the program level. In J.K. Phillips (ed.), *Building bridges and making connections.* (Reports of the Northeast Conference on the Teaching of Foreign Languages.) Middlebury, VT. 154–78.

Wesche, M.B. 1981. Communicative testing in a second language. *CMLR* 37: 551–71.

Journal
Language Testing.

language typology [Grk *typós* 'model, pattern']

Classification of languages based on grammatical characteristics, i.e. ignoring genetic or geographical connections. The classical typology based on morphological criteria comes from A.W. von Schlegel's distinction between **analytic** and **synthetic languages**: in analytic languages (⇒ *also* **isolating language**), such as Classical **Chinese**, the grammatical relations between words in a sentence are expressed by independent syntactic form elements (e.g. prepositions), while in synthetic languages they are expressed by dependent morphological units (see Schlegel 1818). In the synthetic languages, Schlegel distinguishes between **agglutinating languages**, in which grammatical and lexical morphemes with simple semantic components are simply affixed to each other (e.g. **Turkish**), and **inflectional languages**, whose words cannot be analyzed into single morphemes with simple semantic meaning and which sometimes demonstrate phenomena such as root or stem alternation (e.g. **Sanskrit**). Humboldt (1836) added the term 'polysynthetic languages,' (⇒ **polysynthesis**) in which a word often combines several word stems with very specific semantic meaning (e.g. **Iroquoian**) (*also* ⇒ **incorporating language**). In this early stage of language typology, value judgments were also attached to each type: the richness of forms in the inflectional languages was considered a sign of greater development, while the isolating and agglutinating languages were seen as less developed stages on their way to becoming inflectional languages. For a history of the research on language typology, see Haarman (1976). The main objections against this traditional, primarily morphological, typology are based on the lack of theoretical agreement about the nature of the elements (such as **syllable**, **morpheme**, **word**) and properties (such as **intonation**, **concatenation**) in question, as well as its too categorical (as opposed to gradual) nature, which does not sufficiently take into consideration the interdependence of phonological, morphological, and syntactic criteria.

The syntactic approaches to typology owe the most to Greenberg (1963), who developed a typology of word order types (⇒ **universals**). Other syntactic properties, such as the system of grammatical relations (e.g. **ergative** vs **nominative languages**) have also been used as the basis for language typology. For more recent approaches and terminological suggestions, see Altmann and Lehfeldt (1973), Lehmann (1978), and Vennemann (1982).

References
Altmann, G. and W. Lehfeldt. 1973. *Allgemeine Sprachtypologie: Prinzipien und Meßverfahren.* Munich.

Comrie, B. 1981. *Language universals and language typology.* Oxford. (2nd edn 1989.)

Croft, W. 1990. *Typology and universals.* Cambridge.

Finck, F.N. 1909. *Die Haupttypen des Sprachbaus.* Leipzig. (Repr. 5th edn Darmstadt, 1965.)

Greenberg, J.H. 1960. A quantitative approach to the morphological typology of language. *IJAL* 26.

——— 1963. Some universals of grammar with particular reference to the order of meaningful elements. In his *Universals of language.* Cambridge.

——— 1974. *Language typology: a historical and analytical overview.* The Hague.

Haarman, H. 1976. *Grundzüge der Sprachtypologie: Methodik, Empirie und Systematik der Sprachen Europas.* Stuttgart.

Hawkins, J.A. 1986. *A comparative typology of English and German: unifying the contrasts.* Austin, TX.

Humboldt, W. 1836. *Über die Verschiedenheit des menschlichen Sprachbaus.* Berlin. (Repr. in *Werke*, ed. A. Flitner and K. Gields. Darmstadt. Vol. 3, 144–367.)

Lehmann, W.P. (ed.) 1978. *Syntactic typology: studies in the phenomenology of language.* Austin, TX.

——— (ed.) 1990. *Language typology 1987: systematic balance in language.* Amsterdam and Philadelphia, PA.

——— and H.-J. Herwitt. 1991. *Language typology 1988: typological models in reconstruction.* Amsterdam and Philadelphia, PA.

Mallison, G. and B.J. Blake. 1981. *Language typology: cross-linguistic studies in syntax.* Amsterdam.

Nichols, J. 1992. *Linguistic diversity in space and time.* Chicago and London.

Ramat, P. 1987. *Linguistic typology*. Berlin.

Sapir, E. 1921. *Language*. New York.

Schlegel, A.W. von 1818. *Observations sur la langue et la littérature provençales*. Paris.

Schmidt, P.W. 1926. *Die Sprachfamilien und Sprachkreise der Erde*. Heidelberg.

Schopen, T. (ed.) 1985. *Language typology and syntactic description*, 3 vols. Cambridge.

Schwegler, A. 1990. *Analyticity and syntheticity: a diachronic perspective with special reference to the Romance languages*. Berlin and New York.

Shibatani, M. *et al*. (eds). 1995. *Approaches to language typology*. Oxford.

Vennemann, T. 1982. Agglutination – Isolation – Flexion: zur Stimmigkeit typologischer Parameter. In U. Wandruszka (ed.), *Festschrift für H. Stimm*. Tübingen.

Journals
Sprachtypologie und Universalienforschung.
Linguistic Typology.
⇒ **classification of languages**, **universals**

langue d'oc ⇒ **French**

langue d'oïl ⇒ **French**

langue vs parole

A term introduced in de Saussure's *Cours de linguistique générale* to distinguish between language (Fr. *langue*) as an abstract system of signs and rules, and the spoken word (Fr. *parole*) as the concrete realization of language as it is used. *Langue* is characterized as a static system of symbols with broad (social) value, due to the invariant and functional nature of its elements. Instances of *parole* are based on this system of *langue* and vary according to register, age, dialect, among other factors. The goal of structuralist linguistics is to research the systematic regularities of *langue* using data from *parole* (⇒ **corpus**), while *parole* itself can be researched in various disciplines, like **phonetics**, psychology, and physiology. This requirement for autonomy in a purely theoretical inner-linguistic view of language, such as that proposed by Chomsky with **competence vs performance**, has met with much criticism and has been heavily revised. (⇒ *also* **communicative competence**, **pragmatics**, **sociolinguistics**). The type of difference described between *langue* and *parole* has taken many forms: among them, **ergon vs energeia** (W. von Humboldt), *Sprache* vs *Rede* (H. Paul), *Sprachsystem* vs *aktualisierte Rede* (G. v.d. Gabelentz), *Sprachgebilde* vs *Sprechakt* (K. Bühler), register vs use, type vs token (⇒ **type-token-relationship**). (M.A.K. Halliday).

References
Antal, L. 1990. Langue *and* parole or *only* parole? *Historiographia Linguistica*. 17.357–267.

Bühler, K. 1934. *Sprachtheorie*. Jena.

Gabelentz, G. v.d. 1891. *Die Sprachwissenschaft: ihre Aufgaben, Methoden und bisherigen Ergebnisse*. (Rev. repr. of the 1901 2nd edn. Tübingen, 1972.)

Halliday, M. A.K. 1961. Categories of the theory of grammar. *Word* 17.241–92.

Humboldt, W. von 1963. *Schriften zur Sprachphilosophie*. Darmstadt.

Paul, H. 1880. *Prinzipien der Sprachgeschichte*. (9th edn Tübingen, 1975.)

Saussure, F. de. 1916. *Cours de linguistique générale*, ed. C. Bally and A. Sechehaye. Paris. (*Course in general linguistics*, trans. R. Harris. London, 1983.)
⇒ **competence vs performance**

Laotian ⇒ **Cam-Thai**

Lapp

Group of **Uralic** languages, probably **Finno-Ugric**, spoken in northern Scandinavia, with fewer than 30,000 speakers. There are three main dialect groups. First literary documents date from the seventeenth century.

Reference
Lagercrantz, E. 1929. *Sprachlehre des Nordlappischen*. Oslo.

laryngeal

1 Obsolete general (and misleading) term for **glottal**, **pharyngeal**, and pharyngealized **speech sounds** (⇒ **secondary articulation**).

2 **Speech sound** found in the **Mon-Khmer** language Sedang indicated by the diacritic notation ‹~› (⇒ **articulatory phonetics**).

References
⇒ **phonetics**

laryngeal theory

Widely accepted hypothesis concerning the **reconstruction** of a portion of basic **Indo-European**. In general, three consonantal **laryngeals** (notation: h_1, h_2, h_3) are reconstructed. The existence of laryngeals is surmised based on morphological structural evidence. Moreover, these phonemes can be inferred from reflexes in individual languages: for example, **compensatory lengthening** of tautosyllabic vowels accompanied by a simultaneous change in vowel coloring are found in IE *e* to *a* (in certain languages, e.g. Greek) in the environment of h_2, and to *o* in the environment of h_3; in **Hittite**, h_2 has been retained in many positions as a consonantal phoneme. The workings of the morphological system of Indo-European, which is characterized by the phenomenon of **ablaut**, is made more transparent in view of the laryngeal theory. Accordingly, the verbal present singular in Indo-European had an *e*-grade ablaut form (cf. Lat. *est*, Hit. *eszi* 'is'). The

Latin verb *pasco* ('I protect') which corresponds to Hit. *pahsmi* shows no *e* and would, therefore, have to be considered an exception. Laryngeal theory, however, explains the verb as deriving from *peh_2*- with *e*-grade ablaut. In Latin and Hittite, this laryngeal colors the *e* to *a*; in Latin h_2 disappears with compensatory lengthening; in Hittite it is retained as an *h*. De Saussure's structurally motivated theory was empirically proven in the early twentieth century with the deciphering of Hittite, when *h* was found in places where the laryngeal h_2 had been reconstructed by de Saussure, who spoke of 'coéfficients sonantiques.'

References

Bammesberger, A. (ed.) 1988. *Die Laryngaltheorie und die Rekonstruktion des urindogermanischen Laut- und Formensystems.* Heidelberg.

Beekes, R.S.P. 1969. *The development of the Proto-Indo-European laryngeals in Greek.* The Hague.

Kuryłowicz, J. 1927. ə *indoeuropéen et ʒhittite: symbolae grammaticae in honorem Ioannis Rozwadowski.* Cracow.

Lindeman, F.O. 1988. *Introduction to the 'Laryngeal theory.'* Oxford.

Saussure, F. de. 1879. *Mémoire sur le système primitif des voyelles dans les langues indoeuropéennes.* Leipzig.

Schrijver, P. 1991. *The reflexes of the Proto-Indo-European laryngeal in Latin.* Amsterdam and Atlanta, GA.

Winter, W. (ed.) 1965. *Evidence for laryngeals.* London.
⇒ **Indo-European**

larynx

Organ that protects the vocal cords and lies between the **resonance chamber** and the trachea (wind pipe). (⇒ *also* **articulatory phonetics**)

References
⇒ **phonetics**

Larzac ⇒ Celtic

lateral [Lat. *lateralis* 'of/on the side of a body']

Speech sound classified according to its manner in which the airstream bypasses its obstruction (namely, around openings on either side of the tongue) in contrast with **medians**. For example, in the **approximants** [1] and [ɬ] in Brit. Eng. [lutɬ] *little* and in the **fricative** [ɬ] and the approximant [1] in [-ɬa] 'wasteful' or [-la] 'to come' in the **Sino-Tibetan** language Yi. In Yaragia, a language spoken in New Guinea, there is a velar lateral. Laterals can function as nuclei (⇒ **nucleus**) of syllables, e.g. [1] in **Czech** ['pl̩zen] 'Pilsen.' In English, laterals are formed with the pulmonary **airstream mecha-** nism. The **Khoisan** language of Nama has lateral **clicks**.

References
⇒ **phonetics**

lateralization

In **neuropsychology**, functional specialization of both hemispheres of the brain with regard to information processing and, in particular, **language processing**. Lateralization of such functions differs from individual to individual and varies according to ability (thus, for example, receptive abilities seem to be less strongly lateralized than expressive ones). In spite of such variation, the global assignment of specific processing abilities to particular hemispheres has been confirmed: analytical processes tend to be left-brain, and synthetic (or holistic) processes right-brain. Thus, syntactic and phonological processes are ascribed rather to the left hemisphere, while processing of pragmatic information, the recognition and comprehension of sentence melody as well as the recognition of non-linguistic sounds have been ascribed more to the right hemisphere. The specialization of analytical and holistic processes leads to differences in the lateralization of individual abilities and skills. For instance, people who have been educated in music will tend to process melodies in the left hemisphere, while those with no such education will use the right half of their brain. Due to the fact that the neural pathways for hearing and vision are both ipsi- and contralateral (because of cross-over), information can be picked up by both sides, but it will be processed primarily contralaterally. Hence, lateralization does not mean that only one hemisphere is specialized for one function, but rather that the hemisphere that is most strongly specialized for a particular ability suppresses the same specialization in the other hemisphere. In cases involving brain lesion, depending on the type and extent of injury as well as the age of the patient, it is possible that the intact hemisphere may mediate or may, to a certain extent, take over the specific function: for example, the right hemisphere has considerable auditive processing and also a rudimentary expressive potential, which in case of damage to the left hemisphere may be activated.

Since lateralization is hard to determine in healthy people on account of the constant exchange of information between both hemispheres, lateralization is frequently studied in experiments in which a certain half of the brain is specifically stimulated (e.g. through dichotic listening in which stimuli are delivered with headphones to each ear and are essentially processed contralaterally owing to the crossing of auditory paths; in such cases, a 'right-ear effect' occurs when the stimuli are of a linguistic nature, and a 'left-ear effect' when the stimuli are of a non-linguistic nature). Further indications of lateralization can be seen in patients with brain lesion (such as in acquired **language disorder**, ⇒ **aphasia**), indications in patients in whom one hemisphere has been anesthetized (Wada test), in whom the connection between the hemispheres has been missing since birth or had to be cut off (e.g. to control seizures in case of epilepsy; split-brain patient) or in whom the cerebral cortex has been surgically removed.

The position held by Lenneberg (1967) that both hemispheres show the same potential at birth (i.e. are 'equipotential') and that lateralization comes about in the course of childhood, has since been disproven. At birth, there is not only a physical asymmetry between both halves of the brain (in which the left half is normally larger than the right half), but also a functional asymmetry. Thus, in dichotic listening tests, babies of three weeks already demonstrate the 'right-ear effect' when they hear nonsense syllables, and the 'left-ear effect' when they hear music. Lenneberg's assumption of a 'sensitive' or 'critical' (biologically determined) phase for the acquisition of language which is completed in puberty, is discussed controversially (e.g. in studies about fluctuating deafness leading to particular linguistic deficits or through case studies; see Curtiss 1977; for a summary of arguments cf. Aitchison 1989: 84–90).

References
Aitchison, J. 1989. *The articulate mammal: an introduction to psycholinguistics*, 3rd edn. London.
Bishop, D. 1988. *Language development after focal brain damage*. In D. Bishop and K. Mogford (eds), *Development in exceptional circumstances*. Edinburgh. 203–20.
Bryden, M. 1982. *Laterality: functional asymmetry in the intact brain*. New York.
Curtiss, S. 1977. *Genie*. New York.
Geschwind, N. and A.M. Galaburda. 1985. Cerebral lateralization: biological mechanisms, associations, and pathology. *Archives of Neurology* 42.428–59.
Goodman, R. 1987. The developmental neurobiology of language. In W. Yule and M. Rutter (eds), *Language development and disorders*. Oxford. 129–45.
Harris, L.J. 1981. Sex-related variations in spatial skill. In L.S. Liben *et al.* (eds), *Spatial representation and behavior across the life span*. New York and London. 83–125.
Lenneberg, E.H. 1967. *Biological foundations of language*. New York.

Levy, J. and C. Tevarthen. 1977. Perceptual, semantic and phonetic aspects of elementary language processes in split-brain patients. *Brain* 100.105–18.
Neville, H. *et al.* 1992. Fractionating language: different neural subsystems with different sensitive periods. *Cerebral Cortex* 2.244–58.
Wada. J.A. *et al.* 1975. Cerebral hemispheric asymmetries in humans: cortical speech zones in 100 adult and 100 infant brains. *Archives of Neurology* 32.239–46.
Wray, A. 1991. *The focusing hypothesis: the theory of left brain lateralised language re-examined*. Amsterdam and Philadelphia, PA.
⇒ **language and brain**

Latin

Original dialect of the territory of Latium (Rome) belonging to the **Italic** branch of the **Indo-European** language family; it is one of the oldest attested languages of the Indo-European group. The earliest attestations (inscriptions, names) date from the preliterary period (600–240 BC). The period of 'Classical Latin' is generally considered to date from 100 BC to AD 14. During the Late Antiquity (200–600) separate spoken dialects developed in the Roman provinces, which differ from literary Latin primarily through lexical and phonological changes (cf. Vulgar Latin): for example, ‹c›, originally pronounced as [k], became pronounced as [ts] before palatals, cf. [kikeroː] > [tsitesroː] 'Cicero.' Latin is the basis for the **Romance languages** (**French**, **Italian**, **Spanish**, **Portugese**, **Rumanian**, and **Rhaeto-Romance**), all spoken in originally Latin-speaking territories. During the middle ages, 'Medieval Latin' was used for education, church, and government; Classical Latin was revived in the fifteenth century by the humanists. For the influence of Latin on English, ⇒ **borrowing**.

Characteristics: word accent (with few exceptions) on the **penultimate syllable**; vowel quantity is phonologically relevant; synthetic–inflectional morphology (canto, cantas, cantat 'I sing, you sing, he/she/it sings') with frequent **syncretism** of forms; no article and no personal pronoun for the third persons; free word order (sometimes stylistically motivated). On the structural changes from Latin to the **Romance languages**, ⇒ **French**, **Italian**, **Portuguese**, **Spanish**.

References
Allen, W.S. 1975. *Vox latina: a guide to the pronunciation of classical Latin*. Cambridge. (2nd edn 1978.)
Coleman, R. (ed.) 1991. *New studies in Latin linguistics*. Amsterdam and Philadelphia, PA.
Devoto, G. 1971. Studies of Latin and languages of ancient Italy. In T.A. Sebeok (ed.), *Current trends*

in linguistics. The Hague. Vol. 9, 817–34.

Grandgent, C.H. 1907. *An introduction to Vulgar Latin*. Boston, MA.

Herman, J. (ed.) 1994. *Linguistic studies on Latin*. Amsterdam and Philadelphia, PA.

Kent, R.G. 1945. *The sounds of Latin*. Baltimore, MD.

———— 1946. *The forms of Latin*, Baltimore, MD.

Palmer, R.L. 1954. *The Latin language*. London.

Pinkster, H. 1990. *Latin syntax and semantics*. London.

Strunk, K. (ed.) 1973. *Probleme der lateinischen Grammatik*. Darmstadt.

Woodcock, E.C. 1958. *A new Latin syntax*. London.

Grammars

Ernout, A. and F. Thomas. 1984. *Syntaxe latine*. Paris.

Leumann, M., J.B. Hofmann, and A. Szantyr. 1963/72. *Lateinische Grammatik*, 2 vols. Munich.

Rubenbauer, H., J.B. Hofmann, and R. Heine. 1975. *Lateinische Grammatik*. (11th edn 1980.) Bamberg.

History

Collart, J. 1967. *Histoire de la langue latine*. Paris.

Ernout, A. 1953. *Morphologie historique du latin*. Paris.

Kurzová, H. 1993. *From Indo-European to Latin: the evolution of a morphosyntactic type*. Amsterdam and Philadelphia, PA.

Panagl, O. and T. Krisch (eds) 1992. *Latein und Indogermanisch: Akten des Kolloquiums der Indogermanischen Gesellschaft, Salzburg 1986*. Innsbruck.

Dictionaries

Lewis, C. and C. Short. 1879. (Repr. 1975). Oxford.

Oxford Latin dictionary. 1968. 2 vols. Oxford.

Thesaurus linguae Latinae. 1900–90. Leipzig and Stuttgart.

Etymological dictionaries

Ernout, A. and A. Meillet. 1959. *Dictionnaire étymologique de la langue latine*, 4th edn. Paris.

Walde, A. and J.B. Hofmann. 1965. *Lateinisches etymologisches Wörterbuch,*. 3 vols. 4th edn. Heidelberg.

Handbooks

Hammond, M. 1976. *Latin: a historical and linguistic handbook*. New Haven, CT.

Holtus, G., M. Metzeltin, and C. Schmitt (eds) 1987. *Lexikon der romanistischen Linguistik*, vol. 2. Tübingen.

Bibliography

Cousin, J. 1951. *Bibliographie de la langue latine, 1880–1948*. Paris.

Journals

Glotta

Latinitas

Probus

⇒ **classification of languages**, **Indo-European**, **Romance languages**

Latin-Faliscan ⇒ Italic

Latvian

Baltic language with approx. 1.5 million speakers in Latvia. Religious literature dates to the Reformation, secular literature exists since the eighteenth century. The orthography is based on the **Latin** alphabet with diacritic marks, including ‹ņ›, ‹ķ›, ‹ģ›, ‹ļ›. Stress on the first syllable. Long and short vowels with distinctive intonation (including glottal narrowing) even after the accented syllable. Complex morphology. No distinction between singular and plural in the third person verb forms, as in **Lithuanian**.

References

Endzelīns, J. 1951. *Latviešu valodas gramatika*. Riga.

———— 1922. *Lettische Grammatik*. Riga.

Eiche, A. 1983. *Latvian declinable and indeclinable participles: their syntactic function, frequency and modality*. Stockholm.

Fennel, T.G. and H. Gelsen. 1980. *A grammar of modern Latvian*. The Hague.

Mülenbachs, K. 1923–1932. *Latviešu valodas vārdnīca. Rediģējis, papildinājis, turpinājis J. Endzelīns*. 4 vols. Riga (Repr. Chicago 1953). Vols. 5 and 6: J. Endzelīns and E. Hauzenberga. 1934–46. *Papildinājumi un labojumi K. Mülenbacha Latviešu valodas vārdnīcai*. Riga (Repr. Chicago 1956).

Mūsdienu latviešu literārās valodas gramatika. 1959/62. 2 vols. Riga.

Rūķe-Draviņa, V. 1977. *The standardization process in Latvian: sixteenth century to the present*. Stockholm.

Dictionaries

Latviešu literās valodas vārdnīca. 1972. Vol. 6 1986. Riga.

Latviešu valodas vārdnīca. 1987. Riga.

Metuzāle-Kangere, B. 1985. *A derivational dictionary of Latvian. Latviešu valodas atvasiknājumu vārdnīca*. Hamburg.

Soikane-Trapāne, M. 1987. *Latvian basic and topical vocabulary/Latviešu valodas pamata un tematisks vārdu krājums* (3rd printing). Lincoln, NE.

Turkina, E. 1963. *Latvian–English dictionary/Latviešu–Anglu vārdnīca*, ed. M. Andersone. (3rd edn, repr.) Riga.

Etymological dictionary

Karulis, K. 1992. *Latviešu etimoloģijas vārdnīca*, 2 vols. Riga.

law of three morae [Lat. *mora* 'time necessary'] (*also* law of three syllables)

1 Law that governs **stress** relationships in **Greek**, according to which no more than three unstressed morae (= the unit of measurement for a short syllable; ⇒ **mora**) may follow the main stressed syllable of a word.

2 Hypothesis in **Indo-European** linguistics that attempts to explain the long final **vowels** of **Gothic**, according to which in Indo-European

and Proto-**Germanic** long vowels in secondary syllables had two morae with acute and three morae with circumflex **accent**[2]. Vowels of three morae in final syllables came about especially by contraction, e.g. in the genitive singular of IE *ā*: *$g^heb^hâs$ < -ā-es* 'of the gift'; these were preserved in Gothic as long vowels, e.g. *gibos* 'of the gift,' in contrast to syllables of two morae, which were shortened.

References
Krause, W. 1968. *Handbuch des Gotischen*, 3rd rev. edn. Munich.
⇒ **comparative linguistics**

law of three syllables ⇒law of three morae

lax ⇒ tense vs lax

Laz ⇒ South Caucasian

lect [Grk *léktos* 'chosen, picked out; word, expression']

Term introduced in American **variational linguistics** to designate regional, social, and other types of language varieties. In compound words (e.g. **sociolect**, **dialect**, **idiolect**, **isolect**, etc.), the first element indicates the type of variety.

left-branching construction

A type of phrase structure construction. In a left-branching structure in a **tree diagram** each node which branches into constituents *A* and *B* is of the type that only *A*, the left branch, can contain any further branching. An English example of such a construction is [[[*Mary's*] *sister's*] *book*].

Reference
Chomsky, N. 1965. *Aspects of the theory of syntax.* Cambridge, MA.

left vs right dislocation

Term introduced by Ross (1967) for syntactic constructions in which a constituent, usually a noun phrase or an adpositional phrase, is moved to the beginning or the end of the sentence and the original position is marked by a pronominal element. These kinds of dislocations are particularly characteristic of colloquial speech.

Left and right dislocations serve various functions. Left dislocations can be used, for example, to emphasize information (⇒ **topic vs comment**, **theme vs rheme**): 'Spiders, I can't stand them'. Right dislocations often clarify the reference of a constituent: 'He'll be here tomorrow, my brother'.

References
Ashby, W. 1988. The syntax, pragmatics, and sociolinguistics of left- and right-dislocations in French. *Lingua* 75.203–29.

Cinque, G. 1977. The movement nature of left dislocation. *LingI* 8.147–63.
Geluykens, R. 1991. *From discourse process to grammatical construction: on left dislocation in English.* Amsterdam and Philadelphia, PA.
Gundel, J.K. 1975. Left dislocation and the role of topic–comment structure in linguistic theory. *WPL* 18.
Jansen, F. (ed.) 1978. *Studies in fronting.* Lisse.
Keenan, E.O. and E. Schieffelin. 1967. Foregrounding referents: a reconsideration of dislocation in discourse. *PBLS* 2.240–57.
Primus, B. 1993. Word order and information structure: a performance-based account of topic positions and focus positions. In J. Jacobs *et al.* (eds), *Syntax: an international handbook of contemporary research.* Berlin. 880–96.
Rodman, R. 1974. On left dislocation. *PIL* 7.437–66.
Ross, J.R. 1967. Constraints on variables in syntax. Dissertation, Cambridge, MA.
⇒ **word order**

Leipzig School ⇒ Neogrammarians

lemma [Lat. 'title,' from Grk *lēmma* 'anything received'] (*also* catchword)

Entry or individual listing in a lexicon or a dictionary.

lemmatization

In **lexicography** the reduction of the inflectional form of a word to its base form and the elimination of **homography**. In **computational linguistics**, lemmatization attempts to assign each word form a uniform heading under which related textual elements are ordered. In this sense, lemmatization is needed to produce indexes, concordances, and lists of individual authors or textual corpora.

References
⇒ **computational linguistics**, **lexicography**

lengthening vs shortening

Increase vs decrease in the **quantity** of a **segment**, usually a **vowel**. (⇒ *also* **gemination**, **phonetics**, **phonology**, **quality**, **sound change**, **tense vs lax**)

lenis ⇒ fortis vs lenis

lenisization ⇒ weakening

Lepontic ⇒ Celtic

letter

Written sign that stands alone or together with other such written signs to represent linguistic sounds or series of sounds (which are generally not syllables and do not have the length of morphological units) or also numbers. Thus, ⟨n⟩ in Eng. *pin* stands alone for [n] or /n/; ⟨n⟩ in Eng. *angle* appears together with the following ⟨g⟩ for [ŋ]. In some cases the principle seems contradictory as, for example, in Fr. *aux* (an amalgam of *ail* 'garlic' + plural), where the four letters together stand for the sound [o] and thus represent both a syllable and a morphological unit. Two letters of a base alphabet (e.g. the Latin alphabet) may be used in another ortho-graphic system as a single letter or may merge into a single letter: ⟨ch⟩ in **Czech** and ⟨ij⟩ in **Dutch** count as one letter; **German** ⟨ß⟩ is derived from a **ligature** of ⟨ſ⟩ and ⟨ȝ⟩ in Gothic type. In Ancient **Greek** ⟨ϛ⟩ is only used as the character for the number *6*, ⟨π⟩ renders [p] or, with the **diacritic** as ⟨π'⟩, the number *80*.

While the names of the letters of the Greek alphabet can be traced back to Semitic mean-ings (*alpha* 'ox,' *beta* 'house,' *delta* 'wing of a door,' *jota* 'hand'), those of the Latin alphabet are based on sounds. Letters representing **plo-sives** were named after the sound itself fol-lowed by an *e* (pronounced [iː] in English), though *k* and *q* are the notable exceptions. It is believed that *f, l, m, n, r,* and *s* did not originally have their own names; *ha,* the Classical Latin name for *h,* is of unknown origin. All other Latin letters were borrowed from the Greek alphabet or other sources. [fau] as a name for *v* has been in use since Priscian (fifth/sixth cen-tury); the name [iks] for *x,* also of unknown origin, came on the scene later; the name [jot] for *j* came into general use in the thirteenth century.

References
Hammarström, M. 1920. *Beiträge zur Geschichte des etruskischen, lateinischen und griechischen Alphabets.* Helsinki.
⇒ **graphemics, writing**

level

1 Levels of linguistic description, such as **pho-nology, morphology, syntax, semantics,** each of which is characterized by its own specific inventory of units (⇒ **phonemes, morphemes,** etc.), specific types of rules and analytical procedures. (⇒ *also* **stratificational gram-mar**)

2 Language of stylistic level; language variants which are determined by regional, sociological, or rhetorical norms. (⇒ *also* **register**)

Reference
Hartmann, R.R.K. 1973. *The language of linguistics: reflections on linguistic terminology with partic-ular reference to 'level' and 'rank.'* Tübingen.

level I affix ⇒ **lexical phonology**

level II affix ⇒ **lexical phonology**

leveling ⇒ **analogy**

levels of adequacy

The criterion developed by N. Chomsky for evaluating grammatical descriptions of natural languages. There are three distinct levels: observational adequacy, descriptive adequacy, and explanatory adequacy. Observational ade-quacy describes those grammars which present the primary linguistic data correctly and com-pletely. A grammar is descriptively adequate if it accounts for the intuitions and competence (⇒ **competence vs performance**) of the speak-er regarding the regularity and rules of the language. The comprehensive requirements for explanatory adequacy are met if the grammat-ical description is handled in accord with a linguistic theory which specifies linguistic uni-versals (⇒ **universal grammar**) and also sup-ports a theory of **language acquisition**. Such a theory provides the basis on which the most adequate explanatory grammar can be chosen from several descriptively adequate grammars.

References
Chomsky, N. 1964. *Current issues in linguistic theory.* The Hague.
—— 1965. *Aspects of the theory of syntax.* Cam-bridge, MA.
Kimball, J.P. 1973. *The formal theory of grammar.* Englewood Cliffs, NJ.
Lepore, E. 1979. The problem of adequacy in linguistics. *TL* 6.162–72.

lexeme [combined from *lexicon* + *eme*]

Basic abstract unit of the **lexicon**[2] on the level of langue (⇒ **langue vs parole**) which may be realized in different grammatical forms such as the lexeme *write* in *writes, wrote, written.* A lexeme may also be a part of another lexeme, e.g. *writer, ghostwriter,* etc. In its broader sense, 'lexeme' is also used synonymously for 'word' to denote a lexical unit or element of the vocabulary. (⇒ *also* **morphology**)

References
⇒ **word formation**

lexical access ⇒ **mental lexicon**

lexical category [Grk *léxis* 'word']

In the **aspects model** of **generative grammar** those category symbols (*N, Adj, V, Art*) found on the left side of the lexicon rule which are replaced by **lexical formatives** (i.e. words in the **lexicon**[3]) in the process of derivation.

References
⇒ **transformational grammar**

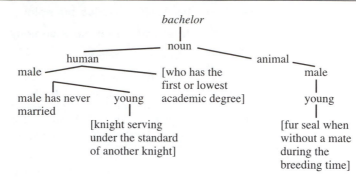

lexical decomposition

In **generative semantics**, a procedure applied especially to **causatives** for the semantic description of lexical units by deriving them from an inventory of smallest (possibly universal) basic expressions (⇒ **semantic primitives**), which on the basis of their internal syntactic structure constitute the complete meaning of the lexemes, e.g., *to kill* is 'decomposed' into CAUSE – BECOME – NOT – ALIVE. For the problematization and critique of the approach, ⇒ **generative semantics**. Nevertheless, lexical decomposition is also applied in other approaches, for the principle of decomposition is only incompatible with a concept of integrality.

References
Bartsch, R. and T. Vennemann. 1972. *Semantic structures: a study in the relation between semantics and syntax.* (2nd edn 1973.) Frankfurt.
Dowty, D.R. 1979. *Word meaning and Montague grammar: the semantics of verbs and times in generative semantics and Montague's PTQ.* Dordrecht.
Fillmore, C.J. 1968. Lexical entries for verbs. *FL* 4.373–93.
——— 1969. Types of lexical information. In F. Kiefer (ed.), *Studies in syntax and semantics.* Dordrecht. 109–37.
Fillmore, C.J. and T.D. Langendoen (eds) 1971. *Studies in linguistic semantics.* New York. 1–118.
Lakoff, G. 1970. Natural logic and lexical decomposition. *CLS* 6.340–62.
McCawley, J.D. 1968. Concerning the base component of a transformation grammar. *FL* 4.243–69.
——— 1988. *The syntactic phenomena of English.* 2 vols. Chicago, IL.
Schulze, W. 1985. *Semantic primitives and categories.* Utrecht.
Wierzbicka, A. 1972. *Semantic primitives.* Frankfurt.
Yamanashi, M. 1971. *Some notes on decomposition.* Ann Arbor, MI.
⇒ **generative semantics**

lexical diffusion

Hypothesis according to which **sound change** takes place in a few words and then spreads successively (through quasi-analogous generalizations) to all words concerned. This view, propounded by **dialect geography** against the concept of sound change of the Neogrammarians, was reintroduced into linguistic discussions at the end of the 1960s with renewed vigor.

References
Chen, M. and W.S.-Y. Wang. 1975. Sound change: actuation and implementation. *Lg* 51.255–81.
Labov, W. 1981. Resolving the neogrammarian controversy. *Lg* 57.267–308.
Wang, W.S.-Y. 1969. Competing changes as a cause of residue. *Lg* 45.9–25.
——— (ed.) 1977. *The lexicon in phonological change.* The Hague.
⇒ **sound change**

lexical entry

In **generative grammar**, the representation of **lexical formatives** in the **lexicon**[3] as **tree diagrams** composed of a phonetic-phonological, a syntactic, and a semantic component. The semantic component consists of the set of readings of a lexeme (cf. the four distinct readings for the lexical entry of Eng. *bachelor* which are distinguished from each other through the specification of semantic markers (in parentheses), **distinguishers** (in brackets) and, as required, **selection restrictions**.

The purpose, content, and form of the lexical entry varies according to the given grammatical and theoretical framework: for example, in the **lexicalist vs transformationalist hypothesis** it is necessary to distinguish between simple and complex lexical entries.

Reference
Katz, J.J. and J.A. Fodor. 1963. The structure of a semantic theory. *Lg* 39.170–210.

lexical field (*also* semantic field)

Term introduced by Trier (1931) to denote a set of semantically related words whose meanings delimit each other and are said to cover a whole conceptual or objective field without gaps (similar to a mosaic). This largely intuitive term has been made more precise at the formal level to denote a class of paradigmatic elements (see Corseriu 1967) and at the content level as a definite structure that can be described with the aid of **componential analysis** and **semantic relations**.

References

Coseriu, E. 1967. Lexikalische Solidaritäten. *Poetica* 1.293–303. (Repr. in W. Kallmeyer *et al.* (eds), *Lektürekolleg zur Textlinguistik*, vol. II: *Reader*. 1974. Frankfurt a.M. 74–86.)

Trier, J. 1931. *Der deutsche Wortschatz im Sinnbezirk des Verstandes: die Geschichte eines sprachlichen Feldes*, vol. I: *Von den Anfängen bis zum Beginn des 13. Jahrhunderts*. Heidelberg.

—— 1934. Das sprachliche Feld: eine Auseinandersetzung. *Neue Jahrbücher für Wissenschaft und Jugendbildung* 10.248–49.

⇒ **lexical field theory**

lexical field theory (*also* semantic field theory)

A predominantly semantic theory of the German structuralist school (⇒ **structuralism**) according to which a word does not exist in isolation in the consciousness of the speaker/ hearer, but always forms a structured set of elements together with other conceptually related words that have a reciprocal influence on each other. Lexical field theory, first associated primarily with J. Trier, reflects the general linguistic tendency to move from an isolating, atomistic, discrete view to a holistic, systematic approach. Both de Saussure's concept of 'system' and the influences of Gestalt psychology as well as Cassirer's theory of cognition have influenced the development of lexical field theory. The following premises are fundamental to Trier's lexical field theory. (a) The **meaning** of an individual word is dependent upon the meaning of the rest of the words of the same lexical or conceptual field (cf. the musical scale). (b) An individual lexical field is constructed like a mosaic with no gaps; the whole set of all lexical fields of a language reflects a self-contained picture of reality. (c) If a single word undergoes a change in meaning, then the whole structure of the lexical field changes. Consequently, the isolated historical study of words can be superseded by the study of lexical fields. In addition to this paradigmatic concept, a syntagmatic concept of field was developed very early on by Porzig (⇒ **inherent semantic relation**). Multiple criticism (see Kandler 1959; Öhmann 1959; Betz 1954) has led to differentiations and modifications of lexical field theory. A more detailed formulation of the terminology and subject matter brought about

the development of **componential analysis** (see Baumgärtner 1967), which on the one hand made the semantic analysis of individual lexemes more systematic and on the other hand also brought syntagmatic aspects into consideration. Both the troublesome problem of selecting a criterion for determining whether or not a particular element belongs to a lexical field and the problem of differentiation, i.e. whether a particular element occupies its own position in the lexical field, have in the meantime been brought closer to a solution by introducing the concept of **semantic relations** for structuring the lexical field.

References

Baumgärtner, K. 1967. Die Struktur des Bedeutungsfeldes. In H. Moser *et al.* (eds), *Satz und Wort im heutigen Deutsch*. Düsseldorf. 165–97.

Betz. W. 1954. Zur Überprüfung des Feldbegriffs. *ZVS* 71.189–98.

Coseriu, E. 1967. Lexikalische Solidaritäten. *Poetica* 1.293–303. (Repr. in W. Kallmeyer *et al.* (eds) *Lektürekolleg zur Textlinguistik*, vol. II: *Reader*. Frankfurt a.M. 1974. 74–86.)

Geckeler, H. 1971. *Strukturelle Semantik und Wortfeldtheorie*. Munich.

—— (ed.) 1978. *Strukturelle Bedeutungslehre*. Darmstadt.

Gipper, H. 1975. Sind sprachliche Felder formalisierbar? In H. Beckers and H. Schwarz (eds), *Gedenkschrift für Jost Trier*. Cologne. 116–49.

Grandy, R.E. 1987. In defense of semantic fields. In E. LePore (ed.), *New directions in semantics*. London. 259–80.

Kandler, G. 1959. Die 'Lücke' im sprachlichen Weltbild. In H. Gipper (ed.), *Zur Synthese von 'Psychologismus' und 'Soziologismus': Festschrift für L. Weisgerber*. Düsseldorf. 256–70.

Karcher, G.L. 1979. *Kontrastive Untersuchung von Wortfeldern im Deutschen und Englischen*. Frankfurt.

Lehrer, A. 1974. *Semantic fields and lexical structure*. Amsterdam.

—— 1978. Structures of the lexicon and transfer of meaning. *Lingua* 45.95–123.

Lipka, L. 1980. Methodology and representation in the study of lexical fields. In D. Kastovsky (ed.), *Perspektiven der lexikalischen Semantik: Beiträge zum Wuppertaler Semantikkolloquium vom 2.–3. Dezember 1977*. Bonn. 93–114.

Lutzeier, P.R. 1981. *Wort und Feld*. Tübingen.

—— 1983. The relevance of semantic relations between words for the notion of lexical fields. *TL* 10.147–78.

—— (ed.) 1993. *Studien zur Wortfeld theorie*. (*Studies in lexical field theory*.) Tübingen.

Öhmann, S. 1959. *Wortinhalt und Weltbild*. Stockholm.

Sansome, R. 1986. Connotation and lexical field analysis. *Cahiers de Lexicologie* 49.13–33.

Schmidt, L. (ed.) 1973. *Wortfeldforschung: zur Geschichte und Theorie des sprachlichen Feldes*. Darmstadt.

Trier, J. 1931. *Der deutsche Wortschatz im Sinnbezirk des Verstandes: die Geschichte eines sprachlichen Feldes*. vol. I: *Von den Anfängen bis zum Beginn des 13. Jahrhunderts*. Heidelberg.
—— 1934. Das sprachliche Feld: eine Auseinandersetzung. *Neue Jahrbücher für Wissenschaft und Jugendbildung* 10.428–49.
—— 1973. *Aufsätze und Vorträge zur Wortfeldtheorie*. Darmstadt.
⇒ **semantics**

lexical formative

In **generative grammar** the smallest semantic-syntactic unit of the lexicon (*book, sing-, old*) which is incorporated into the **deep structure** via lexicon rules. They are differentiated from grammatical formatives, which represent categories like **tense** and **number**. Lexical formatives are relevant in the application of transformational and interpretative components.

References
⇒ **transformational grammar**

Lexical-Functional Grammar (*abbrev.* LFG)

A generative theory from the class of **unification grammars** that was developed by J. Bresnan and R. Kaplan at the end of the 1970s, and was influenced by **relational grammar**. The most comprehensive description of the theory is to be found in Bresnan (1982). Lexical-Functional Grammar (LFG) attaches great meaning to the grammatical relations like subject, direct object, and indirect object, and includes them in a small class of universal grammatical functions (together with other syntactic roles, such as **adjunct** and **free adjunct**). These grammatical functions are the primitive concepts in LFG. LFG's point of departure is that many of the syntactic regularities which were described by transformations in **transformational grammar**, are of a lexical nature and, therefore, can be represented in the lexicon. The grammatical formalism of LFG distinguishes two levels of syntactic representation, constituent structure and functional structure, which are generated in parallel from the annotated phrase structure rules of the grammar. Without annotations, (i.e. feature equations that make up the functional structure), these rules are **context-free rules**, which generate local trees with atomic category symbols. They are governed by a version of **X-bar theory**. The functional structure of a constituent is a feature structure in the sense of **unification grammar**. Grammatical functions like SUBJ (subject), OBJ2 (indirect object) and PRED (predicate) as well as morphosyntactic features like CASE, NUM (number), and TENSE are attributes of the functional structure. An attribute can have an atomic symbol, a semantic predicate expression or a feature structure as a value. By means of two special variables, the feature equations in the phrase structure rules dictate the coreference between the feature structures of the nodes of the local tree and the attributes of the functional structure. The functional structure of the mother constituent is indicated by the symbol '↑', the functional structure of the daughter constituent, with the symbol '↓'. For example, the equation (↑OBJ2) = under the categorial symbol *NP* in a verb phrase rule means that the functional structure of the noun phrase is coreferent with the value of the attribute OBJ2 in the functional structure. The phrase structure rules of LFG overgenerate structures. The structures must satisfy three global wellformedness constraints which function as filters. (a) The principle of functional uniqueness states that every attribute in a functional structure may possess only one value. (b) The principle of functional completeness states that a functional structure is locally complete when it contains all the governable grammatical functions that its predicate governs. (c) The principle of functional coherence states that in every substructure of the functional structure, all governable grammatical functions are governed by the predicate of the substructure. Subcategorization ensues from the attribute PRED in the lexical entry, in which only the grammatical function of the obligatory and optional complements are specified, not their syntactic category. In LFG many syntactic relations described by transformations in transformational grammar (e.g. those between sentences with transitive verbs and the corresponding sentences with passive, middle, or causative verbs) are produced in the lexicon rather than the syntax. Lexical rules relate the corresponding verb classes and produce the correspondences between the complement position in the PRED attribute. Non-local dependencies, e.g. in *wh*-questions and topicalization, were originally dealt with by feature transmission. A newer version of LFG treats non-local dependencies through **functional uncertainty** (see Kaplan and Zaenen 1989). The functional structure of a sentence, especially the predicate expression that is the value of the attribute PRED, is the basis for semantic interpretation. Halvorsen (1983) suggests a semantic component borrowed from **Montague grammar**. Fenstad *et al.* (1987) use functional structure for the encoding of situational schemata, feature-based representations of meaning, which can be interpreted by using **situation semantics**. LFG was used for many descriptions of individual languages, e.g. English

(Bresnan 1982), for Warlpiri (Simpson and Bresnan 1983), Chichewa, Japanese, and Serbo-Croatian (Iida *et al.* 1987). It also serves as the basis for the implementation of numerous computational natural language systems on the computer, e.g. Reyle and Frey (1983), Block and Haugeneder. (1988), and Kaplan and Maxwell (1988).

References
Block, H.U. and H. Haugeneder. 1988. An efficiency-oriented LFG parser. In U. Reyle and C. Rohrer (eds), *Natural language parsing and linguistic theories*. Dordrecht. 149–76.
Bresnan, J. 1982. Control and complementation. In J. Bresnan (ed.), *The mental representation of grammatical relations*. Cambridge, MA. 282–390.
Dalrymple, M. 1993. *The syntax of anaphoric binding*. Chicago, IL.
Fenstad. J.E., P.K. Halvorsen, T. Langholm, and J. van Benthem. 1987. *Situations, language and logic*. Dordrecht.
Halvorsen, P.K. 1983. Semantics for Lexical-Functional Grammar. *LingI* 14.567–615.
Horn, G.M. 1983. *Lexical-Functional Grammar*. Berlin and New York.
Iida, M., S. Wechsler, and D. Zec (eds) 1987. *Working papers in grammatical theory and discourse structure*. Stanford, CA.
Kaplan, R.M. and J.T. Maxwell. 1988. Constituent coordination in Lexical-Functional grammar. *COLING 88* 1.303–5.
Kaplan, R.M. and Z. Zaenen. 1989. Long-distance dependencies, constituent structure, and functional uncertainty. In M. Baltin and A. Kroch (eds), *Alternative conceptions of phrase structure*. Chicago, IL. 17–42.
Kiss, T. 1993. Lexical-Functional Grammar. In J. Jacobs *et al.* (eds) *Syntax: an international handbook of contemporary research*. Berlin and New York. 581–600.
Reyle, U. and W. Frey. 1983. A Prolog implementation of Lexical-Functional Grammar. *IJCAI* 83.693–5.
Simpson, J. and J. Bresnan. 1983. Control and obviation in Warlpiri. *NL&LT* 1.49–64.
Simpson, J. 1991. *Warlpiri morpho-syntax: a lexicalist approach*. Dordrecht.

lexical insertion (rule) (*also* lexicon rule)

In the Extended Standard Theory of **transformational grammar**, the substitution of the preterminal symbols (*N, Adj, V*, etc.) in the **deep structure** with **lexical formatives** (i.e. words) from the **lexicon**[3]. The final chain of **derivation** over which the semantically neutral **transformations** operate, is attained through lexical insertion rules. In contrast to Chomsky's lexical insertion rules in the basic part of the grammar, the adherents of **generative semantics** advocate substituting the **semantic primitives** with lexical units before and after the application of transformations.

References
Chomsky, N. 1965. *Aspects of the theory of syntax.* Cambridge, MA.
McCawley, J.D. 1968. Lexical insertion in a transformational grammar without deep structure. *CLS* 4.71–80.

lexical meaning vs grammatical meaning

(*also* word meaning vs formal/functional/structural meaning)

Lexical meaning is that aspect of **meaning** which is codified in a lexicon or a dictionary, can be semantically analyzed, and, together with the grammatical elements of meaning (such as **mood**, **tense**, comparison ($\Rightarrow$ **degree**)) yields the whole meaning of a linguistic expression. Normally lexical meaning consists of an open class of elements, whereas grammatical meaning is restricted to a closed class of elements. Thus, the lexical meaning of *rich* might be indicated in the dictionary as 'having wealth,' while the grammatical semantic feature [+ comparison] would yield the lexeme *richer*, meaning roughly 'having more wealth.' The distinction between the two types is not always clear.

Reference
Testen, D., V. Mishra, and J. Drogo (eds) 1984. *Papers from the parasession on lexical semantics.* Chicago, IL.

lexical phonology

Approach in **phonology** developed by P. Kiparsky and others that divides the lexicon into levels within which the different means of **word formation** and **inflection** in a language interact with a predetermined set of cyclically applying phonological rules in order to derive word structures. **Affixes** of the first level (level I) together with their stem undergo phonological processes such as word stress, assimilation, vowel shortening (cf. Eng. *párent* and *parént+al*; *il+legal*, *im+possible*, but *in+efficient*; *opáque*, but *opac+ity*). The output of each level always forms a possible word stem, whose internal structure is visible to that level, but which, owing to the deletion of the original bracketing, is inaccessible to higher levels which are organized according to their own characteristic phonological rules. Typical for stems serving as a base for level II affixes and compounds is their phonological as well as semantic transparency (cf. Eng. *non-legal*; *opáque-ness*, *teeth-marks*). Regular inflection (cf. Eng. *cat-s* vs *teeth*, or *brother-s* vs *brethren*) comprises the third and last level. Irregular inflection corresponds to the phonological processes of the first level.

References
Allen, M. 1978. Morphological investigations. Dissertation, University of Connecticut.
Kiparsky, P. 1982a. Lexical morphology and phonology. In I.S. Yange (ed.), *Linguistics in the morning calm*. Seoul. 3–91.
—— 1982b. From cyclic phonology to lexical phonology. In H. van der Hulst and N. Smith (eds), *The structure of phonological representation*. Dordrecht. 131–75.
Pesetsky, D. 1979. Russian morphology and lexical theory. Dissertation, Cambridge, MA.
Siegel, D. 1974. Topics in English morphology. Dissertation, Cambridge, MA.

lexical relation ⇒ thematic relation

lexical solidarities

Term coined by Coseriu (1967) to denote syntagmatic relations of meaning between linguistic elements in contrast to restrictions on usage. The examination of **semantic relations** in syntagmatic constructions is traced to Porzig (1934), who described these relations as **inherent semantic relations**. Lexical solidarities concern directed ('oriented') semantic relations between a determining lexeme (e.g. *blond*) and a determined lexeme (e.g. *hair*). Coseriu distinguishes between three types of lexical solidarities which are independent of the semantic status of the determining element. The semantic determination of the determined lexeme is a function of the determining lexeme: (a) in affinity with a class-forming feature (classeme), e.g. [of animals] in the verb *graze*; (b) through selection of a superordinate feature (**archilexeme**), e.g. [for travel] with *ship* in the context of *train, car, boat, bus*; and (c) through implication of the whole lexeme, e.g. *calico* is (in a non-figurative sense) restricted to *cat*, i.e. it implies *cat* as a determined lexeme.

References
Coseriu, E. 1967. Lexikalische Solidaritäten. *Poetica* 1.293–303.
Porzig, W. 1934. Wesenhafte Bedeutungsbeziehungen. *PBB* 58.70–97.
⇒ **selection restrictions**

lexical hypothesis ⇒ lexicalist vs transformationalist hypothesis

lexicalist vs transformationalist hypothesis (*also* lexicalist vs syntactic hypothesis)

Different strategies for describing the processes of word and sentence formation in the framework of **generative grammar**. In **morphology** the transformationalist position, based on Chomsky (1970), operates on the assumption that word formation and the production of sentences display similar characteristics as far as **recursiveness** and generativity are concerned; moreover, numerous syntactic-semantic characteristics of complex words can be predicted on the basis of their underlying **lexemes**. Drawing upon the postulate of the economy of the **lexicon**[3] in a generative framework, the proponents of the transformationalist hypothesis argue for describing complex morphological structures as the transition of a syntactic deep structure to a correspondingly complex morphological form in the surface structure. The lexicon is viewed as a collection of all irregularities and is thereby relieved of having to describe morphological processes as regular transformational processes. Various facts weaken this 'syntactic' position (see Motsch 1977): the restriction of potentially possible formations by competing terms already in the lexicon (e.g. *brush : to brush* vs *broom : *to broom/sweep*) can no more be justified through syntactic rules than semantic restrictions (e.g. *apish* vs **cattish*, *grassy* vs *?oaty*), the different degree to which regularities can be exploited, and pragmatically motivated problems of grammaticality (*to hammer* vs **to spanner*) seem to be more relevant. Like the effect of analogous processes in word formation, such problems can be more adequately described in the framework of a lexicalist theory which lists simple as well as complex words in the same manner in the lexicon. The *de facto* existing relationships and regularities are taken into account through **redundancy rules**, which formulate systematically predictable information within the processes of word formation. According to the lexicalist position, in the description of syntactic processes a syntactic relationship between two types of constructions (e.g. active-passive or the English dative alternation *I gave him the book* vs *I gave the book to him*) is represented by a lexical rule that operates on lexical entries (or on lexically unspecified sentence forms), whereas the classic transformational representation operates using transformational rules over lexically specified **phrase markers**. Lees (1960) represents the transformationalist position, while Jackendoff (1975) and Aronoff (1976) hold the lexicalist position. The controversy also continues in recent generative syntax theories. Hoekstra *et al.* (1980) and Moortgat *et al.* (1981) provide overviews of the development of these hypotheses.

References
Aronoff, M. 1976. *Word formation in generative grammar*. Cambridge.
Bartsch, R. 1981. Semantics and syntax of nominal-

izations. In J. Groenendijk *et al.* (eds), *Formal methods in the study of language*. Amsterdam. Vol. 1, 1–28.

Chomsky, N. 1965. *Aspects of the theory of syntax*. Cambridge, MA.

——— 1970. Remarks on nominalization. In R.A. Jacobs and P.S. Rosenbaum (eds), *Readings in English transformational grammar*. Waltham, MA. 184–221.

Hoekstra, T., H. van der Hulst, and M. Moortgat (eds) 1980. *Lexical grammar*. Dordrecht.

Jackendoff, R. 1975. Morphological and semantic regularities in the lexicon. *Lg* 51,639–71.

Kastovsky, D. 1977. Problems of word-formation. In C. Gutknecht (ed.), *Grundbegriffe und Hauptströmungen der Linguistik*. Frankfurt. 301–35.

——— 1977. Word formation, or: At the crossroads of morphology, syntax, semantics, and the lexicon. *FL* 10.1–33.

Lees, R.B. 1960. *The grammar of English nominalizations*. Bloomington, IN.

——— 1970. Problems in the grammatical analysis of English nominal compounds. In M. Bierwisch and K.E. Heidolph (eds), *Progress in linguistics*. The Hague. 174–86.

Moortgat, M., H. van der Hulst, and T. Hoekstra (eds) 1981. *The scope of lexical rules*. Dordrecht.

Motsch, W. 1977. Ein Plädoyer für die Beschreibung von Wortbildung auf der Grundlage des Lexikons. In H. Brekle and D. Kastovsky (eds), *Perspektiven der Wortbildungsforschung*. Bonn. 180–202.

Selkirk, E.O. 1982. *The syntax of words*. Cambridge, MA.

lexicalization

1 Synchronically, the adoption of a word into the lexicon of a language as a usual formation that is stored in the lexicon and can be recalled from there for use. Belonging to this lexicon are base words (*fence, lion*) as well as complex words (*cookbook, fireman*) which the language holds ready as denotations for required concepts. Also set syntactic phrases that are similar to words in a particular meaning (*sour cream, at death's door*) belong to the lexicon of a language. In contrast to lexicalization, **nonce words** (*test-tube baby, space glove*) are produced according to standard rules of **word formation** and are instantly comprehensible; they are, however, not usually a permanent part of the lexicon. (⇒ *also* **productivity**)

2 Diachronically, the historical process (and result) of **semantic change**, in which the original meaning can no longer be deduced from its individual elements (cf. *neighbor* < OEng. nēahgebūr 'near dweller'). Fully lexicalized expressions form a (new) semantic unit; their original **motivation** can only be deduced etymologically. This process is often also called **idiomatization**, to distinguish it from lexicalization.

References
⇒ **word formation**

lexicography

Theory and practice of compiling dictionaries. Lexicography provides the principles necessary for documenting the **vocabulary** of a language, a dialect or a profession by drawing on **lexicology** with its theoretical bases and materials for lexicographic codification and by taking practical concerns such as marketability, user-friendliness, etc. into consideration. The form of presentation depends on whether one intends to compile a single or multi-language lexicon, a diachronic or synchronic record of a specific vocabulary, or a descriptive or prescriptive reference work. The distinct purpose of the individual types of dictionaries determines how the materials are to be organized. While alphabetic ordering is by far the most frequent type, some dictionaries are systematically compiled according to semantic principles. A variant of alphabetic indexing is the so-called 'backwards dictionary' which is based on rhyme dictionaries of the Middle Ages. Entries (⇒ **lemma**) are ordered alphabetically according to their final letters or syllables. This type of dictionary is particularly useful, since morphological relationships between words become transparent through their presentation. In contrast to these paradigmatically oriented dictionaries, style dictionaries codify the material according to syntagmatic principles by listing catchwords within syntactic constructions (e.g. **idioms** or phrases). So-called 'valence dictionaries' are also syntactically oriented; verbs, nouns, or adjectives are compiled according to their **valence** (i.e. their compatibility with obligatory complements).

References
Bergenholtz, H. (ed.). 1995. *Manual of specialised lexicography*. Amsterdam.

Burchfield, R.W. (ed.) 1987. *Studies in lexicography*. Oxford.

Hartmann, R.R.K. (ed.) 1986. *The history of lexicography*. Amsterdam.

Hausmann, F.J., P. Reichmann, H.E. Weigand, and L. Zgusta (eds) 1989–91. *Wörterbucher. Dictionnaires. Dictionaries*. 3 vols. Berlin and New York.

Ilson, R.F. (ed.) 1985. *Dictionaries, lexicography and language learning*. Oxford.

——— (ed.) 1986. *Lexicography: an emerging international profession*. Manchester.

Jackson, H. 1988. *Words and their meaning*. London.

Jones, R.L. and S.P. Sondrup. 1989. Computer-aided lexicography. In I.S. Bátori, W. Lenders, and W. Putschke (eds), *Computerlinguistik*. Berlin. 490–518.

Landau, S.I. 1989. *Dictionaries: the art and craft of lexicography*. Cambridge.

McDavid, R.I. and A.R. Duckert (eds) 1973. *Lexico-graphy in English*. New York.

Svensén, B. 1993. *Practical lexicography: principles and methods of dictionary making*, trans. J. Sykes and K. Schofield. Oxford.

Tomaszczyk, J. and B. Lewandowska-Tomaszczyk (eds) 1990. *Meaning and lexicography*. Amsterdam and Philadelphia, PA.

Wierzbicka, A. 1985. *Lexicography and conceptual analysis*. Ann Arbor, MI.

Zgusta, L. 1971. *Manual of lexicography*. The Hague.

—— (ed.) 1992. *History, languages, and lexicographers*. Tübingen.

Bibliography
Zgusta, L. and D.M.T.C. Farina. 1987. *Lexicography today: an annotated bibliography of the theory of lexicography*. Tübingen.

Journals
International Journal of Lexicography.
Lexicographica.

lexicology

Subdiscipline of linguistics or, more specifically, **semantics** that investigates and describes the structure of the vocabulary of a language. Lexicology also examines linguistic expressions for their internal semantic structure and the relationships between individual words or lexical units. The findings of lexicology may be codified by **lexicography** (i.e. the technique of preparing dictionaries), although the relationship between both areas is not necessarily close. (⇒ *also* **lexical field theory, semantic relation**)

References
Aitchison, J. 1987. *Words in the mind: an introduction to the mental lexicon*. Oxford.

Carter, R. 1987. *Vocabulary: applied linguistic perspectives*. London.

Cruse, D.A. 1986. *Lexical semantics*. Cambridge.

Lipka, L. 1992. *An outline of English lexicology*, 2nd edn. Tübingen.

Schwarze, C. and D. Wunderlich (eds) 1985. *Handbuch der Lexikologie*. Königstein.

Roey, J. van 1990. *French–English contrastive lexicology: an introduction*. Leuven.

Journal
Lexicology.
⇒ **lexical field theory, semantic relation, semantics**

lexicon [Late Grk *lexicón* (sc. *biblión*) 'book of or for words']

1 An alphabetically or semantically ordered list of words for a language, **dialect**, or **sociolect**, or a list of terminology for a specific discipline. Such lists are generally compiled as reference works. (⇒ *also* **lexicography, vocabulary**)

2 In its most general sense, the level of description which codifies the morphological and semantic aspects (i.e. the forms and meanings) of the vocabulary of a language which cannot be derived from the regularities of the linguistic system.

3 In **transformational grammar**, one of the basic components of grammar in the form of a subordinated list of all **lexical formatives**. The **lexical entry** consists of a phonetic-phonological description in the form of a **matrix** of **distinctive features** to which a selection of specific syntactic features is correlated (⇒ **complex symbol**) (see Chomsky 1965).

4 In **generative semantics**, the lexicon is composed of syntactically structured complexes of the smallest semantic building blocks (⇒ **semantic primitive**) to which corresponding phonological realizations are assigned. (⇒ *also* **lexicalist vs transformationalist hypothesis**)

References
Aitchison, J. 1987. *Words in the mind: an introduction to the mental lexicon*. Oxford.

Botha, R.P. 1968. *The function of the lexicon in transformational generative grammar*. The Hague.

Chomsky, N. 1965. *Aspects of the theory of syntax*. Cambridge, MA.

Gruber, J. 1967. *The functions of the lexicon in formal descriptive grammars*. Santa Monica, CA.

Hüllen, W. and R.A.I. Schulze, (eds) 1988. *Understanding the lexicon: meaning, sense and world knowledge in lexical semantics*. Tübingen.

Jackendoff, R. 1975. Morphological and semantic regularities in the lexicon. *Lg* 51.639–71.

McCawley, J.D. 1968. Lexical insertion in a transformational grammar without deep structure. *CLS* 4.71–80.

Steinberg, D.D. and L.A. Jakobovits (eds) 1971. *Semantics: an interdisciplinary reader in philosophy, linguistics and psychology*. Cambridge.

Stowell, T. and E. Wehrli (eds) 1992. *Syntax and the lexicon*. New York.

lexicon rule ⇒ lexical insertion (rule)

lexicostatistics

The quantitative description of the vocabulary of a specific language, the frequency of specific devices or the stylistic characteristics of different texts. Lexicostatistical data are gathered by means of data processing. (⇒ *also* **computational linguistics, glottochronology, statistical linguistics**)

References
Dyen, I. 1975. *Linguistic subgrouping and lexicostatistics*. The Hague.

Gudschinsky, S.C. 1956. The ABCs of lexicostatistics (glottochronology). *Word* 12.175–210.

Hymes, D. 1960. Lexicostatistics. *Current Anthropology* 1.3–44.

———— 1960. More on lexicostatistics. *Current Anthropology* 1.338–45.

Lehmann, W.P. 1962. *Historical linguistics: an introduction*. New York. (2nd edn 1973.)

Smith, R.N. 1973. *Probabilistic performance models of language*. The Hague.

Swadesh, M. 1952. Lexicostatistic dating of prehistoric ethnic contacts. *Proceedings of the American Philological Society* 96.452–63.

⇒ **frequency dictionaries**

Lezgian ⇒ North-East Caucasian

LFG ⇒ Lexical-Functional Grammar

liaison [Fr. 'connection']

Pronunciation rule in **French** according to which a normally silent consonant at the end of a word is articulated if it occurs between one word with a final vowel sound and another with an initial vowel sound, cf. *les parents* [1e parã] 'the parents' vs *les amis* [1ez amis] 'the friends.'

References
Klausenburger, J. 1984. *French liaison and linguistic theory*. Göttingen.
⇒ **French, syllable**

ligature

The merging of two or more letters (often for aesthetic reasons) from which a single, independent form is derived. The French ligature ‹œ› is motivated from ‹o› and ‹e› for [œ] or /œ/. Forming ligatures is one way of increasing the inventory of the letters (cf. also the development of ‹w› from ‹vv› or, in Danish, ‹æ› from ‹ae›).

References
⇒ **graphemics, writing**

linearity

1 The relationship between **phonemes** and corresponding **phones** in the realization of a linguistic expression. (⇒ **biuniqueness**)

2 A property of natural languages, linearity refers to the one-dimensional ordering and chronological ordering of linguistic elements during communication.

line spectrum

Result of a **spectral analysis** of **sounds** or vowels, i.e. of periodic sound waves. The wideband **spectrogram** shows regular vertical lines in contrast to a spectrogram of noise. (⇒ *also* **phonetics**)

References
⇒ **phonetics**

lingo

Usually facetious designation for **jargon** or **cant**. (⇒ *also* **slang**)

lingua franca [from Italian; Lat. *lingua* 'tongue, language,' *franca* 'Franconian']

1 Oldest attested **pidgin**, a trade language of the eastern Mediterranean coast which is based on Provençal (⇒ **Occitan**) and **Italian** and incorporates linguistic elements from **Greek** and **Arabic**. The original 'Lingua Franca' arose during the period of the Venetian and Genovese economic domination in the Levantine countries and was spoken until the nineteenth century. (⇒ *also* **Sabir**)

2 General term for a second acquired language system that serves as a means of communication between speakers of different first languages (or extremely distinct dialects), e.g. Latin (in the middle ages) and Arabic (as the universal language of Islam), as well as naturally or artificially mixed languages having arisen from several individual languages (⇒ **Esperanto, koiné, pidgin, interlingua**).

References
Samarin, W.J. 1962. Lingua francas, with special reference to Africa. In F.A. Rice (ed.), *Studies of the role of second languages in Africa and Latin America*. Washington, DC. 54–64.

———— 1987. Lingua franca. In U. Ammon *et al.* (eds), *Sociolinguistics: an international handbook of the science of language and society*. Berlin and New York. 371–4.
⇒ **creole, pidgin**

lingual

Speech sound classified according to its **articulator** (lingua = tongue). In vowels, a distinction is drawn between front, mid, and back. (⇒ *also* **articulatory phonetics**)

linguistic area

An area with a group of geographically proximal languages which are either genetically unrelated or only marginally related and which, on the basis of mutual influence (⇒ **adstratum, language contact**), show signs of convergence that help to delineate them as structurally different from other neighboring and/or genetically related languages.

Reference
Masica, C.P. 1976. *Defining a linguistic area: South Asia*. Chicago, IL.

linguistic atlas

Panregional collection of systematically ascertained dialectal differences in the form of linguistic maps (⇒ **dialect mapping**). Linguistic atlases originated during the Neogrammarian period (⇒ **Neogrammarians**).

References
Allen, H.B. 1973–6. *The linguistic atlas of the Upper Midwest*, 3 vols. Minneapolis, MN.
Avanesov, R.I. and S.V. Bromlej. 1986– . *Dialektologiceskij atlas russkogo jazyka*. Vol. 2 1989. Moscow.
Deutscher Sprachatlas. 1927–56. Comp. by F. Wrede *et al*. 23 vols. Marburg.
Deutscher Wortatlas. 1951–80. 22 vols. Wiesbaden.
Gillierón, J. and E. Edmont. 1902–10. *Atlas linguistique de France*. Paris.
Hotzenköcherle, R. (ed.) 1962– . *Sprachatlas der deutschen Schweiz*. Bern.
Jaberg, K. and J. Jud. 1928–40. *Sprach- and Sachatlas Italiens und der Südschweiz*, 8 vols. Zofingen.
Kolb, E. 1964. *Phonological atlas of the northern region*. Bern.
Kurath, H. 1949. *A word geography of the eastern United States*. Ann Arbor, MI.
Kurath, H., M. Hanley, B. Bloch, and G.S. Lowman Jr. 1939–43. *Linguistic atlas of New England*, 3 vols. Providence, R.I.
Mather, J.Y. and H.H. Speitel. 1975–7. *Linguistic atlas of Scotland*, 2 vols. London.
Moseley, C. and R.E. Asher (eds) 1994. *Atlas of the world's languages*. London.
Orton, H. 1960. An English dialect survey: linguistic atlas of England. *Orbis* 9.331–48. (Repr. in H.B. Allen and G. Underwood (eds), *Readings in American dialectology*. New York, 1971. 230–44.)
—— 1962. *Survey of English dialects: an introduction*. Leeds.
Orton, H. and M. Barry (eds) 1969–71. *Survey of English dialects: the basic material*, vol. 2 (3 parts): *The West Midland counties*. Leeds.
Orton, H. and W. Halliday (eds) 1962–3. *Survey of English dialects: the basic material*, vol. 1 (3 parts): *The six northern counties and the Isle of Man*. Leeds.
Orton, H. and P.M. Tilling (eds) 1969–71. *Survey of English dialects: the basic material*, vol. 3 (3 parts): *The East Midland counties and East Anglia*. Leeds.
Orton, H. and M.F. Wakelin (eds) 1967–8. *Survey of English dialects: the basic material*, vol. 4 (3 parts): *The southern counties*. Leeds.
Orton, H. and N. Wright. 1974. *A word geography of England*. London.
Orton, H., S. Sanderson, and J. Widdowson. 1978. *Linguistic atlas of England*. London.
Wakelin, M.F. 1972. *English dialects: an introduction*. London.
Weigner, A. *et al*. (eds) 1975– . *Atlas linguarum europae*. Vol. 1, 4 1990. Assen.
Veith, W. *et al*. 1984– . *Kleiner deutscher Sprachatlas*. Vol. 1, 2. hitherto. Tübingen.
Veith, W. and W. Putschke, (eds) 1989. *Sprachatlas des Deutschen: laufende Projekte*. Tübingen.
⇒ **dialectology**

linguistic awareness

Linguistic awareness in the sense of 'knowledge about language' or ability to make metalinguistic judgments about linguistic expressions constitutes an important area of study in **transformational grammar**, insofar as such linguistic intuition can be considered an expression of underlying competence. Investigations in **psycholinguistics** have, however, shown that judgments about the **grammaticality** of sentences are a type of linguistic performance and can be influenced just as much by performance factors as other linguistic activities (see Levelt 1972; Ericsson and Simon 1980; Carroll *et al*. 1981). In regard to the possible influence of linguistic awareness on child language development, the seminal investigations of Gleitman *et al*. (1972) have stimulated numerous studies and experiments. Five areas of metalinguistic research can be differentiated: (a) judgments about grammaticality and **acceptability**; (b) segmentation; (c) linguistic transformations and manipulations; (d) production and comprehension of **ambiguity** (e.g. in jokes, metaphors, or riddles); and (e) conceptualization of language, i.e. dissociation of word and referent (see Sinclair *et al*. 1978). The assumption that a single metalinguistic ability underlies the different metalinguistic forms of expression is debated. The importance of linguistic awareness in acquiring **deictic expressions** attests to experimental findings (see Böhme 1983).

References
Böhme, K. 1983. Children's use and awareness of German possessive pronouns. Dissertation, Nijmegen.
Carroll, J.M., T.G. Bever, and C.R. Pollack, 1981. The non-uniqueness of linguistic intuitions. *Lg* 57.368–83.
Ericsson, K.A. and H.A. Simon. 1980. Verbal reports as data. *PsychologR* 87.215–51.
Gleitman, L.R., H. Gleitman, and E.F. Shipley. 1972. The emergence of the child as grammarian. *Cognition* 1.137–64.
Hakes, D.T. 1980. *The development of metalinguistic abilities in children*. Berlin.
Levelt, W.J.M. 1972. Some psychological aspects of linguistic data. *LingB* 17.18–30.
Sinclair, A., R.J. Jarvella, and W.J.M. Levelt. 1978. *The child's conception of language*. Berlin.
⇒ **competence vs performance**, **language comprehension**, **psycholinguistics**

linguistic criticism

An evaluation of language as (a) style criticism (**stylistics**), (b) evaluation of **linguistic norms** (e.g. elaborate vs restricted code (⇒ **code theory**, **nominal style**), (c) evaluation of the properties of the linguistic system (e.g. holes in lexical fields, ⇒ Sapir–Whorf hypothesis). Scientific language criticism is based mainly on functional criteria and is the basis of the politics of language. Journalistic criticism of language is mainly a demythologizing of how language is used as an instrument of control as well as of communication. In **ordinary language philosophy**, language criticism serves to determine linguistically conditioned philosophical pseudo-problems; cf. L. Wittgenstein's 'all philosophy is language criticism' (*Tractatus Logico-Philosophicus*, 4.0031).

References
Eco, U. 1977. *A theory of semiotics*. London.
Fowler, R. 1981. *Literature as social discourse: the practice of linguistic criticism*. London.
——— 1986. *Linguistic criticism*. Oxford.
Wittgenstein, L. 1981. *Tractatus logico-philosophicus*. trans. C.K. Ogden. London.

linguistic determinism

Hypothesis put forth by B.L. Whorf (1897–1941) on the basis of his research into the dialects of **Hopi**, which claims that each individual language determines the perception, experience, and action of its speakers, and therefore speakers necessarily develop world views that differ to the same degree that their languages differ structurally. Thus language is not viewed primarily as a means of communication, but rather as an unconscious 'background phenomenon' which in large part determines individual thought.

References
⇒ Sapir–Whorf hypothesis

linguistic geography ⇒ dialect geography

linguistic norms

Social expectations, which determine the forms of suitable linguistic interaction within the boundaries of the linguistic system. Linguistic norms govern the fundamental conditions of communication (**maxims of conversation, acceptability, comprehensibility**) and in special situations curb the choice and organization of linguistic means like the form of the **illocution**, the choice of words, complexity of sentences, and pronunciation. Situative norms refer to functional and thematic appropriateness (e.g. for types of text for public/private, or oral/written speech), to correct speech in social roles and institutions, to age, and to gender roles, among others. Linguistic norms are based either implicitly on a consensus of the speakers, or they are explicitly determined and legitimized by criteria such as circulation, age, structural accordance, and purpose. The demarcation of linguistic norms and rules of a linguistic system is methodically difficult, since the existence of implicit linguistic norms can only be deduced from usage.

References
Bartsch, R. 1987. *Norms of language: theoretical and practical aspects*. London.
Crowley, T. 1991. *Proper English? Readings in language, history and cultural identity*. London.
Joseph, J.E. 1987. *Eloquence and power: the rise of language standard and standard languages*. London.
Khubchandani Lachman, M. 1983. *Plural languages, plural cultures: communication, identity, and sociopolitical change in contemporary India*. Honolulu.
Lewis, D. 1969. *Convention: a philosophical study*. Cambridge, MA.
Milroy, J. *et al.* 1985. *Authority in language: investigating language prescription and standardisation*. London.
Verdoodt, A. and R. Kjolseth (eds) 1976. *Language in sociology*. Louvain.

linguistic relativity ⇒ Sapir–Whorf hypothesis

linguistic standardization

The establishment and standardization of **jargon**, which is controlled internationally by the IOS (International Organization for Standardization). The choice, standardization, and formation of terminology is made according to standardized rules, such as the extent to which the term can be systematized, morphological **motivation**, **pronunciation**, and brevity.

linguistic theory

General theoretical premise for the linguistic description of natural languages. Through abstracting from individual observances in individual languages, linguistic theory designs models for the description of general grammatical properties of all natural languages (⇒ **universals**); origin, function, structure, rules, tendencies of change of linguistic systems are considered from linguistic, psychological, sociological, and other aspects and placed in an axiomatically based context. Approaches to a linguistic theory that is comprehensive in this sense are to be found in Lieb (1977) and Bartsch and Vennemann (1982). Other uses of the term linguistic theory refer to the 'theory of linguistic description' (e.g. Chomsky 1965); to the grammatical description itself (Lakoff 1965), to the description of competence (⇒ **competence vs performance**; Chomsky 1965) as well as to the methodology of linguistics.

References
Bartsch, R. and T. Vennemann. 1982. *Grundzüge der*

Sprachtheorie: eine linguistische Einführung. Tübingen.

Chomsky, N. 1965. *Aspects of the theory of syntax.* Cambridge, MA.

Cole, R.W. (ed.) 1977. *Current issues in linguistic theory.* Bloomington, IN.

Lakoff, G. 1965. Irregularity in syntax. Dissertation, New York.

Lieb, H.H. 1974/6. Grammars as theories: the case for axiomatic grammar. *TL* 1.39–115.

—— 1977. *Outline of integrational linguistics.* Berlin.

Newmeyer, F. 1986. *Linguistic theory in America,* 2nd edn. Orlando, FL.

⇒ **linguistics**

linguistics

Scientific discipline with the goal of describing language and speech in all relevant theoretical and practical aspects and their relation to adjoining disciplines. Insofar as linguistics deals with human languages as a sign system, it can be understood as a subdiscipline of general **semiotics**. Because of the object of its study and the investigational methods appropriate to it, linguistics has characteristics of both the natural sciences and the social sciences. Depending on the interests of the investigator, linguistics can be divided into general linguistics, which attempts to develop theories explaining general universal regularities of language (⇒ **universals, language typology**), and **applied linguistics**, which investigates problems dealing with specific languages. The various subfields of linguistics result from the different aspects of language investigated. (a) When the structure of language as a sign system is examined, the subfields **phonology, morphology, word formation, syntax, semantics, pragmatics,** and **text linguistics** result. (b) These specific subdisciplines can be used to study language synchronically (i.e. in respect to one specific language state) or diachronically, when the historical development of a language is studied (⇒ **synchrony vs diachrony, language change**). (c) Individual conditions of language production and perception are treated in **psycholinguistics** or **neurolinguistics** (⇒ also **language acquisition, language disorder**). (d) The relationship between language and its social/sociological setting is addressed by **sociolinguistics** and **ethnolinguistics**. (e) The fields listed in (d) overlap with aspects of regional variants and influences (⇒ **dialect, dialectology**). (f) Topics covered by **applied linguistics** include problems of foreign-language instruction (⇒ **foreign language pedagogy**), translation, **machine-aided translation** (⇒ **computational linguistics**) and language planning (⇒ **language contact**).

References

Akmajian, A., R. Demers, and R.M. Harnish, 1979. *Linguistics: an introductory survey,* (3rd edn. 1990) Oxford.

Atkinson, M., D. Kilby, and I. Roca. 1988. *Foundations of general linguistics,* 2nd edn. London.

Bloomfield, L. 1933. *Language.* New York.

Dinneen, F.P. 1967. *An introduction to general linguistics.* New York.

Droste, F.G. and J.E. Joseph (eds) 1989. *Mainstreams in today's linguistics.* Amsterdam.

Fromkin, V. and R. Rodman. 1974. *An introduction to language,* 5th edn. New York.

Gethin, A. 1990. *Antilinguistics: a critical assessment of modern linguistic theory and practice.* Oxford.

Gleason, H.A. 1955. *An introduction to descriptive linguistics.* New York. (Rev. edn 1961.)

Hockett, C.F. 1958. *A course in modern linguistics.* New York.

Jakobsen, R. and M. Halle, 1956. *Fundamentals of language.* The Hague. (2nd rev. edn 1975.)

Langacker, R.W. 1967. *Language and its structure.* New York.

—— 1972. *Fundamentals of linguistic analysis.* New York.

Lyons, J. 1968. *Introduction to general linguistics.* Cambridge.

—— 1981. *Language and linguistics: An introduction.* Cambridge.

Martinet, A. 1965. *La linguistique synchronique, études et recherches.* Paris.

—— (ed.) 1969. *La linguistique.* Paris.

—— 1989. Linguistique générale, linguistique structurale, linguistique fonctionelle. *Linguistique* 25.245–54.

Newmeyer, F.J. (ed.) 1988. *Linguistics: the Cambridge survey,* 4 vols. Cambridge.

Pedersen, M. 1962. *The discovery of language.* Cambridge, MA.

Robins, R.H. 1989. *General linguistics: an introductory survey,* 4th edn. London.

History

Andresen, J.T. 1990. *Linguistics in America 1769–1924: a critical history.* London.

Antonsen, E.H. (ed.) 1990. *The Grimm brothers and the Germanic past.* Amsterdam and Philadelphia, PA.

Beaugrande, R. de. 1991. *Linguistic theory: the discourse of fundamental works.* London.

Bohas, G., J.-P. Guillaume, and D.E. Kouloughli. 1990. *The Arabic linguistic tradition.* London.

Cannon, G. 1990. *The life and mind of Oriental Jones.* Cambridge.

Goldziher, I. 1994. *On the history of grammar among the Arabs,* ed. K. Devenyi *et al.* Amsterdam.

Harris, R. 1990. *Language, Saussure and Wittgenstein.* London.

—— (ed.) 1993. *British linguistics in the nineteenth century.* London.

Harris, R. and T.J. Taylor. 1989. *Landmarks in linguistic thought: the Western tradition from Socrates to Saussure.* London.

Itkonen, E. 1991. *Universal history of linguistics:*

India, China, Arabia, Europe. Amsterdam and Philadelphia, PA.

Koerner, E.F.K. 1989. *Practicing linguistic historiography.* Amsterdam and Philadelphia, PA.

Kühlwein, W. (ed.) 1970/1. *Linguistics in Great Britain.* 2 vols. Tübingen.

Law, V. 1990. Language and its students: the history of linguistics. In N.E. Collinge (ed.) *An encyclopedia of language.* London. 784–842.

―――― (ed.) 1993. *History of linguistic thought in the Early Middle Ages.* Amsterdam and Philadelphia, PA.

Lepschy, G. (ed.) 1994. *History of linguistics,* vol. 1: *The eastern tradition of linguistics*; vol. 2: *Classical and medieval Europe.* London.

Malmberg, B. 1991. *Histoire de la linguistique de Sumer à Saussure.* Paris.

Matthews, P.H. 1993. *Grammatical theory in the United States from Bloomfield to Chomsky.* Cambridge.

Mauro, T. de and L. Formigari, (eds) 1993. *Italian studies in linguistic historiography.* Münster.

Nerlich, B. 1991. *Semantic theories in Europe, 1830–1930: from etymology to contextuality.* Amsterdam and Philadelphia, PA.

Owens, J. 1988. *The foundations of grammar: an introduction to Medieval Arabic grammatical theory.* Amsterdam and Philadelphia, PA.

―――― 1990. *Early Arabic grammatical theory.* Amsterdam and Philadelphia, PA.

Parret, H. (ed.) 1976. *History of linguistic thought and contemporary linguistics.* The Hague.

Robins, R.H. 1985. *A short history of linguistics,* 2nd edn. London.

―――― 1988. History of linguistics. In F. Newmeyer (ed.), *Linguistics: the Cambridge survey.* Cambridge. Vol. 1, 462–84.

Scharfe, H. 1977. *Grammatical literature.* (A history of Indian literature, Vol. 5.) Wiesbaden.

Sebeok, T.A. 1966. *Portraits of linguists: a biographical sourcebook for the history of Western linguistics, 1746–1963,* 2 vols. Bloomington, IN.

―――― 1975. *Current trends in linguistics,* vol. 13: *Historiography of linguistics,* The Hague.

Bibliographies

Bibliographie linguistique – Linguistic bibliography. Utrecht and Antwerp. 1939ff.

Bibliographie linguistischer Literatur. 1975ff. *Bibliographie zur allgemeinen Linguistik und zur anglistischen, germanistischen und romanistischen Linguistik.* Frankfurt.

Koerner, E.F.K. 1978. *Western histories of linguistic thought: an annotated chronological bibliography, 1822–1976.* Amsterdam.

Rice, F. and A. Guss (eds) 1965. *Information source in linguistics: a bibliographical handbook.* Washington, DC.

Dictionaries and reference books

Asher, R.E. and J.M.Y. Simpson (eds) 1994. *The encyclopedia of language and linguistics,* 10 vols. Oxford.

Bright, W. (ed.) 1992. *International encyclopedia of linguistics,* 4 vols. New York and Oxford.

Collinge, N.E. 1990. *An encyclopedia of language.* London.

Crystal, D. 1991. *A dictionary of linguistics and phonetics,* 3rd edn. Oxford.

―――― 1987. *The Cambridge encyclopedia of language.* Cambridge.

―――― 1993. *An encyclopedic dictionary of language and languages.* Oxford.

―――― 1995. *The Cambridge encyclopedia of the English language.* Cambridge.

Dubois, J. *et al.* 1973. *Dictionnaire de linguistique.* 2nd edn. 1994. Paris.

Ducrot, O. and J.-M. Schaeffer. 1995. *Nouveau dictionnaire encyclopédique des sciences du langage.* Paris.

Hartmann, R.R.K. and F.C. Stork. 1972. *Dictionary of language and linguistics.* Barking, Essex.

Malmkjaer K. (ed.) 1991. *The linguistics encyclopedia.* London.

Meetham, A.R. and R.A. Hudson (eds) 1969. *Encyclopaedia of linguistics, information and control.* Oxford.

Nash, R. (ed.) 1968. *Multilingual lexicon of linguistics and philology.* Coral Gables, FL.

Pei, M. 1966. *Glossary of linguistic terminology.* New York.

Trask, R.L. 1993. *A dictionary of grammatical terms in linguistics.* London.

Vachek, J. and J. Dubsky. 1966. *Dictionnaire de linguistique de l'école de Prague.* Utrecht and Antwerp.

Journals

Folia Linguistica.
Historiographia Linguistica.
International Journal for the History of Linguistics.
International Review of General Linguistics.
Journal of Linguistics.
Language.
Languages.
Lingua.
Linguistics.
La Linguistique.
Studies in Language.
Voprosy jazykoznanija.
Word.

⇒ **comparative linguistics**

linking morpheme

Morphological elements (usually single vowels or consonants) that occur between two immediate constituents and thereby create **compounds** and **derivations**. English has few linking morphemes, the most common one being *-s-* (derived from the possessive case), e.g. *bullring* vs *bull's eye*. In some languages, such as German, linking morphemes are commonly used in **word formation**. (⇒ *also* **epenthesis, morphology**)

References

Plank, F. 1976. Morphological aspect of nominal compounding in German and certain other lan-

guages. *Salzburger Beiträge zur Linguistik* 2.201–19.
⇒ **word formation**

linking vowel (*also* connecting vowel)

A collective term for stem-forming suffixes of different origins and with different functions. Linking vowels function in nouns and verbs to mark stem classes (⇒ **stem vowel**) and, in some languages, to connect morphemes (⇒ **linking morpheme**).

References
⇒ **morphology**

liquid

Umbrella term for *l*- and *r*-sounds.

References
⇒ **phonetics**

LISP

Acronym for list processing language, a functional **programming language** for symbolic processing based semantically on the lambda calculus which has established itself as a standard programming language in **computational linguistics** and **artificial intelligence**. LISP is distinguished (a) by the use of a minimal syntax based on the principle of the operator–operand combination with circumfixed parentheses – '(+1 2)' – which provides a great degree of flexibility; (b) by the use of a single data structure (lists) for representing programs and data; and (c) by the free use of recursion. These features are useful in programming partially specified problem areas, such as those undergoing theoretical development, and in specifying representational languages. Since its introduction in 1956 by J. McCarthy, LISP has been developed in numerous stages including a practical (commercial) use.

References
McCarthy, J. *et al.* 1962. *LISP 1.5 programmer's manual.* Cambridge, MA.
Norrig, P. 1992. *Paradigms of artificial intelligence programming: case studies in common LISP.* San Mateo, CA.
Steel, G. 1990. *Common LISP: the language,* 2nd edn. Bedford.

list processing language ⇒ LISP

literacy

1 The ability to read or write. The teaching of literacy is considered a major goal of industrialized nations with universal education. The rates of illiteracy vary widely among countries, depending partly upon how it is measured and how it is defined.

References
Arnove, R.F. and H.J. Graff (eds) 1987. *National literacy campaigns: historical and comparative perspectives.* New York.
Baynham, M. 1994. *Literacy practices: investigating literacy in social contexts.* London.
Bissex, G.L. 1980. *Gnys at wrk: A child learns to read and write.* Cambridge, MA.
Downing, P., S.D. Lima, and M. Noonan (eds) 1991. *The linguistics of literacy.* Amsterdam and Philadelphia, PA.
Elley, W.B. 1992. *How in the world do students read?* International Association for the Evaluation of Educational Achievement.
Fliegel, R. 1987. The codes of literacy. *DI* 47:9.3411A.
Goldman, S.R. and H.T. Trueba (eds) 1987. *Becoming literate in English as a second language.* Norwood, NJ.
Goodman, K. 1982. *Language and literacy,* 2 vols. Boston.
Holdaway, D. 1979. *The foundations of literacy.* Exeter, NH.
Krashen, S. 1988. Free reading and the development of literacy. In L.M. Hyman and C.N. Li (eds), *Language, speech and mind: studies in honour of Victoria A. Fromkin.* London. 224–38.
Lazere, D. 1987. Literacy and mass media: the political implications. *NLH* 18:2.237–55.
Olson, D.R., N. Torrance, and A. Hildyard (eds) 1985. *Literacy, language, and learning: the nature and consequences of reading and writing.* Cambridge.
Olsen, D.R. and N. Torrance (eds) 1991. *Literacy and orality.* Cambridge.
Schneider, W. and J.C. Näslund. 1993. The impact of early metalinguistic competencies and memory capacity on reading and spelling in elementary school: results of the Munich longitudinal study on the genesis of individual competencies (LOGIC). *European Journal of Education* 8.273–87.
Sledd, J. 1986. Permanence and change in standard American English. In G. Nickel and J. Stalker (eds), *Problems of standardization and linguistic variation in present-day English.* Heidelberg. 50–8.
Smith, F. 1983. *Essays into literacy.* Exeter, NH.
—— 1984. *Joining the literacy club.* Victoria, BC.
Street, B.W. 1986. *Literacy in theory and practice.* Cambridge.
—— (ed.) 1993. *Cross-cultural approaches to literacy.* Cambridge.
Verhoeven, L. (ed.) 1994. *Functional literacy: theoretical issues and educational implications.* Amsterdam and Philadelphia, PA.
Walker, R.W. 1987. Towards a model for predicting the acceptance of vernacular literacy by minority-language groups. *DAI* 48:6.1445A.
Williams, G.L. 1987. Literacy acquisition in retrospect: a composite view of academicians and professionals. *DAI* 47:7.2527A.
Williams, J. and G. Snipper. 1990. *Literacy and bilingualism.* London.
Yaden, D.B. and S. Templeton (eds) 1986. *Meta-*

linguistic awareness and beginning literacy: conceptualizing what it means to read and write. Portsmouth, NH.

Zuanelli, E. 1989. *Literacy in school and society: multidisciplinary perspectives.* New York.

Journal
Literacy and bilingualism.

2 Transcribing or retranscribing a language into an **alphabetic writing system**, e.g. the Latinization (= Romanization) of **Chinese** with the Pīn writing system or of **Japanese** with either the Kunrei-siki or Hepburn writing systems. (⇒ *also* **transcription**)

literal paraphasia ⇒ **paraphasia**

literary language

1 **Written language** as opposed to **spoken language**.

2 In works of literature, a highly stylized and variably contrived (panregional) language as opposed to everyday, colloquial language (⇒ **colloquial speech**). Literary language is subject to less strict grammatical norms and makes no claims to authenticity and utility or to economy or semantic clarity.

References
Carter, R.A. and W. Nash. 1990. *Seeing through language: an introduction to styles of English writing.* Oxford.
Fowler, R. 1981. *Literature as social discourse.* London.
Fowler, R. (ed.) 1987. *A dictionary of modern critical terms.* 2nd edn. London.
Sebeok. T.A. (ed.) 1958. *Style in language.* Cambridge.
⇒ **stylistics**

Lithuanian

Baltic language with about 5 million speakers in Lithuania. Religious literature has existed since the sixteenth century; a comprehensive secular literature since the nineteenth century. Latin alphabet with diacritics, including ‹ė›, ‹į›, ‹ŲŲ›. Movable accent. Long and short vowels with distinctive intonations. Complex morphology. Distinction between [±definite] with attributive adjectives. As in **Latvian**, inflectional future tense. In some dialects, dual forms with nouns, pronouns, adjectives, and verbs.

References
Dambriūnas, L., A. Klimas, and W.R. Schmalstieg. 1980. *Introduction to modern Lithuanian,* 3rd edn. Brooklyn, NY.
Schmalstieg, W.R. 1988. *A Lithuanian historical syntax.* Columbus, OH.

Grammars
Lietuvių kalbos gramatika. 1965–76. 3 vols. Vilnius.

Tekorienė, D. 1990. *Lithuanian basic grammar and conversation.* Kaunas.

Dictionaries
Dabartinės kalbos Lietuvių žodynas. 1993. Vilnius.
Kurschat, A. 1968–73. *Litauisch-deutsches Wörterbuch.* 2 vols. Göttingen.
Lietuvių kalbos žodynas. 1968– . Vol. 15, 1991. Vilnius.
Piesarkas, B. and B. Svecevicius. 1995. *Lithuanian dictionary.* London.
Robinson, D.F. 1976. *Lithuanian reverse dictionary.* Columbus, OH.

Etymological dictionary
Fraenkel, E. 1962–5. *Litauisches etymologisches Wörterbuch,* 2 vols. Heidelberg.

Bibliography
Lietuvos TSR bibliografija. 1969– . 3 vols. Vilnius.

litotes [Grk *lītótēs* 'plainness, simplicity']

Rhetorical **trope** which replaces a stressed, positive expression by the negation of the opposite, e.g. *not (exactly) small* = '(rather) large.' Litotes expresses understatement that intensifies meaning, as in *He is not the wisest man in the world* when we mean 'He is a fool' (Peacham, *The Father of Eloquence,* 1577).

References
⇒ **figure of speech**

Liv ⇒ **Finno-Ugric**

loan translation

1 In the narrower sense: the process and result of a one-to-one translation of the elements of a foreign expression into a word in one's own language: Eng. *Monday* for Lat. *dies lunae,* Eng. *accomplished fact* for Fr. *fait accompli.*

2 In a broader sense: (a) a loose translation of the foreign concept into one's own language, e.g. Ger. *Wolkenkratzer* (lit.: 'cloud scratcher') for Eng. *skyscraper*; or (b) an adoption of the foreign concept into one's own language, e.g. Eng. *brotherhood* for Lat. *fraternitas.* (⇒ *also* **borrowed meaning, borrowing, calque, loan word**)

References
⇒ **borrowing**

loan word

1 In the narrower sense: in contrast with **foreign word**, words borrowed from one language into another language (⇒ **borrowing**), which have become lexicalized (= assimilated phonetically, graphemically, and grammatically) into the new language: Eng. *picture* < Lat. *pictura,* Ger. *flirten* ('to flirt') < Eng. *flirt.*

2 In the broader sense: an umbrella term for **foreign word** and loan word (in the above-mentioned sense). Here, a distinction is drawn

between lexical and semantic **borrowings** (⇒ **calque**): in lexical borrowings the word and its meaning (usually together with the 'new' object) are taken into the language and used either as a foreign word (= non-assimilated loan) like *Sputnik*, *paté*, and *rumba*, or as an assimilated loan word (in the narrower sense).

References
⇒ **borrowing**

local tree

Part of a **tree diagram** with only one branching node. A local tree comprises the branching node and its daughter nodes.

localist hypothesis [Lat. *locus* 'place']

Hypothesis that all linguistic expressions, both in form and content, are based on a pattern of locational/spatial expressions. The justification for this approach is relatively non-linguistic, resting instead on the inarguable relevance of spatial experience in the development of cognitive abilities. In all languages there are areas for which the theory is apparently correct, such as prepositions of spatial relations which are also used temporally (*in the house/in an hour*), but the reverse is never the case. If the **dative** case is interpreted as a specialized locative, this seems to present a plausible explanation why so many languages express possessive relationship with the dative, e.g. Lat. *Liber est mihi*, lit. 'book is me (dat.)' = 'The book is mine' or 'I have the book' (i.e. The book is with me). This approach runs into problems, however, when it comes to categories such as **tense**, **aspect**, and in basic cases such as **nominative**. (⇒ *also* **case, case grammar**)

References
Anderson, J.M. 1971. *The grammar of case: towards a localistic theory*. Cambridge.
—— 1987. Case grammar and the localist hypotheses. In R. Dirven and G. Rudden (eds), *Concepts of case*. Tübingen. 103–21.
—— 1988. *The localist basis for syntactic categories*. Duisburg.
Girke, J. 1977. Probleme einer lokalistischen Kasustheorie. *Archiv für das Studium der neueren Sprachen und Literaturen* 214.61–70.
Hjelmslev, L. 1935. *La catégorie des cas*. Munich. (Repr. 1972.)
Lyons, J. 1977. *Semantics*. Cambridge. Vol. 2, ch. 5.7.
Miller, J.E. 1985. *Semantics and syntax: parallels and connections*. Cambridge.
⇒ **case grammar**

locative

1 Morphological **case** in some languages which serves to identify location; e.g. Turkish *ev* 'house' vs *evde* 'in the house.' Some rem-

nants of the locative can be found in Latin, where its function has been taken over mostly by the **ablative** or prepositional constructions.

References
⇒ **case**

2 Term for the **semantic role** of location in **case grammar**.

locative clause

Semantically defined dependent clause functioning as an **adverbial** to indicate place, direction, or areal extent of the state of affairs described by the verb. They are introduced by such spatial adverbs as *where, wherever, whence*: *He sailed wherever the winds took him.*

locution [Lat. *locutio* 'the act of speaking, speech']

In Austin's **speech act theory** (1962), a part of every speech act that comprises the articulation of linguistic forms (**phonetic act**), the production of words and strings of words in a particular grammatical order (**phatic act**) and the reference to objects and states of affairs in the world by means of language (**rhetic act**). Searle (1969) subsumes the phonetic and phatic act under **utterance act**, while the rhetic act corresponds to his propositional act. (⇒ **proposition**) (⇒ *also* **illocution, perlocution, proposition**)

References
Austin. J.L. 1962. *How to do things with words*. Oxford.
Searle, J.R. 1968. Austin on illocutionary acts. *Philosophische Rundschau* 77.405–24.
—— 1969. *Speech acts: an essay in the philosophy of language*. Cambridge.
⇒ **speech act theory**

logic ⇒ **deontic logic, epistemic logic, formal logic, intensional logic, model logic, predicate logic, propositional logic, temporal logic**

logical connective (*also* logical particle)

In **formal logic**, designation for logical elements such as *and, or, not, if ... then, if and only if* (⇒ **equivalence**) that connect elementary sentences with complex propositions whose **truth value** is functionally dependent on the truth value of the elementary sentences (⇒ **truth table**). There is a distinction between (a) one-place logical connectives (⇒ **negation**) and (b) two-place logical connectives (⇒ **conjunction**[3], **disjunction, implication**), each of which connects at least two elementary propositions into a new complex proposition. Although logical connectives correspond to words or groups of words that are traditionally considered **conjunctions**[1] in everyday language, not all conjunctions in the linguistic sense can be considered logical **operators**, that is, truth-functional connections (e.g. *for* and *because* are not logical connectives). Moreover, their logical meaning corresponds only partially to their use in natural languages.

References
Gazdar, G. 1979. *Pragmatics*. New York.
⇒ **formal logic**

logical constant

Umbrella term for all logical elements which, on the basis of their semantic clarity and invariable meaning and function, determine the logical structure of propositional connections. **Logical connectives**, **operators**, and **quantifiers** are all types of logical constants.

References
⇒ **formal logic**

logical form

A level of syntactic representation in **Government and Binding theory** which operates between **surface structure** and semantic interpretation. Various rules operate between surface structure and logical form (LF). Syntactic constraints apply to these rules, so logical form is a syntactic level of representation. Logical form disambiguates the semantics of a sentence. At the level of logical form, the scope relationships between operators are syntactically represented by **c-command** relationships: an operator (e.g. a quantifier or question word) has scope over a constituent X when the operator c-commands the constituent X at logical form. Thus the sentence *everyone₁ loves someone₂* can be transformed by quantifier raising to *someone₂ [everyone loves -₂]*, which is interpreted by semantic rules as *there is an X, and for every Y (it is true) Y loves X.*

References
Carrico, J. de 1983. On quantifier raising. *LingI* 14.343–6.
Chomsky, N. 1981. *Lectures on government and binding*. Dordrecht.
Higginbotham, J. 1983. Logical form, binding and nominals. *LingI* 14.395–420.
Hornstein, N. 1984. *Logic as grammar*. Cambridge, MA.
——— 1994. *Logical form*. Oxford.
Huang, C.T.J. 1982a. Move wh in a language with wh-movement. *LRev* 1.369–416.
——— 1982b. Logical relations in Chinese and the theory of grammar. Dissertation, Cambridge, MA.
Huang, C.T. and R. May (eds) 1991. *Logical structure and linguistic structure*. Dordrecht.
Kayne, R. 1981. Two notes on the NIC. In A. Belletti, L. Brandi, and L. Rizzi (eds), *Theory of marked-*

ness in generative grammar. Pisa. 317–46.
Ladusaw, W. 1983. Logical form and conditions on grammaticality. *Ling&P* 6.373–92.
May, R. 1977. The grammar of quantification. Dissertation, Cambridge, MA.
——— 1985. *Logical form: its structure and derivation*. Cambridge, MA.
Williams, E. 1977. Discourse and logical form. *LingI* 8.101–39.

logical grammars

In **computational linguistics**, generative grammar formalisms taken from logic programming. **Definite clause grammar**, **metamorphosis grammar**, and **extraposition grammar** also belong in this category.

logical implication ⇒ implication

logical language ⇒ formal language

logical particle ⇒ logical connective

logical semantics

Originally used as a designation for semantic investigations on artificially constructed languages in the framework of **formal logic**; in more recent linguistic models, logical semantics refers to the description of semantic structures in natural languages, to the degree that they are implemented with the tools of mathematical logic (= formal logic). The artificial languages, developed since the middle of the nineteenth century by Boole, De Morgan, and Frege, have the following advantages over natural languages: clarity, exactness, and a one-to-one correspondence of syntactic and semantic structures. An attempt to transfer the principles of semantic interpretation developed for artificial languages to natural languages is undertaken primarily by Montague in his **Montague grammar**.

References
Frege, G. 1879. *Begriffsschrift: eine der arithmetischen nachgebildete Formalsprache des reinen Denkens*. Halle.
Landman, F. and F. Veltman (eds) 1984. *Varieties of formal semantics*. Dordrecht.
Reichenbach, H. 1947. *Elements of symbolic logic*. New York.
Rosner, M. and R. Johnson. 1992. *Computational linguistics and formal semantics*. Cambridge.
Russell, B. 1905. *The theory of descriptions*. New York.
Von Benthem, H. 1986. *Essays in logical semantics*. Dordrecht.
Wittgenstein, L. 1921. *Tractatus logico-philosophicus*. London.
⇒ **categorial grammar**, **formal logic**, **intensional logic**, **Montague grammar**

logical type ⇒ **type theory**

logistics ⇒ **formal logic**

logogram ⇒ **logography**

logography [Grk *lógos* 'expression,' *gráphein* 'to write']

Writing system in which the meaning of individual linguistic expressions (individual words) is expressed by graphic signs (logogram) whereby, in contrast with **ideography** and **pictography**, a constant number of phonemic complexes (ideally one complex) is assigned to each sign. Logograms can be read in a similar manner as alphabetic writing systems. **Chinese** is written logographically with Chinese characters. Signs like ‹$› for *dollar*, ‹£› for *pound*, and ‹+› for *plus* are logograms.

References
⇒ **writing**

logophoricity [Grk *phérein* 'to bear, to carry']

Term introduced by C. Hagège to denote a specific type of reference characteristic to a number of West African languages like Ewe, **Yoruba**, and **Igbo**. In comparison to **reflexive reference**, reciprocal reference, and so-called **switch reference** (Wiesemann 1986: 438), logophoric reference can be seen as a form of grammaticalized coreference since it underlies more specific conditions of antecedent choice than anaphoric reference. Logophoric pronouns are distinct from anaphoric pronouns in that they have as their antecedent the person whose speech, thoughts, feelings, general state of consciousness, or point of view is being reported (**empathy**). The phenomenon of logophoricity was actually already known in Latin grammar, since Latin has the logophoric use of the reflexive pronoun as 'indirect reflexivization.'

References
Hagège, C. 1974. Les pronoms logophoriques. *BSLP* 69.287–310.

Sells, P. 1987. Aspects of logophoricity. In A. Zaenen (ed.), *Studies in grammatical theory and discourse structure*, vol. 2: *Logophoricity and bound anaphora*. Stanford, CA.

Wiesemann, U. 1986. Grammaticalized coreference. In U. Wiesemann (ed.), *Pronominal systems*. Tübingen. 437–61.

Logudorese ⇒ **Sardinian**

London school ⇒ **Firthian linguistics**

long consonant ⇒ **geminate**

long-term memory ⇒ **memory**

long vs short

Property of **speech sounds**. Occasionally the speech sounds themselves are referred to as 'longs' or 'shorts.' (⇒ *also* **quantity**).

loss with compensatory lengthening ⇒ **compensatory lengthening**

Low German ⇒ **German**

low variety ⇒ **high vs low variety**

lower case ⇒ **capital vs small**

lowering ⇒ **breaking**

LP rule ⇒ **ID/LP format**

LTM (long-term memory) ⇒ **memory**

Luba ⇒ **Bantu**

LUG ⇒ **Lexical Unification Grammar**

Luo ⇒ **Chari-Nile languages**

Luvian ⇒ **Anatolian**

Lycian ⇒ **Anatolian**

Lydian ⇒ **Anatolian**

M

Maban ⇒ **Nilo-Saharan**

Macedonian

South **Slavic** language with approx. 1.2 million speakers in Macedonia and approx. 100,000 speakers in northern Greece. Macedonian has been standardized since 1945 and is written in the Cyrillic alphabet with the additional letters ⟨S⟩, ⟨Ѓ⟩, ⟨Ќ⟩.

Characteristics: in polysyllabic words, stress on the antepenultimate syllable, three different postclitic definite articles, pronominal anticipation of the determined object.

References
Elson, M.J. 1989. *Macedonian verbal morphology: a structural analysis*. Columbus, OH.
Koneski, B. 1967–81. *Gramatika na makedonskiot literaturen jazik*, Parts 1 and 2. Skopje.
—— 1983. *A historical phonology of the Macedonian language*. Heidelberg.
Lunt, H.G. 1952. *A grammar of the Macedonian literary language*. Skopje.
Stamatoski, T. 1986. *Borba za makedonski literaturen jazik*. Skopje.

Dictionaries
Crvenkovski, D. 1976. *Makedonsko–angliski rečnik* (Macedonian–English dictionary). Skopje.
Koneski, B. (ed.) 1961–6. *Rečnik na makedonskiot literaturen jazik*, 3 vols. (Repr. 1986 in one vol.) Skopje.

Journal
Makedonski Jazik.

machine-aided translation (*also* automatic translation, computer translation, machine translation)

Transmission of a natural-language text into an equivalent text of another natural language with the aid of a computer program. Such programs have (with varying specializations and success) lexical, grammatical, and, in part, encyclopedic knowledge bases. Machine-aided translation consists of three components: (a) analysis of the source language by means of **parsing**; (b) transfer: the transmission of information from the source language into the target language; (c) synthesis: the generation of the target language. The systems vary according to whether they translate directly from one language into another or whether the text in the source language must first be translated into a neutral **interlingua** and then into the target language, which makes particular sense if the source language is to be translated into several target languages. Linguistic problems associated with machine-aided translation arise principally from the different lexical structure of the given vocabularies (e.g. Ger. *kennen, können, wissen* for Eng. *know*), from various grades of grammatical differentiation (e.g. **aspect** differentiation in Slavic as compared to Germanic languages), from need for encyclopedic knowledge to disambiguate ambiguous forms, and from the necessity to rely on experience and standard assumptions when interpreting **vagueness**. Programs for machine-aided translation have been applied with fair success; in most cases, however, it is necessary to pre- and post-edit the texts.

References
Alpac Report. 1966. Language and machines: computers in translation and linguistics. Washington, DC.
Arnold, D. *et al.* 1993. *Machine translation*. Oxford.
Bátori, I. and H.J. Weber (eds) 1986. *Neue Ansätze in maschineller Sprachübersetzung: Wissensrepräsentation und Textbezug / New approaches in machine translation: knowledge representation and discourse models*. Tübingen.
Hutchins, W.J. and H. Somers (eds) 1992. *Machine translation*. New York and London.
Laffling, J. 1991. *Toward high precision machine translation*. Berlin and New York.
Lewis, D. 1985. The development and progress of machine translation systems. *ALLC Bulletin* 5.40–52.
Marchuk, Y.M. 1989. Machine-aided translation. In I.S. Bátori, W. Lenders, and W. Putschke (eds), *Computational linguistics: an international handbook of computer-oriented language research and applications*. Berlin and New York. 682–7.
Maxwell, D. *et al.* (eds) 1989. *New directions in machine translation*. Dordrecht.
Melby, A. 1989. Machine translation: general development. In I.S. Bátori, W. Lenders, and W. Putschke (eds), *Computational linguistics: an international handbook of computer-oriented language research and applications*. Berlin and New York. 622–8.
Newton, J. (ed.) 1992. *Computers in translation: a practical appraisal*. London.
Nirenburg, S. (ed.) 1987. *Machine translation*. Cambridge.
Slocum, J. (ed.) 1985. Special issue on machine translation. *CL* 11: 1.
Tsjuii, J. 1989. Machine translation: research and trends. In I.S. Bátori, W. Lenders, and W. Putschke

(eds), *Computational linguistics: an international handbook of computer-oriented language research and applications.* Berlin and New York. 652–69.

Journal
Machine Translation.

machine language

Based on the **binary** code, a notational convention for computer programs that is specially established for every microprocessor. In order to function, programming texts of programming languages must be translated into the computer language of the particular microprocessor by a **compiler** or **interpreter**.

Reference
Struble, G. 1975. *Assembly language programming.* Reading, MA.

machine-readable corpus

A collection of texts of written or spoken language that are stored in computers and can be evaluated by computer on the basis of word occurrences, word frequencies, word contexts, etc.

References
Chisholm, D. 1985. Computer-assisted research in German language and literature since the mid-seventies. *GQ* 58.409–22.
────── 1986. Post-renaissance German. *LLC* 1.188–189.
Hoffman, C.W. 1985. German research tools. *Monatshefte* 77.292–301.
Van Halteren, H. and T. van den Heuvel. 1990. *Linguistic exploitation of syntàctic databases.* Amsterdam.

machine translation ⇒ machine-aided translation

Macro-Carib ⇒ Carib

macrolinguistics [Grk *makrós* 'long, large']

1 Synonym for **ethnolinguistics**.

2 Scientific investigation of language in the broadest sense, i.e. in the context of all related disciplines such as sociology, psychology, and philosophy. A central subdiscipline of macrolinguistics is **microlinguistics**, linguistics in the narrower sense, which deals with the description and explanation of a language system.

Macro-Siouan ⇒ Siouan

macro speech act ⇒ text function

macrostructure

A term from **text linguistics** (van Dijk) for the global semantic and pragmatic structure of a text. The macrostructure of a text, which includes phonological, graphological, and lex-

icogrammatical patterning, refers to the largest-scale patterns, which are the means whereby texts can be classified into different text types, such as narrative, exposition, lyric poem, and so on. While the patterning of sentences and propositions constitutes the semantic macrostructure, the individual speech acts (⇒ **speech act classification**, **speech act theory**) and sequences of speech acts constitute the pragmatic macrostructure, the 'macro-speech act' which is to be understood as the **illocution** of the text (**text function**).

References
Garcia-Berrio, A. *et al.* 1988. Compositional structure: macrostructures. In J.S. Petöfi (ed.), *Text and discourse constitution.* Berlin. 170–211.
Van Dijk, T.A. 1980. *An interdisciplinary study of global structures in discourse, interaction and cognition.* Hillsdale, NJ.
────── 1981. *Studies in the pragmatics of discourse.* The Hague.
Van Dijk, T.A. and W. Kintsch. 1983. *Strategies of discourse comprehension.* Orlando, FL.
⇒ **argumentation**, **narrative analysis**

macrosyntax

A term from text grammar (⇒ **discourse grammar**) to describe the **cohesion** of texts, for example **textphoric**. (⇒ *also* **transphrastic analysis**, **text linguistics**)

References
Chatman, S. 1978. *Story and discourse.* Ithaca, NY.
Genette, G. 1980. *Narrative discourse: an essay on method.* trans. J.E. Lewin. Ithaca, NY.
⇒ **discourse grammar**

Magyar ⇒ Hungarian

Maiduan ⇒ Penutian

main clause (*also* independent clause)

In a complex sentence, the clause that is structurally independent, i.e. that does not function as a part of speech for another clause. The distinction between main and **subordinate clause** (a clause that is dependent and embedded) is only useful in complex sentences, in which the term 'main clause' corresponds to the **matrix sentence** in which subclauses (⇒ **constituent clauses**) are embedded. As a rule only main clauses have illocutionary force. The distinction between main clause and subordinate clause, while problematic, has been usual since the second half of the eighteenth century.

References
⇒ **subordinate clause**

main verb

Semantically and syntactically motivated subset of verbs which have their own lexical meaning and form the syntactic head of the **predicate** or **verb phrase**. (⇒ *also* **auxiliary**, **copular verb**, **valence**)

Maipuran ⇒ **Arawakan**

(major) constituent

Relatively independent basic structural element of a **sentence**; the exact number and function of constituents depends on the particular language. The determination and classification of constituents depends on the theoretical assumptions of the syntactic approach employed. An operational definition can be given as follows. (a) Constituents can appear before the finite verb in declarative sentences (⇒ **topicalization**). (b) They can be moved around in the sentence (as a unit, if they are complex). Thus the **substitution test** shows that **attributes** are not constituents since they cannot be moved from their **antecedent**. (c) Constituents can be replaced by single words or **pronouns** through **substitution**. This operational definition does not coincide with the traditional definition of constituents, where syntactic and functional aspects are also considered, cf. the traditional definitions of **subject**, **object**, **predicate**, and **adverbial**. For a different definition of constituent, ⇒ **valence**. Constituents include single words (*today*, *works*, *she*), **phrases** (*in the morning*, *the new book*, *without a doubt*), and **constituent clauses**.

Makah ⇒ **Wakashan**

Malagasy

Group of closely related **Malayo-Polynesian** languages in Madagascar; the Merina dialect is the official language of Madagascar (about 10 million speakers).

Characteristics: word order VOS; well-developed voice system.

References
Dez, J. 1980. *Structures de la langue malgache*. Paris.
Domenichini-Ramiaramanana, B. 1976. *Le Malgache: essai de description sommaire*. Paris.
Faublée, J. 1946. Introduction au malgache. *Langues de l'Orient* 1:3.
Rabenilaina, R.-B. 1983. *Morpho-syntaxe du malgache*. Paris.

malapropism [Fr. *mal à propos* 'not to the purpose, inappropriate']

A misuse of words, e.g. *the aggravator in the washing machine* for *the agitator*, or *a detestable wrench* for *an adjustable wrench*. (⇒ **play on words**, **faux amis**)

References
Fay, D. & A. Cutler, 1977. Malapropism and the

structure of the mental lexicon. *LingI* 8.505–20.
Zwicky, A.M. 1982. Classical malapropisms and the creation of a mental lexicon. In L.K. Obler *et al.* (eds), *Exceptional language and linguistics*. New York.

Malay ⇒ **Malayo-Polynesian**

Malayalam ⇒ **Dravidian**

Malayo-Polynesian (*also* Austronesian)

Language group comprising approx. 500 languages with over 170 million speakers spread throughout Madagascar, South-East Asia, Indonesia, and the Pacific Islands. These languages can be divided into two main groups: East Malayo-Polynesian (or **Oceanic**, containing the languages of Polynesia, Micronesia, and Melanesia) and West Malayo-Polynesian (including the languages of Indonesia, the Philippines, Taiwan, Madagascar, and parts of South-East Asia). The most important languages belong to the West Malayo-Polynesian group: **Indonesian** (about 100 million speakers, also as second language), **Javanese** (about 66 million speakers), Sundanese (about 17 million speakers), Malay (about 12 million speakers), **Tagalog** and Cebuano in the Philippines (about 13 million each), **Malagasy** (about 10 million speakers). Included among the less widespread languages of the East Malayo-Polynesian group are Fijian (about 300,000 speakers) and Samoan (about 200,000 speakers).

Scholars in the eighteenth century suspected that many of the languages of the Indian and Pacific Oceans actually belonged to a common linguistic group; Dempwolff (1934–8) undertook a successful historical reconstruction which is today fairly far advanced, if not uncontroversial. Benedikt (1975) has attempted to combine the Malayo-Polynesian languages with the **Cam-Thai** group to form a more comprehensive language family, **Austro-Thai**.

Characteristics: most of the languages have a fairly simple sound system, complex voice constructions and verb-initial word order (VSO, VOS). In the Oceanic territory **noun class** systems and **ergative** structures have developed.

References
Benedikt, P.K. 1975. *Austro-Thai: language and culture*. New Haven, CT.
Blust, R. 1988. *Austronesian root theory*. Amsterdam and Philadelphia, PA.
Dahl, O.C. 1973. *Proto-Austronesian*. Lund.
Dempwolff, O. 1934–8. *Vergleichende Lautlehre des austronesischen Wortschatzes*. Berlin. (Repr. Nendeln 1969.)
Durie, M. 1985. *A grammar of Acehnese*. Dordrecht.
Dyen, I. 1965. *A lexicostatistical classification of the Austronesian languages*. Bloomington, IN.

Lenches, E.P.Y. 1976. *Cebuano case grammar.* 2 vols. Washington, DC.

Schumacher, W.W. *et al.* 1992. *Pacific rim: Austronesian and Papuan linguistic history.* Heidelberg.

Sebeok, T.A. (ed.) 1971. *Current trends in linguistics,* vol. 8: *Oceania.* The Hague.

Journals
Oceanic Linguistics.
Pacific Linguistics.

Maltese ⇒ **Arabic, European languages**

Mam ⇒ **Mayan languages**

Manchu ⇒ **Tungusic**

Mandarin ⇒ **Chinese**

Mande

Branch of the **Niger-Congo** languages with approx. twenty-five languages in West Africa; the most important languages: Bambara (Mali, about 2.5 million speakers), Mende (Sierra Leone, about 1.2 million speakers).

Characteristics: In contrast to other Niger-Congo languages, the Mande languages have no noun classes; however, remnants of an old class system can be seen in the consonant-initial alternations. **Tonal languages** (tone used to mark grammatical categories), velarized consonants (e.g. [k͡p] in *Kpelle*), grammatical distinction between absolute and relational nominals, development of various syllabaries. (⇒ *also* **African languages**)

References
Brauner, S. 1975. *Lehrbuch des Bambara.* Leipzig.
Creissels, D. 1983. *Eléments de grammaire de la langue mandinka.* Grenoble.
Kastenholz, R. 1988. *Mande languages and linguistics, compiled and (partially) annotated.* Hamburg.
Welmers, W.E. 1971. Niger-Congo, Mande. In T.A. Sebeok (ed.), *Current trends in linguistics.* Vol. 7, 113–40.
—— 1973. *African language structures.* Berkeley, CA.
⇒ **African languages**

Manichean ⇒ **Iranian**

manner of action ⇒ **Aktionsart**, **aspect**

manner of articulation

The way in which the airstream is modified during the **articulation** of a **consonant**: either (oral or nasal) **stop**, **fricative** (both **median** and **lateral**), **affricate**, **approximant** (both median and lateral), **flap**, or **trill**. (⇒ *also* **articulatory phonetics**)

Mansi ⇒ **Finno-Ugric**

Manx ⇒ **Celtic**

mapping ⇒ **function**

Mapuche ⇒ **Andean**

Marathi

Indo-Aryan language with approx. 45 million speakers, heavily influenced by the **Dravidian** languages (Kannada, Telugu).

References
Bertensen, M. and J. Nimbkar. 1975. *A Marathi reference grammar.* Philadelphia, PA.
Chitnis, V. 1979. *An intensive course in Marathi.* Mysore.
Kale, K. and A. Soman. 1986. *Learning Marathi.* Pune.
Pandharipande, R. 1989. *Marathi.* London.
⇒ **Indo-Aryan**

Dictionary
Sirmokadam, M.S. and G.D. Khanolkar. 1970–89. *The new standard dictionary Marathi–English–Marathi,* 3 vols. Bombay.

Mari ⇒ **Finno-Ugric**

marked vs unmarked

In **Prague School** phonology, a representational form developed to describe linguistic units on the basis of the presence or absence of the smallest semantically significant features. The element containing the feature is designated by [+A], the element without the feature is designated by [–A] ([A] standing for every possible linguistic feature). For further developments in more recent descriptive models, ⇒ **markedness**.

References
⇒ **markedness**

markedness

The concept of markedness is concerned with the distinction between what is neutral, natural, or expected (= unmarked) and what departs from the neutral (= marked) along some specified parameter. It was introduced in linguistics by the **Prague School** (L. Trubetzkoy, R. Jakobson) for evaluating the members of an oppositional pair as 'marked' (having some kind of feature) or 'unmarked' (having no features). An example: according to Jakobson (1936), in the opposition nominative vs accusative, the accusative is the marked case, because it indicates the presence of an affected entity (i.e. a direct object) while the nominative does not have this feature, i.e. it signals neither the presence nor the absence of such an entity. Unmarked elements also exhibit many of the following characteristics (see Greenberg 1966;

Mayerthaler 1980): they are expressed by simpler means, they occur more frequently in the languages of the world, they are learned earlier in first language acquisition, and are less often the 'target' or 'goal' of processes such as **language change**. Generative **transformational grammar** has contributed much towards a better understanding of the concept of markedness. Chomsky and Halle (1968) evaluate phonological feature descriptions by means of markedness conventions. With the opposition [± rounded], for example, the unmarked feature is [– rounded] for front vowels and [+ rounded] for back vowels. According to this markedness rule, the vowel /y/, a rounded front vowel, is more marked than /u/, a rounded back vowel. On the basis of this convention, phonological systems, word representations, and processes can be compared to one another and evaluated according to their markedness (⇒ **natural phonology**). In syntax, the concept of markedness is applied within recent generative **transformational grammar** (⇒ **core grammar**), within **natural generative grammar**, as well as for syntactic universals (cf. **hierarchy universals**). In semantics, most of the characteristics mentioned above for unmarked categories hold for **prototypes**. Markedness asymmetries have been shown to hold not only for binary systems but also for larger sets of elements yielding markedness hierarchies (e.g. nominative ‹ accusative ‹ dative ‹ genitive, see Primus 1987; singular ‹ plural ‹ dual, see Greenberg 1966). An important principle of markedness theory is the **iconicity** between form units and their corresponding meanings. Mayerthaler (1981) proposes a principle of morphological iconism, according to which semantically unmarked elements are coded morphologically more simply than marked elements. The idea that the markedness of linguistic units corresponds more or less exactly to cognitive-psychological complexity or simplicity can already be found in the first proposals of markedness theory, and is still focal in research on naturalness and markedness.

References
Belleti, A., L. Brandi, and I. Rizzi (eds) 1981. *The theory of markedness in generative grammar.* Pisa.
Bruck, A. *et al.* (eds) 1974. Parasession on natural phonology. *CLS* 11.
Chomsky, N. and M. Halle. 1968. *The sound pattern of English.* New York.
Eckmann, F.R., E.A. Moravcsik, and J.R. Wirth (eds) 1986. *Markedness.* New York.
Greenberg, J.H. 1966. *Language universals with special reference to feature hierarchies.* The Hague.
Haiman, J. (ed.) 1984. *Iconicity in syntax.* Amsterdam.
Herbert, R.K. 1986. *Language universals, markedness theory and natural phonetic processes.* Berlin.
Hooper, J.B. 1976. *An introduction to natural generative phonology.* New York.
Jakobson, R. 1936. Beitrag zur allgemeinen Kasuslehre: Gesamtbedeutungen der russischen Kasus. *TCLP* 6.240–88.
——— 1968. *Child language: aphasia and phonological universals.* The Hague.
Mayerthaler, W. 1981. *Morphologische Natürlichkeit.* Frankfurt. (Trans. as *Morphological markedness.* Ann Arbor, MI, 1986.)
Primus, B. 1987. *Grammatische Hierarchien.* Munich.
Stampe, D. 1969. The acquisition of phonetic representation. *CLS* 5.443–54.
Tomic, O.M. 1989. *Markedness in synchrony and diachrony.* Berlin.
Trubetzkoy, L. 1969. *Principles of phonology*, trans. C.A.M. Baltaxe. Berkeley, CA.
Vennemann, T. 1972. Sound change and markedness theory: on the history of the German consonant system. In R.P. Stockwell and R. Macaulay (eds), *Linguistic change and generative theory.* Bloomington, IN. 230–75.
——— 1983. Causality in language change: theories of linguistic preferences as a basis for linguistic explanations. *FolH* 4.5–26.

markerese

Term devised by D. Lewis from the English word *marker* (in analogy to *Japanese, Chinese,* etc.) to denote the metalinguistic language of features primarily used in **interpretive semantics** and **generative semantics** for the description of meaning. In Lewis' view, markerese cannot fulfill its function, because it is nothing more than an imprecise artificial language which itself requires an interpretation. Semantic description cannot, according to this view, be exhausted by mere translation, but rather must be apparent in the specification of models oriented towards reality. (⇒ *also* **model-theoretic semantics**)

Reference
Lewis, D. 1970. General semantics. *Synthese* 22.18–67.

Markov model ⇒ Markov process

Markov process

Formally, this is a kind of **stochastic grammar**, more exactly a **finite state automaton**, all of whose states are final and whose transitions are weighted by the probabilities of traversing them. Named after the Russian mathematician A.A. Markov (1856–1922), they incorporate a 'finite state assumption', i.e. that future states may be predicted from the present one alone, with no history. Markov applied his technique to analyze the distribution of vowels and consonants in Pushkin's novella *Eugene Onegin*.

For applications in speech recognition, ⇒ **hidden Markov model**.

References
Chomsky, N. 1957. *Syntactic structures*. The Hague.
Damerau, F.J. 1971. *Markov models and linguistic theory*. The Hague.

Marrism

Linguistic theory founded in the 1920s by the Soviet archaeologist and linguist N.J. Marr (1864–1934) in which all linguistic development is represented as a reflection of economic relationships, and language itself is seen as a phenomenon of the social superstructure. The foundation of his linguistic view, oriented towards historical materialism, was his belief that Caucasian was the **proto-language** of Europe. This belief is known as the 'Japhetic theory.' Marr's influence on Soviet linguistics extends into the 1950s, when J.W. Stalin, in his article 'Marxism and questions of linguistics' (1950), refuted Marr's superstructure theory and declared language to be independent of human productivity. (⇒ *also* **materialistic language theory**, **reflexion theory**)

References
Marr, N.J. 1923. *Der japhetitische Kaukasus und das dritte ethnische Element im Bildungsprozeß der mittelländischen Kultur*. Berlin.
Rosse-Landi, F. 1973. *Linguistics and economics*. The Hague.
Simmons, E.J. (ed.) 1951. *The Soviet linguistic controversy*. New York.
Stalin, J.W. 1950. Marxism and questions of linguistics. *Pravda*, 20 June 1950.
Thomas, L.L. 1957. *The linguistic theories of N.J. Marr*. Berkeley, CA.

masculine ⇒ gender

mass communication

Form of public communication conditioned by technical means of communication such as the press, radio, film, and television. Mass communication is characterized by a high degree of communicative distance between a heterogeneous 'audience' and a group of anonymous 'communicators' (announcers, copy writers, moderators, editors, producers) who direct the communication process in different ways. An important aspect of this communicative structure is the asymmetrical distribution of the speaker/hearer roles that precludes a direct interchange between the participants and may consequently bring about confusion with regard to the intentions and effects of communication ('one-way communication'). The particular

conditions, structures, and effects of mass communication are studied in several disciplines, for example, communication science, sociology, political science, and **information theory**. The goal of linguistic research, in particular that of **text linguistics**, is to describe particular **text types** such as **interviews**, news reports, or other forms of **journalistic language**, to analyze the characteristic mixture of informative, entertaining, and persuasive **text functions** (as is the case for **advertising language**), or to analyze political speeches using the methods of **statistical linguistics**, **content analysis**, **argumentation theory**, **stylistics**, or **rhetoric**.

References
Bell, A. 1984. Language style as audience design. *LSoc* 13.145–204.
van Dijk, T.A. (ed.) 1985. *Discourse and communication: new approaches to the analysis of mass media, discourse and communication*. Berlin.
Fowler, R. 1991. *Language in the news: discourse and ideology in the British press*. London.
Hargrave, A.M. (ed.) 1991. *A matter of manners? The limits of broadcasting language*. London.
McQuail, D. 1983. *Mass communication theory*. London.
Murdock, G. 1985. *Mass communication and the advertising industry*. Paris.
Schmidt, R. and J.F. Kess. 1986. *Television advertising and televangelism: discourse analysis of persuasive language*. Amsterdam.
Schramm, W. and D.F. Roberts, (eds) 1971. *The process and effects of mass communication* (rev. edn). Urbana, IL.
⇒ **advertising language**, **journalistic language**

mass noun

Noun which has no **number** distinction and cannot be immediately combined with a **numeral** (e.g. *three rice), as opposed to **count nouns** such as *dress*: *three dresses*. Among mass nouns, a distinction can be made between nouns which refer to elements (*rock, wood, water*) and those which refer to **collectives** (*cattle, rice, brush*). When mass nouns referring to elements are used in the plural, their meaning changes, cf. *wood* vs *woods*, *fish* vs *fishes*.

Reference
Pelletier, F.I. (ed.) 1979. *Mass terms: some philosophical problems*. Dordrecht.

Massai ⇒ Afro-Asiatic

matched guise technique

A process developed by W.E. Lambert to measure the attitude of speakers towards other languages with the greatest possible accuracy. In this test, multilingual speakers are recorded reciting a single text with different voices, so that the hearers do not recognize those voices as belonging to the same speakers. The hearers are then asked to characterize the speakers according to their social status, education, trustworthiness, amiability, etc. In this test, language samples are taken from a single multi(dia)lectal speaker, so that the evaluation of language varieties is not adversely affected by the influence of uncontrollable idiosyncratic characteristics of a given speaker.

References

Giles, H. *et al.* 1987. Research on language attitudes. In V. Ammon (*et al.*) (eds), *Soziolinguistik/ Sociolinguistics*. Berlin and New York. 585–98.

Lambert, W.E. 1967. A social psychology of bilingualism. *Journal of Social Issues* 23.91–108. (Repr. in J.B. Pride and J. Holmes (eds) 1972. *Sociolinguistics*. Harmondsworth. 336–49.)

—— 1974. Culture and language as factors in learning and education. In F.E. Aboud and R.D. Meade (eds), *Cultural factors in learning and education*. Bellingham, WA. 231ff.

material implication ⇒ implication

material noun

Semantically defined class of nouns which refer to materials: *chalk*, *wood*, *marble*. Material nouns are **mass nouns**, i.e. nouns which have no **plural** form or whose plural forms do not refer to the material itself, but to something else, cf. *wood* vs *woods*.

materialistic language theory

Referring to dialectical and historical materialism, the materialistic language theory attempts to explain, within the framework of Marxist–Leninist linguistic views, the essence and development of language, primarily through its function in the social activity of the working person. (⇒ *also* **Marrism**, **reflection theory**)

mathematical linguistics

The representation of linguistic systems and processes with the aid of mathematics (e.g. **logic**, **set theory**, algebra, **formal language theory**, statistics, among others). In **computational linguistics** the methods of mathematical linguistics gained particular significance and influence. Algebraic linguistics and **statistical linguistics** are subdisciplines of mathematical linguistics.

References

Gladji, A.V. and I.A. Mel'cuk. 1973. *Elements of mathematical linguistics*. The Hague.

Gross, M. and A. Lentin. 1967. *Notions sur les grammaires formelles*. Paris.

Harris, Z. 1991. *A theory of language and information: a mathematical approach*. Oxford.

Landman, F. 1991. *Structures for semantics*. Dordrecht.

Partee, B., A. ter Meulen, and R. Wall. 1990. *Mathematical methods in linguistics*. Dordrecht.

Weinberg, A.S. 1988. Mathematical properties of grammars. *CLS* 1.416–92.

⇒ **Montague grammar**

mathematical logic ⇒ formal logic

matrix [Lat. *matrix* 'parent tree']

Two dimensional tabular representation taken from geometry which is used in linguistics to describe phonological, syntactic, semantic and other units using **features**. For an example, see the analysis of kinship terms in **componential analysis**.

matrix sentence

Term introduced by R.B. Lees indicating a superordinate sentence in which partial sentences (⇒ **constituent clauses**) are embedded (⇒ **embedding**). Matrix sentences correspond to the traditional term **main clause** in as far as the S-node of the main clause is not dominated by S; i.e. each complex sentence contains only one main clause, but sometimes several matrix sentences as embedded structures for constituent clauses.

Reference

Lees, R.B. 1960. *The grammar of English nominalizations*. Bloomington, IN.

maxim of conversation

Term introduced by H.P. Grice in a 1967 lecture (see Grice 1975) to denote those requirements accepted as reasonable for effective communication which, if violated, could cause a breakdown in communication. Drawing on Kant's four logical functions of reason, Grice postulates four maxims of conversation: (1) maxim of quantity (make your contribution as informative as necessary for the current purposes of the exchange, but no more informative than necessary); (2) maxim of quality (try to make your contribution one that is true: do not say what you believe to be false; do not say anything for which you lack adequate evidence); (3) maxim of relevance (make your contribution relevant); and (4) maxim of manner (be clear, avoid ambiguity; be brief and orderly). Grice derives these conversational maxims from his cardinal maxim, the so-called 'co-operative principle': 'Make your contribution such as is required, at the stage at which it occurs, by the accepted purpose or direction of the talk exchange in which you are engaged.' The function of indirect speech acts, conversational implicatures, (⇒ **implicature**), and comprehension of irony, among other matters, can be described with the aid of these maxims of conversation. See Keenan (1976) on the possible linguistic and cultural relativity of maxims of conversation. (⇒ *also* **conversation analysis**)

References
Cole, P. 1975. The synchronic and diachronic status of conversational implicature. In P. Cole and J. Morgan (eds), *Syntax and semantics*, vol. 3: *Speech acts*. New York. 257–91.
Gazdar, G. 1977. *Implicature, presupposition and logical form.* Bloomington, IN.
—— 1979. *Pragmatics: implicature, presupposition, and logical form.* New York.
Gordon, D. and G. Lakoff. 1971. Conversational postulates. *CLS* 7.63–84. (Repr. in P. Cole and J. Morgan (eds), *Syntax and semantics*, vol. 3: *Speech acts*. New York, 1975. 83–106.)
Grice, H.P. 1975. Logic and conversation. In P. Cole and J. Morgan (eds), *Syntax and semantics*, vol. 3: *Speech acts*. New York. 41–58. (Orig. 1968.)
—— 1989. *Studies in the way of words.* Cambridge, MA.
Hall, K. *et al* (eds) 1990. *PBLS* 16: *general session and parasession on the legacy of Grice.* Berkeley, CA.
Horn, L.R. 1973. Greek Grice: a brief survey of proto-conversational rules in the history of logic. *CLS* 9.205–14.
—— 1990. Hamburgers and truth: why Gricean explanation is Gricean. *Papers of the BLS Parasession on the legacy of Grice,* 16.4411–28. Berkeley, CA.
Keenan, E.O. 1976. On the universality of conversational implicature. *Language and society* 5.67–80.
Leudar, I. and P.K. Browning. 1988. Meaning, maxims of communication and language games. *Language and Communication* 8.1–16.
Levinson, S.C. 1983. *Pragmatics.* Cambridge.
McCawley, J.D. 1978. Conversational implicature and the lexicon. In P. Cole (ed.), *Pragmatics.* New York. 245–59.
Murphy, J., A. Rogers, and R. Wall (eds) 1977. *Proceedings of the Texas conference on performatives, presuppositions and conversational implicatures.* Washington, DC.
⇒ **conversation analysis**

maximal projection

Those constituents in **X-bar theory** that are projected to the highest level and therefore are phrasal categories. For example, the **noun phrase** *the road from New York to San Francisco* is a maximal projection of the lexical item *road.* Similarly, *from New York* is a maximal projection of the preposition *from,* and *to San Francisco* is a maximal projection of *to.* In general, category X-phrase is a maximal projection of X, when X is dominated by X-phrase and no other Y-phrase stands between X and X-phrase. That is to say, every Y-phrase which dominates X also dominates X-phrase. Thus the above noun phrase is a maximal projection of the noun *road,* but not of *San Francisco,* because the prepositional phrase *from New York* stands in between *New York* and the complex noun phrase.

References
⇒ **X-bar theory**

Maya writing

Hieroglyphic writing system (⇒ **hieroglyphics**) of the Mayans in Meso-America, only partially deciphered.

References
Kelley, D.H. 1976. *Deciphering the Maya script.* Austin, TX.
Thompson, J.E.S. 1950. *Maya hieroglyphic writing.* Washington, DC.
—— 1991. *A catalog of Maya hieroglyphs.* Norman, OK.

Mayan languages

Group of twenty-eight languages in Central America broken down into four groups: Huastec, Yucatec, Western Mayan, and Eastern Mayan. The largest languages are Quiché or Achi (about 700,000 speakers), Mam, Kakchiquel, Kekchi (about 400,000 speakers each) in Guatemala, and Yucatec (about 600,000 speakers) in Yucatán. The languages form a geographically closed group, with the exception of Huastec in the north, and are grouped with the **Penutian** languages of North America to form the Macro-Penuti family. Jacaltec (Guatemala, about 20,000 speakers) and Tzeltal (Mexico, about 100,000 speakers) have been especially well researched; the generally accepted internal classification was established by T. Kaufmann.

Characteristics: relatively complex consonant system (glottalized stops and affricates), tonal languages are rare. Developed numeral classifiers which occur in various positions, including articles. The verb agrees with the subject and object according to the **ergative** pattern (two affix types: A-prefixes – subject of the transitive sentence; B-affixes – subject of the intransitive and object of the transitive sentence); also accusative systems when the verb is not in the preterite or a subordinate clause. The A-prefixes also serve as possessive prefixes with nouns: possessive sentence construction. Word order generally VSO or VOS.

Independently developed writing systems (so-called 'hieroglyphs' which up to now have only been partially deciphered, probably a mix of phonemic and ideographic characters). First written sources in Spanish-influenced orthography dating from the sixteenth century, especially famous is the *Popol Vuh* (Book of the Council) in Quiché, based on an old codex. (⇒ *also* **North and Central American languages**)

References
Campbell, L. 1977. *Quichean linguistic prehistory.*
  Berkeley, CA.
Craig, C.G. 1977. *The structure of Jacaltec.* Austin,
  TX.
Day, C. 1973. *The Jacaltec language.* The Hague.
England, N.C. 1983. *A grammar of Mam, a Mayan
  language.* Austin, TX.
England, N.C. and S.R. Elliott (eds) 1990. *Lecturas
  sobre la lingüística Maya.* Woodstock, VT.
Furbee-Losee, L. 1976. *The correct language: Tojo-
  labal. A grammar with ethnographic notes.* New
  York and London.
Kaufmann, T. 1971. *Tzeltal phonology and morphol-
  ogy.* Berkeley, CA.
Tozzer, A.M. 1921. *A Maya grammar.* Cambridge,
  MA.
Weisshar, E. 1986. Quiché. *StL* 20.63–74.

Journals
Journal of Mayan Linguistics.
Mayan Linguistic Newsletter.
⇒ **North and Central American languages**

Mazahua ⇒ **Oto-Mangue**

meaning

Central semantic notion defined and used differently depending on the theoretical approach.
At least two reasons account for the various
uses of the term: on the one hand, meaning is
not only a linguistic problem but is also a
central issue in philosophy, psychology, sociology, **semiotics**, jurisprudence, and theology,
among others; on the other hand, the use of
other terms (e.g. 'content,' 'reference,' 'sense,'
'signification,' 'designation,' etc.), coupled
with the adoption of some foreign terms (e.g.
Ger. *Sinn, Bedeutung*), has led to numerous
overlappings. Four major factors of linguistic
communication can be taken as points of reference for defining meaning: (a) the material
(phonetic or graphemic) side of the linguistic
expression; (b) cognitive aspects involved in
the production of abstract concepts or in the
awareness of perceptive content; (c) objects,
characteristics and states of affairs in the real
world which are referred to through linguistic
expressions; (d) the speaker and the specific
situational context in which linguistic expressions are used. The fact that these factors are
taken into account and weighed out to varying
degrees accounts for the multiplicity and heterogeneity of the many definitions of meaning
that underlie the various semantic theories.
Thus, de Saussure's concept of meaning may be
considered a psychological interpretation, inasmuch as he equates meaning in a static way to
the result of signifying, namely to the mental
image; meaning is understood to be a mental
phenomenon. The latter is substantiated by
holistic interpretations of meaning. The holistic
aspect contrasts with the traditional linguistic
interpretation in which meaning is viewed as
something to be broken down or parsed (⇒
componential analysis), while the mental
aspect contrasts with the traditional linguistic-
philosophical interpretation in which meaning
is seen as something objective (⇒ **extension**,
referential semantics). In the behaviorists'
view (⇒ **behaviorism**), Bloomfield and Skinner, among others, try to provide a causal basis
for the origin of meaning by reconstructing
meaning from the observable, situational circumstances as well as from the reactions of the
listener. Speaker, listener, and situation are
even more crucial in Wittgenstein's notion of
meaning found in the so-called 'theory of use'
(1953: 20): 'The meaning of a word is its use
in the language.' (⇒ **meaning as use**) Compare
Leisi's (1952) approach, which is similar.

If meaning is interpreted as the process of
referring to the real world, then meaning is
defined as the set of extralinguistic objects and
states of affairs which are denoted by a particular linguistic expression. While the above-
mentioned approaches to the description of
meaning incorporate extralinguistic phenomena
in their definitions of meaning (consciousness,
mental models, behavior, use, reality), the
notion of meaning in structural semantics rests
upon intralinguistic, systemic laws: meaning
arises from the set of semantic relations within
the lexicon like **synonymy**, **antonymy** (⇒
semantic relations, **lexical field theory**) and
the placement of individual expressions within
this system. Yet without mention of extralinguistic reality and the user of language, such
a description remains incomplete.

In semantic descriptions numerous terminological differences in the notion of meaning
come into play: lexical meaning (⇒ **lexical
meaning vs grammatical meaning**), **denotation**, **connotation**, extension, **intension**, **logical semantics**. Independent of the different
notions of meaning held by various scholars
and schools, two basic issues are discussed in
every model: on the one hand, the relationship
between lexical and sentential semantics (**sentence meaning**), i.e. how can the whole meaning of a sentence be explained by the meaning
of the individual elements and how can the
grammatical relations between them be
explained (⇒ **principle of compositionality**)?
On the other hand, the problem of delineating
semantic, syntactic, and pragmatic aspects of
meaning or the problem of the interdependence
between these aspects, which is particularly
relevant in the distinction between sentence
meaning and utterance meaning.

References
Cohen, L.J. 1962. *The diversity of meaning*. London.
Droste, F.G. 1987. Meaning and concept: a survey. *Leuvense Bijdragen* 76.447–73.
Dummett, M.A.E. 1975. What is a theory of meaning? In S. Guttenplan (ed.), *Mind and Language: Wolfson College Lectures, 1974*. Oxford. 97–138.
────── 1976. What is a theory of meaning? (II). In G. Evans and J. McDowell (eds), *Truth and meaning: essays in semantics*. Oxford. 67–137.
Fodor, J.D. 1977. *Semantics*. New York.
Garza-Cuarón, B. 1991. *Connotation and meaning*. Berlin and New York.
Horwich, P. 1990. Wittgenstein and Kripke on the nature of meaning. *Mind and Language* 5.105–21.
Hudson, R. 1995. *Word meaning*. London.
Kefer, M. and J. van der Auwera (eds) 1992. *Meaning and grammar*. Berlin and New York.
Leech, G.N. 1974. *Semantics*. Harmondsworth.
Leisi, E. 1952. *Der Wortinhalt: seine Struktur im Deutschen und Englischen*. Heidelberg. (5th edn 1975.)
Lyons, J. 1977. *Semantics*, 2 vols. Cambridge.
────── 1981. *Language, meaning and context*. London.
Ogden, C.K. and I.A. Richards. 1923. *The meaning of meaning*. New York. (10th edn London, 1966.)
Palmer, F. 1976. *Semantics: a new outline*. Cambridge.
Putnam, H. 1975. The meaning of meaning. In K. Gunderson (ed.), *Language, mind and knowledge*. Minneapolis, MN. 131–93. (Also in H. Putnam, *Mind, language and reality: philosophical papers*. Cambridge. Vol. 2, 215–71.)
Ullmann, S. 1951. *The principles of semantics*. Oxford. (2nd edn 1957.)
Wittgenstein, L. 1953. *Philosophical investigations*. Oxford. (Repr. 1963.)
⇒ **semantics**

meaning as use

Semantic theory developed by Wittgenstein (1953) in connection with **ordinary language philosophy** according to which the meaning of a linguistic expression is equivalent to its function or use within a known context: 'For a *large* class of cases – though not for all – in which we employ the word 'meaning' it can be defined thus: the meaning of a word is its use in the language.' Wittgenstein's abandonment of the psychological and mental aspects of the concept of meaning as well as of the referential relation to reality is the foundation of a pragmatic understanding of the concept of meaning; the rule-governed use of linguistic expressions corresponds to their meaning. This identification of use with meaning has not remained without criticism (see Antal, Pitcher, and Katz).

References
Antal, L. 1963. *Questions of meaning*. The Hague.
────── 1964. *Content, meaning and understanding*. The Hague.

Katz, J.J. 1966. *The philosophy of language*. New York.
Pitcher, G. 1964. *The philosophy of Wittgenstein*. Englewood Cliffs, NJ.
Wittgenstein, L. 1953. *Philosophical investigations*. Trans. G.E.M. Anscombe. Oxford.

meaning postulate

Term introduced by Carnap (1952) to designate a type of general semantic rule which describes a semantic relation between predicates in an artificial language of formal logic. Applied to natural languages, a meaning postulate establishes semantic constraints between different expressions that can be formulated in the form of meaning relations such as **synonymy**. Seen language-internally, an expression of a language is semantically described, when all of the meaning postulates that refer to it have been formulated. Within the scope of **generative semantics** (see Lakoff 1970), meaning postulates serve to describe the semantic relations between **semantic primitives** (i.e. basic semantic expressions). In **Montague grammar**, meaning postulates serve to limit the concept of interpretation: only those interpretations which make all meaning postulates true in at least one possible world are permitted.

References
Carnap, R. 1952. Meaning postulates. *PhS* 3.65–73.
Johnson-Laird, P.N. 1984. Semantic primitives or meaning postulates: mental models or propositional representations. In B.G. Bara and G. Guida (eds), *Computational models of natural language processing*. Amsterdam. 227–46.
Katz, J.J. and R.I. Nagel. 1974. Meaning postulates and semantic theory. *FL* 11.311–40.
Lakoff, G. 1970. Natural language and lexical decomposition. *CLS* 6.340–62.
Montague, R. 1970. Universal grammar. *Theoria* 36.373–98. (Repr. in *Formal philosophy: selected papers of R. Montague*, ed. R.H. Thomason. New Haven, CT, 1974. 222–46.)
────── 1973. The proper treatment of quantification in ordinary English. In J. Hintikka, J.M.E. Moravcsik, and E. Suppes (eds), *Approaches to natural language*. Dordrecht. 221–42. (Repr. in *Formal philosophy: selected papers of R. Montague*, ed. R.H. Thomason. New Haven, CT, 1974. 247–70.)
Schnelle, H. 1973. Meaning constraints. *Synthese* 26.13–37.

media ⇒ tenuis vs media

median [Lat. *medius* 'central, middle']

Speech sound classified according to the way in which the airstream bypasses its obstruction (namely over the center (= median) of the oral cavity in contrast with **lateral**).

References
⇒ **phonetics**

mediation

Process in learning theory that is used in psycholinguistics as an explanatory model for problems of language acquisition, especially those concerning the formation and use of concepts. The term 'mediation' refers to the internal processing of stimuli and denotes non-observable cases of mediation between initial stimulus and final responses. Mediation operates via cerebral processes that bring about new modes of behavior as a reaction to a particular stimulus simultaneously as proprioceptive stimuli. Thus, Bousfield (1961) differentiates the conditioning process in acquiring meaning (which, according to the behaviorist explanation, rests on a coupling of objects with (linguistic) signs), by positing silent repetition of the heard words as a mediating behavioral unit which, for its part, possesses a stimulus character. This theory of mediation, which is based on verbal **associations**, is in direct opposition to C.E. Osgood's much-discussed approach of emotionally controlled processes of mediation. Underlying this latter approach is the technique of **semantic differentials**.

References
Bousfield, W.A. 1961. The problem of meaning in verbal learning. In C.N. Cofer (ed.), *Verbal learning and verbal behavior*. New York. 81–91.
Fodor, J.A. 1965. Could meaning be an r$_m$? *JVLVB* 4.73–81.
Jenkins, J.J. 1965. Mediation theory and grammatical behaviour. In S. Rosenberg (ed.), *Directions in psycholinguistics*. New York. 66–90.
Miron, M.S. 1971. The semantic differential and mediation theory. *Linguistics* 66.77–89.
Osgood, C.E. 1962. Studies on the generality of affective meaning systems. *AmP* 17.10–28.
———— 1971. Where do sentences come from? In D.D. Steinberg and L.A. Jakobovits (eds), *Semantics*. Cambridge. 497–529.
⇒ **meaning**, **psycholinguistics**, **semantic differential**

medio-dorsal ⇒ dorsal

medio-dorso-velar ⇒ articulation

Megheno-Rumanian ⇒ Rumanian

mellow ⇒ strident vs non-strident

memory

Place of recording, interpretation, storing, and recall of information. In view of different functions, storage of information, capacity, and principles of processing, as a rule three types of memory are differentiated. (a) In sensory information storage (SIS) a complete picture of the experiential segment perceived by the sensory organs is represented (with a duration of only 0.1–0.5 seconds). (b) In the short-term memory (STM; occasionally equated with working storage) only information needed for a short period of time and information that is categorized for continual storage, is stored (with a duration of approximately 10 seconds). Short-term memory is considered the co-operative part of the controlled processing of information; here, for a short period of time, a simultaneous overview of organized information is possible in specifically encoded units (⇒ **chunking**). Forgetting information can presumably be attributed both to a disintegration over time as well as to **interference** of other offered material. The limited storage capacity of the short-term memory is of consequence for the **acceptability** of complex syntactic structures. (c) The long-term memory (LTM) has at its disposal an unlimited capacity and guarantees the storage and reproducibility (activated through specific stimuli) of learned experiences: vocabulary and the set of linguistic rules are stored here.

References
Anderson, J.R. 1976. *Language, memory, and thought*. Hillsdale, NJ.
Bartlett, F.C. 1932. *Remembering: a study in experimental and social psychology*. London.
Carroll, D.W. 1986. *Psychology of language*. Monterey, CA.
Clark, H.H. and E.V. Clark. 1977. *Psychology and language: an introduction to psycholinguistics*. New York.
Gathercole, S.E. and A.D. Baddeley. 1993. *Working memory and language*. Hillsdale, NJ.
Harriot, P. 1974. *Attributes of memory*. London.
Howard, D.V. 1983. *Cognitive psychology: memory, language, and thought*. New York.
Lindsay, P.H. and D.A. Norman. 1977. *Human information processing*. New York.
Wanner, E. 1974. *On remembering, forgetting, and understanding sentences*. The Hague.
⇒ **artificial intelligence**, **cognitive linguistics**, **language and brain**, **psycholinguistics**, **text processing**

Mende ⇒ Mande

Menomini ⇒ Algonquian

mental lexicon

Term referring to the lexicon in the human mind. The entries for each lexical item specify the word meaning, the syntactic category, the argument structure, the morphological form and the phonological segments. It is still under debate, for example, whether words are stored as wholes or as morphemes and how much syntactic and semantic information is associated with them. The mental lexicon plays an important role in processing: e.g. in **language comprehension** in word recognition, i.e. lexical access (in the matching of sounds against possible words) and in the narrowing down of the possibilities to one word. Furthermore, in the discussion about autonomous and interactive models, the mental lexicon is the place where, due to the nature of the entries, information of various kinds (morphological, syntactic, and semantic) may influence the comprehension process and thus favor an interactive model. In **language production**, the entries in the mental lexicon likewise play a part in word retrieval. Experiments to obtain insights about the organization of the mental lexicon are, for example, lexical decision tasks, in which the subject is asked to decide as quickly as possible whether a sequence of sounds or letters is a word or not. Experiments for lexical access as an autonomous or interactive process are, for instance, word or phoneme monitoring: in these experiments the subject is asked to react as soon as the relevant item appears. It is assumed that the reaction time is shorter if the items preceding the target item are not complex in phonological or semantic structure.

References
Aitchison, J. 1987. *Words in the mind: an introduction to the mental lexicon.* Oxford.
Altmann, G.T.M. (ed.) 1990. *Cognitive models of speech processing.* Cambridge, MA.
Bresnan, J. (ed.) 1982. *The mental representation of grammatical relations.* Cambridge, MA.
Dunbar, G. 1991. *The cognitive lexicon.* Tübingen.
Emmorey, K.D. and V.A. Fromkin. 1988. The mental lexicon. In F. Newmeyer (ed.), *Linguistics: the Cambridge survey.* Cambridge. Vol. 3, 124–49.
Fodor, J.A. 1978. *Modularity of mind.* Cambridge, MA.
Forster, K.I. 1981. Priming and the effects of sentence and lexical contexts in naming times: evidence for autonomous lexical processing. *Quarterly Journal of Experimental Psychology* 33.465–95.
Halle, M., J. Bresnan, and G.A. Miller (eds) 1978. *Linguistic theory and psychological reality.* Cambridge, MA.
Henderson, L. 1985. Towards a psychology of morphemes. In A.W. Ellis (ed.), *Progress in the psychology of language.* London. Vol. 1, 15–72.
Johnson-Laird, P.N. 1983. *Mental models.* Cambridge, MA.
Kintsch, W. 1974. *The representation of meaning in memory.* Hillsdale, NJ.
Kohn, S.A. *et al.* 1987. Lexical retrieval: the tip of the tongue phenomenon. *Applied Psycholinguistics* 8.245–66.
Levelt, W.J.M. 1989. *Speaking: from intention to articulation.* Cambridge.
Marslen-Wilson, W. 1987. Functional parallelism in spoken word recognition. *Cognition* 25.71–102.
—— (ed.) 1989. *Lexical representation and process.* Cambridge, MA.
Marslen-Wilson, W. and A. Welsh. 1978. Processing interactions and lexical access during word recognition in continuous speech. *Cognitive Psychology* 10.29–63.
Martin, N., R.W. Weisberg, and E.M. Saffran. 1989. Variables influencing the occurrence of naming errors: implication for models of lexical retrieval. *Journal of Memory and Language* 28.462–85.
Mehler, J. *et al.* 1982. *Perspectives on mental representation.* Hillsdale, NJ.
⇒ **language comprehension, language production**

mentalism

Psychological and philosophical concept picked up and developed by Chomsky (1965) and modeled after Descartes' and von Humboldt's **rationalism**. Mentalism attempts to describe the internal (innate) language mechanism that provides the basis for the creative aspect of language development and use. In this program, Chomsky turns against the empirical approach of **American structuralism** (Bloomfield) and, especially, against Skinner's behaviorist interpretation of language (⇒ **behaviorism**), since both positions accept only immediately observable linguistic data as their object of investigation. By limiting the object of investigation to physically perceivable or physically measurable data, linguistic description is reduced to purely surface phenomena. Chomsky supports his mentalist concept in two ways: first, by assuming a grammar with an underlying **deep structure**; and second, with regard to language acquisition and the development of linguistic competence, by presupposing an inborn (universal) mechanism ('device') that provides a basis for language development (**Cartesian linguistics**). The following observations of child language acquisition speak against the antimentalist interpretation, namely, that the process of language learning can be explained solely as **conditioning** through drill or, according to the **stimulus-response** theory, through **association** and generalization: (a) the rapidity with which a child learns to command the grammar of his/her language in three to four years; (b) the complexity of the grammar to be learned; (c) the imperfect relationship between input (= the partially defective language data offered by the social milieu) and output (= the grammar derived from these data); (d) the uniformity of results in all languages; and (e) the process itself, which has little to do with an individual's intelligence. These data can only be adequately explained by assuming an inborn **language acquisition device**, on the basis of which competence (⇒ **competence vs performance**) develops through experience and the maturation of this basic inborn psychological structure (⇒ **nativism**). In this sense, **transformational grammar** attempts to explain both the process of language acquisition and especially the creative aspect of language acquisition, that is, the ability of a competent speaker to produce a potentially infinite number of sentences. For a more detailed explanation and critique of Chomsky's mentalist interpretation, see Putnam (1967).

References
Chomsky, N. 1959. Verbal behavior. (A discussion of B.F. Skinner, 1957.) *Lg* 35.26–58.
——— 1965. *Aspects of the theory of syntax*. Cambridge, MA.
——— 1968. *Language and mind*. New York.
——— 1975. *Reflections on language*. New York.
Katz, J.J. 1964. Mentalism in linguistics. *Lg* 40.124–37.
——— 1966. *The philosophy of language*. New York.
Lenneberg, E.H. 1967. *Biological foundation of language*. New York.
Matthews, P. 1990. Language as a mental faculty: Chomsky's progress. In N.E. Collinge (ed.), *An encyclopedia of language*. London. 112–38.
McNeill, D. 1966. Developmental psycholinguistics. In F. Smith and G.A. Miller (eds), *The genesis of language*. Cambridge, MA. 15–84.
Putnam, H. 1967. The 'innateness hypothesis': an explanatory model in linguistics. *Synthese* 17.12–22.
Watt, W.C. 1974. Mentalism in linguistics. *Glossa* 8.3–40.
⇒ **language acquisition, psycholinguistics**

mention vs use ⇒ **object language vs metalanguage**

Merina ⇒ **Malagasy**

mesolect ⇒ **acrolect**

Messapic ⇒ **Indo-European**

metachrony [Grk *metá* 'between,' *chrónos* 'time']

L. Hjelmslev's complementary term to diachrony (⇒ **synchrony vs diachrony**): While diachronic studies (in his view) treat primarily the influence of extralinguistic factors on individual processes of language development, metachrony describes language change in a functional aspect as a succession of different language systems.

Reference
Hjelmslev, L. 1928. *Principes de grammaire générale*. Copenhagen.

metacommunication

Communication about communication, i.e. communication of speakers about language (in the sense of language/competence) or about speech (in the sense of 'parole' or speech acts, ⇒ **langue vs parole, speech act theory**). Two types of metacommunication are usually distinguished: scientific metacommunication, which includes all forms of linguistic investigation; and everyday metacommunication. The human ability to use metacommunication to understand both the content and intention of linguistic utterances is a large part of **communicative competence**. Investigations in metacommunication that pertain to pragmatic and psycholinguistic factors can be divided into two groups: (a) explicit metacommunication, where the speaker refers to an immediate utterance and expands or modifies it by correcting it, making it more precise, taking a position in reference to it, adding commentary and the like; (b) implicit metacommunication, which corresponds to Watzlawick's **analogue communication**. This refers to the relational aspects between communication partners which occur primarily through non-verbal body language. Since an excess of metacommunication can be a symptom of a distortion of the relationship between communication partners, and because the inability to use metacommunication has proved to be a serious disadvantage in therapy for communication disorders, the investigation of the functions and means of metacommunication is the common object of study both for linguists and for psychologists.

Reference
Watzlawick, P., J.H. Beavin, and D.D. Jackson. 1967. *Pragmatics of human communication: a study of interactional patterns, pathologies, and paradoxes*. New York.

metagrammar ⇒ **metarule**

metalanguage

Second-level language (also called language of description) by which natural language (object language) is described. (⇒ **object language vs metalanguage**)

Reference
Riley, K. 1987. The metalanguage of transformational syntax: relations between jargon and theory. *Semiotica* 67.173–94.

metalepsis

A rhetorical **trope**. The replacement of a word by a contextually incorrectly used part synonym (⇒ **synonymy**). This is found especially with mistranslation and the incorrect equating of two words which have similar though not identical meaning.

References
⇒ **figure of speech, stylistics**

metalinguistics

1 Theoretical discipline that deals with the investigation of **metalanguages** (⇒ **object language vs metalanguage**) which describe natural languages. The task of metalinguistics includes the development of a general theory of grammar which aims to discover all characteristic features of natural languages.

2 Interdisciplinary investigation of the interrelationships between language, thought, behavior, and reality; that is, between the formal structure of a language and the entire culture of the society in which that particular language is spoken. (⇒ *also* **ethnolinguistics**)

References
Botha, R.P. 1992. *Twentieth-century conceptions of language*. Oxford.
⇒ **Sapir–Whorf hypothesis**

metamorphosis grammar

As a precursor to **definite clause grammar** in **computational linguistics**, a formalism in which every substitution rule has the following form: 'Substitute a particular series of tree diagrams for a particular series of tree diagrams.'

Reference
Colmerauer, A. 1978. Metamorphosis grammar. In L. Bolc (ed.), *Natural language communication with computers*. Berlin. 133–88.

metaphor [Grk *metaphorá* 'transference']

Term taken from ancient **rhetoric** for a 'figure of speech.' Metaphors are linguistic images that are based on a relationship of similarity between two objects or concepts; that is, based on the same or similar **semantic features**, a denotational transfer occurs, e.g. *The clouds are crying* for *It's raining*. Metaphor is also frequently described as a shortened comparison, in which the comparison is nonetheless not explicitly expressed. Metaphors may appear in the context of a sentence as nouns, verbs, or adjectives, e.g. *bull's eye* for *center of the target*, *sharp criticism* for *strong criticism*, *to peel one's eyes* for *to watch out for something*. In contrast to **idioms**, the literal reading of a metaphor (in a 'positive' context) results in a **contradiction**. More recent approaches view metaphors not as a purely semantic phenomenon, but rather see them in connection with their use or establish them at the cognitive, conceptual level. Seen historically, metaphors are a source of new lexical formations in which the 'transferred' meaning is either added to the original meaning (e.g. *pansy* 'flower' or 'effeminate male') or displaces the old meaning partially or completely (e.g. *keen*, which origi-

nally meant 'bold, powerful'; *blank* originally 'white'; *crop* originally 'cluster, bunch, ear [of corn]'). In many cases, originally metaphoric denotations are no longer perceived as such (e.g. *miscarriage*).

References
Aarts, J.M. and J.P. Calbert. 1979. *Metaphor and non-metaphor*. Tübingen.
Ankersmit, F.R. and J.J.A. Mooij (eds) 1992. *Knowledge and language*, vol. 3: *Metaphor and knowledge*. Dordrecht.
Christopher, M. 1983. A new model for metaphor. *Dialectica* 37.285–301.
Cooper, D.E. 1986. *Metaphor*. Oxford.
Derek, B. 1969. Prolegomena to a linguistic theory of metaphor. *FL* 5.34–52.
Kittay, E. 1987. *Metaphor: its cognitive force and linguistic structure*. Oxford.
Kittay, E. and A. Lehrer. 1981. Semantic fields and the structure of metaphor. *SLang* 5.31–63.
Lakoff, G. 1985. Metaphor, folk theories, and the possibilities of dialogue. In M. Dascal and H. Cuyckens (eds), *Dialogue: an interdisciplinary approach*. Amsterdam. 57–72.
——— 1987. Image metaphors. *Metaphor and Symbolic Activity* 2.219–22.
Lakoff, G. and M. Johnson. 1981. *Metaphors we live by*. Chicago.
Lakoff, G. and M. Turner. 1989. *More than cool reason: a field guide to poetic metaphor*. Chicago, IL.
Martinich, A.P. 1984. A theory for metaphor. *Journal of Literary Semantics* 8. 35–56.
Miall, D. 1982. *Metaphor: problems and perspectives*. Brighton.
Mooij, J.J. 1976. *A study of metaphor*. Dordrecht.
Ortony, A. (ed.) 1979. *Metaphor and thought*. Cambridge.
Papproté, W. and R. Dirven (eds) 1985. *The ubiquity of metaphor: metaphor in language and thought*. Amsterdam.
Thomas, J.-J. 1987. Metaphor: the image and the formula. *Poetics Today* 8.479–501.

Bibliographies
Shibles, W.A. 1971. *Metaphor; an annotated bibliography and history*. Whitewater, WI.
Van Noppen, J.P. and E. Hols. 1991. *Metaphor*, vol. II: *A classified bibliography of publications*. Amsterdam and Philadelphia, PA.
Van Noppen, J.P., S. de Knop, and R. Jongen. 1985. *Metaphor: a bibliography of post-1970 publications*. Amsterdam.

metaplasm

Umbrella term for sound changes occurring for reasons of euphony or metrics and which often lead to double forms: *I cannot → I can't*; *I do not know → I don't know*; *The man, that hath no music in himself and is not mov'd with concord of sweet sounds is fit for treason. Isn't he? Yes, it's right.*

metarules

Rules which generate grammar rules as well as rules for a metagrammar, which generates an object grammar. In **Generalized Phrase Structure Grammar** (GPSG), metarules are introduced to derive **phrase structure rules** from other phrase structure rules. Thus, it is possible to describe syntactic regularities as relations between groups of rules. In the current version of GPSG, metarules derived ID rules from other ID rules. A metarule contains an input and output schema. The input schema must contain variables so that the metarule can be applied to a class of rules.

References
Flickinger, D. 1983. Lexical heads and phrasal gaps. In M. Barlow, D. Flickinger, and M. Wescoat (eds), *Proceedings of the second West Coast conference on formal linguistics*. Stanford, CA. 89–101.
Gazdar, G. *et al.* 1985. *Generalized Phrase Structure Grammar*. Cambridge, MA.
Shieber, S. *et al.* 1983. Formal constraints on metarules. *ACL Proceedings* 21.22–7.
Thompson, H.S. 1982. Handling metarules in a parser for GPSG. In M. Barlow, D. Flickinger, and J. Sag (eds), *Developments in Generalized Phrase Structure Grammar*. Bloomington, IN. 26–37.
Uszkoreit, H. and S. Peters. 1986. On some formal properties of metarules. *L&P* 9.477–94.

metathesis [Grk *metáthesis* 'transposition, change']

Switching of consonants within etymologically related words: *nuclear* vs *nucular*, *Christian* vs *Kirsten*, Eng. *burn* vs Ger. *brennen*. Apart from such individual cases, 'regular' forms of metathesis can be attributed primarily to syllable structure, e.g. adaptation to universally preferred sound sequences in syllables. In South and West **Slavic** there is regular metathesis of **liquids** *vis-à-vis* Proto-Slavic, cf. PSlav. **berza* 'birch' with Church Slavic. *brĕza*, Serb. (⇒ **Serbo-Croatian***)* *breza*, **Polish** *brzoza*, **Czech** *bříza*.

References
⇒ language change, sound change

metonymy [Grk *metōnymía* 'change of name']

The replacement of an expression by a factually related term. The semantic connection is of a causal, spatial, or temporal nature and is therefore broader than **synecdoche**, but narrower than **metaphor**. Common types of substitution are author/work – *to read Jane Austen*; product/material – *to wear leather*; container/contents – *to have a cuppa*; place/resident – *The White House*.

References
Ruwet, N. 1975. Synecdoque et métonymie. *Poétique* 6.371–88.
⇒ rhetoric, trope

metrical phonology

Concept of accent (⇒ **stress**^{2}) proposed by M. Liberman that sees accent as a relation between strong and weak nodes of a metrical tree. Metrical phonology was later used to describe other phonological phenomena and is a concept in **non-linear phonology**.

References
Booij, G.E. 1983. Principles and parameters in prosodic phonology. *Linguistics* 21.249–80.
Giegerich, H. 1985. *Metrical phonology and phonological structure: German and English*. Cambridge.
Goldsmith, J.A. 1990. *Autosegmental and metrical phonology*, Oxford.
Hogg, R. and C.B. McCully. 1987. *Metrical phonology: a coursebook*. Cambridge.
Liberman, M. and A.S. Prince. 1977. On stress and linguistic rhythm. *LingI* 8.249–336.
Van der Hulst, H. and N. Smith (eds) 1982. *The structure of phonological representations*, 2 vols. Dordrecht.
────── (eds) 1989. *Features, segmental structures and harmony processes*, 2 vols. Dordrecht.

Miao-Yao

Language family in South-East Asia with four languages, spoken in numerous linguistic islands stretching from southern China to Thailand. Largest language is Mien (Yao), with approx. 1 million speakers. Benedict (1975) suspects a relationship to **Austro-Thai**.

References
Benedict, P.K. 1975. *Austro-Thai: language and culture*. New Haven, CT.
Haudricourt, A.G. 1971. *Les Langues miao-yao: Asie de Sud-Est et Monde Insulindien*, vol. 2. Paris.

microlinguistics [Grk *mikrós* 'small']

Science dealing with the structure of language as an autonomous sign system. This restriction to 'internal' linguistics, as is the case with **structuralism**, requires that a language system be abstracted and dealt with separately from extralinguistic approaches (i.e. those referring to such disciplines as philosophy, sociology, psychology, and logic). Microlinguistics is a subdiscipline of **macrolinguistics**.

mid vowel ⇒ vowel

middle verb

1 Verbs which can neither form a passive nor be combined with modal adverbs (*resemble, cost, fit, weigh*), e.g. *This car costs a lot of money* : **A lot of money is costed by this car*;

This car costs voluntarily a lot of money.

2 Verbs with passive-like meaning such as in *The door opened.*

middle voice

Verbal **voice** contrasting with **active** and **passive** which is found in **Sanskrit** and classical **Greek**. The middle voice is semantically similar to reflexive constructions in that it describes an action which is performed by the subject for his/her own benefit or in which the subject affects itself: Grk *loúo* (act.) 'I wash' vs *loúomai* (mid.) 'I wash myself.' There is also a middle construction without an agent subject: *didáskō* (act.) 'I teach' vs *didáskomai* (mid.) 'I have myself taught,' which is similar to passive in meaning. Many **Indo-European** languages developed passives from middle-voice forms (see the typological-historical summary of Kemmer 1993).

References

Anderson, P.K. 1991. *A new look at the passive.* Frankfurt.

Collinge, N.E. 1963. The Greek use of the term 'middle' in linguistic analysis. *Word* 19.232–41.

Fox, B. and P.J. Hopper (eds) 1994. *Voice: form and function.* Amsterdam.

Jasanoff, J.H. 1978. *Stative and middle in Indo-European.* Innsbruck.

Kemmer, S.E. 1993. *The middle voice: a typological and diachronic study.* Amsterdam.

Lehmann, W.P. 1974. *Proto-Indo-European syntax.* Austin, TX.

Mien ⇒ Miao-Yao

mildly context-sensitive languages

In **formal language theory**, a class of languages which properly includes context-free (CF) languages (⇒ **context-free grammar**) and which is powerful enough to describe **reduplication** and the cross-serial dependencies of Dutch verb phrases (VPs), two non-CF phenomena. **Tree-adjoining grammar**, **head-grammar**, and combinatory categorial grammars have been shown to be equivalent and mildly context-sensitive.

Reference

Joshi, A., K. Vijay-Shankar, and D. Weir. 1991. The convergence of mildly context-sensitive grammar formalisms. In P. Sells, S. Shieker, and T. Wasow (eds), *Foundational issues in natural language processing.* Cambridge.

Min ⇒ Chinese

Mingrelian ⇒ South Caucasian

minimal pair

Two expressions (words or morphemes) of a language with different meanings that are distinguished by only one **phoneme**; e.g. Eng. *mail* vs *nail*, Fr. *père* 'father' vs *mère* 'mother,' Span. *tu* 'your' vs *su* 'his/her,' Ger. *Gasse* 'lane' vs *Kasse* 'cashier.' Contrasting minimal pairs is a basic procedure in establishing the phonemic inventory of a language.

References
⇒ **phonology**

minor sentence

Incomplete utterance that is usually dependent on the context: *Two tickets please! – The same for me!* Minor sentences are as a rule interpreted as elliptic (⇒ **ellipsis**); however, this analysis is of limited value in such linguistic contexts as advertisements, film titles, or newspaper headlines.

Miwok-Costanoan ⇒ Penutian

Mixe ⇒ Mixe-Zoque

Mixe-Zoque

Language group of Central America with eight languages; the largest are Mixe (about 78,000 speakers) and Zoque (about 38,000 speakers) in southern Mexico.

Characteristics: relatively simple consonant system, complex vowel system (nine vowels including up to three length distinctions); vowels also glottalized and aspirated (complex syllable nuclei). Complex verb morphology.

References
⇒ **North and Central American languages**

mixed language

Language developed through the contact of a **European language** with that of a non-European language group. Historically, mixed languages arise from **English**, **French**, and **Spanish** through the adoption of foreign vocabulary elements and an extensive simplification of the grammar. (⇒ **bilingualism, code-switching, creole, lingua franca, pidgin, Sabir**)

Mixtec ⇒ Oto-Mangue

Moban ⇒ Nilo-Saharan

modal adverb [Lat. *modus* 'measure, mode, manner']

Semantically defined subset of adverbs which express the subjective evaluation of the speaker towards a state of affairs. This evaluation refers to modal aspects, the degree of reality expressed by the utterance (e.g. *probably, hopefully, possibly*), or to emotional aspects (e.g. *luckily, unfortunately, thank God*). On the syntactic functions of modal adverbs, ⇒ **sentence adverbial**. (⇒ also **adverbial**)

References
⇒ **particle, sentence adverbial**

modal auxiliary [Lat. *auxiliaris* 'giving aid'] (*also* helping verb)

Semantically defined subset of **verbs** which express modal meaning in connection with an infinitive of a main verb: *can, want, must, should, may, shall, will, would* as well as some marginal ones (*dare, ought to,* etc.). The two main functions of modal verbs are (a) specification of the semantic relationship between the subject and the action described by the verb, such as 'suspicion' (*She might/could be right*), 'necessity' (*She must/has to go*), 'permission' (*She can/may stay*), (b) expression of the speaker's subjective attitude towards the utterance; i.e. they can serve as paraphrases of verbal mood, cf. *Sleep!* vs *You should sleep*. (⇒ *also* **auxiliary, modality**). Etymologically, most modal auxiliaries in the Germanic languages including English derive from **preterite-presents**, which explains the irregularity of their formation.

References
Coates, J. 1983. *The semantics of the modal auxiliaries*. London.
Klinge, A. 1993. The English modal auxiliary: from lexical semantics to utterance interpretation. *JL* 29.291–357.
Quirk, R. *et al.* 1985. *A comprehensive grammar of the English language*. London and New York.

modal clause

Semantically defined dependent clause which functions syntactically as an adverbial complement for indicating how that which is described in the main clause happens or the circumstances accompanying it: *He spared her by taking the blame himself*. The term 'modal clause' is often used as an overall term for **instrumental, comparative, proportional,** and **restrictive clauses**.

modal logic

Special form of a philosophical logic that, in addition to logical expressions such as **logical particles** (*and, or,* and others) and **operators** in **formal logic**, also uses modal expressions such as *it is possible/impossible/necessary* by introducing appropriate operators into the semantic analysis.

References
Bull, R.A. and K. Segerberg. 1984. Basic modal logic. In D. Babbay and F. Guenthner (eds), *Handbook of philosophical logic*. Dordrecht. Vol. 2, 1–88.

Hintikka, J. 1969. Deontic logic and its philosophical morals. In *Models for modalities*. Dordrecht. 184–214.
Hughes, G.E. and M.J. Cresswell. 1968. *An introduction to modal logic*. London.
⇒ **intensional logic**

modal particle

Subgroup of particles, especially analysed for German ('Abtönungspartikeln', e.g. *aber, auch, bloß, denn*) which fit the content of an utterance to the context of speech. They have no lexical meaning and contribute nothing to the propositional meaning of a sentence. Modal particles may occur also in other functions, as adverbs (*vielleicht* 'perhaps'), adjectives (*einfach* 'simple'), scalar particles (*nur* 'only'), or conjunctions (*aber* 'but'). An application of the German research – to other languages is still lacking.

References
Bublitz, W. 1978. *Ausdrucksweisen und Sprechereinstellung im Deuschen und Englischen*. Tübingen.
Doherty, M. 1987. *Epistemic meaning*. Berlin.
König, E. and S. Requardt. 1991. A relevance-theoretic approach to the analysis of modal particles in German. *Multilingua* 10.63–77.
Nehls, D. 1989. German modal particles rendered by English auxiliary verbs. In H. Weydt (ed.), *Sprechen mit Partikeln*. Berlin.
Thurmair, M. 1989. *Modalpartikeln und ihre Kombinationen*. Tübingen.
Weydt, H. (ed.) 1979. *Die Partikeln der deutschen Sprache*. Berlin.
⇒ **particle**

modal subordination

Semantic form of subordination: sentences not syntactically subordinated in a text may be modally (and thus semantically) subordinated, if – for the purpose of their interpretation – they are assumed to be within the scope of a modal operator present in the context. Compare (a) the interpretation of a declarative sentence as a conditioned assertion following a conditional sentence (*When fall comes, the days get shorter. The leaves begin to change color*) and (b) the obligatory modalization of a sentence with a textual anaphor referring to a preceding modalized sentence (*Robert should build a greenhouse. He could fill it with exotic plants*).

References
Roberts, C. 1987. Modal subordination, anaphora, and distributivity. MA dissertation, University of Amherst, MA.
⇒ **modal logic**

modality

Semantic category which expresses the attitude of the speaker towards that expressed in the sentence. In this wider sense, modality refers not only to the morphologically formed moods of **indicative**, **subjunctive**, and **imperative**, but also to the different **sentence types** (statement, question, command). Appropriately, modality can be expressed through a variety of formal and lexical means in conjunction with contextual factors: (a) morphological **mood** of the verb; (b) lexical means such as **sentence adverbials** (*hopefully*, *maybe*), **modal auxiliaries** (*can*, *must*, *may*); (c) syntactic means such as paraphrases with *would* as well as constructions with *have* + inf., e.g. *I have to work*. On logical aspects of modality, ⇒ **deontic logic, epistemic logic, modal logic**.

References
Bybee, J. and S. Fleischmann (eds) 1995. *Modality in grammar and discourse*. Amsterdam and Philadelphia, PA.
Bybee, J., R. Perkins, and W. Pagliuca. 1994. *The evolution of grammar: tense, aspect and modality in the languages of the world*. Chicago, IL.
Gonda, J. 1980. *The character of the Indo-European moods*, 2nd edn. Wiesbaden.
Lyons, J. 1977. *Semantics*. Cambridge. Vol. 2, ch. 17.
Palmer, F.R. 1986. *Mood and modality*. Cambridge.
Perkins, M.R. 1983. *Modal expressions in English*. London.
⇒ **tense**

model

1 Generally, a (formal) representation in scientific studies of important structural and functional properties of the real world based on abstraction and idealization. Based on the analogy between models and some aspects of the object of study, predictions can be made about the rule-orderedness of the object of study that are not immediately apparent through observation (cf. N. Chomsky's model for describing linguistic competence (⇒ **competence vs performance**) in the form of an **automaton** that is capable of simulating the linguistic creativity of humans.) To the degree that models are hypotheses about reality, they require (experimental) examination of the object of study in order to be verified. The term 'model' is often used synonymously with **grammar** or grammar theory.

Reference
Chomsky, N. 1965. *Aspects of the theory of syntax*. Cambridge, MA.

2 In **predicate logic**, basic term in **model-theoretic semantics**. A model here consists of a range of individuals E and a model function f that assigns a categorically proper extension to every basic expression in the language. Every model recursively yields a linguistic inter-

pretation that describes a logically dependable interpretation of their expressions.

model-theoretic semantics (*also* Tarskian semantics)

Based on the work of A. Tarski and others, model-theoretic semantics is a concept of semantic interpretation in formal-logical languages developed by logicians for **logical semantics** which permits conditions of 'truth' and 'satisfaction' to be described recursively (⇒ **recursiveness**). An important basic principle of model-theoretic semantics is the strict distinction between a (formal) object language, to be semantically interpreted, and a metalanguage, in which semantic predicates like 'false' or 'true' are introduced (⇒ **object language vs metalanguage**). Procedure in model-theoretic semantics is characterized by specifying an interpretation that consists of a 'set of individuals' E, in which well-formed expressions of this language are interpreted with the aid of an interpretational function g. The values of g are then the **extensions** of the expressions belonging to them. Such a function g assigns, for example in **predicate logic**, elements of E to the individual terms, subsets of E to the one-place predicate constants, and **truth values** as extensions to the closed formulae. One advantage of model-theoretic semantics is that it allows semantic relationships between closed formulae to be realized. This is of particular interest for linguistics. Its restriction to **sentence semantics**, however, indicates its limits for linguistic purposes. The approach of model-theoretic semantics is also the basis of **Montague grammar**, in which the concepts of model-theoretic semantics, now relativized through the contextual factors of **possible worlds**, are drawn on for the characterization of truth, satisfaction, and inference in statements in natural languages.

References
Bunt, H.C. 1985. *Mass terms and model-theoretic semantics*. Cambridge.
Kamp, H. and U. Reyle. 1993. *From discourse to logic: introduction to model-theoretic semantics of natural language, formal logic and discourse representation theory*. Dordrecht.
Meulen, A. ter. (ed.) 1983. *Studies in model theoretic semantics*. Dordrecht.
Tarski, A. 1935. Der Wahrheitsbegriff in den formalisierten Sprachen. *Studia Philosophica* 1.261–405. (Repr. as Eng. trans. in Tarski 1956.)
—— 1944. The semantic conception of truth. *Philosophy and Phenomenological Research* 4.341–75. (Repr. in Tarski 1956.)
—— 1956. *Logic, semantics, metamathematics: papers from 1923 to 1938*. Oxford.

modi significandi [Lat. 'manners of designating']

In medieval linguistics, those aspects of meaning and denotation that were significant for the classification of **parts of speech**. The modi significandi go back to the general logical base concepts of Aristotle, i.e. substance, quality, quantity, relation, place, time, position, possession, action, suffering. According to these modi significandi, nouns were defined as 'substances with properties,' verbs as 'properties of action or suffering.' (⇒ **parts of speech**)

References
Bursill-Hall, G.L. 1971. *Speculative grammarians of the middle ages: the doctrine of 'partes orationis' of the Modistae*. The Hague.
Kaczmarek, L. 1993. *Modi significandi und ihre Destruktionen*. Amsterdam and Philadelphia, PA.
⇒ **linguistics**

modification [Lat. *modificare* 'to measure correctly']

1 In **word formation**, semantic differentiation of the **base morpheme** through word-formation morphemes, especially through **prefixes**. In this process, the original word class (in contrast to **transposition**) can remain the same: *fix* vs *prefix*, *cover* vs *discover*; *dog* vs *doggy*. Other types of modification involve shifts in stress (e.g. *réfuse* vs *refúse*), **suppletivism** (*go* > *went*), **mutation**.

References
⇒ **word formation**

2 ⇒ **complementation and modification**

modifier (*also* determiner)

Linguistic expression which more closely specifies or determines the meaning of another expression (⇒ **head**) semantically and syntactically: *long book*, where *book* is the head and *long* is the modifier describing the book. Syntactically, the **constituent** made up of a modifier and its head are of the same form class as the head (⇒ **endocentric construction**). In English, nouns are typically modified by adjectives (*long book*) or prepositional phrases (*the book on the table*), and verbs by adverbs (*read quickly*). A modifier can be either prespecifying or postspecifying, depending on whether it precedes or follows the head. While Bloomfield (1933) uses the term modifier only for attributive constructions, Trubetzkoy (1939) uses it for the relationship between verb and object, and Bartsch and Vennemann (1980) use it for the relationship between subject and predicate verb. The terminology for the two elements involved is diverse: 'head/center' vs 'attribute' (Bloomfield), 'head center' vs 'modifier' (Fries), 'déterminé' vs 'déterminant' (Trubetzkoy), 'operator vs operand' (Bartsch and Vennemann), and 'head' vs 'modifier' (Lyons). (*also* ⇒ **complementation and modification**)

References
Bartsch, R. and T. Vennemann. 1982. *Grundzüge der Sprachtheorie*. Tübingen.
Bloomfield, L. 1933. *Language*. New York.
Fries, C.C. 1927. *The structure of English: an introduction to the construction of English sentences*. (5th edn New York, 1964.)
Lyons, J. 1968. *Introduction to theoretical linguistics*. Cambridge.
Seiler, H. 1978. Determination: a functional dimension of inter-language comparison. In H. Seiler (ed.), *Language universals*. Tübingen. 301–28.
Trubetzkoy, N. 1939. Le rapport entre le déterminé, le déterminant et le défini. In *Mélanges de linguistique, offers à Charles Bally*. Geneva. 75–82.
Zwicky, A.M. 1985. Heads. JL21.1–29.

Modistae ⇒ speculative grammarians

modularity

Term taken from computer technology for a concept of subsystems with specific tasks which, due to the fact that they function independently, can to a large extent be isolated. The modular structure of parts of a whole is discussed, among other things, in **neuropsychology**, in particular in linguistics by Chomsky (e.g. 1980) and in **psycholinguistics**, in particular because of the modularity hypothesis by Fodor (1983). In connection with modularity, it has been pointed out that certain impairments of the brain may cause selective **language disorder** or **developmental language disorder** (e.g. Curtiss 1988; see also **language and brain**). According to Chomsky (1975, 1980), grammatical regularities are not based on general cognitive principles, but on principles that are specific for language. Thus, grammatical knowledge (the formal grammar or formal competence, ⇒ **competence vs performance**) is independent of other kinds of knowledge. 'Grammar' is conceptualized as a module (next to other modules such as visual perception) and consists of a set of autonomous subsystems, each with its own criteria for well-formedness. For Fodor (1983), modules are characterized by the co-occurrence of the following properties: they are input-systems; they operate within specific domains ('domain specificity'); they operate automatically as soon as a stimulus occurs, which makes them comparable to reflexes ('mandatory operation,' 'stimulus-driven'); the information is encapsulated so that the internal workings cannot be influenced or accessed from the outside, but only their output; they operate extremely fast and with shallow output (e.g. of the sort yes/no); they are considered to be 'hardwired' with a fixed neural architecture and display particular patterns when the system breaks down (for instance, due to a lesion). Fodor considers modules to be particular systems in information processing. For instance, input-systems in speech perception (e.g. perception of linguistic sounds in contrast to non-linguistic noise), 'central processing,' like problem-solving, which has access to information from various domains, is not considered to be modular. For a critical discussion, see Fodor (1985), Garfield (1987), and from a developmental perspective Bates *et al.* (1988) and Karmiloff-Smith (1992).

References
Bates, E. *et al.* 1988. *From first words to grammar.* Cambridge.
Bock, J.K. and A.S. Kroch 1989. The isolability of syntactic parsing. In G. Carlson and M.K. Tanenhaus (eds), *Linguistic structure in language processing.* Dordrecht. 157–96.
Chomsky, N. 1975. *Reflections on language.* Cambridge, MA.
——— 1980. *Rules and representations.* Oxford.
Curtiss, S. 1988. Abnormal language acquisition and the modularity of language. In F. Newmeyer (ed.), *Linguistics: the Cambridge survey*, Cambridge. Vol. 2, 96–111.
Everaert, M. *et al.* (eds) 1988. *Morphology and modularity.* Berlin and New York.
Fodor, J. 1983. *The modularity of mind.* Cambridge, MA.
——— 1985. Precis of the modularity of mind. *The Behavioral and Brain Sciences* 8.1–42.
Frazier, L. 1988. Grammar and language processing. In F. Newmeyer (ed.), *Linguistics: the Cambridge survey.* Cambridge. Vol. 2, 15–34.
Garfield, J.L. (ed.) 1987. *Modularity in knowledge representation and natural-language understanding.* Cambridge, MA.
Karmiloff-Smith, A. 1992. *Beyond modularity: a developmental perspective on cognitive science.* Cambridge, MA.
Linebarger, M.C. 1989. Neuropsychological evidence for linguistic modularity. In G. Carlson and M.K. Tanenhaus (eds), *Linguistic structure in language processing.* Dordrecht. 197–238.
Marr, D. 1982. *Vision.* New York.
Marshall, J. 1984. Multiple perspectives on modularity. *Cognition* 17.209–42.
Neville, H. *et al.* 1992. Fractionating language: different neural subsystems with different sensitive periods. *Cerebral Cortex* 2.244–58.
Roeper, T. 1988. Grammatical principles of first language acquisition: theory and evidence. In F. Newmeyer (ed.), *Linguistics: the Cambridge survey.* Cambridge. Vol. 2, 35–52.
Schwartz, M.F. 1990. *Modular deficits in Alzheimer-type dementia.* Cambridge, MA.
Smith, N. and I. Tsimpli. 1995. *Language learning and modularity.* Oxford.
Yamada, J. 1990. *Laura: a case for modularity of language.* Cambridge, MA.
⇒ **language and brain**

Mohave ⇒ **Hokan**

Molala ⇒ **Penutian**

Mon ⇒ **Mon-Khmer**

moneme [Grk *mónos* 'solitary, only']

Term introduced by Martinet (1960) for the smallest unit of language consisting of content and phonetic form that cannot be broken down further into smaller meaningful units. With regard to function, Martinet distinguishes between the open class of lexical monemes, the so-called '**semantemes**,' whose meaning is codified in the lexicon, and the closed class of grammatical monemes, which he calls 'morphemes,' and further between functional monemes (prepositions), autonomous monemes (free, nonconjugatable or nondeclinable: *today, sadly*), and independent monemes (case, tense). Compared with the terminology introduced by **American structuralism** and now established, Martinet's 'moneme' corresponds to the otherwise common term **morpheme**, his 'semanteme' to free lexical morphemes, his 'morpheme' to bound grammatical morphemes.

References
Martinet, A. 1960. *Eléments de linguistique générale.* Paris. (2nd rev. and exp. edn 1967.)
⇒ **morphology**

Mongolian

Branch of **Altaic** with twelve languages and approx. 3 million speakers in central Asia. Classical Mongolian, with a writing tradition dating back to the thirteenth century, is still used as the written language for these closely related languages.

References
Binnick, R.I. 1981. *On the classification of the Mongolian languages.* Toronto.
Grønbech, K. and J.R. Krueger. 1993. *An introduction to classical (literary) Mongolian*, 3rd corrected edn. Wiesbaden.
Poppe, N. 1955. *Introduction to Mongolian comparative studies.* Helsinki.
——— 1970. *Mongolian language handbook.* Washington, DC.
——— 1974. *Grammar of written Mongolian*, 4th unrev. printing. Wiesbaden.
Spuler, B. and H. Kees (eds) 1964. *Mongolistik.* (Handbuch der Orientalistik 5.2.) Leiden.
Vietze, H.-P. 1969. *Lehrbuch der mongolischen Sprache.* Munich. (5th edn Leipzig, 1987.)

Dictionary
Hangin, G. 1986. *A modern Mongolian–English dictionary.* Bloomington, IN.

monitor model

In **second language acquisition**, a hypothetical model developed by Krashen (1981), according to which language production in a second language is overseen by a type of controlling mechanism ('monitor') which checks for correctness of forms. The extent of this monitoring (which varies according to the type of language learner) is believed to have an effect on the nature of foreign language acquisition. Hence, Krashen distinguishes between 'learning' (heavy reliance upon the monitor) and 'acquisition' (little reliance upon the monitor). (⇒ *also* **natural approach**)

References
Colson, J.-P. 1989. *Krashens monitortheorie: een experimentele studie van het Nederlands als vreemde taal / La Théorie du moniteur de Krashen: une étude expérimentale du néerlandais, langue étrangère*. Leuven.
Krashen, S.D. 1981. *Second language acquisition and second language learning*. Oxford.
——— 1985. *The input hypothesis: issues and implications*. London.
McLaughlin, B. 1987. *Theories of second language learning*. London.
⇒ **second language acquisition**

Mon-Khmer

Language group in South-East Asia with approx. 140 languages belonging to the **Austro-Asiatic** language family; the most important languages are **Vietnamese** (about 50 million speakers) and Khmer (Cambodian, about 7 million speakers). Some have a long writing tradition (Mon and Khmer on the basis of Indian writing, Vietnamese on the basis of **Chinese**).

References
Bauer, C. 1992. *A grammar of spoken Mon*. Wiesbaden.
Jacob, J.M. 1968. *Introduction to Cambodian*. Oxford.
Sacher, R. and N. Phan. 1985. *Lehrbuch des Khmer*. Leipzig.
Thompson, L.C. 1991. *A Vietnamese reference grammar*, 2nd printing. Honolulu.
Thongkum, T.L. *et al.* (eds) 1979. *Studies in Tai and Mon-Khmer phonetics and phonology in honour of Eugenie J.A. Henderson*. Bangkok.

Bibliography
Shorto, H.L., J.M. Jacob, and E.H.S. Simmonds (eds) 1963. *Bibliographies of Mon-Khmer and Tai linguistics*. London.

monolingualism [Grk *mónos* 'only,' *lingua* 'tongue, language']

1 Command of only one language as opposed to **bilingualism** or **multilingualism**[1].

2 The use of only one language in a society, as opposed to **multilingualism**[2].

monophonematic classification

In the phonological analysis of a language, the attribution of two sounds to one **phoneme**. Cf. in contrast **polyphonemic classification**.

References
⇒ **phonology**

monophthong [Grk *monóphthongos* 'with one sound, single vowel']

In contrast with a **diphthong**, a vowel during whose articulation the **articulators** remain in place and maintain an audibly constant sound **quality**.

References
⇒ **phonetics**

monophthongization

Process of **sound change** motivated by articulation through which diphthongs are simplified to long vowels. It usually involves a reciprocally structured assimilation of both vocalic segments, which can also be influenced by corresponding following consonantal sounds and stress, cf. the change of **Germanic** *ai* and *au* respectively to the monophthongs *ā*, *ī* from Old through Middle English times (OE *stān* vs Goth. *stains*; Mod. Eng. *eye* < ME *eighe* < OE *ēage* < Gmc *augōn-*). (⇒ *also* **Great Vowel Shift**)

References
⇒ **sound change**

monosemy [Grk *sēma* 'sign']

1 Typical property of morphemes in **agglutinating languages** (e.g. **Turkish**) which expresses exactly one meaning component (⇒ **agglutination**). In contrast, ⇒ **inflection**. (⇒ *also* **language typology**)

2 An expression is monosemic if it has exactly one meaning, as opposed to **polysemy**, in which an expression may have more than one meaning. As a rule, monosemy is characteristic only of scientific terminology or artificial languages, but not of the vernacular. (⇒ *also* **meaning**, **semantics**)

Montague grammar

Concept of grammar named after its founder, the American logician and language theoretician Richard Montague (1932–71), which follows in the logical tradition of Frege, Tarski, Carnap, and others. Montague's premise is that between artificial (formal) and natural (human) languages there is no theoretically relevant difference. This leads to his attempt at demonstrating the logical structures of natural languages and at describing them by means of universal algebra and mathematical (**formal**) **logic**. In his precise, but very condensed sketches (of particular influence were his works Montague 1970 and Montague 1973, abbrev. PTQ), Montague proceeds from a syntax oriented along the surface structure of sentences, which he represents in the form of a modified **categorial grammar**. Parallel to this syntactic system of putting together simple into complex structures, complex meanings are also constructed from simple meanings, corresponding to the Fregean principle of meaning (⇒ **principle of compositionality**), according to which the whole meaning of a sentence can be determined recursively as a function of the meaning of its well-formed parts. For this purpose, in Montague (1973) the expressions of natural language are translated into the semantically interpreted language of **intensional logic** through a system of translation rules. These rules are a kind of formalization of an intersubjective language competence. The interpretation of this logical language (which is simple type logic expanded by intensional, modal and temporal operators) is conducted on a model-theoretic basis (⇒ **model-theoretic semantics**), i.e. each meaningful expression is attributed exactly one **intension**, which, depending on different situations (**possible worlds** or reference points) provides an **extension** (an object of reference) for the expression. From this concept follows the consequential methodological principle of semantic compositionality: the meanings of expressions form context-independent semantic blocks that alone contribute to the construction of the complete meaning of a sentence. This principle has proved to be extremely fruitful in the analysis of **noun phrases** (uniform treatment of terms for individual entities and quantifier phrases, ⇒ **quantification**). However, for a number of grammatical phenomena it runs into difficulties; the most important examples are the so-called *donkey*-sentences: The expression *a donkey*, to be understood in PTQ in the sense of the existential operator (⇒ **operator**) obtains a generalizing function in the sentence *Any man who owns a donkey beats it* (Geach 1962). Today, Montague grammar, next to **transformational grammar**, is one of the prevalent paradigms of theoretical linguistics, especially in its further developments. (⇒ *also* **discourse representation theory**, **situation semantics**)

References
Cann, R. 1992. *Formal semantics*. Cambridge.

Frosch, H. 1993. Montague-Grammatik. In J. Jacobs *et al.* (eds), *Syntax: an international handbook of contemporary research*. Berlin and New York. 413–29.
Geach, P. 1962. *Reference and generality: an examination of some medieval and modern theories*. Ithaca, NY.
Montague, R. 1970a. English as a formal language. In B. Visentini *et al.* (eds), *Linguaggi nella società e nella tecnica*. Milan.
—— 1970b. Universal grammar. *Theoria* 36.373–98.
—— 1973. The proper treatment of quantification in ordinary English. In J. Hintikka, J.M.E. Moravcsik, and E. Suppes (eds), *Approaches to natural language*. Dordrecht. (abb. PTA).
—— 1974. *Formal philosophy*, ed. R.H. Thomason. New Haven, CT.
Muskens, R. 1990. Going partial in Montague grammar: using programming concepts in deontic reasoning. In R. Bartsch *et al.* (eds), *Semantics and contextual expression*. Dordrecht. 175–220.

Anthologies
Davidson, D. and G. Harman (eds) 1972. *Semantics of natural language*. Dordrecht.
Groenendijk, J. *et al.* (eds) 1981. *Formal methods in the study of language*, 2 vols. Amsterdam.
Guenthner, F. and S.J. Schmidt. 1976. *Formal semantics and pragmatics for natural languages*. Dordrecht.
Guenthner, F. and C. Rohrer (eds) 1978. *Studies in formal semantics*. Amsterdam.
Kasher, A. (ed.) 1976. *Language in focus: foundations, methods and systems*. Dordrecht.
Keenan, E.L. (ed.) 1975. *Formal semantics of natural language*. Los Angeles, CA.
Partee, B. (ed.) 1976. *Montague grammar*. New York.

Bibliography
Petöfi, J.S. (ed.) 1978. *Logic and the formal theory of natural language: selected bibliography*. Hamburg.
⇒ **categorial grammar**, **intensional logic**

mood

Grammatical category of verbs which expresses the subjective attitude of the speaker towards the state of affairs described by the utterance. Most languages have independent paradigms for the **indicative** mood (a neutral category), the **subjunctive** for expressing unreal states, and the **imperative** for expressing commands. Some languages have other subtypes of moods such as the **conditional** in **French** for expressing a possible reality, the **optative** in **Greek**, **Turkish**, and **Finnish** for expressing fulfillable wishes, the dubitative in Turkish for expressing a suspicion, the **energetic** in **Arabic** for expressing an emphatic assertion.

The formulation of modality is not limited to the corresponding morphological verb forms, but can also be expressed lexically, as with

modal auxiliaries (*want*, *can*, etc.) and **sentence adverbials** (*hopefully*, *maybe*); cf. the semantic category of **modality**.

References
⇒ **modality**

mood of affirming ⇒ rule of inference

mood of denying ⇒ rule of negative inference

mora [Lat. *mora* 'time necessary, needed']

Phonological measurement for a short syllable that consists of a short vowel and (at most) one consonant. Syllables with a long vowel or with a short vowel and two or more consonants consist of two morae. According to another definition, light syllables that end in a short consonant consist of one mora, while all other syllables are heavy and consist of two morae. (⇒ *also* **law of three morae**)

Reference
Hyman, L. 1985. *A theory of phonological weight*. Dordrecht.

Mordva ⇒ Finno-Ugric

morph [Grk *morphé* 'form, shape']

The smallest meaningful phonetic segment of an utterance on the level of parole which cannot yet be classified as a representative of a particular **morpheme** (on the level of langue (⇒ **langue vs parole**). If two or more morphs have the same meaning but a different distribution then they belong to the same morpheme and are called **allomorphs** of that morpheme. Thus *-able*, as in *conceivable*, and *-ible*, as in *edible* constitute two different phonetic representations of an abstract suffix meaning roughly 'able.' Homonymic morphs, such as *-er* (⇒ **homonymy**), are allomorphs of different morphemes, namely 'comparative' (e.g. *harder*) and 'agentive' (e.g. *worker*). The distinction between morph, allomorph, and morpheme is analogous to that of **phone**, **allophone**, and **phoneme** in phonology.

References
⇒ **morphology**

morpheme

Theoretical basic element in structural language analysis, analogous to **phoneme**: the smallest meaningful element of language that, as a basic phonological and semantic element cannot be reduced into smaller elements, e.g. *book*, *three*, *it*, *long*. Morphemes are abstract (theoretical) units. They are represented phonetically and phonologically by **morphs** as the smallest meaningful, but unclassified, segments of

meaning. If such morphs have the same meaning and a complementary distribution or if they stand in free variation, then they are said to be **allomorphs** of the same morpheme, e.g. the allomorphs of the plural morpheme 's' are /s/, /z/, /iz/ as in *books*, *radios*, and *houses*, though *-s*, *-en*, and *-ø* (as in *doors*, *oxen*, and *sheep*) constitute allomorphs of an abstract plural morpheme. Thus, only in particular cases do morphemes actually correspond to the grammatical category of **word** (*word*, *we*, *soon*); morphemes must be principally distinguished from the phonetic unit of **syllable**: syllables are concrete sound segments of a word on the level of parole, while morphemes are abstractions on the level of langue (⇒ **langue vs parole**); any formal correspondence between morphemes and syllables is coincidental, cf. *rent control*, but: *rent-al* vs *tor-rent*. A syllable can consist of several morphemes: cf. *thought*, which can be analyzed as containing the four morphemes 'think' (as its lexical meaning (⇒ **lexical meaning vs grammatical meaning**)), 'tense,' 'person,' and 'number,' while *today* consists of two syllables but constitutes only one morpheme. Depending on the aspect of the study one can discern various typologies of classification and differentiation of morphemes. (a) Regarding the postulate of the unity of form and meaning a distinction must be drawn between (i) discontinuous morphemes, in which two or more morphs separated by other elements yield the morpheme's meaning (as in Ger. *ge* + *lieb* + *t*, where *ge-* and *-t* together mark the participle) and (ii) the so-called **portmanteau morphemes** in which the smallest meaningful segments carry several meanings (cf. the analysis above of *thought* or Fr. *au* that is a blend of the morphs *à* and *le*). (b) Regarding their semantic function one distinguishes between (i) lexical morphemes (⇒ **lexeme**), that denote objects, state of affairs, etc. of the extralinguistic world and whose relations are studied in **semantics** and **lexicology** and (ii) grammatical morphemes (also: inflectional morphemes) that express the grammatical relations in sentences and are studied in **morphology** (in the narrow sense) and **syntax**. (c) Regarding their occurrence or their independence one distinguishes between (i) free **morphemes** (also: **roots** or **bases**), which may have both a lexical (*book*, *red*, *fast*) as well as a grammatical function (*out*, *and*, *it*) and (ii) bound morphemes, in which it is a matter of either a lexical stem morpheme (e.g. *typ-* in *type*, *typical*) and inflectional morphemes (as in verb endings) or derivational morphemes of **word formation** (as *un-*, *-able*, *-ness*) (⇒ **affix**). Also, so-called 'cranberry morphemes' (as *cran-* in *cranberry*)

(⇒ **semimorpheme**) are bound morphemes whose synchronic meaning is reduced to its distinctive function. This structuralist morpheme analysis, which is based primarily on **distribution** and operational processes of analysis, is limited by the changes in the forms that are not caused by relations of order, but rather are characterized by sound changes (⇒ **mutation**), cf. the formation of the past tense in Eng. *run : ran.* See Matthews (1974) for a summary and critical view of these analyses. The relevance of the classical concept of morpheme to the description of word formation is doubted by Aronoff (1976), who eventually discards it. Accordingly, the lexicon does not consist of morphemes but rather of finished words of the language. According to Aronoff, outside the words in which they occur, morphemes have no independent existence: they are constituents of words. **Word formation rules** are interpreted as transformational operations within the lexicon that take a word as input and transform the same into a new word with phonologically, semantically, and syntactically determined characteristics. See Di Sciullo and Williams (1987) for criticisms of Aronoff's approach. In contrast to Aronoff, they posit combinatory word formation processes that combine morphemes into words.

References
Aronoff, M. 1976. *Word formation in generative grammar.* Cambridge, MA.
Di Sciullo, A.M. and E. Williams. 1987. *On the definition of word.* Cambridge, MA.
Matthews, P.H. 1974. *Morphology: an introduction to the theory of word-structures.* Cambridge. (2nd edn 1991.)
⇒ **morphology**, **word formation**, **word formation rules**

morphemics

1 In the broad sense, synonymous term for **morphology**.

2 In the narrow sense, term denoting synchronic **morphology** as opposed to historical **word formation**.

morphological analysis

Analysis and description of the (variant) forms, the occurrence, and the function of **morphemes** as the smallest meaningful elements of a language. (⇒ *also* **morphology**)

References
⇒ **morphology**

morphological feature

The conjugational and declensional features of language that mark an expression for inflection, i.e. that indicate **person**, **number**, **tense**, and so on in verbs, and **case** and **gender** in nouns.

References
⇒ **morphology**

morphological reanalysis ⇒ analogy

morphologization

Change of a phonological rule into a morphological regularity through the loss of an originally present phonetic motivational factor. Thus, the plural formation by **umlaut** (*foot : feet*), which was originally conditioned by an *-i-* in the following syllable (Proto-**Germanic** **fotiz*), became productive in **German**, after this conditioning factor had been lost and the umlaut came to be directly connected with the category of plural (e.g. *Hand – Hände* 'hand – hands'); in English, umlaut was not morphologized; there remained only a few isolated cases (see above and, e.g. *mouse : mice*).

References
Bybee, J. 1985. *Morphology: a study of the relation between meaning and form.* Amsterdam.
Dressler, W.U. 1985. *Morphology: the dynamics of derivation.* Ann Arbor. MI.
Klausenburger J. 1979. *Morphologization: studies in Latin and Romance morphophonology.* Tübingen.
Maiden, M. 1991. *Interactive morphology.* London.
Wurzel, W. 1984. *Flexionsmorphologie und Natürlichkeit.* Berlin.
⇒ **grammaticalization, morphophonemics, natural phonology**

morphology

Term coined by J.W. von Goethe to designate the study of form and structure of living organisms which was taken up by linguistics in the nineteenth century as a cover term for **inflection** and **word formation**. In **school grammar**, morphology corresponds to the study of forms, i.e. the subdisciplines of inflection as well as of the study of word classes and their classificational criteria. In various ways word formation is treated as an independent discipline beside morphology or as a further subdiscipline of morphology. Hockett (1954) distinguishes between three types of morphological models: (a) the **item-and-arrangement grammar** (= combinatory morphology) pursued in **American structuralism** with consideration to **distribution**; (b) the concept of an **item-and-process grammar** (= process morphology) which is fundamental to **generative grammar** and in which basic abstract forms are transformed into their surface structure forms; and (c) the word-and-paradigm model (= **paradigm morphology**), which posits not the morpheme, but the **word** as the basic element of morphological description. The basic concepts of morphology in recent linguistics were developed in the framework of **structuralism** (cf. above under (a)). Here, morphology consists of the study of form, inner structure, function, and occurrence of a **morpheme** as the smallest meaningful unit of language. Based on experimental methods of analysis (⇒ **operational procedures**) the morpheme inventory as well as the possible morpheme combinations are described; the transition to syntax is just as continuous as the boundary with phonology (⇒ **morphophonemics**). Further goals of morphological analysis are: (a) the development of criteria that determine **parts of speech**; (b) the description of regularities in inflection (⇒ **declension**, **conjugation**, and **comparison**); (c) the study of grammatical categories like **tense**, **mood**, and others, and their linguistic correlates; (d) in **word formation**, the study of the basic elements, combinatory principles, and semantic function of new word formations; (e) in contrastive linguistics, the development of criteria for determining typological relations between genetically related and nonrelated languages (⇒ **language typology**).

References
Andersen, H. 1980. Morphological change. In J. Fisiak (ed.), *Historical morphology*. The Hague. 1–50.
Anderson, S. 1988. Morphological theory. In F. Newmeyer (ed.), *Linguistics: the Cambridge survey*. Cambridge. Vol. 1, 146–91.
——— 1992. *A-morphous morphology*. Cambridge.
Aronoff, M. 1992. *Morphology now*. Albany, NY.
——— 1994. *Morphology by itself*. Cambridge, MA.
Bauer, L. 1988. *Introducing linguistic morphology*. Edinburgh.
Bloomfield, L. 1933. *Language*. New York.
Booij, G. and J. van Marle, (eds) 1991/3. *Yearbooks of morphology 1991–1993*, 3 vols. Dordrecht.
Bybee, J. 1985. *Morphology: a study of the relations between meaning and form*. Amsterdam.
Carstairs-McCarthy, A. 1992. *Current morphology*. London.
Dressler, W.U. *et al.* (eds) 1990. *Contemporary morphology*. Berlin and New York.
Fisiak, J. (ed.) 1980. *Historical morphology*. The Hague.
Greenberg, J. (ed.) 1978. *Universals of human language*, vol. 3: *Word structure*. Stanford, CA.
Hall, C.J. 1991. *Morphology and mind: a unified approach to explanation in linguistics*. London.
Hammond, M. and M. Noonan. 1988. *Theoretical morphology*. London.
Harris, Z.S. 1951. *Methods in structural linguistics*. Chicago, IL.
Hockett, C.F. 1954. Two models of grammatical description. *Word* 10.210–34.
Jensen, J. 1990. *Morphology: word structure in generative grammar*. Amsterdam.

Katamba, F. 1993. *Morphology*. Basingstoke.
Kilani-Schoch, M. 1988. *Introduction à la morphologie naturelle*. Paris.
Kilbury, J. 1976. *The development of morphophonemic theory*. Amsterdam.
Lieber, R. 1992. *Deconstructing morphology: word formation in syntactic theory*. Chicago, IL.
Matthews, P. 1974. *Morphology: an introduction to the theory of word-structure*. Cambridge. (2nd edn 1991.)
Mel'čuk, I. 1993. *Cours de morphologie générale*, vol. 1: *Introduction et première partie: le mot*. Montreal.
Mugdahn, J. and C. Lehmann. 1995. *Morphology: an international handbook*. Berlin and New York.
Nida, E. 1946. *Morphology: the descriptive analysis of words*. Ann Arbor, MI. (2nd edn 1949.)
Spencer, A. 1991. *Morphological theory: an introduction to word structure in generative grammar*. Oxford.
Szpyra, J. 1989. *The phonology–morphology interface*. London.

Bibliography
Beard, R. and B. Szymanek. 1988. *Bibliography of morphology 1960–1985*. Amsterdam and Philadelphia.

morphonemics ⇒ **morphophonemics**

morphophoneme (*also* alternation)

Term introduced by Trubetzkoy (1929) to denote phonological units whose different elements represent **allomorphs** of a particular **morpheme**, e.g. in English, the different variants of the plural morpheme /-s, -z, -iz, -en, -Ø/ in *cats*, *dogs*, *horses*, *oxen*, *sheep*. Morphophonemes are abstract entities that underlie different allomorphs. (⇒ *also* **morphophonemics**)

References
Trubetzkoy, N.S. 1929. Zur allgemeinen Theorie der phonologischen Vokalsysteme. *TCLP* 1.39–67.
⇒ **morphophonemics**

morphophonemics (*also* morphonemics)

Intermediary level of analysis between **phonology** and **morphology** in which the phonological regularities in the framework of morphology, especially the systematic phonological variants of **morphemes** (⇒ **allomorph**) and the conditions of their occurrence, are described (e.g. the two phonetic variations of the past tense morpheme *-ed* in *stayed* [steːd] vs *heaped* [hiːpt]; further examples under **morphophoneme**). This concept of an abstract phonological level underlying the concrete expressive form was first developed by Trubetzkoy (1929, 1931) and further developed by N. Chomsky in his **transformational grammar**, in which rules are posited that guarantee the transfer of an abstract morphophonological (deep) structure (⇒ **deep structure**) (= a systematic phonemic level) into the concrete phonetic realization of the **surface structure**. In **natural generative grammar** morphophonological variants are stored in the **lexicon**.

References
Chomsky, N. and M. Halle. 1968. *The sound pattern of English*. New York.
Gussmann, E. (ed.) 1983. *Phono-morphology: studies in the interaction of phonology and morphology*. Dublin.
Kilburn, J. 1974. The emergence of morphophonemics: a survey of theory and practice from 1876 to 1939. *Lingua* 33.235–52.
Kuryłowicz, J. 1968. The notion of morpho(pho)-neme. In W.P. Lehmann and Y. Malkiel (eds), *Directions for historical linguistics*. Austin, TX. 65–81.
Maiden, M. 1991. *Interactive morphonology: metaphony in Italy*. London.
Martinet, A. 1965. De la morphonologie. *Linguistique* 1.15–30.
Trubetzkoy, N.S. 1929. Zur allgemeinen Theorie der phonologischen Vokalsysteme. *TCLP* 1.39–67.
—— 1931. Gedanken über Morphophonologie. *TCLP* 4.160–3.

morphosyntax

Procedures of language for representing syntactic features by morphological means, i.e. through the presence of bound **morphemes**, such as flexives or clitics (⇒ **cliticization**), as opposed to using purely combinatory processes that indicate the syntactic features of a linguistic expression by its position or by its combination of free morphemes, such as prepositions or adverbs.

References
⇒ **inflection**, **morphology**

Morse code ⇒ alphabet²

Mossi ⇒ Gur

motion [Lat. *motio* 'movement']

Explicit derivations that denote female counterparts of male designations by the addition of various **suffixes**, cf. *actress*, *aviatrix*. Examples of the reverse process (e.g. *widower < widow*) are very rare. In English, the derivation of female from male forms through suffixation is generally not productive; it is, instead, being replaced by compounding (e.g. *chairwoman* vs *chairman*) or being leveled out completely (e.g. *chair*, *manager*, *mail carrier*).

References
⇒ **word formation**

motivation

A word form is motivated if its whole meaning can be ascertained from the sum of the meanings of its individual elements, e.g. *bookstore*, *garbageman*, *movie theater*. Synchronically, there are several levels of motivation: full motivation (*wine cellar*), partial motivation (*housecoat*), and complete **lexicalization** (*mincemeat*). **Nonce words** are always completely motivated because they are rule-governed.

References
⇒ **word formation**

motor aphasia ⇒ aphasia, Broca's aphasia

motor theory of speech perception

Hypothesis developed by A.M. Liberman about the connection between the divisional distinction of linguistic perception of sounds and the phonological structure of language. Liberman assumes that, on the basis of an observable feedback effect through silent repetition of the heard sound, a hearer's speech perception is directed by the articulatory processes necessary for production of the corresponding sounds.

References
Lane, H. 1965. The motor theory of speech perception: a critical review. *PsychologR* 72.275–309.
Liberman, A.M. 1967. *Intonation, perception, and language*. Cambridge, MA.
Liberman, A.M. *et al*. 1963. *A motor theory of speech perception*. Stockholm.
⇒ **psycholinguistics**

move-α

A general movement rule in newer versions of **transformational grammar** which replaces construction-specific **transformations**. In the standard theory (⇒ **aspects model**) there were specific transformations like passive transformations, question-forming transformations and **raising**; there now exists just one rule: move-α. Earlier construction-specific properties of the respective movement rules must now be the result of the interaction between the lexical properties of the category inserted into the construction on the one hand, and the general constraints on movement rules on the other hand. For example, *wh*-movement, NP-movement, and **Chomsky adjunction** are different subtypes of move-α, which are differentiated according to the landing sites of the movement. In Chomsky's **Government and Binding theory**, there is a distinction between a 'representational' and a 'derivational' interpretation of move-α. In the former, move-α is understood as a structural relationship between an antecedent and a (co-indexed) trace; in the latter, move-α is interpreted in terms of the derivational history between **deep structure** and **surface structure**.

References
Cinque, Guglielmo. 1990. *Types of A-bar Dependencies.* Cambridge, MA.
⇒ **transformational grammar**

movement transformation (*also* reordering transformation, permutation transformation)

A type of **transformation** where a **constituent** in the **tree diagram** is moved to a new position and the original constituent is deleted. (⇒ **transformational grammar**)

multidimensional opposition ⇒ **opposition**

multilingualism [Lat. *multī* 'many,' *lingua* 'tongue; language']

1 Ability of a speaker to express him-/herself in several languages with equal and native-like proficiency. In practice, proficiency in one language usually dominates. (⇒ **bilingualism**)

2 Coexistence of several languages within a politically defined society as, for example, in India, Canada, or Switzerland. Stewart (1964) designed a framework with four criteria to classify multilingual societies, namely: (a) the degree of language standardization; (b) the degree of social and linguistic autonomy; (c) the linguistic tradition; and (d) the strength of the spoken language. Through a combination of these features he arrived at a scale of possible varieties ranging from **pidgin**, **creole**, **dialect**, **vernacular** (i.e. native language), **artificial language** (i.e. **interlingua**), classical language to **standard language**. These language types and their distinctive functions (e.g. official, international, literary, familiar uses) form a basis for **language planning**. (⇒ **language contact**)

References
Alladina, S. and V. Edwards (eds). 1991. *Multilingualism in the British Isles.* 2 vols. London.
Edwards, J. 1994. *Multilingualism.* London.
Harlech-Jones, B. 1991. *You taught me language.* Oxford.
Oksaar, E. (ed.). 1987. *Soziokulturelle Perspektiven von Mehrsprachigkeit und Spracherwerb / Sociocultural perspectives of multilingualism and language acquisition.* Tübingen.
Pattanayak, D.P. 1984. Language policies in multilingual states. *PJL* 14–15:2–1.75–84.
Stewart, W. 1964. A sociolinguistic typology for describing national multilingualism. *Lg* 40.526–31.
Wolfson, N. 1989. *Multilingualism.* Hove.
⇒ **language contact, literacy, sociolinguistics**

multiple-branching construction

A type of phrase structure construction. A constituent forms a multiple-branching construction if it directly dominates similar constituents which do not relate to it in any other way. For example, in *Sam, Louis, and the neighborhood children gathered nuts*, *Sam, Louis and the neighborhood children* forms a multiply branching construction of NP constituents.

Reference
Chomsky, N. 1965. *Aspects of the theory of syntax.* Cambridge, MA.

Munda

Language group belonging to the **Austro-Asiatic** languages. The ten languages comprising this group are spoken in a few linguistic islands in India; the largest language is Santali (about 4 million speakers).

Characteristics: morphology and syntax influenced by other **Indo-Aryan** languages, prefixes, infixes, and suffixes. Word order SOV. Many lexical borrowings.

References
Bhattacharya, S. 1975. *Studies in comparative Munda linguistics.* Simla.
Hoffmann, J. and A. van Emelen, 1950. Encyclopaedia Mundarica, 13 vols. Patna.
MacPhail, R.M. 1964. *An introduction to Santali.* Benagaria.
Zide, N.H. 1978. *Studies in the Munda numerals.* Mysore.

murmuring (*also* breathy voice)

In **articulatory phonetics** a murmuring sound such as that found in **Hindi** and **Igbo**. They are notated with two subscript dots, e.g. [a̤], [d̤] (see the IPA chart, p. xix)

References
⇒ **phonetics**

musical accent ⇒ **pitch accent**

musical stress ⇒ **stress**[2]

Muskogean

Branch of the **Gulf languages** of North America containing approx. ten languages in the southeastern United States; a number of now extinct languages are possibly related as well. The most important language today is Chocktaw (about 10,000 speakers).

Characteristics: three series of pronominal affixes, which can be given different semantic roles (agent; patient or possessor of some trait; recipient); thus it is to be grouped with the **active languages**. (⇒ *also* **North and Central American languages**)

References
Haas, M. 1979. South-Eastern languages. In L. Campbell and M. Mithun (eds), *The languages of*

native America: historical and comparative assessment. Austin, TX. 299–326.

Munro, P. and L. Gordon. 1982. Syntactic relations in western Muskogean. *Lg* 58.81–115.

⇒ **North and Central American languages**.

mutation [Lat. *mutatio* 'change']

In **word formation**, **sound change** in the stem forms. A distinction is drawn between (a) vowel change by **ablaut** (*ring* : *rang*) or **umlaut** (*man* : *men*), and (b) consonant change by **grammatical alternation** (*bring* : *brought*).

mutative ⇒ **durative vs nondurative, imperfective vs perfective**

mute [Lat. *mutus* 'lacking the faculty of speech, dumb']

Umbrella term taken from Latin and Greek grammar for the tenues (*p*, *t*, *k*) and the mediae (*b*, *d*, *g*) (⇒ **tenuis vs media**). As 'silent' sounds they are differentiated from **sonants** in that they cannot form the **nucleus**[2] of syllables.

mutism

In psychiatry, term referring to the effects of a psychoneurotic disturbance which, after the onset of **language acquisition**, can lead to muteness in children and adults ('total mutism'), or to a refusal of children to speak to particular persons in particular situations ('elective mutism'). In adults, post-traumatic or traumatic mutism may be a consequence of a trauma or lesion on the brain stem.

References
⇒ **language disorder**, **neurolinguistics**.

Mycenaean ⇒ **Greek**

N

Na-Dené

Language group in North America with over twenty languages in the northwest and south of the continent; the largest language is **Navajo** (approx. 140,000 speakers). The Na-Dené languages are divided into Haida (approx. 300 speakers), Tlingit (approx. 2000 speakers), and the large Athabaskan language family (including the Navajo and Apache languages).

Characteristics: **tonal languages** (usually two tones), often with complex consonant systems; many nouns derived from verbs, distinction between active and stative verbs; rich **aspect** and voice systems, tendency towards **polysynthesis** and **descriptivity**.

References
Cook, E. and K. Rice (eds) 1988. *Athapaskan Linguistics*. Berlin.
Enrico, J. 1989. The Haida language. In G.G.E. Scudder and N. Gessler (eds), *The outer shores*. Victoria. 223–47.
Golla, V.K. 1964. An etymological study of Hupa noun stems. *IJAL* 30.108–17.
Hymes, D.H. 1956. Na-Dené and positional analysis of categories. *AA* 58.623–8.
Krauss, M.E. 1979. Na-Dené and Eskimo-Aleut. In L. Campbell and M. Mithun (eds), *The languages of native America: Historical and comparative assessment*. Austin, TX. 803–901.
Liedtke, S. 1994. Na-Dene and other language groups. *LDDS* 8.
Narsh, C.M. and G.L. Story. 1973. *Tlingit verb dictionary*. Fairbanks.
Pinnow, H.-J. 1976. *Geschichte der Na-Dené-Forschung*. Berlin.
—— 1990. *Die Na-Dené-Sprachen im Lichte der Greenberg-Klassifikation*. Nortorf.
Rice, K. 1988. *A Grammar of Slave*. Berlin.
⇒ **North and Central American languages**

Nahali ⇒ language isolate

Nahuatl

Classical Nahuatl, an **Uto-Aztecan** language, was the language of the Toltec and Aztec empires; immediately related languages are spoken today in Mexico by approx. 1.2 million speakers. Our knowledge of Classical Nahuatl comes primarily from several codices that were written with the assistance of Spanish missionaries (particularly Bernhardino de Sahagun) in the sixteenth century. In 1528 the first printed book, *Annals of Tlatelolco*, appeared in an orthography influenced by Spanish.

Characteristics: relatively simple sound system; weak noun–verb distinction; predicates used nominatively have the nominalizing suffix *-tl* and can always be used predicatively; when used non-predicatively they receive the 'article' *in-*. Strong tendency towards **incorporation** and nominal composition. Complex verb morphology (four verb classes with different paradigms).

References
Andrews, J.R. 1975. *Introduction to classical Nahuatl*. Austin, TX.
Launey, M. 1981. *Introduction à la langue et littérature aztec*. Paris.
Wohlgemuth, C. 1981. *Grammatica Nahuatl*. Mexico City.

Nakh ⇒ North-East Caucasian

Nakho-Dagestanian ⇒ North-East Caucasian

Nama ⇒ Afro-Asiatic, Khoisan

name ⇒ proper noun

narrative analysis [Lat. *narrare* 'to relate, tell']

An area of **text linguistics** which deals with the analysis and text typology of narrative texts, i.e. stories, everyday narratives, fairy tales, literary types of text. Narrative analysis finds its roots in Russian formalism (Vladimir Propp) and is developed from the narrative theory of structural literary theory (Roland Barthes, Claude Bremond), it occupies the middle ground between linguistics and literature studies nowadays. The point of departure for research is the acceptance of abstract narrative structures as the basis of the narrative text which are formed in a hierarchical fashion from narrative categories.

References
Bremond, C. 1973. *Logique de récit*. Paris.
Britton, B. K. and A.D. Pellegrini (eds) 1990. *Narrative thought and narrative language*. Hove.
Fleischman, S. 1990. *Tense and narrativity*. London.
Genot, G. 1979. *Elements of narrativics, grammar in narrative, narrative in grammar*. Hamburg.
Goffman, E. 1981. *Forms of talk*. Philadelphia, PA.
Greimas, A.-J. 1990. *Narrative semiotics and cognitive discources*. London.
Labov, W. and J. Waletzky. 1967. Narrative analysis: oral versions of personal experience. In J. Helm

(ed.), *Essays on the verbal and visual arts*, Seattle, WA. 12–44.

Prince, G. 1983. *Narratology: the form and functioning of narration*. The Hague.

Propp, V. 1928. *Morphology of the folktale*, 2nd rev. edn. by L.A. Wagner 1968. Austin.

Rumelhart, D.E. 1975. Notes on a schema for stories. In D. Bobrow *et al.* (eds), *Representation and understanding*. New York.

Thorndyke, P.W. 1977. Cognitive structures in comprehension and memory of narrative discourse. *CPsy* 9.77–110.

Toolan, M.J. 1988. *Narrative: a critical linguistic introduction*. London.

narrative structure

The specific structure of the texts of narratives, especially everyday narratives. In contrast with other kinds of texts, e.g. descriptive or argumentative texts (⇒ **argumentation**), narrative structures consist of plots and events that are ordered in a specific way according to chronology or causality. They develop from a text theme, an interesting event, with the hierarchical connection of the basic narrative categories: 'complication' (the composition of the plot), 'resolution' (the disentanglement of the complication), and 'evaluation' (the position of the narrator). Specific structural features work within the frame of a **text typology** to establish an individual kind of text like a fairy tale, novel, history. (⇒ **story grammar**, **superstructure**, **thematic development**)

References
⇒ **narrative analysis**

nasal

1 In contrast with an oral sound, a speech sound in which the **velum** is lowered, such that pulmonic air can escape either completely or partly through the nasal passage. If at the same time there is no oral closure then nasalization occurs, the resulting sounds are nasalized sounds, e.g. in French [bõ] 'good.'

2 In the narrower sense, a sound in which the velum is raised such that pulmonic air passes only through the nasal passage, e.g. [n] and [ŋ] in ['ɪŋlənd] *England*, [nayn] *nine*, [θɪŋk] *think*, [m] as in [maɪ'æmi] *Miami* (⇒ **articulatory phonetics**). (⇒ *also* **phonetics**)

References
⇒ **phonetics**

nasal harmony (*also* nasalization)

Widespread phonological regularity in which a **nasal** in a syllable-final position assumes the **place of articulation** of the following consonant in the same word: Lat. *inperfectus > *imperfectus* ('incomplete'), Eng. *ankle* ([n] > [ŋ]). Nasal harmony is a natural phonological rule (⇒ **natural phonology**) that can be explained phonetically as a process of articulatory simplification.

References
⇒ **markedness**

nasalization ⇒ **nasal harmony**

Nashī ⇒ **Arabic**

national language

In the broad sense, the full set of all regional, social, and functional, spoken and written variants of a historically and politically defined linguistic community. In the narrow sense, the **standard language** as opposed to the **literary language** (**dialect** and **sociolect** necessarily excluded) of a historically and politically defined linguistic community. In both interpretations the term is problematic, since frequently 'nation' and 'language' are not congruent for political or historical reasons. Consider, for example, the situation in multilingual countries such as the United States (⇒ **multilingualism**), or the use of 'German' to describe the language spoken in Germany, Austria, Switzerland, and Luxemburg.

References
Chiappelli, F. (ed.) 1985. *The fairest flower: the emergence of linguistic national consciousness in Renaissance Europe*. Florence.

Clyne, M. 1991. *Pluricentric languages: differing norms in different nations*. Berlin and New York.

Fishman, J.A. 1984. On the peculiar problems of smaller national languages. *PJL* 14–15:2–1.40–5.

native speaker [Lat. *nativus* 'acquired by birth, inborn']

Literally, a person who learned a language as a child. In **transformational grammar**, 'native speaker' refers to a representative **ideal speaker/listener** of a linguistic community. (⇒ *also* **competence vs performance**)

References
Davies, A. 1991. *The native speaker in applied linguistics*. Edinburgh.
⇒ **competence vs performance**, **transformational grammar**

nativism

Philosophical and psychological position which holds that cognitive development of humans arises from 'innate (= inborn) ideas.' Some linguists, such as N. Chomsky (who has continued the tradition of the rationalistic interpretations of Descartes, Humboldt, and others), have recently taken a nativist position (⇒ **mentalism**). **Empiricism** presents an opposing view, namely that the psychological development of humans arises primarily from experience and learning.

References
⇒ **mentalism**

natural approach

Approach to language instruction developed by T. Terrell (with S.D. Krashen), and based on Krashen's **second language acquisition** theory. Krashen offers five interrelated hypotheses regarding language acquisition: (1) 'Acquisition/learning hypothesis', where two types of linguistic knowledge can be distinguished: 'acquired' and 'learned.' Acquired knowledge is used unconsciously and automatically in language comprehension and production, learned knowledge is used in careful speech or 'edited' writing. (2) 'Monitor hypothesis': every language learner has a built-in 'monitor' (⇒ **monitor model**) which is used to 'edit' one's speech or writing. (3) 'Input hypothesis': acquisition occurs only when the language learner comprehends natural language. Input, if it is to be acquired, must be comprehensible. (4) 'Natural order hypothesis': morphology and syntax are acquired according to a 'natural,' predictable order. (5) 'Affective filter hypothesis': language acquisition occurs only in nonthreatening environments. When a language learner is placed in a stressful or otherwise unfavorable learning environment, an 'affective filter' is raised, which prevents the learner from acquiring language. Drawing on these five hypotheses, Terrell developed six guiding principles for the natural approach: (1) comprehension is an essential precondition to production; (2) speech emerges in stages; (3) the emergence of speech is characterized by grammatical errors; (4) speech is promoted when language learners work in pairs or in groups; (5) language is only acquired in a low-anxiety environment; (6) the goal of language learning is proficiency in communication skills. Krashen's later studies increasingly acknowledge the importance of explicit grammar explanation and emphasize reading as a strategy for vocabulary acquisition. The natural approach has become a well-established approach in foreign-language instruction. (⇒ *also* **language pedagogy**, **second language acquisition**)

References

Brown, J.M. and A.S. Palmer. 1988. *The listening approach: methods and materials for applying Krashen's input hypothesis*. New York.

Krashen, S.D. 1982. *Principles and practice in second language acquisition*. New York.

——— 1985. *The input hypothesis: issues and implications*. London.

Krashen, S.D. and T. Terrell. 1983. *The natural approach: language acquisition in the classroom*. Oxford.

Richards, J.C. and T.S. Rodgers. 1986. *Approaches and methods in language teaching*. Cambridge.

Terrell, T.D. 1977. A natural approach to second language acquisition and learning. *MLJ* 61.325–36.

natural class

Set of sounds (**phones**) for which it is the case that fewer **features** are required to describe the class as a whole than to describe any given member of the class, e.g. [p, b, m] form the class of bilabial consonants in English.

natural generative grammar

General language theory developed by R. Bartsch and T. Vennemann (1972) on the basis of **categorial grammar**. The following theoretical principles, most of which resulted from objections to generative **transformational grammar**, underlie natural generative grammar. (a) The objective of description is not the unconscious linguistic knowledge of a competent speaker, but rather the grammatical process through which semantic, syntactic, and phonological representations are related to each other (⇒ **semantics**, **syntax**, **phonology**). The empirical verifiability and justification of the hypothesis is guaranteed by the observation of regularities in language acquisition, use, and change. (b) The syntax is formulated categorically on the basis of **predicate logic**, expanded to include intensional predicates and pragmatic sentence operators (⇒ **logical connective**). In this way, syntactic structures are not represented through a coincidental coexistence of constituents, but rather through logical relations of operator-operand, which can be directly interpreted semantically. (c) This modified categorial grammar is also the basis for the development of a universal word order syntax which follows the principle of natural serialization (⇒ **word order**). This principle states that all languages of the world exhibit either operator–operand or operand–operator ordering or at least tend to develop in one or the other direction. (d) A distinction is made between a word-based semantics built on **meaning postulates**, and a sentence-based semantics, homomorphic with the syntax; the logical semantic representation is in keeping with the cognitive (and therefore universal) structures which are the foundation of human perception, recognition, classification, speech, and understanding. (e) In contrast to transformational grammar, a strict distinction is made between **morphology** and phonology; the phonological description is built on phonetically plausible and universally valid rules, e.g. **nasal harmony** (⇒ *also* **mark-edness**, **natural phonology**). (f) Natural generative grammar encompasses not only synchronic linguistic theory, but also a complementary diachronic theory (⇒ **synchrony vs diachrony**), the so-called 'theory of language change,' whose universal and prognostic characteristics are made especially valid in the areas of word order and **sound change**. (g) The 'strong naturalness condition' states that all phonological representations are realized through phonological **features** in the **surface form**; that the logical operator–operand relations, which are the basis for semantic representations, correlate with essential human cognitive (linguistic) capabilities; and that no semantically uninterpretable medial steps are allowed in syntactic derivations.

References
Bartsch, R. and T. Vennemann. 1972. *Semantic structures: a study in the relation between semantics and syntax*. Frankfurt.
Hooper, J.B. 1976. *An introduction to natural generative phonology*. New York.
Rudes, B.A. 1976. Lexical representation and variable rules in natural generative phonology. *Glossa* 10.111–50.
Vennemann, T. 1974. Words and syllables in natural generative grammar. In A. Buck *et al.* (eds), *Papers from the parasession on natural phonology 1974*. Chicago, IL. 346–74.

natural language

Term for languages which have developed historically and which are regionally and socially stratified, as opposed to **artificial language** systems, which are used for international communication (⇒ **planned language**) or for formulating complex scientific statements. (⇒ **computational linguistics**) Natural languages differ from artificial languages particularly in their lexical and structural polysemy, the potential ambiguity of their expressions, and in their susceptibility to change through time.

natural method ⇒ **direct method**

natural order hypothesis ⇒ **natural approach**

natural phonology

Model developed in particular by D. Stampe and W.U. Dressler as a critical alternative to generative **phonology**. The basic units of natural phonology are not **phonemes** or **distinctive features**, but rather 'natural' phonological processes such as final devoicing, nasalization (⇒ **nasal harmony**), and **labialization**. According to the natural phonological viewpoint, such (potentially universally valid) processes are not

part of language acquisition *per se*, but rather are an integral part of the human capacity for language. The acquisition of a phonological system takes place through suppression and limitation of cumbersome articulatory and perceptive processes; in this way, final devoicing has been eliminated from English in the course of language acquisition. Natural phonological processes are irreversible, thus there is no such thing as 'denasalization' or 'final voicing.' (⇒ *also* **distinctive feature theory**, **markedness**)

References
Dogil, G. 1981. Elementary accent systems. In W.U. Dressler *et al.* (eds), *Phonologica*. Innsbruck.
Donegan, P. and D. Stampe. 1979. The study of natural phonology. In D. Dinnsen (ed.), *Current approaches to phonological theory*. Bloomington, IN. 126–73.
Dressler, W.U. 1984. Explaining natural phonology. *PY* 1.29–53.
——— 1985. *Morphonology: the dynamics of derivation*. Ann Arbor, MI.
Hurch, B. and R. Rhodes (eds) 1995. *Natural phonology: the state of the art*. Berlin.

natural serialization ⇒ **word order**

Navaho ⇒ **Navajo**

Navajo (*also* Navaho)

Na-Dené language from the Athabaskan family, belonging to the Apache languages, with approx. 140,000 speakers, esp. in Arizona.
Characteristics: **tonal language** (high and low tone) with complex consonant system. The verbs are morphologically complex (subject agreement, marking of aspect, mood, evidentiality, etc.); many **portmanteau morphemes** and **suppletive** formations. The numeral system is complex, with a dual, and plural forms marked on the verb that express repeated events or difference of the participants. Like many other Apache languages, Navajo possesses **classifying verbs** as well as a **switch reference** system (differentiation between **proximate vs obviative** personal pronouns.

References
Young, R.W. and W. Morgan. 1987. *The Navajo language. A grammar and colloquial dictionary*. 2nd edn. Albuquerque, NM. (Repr. 1991).
⇒ **Na-Dene**, **North and Central American languages**

necessitation ⇒ **allegation**

negation [Lat. *negare* 'to say that … not, deny']

1 In **formal logic**, logical particles – defined as one-place predicates by the **truth tables** – that convert the **truth value** of a proposition p into its opposite truth value (notation: $\neg p$ or $\sim p$);

that is, $\neg p$ is true if and only if p is false and vice versa. *Tokyo is the capital of Japan* is true if and only if *Tokyo is not the capital of Japan* is false. The term 'negation' refers both to the one-place sentence operator *it is not the case that* or *not* as well as to the proposition defined thereby. The following (two-value) truth table represents a definition of negation:

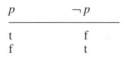

Since logical negation is basically sentence negation, the clearest everyday paraphrase for it is *it is not the case that p* ($\Rightarrow$ **presupposition test** for negation as a criterion for defining **presuppositions**).

2 In contrast with logical negation, natural language negation functions not only as sentence negation, but also primarily as clausal or constituent negation: *She did not pay* (= negation of **predication**), *No one paid anything* (= negation of the subject NP), *He paid nothing* (= negation of the object NP). Here the **scope** (= semantic coverage) of negation is frequently polysemic or dependent on the placement of negation, on the sentence stress ($\Rightarrow$ **stress, prosody**) as well as on the linguistic and/or extralinguistic context. Natural language negation may be realized in various ways: (a) lexically with adverbs and adverbial expressions (*not, never, by no means*), indefinite pronouns (*nobody, nothing, none*), co-ordinating conjunctions (*neither ... nor*), sentence equivalents (*no*), or prepositions (*without, besides*); (b) morphologically with prefixes (*in + exact, un + interested*) or suffixes (*help + less*); (c) intonationally with contrastive accent (in *Jacob is not flying to New York tomorrow* the negation can refer to *Jacob, flying, New York*, or *tomorrow* depending which elements are stressed); (d) idiomatically by expressions like *For all I care, ...* Formally, three types of negation are differentiated: (a) internal (= strong) negation, the basic type of natural language negation (e.g. *The King of France is not bald*); (b) external (= weak) negation, which corresponds to logical negation (e.g. *It's not the case / it's not true that p*); (c) contrastive (= local) negation, which can also be considered a pragmatic variant of strong negation to the degree that stress and the corresponding modifying clause are relevant to the scope of the negation (e.g. *The King of France is not bald, but rather wears glasses*). The linguistic description of negation has proven to be a difficult problem in all grammatical models

owing to the complex interrelationship of syntactic, prosodic, semantic, and pragmatic aspects.

References
Dahl, Ö. 1993. Negation. In J. Jacobs *et al.* (eds), *Syntax: an international handbook of contemporary research*. 914–22. Berlin and New York.
Gazdar, G. 1979. *Pragmatics*. New York.
Haegeman, L. 1995. *The syntax of negation*. Cambridge.
Horn, L.R. 1989. *A natural history of negation*. Chicago, IL.
Jackendoff, R.S. 1969. An interpretative theory of negation. *FoLi* 5.218–41.
——— 1972. *Semantic interpretation in generative grammar*. New York.
Kahrel, P. and R. van den Berg (eds) 1994. *Typological studies in negation*. Amsterdam and Philadelphia, PA.
Klima, E.S. 1964. Negation in English. In J.A. Fodor and J.J. Katz (eds), *The structure of language*. Englewood Cliffs, NJ. 246–323.
Sgall, P. *et al.* 1973. *Topic, focus and generative semantics*. Kronberg.
Stockwell, R.P., R. Schachter, and H. Partee. 1968. *Integration of transformational theories on English syntax*, 2 vols. Los Angeles, CA.
Tottie, G. 1991. *Negation in English speech and writing: a study in variation*. New York.
Welte, W. 1978. *Negationslinguistik: Ansätze zur Beschreibung und Erklärung von Aspekten der Negation im Englischen*. Munich.

Bibliography
Seifert, S. and W. Welte. 1987. *A basic bibliography on negation in natural language*. Tübingen.

3 In **unification grammar**, the logical complement of a **feature structure**.

negative transfer $\Rightarrow$ **interference**

negative transportation

Syntactic process in a certain class of verbs with complement clauses (*to think, to believe, to expect*) in which the **negation** of the **matrix sentence** can also be interpreted as the negation of the complement clause: the sentence *Philip doesn't think that Caroline is home* can be read two ways: (a) *Philip doesn't think: Caroline is home*; and (b) *Philip thinks: Caroline isn't home*; i.e. in (b) the negation is 'transported' out of the matrix sentence into the complement clause.

Nenets $\Rightarrow$ **Uralic**

Neogrammarians (*also* Junggrammatiker, Leipzig School)

A group of linguists in Leipzig in the 1870s whose positivistic view of language was aimed against the metaphysical and biological views of the previous epoch. Leading representatives of this approach included K. Brugmann, H. Osthoff, B. Delbrück, E. Sievers, K. Verner, A. Leskien, H. Paul, O. Behaghel. The name, used derogatorily by the older generation, stems from F. Zarncke and is first attested in Osthoff and Brugmann (1878). The beginning of the Neogrammarian school is considered to be the publication dates of K. Verner's 1877 explanation of apparent exceptions to **Grimm's Law**, A. Leskien's 1876 investigations of declension, in which the postulate of the inviolability of **sound laws** is formulated, and above all H. Paul's *Prinzipien der Sprachgeschichte* ('Principles of the history of language'), published in 1880.

The works of the Neogrammarians, inasmuch as they pertain to general linguistics, can be characterized by the following aspects. (a) The object of linguistic investigation is not the language system, but rather the language as it is localized in the individual, and therefore is directly observable ($\Rightarrow$ **idiolect**). This is seen as a psychological as well as a physical activity. (b) Autonomy of the sound level: according to the postulate of observability of the material (instead of abstractions), the sound level is seen as the most important level of description, and absolute autonomy of the sound level from **syntax** and **semantics** is assumed. (c) Historicism: the chief goal of linguistic investigation is the description of the historical change of a language. This almost exclusive interest in the diachronic development of language ($\Rightarrow$ **synchrony vs diachrony**) is documented in the large number of comparative historical compendia (cf. Leskien, Osthoff and Brugmann, and others), which excel in their wealth of facts as well as in the exactness of their methods of reconstruction. (d) Inviolability of sound laws: this much-debated postulate, patterned after the natural sciences, is not based on empirical findings, but rather is an *a priori* assumption, made to ensure the uniformity of the investigatory methods of linguistics and the natural sciences. (e) **Analogy**: wherever the premise of the inviolability of sound laws fails, analogy is applied as an explanation, i.e. exceptions are understood to be a (regular) adaptation to a related form.

Despite their strong repercussions, the methods and goals of the Neogrammarian view of language have been criticized from various quarters and with various emphases. Such criticism has been aimed especially at the following: reduction of the object of investigation to the idiolect; restriction to the description of surface phenomena (sound level); overvaluation of historical languages and neglect of contemporary ones; description of individual processes instead of systemic connections.

References
Jankowsky, K.R. 1972. *The Neogrammarians: a re-evaluation of their place in the development of linguistic science.* The Hague.
——— 1990. The neogrammarian hypothesis. In E.C. Polomé (ed.), *Research guide on language change.* Berlin. 223–39.
Leskien, A. 1876. *Die Deklination im Slavisch-Litauischen und Germanischen.* Leipzig.
Osthoff, H. and K. Brugmann. 1878. *Morphologische Untersuchungen auf dem Gebiet der indogermanischen Sprachen,* part 1. Leipzig.
Paul, H. 1880. *Prinzipien der Sprachgeschichte.* Tübingen. (9th edn 1975.)
Steinthal, H. 1890–1. *Geschichte der Sprachwissenschaft bei den Griechen und Römern mit besonderer Rücksicht auf die Logik,* 2 vols. Berlin. (Repr. Hildesheim, 1961.)
Vennemann, T. and T.H. Wilbur (eds) 1972. *Schuchardt, the Neogrammarians, and the transformational theory of phonological change.* Frankfurt.
Verner, K. 1877. Eine Ausnahme der ersten Lautverschiebung. *ZVS* 23.97–130.
Wilbur, T.H. (ed.) 1977. *The Lautgesetz-controversy: a documentation.* Amsterdam and Philadelphia, PA.
$\Rightarrow$ **linguistics, sound law**

neo-Humboldtianism $\Rightarrow$ **ethnolinguistics**

neologism [Grk *néos* 'new,' *lógos* 'expression']

1 Newly formed linguistic expression (word or phrase) that is recognized by at least part if not all of a language community as the way to denote a new object or state of affairs, be it in technology, industry, politics, culture, or science. Formally, a distinction is drawn between (a) the formation of new expressions on the basis of already available morphological means and word formation rules (e.g. *user-friendly, data bank, decriminalize*), (b) semantic transfer (e.g. *computer virus*), (c) loans from other languages (*sauté, mesa*); these three sources cannot always be separated exactly (cf. *academic milieu*); and (d) expressions with a constituent used metaphorically (e.g. *child's play*). ($\Rightarrow$ *also* **word formation**)

References
Algeo. J. (ed.). 1993. *Fifty years among the new words. A dictionary of neologisms, 1941–1991.* Cambridge.
Green, J. 1991. *Neologisms: new words since 1960.* London.
Special issue on 'neologisms.' 1974. *Langue* 8.36.

2 In **neurolinguistics**, term referring to new content words that have been fabricated by an individual according to language-specific phonotactic rules, but do not belong to the lexicon.

Their relationship to actual or intended words is often unclear (e.g. *spork*), though some new forms may be transparent (e.g. *picture box* for 'television set'). Neologisms are observed in aphasics (especially those with **Wernicke's aphasia**) as well as in children with **specific language impairments**. (⇒ *also* **paraphasia**)

neologistic paraphasia ⇒ **neologism²**, **paraphasia**

Neo-South Arabic ⇒ **Semitic**

Nepali ⇒ **Indo-Aryan**

nesting

In the semantic theory of U. Weinreich, a construction consisting of two constituents whose semantic features, when taken together, do not result in a **cluster** (i.e. a subset). If *to write* has the features [*a, b*] and *letter* the features [*c, d*], then the phrase *to write a letter* is a 'nesting' construction. Presumably, nesting allows for more convincing derivations of sentence meaning. (⇒ *also* **interpretive semantics**)

Reference
Weinreich, U. 1966. Explorations in semantic theory. In T.A. Sebeok (ed.), *Current trends in linguistics*. The Hague. Vol. 3, 395–477.

network

Term developed by Radcliffe-Brown (1940) which, in contrast to the structural-functionalistic terms 'class,' 'social group,' etc., places social interaction in the center. Every person has a set of relational partners with whom he/she participates in interactional exchanges; if one considers all persons to be 'points' and the social relations that are realized between them to be 'lines,' an individual 'network' develops. All persons involved in such a network are in turn likewise embedded in social networks, which may in part mutually overlap. The whole set of all social transactions within a speech community can be construed to be a complex network of individual social relations, in which individual social groups are characterized each by specific network structures. The more members of an individual network are involved in relations outside the larger network, the more 'tightly woven' the networks become. Furthermore, networks become all the more 'multiplex' as more and more diverse relations are based within the individual networks (e.g. when co-workers, who also happen to be friends, meet regularly for outside activities or live in the same neighborhood).

In such networks social cohesion develops and culture- and group-specific systems of values, shared knowledge, shared attitudes, as well as patterns of behavior are established, which in turn manifest themselves linguistically. This concept is therefore of central importance for empirical studies of linguistic behavior and for studies of the processes of linguistic change: precisely those interactional relations that are responsible for (group-specific) conformity in behavior (though which do not necessarily correlate with a particular special class or ethnic group) are used as a starting point to determine group divisions. (⇒ *also* **sociolinguistics**)

References
Boissevain, J. 1974. *Friends of friends: networks, manipulators, and coalitions*. London.
—— 1987. Social network. In U. Ammon *et al.* (eds), *Soziolinguistik/Sociolinguistics: an international handbook of the science of language and society*. Berlin. 164–9.
Milroy, L. 1980. *Language and social networks*. Oxford.
Radcliffe-Brown, A.R. 1940. On social structure. *Journal of the Royal Anthropological Institute*. 70.1–12.

neurolinguistics

Interdisciplinary field concerned with the study of language processing and representation of language in the brain. Closely allied with **psycholinguistics**, **cognitive linguistics**, and a subdiscipline of **neuropsychology**, neurolinguistics studies disturbances in language comprehension and/or production associated with known central nervous system pathologies (⇒ **articulation disorder**, **developmental language disorder**, **language disorder**, **aphasia**) or designs experiments, such as those involving dichotic listening, to test various processing models. Electrophysiological data, imaging, and 'on-line' measurement of memory phenomena are increasingly useful to research in this field.

References
Arbib, M., D. Caplan, and J. Marshall (eds) 1982. *Neural models of language processes*. New York.
Bouton, C.P. 1991. *Neurolinguistics: historical and theoretical perspectives*. New York.
Caplan, D. 1987. *Neurolinguistics and linguistic aphasiology*. Cambridge.
Hecaen, H. and J. Dubois. 1969. *La naissance de la neuropsychologie du langage: 1825–1865*. Paris.
Lenneberg, E. 1967. *Biological foundations of language*. New York.
Lenneberg, E.H. and E. Lenneberg. 1975. *Foundation of language development: a multidisciplinary approach*, 2 vols. New York.
Luria, A. 1976. *Basic problems of neurolinguistics*. The Hague.
⇒ **neuropsychology**

neuropsychology

Interdisciplinary field encompassing psychology, linguistics, neurology, and others, in which the relationships between the functions of the central nervous system and psychological processes are studied. Neuropsychology subsumes the problems and methods of **neurolinguistics**, but with a greater clinical interest and an effort to describe language functions in the broader context of other psychological processes.

References
Caramazza, A. (ed.) 1990. *Cognitive neuropsychology and neurolinguistics*. Hove.
———— 1991. *Issues in reading, writing and speaking: a neuropsychological perspective*. Dordrecht.
Coltheart, M. *et al.* (eds) 1987. *The cognitive neuropsychology of language*. Hove.
Eccles, J. 1973. *The understanding of the brain*. New York.
Hecaen, H. and M. Albert. 1978. *Human neuropsychology*. New York.
Weigl, E. and M. Bierwisch. 1970. Neuropsychology and linguistics. *FL* 6.1–18.

neuter [Lat. *neuter* 'neither one nor the other']
⇒ **gender**

neutral vowel ⇒ schwa

neutralization

Prague School term for suspension of a phonological **opposition** in particular positions. In English, the opposition of short and long vowels is neutralized in word-final position under stress, long vowels being the realizations of the corresponding **archiphonemes**. Thus there are no [ti], [rɔ] and [sju], but only [tiː], [rɔː] and [sjuː], respectively.

References
Akamatsu, T. 1988. *The theory of neutralization and the archiphoneme in functional phonology*. Amsterdam.
Davidsen-Nielsen, N. 1978. *Neutralization and archiphoneme: two phonological concepts and their history*. Copenhagen.
⇒ **phonology**

neutralized opposition ⇒ opposition

nexus [Lat. *nexus* 'binding together; bond']

Syntactic type of predicative joining in Jespersen's (1937) theory (e.g. *The book is expensive*) which Jespersen distinguishes from **junction**, which is attributive. The fact that nexus constructions can be turned into junctions corresponds to the transformational relationships between both types: *the expensive book - The book is expensive*.

Reference
Jespersen, O.P. 1937. *Analytic syntax*. Copenhagen.

Niger-Congo

Large language family of the **Niger-Kordofanian** group postulated in 1927 by D. Westermann and in 1949–54 by J.H. Greenberg, already recognized in 1854 by S. Koelle. Divided into six branches: **West Atlantic**, **Mande**, **Gur**, **Kwa**, **Benue-Congo**, and **Adamawa-Ubangi**; Kwa and Benue-Congo are today grouped into one branch, Benue-Kwa.

Characteristics: almost all are **tonal languages**. **Noun class** systems are common.

References
Bendor-Samuel, J.T. 1971. Niger-Congo, Gur. In T.A. Sebeok (ed.), *Current trends in linguistics*. The Hague. Vol. 7, 141–78.
Greenberg, J.H. 1966. *The languages of Africa*. Bloomington, IN. (2nd edn 1966.)
Ladefoged, P. 1968. *A phonetic study of West African languages*. Cambridge.
Welmers, W.E. 1971. Niger-Congo, Mande. In T.A. Sebeok (ed.), *Current trends in linguistics*. The Hague. Vol. 7, 113–40.
———— 1973. *African language structures*. Berkeley, CA.
⇒ **African languages**

Niger-Kordofanian

Language group in Africa with several hundred languages and approx. 300 million speakers, first postulated by Greenberg (1963). The group is divided into two families, **Niger-Congo** and the much smaller **Kordofanian**. It is possible that the **Mande** languages, grouped with the Niger-Congo languages, and the Kadugli languages, grouped with Kordofanian, are separate branches. An important similarity between them is the fact that **noun class** systems are widely found among them.

References
Bendor-Samuel, J. (ed.) 1988. *The Niger-Kordofanian-Congo language family*. Berlin.
Bennett, P.R. and J.P. Sterk. 1977. South-Central Niger-Congo: a reclassification. *Studies in African Linguistics* 8.241–73.
Greenberg, J.H. 1963. *The languages of Africa*. Bloomington, IN. (2nd edn 1966.)
Schadeberg, T.C. 1981. *A survey of Kordofanian*, 2 vols. Hamburg.
Wolff, P.P. de *et al.* 1981. Niger-Kordofanisch. In B. Heine *et al.* (eds), *Die Sprachen Afrikas*. Hamburg. Vol. I, 45–128.
⇒ **African languages**

Nilo-Saharan

Language group postulated by Greenberg (1963) with numerous languages in central Africa, often widely spread geographically. Convincing evidence for the relatedness of these languages is still lacking. The following groups are considered to be branches of this group: **Songhai**, **Saharan**, Maban (four languages in Chad), Koman (six languages in Ethiopia and Sudan), Fur (a relatively isolated language in Sudan), and the large group of **Chari-Nile languages**.

References
Bender, M.L. (ed.) 1983. *Nilo-Saharan language studies*. East Lansing, MI.
—— 1989. *Topics in Nilo-Saharan linguistics*. Hamburg.
Greenberg, J.H. 1963. *The languages of Africa*. Bloomington, IN. (2nd edn 1966.)
Schadeberg, T. 1981. Nilosaharanisch. In B. Heine *et al.* (eds), *Die Sprachen Afrikas*. Hamburg. vol. II, 263–328.

Individual languages
Creider, C.A. and J.A. Creider 1989. *A grammar of Nandi*. Hamburg.
Jakobi, A. 1990. *A Fur grammar: phonology, morphophonology and morphology*. Hamburg.
Vossen, R. 1987. *Towards a comparative study of the Maa dialects of Kenya and Tanzania*, trans. M. Frank. Hamburg.
Werner, R. 1987. *Grammatik des Nobiin (Nilnubisch)*. Hamburg.
⇒ **African languages**

Nilotic ⇒ **Chari-Nile languages**

Nivkh ⇒ **Paleo-Siberian**

node [Lat. *nodus* 'knot']

Nodes are those points in a **tree diagram** where there is branching, or the end points, which can be marked by S, NP, VP, N, etc.

noeme [Grk *nóēma* 'thought']

In the framework of Bloomfield's classification of linguistic expressions according to lexical and grammatical basic elements, the noeme is the 'meaning' of a **glosseme** (= smallest meaning-bearing unit).

Reference
Bloomfield, L. 1933. *Language*. New York.

nomen acti [Lat. *nomen* 'name,' *actuna* 'done']

Term for deverbal nouns that denote the result of the action denoted by the verb: *establishment*, *examination*. (⇒ *also* **deverbative**)

References
⇒ **word formation**

nomen actionis [Lat. *actio* 'action, deed']

Term for nouns derived (mostly from verbs) that refer to actions or processes. They are formed through both implicit and explicit **derivation**: *slap*, *presentation*.

References
⇒ **word formation**

nomen agentis [Lat. *agens* 'acting']

Term for nouns (usually derived from verbs) that refer to the performer of the action they describe. The most frequent type in modern English is formed with the agentive suffix *-er*: *dancer*, *player*.

References
⇒ **word formation**

nomen appellativum ⇒ **common noun**

nomen proprium ⇒ **proper noun**

nominal ⇒ **noun phrase**

nominal aphasia ⇒ **aphasia**

nominal construction ⇒ **functional verb structure**

nominal definition ⇒ **definition**

nominal sentence

Sentence composed solely of **nouns**. Nominal sentences are a special case of **ellipsis**, e.g. *Life, a dream*.

nominal style

Frequent use of derived nouns instead of verbs, depending on the reforming and reduction of sentences to groups of nouns. Characteristic **elements of style** are **nominalization**, e.g. *the breakdown of talks* instead of *talks break down*, **compounds**, relational adjective, e.g. *parental agreement* instead of *the parents agree*.

References
Burke, K.A. 1945. *A grammar of motives*. Berkeley, CA.
Sappan, R. 1987. *The rhetorical–logical classification of semantic changes*. Braunton.
Ullmann, S. 1962. *Semantics: an introduction to the science of meaning*. Oxford.
⇒ **stylistics**

nominalization

1 Broadly speaking, every derivation of nouns from another word class, e.g. from verbs (*feeling* vs *feel*) or adjectives (*redness* vs *red*), but also from another noun (*womanhood* vs *woman*).

2 Productive process of **word formation** through which words of all word classes can be used as nouns. In contrast to **conversion**[2] (*hit* < (*to hit*), **lexicalization** is not an underlying phenomenon of nominalization. Normally, nominalization concerns adjectives (including participles) that appear as abstract concepts (*the inconceivable*), or as nouns denoting persons

(*one's contemporaries*; *the good, the bad, the ugly*; *those initiated*), where the resulting word keeps its attributive adjectival function. Also verbs and verb phrases frequently appear as gerunds in nominal phrases: *swearing, twiddling one's thumbs*. Virtually any word can be nominalized: conjunctions (*no ifs, ands, or buts*) adverbs (*the here and now*), particles (*a resounding no*), or parts of words (*an ism*).

References
Koptjevskaja-Tamm, M. 1993. *Nominalizations*. London.
Olsen, S. 1988. Das substantivierte Adjektiv im Deutschen und Englischen. *FoLi* 22.337–72.
Zucchi, A. 1993. *The language of propositions and events: issues in the syntax and the semantics of nominalization*. Dordrecht.

3 ⇒ **lexicalist vs transformationalist hypothesis**

nominative [Lat. *nominare* 'to name'] (*also* casus rectus)

Morphological **case** in nominative languages which as casus rectus usually has a zero form and marks the **subject** of the sentence. The nominative can also occur in predicative nouns (*He is a teacher*) or outside the sentence frame (*Kids, please quiet down*). For objects in the nominative, see Timberlake (1974).

References
Timberlake, A. 1974. *The nominative object in Slavic, Baltic and West Finnic*. Munich.
Zubin, D.A. 1982. A quantitative study of the meaning of the nominative in German. In W. Abraham (ed.), *Satzglieder im Deutschen*. Tübingen. 245–60.
⇒ **case**, **subject**

nominative language (*also* accusative language)

Language type in the framework of **relational typology** (vs **active** and **ergative**) to which all European languages, except Basque and the Caucasian languages, belong. Assuming that in simple transitive and intransitive sentences the **thematic relations** of **agent** and **patient** are the most basic, one can define a nominative language as follows: the unmarked **case** of these languages, the **nominative**, expresses in general both the sole argument of intransitive verbs and the agent of transitive verbs. The **accusative** serves to indicate the patient of transitive verbs. This situation can be illustrated as follows:

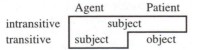

	Agent	Patient
intransitive	subject	
transitive	subject	object

(⇒ *also* **ergative language**)

References
⇒ **ergative language**, **relational typology**

nonce word

Spontaneous **coining** of usually strongly context-bound new formations to designate new or until now unknown objects or states of affairs or to express the specific attitude of a speaker towards the referent. Nonce words arise through the creative application of word formation rules to lexical elements. They have various text-specific functions, for example, economizing on the number of words needed to describe a concept (*antidisestablishmentarianism*), filling in conceptual/lexical gaps (*space walk*), or creating stylistic effects, such as those employed by Lewis Carroll (*Jabberwocky*). As a rule, the statistical frequency of such formations being used again determines whether they will make the transition from the creation of a one-time **neologism** to a lexicalized word codified in a dictionary. In psycholinguistics, nonce words are often used in elicitation tasks, e.g. in **language acquisition**, to examine the mastery of grammatical rules by children. The most famous study is about inflectional rules in young children by Berko (1958).

References
Berko, J. 1958. The child's learning of English morphology. *Word* 14.150–77.
⇒ **neologism**

nondistributive reading ⇒ distributive vs nondistributive reading

non-finite construction [Lat. *finitus* 'bounded, limited']

Comprehensive term for syntactic structures with sentential **non-finite verb form** as their **head**.

non-finite verb form

Unconjugated verb form, i.e. verb form not specified in respect to **person**, **number**, **tense**, **mood**, and **voice**, which shows an affinity to nominals and adjectives, e.g. *solving a problem, a solved problem*. In **Latin**, the gerund (e.g. *genus dicendi* 'the way of talking'), **gerundive** (e.g. Lat. *librum scribendum est* 'the book must be written'), and **supine** (e.g. *hoc est incredibile dictu* 'that sounds incredible') are considered to be non-finite, in addition to the usual **infinitive**, present **participle** and past participle. (⇒ *also* **finite verb form**) non-fluent aphasia ⇒ aphasia, Broca's aphasia

non-headed construction ⇒ exocentric construction

non-kernel sentences

In earlier versions of **transformational grammar**, sentences generated from **kernel sentences** by transformations.

References
⇒ **transformational grammar**

non-lexicalized compound

1 In general, newly formed **compounds** that arise from phrases: *forget-me-not, pain-in-the-neck, car-of-the-month competition*. The boundary with **composition** is continuous.

2 Multi-elemental words that can be analyzed as preposition + noun (*instead*), adverb + preposition (*upon*), and the like.

non-linear phonology

Umbrella term for the different hypotheses of modern generative **phonology** that have broken with the strictly linear ordering of segments. **Autosegmental phonology**, **metrical phonology**, and **dependency phonology** are founded on three such hypotheses.

References
Durand, J. 1986. *Dependency and non-linear phonology*. London.
───── 1990. *Generative and non-linear phonology*. London.
Van der Hulst, H. and N. Smith. 1982. *The structure of phonological representations*. Dordrecht.
───── 1985. *Advances in non-linear phonology*. Dordrecht.

non-monotonic logic (*also* non-monotonic reasoning)

Classical logics are all monotonic, which is to say adding to a set of axioms adds to (or at least retains), the set of theorems. New axioms cannot invalidate old theorems. Natural reasoning (⇒ **commonsense reasoning**), in contrast, is non-monotonic: new knowledge can invalidate conclusions drawn beforehand. A significant problem arises in non-monotonic logic since the body of knowledge needs constant revision in order to stay free of contradictions; the discovery and elimination of such contradictions is effected in truth-maintenance systems. (⇒ *also* **default reasoning**)

References
Bobrow, D. 1980. *AI* 13. Special issue on non-monotonic logic. Cambridge, MA.
Ginsberg, M. 1987. *Readings in nonmonotonic reasoning*. Los Altos, CA.

Reinfrank, M. *et al.*, eds. 1989. *Nonmonotonic reasoning*. Berlin.

non-monotonic reasoning ⇒ non-monotonic logic

non-strident ⇒ strident vs non-strident

non-terminative ⇒ telic vs atelic

non-verbal communication [Lat. *verbum* 'word']

All non-linguistic phenomena in inter-human communication processes which are studied in psychology (or psychiatry), sociology, ethnology, and linguistics (to the extent that spoken language can only be fully understood and described by considering non-linguistic communication). Two distinctions are made in the signals of non-verbal communication: (a) vocal features such as the volume and pitch of the human voice, the rhythm of speech, laughing, coughing, etc., the study of which is collectively called **paralinguistics** (occasionally, 'paralinguistics' is used to refer to all types of non-verbal communication); (b) non-vocal (motor) phenomena such as mimicry, gestures, body language, eye contact, external appearance, and clothing, the study of which is also collectively known as **kinesics**. Structurally determined and freely variable components, which may overlie linguistic communication (such as intonation and speech tempo) or occur independently of it, are found together in both domains. Fundamental to the description of non-verbal communication is the question of the 'character of the code,' that is, the systematic nature of non-verbal communication which suggests a distinction between intentionally directed non-verbal communication and unconscious, independent behavior having no communicative intention. In analogy to the structural characteristics of verbal codes, Trager (1958) and Birdwhistell (1954) interpret vocal, gesticulatory, and mimic phenomena as communicative systems, while various functional approaches (above all those of Ekman and Friesen 1969 and Scherer (1978) try to describe the purpose and effect of non-verbal communication within the scope of all types of communication and to describe their mutual conditions and dependencies. Scherer (1978) distinguishes between four 'parasemantic' functions of non-verbal communication: (a) in 'substitution,' the non-verbal signal replaces the verbal semantic content, e.g. nodding one's head in agreement instead of saying *yes*; (b) in 'amplification,' non-verbal communication serves to make the verbal expression clearer, e.g. directional gesture together with *over* *there*; (c) in 'contradiction,' an inconsistency arises between the non-verbal communication and the verbal content, e.g. nodding one's head in agreement while refusing or denying something (⇒ **double-bind theory**); (d) in 'modification,' verbal content regarding the speaker's attitude is changed, e.g. ironic laughing while stating agreement. (⇒ *also* **animal communication**, **face-to-face interaction**, **semiotics**, **sign language**)

References
Argyle, M. 1975. *Bodily communication*. London.
Birdwhistell, R.L. 1954. *Introduction to kinesics*. Louisville, KY.
—— 1970. *Kinesics and context*. Philadelphia, PA.
Capella, J.N. and M.T. Palmer, 1989. The structure and organisation of verbal and nonverbal behaviour: data for models of reception. *JLSP* 8.167–92.
Ekman, P. and W.V. Friesen. 1969. The repertoire of nonverbal behaviour: categories, origins, usage and coding. *Semiotica* 1.49–98.
Ellgring, H. 1981. Nonverbal communication: a review of research in Germany. *German Journal of Psychology* 5.59–84.
Feldman, R.S. and B. Rimé. 1991. *Fundamentals of nonverbal behavior*. Cambridge.
Harper, R.G., A.N. Wiens, and J.D. Matarazzo. 1978. *Nonverbal communication: the state of the art*. New York.
Hinde, R.A. (ed.) 1972. *Non-verbal communication*. Cambridge.
Key, M.R. (ed.) 1980. *The relationship of verbal and nonverbal communication*. The Hague.
—— (ed.) 1982. *Nonverbal communication today: current research*. The Hague.
Knapp, M.L. 1978. *Nonverbal communication in human interaction*, 2nd exp. edn. New York.
Laver, J. and P. Trudgill. 1979. Phonetic and linguistic markers in speech. In K.R. Scherer and H. Giles (eds), *Social markers in speech*. Cambridge. 1–32.
Papousek, H., M. Papousek, and U. Jurgens (eds) 1992. *Nonverbal vocal communication*. Cambridge.
Patterson, M.L. 1983. *Nonverbal behavior: a functional perspective*. New York.
Poyatos, F. (ed.) 1992. *Advances in non-verbal communication: sociocultural, clinical, esthetic and literary perspectives*. Amsterdam and Philadelphia, PA.
Scherer, K.R. 1970. *Non-verbale Kommunikation: Ansätze zur Beobachtung und Analyse der außersprachlichen Aspekte von Interaktionsverhalten*. Hamburg.
—— 1978. Die Funktionen des nonverbalen Verhaltens im Gespräch. In D. Wegner (ed.), *Gesprächsanalysen*. Hamburg. 273–95.
—— 1982. *Vokale Kommunikation: nonverbale Aspekte des Sprachverhaltens*. Weinheim.
Scherer, K.R. and P. Ekman (eds) 1982. *Handbook of methods in nonverbal research*. Cambridge.
Scherer, K.R. and H.G. Wallbott (eds) 1979. *Non-*
verbale Kommunikation. Weinheim. (2nd edn 1984.)
Trager, G.L. 1958. Paralanguage: a first approximation. *SiL* 13.1–12.
Umiker-Sebeok, J. and T.A. Sebeok (eds) 1981. *Semiotic approach to nonverbal communication*. The Hague.
Weitz, S. (ed.) 1974. *Nonverbal communication*. New York.
Wolfgang, A. (ed.) 1979. *Nonverbal behavior: applications and cultural implications*. New York.

Journal
Journal of Nonverbal Behavior.
⇒ **animal communication**, **face-to-face interaction**, **semiotics**, **sign language**

Nootka ⇒ **Salishan**

Nordic ⇒ **Scandinavian**

normative grammar ⇒ **prescriptive grammar**

North and Central American languages

Before colonization, about 200–300 languages were spoken in North America by approx. 1.5 million inhabitants; these languages can be divided into numerous language families and **language isolates**.

History of research: the first important attempt at classifying these languages was made by Powell (1891), who counted fifty-eight language families based on comparing word lists. Under F. Boas, the first volume of the *Handbook of American Indian Languages* appeared with detailed descriptions of individual languages, influencing **American structuralism**. Sapir assumed six major language groups in 1929. Subsequently, Sapir's groupings were largely given up in favour of smaller but more certain classifications, but groupings remain controversial. Campbell and Mithun (1979) cautiously assume thirty-two language families and thirty language isolates. In contrast, Suarez (1983) suggests seven language families and seven isolates, and Greenberg (1956, 1987) assigns all languages of North, Central and South America, with the exception of the **Na-Dené** and **Eskimo-Aleut** languages, to one large **Amerindian** group. According to Greenberg, the speakers of Amerindian represent the oldest wave of immigrants, followed by speakers of Na-Dené and Eskimo-Aleut. In Central America about seventy native languages are spoken today by over 7.5 million speakers. Research into these languages started in the sixteenth and seventeenth centuries with missionaries (grammars, dictionaries, development of writing systems, and collection of texts). The first attempts at classification were carried out by L. Hervas y Panduro (1800–5), F.

Pimentel (1874) and C. Thoman and J.A. Swanton (1911). More modern linguistic investigation began around 1930.

References
Boas, F. (ed.) 1911, 1922, 1933–8. *Handbook of American Indian languages*, 3 vols. New York.
Campbell, L. and M. Mithun (eds). 1979. *The languages of native America: historical and comparative assessment*. Austin, TX.
Cook, E.-D. and D.B. Gerdts (eds) 1984. *The syntax of native American languages*. Orlando, FL.
Edmonson, M. 1984. Supplement to *The Handbook of Middle American Indians*, vol. 2: *Linguistics*. Austin, TX.
Greenberg, J. 1960. The general classification of Central and South American languages. In A. Wallace (ed.) *Selected Papers of the Fifth International Congress of Anthropological and Ethnological Sciences*. 791–4. Philadelphia.
—— 1987. *Language in the Americas*. Stanford, CA.
Liedtke, S. 1995. *The languages of the 'First Nations'. A comparison in ethnolinguistic perspective*. Munich.
Pinnow, H.-J. 1964. *Die nordamerikanischen Indianersprachen*. Wiesbaden.
Powell, J.W. 1891. *Indian linguistic families of America north of Mexico*. US Bureau of American Ethnology, seventh annual report.
Sebeok, T.A. (ed.) 1973. *Current trends in linguistics*, vol. 10: *Linguistics in North America*. The Hague and Paris.
—— 1977. *Native languages of the Americas*. New York.
Suarez, J.A. 1983. *The Meso-American Indian languages*. Cambridge.
Wauchope, R. 1964. *Handbook of Middle American Indians*, vol. 5: *Linguistics*. Austin, TX.

Journal
International Journal of American Linguistics (previously *American Anthropologist*).
⇒ **classification of languages**

North-East Caucasian (*also* Nakho-Dagestanian)

Language group in the northeastern Caucasus which consists of the Nakh group (three languages; largest language Chechen, approx. 700,000 speakers) and the larger Dagestanian group (about thirty languages; largest language Avar, approx. 500,000 speakers). Dagestanian itself can be further subdivided into the following branches: Avaro-Andi (north), Cezian (west), Lako-Dargwa (central), and Lezgian (south).

Characteristics: relatively rich vowel system, glottalized and sometimes pharyngealized consonants. Elaborated system of noun classification (⇒ **noun class**) (up to ten gender classes). Rich case system (**ergative**).

References
Dumézil, G. 1932. *Introduction à l'étude comparative des langues caucasiennes du nord*. Paris.
Kibrik, A.E. *et al*. 1977. *Opyt strukturnogo opisanija arčinskogo jazyka*. Moscow.
Schulze, W. 1988. Noun classification and ergative construction in East Caucasian languages. In F. Thordarson (ed.) *Studia caucasologica*. Oslo. 251–74.
Smeets, R. and D.M. Job. 1994. *The indigenous languages of the Caucasus*, vol. 3: *The North-East Caucasian languages I*. New York.
⇒ **Caucasian languages**

North Germanic ⇒ Germanic, Scandinavian

North-West Caucasian (*also* Abkhazi-Adyge)

Language group in the northwestern Caucasus with approx. 600,000 speakers and five languages: Abkhaz, Abaza, Adyge, Kabard, and the nearly extinct Ubykh in Turkey.

Characteristics: these languages are known for their very simple vowel system (only two vowels are hypothesized) which contrasts with a very rich consonant system with up to eighty sounds. Simple case system (**ergative**), complex verb conjugation and agreement. Gender system (masculine, feminine, impersonal).

References
Colarusso, J. 1975. *The Northwest Caucasian languages: a phonological survey*. Cambridge, MA.
Hewitt, B.G. 1979. *Abkhaz*. Amsterdam.
—— (ed.) 1989. *The indigenous languages of the Caucasus*, vol. 2: *The North-West Caucasian languages*. Delmar, NY.
⇒ **Caucasian languages**

Norwegian

North **Germanic** (**Scandinavian**) language with approx. 4.5 million speakers; since 1907, Norwegian has consisted of two officially recognized forms, Bokmål 'book language' (formerly Ricksmål 'language of the empire'), a Norwegianized version of **Danish** spoken by 20 per cent of the population, primarily in the central and western parts of the country, and Landsmål 'language of the country' (now called Nynorsk 'new Norwegian'). The reasons for this division are rooted in the earlier influences of Low German (⇒ **German**), **Swedish**, and Danish, the latter introduced in 1397 as the language of government and in 1739 as the official language in school instruction. Since 1892 both languages have received equal treatment in schools; this conflict still has not yet been resolved in spite of several attempted reforms.

Characteristics: both variants have distinctive tone; while Bokmål (like Danish and

Swedish) has only the grammatical **genders** of masculine and neuter, Landsmål also has a feminine gender. SVO word order in main and relative clauses.

References
Breito, O. 1970. *Nynorsk grammatikk*. Oslo.
Haugen, E. 1966. *Language conflict and language planning: the case of modern Norwegian*. Cambridge, MA.
Haugen, E. and K.G. Chapman. 1982. *Spoken Norwegian*, 3rd edn. New York.
Næs, O. 1972. *Norsk grammatikk*, 3rd edn. Oslo.
Strandskogen, A.-B. and R. Strandskogen. 1994. *Norwegian: an essential grammar*, trans. B. White. London.

Dictionary
Norwegian dictionary. 1994. London.

notation [Lat. *notatio* 'a letter, symbol, etc. representing a word etc.']

System of signs or symbols in a descriptive language, such as is used in **formal logic**, mathematics and chemistry. In linguistics, various notational systems are used, such as the International Phonetic Alphabet (IPA) or the notational conventions borrowed from formal logic and **set theory** used for semantic and syntactic descriptions. (⇒ table of symbols on p. xvii)

notion [Lat. *notio* 'concept, idea'] (*also* concept)

Idea which is conceived through abstraction and through which objects or states of affairs are classified on the basis of particular characteristics and/or relations. Notions are represented by **terms**. They can be defined like **sets**: (a) extensionally, by an inventory of the objects that fall under a particular concept; and (b) intensionally, by indication of their specific components. The current equating of 'notion' with 'meaning' or with Frege's **'sense'** ('Sinn') rests upon an intensional definition of 'notion.' (⇒ *also* **definition, intension**)

noun [Lat. *nomen* 'name'] (*also* **substantive**)

Important syntactic category which makes up the majority of items in the English vocabulary. Nouns are marked morphologically in many **Indo-European** languages by the categories **gender, number**, and **case**. As the **nucleus** of **noun phrases**, they can be modified by attributes. Semantically, they are either **concrete** or **abstract**: concretes include **proper nouns** (*Mary, Boston, Mozart*), **common nouns** (*person, cat, singer*), **collectives** (*mountain range, cattle*), and other **mass nouns** (*wine, gold, blood*). Abstracts indicate properties (*loyalty*), events (*dreams*), relationships (*animosity*),

measurements (*hour, mile*). For relevant information on word formation in nouns, ⇒ **composition, nominalization, word formation**; for stylistic aspects ⇒ **nominal style**. (⇒ *also* **declension, noun phrase**)

Reference
Schachter, P. 1985. Parts of speech systems. In K. Shopen (ed.), *Language typology and syntactic description*. Cambridge. Vol. 1, 3–61.

noun class

Broadly defined, any classification of nouns according to semantic aspects such as animate/inanimate (⇒ **animate vs inanimate**), concrete (⇒ **concrete noun**), abstract (⇒ **abstract noun**), masculine/feminine/neuter, dimensions, consistency. More narrowly defined, such classifications which are not based on natural **gender**, i.e. are neither masculine nor feminine. In contrast to gender systems, languages with noun classes often have significantly more classes, e.g. in the **Niger-Congo** languages (such as **Bantu, West Atlantic**), with up to twenty classes which are often grouped in singular/plural pairs. Classificational systems may be overt or covert, depending on whether the classifier itself appears directly on the noun or not. Often the classification is more or less semantically motivated, with the distinction between animate and inanimate playing a major role. (⇒ *also* **classifying language**)

References
Craig, C. 1986. *Noun classes and categorization*. Amsterdam.
Heine, B. 1982. African noun class systems. In: *Apprehension*, ed. by H. Seiler & F. Stachowiak. Vol. 2. Tübingen.
Royen, G. 1929. *Die nominalen Klassifikationssysteme*. Vienna.
Seiler, H. and F.J. Stachowiak (eds) 1982. *Apprehension: das sprachliche Erfassen von Gegenständen*. Tübingen.
Schulze, W. 1992. Die ostkaukasischen Klassenzeichen. In C. Paris (ed.), *Caucasologie et mythologie comparée*. Paris. 335–62.
⇒ **gender**

noun phrase (*also* nominal, NP)

Grammatical category (or **phrase**) which normally contains a noun (*fruit, happiness, Phil*) or a pronoun (*I, someone, one*) as its **head** and which can be modified (= specified) in many ways. Possible modifiers include: (a) **adjuncts**, which in the form of **adjective phrases** in English are usually placed before the noun (*very good beer*) and as **appositions** after the noun (*my friend Phil*); (b) complements in the form of a genitive attribute (*Phil's house*), a **prepositional phrase** (*the house on the hill*), or a relative clause (*the family that* *lives next door*). Noun phrases can function in a sentence as **subjects** or **objects** or can appear as part of a prepositional phrase which itself functions as an object or an **adverbial**.

Semantically there are definite and indefinite noun phrases. **Definiteness** is inherent to **proper nouns**, but can sometimes be shown with a **determiner** (*the Rocky Mountains, the Mississippi* vs *Caroline, Chicago*). Indefinite noun phrases in turn can be either specific or non-specific, cf. *Philip saw a whale yesterday* (a specific one) vs *Philip would like to see a whale some time* (any whale). Both definite and indefinite noun phrases can be used generically (⇒ **generic**).

In **Government and Binding theory**, noun phrases are now seen as being embedded in a **determiner phrase** (DP) with a determiner as head.

References
Abney, S.P. 1987. The English noun phrase in its sentential aspect. Dissertation, MIT, Cambridge, MA.
Andrews, A. 1985. The major functions of the noun phrase. In T. Shopen (ed.), *Language and typology and syntactic description*, vol. 1: *Clause structure*. Cambridge. 64–154.
Bach, E. 1968. Nouns and noun phrases. In E. Bach and R.T. Harms (eds), *Universals in linguistic theory*. New York. 90–122.
Donnellan, K. 1970. Proper names and identifying descriptions. *Synthese* 21.335–58.
Ehrich, V. 1991. Nominalisierungen. In D. Wunderlich (ed.) *Semantik/Semantics: an international handbook of contemporary research*. Berlin. 441–56.
Giorgi, A. and G. Longobardi. 1991. *The syntax of noun phrases: configuration, parameters and empty categories*. Cambridge.
Jackendoff, R.S. 1977. *X-syntax: a study of phrase structure*. Cambridge, MA.
McCawley, J.D. 1969. Where do noun phrases come from? Repr. in D.D. Steinberg and L.A. Jakobovits (eds), *Semantics*. Cambridge, 1971. 217–31.
Olsen, S. 1991. Die deutsche Nominalphrase als 'Determinansphrase'. In S. Olsen and G. Fanselow (eds), *DET, COMP und INFL: zur Syntax funktionaler Kategorien und grammatischer Funktionen*. Tübingen. 35–56.

NP ⇒ noun phrase

NP-movement

The movement of a NP to an **argument position**. The trace (⇒ **trace theory**) left behind by the NP-movement is an empty anaphor (⇒ **anaphora**). (⇒ also **binding theory, Government and Binding theory, wh-movement**)

References
⇒ **trace theory**

n-tuple

In **set theory**, designation for an ordered set of elements of an undetermined number, where *n* symbolizes the variable for the number of elements. In contrast to simple **sets**, for which it is the case that {a,b}={b,a}, in the tuple the order of the elements is firm, i.e. {a,b} ≠ {b,a}.

References
⇒ **set theory**

Nubian ⇒ Chari-Nile languages

nuclear sentence ⇒ kernel sentence

nuclear stress ⇒ syllable, accent[2]

nucleus [Lat. *nucleus* 'kernel; central part of something']
1 In L. Tesnière's **dependency grammar**, a semantic-syntactic term for the syntactic node of a sentence and its additional semantic functions. As the 'constituent cell' of a sentence its structure in the **tree diagram** is more complex than that of simple nodes.

References
⇒ **dependency grammar**

2 (*also* syllable nucleus) In **syllable** structure, the element that forms the peak of the syllable. As a rule, the nucleus consists of vowels, though occasionally it can also consist of the syllabic version of a consonant: e.g., syllabic [n̩] in *thinking*, if pronounced as [θɪŋkn̩], or [s] in *pst!*

References
⇒ **syllable**

3 ⇒ **nucleus vs satellite**

4 ⇒ **head**[2]

nucleus vs satellite [Lat. *satelles* 'escort, attendant']

In an **endocentric construction**, term for the **antecedent** (*also*: center, **head**) that is semantically specified (modified) by an attributive element (*also*: **determiner, modifier**). In the sentence *She sings very well, well* is the nucleus of the satellite *very well* and *sings* is the nucleus of the satellite *sings very well*.

References
⇒ **complementation and modification**

number

Grammatical category of nouns which marks quantity. Number can also be applied to other parts of speech (⇒ **adjective, pronoun, finite verb form**) through **agreement**. The most common categories of number are **singular** and **plural**; there are also systems which have a dual (⇒ **Greek, Sanskrit**, and **Gothic**) and a trialis (e.g. some South-West Pacific languages). In some languages there is a **paucalis** for indicating a small number, as in **Arabic**.

Another kind of more complicated number system can be found in languages which differentiate between a basic form (collective) which is indifferent in respect to number, and a more complicated derived form for single entities (singulative) (⇒ **Breton**). Often not all nouns in a language can occur in all numbers (cf. **single-only**, **plural-only**, **mass nouns**). **Classifying languages** generally have no formal number system.

References

Bartsch, R. 1973. The semantics and syntax of number and numbers. In P. Kimball (ed.), *Syntax and Semantics*. New York. Vol. 2, 51–93.

Greenberg, J.H. 1988. The first person inclusive dual as an ambiguous category. *SLang* 12.1–19.

Hurford, J.R. 1987. *Language and number: the emergence of a cognitive system*. Oxford.

Reid, W. 1991. *Verb and noun number in English: a functional explanation*. London.

Wickens, M.A. 1991. *Grammatical number in English nouns: an empirical and theoretical account*. Amsterdam and Philadelphia.

numeral

Class of words consisting primarily of adjectives (*six months*, *double fault*, *threefold problem*) as well as substantives (*a dozen eggs*, indefinite pronouns (*all*, *both*, *many*, *few*), and adverbials (*He called twice already*). Semantically they form a uniform group inasfar as they designate numbers, quantities, and any other countable divisions. However, because their morphological and syntactic behavior varies in respect to declension, newer grammars classify them differently, relegating them in part to pronouns, in part to adjectives. A basic division is made between definite and indefinite (*ten* vs *several*), where the definite numerals can be divided into the following subgroups: (a) cardinals – *one*, *two*, *three*; (b) ordinals – *first*, *second*, *third*; (c) **distributives** – *six each*; (d) iteratives – *once*, *twice*, *thrice*; (e) multiples – *eightfold*; (f) collective numerals – *a dozen*; and (g) fractions – *a tenth*. For a lengthy bibliography, see Kraus (1977).

References

Gvozdanovič, J. 1991. *Indo-European numerals*. Berlin and New York.

Hurford, J.R. 1975. *The linguistic theory of numerals*. London.

——— 1987. *Language and number: the emergence of a cognitive system*. Oxford.

Kraus, H. 1977. *Das Numerus-System des Englischen*. Tübingen.

Ross, A.C. (ed.) 1981. *Indo-European numerals*. The Hague.

Nuorese ⇒ **Sardinian**

Nynorck ⇒ **Norwegian**

O

object [Lat. *obiectum* 'something presented to the senses,' past participle of *obicere* 'to throw in the way']

Syntactic function in **nominative languages** which, depending on the language, is marked either morphologically (e.g. by an **oblique case**) or positionally (e.g. after the subject) and which generally denotes a thing or state of affairs which is affected by the event denoted by the verb. The number and types of objects are language-specific and their occurrence in the sentence is determined by the **valence** of the verb. Objects are generally divided into **direct**, **indirect** and **prepositional objects** (also called **oblique objects**). Objects in English can be realized as **noun phrases**, **infinitive constructions**, **gerunds**, or **dependent clauses** (⇒ **object clause**). (⇒ *also* **case**, **syntactic function**)

References
Plank, F. (ed.) 1984. *Objects*. London
⇒ **case**, **direct object**, **indirect object**, **syntactic function**

object clause (*also* complement clause)

Subordinate clause (⇒ **constituent clause**) which functions syntactically as an object. In English these include: (a) **relative clauses**: *Wherever you go, there you are*; (b) dependent clauses introduced by an **interrogative pronoun** (*Do you know who that is standing over there?*) or a subordinating conjunction (*She asked herself whether she had done the right thing or not*); (c) dependent clauses without a conjunction: *She wished she were in Athens*; (d) infinitive constructions: *He was glad to have been there at all*.

References
⇒ **subordinate clause**

object language vs metalanguage

Known since ancient times and made more precise in **formal logic** of the twentieth century, the terms 'object language' and 'metalanguage' form a useful distinction for talking about different levels of propositions. Propositions about non-linguistic states of affairs, for example, *London is situated on the Thames* is a proposition in the object language, while *'London' is a proper name of two syllables* is an example of metalanguage. In a metalinguistic description, the example in the object language is marked graphemically by quotation marks, italics, or underlining. This convention corresponds to the language-philosophical distinction between *use* and *mention*. In *London is situated on the Thames* the expression *London* is being used to name a specific English city, while in *'London' is a proper name of two syllables* one is citing, or mentioning the word *London* as an example of a proper name. This metalinguistic hierarchical distinction can be drawn over several levels, thus the definitions and explanations of this dictionary entry (or of the whole dictionary itself) are meta-metalinguistic descriptions of the metalinguistic use of linguistic terminology that is used to describe expressions in the object language. Two languages are in an object-language–metalanguage relation if statements about expressions in the one language are made in the other language, such as might be found in an English language grammar of German. The differentiation between levels of propositions is necessary to avoid so-called **semantic antinomies**, like those of the paradox of the Cretan who maintains 'All Cretans are liars.'

References
Quine, W.V.O. 1940. *Mathematical logic*. New York (Rev. edn Cambridge, MA, 1951.)
⇒ **formal logic**

obligatory vs optional [Lat. *obligatio* 'the state of being legally etc. liable,' *optio* 'choice']

Property of rules which specifies the conditions of their application. The distinction applies to all levels of description and has an important role in the syntactic and semantic description of sentence structure based on verb **valence**. In contrast to valence-independent elements in a sentence, such as **free adjuncts** and attributes, actants which depend on valence can be divided into two groups: valence positions which must be filled and those which do not need to be filled under certain conditions (i.e. optional); cf. *Caroline is writing a letter to her mother* vs *Caroline is writing (something)*, but *Caroline gave her mother a present* vs **Caroline gave her mother*. This structurally based distinction refers exclusively to grammatical completeness or wellformedness; it does not always correspond to semantic–pragmatic factors such as completeness and differentiation of information. For other uses of this distinction, ⇒ *also* **free variation** and **transformations**.

Reference
Sanders, G.A. 1977. On the notions 'optional' and 'obligatory' in linguistics. *Ling* 195.5–47.

oblique case [Lat. *obliquus* 'slanting']

Term for the **genitive**, **dative**, **accusative** and **ablative** cases which depend on the verb, as opposed to the **casus rectus**.

References
⇒ **case**

oblique object

Syntactic function filled by a **noun phrase** in an **oblique case** other than the **accusative** or **dative**, or by a prepositional or adpositional phrase: Ger. *Er klagte den Mann des Mordes an* (gen.) 'He accused the man of murder.' Oblique objects are not considered to be among the primary syntactic functions of a language such as subject or direct object, which can be seen by the fact that only in a few languages do they require verb agreement or occur as antecedents for reflexive pronouns (⇒ **hierarchy universal**). Specific semantic functions include: **agent** (in passive constructions), **benefactive**, **locative** and other semantic categories which are not directly related to the action expressed in the predicate.

References
⇒ **object**, **syntactic function**

observational adequacy ⇒ levels of adequacy

obstruent [Lat. *obstruere* 'to block up, impede']

Speech sound classified according to the way in which it is formed (namely by forcing air through the **resonance chamber** and allowing it to bypass its obstruction medially (**median**)). Obstruents are median occlusives that include the affricates and median fricatives. (⇒ *also* **articulatory phonetics**)

References
⇒ **phonetics**

Ob-Ugric ⇒ Finno-Ugric

obviative ⇒ proximate vs obviative

occasional meaning ⇒ connotation[1]

occasional vs usual word formation

In **word formation**, the distinction drawn between **neologisms** (created according to productive **word formation rules**) that sponta-

neously arise from a momentary need and within a strongly limited context and such expressions that are codified in the lexicon and already belong to the lexical inventory of a language. Since occasional word formations can frequently become incorporated into the usual inventory of a language, the boundary between both areas is fuzzy. (⇒ *also* **nonce word**, **lexicalization**)

References
⇒ **word formation**

Occitan

Gallo-**Romance language** spoken in southern France somewhat south of the line Garonne–Grenoble. The striking demarcation of the Gallo-Romance linguistic territory can be attributed among other reasons to the large number of Franconian settlers in northern France (⇒ **superstratum**). During the Middle Ages, Occitan was an important language of culture, but became increasingly supplanted by the more dominant **French**. Since the nineteenth century there have been various movements for the renewal of Occitan as a literary and trade language (cf. F. Mistral, L. Alibert). Occitan can be divided into North Occitan and Middle Occitan (Provençal); Gascon is in many ways a separate dialect. Today the active speakers of Occitan number about 2 million.

References
Alibert, L. 1935. *Gramatica occitana*. Toulouse.
Anglade, J. 1921. *Grammaire de l'ancien Provençal ou ancienne langue d'Oc*. Paris.
Bec, P. 1973. *Manuel pratique d'occitan moderne*. Paris.
Holtus, G., M. Metzeltin, and C. Schmitt (eds) 1989. *Lexikon der romanistischen Linguistik*, vol. 5, Tübingen.
Jensen, F. 1986. *The syntax of medieval Occitan*, Tübingen.
Kremnitz, G. 1981. *Das Okzitanische: Sprachgeschichte und Soziologie*. Tübingen.
Rohlfs, G. 1970. *Le Gascon*, 2nd rev. edn. Tübingen.

Dictionaries
Alibert, L. 1965. *Dictionnaire occitan–français*. Toulouse.
Mistral, F. 1879–1886. *Lou tresor d'ou Felibrige ou Dictionnaire, provençal–français*, 2 vols. Aix-en-Provence, Avignon, Paris.

Bibliographies
Berthaud, P.-L. 1946. *Bibliographie occitane 1919–1942*. Paris.
Klingebiel, K. 1986. *Bibliographie linguistique de l'ancien Occitan 1960–1982*. Hamburg.

occlusive

A non-nasal **stop**.

occurrence

Concrete realization of a basic abstract linguistic unit in the form of an actual utterance. An occurrence is the result of a performance act on the basis of underlying language competence (⇒ **competence vs performance**). Thus, in spoken language, linguistic utterances are phonetic actualizations (i.e. occurrences) of an underlying abstract phonological structure. This distinction between aspects of *parole* vs aspects of *langue* (⇒ **langue vs parole**) corresponds to the opposition **etic vs emic analysis**, as well as the **type–token relation**.

Oceanic

Collective term for the languages of the southeast Asian islands, New Guinea, Australia, and the Pacific Islands. The most important language groups in this area are **Malayo-Polynesian**, which is spread over nearly the entire Pacific, the southeast Asian islands, and Madagascar and is probably related to the southeast Asian languages, the **Australian languages**, and the **Papuan** languages, the numerous language families in New Guinea and the nearby islands, whose genetic affiliation has not yet been completely explained. Research on this group was first focused on the Malayo-Polynesian languages, while the important investigation of the Australian and Papuan languages was not seriously begun until the 1960s. (⇒ *also* **dialect geography**)

References
Holmer, N.M. 1966. *Oceanic semantics: a study in the framing of concepts in the native languages of Australia and Oceania*. Uppsala.
Wurm, S.A. 1982. *Papuan languages of Oceania*. Tübingen.

Bibliography
Kleineberger, H.R. 1957. *Bibliography of Oceanic linguistics*. London.

Journal
Oceanic Linguistics.

off-glide ⇒ **on-glide vs off-glide**

Ojibwa ⇒ **Algonquian**

Okanogan ⇒ **Salishan**

Old Bulgarian ⇒ **Old Church Slavic**

Old Church Slavic (*also* Old Church Slavonic, Old Bulgarian)

Language of the oldest written **Slavic** documents, based on the dialect of Thessalonica. The documents date from the ninth century and are liturgical in character, which led to the most common designation Old Church Slavic. They were written first in the **Glagolitic**, then in the **Cyrillic** script.

Characteristics: generally open syllables; the front and back nasal vowels ę and ǫ are distinguished; the two *jer*-sounds ʼb and b are also distinguished; complex inflectional system with alternations; no definite article.

References
Diels, P. 1932–4. *Altkirchenslavische Grammatik*, 2 vols. Heidelberg. (2nd edn 1963.)
Gardiner, S.C. 1984. *Old Church Slavonic: an elementary grammar*. Cambridge.
Lunt, H.G. 1974. *Old Church Slavonic grammar*, 6th edn. The Hague.
Schmalstieg, W.R. 1983. *Introduction to Old Church Slavic*, 2nd rev. edn. Columbus, OH.
Trubetzkoy, N.S. 1954. *Altkirchenslavische Grammatik: Schrift-, Laut- und Formensystem*. Graz, Vienna, Cologne (2nd edn 1968.)
Vaillant, A. 1964. *Manuel du vieux slave*, 2 vols, 2nd edn. Paris.

Dictionaries
Sadnik, L. and R. Aitzetmüller. 1955. *Handwörterbuch zu den altkirchenslavischen Texten*. Heidelberg. (Repr. 1989.)
Slovník jazyka staroslověnského (Lexicon linguae palaeoslovenicae). 1966–. Vol. IV– 1994. Prague.

Etymological dictionary
Etymologický slovník jazyka staroslověnského. 1989–. Fasc. 3 – g 1992. Ed. E. Havlová. Prague.

Journal
Palaeobulgarica.

Old Church Slavonic ⇒ **Old Church Slavic**

Old High German consonant shift (*also* Second Sound Shift)

Changes in the consonant system of Proto-**Germanic** that led to the separation of Old High German from the group of the other Germanic languages and dialects. (a) The voiceless stops *p*, *t*, *k* are shifted, depending on their position, to (i) **affricates** initially, medially, and at the end of a word after a consonant as well as in **geminates**; cf. Proto-Germanic **to*, Eng. *to*, Ger. *zu*; Proto-Germanic **hert-*, Eng. *heart*, Ger. *Herz*. The different affricates did not all have the same regional extension; (ii) voiceless **fricatives** after vowels medially and at the end in the entire German-speaking region, cf. Proto-Germanic **lētan*, Eng. *let*, Ger. *lassen*; Proto-Germanic **fat*, Eng. *vat*, Ger. *Faß*. (b) The voiced stops *b*, *d*, *g* (which in Proto-Germanic had developed from the voiced fricatives, ⇒ **Grimm's Law**) in Upper German, especially Bavarian, are shifted to the corresponding voiceless stops, with strong regional differentiation (these voiceless stops, however, were later mostly weakened again), cf. Old Saxon (Low German) *beran*, *bindan*, *giban*, Old High German (Bav.) *peran, pindan, kepan*. (c) The voiceless fricative [θ] becomes the voiced stop [d], cf. Eng. *brother*, Ger. *Bruder*. (On details on the different extension in the German dialects, see Braune and Mitzka 1953: 83–90). Shifted forms are here and there attested in names as early as the sixth century AD (*Attila* > *Etzel*); the fifth to eighth centuries AD are generally regarded as the time of the rise and spread of the Old High German consonant shift. Opinions on the geographical origin and on the spread vary considerably. As the Old High German consonant shift occurred most consistently with the Bavarians and the Alemans, whereas its influence became weaker further north, the traditional 'monogenetic' view regards the south as the origin of this sound change (in contrast to this, see the assumptions of generative phonology (King 1969)); 'polygenetic' approaches (see Schützeichel 1956), however, proceed from specific, autochthonous developments of the sound shift in several regions simultaneously. An alternative view can be found in Vennemann (1984).

The common interpretations of the Old High German sound shift are also contested by a new view: Vennemann's 'bifurcation theory' (1984) says that Low German and High German are two different developments from Proto-Germanic and that High German is not, as hitherto assumed, a development from an earlier Low German sound system ('succession theory'). This view is based on a new reconstruction of Germanic that proceeds not from the Indo-European sound system (⇒ **Indo-European**), but from the state of historically attested languages, and emphasizes language-typological considerations of plausibility.

References
Braune, W. and W. Mitzka. 1953. *Althochdeutsche Grammatik*. (10th edn 1961). Tübingen. 83–90.
Draye, L. 1986. Niederländisch und Germanisch: Bemerkungen zu Theo Vennemanns neuer Lautverschiebungstheorie aus niederlandistischer Sicht. *PBB* 108.180–9.
King, R. 1969. *Historical linguistics and generative grammar*. Frankfurt.
Merlingen, W. 1986. Die Vennemannsche Lautverschiebungstheorie. *PBB* 108.1–15.
Penzl, H. 1986. Zu den Methoden einer neuen germanischen Stammbaumtheorie. *PBB* 108.16–29.
Sanjosé-Messing, A. 1986. ₊Tʰ – ₊T – ₊D₀? Kritische Anmerkungen zu Vennemanns Rekonstruktion des vorgermanischen Konsonantensystems. *PBB* 108.172–9.
Schützeichel, R. 1956. Zur althochdeutschen Lautverschiebung am Mittelrhein. *ZM* 24.112–24.
———— 1961. *Die Grundlagen des westlichen Mittel-*

deutschen: Studien zur historischen Sprachgeographie. Tübingen. (2nd rev. edn 1976.)
Stechow, A. von 1986. Notizen zu Vennemanns Anti-Grimm. *PBB* 108.159–71.
Vennemann, T. 1984. Hochgermanisch und Niedergermanisch: die Verzweigungstheorie der germanisch-deutschen Lautverschiebungen. *PBB* (T) 106.1–45.
———— 1985. The bifurcation theory of the Germanic and German consonant shifts: synopsis and some further thoughts. In J. Fisiak (ed.), *Papers from the sixth International Conference on Historical Linguistics*. Amsterdam. 527–47.
———— 1988. Die innergermanische Lautverschiebung und die Entstehung der germanischen und deutschen Dialekte. In M.A. Jazayery and W. Winter (eds), *Languages and cultures: Studies in honor of Edgar C. Polomé*. Berlin.
———— 1994. Dating the division between high and low Germanic: a summary of arguments. In T. Swan, E. Mørck and O.J. Westvik (eds), *Language change and language structure. Older Germanic languages in a comparative perspective*. Berlin and New York. 271–302.

Old Indic ⇒ **Sanskrit**

Old Irish ⇒ **Gaelic**

Old Persian ⇒ **Iranian**

Old Prussian

Baltic language which died out in the eighteenth century.

References
Caffrey, J.F. 1989. *Dialectal differentiation in Old Prussian*. Ann Arbor, MI.
Endzelīns, J. 1943. *Senprūšu valoda: levads, gramatika un leksika*. Riga.
Schmalstieg W.R. 1974. *An Old Prussian grammar: the phonology and morphology of the three catechisms*. University Park, PA.
———— 1976. *Studies in Old Prussian: a critical review of the relevant literature in the field since 1945*. University Park, PA and London.
Trautmann, R. 1910. *Die altpraußischen Sprachdenkmäler. Einleitung, Texte, Grammatik, Wörterbuch*. Göttingen. (Repro. Göttingen 1970).

Dictionary
Toporov, V.J. 1975– . *Prusskij jazyk: slovar'* Vol. 5, 1984. Moscow,

Etymological dictionary
Mažiulis, V. 1988–. *Prūsų kalbos: etimologijos žodynas*. Vol. 2, 1993. Vilnius.

Bibliography
Kubicka, W. 1967. Bibliografija języka staropruskiego. *Acta Balto-Slavica* 5.257–311.
⇒ **Baltic**

Old Slavic ⇒ Old Church Slavic

Old South Arabic ⇒ Semitic

Omotic

East African branch of **Afro-Asiatic** postulated by H. Fleming in 1969, earlier considered to be West Cushitic and thus belonging to the **Cushitic** languages. There are some two dozen languages with about 1.3 million speakers.

Reference
Bender, M.L. 1975. *Omotic: a new Afroasiatic language family*. Carbondale, IL.

one-dimensional opposition ⇒ opposition

Oneida ⇒ Iroquoian

on-glide vs off-glide

Beginning vs end phase in the **articulation** of a **speech sound**; the movement of the articulatory organs (⇒ **articulator**) from or to their resting position. A distinction is drawn between strong and weak on- and off-glides. Most speech sounds show weak off-glides, the exception being postaspirated, postnasalized, or affricated **plosives** (⇒ **aspiration**, **affrication**), including the **glottal stop**. Strong on-glide occurs in non-preaspirated, non-prenasalized plosives. (⇒ *also* **glottalization**)

References
⇒ **phonetics**

onomasiology [Grk *ónoma* 'name']

Subdiscipline of **semantics** that, beginning with concepts and states of affairs, studies linguistic expressions (i.e. words or word forms) which refer to these concepts or states of affairs in the real world. To the extent that the geographic distribution of particular words (⇒ **word atlas**) has a bearing on the designation of objects, onomasiology is pursued by dialectologists (⇒ **dialectology**). Similarly, conceptual dictionaries or **thesauruses** are compiled according to onomasiological principles. (⇒ *also* **semasiology**)

References
Baldinger, K. 1964. Sémasiologie et onomasiologie. *Revue de Linguistique Romane* 28.249–72.
Mawson, C.O.S. 1911. *Roget's international thesaurus*. (4th edn, rev. by R.L. Chapman. New York, 1977.)
Roget, P.M. 1852. *Thesaurus of English words and phrases*. (Newly ed. by S.M. Lloyd. Harlow, 1982.)

onomastic affix

Derivational prefix or suffix used to form names of persons or places: e.g. *Mc-* (*McGregor*), *Fitz-* (*Fitzgerald*), *-sen* (*Olsen*), *-by* (*Hornsby*), *-land* (*Oakland*), *-ford* (*Hartford*), and so on.

References
⇒ **onomastics, word formation**

onomastics

Scientific investigation of the origin (development, age, etymology), the meaning, and the geographic distribution of names (⇒ **proper noun**). Onomastic subdisciplines include **anthroponymy** (the study of personal names), **hydronymy** (the study of names of bodies of water), and **toponymy** (the study of geographic place-names), among others. Because place-names and personal names are among the oldest and most transparent linguistic forms, they are an important source of hypotheses about the history of language, **dialect geography** and **language families**. More recently, **sociolinguistics** (name-giving and use in society), **psycholinguistics** (psycho-onomastics and the physiognomy of names), **pragmalinguistics**, and **text linguistics** have taken an active interest in onomastics. Onomastics also offers new insights into historical processes (pre- and early history, folklore, among others) as well as geography and natural history.

References
Becker, D.W. 1964. *Indian place names in New Jersey*. Cedar Grove, NJ.
Eichler, E. *et al.* (eds). 1995. *Name studies. An international handbook of onomastics*. Berlin and New York.
Green, E. and R.M. Green. 1971. Place-names and dialects in Massachusetts: some complementary patterns. *Names* 19.240–51.
Grubbs, S. 1971. The opposite of white: names for Black Americans. In P. Maranda and E. Köngäs (eds), *Structural analysis of oral tradition*. Philadelphia, PA. 25–32.
Gudde, E.G. 1969. *California place names: the origin and etymology of current geographical names*. Berkeley, CA.
McArthur, L.L. 1986. Another approach to place-name classification. *Names* 34:2.238–41.
Metcalf, A. 1985. Introduction: special issue on names in dialect. *Names* 33:4.213–25.
Ramsay, R.L. 1952. *Our storehouse of Missouri place names*. Columbia, MO.
Read, A.W. 1970. The prospects in a national place-name survey for the United States. *Names* 18.201–7.
Reaney, P.H. and R.M. Wilson. 1991. *A dictionary of English surnames*. London.
Rich, J.S. 1981. Landscapes and the imagination: the interplay of folk etymology and place names. *SFQ* 45.155–62.
Shirk, G.H. 1965. *Oklahoma place names*. Norman, OK.
Stewart, G.R. 1967. *Names on the land: a historical*

account of place naming in the United States, 3rd edn. Boston, MA.

Upham, W. 1969. *Minnesota geographical names: their origin and significance*. St Paul, MN.

Utley, F.L. 1969. A survey of American place-names. *Onoma* 14.196–204.

Vogel, V.J. 1986. The influence of historical events upon place names. In E. Callary (ed.), *From Oz to the onion patch*. Dekalb, IL. 47–58.

Woolf, H.B. 1939. *The Old Germanic principles of name-giving*. Baltimore, MD.

Bibliography
Lawson, E.D. 1986. Personal names: a hundred years of social science contributions. (Onomastic bibliography.) *Names* 34:1.89–90.

onomatopoeia [Grk *onomatopoiía* 'the coining of a name or word in imitation of a sound']

The formation of words through the imitation of sounds from nature, e.g. *cock-a-doodle-doo*, *meow*, *splash*. The same sound may be represented differently in other languages, e.g. *cock-a-doodle-doo* is *kikeriki* in German and *cocorico* in French. The natural motivation of such words is an exception to the basic **arbitrariness** of the linguistic symbol and should not be understood as evidence of the onomatopoeic origin of language. (⇒ *also* **sound symbolism**)

References
Kakehl, H. 1990. Systematic investigation of onomatopoeic expressions. *PICL* 14.348–50.
⇒ **sound symbolism**

onset ⇒ syllable

onset of voicing ⇒ glottalization

opacity constraint ⇒ specified subject condition

opaque context ⇒ opaque vs transparent context

opaque vs transparent context [Lat. *opacus* 'shady, dark']

Contexts whose **truth values** are influenced by the free substitutability of expressions with the same extension are 'referentially opaque' (or 'oblique') (Quine 1960: 141) in contrast to 'transparent' contexts. In the following example from Quine (1953: 143), an opaque context is created by the use of the modal adverb *necessarily*. The statement *It is necessarily the case that 9 is greater than 7* is true, while the statement *It is necessarily the case that the number of planets is greater than 7* is false, although both expressions *9* and *the number of planets* have the same **extension**, namely the number 9. Other opaque contexts in which two expressions with an identical extension or **meaning (i.e. denotation**, see Frege 1892) and

a different **sense** (⇒ **intension**) cannot be freely substituted are contexts of knowledge and belief, that is, contexts of 'propositional attitudes' which are set by verbs such as *know*, *believe*, *fear* (⇒ **intensional context**). The context *it is true that S* is an example of a transparent context.

References
Frege, G. 1892. Über Sinn und Bedeutung. *Zeitschrift für Philosophie und philosophische Kritik* (new series) 100.25–50. (Repr. in his *Kleine Schriften*, ed. I. Angelelli. Darmstadt, 1967. 143–62. Eng. trans. in *Translations from the philosophical writings of Gottlob Frege*, ed. P. Geach and M. Black. Oxford, 1960.

Jackendoff, R. 1983. *Semantics and cognition*. Cambridge, MA.

Kaplan, D. 1969. Quantifying. In D. Davidson and J. Hinitikka (eds), *Words and objections*. Dordrecht. 206–42.

Linsky, L. 1971. Reference and referents. In D.D. Steinberg and L.A. Jakobovits (eds), *Semantics*. Cambridge, MA. 76–85.

Partee, B.H. 1970. Opacity, reference and pronouns. *Synthese* 21.359–85.

Quine, W.V.O. 1953. *From a logical point of view*. Cambridge, MA.

―――― 1960. *Word and object*. Cambridge, MA.
⇒ **intension**, ⇒ **reference**

open ⇒ closed vs open

open-class word ⇒ autosemantic word

operational definition ⇒ definition

operational procedures (*also* **discovery procedures**)

Experimental analytical procedures in structural linguistics used both to determine and portray linguistic regularities, as well as to establish and test linguistic hypotheses and theories. By deleting, replacing, adding, or reordering linguistic elements in a set context (word, sentence, or text), regularities which are at first intuitively understood can be made more objective, and these linguistic regularities can be described, based on the procedures which are used to determine them. Consider, for example, the definition of **phonemes** as minimal sound elements whose 'exchange' results in a difference in meaning (*bed* vs *red*), or the determination of **major constituents** as elements which can be moved (commuted). There are a number of tests which are included in the category of operational procedures: (a) the **commutation test**, (b) the **substitution test**, (c) the **reduction test**, and (d) the **contact test**. While linguistic investigations have long been based on such heuristic procedures, the concept of analysis represented by taxonomic **structuralism** is in the main responsible for its systematization. When these procedures are compared to experimental approaches in the natural sciences, the fact is often overlooked that in these linguistic tests, the judgment of grammaticality still relies on the intuition of the investigator or the informant, and thus is not purely 'objective' in the scientific sense, but a matter of the linguistic intuition of those performing the analysis. The same is the case in the study of dead languages. In the framework of generative **transformational grammar**, the procedures which are used in structuralist investigations as heuristic tests are formulated as elementary transformations. In this regard, the transformations **deletion, adjunction, substitution**, and **permutation** correspond to the **reduction test**, the **contact test**, the **substitution test** and the **commutation test**.

References

Bloch, B. 1948. A set of postulates for phonetic analysis. *Lg* 24.3–46.
Glinz, H. 1952. *Die innere Form des Deutschen*. Bern.
Harris, Z.S. 1951. *Methods in structural linguistics*. Chicago, IL. (Repr. as *Structural linguistics*.)
Hjelmslev, L. 1961. *Prolegomena to a theory of language*, trans. F. Whitfield. Madison, WI.
Longacre, R.E. 1960. String constituent analysis. *Lg* 36.63–88.
——— 1968. *Grammar discovery procedures: a field manual*. The Hague.
Nida, E. 1951. A system for the description of semantic elements. *Word* 7.1–14.
Postal, P.M. 1964. *Constituent structure: a study of contemporary models of syntactic description*. Bloomington, IN.
Wells, R.S. 1947. Immediate constituents. *Lg* 23.71–117.

operative sense ⇒ **eidetic vs operative sense**

operator

1 Generally, (a) an instrument or process for carrying out an operation, or (b) a symbol that signals a direction for a particular operation.

2 In **formal logic**, 'operator' is in the broadest sense a collective term for **quantifier**, logical predicate and logical particle (⇒ **logical connective**); in the narrower sense the collective term (and frequent synonym) for quantifiers: operators are linguistic expressions (or their symbolizations) that serve to specify (= quantify) sets: *all, none, every*, among others. An operator connects a **variable** to a complete proposition. One differentiates between the following. (a) The existential operator (also

existential quantifier) symbolized by $\bigvee$ or $\exists$ and read as: 'there is at least one element x in set S for which it is the case that …'; e.g. *Some people are late risers* is symbolized by $\bigvee xL(x)$. The existential operator expresses a particular case and is in the truth-functional relation of **disjunction** (cf. the mnemotechnically motivated symbolization: (small) $\vee$ for disjunction, (big) $\bigvee$ for existential operator). Through negation the existential operator can be carried over to the universal operator (cf. (b) below): *Some people are late risers* corresponds to the expression *Not all people are late risers* (notation: $\bigvee x(Lx) \equiv \neg\bigwedge x(\neg Lx)$). However, in contrast to the universal operator the existential operator presupposes the existence of the designated objects in the real world (⇒ **presupposition**). (b) The universal operator (or universal quantifier), symbolized by $\bigwedge$ or $\forall$, and read as: 'for all elements x in set S it is the case that …'. Everyday language example: *All humans are mortal* symbolized by $\bigwedge x(Hx \rightarrow Mx)$ where H = humans and M = mortal. The universal operator expresses a generalization and is in the truth-functional relation of **conjunction** (cf. the mnemotechnically motivated symbolization: (small) $\wedge$ for conjunction, (big) $\bigwedge$ for the universal operator). The proposition *All humans are mortal* is, for a finite set S, equivalent to an enumeration of all elements, i.e. *a and b and c … are mortal*. Through this parallel, the distributive reading of the universal operator is confirmed: i.e. 'for every single element it is the case that' (in contrast to the collective reading of *all*). (c) The iota operator symbolized by iota (ι), the ninth letter of the Greek alphabet, or by i, and read as 'that element x for which it is the case that …'. The iota operator serves to identify a particular entity by means of a characteristic that is true only of this entity (⇒ **definite description**), e.g. to be the composer of 'The Magic Flute': $\iota x(Cx)$: 'that element x of the set S that has the characteristic of being the composer of 'The Magic Flute.' (d) The lambda operator, symbolized by lambda (λ), the eleventh letter of the Greek alphabet, and read as 'those xs for which it is the case that …'; e.g. $\lambda x(Lx)$: *those people who are late risers*. The lambda operator forms class names, i.e. complex one-place predicates, out of propositional functions (= open formulae).

References
⇒ **formal logic**

3 For the use of 'operator' in **language acquisition** theory, cf. **pivot grammar**.

operator–operand relation ⇒ **complementation and modification**

opposition

Fundamental concept introduced by the **Prague School** especially for **phonology**: two sounds are in a relation of phonological opposition if they alone are capable of differentiating two otherwise phonologically identical words with different meanings (e.g. /t/ and /d/ in *tier* vs *deer*, *tank* vs *dank* (⇒ **minimal pair**). They are not necessarily considered the smallest units capable of semantic differentiation since they themselves can be further analyzed as bundles of **distinctive features**. Since Trubetzkoy, a distinction is drawn in distinctive feature analysis between the following oppositions. Depending on the relation of opposition to the whole phonological system, there is: (a) *multidimensional opposition*: features common to both elements also occur in other phonemes (e.g. /p/ and /t/ since /k/ also has the features [+stop, –voiced]); (b) *one-dimensional* (= bilateral) *opposition*: features common to both elements do not occur in any other phoneme of the language (e.g. /b/ and /p/, since no further phonemes share the features [+consonant, +bilabial]); (c) *isolated opposition*: the opposition found in two elements does not occur anywhere else within this system (e.g. /p/ vs /ʃ/); (d) *proportional opposition*: the opposition found in two elements is repeated in other phoneme pairs in the language (e.g. /d/ : /t/, /b/ : /p/, /g/ : /k/, all differentiated by [±voiced]). Depending on the relation between the individual opposition pairs there is: (e) *privative opposition*: pairs are distinguished by only one feature (e.g. **voiced vs voiceless consonants**); (f) *gradual opposition*: elements are distinguished by varying degrees of a feature as, for example, in the description of the **vowels** according to varying degrees of openness; (g) *equipollent opposition*: pairs are distinguished by several different features, i.e. they are neither privative nor gradual, but rather have the same logical value (e.g. /b/ : /d/, /v/ : /g/). With regard to the validity of opposition, a distinction is drawn between (h) *constant*, i.e. unrestricted, *effective opposition* and (i) *neutralized opposition* (⇒ **neutralization**), both of which can be suspended in particular positions. For parallels in phoneme strings with the same types of opposition, ⇒ **correlation**. The principles of opposition are also used in morphological and semantic analysis (⇒ **componential analysis).**

References
⇒ **phonology**

optative [Lat. *optare* 'to choose']

Subcategory of verbal **mood** present in, e.g. **Greek** which expresses fulfillable wishes. While Greek has an independent paradigm for the optative, other languages express it by means of the **subjunctive**: *Long live the Queen!*

References
⇒ **modality**

optional ⇒ **obligatory vs optional**

oral [Lat. *os*, gen. *oris* 'mouth']

Speech sound which, in contrast to a **nasal**, is formed without the use of the nasal cavity (i.e. with a raised **velum**). With the exception of [m], [n], and [ŋ], all consonants and vowels in English are orals. (⇒ *also* **articulatory phonetics**)

References
⇒ **phonetics**

oral proficiency interview ⇒ **proficiency**

ordering of rules ⇒ **extrinsic vs intrinsic ordering of rules**

ordinary language philosophy

Linguistic theory of analytical philosophy represented by Ryle, Wittgenstein (in his later years), Strawson, Austin, Searle, and others, which – in contrast to **logical semantics** – takes everyday (colloquial) language as the basis for investigating philosophical and linguistic problems. Following Wittgenstein's equation of meaning with use, ordinary language philosophy investigates the origin of meaning and the functioning of linguistic communication through observation and analysis of linguistic transactions in pragmatic contexts. (⇒ *also* **speech act theory**)

References
Austin, J.L. 1962. *How to do things with words*. Oxford.
Keith, G. 1977. *J.L. Austin: a critique of ordinary language philosophy*. Hassocks.
Rorty, R. (ed.) 1967. *The linguistic turn*. Chicago, IL.
Strawson, P.F. 1952. *Individuals: an essay in descriptive metaphysics*. London.
—— 1971. *Logico-linguistic papers*. London.
Wittgenstein, L. 1953. *Philosophical investigations*. Oxford.

organon model of language [Grk *órganon* 'instrument, tool']

Linguistic and semiotic model designed by K. Bühler in his *Sprachtheorie* ('Theory of Language') (1934:28) and founded on Plato's metaphor of language as *organon*, i.e. 'tool,' by

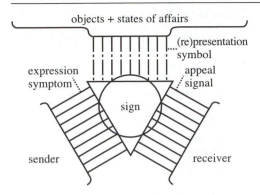

objects + states of affairs

(re)presentation
symbol

expression
symptom

appeal
signal

sign

sender   receiver

means of which 'one person (i.e. sender) communicates to another person (i.e. receiver) about the things being communicated.' Bühler distinguishes three factors constituting signs that correspond to these three functions of the linguistic sign. The linguistic sign is (a) a 'symptom' inasmuch as it 'expresses the profound psyche of the speaker' (⇒ **expressive function of language**); (b) a 'signal' inasmuch as it is an appeal to the receiver (⇒ **appellative function of language**); (c) a 'symbol' inasmuch as it refers to objects and states of affairs in reality (⇒ **representational function of language**). (⇒ *also* **axiomatics of linguistics**, **functional grammar**, **Prague School**)

References
Bühler, K. 1934. *Sprachtheorie*. Jena. (Repr. Stuttgart, 1965.)
Innis, R.E. (trans.) 1982. *Karl Bühler: semiotic foundations of language theory*. New York.

origin of language

There are various hypotheses or assumptions about the origin of language, none of which can be verified through linguistic theory. Relatively certain knowledge about language goes back approx. 5,000 to 6,000 years, but the development of humankind stretches over an assumed period of a million years. Thus, all hypotheses on language origin such as, among others, (a) the 'onomatopoeic' theory (imitation of animal sounds, ⇒ **onomatopoeia**), (b) the 'interjective' theory (origin of language in the expression of emotions), or (c) the 'synergastic' theory (origin of language through co-operation in work) remain completely speculative and confirm J. Herder's paradoxical formulation: 'Humans are only human through language, but in order to invent language, they would already have to be human' (*Gesammelte Schriften*, VII, 47).

References
Armstrong, D.F. *et al.* 1995. *Gesture and the nature of language*. Cambridge.

Bickerton, D. 1990. *Language and species*. Chicago, IL.
Harnad, S., H. Steklis, and J. Lancaster (eds) 1976. *Origins and evolution of language and speech*. New York.
Hawkins, J.A. and M. Gell-Mann (eds). 1992. *The evolution of human language*. Reading, MA.
Herder, J.G. 1772. *Abhandlung über die Ursprünge der Sprache*. Berlin.
Hockett, C.F. 1960. The origin of speech. *Scientific American* 203.88–96.
Landsberg, M.E. (ed.) 1988. *The genesis of language: a different judgement of evidence*. Berlin and New York.
Lenneberg, E.H. (ed.) 1964. *New directions in the study of language*. Cambridge, MA.
——— 1967. *Biological foundations of language*. New York.
Lenneberg, E.H. and E. Lenneberg (eds) 1976. *Foundations of language development: a multidisciplinary approach*, Vol. I. New York.
Lieberman, P. 1975. *On the origins of language: an introduction to the evolution of human speech*. New York.
Puppel, S. (ed.). 1995. *The biology of language*. Amsterdam and Philadelphia.
Raffler-Engel, W. von, J. Wind, and A. Jonker (eds) 1989. *Studies in language origins*, vol. 2. Amsterdam and Philadelphia.
Rosenkranz, B. 1971. *Vom Ursprung der Sprache*, 2nd edn. Heidelberg.
Rousseau, J.-J. and J.G. Herder. 1986. *On the origin of language*, trans. J.H. Moran and A. Gode. Chicago, IL.
Wescott, R.W. (ed.) 1974. *Language origins*. Silver Spring, MD.
Wind, J. *et al.* (eds) 1989–94. *Studies in language origins*, 3 vols. Amsterdam and Philadelphia.
——— *et al.* (eds) 1991. *Language origin: a multidisciplinary approach*. Dordrecht.

Bibliography
Hewes, G.W. 1974. Abridged bibliography on the origin of language. In *Language origins*. R.W. Wescott (ed.), 239–86. Silver Spring, MD.

origo ⇒ **I–now–here origo**

ornative [Lat. *ornare* 'to equip, finish']
Semantically defined type of derived verbs (usually from nouns) whose meaning can be paraphrased by 'furnished with something,' (*to*) *salt*, (*to*) *gag*, (*to*) *arm*, (*to*) *label*, and so on.

References
⇒ **word formation**

Oromo ⇒ **Cushitic**

orthoepy ⇒ **standard pronunciation**

orthography [Grk *orthós* 'right, correct,' *gráphein* 'to write'] (*also* spelling)
The study and/or instruction of systematic and

uniform transcription with letters (⇒ **gra-phemes**) and **punctuation**. The orthographic system of a given language is the result of different and, at times, controversial principles. The problems of English orthography can be seen as the result of overlapping and, often, incompatible principles. (a) *Phonetic principle*: every spoken sound should correspond exactly to one written character. This principle constitutes only a basic tendency in natural languages. Thus, the written sign ‹c› represents [s] and [k], as in *circle*. (b) *Phonological principle*: a single written sign should correspond to every phoneme. The allophones [t] and [ɾ] are realized orthographically with the same sign ‹t›, as in American English *late* vs *later*. (c) *Etymological principle* (⇒ **etymology**): etymologically related words should be spelled analogously. This idea can generally be traced to the interests of nineteenth-century spelling reformers who changed words like *dette* and *receit* to *debt* and *receipt*, respectively, to reflect etymology. (d) *Historical principle*: orthography should remain static over time. Thus, relics from earlier stages in the language are found (e.g. ‹gh› in *bought* represents a former fricative /χ/, which is no longer pronounced). (e) *Homonymy principle*: different words that sound alike should be spelled differently (thus, the differentiation of *plane* vs *plain*, though both words come from Latin *plānus*). (f) *Principle of economy*: superfluous letters should be dropped (e.g. *judge*, but *judgment*). (g) *Principle of aesthetics*: for various reasons, some letter combinations may not be doubled, such as certain consonants in word-final position (*bet*, but *bettor*; *pin* but *pinned*). (h) *Pragmatic principle*: for pragmatic reasons, some words (proper nouns and the pronoun *I*) are capitalized. All of these 'principles' are merely tendencies; the numerous non-systematic deviations make learning the orthography of the given language more difficult. Thus, discussions about orthographic reform are of interest not only to linguists, but also to those involved in making educational and political decisions because the practical orthography used and required by the speech community often differs from that demanded by linguists.

References
Carney, E. 1994. *A survey of English spelling*. London.
Levitt, J. 1978. The influence of orthography on phonology: a comparative study (English, French, Spanish, Italian, German). *Linguistics* 208.43–67.
⇒ **writing**

Oscan-Umbrian ⇒ **Italic**

oscillogram [Lat. *oscillum* 'something that moves to and fro, a swing']

Resulting graphic representation of the oscillograph, a recording machine used in **experimental phonetics** to record electronically the fluctuations in acoustic air pressure (⇒ **spectrograph**).

References
⇒ **phonetics**

Ossete ⇒ **Iranian**

Ostyak ⇒ **Finno-Ugric**

Oto-Mangue

Language group in Central America consisting of approx. twenty-five languages, which, according to Suarez (1983), break down into eight branches, spoken in Central Mexico with some outlying groups in Nicaragua. The largest languages are Otomi and Zapotec (about 400,000 speakers each), Mixtec (about 300,000 speakers), and Mazahua (about 300,000 speakers).

Characteristics: typically fairly complex sound systems, mostly **tonal languages** (especially in the Mexican province Oaxaca) with up to five distinctive tones (in Usila Chinantecan); register and contour tones, as well as **downstep** and upstep; tonality has helped make whistle languages possible. Relatively simple morphology, hardly any derivation, no case, hardly any number distinction. The verb is fairly complicated, with aspectual and personal affixes. Some Mixtecan languages have **noun class** systems. Word order: mostly VSO or SVO, VOS and SOV also occur. (⇒ *also* **North and Central American languages**)

References
Hess, H.H. 1968. *The syntactic structure of Mezquital Otomi*. The Hague.
Hopkins, N.A. and K. Josseraud (eds) 1979. *Estudios lingüísticos en lenguas otomangues*. Mexico.
⇒ **North and Central American languages**

Otomi ⇒ **Oto-Mangue**

oxymoron [Grk *oxýmōron* 'pointedly foolish']

A **figure of speech** of semantic abbreviation. A paradoxical connection of two opposite terms within a word or within a phrase, e.g. *dry humor* (from Lat. *humor* 'moisture'), *terribly nice*. (⇒ *also* **antithesis**)

References
⇒ **figure of speech**

P

Paez ⇒ **Chibchan-Paezan**

Pahlavi ⇒ **Iranian**

Palaic ⇒ **Anatolian**

palatal [Lat. *palatum* 'the roof of the mouth']
Speech sound classified according to its **place of articulation** (hard palate), e.g. [j] in [jɛs] *yes* and [ɲ] in Ital. ['baɲo] *bagno* 'bath.' (⇒ *also* **articulatory phonetics**, **palato-alveolar**, **phonetics**)

References
⇒ **phonetics**

palatalization
Change, conditioned through assimilation, in the **place of articulation** of consonants and vowels towards the hard palate (⇒ **secondary articulation**). In consonants it usually involves dentals or velars with a neighboring front vowel (mostly *i, y*), cf. e.g. the palatalization of Lat. [k] in *centum* [kentum] > Ital. *cento* [tʃento]. In vowels, palatalization generally involves a fronting of back vowels (⇒ **vowel harmony**).

References
⇒ **phonetics**

palate
The concave region of bony cartilage that covers the oral cavity and is connected behind the alveolus.

palato-alveolar
Alternate (see IPA chart, p. xix) term for **lamino-post-alveolar**.

palatogram
Contact diagram of the tongue reflexes against the palate in the **articulation** of **speech sounds**.

palatolalia [Grk *lalia* 'talk']
Term referring to an articulatory disorder due to an impairment of the palate (in most cases, cleft palate). Palatolalia may be combined with a disturbance in voice quality (palatophonia) or nasalization (⇒ **rhinophonia, rhinolalia**). This term is not currently used in North America.

References
⇒ **articulation disorder**

palatophonia ⇒ **palatolalia**

Paleo-Siberian
A group of small languages in northeastern Asia that do not form an established language family. Included in this group on purely geographical grounds are Gilyak (Nivkh, about 2200 speakers), Yukagir, and the Chukotko-Kamchatkan language family, whose largest language, Chukchi (about 11,500 speakers), is an **ergative language**. Ket (about 1,200 speakers), spoken along the Yenisey River, is typologically deviant (**tonal language**, very complex verb morphology).

References
Comrie, B. 1981. *The languages of the Soviet Union.* Cambridge.

Pali ⇒ **Indo-Aryan**

palilalia [Grk *páli* 'back(wards),' *lalía* 'talk']
In **neurolinguistics**, within the domain of **language disorders**, term referring to the continuous, involuntary repetition of words. This term is not currently used in North America.

References
⇒ **language disorder**

palindrome [Grk *palindrómos* 'running back again']
A term for a word or phrase that reads the same backwards and forwards, e.g. *able was I ere I saw Elba* and the name *Otto*. This is a special type of **anagram**.

Pama-Nyungan languages ⇒ **Australian languages**

panchronic [Grk *pãn-* 'all, the whole,' *chrónos* 'time']
Term used by de Saussure to indicate the approach to language which sees linguistic regularities in a language which are not subject to change through time. (⇒ *also* **universals**)

References
Jakobson, R. 1968. *Child language. Aphasia and phonological universals.* The Hague.
Saussure, F. de. 1916. *Cours de linguistique générale*, ed. C. Bally and A. Sechehaye. Paris. (*Course in general linguistics*, trans. R. Harris. London, 1983.)

Panjabi

Indo-Aryan language with approx. 45 million speakers in India and Pakistan.

Characteristics: **tonal languages**; three writing systems (Gurumukhi, **Persian**, Devanāgarī).

References
Bhatia, M. 1985. *An intensive course in Punjabi.* Mysore.
Bhatia, T. 1988. *Panjabi.* London.

Dictionaries
Bailey, T.G. 1919. *An English–Panjabi dictionary.* (Repr. Delhi 1976).
Sandhi, B.S. 1982. *English–Punjabi* dictionary. Chandigarh.
Singh, G. *et al.* 1981. *Panjabi–English dictionary.* 3rd edn. Amritsar.

Bibliography
Koul, O. and M. Bala. 1992. *Punjabi language and linguistics: an annotated bibliography.* New Delhi.

Panoan

Language family with approx. fifty languages; postulated by Greenberg (1987).

References
Greenberg, J.H. 1987. *Language in the Americas.* Stanford, CA.
Key, M.R. 1968. *Comparative Cavineña phonology and notes on Pano–Tacanan relationship.* The Hague and Paris.
Klein, H.M. 1988. *Toba.* London.
⇒ **South American languages**

Papuan

Collective term for approx. 760 languages (with about 3 million speakers) in New Guinea and nearby islands; the most important language is Enga (about 150,000 speakers in the western highlands of Papua New Guinea). It has not yet been established whether or not all Papuan languages belong to a single group, the Indo-Pacific family, as postulated by Greenberg (1971). With a few exceptions, research on this group did not begin until the 1950s. Today the first good grammars are finally available and the classification of these strongly diverging languages is proceeding.

Characteristics: complex verbs, (marking for person, tense, aspect, mood, direction, **serial verb construction**, circumstances of the action, emphasis, **sentence mood**, etc.) Extensive **switch-reference** systems. **Noun class** systems (up to ten classes) with agreement. Often **ergative languages**. Word order: usually SOV.

References
Foley, W.A. 1986. *The Papuan languages of New Guinea.* Cambridge.

Greenberg, J. 1971. The Indo-Pacific hypothesis. In T.A. Sebeok (ed.) *Current trends in linguistics.* The Hague. Vol. 8, 808–71.
Haiman, J. 1980. *Hua: a Papuan language of the Eastern Highlands of New Guinea.* Amsterdam.
Roberts, J. 1987. *Amele.* London.
Schumacher, W.W. *et al.* 1992. *Pacific rim: Austronesian and Papuan linguistic history.* Heidelberg.
Wurm, S.A. 1982. *Papuan languages of Oceania.* Tübingen.

Dictionary
Haiman, J. 1991. *A dictionary of Hua.* Wiesbaden.

paradigm [Grk *parádeigma* 'pattern, model']

1 Set of word forms which together form a **declension** or **conjugation** pattern.

References
⇒ **inflection**

2 Expressions of the same word category which are mutually interchangeable at the vertical level. They stand in contrast to elements which can be segmented at the horizontal level (⇒ **syntagms**). (⇒ *also* **paradigmatic vs syntagmatic relationship**)

paradigm morphology

Traditional approach of research in **morphology** where the word is seen as the central unit of grammatical description (in contrast to **item and arrangement grammar**, which posits the **morpheme** as the smallest unit of description.) The paradigm results from such grammatical (morphosyntactic) categories as **tense** and **mood** for verbs, **gender** and **case** for nouns. It can also result from the various word forms of a lexeme which are formed by the stem and all inflectional endings. For a more exact theoretical distinction between this model and **item and arrangement grammar**, see Matthews (1974).

References
Hockett, C.F. 1954. Two models of grammatical description. *Word* 10.210–34.
Matthews, P. 1972. *Inflectional morphology.* Cambridge.
——— 1974. *Morphology.* Cambridge. Ch. 8. (2nd edn 1991.)

paradigmatic leveling ⇒ analogy

paradigmatic vs syntagmatic relationship

Basic linguistic relationships which describe the complex structure of a language system. Paradigmatic relationships between linguistic elements can be established by use of the **substitution test** at the vertical level. Thus the initial consonants in *beer, deer, peer* form a paradigmatic class, as well as words such as *today* and *tomorrow* in the sentence: *She will arrive today/tomorrow.* Syntagmatic relationships are defined by the ability of elements to be combined horizontally (linearly), e.g. the relationship between *She will arrive* and *today*. De Saussure (1916) called paradigmatic relationships 'associative' relationships, because they represent the relationship between individual elements in specific environments with such elements in the memory which can potentially replace them. Paradigmatic relationships are based on the criteria of selection and distribution of linguistic elements, and are, for example, the basis for establishing the **phoneme inventory** of a language through the construction of **minimal pairs**, the replacement of sounds in an otherwise constant environment that leads to a difference in meaning. Elements which are related to each other paradigmatically can potentially occur in the same context but are mutually exclusive in an actual concrete context because they stand in **opposition** to one another. The distinction between paradigmatic and syntagmatic relationships is relevant to all levels of description; cf. in **semantics** the paradigmatic **semantic relations** (such as **synonymy** and **antonymy**) vs the syntagmatic relations between lexemes in **selectional restrictions**. (⇒ *also* **structuralism**)

References
Happ, H. 1985. *Paradigmatisch – syntagmatisch.* Heidelberg.
Saussure, F. de. 1916. *Cours de linguistique générale*, ed. C. Bally and A. Sechehaye. Paris. (*Course in general linguistics*, trans. R. Harris. London, 1983.)

paragrammatism [Grk *pará* 'beside, along; in transgression of,' *grámma* 'writing']

In **neurolinguistics** and **speech-language pathology**, a term referring to a feature of acquired **language disorder**, with language-specific characteristics (see also Bates *et al.* 1987). In English, paragrammatism is characterized by substitution errors of function words. The term, introduced by K. Kleist in 1914, was identified as a feature of **Wernicke's aphasia** in contrast with **agrammatism** in **Broca's aphasia** (see de Bleser 1987). Paragrammatism, for a time, was considered a virtual synonym for Wernicke's aphasia. This strict association can no longer be maintained, since a given patient may produce agrammatical utterances in spontaneous speech and paragrammatical utterances in experimental situations (see Heeschen 1985).

References
Bates, E. *et al.* 1987. Grammatical morphology in aphasia: evidence from three languages. *Cortex* 23.545–74.
Bleser, R. de. 1987. From agrammatism to paragrammatism: German aphasiological traditions and grammatical disturbances. *Cognitive Neuropsychology* 4.187–256.
Heeschen. C. 1985. Agrammatism vs paragrammatism: a fictitious opposition? In M.L. Kean (ed.), *Agrammatism*. Orlando, FL. 207–48.
Kolk, H. and C. Heeschen. 1992. Agrammatism, paragrammatism and the management of language. *Language and Cognitive Processes* 7.89–129.

paralalia [Grk *lalía* 'talk']

A specific form of **dyslalia** in which one sound is consistently substituted for another, in particular a sound that is acquired later replaced by a sound acquired earlier (e.g. /s/ is used for /d/ or /f/). This term is not used in North America.

paralanguage ⇒ **paralinguistics, kinesics**

paralexeme

A.J. Greimas' term for **compound** words (Fr. *arc-en-ciel* 'rainbow') as opposed to non-compound words or simple lexemes, such as Fr. *étoile* 'star.'

Reference
Greimas, A.J. 1965. *La sémantique structurale.* Paris.

paralinguistics

Within the comprehensive science of communication, paralinguistics deals with the investigation of phonetic signals of non-verbal character (i.e. signals that cannot be linguistically segmented) as well as with their communicative functions. Such paralinguistic factors are, for example, particular types of **articulation** and **phonation** (breathing, murmuring, whispering, or clearing one's throat, crying, and coughing), individual types of language (pitch, timbre, rhythm of speech) and **intonation**. A distinction can be drawn between language-specific vs language-independent signals as well as between language-associated vs separate signals. Many researchers include the investigation of non-vocal, non-verbal actions (⇒ **kinesics**) in paralinguistics. (⇒ *also* **nonverbal communication, prosody**)

References
Abercrombie, D. 1968. Paralanguage. Repr. in J. Laver and S. Hutcheson (eds), *Communication in face to face interaction*. Harmondsworth, 1972. 64–70.
Argyle, M. 1967. *The psychology of interpersonal behavior*. Harmondsworth.
——— 1969. *Social interaction.* London.
Birdwhistell, R.L. 1954. *Introduction to kinesics.* Louisville, KY.

Crystal, D. 1974. Paralinguistics. In T.A. Sebeok (ed.), *Current trends in linguistics*. The Hague. Vol. 12, 265–96.

—— 1975. *The English tone of voice: essays in intonation, prosody and paralanguage*. London.

Crystal, D. and R. Quirk. 1964. *Systems of prosody and paralinguistic features in English*. The Hague.

Ekmann, P. and W.V. Friesen. 1969. The repertoire of nonverbal behaviour: categories, origins, usage and coding. *Semiotica* 1.49–98.

Grassi, L. 1973. Kinesic and paralinguistic communication. *Semiotica* 7.91–6.

Laver, J. and S. Hutcheson (eds) 1972. *Communication in face to face interaction*. Harmondsworth.

Poyatos, F. 1993. *Paralanguage: a linguistic and interdisciplinary approach to interactive speech and sounds*. Amsterdam and Philadelphia, PA.

Scherer, K.R. 1970. *Non-verbale Kommunikation: Ansätze zur Beobachtung und Analyse der außersprachlichen Aspekte von Interaktionsverhalten*. Hamburg.

Scherer, K.R. and P. Ekman (eds) 1982. *Handbook of methods in nonverbal research*. Cambridge.

Trager, G.L. 1958. Paralanguage: a first approximation. *SiL* 13.1–12.

Watzlawick, P., J.H. Beavon, and D.D. Jackson. 1967. *Pragmatics of human communication: a study of interactional patterns, pathologies and paradoxes*. New York.

Bibliography
Davis, M. 1982. *Body movement and nonverbal communication: an annotated bibliography, 1971–1980*. Bloomington, IN.

parallelism [Grk *parallēlismós* 'placing side by side']

A **figure of speech** of repetition for syntactically similar constructions of co-ordinated sentences or phrases, e.g. *Time is passing, Johnny Walker is coming*. (⇒ *also* **chiasm**)

References
⇒ **figure of speech**

parameter

In **transformational grammar**, a variable (= parameter) in the rules or constraints of **universal grammar**, whose value is determined for individual languages. The determination and setting of the values of a particular parameter implies a grammar for a specific language that is consistent with universal grammar: the learner chooses a particular option for a specific language from within the framework of universal grammar. Such a system of universal principles and parameters must also be consistent with theories of **language acquisition**. Thus, it is often assumed that universal grammar assigns forms an unmarked value which can be changed in the course of language acquisition on the basis of external evidence (i.e. the data). According to the current range of the grammar,

the syntactically most local domain is assumed to be unmarked; it will be broadened to a less local domain, if there is a conflict with the data of the individual language (cf. **domain extension**). Parameters allow core grammatical problems to be formulated more flexibly by leaving certain details 'open' (see Yang 1983 on binding theory). On the other hand, parameters also interact with specific prognoses about language acquisition mechanisms and with theories of the **markedness** of individual languages (see Manzini and Wexler 1988).

References
Hyams, N. (ed.) 1986. *Language acquisition and the theory of parameters*. Dordrecht.

Manzini, R. and K. Wexler. 1988. Parameters, binding theory and learnability. *LingI* 18.413–44.

Roeper, T. and E. Williams (eds) 1987. *Parameter setting*. Dordrecht.

Yang, D.W. 1983. The extended binding theory of anaphors. *LangR* 19.169–92.

paraphasia [Grk *phásis* 'utterance, expression']

In **neurolinguistics**, term denoting a characteristic of patients with **aphasia** (in particular **Wernicke's aphasia**). Three kinds of paraphasia are traditionally distinguished: (a) *phonemic or literal paraphasia*: the simplification of consonant clusters (e.g. 'paghetti' for *spaghetti*), the permutation of sounds (e.g. 'lispper' for *slipper*), or the anticipation of a later sound (e.g. 'partender' for *carpenter*); (b) *semantic or verbal paraphasia*: the choice of a word of the same syntactic category with a close semantic relation to the intended word ('cup' for *kettle*); such paraphasia can be evoked by visual associations (e.g. 'banana' for *sausage*); (c) *neologistic paraphasia* (⇒ **neologism**). (⇒ *also* **paragrammatism**)

References
Butterworth, B. 1979. Hesitation and the production of verbal paraphasias and neologisms in jargon aphasia. *B&L* 8.133–61.

Caplan, D. 1987. *Neurolinguistic and linguistic aphasiology*. Cambridge.

Freud, S. 1891. *Zur Auffassung der Aphasien*. Vienna.

—— 1901. *Psychopathologie des Alltagslebens*. Vienna.

Fromkin, V. (ed.) 1973. *Speech errors as linguistic evidence*. The Hague.

—— (ed.) 1980. *Errors in linguistic performance*. New York.

paraphrase

1 Used idiomatically in the sense of 'rewording': a means for explaining, clarifying, or interpreting original communicative intentions.

2 Heuristic term for indicating **synonymy**

between sentences (linguistics) as well as propositions (logic). (a) In the framework of **propositional logic**, paraphrase is identical with bilateral **implication** or **equivalence** relations: sentence 1 is a paraphrase of and equivalent to sentence 2 when S_1 implies S_2 and S_2 implies S_1 (formally $(S_1 \to S_2) \ X \ (S_2 \to S_1)$), e.g. *Philip is older than Caroline* implies *Caroline is younger than Philip*. (b) In the framework of generative **transformational grammar**, two sentences are paraphrases of a common **deep structure** if they have the same semantic meaning and are derived by different **transformations** which do not change meaning (e.g. **passive transformation**). Paraphrases are typically divided into syntactic paraphrases – *I'll give it to them tomorrow* vs *Tomorrow I'll give it to them*); lexical paraphrases – *bachelor* vs *unmarried man*; deictic paraphrases – *Louise lives in New York* vs *Louise lives there*; and pragmatic paraphrases – *Please close the window* vs *It's cold in here*.

References

Chafe, W.L. 1971. Directionality and paraphrase. *Lg* 47.1–26.

Gleitman, L.R. and H. Gleitman. 1970. *Phrase and paraphrase: some innovative uses of language*. New York.

Nolan, R. 1970. *Foundations for an adequate criterion of paraphrase*. The Hague.

Smaby, R.A. 1971. *Paraphrase grammars*. Dordrecht.

parasite vowel ⇒ **anaptyxis**

parasitic gap

An **empty position** which does not result directly from a **movement transformation** but which is licensed secondarily by another transformation that does not itself affect the parasitic gap. Thus in the following ungrammatical sentence, the gap denoted by 'e' (empty) is licensed when the object of the matrix sentence undergoes *wh*-**movement**: **Philip filed the book without reading* e (e = *it* = *the book*) vs *Which book did Philip file without reading* e (*it*)?

References

Chomsky, N. 1982. *Some concepts and consequences of the theory of government and binding*. Cambridge, MA.

Engdahl, E. 1983. Parasitic gaps. *Ling&P* 6.5–34.

—— 1985. Parasitic gaps, resumptive pronouns and subject extractions. *Linguistics* 23.3–44.

Felix, S. 1983. Parasitic gaps in German. In W. Abraham (ed.), *Erklärende Syntax des Deutschen*. Tübingen. 173–200.

Kayne, R. 1984. *Connectedness and binary branching*. Dordrecht.

Koster, J. 1987. *Domains and dynasties: the radical*

autonomy of syntax. Dordrecht.

Pesetsky, D.M. 1982. Paths and categories. Dissertation MIT, Cambridge, MA.

Tellier, C. 1991. *Licensing theory and French parasitic gaps*. Dordrecht.

⇒ **transformational grammar**

parasitic vowel ⇒ **anaptyxis**

parataxis [Grk *parátaxis* 'placing side by side'] (*also* **co-ordination**)

Syntactic conjoining of sentences through co-ordination (as opposed to subordination, ⇒ **hypotaxis**). This structural equivalence is marked in English by the use of co-ordinating conjunctions (*and*, *or*) or through **juxtaposition** (⇒ **asyndeton**) with corresponding intonation.

parenthetic(al) expression [Grk *pará* 'beside,' *énthesis* 'insertion']

Expression (word, phrase, clause) inserted into a sentence from which it is structurally independent: *Her new boyfriend – his name is Jacob – will be coming over tonight*. In a wider sense **interjections**, **vocatives**, and parenthetic sentences are parentheticals.

References

Corum, C. 1975. A pragmatic analysis of parenthetic adjuncts. *CLS* 11.133–44.

Emonds, J. 1974. Parenthetical clauses. In C. Rohrer and N. Ruwet (eds), *Actes du colloque Franco-Allemand de grammaire transformationelle*. Tübingen. Vol. I, 192–205.

parenthetical verbs

Class of verbs (such as *to assume*, *to suspect*) whose use leads to polysemic utterances: *I assume that he's coming today* can be interpreted either as a 'suspicion' or as a '(cautious) statement'; the latter is a case of parenthetic use. (⇒ *also* **sentence adverbial**)

Reference

Urmson, J.O. 1952. Parenthetical verbs. *Mind* 61.192–212.

parisyllabic word [Lat. *par* 'equal']

A word which has the same number of syllables in all inflectional forms of the singular and plural (e.g. *tree – trees*). Words which have a different number of syllables in some paradigmatic positions are termed imparisyllabic words, (e.g. *house – houses*).

parole ⇒ **langue vs parole, performance**

paronomasia ⇒ **pun**

paronymy [Grk *ónyma* 'name']

1 Phonic similarity between two expressions

from different languages, e.g. Eng. *summer* and Ger. *Sommer*.

2 In **word formation**, obsolete term for **derivations** of the same word **stem**: *work, worker, workable*.

paroxytone

In **Greek**, a word which carries **penultimate** stress: *analogía* 'analogy.'

parser

Computer programs for syntactic analyses (⇒ **parsing**^{2}).

parsing

1 Description of the syntactic structure of sentences using elementary units such as **morphemes, words, phrases** and their mutual interrelationships. The goals and methods of parsing are dependent on the grammatical theory in question. Thus the point of departure for parsing in **traditional grammar** is the relationship of **subject** to **predicate**; in structural linguistics, the breaking down of sentences into their immediate **constituents**; in **dependency grammar**, the dependency relationships of the individual elements of the sentence to the verb; and in communicative-grammar approach, the relationship between previously known and new information (⇒ **theme vs rheme, functional sentence perspective**). On processes of parsing, ⇒ **operational procedures**.

2 Machine-aided syntactic analysis of language for checking whether a particular word chain (e.g. a sentence) corresponds to the rules of a particular (formal or natural) language. If this is the case, then a representation of the syntactic (and/or semantic) structure (e.g., as a phrase structure diagram) for the word chain is produced. The linguistic basis of parsing may consist of very distinct grammar formalisms (or conceptual structures) such as **Generalized Phrase Structure Grammar** (GPSG), **Lexical Functional Grammar** (LFG), and the like. Also, the parsing strategy (the application of rules) may vary: 'top-down' (from the sentence node to the terminal symbols) or 'bottom-up' (from the terminal symbols to the sentence node); alternatively, the parser can seek to satisfy a rule hypothesis until it can go no further ('depth first') or at every point first check all possibilities ('breadth first'), every strategy or combination of partial strategies having its advantages and disadvantages. Lexical and structural ambiguity is a main cause of difficulties in parsing natural language utterances. Computer programs for syntactic analysis are called 'parsers.' These are employed in

machine-aided translation, dialogue systems, and the like. (⇒ *also* **ATN grammar, chart, definite clause grammar**)

References
Aho, A. and J.D. Ullman. 1972. *The theory of parsing, translation, and compiling*, vol. 1: *Parsing*. Englewood Cliffs, NJ.
Altmann, G., (ed.) 1989. *Parsing and interpretation*. Special issue of *Language and Cognitive Processes*, vol. 4. Hove and London.
Berwick. R.C., S.P. Abney and C. Tenny (eds) 1991. *Principle-based parsing*. Dordrecht.
Dowty, D., L. Karttunen, and A. Zwicky (eds) 1985. *Natural language parsing*. Cambridge.
Earley, J. 1970. An efficient context-free parsing algorithm. *Communications of the ACM* 6.94–102.
Kaplan, R. 1973. A general syntactic processor. In R. Rustin (ed.), *Natural language processing*. Englewood Cliffs, NJ.
Kay, M. 1982. Algorithm schemata and data structures in syntactic processing. In S. Allén (ed.), *Text processing*. Stockholm. 327–58.
King, M. (ed.) 1983. *Parsing natural language*. London.
Marcus, M. 1980. *A theory of syntactic recognition for natural language*. Cambridge, MA.
Reyle, U. and C. Rohrer (eds) 1988. *Natural language parsing and linguistic theories*. London.
Small, S. and C. Rieger. 1982. Parsing and comprehending with word experts. In W.G. Lehnert and M.H. Ringle (eds), *Strategies for natural language processing*. London. 89–147.
Thompson, H. and G. Ritchie. 1984. Implementing natural language parsers. In T. O'Shea and M. Eisenstadt (eds), *Artificial Intelligence: tools, techniques and applications*. New York. 245–300.
Tomita, M. (ed.) 1991. *Current issues in parsing technology*. Boston and Dordrecht.
Vincenzi, M. de. 1991. *Syntactic parsing strategies in Italian: the minimal chain principle*. Dordrecht.
Winograd, T. 1983. *Language as a cognitive process*, vol. 1: *Syntax*. Reading, MA.

part of speech

Result of the classification of the words of a given language according to form and meaning criteria. Such classifications reach back into antiquity. Because of the different classificatory approaches, the number of parts of speech in the various grammars varies between two and fifteen. The two classes of 'ónoma' (= names; nouns) and 'rhēma' (= statements; verbs) of Plato are the result of a logical syntactic analysis (⇒ **argument, predicate**) and represent both noun and subject as well as verb and predicate, respectively. Aristotle added a third group to these two parts of speech, the group of 'indeclinables.'

Our current classification is based primarily on the teachings of the grammarian Dionsyios Thrax (first century BC), who proposed eight parts of speech: **noun, verb, adjective, article, pronoun, preposition, adverb**, and **conjunction**. In principle, all such divisions have as their basis the following three considerations, whose emphasis or lack thereof is the cause for the diverging analyses of many grammarians: (a) **morphology**: the distinction between inflected (noun, adjective, verb, pronoun) and non-inflected (adverb, conjunction, preposition) words; (b) **syntax**: for example, the ability to modify nominal or verbal elements (adjective vs adverb), to take an article (noun vs pronoun), to require a certain case of nouns or pronouns through **government** (preposition vs conjunction); (c) **semantics**: conceptual–categorial aspects – the three basic parts of speech, noun, adjective and verb, are based on the logical categories 'substance,' 'property,' and 'process,' while conjunctions and prepositions are based on the category 'relation.'

Most of the criticism of parts of speech is directed at the unevenness of the classificatory criteria, which are partially contradictory or overlapping, for example, the **numerals**, which on the basis of common lexical features (= terms for numbers and quantities) form an independent group, while the individual representatives behave syntactically as nouns (*thousands of people*), adjectives (*one book*), indefinite pronouns (*many*), or adverbs (*He called twice*). In addition, words can change historically from one category to another through **conversion**.

It must be remembered that words which sound the same due to **homophony** must often be assigned to different parts of speech according to usage, e.g. *sound*, which can occur as a noun (*a loud sound*), a verb (*to sound like ...*), and an adjective (*a sound reason*). In generative **transformational grammar**, the classification follows distributional criteria: all linguistic units which are interchangeable in the **deep structure** for the same lexical constituent belong to the same category. In **categorial grammar**, however, only the nouns form an independent category, all other categories being defined according to the way and manner they, combined with nouns, form sentences.

References
Magnusson, R. 1954. *Studies in the theory of the parts of speech*. Lund.
Shopen, T. (ed.) 1985. *Language typology and syntactic description*, vol. 3: *Grammatical categories and the lexicon*. Cambridge.

part–whole relation (*also* partonymy relation)

Semantic relation between linguistic expressions that designates the relation of a part to the whole or possessive relations: *A possesses B.* The part–whole relation is very similar to **inclusion**. Like true inclusion, it is asymmetric; but unlike inclusion, it is not transitive, e.g. *An arm has a hand* and *A hand has five fingers*, but not **An arm has five fingers* (⇒ **symmetrical relation, transitive relation**). **Selection restrictions** between certain verbs (*have, possess*) and different noun classes (*A cat has a long tail*, but not **A long tail has a cat*) cannot be described in **componential analysis** with binary features, but rather only with relational features.

References
Bendix, E.H. 1966. *Componential analysis of general vocabulary: the semantic structure of a set of verbs in English, Hindi, and Japanese*. The Hague.
Bierwisch, M. 1965. Eine Hierarchie syntaktisch-semantischer Merkmale. *Stgr* 5.29–86.
Cruse, D.A. 1979. On the transitivity of the part-whole relation. *JL* 15.29–38.
Kiefer, F. 1966. Some semantic relations in natural language. *FL* 2.228–40.

Parthian ⇒ Iranian

participial construction

Non-finite sentential expression composed of a **participle** and **modifiers**: *Demoralized by so many failures, he finally gave up.* Participial constructions can function semantically as temporal, modal, or causal complements, as well as **attributes**. They can be paraphrased (⇒ **paraphrase**) by corresponding **subordinate clauses**.

participle [Lat. *particeps* 'having a share in, participating']

Non-finite verb form, in English the present participle and past participle: *doing* vs *done*. Participles have properties of both nouns and verbs. In keeping with their verbal character, participles govern objects and give temporal and aspectual information (⇒ **tense, aspect**). The present participle designates the course of a process, while the past participle describes its result or effect(s). In addition, participles serve to form compound tenses (*He has come, He was coming*); the past participle is also used in forming passives (*The book was written*). Nominal features are: (a) it can be declined as an adjective in some languages; (b) it forms antonyms, e.g. *fitting* vs *unfitting*, *satisfied* vs *dissatisfied*; (c) it forms **compounds**, such as *far-reaching, near-sighted*; (d) it can be used both attributively and predicatively, e.g. *a much-read book* vs *The book is much read*; (e) it is used in forming **gerunds**, e.g. *reading books is good for you.*

particle [Lat. *particula* 'small part'] (*also* function/structural word)

1 Wide-reaching term, including all indeclinable word classes such as **adverbs, conjunctions, prepositions** and other particle classes such as **scalar particles, discourse markers, modal particles, negation, interjections**.

2 In a narrower sense: all invariant words which are not adverbs, conjunctions or prepositions, i.e. scalar particles, discourse markers, modal particles and interjections. They have weak lexical meaning and are ambiguous; a characteristic is the overlapping of the individual functions. (⇒ *also* **modal particle**)

References
Dikken, M. den 1995. Particles. *On the syntax of the verb-particle, triadic and causative constructions.* Oxford.
⇒ **discourse marker, interjection, modal particle, scalar particle**

Bibliography
Weydt, H. 1987. *Partikel-Bibliographie: internationale Sprachenforschung zu Partikeln und Interjektionen.* Frankfurt.

partitive

Morphological **case** in some languages (e.g. **Finnish**) which expresses 'a part of'; e.g. *eat a fish* vs *eat some fish*. The partitive is often expressed with the **genitive** case and can also take on a number of other meanings and functions.

References
⇒ **case**

partonymy relation ⇒ **part-whole relation**

Pashto

Iranian language in Afghanistan and Pakistan (about 10 million speakers), official language of Afghanistan.
   Characteristics: phonologically and morphologically more complicated than **Persian**, structured ergatively (⇒ **ergative language**) in the preterite. Word order: strictly SOV.

References
Lorenz, M. 1979. *Lehrbuch des Pashto (Afghanisch).* Leipzig.
Lorimer, D.L.R. 1915. *A syntax of colloquial Pashto.* Oxford.
Penzl, H. 1955. *A grammar of Pashto.* Washington, DC.
Shafeev, D.A. 1964. *A short grammatical outline of Pashto.* Bloomington, IN and The Hague. (= *IJAL* 30:3, pub. 33.)

Etymological dictionary
Morgenstierne, G. 1927. *An etymological vocabulary of Pashto.* Oslo.
⇒ **Iranian**

passive

Verbal **voice** contrasting with the **active** and in some languages the **middle voice**. Passive constructions describe the action expressed by the verb semantically from the point of view of the **patient** or another non-agentive semantic role. In this process the **valence** of the verb when used actively is usually changed: the subject becomes a prepositional object, usually optional, and an object, usually the direct object, becomes the subject: *A neighbor saw the robber*; *The robber was seen by a neighbor*. The passive is not the basic, or unmarked voice, as it is morphosyntactically the more complex construction (the passive is usually formed by specific auxiliaries or verb affixes) and is also subject to certain restrictions. The restrictions for forming the passive depend on the language; in English, for example, **middle verbs** (*cost, weigh*) as well as sentences with **cognate objects** (*He died a cruel death* vs **A cruel death was died by him*) cannot form passives.

References
⇒ **middle voice, voice**

passive articulator ⇒ **place of articulation**[1]

passive transformation ⇒ **voice**

past perfect (*also* pluperfect)

Verbal **tense** formed in English with *had* + past participle. In some uses the past perfect indicates the end point of an event in the past (*Caroline had finally achieved her goal*). In complex sentences the past perfect is used as a relative tense which marks anteriority of an event relative to another event that was completed in the past: *When we got to the station, the train had already departed*. (⇒ *also* **sequence of tenses**)

References
⇒ **tense**

past tense ⇒ **imperfect, preterite**

patient [Lat. *patiens* 'bearing, suffering']

Semantic role (⇒ **thematic relation**) of elements which are affected by the action of the verb, in contrast to the **agent**, which is the performer of the action. In **nominative languages** such as English, the patient is usually marked as the **direct object**. (⇒ *also* **case grammar**)

References
⇒ **case grammar**

patois

1 In **French**, term for a non-written regional dialect that is restricted to the most narrow social occasions.

2 Designation for a mixture of a regional **dialect** and **standard language** usually found in rural areas.

PATR (acronym for **parsing** and **translation**)

A grammatical formalism in **generative grammar** from the family of **unification grammars**. PATR was created and first used by Shieber as a computer language for the development of unification grammar. Context-free **phrase structures** and **feature structures** are kept distinct in the syntactic representations and rules. PATR is the simplest of the formalisms in unification grammar and is often used.

References
Hirsch, S. 1988. P-PATR: a compiler for Unification-based Grammars. In V. Dahl and P. Saint-Dizier (eds), *Natural language understanding and logic programming*. Amsterdam. 63–78.
Karttunen, L. 1986. D-PATR: a development environment for Unification-based Grammars. *COLING* 86.74–80.
Shieber, S.M. 1984. The design of a computer language for linguistic information. *COLING* 84.362–6.
——— *et al.* 1983. The formalism and implementation of PATR-II. *Research on interactive acquisition and use of knowledge. SRI International.* Menlo Park, CA. 39–79.

PATR-II ⇒ PATR

pattern drill ⇒ pattern practice

pattern practice (*also* pattern drill)

In foreign-language instruction, especially in the **audio-lingual method**, a short sample text (usually a sentence) that is changed by inserting other words or grammatical elements. This type of language exercise, which is based on imitation and analogy, is believed to lead to the development of syntagmatic habits.

paucalis [Lat. *pauci* 'few']

Subcategory of **number** for indicating a small number of objects, e.g. in Arabic.

pause

1 Brief interruption of the articulatory process between consecutive linguistic units such as sounds, syllables, morphemes, words, phrases, and sentences. Pauses are **suprasegmental features**. (⇒ *also* **intonation**)

2 ⇒ **interruption**

p-Celtic ⇒ Celtic

PDA ⇒ push-down automaton

peak ⇒ nucleus[2]

pedagogical grammar

Grammatical textbook or handbook for students or teachers of language that presents the grammar (usually **prescriptive grammar**) in a pedagogically based approach. Such handbooks are characterized above all by the selection of specific grammar items which are introduced in the form of an outline and are accompanied by explanatory notes on grammatical forms and usage.

References
Engels, L.K. 1977. *Pedagogical grammars*. Trier.
Leitner, G. (ed.) 1986. *The English reference grammar*. Tübingen.

pejorative [Lat. *peior*, used as comparative of *malus* 'bad']

Semantic characteristic of linguistic expressions which invoke negative **connotations**: such derogatory meaning components can be created by new formations (e.g. *wet-backs* for 'illegal Mexican immigrants'), by **meaning** change, (e.g. *dame*, originally '(noble) lady'), as well as by **prefixes** such as *mal-*, *pseudo-*.

Pennsylvania Dutch

Language variety in North America based on Middle **German** dialects, spoken today by approx. 700,000 descendants of German immigrants who came to America in the eighteenth century from the Rhine valley and the Palatinate. It is used as the colloquial and ritual language, but also as the spoken and written poetic language. The American term *Dutch* is an incorrect rendering of *deutsch* 'German'; it has nothing to do with **Dutch** as the name for the language spoken in the Netherlands.

Reference
Enninger, W. *et al.* (eds) 1986–9. *Studies of the languages and the verbal behavior of the Pennsylvania Germans*, 2 vols. Göttingen.

penthouse principle

A syntactic principle formulated by Ross (1973) and based on the theory that 'more goes on upstairs than downstairs.' It states that there can be syntactic processes which only occur in main clauses (⇒ **root transformation**), but none which only occur in subordinate clauses.

Reference
Ross, J.R. 1973. The penthouse principle and the order of constituents. In C. Corum, T.C. Smith-Stark, and A. Weiser (eds), *You take the high node*

and I'll take the low node: papers from the comparative syntax festival. The differences between main and subordinate clauses. Chicago, IL. 397–422.
⇒ **transformational grammar**

penultimate

The second to last syllable of a word.

Penutian

Language group of North America whose reconstruction is still debated. In total there are over a dozen highly diversified languages, (Tsimshian, Chinookan, Takelma-Kalapuyan, Alsea, Siuslaw, Coosan, Sahaptian, Klamath, Molala, Maiduan, Wintuan, Yokuts, Miwok-Costanoan, Zuni), few of which have more than 2,000 speakers; the largest language groups are Tsimshian in British Columbia and Sahaptian in Oregon and Washington state. Macro-Penutian is a substantially larger group which also includes the **Gulf languages** and the Central American languages such as **Mayan**.

Characteristics: complex consonant system, typically with a series of glottalized plosives; implosives also occur. **Vowel harmony**. Rich case system, often **ergative**, complex verbs (derivation, voices, aspect, and mood markers, but rarely agreement). Morphological type: **inflectional**, reduplication, and root inflection sometimes occur. Relatively free word order. Occasionally dual forms in the pronominal system, **noun classes**.

References
Barber, M.A.R. 1964. Klamath grammar. Berkeley, CA.
Barker, M.A. 1981. *Klamath grammar*. Berkeley, CA.
Buckley, E. 1987. Coast Oregon Penutian: a lexical comparison. In *Papers from the third Annual Pacific Linguistics Conference*. Eugene, OR.
Delancey, S. 1987. Klamath and Wintu pronouns. *IJAL* 53.461–4.
—— *et al*. 1987. Some Sahaptian–Klamath–Tsimshianic lexical sets. In W. Shipley (ed.), *In honor of Mary Haas: from the Haas festival conference on Native American linguistics*. Berlin and New York. 195–224.
Dunn, J.E. 1979. *A reference grammar for the Coast Tsimshian languages*. Ottawa.
Gamble, G. 1978. Wikchamni grammar. Berkeley, CA.
Hinton, L. 1994. *Flutes of fire: essays on California Indian languages*. Berkeley, CA.
Hymes, D.H. 1955. The language of the Kathlamet Chinook. Dissertation, Indiana University.
—— 1957. Some Penutian elements and the Penutian hypothesis. *SJA* 13.69–87.
Liedtke, S. 1994a. Penutian cognate sets. *LDDS* 4.
—— 1994b. Penutian, Mayan and Quechua. *LDDS* 10.
Pitkin, H. 1984. *Wintu grammar*. Berkeley, CA.
Shipley, W.E. 1964. *Maidu grammar*. Berkeley, CA.
Silverstein, M. 1979. Penutian: an assessment. In L. Campbell and M. Mithun (eds), *The languages of native America: historical and comparative assessment*. Austin, TX. 650–91.
Swadesh, M. 1956. Problems of long-range comparison in Penutian. *Lg* 32.17–41.

Dictionary
Callaghan, C.A. 1987. Northern Sierra Miwok dictionary. Berkeley, CA.

Bibliography
Golla, V. (to appear 1995). Penutian linguistic studies: a bibliography. *IJAL*.

perception theory

Phonetic study of the processes and conditions of speech perception (⇒ **acoustic phonetics**, **motor theory of speech perception**).

References
Pisoni, D. and P.A. Luce. 1986. Speech perception: research, theory and the principal issues. In E. Schwab and H. Nusbaum (eds), *Pattern recognition by humans and machines*. Orlando, FL. Vol. 1, 1–50.
⇒ **phonetics**

percolate [Lat. *percolare* 'to put through a filter, strain']

A term from **X-bar theory** which expresses the agreement of the morphosyntactic or semantic features of a phrase with the corresponding features of its lexical **head**. For example, in the phrase *the delicious cream doughnuts*, the feature [+plural] percolates or 'drips down' from the NP-node through the non-maximal projection of N, *delicious cream doughnuts*, and on to the lexical head, *doughnuts*, where it is realized phonologically as the inflected form, i.e. by *-s*. Many different formal mechanisms have been suggested for the percolation of individual features, cf. **Generalized Phrase Structure Grammar**, **Head-Driven Phrase Structure Grammar**.

References
⇒ **X-bar theory**

perfect

1 Term for a verbal category linked to **tense** and **aspect**.

2 (*also* present perfect) In English, the perfect is formed with the auxiliary *have* and the past participle of the main verb and denotes an action as having begun in the past, but extending up to the present (either as a continuing process or in repetition): *I have lived here all my life*; *She has given ten lectures this month*; or some result of which is relevant to the present: *She has just taken her exam* (*and is now waiting for the results*). In American

English, there is the tendency to use the simple past instead of the present perfect.

References
Dik, S. 1989. *The theory of functional grammar*, part I: *The structure of the clause*. Dordrecht.
Fenn, P. 1987. *A semantic and pragmatic examination of the English perfect*. Tübingen.
McCoard, R.W. 1978. *The English perfect: tense-choice and pragmatic inferences*. Amsterdam.
Michaelis, L. A. 1994. The ambiguity of the English present perfect. *JL* 30.111–57.
Quirk, R. *et al*. 1985. *A comprehensive grammar of the English language*. London.
⇒ **aspect**, **tense**

perfective ⇒ **imperfective vs perfective**

performance

Chomsky's term for the concrete individual linguistic event. Performance is based on the notion of competence as the intuitive knowledge of the **ideal speaker/listener** about the regularities of the language. The term 'performance' overlaps with de Saussure's term *parole* to a great extent. (⇒ **competence vs performance**, **langue vs parole**)

References
⇒ **competence vs performance**

performative analysis

Hypothesis developed by Ross (1968) to describe illocutionary forces within the framework of **transformational grammar**. On the basis of syntactic observations of declarative sentences, Ross attempted to derive all sentences from a unified deep structure that had one performative sentence as a matrix sentence (**hypersentence**), consisting of a subject (= first person) + a performative verb + an indirect object (= second person); the performative sentence, if need be, would be eliminated via deletion rules in the subsequent derivation of the uttered sentence. However, since the identity of speaker, addressee, and illocutionary force are dependent upon the given utterance situation, the performative analysis constitutes an (inadequate) syntacticization of pragmatic phe-

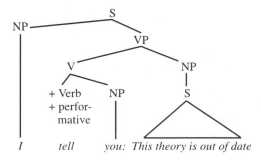

nomena. For criticism of the performative analysis cf. Gazdar (1979). Sadock (1985) and McCawley (1985) have recently attempted to salvage the performative analysis, at least in part.

References
Boer, S.E. and W.G. Lycan. 1980. A performadox in truth-conditional semantics. *Ling&P* 4.71–100.
Fraser, B. 1974. An examination of the performative analysis. *PIL* 7.1–40.
Gazdar, G. 1979. *Pragmatics: implicature, presupposition, and logical form*. New York.
Lakoff, R. 1972. Language in context. *Language* 48.907–27.
McCawley, J.D. 1985. What price the performative analysis? *University of Chicago Working Papers in Linguistics*. 1.43–64.
Ross, J.R. 1968. On declarative sentences. In R.A. Jacobs and P.A. Rosenbaum (eds), *Readings in English transformational grammar*. Waltham, MA. 222–72.
Sadock, J.M. 1968. Hypersentences. Dissertation, University of Illinois, Urbana.
———— 1974. *Toward a linguistic theory of speech acts*. New York.
———— 1985. On the performadox, or a semantic defense of the performative hypothesis. *University of Chicago Working Papers in Linguistics* 1.160–9.

performative antinomy

Performative antinomies are the illocutionary counterparts to the propositional (**semantic**) **antinomy** in the liar's statement: *This statement is false*, which is true only if it is false. Analogously, an order like *Don't obey this order* is obeyed if and only if it is not obeyed. (⇒ *also* **double-bind theory**)

References
Lakoff, G. 1972. Performative antinomies. *FL* 8.569–72.
Vanderveken, D. 1980. Illocutionary logic and self-defeating speech acts. In J.R. Searle, F. Kiefer, and M. Bierwisch (eds), *Speech-act theory and pragmatics*. Dordrecht. 247–72.

performative utterance

J.L. Austin's term which, in the first stage of his **speech act theory**, refers to utterances in the uttering of which, in appropriate circumstances, one performs particular actions. Performatives contrast with **constative** utterances, which describe actions or states. In developing his speech act theory further, Austin downplayed this distinction of two different utterance types in favor of a distinction between two different aspects of speech acts, the locutionary and illocutionary. The original distinction between performative and constative became increasingly problematic as Austin began to present all utterances as performative utterances in some respect or other. However, the distinction between (a) implicit (or primary or primitive) performative utterances and (b) explicit performative utterances remains. With the primary (implicit) utterance of *you're mistaken*, one can just as easily assert that the addressee is mistaken as with the explicit utterance of *I assert that you're mistaken*. Primary performative utterances in general have no lexical illocutionary indicators (⇒ **illocution**); in contrast, explicit performative utterances usually have the form of a matrix sentence with a **performative verb** in the first person present indicative, an indirect object denoting the addressee, and an embedded sentence. The self-reference of the explicit performative utterance can be highlighted by insertion of *hereby*: *I (hereby) christen this ship the 'Queen Mary.'*

References
Austin, J.L. 1963. Performative – constative. In C.E. Caton (ed.) *Philosophy and ordinary language.* Urbana, IL. 22–54.
⇒ **speech act theory**

performative verb

Semantically and pragmatically defined class of verbs (e.g. *to promise*, *to command*, *to christen*, *to swear*, among others), the use of which in explicitly performative utterances causes precisely that action to be carried out that is expressed by the particular verb. Performative verbs are distinguished from perlocutive verbs such as *to provoke*, *to convince*, *to humble*, which cannot be used performatively (*?I hereby convince you to vote democratic*) and instead describe reactions partly under the control of the addressee. Not all illocutionary verbs, that is, verbs that denote **illocutions**, are performative verbs. For example, *to threaten* is an illocutionary, but not a performative verb. This distinction is supported by the fact that only performative verbs can be used with *hereby*: *I hereby promise you that …* vs **I hereby threaten you that …*.

References
Vanderveken, D. 1990–1. Meaning and speech acts, 2 vols. Cambridge.
⇒ **performative analysis, pragmatics, speech act theory**

peripheral ⇒ compact vs diffuse

periphrasis [Grk *períphrasis* 'circumlocution']

Substitution of more words for fewer. In periphrasis a word is replaced by an expanded and more colorful expression for the purpose of linguistic variation, accentuation, or explanation, e.g. Berlin was 'the divided city,' Ireland is 'the Emerald Isle.' **Definition** is a special type of periphrasis.

periphrastic verb forms

Term from **Latin** grammar for verb forms that are not strictly morphological, but include additional 'helping verbs' (**auxiliaries**). Latin has at least two formations, the **supine** (*laudaturus sum* 'I am about to praise') and the **gerundive** (*laborandum est* 'one must work'). In English virtually all tenses are formed periphrastically, the only synthetic (= non-periphrastic) tenses being the present and the simple past (*I am*, *I was* vs *I have been*, *I will be*).

perispomenon [Grk *perispōménos*, participle of *perispãn* 'pronounce with a circumflex accent']

In Greek, a word with circumflex accent, presumably reflecting a rise–fall intonation on the last **syllable**, e.g. *philõ* 'I love.' (⇒ *also* **properispomenon**)

perlocution [Lat. *per-* 'through,' *loqui* 'to talk, speak']

In **speech act theory**, an aspect of speech acts that includes the causal effects (intentionally) brought about by a speaker by way of his/her utterance. Perlocutionary acts consist in achieving effects in the hearer through the performance of an illocutionary act, for example, in cheering someone up by asserting that he/she did an excellent job. Just what perlocutionary effects are achieved, in the uttering of a particular illocution in context, may vary widely in differing circumstances.

References
⇒ **speech act theory**

Permic ⇒ Finno-Ugric

permutation [Lat. *permutare* 'to exchange']

1 Generally, the reordering of **constituents**. In the framework of generative **transformational grammar**, a formal two-step operation (⇒ **operational procedures**) by which an element is placed in another position via **substitution**, and then deleted in its original position.

References
⇒ **transformational grammar**

2 In **word order** and linear **syntax**, term for reordering processes such as **extraposition** and **topicalization**.

References
⇒ **word order**

permutation transformation ⇒ **movement transformation**

perseverative assimilation ⇒ **assimilation**

Persian (*also* Farsi)

Largest **Iranian** language (about 50 million speakers), official language of Iran, in addition approx. 5 million speakers in Afghanistan (Dari dialect) and 2.2 million speakers in Tajikistan. Modern Persian, of which the first documentation occurs in the eighth century, is not a direct descendant of a Middle Iranian dialect. The lexicon was strongly influenced by **Arabic**. Around AD 1300 a supraregional standard (Classical Persian) developed with a comprehensive literature; it was the court language of both the Ottoman Empire and northern India (Mogul Dynasty). Arabic script is used with a few additional characters.

Characteristics: relatively simple sound system. Morphology: the **Indo-European** nominal and verbal inflection was almost completely lost and replaced by analytical constructions and enclitic pronouns. Differential object marking (marking of specific objects). Nominal syntagms can consist of the structure modifier – head – modifier. The modifier following the head is linked to it with an *e*, the so-called *ezāfe*: *īn mīz-e-bozorg* 'this big table.' Word order: SOV.

References
Towhīdī, J. 1974. *Studies in the phonetics and phonology of modern Persian*. Hamburg.
Windfuhr, G.L. 1979. *Persian grammar: history and state of its study*. The Hague.

Grammars
Bātenī, M.R. 1370 (= 1991). *Towsīfe saxtemāne dasturīe zabāne fārsī*. 4th edn. Tehran.
Boyle, J.A. 1966. *Grammar of modern Persian*. Wiesbaden.
Clair-Tisdall, W.S. 1923. *Modern Persian conversation grammar*. London.
Lambton, A.K.S. 1986. *Persian grammar*, Reissue (with corrections and repagination). Cambridge.
Lazard, G. 1957. *Grammaire du persan contemporain*. Paris.
Rastorgueva, V.S. 1963. A short sketch of Tajik grammar. Transl. and ed. by H.H. Paper. *IJAL* Part II. (Repr. Bloomington, IN 1992).
———— 1964. *A short sketch of the grammar of Persian*. Bloomington, IN and The Hague. (= *IJAL* 30:1, pub. 29.)

Dictionaries
Aryanpur Kashani, A. 1986. *Combined new Persian–English and English–Persian dictionary*. Lexington.
Dekhodā, A.A. 1334/1962. *Loghatnāme*. Tehran.
Haim, S. 1985. *New Persian–English dictionary*, 6th impr., 2 vols. Teheran.
Hübschmann, H. 1895. *Perische Studien*. Straßburg

(additions and corrections to Horn).
Steingass, F. 1892. A comprehensive Persian–English dictionary. (8th impr. 1988.) London.

Etymological dictionary
Horn, P. 1893. *Grundriss der neupersischen Etymologie*. Strasburg.
⇒ **Iranian**

person

Morphological category of the verb used to mark the singular and plural finite verb forms as 'speakers' (first person), 'addressees' (second person), or a 'person, state or thing' referred to in the utterance (third person). In the first person plural, two different interpretations are possible: an inclusive interpretation, in which the speaker is included, and an exclusive interpretation, in which the speaker is not included. Some languages express this distinction morphologically (⇒ **inclusive vs exclusive**). On different uses of forms of address, ⇒ **pronominal form of address**.

References
⇒ **personal pronoun, pronominal form of address**

person hierarchy

Hierarchical ordering of the verbal categories of **person** which in some languages is important to the grammar. The typical hierarchy is first–second–third person (as in **Guaraní**); second–first–third also occurs (as in **Algonquian**).

References
⇒ **hierarchy universal**

personal pronoun

Subgroup of **pronouns** which refer to persons, either speakers (*I*, *we*), addressees (*you*) or other persons/things (*he*, *she*, *it*) (⇒ **inclusive vs exclusive**). Three types of personal pronouns can be distinguished according to use: (a) anaphoric pronouns (= the antecedent precedes the pronoun): *Philip is looking for his knife, which he desperately needs*; (b) cataphoric pronouns (the antecedent follows the pronoun): *Before she said anything, Caroline thought about it a long time*; and (c) exophoric pronouns (the antecedent stands outside of the sentence): *Caroline is glad that he is coming*. The use of pronouns is subject to certain language-specific restrictions. Nevertheless, one general tendency is that pronouns cannot be used in the same clause as the **antecedent** they refer to; in such situations, **reflexive pronouns** are used (e.g. *Philip₁ brushed *him₁/himself₁ off*). In addition, personal pronouns (just as all pronouns in general) tend to follow their antecedents (⇒ **anaphora**), so that cataphoric pronouns occur more rarely and are subject to greater restrictions than anaphoric pronouns. In older forms of **transformational grammar**, personal pronouns are derived from pronominalizing **transformations** which replace a noun phrase by a pronoun if both elements have identical reference. In more recent forms of transformational grammar personal pronouns are not handled by transformations, but rather by **binding theory**.

References
Bach, E. 1970. Problominalization. *LingI* 1.121ff.
Ingram, D. 1978. Typology and universals of personal pronouns. In J.H. Greenberg *et al.* (eds), *Universals of human language*. Stanford, CA. 213–47.
Jackendoff, R.S. 1972. *Semantic interpretation in generative grammar*. Cambridge, MA.
Kreimann, J. and A.E. Ojeda (eds) 1980. *Papers from the parasession on pronouns and anaphora of the Chicago Linguistic Society*. Chicago, IL.
Langacker, R. 1966. On pronominalization and the chain of command. Repr. in D.A. Reibel and S.A. Schane (eds), *Modern studies in English: readings in transformational grammar*. Englewood Cliffs, NJ, 1969. 160–87.
Lasnik, H. 1976. Remarks on coreference. *LingA* 2.1–22.
Partee, B.H. 1970. Opacity, reference and pronouns. *Synthese* 21.359–85.
Postal, P.M. 1971. *Cross-over phenomena: a study in the grammar of coreference*. New York.
—— 1972. A global constraint on pronominalization. *LingI* 3.35–60.
Ross, J.R. 1967. On the cyclic nature of English pronominalization. Repr. in D.A. Reibel and S.A. Schane (eds), *Modern studies in English: readings in transformational grammar*. Englewood Cliffs, NJ, 1969. 187–200.
⇒ **anaphora**, **binding theory**, **reflexive pronoun**

persuasive

A term from **rhetoric** for a communicative act in which the listener is convinced to relinquish one opinion and to adopt another against his/her real or supposed resistance. The spectrum of persuasive speech extends from argumentative **discourse** and legal defence to advertising and political propaganda. In accordance with its appellative intention (⇒ **text function**), persuasive speaking is carefully planned and characterized by the most effective employment of linguistic means possible. (⇒ **advertising language**, **mass communication**)

References
Brown, J.A.C. 1963. *Techniques of persuasion*. Harmondsworth.
Chase, S. 1954. *The power of words*. New York.
Hawthorn, J. (ed.) 1987. *Propaganda, persuasion and polemic*. London.
Hovland, C.J. *et al.* 1953. *Communication and persuasion*. New Haven, CT.
Mey, J.L. 1985. *Whose language? A study in linguistic pragmatics*. Amsterdam.
Mulholland, J. 1994. *A handbook of persuasive tactics*. London.
Sandell, R. 1977. *Linguistic style and persuasion*. New York.
Stevenson, C.L. 1944. *Ethics and language*. New Haven, CT.
⇒ **rhetoric**

pharyngeal [Grk *phárynx* 'throat']

Speech sound classified according to its **place of articulation** (**pharynx**). Because of limitations to moving the pharynx, there are generally only two pharyngeals: the fricatives [ħ] and [ʕ]. Both occur in **Arabic**: [ħiˈnːaːʕ] 'henna,' [ˈʕiːsaː] 'Jesus.' (⇒ *also* **articulatory phonetics**)

References
⇒ **phonetics**

pharyngeal dysglossia ⇒ dysglossia

pharyngealization ⇒ secondary articulation

pharynx

Chamber located between the root of the tongue and the back of the throat and between the larynx and the nasal cavity.

phatic act [Grk *phátis* 'speech']

In J.L. Austin's **speech act theory**, a phatic act consists in the production of words and strings of words in a particular construction with a particular intonation. Together with the **phonetic act** (= utterance of speech sounds) and the **rhetic act** (= use of words with a certain meaning, i.e. a certain sense and a certain reference), the phatic act is subsumed under the locutionary act (**locution**).

References
⇒ **speech act theory**

phatic communion

B. Malinowski's term for communicative acts that fulfill an exclusively social function, that is, acts that serve to confirm 'ties of union,' such as the more or less formal inquiry about one's health, remarks about the weather, or comments about trivial matters.

References
Laver, J. 1975. Communicative functions of phatic communion. In A. Kendon *et al.* (eds), *Organization of behaviour in face-to-face interaction*. The Hague and Paris. 215–38.
Malinowski, B. 1923. The problem of meaning in primitive languages. In C.K. Ogden and I.A. Richards, *The meaning of meaning* (appendix). London. 296–336.

Schneider, K. 1988. *Small talk: analyzing phatic discourse*. Marburg.

phenotype [Grk *phainómenon* 'that which appears']

Term which S. Šaumjan took from the study of inheritance and applied to **semiotics**. The term 'phenotype' refers to any outward manifestation of natural language that can be measured by empirical observation. This concrete linear linking of linguistic expressions is governed by correspondence rules with the **genotype**, the ideal, universal linguistic level which underlies all phenotypes. (⇒ *also* **applicational-generative model**)

References
⇒ **applicational-generative model**

philosophical grammar ⇒ general grammar

philosophy of language

In the framework of philosophy, a multitude of approaches and directions that are concerned with questions on the origin, characteristics, way of functioning and achievement of language. For the solution of the predominantly interdisciplinary problems logical, psychological, linguistic, biological, sociological, and other investigations and insights need to be taken into account. A central question of contemporary language philosophy is the connection between philosophical insight and knowledge on the one hand and the form and structure of language on the other, as was discussed especially in 'Analytical Philosophy,' with its interest in logical analysis. (⇒ **language criticism, ordinary language philosophy, origin of language**)

References
Black, M. 1949. *Language and philosophy*. Ithaca, NY.
Borgmann, A. 1974. *The philosophy of language*. The Hague.
Bühler, K. 1934. *Sprachtheorie*. Jena.
Coseriu, E. 1969. *Die Geschichte der Sprachphilosophie von der Antike bis zur Gegenwart*, 2 vols. Tübingen.
Dascal, M. *et al.* (eds) 1992/3. *Philosophy of language: an international handbook of contemporary research*. Vol. 1. Berlin and New York.
Gabbay, D. and F. Guenthner (eds) 1989. *Handbook of philosophical logic*, vol. 4: *Topics in the philosophy of language*. Dordrecht.
Grewendorf, G. and G. Meggle (eds) 1974. *Linguistik und Philosophie*. Frankfurt.
Heintel, E. 1975. *Einführung in die Sprachphilosophie*. Darmstadt.
Jespersen, O. 1925. *The philosophy of language*. London.
Meulen, A. ter. 1988. Linguistics and the philosophy of language. In F. Newmeyer (ed.), *Linguistics: the Cambridge survey*. Cambridge. Vol. I, 430–46.
Rorty, R. 1967. *Linguistic turn*. Chicago, IL.
Searle, J.R. (ed.) 1971. *The philosophy of language*. Oxford.
Stegmüller, W. 1969. *Hauptströmungen der Gegenwartsphilosophie*, vol. 1. Stuttgart (7th rev. edn 1989.)
Tugendhat, E. 1976. *Einführung in die sprachanalytische Philosophie*. Frankfurt.

Phoenician ⇒ Semitic

phonation [Grk *phōnḗ* 'sound; voice']

One of four processes involved in the formation of **speech sounds** that refers to the different positions of the **vocal cords** and **glottis**. Five different positions play a role in phonation: (a) the glottis is open in voicelessness (⇒ **voiced vs voiceless**); (b) the vocal cords form a crevasse and vibrate with normal voicing; (c) when whispering quietly, the vocal cords are tightly constricted in the front and form a crevasse in the back; with laryngeal sounds there is added vibration; (d) in **murmuring**, the vocal cords are not constricted and they vibrate; and, as in loud whispering, they form a triangle; (e) if the glottis is closed, there is no phonation. A **glottal stop** is achieved by closing and reopening the glottis. Different **pitches** are produced by vibrating the vocal cords. Some think that accent (⇒ **stress**[2]) is brought about by varying the pressure of the pulmonic air; differences in quality are caused by varying the duration of the sound formation (⇒ **intonation, quantity**).

References
⇒ **phonetics**

phone

1 In **acoustic phonetics**, unit for measuring subjectively perceived volume that corresponds to 1,000 Hertz on a scale of normal sound.

2 (*also* **segment, speech sound**) In **phonology**, the smallest phonetic unit uncovered through **segmentation** of a spoken language (*parole*, ⇒ **langue vs parole**) that has not yet been classified as a representative of a particular **phoneme**. Phones are notated in brackets: [foːn].

phoneme

1 Since the end of the nineteenth century, term used to denote the smallest sound units that can be segmented from the acoustic flow of speech and which can function as semantically distinctive units (notation: phonetic symbol between slashes, e.g. /a/). The inventory of phonemes in a given language can be determined by: (a) finding **minimal pairs**, i.e. two words with

different meanings that differ by a single phonetic element (e.g. /g/ vs/ /k/ in *gap* : *cap*, /m/
vs /t/ in *map* : *tap*); (b) using **commutation
tests** to isolate the phonetic elements (e.g. [g, k,
m, t]) as word-initial consonants through syntagmatic segmentation and identifying them as
phonemes through paradigmatic classification
based on their substitutability in otherwise
similar environments. In other words, the fact
that each of the four expressions has a different
meaning is signaled alone by the different
initial consonants. (c) Phonemes are, however,
not the smallest units of phonetic description,
for each phoneme represents a class of phonetically similar sound variants, the **allophones**,
which cannot be contrastively substituted for
each other, i.e. cannot stand in semantically
distinctive **opposition**. These allophones may
be realized coincidentally as independent variants unaffected by their phonetic environment
(⇒ **free variation**). If allophonic differences
are phonotactic (i.e. conditioned according to
their placement/environment), language-
specific, and in complementary **distribution**,
then the allophones are said to be 'combinatory
variants.' Such phonetic variants cannot be
freely substituted for one another. (d) Phonemes can be represented as bundles of distinctive (i.e. phonologically relevant) **features** (e.g.
/p/ as [+stop, +bilabial –voiced, –nasal]. From
the large number of articulatory and acoustic
characteristics theoretically available as distinctive features, each language takes only a
small number. The various definitions of what
constitutes a phoneme are by no means standard; rather, depending on the theoretical thrust
and perspective, the following functional
aspects are stressed in the analysis: in the
Prague School the semantically distinctive
function, and in **American structuralism** the
distributional conditions and **operational procedures** required to ascertain phonemes. For a
discussion of the concept of 'phoneme' in
generative phonology, ⇒ **phonology**.

2 A more recent use of 'phoneme' is essentially unrelated to that found in linguistic technical literature. In the production of artificial
language, 'phoneme operators' are machines
that produce speech sounds. During this production, the frequency and volume of individual sounds can be modified in very small
increments. Because of the modifiability of
these individual sounds, technicians speak of
'phonemes,' even though such 'phonemes' do
not correspond to those in a phonetic class of
articulatory phonetics.

References
⇒ **phonology**

phoneme analysis

Process for determining the **phonemes** of a
language, their characteristics, relations, and
combinatory rules in the framework of a particular language theory. The proceedings of the
Prague School (N. Trubetzkoy, R. Jakobson)
are based on the functional aspect of phonemes
and their characteristics as semantically distinctive elements of language and primarily on the
analysis of their distinctive **oppositions**. **American structuralism** (principally L. Bloomfield,
Z.S. Harris) attempts to determine the phonemic inventory by establishing the possible
environments in which phonemes occur.
Regardless of divergences in the theoretical
approaches, certain procedures are fundamental
to any (structuralist) phonemic analysis: the
smallest distinctive sound units are identified
and classified according to their **distribution**
and phonetic similarities to other phonemes
through **segmentation** of the air stream and
substitution of different phonemes. Substitution tests are performed on **minimal pairs**, e.g.
[gæb] vs [kæb] vs [tʰæb]. Sound units that can
be substituted in the same position but are
semantically distinctive are identified as phonemes. Differences between relevant (= distinctive) and irrelevant (= redundant) features of
phonemes of a language, their distribution in
different positions (initial, medial, final), as
well as the rules governing their possible combinations are determined by constantly refining
the process of segmentation and classification.
For a criticism of classical phoneme analysis,
see Chomsky and Halle (1965). (⇒ *also* **allophone, distribution, neutralization, opposition, phonemic inventory, phonology**)

References
Chomsky, N. and M. Halle. 1965. Some controversial
    questions in phonological theory. *JL* 1.97–138.
⇒ **phonology, Prague School**

phoneme distance

Degree of relatedness between two or more
phonemes based on the number of common or
different **distinctive features**. All phonemes
can be distinguished by at least one (acoustic or
articulatory) feature. For details on the conceptual system developed by N. Trubetzkoy to
describe the relationships, ⇒ **opposition**.

References
⇒ **phonology**

phoneme system

The overall pattern of characteristics and relationships of the phonemes in the **phonemic
inventory** of a given language. The phonological characteristics of the phonemes and

their **allophones** are described by articulatory or acoustic features, the interrelationships between phonemes through **oppositions**.

References
⇒ **phonology**

phonemic feature ⇒ distinctive feature

phonemic inventory

The set of phonemes of a given language as determined by a phonological analysis of that language. Every language takes a limited number of articulatory/acoustic features from a virtually unlimited number of possibilities. For most known languages the inventory contains thirteen to seventy-five phonemes (see Hockett 1958: 93). The phonetic characteristics of individual members of the inventory are, as a rule, given through matrices showing articulatory or acoustic features. Jakobson and Halle (1956) have provided a universal phonemic inventory.

References
Hockett, C.F. 1958. *A course in modern linguistics.* New York.
Maddieson, I. 1984. *Patterns of sounds.* Cambridge.
Jakobson, R. and M. Halle. 1956. *Fundamentals of language.* The Hague. (2nd rev. edn 1975.)
⇒ **phonology**

phonemic paraphasia ⇒ aphasia, paraphasia

phonemic script ⇒ phonography²

phonemic theory ⇒ phonology

phonemic variant ⇒ allophone

phonemics

1 Synonym for **phonology**.

2 Because of the historical connotations that since the time of the Neogrammarians were attached to the term **phonology**, which today is used for synchronic and diachronic studies, 'phonemics' was first used by the American structuralists for 'synchronic phonology.' This designation was also meant to distinguish the American structuralist approach from that of the European structuralists, especially those of the **Prague School**.

References
⇒ **phonology**

phonemization

In diachronic **phonology** process and result of the development of a phonological variant (⇒ **allophone**) into a **phoneme**. (⇒ *also* **sound change**)

phonetic act

In J.L. Austin's **speech act theory**, the partial speech act that consists in the production of language sounds or complex sound forms. Together with the **phatic act** and the **rhetic act**, the phonetic act constitutes the locutionary act (**locution**).

References
⇒ **speech act theory**

phonetic relationship (*also* phonetic similarity)

Characteristic of sound variants that belong to one and the same **phoneme**. The phonetic relationship cannot be defined exactly operationally; rather, in many cases it requires intuition or is independent of differences in the language used to describe the sounds. A phonetic relationship in complementary distribution is, as a rule, a criterion for considering two sound variants as belonging to one and the same phoneme.

References
⇒ **phonology**

phonetic similarity⇒ phonetic relationship

phonetic symbolism ⇒ sound symbolism

phonetic transcription

A system of symbols used for the written notation of spoken language. A distinction must be drawn between non-alphabetic (= analphabetic) systems (⇒ **visible speech**), as developed by A.M. Bell, O. Jespersen, and K.L. Pike, and alphabetic systems. Among the last group are most of the alphabets for phonetic transcription developed since the nineteenth century, which are mainly of historical value. The IPA (International Phonetic Alphabet) developed by the International Phonetic Association, which is now in widespread use, is based primarily on the Latin alphabet (see chart, p. xix). Additional letters from Greek, reversed letters, and newly developed letters and diacritics (such as those needed to indicate long vowels and consonants, nasalization, and so on) are also part of the alphabet. As in the transcriptional system of D. Jones (1914), a distinction is made with regard to the degree of differentiation between 'narrow' and 'broad' transcriptions (e.g. [tʰæp⁻] is narrow and [tæp] is broad). More recently, some modified or expanded transcriptional alphabets have been designed for special needs based on the IPA. Pullum & Ladusaw (1986) offer a good overview; the phonetic transcriptions in this dictionary are based on the system outlined in their book.

References

International Phonetic Association. 1989. *The principles of the International Phonetic Association.*

Jones, D. 1914. *Outline of English phonetics.* London.

Kuglerkruse, M. 1985. *Computer phonetic alphabet.* Bochum.

Ladefoged, P. 1990. The revised International Phonetic Alphabet. *Language* 66.550–2.

Passy, P. and D. Jones. 1921. *L'Écriture phonétique internationale*, 3rd edn. Cambridge.

Pullum, G.K. and W.A. Ladusaw. 1986. *Phonetic symbol guide.* Chicago, IL.

Bibliography

Wellisch, H. 1975. *Transcription and transliteration: an annotated bibliography on conversion of scripts.* Silver Spring, MD.
⇒ **phonetics**

phonetics

Linguistic subdiscipline that studies the phonetic aspect of speech with regard to the following processes: (a) articulatory–genetic sound production (⇒ **articulatory phonetics**); (b) structure of the acoustic flow (⇒ **acoustic phonetics**); and (c) neurological–psychological processes involved in perception (⇒ **auditory phonetics**). An understanding of anatomy, physiology, neurology, and physics is fundamental to these studies. In contrast to **phonology**, phonetics studies the concrete articulatory, acoustic, and auditory characteristics of all the possible sounds of all languages. Instrumental phonetics makes use of electronic equipment, whereas **experimental phonetics** involves empirical and experimental processes.

References

Abercrombie, D. 1966. *Elements of general phonetics.* Edinburgh.

Asher, R.E. and E.J.A. Henderson (eds) 1981. *Towards a history of phonetics.* Edinburgh.

Catford, J.C. 1988. *A practical introduction to phonetics.* Oxford.

Clark, J. and C. Yallop. 1995. *An introduction to phonetics and phonology.* 2nd edn. Oxford.

Jespersen, O. 1904. *Lehrbuch der Phonetik.* Leipzig.

Jones, D. 1922. *An outline of English phonetics*, 2nd edn. Berlin.

Knowles, G. 1987. *Patterns of spoken English: an introduction to English phonetics.* London.

Ladefoged, P. 1971. *Preliminaries to linguistic phonetics.* Chicago, IL.

——— 1975. *A course in phonetics.* 3rd edn 1993. Fort Worth, TX and Philadelphia, PA.

Laver, J. 1994. *Principles of phonetics.* Cambridge.

MacMahon, M.K.C. 1990. Language as available sound: phonetics. In N.E. Collinge (ed.), *An encyclopedia of language.* London. 3–29.

Pike, K.L. 1943. *Phonetics.* Ann Arbor, MI.

Pompino-Marshall, B. 1992. *Einführung in die Phonetik.* Berlin and New York.

Thomas, J.M.C., L. Bouquiaux, and F. Cloarec-

Heiss. 1976. *Initiation à la phonétique.* Paris.

Trask, R.L. 1995. *A dictionary of phonetics and phonology.* London.

Bibliography

Laver, J. 1979. *Voice quality: a classified research bibliography.* Amsterdam.

Journal

Zeitschrift für Phonetik, Sprachwissenschaft und Kommunikationsforschung.

phonogram ⇒ phonography

phonography

1 In **experimental phonetics**, the recording of spoken language by means of records and tapes (phonograms).

2 (*also* phonemic script) Writing system whose signs relate to phonological units. All alphabetic writing systems and syllabic scripts are phonographic; however, only alphabetic writing systems come close to a one-to-one correspondence between sound (**phoneme**) and written sign. **Letters** or letter clusters as well as syllabograms are called phonograms. The purest form of phonography is found in the IPA (⇒ **phonetic transcription**) in which, as a rule, each sign corresponds to a single sound.

References
⇒ **phonetic transcription, writing**

phonological component

In generative **phonology** the set of rules that phonetically interpret the underlying phonological form of sentences.

References
⇒ **phonological rule**

phonological disorder

Type of **developmental language disorder** wherein the child has difficulty learning language-specific speech sound categories, but seems capable of producing the requisite phonetic forms. This type of disorder may or may not be accompanied by atypical development in other linguistic domains. It has recently been distinguished from non-standard pronunciation patterns which result from a limited phonetic repertoire due to structural or neural deficiencies. (⇒ **articulation disorder**)

References

Benthal, J. and N. Bankson, 1988. *Articulation and phonological disorders*, 2nd rev. edn. Englewood Cliffs, NJ.

Elbert, M. and J. Gierut. 1986. *Handbook of clinical phonology.* San Diego, CA.

Grunwell, P. 1987. *Clinical phonology.* London.

phonological rule

In generative **phonology**, type of transformational rule (⇒ **transformation**) that transfers the phonological representation of sentences into the phonetic transcription. Phonological rules are in the form of: $A \rightarrow B/X$____Y, i.e. 'replace segment A with element B in the environment of immediately following X and immediately preceding Y.' (⇒ *also* **phonology**, **transformational grammar**)

References

Anderson, S. 1974. *The organization of phonology.* New York. 51–62.

Blomberger, S. and M. Halle. 1989. Why phonology is different. *LingI* 20.51–70.

phonologically conditioned

In **morphology**, such morpheme variants (⇒ **allomorph**) whose occurrence is determined by the phonological environment. For example, in American English intervocalic [t] is pronounced as a flap [ɾ], e.g. [bæɾər].

References

⇒ **lexical phonology**

phonological transcription

A transcription of language on the basis of its phonologically relevant elements (notation: phonetic symbol between slashes), using symbols from the phonetic alphabet. In contrast with a **phonetic transcription** which indicates every perceivable (allophonic) distinction in sounds as accurately as possible, a phonological transcription is restricted to the linguistically significant differences, i.e. both allophones in **free variation** (such as the difference between a front trilled *r* [r] and a back trilled *r* [ʁ] in German) and in **complementary distribution** (e.g. aspirated voiceless vs non-aspirated voiceless stops in English) are indicated by the same phonetic symbol in the transcription.

References

⇒ **phonetic transcription**

phonologization ⇒ morphologization

phonology (*also* **phonemics**, phonemic theory)

Linguistic subdiscipline concerned with semantically relevant speech sounds (⇒ **phoneme**), and their pertinent characteristics, relations, and systems viewed synchronically and diachronically. Today, the term 'phonology' is used in this broadly defined sense and is differentiated at the same time from **phonetics** as the scientific study of the material aspect of speech sounds. Other definitions of phonology are only of peripheral or historical interest. The term was, at one time, used synonymously with phonetics. The French continue to draw a distinction between autonomous phonology

and **prosody**, while in American linguistics phonology is occasionally used as an umbrella term for phonetics and phonemics.

(a) *Structuralist phonology*: structurally oriented phonology started with N. Trubetzkoy (⇒ **Prague School**) and quickly developed in several directions. While Trubetzkoy was concerned with the functional aspect of phonemic analysis, the principle of the opposition of phonemes as the basis of his phonological work, **American structuralism** bases its concept of phoneme largely on distributional criteria (see Bloomfield 1933; Harris 1951). Common to both varieties is the way in which phonology is understood as an autonomous level of linguistic description in contrast to generative phonology (see Chomsky & Halle 1968, among others). Phonology is considered a basic discipline of structuralist language analysis (⇒ **operational procedure**). This is particularly the case for the functional principle of distinctiveness (⇒ **distinctive feature**, **opposition**), the analytical process of **segmentation** and **classification**, but especially for the concept of the phoneme as a bundle of distinctive features and for the hypothesis of a universal inventory of phonological features as the basis for describing all languages of the world (see Jakobson & Halle 1956).

(b) *Generative phonology*: in contrast to the structuralist interpretation of phonology as an autonomous level of linguistic description, in the framework of **generative grammar**, phonology refers to phonetic, phonological, and syntactic–morphological regularities (= systematic phonology). Instead of the phoneme, distinctive features of a universal character are considered the basic units of the phonological description (⇒ **distinctive feature theory**). On the basis of relatively abstract and stable **underlying forms**, the phonetic variants of the **surface structure** are derived from extrinsically ordered rules (cf. /fɪʃd/ as the underlying form of /fɪʃt/.

(c) From the criticism of classical transformational concepts 'natural phonology' and 'natural generative phonology' have developed. These concepts are based on the belief in a strict division of the two levels of phonology and morphology (see Hooper 1976; Dressler 1984).

(d) The problems of generative phonology in the description of **suprasegmental features** have recently led to a paradigm change towards **non-linear phonology**. The methods and results of phonological theories are a prerequisite and challenge for numerous studies in neighboring (applied) disciplines such as **psycholinguistics** (especially in **language acquisition** and language loss, ⇒ **aphasia**), **contrast-**

ive analysis, as well as in **writing** and spelling problems.

References
General and introductions
Archangeli, D. and D. Pulleyblank. 1994. *Grounded phonology*. Cambridge, MA.
Carr, P. 1993. *Phonology: an introduction*. Basingstoke.
Dinnsen, D.A. 1979. *Current approaches to phonological theory*. Bloomington, IN.
Durand, J. and F. Katamba (eds) 1994. *New frontiers in phonology*. London.
Ferguson, C.A. 1977. New directions in phonological theory: language acquisition and universals research. In R.W. Cole (ed.), *Current issues in linguistic theory*. Bloomington, IN.
Fisiak, J. (ed.) 1992. *Phonological investigations*. Amsterdam and Philadelphia.
Fudge, E. 1990. Language as organised sound: phonology. In N.E. Collinge (ed.), *An encyclopedia of language*. London. 30–67.
Giegevich, H.J. 1992. *English phonology*. Cambridge.
Katamba, F. 1989. *An introduction to phonology*. London.
Kaye, J. 1989. *Phonology: a cognitive view*. Hillsdale, NJ.
Lass, R. 1984. *Phonology: an introduction to basic concepts*. Cambridge.
Vennemann, T. 1986. *Neuere Entwicklungen in der Phonologie*. Berlin.
Vihmann, M. 1995. *The origins of phonology*. Oxford.

Phonological theory
Anderson, J.M. and C.J. Ewen, 1987. *Principles of dependency phonology*. Cambridge.
Anderson, S.R. 1985. *Phonology in the twentieth century*. Chicago, IL.
Basbøll, H. 1988. Phonological theory. In F. Newmeyer (ed.), *Linguistics: the Cambridge survey*. Cambridge. Vol. 1, 192–216.
Durand, J. (ed.) 1986. *Dependency and non-linear phonology*. London.
Fischer-Jørgensen, E. 1975. *Trends in phonological theory: a historical introduction*. Copenhagen.
Foley, J. 1977. *Foundations of theoretical phonology*. Cambridge.
Goldsmith, J. 1994. *The handbook of phonological theory*. Oxford.
Hogg, R. and C.B. McCully, 1987. *Metrical phonology*. Cambridge.
Kramsky, J. 1973. *The phoneme: introduction to the history and theories of a concept*. Munich.
Makkai, V.B. (ed.) 1972. *Phonological theory: evolution and current practice*. Lake Bluff, IL.
Vennemann, T. 1978. Universal syllabic phonology. *TL* 5.175–251.

Structuralist phonemic theory
Bloomfield, L. 1933. *Language*. New York.
Harris, Z.S. 1951. *Methods in structural linguistics*. Chicago, IL. (Repr. as *Structural linguistics*.)
Hockett, C.F. 1955. *Manual of phonology*. Bloomington, IN.
———— 1958. *A course in modern linguistics*. New York.
Jakobson, R. and M. Halle. 1956. *Fundamentals of language*. The Hague. (2nd rev. edn 1975.)
Twaddell, W.F. 1935. On defining the phoneme. Suppl. to *Lg* 16. (Also in M. Joos (ed.), *Readings in linguistics*, 4th edn. Chicago, IL, 1966.)
Trubetzkoy, N. 1939. *Grundzüge der Phonologie*. Göttingen. (4th edn 1967.)

Generative phonology
Chomsky, N. and M. Halle. 1968. *The sound pattern of English*. New York.
Dell, F. 1980. *Generative phonology and French phonology*, trans. C. Cullen. Cambridge.
Durand, J. 1990. *Generative and non-linear phonology*. London.
Foley, J. 1977. *Foundations of theoretical phonology*. Cambridge.
Helff, B. 1970. Generative phonology. *LingB* 86–116.
Hooper, J.B. 1976. *An introduction to natural generative phonology*. New York.
Hyman, L.M. 1975. *Phonology: theory and analysis*. New York.
Kenstowicz, M. and C. Kisseberth. 1977. *Topics in phonological theory*. New York.
Kiparsky, P. 1981. *Explanation in phonology*. Dordrecht.
Roca, I. 1994. *Generative phonology*. London.
Schane, S. 1973. *Generative phonology*. Englewood Cliffs, NJ.
Sommerstein, A.H. 1977. *Modern phonology*. London.
Van der Hulst, H. and N. Smith. 1982. *The structure of phonological representation*. Dordrecht.

Phonology and psycholinguistics
Dressler, W.U. 1984. Explaining natural phonology. *PY* 1.29–53.
Linell, P. 1979. *Psychological reality in phonology*. Cambridge.

Historical phonology
Fisiak, J. (ed.) 1978. *Recent developments in historical phonology*. The Hague.
King, R. 1969. *Historical linguistics and generative grammar*. Englewood Cliffs, NJ.
Martinet, A. 1955. *Economie des changements phonétiques*. Bern.

⇒ **phonetics, syllable**

phonostylistics

A branch of **stylistics** which investigates the expressively stylistic properties of articulation and intonation.

phonotactics

Study of the sound and phoneme combinations allowed in a given language. Every language has specific phonotactic rules that describe the way in which phonemes can be combined in different positions (initial, medial, and final).

For example, in English the stop + fricative cluster /gz/ can only occur in medial (*exhaust*) or final (*legs*), but not in initial position, and /h/ can only occur before, never after, a vowel. The restrictions are partly language-specific and partly universal.

References
⇒ **phonology**

phonotagm

Phonotactic unit (⇒ **phonotactics**) that concerns the phonological structure of morphemes as phoneme combinations. Phonotagms are morphologically relevant phoneme combinations that – in contrast with **phonotagmemes** – are not semantically relevant, e.g. devoicing of voiced stops after a voiceless consonant (*fished*).

phonotagmeme

Phonotactic unit (⇒ **etic vs emic analysis**) that constitutes a morphologically relevant combination of phonemes on the level of parole (⇒ **langue vs parole**) and which – in contrast to **phonotagms** – is semantically distinct from other phonotagms, e.g. **ablaut** in *sing* vs *song*. (⇒ *also* **phonotactics**)

phrase [Grk *phrásis* 'expression']

1 Term for word groups without a finite verb that belong together syntactically. In contrast, the term 'clause' denotes a syntactic construction with a finite verb; thus clause stands hierarchically between phrase and **sentence**. (⇒ **X-bar theory**)

2 In **phrase structure grammar**, the term 'phrase' stands for a set of syntactic elements which form a **constituent** (= relatively independent group of words). The most important phrases are **noun phrases** (consisting of nominal expressions with corresponding attributive modifiers: *Philip, good old Philip, he, Philip, who is a dreamer*), **verb phrases** (*dreams, sees the fire, thinks that he's right*), **prepositional phrases** (*on the table*) among others. (⇒ *also* **adjective phrase, determiner phrase**)

phrase marker

The representation of the **phrase structure** of a sentence by a **tree diagram** or by **labeled bracketing**.

phrase structure (*abbrev.* PS)

The result of an **immediate constituent analysis** of a phrase. The PS of a sentence is the result of the hierarchical ordering of its constituents, as depicted in a **tree diagram**.

References
⇒ **phrase structure grammar**

phrase structure diagram ⇒ tree diagram

phrase structure grammar

A type of grammar from the **American structuralists**. Phrase structure grammars describe the syntactic structure of sentences as constituent structures, i.e. as a hierarchy of ordered constituents. Insights gained from optional rules (⇒ **obligatory vs optional**) justify the individual steps of **segmentation** and **classification**, upon which the establishment of the constituent structure of a language is based. Within the framework of **transformational grammar**, this type of grammar, originally formulated as a recognition grammar within the framework of generative grammar undergoes a strong formalization as well as a partial reinterpretation: the static, analytically descriptive rules can be interpreted as **rewrite rules**, e.g. $S \rightarrow NP + VP$ corresponds to 'a sentence consists of a noun phrase and a verb phrase' (⇒ **phrase structure rules, generative grammar**). A phrase structure grammar which operates strictly at **surface structure** cannot adequately capture a string of syntactic–semantic problems, e.g. **discontinuous elements**, *Philip called his brother up*, or **ambiguity**, *the discovery of the student* ('the student was discovered' or 'the student discovered something'); the paraphrase relationship between sentences, e.g. the paraphrase relationship between active and passive sentences. Generative grammar uses these difficulties in its own defense, to assign sentences complex syntactic representations, which are mediated by transformations. (⇒ *also* **X-bar theory, Generalized Phrase Structure Grammar**)

References
Bar-Hillel, Y., M. Perles, and E. Shamir. 1961. On formal properties of simple phrase structure grammars. *ZPSK* 14.143–72.
Bhatt, C. *et al.* (eds) 1990. *Syntactic phrase structure phenomena in noun phrases and sentences*. Amsterdam.
Borsley, R.D. 1993. Phrase structure grammar. In J. Jacobs *et al.* (eds), *Syntax: an international handbook of contemporary research*. Berlin and New York. 570–80.
Chomsky, N. 1957. *Syntactic structures*. The Hague.
——— 1965. *Aspects of the theory of syntax*. Cambridge, MA.
Gazdar, G. and G.K. Pullum. 1985. *Generalized Phrase Structure Grammar: a theoretical synopsis*. Cambridge, MA.

Leffel, K. and D. Bouchard (eds) 1991. *Views on phrase structure*. Dordrecht.

Postal, P.M. 1964a. *Constituent structure: a study of contemporary models of syntactic description*. Bloomington, IN.

—— 1964b. Limitations of phrase structure grammars. In J.A. Fodor and J.J. Katz (eds), *Readings in the philosophy of language*. Englewood Cliffs, NJ. 137–54.

Rothstein, S. (ed.) 1992. *Perspectives on phrase structure: heads and licensing*. New York.

⇒ **universal grammar**

phrase structure rules

Phrase structure rules are **rewrite rules** for constituents of the form $A \rightarrow X_1 \dots X_n$, e.g. $S \rightarrow NP + VP$. This rule should be read as an instruction to replace the sentence symbol S with a **noun phrase** (NP) and a **verb phrase** (VP). Thus, the symbol to the left of the arrow is replaced by the symbols to the right of the arrow. Parentheses are used to denote optional elements, and curly brackets are used for alternatives. Phrase structure rules can also be read as specifying the relationship of immediate dominance in a well-formed **tree diagram**. In the above example, S has the symbols NP and VP respectively as immediate constituents. Phrase structure rules are subject to a set of formal constraints: there must always be a single symbol to the left of the arrow which is replaced by one or more symbols (a **chain**) to the right of the arrow. It follows that neither the right symbol nor the left symbol may be zero, e.g. neither $0 = Adj + N$ nor $S = 0$ are possible. Also a chain cannot consist of nothing, nor can deletions follow in the derivation. Transpositions are also prohibited; $NP + VP \rightarrow VP + NP$ is ruled out. These restrictions are necessary to ensure that each phrase structure rule corresponds to a branching in the tree diagram. The duplication of the phrase structure rules by the tree diagram ensures the reconstructability of the derivational process. The basic components of **generative grammar** are derived from phrase structures rules. PS-rules are usually context-free, i.e. their use is independent of the environment of the symbols. **Context-free rules** are distinguished from **context-sensitive rules**, especially in the earlier versions of generative grammar. For example, a context-sensitive phrase structure rule for the verb *visit* would be $V \rightarrow V_{trans}/\#N_{dir\ obj}$: replace a verb by a transitive verb if a direct object noun follows, e.g. *Philip visits Caroline*. (⇒ *also* **phrase structure grammar**)

References
⇒ **phrase structure grammar**

phraseology ⇒ **idiomatics**

Phrygian ⇒ **Indo-European**

phylum ⇒ **language family**

pictogram ⇒ **pictography**

pictography [Lat. *pictum* 'painted,' Grk *gráphein* 'to write']

Graphemic system in which linguistically independent concepts or meanings of linguistic utterances are expressed in pictorial signs (pictograms), whereby an individual sign can stand for complex concepts or whole meanings. Writing systems such as those used by the Alaskan Eskimos, and international symbols, like those used at airports and at the Olympic Games, are pictograms. (⇒ *also* **ideography**)

References
⇒ **writing**

pidgin (*also* hybrid language)

The term 'pidgin' is probably a corruption of the English word *business*, as pronounced by the indigenous Chinese, and designates a **mixed language** that arises in situations where speakers of different languages are unable to understand each other's native language and, therefore, need to develop a common means of communication. In such situations, the structure and vocabulary of the individual native languages are reduced over time, in order to bring about general, mutual understanding. Gradually, a functional mixed language develops from the rudimentary contact language and is learned along with one's native language.

Pidgins developed principally in the European colonies during the height of European colonization. The dominant European languages became the primary source for vocabulary. Linguistically, pidgins are characterized by a limited vocabulary, a greater use of paraphrase and metaphor, a simplified phonological system, and a reduced morphology and syntax. It is also interesting to note, especially in view of naturalness theory and **universals**, that pidgin language systems are remarkably similar, regardless of whether they are related (English pidgins) or unrelated (English vs French pidgins). Pidgins that develop into full-fledged native languages are called **creoles**.

References
Arends, J., P. Muysken, and N. Smith (eds) 1995. *Pidgins and creoles: an introduction*. Amsterdam and Philadelphia.

Decamp, D. 1971. The study of pidgin and creole languages. In D. Hymes (ed.), *Pidginization and creolization of languages*. Cambridge. 13–39.

Decamp, D. and I.F. Hancock (eds) 1974. *Pidgins*

and creoles: current trends and prospects. Washington, DC.

Ferguson, C.A. 1971. Absence of copula and the notion of simplicity: a study of normal speech, baby talk, foreigner talk, and pidgins. In D. Hymes (ed.), *Pidginization and creolization of languages*. Cambridge. 141–50.

Foley, W., 1988. Language birth: the processes of pidginization and creolization. In F.J. Newmeyer (ed.), *Linguistics: the Cambridge survey*, vol. 4: *Language: the socio-cultural context*. Cambridge. 162–83.

Hall, R.A. 1966. *Pidgin and creole languages*. Ithaca, NY.

Hancock, I. 1987. History of research on pidgins and creoles. In U. Ammon *et al.* (eds), *Soziolinguistik/ Sociolinguistics: an international handbook on the science of language and society*. Berlin. 459–69.

Holm, J. 1988–9. *Pidgins and creoles*, 2 vols. London.

Hymes, D. (ed.) 1971. *Pidginization and creolization of languages*. Cambridge.

Meisel, J. (ed.) 1977. *Langues en contact: pidgins/ creoles; languages in contact*. Tübingen.

Mühlhäusler, P. 1986. *Pidgin and creole linguistics*. Oxford.

Reinecke, J.E. 1971. Tay Bói: notes on the Pidgin French spoken in Vietnam. In D. Hymes (ed.), *Pidginization and creolization of languages*. Cambridge. 43–56.

Romaine, S. 1988. *Pidgin and creole languages*. London.

Singler, J.V. (ed.) 1990. *Pidgin and creole tense–mood–aspect systems*. Amsterdam and Philadelphia.

Todd, L. 1975. *Pidgins and creoles*. London. (2nd edn 1990).

Valdman, A. (ed.) 1977. *Pidgin and creole linguistics*. Bloomington, IN.

Verhaar, J. (ed.) 1990. *Melanesian and Tok Pisin: proceedings of the First International Conference on Pidgins and Creoles in Melanesia*. Amsterdam and Philadelphia.

Whinnom, K. 1965. The origin of European-based pidgins and creoles. *Orbis* 14.509–27.

——— 1971. Linguistic hybridization and the special case of pidgins and creoles. In D. Hymes (ed.), *Pidginization and creolization of languages*. Cambridge. 91–115.

Bibliography
Reinecke, J. *et al.* (eds) 1975. *A bibliography of pidgin and creole languages*. Honolulu.
⇒ **creole**

pied piping

The optional movement of a NP or PP containing the item which is affected by a movement rule, described by Ross (1967). For example, normally, a relative pronoun is the first word in the relative clause, e.g. *the lady, whom I saw pictures of*. In a pied-piping construction, the whole phrase (NP) which includes the relative pronoun can be in initial position: *the lady, pictures of whom I saw*.

References
Klein, E.C. 1993. *Toward second language acquisition: a study of null-prep*. Dordrecht.

Moritz, L. and D. Valois. 1994. Pied-piping and specifier–head agreement. *LingI* 25.667–707.

Ross, J.R. 1967. Constraints on variables in syntax. Dissertation, MIT, Cambridge, MA. (Repr. as *Infinite Syntax!* Norwood, NJ, 1986.)

Van Riemsdijk, H. 1985. Zum Rattenfängereffekt bei Infinitiven in deutschen Relativsätzen. In W. Abraham (ed.), *Erklärende Syntax des Deutschen*. Tübingen. 75–97. (Eng. rev. in J. Toman (ed.), *Studies in German grammar*. Dordrecht, 1985. 165–93).

Pima-Papago ⇒ Uto-Aztecan

pitch

1 In **acoustic phonetics**, the number of tonal oscillations per second, or in **auditory phonetics** the auditory characteristics corresponding to the different tonal oscillations.

2 In **phonology**, **suprasegmental feature** of linguistic expressions. In **tonal languages**, pitch is distinctive. (⇒ **pitch accent**)

References
⇒ **phonetics**

pitch accent (*also* musical accent)

Word accent in which the change of pitch is distinctive, as in **Serbo-Croatian** and in **Swedish** (e.g. *tanken* with falling pitch on the first syllable 'tank,' with falling–rising pitch on the first syllable 'thought'). In contrast to **stress accent**, the change in pitch is distinctive and, in contrast with **tonal languages** only one syllable per word has distinctive tone. (⇒ *also* **stress**[2])

Reference
Bruce, G. 1977. *Swedish word accents in sentence perspective*. Lund.

Pitjantjatjara ⇒ Australian languages

pivot grammar

Proposed by M.D.S. Braine, the distributional analysis of utterances in child language which are devoid of reference to the utterance meaning. In pivot grammar, frequently occurring closed-class words (primarily function words, 'pivots' or 'operators,' such as *more*, *than*, *also*) are distinguished from open-class words (nouns, verbs, and the like). In contrast to words of the second class, 'pivots' determine positional restrictions: thus, in utterances of two words, they can occur either only in the first or in the second position, and may not co-occur or stand alone. For criticism of this analysis, see Miller (1976); for a revision of this analysis, cf. Braine (1976).

References
Braine, M.D.S. 1963a. The ontogeny of English phrase structure. *Lg* 39.1–13.
—— 1963b. On learning the grammatical order of words. *PsychologR* 70.323–48.
—— 1976. Children's first word combinations. *MRCD* 41:164.
McNeill, D. 1970. Developmental psycholinguistics. In F. Smith and G.A. Miller (eds), *The genesis of language*. Cambridge, MA. 15–84.
Miller, M. 1976. *Zur Logik der frühkindlichen Sprachentwicklung*. Stuttgart.
Miller, W. and S. Ervin. 1964. The development of grammar in child language. In U. Bellugi and R. Brown (eds), *The acquisition of language. MRCD* 29:92.9–34.

place of articulation (*also* point of articulation)

1 In the narrow sense (*also* passive articulator), upper and back parts of the oral cavity (upper lips, teeth, **palate**, **uvula**, etc.), which can be completely or partially contacted by one of the (relatively mobile, active) articulatory organs (⇒ **articulator**). In contrast to the articulatory organs, the places of articulation are relatively stationary. (Although the uvula can vibrate, it is still a potential goal for some of the articulatory organs.)

2 In the broad sense, constriction of the airstream during **articulation**, due to the contact or proximity of an articulatory organ with a place of articulation in the narrow sense. (⇒ *also* **articulatory phonetics**)

References
⇒ **phonetics**

placeholder ⇒ dummy element

placement of the tongue

In **vowels** a distinction is drawn regarding the degree of openness of the front of the **resonance chamber** (of the oral cavity) between a high (e.g. [i]), high-mid (e.g. [e]), mid (e.g. [ə]), low-mid (e.g. [ɛ]), and low (e.g. [a]), placement of the tongue. One generally speaks of (e.g. in the IPA) closed, half-closed, mid, half-open, and open vowels, respectively.

References
⇒ **phonetics**

plane

Term used by F. de Saussure and L. Hjelmslev for the division of a language system into a level (plane) of expression and a level of content. (⇒ **expression plane vs content plane**)

planned language

In contrast to natural language, an artificially created linguistic system for the purpose of international understanding (⇒ **interlingua**).

Plateau ⇒ Benue-Congo

play on words

A playful change of a word with the intention of causing surprise. It is a frequently used **figure of speech** in fashionable literature and advertising language. A play on words can come into existence (a) through the change in meaning, and therefore from **homonymy** and **polysemy**, (b) through the change of word forms and the rearranging of sound, e.g. an **anagram**, the rearranging of syllables or of morphemes, (c) by **blend**. (⇒ *also* **pun, polyptoton, malapropism**)

References
Chiaro, D. 1992. *The language of jokes: analysing verbal play*. London.
Redfern, W. 1984. *Puns*. Oxford.

pleonasm [Grk *pleonasmós* 'superabundance, excess']

The addition of a superfluous expression which is already included in that which is said, e.g. *three a.m. in the morning* (⇒ **solecism**). As any **figure of speech**, pleonasm can serve to strengthen a statement, e.g. *I saw it myself, with my own eyes*. A related form of semantic redundancy is **tautology**, the repetition of the same word or sentence. Expressions like *boys will be boys* only appear to be pleonastic. (⇒ *also* **emphasis**)

References
⇒ **figure of speech**

plerematics [Grk *plérēs* 'full']

In **glossematics**, the study of the content plane of language (⇒ **expression plane vs content plane**).

plereme

1 In **glossematics** the smallest ('complete') unit on the semantic level which, together with its features, is classified as a **glosseme**. Pleremes correspond to **semantic features** in **componential analysis**.

2 Synonym for **morpheme**. In this context, the expression form of a plereme is the **moneme**, and its content is the **sememe**.

References
⇒ **glossematics**

plexus [Lat. '*intertwined*']

Syntactic process in L. Tesnière's **dependency grammar**. Plexus is a result of overlapping **connections** within a stemma when sentence

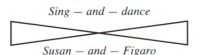

Sing — and — dance

Susan — and — Figaro

parts that have arisen by **junction** are subjected to a junction with different elements. For example, *Susan and Figaro sing and dance.*

References
⇒ **dependency grammar**

plosive [Lat. *plaudere* 'to make a clapping sound']
1 Non-nasal **speech sound** (**stop**) formed with the pulmonic **airstream mechanism** by closure of the oral cavity.
2 ⇒ **glottal stop**
3 Sound that is either an **implosive** or a **click**.

pluperfect ⇒ **past perfect**

plural
Subcategory of **number** of nouns and verbs which usually serves to indicate the presence of more than one element, but which can also have an individualizing function with certain **common nouns** (*rock* : *rocks*) and **collective nouns** (*people* : *peoples*). There are also **plural-only nouns** (*scissors*, (*eye*)*glasses*, *the Alps*). In English, most plurals are formed by adding *-(e)s* (*cats*, *dogs*, *bosses*); other types of plural formation include foreign suffixes (*phenomenon* : *phenomena*) and changes in the stem (*mouse* : *mice*). (⇒ *also* **mutation**)

References
Greenberg, J. 1974. Numeral classifiers and substantial number: problems in the genesis of a linguistic type. *PICL* 11.17–37.
Link, G. 1983. The logical analysis of plurals and mass terms. In R. Bäuerle *et al.* (eds), *Meaning, use and interpretation.* Berlin and New York.
Schein, B. 1993. *Plurals and events.* Cambridge, MA.
Unterbeck, B. 1993. *Kollektion, Numeralklassifikation und Transnumerus.* Frankfurt-on-Main.

plural of majesty
Manner of expression used by kings, queens, princes, etc., where the speaker refers to him/herself in the plural (*we* instead of *I*) and/or was addressed or spoken of in the plural (cf. Ger. *Eure Majestät* 'Your Majesty').

Reference
Dryry, D. 1986. The lofty and/or assumptive 'we'. *Verbatim* 7:3.11–13.

plural of modesty (*also* editorial we)
Use of plural form *we* instead of *I* or *you* where the speaker includes the speaker/reader, but actually means only him/herself or the addressee: *We will only mention this point in passing*; or with children: *Now it's time for us to go to bed!* (⇒ *also* **plural of majesty**)

plural-only noun (*also* plurale tantum)
Noun which can only occur in the **plural**. In English, there are a number of such nouns: *scissors*, (*eye-*)*glasses*, *measles*, *the Alps*, *shorts*.

plurale tantum ⇒ **plural-only noun**

point of articulation ⇒ **place of articulation**

polarity
1 Cover term for **semantic relations** which categorize the vocabulary according to particular dimensions of semantic opposition (⇒ **antonymy, incompatibility, complementarity, conversion**).
2 Characteristic of antonymous adjectives like *short* : *long, easy* : *difficult, light* : *dark* whose systematic difference in meaning can be described by the **semantic feature** [±polarity]. Assertions cannot be made about a particular state of affairs from a single perspective using a polar adjective pair, e.g. a thing cannot be both short and long. The restrictions on the use of polar expressions are notable, e.g. in unmarked questions (*How old are you?*, but not **How young are you?*) and in nominalizations (*the height of the building/mountain* but not **the lowness of the building/mountain*).

References
Cruse, D.A. 1977. The pragmatics of lexical specificity. *JL* 13.153–64.
Lehrer, A. 1985. Markedness and antonymy. *JL* 21.397–429.
⇒ **Semantic relations**

Polish
West **Slavic** language with approx. 42 million speakers, predominantly in Poland (about 35 million speakers) and the United States (about 6 million speakers). Polish has existed as a written language since the fourteenth century, attested in the Papal Bull of Gniezno, which contains over 400 names. The oldest complete text, Kazania Świętokrzyskie 'Holy Cross sermons' dates from the fourteenth century. Polish literature flowered during the sixteenth century. Today Polish is written in the Latin alphabet with diacritics and special characters: ‹ł, Ł›, ‹ż, Ż›.

Characteristics: word stress, with a few exceptions, on the penultimate syllable; nasal vowels, which occur in word-final position and before fricatives, e.g. *Wałęsa* [va'wēsa], *są* [sąɔ̃] 'are'; palatalization distinct for velars and labials; three-way distinction (dental, alveolar, prepalatal) for affricates and fricatives, morphologically expressed distinction in the nominal system of [±masculine animate] in the singular, and of [±masculine human] in the plural, verbal forms with conjunctions and certain particles: *coś powiedieła* vs *co powiedziełaś* 'What did you (fem. informal) say.'

References
Brooks, M.Z. 1975. *Polish reference grammar.* The Hague.
Klemensiewicz, Z. 1961–72. *Historia języka polskiego*, 3 vols. Warsaw (4th edn 1980.)
Schenker, A. 1954. Polish conjugation. *Word* 10.469–81.
———— 1964. *Polish declension.* The Hague.
Stieber, Z. 1973. *A historical phonology of the Polish language.* Heidelberg.
Szober, S. 1971. *Gramatyka języka polskiego*, 12th edn. Warsaw.
Westfal, S. 1985. *The Polish language.* London.

Dictionary
Doroszewski, W. (ed.) 1958–69. *Słownik języka polskiego*, 11 vols. Warsaw.

Etymological dictionary
Brückner, A. 1974. *Słownik etymologiczny języka polskiego*, 3rd edn. Warsaw.

Bibliography
Urbanczyk, S. (ed.) 1978. *Encyklopedia wiedzy o języku polskim.* Wrocław.
⇒ **Slavic**

politeness

Umbrella term for a combination of interpersonal considerations and linguistic choices affecting the form and function of linguistic interactions. Analysts from diverse fields – **pragmatics, sociolinguistics,** and anthropology – argue that the specific ways in which speakers, as interactants, perform speech acts (⇒ **speech act classification, speech act theory**) such as requests, commands, elicitations and offers, both express and reflect the nature of the relationship between them. Fluent speakers of a language have therefore learned (automatically) to take great care over, for example, how to phrase impositive requests. A central concept of politeness theory is 'face', which is taken to be important to individuals in both a positive and negative aspect. One preserves the negative face of an interactant by impeding or interfering with his/her actions and values as little as possible; one attends to the positive face of an interactant by endorsing and supporting the

interactant's presumed positive self-image as much as possible. Acts which involve the speaker in breaking away from either of these face-maintaining tendencies are known as 'face-threatening acts.' Ordering someone to do something is *prima facie* threatening to that person's negative face; so, where other factors allow it, politeness considerations usually lead us to mitigate and minimize, linguistically, the degree of overt imposition: *I'm sorry to bother you, but would you mind ... ?*; *Phil, I'm afraid I need you to....* Positive face is reflected in numerous 'other-appreciative' conversational gambits: *I just love that sweater you're wearing*; (*It was*) *good talking to you*; *I'm sure you'll do just fine*; *Have a nice day!* One of the most interesting aspects of face and politeness, and their conventional encoding in the patterns of grammar and usage associated with particular kinds of speech acts, is that they differ from culture to culture and from language to language in ways that are difficult to calibrate. This has major consequences for truly felicitous cross-cultural communication. One can be near-native in one's fluency in a foreign language and yet, if one does not have control of the pragmatics of politeness in the language, sound offensively abrupt in one's requests or ludicrously flattering in one's compliments.

References
Blum-Kulka, S. and G. Kasper. 1990. Special issue on 'politeness.' *JPrag* 14:2.
Brown, P. and S. Levinson, 1987. *Politeness.* Cambridge.
Leech, G.N. 1983. *Principles of pragmatics.* London.
Sifianou, M. 1992. *Politeness phenomena in England and Greece: a cross-cultural perspective.* Oxford.
Watts, R.J., S. Ide, and K. Ehlich (eds) 1992. *Politeness in language: studies in its history, theory and practice.* Berlin and New York.

Polynesian

Approx. thirty closely related languages of the **Malayo-Polynesian** family, spoken in the Polynesian Islands.

Characteristics: extremely reduced sound system (e.g. Hawaiian has thirteen phonemes). Word order: VSO; tendency towards ergativity (⇒ **ergative language**).

References
Chung, S. 1978. *Case marking and grammatical relations in Polynesian.* Austin, TX.
Krupa, V. 1973. *Polynesian languages.* The Hague.
———— 1982. *The Polynesian languages: a guide.* London.
Seiter, W.J. 1980. *Studies in Niuean syntax.* New York.

polyphonemic classification (*also* biphonemic classification)

In phonological analysis, the classification of two consecutive, articulatorily different sounds as two different **phonemes**. In contrast, ⇒ **monophonemic classification**.

References
⇒ **phonology**

polyptoton [Grk *polýptōton* 'employment of the same word in various cases']

The double play of varying sound and contrasting meaning in many aphorisms is achieved through the use of polyptoton: *Few men speak humbly of humility, chastely of chastity, skeptically of skepticism* (Pascal). The rhetorical repetition of a word with different intonation or inflection, e .g. *my own heart's heart, and my ownest own, farewell* (Tennyson). (⇒ *also* **pun**)

References
⇒ **figure of speech**

polysemy [Grk *sēma* 'sign']

Term coined by Bréal (1897). One speaks of 'polysemy' when an expression has two or more definitions with some common features that are usually derived from a single basic meaning. A distinction is traditionally drawn between polysemy and **homonymy**. The different meanings of **homonyms** can be traced to different etymological roots (thus different words are involved), whereas the semantic variants of polysemic expressions go back to a single root (see Heger 1963). However, the etymological criterion is vague and, if applied consistently, leads to conclusions which run counter to intuition. The distinction between polysemy and homonymy cannot be drawn precisely. This is abundantly clear in the way the same word may be listed as a polysemic expression in one dictionary, but as a homonym in another. The distinction frequently involves the question of **ambiguity** (see Fries 1980).

References
Bartsch, R. 1984. The structure of word meanings: polysemy, metaphor, metonymy. In F. Landman and F. Veltman (eds), *Varieties of formal semantics*. Dordrecht. 25–54.
Bréal, M. 1897. *Essai de sémantique: science des significations*. Paris.
Heger, K. 1963. Homographie, Homonymie und Polysemie. ZRPh 79.471–91.
Lakoff, G. 1982. *Categories and cognitive models*. Trier.
Lyons, J. 1977. *Semantics*, 2 vols. Cambridge.
Ruhl, C. 1975. Polysemy or monosemy: discrete meanings or continuum? In R.W. Fasold and R.W. Shuy (eds), *Analyzing variation in language*. Washington, DC. 184–202.
Ullmann, S. 1962. *Semantics: an introduction to the science of meaning*. Oxford.

Bibliography
Fries, N. 1980. *Ambiguität und Vagheit: Enführung und kommentierte Bibliographie. (Annotated bibliography.)* Tübingen.
⇒ **semantics**

polysyndeton

The use of more conjunctions than ordinary usage demands. Stephen Crane employed a polysyndeton in writing *The horizon narrowed and widened, and dipped and rose, and at all times its edge was jagged with waves*. A polysyndeton can either emphasize the length of items enumerated or underscore the distinctiveness of each item from the others.

References
⇒ **figure of speech**

polysynthesis

Phenomenon common, among others, to some native American languages, where complex words are formed from morphemes of different types. Polysynthesis may involve **incorporation**, but need not necessarily do so. But in contrast to **incorporation**, these morphemes occur only as bound morphemes, never as free morphemes (e.g. the one-word sentence from Onondage (⇒ **Iroquoian**) *a?akwan,ohsahnin,ony,ó?* 'we are buying the houses' with the verb root *-hnin,o-* 'to buy,' the subject *-akwa-* 'we,' and the object *-n,ohsa-* 'house' with the plural marker *-ny,ó-*, which can only occur as elements of complex words.

References
Mithun, M. 1983. The genius of polysynthesis. In J.S. Thayer (ed.), *North American Indians: humanistic perspectives*. Norman, OK.
Sasse, H.-J. 1988. Der irokesische Sprachtyp. ZS 7.173–213.

polysynthetic construction ⇒ **incorporating language**, **polysynthesis**

polysystemic phonology ⇒ **prosody**

Port Royal grammar

A general theoretical grammar, the *Grammaire générale et raisonnée*, written by A. Arnauld and E. Lancelot within the framework of French rationalism and named after the famous seventeenth-century Parisian abbey and schools of Port Royal. Reprinted as late as 1830, the Port Royal grammar attempts to develop grammatical categories on the basis of Greek, Latin, Hebrew, and modern European languages which would be valid for all languages (⇒ *also* **general grammar**). For the foundation and justification of his model of generative **transformational grammar**, N. Chomsky referred to this concept of universal grammar. (⇒ *also* **Cartesian linguistics, rationalism**)

References
Arnauld, A. and E. Lancelot. 1660. *Grammaire générale et raisonnée*. Paris. (*A general and rational grammar, translated from the French of Messieurs de Port Royal*. London, 1753.)
Chomsky, N. 1966a. *Topics in the theory of generative grammar*. The Hague.
—— 1966b. *Cartesian linguistics: a chapter in the history of rationalist thought*. New York.
—— 1968. *Language and mind*. New York.
Donze, R. 1971. *La grammaire générale et raisonnée de Port-Royal*, 2nd edn. Bern.
Harris, R. and T.J. Taylor. 1989. *Landmarks in linguistic thought*. London. Ch. 8.
Tsiapera, M. and G. Wheeler. 1993. *The Port-Royal grammar: sources and influences*. Münster.

portmanteau morpheme [Fr. *portemanteau* 'clothes-stand']

Term introduced by C.F. Hockett to denote phonomorphological units that blend several otherwise distinct morphemic units together, cf. Fr. *au* (= blend of *à + le*) which contains the meanings of 'dative,' 'definite,' 'masculine,' and 'singular.'

References
Hockett, C.F. 1947. Problems of morphemic analysis. *Lg* 23.321–43.
⇒ **morphology**

Portuguese

Language belonging to the Ibero-Romance (⇒ **Romance languages**) branch of **Indo-European**, the first language of approx. 140 million speakers in Portugal, Madeira, the Azores, and Brazil. Portuguese has fewer dialectal variations than the other Romance languages. The pronunciation and standard written form of Portuguese is based on the language of Lisbon and Coimbra. Historically, Portuguese derives from Galician Portuguese in northern Portugal and in what is now Spanish Galicia (Gallego). The pronunciation in Brazil differs in many ways from that in Portugal.

Characteristics: special characteristics of Portuguese include a number of nasalized vowels (with numerous diphthongs and triphthongs); two /r/ phonemes (dental and uvular); no marking of word boundaries with correspondingly strong tendencies towards assimilation and **sandhi**. The inflectional morphology includes a synthetically formed past perfect as well as a declinable infinitive.

References
Costa Campos, M.H. and M.F. Xavier. 1991. *Sintaxe e semântica do Português*. Lisbon.
Holtus, G., M. Metzeltin, and C. Schmitt (eds) 1994. *Lexikon der romanistischen Linguistik*, vol. 6, 2.130–692. Tübingen.
Mateus, M.H.M. *et al.* 1990. *Fonética, fonologia e morfologia do Português*. Lisbon.
Mattoso Câmara, Jr, J. 1972. *The Portuguese language*, trans. A.J. Naro. Chicago, IL.
Thomas, E.W. 1974. *A grammar of spoken Brazilian Portuguese*. Nashville, TN.
Vâzquez Cuesta, P. and M.A. Mendes da Luz. 1971. *Gramática portuguesa*, 3rd edn, 2 vols. Madrid.

History and dialectology
Leite de Vasconcellos, J. 1901. *Esquisse d'une dialectologie portugaise*. (2nd edn Lisbon, 1970.)
Messner, D. 1990. *História do léxico Português*. Heidelberg.
Teyssier, P. 1980. *Histoire de la langue portugaise*. Paris. (Also pub. as *Historia da lingua portuguesa*. Lisbon, 1982.)
Williams, E.B. 1938. *From Latin to Portuguese: historical phonology and morphology of the Portuguese language*. Philadelphia, PA. (2nd edn 1962.)

Dictionaries
Almeida Costa, J. and A. Sampaio e Melo. 1952. *Dicionário da lingua portuguesa*. Lisbon. (6th edn 1984.)
Da Cunha, A.G. 1982. *Dicionário etimologico Nova Fronteira da lingua portuguesa*. Rio de Janeiro.
De Morais, A. 1949–59. *Grande dicionário da lingua portuguesa*, 11 vols, 10th edn. Lisbon. (1st edn 1789.)

Bibliography
Dietrich, W. 1980. *Bibliografia da língua Portuguesa do Brasil*. Tübingen.

positional fields (*also* topological fields)

Umbrella term for topological sections in German clauses which result from the positional characteristics of the finite and infinite parts of the verb; thus, in a propositional clause (⇒ **proposition**) with the finite verb form in second position, the positional field before the finite verb is termed *Vorfeld* 'front field' or 'prefield,' the position after the brace-closing element *Nachfeld* 'end field,' 'final field,' or 'postfield' and the section between the finite verb and the brace-closing element *Mittelfeld* 'inner field'; cf. *Niemand* (front field) *hat* (brace-opening element) *den Aufruf* (inner field) *gehört* (brace-closing element) *heute nacht* (end field) 'Nobody heard the summons tonight.' (⇒ *also* **brace construction, dislocation, exbraciation, topicalization**)

References
Haftka, B. 1993. Topologische Felder und Versetzungsphänomene. In J. Jacobs *et al.* (eds), *Syntax. An international handbook of contemporary research*. Berlin and New York. 846–66.
Lohnes, W. and F.W. Strothmann. 1967. *German: a structural approach*. New York.

Olsen, S. 1982. On the syntactic description of German: Topological fields vs X-theory. In D. Welte (ed.), *Sprachtheorie und angewandte Linguistik*. Tübingen. 29–45.

Reis, M. 1981. On justifying topological frames: 'Positional fields' and the order of nonverbal elements in German. *DRLAV* 22/23.59–85.

⇒ **brace construction, dislocation, exbraciation, topicalization, word order**

positive ⇒ **degree**

positivism ⇒ **Neogrammarians**

possessive compound ⇒ **bahuvrihi**

possessive pronoun

Subgroup of **pronouns**. The term 'possessive pronoun' is misleading, since it refers not only to possession (*my/your book*) but also to general relations between things: *his pity, her father, our conviction.*

possible word

Morphological approach (⇒ **word formation**) developed by Fanselow (1985) that restricts the possibilities for forming and interpreting new words based on semantic and logical principles, in order to arrive at a definition of 'a possible complex word.' In the modular interaction of general semantic interpretative processes with the formal word structures, only those semantic representations are characterized as well formed which stand in unison with a correlation between syntactic categories and semantic types that is motivated independently by type logic.

References
Fanselow, G. 1985. What is a possible complex word? In J. Toman (ed.), *Studies in German grammar*. Dordrecht. 289–318.
——— 1988. 'Word syntax' and semantic principles. In G. Booij and J. van Marle (eds), *Yearbook of morphology*. Dordrecht. 95–122.

possible world

(Metaphoric) term attributed to G.W. Leibniz (1646–1716) which assumes real situations to be hypothetically different and attempts to group all such situations or conditions into a plausible whole. In **model-theoretic semantics**, the interpretational function is relativized to possible worlds, for in order to establish whether the **proposition** of a statement is true or false, it is necessary to know the composition of the given world to which the statement refers. The status of the possible world as an undefined basic term is controversial: frequently, a definition is proposed depending on the set of propositions which holds true for a given world. In so-called 'classic' possible worlds, all

logical connectives have a customary (set) interpretation, whereas so-called 'non-classical' possible worlds do not. The latter were proposed by M.J. Cresswell to encompass phenomena in **intensional contexts**. (⇒ *also* **intensional logic, Montague grammar**)

References
Bruner, J. 1986. *Actual minds, possible worlds*. Cambridge, MA.
Cresswell, M.J. 1972. Intensional logics and logical truth. *JPL* 1.2–15.
——— 1994. *Language in the world*. Cambridge.
Hintikka, J. 1969. *Models for modalities*. Dordrecht.
Hughes, G.E. and M.J. Cresswell. 1968. *An introduction to modal logic*. London.
Kripke, S.A. 1963. Semantical considerations on modal logic. *Acta Philosophica Fennica*. 16.83–94.
——— 1972. Naming and necessity. In D. Davidson and G. Harman (eds), *Semantics of natural language*. Dordrecht. 253–355, 762–9.
Lewis, D. 1970. General semantics. *Synthese* 22.18–67.
——— 1973. *Counterfactuals*. Oxford.
Lutzeier, P.R. 1981. Words and worlds. In J. Eikmeyer and H. Rieser (eds), *Words, worlds, and contexts: new approaches in word semantics*. Berlin. 75–106.
Montague, R. 1974. *Formal philosophy: selected papers*, ed. R.H. Thomason. New Haven, CT.

post-alveolar

Speech sound classified according to its **place of articulation** (behind the **alveolar ridge**), e.g. [ʂ], [ʃ], [ɳ] in Swedish [fɔʂ] 'waterfall', [ʃøː] 'lake, sea', [baːɳ] 'child.' (⇒ *also* **articulatory phonetics, lamino-post-alveolar, retroflex**)

References
⇒ **phonetics**

Post-Bloomfieldian linguistics ⇒ **American structuralism**, *also* **distributionalism**

post-dorsal ⇒ **dorsal**

post-dorsal velar ⇒ **articulation**

posteriority [Lat. *posterior* 'later']

Temporal relationship in complex sentences between several actions: the action described in the dependent clause occurs after the action of the main clause: *They kept calling him until he finally heard them.* (⇒ **sequence of tenses**)

postposition ⇒ **adposition**

potential [Lat. *potentialis* from *potentia* 'dynamics; state of that which is not yet fully realized']

Verbal **mood** which characterizes an action as possible or probable. The **Indo-European** languages have no separate paradigm for this mood, using mainly the **subjunctive** to express it, e.g. the Latin subjunctive *existimem* 'I would suspect.'

PP ⇒ **prepositional phrase**

pragmalinguistics [Grk *prāgma* 'deed, act']

1 Synonym for **pragmatics** or pragmatically oriented studies in **text linguistics** and/or **sociolinguistics**.

2 Communication-oriented subdiscipline of a so-called 'social pragmatics' that describes the linguistic signs and their combination in the process of linguistic communication and attempts to complement them with the component of 'action.' In this connection, pragmalinguistics is subsumed under **psycholinguistics** and **sociolinguistics**, whereas linguistic pragmatics is generally associated with **syntax** and **semantics**.

Reference
Mey, J.L. (ed.) 1979. *Pragmalinguistics: theory and practice*. The Hague.

pragmatics

A subdiscipline of linguistics developed from different linguistic, philosophical and sociological traditions that studies the relationship between natural language expressions and their uses in specific situations. The term pragmatics comes from Morris' (1938) general theory of signs: in this semiotic model (**semiotics**), pragmatics refers to the relationship of the **sign** to the sign user. In linguistics the distinction between pragmatics and semantics and syntax on the one hand and, in a broader sense, between pragmatics and sociolinguistics on the other hand depends wholly on the particular theory. Pragmatics can hardly be considered an autonomous field of study (as is the case for **phonology**, for example). In British-American linguistics, the term 'pragmatics' has only been in use for a relatively short time; this area was previously subsumed under the term '**sociolinguistics**'. The distinction between pragmatics and **semantics**, both of which investigate different aspects of linguistic **meaning**, is even less clear-cut. While semantics is concerned with the literal and contextually non-variable meaning of linguistic expressions or with the contextually non-variable side of the **truth conditions** of **propositions** or sentences, pragmatics deals with the function of linguistic utterances and the propositions that are expressed by them, depending upon their use in specific situations. Consequently, issues such as whether **deixis** is a pragmatic or semantic phenomenon are controversial; as a way of

placing utterances in contexts **deictic expressions** are part of pragmatics, as factors in establishing the truth conditions of sentences they are part of (indexical) semantics. Similar uncertainties arise with regard to **topicalization**, **theme vs rheme** structure and **presupposition**, among others. In the early 1970s, pragmatics became almost exclusively identified with **speech act theory**. Later it was concerned above all with empirical studies in **conversation analysis**, drawing on Grice's (1975) **maxims of conversation**. It has also dealt with issues involving the differentiation of pragmatics and semantics (as in the case of deixis and presupposition mentioned above). As a result of a growing awareness of the close interaction of meaning and use, there has been a recent trend towards treating them together under the heading of a more broadly conceived semantics, especially in formally oriented work such as 'situation semantics' (Gawron and Peters 1990) and 'illocutionary logic' (Vanderveken 1990–1), which integrate complex circumstances and speech act theory, respectively, into semantics.

References
Blum-Kulka, S. and G. Kasper (eds) 1989. *Cross-cultural pragmatics: requests and apologies*. Hove.

Bühler, K. 1934. *Sprachtheorie*. Jena. (Repr. Stuttgart, 1965.)

Burkhardt, A. (ed.) 1990. *Speech acts, meaning and intentions: critical approaches to the philosophy of John R. Searle*. Berlin and New York.

Cole, P. (ed.) 1978. *Syntax and semantics*, vol. 9: *Pragmatics*. New York.

Davis, S. (ed.) 1991. *Pragmatics: a reader*. Oxford.

Franck, D. 1979. Seven sins of pragmatics: theses about speech act theory, conversational analysis, linguistics and rhetoric. In H. Parret, M. Sbisa and J. Verschueren (eds), *Possibilities and limitations of pragmatics*. Amsterdam. 225–36.

Gawron, J.M. and S. Peters. 1990. Some puzzles about pronouns. In R. Cooper *et al.* (eds), *Situation theory and its applications*. Stanford, CA. Vol. 1, 395–431.

Green, G.M. 1988. *Pragmatics and natural language understanding*. Hove.

Grice, H.P. 1975. Logic and conversation. In P. Cole and J.L. Morgan (eds), *Syntax and semantics*, vol. 3: *Speech acts*. New York. 41–58. (Orig. 1968.)

Gumperz, J. and D. Hymes (eds) 1972. *Directions in sociolinguistics: the ethnography of communication*. New York.

Hickey, L. (ed.) 1989. *The pragmatics of style*. London.

Hymes, D. 1968. The ethnography of speaking. In J.A. Fishman (ed.), *Readings in the sociology of language*. The Hague. 99–138.

Leech, G. 1983. *Principles of pragmatics*. London and New York.

Levinson, S.C. 1983. *Pragmatics*. Cambridge.

Mey, J. 1993. *Pragmatics. An introduction*. Oxford.

Morris, C.W. 1938. *Foundations of the theory of signs*. Chicago, IL.

Olesky, W. (ed.) 1989. *Contrastive pragmatics*. Amsterdam.

Schegloff, E.A. and H. Sacks, 1973. Opening up closings. *Semiotica* 8.289–327.

Stalnaker, R.C. 1970. Pragmatics. *Synthese* 22.272–89.

Steiner, E.H. and R. Veltman (eds) 1988. *Pragmatics, discourse and text*. London.

Vanderveken, D. 1990–1. *Meaning and speech acts*, 2 vols. Cambridge.

Watzlawick, P., J.H. Beavin, and D.D. Jackson. 1967. *Pragmatics of human communication: a study of interactional patterns, pathologies, and paradoxes*. New York.

Wierzbicka, A. 1991. *Cross-cultural pragmatics: the semantics of human interaction*. Berlin and New York.

Bibliography

Verschueren, J. 1978. *Pragmatics: an annotated bibliography*. Amsterdam.

Journal

Journal of Pragmatics.

⇒ **communicative competence**, **deictic expression**, **maxim of conversation**, **ordinary language philosophy**, **performative analysis**, **politeness**, **presupposition**, **reference**, **semantics**, **speech act theory**, **word order**

Prague School (*also* **functional grammar**, **functional linguistics**, **functionalism**)

Branch of European **structuralism** arising from the Prague Linguistic Circle, which was founded in 1926 by V. Mathesius, B. Trnka, J. Vachek and others. The theses of this school were first presented at a Slavicist conference in The Hague (1928), and it has referred to itself as the 'Prague School' since the Amsterdam Phonetics Conference of 1932. In contrast to other branches of structuralism, especially **glossematics**, with its emphasis on form, the Prague School regarded language primarily as a functional means of communication whose structural **sign** system can be described through observation of concrete linguistic material in particular moments of use. The Prague School, therefore, abandons De Saussure's strict separation of *langue* and *parole* (⇒ **langue vs parole**), and also the primacy of **synchrony vs diachrony**, as it attempts to explain **language change** with structural principles.

Premises common to the Prague School and the structuralist schools are (a) the decisive break from the positivistic atomism of the **Neogrammarians**, and (b) the representation of language as system and of linguistics as an autonomous science (independent of psychology, philosophy and other disciplines). Charac-teristic of the Prague School's scientific procedure and also of its most decisive influence on the development of linguistics is its orientation towards the concept of 'functionalism.' The starting point of analysis is the intention of the speaker expressed through linguistic **utterances**; the analysis, then, begins with the 'function' of the utterance in order to describe its 'form.' The concept of function appears in various guises in all important areas of Prague School research, e.g. in the applications of **functional sentence perspective**, which sees the **theme–rheme** structure of a text as a structural principle, and especially in the **phonology** as conceived by Trubetzkoy (1890–1938) and further developed by Jakobson.

The theoretical foundations and practical representations of this approach, such as **binary opposition**, **distinctive feature**, **opposition** and the **phoneme**, were summarized in Trubetzkoy's posthumously published *Grundzüge der Phonologie* ('Principles of Phonology') and supplemented by Jakobson, who postulated a universal inventory of phonetic/phonological features for all languages. Of lasting influence on generative **transformational grammar** is the level of **morphophonemics**, introduced by Trubetzkoy, within which the alternating phonological form of morphological units is described. Since the 1950s, Prague School linguists, such as J. Vachek (b. 1909) and J. Firbas (b. 1921), have been primarily concerned with the syntactic, semantic and stylistic problems of English and the Slavic languages.

References

Bühler, K. 1934. *Sprachtheorie*. Jena.

Garvin, P.L. 1964. *A Prague School reader on esthetics, literary structure and style*. Washington, DC.

Grossman, R.E. *et al.* (eds) 1975. *Papers from the parasession on functionalism*. Chicago, IL.

Jakobson, R. and M. Halle. 1956. *Fundamentals of language*. The Hague.

Jespersen, O. 1924. *The philosophy of grammar*. London.

Luelsdorff, P. (ed.) 1994. *The Prague School of structural and functional linguistics*. Amsterdam and Philadelphia.

Luelsdorff, P.A., J. Panevová, and P. Sgall (eds) 1994. *Praguiana 1945–1990*. Amsterdam and Philadelphia.

Martinet, A. 1955. *Economie des changements phonétiques*. Bern.

Stunova, A. 1990. The Prague School as leitmotif in the communicative approach to language. *IJSL* 86.143–9.

Trubetzkoy, N. 1939. *Grundzüge der Phonologie*. Göttingen.

Vachek, J. 1966. *The linguistic school of Prague: an*

introduction to its theory and practice. Bloomington, IN.
⇒ **structuralism**

Prakrit ⇒ **Indo-Aryan**

predicate [Lat. *praedicare* 'to declare; make mention of,' corresponds to Grk *rhēma*]

1 In **school grammar** a verbal **constituent** which, in conjunction with the subject, forms the minimal statement of an utterance. The predicate expresses actions, processes, and states that refer to the subject (⇒ **predication**). It consists of simple or compound verb forms or of a **copular verb** and a **predicative complement**. The predicate is linked to the subject through **agreement** and determines the number and kind of obligatory **complements** (⇒ **obligatory vs optional**) through **valence** of the verb. The position of the **finite verb form** in English depends on the sentence type: verb first in interrogatives (except *wh*-questions) and **imperatives**, otherwise after the subject. Communicatively, the predicate usually refers to new, unknown information, in contrast to the subject, which generally refers to known or previously mentioned information (⇒ **theme vs rheme**, **topic vs comment**).

The predicate is not the same thing as the **verb phrase** in generative **transformational grammar**, since, unlike the VP, in the **tree diagram** it dominates not only the verb, but also all elements (⇒ **objects**) dependent on the verb. (⇒ *also* **part of speech**, **subject vs predicate**)

2 In **formal logic**, especially **predicate logic**, the linguistic expression which, together with the expressions for the **arguments**, forms a **proposition**. The following expressions are (logical) predicates: (a) *x sleeps / x is young / x was an atheist / x are reassured / x is thirsty*; (b) *x is younger than y / x loves y*; (c) *x lies between y and z / x points to y through z*. Depending on the number of positions for arguments, predicates in (a) are one-place (they indicate characteristics of their argument), those in (b) and (c) are multi-place (they express relations between arguments). **Generative semantics** is based on this definition of predicate.

3 ⇒ **semantic primitive**

predicate calculus ⇒ **predicate logic**

predicate clause

Dependent clause which fulfills the syntactic function of a **predicate noun**: *He's like he's always been.*

predicate logic (*also* predicate calculus)

In **formal logic**, a theoretical system for describing the inner structure of **propositions**. While propositional logic only analyzes the meaning of **logical connectives** in truth-functional propositions based on the **truth values** of the propositional clauses, predicate logic differs in that it analyzes the internal make-up of propositions and expands on them by introducing generalized propositions (**existential propositions** and **universal propositions**). Predicates in the logical sense assign properties to individuals. Simple propositions consist of names for individuals and predicates, wherein a distinction is drawn between one-place and multi-place predicates, cf. *Philip daydreams* (one-place) vs *Philip is giving Caroline a book* (three-place). Simple propositions can be expanded by being generalized into complex propositions that indicate to how many individuals the predicate of the simple proposition applies. In such cases, the names of the simple propositions are replaced by variables and the variables are connected by **quantifiers** (⇒ **operator**). For example: *Philip daydreams* $\bigvee (x(x\ daydreams)$, read as 'there is at least one x, for which it is true that x daydreams.' This type of **quantification** is carried out by the existential quantifier or the universal quantifier ('for all x it is true that y'). Natural-language sentences are frequently ambiguous when quantified owing to the different **scope** of the quantifier. This ambiguity can be translated into unambiguous readings in propositional logic, cf. *Everybody loves somebody* in the sense of $\bigvee x \bigwedge y$ (x is a person and y loves x) or in the sense of $\bigwedge y \bigvee x$ (y loves x and x is a person). Based on the suppositions that the system of predicate logic corresponds to the underlying logical structure of natural-language sentences and that this 'semantic deep structure,' in turn, corresponds to the structure of extralinguistic states of affairs, predicate logic can be considered a fundamental metalanguage among more current semantic models (such as **categorial grammar**, **generative semantics**, **Montague grammar**, **natural generative grammar**).

References
Gamut, L.T.F. 1991. *Logic, language, and meaning*, vol. 1: *Introduction to logic*. Chicago, IL.
Marciszewski, W. 1992. *Logic from a rhetorical point of view*. Berlin and New York.
⇒ **formal logic**

predicate noun ⇒ **predicative complement**

predication

1 Process and result of assigning properties to

objects or states of affairs. Objects are specified by predication according to quality, quantity, space, time, etc. or are placed in relation to other objects. Predication is the basis of all forms of proposition. Linguistically it is realized by **predicates**.

2 In J.R. Searle's **speech act theory**, part of the speech act which, together with **reference**, forms a propositional speech act (⇒ **propositional act**). While the speaker refers to objects and states of affairs in the real world with reference acts, predication is used to assign these referents certain properties.

3 Relationship between subject and predicate (in linguistics) or between arguments and predicate in (**formal**) **logic**.

4 ⇒ **topic vs comment**.

predicative adjunct ⇒ **predicative complement**

predicative complement (*also* predicative adjunct)

Nominal **complement** which in some sentence patterns forms the predicate of the sentence in conjunction with a semantically weak **copular verb** such as *to be, to stay, to become, to seem*. Depending on its form, there are three types of predicative complements: (a) predicate nouns: *He is my friend*: (b) predicate adjectives: *It's getting dark*; and (c) **predicate clauses**: *What we didn't reckon with was that he would abandon us so quickly*. Depending on syntactic and semantic relations, predicative complements are divided into (1) predicative nominatives: *Philip is a student* and (2) predicative objects: *We consider him a gifted scientist*.

pre-dorsal ⇒ **dorsal**

pre-dorsal palatal ⇒ **articulation**

preference

In **conversation analysis**, the structural **markedness** of options such as those in **adjacency pairs** (e.g. an invitation followed by acceptance or decline). The unmarked preferred option (such as acceptance) has a less complex structure than the marked, non-preferred option (decline), for example:

A: *Why don't you come for dinner tonight?*
B: *Love to. Shall I bring something?*
vs
A: *Why don't you come for dinner tonight?*
C: *Sorry. [pause] Would love to, but I've got to work . . .*

C's turn is more complex in its structure because of the excuse, the delay (or significant

pause, ⇒ **interruption**), and the reasoning. Furthermore, preferred and non-preferred options differ in their position within the turn: the preferred option is realized early while the non-preferred option is realized late. For a different point of view on such interchanges, cf. remedial **interchange**.

References
Atkinson, J.M. and J. Heritage (eds) 1984. *Structures of social action*. Part II: *Preference organization*. Cambridge. 57–164.
Pomerantz, A. 1978. Compliment responses. In J. Schenkein (ed.), *Studies in the organization of conversation*. New York. 79–112.
Schegloff, E., G. Jefferson, and H. Sacks. 1977. The preference for self-correction in the organization of repair in conversation. *Lg* 53.361–82.
⇒ **maxim of conversation**, **repair**, **sequential organization**

prefix

A subclass of bound word-forming elements that precede the **stem**. Unlike **suffixes**, which are generally associated with a particular word class and create new words of that class (e.g. *-er* derives nouns from verbs, cf. *swimmer*), prefixes cannot be associated with a fixed category and tend to attach to one of two larger categories: verbs (*be-, de-, dis-, en-, mis-, re-, under-*, and so on) and substantives (i.e. nouns and adjectives) (*in-, non-, un-*, and so on), always producing verbs and substantives respectively (cf. *misrepresent, unwise*). **Lexemes** are transformed into words of various classes through the processes of **conversion**[2] and **derivation**. The question of whether nominal and adjectival bases are verbalized by the prefix (*encage* < *cage, endear* < *dear*) or by the conversion of the nominal and adjectival stem into a verb with subsequent prefixation has been debated. (⇒ *also* **particle**)

References
Lieber, R. 1981. *On the organization of the lexicon*. Bloomington, IN.
Selkirk, E. 1982. *Syntax of words*. Cambridge, MA.
Williams, E. 1981. Argument structure and morphology. *LRev* 1.81–114.
Wunderlich, D. 1987. An investigation of lexical composition: the case of German be-verbs. *Linguistics* 25. 283–331.
⇒ **derivation**, **word formation**

prefixation

Essential process of **word formation** in which an **affix** is attached to the beginning of a **stem**. The classification of prefixes is debated: on the one hand, prefixation, like **suffixation**, is considered a main type of **derivation**; on the other hand, prefixation is seen as a third main type of word formation next to derivation (= suffixation) and **composition**.

References
⇒ **derivation**

preposition [Lat. *praeponere* 'to place in front of']

Uninflected **part of speech** (usually) developed from original adverbs of place. Like adverbs and some conjunctions, prepositions in their original meaning denote relations between elements regarding the basic relations of locality (*on, over, under*), temporality (*before, after, during*), causality (*because of*), and modality (*like*). In all modern European languages, prepositions occur not only in the adverbial, but also in the verbal domain. (⇒ *also* **prepositional phrase**)

References
Zelinsky-Wibblet, C. (ed.) 1993. *The semantics of prepositions*. Berlin and New York.

Bibliography
Gumier, C. 1981. *Prepositions: an analytical bibliography*. Amsterdam.

prepositional object (*also* **oblique object**)

Object of a **preposition** which is determined by the **government** of the verb: *He believes in ghosts*, where the preposition *in* is required in this case by the verb *to believe*. (⇒ *also* **prepositional phrase**)

References
⇒ **syntactic function**

prepositional phrase (*abbrev.* PP)

Complex syntactic category with differing categorial representations: *along the steep road* (**preposition + noun phrase**), *since yesterday* (preposition+ **adverb**), *hereby, hitherto* (pro-prepositional phrase). Prepositional phrases function primarily as **adverbials** (*Phil went hiking in the mountains*), **attributes** (*The cabin in the mountains*) and **objects** (*Phil thinks a lot about the mountains*). The internal structure of prepositional phrases as well as their position and function in a sentence are analyzed differently depending on the theoretical approach.

Reference
Wunderlich, D. 1984. Zur Syntax der Präpositionalphrasen im Deutschen. *ZS* 3.65–99.

prescriptive grammar (*also* normative grammar)

Form of grammatical description with the goal of instruction in the proper use of language and which is influenced by historical, logical and aesthetic considerations. Based on the example of other languages (for **Indo-European** languages, usually **Latin**), on the language of poets, writers, and scholars, certain researchers and institutions (for example, the Académie Française in Paris, Duden in Mannheim, Germany) attempt to codify a language in a binding fashion, which is considered 'good style,' and is regarded as 'right' or 'wrong.' A reaction against such grammars can be seen in the grammars based on **descriptive linguistics**, which do not attempt to be regulative, but which represent various linguistic variants without evaluating them as 'right' or 'wrong.' As a rule, prescriptive grammars lag behind the development of theoretical, or descriptive grammars. This was apparent, for example, in the gradual replacement of traditional language-teaching methods (e.g. **grammar-translation method**) with language-teaching methods influenced by **structuralism** (e.g. **audio-lingual method**). The selection of a basic grammar model (above all the question of whether one should use *one* model or integrate various approaches) has led to intense controversies, all the more so since there is no consensus about the general goals of language instruction. The inventory of the pedagogical goals of native-language grammar instruction extends from a 'view of formal structure and regularities of language,' a 'capacity for language analysis' and the 'enhancement of linguistic competence' to the 'capacity for language criticism,' the 'development of logical thinking' and 'emancipation,' etc. These global statements are overlaid with very different extralinguistic factors such as pedagogical, educational psychological, sociocultural, educational political, and institutional expectations. (⇒ **linguistic norms, school grammar**)

References
Alexander, L.G. 1989. *Longman English grammar*. London.
⇒ **linguistic norms**

present

Verbal **tense** which has various temporal functions such as (a) expressing single or repeated events in the present; (b) general timeless states of affairs, especially in sayings, mathematical or logical propositions (*three times three equals nine*) and headlines (= general present); (c) events and states of affairs that are in the past but continue to effect the present: *Socrates teaches that …*; (d) events in the past that are made 'present' by using the present tense (= historical present): *… and then he says … and then I say …*

References
⇒ **tense**

present perfect ⇒ perfect²

prespecifying vs postspecifying ⇒ word order

presupposition

Self-evident (implicit) assumption about the sense of a linguistic expression or utterance. The term, taken from the analytical philosophy of language (Frege, Russell, Strawson), has been the subject of intensive debate in linguistics since 1970 and has led to some very distinct definitions. On the one hand, the term is unclear because the transfer of logical concepts to natural languages is not governed by an algorithmic set of transfer rules and, on the other hand, because the relationship between logic and linguistics and the role of both in the analysis of natural languages is, at best, unclear (see Garner 1971).

The following definition is fundamental to the concept of presupposition in logic: S_1 presupposes S_2 exactly if S_1 implies S_2 and if not-S_1 also entails S_2. For example, *The present king of France is bald* or *is not bald* presupposes *There is presently a king of France* (Russell's example). Various characteristics of or ideas about presupposition can be derived from this definition: (a) presuppositions are conditions that must be fulfilled so that a statement can be assigned a **truth value** (see Strawson 1952); (b) presuppositions remain constant under negation; (c) presuppositions refer to assertions (= **declarative sentences**). Investigations in this area dealt at first with the conditions of existence or individuality of particular expressions functioning as subjects (in the above example: *the king of France*); thus, the analysis concentrated primarily on **proper nouns** and (**definite**) **descriptions**. Since the phenomenon of presupposition is covered by a series of long-known problems in grammatical investigations (such as emphatic structure, **subordination**, **topic vs comment**, emotive vs connotative meaning (⇒ **connotation**), the term was used partly synonymously with these corresponding linguistic concepts: cf. 'quasi-implication' in Bellert (1969), 'covert categories' in Fillmore (1969), 'subordination' in McCawley (1968), '**selectional restrictions**' in Chomsky (1965).

The transfer of the concept of presupposition from logic to linguistics was influenced both by Strawson (1950) and by Austin's and Searle's **speech act theory** and has brought about various controversies. (a) Are presuppositions relations between sentences, utterances, or attitudes of the speaker/hearer? (b) Are they logico-semantic, functional relations of truth values and therefore context-independent elements of meaning specific to the level of *langue* (⇒ **langue vs parole**) or are they context-dependent, pragmatic conditions of the use of linguistic expressions, dependent upon linguistic behavior and conventions on the level of *parole* (Searle, Seuren, Fillmore, Wilson)? All these attempts at delineating and ordering are, in the last analysis, aimed at modeling the concept of presupposition after one or more levels of language. In the case of (a), syntactic or constructionally based presupposition, there are difficulties regarding the dependence of presupposition on such phenomena as **focus**, **topicalization**, and **subordination**. With (b), semantically and lexically based presupposition, one must determine whether it is a matter of inherent semantic features or selection restrictions. And as far as (c), pragmatically based presuppositions (which correspond to Searle's **felicity conditions**), are concerned, it remains questionable to what extent they are open to internal linguistic description (⇒ **implicature, invited inference**). The following linguistic indicators are suspected to be so-called 'P-inducers,' that is, consistently likely to result in the same presuppositions in all conceivable contexts: definite **noun phrases**, **factive predicates**, **quantification**, **conjunctions**, **particles**, the theme–rheme division of sentences (⇒ **theme vs rheme**), emphatic structure, subordination, **subcategorization**, or selection restrictions (see Reis 1977).

Investigations on presupposition have played and continue to play a central role in linguistic approaches and in questions concerning the delineation of the linguistic disciplines. This has been especially apparent in the discussion and delineation of **interpretive semantics** vs **generative semantics**, **logic** vs **linguistics**, linguistics vs **pragmatics**, and linguistic vs encyclopedic knowledge, as well as in questions regarding textual coherence (⇒ **coherence, cohesion**) and in the investigation of text constituents in **text linguistics**. In everyday language, the misuse of presupposition may lead to the manipulation of language, for example, when the cross-examiner asks the defendant *When will you stop beating your wife?* Denying an apparently obvious supposition is frequently less easy than contradicting an explicit statement. (⇒ *also* **conversation analysis, formal logic**)

References
Bellert, I. 1969. Arguments and predicates in the logicosemantic structure of utterances. In F. Kiefer (ed.), *Studies in syntax and semantics*. Dordrecht. 109–37.

Chomsky, N. 1965. *Aspects of the theory of syntax.* Cambridge, MA.

Fillmore, C.J. 1969. Types of lexical information. In: F. Kiefer (ed.), *Studies in syntax and semantics.* Dordrecht. 109–37.

Frege, G. 1892. Über Sinn und Bedeutung. *Zeitschrift für Philosophie und philosophische Kritik,* new series 100.25–50. (Repr. in *Kleine Schriften,* ed. I Angelelli. Darmstadt, 1967. 143–62.)

Garner, R. 1971. Presupposition in philosophy and linguistics. In C.J. Fillmore and T.D. Langendoen (eds), *Studies in linguistic semantics.* New York. 23–42.

Gazdar, G. 1977. *Implicature, presupposition and logical form.* Bloomington, IN.

——— 1979. *Pragmatics.* New York.

Hausser, R. 1976. Presuppositions in Montague grammar. *TL* 3.245–80.

Jackendoff, R.S. 1972. *Semantic interpretation in generative grammar.* New York.

Keenan, E.L. 1971. Two kinds of presupposition in natural language. In C. Fillmore and D.T. Langendoen (eds), *Studies in linguistic semantics.* New York. 45–52.

Kempson, R.M. 1975. *Presupposition and the delimitation of semantics.* London.

Kiparsky, P. and C. Kiparsky. 1970. Fact. In M. Bierwisch and K.E. Heidolph (eds), *Progress in linguistics.* The Hague. 143–73.

McCawley, J.D. 1968. The role of semantics in a Grammar. In: E. Bach and R. Harms (eds), *Universals in linguistic theory.* New York. 125–204.

Murphy, J., A. Rogers, and R. Wall (eds) 1977. *Proceedings of the Texas conference on performatives, presuppositions and conversational implicatures.* Washington, DC.

Oh, C.-K. and D.A. Dineen (eds) 1979. *Presupposition.* New York.

Petöfi, J.S. and D. Franck (eds) 1973. *Präsuppositionen in Philosophie und Linguistik.* Frankfurt.

Reis, M. 1974. Präsuppositionen in Philosophie und Linguistik: Anmerkungen zur Anthologie von J.S. Petöfi und D. Franck, *Präpsuppositionen in Philosophie und Linguistik. DSp* 4.287–304.

——— 1977. *Präsuppositionen und syntax.* Tübingen.

Russell, B. 1905. On denoting. *Mind* 30.479–93.

Searle, J.R. 1969. *Speech acts: an essay in the philosophy of language.* Cambridge.

Seuren, P.A.M. 1985. *Discourse semantics.* Oxford.

Strawson, P.F. 1950. On referring. *Mind* 67.320–44.

——— 1952. *Introduction to logical theory.* London.

Von Fraassen, B.C. 1968. Presupposition, implication and self-reference. *JP* 65. 136–52. (Repr. in J.S. Petöfi and D. Franck (eds), *Präsuppositionen in Philosophie und Linguistik.* Frankfurt, 1973. 109–37.)

——— 1971. *Formal semantics and logic.* New York.

Wilson, D. 1975. *Presuppositions and non-truth-conditional semantics.* London.

Bibliography
Petöfi, J.S. (ed.) 1978. *Logic and the formal theory of natural language: selective bibliography.* Hamburg.

⇒ **conversation analysis, formal logic, pragmatics**

presupposition test

In order to distinguish **presupposition** from **assertion**, **implicature**, **maxims of conversation** and speech acts (⇒ **speech act theory**), the following tests for monologues and dialogues or a combination thereof may be used (see Altmann 1976). (a) Negation test to determine assertion and presupposition: by definition, presupposition remains constant under (heavy) **negation**, while assertion and implicature convert to their opposites. However, only under certain conditions is the negation test sufficient, since negation in natural languages corresponds to logical negation only in assertions. Moreover the **scope** (i.e. elements of the sentence covered by the negation) is frequently ambiguous depending on **stress** and/or context. The negation of *Caroline painted the picture*, namely *Caroline didn't paint the picture*, may refer – depending on the reading – to *Caroline*, to *the picture*, or to the whole situation. Especially in sentences with **particles**, a correct reading of the negation is clearly not always possible (strong, weak, or contrastive negation?) (see Seuren 1985). (b) Variation of the speech act type with non-variation of the proposition to determine the proposition: *Is the present king of France bald?* presupposes *There is presently a king of France.* (c) Conjunction test with *and*: individual aspects of meaning (assertion, proposition, conversational **implicature**) are placed before or after the given utterance, i.e. conjoined by *and*. This test is based on the fact that presuppositions of grammatical sentences can be placed before and conversational implicatures after the conjunction, while both positions are possible for assertions. (d) Contradiction test with *but*: explicit contradiction of that which is presupposed in the previous utterance results in an ungrammatical sentence.

References
⇒ **presupposition**

preterite [Lat. *praeteritum* 'gone by; that has occurred in the past'] (*also* **imperfect**, past tense)

1 Term for past tense in languages that do not distinguish between **aorist**, **imperfect**, and **perfect**, as does, for example, Classical **Greek**. The preterite describes something that is completed before the speech act it occurs in, and is thus primarily used for epic narrative, i.e. recounting series of events.

2 In older usage, term used collectively for the perfect, imperfect, and past perfect.

preterite-present

Verb whose original **Indo-European** preterite form has taken on a present-tense meaning. The reinterpretation of tense and meaning is based on the aspectual character of the Indo-European tense system (⇒ **aspect**): the basic inventory and model for preterite-present verbs are found in the Indo-European perfect stem which denotes a condition caused by a previously occurring action: Grk *oĩda* 'I have seen,' therefore: 'I know.' The preterite of this class of originally strong verbs (i.e. verbs with a regular stem vowel change, ⇒ **ablaut**) is newly formed by analogy with weak verbs (⇒ **strong vs weak verb**). Characteristics of the preterite-present verbs are (a) vowel differentiation in the singular and plural present tense (former preterite), cf. OE *cann/cunnon* '(I) can / (we) can,' vs OE *singa/singan*' (I) sing / (we) sing' and (b) the third person singular present is endingless: *he may, she can* vs *he does*. Preterite-present verbs get their specific meaning from their syntactic use as **modal auxiliary** verbs.

References
⇒ **historical grammars**

primacy relation

Relation described by Langacker (1966) between **nodes** in a **tree diagram**: two nodes A and B are in a relation of primacy, if (a) in the linear chain node A precedes node B and (b) node A commands node B, i.e. neither A nor B dominate each other, and the S-node which immediately dominates node A also dominates the node B. See the following tree diagram, in which node A precedes node B (precedence relation) and node A commands the nodes X and B:

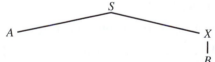

The primacy relation plays an important part in transformation processes such as pronominalization (see Langacker), but also generally in constraints for the application of rules (Reis 1974).

References
Langacker, R.W. 1966. On pronominalization and the chain of command. In D.A. Reibel and S.A. Schane (eds), *Modern studies in English: readings in transformational grammar*. Englewood Cliffs, NJ. 160–86.

Reis, M. 1974. Syntaktische Hauptsatzprivilegien und das Problem der deutschen Wortstellung. *ZGL* 2.299–327.
⇒ **transformational grammar**

primary stress ⇒ **stress**^{2}

primate communication ⇒ **animal communication**

primate language ⇒ **animal communication**

primitive predicate ⇒ **semantic primitive**

principle of abstractive relevance

Basic principle of K. Bühler's (linguistic) sign theory, postulated in analogy to N. Trubetzkoy's theory and exemplified by the distinction between phonetics and phonology: the constitution of the sign as a sign does not occur on the basis of its materially perceptible characteristics (i.e. the phonetic variety in its articulation), but rather on the basis of its 'diacritically effective' features which are relevant for distinguishing meaning. (⇒ *also* **axiomatics of linguistics, distinctive feature**)

References
Bühler, K. 1934. *Sprachtheorie*. Jena. (Repr. Stuttgart 1965.)
Innis, R.E. (trans.) 1982. *Karl Bühler: semiotic foundations of language theory*. New York.
Trubetzkoy, N. 1929. Zur allgemeinen Theorie der phonologischen Vokalsysteme. *TCLP* 1.39–67.
⇒ **axiomatics of linguistics**

principle of compositionality (*also* Frege's principle of meaning, Fregean principle)

Principle usually ascribed to G. Frege (1848–1925) according to which the whole meaning of a sentence can be described according to the functional interdependency of the meanings of its well-formed parts. The methodological premise, that the semantic description of complex expressions in natural language can be conceived such that the meaning of these expressions (in particular sentences) can be reconstructed from the meanings of their individual elements and their syntactic relationship to one another, is based upon this empirical assumption. To this extent, the application of the principle of compositionality presupposes a syntactic analysis and yields, in the case of sentences, their **sentence meanings** but not the utterance meanings (⇒ **meaning, utterance**). Possible problems with the principle of compositionality may be evident in **idioms, metaphors**, and **intensionality. Categorial grammar** and **Montague grammar** are based on the principle of compositionality.

References
Frege, G. 1962. *Funktion, Begriff, Bedeutung*, ed. G. Patzig. Göttingen. (4th edn 1975.)
Partee, B.H. 1984. Compositionality. In F. Landman and F. Veltman (eds), *Varieties of the Fourth Amsterdam Colloquium, September 1982*. Dordrecht. 281–311.
Seuren, P.A.M. 1985. *Discourse semantics*. Oxford.
⇒ **categorial grammar, formal logic, intensional logic, Montague grammar**

principle of cyclic rule application

A provision for the repeated application of **transformations** in **transformational grammar**. According to the principle of cyclic rule application, syntactic and phonological rules operate from bottom to top, i.e. they begin on the lowest level of the **tree diagram** and then move to the next highest level until they reach the highest cyclic node, the **matrix sentence**. The application of a cyclic rule within a **cyclic node** assumes that no other cyclic rules have been applied to a higher cyclic node. According to the goal of formulating universal restrictions for the grammars of all natural languages, Chomsky (1968) postulated that the cyclic principle was an inherent organizational principle of universal grammar. In syntactic theory, **trace theory** has shown that the empirical predictions of the cyclic principle can also be derived from other **constraints** on **transformations** (see Freidin 1978). In phonology as well there are attempts to replace the cyclic principle with other restrictions (see Kiparsky 1982). (⇒ *also* **transformational grammar**)

References
Chomsky, N. 1965. *Aspects of the theory of syntax*. Cambridge, MA.
——— 1968. *Language and mind*. New York.
Freidin, R. 1978. Cyclicity and the theory of grammar. *LingI* 9.519–49.
Kiparsky, P. 1982. From cyclic phonology to lexical phonology. In H. van der Hulst and N. Smith (eds), *The structure of phonological representation*, part 1. Dordrecht. 131–75.
Pelletier, F.J. 1980. The generative power of rule orderings in formal grammars. *Linguistics* 18.17–72.
Pullum, G. 1979. *Rule interaction and the organization of a grammar*. New York.
Ross, J.R. 1967. On the cyclic nature of English pronominalization. In *To honor Roman Jakobson: essays on the occasion of his seventieth birthday, 11 October 1966*. The Hague. Vol. 3, 1669–82.
Rudin, C. 1981. 'Who what to whom said': an argument from Bulgarian against cyclic wh-movement. *PCLS* 17.353–60.
Soames, S. and D.M. Perlmutter. 1979. *Syntactic argumentation and the structure of English*. Berkeley, CA.
Williams, E. 1977. Rule ordering in syntax. Dissertation, Bloomington, IN.

——— 1982. The NP-cycle. *LingI* 13.277–95.
⇒ **constraints, transformational grammar**

principle of directionality

A syntactic rule for co-ordinating structures. The first of two co-referential constituents can be deleted in a co-ordinating structure only if the constituent appears in the right-hand branch of a node in a **tree diagram**, whereas the second element can be deleted only if it branches to the left. For example, *Philip looks for Caroline and Philip finds Caroline* can become *Philip looks for and finds Caroline* because the first instance of *Caroline* occurs to the right of *looks for* and the second instance of *Philip* occurs to the left of *looks for*. (⇒ **gapping**)

References
⇒ **co-ordination, transformational grammar**

principle of expressibility ⇒ speech act theory

principle of least effort ⇒ Zipf's law

private language

Concept used by differing schools in philosophy (of language) comprising the idea that there is a language distinct from public language whose expressions refer exclusively to personal experiences and consciousness to such a degree that they cannot be understood by anyone but the speaker him-/herself. With various arguments, Wittgenstein, in his *Philosophical Investigations*, disputes the very consistency of the notion.

References
Chomsky, N. 1986. Questions about rules. In N. Chomsky (ed.), *Knowledge of language: it's nature, origin, and use*. New York. 221–75.
Jones, C.R. (ed.) 1971. *The private language argument*. London.
Kripke, S. 1982. *Wittgenstein on rules and private language*. Oxford.
Wittgenstein, L. 1953. *Philosophical investigations*. Oxford.

private speech ⇒ internal language

privative [Lat. *privare* 'to rob or deprive of']

Semantically defined class of derived verbs whose meaning can be paraphrased as 'removal of something': *detoxify, unburden, behead, disinfect*, etc.

privative opposition ⇒ opposition

PRO

An abstract element in **surface structure**, which, as a phonologically empty category, syntactically represents the logical subject of an infinitive (⇒ **projection principle**). Infinitival clauses are treated as whole sentences on the basis of the abstract representation of the subject by PRO (⇒ **complementizer**). In contrast to the empty category marked by pro, the PRO element is always ungoverned, i.e. it occupies a position which no case-bearing NP could occupy. The distribution and semantic content of PRO is governed by the theory of control.

References
Vanden Wyngaerd, G.J. 1994. *PRO-legomena: distribution and reference of infinitival subjects.* Berlin and New York.
⇒ **control**

pro-adverb ⇒ pronominal adverb

probabilistic grammar

Grammatical model developed by Salomaa (1969) and Suppes (1972) to describe social, regional, diachronic and situative variants in natural languages. On the basis of statistical hypotheses that are strongly supported by empirical evidence, every linguistic rule is assigned a degree of probability that predicts its occurrence within the framework of a 'relational grammar' which encompasses one of each variant. The development of such grammars, arranged according to probabilities, has proved to be a useful instrument for describing the processes of language change and language acquisition.

References
Salomaa, A. 1969. Probabilistic and weighted grammars. *IC* 15.529–44.
Sankoff, D. (ed.) 1978. *Linguistic variation: models and methods.* New York.
Suppes, P. 1972. Probabilistic grammars for natural languages. *Synthese* 22.95–116. (Repr. in D. Davidson and G. Harman (eds), *Semantics of natural language.* Dordrecht. 741–62.)
⇒ **variational linguistics**

problominalization (*also* Bach–Peters paradox)

Humorous term coined by Bach (1970) formed from contamination of probl(em) and (pron)ominalization which refers to certain difficulties in the derivation of pronouns from the deep structure. (⇒ *also* **personal pronoun**)

References
Bach, E. 1970. Problominalization. *LIn* 1. 121ff.
Karttunen, L. 1971. Definite descriptions with crossing coreference: a study of the Bach–Peters paradox. *FL* 7.157–82.

process vs action

Semantic distinction of verbs, often handled as an **aspect** distinction. Process verbs describe dynamic events that are not caused by an **agent**: *bloom, grow, rise.* They are usually intransitive.

Actions, on the other hand, are caused by an agent; they can occur in the **imperative** and can be combined with certain modal **adverbs**: *dance joyfully.* (⇒ *also* **stative vs active**)

References
⇒ **aspect**

prochievement test ⇒ language test

proclitic

Phonetic merging of a weakly stressed or unstressed word to the following word, as a rule with simultaneous phonetic weakening, cf. Fr. *l'enfant* 'child.' Proclitics are virtually non-existent in English. (⇒ *also* **enclitic**)

procope

Diachronic or synchronic loss of one or more speech sounds at the beginning of a word, cf. *bishop* < Grk *episkopos.* (⇒ *also* **aphesis**)

pro-drop language

A language in which an empty subject position that has been motivated by the **projection principle** and which has pronominal, i.e. referential, properties can appear in a finite sentence. Examples of such languages are **Italian** and **Spanish**, but not **English**, **German**, or **French**. For example, compare Italian [pro *mangia*] with English *[pro *eats*] for *he eats*. The pronoun *he* cannot be dropped in English.

References
Adams, M. 1987. From Old French to the theory of pro-drop. *NL&LT* 5.1–32.
Chomsky, N. 1981. *Lectures on government and binding.* Dordrecht.
——— 1982. *Some concepts and consequences of the theory of government and binding.* Cambridge, MA.
Perlmutter, D.M. 1971. *Deep and surface structure constraints in syntax.* New York.
Picallo, M.C. 1984. The INFL node and the null subject parameter. *LingI* 15.75–102.
Platzack, C. 1985. The Scandinavian languages and the null subject parameter. *Working Papers in Scandinavian Syntax* 20.1–65. Trondheim. (Repr. in *NL&LT* 5(1987).377–401.)
Rizzi, L. 1982. Negation, wh-movement and the null subject parameter. In L. Rizzi (ed.), *Issues in Italian syntax.* Dordrecht. 117–84.
——— 1986. Null objects in Italian and the theory of PRO. *LingI* 17.501–57.

pro-drop parameter

The parameter which determines whether a language is a **pro-drop language** or not. A positive setting of the parameter allows an empty pro-element to be identified by its governor. This is the case in pro-drop languages.

References
⇒ **pro-drop language**

productivity

Ability of word-forming elements to be used to form new linguistic expressions. Productivity is a gradient concept that is broken down into unproductive elements (e.g. *be-*, cf. *behead*), occasionally productive (or 'active') elements (e.g. *-ify* and *-ese*, cf. *beautify* and *motherese*), and highly productive elements (e.g. *re-* and *-er*, cf. *retry*, *player*). The explanation and description of productivity is controversial: on the one hand, **neologisms** and their immediate comprehensibility parallel syntactic 'creativity,' but on the other hand, even as highly productive processes, they are, as a rule, not free of lexical gaps and exceptions (e.g. **topwards* vs *sidewards*, **teen-something* vs *twenty-something*, *'writable* vs *readable*). (⇒ *also* **word formation**)

References
Aronoff, M. 1976. *Word formation in generative grammar*. Cambridge, MA.
Baayen, H. 1992. Quantitative aspects of morphological productivity. In G. Booij and J. van Marle (eds), *Yearbook of morphology 1991*. Dordrecht. 109–49.
Baayen, H. and R. Lieber. 1991. Productivity and English derivation. *Linguistics* 29.801–43.
Frauenfelder, U. and R. Schreuder. 1992. Constraining psycholinguistic models of morphological processing and representation: the role of productivity. In G. Booij and J. van Marle (eds), *Yearbook of morphology 1991*. Dordrecht. 165–83.
Kastovsky, D. 1986. The problem of productivity in word formation. *Linguistics* 24.585–600.
Marle, J. van. 1992. The relationship between morphological productivity and frequency. In G. Booij and J. van Marle (eds), *Yearbook of morphology 1991*. Dordrecht. 151–63.
⇒ **word formation**

proficiency

The ability to function competently in one's native or in a second language, involving a sense for appropriate linguistic behavior in a variety of situations. Since the late 1960s, the proficiency movement has played a dominant role in foreign language instruction in the United States and Canada. The ACTFL (American Council on the Teaching of Foreign Languages) provisional proficiency guidelines, first disseminated in 1982, were developed in cooperation with American and international government, business and academic groups, and represent an adaptation of a scale formulated by linguists at the United States Foreign Service Institute in the early 1950s. The ACTFL guidelines outline levels for proficiency in the four skills of speaking, writing, listening, and reading. The levels (Novice Low, Mid, High; Intermediate Low, Mid, High; Advanced, Advanced High, and Superior; the Distinguished level also applies to the reading and listening skills) establish parameters for determining the degree of proficiency in the different skills. Oral proficiency, one of the key goals of the proficiency movement, is measured by the 'oral proficiency interview,' a test administered by a specialist trained in identifying the linguistic functions, contexts, text types, and accuracy levels characteristic of the different levels of proficiency. (⇒ *also* **second language acquisition**)

References
American Council on the Teaching of Foreign Languages. 1986. *ACTFL proficiency guidelines*. New York.
Carroll, J.B. 1967. Foreign language proficiency levels attained by language majors near graduation from college. *Foreign Language Annals* 1.131–51.
Higgs, T.V. (ed.) 1984. *Teaching for proficiency: the organizing principle*. Lincolnwood, IL.
Van Patten, B. and J.F. Lee. 1995. *Making communicative language teaching happen*. New York.

pro-form (*also* pronominal copy, **substitute**)

Linguistic elements which refer primarily to nominal **antecedents**. They represent other elements by referring to them regressively (⇒ **anaphora**) or progressively (⇒ **cataphora**), depending on whether or not the antecedent has been named previously or not. They reflect various aspects of their antecedent depending on their categorial function: **person**, **number**, **gender**, and **case** are expressed to various degrees by pronominals, while **pronominal adverbs** refer to semantic aspects such as location (*there*), temporality (*then*), causality (*for that reason*), and modality (*like*, *thus*).

References
⇒ **anaphora**, **reference**, **textual reference**

programming language

Formal (artificial) language used in computers and designed for formulating tasks and solving problems (⇒ **algorithm**, **formal language**). An executable program ('source code') written in a programming language is translated by a **compiler** or **interpreter** into a **machine language** ('object code'). Every (higher-level) programming language is conceived for working on certain types of problems, e.g. ALGOL ('algorithmic language') principally for mathematical problems, COBOL ('common business-oriented language') for business-oriented problems. FORTRAN ('formula translation system') for non-numeric scientific problems. In the framework of **computational linguistics**, **LISP** (e.g. for **ATN grammars**) and **PROLOG** (for **definite clause grammar**) play an important role.

References
Clocksin, W.F. and C.S. Mellish. 1981. *Programming in PROLOG*. Berlin (2nd edn 1984.)
Garner, M. 1987. *Artificial languages: a critical history*. London.
Wechselblat, R.L. (ed.) 1981. *History of programming languages*. London.
Winston, P.H. and B.K.P. Horn, 1981. *LISP*. Reading, MA. (2nd edn 1984.)

progressive (*also* continuative, continuous)

Verbal **aspect** which indicates an action as taking place over a longer period of time relative to an implicitly or explicitly stated time of reference: Eng. *John was singing* (*when I came in*); Span. *Juan está cantando*, Icelandic *Jón er að syngja*. In some languages (such as English) this category is grammaticalized so that the use of the progressive is obligatory for expressing progressive meaning, although such forms can also acquire other meanings depending on the context: *She is constantly smoking* (emotive meaning implying disapproval or annoyance).

References
Leech, G.N. 1971. *Meaning and the English verb*. London.
Schopf, A. (ed.) 1974. *Der englische Aspekt*. Darmstadt.
Vlach, F. 1981. The semantics of the progressive. In P.J. Tedeschi and A. Zaenen (eds), *Tense and aspect*. New York. 271–92.

progressive assimilation ⇒ assimilation

prohibitive

Verbal **mood** used to prohibit the addressee from doing something. In **Latin**, the prohibitive is expressed by the perfect subjunctive: *ne dubitaveris* 'do not doubt!'

References
⇒ **modality**

projection

1 The process by which **presuppositions** of simple sentences are transmitted to complex sentences.

References
⇒ **presupposition**

2 In Chomsky's **Government and Binding theory**, a mapping of syntactic-semantic properties, as they are stated in the lexicon, onto other levels of syntactic representation.

References
Baker, Mark. 1988. *Incorporation: a theory of grammatical function changing*. Chicago, IL.
Dowty, David. 1991. Thematic proto-roles and argument selection. *Language* 67: 547–619.
Grimshaw, Jane. 1990. *Argument structure*. Cambridge, MA.
Jackendoff, Ray. 1990. *Semantic structure*. Cambridge, MA.
⇒ **projection principle**

projection principle

1 A term introduced in Chomsky's **Government and Binding theory** which links together the levels of syntactic description (**surface structure**, **deep structure**, and **logical form**). The projection principle states that a node which is present at one of these levels must be present at all levels. Therefore a **movement transformation** must leave behind an empty category (⇒ **empty category principle**) because the position in deep structure from which it was moved must correspond to an (empty) position in surface structure. (⇒ **trace theory**)

2 A principle of GB theory that connects syntactic structures with lexical entries: the logical valence of predicates, which is established in the lexicon, must be represented at all syntactic levels of representation. As a result of this principle, semantically implied arguments of a verb that are not realized phonologically are represented syntactically as an empty category.

The so-called 'extended' projection principle additionally requires that every clause projects a subject position, even if this position does not belong to the logical valence of the predicate. (⇒ **raising**)

References
Chomsky, N. 1981. *Lectures on government and binding*. Dordrecht.
⇒ **control, pro-drop language, transformational grammar**

projection rule

In Katz and Fodor's (1963) theory of **interpretive semantics**, a semantic operation which arrives at the interpretation of the whole meaning of a sentence through the step-by-step 'projection' of the meaning of the individual **constituents** from the lowest level of derivation to the next higher level. Thus, projection rules function over the hierarchic relations of the constituents in the deep structure. According to Katz and Fodor, projection rules simulate the cognitive process in which the speaker and hearer comprehend the whole meaning of the sentence, using their knowledge of the **lexicon** (i.e. of the meaning of the individual elements) and of the syntactic relations. The process in which projection rules are applied is known as **amalgamation**.

Reference
Katz, J.J. and J.A. Fodor. 1963. The structure of a semantic theory. *Lg* 39.170–210.

projectivity

Term taken from mathematics which refers in linguistics to structures whose **tree diagram** and **labeled bracketing** are equivalent. This applies in the example *Anne has promised the count a night of love*, but not to the sentence *Has Anne promised the count a night of love?*, because the discontinuous elements *has* and *promised* would have to be expressed in the tree diagram by crossing branches, which cannot be expressed in brackets (see diagram below).

prolepsis [Grk *prólēpsis* 'taking beforehand']

1 An argumentative **figure of speech**. The anticipation of an argument with the goal of tactical compromise, frequently in the form of a rhetorical question and answer. (⇒ **concession**)

2 Syntactic construction in which one element (usually the subject) is 'anticipated' and placed at the beginning of the sentence outside the sentence frame and then expressed in the sentence by a pro-form, usually a pronoun: *Now my boss, he wouldn't put up with that sort of thing* (⇒ **left vs right dislocation**).

References
⇒ **figure of speech**

PROLOG

Programming language (name derived from Fr. *programmation en logique* and Eng. *programming in logic*) that realizes the principles of logical programming, that is, the execution of a program is conceived as carrying out a proof. This is based on the more general view that problem-solving may be construed as proving that certain target conditions can be met. PROLOG has been under development con-

currently in Marseille and Edinburgh since the early 1970s and has played an increasingly important role in **computational linguistics** since the mid-1980s.

References
Clocksin, W.F. and C.S. Mellish. 1981. *Programming in PROLOG*. Berlin (2nd edn 1984.)
Gazdar, G. and C.S. Mellish. 1989. *Natural language processing in PROLOG*. Reading, MA.
Kowalski, R. 1979. *Logic for problem solving*. New York.
Pereira, F. and S. Shieber. 1987. *PROLOG and natural language analysis*. Stanford, CA.

prominence

In the study of **suprasegmental features**, a term encompassing **stress**[2], duration, and **tone**. These features are always present to some degree in all utterances; the prominence of a unit is therefore relative to that of other units.

pronominal adverb (*also* pro-adverb)

Term used in a variety of ways which in general refers to linguistic elements which stand syntactically as **pro-forms** for prepositional phrases (**objects** or **adverbials**): *thereon, hereby, hitherto, hereafter*.

pronominal copy ⇒ pro-form

pronominal form of address

Pronominal expressions used for addressing the hearer; languages which make use of these generally have at least two forms whose use depends on the status of and relationship between the speakers. Investigations into the connection between social and linguistic aspects of pronominal forms of address have uncovered a series of regularities among most languages. The use of pronominal forms of address is dependent not only on a vertical status hierarchy ('higher' vs 'lower'), but also on a horizontal dimension of 'solidarity' (i.e. belonging to a common 'group') or relational intimacy. Both dimensions intersect inasfar as the pronoun used symmetrically in intimate situations (e.g. Fr. *tu*, Ger. *du* 'you') is identical with the pronoun used in an asymmetrical

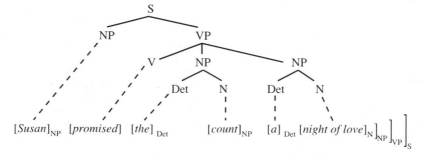

social situation from 'higher to lower,' while the more distant form (Fr. *vous*, Ger. *Sie* 'you') is used symmetrically in less intimate situations as well as for the address from 'lower to higher' socially. Research on pronominal forms of address has recently focused primarily on pragmatic, sociological, and ethnological aspects. (⇒ *also* **honorific**)

References
Braun, F. 1988. *Terms of address*. Berlin.
Brown, R. and A. Gilman. 1968. The pronouns of power and solidarity. In J.A. Fishman (ed.), *Readings in the sociology of language*. The Hague. 252–75.
Brown, R. and S. Levinson. 1978. Universals of language usage: politeness phenomena. In E.N. Goody (ed.), *Questions and politeness: strategies in social interaction*. Cambridge.
Ervin-Tripp, S.M. 1964. Imitation and structural change in children's language. In E.H. Lenneberg (ed.), *New directions in the study of language*. Cambridge, MA. 163–89.
Hymes, D. (ed.) 1964. *Language in culture and society: a reader in linguistics and anthropology*. New York.
Metcalf, G.J. 1938. *Form of address in German (1500–1800)*. Washington, DC.
Silverberg, W.V. 1940. On the psychological significance of 'du' and 'Sie.' *Psychoanalytic Quarterly* 9.509–25.

Bibliography
Braun, F., A. Kohz, and K. Schubert. 1986. *Anredeforschung: kommentierte Bibliographie zur Soziolinguistik der Anrede*. Tübingen.
⇒ **politeness**

pronominalization ⇒ personal pronoun

pronoun (*also* shift word)

Part of speech named for its function of standing for ('pro') the noun. Pronouns form a very heterogeneous group in regard to syntax and semantics. All pronouns share the property of **deixis**, but differ from nominal expressions in that nominal expressions such as **proper nouns** always refer to the same elements in the real world, independent of the specific speaker context, while pronouns refer to various objects in the real world in a way that is dependent on the specific linguistic context of the utterance. Thus, the proper name *Mozart* usually refers to the same individual, irrespective of the linguistic context, while the reference of a pronoun like *he* can only be determined from the context of the utterance, i.e. the man last mentioned, the individual pointed to by the speaker, etc. Morphologically, pronouns in inflectional languages generally have a complex inflectional pattern and are subject to **agreement** with their antecedents. Pronouns are divided into several syntacto-semantic subgroups, including **perso-**nal, **reflexive**, **possessive**, **demonstrative**, **indefinite**, **interrogative**, and **relative pronouns**, as well as **pronominal adverbs**.

References
⇒ **anaphora**, **clitics**, **personal pronoun**

pronunciation

One generally speaks of the pronunciation of a language with regard to a **speech community**. Often this refers to the conventions of the **writing** system, and one speaks of the pronunciation of a letter or a word. (⇒ *also* **prescriptive grammar**, **standard pronunciation**)

References
⇒ **standard pronunciation**

proper name ⇒ proper noun

proper noun (*also* name, nomen proprium, proper name)

Semantically defined class of nouns that unequivocally identifies objects and states of affairs within a given context. By designating an object or a state of affairs in a given statement, proper nouns replace deictic, or pointing, gestures such that direct **reference** to that object or state of affairs is made. Whether proper nouns have meaning and how they differ from **generic** names and (**definite**) **descriptions** has been open to much debate. **Onomastics**, in its narrower sense, deals with proper nouns and differentiates them into personal names, place names, and names of bodies of water, among others.

References
Allerton, D.J. 1987. The linguistic and sociolinguistic status of proper names. *JPsyR* 11.61–92.
Conrad, B. 1985. On the reference of proper names. *ALH* 19.44–124.
Kripke, S. 1972. Naming and necessity. In D. Davidson and G. Harman (eds), *Semantics of natural language*. Dordrecht. 253–355, 762–9.
Kuryłowicz, J. 1956. La position linguistique du nom propre. *Onomastica* 2.1–14.
Searle, J.R. 1969. *Speech acts: an essay in the philosophy of language*. Cambridge.
⇒ **onomastics**

properispomenon [Grk *properispómenos*, participle of *properispán* 'to pronounce the penultimate syllable with a circumflex accent']

In Greek, a word with circumflex accent, presumably reflecting a rise–fall intonation on the penultimate syllable. e.g. *dōron* 'gift.' (⇒ *also* **perispomenon**)

proportional analogy ⇒ **analogy**

proportional clause

Semantically defined modal clause functioning as an adverbial modifier to indicate a dependency relationship proportional to the state of affairs expressed in the main clause. They are introduced by *the* + comparative in both the dependent and independent clauses: *The closer they came to the city, the more excited they became.*

proportional opposition ⇒ **opposition**

proposition [Lat. *propositio* 'statement of the facts or substance of a case']

Term adopted by **semantics** and **speech act theory** from philosophy and **formal logic** (where a proposition is usually designated by 'that p'). By 'proposition' one usually understands the language-independent common denominator of the meaning of sentences which express the factuality of a given state of affairs. In appropriate utterances of the sentences *Phil smokes habitually.* / *Does Phil really smoke habitually?* / *It is not true that Phil smokes habitually.* / *If Phil smokes habitually, then he will not live much longer*, every time the same **reference** (i.e. to Phil) and the same **predication** (i.e. of habitual smoking) is made, quite independent of the illocutionary force (assertion, question, denial, etc.). Thus, a proposition is the semantic kernel of a sentence that determines its **truth conditions**, regardless of the syntactic form and lexical filling of the given form of expression. A distinction is drawn between 'coarser' concepts of proposition, according to which, for example, all logically true sentences denote the same proposition, and 'finer' concepts of proposition, in which this is not the case. While older semantic models (cf. **possible world** semantics) conceived of propositions as unstructured units, the need for a structured concept of proposition in linguistics is now more and more accepted (cf. **situation semantics**). Since propositional acts (i.e. acts of expressing a proposition) are always constituents of illocutionary acts (**illocution**) and therefore cannot occur independently, they must be distinguished from **statements** (i.e. illocutionary acts) in which propositions are asserted and not just expressed.

References
Austin, J.L. 1950. Truth. *Proceedings of the Aristotelian Society* 24. (Repr. in his *Philosophical papers*. Oxford, 1961. 117–33.)
Barwise, J. and J. Etchemendy. 1987. *The liar: an essay in truth and circularity*. Oxford.
Cresswell, M.J. 1973. *Logic and languages*. London, Chs 3–4.
—— 1985. *Structured meanings: the semantics of propositional attitudes*. Cambridge, MA.
Kearns, J.T. 1972. Propositions and truth in natural languages. *Mind* 81.225–43.
Nuchelmans, G. 1973. *Theories of propositions*. Amsterdam.
Russell, B. and A.N. Whitehead. 1910/13. *Principia mathematica*. Cambridge.
Searle, J.R. 1969. *Speech acts: an essay in the philosophy of language*. Cambridge.
Stalnaker, R.C. 1984. *Inquiry*. Cambridge, MA.
—— 1985. Propositions. In A.P. Martenich (ed.), *The philosophy of language*. Oxford. 373–80.

propositional calculus ⇒ **propositional logic**

propositional island constraint (*also* tensed-S-condition, *wh*-island constraint)

A **constraint** proposed by N. Chomsky on the use of **transformational rules**. In a structure such as $[\ldots X \ldots [_S \ldots Y \ldots] \ldots X \ldots]$ no rules can refer to both X and Y, if S contains a finite verb, unless X is in the COMP position (**complementizer**) of S. The propositional island constraint refers above all to sentences introduced by question words. Compare, for example, *What* (= X) *did she say* – (= X in COMP) *she saw* – (= Y)? with **Philip* (= X) *is likely that* – (= Y) *will leave early*.

References
⇒ **constraints**, *wh* -**island constraint**

propositional logic

Propositional logic as an elementary part of **formal logic** investigates the connection of simple (not analyzed) **propositions** to complex propositions. This connection occurs through the **logical connectives** such as *and* and *or*. Here it is a matter (in contrast with **intensional logic**) of an extensional approach in which the actual semantic relations between the propositions are not taken into consideration in favor of studying the extensional rules for connecting propositions that are defined by the **truth tables**: the truth or falsity of complex propositions is the value of a logical function of the truth or falsity of the individual component propositions. The most important propositional connections between two propositions p and q are (a) **conjunction**: *p and q* (notation: $p \wedge q$); (b) **disjunction**: *p or q* (notation: $p \vee q$); (c) **implication**: *if p, then q* (notation: $p \rightarrow q$); (d) **equivalence**: *p is equivalent to q* (notation: $p \leftrightarrow q$); (e) **negation**: *not p* (notation: $\neg p$). Numerous more recent interpretations of language description are based on the terminology and rules of propositional logic and **predicate** logic. ($\Rightarrow$ *also* **generative semantics, Montague grammar**)

prosiopesis $\Rightarrow$ **aphesis**

prosodeme [new formation after Grk *prós* 'besides, in addition to,' *oidé* 'song,' *-em* = suffix denoting functional units]

Phonological unit encompassing one or more (segmental) phonemes which is, therefore, considered a **suprasegmental feature**, such as **intonation, stress², juncture**.

References
$\Rightarrow$ **suprasegmental feature**

prosodic feature

Feature that refers to units greater than a **phoneme**, thus to **syllables**, **words**, and **sentences**. ($\Rightarrow$ *also* **intonation, juncture, prosody, stress², suprasegmental feature**)

References
$\Rightarrow$ **suprasegmental feature**

prosodics

The study of **prosody**.

prosody [Grk *prosōidía* 'song sung to a musical instrument; variation in pitch']

Linguistic characteristics such as **stress²**, **intonation**, **quantity**, and **pauses** in speech that concern units greater than the individual phonemes. Prosody also includes speech tempo and rhythm. ($\Rightarrow$ *also* **suprasegmental feature**)

References
Selkirk, E.O. 1984. *Phonology and syntax: the relation between sound and structure*. Cambridge, MA.
$\Rightarrow$ **suprasegmental feature**

protasis vs apodosis

In **rhetoric**, the distinction between the 'tension-creating' (protasis) and the 'tension-relaxing' (apodosis), components of an antithetical idea or sentence. Structurally, protasis and apodosis can be in a relation of **coordination** or **subordination**.

References
$\Rightarrow$ **rhetoric**

prothesis [Grk *prósthesis* 'addition']

Insertion of a sound (usually a vowel), at the beginning of a word through motivation of the given **syllable** structure. For example, initial /sp, st, sk/ clusters in **Latin** were broken up in **Spanish** and **French** by a prothetic e; cf. Lat. *spiritus, stella, schola* : Span. *espíritu, estrella, escuela* : Fr. *esprit, étoile, école* 'spirit,' 'star,' 'school.'

References
$\Rightarrow$ **language change, sound change**

proto-language

Term indicating an early stage of a language or language family that is not historically attested but rather reconstructed through the comparative method (e.g. **Indo-European**). ($\Rightarrow$ *also* **comparative linguistics, historical linguistics, genetic tree theory, reconstruction**)

prototype [Grk *prótos* 'first,' *týpos* 'form, shape; image']

The prototype is (a) the model or proto-image of all representatives of the meaning of a word or of a 'category.' Thus, Shakespeare can be regarded as the or a prototype, as the 'best example' of the category *poet*. But it is only in exceptional cases that an individual 'best example' exists, and even this only becomes such a one by virtue of its typical features. Thus, a prototype is (b) the bundle of typical features of a category. The prototype of *bird* can be any given sparrow, but also an eagle; a penguin, however, is a less 'good' bird, as it lacks some of the typical features, such as the ability to fly. (c) The features themselves can also be more or less typical, i.e. they can have a higher or lower 'cue validity'; thus, *twittering* is less typical and specific to birds than *flying* (*by one's own strength*). The determination of the typical features of a category is the task of lexical **semantics**, and, as prototype theory has been extended to grammatical categories, also of **grammar**. In principle, the typical features of a category do not correspond to the necessary and sufficient conditions of the membership in a category; thus, *melon* is no typical *berry*, although botanically it is classified as such. The meaning of a word is thus an 'idealized cognitive model' (ICM) or a social **stereotype**. The main question is always whether a central, most typical feature, i.e. a 'basic meaning,' can be found. To the degree that this is impossible, the prototypically organized structure of a word meaning disintegrates into 'prototypical effects.'

References
Coleman, L. and P. Kay, 1981. Prototype semantics: the English word LIE. *Language* 57.26–44.
Fillmore, J.C. 1975. An alternative to checklist theories of meaning. In C. Cogen *et al.* (eds), *Proceedings of the first annual meeting of the Berkeley Linguistic Society*. Berkeley, CA. 123–31.
—— 1982. Towards a descriptive framework for spatial deixis. In R.J. Jarvella and W. Klein (eds), *Speech, place and action*. London. 31–59.
Geeraerts, D. 1983. Prototype theory and diachronic semantics: a case study. *IF* 88.1–32.

Janicki, K. 1990. On the predecessors of prototype linguistics. *Nordlyd*, 16.59–71.

Kleiber, G. 1990. *La sémantique du prototype: catégories et sens lexical*. Paris.

Lakoff, G. 1987. *Women, fire and dangerous things: what categories reveal about the mind*. Chicago and London.

Rosch, E. 1973. Natural categories. *CPsy* 4.328–50.

―――― 1978. Principles of categorization. In E. Rosch and B. Lloyd (eds), *Cognition and categorization*. Hillsdale, NJ. 27–48.

Taylor, J.R. 1991. *Linguistic categorization*. Oxford.

Tsohatsidis, S. 1990. *Meaning and prototypes: studies in linguistic categorization*. London.

⇒ **stereotype**

Provençal ⇒ Occitan

proxemics [Lat. *proximum* 'neighborhood, vicinity']

Word coined by E.T. Hall from *prox-* and *-emic* (⇒ **etic vs emic analysis**) to designate studies dealing with the differing perception and interpretation of spaces and its influence on communicative behavior in various cultural spheres. Proxemics (like **kinesics**) is a newer subdiscipline of communication science, which treats non-linguistic aspects of **communication**.

References

Hall, E.T. 1963. Proxemics: the study of man's spatial relations. In I. Galston (ed.), *Man's image in medicine and anthropology*. New York.

―――― 1963. A system for the notation of proxemic behavior. *AA* 65.1003–26.

―――― 1969. *The silent language*. New York.

Watson, O.M. 1974. Proxemics. In T.A. Sebeok (ed.), *Current Trends in Linguistics*. The Hague. Vol. 12, 311–44.

proximate vs obviative

Category of the **personal pronoun** systems in some languages (e.g. **Algonquian, Na-Dené**): personal pronouns are proximate if they refer to an object that has just been mentioned in the discourse; if they do not refer to something just mentioned, they are obviative.

PS ⇒ phrase structure

pseudomorpheme

Lexicalized **morpheme** occurring in lexicalized expressions in only one environment and whose basic meaning can no longer be analyzed synchronically, e.g. *-gin* in *begin*. If such a pseudomorpheme occurs in **compounds** with free **morphemes**, then it is called a **semimorpheme** (cf. *cran-* in *cranberry*).

psycholinguistics

Interdisciplinary area of research concerned with the processes of **language production**, **language comprehension**, and **language acquisition**, in which **neurolinguistics**, **discourse analysis**, **sociolinguistics**, cognitive psychology, cognitive science, and **artificial intelligence** are closely allied. The central issues of psycholinguistics were taken up as early as the end of the nineteenth and beginning of the twentieth centuries by Steinthal, Wundt and Bühler. The designation, concept, and program of psycholinguistics was developed in the summer of 1953 in a seminar at the Linguistics Institute of Indiana University by American psychologists and linguists (see Osgood & Sebeok 1954). It was determined that the linguistic structures discovered by linguists could be studied using the methods and theories of (experimental) psychology.

Two important directions based on different assumptions about the relationship between language and cognition can be distinguished. (a) The first direction is oriented towards more recent linguistic theories (especially as a consequence of Chomsky's work on **transformational grammar** in the 1960s and 1980s). It views grammar as an autonomous cognitive system (⇒ **modularity**) and concerns itself with proving the psychological reality of linguistic constructs (⇒ **click**^{2}). (b) The second direction is more closely oriented towards models in cognitive psychology, in particular towards approaches that assume a more intensive interaction between the individual levels of linguistic description or between cognitive systems. In the 1980s models were tested that assumed a parallel processing of information in closely intertwined systems (⇒ **connectionism**). For an overview, see Weissenborn & Schriefers (1987).

References

Aitchison, J. 1989. *The articulate mammal: an introduction to psycholinguistics*, 3rd rev. edn. London.

Appel, G. and H. Dechert (eds) 1991. *A case for psycholinguistic cases*. Amsterdam and Philadelphia.

Blumenthal, A.L. 1970. *Language and psychology: historical aspects of psycholinguistics*. New York.

Bresnan, J. (ed.) 1981. *The mental representation of grammatical relations*. Cambridge, MA.

Bühler, K. 1934. *Sprachtheorie*. Jena. (Repr. Stuttgart, 1965.)

Carroll, D.W. 1986. *Psychology of language*. Belmont, CA.

Chomsky, N. 1968. *Language and mind*. New York.

Clark, H.H. and E.V. Clark. 1977. *Psychology and language: an introduction to psycholinguistics*. New York.

Flores d'Arcais, G.B. and W.J.M. Levelt (eds) 1970. *Advances in psycholinguistics*. New York.

Fodor, J.A., T.G. Bever, and M.F. Garrett. 1974. *The*

psychology of language. New York.

Garman, M. 1990. *Psycholinguistics*. Cambridge.

Garnham, A. 1985. *Psycholinguistics: central topics.* London.

Gernsbacher, M.A. (ed.) 1994. *Handbook of psycholinguistics*. San Diego, CA.

Glucksberg, S. and J. Danke. 1975. *Experimental psycholinguistics: an introduction.* New York.

Johnson-Laird, P.N. 1983. *Mental models.* Cambridge, MA.

Kess, J. F. 1991. *Psycholinguistics: psychology, linguistics and the study of natural languages.* Amsterdam and Philadelphia.

Lenneberg, E.H. 1967. *Biological foundations of language*. New York.

Lenneberg, E.H. and H.E. Lenneberg (eds) 1976. *Foundations of language development: a multidisciplinary approach*, vol. 1. New York.

Levelt, W.J.M. 1974. *Formal grammars in linguistics and psycholinguistics*, vol. 3: *Psycholinguistic applications*. The Hague.

—— 1989. *Speaking: from intention to articulation*. Cambridge, MA.

McWhinney, B. and E. Bates (eds) 1989. *The cross-linguistic study of language processing*. Cambridge.

Miller, G. and P.N. Johnson-Laird. 1976. *Language and perception*. Cambridge, MA.

Murray, D.J. 1990. On the early history of psycholinguistics. *Historiographia Linguistica* 17.369–81.

Osgood, C and T.A. Sebeok (eds) 1954. *Psycholinguistics: A survey of theory and research problems*. Baltimore, MD.

—— (eds) 1965. *Psycholinguistics: a survey of theory and research problems*. Bloomington, IN.

Prideaux, G.D. 1985. *Psycholinguistics: the experimental study of language*. London.

Reed, S.K. 1982. *Cognition: theory and applications*. Monterey, CA.

Rosenberg, S. (ed.) 1982. *Handbook of applied psycholinguistics*. Hillsdale, NJ.

—— (ed.) 1987. *Advances in applied psycholinguistics*, 2 vols. Cambridge.

Slobin, D.I. 1979. *Psycholinguistics*, 2nd edn. Glenview, IL, and London.

Steinberg, D.D. 1993. *An introduction to psycholinguistics*. London.

Tannenhaus, M.K. 1988. Psycholinguistics: an overview. In F. Newmeyer (ed.), *Linguistics: the Cambridge survey*. Cambridge. Vol. 3, 1–37.

Weissenborn, J. and H. Schriefers. 1987. Psycholinguistics. In U. Ammon *et al.* (eds), *Soziolinguistik/ Sociolinguistics*. Berlin. 470–87.

Bibliographies

Prucha, J. 1972. *Information sources in psycholinguistics: an interdisciplinary bibliographical handbook*. The Hague.

Sheldon, A. 1977. Bibliography of psychological, linguistic, and philosophical research on the psychological reality of grammar. *Minnesota Working Papers in Linguistics and Philosophy of Language* 4.169–79.

Journals

Journal of Psycholinguistic Research.

Applied Psycholinguistics.

International Journal of Psycholinguistics.

⇒ **connectionism**, **modularity**, **language acquisition**, **language processing**, **language production**, **parsing**, **speech error**, **speech perception**, **translation**

psychological object ⇒ focus

psychology of language ⇒ psycholinguistics

pulmonic [Lat. *pulmo* 'lungs']

1 Of or referring to the lungs.

2 Sounds formed with the pulmonic **airstream mechanism**. Most sounds in English, except stop consonants, are formed with the pulmonic airstream mechanism.

References
⇒ **phonetics**

pulmonic airstream mechanism ⇒ airstream mechanism

pun (*also* paronomasia)

A **figure of speech** of repetition. A **play on words** through the coupling of words that sound similar but which are very different semantically and etymologically, e.g. *Is life worth living? That depends on the liver.* (⇒ **figura etymologica**, **polyptoton**)

References
Redfern, W. 1984. Puns. Oxford.
Ross, E. 1991. Aspects of the interpretation of puns in newspaper advertisements. In C. Feldbusch *et al.* (eds), *Neue Fragen der Linguistik*. Tübingen. Vol. 2, 439–46.

punctual (*also* achievement)

Verbal **aspect** included among the non-duratives (⇒ **durative vs non-durative**): punctual verbs refer to a sudden change in a situation and thus cannot be combined with temporal modifiers denoting duration: **He found the key for an hour/an hour long.*

References
⇒ **aspect**

punctuation

Rules for the optical arrangement of **written language** by means of non-alphabetic signs such as periods, commas, and exclamation marks. Such delimiting symbols clarify both grammatical and semantic aspects of the text. They indicate quotes, direct speech and contractions, and can reflect the intonation of spoken language.

push chain vs drag chain

Terms from the structuralist theory of **language change** (⇒ **structuralism**) that denote phonologically motivated **sound changes** (⇒ *also* **sound shift**). 'Push' in the sense of system pressure occurs when a phoneme /X/ encroaches on the allophonic field of a phoneme /Y/, which, in turn, moves over to the field of phoneme /Z/. The **Great Vowel Shift** in English is an example of this phenomenon. In this way, sound changes of this type preserve phonological distinctions. On the other hand, a gap in the phonological system can bring about a 'drag chain' which causes the **empty slot** to be filled by a new phoneme and, thus, 'improves' the system in the sense that it brings about preferred symmetry within the system.

References
King, R.D. 1969. Push-chains and drag-chains. *Glossa* 3.3–21.
Martinet, A. 1952. Function-structure and sound change. *Word* 8.1–32.
—— 1955. *Economie des changements phonétiques*. Bern.

push-down automaton (*abbrev.* PDA; *also* push-down stack automaton, stack automaton)

This is an **automaton** which has, in addition to the states and transitions of a **finite state automaton**, a push-down memory, i.e. one in which most recently stored information must be retrieved first. Chomsky proved that PDAs are essentially equivalent to **context-free grammars**. (⇒ **formal language theory**)

Reference
Hopcroft, J. and J. Ullman. 1979. *Introduction to automata theory, languages and computation*. Reading, MA.

push-down stack automaton ⇒ push-down automaton

Putenghua ⇒ Chinese

Q

q-Celtic ⇒ **Celtic**

qualitative ablaut ⇒ **ablaut**

quality (*also* timbre)

Umbrella term for all articulatory and acoustic characteristics of **speech sounds** that do not involve **quantity**; particularly in **vowels**, e.g. degree of openness and rounding. (⇒ *also* **articulatory phonetics**, **distinctive feature**, **open vs closed**, **phonetics**, **rounded vs unrounded**)

References
⇒ **phonetics**

quantification

In **formal logic**, quantification refers to the specification of for how many objects in a certain set a predicate is valid. Quantification is determined by **quantifiers** (⇒ **operator**) which connect freely occurring variables in a sentence. A distinction is made between the existential quantifier, which says that the predicate in question is valid for at least one object in the given set, and the universal operator, through which the predicate in question is assigned to all elements of the underlying set of individuals. In quantification, the logical analysis is abstracted from the many colloquial interpretations, which may appear as the expressions *several, some, many*, by rendering these expressions non-distinctive through the existential operator. On the other hand, ambiguities such as those found in the colloquial statement *Everybody loves somebody* can be specified in formal logic by illuminating the different **scopes** of the quantifying expressions. Such specifications constitute an important area of investigation for linguistic descriptions. Compare the approach of **generative semantics** (Lakoff 1971; Partee 1970) as well as the corresponding proposals of **categorial grammar** and **Montague grammar**, specifically Montague's milestone essay of 1973, 'The proper treatment of quantification in ordinary English.' (abbrev. PTQ)

References
Altham, J.E.J. 1971. *The logic of plurality*. London.
Bartsch, R. 1973. The semantics and syntax of number and numbers. In P. Kimball (ed.), *Syntax and semantics*. New York. 51–93.
Bellert, I. 1971. On the use of linguistic quantifying operators in the logico-semantic structure of representation of utterances. *Poetics* 2.71–86.
Cushing, S. 1982. *Quantifier meanings: a study in the dimensions of semantic competence*. Amsterdam.
Hausser, R.R. 1974. *Quantification in an extended Montague grammar*. Austin, TX.
Horn, L.R. 1972. *On the semantic properties of logical operators in English*. Los Angeles, CA.
Jackendoff, R.S. 1968. Quantifiers in English. *FL* 4.422–42.
Keenan, E.L. 1971. Quantifier structures in English. *FL* 7.255–84.
Lakoff, G. 1971. On generative semantics. In D.D. Steinberg and L.A. Jakobovits (eds), *Semantics*. Cambridge, MA. 232–96.
Levin, H. 1982. *Categorial grammar and the logical form of quantification*. Naples.
Löbner, S. 1986. Quantification as a major module of natural language semantics. In J. Groenendijk and M. Stokhof (eds), *Information, interpretation, and inference: selected papers of the fifth Amsterdam colloquium*. Dordrecht. 53–85.
May, R.C. 1978. *The grammar of quantification*. Cambridge, MA.
Montague, R. 1973. The proper treatment of quantification in ordinary English. In J. Hintikka, J.M.E. Moravcsik, and E. Suppes (eds), *Approaches to natural language*. Dordrecht. 221–42. (Repr. in *Formal philosophy: selected papers of R. Montague*, ed. R.H. Thomason. New Haven, CT, 1974. 247–70.)
Partee, B.H. 1970. Negation, conjunction, and quantifiers: syntax vs semantics. *FL* 6.153–65.
Pelletier, F.J. 1979. *Mass terms: some philosophical problems*. Dordrecht.
Van der Auwera, J. (ed.) 1980. *Determiners*. London.
⇒ **formal logic**

quantifier

1 In **predicate logic**, a frequently used synonym for **operator** in the narrower sense, that is, an umbrella term or synonym for the universal quantifier and the existential quantifier.

2 Linguistic term taken from **predicate logic** that designates **operators** that specify or quantify a set and are expressed in everyday language by indefinite adjectives or pronouns (*all, some, several*, and others), numerals (*one, two, three*, etc.), the definite article (*The books are expensive*), or indefinite plurals (*Books are expensive*). In **transformational grammar** quantifiers are derived from noun phrases in the **deep structure**, in **generative semantics** they are introduced as higher-order **predicates**. In

Montague grammar quantifying phrases like *all humans* denote sets of properties such that a universal proposition like *All humans are mortal* can be analyzed as simple predication: 'mortal' is a property that belongs to the set of properties that apply to all humans. This analysis corresponds to the syntactic structure of natural-language sentences and presents an important example of the methodological principle of compositionality in grammar theory and semantics (⇒ **principle of compositionality**). It is a point of departure for more recent research on the semantics of natural-language quantifiers (see Barwise and Cooper 1981; Benthem and Meulen 1985).

References
Bartsch, R. 1973. The semantics and syntax of number and numbers. In P. Kimball (ed.), *Syntax and semantics*. New York. Vol. 2, 51–93.
Barwise, J. and R. Cooper, 1981. Generalized quantifiers and natural language. *Ling&P* 4.159–219.
Lakoff, G. 1971. On generative semantics. In D.D. Steinberg and L.A. Jakobovits (eds), *Semantics*, Cambridge, MA. 232–96.
Van Benthem, J. and A. ter Meulen (eds) 1985. *Generalized quantifiers in natural language*. Dordrecht.
Van der Auwera, J. (ed.) 1980. *Determiners*. London.
Westerståhl, D. 1989. Quantifiers in formal and natural language. In D. Gabbay and F. Guenthner (eds), *Handbook of philosophical logic*. Dordrecht. Vol. 4, 1–131.

quantifier floating

The placement of quantifiers such as *all* and *both* at a distance, so that they are separated by other elements from their 'source NP,' *Who (all) was all there? They (both) were both infatuated with Rome.* (⇒ also **quantification**, **quantifier**)

References
Partee, B.H. (ed.) 1976. *Montague grammar*. New York.
Vater, H. 1980. Quantifier floating in German. In J. van der Auwera (ed.), *The semantics of determiners*. London. 232–49.

quantifier raising ⇒ raising

quantitative ablaut ⇒ ablaut

quantitative linguistics ⇒ statistical linguistics

quantity

Prosodic characteristic of **speech sounds** that so far has only been physically measured in approximate values, since objective parameters for boundaries between individual speech sounds cannot be ascertained owing to the fact that speech proceeds in an uninterrupted flow. While the absolute duration of speech sounds depends on the speech tempo and one's personal way of speaking, the relative duration may function to differentiate meaning, for example in English the opposition of long and short vowels (e.g. *heed* vs *hid*) that is accompanied by qualitative characteristics (⇒ **quality**). Three distinctive qualities are found, for example, in **Estonian**. Long and short consonants as well as long and short vowels are found, for example, in Greenlandic: [maːˈnːa] 'now,' [maˈna] 'this,' [uːˈnɛq] 'burn' [unːˈɛq] 'leather,' [aːˈnɑq] 'stepmother,' [aˈnɑq] 'excrement.' Long consonants (**geminates**) can also be differentiated from short ones in that they are formed when pulmonic (or in the case of **ejectives**, pharyngeal) air is forced with great pressure through the resonance chamber. (⇒ **fortis vs lenis**)

References
⇒ **phonetics**

Quechua

Group of languages spoken from Columbia to Chile (about 7 million speakers); the largest language is the dialect of Cuzco (about 1 million speakers). Together with Aymara it is supposed to form the Quechumaran branch of the **Andean** languages. There are also links with **Penutian**.

Characteristics: complex sound system (five places of articulation and three types of articulation for plosives – normal, aspirated, glottalized). Verbs are morphologically complex, with suffixes indicating person, tense, various voices, mood, etc. Case system with about ten cases; there are also possessive suffixes and various suffixes to express diminutives, coordination, focus, and topicalization. Number markers are rare and first occurred as a result of **Spanish** influence.

References
Adelaar, W.F.H. 1977. *Tarma Quechua: grammar, texts, dictionary*. Lisse.
Bills, G.D. *et al.* 1969. *An introduction to spoken Bolivian Quechua*. Austin, TX, and London.
Cerron-Palomino, R. 1987. *Lingüística Quechua*. Cuzco.
Cole, P. 1982. *Imbabura Quechua*. Amsterdam.
Levinson, S.H. 1976. *The Inga language*. The Hague
Liedtke, S. 1994. Penutian, Mayan and Quechuan. *LDDS* 10.
Parker, G.J. 1969. *Ayacucho Quechua grammar and dictionary*. The Hague.
Weber, D.J. 1983. *A grammar of Huallaga (Huana-*

co) Quechua. Los Angeles.
⇒ **South American languages**

Quechumaran ⇒ Andean, Quechua

queclarative

J.M. Sadock's term, derived from *question + declarative*, for sentences that are formulated as interrogatives, but are interpreted as declarative sentences in certain contexts, e.g. *Are you crazy?* with the suggested meaning 'your behavior or claim is ridiculous and unsupportable.'

Reference
Sadock, J.M. 1971. Queclaratives. *CLS* 7.223–31.

question

A type of **illocution** that attempts to elicit particular information, typically in the form of an **answer**. (⇒ *also* **interrogative**)

question tag ⇒ tag question

Quiché ⇒ Mayan languages

quotative

Sentence mood which characterizes sentence content as 'known through hearsay' and which therefore relieves the speaker of any responsibility for the accuracy of what was said. In many languages the quotative is its own morphological category; in other languages other modal categories subsume the quotative function. Note, for example, the use of the subjunctive in the English sentence *Phil said he would dine with us tomorrow evening*. (⇒ *also* **direct vs indirect discourse**, **evidentiality**)

References
Palmer, F.R. 1986. *Mood and modality*. Cambridge.
⇒ **direct vs indirect discourse**, **evidentiality**, **modality**

R

radical [Lat. *radix* 'root']

1 **Speech sound** classified according to its **articulator** (*radix* = root of the tongue). As a rule, radicals are divided into **uvulars** (e.g. [ʁ]) and **pharyngeals** (e.g. [ħ], [ʕ]), depending on their **place of articulation**. (⇒ *also* **articulatory phonetics, phonetics**)

References
⇒ **phonetics**

2 ⇒ **Chinese writing**

Rain Forest Bantu ⇒ **Bantu**

raising

In **transformational grammar**, a rule for deriving certain **infinitive constructions** by which the subject noun phrase of an embedded sentence is 'raised' into the subject or object position of the matrix sentence in the transition from **deep structure** to **surface structure**. The rest of the sentence is marked as 'infinitive.' The so-called **accusative plus infinitive constructions** were considered to be cases of raising in the early phases of transformational grammar: *Caroline let/heard her brother come*, in which the 'logical' or deep structure subject of *come* is raised to the 'grammatical' or surface structure object of *let/hear* (see Postal 1974). In later theories, object raising was discarded in favor of a non-transformational analysis. Constructions with auxiliary-like expressions are described as raising into the subject position: *Philip seems [– to read a lot]*. Whereas in constructions with **control** of a logical argument of the infinitive, the matrix verb (= control verb) must have a semantic argument as 'controller,' it is a characteristic of raising constructions that the grammatical subject of the matrix predicate is not the logical subject of the matrix verb (the so-called raising verb), but only of the embedded verb. This becomes clear in the paraphrase *It seems that Philip reads a lot*, in which *Philip* is not the logical argument of the raising verb *seem*. In the movement of quantified expressions to a structurally higher position in the **logical form**, one also speaks of (quantifier) raising.

References
Bech, G. 1955/7. *Studien über das deutsche Verbum infinitum*, 2 vols. Copenhagen. (Repr. Tübingen, 1983.)

Olsen, S. 1981. *Problems of 'seem/scheinen' constructions and their implications for the theory of predicate sentential complementation*. Tübingen.
Postal, P.M. 1974. *On raising: one rule of English grammar and its theoretical implications*. Cambridge, MA.
⇒ **transformational grammar**

raising vs lowering

Sound change in vowels that results from a change in the **place of articulation** through a higher or lower tongue position (⇒ **vowel chart**); usually conditioned through assimilation to neighboring high/low vowels (⇒ **umlaut, vowel harmony**) or consonants; to be sure, some environment-free raising (particularly in the lower long vowels) and lowering (particularly in the higher extreme vowels in informal, 'careless' speech) are possible.

Reference
Donegan, P.J. 1978. *On the natural phonology of vowels*. Columbus, OH.
⇒ **sound change**

Rajasthani ⇒ **Indo-Aryan**

range ⇒ **function**

rapid speech vs slow speech

Different word forms can emerge from rapid speech when compared with slow speech. For example, *perhaps* in clearly articulated slow speech becomes **'praps'** in rapid speech.

rationalism [Lat. *ratio* 'the faculty of reason']

Seventeenth century branch of philosophy based on the philosophies of R. Descartes and G.W. Leibniz, which admits reason as the sole source of human knowledge. N. Chomsky sees so-called '**Cartesian linguistics**' as continuing the tradition of rationalism, especially in reference to (a) the concept of 'innate ideas,' (b) the idea of language as a specifically human activity, (c) the emphasis on the creative aspect of language use, and (d) the distinction between outer and inner forms of language (i.e. between **surface structure** and **deep structure**). (⇒ *also* **mentalism, Port Royal grammar**)

References
⇒ **mentalism, transformational grammar**

reading

Analytic–synthetic process in which (a series

of) written signs is converted through interpretation into information. This sensual reconstruction is a complex neurophysiological process (⇒ **neurolinguistics**) in which the optic-perceptive and articulatory components function more or less simultaneously with the perception of lexical meanings and the recognition of syntactic structures, or these components may mutually influence each other through a process of feedback (see Pirozzolo & Wittrock 1981). The process of reading is supported by the probability structure of language and writing (⇒ **Zipf's law**) as well as by redundancy on all descriptive levels. Such redundancies may include the aesthetic characteristics of the form of written symbols, morphological redundancy (e.g. the grammatical redundancy in Span. *los libros nuevos*), or **valence** relationships on the level of syntax. (⇒ *also* **language comprehension**)

References
Barnett, M.A. 1989. *More than meets the eye: foreign language reading theory and practice.* Englewood Cliffs, NJ.
Bernhardt, E.G. 1991. *Reading development in a second language.* Norwood, NJ.
Grellet, F. 1981. *Developing reading skills.* Cambridge.
Grey, W.S. 1956. *The teaching of reading and writing: an international survey.* Paris (UNESCO).
Just, M.A. and P.A. Carpenter. 1980. A theory of reading: from eye fixation to comprehension. *PsychologR* 87.329–54.
Kieras, D.E. and M.A. Just (eds) 1984. *New methods in reading comprehension research.* Hillsdale, NJ.
Lee, J.F. and D. 1988. Musumeci. On hierarchies of reading skills and text types. *MLJ* 72: 173–187.
Pearson, P.D. (ed.) 1984. *Handbook of reading research.* New York.
Pirozzolo, F.J. and M.C. Wittrock (eds) 1981. *Neuropsychological and cognitive processes in reading.* London.
Swaffar, J., K. Arens and H. Byrnes. 1991. *Reading for meaning. An integrated approach to language learning.* Englewood Cliffs, NJ.
Weaver, W.W. 1977. *Towards a psychology of reading and language.* Athens, OH.

Bibliography
Fay, L.C. *et al.* (eds) 1964. *Doctoral studies in reading.* Bloomington, IN.
⇒ **language comprehension**, **literacy**

readjustment component (*also* readjustment rule)

Grammatical component in **transformational grammar** that contains the rules that operate between the syntactic and the **phonological components** and supply the **formative** of the terminal syntactic chains with the correct inflectional features in the surface structure.

References
⇒ **transformational grammar**

readjustment rule ⇒ **readjustment component**

real definition ⇒ **definition**

reanalysis

The reorganization of a **tree diagram** in which the terminal **nodes** remain identical, but the hierarchical analysis of the construction is changed. For example, the controlled infinitive construction is described by a reanalysis rule which derives the **surface structure** by the **deletion** of an embedded sentence (⇒ **embedding**) in the **deep structure** where the embedded verb forms a constituent with the once embedded matrix verb.

Reference
Haegeman, L. and H. van Riemsdijk. 1986. Verb projection raising, scope, and the typology of movement rules. *LingI* 17.417–66.

reasoning ⇒ **argumentation**

received pronunciation ⇒ **standard pronunciation**

receptive aphasia ⇒ **aphasia**, **Wernicke's aphasia**

recessive [Lat. *recedere* 'to draw back, move away'] (*also* ergative verb or **unaccusative**)

Intransitive interpretation of verbs like *break*, *roll* and *boil* which also have transitive interpretations, e.g. *The sun is melting the ice* vs *The ice is melting*. Recessives stand in converse relation to **causatives**. (⇒ *also* **unaccusative**)

References
⇒ **causative**

recipient

Semantic role in **case grammar** for the participant (usually animate) that is affected indirectly by the action expressed by the verb. Recipient includes the receiver in verbs which describe a change of possession (*They contribute money to various causes*) and the addressees with verbs of communication (*They told us stories about their stay abroad*) and are usually expressed as an **indirect object**. (⇒ *also* **dative**)

References
⇒ **case grammar**

recipient design

In **conversation analysis**, term referring to the fact that – in their choice of verbal and nonverbal devices (e.g. gazing) – speakers orient themselves towards the expectations of the listeners. Thus, **turns** are constructed inter-actively. For excellent examples, see Goodwin (1979, 1981).

References
Goodwin, C. 1979. The interactive construction of a sentence in natural conversation. In G. Psathas (ed.), *Everyday language.* New York. 97–122.
―――― 1981. *Conversational organization.* New York.
Sacks, H., E. Schegloff, and G. Jefferson. 1974. A simplest systematics for the organisation of turn-taking for conversation. *Lg* 50.696–735.

reciprocal assimiliation ⇒ **assimilation**

reciprocal pronoun ⇒ **reciprocity**

reciprocity [Lat. *reciprocus* 'moving back-wards and forwards']

Term for a bilateral relationship between two or more elements; in English, reciprocity can be expressed by reciprocal pronouns (*one another*, *each other*): *Philip and Caroline love each other.* The use of reciprocal pronouns is subject to the same kinds of restrictions as **reflexive pronouns.** (⇒ *also* **binding theory**)

References
Baldi, P. 1975. Reciprocal verbs and symmetric predicates. *LingB* 36.13–20.
Fiengo, R.W. and H. Lasnik. 1973. The logical structure of reciprocal sentences in English. *FL.* 9.447–68.
Langendoen, T. 1978. The logic of reciprocity. *LingI* 9.177–97.
Lichtenberk, F. 1985. Multiple uses of reciprocal constructions. *Australian Journal of Linguistics* 5.19–41.
⇒ **binding theory**

reconstruction

Procedure for determining older, non-recorded, or insufficiently attested stages of a language. Proceeding from our knowledge of possible (e.g. phonetic) types of change (⇒ **sound change**), (pre)historic language systems are reconstructed little by little on the basis of synchronic linguistic data. Such data consist in alternating, varying forms that can be system-atically traced back to historically invariable structures. Depending on whether such syn-chronic alternations can be observed in one language or between several genetically related languages, two methods of reconstruction are distinguished. (a) *Internal* (or language-internal) *reconstruction*: historical character-istics of structures are reconstructed on the basis of systematic relationships within a given language. Apart from **ablaut** and **Verner's law**, the best example for internal reconstruction is **laryngeal theory**: in 1879, F. de Saussure hypothesized the existence of Indo-European

laryngeals based on internal structural aspects. His theory was later corroborated through actual evidence of such traces in newly dis-covered **Hittite**. (b) *External* (comparative) *reconstruction*: reconstruction takes place by comparing particular phenomena in several related (or presumably related) languages. Comparative reconstruction became particu-larly significant and its methods underwent refinement in the nineteenth century with the elucidation of the Indo-European **obstruent** (= **stops** and **fricatives**) system, which was recon-structed by comparing the consonantal systems of the individual **Indo-European** languages (⇒ **Grimm's law**, **Verner's law**). Comparative reconstruction forms the foundation of **com-parative linguistics** and was used primarily by the **Neogrammarians** in connection with their thesis of the regularity of **sound laws**.

References
Baldi, P. (ed.) 1990. *Linguistic change and recon-struction methodology.* Berlin and New York.
Beekes, R. *et al.* 1992. *Rekonstruktion und relative Chronologie: Akten der VIII. Fachtagung der Indogermanischen Gesellschaft, Leiden.* Innsbruck.
Eichner, H. 1988. Sprachwandel und Rekonstruktion. In C. Zinko (ed.), *Akten der 13. Österreichischen Linguistentagung.* Graz. 10–40.
Fox, A. 1995. *Linguistic reconstruction. An introduc-tion to theory and method.* Oxford.
Haas, M.R. 1966. Historical linguistics and the genetic relationship of languages. In T.A. Sebeok (ed.), *Current trends in linguistics.* The Hague. Vol. 3, 113–153.
Hock, H.H. 1986. *Principles of historical linguistics.* Berlin and New York. (2nd edn, rev. and updated 1991.)
Hoenigswald, H.N. 1960. *Language change and linguistic reconstruction.* Chicago.
―――― 1973. The comparative method. In T.A. Sebeok (ed.), *Current trends in linguistics.* The Hague, Vol. 11, 51–62.
Incontri Linguistici 1984. *Problemi della ricos-truzione: un dibattito.* Vol. 9, 67–152.
Lehmann, W.P. 1962. *Historical linguistics: an intro-duction.* New York. (2nd edn 1973.)
Lehmann, W.P. and H.-J. Herwitt. 1991. *Language typology 1988: typological models in reconstruc-tion.* Amsterdam and Philadelphia.
Marchand, H. 1956. Internal reconstruction of pho-nemic split. *Lg* 32.245–53.
Meillet, A. 1925. *La méthode comparative en linguis-tique historique.* Oslo.
Pedersen, H. 1962. *The discovery of language.* Bloomington, IN. (Repr. from *Linguistic science in the nineteenth century.* Cambridge, 1931.)
⇒ **Indo-European, language change, linguistics**

recoverability

A **constraint** on **deletion** that ensures that no change in meaning occurs. After the deletion has taken place, the basic structure must always be visible at **surface structure**. The sentence (i) *Philip is bigger than Caroline* can be seen as the result of a permissible deletion in the sentence (ii) *Philip is bigger than Caroline is big* because the elements are deleted according to precise conditions and the recoverability of (ii) from (i) is guaranteed.

References
⇒ **constraint, transformation**

recurrence [Lat. *recurrere* 'to run back, return']

A term from **text linguistics**. The repetition of the same linguistic elements, e.g. syntactic categories or referentially identical words; also the repetition of the root of one word in other words (partial recurrence; ⇒ **figure of speech, polyptoton, pun**). Recurrence is important for **cohesion** and **coherence** in a text.

References
Beaugrande, R. de 1980. *Text, discourse, and process: toward a multidisciplinary science of texts.* London.
Harris, Z.S. 1952. Discourse analysis. *Language* 28.1–30.
Koch, W.A. 1966. *Recurrence and a three-modal approach to poetry.* The Hague.
Petöfi, J.S. 1973. Towards an empirically motivated grammatical theory of verbal texts. In J.S. Petöfi *et al.* (eds), *Studies in text grammar.* Dordrecht. 205–75.
⇒ **discourse grammar, figure of speech, text linguistics**

recursive definition ⇒ **recursive rule**

recursive rule

A type of rule taken from mathematics that is formally characterized by the fact that the symbol to the left of the arrow also occurs to the right: e.g. $N \rightarrow AP + N$. Here N is the recursive element, which ensures that the rule can be used on itself. Wherever the symbol N occurs, the expression to the right of the arrow can be inserted, which in turn contains the symbol N.

References
⇒ **recursiveness**

recursiveness

A term from mathematics used in linguistics for the formal properties of grammars, which use a finite inventory of elements and a finite group of rules to produce an infinite number of sentences. In this respect, such a grammatical model is able to grasp human competence (⇒ **competence vs performance**) which is characterized by creativity. Although Chomsky formalized recursiveness through generalized

transformations in *Syntactic structures* (1957), in the so-called **aspects model** of the standard theory (1965), he generates it in **deep structure** by **phrase structure rules**. The source of recursiveness is considered to be **embedding**, since all recursive constructions (attributive adjectives, prepositional attributes) can be traced back to relative clauses. For example, *the interesting book* ⇔ *the book that is interesting, the hood of the car* ⇔ *the hood that belongs to the car.* The only essential recursive rule in deep structure, from which all surface-structure recursive constructions are derived, is $NP \rightarrow NP + S$. Since **generative semantics** could not formulate semantically motivated derivations satisfactorily, the sole source for the generation of recursive structures was phrase structure rules. Thus *the interesting book* is generated with the help of $NP \rightarrow Det\ N$ and the recursive rule $N \rightarrow AN$.

References
Bar-Hillel, Y. 1953. On recursive definitions in empirical science. In *Proceedings of the eleventh international congress of philosophy.* Brussels. Vol. 5, 10–165.
Chomsky, N. 1957. *Syntactic structures.* The Hague.
——— 1965. *Aspects of the theory of syntax.* Cambridge, MA.
⇒ **transformational grammar**

reduction

1 Operational procedure in parsing: the shortening of complex sentence structures to the minimal obligatory structure. (⇒ *also* **reduction test**)

2 The result of a **transformation** in which a complex element is replaced by a simple element, e.g. **pronominalization**. (⇒ *also* **substitution**)

3 In **phonetics** and **phonology**, the weakening of vowels (⇒ **apocope, syncope**) or consonants.

reduction test

Experimental analytic procedure in structural linguistics which is used to discover the most basic sentence structures (⇒ **kernel sentence**) as well as to distinguish between optional and obligatory sentential elements. Thus in the sentence: (*At that time,*) *Goethe already resided in Strassburg,* the elements in parentheses can be eliminated, whereas *in Strassburg* cannot be eliminated, since it is an adverbial required by the **valence** of the verb *to reside.* (⇒ *also* **operational procedures**)

redundancy (*also* hypercharacterization)

1 In general, excess information, that is, information expressed more than once and which

hence could easily be forgone in some occur-rences. However, since linguistic communica-tion is constantly hampered by disruptive noises, idiolectal and other variation, inatten-tion and misinterpretation, language has devel-oped into a means of communication charac-terized by a great degree of redundancy. This is apparent on all levels of linguistic description, perhaps most clearly in the plethora of morpho-logical markings (e.g. in Spanish the plural is morphologically realized throughout all end-ings in the NP *los árboles verdes*) and in lexical repetition. Redundancy is also intentionally used for rhetorical purposes: e.g. *Each and every one was there*.

2 In **phonology** 'redundancy' is occasionally used as a term to contrast with 'distinctiveness' (⇒ **distinctive feature**).

3 In **information theory**, redundancy corre-lates in a statistically verifiable manner with the probability of occurrence of the particular ele-ment of information, that is, the more probable the occurrence of a particular sign, or the more frequently a particular expression is used, the less information value it has.

References
⇒ **information theory**

redundancy rules

A type of rule in **transformational grammar** for the specification of general regularities. They take the form of **rewrite rules** and state 'If feature A exists, then insert feature B.' Such generalizations affect morphological, syntactic, and semantic properties. They help simplify lexical entries, because they specify predictable features. For example, phonological redun-dancy specifies the predictability of phonetic–phonological features in a general way: [+nasal] → [+voiced] since voicing correlates with nasality.

References
Jackendoff, R. 1975. Morphological and semantic regularities in the lexicon. *Lg* 51.639–71.
⇒ **phonology**, **transformational grammar**

reduplication

Doubling of initial syllables of a **root** or **stem** with or without a change in sound to express a morphosyntactic category, e.g. the formation of the perfect in a number of **Indo-European** verbs (Lat. *tango – tetigī* 'I touch – I touched'; Goth. *haitan – haíhait* 'to be called – was called') or plural formation in **Indonesian**. In **word formation**, repetition of morphemes indicates a strengthening of the expression: Lat. *quisquis* 'whoever,' Eng. *goody-goody*.

References
Marantz, A. 1982. Re reduplication. *LingI* 13.435–82.
⇒ **sound symbolism**, **word formation**

reference

1 In traditional semantics, reference is the relation between the linguistic expression (name, word) and the object in extralinguistic reality to which the expression refers (⇒ **semi-otic triangle**). The division between **denota-tion** and **extension** seems to be problematic in this case.

2 In J.R. Searle's **speech act theory**, which was developed along the lines of Strawson, language use and the speaker are brought into play. In this case, the speaker makes reference to the intra- and extralinguistic context by using linguistic and non-linguistic means, which, together with **predication**, constitute a partial act in the execution of a propositional speech act. By means of referential expressions (partic-ularly personal pronouns, proper nouns, nom-inal expressions), the speaker identifies objects of reality, about which he/she says something. Distinctions are drawn between the following forms of reference: (a) situation-dependent ref-erence expressed through **pronouns**, definite **articles**, deictic expressions (⇒ **deixis**), 'incomplete' designations, and also through gestures; (b) situation-independent reference expressed through personal names (⇒ **proper noun**) and 'complete' designations; (c) situation-defining reference expressed through illocutive expressions (⇒ **illocution**; ⇒ *also* **anaphora**). On the one hand, the properties of reference make the relations and distinctions of **meaning** and extension apparent, and, on the other hand, a more exact understanding of the role of reference in communication are cur-rently of particular linguistic interest. The issue of reference is especially important for appro-priate semantic interpretations that rely on the descriptive models of **generative grammar** (⇒ **binding theory**).

References
Atkinson, M. 1979. Prerequisites for reference. In E. Ochs and B.B. Schieffelin (eds), *Developmental pragmatics*. New York. 229–49.
Barwise, J. 1991. Situationen und Kleine Welten. In A.V. Stechow and D. Wunderlich (eds), *Semantik/ Semantics: an international handbook of contem-porary research*. Berlin. 80–9.
Bellert, I. 1972. On a condition of the coherence of texts. *Semiotica* 2.335–63.
Clark, H.H. and C.R. Marshall. 1981. Definite refer-ence and mutual knowledge. In A.K. Joshi, B.L. Webber, and I.A. Sag (eds), *Elements of discourse understanding*. Cambridge. 10–53.
Clark, H.H. and G.L. Murphy. 1982. Audience design

in meaning and reference. In J.-F. LeNy and W. Kintsch (eds), *Language and comprehension.* Amsterdam. 287–99.

Clark, H.H., R. Schreuder, and S. Buttrick. 1983. Common ground and the understanding of demonstrative reference. *JVLVB* 22.245–58.

Conrad, B. 1985. On the reference of proper names. *ALH* 19.44–124.

Cresswell, M.S. 1991. Die Weltsituation. In A.V. Stechow and D. Wunderlich (eds), *Semantik/ Semantics: an international handbook of contemporary research.* Berlin. 71–9.

Dik, S. 1968. Referential identity. *Lingua* 21.70–97.

Donnellan, K. 1966. Reference and definite descriptions. *Philosophische Rundschau* 75.281–304.

Lieb, H.H. 1979. Principles of semantics. In F. Henny and H. Schnelle (eds), *Syntax and semantics,* vol. 10: *Selections from the third Groningen round table.* New York. 353–78.

Linsky, L. 1967. *Referring.* London.

———— 1971. Reference and referents. In D.D. Steinberg and L.A. Jakobovits (eds), *Semantics.* Cambridge, MA. 76–85.

Marslen–Wilson, W., E. Levy, and L.K. Tyler. 1982. Producing interpretable discourse: the establishment and maintenance of reference. In R. Jarvella and W. Klein (eds), *Speech, place, and action: studies in deixis and related topics.* Chichester. 339–78.

Quine, W.V.O. 1973. *The roots of reference.* La Salle.

Recanati, F. 1993. *Direct reference.* Oxford.

Russell, B. 1905, On denoting. *Mind* 14.479–93.

Schwarz, D.S. 1979. *Naming and referring: the semantics and pragmatics of singular terms.* Berlin.

Searle, J.R. 1969. *Speech acts: an essay in the philosophy of language.* Cambridge.

Shadbolt, N. 1983. Processing reference. *JoS* 2.63–98.

Smith, B. 1978. Frege and Husserl: the ontology of reference. *Journal of the British Society for Phenomenology* 9.111–25.

Strawson, P.F. 1950. On referring. *Mind* 67. 320–44.

Vater, H. 1986. *Einführung in die Referenzsemantik.* Cologne.

Wettstein, H.K. 1984. How to bridge the gap between meaning and reference. *Synthese* 58.63–84.

⇒ **anaphora**, **textual reference**

referent (*also* **denotatum**^{2}, designatum)

Object or state of affairs in extralinguistic reality or also a linguistic element to which the speaker or writer is referring by using a linguistic sign (**noun phrases**, possibly also **adjective phrases**, **verb phrases**).

References
⇒ **reference**

referential index

A formal convention, a referential index marks the same or different **referents** of a text through numbers or small Roman letters. In the sentences (1) *Philip*$_1$ *promised me*$_2$ [*to come to London*$_1$] and (2) *Philip*$_1$ *helped me*$_2$ [*to come to London*$_2$] the subject of [*to come to London*] in (1) is referentially identical with *Philip*, in (2) with the speaker of the sentence.

referential reading ⇒ attributive vs referential reading

referential semantics

As a 'language-external' discipline, referential semantics investigates and describes the conditions and rules that govern the way language is used to refer to the extralinguistic world. Whereas a content-oriented semantics is concerned with the language-internal relations of linguistic expressions (⇒ **semantic relations**), referential semantics, developed primarily within the framework of **speech act theory**, investigates the specific ways in which a speaker refers to the space–time structure of a given speech situation (⇒ **deixis**), establishes relations, or refers to objects or ideas. (⇒ *also* **I–now–here origo**, **reference**)

References
⇒ **reference**, **speech act theory**

reflection theory

In Marxist linguistic theory, the teaching that language is the expression or the ideal reflection of objective reality through human consciousness. Linguistic **signs** are seen as the material realizations of mental images, i.e. concepts or assertions. The inquiry into the relationship between linguistic expressions and their mental counterparts is the task of **semantics**. (⇒ *also* **Marrism**, **materialistic language theory**)

References
⇒ **Marrism**

reflexive pronoun [Lat. *reflexus* 'bent or curved back']

Subgroup of **pronouns** which are used when the pronoun is coreferential with the subject of the clause it is used in: *Philip*$_1$ *defended himself*$_1$. Reflexive pronouns are often handled as special cases of **personal pronouns**, since in many languages they have the same grammatical forms, particularly in the first and second persons (Fr. *je me lave* 'I wash myself' vs *il me lave* 'he washes me'). There are some languages, however, where reflexivity is not expressed by pronouns but rather by verbal affixes (see Sells *et al.* 1987). In older forms of generative **transformational grammar**, reflexive pronouns are derived from a pronominalization transformation which replaces a full **noun phrase** with a reflexive pronoun when two elements in a text are coreferential. In more recent approaches of transformational grammar, reflexive pronouns are not handled by **transformations**, but rather by **binding theory**.

Unlike English, some languages (e.g. **German**, **French**) have verbs that can only be used reflexively: Ger. *sich schämen* 'to be ashamed.' Also, many languages can use reflexive pronouns to describe reciprocal relationships and actions, where English uses reciprocal pronouns such as *each other, one another*, etc. (⇒ *also* **anaphora**, **reciprocity**)

References
Edmondson, J. 1978. Ergative languages, accessibility hierarchies, governing reflexives and questions of formal analysis. In W. Abraham (ed.), *Valence, semantic case and grammatical relations*. Amsterdam. 633–60.
Everaert, M. 1986. *The syntax of reflexives*. Dordrecht.
Faltz, L.M. 1977. *Reflexivization: a study in universal syntax*. Ann Arbor, MI.
Geniusiene, E. 1988. *The typology of reflexives*. Berlin.
Jackendoff, R.S. 1972. *Semantic interpretation in generative grammar*. Cambridge, MA.
Kubinski, W. 1987. *Reflexivization in English and Polish: an arc pair grammar analysis*. Tübingen.
Nedjalkov, V.P. 1980. Reflexive constructions: a functional typology. In G. Brettschneider and C. Lehmann (eds), *Wege zur Universalienforschung*. Tübingen. 222–8.
Ruszkiewicz, P. 1984. *Aspects of reflexivization in English*. Katowice.
Sells, P., A. Zaenen, and D. Zec. 1987. Reflexivization variation: relations between syntax, semantics, and lexical structure. In M. Iida, S. Wechsel, and D. Zec (eds), *Working papers in grammatical theory and discourse structure: interactions of morphology, syntax and discourse*. Stanford, CA. 169–238.
Zribi–Hertz, A. 1989. Anaphor binding and narrative point of view: English reflexive pronouns in sentence and discourse. *Lg* 65.695–727.

reflexive relation

In **formal logic**, the characteristic of a two-place relation R in a set S, which is true if every element x in S is in the relation R with itself (notation: $R(x,x)$). This is true, for example, for the relation of identity: every element is identical to itself. A relation R is non-reflexive in the cases where $R(x,x)$ is not true for every element. This is, for example, the case in the relation of punishment, for not every individual punishes him/herself. One must distinguish between a non-reflexive relation R and a so-called irreflexive relation R', in which it is the case that for all elements $\neg R'(x,x)$. Compare the (irreflexive) relation of being married: No one gets married to oneself.

References
⇒ **formal logic**, **set theory**

reflexivity

1 Property of syntactic constructions where two **arguments** of an action or relationship described by a single **predicate** have identical **reference**. Reflexivity can be expressed by a **reflexive pronoun** (*Philip hurt himself*) or by verbal affixes, as in Dyirbal (⇒ **Australian languages**): *–ɲu* in *bayi buybayir-ɲu* 'he hides (himself).'

References
Helke, M. 1979. *The grammar of English reflexives*. New York.
⇒ **reflexive pronoun**

2 Property of human language to refer to itself, as in citations of words, for example. (⇒ *also* **metalanguage**)

reflexivization ⇒ **reflexive pronoun**

regional dictionary ⇒ **dialect dictionary**

register

Manner of speaking or writing specific to a certain function, that is, characteristic of a certain domain of communication (or of an institution), for example, the language of religious sermons, of parents with their child, or of an employee with his/her supervisor. Registers play a prominent role in Halliday's school of Systemic Functional Grammar. (⇒ **systemic linguistics**)

Reference
Biber, D. 1995. *Dimension of register variation. A cross-linguistic comparison*. Cambridge.
Halliday, M.A.K. *et al.* 1964. *The linguistic sciences and language teaching*. London.

regressive assimilation ⇒ **assimilation**

regulative rule

Rules of behavior that regulate forms of behavior which exist independently of those rules (e.g. interpersonal relationships or street traffic or table manners), in contrast to **constitutive rules** which define forms of behavior. See Searle (1969: ch. 2.5).

References
Searle, J.R. 1969. *Speech acts: an essay in the philosophy of language*. Cambridge.
⇒ **speech act theory**.

reification [Lat. *res* 'thing']

A term coined by Lakoff (1968) to denote the

(systematic) semantic relations between the abstract meaning of a lexeme (e.g. *dissertation*) and the 'concretization' derivable from it: *His dissertation deals with the philosophy of language* vs *His dissertation has more than 500 pages*, where the first sentence refers to the concept 'dissertation,' whereas the second refers to its material realization.

Reference
Lakoff, J.D. 1968. The role of semantics in a grammar. In E. Bach and R.T. Harms (eds), *Universals in linguistic theory*. New York. 124–169.

relation

1 In **set theory** and **formal logic**, the relation between at least two elements of an ordered pair: *Philip is bigger than Caroline* (notation: larger than (x, y) or $L(x, y)$. Depending on the number of places, relations are created between two, three, or more objects, individuals, or states of affairs, the order of the elements not being arbitrary. In natural language, syntactic–semantic relations in a sentence are determined by the valence of the verbal expressions, cf. *x loves y, x falls between y and z*, and expressed by noun phrases (and any corresponding case markers). For special characteristics of relation, ⇒ **symmetrical relation**, **transitive relation**, **reflexive relation**, **connex relation**, **converse relation**; for relation in syntax, ⇒ **dependence**, **domination**, **constituency**; for relation in semantics, ⇒ **semantic relation**. (⇒ *also* **set theory**)

References
⇒ **formal logic**, **set theory**

2 ⇒ **syntactic function**

relation judgment

In **formal logic**, a judgment in which a relation between two or more objects with regard to size, serial order, placement in space and time, relatedness, among others, is expressed, for example, *Philip is older than Caroline* or *Philip is the brother of Caroline*.

relational adjective ⇒ adjective

relational expression

A noun with a one-place argument, such as *father (of)*, *foot (of)*, *president (of)*. In many languages relational expressions differ syntactically and morphologically from non-relational expressions, for example by having distinct possessive constructions (⇒ **alienable vs inalienable possession**).

relational grammar

Model of a universal grammar put forward by D.M. Perlmutter, P.M. Postal, and D.E. Johnson, among others, as an alternative to **transformational grammar**. A basic assumption of relational grammar is that grammatical relations (such as subject and object) play a central role in the syntax of natural languages. This distinguishes relational grammar from universal grammar models that use concepts of constituent structure for syntactic rules and the definition of grammatical relations. Because no universally valid definition of grammatical relations can be given (⇒ **syntactic function**), transformational grammar of the 1960s did not succeed in describing universal phenomena (such as the **passive**) as uniform phenomena of all languages. This motivated two basic assumptions of relational grammar: (a) grammatical relations are primitives which cannot be further defined; and (b) representations in terms of syntactic constituent structure are not suited for describing universal phenomena. Instead, sentences are analyzed by means of relational networks. These contain at least one sentence node, from which 'arcs' for the predicate and its arguments proceed. Each major constituent of the sentence stands in precisely one grammatical relation to its dominating sentence node at every level of description. The most important grammatical relations are: **subject** (or 1-relation), **direct object** (2-relation), **indirect object** (3-relation), **genitive**, **locative**, **instrumental**, and **benefactive**. The following arc diagram illustrates the relational network of the sentence *That book was reviewed by Louise* (see Perlmutter 1983.16):

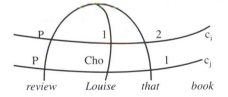

$1, 2$ and P represent the grammatical relations 'subject,' 'direct object,' and 'predicate' on two syntactic levels, which are represented by co-ordinate arcs (c_i, c_j). The network depicted here reconstructs the passive construction as follows: The direct object of the c_i level becomes the subject of the c_j level, and the subject of the c_i level does not have a grammatical relation to the predicate at c_i level but instead functions as a 'chômeur' (French for 'unemployed person'). The constituent structure of the sentence, the linear order and the morphological marking of the sentence elements are not represented.

Specific to relational grammar is the assumption of several successive syntactic levels and thus of several grammatical relations which an element in a given sentence bears to the sentence node. This is a natural consequence of the theoretical assumptions of relational grammar pertaining to grammatical relations, and tries to capture the fact that in many cases an element cannot be identified as the bearer of a certain grammatical relation, but rather has properties of both subject and object (⇒ **inversion, unaccusative**). Relational grammar has concentrated on phenomena such as passive, verb agreement, and reflexives, and has established **hierarchy universals** for their description. A more recent development in relational grammar is 'Arc Pair Grammar' (see Johnson and Postal 1980; Kubinski 1988).

References
Blake, B. 1990. *Relational grammar*. London.
Johnson, D.E. 1976. *Towards a theory of relationally based grammar*. Bloomington, IN.
—— 1977. On relational constraints on grammar. In P. Cole and J.M. Saddock (eds), *Syntax and semantics*, vol. 8: *Grammatical relations*. New York. 151–77.
Johnson, D.E. and P.M. Postal. 1980. *Arc pair grammar*. Princeton, NJ.
Kubinski, W. 1988. *Reflexivization in English and Polish: an arc pair grammar analysis*. Tübingen.
Oppenrieder, W. 1993. Relationale Grammatik. In *Syntax: an international handbook of contemporary research*. Berlin and New York. 601–9.
Perlmutter, D.M. 1980. Relational grammar. In E.A. Moravcsik and J.R. Wirth (eds), *Syntax and semantics*, vol. 13: *Current approaches to syntax*. New York. 195–229.
—— (ed.) 1983. *Studies in relational grammar*, vol. 1. Chicago, IL.
Perlmutter, D.M. and C. Rosen (eds) 1984. *Studies in relational grammar*, vol. 2. Chicago, IL.
Postal, P.M. and B.D. Joseph (eds) 1990: *Studies in Relational Grammar*, vol. 3. Chicago, IL.

Bibliography
Dubinsky, S. and C.G. Rosen. 1987. *A bibliography on Relational Grammar*. Bloomington, IN.

relational typology

Classification of the world's languages according to 'fundamental relations,' i.e. according to how their **constituents** are encoded into **nominative**, **ergative**, and **active languages**.

References
Plank, F. (ed.) 1985. *Relational typology*. Berlin and New York.
Primus, B. 1994. Relational typology. In *Syntax: an international handbook on contemporary research*. Vol. 2. Berlin and New York. 1076–109.
⇒ **ergative language**

relative adjective ⇒ adjective

relative clause

Subordinate clause which is dependent on a **noun** or **pronoun**, is usually introduced by a **relative pronoun** or relative adverb, and can refer to various elements (or even a whole sentence) except for the **predicate**. Depending on the semantic/pragmatic function, a distinction is usually made between defining/restrictive and amplifying/non-restrictive relative clauses. Restrictive clauses limit the set of possible objects the noun specified by the clause can refer to: *Here is the book that you were looking for* (*and none other than that one*), while amplifying clauses specify their referent more exactly: *Napoleon, who came from Corsica, was exiled to Elba*. These two types of clause, which often allow for two or more interpretations, can be distinguished from one another by examining the following characteristics of the surface structure: in restrictive clauses, which are always a part of a definite description, the referent can be emphasized by using a demonstrative pronoun (*that book, which*), while in non-restrictive clauses the referent is often a proper noun or personal pronoun, and the whole sentence can usually be modified by adding words or phrases such as *apparently* or *as is well known*, which underline its purely attributive character. In addition, non-restrictive clauses are optional, while defining clauses are obligatory. This distinction is also supported by various intonational properties.

References
Bartsch, R. 1976. *Syntax and semantics of relative clauses*. Amsterdam.
Downing, B.T. 1978. Some universals of relative clause structure. In J.H. Greenberg *et al.* (eds), *Universals of human language*. Stanford, CA. 375–418.
Helgander, J. 1971. *The relative clause in English and other Germanic languages: a historical and analytical survey*. Göteborg.
Keenan, E.L. 1985. Relative clauses. In T. Shopen (ed.), *Language typology and linguistic description*. Cambridge. Vol. 2, 141–70.
Kleiber, G. 1987. *Relatives restrictives et relatives appositives: une opposition* 'introuvable.' Tübingen.
Lehmann, C. 1984. *Der Relativsatz*. Tübingen.
Prideaux, G. and W.J. Baker. 1987. *Strategies and structure: the processing of relative clauses*. Amsterdam.

relative pronoun

Subgroup of **pronouns** which refer to an immediately preceding noun, **noun phrase**, clause, or sentence and which serve to introduce attributive subordinate (relative) clauses (⇒ **relative**

clause, **subordinate clause**). In English, relative pronouns include *who, whom, which, that*.

relator

In **formal logic**, a **predicate** with at least two **empty slots**, that is, one that requires at least two **arguments** (notation: *aRb*); cf. the **relation judgment** *Caroline is the sister of Philip*, where 'be-sister-of' is the relator.

References
⇒ **formal logic**

relevance [Lat. *relevare* 'to reduce the load of, alleviate']

The relevance of an entity for a particular goal is a measure of how much the entity contributes to the attainment of the goal. If it does not contribute anything, then it is considered to be irrelevant to that goal. If it is a necessary condition for it, then it is maximally relevant. In linguistic investigations, it is the relevance of an utterance for the mutually recognized purpose of **discourse** which is of particular interest. Grice's maxim of relevance states simply: 'Be relevant.' The response *Here's five dollars* to the utterance *I'm hungry* is relevant only in a situation in which one can buy oneself something to eat for five dollars, but not, for example, in the middle of a forest. (⇒ **maxim of conversation**)

References
Blass, R. 1990. *Relevance relations in discourse: a study with special reference to Sissala*. Cambridge.
Sperber, D. and D. Wilson. 1986. *Relevance: communication and cognition*. Cambridge, MA.
Werth, P. 1985. The concept of 'relevance' in conversational analysis. In P. Werth (ed.), *Conversation and discourse*. London. 129–54.

relevant feature

In structural **phonology**, phonological features which in an individual language are distinctive, i.e. cause a difference in meaning, such as in English the feature of **voiced vs voiceless** with stops, which distinguish /b, d, g/ from /p, t, k/, e.g. *beer* /biːr/ vs *peer* /piːr/. Aspiration is not relevant in English (e.g. *tar* vs *star*, [tʰar] vs [star]). (⇒ *also* **distinctive feature**)

relic area ⇒ enclave

reordering transformation ⇒ movement transformation

repair

In **conversation analysis**, those techniques that participants in conversations employ in order to achieve a smooth functioning of the interaction. Utterances need to be 'repaired' when the speaker has problems finding the right word or makes a mistake (see Schegloff *et al.* 1977). Repairs may be initiated or undertaken by the same or the next speaker. Since the organization of repairs is subordinate to the system of **turn-taking** (see Schegloff 1979), repair may lead to an impairment of the **sequential organization**; for instance, the sequentially implied next turn may have to be postponed (⇒ **adjacency pair**, **conditional relevance**). For this reason a self-initiated repair within the same turn is preferred over other alternatives (⇒ **preference**).

References
Goodwin, C. 1981. *Conversational organization: interaction between speaker and hearer*. New York.
Jefferson, G. 1984. On embedded and exposed corrections. *StL* 14.58–68.
Schegloff, E. 1979. The relevance of repair to syntax-for-conversation. In T. Givón (ed.), *Syntax and semantics*, vol. 12: *Discourse and syntax*. New York. 261–86.
Schegloff, E., G. Jefferson, and H. Sacks, 1977. The preference for self-correction in the organization of repair. *Lg* 53.361–82.
Selting, M. 1988. The role of intonation in the organization of repair and problem handling sequences in conversation. *JPrag* 12.293–322.
⇒ **conversation analysis**

representational function of language

Besides the **expressive function of language** and **appellative function of language**, one of the three subfunctions of the linguistic sign in K. Bühler's **organon model of language**. The representational function of language refers to the relation between the linguistic sign and the object or state of affairs that it represents as a 'symbol.' (⇒ *also* **axiomatics of linguistics**)

Reference
Bühler, K. 1990. *Theory of language: the representational function of language*, trans. D.F. Goodwin. Amsterdam and Philadelphia.

resonance

An increase in the strength of sound waves through a co-oscillation of other sources of sound whose own frequency is identical with the frequency of the primary sound source. In this manner, certain frequencies increase in speaking and singing by a change in the size and shape of the **resonance chamber**.

References
⇒ **phonetics**

resonance chamber

Term taken from musicology (referring to wind instruments) for the anatomical region in which **speech sounds** are articulated: the upper laryngeal region, the pharyngeal, nasal, and oral cavities. These four resonance spaces are bordered by the vocal cords towards the inside of the body and the opening of the nose and mouth towards the outside of the body.

resonant ⇒ sonorant

restricted code ⇒ code theory

restrictive

Semantic property of **conjunctions** (*but*, *only*), **adverbs** (*at least*), or **relative clauses** (*the book that you're looking for is on the table*) which express some sort of limitation relative to the statement in question.

restrictive clause

Semantically defined modal clause which functions as an adverbial modifier to express limitation on that which is expressed in the main clause. They are usually introduced by such conjunctions as *as far as*, *except that*: *As far as I know, he's been retired for years.*

restructuring

Term used in **transformational grammar** for the change of underlying forms in a process of linguistic change. Restructuring always occurs when a linguistic change (e.g. a **sound change**) does not result in synchronously alternating surface forms. Consequently, this innovation cannot be acquired by children as a new or modified rule or series of rules, but rather takes place as a reorganization of the grammar; the original innovations are then understood to be part of the underlying forms.

References
King, R. 1969. *Historical linguistics and generative grammar.* Frankfurt.
Traugott, E.C. 1976. On the notion restructuring in historical syntax. In D.D. Bornstein (ed.), *Reader in the theory of grammar: From the seventeenth to the twentieth century.* Cambridge. 94–103.
Vennemann, T. 1974. Restructuring. *Lingua* 33.137–56.

resultative (*also* accomplishment, achievement, conclusive, delimitative, **effective**, **egressive**, finitive, telic, terminative)

Verbal **aspect** which forms a subclass of nonduratives (⇒ **durative vs non-durative**). Resultatives are verbs which refer to an event that comes to a conclusion, e.g. *to kill*, *to cut up*, *to burn down*, *to find*, *to eat an apple*. Resultative verbs or constructions can be recognized from the fact that their imperfective variants (*He was eating an apple*) do not logically imply the perfective variant: **He ate the apple.* In contrast, with a non-resultative verb such as *to*

dance (*He was dancing when I entered the room*), the perfective variant follows logically: *He danced.* (⇒ *also* **telic vs atelic**)

References
Nedjalkov, V.P. (ed.) 1988. *Typology of resultative constructions.* Amsterdam.
⇒ **aspect**

retroflex (*also* cacuminal)

Speech sound classified according to its **articulator** (**apical**) and its **place of articulation** (**post-alveolar**). In the articulation of a retroflex, the tip of the tongue is bent towards the top and back of the mouth, e.g. [ʂ], [ɳ], [ɖ] in Swed. [fɔʂ] 'waterfall,' [baɳ] 'child,' [buːɖ] 'table,' [ɚ] in Am. Eng. [doɚ] 'door.' (⇒ *also* **articulatory phonetics**)

References
⇒ **phonetics**

reversivity

Relation of semantic opposition. In contrast to the general relation of **incompatibility**, reversivity is limited to expressions denoting processes. A relation of reversivity is said to exist between two expressions (e.g. *enter* vs *leave*) when both expressions contain an element of change from an initial state to a final state such that the initial state of the first expression corresponds to the final state of the second expression and vice versa. Frequently, reversivity is signaled by prefixes (Engl. ø vs *un-* (*lock* vs *unlock*).

References
Cruse, D.A. 1979. Reversives. *Linguistics* 17. 957–66.
——— 1986. *Lexical semantics.* Cambridge.

Revised Extended Standard Theory ⇒ transformational grammar

rewrite rule

A rule of **transformational grammar** of the type $X \rightarrow Y_1 \ldots Y_n$, where the element to the left of the arrow, X, can be replaced by the elements to the right of the arrow. These rules correspond to the branching in **tree diagrams** (⇒ **phrase structure rules**). There is a difference between context-free rewrite rules and context-sensitive rewrite rules. For example *V → V transitive* / *#NP* is a context-sensitive rule, where / means 'in the environment of' and # the empty space where the transposed element will be placed.

References
⇒ **transformational grammar**

Rhaeto-Romance (also Rhaeto-Romansh)

Collective term for the **Romance languages** and dialects derived from the Vulgar **Latin** spoken in the Alps between St Gotthard and the Gulf of Trieste. The unity of these languages was not recognized until the nineteenth century (G.I. Ascoli, T. Gartner). Today the following divisions are generally recognized: (a) Friulian (East Ladinian: Carnia to the Friulian lowlands, approx. 450,000 speakers); (b) (Central) Ladinian in the valleys surrounding the Sella range, with approx. 27,000 speakers; (c) Romansh (West Ladinian: Graubünden, Switzerland) with approx. 40,000 speakers. Rhaeto-Romance has been the fourth official language of Switzerland since 1938. The Rhaeto-Romance dialects, which fall typologically between **French** and northern **Italian**, differ greatly in terms of morphology and lexicon (numerous dialectal variants) and have been strongly influenced both by neighboring languages as well as by the multilingual nature of their speakers.

References
Billigmeier, R.H. 1979. *A crisis in Swiss pluralism: the Romansh and their relations with the German- and Italian-Swiss in the perspective of a millenium*. The Hague.
Decurtins, A. 1993. *Rätoromanisch: Aufsätze zur Sprach-, Kulturgeschichte und zur Kulturpolitik*. Chur.
—— 1993. *Viarva romontscha: contribuziuns davart il lungatg, sia historia e sia tgira*. Chur.
Ebneter, T. 1994. *Syntax des gesprochenen Räto-romanischen*. Tübingen.
Gregor, D.B. 1982. *Romontsch: language and literature*. Cambridge.
Haiman, J. and P. Beninca. 1992. *The Rhaeto-Romance languages*. London.
Holtus, G. and J. Kiramer. 1986. 'Rätoromanisch' in der Diskussion, 1976–1985. In G.H. Ringger and K. Ringger (eds), *Festschrift für W.T. Elwert*. Tübingen. 1–88.
Holtus, G., M. Metzeltin, and C. Schmitt (eds) 1989. *Lexikon der romanistischen Linguistik*, vol. 3. Tübingen.
Rohlfs, G. 1975. *Rätoromanisch: die Sonderstellung des Rätoromanischen zwischen Italienisch und Französisch. Eine kulturgeschichtliche und linguistische Einführung*. Tübingen.

Grammars
Candinas, T. 1982. *Romontsch sursilvan: grammatica elementara per emprender igl idiom sursilvan*. Chur.
Ganzoni, G.P. 1977. *Grammatica Ladina*. Samedan.

Dictionaries
Dicziunari Rumantsch Grischun. 1939– . Chur. (Vol. 8, 1986–91.)
Dicziunari Tudais-Ch-Rumantsch Ladin. 1944. Chur. (2nd edn 1976.)

Pirona, G.A. *et al*. 1935. *Il nuovo Pirona: vocabolario friulano*. Udine. (2nd edn 1967.)

Bibliography
Iliescu, M. and H. Siller-Runggaldier. 1985. *Rätoromanische Bibliographie*. Innsbruck.

Rhaeto-Romansh ⇒ Rhaeto-Romance

rheme ⇒ comment, focus, theme vs rheme

rhetic act [Grk *rhēma* 'subject of speech, matter; predicate']

In J.L. Austin's **speech act theory**, the performance of a **phatic act** in a manner that establishes the meaning of this act, whereby the meaning of such an act is determined, if one has established, (a) what is being talked about and (b) what is being said about it. This term was replaced by J.R. Searle with the term 'propositional act' (⇒ **proposition**) in his elaboration of Austin's theory.

References
⇒ **speech act theory**

rhetoric [Grk *rhētorikḗ* (*téchnē*)]

Classical rhetoric was a politically and ethically established style of teaching effective public speaking. The system was codified by Aristotle, Cicero, and Quintillian into five departments: 'invention,' 'arrangement,' 'style,' 'memory,' and 'delivery.' Aristotle identified three branches of rhetoric: 'deliberative' – legislative rhetoric, the purpose of which is to exhort or dissuade; 'judicial' or forensic rhetoric, which accuses or defends; 'epideictic' or panegyric rhetoric, which is ceremonial in nature and commemorates or blames. Classical rhetoric considered what is today studied in the domains of **stylistics** and **pragmatics**, and laid the foundations of modern linguistic theory. While medieval and early modern rhetoric retreated into the study of **figures of speech** and **tropes**, the 'new rhetoric' of the last thirty years has been conceptualized as a social-psychologically grounded tool of communication (new rhetoric, Hovland), as a means of researching intelligibility (applied rhetoric), as a theory of argumentation (*nouvelle rhétorique*, Perelman), and as a sociopolitical institution of democratic societies. Within linguistics, rhetoric can be seen as a part of the pragmatically grounded **text linguistics**, characterized by (a) the pragmatic aspects of a speech act, where one is conscious of its effect and **perlocution**, and (b) by the changing text-internal features of a situatively suitable, argumentative and stylistic structure. 'Rhetorical' here means any kind of **persuasive** use of language in private (everyday use) and in the public arena (politics, advertising, law). Rhetoric stands at the interdisciplinary intersection of linguistics, sociology, and language psychology.

References
Aristotle. 1982. *'Art' of rhetoric*, trans. J.H. Freese. Cambridge, MA.
Billig, M. 1987. *Arguing and thinking: a rhetorical approach to social psychology*. Cambridge.
Erickson, K.V. (ed.) 1974. *Aristotle: the classical heritage of rhetoric*. Metuchen, NJ.
Hovland, C.I. *et al.* 1953. *Communication and persuasion*. New Haven, CT.
Kennedy, G. 1963. *The art of persuasion in Greece*. Princeton, NJ.
—— 1980. *Classical rhetoric and its Christian and secular tradition from ancient to modern times*. London.
Lausberg, H. 1960. *Handbuch der literarischen Rhetorik*, 2 vols. Munich. (3rd edn Stuttgart, 1990.)
—— 1963. *Elemente der literarischen Rhetorik*, 2nd rev. edn. Munich. (4th corr. edn 1971.)
Leith, D. and G. Myerson. 1989. *The power of address: explorations in rhetoric*. London.
Levi, J.N. (ed.) 1990. *Language in the judicial process*. New York.
Martin, J.E. 1992. *Toward a theory of text for contrastive rhetoric*. New York.
Medhurst, M.J. 1990. *Cold war rhetoric: strategy, metaphor, and ideology*. New York.
Murphy, J.J. 1974. *Rhetoric in the Middle Ages: a history of rhetorical theory from St. Augustine to the Renaissance*. Berkeley, CA.
Nash, W. 1989. *Rhetoric: the wit of persuasion*. Oxford.
Perelman, C. 1989. *Rhétoriques*. Brussels.
Perelman, C. and L. Olbrechts-Tyteca. 1969. *The New Rhetoric: a treatise on argumentation*, trans. J. Wilkinson and P. Weaver. Notre Dame, IN.
Renwick, J. (ed.) 1990. *Language and the rhetoric of the Revolution*. Edinburgh.
Steinman, M., Jr. 1967. *New rhetorics*. New York.

Bibliography
Vickers, B. 1981. Bibliography of rhetoric studies 1970–1980. *Comparative Criticism* 3.316–22.
⇒ **argumentation**, **figure of speech**, **trope**

rhetorical question

1 In the broad sense, rhetorical questions are all uses of **interrogative** sentences to which the speaker does not expect an answer from the addressee. Some merely serve to raise an issue for discussion, others have the effect of declaring the speaker's preference for one view or expectation over other possible ones: *If winter's here, can spring be far behind?*

2 Rhetorical questions in the narrow sense are those questions that lead the addressee to understand the opposite, in a sense, of its propositional content, that is, the negative assertion in a positive *yes/no*-interrogative (*Is it at all likely that he's really sick?* = 'He is not

sick') and the positive assertion in a negative *yes/no*-interrogative (*Is it at all likely that he isn't really sick?* = 'He is indeed sick') as well as the corresponding negative existential assertion in a positive *wh*-interrogative (*Where can anyone get any peace and quiet?* = 'One cannot get any peace and quiet anywhere') and the corresponding positive universal assertion in a negative *wh*-interrogative (*When has Philip not been in the theater?* = 'Philip is always in the theater'). Occasionally, rhetorically used *wh*-interrogatives have another, contextually determined use, namely, if there is a known exception to the indirectly expressed negative existential or positive universal assertion (*Who shuffles like that around here with a derby, bowtie, and walking stick? – Only Charlie Chaplin shuffles like that . . .*).

3 A **figure of speech** in the form of an apparent question that is used to intensify a corresponding comment (e.g. *Are you blind?*) or request (*Would you like to keep quiet?*). The rhetorical question can be analyzed pragmatically as an indirect speech act. (⇒ **prolepsis**)

rhinolalia [Grk *rhís* 'nose', *lalía* 'talk']

Term referring to both a **voice disorder** and **articulation disorder** in which not only the voice is affected (as in **rhinophonia**) but also the articulation of sounds. This term is not used in North America.

rhinophonia [Grk *phōné*, 'sound, voice']

Term referring to a **voice disorder** caused by a dysfunction of the velum, or physical changes in the nasal cavities.

rhotacism [Grk *rhō̃*, name of the Greek letter ‹ρ›]

1 In the broader sense, every change of a consonant to *r*. This change mostly concerns dental fricatives and *l*. It is found, for example, in numerous **Italian** dialects.

2 In the narrower sense, spontaneous change of Proto-Gmc [z] to West Gmc [r] intervocalically, cf. Goth. *maiza*, OE *māra* 'more'. Synchronic reflexes of this change can still be recognized in the **grammatical alternation** of *r* : *s* in Eng. *was* vs *were* (⇒ **Verner's law**).

3 Speech disorder caused by stuttering of the *r*-sound. (⇒ *also* **language disorder**)

Rickmål ⇒ Danish, Norwegian

right-branching construction

A **phrase structure grammar** construction. A structure is right branching if in the **tree diagram** each node which branches into constituents A and B is of the type that only the right branch, B, may branch.

Reference
Chomsky, N. 1965. *Aspects of the theory of syntax.* Cambridge, MA.

rising ⇒ falling vs rising

rising diphthong ⇒ diphthong, intonation

Ritwan ⇒ Algonquian

Romaji ⇒ Japanese

Romance languages

Branch of **Indo-European** which developed from **Italic**, particularly from **Latin** and its various regional forms in the territories conquered by Rome (Vulgar Latin). A division is generally made between East Romance languages (**Rumanian**, **Italian**) and West Romance languages (Gallo-Romance, Ibero-Romance, and **Rhaeto-Romance** languages) based on phonological and morphological criteria (e.g. voicing or deletion of intervocalic voiceless stops in West Romance and the loss of final [s] in East Romance: Span. *sabéis* vs Ital. *sapete* 'you (pl.) know,' Span. *las casas* vs Ital. *le case* 'the houses'). Included in Gallo-Romance are **French**, **Occitan**, and Franco-Provençal, while **Spanish**, **Portuguese**, **Galician**, and **Catalan** belong to Ibero-Romance. Some of the main factors contributing to the individual development of each territory include substratum and superstratum influences, the date of Romanization, and the extent of relations with Rome. The language which has changed the most from Latin is French, which underwent a thorough typological transformation (heavy loss of inflectional morphology due to the loss of final syllables and their replacement by elements such as personal pronouns, articles, prepositions, auxiliaries). In contrast, the southern Romance languages such as Spanish and Italian, as well as Rumanian, are much closer to Latin. **Sardinian** has a particularly conservative phonological inventory, and does not fit easily into the East/West distinction.

References
Agard, F.B. 1984. *A course in Romance linguistics,* 2 vols. Washington, DC.
Elcock, W.D. 1975. *The Romance languages,* 2nd edn. London.
Hall, R.A., Jr. 1974. *External history of the Romance languages.* New York.
——— 1983. *Proto-Romance morphology.* Amsterdam and Philadelphia.
Harris, M. and N. Vincent. 1988. *The Romance languages.* London. (Repr. 1990.)
Holtus, G., M. Metzeltin, and C. Schmitt (eds) 1987. *Lexikon der romanistischen Linguistik.* Tübingen.

Hope, T.E. 1971. *Lexical borrowing in the Romance languages,* 2 vols. Oxford.
Jensen, F. 1990. *Old French and comparative Gallo-Romance syntax.* Tübingen.
Malmberg, B. 1971. *Phonétique général et romane.* The Hague.
Posner, R. and J.N. Green (eds) 1980–93. *Trends in Romance linguistics,* 5 vols to date. Berlin and New York.
Rohlfs, G. 1971. *Romanische Sprachgeographie.* Munich.
Wright, R. (ed.) 1990. *Latin and the Romance languages in the Early Middle Ages.* London.

Grammar
Meyer-Lübke, W. 1890–9. *Grammatik der romanischen Sprachen,* 3 vols. Leipzig. (Repr. Hildesheim and New York, 1972.)

Bibliography
Romanische Bibliographie (suppl. to *Zeitschrift für romanische Philologie*). Tübingen.

Dictionary
Meyer-Lübke, W. 1935. *Romanisches etymologisches Wörterbuch.* Heidelberg. (5th edn 1972.)

Journals
Probus
Revue de Linguistique Romane.
Romance Philology.
Romanistisches Jahrbuch.
Vox Romanica.
Zeitschrift für romanische Philologie.

Romanian ⇒ Rumanian

Romanization ⇒ transcription, transliteration

Romany

Language of the Gypsies (called Sinti and Roma by themselves), genetically related to the **Indo-Aryan** languages. Since the beginning of the Gypsy migrations, around AD 1000, Romany has been increasingly influenced by other languages.

References
Hancock, I. 1988. The development of Romany linguistics. In M.A. Jazayery and W. Winter (eds), *Languages and cultures: Studies in honor of E.C. Polomé.* Amsterdam.
Turner, R.L. 1926. The position of Romani in Indo-Aryan. *Journal of the Gypsy Lore Society,* 3rd series, 5: 4.145–89. (Repr. in *Collected papers.* London, New York, and Toronto. 251–90.)
Ventzek, T.V. 1983. *The Gypsy language.* Moscow.

root

1 Diachronically, the historical basic form of a word, reconstructed from comparison of related languages and specific sound laws, which cannot be broken down into further elements, and which is seen phonetically and semantically as the basis for corresponding **word families**, e.g.

the (reconstructed) Indo-European root *per-* or *par-* for 'all types of locomotion,' which underlie *fare*, *welfare*, *wayfarer*, *ferry*.

2 Synchronically, synonym for 'free' **morpheme** or **base**. (⇒ *also* **word formation**)

References
⇒ **word formation**

root compound ⇒ verbal vs root compound

root determinative

In historical **word formation**, a no longer transparent derivational element, such as -(*th*)*er*, with an originally serializing function: *father*, *mother*, *brother* or Lat. *pater*, *frater*.

References
⇒ **word formation**

root-isolating language ⇒ isolating language

root noun

Noun that consists of only one free **morpheme** (= root) or of a **base** or **stem** (morpheme) without a recognizable derivational morpheme: *box*, *fin*, *light*.

root transformation

A term coined by J.E. Edmonds to describe transformations that apply to main sentences (main clauses, matrix sentences) rather than embedded sentences (⇒ **embedding**). Non-root transformations can operate at any level of embedding. Examples of root transformations include **imperative transformations** and subject-aux inversion in English questions.

References
Chomsky, N. 1975. *Reflections on language*. New York.
Edmonds, J.E. 1976. *A transformational approach to English syntax*. New York.
Hooper, J.B. and S.A. Thompson. 1977. On the applicability of root transformation. *LingI* 4.465–97.
⇒ **penthouse principle**, **transformational grammar**

rounded vs unrounded

Binary phonological **opposition** in **distinctive feature** analysis based on articulation. Rounded sounds are pronounced with a narrowing of the lips, unrounded with spread lips. The distinction describes the opposition between [y, ø] and [i, e].

References
⇒ **distinctive feature**

rounding ⇒ labialization

rückumlaut

Term (from Ger. 'reverse umlaut') coined by J. Grimm for the change of non-umlauted and umlauted (⇒ **umlaut**) vowels in paradigmatically related *jan*-verbs like OE *sēcan* – *sōhta* 'seek - sought.' Since the umlaut-conditioning *i* in the preterite (cf. Goth. *sōkjan* – *sōkida*) had already disappeared before umlaut was applied, because of pre-Old English **syncope** (OE *sōhta*), this form was never umlauted, so the term is actually misleading. Modern English reflexes can still be found in several verbs, e.g. *bring* – *brought*, *buy* – *bought*, *teach* – *taught*, *tell* – *told*, *think* – *thought*; in other cases, rückumlaut has been leveled out by **analogy**, e.g. *kill* – *killed*, *quake* – *quaked*, *reach* – *reached*, *stretch* – *stretched*, *wake* – *waked*. (⇒ *also* **sound change**)

Reference
Vennemann, T. 1986. Rückumlaut. In D. Kastovsky *et al.* (eds), *Linguistics across historical and geographical boundaries*. Berlin. 701–23.

rule

Basic term in the natural sciences, social sciences, and humanities as well as in various linguistic schools used to describe, explain, or regulate behavior. Depending on the context, the term can be used to describe such varying concepts as norms, (universal) rules of conduct, formal procedures in calculus or natural laws. In the framework of linguistics, the following interpretations can be established. (a) In **school grammar**, rules have the intention of being normative; actually, they are descriptions of regularities and exceptions based on selected examples whereby one is forced to call on readers and speakers to use their intelligence and linguistic intuition to fill in holes left by the sometimes vague formulations. (b) In **descriptive linguistics**, rules are descriptions of regularities that can be empirically observed; they do not have the same normative nature as rules in (a) above, but are still based on a static conception of rule. (c) In contrast to the static understanding of rule outlined above, **transformational grammar** uses a dynamic understanding of rule to describe linguistic competence. It refers to a production process and is an explicit indication of formal operations that are carried out. For technical details, ⇒ **phrase structure rules**, **recursive rule**, **transformation**. (d) Based on Wittgenstein's understanding of meaning, a theoretical understanding of rule oriented around language as act has developed in the framework of semantics and pragmatics since the beginning of the 1970s, which sees language as rule-derived (social) behavior. See J.R. Searle's distinction between **constitutive** and **regulative rules**.

References
Chomsky, N. 1961. On the notion of 'rule of grammar.' In R. Jakobson (ed.), *Structure of language and its mathematical aspects*. Providence, RI. 255–7.
——— 1980. *Rules and representations*. New York.
Gumb, R.D. 1972. *Rule governed linguistic behavior*. The Hague.
Heringer, H.J. (ed.) 1974. *Seminar: der Regelbegriff in der praktischen Semantik*. Frankfurt.
Wheatley, J. 1970. *Language and rules*. The Hague.

rule inversion

Term in (generative) historical **phonology** that denotes the inverse 'reinterpretation' of an original phonological rule. For example, in many varieties of English, postvocalic *r* is vocalic, but becomes non-vocalic in an intervocalic environment. This is also true in spoken language when an 'intervocalic' environment is spontaneously created by a following word that begins with a vowel. The inverse view reinterprets the vocalization of *r*, which does not occur in this environment, as *r*-insertion in hiatus; the original exception then occurs as a new rule. Thus, *r* is even inserted where it, historically, should not appear: *the-idea-r-of-it*, *America-r-and-Europe*.

Reference
Vennemann, T. 1972. Rule inversion. *Lingua* 19.209–42.

rule of inference (*also* mood of affirming)

In **propositional logic**, inference rule for **implication**: if the premises p and p *implies* q are true, then (according to the **truth table**) the conclusion p is also true (notation: p, p $\rightarrow$ q $\Vdash$ q, read as: '*p*. If *p*, then *q*. Therefore *q*'). For example, *Philip lives in San Francisco* (= p), *If Philip lives in San Francisco, then he lives in California* ($p \rightarrow q$), thus: *Philip lives in California* (= $\Vdash q$). See **rule of negative inference** for the formal criteria for distinguishing between **presupposition** and implication.

References
$\Rightarrow$ **formal logic**

rule of negative inference (*also* mood of denying)

In **propositional logic** inference rule for **implication**: if the premise p *implies* q is true and q is false, then p is also false (notation: $\neg q$, p $\rightarrow$ q $\Vdash \neg p$, read as: 'not *q*. If *p*, then *q*. Therefore, not *p*'). For example, *If Philip lives in San Francisco, then he lives in California* ($p \rightarrow q$). *Philip does not live in California* ($\neg q$), thus:

Philip does not live in San Francisco ($\neg p$). The rule of negative inference and the **rule of inference** represent the criteria for formally distinguishing between **presupposition** and **implication**: while both rules apply to implication, only the rule of inference applies to presupposition.

References
$\Rightarrow$ **formal logic**

Rumanian

Balkan Romance branch of East Romance ($\Rightarrow$ **Romance languages**) which is divided into four dialect groups: Daco-Rumanian, Arumanian, Megleno-Rumanian, and Istro-Rumanian. The standard language, based on Daco-Rumanian, contains both a large number of **Slavic** elements ($\Rightarrow$ **adstratum**), and the replacement of the infinitive with the subjunctive, a typical feature of Balkan languages, as well as signs of strong French influence, dating from the beginning of the nineteenth century. There are approx. 25 million speakers of Rumanian.

Characteristics: Rumanian differs from the other Romance languages especially in the area of morphosyntax: remnants of Latin nominal morphology (including the vocative), preservation of the Latin neuter, enclitic definite article (*studentul* 'the student'), the so-called prepositional accusative (*văd pe mama* 'I see mama').

References
Agard, F.B. 1958. *Structural sketch of Rumanian*. Baltimore, MD.
Deletant, D. 1983. *Colloquial Romanian*. London.
Dimitrescu, F. 1978. *Istoria limbii Române*, 2 vols. Bucharest.
Gramatica limbii române. 1966. 2 vols. Bucharest.
Holtus, G., M. Metzeltin, and C. Schmitt (eds) 1989. *Lexikon der romanistischen Linguistik*. Tübingen. Vol. 3, 1–52.
Iordan, I. 1978. *Limba română contemporană*. Bucharest.
Ivănescu, G. 1980. *Istoria limbii române*. Iași.
Mallinson, G. 1986. *Rumanian*. London.
Rosetti, A. 1986. *Istoria limbii române: ediție definitivâ*, vol. I. Bucharest.

Dictionary
Academia Republicii Socialiste Românîa 1913–83. *Dictionarul limbii române*, 12 vols. Bucharest.

Dialectology
Atlasul lingvistic român. Serie nouă. 1956–.
Dahmen, W. and J. Kramer. 1985. *Aromunischer Sprachatlas*. Hamburg.
Wild, B. 1983. *Meglenorumänischer Sprachatlas*. Hamburg.

rune

Scholarly term, taken from Danish in the seventeenth century, denoting the written symbols of the Germanic tribes that were used before the introduction of and, then concurrently with, the Latin writing system. Runes appear to have served magic and profane purposes. While their origins are unclear, it is believed that they developed from a mixed North Etruscan and Latin alphabet. Every rune represents a particular phone that is called by the first letter of its name, but also has a conceptual value (related to its use in magical contexts), cf. *g* 'gift,' *n* 'need,' *s* 'sun.' The earliest attested runes come from Scandinavia (beginning of the second century AD). Some 5,000 inscriptions (3,000 of them in Sweden alone) are known today. (⇒ *also* **writing**)

References

Antonsen, E. 1975. *A concise grammar of the older Runic inscriptions*. Tübingen.
Arntz, H. 1935. *Handbuch der Runenkunde*. Halle. (4th edn 1944.)
Duwel, K. 1968. *Runenkunde*. Stuttgart.
Elliott, R.W.V. 1989. *Runes: an introduction*. 2nd edn. Manchester and New York.
Krause, W. 1970. *Runen*. Berlin.
Krause, W. and H. Jankuhn. 1966. *Die Runen-Inschriften im älteren Futhark*, 2 vols. Göttingen.
Musset, L. 1965. *Introduction à la runologie*. Paris.

Bibliography
Runebibliografi. 1990–1991. *NRun* 5 and 6.
⇒ **writing**

Russian

East **Slavic** language with approx. 150 million speakers, spoken in Russia and many of the former Soviet republics. On the basis of (South Slavic) **Old Church Slavic** and spoken East Slavic, an Old Russian literary language developed that was used until well into the seventeenth century. But the existence of hundreds of birch bark letters found in Novgorod suggests that there may also have been a literary tradition less tied to the church and Old Church Slavic. The most important literary document is the *Slovo o polku Igorevě*, the 'Lay of Igor's Campaign' (1185). The eighteenth century saw the development of modern Russian, in part due to the activities of Peter the Great (1672–1725), whose greatest contribution to the language was the reform of the **Cyrillic** alphabet through the introduction of the *graždánskaja ázbuka* ('people's alphabet'). The last extensive spelling reform occurred in 1917 (including loss of redundant ‹ъ› in word-final position, and the loss of ‹ѣ›, > ‹v›, and ‹и › in all positions.

Characteristics: free word stress, reduction of unstressed vowels, distinction of palatalized vs unpalatalized consonants, verbal categories of number and gender distinguished in the past tense; numerous impersonal constructions;

remnants of Old Church Slavic in the lexicon: e.g. *grad* 'city' in *Leningrad* vs East Slavic *gorod* 'city' in *Novgorod*.

General
Comrie, B. 1996. *The Russian language in the twentieth century*. Oxford.
Hamilton, W.S. 1980. *Introduction to Russian phonology and word order*. Columbus, OH.
Isačenko, A.V. 1980–3. *Geschichte der russischen Sprache*, 2 vols. Heidelberg.
—— 1962. *Die russische Sprache der Gegenwart*, part 1: *Formenlehre*. Halle. (3rd edn 1975.)
Halle, M. 1959. *The sound pattern of Russian*. 's-Gravenhage.
Jones, D. and D. Ward. 1969. *The phonetics of Russian*. Cambridge.

Grammars
Garde, P. 1980. *Grammaire russe*. Paris.
Švedova, N.J. *et al.* (eds) 1980. *Russkaja grammatika*, 2 vols. Moscow.
Wade, T. 1992. *A comprehensive Russian grammar*. Oxford.

Historical grammars
Borkovskij, V.I. and P.S. Kuznecov. 1965. *Istoričeskaja grammatika russkogo jazyka*, 2nd edn. Moscow.
Kiparsky, V. 1963–75. *Russische historische Grammatik*, 3 vols. Heidelberg.

History and dialects
Avanesov, R.I. and S.V. Bromlej. 1986– . *Dialektologičeskij atlas russkogo jazyka*, Vol. 2 1989. Moscow.
Avanesov, R.I. and V.G. Orlova (eds) 1965. *Russkaja dialektologija*, 2nd edn. Moscow.
Comrie, B. and G. Stone. 1978. *The Russian language since the revolution*. Oxford.
Vinokur, G.O. 1971. *The Russian language: a brief history*. Cambridge.

Dictionaries
Harrison, W. and S. le Fleming. 1981. *Russian dictionary*. London.
Slovar' sovremennogo russkogo literaturnogo jazyka. 1950–65. 17 vols. Moscow.
Zaliznjak, A.A. 1977. *Grammatičeskij slovar' russkogo jazyka*. Moscow.

Etymological dictionaries
Preobraženskij, A.G. 1951. *Etymological dictionary of the Russian language*. New York.
Šanskij, N.M. 1963–82. *Etimologičeskij slovar' russkogo jazyka*, 8 vols. Moscow.
Vasmer, M. 1953–8. *Russisches etymologisches Wörterbuch*. Heidelberg. (Russ. trans. and annotation by O.N. Trubačev. Moscow 1964–73.)

Journals
Russian Language Journal.
Russian Linguistics.
Russistik
⇒ **Slavic**

Rwanda ⇒ Bantu

Ryukyu ⇒ Japanese

S

Sabir

The term, from Provençal *saber* ('to know'), designates a trade language that developed on the western coast of the Mediterranean and was based mostly on Provençal (⇒ **Occitan**) mixed with elements from **Spanish**, **Portuguese**, and **Greek**. (⇒ *also* **lingua franca**)

Sahaptian ⇒ Penutian

Saharan

Group of six languages in Nigeria and Chad, grouped by A.N. Tucker and M.A. Bryan as 'East Saharan' and considered by Greenberg (1963) to be a branch of the **Nilo-Saharan** languages. Largest language is Kanuri in northern Nigeria (over 4 million speakers).

Characteristics: **tonal languages**, tone often has grammatical functions. Relatively complex case system, verb agreement. Morphological type: **inflectional**. Word order: SOV; postpositions.

References
Greenberg, J.H. 1963. *The languages of Africa.* Bloomington, IN. (2nd edn 1966.)
Hutchinson, J.P. 1981. *The Kanuri language: a reference grammar.* Madison, WI.
Tucker, A.N. and M. Bryan. 1956. *The non-Bantu languages of north-eastern Africa. (Handbook of African languages, 3).* Oxford.
⇒ **African languages, Nilo-Saharan**

Salish ⇒ Salishan

Salishan

Language family in western North America with approx. thirty languages; the largest languages are Salish and Okanagan in Canada (with about 2,000 speakers each).

Characteristics: extremely rich consonantal system (often eight points of articulation and five manners of articulation), including glottalized consonants and pharyngeals; in contrast, a very simple vowel system (typically three vowels + **schwa** in unstressed syllables). Noun–verb distinction only weakly evident. A sentence often consists of several smaller predications (example: *A bear ate a rabbit* is made into three predications: *x ate y, x is a bear, y is a rabbit*). **Agents** are marked as to whether or not they have control of the action. **Polysynthesis**, highly developed nominal classification (⇒ **noun class**). Typologically similar to the neighboring **Wakashan** languages.

References
Kinkade, M.D. 1975. The lexical domain of anatomy in Columbian Salish. In M. Kinkade *et al.* (eds), *Linguistics and anthropology in honor of C.F. Voegelin.* Lisse. 423–43.
Kuipers, A.H. 1967. *The Squamish language: grammar, texts, dictionary.* The Hague.
—— 1974. *The Shuswap language.* The Hague.
Newman, S. 1976. Salish and Bella Coola prefixes. *IJAL* 42.228–42.
Thompson, L.C. 1979. Salishan and the Northwest. In L. Campbell and M. Mithun (eds), *The languages of native America: historical and comparative assessment.* Austin, TX. 692–765.

Bibliography
Mattina, A. 1989. Interior Salish post-Vogt: a report and bibliography. *IJAL* 55.85–94.
⇒ **North and Central American languages**

Samoan ⇒ Malayo-Polynesian

Samoyedic ⇒ Uralic

San ⇒ Khoisan

Sandawe ⇒ Khoisan

sandhi [Old Indic *saṁ-dhi-* 'putting together']

Term taken from Old Indic grammar (⇒ **Sanskrit**) for the merging of two words or word forms and the resulting systematic phonological changes. Internal sandhi involves two morphemes within a word; external sandhi takes place between two consecutive words. An example of the latter is the variation of the indefinite article in English: *a* with a following consonant and *an* before a vowel (*a book* vs *an egg*).

References
Allen, W.S. 1962. *Sandhi: the theoretical, phonetic and historical basis of wordjunction in Sanskrit.* The Hague.
Napoli, D.J. and M. Nespor. 1979. The syntax of word-initial consonant gemination in Italian. *Lg* 55.812–41.
Vogel, I. 1986. External sandhi rules operating between sentences. In H. Andersen and J. Gvozdanović (eds), *Sandhi phenomena in the languages of Europe.* Dordrecht. 55–64.
⇒ **phonotactics**

414   **Sango**

Sango ⇒ Adamawa-Ubangi

Sanskrit [Skt *saṁskṛtá-* 'put together; well-formed, refined, correct']

Term for various forms of Old **Indo-Aryan**. The oldest form is the language of the Vedas (ritual texts originating before 1000 BC but written down much later), followed by the language of speculative writings such as Brāhmaṇas and theoretical works like the grammar of Pāṇini. The language of the two great epics, the *Mahābhārata* and *Rāmāyaṇa*, dates to the second and first centuries BC. The term Classical Sanskrit is used to denote the language still used today for the language of priests and scholars in India; especially important is the Devanāgarī script developed from the Brāhmi script. In some usage, only the classical language is called Sanskrit, the term Vedic being used for the older form, as this differs in many aspects (e.g. more complex morphology) from the classical language.

Characteristics: rich morphology (for nominals eight cases, three numbers, three genders; for verbs various tenses, moods, and voices); especially in Classical Sanskrit, numerous word compounds. Word order: SOV.

References

General
Burrow, T. 1955. *The Sanskrit language*. London.
Goldmann, R. and S. Sutherland. 1986. *Devarāṇipraveśikā*. San Francisco, CA.
Staal, J.F. 1967. *Word order in Sanskrit and universal grammar*. Dordrecht.
—— (ed.) 1972. *A reader on the Sanskrit grammarians*. Cambridge, MA.
Thumb, A., H. Hirt, and R. Hauschild. 1958–9. *Handbuch des Sanskrit*. Heidelberg.
Wackernagel, J. and A. Debrunner. 1896–1954. *Altindische Grammatik*, 3 vols. (Reprints: vol. I 1978; vol. II,1 1985; vol. II, 2 1987; vol. 3 1975.) Göttingen.
Whitney, W.D. 1896. *Sanskrit grammar, including both the classical language and the older dialects of Veda and Brahmana*. (5th edn 1924.) Leipzig/London. (Reprint Delhi, 1983.)

Vedic
Klein, J.S. 1985. *Toward a discourse grammar of the Rigveda*, 2 vols. Heidelberg.
MacDonell, A.A. 1910. *Vedic grammar*. Strasburg.
—— 1916. *Vedic grammar for students*. Oxford. (Last reprint Delhi, 1990.)
Renou, L. 1952. *Grammaire de la langue védique*. Paris.

Classical Sanskrit
Aklujkar, A. 1991. *An easy introduction to an enchanting language*, 3 vols. with cassettes. University of British Columbia.
Egenes, T. 1989. *Introduction to Sanskrit*, 2 vols. San Diego, CA.

MacDonell, A.A. 1927. *A Sanskrit grammar for students*, 3rd edn. Oxford. (Reprint Delhi, 1987.)
Renou, L. 1968. *Grammaire sanscrite*, 2 vols. Paris. (2nd rev. edn 1984.)

Dictionaries
Apte, V.S. 1959. *Sanskrit–English dictionary*, rev. ed. Poona.
An encyclopedic dictionary of Sanskrit on historical principles. 1979– . Ed. A.M. Ghatage *et al.* Vol. 4, 3 1992–3. Poona.
Böhtlingk, O. von and R. Roth. 1855–75. *Sanskrit Wörterbuch*, 7 vols. (Reprint 1966.) St. Petersburg.
Grassmann, H. 1976. *Wörterbuch zum Rigveda*, 5th repr. Wiesbaden.
Monier-Williams, M. 1899. *A Sanskrit–English dictionary*, new edn, enlarged and improved with the collaboration of E. Leumann, C. Cappeller *et al.* Oxford. (Last reprint Delhi, 1990.)
Schlerath, B. 1980. *Sanskrit vocabulary, arranged according to word-families with meanings in English, German and Spanish*. Leiden.

Etymological dictionaries
Mayrhofer, M. 1956–80. *Kurzgefaßtes etymologisches Wörterbuch des Altindischen/Concise etymological Sanskrit dictionary*. 4 vols. Heidelberg.
—— 1986–. *Etymologisches Wörterbuch des Altindoarischen*. Vol. III. 1995. Heidelberg.

Bibliographies
Dandekar, R.N. 1946–73. *Vedic bibliography*, 3 vols. Bombay and Poona.
Renou, L. 1931. *Bibliographie védique*. Paris.
⇒ **Indo-Aryan**

Santali ⇒ Munda

Sapir–Whorf hypothesis (*also* linguistic determinism, linguistic relativity)

Hypothesis developed by B.L. Whorf (1897–1941) and based on the linguistic approach of his teacher, E. Sapir (1884–1939), which, in its strongest form claims that a language determines the thought and perception of its speakers. Whorf himself called this view the 'linguistic relativity principle.' In other words, just as time, space, and mass (according to Einstein) can be defined only in terms of a system of relationships, human knowledge similarly arises only in relation to the semantic and structural possibilities of natural languages. Through his work with Native American languages, whose vocabularies and grammatical structures deviate considerably from the regularities of Indo-European languages, Whorf came to the conclusion that 'people who use languages with very different grammars are led by these grammars to typically different observations and different values for outwardly similar observations' (Whorf 1956: 20). Whorf's main interest at the time was the **Hopi** language and culture. He worked especially with the linguistic channels for space–time conceptualization in Hopi, with plural formation and peculiarities of counting, and from these observations derived the hypothesis that Hopi has no physical concept of time. The Sapir–Whorf hypothesis stands in accord with von Humboldt's theory of a 'world view' of languages, as is clearly seen in the title of his work on the Kawi languages of Java: *On language: the diversity of human language-structure and its influence on the mental development of mankind*. However, Sapir and Whorf make no explicit reference either to von Humboldt or to contemporary parallel views. The continuing discussion of the function of language in cognitive processes tends increasingly towards assuming a reciprocal relationship between language and thought. For refutation of the strong form of this hypothesis, see Berlin, Berlin and Kay (1969).

References
Berlin, B., E.A. Berlin, and P. Kay. 1969. *Basic color terms: their universality and evolution.* Berkeley, CA.
Gipper, H. 1972. *Gibt es ein sprachliches Relativitätsprinzip? Untersuchungen zur Sapir–Whorf-Hypothese.* Frankfurt.
Grace, G.W. 1987. *The linguistic construction of reality.* London.
Humboldt, W. von. 1836–9. *Über die Kawi-Sprache auf der Insel Java, nebst einer Einleitung über die Verschiedenheit des menschlichen Sprachbaues und ihren Einfluß auf die geistige Entwicklung des Menschengeschlechts,* 3 vols. Berlin. (*On language: the diversity of human language structure and its influence on the mental development of mankind,* trans. P. Heath. New York, 1988.)
Lucy, J.A. 1992. *Language diversity and thought: a reformulation of the linguistic relativity hypothesis.* Cambridge.
Miller, R.L. 1968. *The linguistic relativity principle and Humboldtian ethnolinguistics: a history and appraisal.* The Hague.
Penn, J.M. 1972. *Linguistic relativity versus innate ideas: the origins of the Sapir–Whorf hypothesis in German thought.* The Hague.
Sapir, E. 1921. *Language.* New York.
—— 1931. Conceptual categories in primitive languages. *Science* 74.578.
Steinfatt, T.M. 1989. Linguistic relativity: toward a broader view. In S. Ting-Toomey and F. Korzenny (eds), *Language, communication and culture: current directions.* London. 35–75.
Werlen, I. 1989. *Sprache, Mensch und Welt: Geschichte und Bedeutung des Prinzips der sprachlichen Relativität.* Darmstadt.
Whorf, B.L. 1946. The Hopi language, Toreva dialect. In H. Hoijer (ed.), *Linguistic structures of native America.* New York. 158–83.
—— 1952. *Collected papers on metalinguistics.* Washington, DC.
—— 1956. *Language, thought and reality: selected writings of Benjamin Lee Whorf,* ed. J.B. Carroll. Cambridge, MA.
⇒ **Hopi**

Sardinian

Sardinian is the most archaic and independent of the **Romance languages** and fits in neither the West Romance nor the East Romance groups. In large parts of Sardinia, **Italian** has replaced Sardinian as the main language of literature and commerce. Attempts at reviving Sardinian in the twentieth century have been hampered by the large number of dialects. Spoken by approx. 1 million speakers, Sardinian is divided into two main dialect areas (with numerous subdialects): Central Sardinian (Logudorese, Nuorese) and South Sardinian (Campidanese).

References
Blasco Ferrer, E. 1984. *Storia linguistica della Sardegna.* Tübingen.
—— 1986. *La lingua sarda contemporanea: grammatica del logudorese e del campidanese.* Cagliari.
Holtus, G., M. Metzeltin, and C. Schmitt (eds) 1988. *Lexikon der romanistischen Linguistik.* Tübingen. Vol. 4, 836–935.
Jones, M. 1993. *Sardinian syntax.* London.
Pittau, M. 1972. *Grammatica del sardo-nuorese.* Bologna.
—— 1991. *Grammatica della lingua sarda: varietà logudorese.* Sassari.
Wagner, M.L. 1951. *La lingua sarda.* Bern.

Etymological dictionary
Wagner, M.L. 1960–4. *Dizionario etimologico Sardo,* 3 vols. Heidelberg.

satellite phoneme [Lat. *satelles* 'escort']

Term for **phonemes** that do not form the **nucleus** of a given **syllable.**

References
⇒ **phonology**

Savannah Bantu ⇒ Bantu

scalar particle

Subcategory of **particles** that in English include such words as *only, also, already, still.* Scalar particles indicate alternative degrees that are implicit either from the focus-backgrounding structure (⇒ **topic vs comment**) or the **context.** Thus in the sentence *Only Jacob is coming, only* expresses the exclusion of other background people known from the context. Such particles can also often refer to scalar degrees, such as *Even Jacob is coming,* which focuses on *Jacob* as being particularly high on the scale in question.

Statements modified by scalar particles are generally **presuppositions** or cases of conventional **implicature** (see Karttunen & Peters, 1979).

References
Altmann, H. 1976. *Die Gradpartikeln im Deutschen.* Tübingen.
Fraser, B. 1971. An analysis of *even* in English. In Fillmore, C.J. and D.T. Langendoen (eds), *Studies in linguistic semantics.* New York. 150–78.
Horn, L. 1969. A presuppositional analysis of *only* and *even.* In *Chicago Linguistic Society* 5.98–107.
Jacobs, J. 1983. *Focus und Skalen.* Tübingen.
Karttunen, L. and S. Peters. 1979. Conventional implicatures. In C. Oh and D. Dinneen (eds), *Syntax and semantics,* vol. 11: *Presuppositions.* New York. 1–56.
König, E. 1981. The meaning of scalar particles in German. In Eickmeyer, H.-J. and H. Rieser (eds), *Words, worlds, and contexts.* Berlin.
Taglicht, J. 1984. *Message and emphasis: on focus and scope in English.* London.
⇒ **particle**

scalar verb ⇒ **vectorial vs scalar verbs**

scale and category linguistics ⇒ **systemic linguistics**

scale and category model ⇒ **systemic linguistics**

Scandinavian (*also* Nordic, North Germanic)

Collective term for the **Germanic** languages **Danish**, **Norwegian**, **Swedish**, **Icelandic**, and **Faroese**.

References
Haugen, E. 1976. *The Scandinavian languages: an introduction to their history.* London.
—— 1982. *Scandinavian language structures: a comparative historical survey.* Tübingen.
Ureland, P.S. and I. Clarkson (eds) 1984. *Scandinavian language contacts.* Cambridge.

schema

Generalized knowledge about the sequence of events in particular sociocultural contexts, for example, going to a restaurant, purchasing a ticket, borrowing a book. Such structured everyday knowledge forms an essential basis for human **language comprehension** since it simplifies the interpretation of incomplete or ambiguous information. In this way the processing of stories is directed according to conventionalized knowledge about how stories are usually told, which sequences of occurrences are permissible and logical. Schema information is stored in one's long-term **memory** and can be quickly recalled in the course of processing information. (⇒ **script**)

References
Bartlett, F.C. 1932. *Remembering: a study in experimental and social psychology.* Cambridge.

Minsky, M. 1975. A framework for representing knowledge. In P.H. Winston (ed.), *The psychology of computer vision.* New York. 211–77.
Rumelhart, D.H. 1975. *Introduction to human information processing.* New York.
⇒ **script**

schema-based text comprehension

Numerous approaches of **artificial intelligence** to text comprehension (following work by the English psychologist F.C. Bartlett) proceed from the assumption that processes of text comprehension are based primarily on projecting pre-knowledge that exists in the form of schemas onto the contents in the text that is currently being worked on. This means that text construction is in the main a process of reconstruction (⇒ **frames**, **scripts**).

References
Bartlett, F.C. 1932. *Remembering: a study in experimental and social psychology.* Cambridge.
⇒ **frames**, **scripts**

school grammar (*also* traditional grammar)

A type of grammar first developed in Europe in the eighteenth century, based on Aristotelian logic and ancient Greek and Latin grammars, often as an aid to learning these languages and interpreting classical texts. Its general characteristics are: (a) classification of data into formal categories, e.g. **sentence type**, **part of speech** (since these categories are taken from Greek and Latin, they often cannot be directly transferred onto other languages); (b) classification based on logical, semantic, syntactic, and extralinguistic criteria, with little attention paid to functional aspects of communication; (c) primarily a prescriptive attitude (⇒ **prescriptive grammar**) i.e. concerned with judgments such as 'correct,' 'incorrect,' 'affected,' 'awkward'; (d) usually written rather than spoken language as the subject; (e) grammatical explanations often confusing synchronic and diachronic aspects – a point especially criticized from a structuralist perspective (⇒ **synchrony vs diachrony**, **structuralism**); (f) rules that are not explicit or exhaustive; they appeal to the reader's intuition.

Notwithstanding these methodological restrictions, there is no doubt that all modern linguistic approaches are based on data and results of school grammar or are attempts at systematization of what these grammars presented; see terms such as **hierarchy**, **universals**, **parts of speech**. An example of this type of grammar in English is Curme (1925).

Reference
Curme, G.O. 1925. *English grammar.* New York.

schwa (*also* neutral vowel)

From Hebrew *šəwa*, diacritical vowel sign for a missing vowel or for the unstressed [ə]. In English, schwa is an unstressed vowel produced with the tongue in its (neutral) resting position, e.g. [pəlayt] *polite*. In **Bulgarian** *gălăb* ['gətəb], the first occurrence of schwa is stressed.

Reference
⇒ **phonetics**

scope

In analogy to **formal logic**, where 'scope' denotes the range governed by **operators** (⇒ **logical connective**, **quantifier**), in linguistics 'scope' denotes the range of semantic reference of **negation**, linguistic quantifiers, and **particles**. Corresponding to 'scope' in logic is the constituent that is modified by quantifiers or particles; cf. the adverb *also* in *Louise was also hungry* (*not just thirsty*) vs *Louise was also hungry* (*not just the others*). The interpretation of scope frequently depends on the placement of sentence stress (⇒ **intonation**).

References
Aoun, J. and Y.A. Li. 1993. *Syntax of scope*. Cambridge, MA.
⇒ **formal logic, negation, quantification**

Scots-Gaelic ⇒ Celtic, Gaelic

scrambling

A term coined by J.R. Ross to describe **transformations** which generate **surface structures** with varying word orders from a basic structure. Scrambling also refers to the relationships between the permuted parts of the sentence (⇒ **permutation**).

References
Grewendorf, G. and W. Sternefeld. 1989. *Scrambling and barriers*. Amsterdam.
Riemsdijk, H. van and N. Corver (eds) 1994. *Studies on scrambling: movement and non-movement approaches to free word order*. Berlin and New York.
Ross, J.R. 1967. Constraints on variables in syntax. Dissertation, MIT, Cambridge, MA. (Repr. as *Infinite Syntax!* Norwood, NJ, 1986.)
⇒ **transformational grammar**

script

1 Schema-based approach of **artificial intelligence** for **knowledge representation**, in particular for machine-aided text comprehension. Knowledge about standardized events, including knowledge about typical participants and subevents, is represented in active data structures (scripts), i.e. data structures provided with procedural elements. Scripts are not formal alternatives to **frames**, but rather an orthogonal organizational scheme.

References
Schank, R. 1982. *Dynamic memory*. Cambridge.
Schank, R. and R. Abelson. 1977. *Scripts, plans, goals and understanding*. Hillsdale, NJ.
Schank, R. and C. Riesbeck. 1981. *Inside computer understanding*. Hillsdale, NJ.
⇒ **frame, story grammar**

2 ⇒ **writing**

second language acquisition

Term used with varying meanings: (a) the acquisition of a (first) foreign language; (b) the (essentially) non-directed acquisition of a foreign language in an environment in which that language is used as a trade language; (c) in an even narrower sense, the (essentially) non-directed acquisition of a second language before the acquisition of the first language has been completed.

Second language acquisition research concentrates on the acquisition of a foreign language, in a natural environment as opposed to acquisition directed through classroom instruction (cf. Krashen's distinction between 'language acquisition' and 'language learning'). The following gave the main questions of interest: To what extent does second language acquisition follow an innate system which is independent of the acquisition of one's native (first) language? How great is the similarity between this process of acquisition and that of first language? What role do positive and negative transfer from the native language (and from another earlier-acquired language) play in the acquisition of a second language and the production of errors? Can regularities in second language acquisition help explain the phenomena of **language change** and **language contact** (⇒ **pidgins, creoles**)?

Behaviorist theories (⇒ **behaviorism**) explain second language acquisition according to general laws of behavior modification. Nativistic theories (⇒ **nativism**) tend to assume a language-specific disposition towards learning which, in generative language theory (⇒ **generative grammar**), has been developed into the concept of **universal grammar**. According to the universal grammar hypothesis, the language learner possesses an innate 'knowledge' of how language functions and only needs to set the 'parameters' that are right for the input data (i.e. for the second language in its given environment). The empirical evidence for this theory, according to many researchers in this field, can be explained with little speculation. For this reason, research has recently focused more directly on the perceivable manifestations, cognitive analyzability, and communicative relevance of the linguistic features to be learned as well as on the psychological implications of the linguistic process itself (perception, analysis, storage and recall).

The study of natural second language acquisition is of great significance to foreign-language education, since foreign-language instruction can be most successful only if it is modeled after the principles of natural-language acquisition.

References

Arnaud, P.J.L. and H. Bejoint, (eds) 1992. *Vocabulary and applied linguistics*. Basingstoke.

Bailey, C., M. Long, and S. Peck (eds) 1983. *Second language acquisition studies*. Rowley, MA.

Beebe, L.M. (ed.) 1988. *Issues in second language acquisition: multiple perspectives*. New York.

Chaudron, C. 1988. *Second language classrooms: research on teaching and learning*. Cambridge.

Cook, V. 1993. *Linguistics and second language acquisition*. Basingstoke.

Dechert, H.W. and M. Raupach. 1989. *Transfer in language production*. Hove.

Dulay, H., M. Burt, and S. Krashen. 1982. *Language two*. New York.

Ellis, Rod. 1985. *Understanding second language acquisition*. Oxford.

—— 1991. *Second language acquisition and language pedagogy*. Clevedon.

—— 1994. *The study of second language acquisition*. Oxford.

Eubank, L. 1991. *Point counterpoint: universal grammar in the second language*. Amsterdam and Philadelphia.

Flynn, S. and W. O'Neil (eds) 1988. *Linguistic theory in second language acquisition*. Dordrecht.

Freed, B.F. (ed.) 1991. *Foreign language acquisition research and the classroom*. Lexington, MA.

Gass, S. *et al.* (eds) 1989. *Variation in second language acquisition*, vol. I: *Discourse and pragmatics*. Clevedon.

Gass, S. and L. Selinker. 1992. *Language transfer in language learning*, rev. edn. Amsterdam and Philadelphia.

Gass, S. and J. Schachter (eds) 1990. *Linguistic perspectives on second language acquisition*. Cambridge.

Harley, B. *et al.* 1990. *The development of second language proficiency*. Cambridge.

Hatch, E. (ed.) 1978. *Second language acquisition*. Rowley, MA.

House, J. and S. Blum-Kulka (eds) 1986. *Interlingual and intercultural communication: discourse and cognition in translation and second language acquisition*. Tübingen.

Huebner, T. and C.A. Ferguson (eds) 1991. *Cross-currents in second language acquisition and linguistic theories*. Amsterdam and Philadelphia.

James, A.R. 1988. *The acquisition of a second language phonology*. Tübingen.

Klein, W. 1986. *Second language acquisition*. Cambridge.

Krashen, S. 1981. *Second language acquisition and second language learning*. Oxford.

—— 1982. *Principles and practice in second language acquisition*. New York.

—— 1985. *The input hypothesis: issues and implications*. London.

Labarca, A. and L. Bailey. 1989. *Issues in L2: theory as practice and practice as theory*. Hove.

Larsen-Freeman, D. and M.H. Long. 1991. *An introduction to second language acquisition research*. London.

McLaughlin, B. 1987. *Theories of second language learning*. London.

Odlin, T. 1989. *Language transfer*. Cambridge.

Rutherford, W.E. 1987. *Language universals and second language acquisition*, 2nd edn. Amsterdam and Philadelphia.

Slobin, D. (ed.) 1985. *The cross-linguistic study of language acquisition*. Hillsdale, NJ.

Smith, M.S. 1994. *Second language learning: theoretical foundations*. London.

Van Patten, B. and J.F. Lee. 1990. *Second language acquisition – foreign language learning. Perspectives on research and practice*. Clevedon.

White, L. 1989. *Universal grammar and second language acquisition*. Amsterdam and Philadelphia.

Journals
Second Language Research.
Studies in Second Language Acquisition.
⇒ **applied linguistics**, **interlanguage**, **language acquisition**, **universals**.

second language learning ⇒ second language acquisition

second signaling system

I.P. Pavlov's term for human language in contrast to **animal communication** as the 'first signaling system.' The characteristic function of the second signaling system is the formation of concepts by generalizing of immediate sensory impressions, as represented in the first signaling system. (⇒ *also* **semantic generalization**)

Reference
Pavlov, I.P. 1954. *Essays on the patho-physiology of the higher nervous activity*. Moscow.

second sound shift ⇒ Old High German consonant shift

secondary articulation

Secondary articulation is said to occur when, during the **articulation** of a **speech sound**, the airstream must bypass a second obstruction in the resonance chamber. Types of secondary articulation are as follows: (a) *Labialization*: an occlusion, approaching or rounding of the lips, e.g. [ʃ] vs [ʃ] in Engl. [ʃut] *shoot*; [ʒ] vs [ʒ] in

Abkhazi-Adyge [wӡa] 'ten'; [k̠p] vs [k] and [p] in the **Bantu** language Lingala [k̠paŋga] 'manioc root.' (b) *Palatalization*: the front of the tongue approaching the front of the hard palate, e.g. [m̡] vs [m] in **Russian** [t̡at̡] 'knead,' [m̡at] 'mother'; [ø:] vs [o:] in **German** ['bø:gn̩] 'bows.' (c) *Velarization*: the back of the tongue approaching the back part of the velum, e.g. [ɫ] vs [l̡] in Russ. [ɫuk] 'onion' vs [l̡uk] 'hatch.' (d) *Pharyngealization*: the root of the tongue approaching the back wall of the throat, e.g. [sˁ] vs [s] in Egyptian **Arabic** [sˁe:f] 'summer' vs [se:f] 'sword.' (⇒ *also* **articulatory phonetics**)

References
⇒ **phonetics**

secondary motivation ⇒ **arbitrariness**

secret language
System of language artificially constructed to keep communication secret (e.g. in political resistance movements), to separate a group of secret language speakers from the society at large, or to express solidarity within such a group. The languages of schoolchildren (e.g. pig latin) in which consonants are switched or syllables doubled according to a specific system are types of secret languages.

References
Leslau, W. 1969. *Ethiopian argots*. The Hague.
Opie, I. and P. Opie. 1947. *The lore and language of schoolchildren*. Oxford.

SEE (Seeing Essential English) ⇒ **sign language**

segment [Lat. *segmentum* 'a piece removed by cutting']
A result of linguistic analysis that attempts to isolate minimal linguistic units, such as **phones**, **morphs**, **syllables**, from a language or speech continuum.

segmental feature
In **American structuralism**, such phonological features that can be broken down into further segments, that is, can be individually extracted from a linear series of sounds in the context of speech. Segmentability is a purely theoretical postulate, since speech is realized only as a continuum of sound without natural breaks, so that individual elements cannot be isolated in their articulation or acoustics (⇒ **co-articulation**). For contrast, see the non-segmentable **suprasegmental features**.

References
⇒ **phonology**

segmentation
Elementary analytical process of taxonomic **structuralism** for isolating the smallest linguistic elements, such as **phones**, **morphs**, or **syllables**, among others. The criterion of segmentation is the substitutability of the isolated element with another such element of the same class, e.g. [k] in *cap* [kaep] can be isolated through segmentation and replaced by [g, l, m, n, r, s, t] *gap, lap, map, nap, rap, sap, tap*. Through the complementary process of **classification**, one arrives at a class of consonants that can occur word-initially in English. (⇒ *also* **paradigmatic vs syntagmatic relationship**, **sound**[2])

References
⇒ **operational procedures, phonology, structuralism**

selection ⇒ **collocation**

selectional feature
Class of context-independent syntactic features (i.e. inherent features) of nouns (Chomsky 1965), or semantic features of whole noun phrases (McCawley 1968) that mark the **selection restrictions** between nouns or noun phrases and verbs. These selectional features are formulated as contextual indicators of the verbs. In this analysis, the two-place verb *think* (in its standard reading) can only be used with a [+human] subject and a **prepositional phrase**.

References
Chomsky, N. 1965. *Aspects of the theory of syntax*. Cambridge, MA.
McCawley, J.D. 1968. The role of semantics in a Grammar. In E. Bach and R. Harms (eds), *Universals in linguistic theory*. New York. 125–204.
⇒ **selection restriction, subcategorization**

selection restriction
In Chomsky's grammar model the (non-categorial) semantic–syntactic restrictions on **compatibility** between lexical elements which prevent the derivation of agrammatical sentences like *The stone thinks*. Much debate has centered on the question of whether selection restrictions are of a syntactic or a semantic nature. The violation of selection restrictions often underlies creativity in language and the poetic use of language. (⇒ *also* **inherent semantic relation, metaphor**)

References
Chomsky, N. 1965. *Aspects of the theory of syntax*. Cambridge, MA.

McCawley, J.D. 1968a. Lexical insertion in a transformational grammar without deep structure. *CLS*
4.71–80.
——— 1968b. The role of semantics in a grammar.
In E. Bach and R.T. Harms (eds), *Universals in
linguistic theory*. New York. 124–69.
⇒ **subcategorization**

self-embedded construction

A **phrase structure grammar** construction.
Two phrases S_1 and S_2 form a self-embedded
construction if (a) S_1 is inserted into S_2 so that
elements of S_2 are to the right and the left of S_1,
and (b) S_1 and S_2 are the same type of phrases
(rather than encapsulated constructions). For
example, the phrase (S_1) *who said he was a
tight-rope walker* is embedded in the sentence
(S_2) *She talked to Philip, who admired the man
who said he was a tight-rope walker very
much.*

Reference
Chomsky, N. 1965. *Aspects of the theory of syntax.*
Cambridge, MA.

semanteme [Grk *sēma* 'sign']

Term proposed by A. Noreen that has various
usages in **structural semantics**. It is generally
synonymous with **lexeme** in the sense of 'basic
semantic unit' of the **lexicon**.

Reference
Noreen, A. 1923. *Einführung in die wissenschaftliche
Betrachtung der Sprache*. Halle. .

semantic antinomy [Grk *antinomía* 'conflict of laws'] (*also* semantic paradox)

Contradictory statement(s) whose truth value
cannot be determined. Compare, for example,
the semantic antinomy from classical times
about the (lying) Cretan, who maintained: *All
Cretans are liars*. This statement is true only
when it is false. Such a logical contradiction
can be resolved through the distinction of
different linguistic levels (⇒ **object language
vs metalanguage**) which both occur in this
example; the assertion of the Cretan that *All
Cretans are liars* creates an impermissible
statement about one's self, which can only be
resolved in the object language assertion *All
Cretans are liars* and in the metalinguistic
judgment of this assertion: namely, that it is not
true. (⇒ *also* **formal logic**, **type theory**)

References
Brendel, E. 1992. *Die Wahrheit über den Lügner.*
Berlin and New York.
Kripke, S. 1975. Outline of a theory of truth. *JP*
72.690–716.

Levi, D.S. 1988. The liar parody. *Philosophy*
63.43–62.
Martin, R. (ed) 1970. *The paradox of the liar.* New
Haven, CT.
Tarski, A. 1956. *Logic, semantics, metamathematics.*
Oxford.

semantic change

Changes in the meaning of linguistic expressions, seen from a historical perspective, where
semantic change refers both to changes in the
relation between linguistic signs and extralinguistic reality and to changes in the relations
between signs (⇒ **semantic relation**). Classifying the different types of semantic change
and ascertaining the cause for its rise and spread
was the main goal of semasiological research
(⇒ **semasiology**); various theories for this can
be found in Paul (1880: ch. 4) and Ullmann
(1957: chs 2, 4). The following aspects are
fundamental to most classifications. (a) In **logic**
or **rhetoric**, regarding the relationship of old
and new meaning, one distinguishes between (i)
semantic narrowing: restriction of the semantic
scope or context in which the word may be
used; e.g. OE *hund* 'dog' > Eng. *hound* 'hunt-
ing breed'; (ii) semantic widening: whereas
semantic narrowing refers to the specialization
of the new as opposed to the older semantic
scope, semantic widening is characterized by
generalization; e.g. OE *dogge* 'particular breed
of dog' > Eng. *dog* 'any kind of dog'; (iii)
metaphor: Gmc *['bitraz] 'biting' (derived
from the verb meaning 'to bite') > *bitter* 'harsh
in taste' (examples from Bloomfield 1933:
426–7) (⇒ **catachresis**). Other forms of
semantic transfer are **hyperbole**, **litotes**,
metonymy, and **synecdoche**, among others. In
regard to the causes of semantic change, one
distinguishes between (b) changes in the extralinguistic reality, i.e. changes in states of affairs
or knowledge about states of affairs as is
reflected in expressions like *fee* ('cattle') or
their objects of reference (in this case, 'cattle'
as a commodity); (c) changes in social value: (i)
semantic degeneration, as in Lat. *potio* 'drink'
> Fr. *poison* 'poison'; or (ii) semantic elevation,
as in *marshal* (originally 'keeper of the horses')
(⇒ **euphemism**). (d) Semantic borrowing
through **language contact**: semantic change
occurs through the influence of foreign languages (⇒ **foreign vs second language**), **jargon**, **sociolects**, or **dialects**, in that a lexeme in
a particular language adopts aspects of the
meaning of a lexeme in the other (influencing)
language, as in *write* (originally 'to scratch'),
influenced by Lat. *scribere* (⇒ **loan word**,
borrowed meaning). (e) Intralinguistic causes:
individual examples indicate that there is occa-

sionally a connection between semantic change and a phonetic or grammatical change. To be sure, it is often uncertain whether the phonetic or grammatical change was in fact the precursor to semantic change (⇒ also **folk etymology**). On the other hand, studies in **lexical fields** (see Trier 1931) have shown that within a specific lexical field every change of a lexeme is systematically connected with changes in related ('neighboring') lexemes.

References
Anttila, R. 1972. *An introduction to historical and comparative linguistics*. New York. (2nd rev. edn 1989.)
Bloomfield, L. 1933. *Language*. Chicago, IL. (Repr. 1984.)
Fisiak, J. (ed.). 1985. *Historical semantics – historical word-formation*. Berlin.
Meillet, A. 1921. *Linguistique historique et linguistique générale*. Paris.
Paul, H. 1880. *Prinzipien der Sprachgeschichte*. Tübingen. (9th edn 1975.)
Stern, G. 1931. *Meaning and change of meaning*. Bloomington, IN.
Sweetser, E. 1990. *From etymology to pragmatics*. Cambridge.
Traugott, E.C. 1985. On regularity in semantic change. *Journal of Literary Semantics* 14.155–73.
Trier, J. 1931. *Der deutsche Wortschatz im Sinnbezirk des Verstandes: die Geschichte eines sprachlichen Feldes*, vol. I: *Von den Anfängen bis zum Beginn des 13. Jahrhunderts*. Heidelberg.
Ullmann, S. 1957. *The principles of semantics*. Oxford.
Voyles, J.B. 1973. Accounting for semantic change. *Lingua* 31.95–124.
⇒ **componential analysis**, **historical linguistics**, **language change**, **semantics**.

semantic differential

A process developed by Osgood *et al.* (1957) that attempts to measure the connotative (affective) semantic components of linguistic expressions. This test is administered by presenting subjects with a list of antonymous pairs of related scalar adjectives (e.g. *good – bad*, *happy – sad*). The subjects are asked to differentiate the meaning of a given word by placing it on an associative 'adjective scale.' In one experiment it turned out that several pairs of adjectives correlated indirectly with one another, that is, their scales turned out to be the same for the given word from subject to subject. From the correlations, Osgood derived three 'factors of semantic space' according to which every word can be semantically localized, namely *potency* (strong/weak, hard/soft, etc.), *activity* (active/passive, excitable/quiet, etc.), and *evaluation* (sweet/sour, pretty/ugly, etc.). Osgood's method for measuring meaning

through a factorial analysis has run up against various criticisms, first because of its basically subjective concept of meaning (⇒ **connotation**) and second because of doubts about the principles used in selecting the predetermined adjective scales (Carroll 1964; Weinreich 1958). Its application ranges from linguistic texts to market and opinion studies.

References
Carroll, J.B. 1964. *Language and thought*. Englewood Cliffs, NJ.
Osgood, C.E., G.J. Suci, and P.H. Tannenbaum. 1957. *The measurement of meaning*. Urbana, IL.
Snaider, J. and C.E. Osgood. 1969. *Semantic differential technique: A source-book*. Chicago, IL.
Weinreich, U. 1958. Travels through semantic space. *Word* 14.346–66.
⇒ **meaning, mediation**

semantic entailment ⇒ implication

semantic feature

In **structural semantics** a class of theoretical constructs developed in analogy to the **distinctive features** of **phonology** which are considered to be the smallest semantic units for the description of linguistic expressions and their **semantic relations**, e.g. *walk* [+motion, +on ground, +upright] as opposed to *stroll*, which is further characterized by [+slowly, +portly]. Semantic features are generally expressions found in ordinary spoken language but treated as metalinguistic terms and are (as a rule) placed in brackets (⇒ **componential analysis** for the derivation of semantic features). The theoretical status of semantic features is disputed. They do not directly represent physical characteristics of the real world, but reflect the psychological conditions according to which humans interpret their environment via language. Consider the classic example *the deceased* vs *the corpse*: both expressions denote the same state of affairs/condition in the real world, but in language there is a semantic differentiation, as evidenced by the difference in **I was a good friend of the corpse* vs *I was a good friend of the deceased*. It is also noteworthy that – in contrast to the distinctive features of phonology – there is no universally recognized class of semantic features that can be used in the semantic description of all languages. (⇒ *also* **plereme**, **semantics**, **seme**).

References
Lipka, L. 1979. Semantic components of English nouns and verbs and their justification. *Angol Filológiai Tanulmányok* 12.187–202.
—— 1985. Inferential features in historical

semantics. In J. Fisiak (ed.), *Historical semantics*. Berlin. 339–54.
⇒ **componential analysis**, **semantics**

semantic feature analysis ⇒ componential analysis

semantic field ⇒ lexical field

semantic field theory ⇒ lexical field theory

semantic generalization

In **psycholinguistics**, the experimentally proved mechanism according to which certain reactions of subjects which were conditioned to particular objects were also elicited by presenting the subjects with the linguistic expressions that denote these objects. The same is observed when words that are similar in sound or sense are presented to subjects: a reaction conditioned to a key word is also triggered when synonymous expressions or expressions that are similar in meaning are named.

Reference
Feather, B.W. 1965. Semantic generalization of classical conditioned responses: a review. *PsyB* 63.425–41.

semantic implication ⇒ implication

semantic network

Frequently used form of **knowledge representation** that uses a graph-like notation system. Originally developed to model associative memory, semantic networks have evolved into general knowledge representation schemes. Semantic networks represent by using a hierarchy of concepts organized by a primitive relation such as 'IS A' or 'PART OF.' Further two-place relations (roles) are defined by using these. The main task in developing semantic networks consists in establishing the inventory of semantic relations between concepts. Simple semantic networks are formally a restricted variant of **predicate logic**. Current developments in knowledge representation, such as KL-ONE, are based on semantic networks.

References
Brachman, M. and J. Schmolze. 1985. An overview of the KL-ONE knowledge representation system. *CS* 9.171–216.
Findler, N.V. (ed.) 1979. *Associative networks*. New York.
Quillian, M.R. 1968. Semantic memory. In M. Minsky (ed.), *Semantic information processing*. Cambridge, MA. 227–70.
Schank, R. 1975. *Conceptual information processing*. Amsterdam.
Sowa, J. 1984. *Conceptual structures: information processing in mind and machines*. Reading, MA.

semantic paradox ⇒ semantic antinomy

semantic paraphasia ⇒ paraphasia

semantic pathology

Disruption in the balance of a synchronous language system through **polysemy** and **homonymy**, especially where ambiguous expressions in similar contexts lead to communicative misunderstandings. (⇒ *also* **disambiguation**, **homonym conflict**)

semantic primitive (*also* primitive predicate, atomic concept)

First introduced in **generative semantics** to describe **causative verbs**, semantic primitives are the smallest (possibly universal) basic terms whose relations (i.e. the semantic restrictions on their use) can be described in terms of **meaning postulates** (e.g. *kill* = make-become-not-alive). The idea of describing the meaning of linguistic expressions by means of semantic primitives has lead to various controversies. (⇒ *also* **lexical decomposition**)

References
⇒ **generative semantics**

semantic relation

1 Cover term for all relations that exist between the meanings of expressions (words, sentences) in natural languages. Such relations of meaning concern either (a) syntagmatic wellformedness, i.e. semantic agreement between the subject and the finite verb, e.g. *The rock is fleeing* (ungrammatical in its literal meaning) (⇒ **compatibility**, **selection restriction**, **inherent semantic relation**) or (b) paradigmatically substitutable classes, e.g. *Chicago is a big town/city* (*town* and *city* are in the semantic relation of **synonymy**). The most important semantic relations are **antonymy**, **hyperonymy**, **hyponymy**, **incompatibility**, **complementarity**, **conversion**, **paraphrase**, and **inference**. The semantic relations of individual expressions to (all) other expressions and, subsequently, the semantic structure of the vocabulary of a whole language can be described with the aid of the logical operations of **equivalence**, **implication**, and **negation**. The descriptive methods and the languages involved in such a description depend upon the particular theory that is used; consider, for example, the use of **semantic features** in the **componential analysis** of **structural semantics** or the introduction of basic expressions (⇒ **semantic primitives**) and **meaning postulates** in the framework of **generative semantics**. An even greater precision and independence from phenomena found in individual languages has

been achieved in more recent approaches that attempt to describe semantic relations within the framework of an **artificial language**, such as **Montague grammar**. (⇒ *also* **intensional logic**)

References
Cruse, D.A. 1986. *Lexical semantics*. Cambridge.
Lipka, L. 1990. *An outline of English lexicology* (2nd edn 1992). Tübingen.
Lutzeier, P.R. 1983. The relevance of semantic relations between words for the notion of lexical field. *TL* 10.147–78.
Lyons, J. 1968. *Introduction to theoretical linguistics*. Cambridge.
——— 1977. *Semantics*, 2 vols. Cambridge.
Schnelle, H. 1974. Meaning constraints. *Synthese* 26.13–37.
Ullmann, S. 1957. *The principles of semantics*, 2nd edn. Oxford. (Orig. 1951.)
⇒ **semantics**

2 ⇒ **case grammar**

semantic role (*also* deep case, semantic relation, **thematic relation**) ⇒ **case grammar**

semantic triangle ⇒ **semiotic triangle**

semantics

Term coined by Bréal (1897) for the subdiscipline of linguistics concerned with the analysis and description of the so-called 'literal' **meaning** of linguistic expressions. Depending on the focus, various aspects of meaning may be prominent: (a) the internal semantic structure of individual linguistic expressions, as described by **componential analysis**, **meaning postulates**, or stereotypes (⇒ **stereotype**^{2}, also **prototype**); (b) the semantic relations between linguistic expressions as in **synonymy, antonymy**; (c) the whole meaning of sentences (⇒ **sentence meaning, principle of compositionality**) as the sum of the meaning of the individual **lexemes** as well as the grammatical relations between them; (d) the relation of linguistic expressions – or their meaning – to extralinguistic reality (⇒ **referential semantics**). All questions under (a)–(d) can be examined both diachronically and synchronically.

One traditional area of semantics is the historical semantics of single words (⇒ **semantic change, etymology**). Under the influence of **structuralism**, semanticists began to focus on the **semantic relations** between words and, thus, on the semantic structure of present-day vocabulary. With the development of **generative grammar**, lexically oriented structuralist semantics was expanded to view problems concerning **sentence semantics**; the rivalry between **interpretive semantics** and **gener-**

ative semantics attests to the controversial state of research of the 1960s.

More recent developments in semantics are characterized by an overlap within various areas of linguistic investigation; this applies both to pragmatic aspects of meaning (⇒ **pragmatics, speech act theory, maxim of conversation, presupposition**) as well as to the descriptive approaches of **formal logic** which attempt to define meaning according to truth conditions (⇒ **predicate logic, intensional logic**). Moving away from this preoccupation with truth values, some semanticists have attempted a direct semantic categorization of situations (see Barwise & Perry 1983), a semantic interpretation based on a mathematical concept of **game theory** (see Saarinen 1979), or a dynamism based on a mathematical concept of **catastrophe theory** (see Wildgen 1982). In the meantime, semantics has become more and more a branch of an interdisciplinary 'cognitive science' (⇒ **language and cognition**).

References
Barwise, J. and J. Perry. 1983. *Situations and attitudes*. Cambridge, MA.
Bendix, E.H. 1966. *Componential analysis of general vocabulary: the semantic structure of a set of verbs in English, Hindi and Japanese*. The Hague.
Burling, R. 1964. Cognition and componential analysis: God's truth or hocuspocus? *AA* 66.20–8.
——— 1965. Yankee kinship terminology: a problem in componential analysis. *AA* 67.129–287.
Chafe, W.L. 1970. *Meaning and the structure of language*. Chicago, IL.
Chierchia, G. and S. McConnell-Ginet. 1990. *Meaning and grammar: an introduction to semantics*. Cambridge, MA.
Coseriu, E. and H. Geckeler (eds) 1981. *Trends in structural semantics*. Tübingen.
Cruse, D. 1986. *Lexical semantics*. Cambridge.
Davidson, D. and G. Harman (eds) 1972. *Semantics of natural languages*. Dordrecht.
Dillon, G. 1977. *Introduction to contemporary linguistic semantics*. Englewood Cliffs, NJ.
Eikmeyer, H.-J. and H. Rieser (eds) 1981. *Words, worlds, and contexts*. Berlin.
Fillmore, C.J. and T.D. Langendoen (eds) 1971. *Studies in linguistic semantics*. New York.
Fisiak, J. (ed.) 1985. *Historical semantics: historical word-formation*. The Hague.
Fodor, J.D. 1977. *Semantics: theories of meaning in generative grammar*. New York.
Goodenough, W. 1956. Componential analysis and the study of meaning. *Lg* 32.195–216.
Gruber, J. 1976. *Lexical structures in syntax and semantics*, 2 vols. Amsterdam.
Higginbotham, J. 1985. On semantics. *LingI* 16.537–93.
Hoffmann, T.R. 1993. *Realms of meaning: an introduction to semantics*. London.
Hüllen, W. and R. Schulze (eds) 1988. *Under-*

standing the lexicon: meaning, sense and world knowledge in lexical semantics. Tübingen.

Katz, J.J. 1972. *Semantic theory*. New York.

Kefer, M. and J. van der Auwera (eds) 1992. *Meaning and grammar*. Berlin and New York.

Landman, F. 1991. *Structures for semantics*. Dordrecht.

Leech, G.N. 1974. *Semantics*. Harmondsworth.

Linsky, L. (ed.) 1952. *Semantics and the philosophy of language*. Chicago, IL.

Lipka, L. 1972. *Semantic structure and word formation: verb–particle constructions in contemporary English*. Munich.

—— 1990. *An outline of English Lexicology* (2nd edn 1992). Tübingen.

Lyons, J. 1977. *Semantics*, 2 vols. Cambridge.

Nida, E. 1975. *Componential analysis of meaning: an introduction to semantic structure*. The Hague.

Saarinen, E. (ed.) 1979. *Game-theoretical semantics: essays on semantics by Hintikka, Carlson, Peacocke, Rantala, and Saarinen*. Dordrecht.

Stamenov, M. (ed.) 1991. *Current advances in semantic theory*. Amsterdam and Philadelphia.

Stechow, A. von and D. Wunderlich (eds) 1991. *Semantics: an international handbook of contemporary research*. Berlin and New York.

Steinberg, D.D. and L.A. Jakobovits (eds) 1971. *Semantics: an interdisciplinary reader in philosophy, linguistics and psychology*. Cambridge, MA.

Ullmann, S. 1957. *The principles of semantics*. Oxford.

Wallace, A.F.C. 1965. The problem of psychological validity of componential analysis. *AA* 67.229–48.

Wierzbicka, A. 1992. *Semantics, culture and cognition*. Oxford.

Wildgen, W. 1982. *Catastrophe theoretic semantics: an elaboration and application of René Thom's theory*. Amsterdam.

Zadeeh, F., E.D. Klemke, and A. Jacobson (eds) 1974. *Readings in semantics*. Urbana, IL.

Zaefferer, D. 1991. *Semantic universals and universal semantics*. Berlin and New York.

Bibliographies

Gordon, W.T. 1980. *Semantics: a bibliography, 1965–1978*. London.

Hofmann, T.R. 1975. *Bibliography on the semantics of human language*. Ottawa.

Journals

The Journal of Semantics.

Natural Language Semantics.

⇒ **componential analysis, computational linguistics, formal logic, generative semantics, intensional logic, interpretive semantics, lexicography, lexicology, lexicon, meaning, meaning postulate, onomasiology, prototype, semantic change, stereotype, structural semantics**.

semasiology

1 Obsolete (original) term for **semantics**.

2 Subdiscipline and area of study within semantics that is concerned with the meaning of individual linguistic expressions, the semantic relations between linguistic expressions (⇒

lexical field theory) as well as problems of **semantic change**. In contrast to **onomasiology** (the study of name-giving), semasiology studies the semantic characteristics of linguistic expressions (word forms).

Reference

Baldinger, K. 1980. *Semantic theory: towards a modern semantics*, trans. W.C. Brown, ed. R. Wright. Oxford.

Kronasser, H. 1952. *Handbuch der Semasiologie*. Heidelberg.

⇒ **onomasiology, semantics**

sematology

Term introduced by Bühler (1934) in which linguistics is viewed as the central object of a general theory of signs. In this sense, sematology corresponds to Saussure's **semiology**.

References

Bühler, K. 1934. *Sprachtheorie*. Jena. (Repr. Stuttgart, 1965.)

Innis, R.E. (trans.) 1982. *Karl Bühler: semiotic foundations of language theory*. New York.

⇒ **semiotics**

seme

In A.J. Greimas' semantic theory the basic unit of semantic analysis in the sense of the smallest distinctive component of meaning, by means of which the whole meaning of a linguistic expression is described in a lexicon entry. (⇒ *also* **semantic feature**)

References

Greimas, A.J. 1966. *Sémantique structurale*. Paris.

⇒ **componential analysis**

sememe

1 In **structural semantics** the basic semantic unit of the **lexicon**, which is described via **semes** (i.e. the minimal semantic components). In this sense, a sememe corresponds to the more current term **lexeme**.

2 In Bloomfield's (1933) terminology, the sememe corresponds to the lexical meaning of a **morpheme**.

Reference

Bloomfield, L. 1933. *Language*. New York.

3 In Greimas' (1966) terminology, the combination of the nucleus of the seme (i.e. invariant semantic content) with the contextually determined and variable semes.

Reference

Greimas, A.J. 1966. *Sémantique structurale*. Paris.

semeology ⇒ semiology

semi-affix [Lat. *semi-* 'half']

Cover term for all affix-like derivational elements that also exist as independently occurring stems. The criteria for classifying elements caught up in this transition from free to bound status are a series formation (*fireproof, waterproof, winterproof*) and a generalization of meaning. (⇒ *also* **semi-prefix, semi-suffix**)

semi-morpheme (*also* cranberry morph, unique morpheme)

Lexical morpheme that is attached to one (and only one) **base** morpheme and whose original meaning can no longer be analyzed synchronically, as e.g. *cran-*, in *cranberry*. Pertinent to the classification of a semi-morpheme is that (a) the morpheme with which it occurs can be unequivocally classified, (b) the semi-morpheme has a distinctive function in the paradigm (cf. *cranberry* vs *boysenberry* and *huckleberry*), but (c) does not form a series (by which it would be differentiated from other stems). If a semi-morpheme occurs in derivations, it is called a **pseudomorpheme**.

References
⇒ **morphology**

semiology (*also* **sematology**, semeology, **semiotics**, semology)

Term introduced by Saussure (1916) for the sketch of a general theory of signs subordinate to (social) psychology that studies signs 'within the framework of social life.' Linguistics is a discipline that is important for semiology, but none the less secondary to it, as semiology is concerned with the general properties of all possible signs and also comprises the study of other sign systems, such as **sign language**, forms of politeness, military signals, etc.

References
Lanigan, R.L. 1972. *Speaking and semiology*. Berlin and New York. (2nd edn 1991.)
Saussure, F. de. 1916. *Cours de linguistique générale*. Paris. (*Course in general linguistics*, trans. R. Harris. London, 1983.)
⇒ **semiotics**

semiosis

Term used in **semiotics** to designate the production and interpretation of a **sign**.

semiotic triangle (*also* semantic triangle)

Geometric schema developed by Odgen and Richards (1923) to illustrate the dependent relationship between symbol, thought, and referent; or, in more common terms, sign, meaning, and object (of reference).

Germane to this approach, whose basic ideas are to be found as early as in the works of Parmenides (*c.* 540–470 BC), is the hypothesis that there is no direct relation between the symbol and referent, between the linguistic expression and the state of affairs in the real world; that is, linguistic expressions relate to the real world only through their meaning.

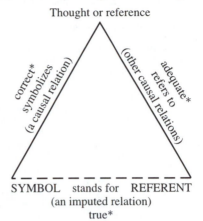

SYMBOL   stands for   REFERENT
(an imputed relation)
true*

Reference
Ogden, C.K. and I.A. Richards. 1923. *The meaning of meaning*. New York.

semiotics (*also* sign theory)

The theory of linguistic and non-linguistic **signs** and signing processes to which the study of natural languages, as the most comprehensive system, is central. Besides language and communication theory, many humanistic disciplines are concerned with theories of non-linguistic signs (aesthetics, graphic design, art, mythology, psychoanalysis, cultural anthropology, religious studies, to name a few). C.W. Morris distinguishes the following areas of study: (a) the syntactic aspect, i.e. the relation between different signs (⇒ **syntax**); (b) the semantic aspect, i.e. the relation between the sign and its meaning (⇒ **semantics**); and (c) the pragmatic aspect, i.e. the relation between the sign and the sign user (⇒ **pragmatics**). (⇒ *also* **semiology**)

References
Bense, M. and E. Walther (eds) 1973. *Wörterbuch der Semiotik*. Cologne.
Bühler, K. 1934. *Sprachtheorie*. Jena. (Repr. Stuttgart, 1965.)
Eco, U. 1976. *A theory of semiotics*. Bloomington, IN.
—— 1984. *Semiotics and the philosophy of language*. Bloomington, IN.
Greimas, A.-J. and J. Courtes. 1979. *Semiotique: dictionnaire raisonné de la théorie du langage*. Paris.
Haarmann, H. 1990. *Language in its cultural embedding: explorations in the relativity of signs and sign systems*. Berlin and New York.
Krampe, M. *et al.* (eds) 1987. *Classics of semiotics*. New York and London.

Manning, P.K. 1987. *Semiotics and fieldwork*. London.

Morris, C.W. 1938. *Foundations of the theory of signs*. Chicago, IL.

—— 1946. *Sign, language and behavior*. New York.

—— 1971. *Writings on the general theory of signs*. The Hague.

Peirce, C.S. 1931–58. *Collected papers of Charles S. Peirce*, ed. C. Hartshorne, P. Weiss, and A.W. Burks. 8 vols. Cambridge, MA.

—— 1955. *Philosophical writings of Peirce*, ed. J. Buchler. New York.

Prower, E. 1990. Linguistics and C.S. Peirce's semiotics: two incompatible paradigms? *Linguistica Silesiana* 11.7–20.

Rey-Debove, J. 1979. *Lexique semiotique*. Paris.

Saussure, F. de. 1916. *Cours de linguistique générale*. Paris. (*Course in general linguistics*, trans. R. Harris. London, 1983.)

Schleifer, R. 1987. *A.J. Greimas and the nature of meaning: linguistics, semiotics and discourse theory*. London and Sydney.

Sebeok, T.A. 1974. Semiotics. In T.A. Sebeok (ed.), *Current trends in linguistics*. The Hague. Vol. 12, 211–64.

—— 1976. *Contribution to the doctrine of signs*. Bloomington, IN.

—— (ed.) 1986. *Encyclopedic dictionary of semiotics*. Berlin, New York, and Amsterdam. (2nd rev. edn 1994.)

—— 1994. *An introduction to semiotics*. London.

—— and I. Smith. 1991. *American signatures: semiotic inquiry and method*. Norman, OK.

—— and J. Umiker-Sebeok (eds) 1987– . *The semiotic web*. Vol. 6 1992. Berlin.

Singh, J. (ed.) 1992. *Semiosis and semiotics: explorations in the theory of signs*. Delhi.

Spinks, C.W. 1991. *Peirce and Triadomania: a walk in the semiotic wilderness*. Berlin and New York.

Tejerea, V. 1988. *Semiotics: from Peirce to Barthes*. Amsterdam and Philadelphia.

Tobin, Y. 1990. *Semiotics and linguistics*. London.

Wolde, E.J. van. 1987. A semiotic analytical model: proceeding from Peirce's and Greimas' semiotics. *Kodikas* 10.195–212.

Bibliographies

Eschbach, A. 1974. *Zeichen – Text – Bedeutung: Bibliographie zu Theorie und Praxis der Semiotik*. Munich.

Eschbach, A. and V. Eschbach-Szabo. 1986. *Bibliography of semiotics, 1975–1985*, 2 vols. Amsterdam.

Eschbach, A. and W. Radler. 1976. *Semiotik-Bibliographie*. Frankfurt.

—— 1977. Kurze Bibliographie zur Geschichte der Semiotik. In R. Posner and H.-P. Reinecke (eds), *Zeichenprozesse: semiotische Forschung in den Einzelwissenschaften*. Wiesbaden. 355–67.

Journals
Kodikas.
Semiotika.
Zeitschrift für Semiotik.
⇒ **language and cognition**

semi-prefix

Prefix-like **word formation** element like *out* in *outsmart* and *outlook*, that forms series and can occur freely in the same form but with a different meaning (*out* 'adverb of location'). The capacity to form a series as well as semantic relatedness are parameters that allow a broad heterogeneous zone between **composition** and **affixation**. (⇒ *also* **semi-suffix**)

semi-suffix

Suffix-like formatives such as *-free* in *lead-free*, *-worthy* in *noteworthy*, and *-like* in *life-like* that form series of words, but (often) still have a corresponding **base morpheme** as well (*free*, *worthy*, *like*). At the same time, there is in many cases a development away from the content of the original word towards generalization. The distinction between suffix and semi-suffix is continuous.

References
⇒ **word formation**

Semitic

Named after Sem, the son of Noah, language family belonging to **Afro-Asiatic**. The oldest attested language is **Akkadian** in ancient Mesopotamia (2500–600 BC). Other branches: North-West Semitic (Phoenician, Ugaritic, **Hebrew**, **Aramaic**), South Semitic (**Arabic**, Old South Arabic, Neo-South Arabic), and Ethiosemitic (**Ge'ez**, Tigrinya, Tigre, **Amharic**, Gurage, Harari).

The relationship between languages such as Hebrew, Arabic, and Aramaic was already recognized by the Jewish grammarians of the Middle Ages. The European study of the Semitic languages dates back to the sixteenth century, the term 'Semitic' was coined by L. von Schlözer in 1781. The turn of the century marked a flurry of research (C. Brockelmann, T. Nöldeke).

Characteristics: a series of emphatic (pharyngealized or glottalized) consonants. Verbal morphology: two **aspects** with different conjugation patterns (perfect vs imperfect with the meaning preterite vs present/future), rich system of voices, subject agreement. Nominal morphology: two-way gender system (masculine/feminine), often three cases (nominative, genitive, accusative; dative and locative can be reconstructed, in the modern languages often no case for the noun), rich number system (dual forms, sometimes collective–singular distinction), so-called 'status constructus' (the governing noun in a genitive construction is marked, cf. Ge'ez *ḥayl* 'power,' *ḥayl- ä səlase* 'power of the trinity', name of the last Ethiopean emperor). Root inflection: the roots consist of a few (usually three) consonants (so-called 'radicals') and are generally inflected by various vowels occurring between them (so-called 'triliterality,' example: from the Arabic radical *k-t-b* 'write' is derived *kitāb* 'book,' *kataba* 'he wrote,' *yaktubu* 'he writes,' *kattāb* 'writer,' *maktab* 'office,' etc.). Foreign words are also made to conform to this system, cf. *film*, pl. *aflām*. Word order: usually VSO, differentiation between nominal clause (without copula) and verbal clause.

References

Bergsträsser, G. 1928. *Einführung in die semitischen Sprachen*. Munich. (*Introduction to the Semitic languages*, trans. P.T. Daniels. Winona Lake, IN, 1983.)

Brockelmann, C. 1908–13. *Grundriß der vergleichenden Grammatik der semitischen Sprachen*. Berlin. (Repr. Hildesheim, 1961.)

Moscati, S.A. *et al.* 1969. *An introduction to the comparative grammar of the Semitic languages: phonology and morphology*. Wiesbaden. (2nd printing.)

Spuler, B. (ed.) 1953. *Semitistik*. (Handbuch der Orientalistik I, Vol. 3.) Leiden. (Repr. 1964.)

Dictionary

Cohen, D. 1970– . *Dictionnaire des racines sémitiques ou attestées dans les langues sémitiques*. Paris and Leuven.

Bibliography

Hospers, J. (ed.) 1973–4. *A basic bibliography for the study of the Semitic languages*, 2 vols. Leiden.

Journals

Journal of Northwest Semitic Languages.
Journal of Semitic Studies.
Journal for Semitics.

semivowel

1 (*also* **glide**[1]) Principally a phonologically defined subclass of **approximants**. A semivowel functions phonologically like a consonant, that is, does not constitute the nucleus of the syllable, e.g. [j] in Eng. ['jɛlɛʊ] *yellow* and [ɟ] in Fr. [ɟit] *huit* 'eight.'

References
⇒ **syllable**

2 In **Old Church Slavic** and in the reconstructed primary stages of contemporary **Slavic** languages, an overshort *ĭ* or *ŭ* (ь or ъ).

semology ⇒ semiology

sense

Frege's (1892) term (Ger. *Sinn*) for the characteristic or quality of the object denoted by the linguistic expression. Frege's distinction of *Sinn* vs *Bedeutung* (translated as *sense* vs *reference*) corresponds to the dichotomies of

meaning vs **referent** or that of **intension** vs **extension**. (⇒ *also* **connotation**, **denotation**)

References

Carl, W. 1994. *Frege's theory of sense and reference*. Cambridge.

Frege, G. 1892. Über Sinn und Bedeutung. *Zeitschrift für Philosophie und philosophische Kritik* (new series) 100.25–50. (Repr. in *Kleine Schriften*, ed I. Angelelli. Darmstadt, 1967 143–62. (Also as: On sense and reference, trans. M. Black. In P. Geach and M. Black (eds), *Translation from the philosophical writings of Gottlob Frege*. Oxford. 56–78.)

⇒ **intension**, **meaning**

sensory aphasia ⇒ aphasia, Wernicke's aphasia

sensory information storage ⇒ memory

sentence

Unit of speech constructed according to language-dependent rules, which is relatively complete and independent in respect to content, grammatical structure, and **intonation**. During the history of linguistics, the vagueness of syntactic and semantic features which define sentences has led to repeated attempts at definitions, of which the following two more recent attempts will be highlighted. According to formal aspects, **American structuralism** (see Bloomfield 1933) provides a strict definition of 'sentence' as the largest independent syntactic form which cannot be embedded in any other syntactic form by any grammatical rule. Described syntactically, the sentence is the result of an analysis that proceeds from the smallest units (**phonemes**) through **morphemes**, **words**, and **phrases** to the synthesis 'sentence.' In **transformational grammar**, a sentence (abbreviated *S*) is the fundamental basis of syntactic analysis, where *S* is defined extensionally by giving the rules that, when applied, will result in the production of sentences. In both of these definitions, a sentence is seen as a unit of langue (⇒ **langue vs parole**), in distinction to sentence as a parole-based concrete utterance, where it becomes especially problematic to identify a sentence, particularly in spoken discourse. Sentences can be classified according to the following aspects. (a) Formally, the position of the verb can be important: in English, verb-initial position is a marker for **interrogatives** or **imperatives**. (b) In reference to communicative-pragmatic functions, **word order**, **mood**, and intonation can be used to indicate four basic types of sentences: **statements**, interrogatives, imperatives and **conditionals** (*if only* ...). (c) Based on varying degrees of complexity of the syntactic structure, sentences can be divided into simple, compound, and complex sentences: simple sentences may contain only one finite verb plus obligatory and optional (⇒ **obligatory vs optional**) **constituents**; compound sentences contain at least two finite verbs, with clauses being joined through **co-ordination**; complex sentences contain at least two finite verbs, with all additional (dependent) clauses being joined to the **main** (= independent) **clause** via **subordination**.

References
Bloomfield, L. 1933. *Language*. New York.
Fabb, N. 1994. *Sentence structure*. London.
Kasher, A. 1976. Sentences and utterances reconsidered. *FL* 8.313–45.

sentence adverbial (*also* adsentential)

Adverbial construction which expresses the subjective attitude of the speaker towards some state of affairs. Sentence adverbials can occur as **modal adverbs** (*hopefully*, *maybe*) or **prepositional phrases**: *Apparently/Surprisingly/Without a doubt she figured it out*. In contrast to modal adverbs, sentence adverbials modify the whole sentence (⇒ **scope**) and have sentential characteristics, i.e. logically they are sentences about sentences. Thus in the utterance *He's probably been sick for a long time*, the statement *He's been sick for a long time* is restricted by the subjective evaluation of the speaker towards the state of affairs: *I suspect it/that*.

References
Allerton, D.J. and A. Cruttenden. 1974. English sentence adverbials. *Lingua* 34.1–30.
Bellert, I. 1977. On semantic and distributional properties of sentential adverbs. *LingI* 8.337–51.
Hetland, J. 1992. *Satzadverbien im Fokus*. Tübingen.
⇒ **adverbial**

sentence meaning

The whole meaning of a sentence as opposed to that of an individual word (⇒ **lexical vs grammatical meaning**). In philosophy and logic, sentence meaning is readily equated with **propositions** or, for the sake of simplicity, with **truth values** and thereby represents qualitatively something different as compared to the meaning of terms and **predicates**. However, this distinction does not generally apply in linguistics, since sentence meaning may be structurally derived from the **principle of compositionality**. To this extent, sentence meaning yields a completely structured whole. Since sentence meaning can be ascertained based only on what has been actually uttered, **stereotypes** or other knowledge about the world are usually necessary to understand sentence meaning. (⇒ *also* **sentence semantics**)

References
⇒ **meaning**, **semantics**

sentence mood

Grammatical category referring to that part of sentential modality which is structurally encoded, for example, by verbal **mood**, such as **indicative** or **imperative**, and by word order. Sentential modality, in turn, is the communicative role played by a sentence's propositional content in discourse (illocutionary force) as expressed by linguistic means. *Please keep quiet!* expresses the sentential modality of a polite request, the sentence mood is imperative.

References
Altmann, H. 1993. Satzmodus. In J. Jacobs *et al.* (eds), *Syntax: an international handbook of contemporary research*. Berlin and New York. 1006–29.
Grewendorf, G. and D. Zaefferer. 1991. Theorien der Satzmodi/Theories of sentence mood. In A. v. Stechow and D. Wunderlich (eds), *Semantik/Semantics: an international handbook of contemporary research*. Berlin. 270–86.
Zaefferer, D. 1990. On the coding of sentential modality. In J. Bechert (ed.), *Toward a typology of European languages*. Berlin. 215–37.
⇒ **focus**, **intonation**

sentence pattern (*also* **atomic sentence**, **kernel sentence**)

Elementary structure of a simple sentence based on the **valence** of the verb which remains after elimination of all structurally unnecessary (i.e. optional) elements. Some very traditional basic sentence patterns in English include: noun + verb (*I think*); noun + verb + direct object (*I see the dog*), noun + verb + indirect object + direct object (*I give the dog a bone*). (⇒ *also* **atomic sentence**, **kernel sentence**, **valence**)

sentence root

The basic state of affairs in a sentence which remains constant regardless of what sentence type (⇒ **declarative sentence**, **interrogative**, **imperative**) it appears in. The sentence root in *Philip is coming / Is Philip coming? / Come, Philip!* describes the state of affairs in which the individual, *Philip*, is attributed with the process of *coming*. In **categorial grammar**, the sentence root is the basic category of sentence, while in **logic** and **speech act theory** it corresponds to **proposition**.

References
Lewis, D. 1970. General semantics. *Synthese* 22.18–67.
⇒ **categorial grammar**

sentence semantics

The description of the semantic structure of sentences based on the meaning of individual lexemes and their syntactic roles in the given sentence. (⇒ also **meaning**, **principle of compositionality**, **sentence meaning**)

sentence type

Distinction in **school grammar** between basic kinds of **sentences**: **declarative**, **imperative**, **interrogative**, **exclamatory**, wish sentences. This typology is based on (a) formal criteria such as position of the finite verb (verb-initial position in interrogative and imperative sentences), **mood** (imperative in imperative sentences), **intonation**, lexical means (⇒ **interrogative pronouns**, **modal particles**) and (b) communicative aspects such as speaker intention (⇒ **speech act theory**). The interplay of formal, lexical, and functional aspects is far more complex than these traditional types suggest.

sentence word

Individual words like *yes*, *thanks*, and *bye* that can appear outside a sentence and have sentential character. Their morphological–syntactic classification (as 'particle' or 'adverb') is unclear, as is their connection to **ellipsis**.

References
⇒ **word formation**

sentential

Property of **participial** and **infinitive constructions** which can be paraphrased with and used in the same way as **clauses**. They are subject to the same syntactic rules as clauses, such as **extraposition**. Thus the sentence *Distressed by their helplessness* (past participle), *the mayor decided to support them more fully* (infinitive) can be paraphrased as (a) *The mayor was distressed by their helplessness*, (b) *The mayor decided* (something); (c) *The mayor will support them more fully*.

sentential infinitive ⇒ infinitive construction

sentential subject clause (*also* sentential subject complement)

Dependent clause which functions syntactically as a subject. Sentential subject clauses in the form of conjunctive clauses are introduced by *that*, *if*, *who*, *how*; they can also be expressed by participial constructions: *It became clear only later that he had no such intentions*; *Helping her (that) can be difficult*. Semantically, sentential subject clauses are modifiers of a semantically empty (usually optional) **dummy element** in the main clause such as *it*, *that*, *the fact that*. (⇒ also **sentential**)

sentential subject complement ⇒ sentential subject clause

sentential subject constraint

A **constraint** on **transformations** suggested by J.R. Ross, whereby no constituent may be moved out of a sentence which is the subject of a clause. For example, [*Who did* [*that Caroline was going out with –*] *bother you?*]. In this respect, subject sentences are 'islands' from which no constituents can be moved.

References
⇒ **constraints**, **island**

sentoid

Term coined by J.J. Katz and P.M. Postal (derived from *sentence*) for structurally unambiguous chains of **formatives**[2]. In contrast to sentences, sentoids are structurally unambiguous readings of the **deep structure** of a sentence and thus can be described by a single structural description. In this analysis, the ambiguous chain of formatives *Men and women with long hair must wear bathing caps* is interpreted as one sentence but as two sentoids, namely as [*men*] and [*women with long hair*] or [*men with long hair*], and [*women with long hair*].

Reference
Katz, J.J. and P.M. Postal. 1964. *An integrated theory of linguistic description*. Cambridge, MA.

sequence of tenses

Fixed order of tenses in complex sentences. This 'relative' use of tenses is strictly regulated in **Latin**. If the actions depicted in the **main** and **relative clauses** are simultaneous, the tense of the dependent clause depends on the tense in the independent clause: **present** in the main clause requires present **subjunctive** in the dependent clause; **preterite** or **past perfect** in the main clause requires perfect subjunctive in the dependent clause. This strict ordering also occurs in English, such as in conditional sentences: *If I knew the answer I wouldn't ask* vs *If I had known the answer I wouldn't have asked*.

sequential organization

In **conversation analysis**, the structuring of a conversation through various types of 'action-sequences' produced by different speakers. It is assumed that sequential organization is a resource for assigning meaning, that is, within a sequence, an utterance brings about one of various expected actions depending on the preceding **turn**, which alternately leads to the expectation of a particular next turn (taken from a limited set of possible next turns). In this manner, participants demonstrate how they have understood the preceding turn. Among such types of sequences, in which the choice of a particular first turn leads to a particular next turn, are **adjacency pairs** (such as question–answer, ⇒ **conditional relevance**) or sequences with preferred options (such as the acceptance of an invitation instead of its decline, ⇒ **preference**). Further evidence for the sequential organization of conversation is provided by expressions that mark misplacements (e.g. *by the way*, ⇒ **discourse markers**). Sequential organization is supported by the 'local' management of **turn-taking** (see Sacks *et al.* 1974). For this reason, in conversation analysis, utterances are not analyzed in isolation, but rather within sequences. This approach distinguishes conversation analysis from other related approaches of **discourse analysis**, such as those of **text linguistics** or **speech act theory**. For impressive examples, see Turner 1976 and Jefferson 1981.

References
Jefferson, G. 1972. Side sequences. In D. Sudnow (ed.), *Studies in social interaction*. New York. 294–338.
────── 1981. The abominable *ne*? In P. Schröder and H. Steger (eds) *Dialogforschung*. Düsseldorf. 53–88.
Turner, R. 1976. Utterance positioning as an interactional resource. *Semiotica* 17.233–54.
Levinson, S. 1983. *Pragmatics*. Cambridge.
Sacks, H., E. Schegloff, and G. Jefferson. 1974. A simplest systematics for the organization of turn-taking for conversation. *Lg* 50.696–735.

Serbian ⇒ Serbo-Croatian

Serbo-Croatian

South **Slavic** language with approx. 15 million speakers of the two main variants, Serbian and Croatian. Serbian is written in the **Cyrillic** alphabet with additional characters ⟨Џ⟩, ⟨Љ⟩, ⟨Њ⟩ and, in contrast to **Macedonian**, ⟨Ћ, ћ⟩, ⟨Ђ, ђ⟩ and is spoken mainly in Serbia. Croatian is written in the Latin alphabet with numerous diacritics and the additional character ⟨đ, Đ⟩ and is spoken mainly in Croatia. Agreement between the Serbs and Croats on the unity of Serbo-Croatian was reached in Vienna in 1850 based on the standard language created by Vuk Karadžić in Vienna (1813–18). Serbian, Croatian, and **Slovene** are to a large extent mutually intelligible.
Characteristics of both variants: short and long vowels with rising and falling tone (in Slavic terminology: 'intonation'); complex tense and **aspect** system. Differences between Serbian and Croatian include: Serb. ⟨e⟩ vs Croat. ⟨je⟩ or ⟨ije⟩, both corresponding to **Old Church Slavic** ⟨ě⟩ in *ded* vs *djed* vs *dědъ* 'grandfather,' *reka* vs *rijeka* vs *rěka* 'river.' Lexical differences: Serb. *krtola* vs Croat. *krompir* 'potato,' Serb. *pozorište* vs Croat. *kazalište* 'theater.'

Reference
Gvozdanović, J. 1980. *Tone and accent in standard Serbo-Croatian*. Vienna.

Grammars
Leskien, A. 1914. *Grammatik der serbokroatischen Sprache*, Vol. I: *Lautlehre, Stammbildung, Formenlehre*. Heidelberg.
Meillet, A. and A. Vaillant. 1969. *Grammaire de la langue serbo-croate*, 2nd edn. Paris.
Partridge, M. 1972. *Serbo-Croat: practical grammar and reader*. 2nd edn. Belgrade.

Dialects and history
Ivić, P. 1958. *Die serbokroatischen Dialekte: ihre Struktur und Entwicklung*, Vol. I: *Allgemeines und die štovakische Dialektgruppe*. 's-Gravenhage.
Popović, I. 1960. *Geschichte der serbokroatischen Sprache*. Wiesbaden.

Dictionaries
Benson, M. (ed.) 1990. *Serbo-Croatian–English dictionary*, 3rd edn. Cambridge.
────── (ed.) 1990. *English–Serbo-Croatian dictionary*. Cambridge.
Rečnik hrvatskoga ili srpskoga jezika. 1880–1976. 23 vols. Zagreb.
Skok, P. 1971–4. *Etimologijski rječnik hrvatskoga ili srpskoga jezika*, 4 vols. Zagreb.
⇒ **Slavic**

Serer ⇒ West Atlantic

serial verb construction

Type of construction that is found predominantly in **isolating languages** such as **Chinese** or the **Kwa** languages of West Africa. A series of verbs or verb–object complexes are juxtaposed without any kind of conjunction, certain verbs having more abstract or grammaticalized meaning, e.g. **Yoruba** *ó gbé e wá* lit. 'he carry it come,' i.e. 'he brings it.'

References
Déchaine, R.-M. 1993. Serial verb constructions. In J. Jacobs *et al.* (eds), *Syntax: an international handbook of contemporary research*. Berlin and New York. 799–925.
Lefebvre, C. (ed.) 1991. *Serial verbs: grammatical, comparative and cognitive approaches*. Amsterdam and Philadelphia.
Lord, C. 1993. *Historical change in serial verb constructions*. Amsterdam and Philadelphia.
Schachter, P. 1974. A non-transformational account of serial verbs. *Studies in African Linguistics*, supp. 5.253–70.

Sebba, M. 1987. *The syntax of serial verbs: an investigation into serialization in Sranan and other languages.* Amsterdam.

Steever, S.B. 1988. *The serial verb formation in the Dravidian languages.* Delhi.

serialization ⇒ word order

set

Basic concept in mathematics and, more specifically, in **set theory**: a set is a collection of elements that have a particular characteristic in common. The elements are contained or included in the set (i.e. in a relation of 'inclusion' to the set) (notation: $x \, \varepsilon \, S$, read as '*x* is an element (or member) of *S*'). Sets can be defined extensionally by naming the number of their elements (enumeration, ⇒ **extension**), the order of the elements being insignificant, or intensionally by indicating the common characteristics of the elements (description) (⇒ **intension, predicate**). In contrast to the everyday language use of the term 'set,' mathematical sets have the following characteristics. (a) Concrete objects as well as abstract concepts and mental constructs like numbers, names and **phonemes** may be elements of sets, which also means that sets, in turn, can be elements of other sets (e.g. the set of all verbs in English is at the same time an element of the set of all word classes in English, if a class is understood as a set of expressions). (b) A set can be empty (empty set, notation: Ø) (e.g. the set of all **clicks** in English). (c) A set can consist of a single element (singleton) (e.g. the set of initial symbols in a **phrase structure grammar** that have only the element *S* for 'sentence' as the initial node). (d) The number of elements of a set can be infinite (e.g. the set of natural numbers or the set of grammatical sentences in English).

The following operations and relations between sets can be distinguished. (e) The identity of sets: two sets *A* and *B* are extensionally 'the same,' if they contain the same elements. (f) **Equivalence**: two sets are equivalent, if they can be mapped onto each other bijectively (⇒ **function**). Equivalence is both a **reflexive relation** and a **symmetric relation** and a **transitive relation**. (g) The union set is that set *S* to which all elements belong that are included in at least one of the two original sets *A* and *B* (notation: $A \cup B := \{x | x \varepsilon A \vee x \varepsilon B\}$). The union set corresponds in **propositional logic** to the inclusive, i.e. to the 'non-exclusive,' *or*, the propositional conjunction of which is true if one or both statements are true (⇒ **disjunction**). See the following **Venn diagram** for $A \cup B$ (with hachure):

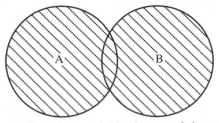

For example: let *A* and *B* be the sets of abstract words and words ending in *-ion* in English. The union set is, then, the set of abstract words or words ending in *-ion* in English (*billion, carrion, nation, onion,* etc.). (h) The intersection set is the set of those elements that are contained both in set *A* and in set *B* (notation: $A \cap B := \{x | x \varepsilon A \wedge x \varepsilon B\}$). For example: if *A* is the set of transitive and *B* the set of irregular verbs in English, then the intersection set of *A* and *B* is the set of transitive and irregular verbs in English (*bind, eat, come*). (i) Difference: the difference is that subset of *A* that contains exactly the same elements in *A* that are not also elements of *B* (notation: $A \backslash B := \{x | x \varepsilon A \wedge x \notin B\}$. The union set of the difference *A\B and B\A* corresponds in propositional logic to the 'exclusive' *or*, the propositional conjunction of which is true only if one of the two statements linked by *or* is true (but not if both are true) (⇒ **disjunction, exclusive disjunction**). See the following Venn diagram for *A\B* (with hachure):

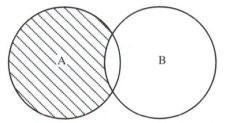

For example: let *A* be the set of the transitive verbs in English and *B* the set of irregular verbs in English. The difference *A\B* is, then, the set of regular transitive verbs in English (e.g. *work*). (j) Subset: a set *A* is a subset of a set *B* if all elements of *A* are also elements of *B* (notation: $A \subset B \leftrightarrow \wedge x(x \varepsilon A \rightarrow x \varepsilon B)$.

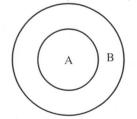

For example: the set of transitive verbs in English is a (true) subset of the verbs of the

English language, that is to say that in the set of English verbs there is at least one verb that is not an element of the subset of English transitive verbs. In propositional logic the subset corresponds to **implication**; in **semantics** 'subset' is germane to the relation of **hyponymy**. (k) Complement: the complement of A with respect to a certain universe of discourse U is the set of all elements that are not elements of A (notation: $\complement_u A$ or A^-). It is the case that $\complement_u A$ = $U\backslash A$, that is, the complement of A with respect to U is the special case of the difference of $A \subset U$.

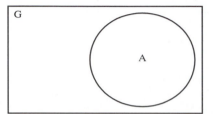

For example: let U be the set of all English words. If A is the set of all English verbs, then the complement of set A is the set of all English words except the verbs. (1) Power set: the power set of a set A is the set of all subsets of A (notation: $\{P(A): = \{x|x \subset A\}\}$). In this case, the number of elements of the power set corresponds to the number 2 raised to the power of the number of elements in the original set: if A contains the three elements $\{a, b, c\}$, then the power set has $P(A)$ $2^3 = 8$ elements: $\emptyset$, $\{a\}$, $\{b\}$, $\{c\}$, $\{a, b\}$, $\{a, c\}$, $\{b, c\}$, $\{a, b, c\}$. (m) Disjunction: two sets A and B are disjunct if their intersection (see (h)) yields the empty set ($= \emptyset$), that is, if they do not have any elements in common. Put formally: $A \cap B = \emptyset$.

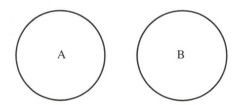

For example: let A be the set of transitive verbs and B the set of intransitive verbs in English; the intersection set is, then, $\emptyset$, since no verb can be both intransitive and transitive at the same time. (n) Cartesian product (named for the French philosopher R. Descartes (1596–1650)): the Cartesian product of two sets A and B is the set of all ordered pairs $\langle x, y \rangle$, wherein x is included in A and y in B, put formally as $A X B = \{\langle x, y \rangle | x \varepsilon A \wedge x \varepsilon B\}$ and read as 'A cross B.'

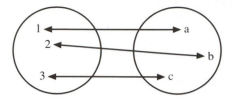

For example: languages with intact inflectional systems use morphological markers for case and number. Let A be the set of grammatical cases in German {nominative, genitive, dative, accusative} and B the set of number {singular, plural}. The Cartesian product of $A X B$ contains all possible combinations {nominative singular, dative plural, etc.}.

References
⇒ **set theory**

set feature

An **extension** of the descriptive apparatus of **unification grammar** for features with more than one value. Set features are used in **Functional Unification Grammar**, **Lexical Functional Grammar**, and **Head-Driven Phrase Structure Grammar**.

References
⇒ **unification grammar**

set phrase ⇒ idiom

set theory

Basic mathematical discipline founded by G. Cantor (1845–1918) concerned with the axiomatization of the theory of **sets**. As a fundamental mathematical and logical discipline set theory, the terminology, and its definitions have found many applications in linguistics, particularly in **computational linguistics**.

References
Cooper, W.S. 1964. *Set theory and syntactic description*. The Hague.
Halmos, R. 1960. *Naive set theory*. Princeton, NJ.
Hockett, C.F. 1966. Language, mathematics, and linguistics. In T.A. Sebeok (ed.) *Current trends in linguistics*. The Hague, Vol. 3, 155–204.
Lipschutz, S. 1955. *Set theory and related topics, including 530 solved problems*. New York.
Mulder, J.W.F. 1968. *Sets and relations in phonology: an axiomated approach to the description of speech*. Oxford.
Suppes, P. 1960. *Axiomatic set theory*. Princeton, NJ.
Wall, R. 1972. *Introduction to mathematical linguistics*. Englewood Cliffs, NJ.
⇒ **formal logic**

shibboleth

From Heb. *shibboleth* ('ear of corn,' 'stream'), shibboleth is a linguistic characteristic that is unique to a certain group and serves to distinguish that group from other groups. The term comes originally from the Book of Judges 12:5–6: 'And the Gileadites took the fords of the Jordan against the Ephraimites. And when any of the fugitives of the Ephraim said, 'Let me go over,' the men of Gilead said to him, 'Are you an Ephraimite?' When he said 'No,' they said to him 'Then say Shibboleth,' and he said 'Sibboleth,' for he could not pronounce it right; then they seized him and slew him at the fords of the Jordan.'

shibilant

In analogy to **sibilant**, term used to denote sounds such as [ʃ] and [ʒ] as well as the corresponding affricates [tʃ] and [dʒ].

References
⇒ **phonetics**

shift word ⇒ **pronoun**

shifter ⇒ **deictic expression**

Shliḥ ⇒ **Berber**

Shona ⇒ **Bantu**

short ⇒ **long vs short, quantity**

short-term memory ⇒ **memory**

shortening ⇒ **lengthening vs shortening**

shuttering ⇒ **dysfluency**

Siamese ⇒ **Thai**

sibilant [Lat. *sibilare* 'to make a hissing sound']

Subclass of auditorily similar **fricatives** as well as corresponding **affricates** that are produced through a narrow opening between the front of the tongue and the front palate. For example [s], [z], [ʃ], [ʒ], in [haʊs] 'house,' [zu] 'zoo' [ʒɑrə] 'genre,' and [ʃɔr] 'shore.'

References
⇒ **phonetics**

Sievers' Law

This term covers two different **sound changes** of **Indo-European** that in more recent literature are differentiated as Sievers' Law I and Sievers' Law II.

1 Sievers' Law I (*also* Sievers–Edgerton's Law): this is a regularity in the syllable structure of Indo-European saying that the semivowels *y* and *w* following a short syllable alternate regularly with *i* (*iy*) and *u* (*uw*) following a long syllable. Thus, the same suffix in **Gothic** appears either as *ji* (= *i+i*) or as *ei* (*ī*)

(= *i+i*) depending on the length of the preceding syllable; cf. *satjiþ* 'sets' vs *sôkeiþ* 'searches'. The original Sievers' Law underwent numerous modifications; the most significant reformulation was made by F. Edgerton.

References
Collinge, N.E. 1985. *The laws of Indo-European*. Amsterdam and Philadelphia. 159–178.
Edgerton, F. 1934. Sievers' law and Indo-European weak grade vocalism. *Lg* 10.235–65.
Seebold, E. 1972. *Das System der indogermanischen Halbvokale: Untersuchungen zum sogenannten 'Sieversschen Gesetz' und zu den halbvokalhaltigen Suffixen in den indogermanischen Sprachen, besonders im Vedischen*. Heidelberg.
Sievers, E. 1878. Zur accent-und lautlehre der germanischen sprachen, II: zum vokalischen auslautsgesetz. *PBB* 5.101–63.

2 Sievers' Law II: this concerns the development of the IE labiovelar *kʷ*. Through **Grimm's Law**, this regularly becomes Proto-Germanic *hʷ* > OHG *h*; cf. IE **akʷa* 'water' > Proto-Germ. **ahwo* > OHG *aha* > NHG *Ache*. However, the development is different in Verner surroundings (⇒ **Verner's Law**); here, the original labiovelar becomes *gw* through Grimm's Law, then Proto-Germ. *u* > OHG *w* or *u*; cf. again IE **akʷa* > Proto-Germ. **agwo*; with *i*-derivation Proto-Germ. **awio* 'of or belonging to water' > OHG *ouwa* > NHG *Aue*. Such word pairs with respectively different sound development of labiovelars depending on the position of the word accent can also be found for Indo-European voiced-aspirated stops. Thus, in summary, this law says that in Verner surroundings the labial component of the Indo-European labiovelar survived, whereas under other conditions the velar component was retained.

References
Seebold, E. 1967. Die Vertretung idg. **gʷʰ-* im Germanischen. *ZVS* 81.104–33.
Sievers, E. 1878. Zur accent- und lautlehre der germanischen sprachen. *PBB* 5.63–164.

Sievers–Edgerton's Law ⇒ **Sievers' Law**[1]

sign

Basic element of a general theory of signs (⇒ **semiotics**). Abstract class of all sensually perceivable **signals** that refer to the same object or state of affairs in the real world. A distinction is made between natural signs (or 'symptoms'), which are founded upon a causal relationship between the sign and the signified (e.g. jaundice as a symptom of a particular illness; ⇒ **index**) and artificial signs (or 'representational signs'), which are based on convention and distinct from language to language (e.g. *yellow* as the denotation for a particular segment of the color spectrum; ⇒ **symbol**).

Linguistic signs have specific basic characteristics (see de Saussure 1916). (a) Bilaterality, that is, every sign has two aspects, the material sign (or 'signifier'), which is realized phonetically or graphemically, and a conceptual sign (or 'signified') (⇒ **signifier vs signified**). In contrast to de Saussure's diadic sign, others, for example C.S. Peirce, assume that the sign has a triadic structure and distinguish between the material sign, the signified, and the speaker. (b) Arbitrariness, that is, the co-ordination between the signifier and the signified is, of course, predetermined by convention, yet nevertheless arbitrary, to the extent that it differs from language to language and the relation between signifier and signified is not motivated. (c) Linearity, that is, as a sensually perceptible signal the linguistic sign exists exclusively within the framework of time.

In sign theory, three or four areas of study are differentiated: (1) the syntactic aspect, or the relation between different signs (⇒ **syntax**); (2) the semantic aspect, or the relation between sign and meaning (⇒ **semantics**); and (3) the pragmatic aspect, or the relation between sign and sign user (⇒ **pragmatics**). (⇒ also **icon**, **organon model of language**, **semiotics**)

References

Bühler, K. 1934. *Sprachtheorie*. Jena. (Repr. Stuttgart, 1965.)
Morris, C.W. 1938. *Foundations of the theory of signs*. Chicago, IL.
—— 1946. *Sign, language and behavior*. New York.
—— 1971. *Writings on the general theory of signs*. The Hague.
Peirce, C.S. 1931–58. *Collected papers of Charles S. Peirce*, ed. C. Hartshorne, P. Weiss and A.W. Burks. 8 vols. Cambridge, MA.
Sangdhansen, H. 1954. *Recent theories on the nature of the language sign*. Copenhagen.
Saussure, F. de 1916. *Cours de linguistique générale*. Paris. (*Course in general linguistics*, trans. R. Harris. London. 1983.)
⇒ **semiotics**

sign language

1 In the broadest sense, gestural systems used by religious or secret societies (i.e. Trappist monks, Freemasons) or hand signals used in sports, auctions, diving, ritual dance, etc. These manual systems do not have the structural complexity or communication range of natural languages.

2 In the narrow sense, 'sign language' refers to the natural languages which have evolved over time in deaf communities throughout the world and used for the same wide range of commu-

nicative purposes as spoken languages. There are national sign languages and their regional dialects, as well as sociolects, style, and register distinctions. The linguistic structure utilizes the visual/gestural modality of the language; sign languages are thus independent of the spoken languages used in the same region. Nevertheless, sign languages have been found to be constrained to 'general restrictions on structure and organization proposed for oral languages' (Padden 1988b).

Modern research on sign languages began relatively recently, beginning with research showing that manual signs, formerly regarded as unanalyzable global units, were composed of a limited set of sublexical units ('aspects' according to Stokoe 1960; 'parameters' according to Klima and Bellugi 1979). Whereas the early studies emphasized that the visual/gestural modality allows for extensive simultaneous as well as sequential production of sublexical elements, more recent research, using autosegmental or hierarchical syllable frameworks, has emphasized the sequential arrangement at the phonological level. (Liddell and Johnson 1989; Sandler 1990; Wilbur 1990; Coulter 1993). Several different notation systems have been developed for sublexical components (Stokoe *et al.* 1965; Prillwitz and Zienert 1990; McIntire *et al.* 1987).

An unusual characteristic of this visual language is the grammatical use of the three-dimensional space around the signer (see Engberg-Pedersen 1993; Lucas 1990). Signals given by the facial expression, head, trunk, and eye gaze have also been found to function linguistically (Baker-Shenk 1983; Liddell 1980; Bergman 1984). The mouthing of word-like elements from the spoken language has been reported to be an important loan element in several European sign languages (see Schermer 1990; Ebbinghaus and Hessmann 1990).

All sign languages studied to date have been found to have a rich morphology. Different groups of verbs can mark subject–object agreement, locative relations, path and manner of motion, and several kinds of temporal aspect (Padden 1988a; Klima & Bellugi 1979; Bergman & Dahl 1990; Supalla 1982; Newport 1988). Engberg-Pedersen (1993) describes verbs in Danish Sign Language in terms of being more or less 'polymorphemic' and temporal relations expressed by means of several different kinds of 'time lines.' Derivational processes for adjectives, verbs, and nouns have been studied (Klima and Bellugi 1979; Bellugi and Newkirk 1981). Syntactical issues have been addressed for American Sign Language (Liddell 1980; Padden 1988a; Fischer and Siple

1990; Lucas 1990) and other sign languages (Brennan and Turner 1994). Several forms of 'contact signing' (Lucas and Valli 1989) are used in communicative situations involving deaf or hearing persons bilingual in both a signed and an oral language (Ahlgren and Hyltenstam 1994). Signs used simultaneously with spoken language in educational situations are not considered a form of deaf sign language but rather a pedagogical system for making the oral language more 'visible' to deaf children (Wilbur 1979). Non-verbal communication of signers has been studied by Reilly *et al.* (1990; 1992).

Deaf children exposed to the language from infancy acquire sign language at a rate and through a process similar to their hearing peers' acquisition of spoken language (Volterra and Erting 1990; Newport and Meier 1985). Sign language is considered by deaf persons to be a core characteristic of Deaf culture (Padden and Humphries 1988). American Sign Language has been accepted as fulfilling the foreign-language requirement in many US universities (Wilcox 1992). An extensive international bibliography of research on sign language can be found in Joachim and Prillwitz (1993).

References

Ahlgren, I. and K. Hyltenstam (eds) 1994. *Bilingualism in deaf education*. Hamburg.

Baker-Shenk, C.L. 1983. A microanalysis of the nonmanual components of questions in American Sign Language. Unpublished dissertation, University of California, Berkeley.

Bellugi, U. and D. Newkirk. 1981. Formal devices for creating new signs in American sign language. *Sign Language Studies* 30.1–35.

Bergman, B. 1984. Non-manual components in signed language: some sentence types in Swedish sign language. In F. Loncke *et al.* (eds), *Recent research on European sign languages*. Lisse. 49–59.

Bergman, B. and Ö. Dahl. 1990. Idiophones in sign language? The place of reduplication in the tense–aspect system of Swedish Sign Language. In C. Bache *et al.* (eds) *Tense–aspect–modality: new data – new approaches.* , The Hague.

Brennan, M. and G. Turner. 1994. *Word-order issues in sign language working papers*. Durham.

Coulter, G.R. (ed.) 1993. *Phonetics and phonology*, vol. 3: *Current issues in ASL phonology*. San Diego, CA.

Deuchar, M. 1984. *British sign language*. London.

Ebbinghaus, H. and J. Hessmann, 1990. German words in German sign language. In S. Prillwitz and T. Vollhaber (eds), *Current trends in European sign language research*. Hamburg. 97–112.

Engberg-Pedersen, E. 1993. *Space in Danish Sign Language*. Hamburg.

Fischer, S. and P. Siple (eds) 1990. *Theoretical issues in sign language research*. Chicago, IL.

Kendon, A. 1989. *Sign languages of Aboriginal Australia*. Cambridge.

Klima, E.S. and U. Bellugi (eds) 1979. *The signs of language*. London.

Lane, H. and F. Grosjean (eds) 1989. *Recent perspectives on American sign language*. Hove.

Liddell, S.C. and R.E. Johnson. 1989. American sign language: the phonological base. *Sign Language Studies* 64.195–277.

Liddell, S.K. 1980. *American sign language syntax*. The Hague.

Lillo-Martin, D.C. 1991. *Universal grammar and American sign language*. Dordrecht.

Lucas, C. (ed.) 1990. *Sign language research: Theoretical issues*. Washington, DC.

Lucas, C. and C. Valli. 1989. Language contact in the American deaf community. In C. Lucas (ed.), *The sociolinguistics of the deaf community*. San Diego, CA. 11–40.

McIntire, M. *et al.* (eds) 1987. Hands and faces: a preliminary inventory for written ASL. *Sign Language Studies* 56.197–241.

Newport, E.L. 1988. Constraints on learning and their role in language acquisition: Studies of the acquisition of American Sign Language. *LangS* 10.147–72.

Newport, E.L. and R.P. Meier. 1985. The acquisition of American Sign Language. In D.L. Stobin (ed.), *The cross-linguistic study of language acquisition*, 2 vols. Hillsdale, NJ.

Padden, C.A. 1988a. *Interaction of morphology and syntax in American Sign Language*. New York.

—— 1988b. Grammatical theory and signed languages. In Frederick Newmeyer (ed.), *Linguistics: The Cambridge survey*. Cambridge. Vol. 2, 250–66.

Padden, C. and T. Humpries. 1988. *Deaf in America*. Cambridge.

Prillwitz, S. and H. Zienert. 1990. Hamburg notation system for sign language: development of a sign writing with computer application. In S. Prillwitz and T. Vollhaber (eds), *Current trends in European sign language research*. Hamburg. 355–79.

Reilly, J.S. *et al.* 1990. Faces: the relationship between language and affect. In V. Volterra and C.J. Erting (eds), *From gesture to language in hearing and deaf children*. Berlin. 128–41.

—— 1992. Affective prosody in American sign language. *Sign Language Studies* 75.113–28.

Sandler, W. 1990. Temporal aspects and ASL phonology. In S. Fischer and P. Siple (eds), *Theoretical issues in sign language research*, vol. 1: *Linguistics*. Chicago. 7–35.

Schermer, T.M. 1990. *In search of language: influences from spoken Dutch on Sign Language of the Netherlands*. Delft.

Stokoe, W. 1960. Sign language structure: an outline of the visual communication systems of the American Deaf. Buffalo, NY.

Supalla, T. 1982. Structure and acquisition of verbs of motion and location in American Sign Language. Unpublished dissertation, University of California, San Diego.

Volterra, V. and C.J. Erting (eds) 1990. *From gesture to language in hearing and deaf children*. Berlin.

Wilbur, R. 1979. *American Sign Language and sign systems*. Baltimore, MD.
—— 1990. Why syllables? What the notion means for ASL research. In S. Fischer and P. Siple (eds), *Theoretical issues in sign language research*, vol. 1. *Linguistics*. Chicago, IL. 81–108.
Wilcox, S. (ed.) 1992. *Academic acceptance of American Sign Language*. Burtonsville.

Dictionary
Stokoe, W.C. *et al.* 1965. *A dictionary of American sign language on linguistic principles*. Washington, DC.

Bibliography
Joachim, G.H.G. and S. Prillwitz. 1993. *International bibliography of sign language*. Hamburg.

sign theory ⇒ semiotics

signal

In **information theory** the state or change of material (acoustic, electromagnetic, or biochemical) systems. Signals are potential carriers of information and, thus, have in and of themselves no symbolic character. They provide for the spatial transmission or temporal indication of information, and their interpretation is dependent on the given signaling system.

References
⇒ **information theory**, **semiotics**

signatum ⇒ signifier vs signified

signeme

Term formed from *sign-* and *-eme*, which is used to refer to all distinctive elements at the various levels of linguistic description.

significant ⇒ signifier vs signified

significative meaning ⇒ connotation[2]

signified ⇒ signifier vs signified

signifier (*also* significant) vs signified (*also* signatum)

Distinction established by F. de Saussure between the form of a linguistic sign and its content, wherein both aspects are of a mental nature and the relation between these two sides of the (linguistic) sign is arbitrary (⇒ **arbitrariness**, **sign**). (⇒ *also* **expression**[2], and cf. **meaning**, **denotatum**)

References
⇒ **arbitrariness**, **sign**

simultaneity

Temporal relationship in complex sentences with several actions, where the action described in the **subordinate clause** occurs simultaneous-

ly with the action in the **main clause**: *When I arrived in New York, it was raining*. (⇒ *also* **sequence of tenses**)

simultaneous interpreting ⇒ interpreting

simultaneous translation ⇒ interpreting

Sindhi ⇒ Indo-Aryan

Singhalese ⇒ Indo-Aryan

single-only noun (*also* singulare tantum)

Noun which can only be used in the singular. These include **mass nouns** (*wood*, *air*), **abstracts** (*righteousness*, *anger*, *ubiquity*), and **collective nouns** (*fruit*, *rice*, *cattle*).

singleton ⇒ set

singular

Subcategory of **number** which refers to single elements (*a house* vs *many houses*), generalizing statements (*Man shall not live by bread alone*), and collective terms (*The wolf's cunning*). Nouns which can only be used in the singular are called **single-only nouns**.

singulare tantum ⇒ single-only noun

singulative

Subcategory of **number** which designates a single entity. In contrast to the **singular**, the singulative is a marked form of a **collective noun**, e.g. **Arabic** *dabbān* 'fly, flies' (unspecified) vs *dabbāne* 'a fly.'

Sinitic ⇒ Sino-Tibetan

Sinn (Ger.) ⇒ sense; *see also* intension, meaning

Sino-Tibetan

Language group of Central and East Asia with approx. 300 languages which are divided into the Sinitic (**Chinese**) and **Tibeto-Burman** branches, all of which have a long written tradition.
    Characteristics: typically **isolating**, monosyllabic **tonal languages**. Remnants of older prefixal morphology are recognizable. No developed distinction between noun and verb.

References
Benedict, P.K. 1972. *Sino-Tibetan: a conspectus*. Cambridge.
McCoy, J. and T. Light (eds) 1986. *Contributions to Sino-Tibetan studies*. Amsterdam and Philadelphia.
Shafer, R. 1974. *Introduction to Sino-Tibetan*. Wiesbaden.

Bibliography
Shafer, R. *et al.* (eds) 1957/63. *Bibliography of Sino-Tibetan languages*, 2 vols. Wiesbaden.

Siouan

Language family of North America with approx. twelve languages; the largest language is Lakhota with approx. 30,000 speakers. E. Sapir grouped them together with **Iroquoian** and **Caddoan** into a Macro-Siouan group.

Characteristics: **sound symbolism** used for making diminutives and/or argumentatives (diminutive: dental fricative; argumentative: velar fricative). **Noun classes** (**animate vs inanimate**), complex verbs with several prefixes, including markers for instrument, ergativity ($\Rightarrow$ **ergative language**) in the personal inflection of the verb, complex possession distinctions (alienable, body parts, and kinship terms are distinguished). Word order: SOV.

References
Chafe, W.L. 1976. *The Caddoan, Iroquoian and Siouan language*. The Hague.
Levin, N.B. 1964. *The Assiniboine language*. Bloomington, IN, and The Hague (= *IJAL* 30:3, pub. 32).
Matthews, G.H. 1965. *Hidatsa syntax*. London.
Rood, D.S. 1979. Siouan. In L. Campbell and M. Mithun (eds), *The languages of native America: historical and comparative assessment*. Austin, TX. 236–98.
Williamson, J.S. 1984. *Studies in Lakhota Grammar*. San Diego, CA.
$\Rightarrow$ **North and Central American languages**

SIS (sensory information storage) $\Rightarrow$ **memory**

sister adjunction

Sister adjunction refers to the relationship between two or more **constituents** which are immediately dominated by the same **node** in a **tree diagram**.

References
$\Rightarrow$ **transformational grammar**

situation semantics

A formal theory of meaning of natural (or artificial) languages based on situation theory and a recent competitor to **possible world** semantics. It was developed in the late 1970s by Barwise with the collaboration of Perry, Cooper, Peters, Etchemendy, and others. It is based upon the following basic assumptions: (a) properties and relations are assumed to be primitives and are not set-theoretically construed from other entities; (b) there is a single world, namely the real one, and not a multitude of possible worlds; (c) well-formed propositions are about this world or its parts, which are called 'situations'; (d) the meaning of a declarative sentence S is a relation between the type of situations in which S is assertively expressed and the type to which those situations belong that are described by it ('relational theory of meaning'). Two phenomena, which were viewed more peripherally in earlier theories, are now considered central to this theory, namely the efficiency of language (i.e. the way one and the same expression has multiple uses) and the partiality of information (i.e. that information is incomplete).

References
Barwise, J. 1989. Situations and small worlds. In J. Barwise (ed.), *The situation in logic*. Stanford, CA. 79–92.
Barwise, J. and J. Etchemendy. 1987. *The liar: an essay in truth and circularity*. Oxford.
Barwise, J. and J. Perry. 1983. *Situations and attitudes*. Cambridge, MA.

slang

British or American variant of carelessly used colloquial language with explicitly social and regional variants. Corresponding to the French **argot**, slang is characterized by the innovative use of common vocabulary as well as newly coined words. Slang corresponds to the older designation **cant** which originally referred to **secret languages** and **sublanguages**.

References
Ayto, J. and J. Simpson. 1992. *The Oxford dictionary of modern slang*. Oxford and New York.
Beale, P. (ed.) 1991. *A concise dictionary of slang and unconventional English, based on the work of E. Partridge*, 9th edn. London.
Berry, L.V. and M. van den Bark. 1953. *The American thesaurus of slang*, 2nd edn. New York.
Butcher, A. and C. Gnutzmann. 1977. Cockney rhyming slang. *LingB* 50.1–10.
Franklyn, J. 1992. *A dictionary of rhyming slang*, 2nd edn. London.
Goldin, H.E. (ed.) 1970. *Dictionary of American underworld lingo*. New York.
Landy, E.E. 1971. *The underground dictionary*. New York.
Major, C. 1971. *Black slang: a dictionary of Afro-American talk*. London.
Partridge, E. 1949. *A dictionary of slang and unconventional English*. London. (8th edn. 1984, reissue 1991.)
—— 1950. *A dictionary of the underworld: British and American*. New York. (3rd edn London, 1968.)
Thorne, T. 1990. *Bloomsbury dictionary of contemporary slang*. London.
Weingarten, J.A. 1955. *An American dictionary of slang and colloquial English*. Brooklyn, NY.

Wentworth, H. and S.B. Flexner (eds) 1975. *Dictionary of American slang*, 2nd rev. edn. New York.

Slavic

Family of **Indo-European** languages which show similarities to the **Baltic** languages, perhaps deriving from a common Balto-Slavic group. There are numerous phonological, morphological, and lexical correspondences between these two language families. The Slavic languages are commonly divided into three groups containing the following official languages: East Slavic (**Russian, Belorussian, Ukrainian**), West Slavic (**Polish, Czech, Slovak, Sorbian**), and South Slavic (**Bulgarian, Macedonian, Serbo-Croatian, Slovene**). **Kashubian** is a member of the West Slavic group, but now has only a few thousand speakers. **Old Church Slavic** in its numerous variants continues to be used in Orthodox Christian services.

Characteristics: virtually all the Slavic languages have a developed **aspect** system for the verb, pairing perfective and imperfective verbs. Imperfectives can be constructed by adding various suffixes. Base verbs are almost invariably imperfective; prefixation renders a verb perfective and usually alters its meaning. Suffixation can provide an exact imperfective partner for a prefixed perfective. All Slavic languages, except Bulgarian and Macedonian, have well-developed case systems.

References
Arumaa, P. 1964–85. *Einführung in das vergleichende Studium der slavischen Sprachen*, 3 vols. Heidelberg.
Bernštejn, S.B. 1961–74. *Očerk sravnitel'noj grammatiki slavjanskix jazykov*, 2 vols. Moscow.
Birnbaum, H. 1975. *Common Slavic: progress and problems in its reconstruction*. Columbus, OH.
Bräuer, H. 1961–9. *Slavische Sprachwissenschaft*. Berlin.
Carlton, T.R. 1991. *Introduction to the phonological history of the Slavic languages*. Columbus, OH.
Comrie, B. and G.G. Corbett (eds) 1993. *The Slavonic languages*. London.
de Bray, R.G.A., de. 1980. *Guide to the Slavonic languages*, 3 vols, 3rd edn. Columbus, OH.
Jakobson, R. 1955. *Slavic languages: a condensed survey*. New York.
Picchio, R. and H. Goldblatt. 1984. *Aspects of the Slavic language question*, 2 vols. Columbus, OH.
Schenker, A.M. and E. Stankiewicz (eds) 1980. *The Slavic literary languages: formation and development*. New Haven, CT.
Shevelov, G.Y. 1964. *A prehistory of Slavic: the historical phonology of Common Slavic*. Heidelberg.
Stone, G. and D. Worth (eds) 1985. *The formation of the Slavonic literary languages*. Columbus, OH.
Panzer, B. 1991. *Die slavischen Sprachen in Gegen-wart und Geschichte: Sprachstrukturen und Verwandtschaft*. Frankfurt-on-Main.
Rehder, P. (ed.) 1991. *Einführung in die slavischen Sprachen*, 2nd rev. edn. Darmstadt.
Vaillant, A. 1950–77. *Grammaire comparée des langues slaves*, 5 vols. Paris.

Bibliographies
Birnbaum, H. and P.T. Merrill. 1983. *Recent advances in the reconstruction of Common Slavic (1971–1982)*. Columbus, OH.
Stankiewicz, E. and D.S. Worth. 1966–70. *A selected bibliography of Slavic linguistics*, 2 vols. The Hague.

Dictionary
Trubačev, O.N. 1974– . *Ėtimologičeskij slovar' slavjanskix jazykov*. Vol. 20, 1994. Moscow.

Journals
International Journal of Slavic Linguistics and Poetics.
Journal of Slavonic Studies.
Slavjanskoe i balkanskoe jazykoznanie.

slip of the tongue ⇒ **speech error**

slogan [Scots 'war cry, battle cry,' from Gaelic *sluaghghairm*, from *sluagh* 'host' + *gairm* 'shout, cry']

A precise and impressingly formulated expression with a **persuasive** function, frequently formed as an elliptic sentence and equipped with **figures of speech** such as advertising slogans (e.g. *Have you driven a Ford lately?*) or political slogans (e.g. *Give me liberty or give me death, Better dead than red*).

References
⇒ **persuasive**

slot ⇒ **empty position**

Slovak

West **Slavic** language with approx. 4.5 million speakers, primarily in Slovakia. After a number of unsuccessful attempts in the early nineteenth century, Slovak became a literary language, in large part due to L. Štúr's (1848) programmatic writings. Since 1968, Slovak has been the language of government in Slovakia and was recognized and used as an official language in former Czechoslovakia from 1945. The writing system is based on the Latin alphabet with numerous diacritics: ⟨l̕⟩, ⟨l'⟩, ⟨ŕ⟩ and, in contrast to **Czech**, ⟨ä⟩, ⟨dz⟩, ⟨dž⟩, ⟨ô⟩.

Characteristics: Syllabic *l* and *r*, both long and short: *vlk* 'wolf' vs *vĺča* 'little wolf'; *srdce* 'heart' vs *hŕba* 'pile.' Stress is on the first syllable, as in Czech. Animacy (⇒ **animate vs inanimate**) is distinguished in masculine declension.

References
Bartoš, J. and J. Gagnaire. 1972. *Grammaire de la langue slovaque*. Bratislava.
Krajčovič, R. 1975. *A historical phonology of the Slovak language*. Heidelberg.
Mistrík, J. 1983. *A grammar of contemporary Slovak*. Bratislava.
Oravec, J. *et al.* 1982/4. *Súčasný slovenský spisovný jazyk*, vol. I: *Syntax*, vol. II: *Morfológia*. Bratislava. (Vol. I 2nd edn 1986.)
Pauliny, E. *et al.* 1981. *Slovenská gramatika*. Bratislava.
Štolc, J. *et al.* 1968–84. *Atlas slovenského jazyka*, vols I–IV. Bratislava.
Swan, O.E. and S. Galova-Lorinc. 1990. *Beginning Slovak*. Columbus, OH.

Dictionary
Slovník slovenského jazyka. 1959–68. 6 vols. Bratislava.
⇒ **Slavic**

Slovene

South **Slavic** language with approx. 1.8 million speakers, primarily in Slovenia, but also in Carinthia (Austria), the northeastern provinces of Italy, and in Croatia. The Freising fragments comprise the oldest sizable written Slavic text, dating from about 1000 AD, and are in Old Slovene, written in the Latin alphabet based on Old High German spelling. The development of a Slovene literature dates from the sixteenth century; Slovene uses the Latin alphabet with additional diacritics.

Characteristics: moveable accent; **tone**; **dual** forms; split relative pronoun; eight-vowel system.

References
Breznik, A. 1982. *Jezikoslovne razpravy*. Ljubljana.
Lencek, R.L. 1982. *The Structure and history of the Slovene language*. Columbus, OH.

Grammar
Svane, G.O. 1958. *Grammatik der slovenischen Schriftsprache*. Copenhagen.

Dictionaries
Kotnik, J. 1967. *Slovensko–angelski slovar*, 6th edn. Ljubljana.
Slovar slovenskega knjižnega jezika. 1970–91. 5 vols. Ljubljana.

Etymological dictionary
Bezlaj, G. 1976–. *Etimološki slovar slovenskega jezika*. Ljubljana.

Bibliography
Lencek, R.L. 1975. *American linguists on the Slovene language: a comprehensive annotated bibliography*. New York.

Journal
Slovene Studies.
⇒ **Slavic**

social dialect ⇒ **sociolect**

social dialectology ⇒ **sociolect, code theory**

social network ⇒ **network**

sociolect (*also* social dialect)

In analogy to 'dialect,' 'sociolect' describes a language variety that is characteristic for a socially defined group. (⇒ **code theory**, **sociolinguistics**)

sociolinguistics

Scientific discipline developed from the co-operation of linguistics and sociology that investigates the social meaning of the language system and of language use, and the common set of conditions of linguistic and social structure. Several areas of sociolinguistic investigation are differentiated. (a) A primarily sociologically oriented approach concerned predominantly with the norms of language use. (When and for what purpose does somebody speak what kind of language or what variety with whom?) Here language use and language attitudes as well as larger and smaller social **networks** are in the foreground. These facets are studied mainly by using quantitative methods; connections between socio-economics, history, culture, ethnic differentiation, social class structure, and language varieties are included in the investigation (⇒ **diglossia**, **code theory**). (b) A primarily linguistically oriented approach that presumes linguistic systems to be in principle heterogeneous, though structured, when viewed within sociological parameters. For an appropriate description of linguistic variation, a new type of rule – differentiated from rules found in **generative grammar** – is proposed, the so-called 'variable rule,' which expresses and establishes the probability that a particular linguistic form will result from the influence of different linguistic and extralinguistic variables, e.g. social class, age, etc. (⇒ **variational linguistics**). The results of this sociolinguistic approach have particularly important implications for the theory of **language change**: in a series of empirical investigations the relevance of social conditions to the processes of language change was demonstrated and proved, such that synchronically present variational structures can be seen as a 'snap shot' of diachronic changes. (c) An ethnomethodologically oriented approach with linguistic interaction as the focal point, which studies the ways in which members of a society create social reality and rule-ordered behaviour. Here a formal distinction must be drawn between **conversation analysis**, which deals with the structure of conversations, and ethnographic conversation analysis (⇒ **ethnography of speaking**), which investigates interactive processes in the production of meaning and understanding (⇒ **contextualization**).

References
Ager, D. 1990. *Sociolinguistics and contemporary French*. Cambridge.
Ammon, J., N. Dittmar, and K.J. Mattheier (eds) 1987. *Sociolinguistics: an international handbook of the science of language and society*, 2 vols. Berlin and New York.
Bell, R.T. 1976. *Sociolinguistics: goals, approaches and problems*. London.
Bierwisch, M. 1975. Social differentiation of language structure. In A. Kasher (ed.), *Language in focus*. Dordrecht. 407–56.
Bolton, K. 1991. *Sociolinguistics today: international perspectives*. London.
Downes, W. 1984. *Language and society*. London.
Fasold, R. 1984. *The sociolinguistics of society*. New York.
Giles, H., N. Coupland, and J. Coupland (eds). 1992. *Contexts of accommodation: developments in applied sociolinguistics*. Cambridge.
Gumperz, J.J. 1982. *Discourse strategies*. Cambridge.
Holmes, J. 1992. *An introduction to sociolinguistics*, London.
Hudson, R.A. 1980. *Sociolinguistics*. Cambridge.
Hymes, D. 1974. *Foundations in sociolinguistics: an ethnographic approach*. Philadelphia, PA.
Labov, W. 1972. *Sociolinguistic patterns*. Philadelphia, PA.
Milroy, L. 1980. *Language and social networks*. Oxford.
Montgomery, M. 1995. *An introduction to language and society*. 2nd edn. London.
Romaine, S. 1982. *Socio-historical linguistics: its status and methodology*. Cambridge.
———— 1994. *Language in society: an introduction to sociolinguistics*. Oxford.
Ryan, E.B. and H. Giles. 1982. *Attitudes towards language variation: social and applied contexts*. London.
Shuy, R.W. 1990. A brief history of American sociolinguistics, 1949–1989. *Historiographia Linguistica* 17.183–209.
Trudgill, P. 1974. *Sociolinguistics: an introduction*. Harmondsworth.
Wardhaugh, R. 1986. *An introduction to sociolinguistics*. Oxford.
Whorf, B.L. 1956. *Language, thought and reality: selected writings of B.L. Whorf*, ed. J.B. Caroll. Cambridge, MA.

Bibliography
Simon, G. (ed.) 1974. *Bibliographie zur Soziolinguistik*. Tübingen.

Journals
International Journal of the Sociology of Language.
Language in Society.

Sociolinguistica.
⇒ **Black English**, **English**, **feminist linguistics**, **terminology**

Sogdian ⇒ Iranian

solecism [Grk *soloikismós* 'incorrectness in the use of language']

A term from **rhetoric** for an infraction of the rules of grammar. Solecism, like **barbarism**, affects the principle of correctness of language, which is the first of the four qualities of style in classical rhetoric.

References
⇒ **figure of speech**, **rhetoric**

solidarity

Term used in **glossematics** for the syntagmatic relation (*not only but also*) which indicates the reciprocal dependence of two elements (⇒ **interdependence**), such as the obligatory simultaneous occurrence of case and number in **Latin**.

References
⇒ **glossematics**

Somali ⇒ Cushitic

sonant [Lat. *sonare* 'to make a sound']

1 Voiced **speech sound** that can function as the nucleus of a syllable, e.g. in [I] and [ŋ] in *given* [gɪvŋ].

2 Voiced speech sound used syllabically, e.g. [i] in [invɛriəbl] *invariable*.

3 **Sonorant**[1] consonant.

References
⇒ **phonetics**

Songhai

Relatively isolated language in Mali and Niger, spoken along the Niger River (about 1 million speakers), the language of the old Songhai Empire. Greenberg (1963) considers it a member of the **Nilo-Saharan** family.

References
Greenberg, J.H. 1963. *The languages of Africa*. Bloomington, IN. (2nd edn 1966.)
Nicolaï, R. 1981. *Les dialectes des songhay*. Paris.

sonorant (*also* resonant, sonant consonant)

1 In the narrower sense, voiced **speech sound** that is not an **obstruent**, that is, all sounds in English except stops or fricatives; [ɔ], [r], [aː] in **Czech** ['dvɔraːk] *Dvořák*; [r], [n], [ɔ] in Czech ['brnɔ] *Brünn* (town name). In ['brnɔ], [r] is a sonant consonant and moreover the nucleus of the syllable, while [ɔ] is a sonant vowel.

References
⇒ **phonetics**

2 In the broader sense, voiced speech sound (⇒ **articulatory phonetics**).

References
⇒ **phonetics**

sonority

Auditory characteristic of a **speech sound**. According to Jespersen (1904), the following ranking of relative sonority can be ascertained when the air pressure is stable: vowels with a low, vowels with a mid, vowels with a high tongue position, *r*-sounds, nasals, and laterals, voiced fricatives, voiced plosives, voiceless fricatives, voiceless plosives.

References
Jespersen, O. 1904. *Lehrbuch der Phonetik*. Leipzig. (7th edn 1912.)
⇒ **phonetics**

sonorization

The substitution of a voiceless consonant by a **homorganic** voiced consonant. For example, [g] in **Dutch** [ʔɪgˈbɛn] *ik ben* 'I am' is a sonorized [k] through assimilation with the following voiced [b]. Sonorization as a historical process is found in **Italian** *strada* vs *strāta*. The opposite process is called devoicing (or 'desonorization'). Examples of this are final devoicing of consonants in **German** [liːp] *lieb* 'dear,' the devoicing of voiced obstruents in absolute final position in **Russian** (e.g. [ˈjuˑgə] 'south' (gen.sg.) with [juˑk] 'south' (nom.).

References
⇒ **phonetics**

Sorbian

West **Slavic** language with two variants: (a) Upper Sorbian in Oberlausitz (Germany) with approx. 35,000 speakers (primarily Catholic); and (b) Lower Sorbian in Niederlausitz (Germany) with approx. 15,000 speakers (primarily Protestants). During the eighth century the Sorbian-speaking territory extended to the Saale River valley. In the **German** dialects spoken in the formerly Sorbian territories, there are a number of words borrowed from Sorbian. Influence of German on Sorbian can be seen in the instrumental, which is formed with the preposition *z* (*ze* 'with'), in contrast to most other Slavic languages.

The first written documents date from the sixteenth century during the course of the Reformation; the first book in Lower Sorbian appeared in 1574, while Bible translations in Upper Sorbian date from 1670. Lower Sorbian has been disappearing since 1930. Both dialects of Sorbian have been protected as minority languages since 1947.

Characteristics: word stress on the initial syllable (as in **Czech**); no distinction of vowel length (as in **Polish**); dual form; uvular *r*.

References
Fasske, H. 1981. *Grammatik der obersorbischen Schriftsprache der Gegenwart: Morphologie*. Bautzen.
Hauptmann, J.G. 1791. *Nieder-Lausitzsche Wendische Grammatica*. Lübben. (Fotomechanical reprint Bautzen, 1984.)
Janas, P. 1984. *Niedersorbische Grammatik*, 2nd edn. Bautzen.
Sorbischer Sprachatlas. 1965– . Bautzen.
Stone, G.C. 1972. *The smallest Slavonic nation: the Sorbs of Lusatia*. London.
⇒ **Slavic**

sound

1 In the narrow sense, a vibration wave causing a disturbance in the pressure and density of the air and having a frequency within the range of 20 to 20,000 oscillations per second that are detectable by the organs of hearing.

2 In the broader sense, general term for the smallest acoustic or articulatory element of spoken language that can be perceived. Since speech and articulation occur in a continuous 'chain' without natural breaks (⇒ **co-articulation**), the concept of a sound being segmentable is merely hypothetical. Only by using special methods of analysis within **phonology** can one arrive at the abstract units of sound, namely **phonemes**, which can be identified as segments of utterances. (⇒ *also* **speech sound**)

References
⇒ **phonetics**

sound change

Historical changes in the sound system of a language. Different types of sound change can be distinguished (see Bartsch and Vennemann 1982). (a) Phonetically motivated changes: a type of change related to the trend towards simplicity in the articulatory effort. (i) Simplification of segments: the inherent complexity of segments is reduced as more complicated articulatory positions disappear, e.g. the simultaneous lowering of the **velum** in the denasalization of nasal vowels. (ii) Sequential simplification: far less articulatory effort achieved by an adjustment of sounds to be more like the surrounding sounds (⇒ **assimilation, umlaut, vowel harmony**), simplification of syllable structure (⇒ **anaptyxis, epenthesis, metathesis, prothesis**), and reductions (**aphesis, apocope**, lenisization (⇒ **weakening**), **syncope**).

(b) Phonologically motivated changes: a type of change related to the trend towards maximal contrast and distinctiveness of speech sounds in the process of communication. This type has been studied foremost by the structuralists: consider, for example, the concept of **push chain vs drag chain**, which operates on the principle of the retention of contrast of different **phonemes**. (c) Changes motivated by language-external factors: a type of change related to social/social-psychological motivation (trend towards maximum radius of communication, optimal individuation in interactions with others, adaptation to norms of specific social groups, and so on) in which idiosyncratic or systematic characteristics of other, more prestigious, varieties are adopted (see also **sound substitution**). (d) Changes motivated by analogy: a type of change related to the trend towards simplifying acquisition, conceptual simplicity and economy, in which the individual words or groups of words are modeled after phonetically similar units or units that belong together conceptually (⇒ **analogy**).

Regarding the manner in which sound changes spread, two aspects can be differentiated. (a) Language-internal spread involves the question of gradual lexical and/or phonetic spread, i.e. whether a sound change occurs at the same time and in the same form for one sound in all environments or if it occurs 'quasi-analogously' only from word to word (⇒ **lexical diffusion**), and whether this happens phonetically in minimal steps (steadily) or in qualitative jumps (abruptly). There is a definite tendency for different modes of spread to fit into different sound change types (e.g. language-external borrowing as a lexically gradual, but phonetically abrupt change). A comprehensive explanation, however, is still lacking (see Labov 1981). (b) Language-external spread concerns the problem of (social) origin and of the social and regional spread of a change, until all speakers of a linguistic community use the new forms in all situations. Here the results of sociolinguistic research (⇒ **sociolinguistics**) are pertinent. (⇒ *also* **historical grammars**, **language change**)

References
Baldi, P. and R.N. Werth (eds) 1978. *Readings in historical phonology*. London.
Bartsch, R. and T. Vennemann. 1982. *Grundzüge der Sprachtheorie*. Tübingen.
Bynon, T. 1977. *Historical linguistics*. Cambridge.
Eckert, P. (ed.) 1992. *New ways of analyzing sound change: quantitative analyses of linguistic structure*. New York.
Fisiak, J. (ed.) 1978. *Recent developments in historical phonology*. The Hague.
Fónagy, I. 1956. Über den Verlauf des Lautwandels. *Acta Linguistica* (Budapest) 6.173–278.
Hagège, C. and A. Haudricourt. 1978. *La phonologie panchronique: comment les sons changent dans les langues*. Paris.
Hock, H.H. 1986. *Principles of historical linguistics*. New York. (2nd edn 1990.)
Jones, C. (ed.) 1993. *Historical linguistics: problems and perspectives*. London and New York.
King, R. 1969. *Historical linguistics and generative grammar*. Frankfurt.
Kiparsky, P. 1968. Linguistic universals and linguistic change. In E. Bach and R.T. Harms (eds), *Universals in linguistic theory*. New York. 170–202.
——— 1970. Historical linguistics. In J. Lyons (ed.), *New horizons in linguistics*. Harmondsworth. 302–15.
Labov, W. 1963. The social motivation of a sound change. *Word* 19.273–309.
——— 1981. Resolving the neogrammarian controversy. *Lg* 57.267–308.
——— 1994. *Principles of linguistic change*, vol. I: *Internal factors*. Oxford and Cambridge.
Labov, W., M. Yaeger, and R. Steiner. 1972. *A quantitative study of sound change in progress*. Philadelphia, PA.
Locke, J.L. 1983. *Phonological acquisition and change*. New York.
Martinet, A. 1955. *Economie des changements phonétiques*. Bern.
Ohala, J. 1992. What's cognitive, what's not, in sound change. *Lingua e Stile* 27.321–63.
Paul, H. 1880. *Prinzipien der Sprachgeschichte*. Tübingen. (9th edn 1975.)
Weinreich, W., W. Labov, and M.I. Herzog. 1968. Empirical foundations of language change. In W.P. Lehmann and Y. Malkiel (eds), *Directions for historical linguistics*. Austin, TX. 95–188.
⇒ **historical grammars**, **language change**, **Neogrammarians**

sound class

Class of phonetically similar sound variants (= **phones**) that can be described on the basis of listening tests according to similar acoustic or articulatory features.

References
⇒ **phonetics**

sound image ⇒ acoustic image

sound law

Central notion of the historical linguistic description of the **Neogrammarians**. The use of this term is based on the assumption that – in analogy to natural scientific regularities – certain sounds of a given language undergo certain phonetic changes in the same way without exception. Such changes have a physiological basis and occur under the same conditions, e.g. the Germanic sound shift (⇒ **Grimm's law**; also **umlaut**, **diphthongization**). In those cases in which exceptions are ascertained in spite of the law, **analogy** and language mixing, i.e. adoptions from other varieties of languages (⇒ **sound substitution**) are considered to be at cause.

References

Collinge, N.E. 1985. *The laws of Indo-European.* Amsterdam and Philadelphia.

Fónagy, I. 1956. Über den Verlauf des Lautwandels. *ALASH* 6.173–278.

Labov, W. 1981. Resolving the neogrammarian controversy. *Lg* 57.267–308.

Paul, H. 1880. *Prinzipien der Sprachgeschichte.* Tübingen. (9th edn 1975.)

Schneider, G. 1973. *Zum Begriff des Lautgesetzes in der Sprachwissenschaft seit den Junggrammatikern.* Tübingen.

Schuchardt, H. 1885. *Über die Lautgesetze: gegen die Junngrammatiker.* Berlin. (Repr. in *Hugo Schuchardt-Brevier: ein Vademecum der allgemeinen Sprachwissenschaft,* ed. L. Spitzer, 2nd edn. Halle, 1928. 51–86.)

Wechssler, E. 1900. Gibt es Lautgesetze? In *Forschungen zur romanischen Philologie: Festschrift für H. Suchier.* Halle. 349–538.

Wilbur, T.H. (ed.) 1977. *The Lautgesetz-controversy: a documentation (1885–86).* Amsterdam.

⇒ **analogy**, **Bartholomae's Law**, **Grassmann's Law**, **Grimm's Law**, **Neogrammarians**, **Sievers' Law**, **sound change**, **Thurneysen's Law**, **Verner's Law**

sound physiology

Articulatory phonetics as practised by the **Neogrammarians**.

sound shift

Term for a set of **sound changes** occurring systematically, so that a whole sound system is shifted. (⇒ *also* **Great Vowel Shift**, **Grimm's Law**, **push chain vs drag chain**)

References
⇒ **sound change**

sound substitution

1 Process in which foreign words are adopted into another language and their sounds assimilated to those in the adopting language. As a rule, sounds of a foreign language that are not found in one's own language system are replaced by those sounds in one's own language that are most similar to the foreign sound, e.g. the imitation of Eng. [ð] and [θ] (written ‹th› for the voiced and voiceless dental fricatives) as Ger. [d] or [z], [t], or [s] in *these* vs *thick*.

2 Sound substitution is also found when sounds are adopted from a prestigious language variety within a given language community, for example in the often haphazard substitution of standard American pronunciation in favor of a sometimes imagined British standard, e.g. [tomaːtoː] instead of [təmeːtoː]. Since this sound substitution happens consciously, it occurs word by word, and is replete with exceptions, the **Neogrammarians** referred to it as a 'process of irregular sound alteration,' as opposed to regular, unconsciously occurring **sound change**. In **historical linguistics**, particularly in the study of place-names, ascertaining regularities in sound substitution between different languages is a significant method for substantiating and dating regional language contact.

References
⇒ **sound change**

sound symbolism (*also* phonetic symbolism, synaesthesia)

Hypothesis about the relationship of linguistic sounds to acoustic or optical phenomena in the extralinguistic world. Sound-symbolic word formations (as in *cuckoo, bang*) raise the question of the psycholinguistic origin of naming extralinguistic states of affairs onomatopoeically (⇒ **onomatopoeia**). Even if sound symbolism is not a universal phenomenon, numerous experiments do appear to demonstrate certain similarities in the way individuals perceive the relationship between language sounds and sensory impressions. Thus, a majority of speakers of different languages attribute the expression *malume* to the round and *takete* to the pointy stick figure (see figures below), though both figures are inherently meaningless (see Köhler 1947).

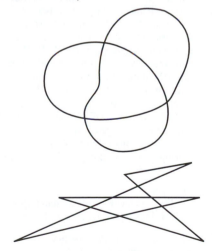

In another experiment, 80 percent of the informants (to whom the expressions *mal* and *mil* were given to mean 'table') indicated that *mal* designated the larger table and *mil* the smaller table (see Sapir 1929). Thus, it seems that high-pitch sounds in many languages designate small objects, while low-pitch sounds generally designate larger objects. International comparative investigations have led some researchers, such as Osgood (1962), to believe in universal sound symbolism.

References

Brown, R. 1958. *Words and things*. Glencoe, IL.
Hinton, L. *et al.* (eds). *Sound symbolism*. Cambridge.
Köhler, W. 1947. *Gestalt psychology*. New York.
Osgood, C.E. 1962. Studies on the generality of affective meaning systems. *AmP* 17.10–28.
Sapir, E. 1929. A study in phonetic symbolism. *JEP* 12.225–39.
⇒ **semantic differential**

source language

1 Language from which one translates into the **target language**.

2 **Native language** of the learner in **second language acquisition**, especially from a contrastive and error-analytic perspective.

South American languages

Research on the South American languages started in the sixteenth century (primarily grammatical descriptions by Spanish and Portuguese missionaries); today the knowledge of individual languages and the reconstruction of language families still has some gaps. Since numerous languages have various names, the exact number of languages in this group is still unknown; usual estimates range from 550 to 2000 with about 11 million speakers (before colonization). Today a large number of languages are either dead or dying out. An important first work on the classification of these languages was undertaken by F.S. Gilij (1782); more recent classifications by Loukotka (latest 1968, with 108 language families), Greenberg (1956; four families with considerable deviation in details), and Suarez (1974, 1982; 82 families). Greenberg (1987) believes that all South American languages as well as the Central American and most North American languages belong to one language group, **Amerindian**.

References

Derbyshire, D.C. and G.K. Pullum (eds) 1986–8. *Handbook of Amazonian languages*, 2 vols. Berlin.
Gilij, F.S. 1780–84. *Saggio di storia americana o sia storia naturale, civile e sacra, de' regni e delle provincie spagnuole de terra ferma nell' America Meridionale*. 4 vols. Rome.
Greenberg, J. 1960. The general classification of Central and South American languages. In: A.

Wallace, (ed.) *Selected Papers of the Fifth International Congress of Anthropological and Ethnological Sciences*. 791–794. Philadelphia.
——— 1987. *Language in the Americas*. Stanford, CA.
Key, M.R. 1979. *The grouping of South American Indian languages*. Tübingen.
Klein, H.E.M. and L.R. Stark. 1985. *South American Indian languages: retrospect and prospect*. Austin, TX.
Loukotka, Č. 1968. *Classification of South American Indian languages*. Los Angeles, CA.
Sebeok, T.A. 1977. *Native languages of the Americas*. New York.
Suarez, B. 1974. South American Indian Languages. *Encyclopaedia Britannica*. 792–9.

South Caucasian (*also* Kartvelian)

Branch of **Caucasian** in the southern Caucasus with four languages: Mingrelian, Laz, Svan, and the largest language **Georgian**.

References

Deeters, G. 1930. *Das khartwelische Verbum, vergleichende Darstellung des Verbalbaus der südkaukasischen Sprachen*. Leipzig.
Harris, A.C. 1985. *Diachronic syntax: the Kartvelian case*. Orlando, FL.
——— (ed.) 1991. *The indigenous languages of the Caucasus*, vol. I: *The Kartvelian languages*. Delmar, NY.
Schmidt, K.H. 1962. *Studien zur Rekonstruktion des Lautstandes der südkaukasischen Grundsprache*. Wiesbaden.

Journal
Bedi Kartlisa.

Spanish

A **Romance language** belonging to the **Indo-European** family which is spoken by approx. 300 million speakers in Spain, Central and South America, the Canary Islands, the United States, and other countries. The basis for the standard language is the Castilian dialect, which developed from the variety of Vulgar **Latin** spoken in Spain during the time of the Roman Empire. Castilian Spanish was spoken only in the northern Cantabrian provinces until the Arabs were expelled from Spain during the 'reconquista.' Some characteristic features of Castilian Spanish include the development of [f] to [h] (possibly due to a **Basque** substratum), the change of [kt] to [tʃ] (Lat. *factum* > Sp. *hecho* 'done') as well as the introduction of the phoneme /x/ (Lat. *filius* > Sp. *hijo* [ixo] 'son'). The standard language has a so-called 'prepositional accusative' for persons (*Veo a Felipe* 'I see Felipe,' but *Veo el libro* 'I see the book'); the lexicon contains numerous **Arabic** elements. The dialect structure of central and southern Spain (Andalucia) became increasingly leveled due to the influence of Castilian

Spanish, while the northern regions show stronger dialectal variation (Leon, Aragon; **Catalan**, **Portuguese**, Galician). The Spanish spoken in South America, which in the written language diverges only slightly from European Spanish, is based phonetically and morphologically on Andalucian.

References

Amastae, J. and L. Elias-Olivares (eds) 1982. *Spanish in the United States*. Cambridge.

Entwistle, W.J. 1962. *The Spanish language, together with Portuguese, Catalan, and Basque*, 2nd edn. London.

Holtus, G., M. Metzeltin, and C. Schmitt (eds) 1992. *Lexikon der romanistischen Linguistik*, vol. 6, 1. Tübingen.

King, L.D. 1992. *The semantic structure of Spanish: meaning and grammatical form*. Amsterdam and Philadelphia.

Lang, M.F. 1990. *Spanish word formation*. London.

Stevenson, C.H. 1970. *The Spanish language today*. London.

Whitley, M.S. 1986. *Spanish/English contrasts*. Washington, DC.

Grammars

Alcina, J. and J.M. Blecua. 1975. *Gramática española*. Barcelona.

Butt, J. and C. Benjamin. 1988. *A new reference grammar of Modern Spanish*. London.

Coste, J. and A. Redondo. 1965. *Syntaxe de l'espagnol moderne*. Paris.

Marcos Marin, F. 1980. *Curso de gramática española*. Madrid.

Real Academica Española. 1973. *Esbozo de una nueva gramática de la lengua española*. Madrid.

History and dialectology

Cotton, E. and J. Sharp. 1986. *Spanish in the Americas*. Georgetown, KY.

Lapesa, R. 1942. *Historia de la lengua española*. Madrid. (9th edn 1981.)

Lipski, J. 1994. *Latin American Spanish*. London.

Menéndez Pidal, R. 1926. *Orígenes del español*. Madrid. (6th edn 1968.)

Penny, R. 1991. *A history of the Spanish language*. Cambridge.

Vidal Sephiba, H. 1986. *Le Judéo-espagnol*. Paris.

Zamora Vicente, A. 1960. *Dialectología española*. Madrid. (2nd edn 1970.)

Dictionaries

Corominas, J. and J.A. Pascual. 1980–91. *Diccionario crítico etimológico castellano e hispánico*, 6 vols. Madrid.

Moliner, M. 1970/1. *Diccionario del uso del español*, 2 vols. Madrid. (2nd edn 1984.)

Real Academia Española. 1992. *Diccionario de la lengua española*, 21st edn. Madrid.

Bibliographies

Bialik Hubermann, G. 1973. *Mil obras de lingüística española e hispanoamericana*. Madrid.

Solé, C.A. 1970. *Bibliografía sobre el español en América 1920–1967*. Georgetown, KY.

⇒ **Romance languages**

specific language impairment

Term referring to significant difficulties with language aquisition which are not accompanied by commensurate delays in cognitive development, sensory-motor deficits, frank neurological pathology, or social–emotional disturbances. The causes and fundamental nature of such impairment are unknown, although in some instances there is evidence of genetic influence. Children with specific language impairment show varying profiles of linguistic ability, but are likely to show developmental asynchronies, that is, divergent rates of learning in the various linguistic domains. Formal aspects of grammar appear to be particularly vulnerable (see Johnston 1988). Symptoms of specific language impairment may persist into adulthood. Earlier terms for this condition are 'childhood aphasia' and '**developmental dysphasia.**' (⇒ *also* **developmental language disorders**)

References

Beitchman, J.H. and A. Inglis. 1991. The continuum of linguistic dysfunction from pervasive developmental disorders to dyslexia. *Psychiatric Clinics of North America* 14.95–111.

Bishop, D.V.M. 1992. The underlying nature of specific language impairment. *Journal of Child Psychology and Psychiatry* 33.3–66.

Clahsen, H. 1991. *Child language and developmental dysphasia: linguistic studies of the acquisition of German*. trans. K. Richman. Amsterdam and Philadelphia.

Fletcher, P. and D. Hall (eds) 1992. *Specific speech and language disorders in children*. London.

Johnston, J.R. 1988. Specific language disorders in the child. In N. Lass *et al.* (eds), *Handbook of speech–language pathology and audiology*. Philadelphia, PA. 685–715.

Neville, H. and S. Coffery. 1993. The neurobiology of sensory and language processing in language-impaired children. *Journal of Cognitive Neuroscience* 5.235–53.

Watkins, R. and M.L. Rice. 1994. *Specific language impairments in children*. Baltimore, MD.

Wyke, M.A. (ed.) 1978. *Developmental dysphasia*. London.

Wyke, M.A., S. Chiat and A. Hirson. 1987. From conceptual intention to utterance: a study of impaired language output in a child with developmental dysphasia. *British Journal of Disorders of Communication* 22.37–64.

⇒ **developmental language disorders**

specific vs non-specific reading

The reference of an indefinite **noun phrase** can be understood either as a definite element of the **extension** of the noun ('specific reading') or as any given element of the extension of the noun ('non-specific reading'). For example, the sentence *A song is sung* has two possible readings:

the first is a statement about a particular song; the second about any song in general. Such ambiguities are especially apparent in verbs of seeking, wishing, etc. (cf. *Philip is looking for a friend*). Interpretations of such readings can often be disambiguated in English through **aspect**: for example, the interpretation of *A song is sung* or *A child cries* can be made clear through the progressive aspect: *A song is being sung* or *A child is crying* (specific reading). In formal approaches, ambiguities are handled by ascertaining differences in the **scope** of the **existential quantifier** ($\Rightarrow$ **operator**).

References
Ioup, G. 1977. Specificity and the interpretation of quantifiers. *Ling&P* 1.233–45.
$\Rightarrow$ **intension**, **Montague grammar**

specified subject condition (*also* opacity constraint)

A **constraint** suggested by Chomsky (1973) on **movement transformations** like *wh-movement* (also for reflexivization later on). No rule can affect *X* and *Y* when they appear in the structure $[...X...[α...Z...Y]...]$, where (a) α is a cyclic node (i.e. S or NP), (b) the subject *Z* is specified by α (i.e. is not under the **control** of *X*), and (c) *X* is not in the COMP position of S. The specified subject condition is replaced by the **binding theory** in Chomsky (1981).

References
Chomsky, N. 1973. Conditions on transformation. In S.R. Anderson and P. Kiparsky (eds), *Festschrift for Morris Halle*. New York. 232–86.
——— 1981. *Lectures on government and binding*. Dordrecht.
$\Rightarrow$ **constraints**, **transformational grammar**

specifier $\Rightarrow$ modifier

spectral analysis [Lat. *spectrum* 'image']

Process in **acoustic phonetics** for determining the acoustic features of **speech sounds** by means of electrical instruments ($\Rightarrow$ **spectrograph**).

References
$\Rightarrow$ **phonetics**

spectrogram

Product of a **spectral analysis** that graphically represents the acoustic features of sounds such as amplitude, **quantity**, frequency. ($\Rightarrow$ *also* **spectrograph**, **visible speech**)

spectrograph

Machine with electric filters that acoustically analyzes (speech) sounds for their frequency, intensity, and **quantity**. The result can be read as varying degrees of dark lines on special light sensitive paper. ($\Rightarrow$ *also* **spectrogram**, **visible speech**)

speculative grammarians (*also* Modistae)

Authors of the medieval treatises on the **modi significandi**, i.e. on the semantic and deictic functions of words and word classes. The most famous of these writers was Thomas of Erfurt, with his extensively transmitted work *Grammatica speculativa* (approx. 1300). In the classical tradition of Aristotle, the speculative grammarians attempted to correlate words and word classes with logical, extralinguistic criteria such as substance, quality, time, and action. The wealth of detail in terminology and definition has had a lasting influence on the systematicity of traditional grammar.

References
Bursill-Hall, G.L. 1971. *Speculative grammarians of the Middle Ages: the doctrine of 'Partes Orationes' of the Modistae*. The Hague.
——— 1972. '*Grammatica speculativa*' of Thomas of Erfurt. London.
Covington, M.A. 1984. *Syntactic theory in the high Middle Ages*. Cambridge.
Harris, R. and T.J. Taylor. 1989. *Landmarks in linguistic thought*. London. Ch. 6.
Pinborg, J. 1972. *Logik und Semantik im Mittelalter: ein Überblick*. Stuttgart-Bad Cannstatt.
Scaglione, A. 1990. The origins of syntax: Descartes (1596–1650) or the Modistae? *PICHoLS* 4/1.339–47.

speech

1 Process and result of oral or written linguistic production.

2 Form for retelling of utterances through (a) literal/direct speech: *She said, 'I am tired'*, (b) dependent (or indirect) speech: *She said she was tired* ($\Rightarrow$ **direct vs indirect speech**).

3 Synonym for Fr. *parole* which designates concrete acts of language as opposed to the language system ($\Rightarrow$ **langue vs parole**).

speech act classification

A typology of speech acts according to their illocutionary force. Diverging critically from Austin (1962), Searle (1975) distinguishes five classes of illocutionary acts and bases his typology upon illocutionary and grammatical indicators as well as upon the relationship of 'word' and 'world' as differently defined by different speech acts: (a) assertives (previously also representatives): the intention of the speaker is to commit him-/herself to the truth of the expressed proposition, cf. *to maintain*, *to identify*, *to report*, *to assert*; (b) directives: the speaker tries to cause the hearer to take a particular action, cf. *to request*, *to command*,

Structure of speech acts

Simultaneous subaspects

	utterance of speech sounds	utterance of words in a particular grammar structure	stating something about something	statement about the use of the proposition	intended consequences of the speech act
Austin (1962)	phonetic act	phatic act	rhetic act	illocutionary act	perlocutionary act
Searle (1969)	utterance act (locution)		proposition act (proposition)	illocutive act (illocution)	perlocutive act (perlocution)

reference to world — predication proposition about world

to beseech, to advise; (c) commissives: the speaker obligates him-/herself to carry out a future action, cf. *to promise, to pledge, to threaten*; (d) expressives: the speaker expresses the attitude specified in the sincerity condition towards the state of affairs expressed in the proposition, cf. *to congratulate, to give condolence, to excuse, to thank*; and (e) declarations: by successfully carrying out a declaration, the speaker brings reality into accord with the propositional content of the declaration, cf. *to define, to christen, to pronounce guilty, to declare a state of war*. A different classification is proposed in Meggle and Ulkan (1992).

References

Austin, J.L. 1962. *How to do things with words*. Oxford.

Meggle, G. and M. Ulkan. 1992. Informatives and/or directives? (A new start in speech act classification.) *Protosoziologie* 4.

Searle, J.R. 1975. A taxonomy of illocutionary acts. In K. Günderson (ed.), *Language, mind, and knowledge: Minnesota studies in the philosophy of science*. Minneapolis, MN. Vol. 7.

⇒ **speech act theory**

speech act theory

Influenced by **ordinary language philosophy**, and particularly by Wittgenstein's theory of **meaning as use**, J.L. Austin (1962) and, later, Searle (1969) developed a systematic account of what people do when they speak (cf. the title of Austin's lectures 'How to do things with words'). According to Austin, it is not individual words or sentences that are the basic elements of human communication, but rather particular speech acts that are performed in uttering words and sentences, namely illocutionary acts (⇒ **illocution**) or speech acts in the

narrow sense. To this extent speech act theory pursues language theory as a part of a comprehensive pragmatic theory of linguistic behavior (⇒ **pragmatics**). Every speech act is comprised of several sub-acts performed simultaneously (cf. the diagram above for an overview of the terminological differences between Austin and Searle).

Searle distinguishes among (a) **utterance acts** (⇒ *also* **locution**): the articulation of linguistic elements in a particular grammatical order; (b) propositional acts (⇒ **proposition**): the formulation of the content of an utterance through **reference** (i.e. reference to an object in the extralinguistic world) and **predication** (attribution of particular characteristics), e.g. *this mushroom* (= reference) *is poisonous* (= predication); (c) illocutionary act: the indication of the way the proposition is to be related to the word and of the communicative function of the speech act as, for example, an assertion, an ascertainment of fact, or a warning. In rare cases the illocutionary function is explicitly expressed by a performative verb in the first person singular present tense indicative (*I hereby warn, maintain, promise* ...). Where this is not the case (as in all non-problematized communicative situations) other means, such as **intonation, accent, sentence mood, adverbs, particles**, or verb **mood**, are illocutionary indicators. In these cases one speaks of 'primary performative' acts. If the literally indicated illocution is different from the actually performed illocution, one speaks of '**indirect**' **speech acts**. Illocutionary acts may have effects that are not conventionally associated with them; if these are intended by the speaker, they are called 'perlocutionary effects,' and the speaker has simultaneously carried out a (d) perlocutionary act (⇒ **perlocution**).

According to Searle, for an illocutionary act to be successfully performed, four kinds of conditions – apart from general input and output conditions (conditions for normal speaking and understanding) – must be characteristically fulfilled. The specific expression of each of these four conditions is decisive for the classification of speech acts: (a) propositional content conditions, (b) preparatory conditions, (c) sincerity conditions, (d) essential conditions. In this scheme, (d) has the format of a **constitutive rule**, while (a)–(c) correspond to **regulative rules**. In formulating 'felicity conditions' (which assure the successful performance of speech acts) as rules for using pertinent illocutionary indicators, Searle also speaks of the 'principle of expressibility,' which alone allows the (basically pragmatic) analysis of speech acts to be equated with the (semantic) analysis of expressions. It should be noted that the relationship between the two is debated. Accordingly, one can distinguish between two diverging lines of thought: a speech act theory that is more semantically oriented (that is concerned with the analysis of expressions that characterize speech acts) and a pragmatically oriented speech act theory (that takes communication processes as its starting point).

References
Austin, J.L. 1962. *How to do things with words.* Oxford.
Bach, K. and R. Harnish. 1979. *Linguistic communication and speech acts.* Cambridge, MA.
Ballmer, T. and W. Brennenstuhl. 1981. *Speech act classification.* Berlin.
Burkhardt, A. (ed.) 1990. *Speech acts, meaning and intentions: critical approaches to the philosophy of J.R. Searle.* Berlin and New York.
Clark, H.H. and T.B. Carlson. 1982. Hearers and speech acts. *Language* 58.332–73.
Cole, P. and J.L. Morgan (eds) 1975. *Syntax and semantics*, vol. 3: *Speech acts.* New York.
Franck, D. 1979. Seven sins of pragmatics: theses about speech act theory, conversational analysis, linguistics and rhetoric. In H. Parret *et al.* (eds), *Possibilities and limitations of pragmatics.* Amsterdam. 225–36.
Fraser, B. 1975. Hedged performatives. In P. Cole and J.L. Morgan (eds), *Syntax and semantics*, vol. 3: *Speech acts.* New York. 187–232.
Grice, H.P. 1968. Logic and conversation. In P. Cole and J.L. Morgan (eds), *Speech acts.* New York. 41–58.
Katz, J.J. 1977. *Propositional structure and illocutionary force.* New York.
Levinson, S.C. 1983. *Pragmatics.* Cambridge.
Sadock, J.M. 1974. *Toward a linguistic theory of speech acts.* New York, San Francisco, and London.

Searle, J.R. 1969. *Speech acts: an essay in the philosophy of language.* Cambridge.
—— (ed.) 1971. *The philosophy of language.* Oxford.
—— 1975a. A taxonomy of illocutionary acts. In K. Gunderson (ed.), *Language, mind and knowledge: Minnesota studies in the philosophy of science.* Minneapolis, MN. Vol. 7. (Repr. in *Expression and meaning.* Cambridge, 1979. 1–29.)
—— 1975b. Indirect speech acts. In P. Cole and J.L. Morgan (eds), *Syntax and semantics*, vol. 3: *Speech acts.* New York. 344–69.
Searle, J.R., F. Kiefer, and M. Bierwisch (eds) 1980. *Speech act theory and pragmatics.* Dordrecht.
Strawson, P.F. 1964. Intention and convention in speech acts. *PhR* 73.439–60.
Streeck, J. 1980. Speech acts in interaction: a critique of Searle. *DPr* 3.133–54.
Tsohatzidis, S.L. (ed.) 1994. *Foundations of speech act theory.* London.
Ulkan, M. 1992. *Zur Klassifikation von Sprechakten: eine grundlagentheoretische Fallstudie.* Tübingen.
Vanderveken, D. 1990–1. *Meaning and speech acts: principles of language use*, 2 vols. Cambridge.
Wittgenstein, L. 1953. *Philosophical investigations.* Oxford.

Bibliographies
Meyers, R.B. and K. Hopkins. 1977. A speech-act bibliography. *Centrum* 5.73–108.
Verschueren, J. 1976. *Speech act theory: a provisional bibliography with a terminological guide.* Bloomington, IN.
—— 1978. *Pragmatics: an annotated bibliography.* Amsterdam.
⇒ **conversation analysis**, **performative analysis**, **pragmatics**

speech community

1 Total set of speakers of the same (native) language. In this definition language and speaker are equated without social or cultural aspects being taken into consideration.

2 In **sociolinguistics**, speech community is related more strictly to interactional conditions: a set of speakers who, through frequent, rule-governed interaction and the use of a common linguistic repertoire of signs (thus not necessarily a single language!) constitute a group. This group is distinguished from others by significant differences in language use.

3 Not so much the 'objective' use of particular linguistic elements, but rather for the 'feeling' of belonging to a group or being in agreement with specific norms is central to this further definition. These norms 'may be observed in overt types of evaluative behavior, and by the uniformity of abstract patterns of variation' (Labov 1972: 121).

4 The term is most radically construed and

at the same time finally resolved in the consistently integrative view of linguistic, social, social-psychological and individual-psychological factors; according to Bolinger (1975: 333), 'there is no limit to the ways in which human beings league themselves together for self-identification, security, gain, amusement, worship, or any of the other purposes that are held in common; consequently there is no limit to the number and variety of speech communities that are to be found in society.' (⇒ also **network**)

References

Bloomfield, L. 1933. *Language*. New York.

Bolinger, D. 1975. *Aspects of language*, 2nd edn. New York.

Gumperz, J.J. 1962. Types of linguistic communities. *AnL* 4.28–40.

Labov, W. 1972. *Sociolinguistic patterns*. Philadelphia, PA.

Le Page, R.B. 1968. Problems of description in multilingual communities. *TPS* 189–212.

⇒ **variational linguistics**

speech comprehension ⇒ **language comprehension**

speech error (*also* Freudian slip, slip of the tongue)

Disruption in the production of speech through a conscious or unconscious linguistic deviation from the apparently intended form of an utterance. Linguistic speech error analysis is based on the hypothesis that the phenomena of deviation observable in different components are limited by the structure of the language and can be described and explained on the basis of grammatical units and regularities and that speech errors cause one to posit inferences to basic mental abilities and representations. The following types of speech errors are distinguished according to their level of linguistic description. (a) Phonological substitutions rest primarily on identical beginning or ending segments, similarity of syllable, or accent structure: e.g. *heft lemisphere* instead of *left hemisphere*; a morphophonological example is *It's not tell ussing anything new* instead of *It's not telling us anything new*. (b) Substitutions based on semantic relationships are based above all on semantic relations like **synonymy**, **antonymy**, or membership in the same **lexical field**: e.g. *unsure* instead of *sure*. The mental reality of both types appears to confirm the linguistic relevance of morphological analyses and of general rules of word formation. (c) Speech errors in the area of syntax relate to serial order errors, whereby each syntactic category remains intact, but the exact morphophonological form accommodates the new context:

Take the freezes out of the steaker instead of . . . *steaks out of the freezer*. (d) Blending of contextually similar words and/or phrases as the result of the intention to say two different (and competing) things usually marks most transitions between changing informational intentions: *Mozart's symphonatas – symphonies* vs *sonatas*. S. Freud's interest in speech errors related above all to the basic psychological mechanisms, the suppressed causes of utterance intentions that compete with each other. (⇒ *also* **error analysis, paraphasia**)

References

Abd-el-Jawad, H. and I. Abu-Salim. 1987. Slips of the tongue in Arabic and their theoretical implications. *LangS* 9.145–71.

Cutler, A. 1982. *Slips of the tongue and language production*. Berlin.

Del Viso, S. 1991. On the autonomy of phonological encoding: evidence from slips of the tongue in Spanish. *JPsyR* 20.161–85.

Dell, G.S. and P.A. Reich. 1981. States in sentence production: an analysis of speech error data. *JVLVB* 20.611–29.

Dittmann, J. 1988. Versprecher und Sprachproduktion: Ansätze zu einer psycholinguistischen Konzeption von Sprachproduktionsmodellen. In G. Blanken (ed.), *Sprachproduktionsmodelle, neuro- und psycholinguistische Modelle der menschlichen Spracherzeugung*. Freiburg. 35–82.

Dressler, W.U., L. Tonelli, and E. Magno Caldognetto. 1990. Phonological paraphasias versus slips of the tongue in German and Italian. In J.-L. Nespoulous (ed.), *Morphology, phonology and aphasia*. New York. 206–12.

Ferber, R. 1991. Slips of the tongue or slips of the ear? On the perception and transcription of naturalistic slips of the tongue. *JPsyR* 20.105–22.

Fodor, J.A. 1983. *The modularity of mind*. Cambridge, MA.

Freud, S. 1901. Zur Psychopathologie des Alltagslebens. *Monatschrift für Psychiatrie und Neurologie* 10.1–13.

—— 1917/89. Vorlesungen zur Einführung in die Psychoanalyse. In A. Mitscherlich *et al*. (eds), *Studienausgabe*. Darmstadt.

Fromkin, V.A. (ed.) 1973. *Speech error as linguistic evidence*. The Hague. (Repr. 1984.)

—— 1980. *Errors in linguistic performances: slips of the tongue, ear, pen and hand*. London.

—— 1988. Grammatical aspects of speech errors. In F. Newmeyer (ed.), *Linguistics: the Cambridge Survey*. Cambridge. Vol. 2, 117–38.

Gerken, L.A. 1992. A slip-of-the-tongue approach to language development. In J. Charles-Luce *et al.*, (eds), *Spoken language: perception, production, and development*. Norwood, NJ.

Jaeger, J.J. 1992. Phonetic features in young children's slips of the tongue. *L&S* 35.189–205.

Kutas, M. and S.A. Hillyard. 1983. Event-related brain potentials to grammatical errors and semantic anomalies. *Memory and Cognition* 11.539–50.

Laubstein, A.S. 1987. Syllable structure: the speech

error evidence. *CJL* 32.339–63.

Meringer, R. and K. Mayer. 1895. *Versprechen und Verlesen: eine psychologisch-linguistische Studie.* Stuttgart.

Meyer, A.S. 1992. Investigation of phonological encoding through speech error analyses: achievements, limitations, and alternatives. *Cognition* 42.181–211.

Picard, M. 1992. Syllable structure, sonority and speech errors: a critical assessment. *FoLi* 26.453–65.

Postma, A. and H.H.J. Kolk. 1993. The covert repair hypothesis: prearticulatory repair processes in normal and stuttered dysfluencies. *Journal of Speech and Hearing Research* 36.472–87.

Safi-Stagni, S. 1990. Slips of the tongue in Arabic. In M. Eid (ed.), *Perspectives on Arabic linguistics.* Amsterdam. Vol. 1, 271–90.

Shattuck-Hufnagel, S. 1992. The role of word structure in segmental serial ordering. *Cognition* 42.213–59.

Stemberger, J.P. 1989. Speech errors in early child language production. *JMemL* 28.164–88.

—— 1992. Vocalic underspecification in English language production. *Lg* 68.492–524.

Ubozono, H. 1989. The mora and the syllable structure in Japanese: evidence from speech errors. *L&S* 32.249–78.

Bibliographies
Cutler, A. 1982. *Speech errors: a classified bibliography.* Bloomington, IN.

Wiedenmann, N. 1992. *Versprecher und die Versuche zu ihrer Erklärung: ein Literaturüberblick.* Trier.

speech island ⇒ enclave

speech-language pathology

The study of the diagnosis and treatment of language, articulation, and voice disorders (⇒ **language disorder**, **developmental language disorder**, **articulation disorder**, **voice disorder**); also, the related professional practice. The term has been used in North America since the 1970s (formerly 'speech pathology'). The domains of speech-language pathology are variously organized in the institutions and professional schools of different cultures and countries. Thus speech-language pathology does not correspond to logopedics or clinical linguistics.

References
Smith, B.R. and E. Leinonen. 1991. *Clinical pragmatics.* London.
⇒ **language disorder**

speech perception ⇒ speech recognition

speech production ⇒ language production

speech recognition

In **computational linguistics** the recognition of linguistic signs and structures on electronic channels, such as the isolation of phones from an acoustically perceivable stream of signs (cf. character recognition for optical media). Speech recognition is necessary for computer language processing, especially for reducing speech to texts (cf. **speech synthesis** for the reverse). Outside linguistics, voice recognition is used in criminal investigations to identify persons on the basis of voice quality.

References
Altmann, G.T.M. (ed.) 1991. *Cognitive models of speech processing: psycholinguistic and computational perspectives.* Cambridge, MA.

Fraser, H. 1992. *The subject of speech perception: an analysis of the philosophical foundations of the information-processing model of cognition.* Basingstoke.

Goodman, J.C. and H.C. Nusbaum (eds) 1994. *The development of speech perception.* Cambridge, MA.

Lobacz, P. 1984. *Processing and decoding the signal in speech perception.* Hamburg.

Waibel, A. and K.-F. Lee. 1990. *Speech recognition.* San Mateo, CA.

speech sound

Abstract unit derived from a continuum of sound that is characterized by the set of its phonetic features (⇒ **phone**).

References
⇒ **phonetics**

speech synthesis

The production of speech sounds by mechanical means, generally from text input. Speech synthesis is now a common technology, used in telephone information systems (in the United States) and in reading machines for the blind. **Speech recognition** reverses the conversion, extracting text from acoustic signals.

Reference
Denes, P. 1973. *The speech chain: the physics and biology of spoken language.* Garden City, NY.

spelling ⇒ orthography

spirant [Lat. *spirare* 'to breathe']

Term denoting **fricatives**, any kind of constrictive, or a **median** without friction.

References
⇒ **phonetics**

spirantization

Replacement of plosives through homorganic **fricatives**. For example, in the **Old High German consonant shift**, where Gmc *p, t, k* are shifted to the double fricatives *ff, zz, hh* initially and after vowels; compare OHG *offan* with OS *opan* 'open,' OHG *mahhon* with OS *makon* 'make.' Spirantization with sonorization is found in the historical development of **Danish**: compare [tʰ] with [ð̞] in Icelandic; [ˈgaːt̪aʰ] with Dan. [ˈgæːð̞ə] 'street.'

References
⇒ **sound change**

spoken language

In terms of its historical development (as well as its importance to **historical linguistics** and **language acquisition**), spoken language is the primary form of communication. Interest in spoken language became gradually intensified in the 1960s. In the first studies, which were almost exclusively contrastive in nature and oriented towards syntax, spoken language was considered either a linguistic system that deviated from the written language and had its own rules or a 'deficient' linguistic system; the most characteristic traits of spoken language are short, often incomplete sentences (free-standing dependent clauses, sentence clipping, **ellipsis**); mixing of sentence structures (**anacoluthon**); frequent use of specific syntactic structures such as **left vs right dislocation**, **hanging topic**, and so on; dominance of **parataxis** vs **hypotaxis** (**co-ordination** vs **subordination**); more frequent use of discourse **particles** (⇒ **discourse marker**), among other characteristics. Through the influence of **speech act theory** and ethnomethodological **discourse analysis**, there has been a greater interest in the communicative function of the typical linguistic devices of spoken language (e.g. **intonation**). Of primary interest are the structural elements of a conversation (the opening and closure of conversation, the system of turn-taking for speaker and hearer, the direction of conversation, and procedures for the production of meaning and the assurance of understanding (**paraphrase**, **repair**, etc.). From this perspective many of the traits of spoken language previously regarded as deficient are shown to be instrumental in the organization and **contextualization** of conversations.

References
Akinnaso, F.N. 1982. On the differences between spoken and written language. *L&S* 25.97–125.
—— 1986. On the similarities between spoken and written language. *L&S* 28.323–59.
Biber, D. 1988. *Variation across speech and writing.* Cambridge.
Brazil, D. 1995. *A grammar of speech.* Oxford.
Chafe, W.L. and D. Tannen. 1987. The relation between written and spoken language. *Annual Review of Anthropology* 16.383–407.
Čmejrková, S. *et al.* (eds) 1994. *Writing* vs *speaking.* Tübingen.
Geluykens, R. 1992. *From discourse processes to grammatical constructions: on left-dislocation in English.* Amsterdam.
—— 1994. *The pragmatics of discourse anaphora in English: evidence from conversational repair.* Berlin.
Redeker, G. 1984. On the differences between spoken and written language. *DPr* 7.43–55.
Schegloff, E.A. 1979. The relevance of repair to 'syntax for conversation.' In T. Givón (ed.), *Syntax and semantics*, vol. 12: *Discourse and syntax.* New York. 261–86.
Schiffrin, D. 1987. *Discourse markers.* Cambridge and New York.
Tannen, D. (ed.) 1982a. *Analysing discourse: text and talk.* Washington, DC.
—— 1982b. *Spoken and written language: exploring orality and literacy.* Norwood, NJ.

spoonerism

Type of **speech error** in which two segments are switched. The term refers to the British clergyman William A. Spooner, who is credited with first noting these kinds of slips of the tongue, e.g. *Take the flea of my cat and leave it at the louse of my mother-in-law* instead of *Take the key of my flat and leave it at the house of my mother-in-law.* Spoonerisms play a role in the evaluation of grammar models: a strict (left-to-right) grammar that sees every word as a stimulus for the word that immediately follows cannot adequately describe speech errors involving such switching of segments.

References
⇒ **speech error**

s-structure ⇒ surface structure

stack automaton ⇒ push-down automaton

stammering ⇒ dysfluency

Standard Average European

Collective term used by B.L. Whorf for all European languages derived from **Indo-European**, whose common grammatical and lexical features he compares to the North American language of the **Hopi**. (⇒ *also* **Sapir–Whorf hypothesis**)

References
⇒ **Sapir–Whorf hypothesis**

standard language

Since the 1970s this term has been the usual designation for the historically legitimated, panregional, oral and written language form of the social middle or upper class. In this sense it is used synonymously with the (judgmental) term 'high variety' (⇒ **high vs low variety**). Because it functions as the public means of communication, it is subject to extensive normalization (especially in the realm of grammar, pronunciation, and spelling), which is controlled and passed on via the public media and institutions, but above all through the school systems. Command of the standard language is the goal of formal language instruction. ($\Rightarrow$ *also* **national language**, **prescriptive grammar**, **orthography**, **standard pronunciation**)

References
Joseph, J. 1984. The elaboration of the emerging standard. *LangS* 6:1.39–52.
Leuvensteijn, J.V. and J. Berns (eds) 1992. *Dialect and standard language in the English, Dutch, German and Norwegian language areas*. Amsterdam.
Nickel, G. and J.C. Stalker (eds) 1986. *Problems of standardization and linguistic variation in present day English*. Heidelberg.
Stein, D. and I. Tieken-Boon. 1993. *Towards Standard English, 1600–1800*. Berlin.

References
$\Rightarrow$ **grammar**, **linguistic norms**, **orthography**, **standard pronunciation**, **stylistics**

standard pronunciation (*also* orthoepy, Received Pronunciation (Brit.))

The customary pronunciation of the educated class; that pronunciation generally taught in formal language instruction.

References
Avanesov, R.I. 1950. *Russkoe literaturnoe proiznošenie*. Moscow.
Avery, P. and S. Ehrlich. 1991. *Teaching American English pronunciation*. Oxford.
Duden. 1962. *Aussprachewörterbuch*. Mannheim.
Jones, D. 1917. *Everyman's English pronouncing dictionary*. London. (New edn by A.C. Gimson and S. Ramsaran. Cambridge 1991.)
Price, G. 1991. *An introduction to French pronunciation*. Oxford.
Warnant, L. 1968. *Dictionnaire de la prononciation française*. Gembloux.

standard theory $\Rightarrow$ aspects model

starred form

A written linguistic expression marked with an asterisk, meaning that the expression is either a **reconstruction** of an unattested expression, as in **Indo-European** *$*b^her$*- root of 'to bear,' or agrammatical, as in **catched* for *caught* or **buyed* for *bought*.

statal passive

Passive voice distinct from the actional passive in some languages (e.g. **German**, **Russian**), which indicates a state resulting from an action rather than the action itself, cf. Ger. *Die Polizei wird gewarnt* 'The police are being warned' with the focus on the action vs *Die Polizei ist gewarnt* 'The police are warned' (i.e. 'have been warned'), with the focus on the state.

statal verb $\Rightarrow$ stative vs active

statement (*also* assertion)

1 Term used by J.R. Ross for statements which in deep structure are dependent on verbs such as *assert, maintain, say*. Thus, the unmarked utterance *Prices are falling* can be derived from *I tell you (that) prices are falling*. This derivation is also considered a **performative analysis**.

2 Synonym for **proposition**.

statistical linguistics (*also* quantitative linguistics)

Experimentally oriented subdiscipline of **mathematical linguistics**. Using statistical methods, statistical linguistics investigates the quantification of linguistic regularities in a controlled fashion. Its methods are used in the production of frequency dictionaries, stylistic text analysis, and in natural-language processing, where it is used to guide parsing and recognition hypothesis.

References
Butler, C.S. 1985. *Statistics in linguistics*. Oxford.
Woods, A., P. Fletcher, and A. Hughes. 1986. *Statistics in language studies*. Cambridge.

Bibliography
Köhler, R. 1995. *Bibliography of quantitative linguistics*. Amsterdam.
$\Rightarrow$ **computational linguistics**, **lexicostatistics**, **mathematical linguistics**

stative verb

Semantically and syntactically defined group of verbs that share the semantic feature [+static] (e.g. *be, own, know, understand*, etc.). Stative verbs (a) are not normally used in the imperative mood (*$^?$Understand me*), (b) do not form true passives (**The book is being owned by him*), (c) cannot occur as predicates in dependent clauses after verbs of telling (**He advised her to understand the lecture*). Adjectives are also subject to this semantic dichotomy (e.g. *old, rich, spontaneous* vs *fast, helpful*). ($\Rightarrow$ *also* **stative** vs **active**)

stative vs active

Basic distinction of **aspect**. Stative verbs such as *know, feel, own* and *be able to* describe properties or relations which do not imply a change in state or motion and which cannot be directly controlled by the entity possessing the property, i.e. stative situations cannot be started, stopped, interrupted, or brought about easily or voluntarily. Related to this is the fact that stative verbs cannot usually occur in the imperative (**Know Louise!*, but *Know [what you're doing] before you go!*) and cannot be combined with such modal adverbs as *voluntarily* or *secretly*.

Active verbs, which include all **process verbs** and **action verbs** such as *wither*, *work*, and *read* imply a change or a transition from one state to another; in the case of action verbs, this is caused by an agent. The distinction stative vs active is relevant not only for verbs but also for subcategories of adjectives (*old*, *rich* vs *fast*, *helpful*), and plays an important role in the grammars of many languages. For example, in many languages, stative verbs cannot occur in the passive; in English, they cannot be used in the **progressive** **He is knowing Phil.* The distinction stative vs active verb is also important in **active languages**.

References
Åquist, L. 1974. A new approach to the logical theory of actions and causality. In S. Stenlund (ed.), *Logical theory and semantic analysis*. Dordrecht. 73–91.
Kenny, E. 1963. States, performances, activities. In E. Kenny (ed.), *Action, emotion and will*. New York. 171–86.
Lee, D.A. 1973. Stative and case grammar. *FL* 10.545–68.
Vendler, Z. 1967. *Linguistics and philosophy*. Ithaca, NY.
⇒ **aspect**

steady-state sounds vs transitional sounds

In early phonetics, the speech process – in analogy to writing the letters of the alphabet – was seen as a series of discrete individual sounds (steady-state sounds) in which the articulatory organs did not move. For the transition from one steady-state sound to another, transitional sounds were hypothesized.

stem

1 Morphemes or morpheme constructions on which inflectional endings (⇒ **inflection**) can appear. Based on this criterion, **base morphemes** (*easy*) as well as **derivations** (*uneasy*, *easiness*) and **compounds** (*easy-going*) are considered word stems.

2 In synchronic language analysis that **base morpheme** that underlies all words of the same **word family** and that is the carrier of the (original) lexical base meaning. Thus, the stem *work* underlies *working*, *worker*, *unworkable*; its **part of speech** and meaning are specified by the word forming morphemes (*-ing*, *un-*, *-able*). (⇒ *also* **morphology**, **word formation**)

References
⇒ **morphology**, **word formation**

stem vowel

In **Latin**, stem vowels, most clearly evident in the genitive plural (*ā*, *ō*, *i*, *u*, *ē*), indicate the declensional class to which a particular substantive (noun or adjective) belongs: *mensārum* (1st declension), *cervōrum* (2nd), *civium* (3rd), *fructuum* (4th), *diērum* (5th). In **Indo-European** distinction is drawn between thematic verbs (those with a theme vowel inserted between the root and the personal ending, e.g. *leg-i-tis*, *leg-u-nt*) and athematic verbs (those in which the personal ending is attached directly to the root, *es-t*, *es-tis*). (⇒ *also* **linking morpheme**, **linking vowel**)

stereotype [Grk *stereós* 'firm, solid,' *typós* 'form, shape, image']

1 Borrowed from sociology and originating in printers' jargon (stereotype 'lines printed tightly together' in contrast with movable type), the term denotes any (pre-)judgments – deeply rooted in emotion and usually unconscious – about a particular group. Stereotypes as 'aids' in judging and leveled primarily at racial, national, religious, or professional groups, may function to defuse situations of personal or public conflict. **Semantic differentials** or **content analysis** provide a linguistic method to determine stereotypes.

References
Lippman, W. 1922. *Public opinion*. London.
Quasthoff, U. 1978. The uses of stereotypes in everyday argument. *JPrag* 2.1–48.
Schaff, A. 1984. The pragmatic function of stereotypes. *JSL* 45.89–100.
⇒ **cliché**

2 In the framework of Putnam's (1975) philosophical theory of semantics, term denoting the collection of semantic associations that are firmly connected with a particular word or the beliefs about characteristics of typical examples of natural classes (e.g. cats, roses, water) in 'normal' situations. These (stereotypical) assumptions may be empirically correct or incorrect (e.g. *gold* has the stereotypical features of 'valuable metal' and 'yellow,' even though as a chemical alloy it is actually white). It therefore follows that not all elements belonging to the **extension** of an expression must necessarily exhibit all of the characteristics of the stereotype: for example, there are possibly also white tigers, even though 'striped' is part of the stereotype of *tiger*. Moreover, not every speaker must know all the stereotypes of an expression to be able to refer successfully to the element designated by it. As demonstrated in the psychological tests of Rosch (1973), stereotypes are the result of the perceptual classification of an inherently structured world through categories established by humans (though in this regard the concept of '**prototype**' is more common). As part of the whole

meaning of linguistic expressions, the concept of 'stereotype' plays – in addition to the concepts of '**intension**' and 'extension' – an important role in more recent semantic theories, specifically in lexical **semantics** and **morphology** (see Eikmeyer and Rieser 1981). Lakoff and Johnson (1981) establish the connection with the first definition of stereotype above, by showing how natural languages have fixed (pre-)judgments and how speakers use them, mostly unconsciously, as a structure for understanding their environment.

References
Clark, E.V. and H.H. Clark. 1979. When nouns surface as verbs. *Lg* 5.767–811.
Dahlgren, K. 1978. The nature of linguistic stereotypes. In D. Farkas (ed.), *Papers from the parasession on the lexicon*. Bloomington, IN. 58–70.
Eikmeyer, H.-J. and H. Rieser. 1981. Meanings, intensions, and stereotypes: a new approach to linguistic semantics. In H.-J. Eikmeyer and H. Rieser (eds), *Words, worlds, and contexts*. Berlin. 133–50.
Lakoff, G. 1982. *Categories and cognitive models*. Trier.
Lakoff, G. and H. Johnson. 1981. *Metaphors we live by*. Chicago, IL.
Leyens, J.-P. *et al.* 1994. *Stereotypes and social cognition*. London.
Putnam, H. 1975. The meaning of meaning. In K. Gundersen (ed.), *Language, mind, and knowledge*. Minneapolis, MN. 131–93.
Rosch, E. 1973. Natural categories. *CPsy* 4.328–50.
――― 1975. Cognitive representations of semantic categories. *JEP* 104.192–233.
⇒ **prototype**

stimulus-response

Central notion of behavioral psychology (⇒ **behaviorism**) according to which human (and thus also linguistic) behavior can be explained or reconstructed after a model of a mechanical apparatus. All forms of experience, ideas, and intentions are interpreted as the result of an interchange between observable stimuli and the corresponding responses. Regarding the reactions, one differentiates between 'immediate' and 'conditioned' reflexes. Immediate reflexes are spontaneous, involuntary reactions to stimuli, such as squinting when bright lights are turned on; conditioned reflexes, on the other hand, are artificial, acquired reactions to stimuli picked up through the process of learning. The first experiment in stimulus-response was undertaken with a dog by the Russian physiologist I. Pavlov (1849–1939), in which it was demonstrated that the immediate natural reflex of salivation when the dog saw its food occurred as a conditioned reflex after corresponding training, when a bell sounded (initially simulta-

neously with the offering of food), itself given as a stimulus. This process is known as classic **conditioning**. This one-dimensional schema is differentiated by taking a non-observable, mediating case of stimulus-response into consideration. Such a modified model of stimulus-response is the basis of the so-called **mediation** theory of meaning.

References
⇒ **behaviorism, mediation**

STM (short-term memory) ⇒ **memory**

stochastic grammar

A grammar of any type (⇒ **formal language theory**) in which rules are assigned probabilities by a probability density function. Stochastic grammars are applied to the problem of **speech recognition**, in which hypotheses must be evaluated with reference to confidence values, and to a range of other problems in which information is unsure. (⇒ **hidden Markov model, Markov process**)

Reference
Wetherell, C. 1980. Probabilistic languages. *Computing Surveys* 12.

stop

Speech sound classified according to its **manner of articulation**, in which at least one closure is formed with the glottis or in the oral cavity: (a) glottal stop [ʔ]; (b) **nasals**[2] [m], [n]; (c) **plosives**[1] [p], [t], [b], [d]; (d) **implosives**[1] [ɓ], [ɗ]; (e) **ejectives** [p']; (f) **clicks** [ʘ], [ǀ]. A **plosive** in which the stop is formed orally and released without friction is called an explosive sound. If the oral release occurs during the formation of non-nasal oral stops (in the cases of (c)–(f)) with friction, then they are called **affricates**. An oral double stop is present in [k͡p], as in **Yoruba** [k͡pe] 'thank you.' Subclasses of stops involve **labialization, palatalization,** velarization, pharyngealization (⇒ **secondary articulation**), **aspiration**, nasalization (⇒ **nasal harmony**), **glottalization**. Further classificatory features are **phonation, articulators,** and **places of articulation**. The use of the term stop is not uniform: at times it refers to (a)–(f), but not (b); at times only to (a) and (c); at times only to (c). (⇒ *also* **articulatory phonetics**)

References
⇒ **phonetics**

story grammar

Expansion of the concept of **generative grammar** from the sentence level to the level of (narrative) texts. In story grammar, the text structure is seen as primary in comparison to the background knowledge. From this stance, a controversy with the proponents of script theory (⇒ **script**) developed in the early 1980s.

References
Black, J. and R. Wilensky. 1979. An evaluation of story grammars. *CSc* 3.213–39.
Budniakiewicz, T. 1992. *Fundamentals of story logic: introduction to Greimassian semiotics.* Amsterdam and Philadelphia, PA.
Mandler, J. and N. Johnson. 1980. On throwing out the baby with the bathwater: a reply to Black and Wilensky's evaluation of story grammars. *CSc* 4.305–12.
Rumelhart, D. 1975. Notes on a schema for stories. In D. Bobrow and A. Collins (eds), *Representation and understanding.* New York. 211–36.
—— 1980. On evaluating story grammars. *CSc* 4.313–16.
⇒ **language processing**

stratic [Lat. *stratum* 'level']

Sociocultural or class-specific feature used in investigations in **dialectology**.

stratificational grammar

Descriptive analysis developed by S.M. Lamb, based on structuralist (⇒ **structuralism**) principles which plays a role in computer linguistics and machine translation. Lamb views language primarily as a highly complex means of communication, whose structure can be described as a relational net of hierarchically ordered systems and subsystems (i.e. strata, ⇒ **stratum**). In sharp contrast to American branches of structuralism, **semantics** functions as the highest stratum, that is, the starting point for linguistic description is meaning, which is restructured from stratum to stratum until it finds its material realization on the **phonetic** level. Lamb (1966) distinguishes six strata for English, two for each of the traditionally described levels: semantics, **syntax**, and **phonology**. The combinatory restrictions on the individual levels are ensured by the so-called 'tactical' rules and, depending on the stratum, Lamb speaks of semotactics, lexotactics, morphotactics, and phonotactics. The linguistic units assigned to each level appear in triads: (a) **sememe, lexeme, morpheme, phoneme**, and others as abstract emic units (⇒ **etic vs emic analysis**); (b) semon, lexon, phonon, among others, as constitutive elements of the abstract units; and (c) sema, lex, **phone**, among others, as the material realization. The terminological neologisms and notational system of stratificational grammar are extremely complex. There is to date no complete representation of a language that exhaustively employs this theoretical apparatus.

References
Hartmann, R.R.K. 1973. *The language of linguistics: reflections on linguistic terminology with particular reference to 'level' and 'rank.'* Tübingen.
Hockett, C.F. 1966. Language, mathematics and linguistics. In T.A. Sebeok (ed.), *Current trends in linguistics*, vol. 3: *Theoretical linguistics.* The Hague. 155–204.
Lamb, S.M. 1966. *Outline of stratificational grammar.* Washington, DC.
Lockwood, D.G. 1972. *Introduction to stratificational linguistics.* New York.
Sampson, G. 1970. *Stratificational grammar: a definition as an example.* The Hague.

Bibliography
Fleming, I. 1969. Stratificational theory: an annotated bibliography. *JEngL* 3.37–65.

stratum

1 **Level** of classification whose elements define the elements of the next highest level. For example, **morphophonemes** are defined by **phonemes**.
2 In S.M. Lamb's **stratificational grammar**, structural levels which are ordered hierarchically and have a systematic character: the lowest level corresponds to **phonology** (= hypophonemic and phonemic stratum); the intermediate level corresponds to **syntax** (= morphemic and lexemic stratum); and the highest level corresponds to **semantics** (= sememic and hypersememic stratum).

References
⇒ **stratificational grammar**

stress

1 In the narrow sense, a **suprasegmental feature** which, together with **pitch**, duration, and **sonority**, makes up the **prominence** of sounds, syllables, words, phrases, and sentences. Articulatory characteristic (⇒ **articulation**): increased muscular activity. Acoustic characteristic: increase in intensity (volume).

2 In the broad sense (*also* 'accent'), the syntagmatic (⇒ **paradigmatic vs syntagmatic relationship**) prominence of a linguistic element. (a) Two basic types of stress are 'dynamic stress' (= 'dynamic accent,' 'expiratory accent,' '**stress accent**' and 'musical stress' (= '**pitch accent**'). Dynamic stress is achieved through intensified muscle activity during articulation (e.g. word accent in English), musical stress through change or distribution of pitch over one or more linguistic elements (e.g. **Swedish**, Classical **Greek**). These two types actually occur together, with one or the other being predominant. (b) According to the prosodic (⇒ **prosody**) unit affected, a distinction is drawn between syllable stress, word or word group

stress, and sentence stress. These units can carry (c) primary (= main), secondary, or weak stress, i.e. varying gradations of emphasis. (d) A further distinction is drawn with regard to the regularity of occurrence: 'fixed stress' refers to those languages in which stress always or almost always occurs on a particular syllable (e.g. the initial syllable in **Czech**, **Lithuanian**, **Hungarian**, and **Finnish**, the penultimate syllable in **Polish**, the final syllable in **French**), and thereby marks word boundaries; 'free stress' is found in **Germanic** languages (generally on the **root** syllable), **Russian**, **Bulgarian**, **Spanish**, and **Italian**. In free-stress languages, stress can be used to distinguish between different **lexemes** (*bláckbird* vs *blàck bírd*), different **parts of speech** (*présent* vs *presént*), or different grammatical categories (Ital. *canto* 'I sing' vs *cantò* 'he/she/it sang').

Stress can have a significant diachronic (⇒ **synchrony vs diachrony**) influence on **sound change**: cf. the 'exceptions' to the Germanic sound shift (⇒ **Grimm's law**), elucidated in **Verner's law**, which resulted from the Proto-Indo-European free stress. (⇒ *also* **intonation**, **metrical phonology**, **phonetics**, **phonology**)

References
Beckmann, M.E. 1986. *Stress and non-stress accent.* Berlin and New York.
Burzio, L. 1994. *Principles of English stress.* Cambridge.
Halle, M. and J.-R. Vergnaud. 1987. *An essay on stress.* Cambridge, MA.
Hayes, B. 1981. *A metrical theory of stress rules.* Bloomington, IN.
——— 1994. *Metrical stress theory.* Chicago, IL.
Liberman, M. and A. Prince. 1977. On stress and linguistic rhythm. *LingI* 8.249–336.
Schmerling, S.F. 1976. *Aspects of English sentence stress.* London.
Visch, E. 1990. *A metrical theory of rhythmic stress phenomena.* Berlin and New York.

Generative theories
Haraguchi, S. 1991. *A theory of stress and accent.* Berlin and New York.
Kenstowicz, M. 1990. Stress and generative phonology. *Rivista di Linguistica* 2.55–86.
⇒ **intonation**, **phonetics**, **suprasegmental feature**

stress accent (*also* dynamic accent, expiratory accent)
Word accent that is distinguished by a greater sound intensity or a non-distinctive change in pitch, as opposed to **pitch accent**. (⇒ *also* **stress**[2])

stress-timed vs syllable-timed
Typological distinction (⇒ **language typology**) to do with the rhythm of a language. In stress-timed languages (e.g. **English**, **German**), the intervals between the stressed syllables tend to be qualitatively even (⇒ **ictus**); in syllable-timed languages (e.g. **French**, **Italian**, **Hungarian**), it is the intervals between individual syllables that tend to be quantitatively even.

Reference
Dauer, R. 1983. Stress-timing and syllable-timing reanalysed. *JPhon* 11.51–62.

strict implication ⇒ **implication**

strident vs mellow ⇒ **strident vs non-strident**

strident vs non-strident [Lat. *stridere* 'to make a high-pitched sound'] (*also* strident vs mellow)
Binary phonological **opposition** in **distinctive feature** analysis, based on acoustically analyzed and spectrally defined criteria (cf. **acoustic phonetics**, **spectral analysis**). Acoustic characteristics: higher/lower noise intensity in the higher/lower, respectively, frequencies. Articulatory characteristics: greater or lesser impediment of friction in the **resonance chamber**, cf. the opposition between [f, s, ʃ] vs [v, z, ʒ].

References
Jakobson, R. *et al.* 1951. *Preliminaries to speech analysis.* Cambridge, MA. 23–6. (6th edn 1965.)
⇒ **phonetics**

string analysis
Method of grammatical analysis of sentences developed by R.E. Longacre and Z.S. Harris within the framework of **tagmemics**. In contrast to **phrase structure grammar**, which assumes a hierarchical structure for sentences, string analysis is based on the hypothesis that language is a linear ordering of individual elements. Every sentence, then, is analyzable as a **kernel sentence** which is surrounded by zero or more **complements** (⇒ *also* **adjunct**); the complements are in turn made up of necessary elements. Each word is classifiable on the basis of its morphosyntactic characteristics, so that sentences can be represented as strings of **category symbols**. On the basis of an open-ended list of axiomatic elementary strings, sentences are parsed into partial strings that can occur to the right or left of the central kernel string. In other words, acceptable sentences are conceived as combinations or expansions of elementary units (**phonemes**, **morphemes**, **words**, **syntagms**, **sentences**).

References
Harris, Z.S. 1962. *String analysis of sentence structure.* The Hague.

Longacre, R.E. 1960. String constituent analysis. *Lg* 36.63–88.

strong vs weak verb

Formal classification of **verbs** in **Germanic** languages according to their pattern of conjugation. This distinction, first suggested J. Grimm, refers to the ability of strong verbs to form the **preterite** (past tense) stem 'on its own' by changing the root vowel (⇒ **ablaut**, e.g. Eng. *see/saw, rise/rose*), as well as the need for weak verbs to employ an additional formal element (a dental suffix realized as *-ed, -d, -t*: *worked, heard, burnt*), ⇒ **irregular verb**. The strong verbs stem from older processes in **Indo-European**, while the weak verbs are a Germanic innovation.

References
Barbour, J.S. 1982. Productive and non-productive morphology: the case of the German strong verbs. *JL* 18.331–54.
Barnes, M. and H. Esau. 1973. Germanic strong verbs: a case of morphological rule extension? *Lingua* 31.1–34.
Bech, G. 1963. *Die Entstehung des schwachen Präteritums*. Copenhagen.
Kern, P.C. and H. Zutt. 1977. *Geschichte des deutschen Flexionssystems*. Tübingen.
Lehmann, W.P. 1943. The Germanic weak preterite endings. *Language* 19.313–19.
Meid, W. 1971. *Das germanische Präteritum*. Innsbruck.
Seebold, E. 1970. *Vergleichendes und etymologisches Wörterbuch der germanischen starken Verben*. The Hague.
Tops, G.A. 1974. *The origin of the Germanic dental preterite: a critical research history since 1912*. Leiden.
Veith, W.H. 1984. The strong verb conjugation in modern English compared with modern German. *LB* 73.39–57.

structural analysis

In **transformational grammar**, the presentation of sentences in the form of a **tree diagram** or **labeled bracketing** as the output of the application of **transformational rules**.

References
⇒ **transformational grammar**

structural meaning ⇒ lexical meaning vs grammatical meaning

structural semantics

Collective term for different descriptive models in lexical semantics, all of which are based on the basic principles of **structuralism**. The common characteristics of these approaches are: (a) the meaning of a word cannot be described in isolation, but is a function of its relation to other lexemes of the same conceptual area (⇒ **lexical field theory**, **semantic relation**); (b) the whole meaning of a word can be analyzed as smaller semantic elements (⇒ **componential analysis**, **lexical decomposition**). As in phonology, this assumption is based on the hypothesis that there is a universal inventory of semantic components from which every individual language makes specific selections. Structural semantics sets out to describe the structure of the lexicon by analyzing individual meanings and semantic relations like **synonymy** and **antonymy**, among others.

References
Bendix, E.H. 1966. *Componential analysis of general vocabulary: the semantic structure of a set of verbs in English, Hindi, and Japanese*. The Hague.
Coseriu, E. 1970. *Einführung in die strukturelle Betrachtung des Wortschatzes*. Tübingen.
Geckeler, H. 1971. *Strukturelle Semantik und Wortfeldtheorie*. Munich.
——— (ed.) 1978. *Strukturelle Bedeutungslehre*. Darmstadt.
——— 1981. Structural semantics. In H.-J. Eikmeyer and H. Rieser (eds), *Words, worlds, and contexts: new approaches in word semantics*. Berlin. 381–413.
Greimas, A.J. 1966. *Sémantique structurale*. Paris.
Leisi, E. 1973. *Praxis der englischen Semantik*. Heidelberg.
Lyons, J. 1963. *Structural semantics: an analysis of part of the vocabulary of Plato*. Oxford.
⇒ **semantics**

structuralism

Collective term for a number of linguistic approaches in the first half of the twentieth century, all based on the work of F. de Saussure, but strongly divergent from one another. Depending on theoretical preconceptions, the term 'structuralism' is used in several ways. In its narrower sense, it refers to the pre-generative phase of linguistics before N. Chomsky's *Syntactic structures*; in its broader sense, to all linguistic theories which focus on an isolated investigation of the language system, which would include generative **transformational grammar**. The most important centers of 'classical' structuralism are (a) the **Geneva School**, concerned primarily with the work of de Saussure, (b) **American structuralism**, following the work of L. Bloomfield, (c) the Copenhagen Linguistic Circle with L. Hjelmslev's **glossematics**, (d) contextualism (⇒ **Firthian linguistics**), centered in London, and (e) the **Prague School**, represented chiefly by N. Trubetzkoy, A. Martinet, and R. Jakobson.

All variations of structuralism have certain theoretical premises in common, which result in part from the influence of **empiricism** and in part from a common reaction against the nineteenth century positivistic atomism of the **Neogrammarians**.

Even though de Saussure did not use the term 'structure' in his posthumously published *Cours de linguistique générale* (1916, based on lecture notes from the years 1906–11), but rather the terms *système* and *mécanisme*, he is none the less recognized as the 'father' and pioneer of structuralism, and his *Cours* is seen as a summary of the fundamental principles of structuralist linguistic description. De Saussure assumes that language is a relational system of formal, not substantial, elements, which can be precisely recorded and exactly represented. He sees research into the internal relations of language as the central task of linguistics and linguistics as an autonomous sicence that has no need to resort to psychology or the social sciences for aid in explanation. The following basic assumptions found in de Saussure's work are viewed as fundamental for structuralist linguistic analysis. (a) 'Language' can be regarded from three aspects as *langue* (⇒ **langue vs parole**) (a particular language stored in the minds of all of its speakers), as *parole* (actual instances of speech in concrete situations), and as *faculté de langage* (⇒ **langage**) (general competence for the acquisition and use of language). In this view, *langue* and *parole* condition each other. The object of linguistic investigation is *langue*, which can only be described through an analysis of the expressions of *parole*. (b) Language (in the sense of *langue*) is regarded as a system of **signs**. Each sign consists of two (mutually conditioning) aspects, the **acoustic image**, and the concept. The connection of these aspects to one another is arbitrary (⇒ **arbitrariness**), i.e. language-specific and dependent on convention. (c) These linguistic signs form a system of values which stand in **opposition** to one another. Each sign is defined by its relation to all other signs in the same system. The fundamental structuralist concept of the 'distinctive principle' is characterized by this principle of 'contrast.' (d) These element relationships can be analyzed on two levels: the syntagmatic level, i.e. the level of linear co-existence; and the paradigmatic level, i.e. the level of interchangeability of elements in a particular position; (⇒ **paradigmatic vs syntagmatic relationship**). (e) Since language (*langue*) is understood to be a system of signs, its analysis must be pursued along strictly synchronic lines, i.e. as the description of a state of affairs that exists at a given time (⇒ **synchrony vs diachrony**). (f) Linguistic analysis is based on a representative **corpus**, whose

regularities are defined by way of two steps, **segmentation** and **classification**, segmentation taking place on the syntagmatic level, classification on the paradigmatic (⇒ *also* **distribution**).

The central level of investigation in structuralism, especially in the Prague School, is **phonology**. Methods of analysis were tested on its inventory of elements and possible combinations. These methods, when applied to the analysis of **syntax**, led to **phrase structure grammar**; the limits of these procedures are shown most clearly in the area of **semantics** (⇒ **componential analysis**, **lexical field theory**).

While 'structuralism' in its narrower sense refers to de Saussure's linguistic theories, in its broader sense it is an umbrella term for approaches in anthropology, ethnology, sociology, psychology, and literary criticism, which – in analogy to linguistic structuralism – concentrate on synchronic analysis rather than on genetic/historical preconditions, in order to expose the universal structures at work under the surface of social relations (see especially R. Barthes, C. Lévi-Strauss).

References
Albrecht, J. 1988. *Europäischer Strukturalismus*. Darmstadt.
Bloomfield, L. 1933. *Language*. New York.
Harris, Z.S. 1951. *Methods in structural linguistics*. Chicago, IL.
——— 1965. Transformational theory. *Lg* 41.363–401. (Repr. in *Papers in structural and transformational linguistics*. Dordrecht, 1970. 531–77.)
Harris, R. 1987. *Reading Saussure*. London.
Hjelmslev, L. 1943. *Omkring sprogteoriens grundlaeggelse*. Copenhagen. (*Prolegomena to a theory of language*, trans. F.J. Whitfield. Baltimore, MD, 1953.)
Holdcroft, D. 1991. *Saussure: signs, systems and arbitrariness*. Cambridge.
Joos, M. (ed.) 1966. *Readings in linguistics*, vol. 1: *the development of descriptive linguistics in America, 1925–1956*. Chicago, IL.
Joseph, J.E. 1990. Bloomfield's (1887–1949) Saussureanism. *Cahiers Ferdinand de Saussure*, 43.43–53.
Koerner, E.F.K. 1990. L. Bloomfield (1887–1949) and the *Cours de linguistique générale*. *Cahiers Ferdinand de Saussure*, 43.55–63.
Mohrmann, C. *et al.* (eds) 1961. *Trends in European and American linguistics, 1930–1960*. Utrecht.
Newmeyer, F.J. *Linguistic theory in America*. Orlando, FL.
Sapir, E. 1921. *Language*. New York.
Saussure, F. de. 1916. *Cours de linguistique générale*. Paris. (*Course in general linguistics*, trans. R. Harris. London, 1983.)
Trubetzkoy, N. 1939. *Grundzüge der Phonologie*. Göttingen.
Von der Gabelentz, G. 1891. *Die Sprachwissen-*

schaft: ihre Aufgaben, Methoden und bisherigen Ergebnisse. Tübingen.
⇒ **American structuralism, distributionalism, linguistics, Prague School**

structure-preserving constraint

A constraint postulated by J.E. Edmonds from the observation that many **transformations** generate structures that could be generated independently of these transformations by the basic rules of the grammar. This became the accepted **constraint** for changes in structure by transformations in later versions of **transformational grammar**. Constituents can only be moved to positions in the **tree diagram** which could have been generated by the **phrase structure rules** independently of the transformations.

Reference
Edmonds, J.E. 1976. *A transformational approach to English syntax*. New York.

structure word ⇒ synsemantic word

stuttering ⇒ dysfluency

style [Lat. *stilus* 'a pointed instrument for incising letters,' metonymically 'pen,' i.e. 'way of writing']

The characteristic use of language in a text. When referring to the speaker, style is more or less the controlled choice of linguistic means, whereas in referring to texts, style is the specific form of language. For the reader or listener, style is the variation (or confirmation) of possible expectations, i.e. the observation and interpretation of linguistic specifics. **Stylistics** has fluctuated in basing its definitions of style on one or the other of these aspects and has correspondingly developed different goals and procedures for description. The following qualifications are generally valid: (a) style is based on individual linguistic elements (**elements of style**); (b) style is a feature of texts (**stylistic features**); (c) style is contingent upon historical, functional, and individual components. (⇒ *also* **usage vs use**)

References
⇒ **stylistics**

stylistic feature

The characteristic property of the language of a text. The stylistic feature is based on the repetition or mixing of **elements of style** and, therefore, on the particulars of the grammatical form, e.g. nominal vs verbal (⇒ **nominal style**), on the vocabulary (e.g. modern, vulgar, graphic), or on the structure of the text (e.g. argumentative, visual, boring). Other derived

styles like telegraphic style, editorial style, or oral style are based on the correspondingly typical element of style of particular classes of text. (⇒ *also* **style**)

References
⇒ **stylistics**

stylistics

Stylistics developed in the nineteenth and twentieth centuries from the traditions of fostering the mother tongue, from **rhetoric** and from the interpretation of literature. Correspondingly, the discipline is quite broad: (a) methodically, stylistics is a procedure for the analysis of texts; (b) normatively, stylistics is a directive for what is right in the use of language; (c) descriptively, stylistics is a text linguistic discipline, which explains the style of a text and sets it in relation to other features of the text (**style**). This newest branch of stylistics forms the foundation for scientific analysis of style as well as for practical stylistics, the standardization of style, and the fostering of the mother tongue. The results of functional stylistics are particularly important for research into the connection between the style and the function of a text (or type of text). Since functionally explicable properties of style are also fundamental for rhetorical texts, stylistics overlaps here with its ancestors and with the modern neighboring discipline of rhetoric.

References
Carter, R. (ed.) 1989. *Language, discourse and literature: an introduction reader in discourse stylistics*. London.
Carter, R.A. and W. Nash. 1990. *Seeing through language: an introduction to styles of English writing*. Oxford.
Chatman, S. (ed.) 1971. *Literary style: a symposium*. Oxford.
Ehrlich, S. 1990. *Point of view*. London.
Enkvist, N.E. 1973. *Linguistic stylistics*. The Hague.
Enkvist, N.E. *et al.* 1967. *Linguistics and style*. London.
Esser, J. 1993. *English linguistic stylistics*. Tübingen.
Gaitet, P. 1991. *Political stylistics*. London.
Haynes, J. 1989. *Introducing stylistics*. London.
———— 1995. *Style*. London.
Hickey, L. (ed.) 1989. *The pragmatics of style*. London.
Jucker, A. 1992. *Social stylistics: syntactic variation in British newspapers*. Berlin.
Ledger, G.R. 1989. *Re-counting Plato: a computer analysis of Plato's style*. Oxford.
Taylor, T.J. 1981. *Linguistic theory and structural stylistics*. Oxford.
Toolan, M.J. 1990. *The stylistics of fiction: a literary-linguistic approach*. London.

Ullman, S. 1973. *Meaning and style: collected papers*. Oxford.

Wales, K. 1990. *A dictionary of stylistics*. London.

Bibliographies

Bailey, R. and D.M. Burton. 1968. *English stylistics: a bibliography*. Cambridge, MA.

Bennett, J.R. 1986. *Bibliography of stylistics and related criticism, 1967–83*. New York.

Journal

Language and Literature.

subcategorization [Lat. *sub* 'under'; Grk *katēgoría* 'predicate']

In Chomsky's **transformational grammar**, a specification of lexical categories (noun, verb) into syntactically and semantically motivated subclasses, which correspond to the compatibility between syntactic functions in the sentence. Regarding the subcategorization of nouns and verbs, one distinguishes between context-free and context-sensitive rules. (a) Context-free subcategorization rules (for nouns) apply independently of the specific use of the lexical item. An example is the complex symbol *book*, which consists of the following subcategorizations [+noun, –living, –human, ...]. (b) Context-sensitive subcategorization rules for verbs, whose subcategorization is dependent on the syntactic context. There is a difference depending on whether it is a question of purely formal properties dependent on the **valence** of the verb or of the semantic–lexical relationships. (i) Strict subcategorization defines the obligatory syntactic framework of the verb, e.g. it differentiates between transitive and intransitive verbs. Strict subcategorization in this sense is strictly local. That is to say, the subcategorization rule relates only to co-constituents of the verb. For example, the rule for the verb *find* is $V \rightarrow [+V +transitive]/[\#NP_A]$; that is: replace a verb by a transitive verb if a direct object follows. (ii) Selectional subcategorization specifies semantic–lexical features, which determine the compatibility between lexemes in a particular syntactic position. Such selectional relationships exist between the verb and the subject of a sentence (**the stone died*), the verb and the object (**Carol drinks stones*), and the verb and the adverb (**Stella willingly weighs a ton*).

References

Chomsky, N. 1965. *Aspects of the theory of syntax*. Cambridge, MA.

Grimshaw, J. 1982. Subcategorization and grammatical relations. In A. Zaenen (ed.), *Subjects and other subjects: proceedings of the Harvard conference on the representation of grammatical relations*. Bloomington, IN. 35–55.

Jacobs, R.A. and P.S. Rosenbaum. 1968. *English

transformational grammar. Waltham, MA.

⇒ **transformational grammar**

subjacency (formed after **adjacency**)

A constraint advanced by N. Chomsky for **movement transformations** whereby a constituent may not be moved over more than one (i.e. *S* or *NP*) node (⇒ **principle of cyclic rule application**). Subjacency means that transformations may only operate on one or at most two adjacent levels, so that a transformation may only move a constituent out of a single subjacency-relevant node. An example of a violation of subjacency is [**The man* [*who I identified the dog* [*which bit* –]]. The subjacency constraint is not uncontroversial. In substance it corresponds to several of Ross' (1967) individual restrictions; the **sentential-subject constraint** (if one assumes that sentential subjects are dominated by S and NP), the complex NP constraint (complex NPs are islands for transformations) and the *wh*-**island constraint**.

References

Ross, J.R. 1967. Constraints on variables in syntax. Dissertation, MIT, Cambridge, MA. (Repr. as *Infinite syntax!* Norwood, NJ, 1986.)

⇒ **constraint**

subject

Main **syntactic function** in **nominative languages**, such as **English**, which is marked morphologically, positionally, and structurally depending on the specific language. The most common morphological marker is the **nominative** case. On other possibilities, see Keenan (1976) and Sridhar (1979). The subject can be marked positionally by initial, unmarked **word order**. In the constituent structure of a sentence, the subject is immediately dominated by the S-node in contrast to the object, which is immediately dominated by the verb or predicate phrase.

The subject **constituent** plays a prominent role in the sentence in so far as it is less likely than an object constituent to be affected by language-specific restrictions (⇒ **hierarchy universal**). Thus the verb usually agrees only with the subject in most languages, which is also the most preferred antecedent for pronouns (⇒ **reflexive pronoun**). The specific semantic role of the subject is that of the **agent** of an action; the subject can take on very different roles, especially in the **passive voice**, e.g. *This information was kept secret by the government until now*. In such cases, where the formal and semantic criteria for the subject do not concur, a distinction is made between the grammatical (i.e. syntactic) subject (*this information*) and the logical subject, which is also termed the underlying subject (*by the government*). In reference to **pragmatics** and communicative aspects, the subject is usually the theme (that which is known) of the sentence, while the predicate is usually the rheme (that which is new) (⇒ **theme vs rheme**).

References

Andrews, A. 1985. The major functions of the noun phrase. In T. Shopen (ed.), *Language and typology and syntactic description*, vol. 1: *Clause structure*. Cambridge. 64–154.

Faarlund, J.T. 1988. A typology of subjects. In M.T. Hammond, E.A. Moravcsik, and J.W. Wirth (eds), *Studies in syntactic typology*. Amsterdam. 193–208.

Fillmore, C.J. 1968. The case for case. In E. Bach and R.T. Harms (eds), *Universals in linguistic theory*. New York. 1–88.

Foley, W. and R.D. van Valin. 1977. On the viability of the notion of 'subject' in universal grammar. *BLS* 3.293–320.

Hasan, R. and P.H. Fries (ed.) 1995. *On subject and theme: a discourse functional perspective*. Amsterdam and Philadelphia.

Johnson, D.E. 1977. On Keenan's definition of 'subject of.' *LingI* 9.673–92.

Keenan, E.L. 1976. Towards a universal definition of 'subject.' In C.N. Li (ed.), *Subject and topic*. New York. 303–34.

Sridhar, S.N. 1979. Dative subjects and the notion of subjects. *Lingua* 49.99–125.

Van Oosten, J. 1977. Subjects and agenthood in English. *CLS* 13.459–71.

Zaenen, A. (ed.) 1982. *Subjects and other subjects*. Bloomington, IN.

⇒ **syntactic function**, **relational grammar**

subject–predicate model ⇒ actor–action model

subject to object raising ⇒ accusative plus infinitive construction

subject vs predicate

Fundamental grammatical relation based on the binary sentence analysis of **school grammar**, which is derived from the logical categories of Aristotle. The interdependence of **subject** and **predicate** is the basic requirement for a sentence as an independent linguistic unit. In contrast to attributive and adverbial relations, in which a one-sided dependence between the modified expression (noun, verb) and the modifier (attributive and adverbial elements) exists, a bilateral dependency holds between the subject and the predicate. The **valence** of the verb (or its **selection restrictions**) determines the choice of the subject, while the subject determines the **agreement** (transference of number and person) between the subject and the verb.

Many objections, based mostly on formal grounds, have been raised against the binary analysis of subject/predicate, which was continued in the division of NP and VP in **transformational grammar**. For instance, the binary analysis cannot be demonstrated, at least in the surface structure, for such sentences as *Jump!* A more serious challenge has been presented by **dependency grammar**, which denies the centrality of the subject–predicate relation and instead considers the verb to be the highest node of the sentence. For a somewhat different analysis of non-Indo-European languages, see Sasse (1987).

References

Bellert, I. 1970. On the semantic interpretation of subject–predicate relations in the sentence of particular reference. In M. Bierwisch and K.E. Heidolph (eds), *Progress in linguistics*. The Hague. 9–26.

Geach, P.T. 1950. Subject and predicate. *Mind* 59.461–82.

Sandmann, M. 1979. *Subject and predicate: a contribution to the theory of syntax*, 2nd edn. Heidelberg.

Sasse, H.-J. 1987. The thetic/categorial distinction revisited. *Linguistics* 25.511–80.

⇒ **subject**

subjunction ⇒ implication, conjunction

subjunctive [Lat. *subiunctivus* (transl. of Grk *hypotaktikós*), from *subiungere* 'to fix under; to attach in a subordinate capacity']

Subcategory of verbal **mood** in many languages, which, in contrast to the neutral **indicative**, portrays the state of affairs described by the verb as 'relative.' It can be used to express a subjective evaluation by the speaker, such as a wish (*If only he were here!*), a doubt or an expression of possibility. Virtually all **Indo-European** languages still possess a morphological subjunctive system, although it is greatly reduced in **English** as compared to **German** and **French**. In many languages, other forms such as **modal auxiliaries** and **sentence adverbials** (*probably*, *maybe*) have taken on some of the functions of the subjunctive.

In English, the subjunctive occurs only in a limited number of constructions: (a) wishes: *If only I had a million dollars!*; (b) some set expressions: *Long live the Queen! Be that as it may ..., God bless!*; (c) clauses containing recommendations, requirements, demands, etc.: *It is recommended that each participant come early*; (d) in hypothetical or unreal sentences as the first element: *If I were benevolent dictator of the world ...* Such sentences are followed by the **conditional** (⇒ **sequence of tenses**).

The form of the subjunctive in English depends on its use. (1) For types (a)–(c), the subjunctive is identical to the infinitive form (without *to*); the main differences are in the forms of *to be*, and in the third person singular, where the indicative adds *-s*: *I demand that he attend/be present* vs *He attends/is present*. (2) For hypothetical constructions, two forms of subjunctive are used: (a) for present or timeless conditions, present subjunctive, identical in form to the past tense with *-ed* (or *were*): *If I were you ...*, *If you worked harder ...*; (b) for conditions in the past, *had* + past participle: *If you had been there ...*, *If you had worked harder.*

Reference
James, F. 1986. *Semantics of the English subjunctive*. Vancouver.
⇒ **conditional, modality**

sublanguage

1 Term coined by Harris (1968) to describe a subset of sentences in a language which can be generated from a special set of grammatical rules, some of which belong to the grammar of the language, others of which are unique to the sublanguage itself. Thus, in the sublanguage of an aviation hydraulics maintenance manual *the*-deletion is required: *Depressurize Ø hydraulic system. Disconnect Ø electrical connector on Ø pressure switch*. Sublanguages are also characterized by constraints on **collocations**. For example, in the sublanguage of stock market reports, intransitive verbs of motion (e.g. *plunge, drop*) are combined only with certain nouns and certain adverbs, while these same combinations are not found in the standard language: *Mines plunged sharply, The gold index dropped sharply*. Recent research in sublanguages has concentrated above all on the facilitation of automated translation, especially between English and French sublanguages.

2 In a broader sense 'sublanguage' refers to those language variants that deviate from the standard language as they arise in various social-, gender-, and age-specific groups as well as in professional and academic groups.

3 Socially determined sublanguages are differentiated from **terminology**-based speech variants, i.e. jargons; but since professionally based groupings frequently overlap with social classes, the transition between sublanguage and jargon is unclear. Following the organization of the **speech community** into social groups, sublanguages are also designated as group, class, or professional languages (⇒ **jargon**). The differences from the standard language lie above all in the vocabularies of the different sublanguages, which were developed according to the interests and needs specific to each

group. This is particularly obvious in the speech of hunters, fishers, miners, vintners, printers, students, beggars, and thieves. While, on the one hand, sublanguages develop their unique variants through the innovative (metaphoric) use of pre-existing expressions in the lexicon and grammar of the mother tongue, they also contribute to the proliferation of new elements in the mother tongue itself, when elements of the sublanguage are adopted into the standard language.

References
Harris, Z. 1968. *Mathematical structures of language*. New York.
────── 1982. Discourse and sublanguage. In R. Kittredge and J. Lehrberger (eds), *Sublanguage: studies of language in restricted semantic domains*. Berlin. 231–6.
Hirschman, L. and N. Sager, 1982. Automatic information formatting of a medical sublanguage. In R. Kittredge, R. and J. Lehrberger (eds), *Sublanguage: studies of language in restricted semantic domains*. Berlin. 27–69.
Kittredge, R. 1982. Variation and homogeneity of sublanguage. In R. Kittredge and J. Lehrberger (eds), *Sublanguage: studies of language in restricted semantic domains*. Berlin. 107–37.
Lehrberger, J. 1986. Sublanguage analysis. In R. Grishman and R. Kittredge (eds), *Analyzing language in restricted domains: sublanguage description and processing*. Hillsdale, NJ. 19–38.
Sagar, N. 1986. Sublanguage: linguistic phenomenon, computational tool. In R. Grishman and R. Kittredge (eds), *Analyzing language in restricted domains: sublanguage description and processing*. Hillsdale, NJ. 1–17.

subordinate clause (*also* constituent clause, dependent clause)

In contrast to the structurally independent **main clause** (*also* **matrix sentence**), a formally subordinate clause, i.e. one that is dependent on a main verb in respect to **word order**, **tense**, and **mood**, as well as **illocution**. Important aspects for classifying subordinate clauses are formal markers (introduced by a conjunction or not), function in the sentence (⇒ **subject, object, adverbial**), as well as semantic considerations (temporal, causal, modal, or conditional clauses).

(a) Formally, dependent clauses introduced by a conjunction are divided into the following: (1) **relative clauses** introduced by a **relative pronoun** (*who, which*) or adverb (*when, where*); (2) relative clauses introduced by an **interrogative** pronoun (*who, how, what*) or interrogative adverb (*when, where*), whose identification is established by the meaning of the finite verb of the main clause (*He wondered where she could be*); they can appear as subjects, objects, or adverbials (and are also called 'free relative clauses'); (3) conjunctive clauses (introduced by subordinating **conjunctions** or pronominal adverbs).

Unpreceded dependent clauses often appear in reported speech (⇒ **direct vs indirect discourse**) (*She says she'll come as soon as she can*). Similar to subordinate clauses are such constructions as **infinitive constructions** (*She promises to come as soon as possible*) and **participle constructions** (*Being heavily under the influence of alcohol, he couldn't remember anything*).

(b) In respect to their function in the main clause: (1) clauses that have sentential functions: *Everyone was glad that she came*; (2) attributive clauses that refer to an antecedent in the main clause (*He refused to give up the hope that she would still come*); (3) clauses which do not refer to specific elements in the main clause, but rather to the clause as a whole: *She's coming tomorrow, which is good news to everyone*.

(c) Semantically subordinate clauses are divided into different groups depending on the conjunction or adverb: temporal, causal, modal, and conditional clauses. The distinction between restrictive vs non-restrictive relative clauses also rests on semantic considerations.

The use of the term 'subordinate clause' is not treated uniformly in all grammars: in the narrower sense, all clauses listed in (c) are considered subordinate clauses; in the broader sense, all forms of dependent sentential syntactic structures are included in the definition. In this definition, subordinate clauses are equivalent to the term **constituent clause** used in generative **transformational grammar**. For universal typological aspects of clauses, see Shopen (1985).

References
Shopen, T. (ed.) 1985. *Language typology and syntactic description*, vol. 2: *Complex constructions*. Cambridge.
⇒ **syntax**

subordinating conjunction ⇒ conjunction

subordination

1 ⇒ **hyponymy**

2 In addition to dependency, **interdependence**, and **co-ordination**, the most important relationship between syntactic elements. A dependency relationship of subordination exists, for example, between predicate and object/adverbials, between heads and modifiers, between main and dependent clauses, as well as between dependent clauses of various degrees of dependency in complex sentence structures. Grammatical terms which are based on subordination include **dependency**, **hypotaxis**, **subordinate clause**, **government**, **valence**.

subordinator ⇒ complementizer

subset ⇒ set

substance

In **glossematics**, the material aspect of the linguistic system (e.g. sound waves, characters of a script); substance refers to the expression plane as well as to the content plane (⇒ **expression plane vs content plane**): the substance of the expression plane is phonetic events (individual unclassified sounds), the substance of the content plane is the set of unordered thoughts and concepts that are differently structured from language to language by the **form** (see Hjelmslev 1943: ch. 9).

References
Hjelmslev, L. 1943. *Omkring sprogteoriens grundlaeggelse*. Copenhagen. (*Prolegomena to a theory of language*, trans. F.J. Whitfield. Baltimore, MD, 1953.)
⇒ **glossematics**

substantive [Lat. *substare* 'to be present, exist']

1 In its narrower sense, a synonym for **noun**.

2 In its broader sense, a comprehensive term for nominals, which some grammars define as all declinable words (**nouns**, **adjectives**, **pronouns**, and **numerals**), but which others define as only nouns and adjectives.

substitute

Element which can replace another element having the same function in certain contexts, e.g. **pronoun** for **noun**, e.g. *The book/It's on the table*.

substitution

1 In generative **transformational grammar**, a formal syntactic operation by which certain **constituents** of a **tree diagram** are replaced by other constituents between the **deep structure** and the **surface structure**. There are two forms of substitution: (a) reduction: an element replaces an original element that is larger: *the old man → he*; (b) expansion: an element replaces an element that is smaller (i.e. the opposite of reduction). All forms of substitution consist of the two elementary **transformations**, **deletion** and **insertion**.

2 Synonym for **substitution test**. (⇒ *also* **operational procedures**)

substitution test

1 In general, an experimental method of analysis in structural linguistics for the establishment of elements which belong to the same grammatical category. Any elements that can be paradimatically substituted for each other, belong to the same class of constituents. (⇒ *also* **operational procedures**)

2 In **glossematics**, substitution tests are used to discover linguistically relevant invariants on the levels of content and expression (⇒ **expression vs content plane**). For example *c* can be substituted for *b* in English, but this phonetic change (expression level) also leads to a change in meaning (content level): *cat* vs *bat*. In German, the difference between the trilled *r* and the uvular *r* is manifested only at the level of expression; this allophonic variation is not important at the level of content.

References
⇒ **glossematics**

substitution theory

A text grammar model by R. Harweg which is based on **syntagmatic substitution** as the basic method of forming a text.

Reference
Harweg, R. 1968. *Pronomina und Textkonstitution.* Munich.

substratum

In **language contact** theory, 'substratum' refers to the native language of an indigenous people influenced by the language of a dominant people as well as to its influence upon the dominating language. Examples of a linguistic substratum include the remnants of **Celtic** in the **Romance languages** or the influence of **Scandinavian** on English. The opposite effect is called a **superstratum**, while the mutual influence of two equally prestigious languages is known as an **adstratum**.

References
⇒ **language contact**

succedent

In **formal logic**, the second part of a complex proposition in a propositional connection (cf. **antecedent**).

suffix [Lat. *suffigere* 'to attach']

Morphological element that is attached finally to free **morpheme** constructions, but does not occur as a rule as a free morpheme. In regard to morphosyntactic function, a distinction is drawn between inflectional suffixes (⇒ **inflec-**

tion) and derivational suffixes (⇒ **derivation, word formation**). The latter serve both for systematic semantic differentiation (e.g. *father*: *fatherhood* (abstract noun), *book*: *booklet* (diminutive)) and for determining word class, e.g. *read, reader, readable* (verb, noun, adjective). As a result, suffixes (in contrast with **prefixes**) are tied to specific word classes, e.g. noun suffixes like *-er, -ity, -ling, -ness, -tion*, and the adjectival suffixes such as *-able, -ive, -ish, -ous*.

References
Selkirk, E. 1982. *The syntax of words.* Cambridge, MA.
⇒ **word formation**

suffixation

The formation of complex words or word forms through the addition of a suffix to the word stem. (⇒ *also* **derivation, inflection**)

References
⇒ **word formation**

Suislaw ⇒ Penutian

Sumerian

Language of ancient Mesopotamia with unknown genetic affiliation; the language with the oldest writing tradition. First written documents (**cuneiform**) 3100 BC; the language was spoken until 2000 BC and was then replaced by **Akkadian**, but remained in use for two further millennia as a written language.

Characteristics: **agglutinating** language with **ergative** case system.

References
Attinger, P. 1993. *Eléments de linguistique sumérienne.* Fribourg and Göttingen.
Civil, M. 1973. The Sumerian writing system: some problems. *Orientalia* n.s. 42.21–34.
Cooper, J.S. 1973. Sumerian and Akkadian in Sumer and Akkad. *Orientalia* n.s. 42.239–46.
Falkenstein, A. 1949/50. *Grammatik der Sprache Gudeas von Lagass̆,* 2 vols. Rome.
———— 1959. *Das Sumerische.* (Handbuch der Orientalistik I, vol. 2.) Leiden.
Gostony, C.-G. 1975. *Dictionnaire d'étymologie sumérienne et grammaire comparée.* Paris.
Hayes, J.L. 1990. *A manual of Sumerian: grammar and texts.* Malibu, CA.
Jacobsen, T. 1988. Sumerian grammar today. *JAOS* 108.123–33.
Michalowski, P. 1980. Sumerian as an ergative language. *Journal of Cuneiform Studies* 32.86–103.
Thomsen, M.L. 1984. *The Sumerian language: introduction to the history and grammatical structure.* Copenhagen.

Sundanese ⇒ Malayo-Polynesian

superdental ⇒ alveolar

superiority condition

Constraint introduced by Chomsky (1973) for transformations according to which a *wh*-element X in the configuration ...Y... [...Z...X...]... may not be moved to Y, if Z can be moved to Y and Z is 'structurally higher' than Y (i.e. Z c-commands X). This restriction blocks the derivation of **I know what_i (=Y) who (= Z) saw t_i (= X)*, as *wh*-movement is applicable to *who* (cf. *I know who_i t_i saw what*) and *who* commands the d-structural position of *what*.

References
Chomsky, N. 1973. Conditions on transformations. In S.R. Anderson and P. Kiparsky (eds), *Festschrift for Morris Halle*. New York. 232–86.
⇒ **transformational grammar**

superlative [Lat. *superlativum*, from *super-ferre* 'to carry to a higher degree']

Morphological category of adjectives which is the highest level of **degree** and in English is formed with the suffix *-est*: *oldest, longest*. When a superlative refers semantically to the highest degree of a property (comparing at least three elements), it is termed a relative superlative: *This theory is the most convincing (of all theories)*. If it refers to a high degree without comparison, it is termed an absolute superlative (*also* **elative**): *This theory is most convincing*.

References
⇒ **degree**

superordinate ⇒ hyperonymy

superordination ⇒ hyperonymy

superstratum [Lat. *stratum* 'level']

In **language contact** theory, the dominant language as well as its influence on the native language of the indigenous people. (⇒ *also* **substratum, adstratum**)

References
⇒ **language contact**

superstructure

A term from **text linguistics** referring to the characteristic semantic structure of a **text type**. The superstructure is at the foundation of the changing text content (**macrostructure**). It can be understood as a conventional schema of ordering that is comprised of text-type typical categories and combination rules. (⇒ *also* **argumentation, narrative structures**)

Reference
Van Dijk, T.A. and W. Kintsch. 1983. *Strategies of discourse comprehension*. Orlando, FL.

supine [Lat. *supinus* 'lying back; upturned']

Abstract verbal form in **Latin** which is derived from verbs of motion. There are two types of supine in Latin: (a) supine I ends in *-tum* and has adjectival meaning, indicating a direction or purpose: *Salutatum venire* 'to come for the purpose of greeting'; (b) supine II ends in *-u* and appears after certain adjectives: *Haec res est facilis intellectu* 'This is easy to understand.'

suppletivism

Completion of a defective inflectional **paradigm** by a lexically similar but etymologically unrelated **stem** morpheme. For instance, the different stem morphemes in the inflectional paradigm of the verb *be, am, is, was, been*, or in Latin the combination of the paradigm of *ferre* 'to carry' from the three suppletive stems *ferro–tuli–latum*.

References
Dressler, W.U. 1986. Suppletivism in word-formation. In J. Fisiak (ed.) *Historical semantics, historical word formation*. Berlin. 97–112.
Matthews, P.H. 1974. *Morphology*. Cambridge. (2nd edn 1991.)
Mel'čuk, I.A. 1976. On suppletion. *Linguistics* 170.54–90.
Osthoff, H. 1900. *Vom Suppletivwesen in den indogermanischen Sprachen*. Leipzig.

suprasegmental feature (*also* prosodic feature)

Term coined by American structuralists for a **distinctive feature** that – unlike a **phoneme** – cannot be segmented individually from linguistic utterances, e.g. differences in **juncture, stress, pitch, accent, prosody, intonation, syllable breaks**.

References
Crystal, D. 1974. Paralinguistics. In T.A. Sebeok (ed.), *Current trends in linguistics*. The Hague. vol. 12, 265–95.
——— 1975. *The English tone of voice: essays in intonation, prosody and paralanguage*. London.
Crystal, D. and R. Quirk. 1964. *Systems of prosodic and paralinguistic features in English*. The Hague.
Lehiste, I. 1970. *Suprasegmentals*. Cambridge, MA.
Wittmann, H. 1970. The prosodic formatives of modern German. *Phonetica* 22.1–10.
⇒ **intonation**

surface structure

1 In a general sense, the directly observable

actual form of sentences as they are used in communication.

2 In the terminology of **transformational grammar**, a relatively abstract sentence structure which results from the application of base rules and **transformational rules** and which is the input for the phonological component. That is, surface structure must undergo phonetic interpretation in order to correspond to (1). At the same time, phonologically identical interpretations can arise from different surface structures. For example, *red roses and tulips* is ambiguous and can be interpreted as [[*red roses*] *and tulips*] or [*red* [*roses and tulips*]]. The basing of the syntactic description of language only on its surface structure is a hallmark of structuralist (⟹ **structuralism**) analysis, e.g. as in **phrase structure grammar**. Phenomena like the following examples have led to the positing of multiple representations, especially in the distinction between surface structure and **deep structure**: (a) The surface structure can be ambiguous (**ambiguity**), e.g. *the choice of the chairman = the chairman chose X* or *the chairman was chosen*. (b) Differing surface structures can be semantically synonymous (**paraphrase**), e.g. *the blue sky* and *the sky which is blue*. (c) Information can be missing from the surface structure and be understood intuitively by the listener, e.g. *Philip promised to come to California*, where it is understood that the logical subject of *to come* is *Philip*. (d) The representation of discontinuous elements, e.g. *Caroline will call me up tomorrow*, where *call* and *up* are syntactically discontinuous but form a single semantic unit. – These problems led to the acceptance of syntactic deep structure, which delineates the abstract basic structure of all grammatical relations and also explicitly contains all information which is necessary for semantic interpretation and for the application of syntactically motivated transformations (**transposition, deletion**). Several revisions of the original model have given rise to a new definition of the syntactic levels: the surface structure is enriched by traces (⟹ **trace theory**) of transpositional transformations and by other **empty positions**, so that the structural information of the deep structure is maintained in the surface structure (⟹ **projection principle**). This new surface structure which contains information from the deep structure is called s-structure. The actual deep structure in this case is called d-structure. In the revised theory, the semantic interpretation originates at surface structure, and since s-structure contains disambiguating information and since ambiguities can only be handled in the semantic component of the grammar, the motivation for a level of d-structure independent of surface structure is lost in trace theory. (⟹ *also* **transformational grammar, surface syntax**).

References

Chomsky, Noam. 1992. *A Minimalist Program for Linguistic Theory.* Cambridge, MA.
⟹ **deep structure, transformational grammar**

surface syntax

Collective term for various directions in syntax research which, in contrast to some stages of generative **transformational grammar**, assumes the syntactic structures of the **surface structure** to be the basis for the interpretation of sentence meaning. Linguistic theories with surface syntax include that of Hudson (1976), **daughter dependency grammar** (so called because it allows not only dependency relations between sister nodes of constituents, e.g. between *new* and *book* in *new book*, but also dependency relations between daughter and mother nodes, as between *new* and *new book*), H.H. Lieb's 'Integrational Linguistics,' as well as **categorial grammar**, which is more or less similar to surface syntax. (⟹ *also* **integrational linguistics, Montague grammar**)

References

Fiengo, R. 1981. *Surface structure: the interface of autonomous components.* New Haven, CT.
Hudson, R. 1976. *Arguments for a non-transformational grammar.* Chicago, IL.
Lieb, H.H. 1977. *Outline of integrational linguistics.* Berlin.

Svan ⟹ South Caucasian

svarabhakti [Old Indic 'vowel part']

Term from **Sanskrit** grammar to denote **epenthesis** before consonants (especially before *r, l, m, n*) which functions as a way to form syllables, e.g. West Gmc **fugl* > Ger. *Vogel* 'bird' (⟹ **anaptyxis**).

Swahili

Bantu language of the East African coast and off-shore islands, official language of Tanzania and Kenya. Used as a **lingua franca** for the East African slave and spice trade, Swahili incorporated numerous **Arabic** and later English words, but has still maintained the typical grammatical structure of a Bantu language. Documents (in Arabic script) since about 1700; from 1890 in Latin alphabet.

References

Adam, H. 1987. *Kiswahili: elementary course with key.* Hamburg.

Ashton, E.O. 1944. *Swahili grammar (including intonation)*. London.

Polomé, E.C. 1967. *Swahili language handbook*. Washington, DC.

Vitale, A.J. 1981. *Swahili syntax*. Dordrecht.

Swedish

Scandinavian language with approx. 9 million speakers in Sweden and Finland. The development of an independent written language dates from Sweden's independence from Denmark (1526) and was strongly influenced by the Bible translation (1541) commissioned by Gustav I.

Characteristics: definite article *-en* as a nominal suffix (from Common Scandinavian), cf. *en dag* vs *dagen* 'a day' vs 'the day.' Word order: SVO.

References
Collinder, B. 1974. *Svensk språklära*. Stockholm.

Holmes, P. and I. Inchliffe. 1993. *Swedish: a comprehensive grammar*. London.

Thorell, O. 1973. *Svensk grammatikk*. Stockholm.

Dictionary
Swedish dictionary. 1995. London.
⇒ **Scandinavian**

switch reference

1 Grammatical coding in subordinate or paratactical clauses (⇒ **subordinate clause**) that expresses whether, for example, the subject of this clause is referentially identical with the subject of the **main clause** or not. The latter case is termed switch reference in a narrower sense; cf. Lango (**Nilo-Saharan**) *Dákó òpòyò ní* ('The woman remembers that') *ècégò dógólà* ('she closed the door,' i.e. the woman herself) vs *òcègò dógólá* ('he/she closed the door,' i.e. someone else). Switch reference is widespread, e.g. in languages of New Guinea, Australia, America, and Africa.

2 In **discourse grammar**, the structured presentation of information from utterance to utterance in a text. The information contained in an utterance can be classified according to different referential domains such as time, place, person, object. The switch reference within these domains is comprehended by means of descriptive categories such as 'introduction', 'reception', 'postponement'. In the framework of **discourse analysis**, the concept of switch reference is used to describe characteristic features of **text types**. One proceeds from the assumption that a specific communicative objective, the 'text question' provides certain 'givens' with regard to the text structure which are then comprehended as models of switch reference (⇒ **coherence**, **text typology**).

References
Finer, D.L. 1985. *The formal grammar of switch reference*. New York.

Givón, T. 1982. Topic continuity in discourse. The functional domain of switch reference. In J. Haiman and P. Munro (eds), *Switch reference and universal grammar*. Amsterdam. 51–82.

Heydrich, W. *et al.* (eds) 1989. *Connexity and coherence*. Berlin.

Marslen-Wilson, W. *et al.* 1982. Producing interpretable discourse: the establishment and maintenance of reference. In R. Jarvella and W. Klein (eds), *Speech, place and action*. New York. 339–78.

Stirling, L. 1993. *Switch reference and discourse representation*. Cambridge.

Tomlin, R.S. 1985. Foreground–background information and the syntax of subordination. *Text* 5.85–122.

syllabary

Generally, the (ordered) inventory of signs in a syllabic writing system.

syllabic law

Sound changes that relate to the prosodic unity (⇒ **prosody**) of the **syllable**, such as **assimilation**.

syllable

Basic phonetic-phonological unit of the word or of speech that can be identified intuitively, but for which there is no uniform linguistic definition. Articulatory criteria include increased pressure in the airstream (⇒ **stress**^{2}), a change in the **quality** of individual sounds (⇒ **sonority**), a change in the degree to which the mouth is opened. Regarding syllable structure, a distinction is drawn between the **nucleus** (= 'crest,' 'peak,' i.e. the point of greatest volume of sound which, as a rule, is formed by vowels) and the marginal phonemes of the surrounding sounds that are known as the head (= 'onset,' i.e. the beginning of the syllable) and the **coda** (end of the syllable). Syllable boundaries are, in part, phonologically characterized by **boundary markers**. If a syllable ends in a vowel, it is an open syllable; if it ends in a consonant, a closed syllable. Sounds, or sequences of sounds that cannot be interpreted phonologically as syllabic (like [p] in *supper*, which is phonologically one **phone**, but belongs to two syllables), are known as 'interludes.'

References
Awedyk, W. 1990. Is a phonetic definition of the syllable possible? *Studia Phonetica Posnaniensia* 2.5–12.

Bell, A. and J.B. Hooper (eds) 1978. *Syllables and segments*. Amsterdam.

Clements, G.N. and S.J. Keyser. 1983. *CV phonol-*

ogy: a generative theory of the syllable. Cambridge, MA.

Hooper, J.B. 1972. The syllable in phonological theory. *Lg* 48.524–40.

Rosetti, A. 1963. *Sur la théorie de la syllabe,* 2nd edn. The Hague.

Vennemann, T. 1974. Words and syllables in natural generative grammar. In A. Buck *et al.* (eds), *Papers from the parasession on natural phonology.* Chicago, IL. 346–74.

—— 1978. Universal syllabic phonology. *TL* 5.175–215.

—— 1988. *Preference laws for syllable structure and the explanation of sound change.* Berlin.

⇒ **accent, intonation, phonetics, phonology**

syllable break

An important prosodic feature (⇒ **prosody**) related to **vowel** length. A distinction is drawn between the close and the loose association of consonants and vowels, depending on the manner in which the consonant 'breaks' the preceding vowel.

References
Trubetzkoy, N. 1939. *Grundzüge der Phonologie.* Göttingen. (4th edn 1967.)
⇒ **syllable**

syllable nucleus ⇒ nucleus²

syllable stress ⇒ stress²

syllable weight

Language-specific characteristic of **syllables** that bear word stress.

Reference
Hyman, L. 1985. *A theory of phonological weight.* Dordrecht.

syllepsis ⇒ zeugma

syllogism [Grk *syllogismós* 'computation, calculation']

A method of **formal logic** to deduce a conclusion from two premises. For example, *If all humans die and Socrates is human, then Socrates will die.* In a correctly formed syllogism, the truth of the conclusion necessarily follows from the truth of the premises. A syllogism is always true on the basis of its structure (⇒ **implication**), even if all its premises are false. (⇒ *also* **argumentation, enthymeme**)

References
⇒ **formal logic**

symbol [Grk *sýmbolon* 'token (serving as proof of identity)']

1 In the semiotics of Peirce (1931), a class of signs in which the relation between the sign and the denoted state of affairs rests exclusively upon convention. The meaning of a symbol is established within a given language or culture. This is the case both for linguistic signs and for gestures (modes of address) or visual representations (e.g. the dove as a symbol of peace). (⇒ *also* **icon, index**)

Reference
Peirce, C.S. 1931–58. *Collected papers of Charles S. Peirce,* ed. C. Hartshorne, P. Weiss, and A.W. Burks. 8 vols. Cambridge, MA.

2 A conventionalized sign used in formal **metalanguages** (e.g. one in the inventory of signs used for grammatical categories in **transformational grammar** (*NP, VP*)), formally prescribed signs (e.g. the double arrow (⇒) indicating a transformation), and conventions for the use of brackets and parentheses.

symbol field of language

In Bühler's (1934) **two-field theory**, the level of the linguistic context in contrast to the **index field of language** of individual communicative situations. Both the symbol field of language and the index field are determined by the given **I–now–here origo**, which functions as the origin of the two co-ordinates. Aids for constructing and understanding the linguistic context can be classified according to how their elements are used in the **synsemantic field of language**, the **sympractical field of language**, or the **symphysical field of language**.

References
Bühler, K. 1934. *Sprachtheorie.* Jena. (Repr. Stuttgart, 1965.)

Innis, R.E. (trans.) 1982. *Karl Bühler: semiotic foundations of language theory.* New York.
⇒ **axiomatics of linguistics**

symbolic logic ⇒ formal logic

symmetrical relation

A two-place relation R for which, with regard to any objects x and y, it is true: $R(x, y) \rightarrow R(y, x)$. This is the case, for example, for the relation of 'being married': if x is married to y, then y is also married to x. If both pairs in the relation cannot be reversed in any case, then the relation is not symmetrical: for example, *x is the sister of y* cannot be reversed to *y is the sister of x*, if $y = [+male]$. A relation R is asymmetric, if there are not two objects x and y for which both $R(x, y)$ as well as $R(y, x)$ is the case; for example, this is the case in the relation 'is the daughter of.'

References
⇒ **formal logic, set theory**

symphysical field of language [Grk *sýmphysis* 'growing together']

Term used by K. Bühler to designate the way

in which inherently context-free utterances are 'affixed to the things' they name, e.g. trademarks on goods, book titles, texts on monuments, and signposts.

References
⇒ **axiomatics of linguistics**

sympractical field of language [Grk *syn-* 'with,' *prãxis* 'action']

Term coined by K. Bühler, inspired by Gestalt psychology, to designate the situative context of utterances. The sympractical field of language comes especially into effect in the interpretation of isolated utterances. When such utterances occur with little or no context, they are, according to Bühler, used empractically (⇒ **empractical use of language**).

References
⇒ **axiomatics of linguistics**

synaeresis

Contraction of two vowels from originally different syllables from between which a consonantal element has been dropped due to **stress**[2] on the root syllable, e.g. Lat. *vidēre* > Span. *ver* 'see.' The opposite process is called **diaeresis**.

References
⇒ **language change**

synaesthesia ⇒ sound symbolism

synaloepha [Grk *synaloiphē* 'stopping of a hiatus, coalescing']

Contraction of two vowels, in which a vowel in final position runs into the following vowel in initial position through (a) **elision** (= loss of both vowels) (e.g. in Fr. masc. article before initial vowel: *l'air* instead of **le air* 'air'), (b) **synaeresis** (= contraction of two contiguous vowels to a **diphthong**) (e.g. Lat. *vidēre* > Span. *ver* 'see'), or (c) **contraction** (= contraction to a single long vowel) (Goth. *maiza*, OE *māra* > Mod. Eng. *more*. (⇒ *also* **language change**)

synapsis [Grk *sýnapsis* 'contact']

In E. Benveniste's terminology, a semantic unit in French consisting of several lexemes that are syntactically related to one another, in which the determined element precedes the determining element and every lexeme retains its original separate individual meaning: *machine-à-coudre* 'sewing machine,' *arc-en-ciel* 'rainbow.'

Reference
Benveniste, E. 1966. *Problèmes de linguistique gén-*

érale. Paris. (*Problems in general linguistics*, trans. M.E. Meek. Coral Gables, FL, 1971.)

syncategorematic word ⇒ synsemantic word

synchrony vs diachrony [Grk *chrónos* 'time']

After the distinction **langue vs parole**, the most important methodological distinction established by F. de Saussure for the interpretation and investigation of language as a closed system. It is only on the axis of simultaneity (i.e. a fixed moment in time) that language can be analyzed as a system of values in which the value of an individual element results from the relational context of all values in the system. Synchrony refers to a state fixed in time, while diachrony refers to changing states of a language between different time periods. While descriptive synchronic research investigates the relationship of individual elements to a balanced linguistic system that can be described structurally, historically oriented diachronic investigations can, according to de Saussure, only address the replacement of single elements by other elements, or the change of individual elements. This devaluation of historical investigation, which was a reaction against the **historical linguistics** advocated by the **Neogrammarians**, was in turn subject to criticism (see W. von Wartburg, A. Martinet, and E. Coseriu). Owing to this, diachronic (historical) linguistics of the structuralist variety is still lively today. Coseriu and post-structuralist linguistic research influenced by W. Labov argue against the distinction synchrony–diachrony as having any basis in reality.

References
Baumgärtner, K. 1969. Diachronie und Synchronie der Sprachstruktur. In H. Moser (ed.), *Sprache: Gegenwart und Geschichte*. Düsseldorf. 52–64.
Coseriu, E. 1958. *Synchronie, Diachronie und Geschichte*. Munich.
Kanngiesser, S. 1972. *Aspekte der synchronischen und diachronischen Linguistik*. Tübingen.
Labov, W. 1965. On the mechanism of linguistic change. In C.W. Kreidler (ed.), *Report on the sixteenth annual round table meeting*. Washington, DC.
Labov, W., W. Weinreich, and M.I. Herzog. 1968. Empirical foundations of language change. In W.P. Lehmann and Y. Malkiel (eds), *Directions for historical linguistics*. Austin, TX. 95–188.
Martinet, A. 1955. *Economie des changements phonétiques*. Bern.
Saussure, F. de. 1916. *Cours de linguistique générale*, ed. C. Bally and A. Sechehaye. Paris. (*Course in general linguistics*, trans. R. Harris. London, 1983.)
Wartburg, W. von. 1946. *Problèmes et méthodes de*

la linguistique. Paris. (2nd rev. edn 1963.)

Zwirner, E. 1969. Zu Herkunft und Funktion des Begriffspaares Synchronie–Diachronie. In H. Moser (ed.), *Sprache: Gegenwart und Geschichte*. Düsseldorf.

syncope [Grk *synkopḗ* 'cutting off']

Loss of an unstressed vowel (or, more rarely, a consonant) within a word. Compare, for example, two common pronunciations of *laboratory*: Am. Eng. /ˈlabrətorɪ/ and Brit. Eng. /laˈborətrɪ/ (⇒ **apocope**).

References
⇒ **language change**

syncretism [Grk *synkrâtos* 'mixed together']

Historical **language change**: formal collapse of different, originally separate grammatical functions, especially apparent in the case system of various languages, thus the **ablative**, **locative**, and **instrumental** in other **Indo-European** languages correspond to the **dative** in **Greek**, while the functions of the instrumental and, in part, those of the locative are subsumed under the ablative in Latin; in German, the **nominative** case has assumed the function of the **vocative**. A result of syncretism is that grammatical categories come to be no longer morphologically marked: for instance, syncretism in the development of English led to the loss of case marking and the stabilization of **word order**.

syndeton [Grk *syndéton* 'bound together']

Connection of linguistic expressions (words, syntagms, or sentences) with the aid of **conjunctions**. (⇒ *also* **asyndeton**)

synecdoche [Grk *synekdochḗ* 'understanding one thing with another']

A rhetorical **trope** that refers to something with a semantically narrower term (particularizing synecdoche) or a broader term (generalizing synecdoche). Examples include *Washington* or *America* for USA, or *we* for I.

References
Burke, K. 1945. *A grammar of motives*. Berkeley, CA.
Ruwet, N. 1975. Synecdoque et métonymie. *Poétique* 6.371–88.
Todorov, T. 1970. Synecdoques. *Communications* 16.26–35.
⇒ **figure of speech**, **trope**

synesis [Grk 'uniting, union']

Interpretation of a syntactic structure according to semantic content instead of grammatical structure, which often results in variation in **agreement**: *A pile* (sg.) *of books were* (pl.) *lying on the table*.

synesthesia [Grk *synaísthēsis* 'joint perception']

The association of stimuli or the senses (smell, sight, hearing, taste, and touch). The stimulation of one of these senses simultaneously triggers the stimulation of one of the other senses, resulting in phenomena such as hearing colors or seeing sounds. In language, synesthesia is reflected in expressions in which one element is used in a metaphorical sense. Thus, a voice can be 'soft' (sense of touch), 'warm' (sensation of heat), or 'dark' (sense of sight).

References
⇒ **metaphor**

synonym [Grk *ónyma* 'name']

In the strictest sense, a word or expression that has the same meaning as another word or expression. In the case of referential words, synonyms have the same referent. For example, *morning star* and *evening star* are synonyms because they both refer to the planet Venus. In the broadest sense, any words that have overlapping meanings are said to be synonyms, e.g. *acquire*, *get*, *obtain*, *receive*, etc. (⇒ *also* **extension**, **intension**, **lexical field theory**, **synonymy**, **thesaurus**)

References
⇒ **synonymy**

synonym dictionary

In the broader sense, any dictionary that provides explanations of the **lexemes** through semantic paraphrases (*mare* 'female horse'). In the narrower sense, a compilation aiming at the inclusion of all synonymous expressions, based on a very broad concept of **synonymy**.

References
Longman synonym dictionary. 1986. London.
Webster's new dictionary of synonyms. 1968. Springfield, MA.
⇒ **lexicography**, **semantics**

synonymy

Semantic relation of sameness or (strong) similarity in meaning of two or more linguistic expressions. In lexicology, grammar, or stylistics it is a term whose interpretations are as varied as the semantic theories in which it is found. The following distinctions are generally made. (a) Complete (absolute, strict, or pure) synonymy: by definition, complete synonymy presupposes the unconditional substitutability of the given expressions in all contexts and refers both to denotative (⇒ **denotatum**) and to connotative (⇒ **connotation**) semantic elements. In the narrow interpretation of this operational definition and in its restriction to a specific linguistic system, it appears that the concept of linguistic economy eliminates, in almost all cases, the possibility of complete synonymy at least in lexemes. (b) Partial synonymy, which refers either to lexemes which can be substituted in some but not all contexts depending on their denotative and connotative meaning (*get/receive a letter*, but not *receive a cold*) or to lexemes with the same denotative meaning that have different connotations depending on regional (*peanuts* vs *goobers*), socio-dialectal (*money, dough, bread, moolah*), political (*team, committee*), stylistic (*room, suite*), or sublinguistic (⇒ **sublanguage**) (*salt, NaCl*) distinctions. The causes of synonymic variation may be traced especially to the fact that the vocabulary of a language is an open system which can rapidly adapt to dialectal, social, and scientific developments. Synonymy comes about through the concurrent development of dialectal and standard, colloquial, and technical variants, through euphemistic tendencies towards circumlocution (e.g. *die* vs *pass away*), through language manipulation (e.g. *free world* vs *the West*) and through the adoption of foreign words (e.g. *following* vs *entourage*). The following constitute operational processes for determining the degree of lexical synonymy: the **substitution test**, which determines the substitutability of synonymous lexemes in sentences of identical syntactic structure; **distribution analysis**, which establishes the distributional limits in particular contexts; and **componential analysis**, which provides descriptions via identical bundles of **semantic features**. Even greater exactness in describing the denotative aspect of synonymy is achieved through the definition in **formal logic** according to which synonymy corresponds to an **equivalence** relation: Two expressions E_1 and E_2 in the same syntactic position are synonymous if E_1 implies E_2 and E_2 implies E_1. In addition, the distinction between **extension** and **intension** makes it possible to differentiate more precisely referential synonymy from sameness of sense. For example, the expressions *morning star* and *evening star* are, to be sure, extensionally equivalent (i.e. both refer to the planet Venus), but are intensionally different (⇒ **intensional logic**). (⇒ *also* **equivalence, implication, paraphrase, semantics, thesaurus**)

References
Carnap, R. 1955. Meaning and synonymy in natural languages. *PhS* 7.33–47.

Jones, K.S. 1987. *Synonymy and semantic classification*. New York.
Mates, B. 1950. Synonymity. *UCPPh* 25.201–26.
Quine, W.V.O. 1951. The two dogmas of empiricism. *PhR* 60.20–43.
——— 1960. *Word and object*. Cambridge, MA.
⇒ **semantics**

synsemantic field of language [Grk *sēma* 'sign']

Term coined by K. Bühler, inspired by Gestalt psychology, to designate the determination of the meaning of individual signs of speech through the verbal context as well as through the associated non-verbal signs (illustrations, mimicry, gesture, music). (⇒ *also* **axiomatics of linguistics, symbol field of language**)

References
⇒ **axiomatics of linguistics**

synsemantic word (*also* closed-class word, function word, structure word, syncategorematic word)

Words which, in isolation, have allegedly no independent lexical meaning (cf. the literal translation of synsemantic, i.e. 'co-signing'). Candidates for these so-called empty or function words are prepositions, conjunctions, derivational elements, and other words or word classes that form more or less closed classes. Synsemantic words, in the wider sense, are polysemic linguistic expressions like the adjective *good*, whose meaning varies with the context, e.g. *His character/the answer/the weather/the food is good*. (⇒ *also* **autosemantic word**)

syntactic affixation

Several recent studies on **word formation** presuppose that certain **affixes** demonstrate selectional characteristics that go beyond the usual word configurations. For example, in the gerund construction *Philip's spraying paint on the wall* the verb assigns its complements their **thematic relation**. For this reason, Toman (1986) and Abney (1987) postulate that affixes such as *-ing* are more closely associated with a syntactic category (*VP* or *S*) than with a lexical stem (such as *V*).

References
Abney, S. 1987. The English noun phrase in its sentential aspect. Dissertation, MIT, Cambridge, MA.
Fabb, N. 1984. Syntactic affixation. Dissertation, MIT, Cambridge, MA.
Toman, J. 1986. A (word-)syntax for participles. *LB* 105.367–408.

syntactic category ⇒ grammatical category, syntactic function

syntactic function (*also* grammatical function, grammatical relation, **part of speech**, syntactic relation)

General term for such notions as 'subject,' 'predicate,' 'object,' 'adverbial,' 'attribute,' whose use is dependent on the specific theory or language type in question. (a) For languages like **Latin** and **German**, which have a well-developed morphological system, syntactic functions are usually indicated by cases. Thus, the **subject** is identified with the nominative complement of the predicate (see school grammars of the above-mentioned languages). (b) For languages like **English** and **French**, in which morphological case occurs only marginally, syntactic functions are defined by their structural and topological relations, e.g. the subject is the noun phrase immediately dominated by the sentence-node (see Chomsky 1965), or as the noun phrase whose basic position is sentence-initial (see Halliday 1967). (c) Syntactic functions have also been associated with semantic roles with other semantic or pragmatic notions: subject is associated with the **agent** of an action (⇒ **case grammar**), the logical subject (⇒ **school grammar**) or the topic or theme of a sentence (⇒ **topic vs comment**, **theme vs rheme**) (see Lyons 1977). (d) Multi-factor definitions have also been proposed (see Keenan 1976) as well as attempts at differentiating several kinds of syntactic functions (⇒ **subject**), because the defining criteria mentioned above often contradict each other, as in the passive (for a critique of syntactic functions along these lines, see Vennemann 1982; Primus 1993). (e) For this reason, syntactic functions are not defined but taken as primitive notions in the framework of **Relational Grammar** and **Lexical Functional Grammar**. The syntactic functions listed above refer to **nominative languages** such as English and cannot be directly applied to **ergative languages** or topic-prominent languages (see Foley and Van Valin 1977). (⇒ *also* **object**)

References

Abraham, W. (ed.) 1978. *Valence, semantic case and grammatical relations*. Amsterdam.
Anderson, J.M. 1972. *A study of grammatical functions in English and other languages*. Edinburgh.
Andrews, A. 1985. The major functions of the noun phrase. In T. Shopen (ed.), *Language and typology and syntactic description*, vol. 1: *Clause structure*. Cambridge. 64–154.
Bresnan, J. (ed.) 1982. *The mental representation of grammatical relations*. Cambridge, MA.

Chomsky, N. 1965. *Aspects of the theory of syntax*. Cambridge, MA.
Cole, P. and J.M. Sadock (eds) 1977. *Grammatical relations*. New York.
Croft, W. 1991. *Syntactic categories and grammatical relations*. Chicago, IL.
Foley, W. and R. van Valin. 1977. On the viability of the notion of 'subject' in universal grammar. *BLS* 3.293–320.
Halliday, M.A.K. 1967. Notes on transitivity and theme in English. *JL* 3:1.37–81, 3:199–244.
Keenan, E.L. 1976. Towards a universal definition of 'subject.' In C.N. Li (ed.), *Subject and topic*. New York. 303–34.
Lyons, J. 1977. *Semantics*, vol. 2. Cambridge.
Marantz, A. 1984. *On the nature of grammatical relations*. Cambridge, MA.
Primus, B. 1993. Syntactic relations. In J. Jacobs *et al.* (eds), *Syntax: an international handbook of contemporary research*. Berlin. Vol. 1, 686–705.
Seiler, H.J. 1970. Semantic information in grammar: the problem of syntactic relations. *Semiotica* 2.321–34.
Vennemann, T. 1982. Remarks on grammatical relations. In S. Yang (ed.), *Proceedings of the 1981 Seoul International Congress of Linguistics*. Seoul.

syntactic hypothesis ⇒ lexicalist vs transformationalist hypothesis

syntactic relation ⇒ syntactic function

syntagm [Grk *sýntagma* 'that which is put together in order']

1 Structured syntactic sequence of linguistic elements formed by **segmentation** which can consist of sounds, words, phrases, clauses, or entire sentences. (⇒ *also* **paradigm**)

2 In a more restricted use by Lyons, linguistic unit lying between word and sentence which has no subject or predicate and thus is similar in character to words.

Reference

Lyons, J. 1968. *Introduction to theoretical linguistics*. Cambridge.

syntagmatic substitution

A term from **discourse grammar** (R. Harweg) for the contextual (syntagmatic) replacement of one expression by another, which is semantically related by coreference (⇒ **co-referentiality**) or **contiguity**. The various forms of syntagmatic substitution are an important means of **cohesion** in a text and serve as a criterion for **text typology**. (⇒ **substitution theory**, **textual reference**, **textphoric**)

syntagmeme

Term used by K. Pike (⇒ **tagmemics**) for a syntactic construction. A syntagmeme consists of a chain of formal grammatical elements (⇒ **tagmeme**).

syntax [Grk *sýntaxis* 'putting together in order, arrangement']

1 Subcategory of **semiotics** which deals with the ordering of and relationships between signs and is abstracted from the relationship of the speaker to the **sign**, the sign to its meaning, and the sign to its extralinguistic reality. (⇒ *also* **semantics**)

2 Subcategory of the grammar of natural languages: a system of rules which describe how all well-formed sentences of a language can be derived from basic elements (⇒ **morphemes**, **words**, **part of speech**). Syntactic descriptions are based on specific methods of sentence analysis (⇒ **operational procedures**) and category formation (⇒ **sentence type**, sentential elements). The boundaries with other levels of description, especially with **morphology** and **semantics**, are fluid, and thus more precise descriptions of them depend on the syntactic theory in question.

References
Borsley, R.D. 1991. *Syntactic theory*. London.
Givón, T. 1984/90. *Syntax: a functional–typological introduction*, 2 vols. Amsterdam.
Jacobs, J. *et al.* (eds) 1993. *Syntax: an international handbook of contemporary research*. Berlin and New York.
Moravcsik, E.A. and J.R. Wirth (eds) 1980. *Syntax and semantics*, vol. 13: *Current approaches to syntax*. New York.

Historical syntax
Fisiak, J. (ed.) 1984. *Historical syntax*. The Hague.
Gerritsen, M. and D. Stein. 1992. *Internal and external factors in syntactic change*. Berlin and New York.

synthetic compound

In Marchand's (1960) terminology, a border case in historical **word formation** between **derivation** and **composition**, in which the first constituent forms not a word, but rather a word group, e.g. *watchmaker*, *heartbreaking*. (⇒ *also* **verbal vs root compound**)

References
Fanselow, G. 1988. Word syntax and semantic principles. In G. Booij and J. van Marle (eds), *Yearbook of morphology*. Dordrecht. 95–122.
Marchand, H. 1960. *The categories and types of present-day English word-formation*. Munich. (2nd edn 1969.)

synthetic language

A type of classification postulated by A.W. Schlegel (1818) under morphological aspects for languages that have the tendency to mark the syntactic relations in the sentence through morphological marking at the word stem; it comprises the subclasses **inflectional languages** and **agglutinating languages**. For the opposite, ⇒ **analytic language**.

References
Schlegel, A.W. 1818. *Observations sur la langue et la littérature provençales*. Paris.
⇒ **language typology**

synthetic speech

'Natural' language that has been imitated in an electro-acoustic process.

systemic linguistics (*also* scale and category linguistics, scale and category model)

Descriptive model for linguistic analysis based on the ideas of J.R. Firth and formulated by M.A.K. Halliday. It proceeds from the notion that linguistic descriptions are abstractions of linguistic forms from linguistic utterances. Between language and the extralinguistic world there exists a close relationship which is produced by the situational context. Therefore, a system of mutually defining and deriving formal units guarantees an adequate and complete linguistic analysis.

Halliday (1961) makes the following distinctions. (a) Three levels: form (**grammar**, **lexicon**), substance (**phonology**, **orthography**), and situational context (**semantics**, which is a function of the relationship between form and context). (b) Four basic categories: unit (the structured element of a given level, e.g. sentence, word, **morpheme**), structure (which reflects the syntagmatic order among units), class (the classification of units according to their function), and system (the paradigmatic order among units of closed classes, e.g. **number** for **nouns** or **verbs**). (c) Three abstraction scales, which produce the relationship between the categories and the observable linguistic data: rank (referring to the hierarchical ordering of units, e.g. morpheme–word–phrase–clause–sentence), exponence (the relationship between the categories and the linguistic data), and delicacy (more exact distinctions on all levels, e.g. the division of clauses into concessive, causal, and others).

References
Eggins, S. 1994. *An introduction to systemic linguistics*. London.
Halliday, M.A.K. 1961. Categories of the theory of grammar. *Word* 17.241–92.
——— 1967. Notes on transitivity and theme in English. *JL* 3.37–81, 3.199–244, 4.179–215.
——— 1973. *Explorations in the function of language*. London.

—— 1985. *An introduction to functional grammar*. London.

Hartmann, R.R.K. 1973. *The language of linguistics: reflections on linguistic terminology with partic-ular reference to 'level' and 'rank.'* Tübingen.

Langendoen, T.D. 1968. *The London School of linguistics: a study of the linguistic theories of B. Malinowski and J.R. Firth*. Cambridge, MA.

T

taboo word [Polynesian *tabu* 'inviolable, consecrated']

A term that is avoided for religious, political, or sexual reasons and is usually replaced by a **euphemism**, e.g. *rest room* or *bathroom* for toilet.

References
Eckler, A.R. 1986/7. A taxonomy for taboo-word studies. *Maledicta* 9.201–3.
Steiner, F. 1967. *Taboo*. Harmondsworth.
Tournier, P. 1975. *The naming of persons*. New York.
Ullmann, S. 1962. *Semantics: an introduction to the science of meaning*. Oxford.
⇒ **euphemism, tabooization**

tabooization

Phenomenon in numerous language communities (e.g. in Africa, Australia, Oceania, and the Americas) where the use of certain words is avoided. One typical example is the name of a deceased person (and all similar-sounding words); rather than using the word, paraphrases or borrowings from other languages are used. This leads to rapid changes in the vocabulary and makes it difficult to study genetic affiliations.

References
Dixon, R.M.W. 1980. *The languages of Australia*. Cambridge.
Elmendorf, W.W. 1951. Word taboo and lexical change in Coast Salish. *IJAL* 17:205–8.
Liedtke, S. 1994. Pointing with lips and name taboo in Native American cultures. *LDDS* 13.
Suarez, J.A. 1971. A case of absolute synonyms. *IJAL* 37:3.192–5.

tachysphemia ⇒ **cluttering**

tactile agnosia ⇒ **agnosia**

tag question (*also* question tag)

Short question added to a statement which requests assurance or affirmation regarding what is expressed in the main clause: *isn't it?* Fr. *n'est-ce pas?* (⇒ *also* **interrogative**)

Tagalog

Malayo-Polynesian language spoken in the Philippines with approx. 13 million speakers and the basis for simplified Philipino, official language of the Philippines.

Characteristics: typical traits of the Philipino languages: verb-initial word order; topical NPs positioned sentence-finally; marking of semantic roles by prepositions; extensive and flexible voice system for topicalization of nominal phrases. Morphologically interesting due to the occurrence of infixes.

References
Ramos, T. 1971. *Tagalog structures*. Honolulu, HI.
Schachter, P. and F.T. Otanes. 1972. *Tagalog reference grammar*. Berkeley, CA.

tagma [Grk *tágma* 'division; arrangement']

In **tagmemics**, the smallest concretely realized grammatical units of linguistic analysis; e.g. **phone, morph**.

tagmatics

The investigation of the special ordering of specific linguistic elements.

tagmeme

1 The smallest functional grammatical element of *langue* (⇒ **langue vs parole**), which bears meaning, as opposed to the **taxeme**, which does not bear meaning.

2 According to K. Pike's definition, the smallest structural element which can be understood as a correlate of grammatical function (= functional slot) and paradigmatic class (= filler class). The original term for these elements was 'grammeme.'

References
⇒ **tagmemics**

tagmemics

Important branch of **American structuralism** that attempts to describe linguistic regularities in connection with sociocultural behavior. The methodological orientation is, on the one hand, characterized by the practical necessities of Bible translation into unresearched 'exotic' languages (compiled by the Summer Institute of Linguistics), and, on the other hand, strongly influenced by L. Bloomfield and the concepts of **descriptive linguistics**. Chief representative of tagmemics is K.L. Pike, whose three-part book, *Language in relation to a unified theory of the structure of human behavior*, was first published in 1954–60. In keeping with his goal of drafting a type of universal taxonomy of human behavior, Pike begins with a tight systematic interweaving of various levels of description.

The smallest functional formal element he calls the '**tagmeme**' (following Bloomfield) and defines it as the correlation of syntagmatic functions (e.g. **subject**, **object**) and paradigmatic fillers (e.g. **nouns**, **pronouns**, or **proper nouns** as possible inserts into subject position) (⇒ *also* **paradigmatic vs syntagmatic relationship**). Tagmemes combine to form **syntagmemes**. The interweaving of hierarchical levels (e.g. for **syntax**: word, phrase, sentence, paragraph, discourse) results from the fact that the elements of a tagmeme on a higher level (e.g. 'sentence') are analyzed as syntagmemes on the next lower level (e.g. 'phrase'). This occurs in the form of multipartite strings by means of **string analysis**, as developed by Z.S. Harris and R.E. Longacre. Principally, all linguistic units are researched under three different theoretical perspectives: (a) under the aspect 'Feature' each unit governs a specific emic structure (⇒ **etic vs emic analysis**), e.g. the **distinctive features** in **phonology**; (b) under the aspect 'Manifestation,' each unit appears as an element of a paradigmatic class of etic forms; (c) under the aspect '**Distribution**,' each unit is assigned to a particular class according to its occurrence.

Modern research in tagmemics focuses primarily on semantic and ethnolinguistic problems, e.g. kinship terms in different languages (⇒ **semantics**, **ethnolinguistics**), especially the inclusion of non-verbal, paralinguistic perspectives in linguistic description. (⇒ **paralinguistics**)

References
Brend, R.M. (ed.) 1974. *Advances in tagmemics*. Amsterdam.
Cook, W.A. 1967. *The generative power of a tagmemic grammar*. Washington, DC.
—— 1969. *Introduction to tagmemic analysis*. New York.
Frank, D.B. 1990. A tagmemic model for the study of language in context. *PICL* 14.2070–2.
Harris, Z.S. 1962. *String analysis of sentence structure*. The Hague.
Longacre, R.E. 1960. String constituent analysis. *Lg* 36.63–88.
—— 1964. *Grammar discovery procedures: a field manual*. The Hague.
—— 1965. Some fundamental insights of tagmemics. *Lg* 41.65–76.
Pike, K.L. 1943. Taxemes and immediate constituents. *Lg* 19.65–82.
—— 1966. A guide to publications related to tagmemic theory. In T.A. Sebeok (ed.), *Current trends in linguistics*. The Hague. Vol. 3, 365–94.
—— 1967. *Language in relation to a unified theory of the structure of human behavior*. The Hague. (Repr. 1971.)
—— 1982. *Linguistic concepts: an introduction to tagmemics*. Lincoln, NE.

—— 1983. *Text and tagmeme*. London.
Waterhouse, V.G. 1974. *The history and development of tagmemics*. The Hague.

Bibliography
Brend, R.M. 1970–2. Tagmemic theory: an annotated bibliography. *JEngL* 4.7–45, 6.1–16.

Takelma-Kalapuyan ⇒ Penutian

Tamashek ⇒ Berber

Tamil

Dravidian language (about 45 million speakers) with the most extensive geographical distribution and oldest literary tradition, spoken in India and Sri Lanka. Independent syllabary developed from the southern Brahmi script of the Aśoka period. The language has a remarkable number of registers for indicating the social status and formality of the speakers.

References
Asher, R. 1983. *Tamil*. Amsterdam.
James, G. 1991. *Tamil lexicography*. Tübingen.
Pope, G.U. 1979. *A handbook of the Tamil language*. New Delhi.

Grammars
Agesthialingom, S. 1977. *A grammar of Old Tamil with special reference to Patirruppattu*. Annamalainagar.
Arden, A.H. 1976. *Progressive grammar of the Tamil language*, rev. A.C. Clayton (5th repr.). Madras.
Lehmann, T. 1989. *A grammar of modern Tamil*. Pondicherry.

Dictionaries
A dictionary of Tamil and English. 1972. Based on Fabricius' 'Malabar-English dictionary,' 4th edn, rev. and enl. Tranquebar.
Pillai, V.V. 1984. *A Tamil–English dictionary*, 9th rev. edn. Madras.
Tamil lexicon. 1982. Publ. under the authority of the University of Madras. 6 vols.

Etymological dictionary
Pavanar, G.D. 1985. *A comprehensive etymological dictionary of the Tamil language*, vol. I, 1. Madras.

Bibliography
Dhamotharan, A. 1978. *Tamil dictionaries: a bibliography*. Wiesbaden.

tap

Speech sound classified according to the way in which it bypasses its obstruction, namely by way of a tapping motion. In contrast to a **flap**, in the formation of a tap, the tip of the tongue strikes against the **place of articulation** directly from its resting position. For example, in [ɾ] in Span. (tap) [ˈpeɾɔ] *pero* 'but' vs (flap) [ˈperɔ] *perro* 'dog.' Often there is no strict distinction between taps and flaps. There are also labial and uvular taps. (⇒ *also* **articulatory phonetics**)

References
⇒ **phonetics**

Tarahumara ⇒ **Uto-Aztecan**

target language

1 The language into which one translates from a **source language**.

2 In **second language acquisition**, the language being learned as opposed to the native language or first language. (⇒ *also* L_1 **vs** L_2)

Tarskian semantics ⇒ **model-theoretic semantics**

tautology [Grk *tautologeĩn* 'to repeat what has been said']

1 In **formal logic**, a complex linguistic expression which, regardless of which possible world it refers to, is always true based on its logical form; for example, *p or not p* (*It's raining or it is not raining*). Tautologies are analytically and logically true propositions; in contrast cf. **contradiction**.

2 ⇒ **pleonasm**

tautosyllabic [Grk *tautós* 'identical']

Belonging to one and the same single **syllable**.

tax [Grk *táxis* 'arrangement']

Term for the smallest concretely realized grammatical units at all levels of description, such as **phone**, **graph**, **morph**.

taxeme

Term coined by L. Bloomfield for the smallest grammatical form unit which bears no meaning, as opposed to the **tagmeme**, which does carry meaning.

References
⇒ **tagmemics**

taxonomic analysis ⇒ **distributionalism**

taxonomic structuralism ⇒ **distributionalism**

teacher-talk

Artificial or stylized language spoken by the second (or foreign) language instructor with the purpose of conveying meaningful information to the language learners. Teacher-talk, which is similar to other forms of caretaker language, is often characterized by shorter sentences, reduced grammar and vocabulary, slower speech tempo, careful articulation, and continual comprehension checks.

Reference
Wing, B.H. The linguistic and communicative func-
tions of foreign language teacher talk. In B. Van Patten, T.R. Dvorak, and J.F. Lee (eds), *Foreign language learning: a research perspective*. Cambridge, MA. 158–73.

telescoped word ⇒ **blend**

telic vs atelic [Grk *télos* 'completion, end'] (*also* aterminative/non-terminative vs terminative, bounded vs non-bounded)

Verbal **aspect** distinction which refers to events with a temporal boundary or limit, e.g. *fly to New York*, *drink a glass of wine*, as telic, and to events without such limits, e.g. *travel by train*, *drink wine* as atelic. (⇒ *also* **resultative vs non-resultative**)

References
Dahl, Ö. 1981. On the definition of the telic–atelic (bounded–nonbounded) distinction. In P.J. Tedeschi and A. Zaenen (eds), *Syntax and semantics*, vol. 14: *Tense and aspect*. New York. 79–90.
Garey, H. 1957. Verbal aspects in French. *Lg* 33.

Telugu ⇒ **Dravidian**, **Marathi**

template

A feature macro in unification grammar which can be called upon within other **feature structures**. Templates were introduced into PATR and are used extensively in **Head-Driven Phrase Structure Grammar**.

References
⇒ **unification grammar**

temporal clause [Lat. *tempus* 'time']

Semantically defined dependent clause functioning as an **adverbial** modifier which refers to the **main clause** in relation to anteriority, posteriority, or simultaneity; they are introduced by such conjunctions as *while, as long as, until, since*: *I watched television while he made dinner*.

temporal logic

A special form of philosophical logic which, in addition to logical expressions such as **logical connectives** (*and*, *or*, and others) and **operators** in **formal logic**, also uses temporal expressions such as *it was the case that* and *it will be the case that* by introducing corresponding operators into the semantic analysis. The extent to which natural-language **tense** can be accommodated by this is under debate.

References
Benthem, J.V. 1983. *The logic of time*. Dordrecht.
Burgess, J.P. 1984. Basic tense logic. In D. Gabbay and F. Guenthner (eds), *Handbook of philosophical logic*. Dordrecht. Vol. 2, 89–133.
Kuhn, T.S. 1989. Tense and time. In D. Gabbay and F. Guenthner (eds), *Handbook of philosophical*

logic. Dordrecht. Vol. 4, 513–52.

Prior, A.N. 1967. *Past, present and future*. Oxford.

Rescher, N. and A. Urquhart. 1971. *Temporal logic*. Vienna.

Rohrer, C. (ed.) 1980. *Time, tense, and quantifiers*. Tübingen.

Bibliography

Bäuerle, R. 1977. Tempus, Zeitreferenz und temporale Logik: Eine Bibliographie, 1940–1976. *LingB* 49.85–105.

tense

Fundamental grammatical (morphological) category of the verb which expresses the temporal relation between a speech act (S) and the state of affairs or event (E) described in the utterance, i.e. which places the event spoken of in relation to the temporal perspective of the speaker. In English the past tense (⇒ **imperfect, preterite**) expresses the temporal relationship of E before S, while the **present** tense expresses simultaneity of E and S. In addition to these absolute tenses there are relative tenses which relate both S and E together to another temporal reference point (R): **past perfect** (E before R before S), **future perfect** (E before R after S), **present perfect** (E before R simultaneous with S). In some languages the temporal distance between E and S or R can also be expressed, e.g. that E is before S but belongs to the same type (Ger. *heute* 'today' + past tense). There are various language-dependent rules for the choice of tense in embedded clauses in relation to the tense in the **main clause**. (⇒ **matrix sentence**, *also* **sequence of tenses**)

Tense systems are language-specific and often encode other sorts of information, such as **aspect** and **mood**. Because of this, the analysis of tense can be fairly complicated, especially when stylistic and pragmatic factors are taken into consideration.

References

Basbøll, H., C. Bache, and C.E. Lindberg (eds) 1994. *Tense, aspect, actionality*. Berlin and New York.

Binnick, R.I. 1991. *Time and the verb: guide to tense and aspect*. Oxford.

Bybee, J. 1985. *Morphology: study of the relation between meaning and form*. Amsterdam.

Bybee, J., R. Perkins, and W. Pagliuca. 1994. *The evolution of grammar: tense, aspect and modality in the languages of the world*. Chicago, IL.

Chung, S. and A. Timberlake. 1985. Tense, aspect, mood. In T. Shopen (ed.), *Language typology and syntactic description*. Cambridge. Vol. 3, 202–58.

Comrie, B. 1985. *Tense*. Cambridge.

Dahl, Ö. 1985. *Tense and aspect systems*. Oxford.

Declerck, R. 1991. *Tense in English: its structure and use in discourse*. London.

Engel, D. 1990. *Tense and text: study of French past tenses*. London.

Erhart, A. 1985. *Zur Entwicklung der Kategorien Tempus und Modus im Indogermanischen*. Innsbruck.

Fleischman, S. 1990. *Tense and narrativity*. London.

Klein, W. 1994. *Time in language*. London.

Reichenbach, H. 1947. *Elements of symbolic logic*. New York.

Rohrer, C. (ed.) 1980. *Time, tense and quantifiers: proceedings of the Stuttgart conference on the logic of tense and quantification*. Tübingen.

Schopf, A. (ed.) 1987. *Essays on tensing in English*, vol. 1: *Reference time, tense and adverbs*. Tübingen.

Strunk, K. 1968. Zeit und Tempus in altindogermanischen Sprachen. *IF* 73.279–311.

——— 1969. 'Besprochene und erzählte Welt' im Lateinischen? Eine Auseinandersetzung mit H. Weinrich. *Gymnasium* 76.289–310.

Tedeschi, T. and A. Zaenen (eds) 1981. *Syntax and semantics*, vol. 14: *Tense and aspect*. New York.

Thieroff, R. and J. Ballweg (eds) 1994. *Tense systems in European languages*. Tübingen.

Vet, C. (ed.) 1985. *Le pragmatique de temps verbaux*. Paris.

Vet, C. and C. Vetters (eds) 1994. *Tense and aspects in discourse*. Berlin and New York.

Weinrich, H. 1964. *Tempus: besprochene und erzählte Welt*. Stuttgart. (4th edn 1985.)

Bibliographies

Bäuerle, R. 1977. Tempus, Zeitreferenz und temporale Logik: eine Bibliographie, 1940–1976. *LingB* 49.85–105.

Brons-Albert, R. 1978. *Kommentierte Bibliographie zur Tempusproblematik*. Trier.

⇒ **universal grammar**

tense vs lax

Binary phonological **opposition** in **distinctive feature** analysis, based on acoustically analyzed and spectrally defined criteria (⇒ **acoustic phonetics**, **spectral analysis**). Acoustic characteristics: clear delineation of the **resonance chambers** on the spectrum with greater vs lesser energy expenditure in frequency and time. Articulatory characteristic: greater vs lesser muscle tension and correspondingly different degree of distortion of the **vocal tract** from its resting position. In many European languages, this distinction corresponds to the opposition **voiced vs voiceless** in consonants or decentralized vs centralized (⇒ **centralization**) and **closed vs open** in vowels. In West African languages, this opposition correlates with the position of the root of the tongue; [ATR] ('advanced tongue root') is used to denote this feature.

References

Wood, S. and T. Petersson. 1988. Vowel reduction in Bulgarian. *FoLi* 22.239–62.

⇒ **phonetics**

tensed form ⇒ finite verb form

tensed-S-condition ⇒ propositional island constraint

tenuis vs media [Lat. *tenuis* 'thin,' *medius* 'middle']

Terms that, in the tradition of Greek and Latin grammarians, denote the difference between 'thin' *p*, *t*, *k* and 'middle' *b*, *d*, *g*. In **Greek** tenuis vs media are in opposition to the **aspirates** *ph*, *th*, *kh*. In **Indo-European** a distinction is drawn between the non-aspirated tenues *p*, *t*, *k* and the mediae *b*, *d*, *g*, on the one hand, and the aspirated mediae *bh*, *dh*, *gh*, on the other. In older literature, the tenues/mediae sounds are lumped together as **mutes**.

References
⇒ **Indo-European**, **phonetics**

Tepehua ⇒ Totonac

Tequistlatec ⇒ Hokan

term [Lat. *terminus* 'boundary']

Taken from **formal logic**, 'term' is an umbrella term for **proper nouns** that denote individuals (like individual humans, animals, places) and **predicates** (that ascribe particular properties to the denoted individuals with proper names). One speaks of individual terms and predicate terms. Terms are the well-formed components of a **proposition** (sentence, formula) and cannot have truth values.

terminal symbol

Symbol used in rule construction for deriving linguistic structures which can only appear to the right of an **arrow**, and thus cannot be broken down into other (non-terminal) symbols. At the syntactic level, terminal symbols are individual words; in **phonology**, terminal symbols are **phonemes** or their phonetic features.

terminative vs aterminative ⇒ durative vs non-durative, resultative, telic vs atelic

terminology

The collection of defined technical terms within a scientific system, which differs from everyday usage in that the terms are defined exactly within a specific system. Methods used in establishing a terminology include narrower definition of terms already present in everyday language (e.g. the linguistic terms **root**, **tree diagram**), neologisms (e.g. **phoneme**, **morpheme**, **lexeme**), or terms borrowed from foreign languages (e.g. **langue vs parole** as opposed to **langage**). On the formation of technical terms in linguistics, see the introductions to linguistic dictionaries.

References
Hartmann, R.R.K. 1973. *The language of linguistics: reflections on linguistic terminology with particular reference to 'level' and 'rank.'* Tübingen.
Mackey, W.F. 1990. Terminology for sociolinguistics. *Sociolinguistics* 19.99–124.
Mugdan, J. 1990. On the history of linguistic terminology. *PICHoLS* 4:149–61.
Sonneveld, H.B. and K.L. Loening (eds) 1993. *Terminology: applications in interdisciplinary communication.* Amsterdam and Philadelphia.
⇒ **sublanguage**

text [Lat. *textus* 'piece of plaited work; fabric']

1 Theoretical term of formally limited, mainly written expressions that include more than one sentence.

2 Term from **text linguistics** and **text theory**. Linguistic form of expression of a communicative act which is individually determined (a) according to pragmatic, text-internal criteria of a communicative intention which is situation-specific and meets a corresponding listener expectation (**text function**), and (b) according to internal textual features, such as boundary signals, grammatical **cohesion**, dominant **text theme**, and content **coherence** (**macrostructure**, **thematic development**). In addition, there are properties of non-verbal signals, such as gesticulation, that constitute 'text' (Koch 1969; Kallmeyer *et al.* 1974). The internal and text-external characteristics of text form its **textuality**.

References
Bellert, I. 1970. On a condition of the coherence of texts. *Semiotica* 2.335–63.
Kallmeyer, W. *et al.* (eds) 1974. *Lektürekolleg zur Textlinguistik*, 2 vols. Frankfurt.
Koch, W. 1969. *Vom Morphem zum Textem.* Hildesheim.
Van Dijk, T.A. 1972. Foundations for typologies of texts. *Semiotica* 6.297–323.
Vitacolonna, L. 1988. 'Text'/'Discourse' definitions. In J.S. Petöfi (ed.), *Text and discourse constitution.* Berlin. 412–39.

3 According to Hjelmslev (⇒ **glossematics**), the total of all linguistic expressions in the sense of a **corpus**.

References
Hjelmslev, L. 1943. *Omkring sprogteoriens grundlaeggelse.* Copenhagen. (*Prolegomena to a theory of language*, trans. F.J. Whitfield. Baltimore, MD, 1953.)

Journal
Text
⇒ **pragmatics**

text analysis

1 In general, any form of grammatical, stylistic, rhetorical, literary-critical description or interpretation of texts.

2 In Harris' article 'Discourse analysis,' which is the first attempt of **text linguistics** to describe the structure of texts using **distribution**, varying word order which appears in the text in the same environment is combined to classes without regard to meaning. The distribution of these equivalence classes in the text represents the structure of the text. (⇒ *also* **discourse analysis**)

Reference
Harris, Z.S. 1952. Discourse analysis. *Lg* 28.1–30.

text basis

The semantic representation of a **text** in the form of sequence of **propositions** or of a **semantic network** made up of concepts. The explicit text basis (Van Dijk) includes not only the propositions expressed in the text, but also their **presuppositions** and the content that is derived by **inference** from reworking the text.

Reference
Van Dijk, T.A. 1980. *Macro-structures: an interdisciplinary study of global structures in discourse, cognitions and interaction.* Hillsdale, NJ.

text constituents

Parts of texts whose function is established in the **coherence** of the text and which have the function of forming the text, e.g. **pro-forms**, **articles**, repetition of words (**recurrence**), ambiguous words which are disambiguated through context.

References
⇒ **discourse grammar**

text criticism

The process and result of investigating older written or printed works, especially poetic ones, with the purpose of reconstructing the original version. When too many original authentic manuscripts are missing, as is especially the case with texts from antiquity and to a certain extent with medieval texts, or when there is a large temporal gap between the earliest preserved version of a text and the date of its original composition, reconstruction of the original text must depend primarily on an exact understanding of the linguistic features of the work as well as the time of its origin and transmission. Important tools for linguistic analysis include **dialectology**, **graphemics**, **phonetics**, **phonology**, as well as any linguistic investigations and descriptions of previous stages of the language, especially **historical grammars** and glossaries, among others.

text function

The dominant communicative function of text. In contrast to possible text effect, text function is conventionally determined and is signaled by linguistic or situational features of **text type**, such as **performative verbs**, headlines, and communication media, among others. In addition to **speech act classification**, Brinker distinguishes five basic communicative functions as the basis for a typology of usage texts: information, appeal, obligation, contact, declaration. (⇒ *also* **macrostructure**, **text theme**)

References
Brinker, K. 1983. Textfunktionen. Ansätze zu ihrer Beschreibung. *ZG* 11.127–148.
Van Dijk, T.A. 1977. *Text and context: explorations in the semantics and pragmatics of discourse.* London.

text generation

The mechanical generation of natural-language sentences or texts from internal representations (semantic representations) encompasses the phase of planning the content ('what to say') as well as the form ('how to say') of assertions. This division of labor is reflected in the system architecture in strategic and in tactical components, respectively. However, language can only be adequately generated if both components interact. The informational resources required for generation and production clearly overlap, but it is an open question as to what degree. In particular, it is unclear to what extent comprehension and production can be seen as inverse processes.

References
Dale, R. 1992. *Generating referring expressions: constructing descriptions in a domain of objects and processes.* Cambridge, MA.
Kempen, G. 1989. Language generation systems. In I.S. Bátori, W. Lenders, and W. Putschke (eds), *Computerlinguistik / Computational linguistics.* Berlin. 471–80.
Levelt, W. 1989. *Production.* Cambridge, MA.
McKeown, K. 1985. *Text generation.* Cambridge.

text linguistics

Linguistic discipline which analyses the linguistic regularities and constitutive features of texts. Text linguistics has developed since the 1960s from its structuralist foundations (**tagmemics**, **text analysis**, the **Prague School**) and has been integrated into the research foundations of **stylistics** and **rhetoric**. The historical significance of text linguistics lies in the fact that it overcame the narrow sentence-specific perspective of linguistics and thereby created a basis for the interdisciplinary study of texts. The development of the discipline is reflected in the various definitions of **text**. If one defines 'text' as a sequence of sentences and thereby a unit of the linguistic system, text linguistics is an expanded sentence grammar and therefore constitutes **discourse grammar**. The methods of sentence analysis are transferred to **transphrastic analysis** and lead to the composition of text grammatical rules of **cohesion**. If one understands 'text' as a communicative unit, further features like **text function** or **text theme** result from text-grammatical regularities. In this broader framework, which includes text grammar, text linguistics includes the following problems: (a) general aspects of structural and functional text constituents, i.e. **textuality**; (b) classification of texts in the framework of a **text typology**; (c) problems concerning the integration of stylistics and rhetoric; (d) interdisciplinary-oriented research in the direction of text reworking and comprehensibility.

References
Beaugrande, R.A. de. 1980. *Text, discourse and process: toward a multidisciplinary science of texts*. London.
———— 1992. *A new introduction to the study of text and discourse*. London.
Beaugrande, R. de and W.-U. Dressler. 1981. *Introduction to text linguistics*. London.
Conte, M.E. *et al.* (eds) 1989. *Text and discourse connectedness: proceedings of the conference on connexity and coherence Urbino, July 16–21, 1984*. Amsterdam.
Dressler, W.U. (ed.) 1978. *Current trends in text linguistics*. Berlin.
Petöfi, J.S. 1979–82. *Text vs sentence*. Hamburg.
Van Dijk, T.A. 1990. The future of the field: discourse analysis in 1990. *Text* 10.133–56.
⇒ **coherence**

text processing

Term denoting the cognitive activities involved in understanding, retaining, and remembering texts. Text processing is not a unilateral process of recording textual content, but rather an active, constructive activity that is directed (a) by the text ('text directed' or 'ascending' processing), (b) by the reader's background knowledge that is stored in schemata ('schema-directed' or 'descending' processing (⇒ **schema**)), and (c) by the intention and interests of the reader as well as his/her assumptions about the writer and the situation. In the model of Kintsch and Van Dijk (1978), the cognitive (re)construction of the text takes place in cyclical processing phases on several levels, beginning with the construction of propositions on

the basis of sentences, beyond logically cohesive, coherent sequences of different hierarchical steps (⇒ **coherence**), to the semantic **macrostructure**, where the text material is, on the one hand, reduced and abbreviated on every level (e.g. through generalization) and, on the other hand, expanded by **inferences**[2].

References
Burghardt, W. and K. Hölker (eds) 1979. *Text processing / Textverarbeitung*. Berlin.
Halliday, M.A.K. 1977. Text as semantic choice in social contexts. In T.A. Van Dijk and J.S. Petöfi (eds), *Grammars and descriptions*. New York. 176–225.
Just, M.A. and P.A. Carpenter (eds) 1977. *Cognitive processes in comprehension*. Hillsdale, NJ.
Kintsch, W. and T.A. Van Dijk. 1978. Toward a model of text comprehension and production. *PsychologR* 85.363–94.
Nilsson, L.G. (ed.) 1979. *Memory processes*. Hillsdale, NJ.
Rickheit, G. and M. Bock (eds) 1983. *Psycholinguistic studies in language processing*. Berlin.
Van Dijk, T.A. 1977. *Text and context: explorations in the semantics and pragmatics of discourse*. London.
Van Dijk, T.A. and W. Kintsch. 1983. *Strategies of discourse comprehension*. Orlando, FL.

text theme

The content core of a **text** which carries its communicative function (**text function**). The text theme develops according to a special text structure which determines the structure of the text (**thematic development**, **macrostructure**). Some text sorts signal the text theme by using a headline.

text theory (*also* textology)

A subdiscipline of linguistic theory. Text theory supplies an explanation for the constitutive properties of **texts** in **text linguistics**. Common to all newer suggestions for a schema is the assumption that texts can only be explained and adequately described if all factors of the communication process are included.

References
Jakobson, R. 1968. Closing statement: linguistics and poetics. In T.A. Sebeok (ed.), *Style in language*. Cambridge, MA.
Petöfi, J.S. 1978. A formal semiotic text theory as an integrated theory of natural languages. In W. Dressler (ed.), *Current trends in text linguistics*. Berlin. 35–46.
Van Dijk, T.A. 1985. *Handbook of discourse analysis*, 4 vols. London.

text types

A term from **text linguistics** for different classes of **texts**. Within the framework of a hierarchical **text typology**, text types are usually the most strongly specified class of texts (e.g. recipes, sermons, interviews), characterized by different internal and external features. Distinctive text-internal features are the use of particular classes of words (e.g. **deictic expressions**, **proper nouns**), forms of **textphoric**, **theme–rheme** alternation, type of style as well as the content and thematic structure (**macrostructure**, **superstructure**, **thematic development**). Text-external elements can be interpreted as complex speech acts that are defined by the factors of the communicative situation like the intention of the speaker, the expectation of the listener, as well as locational, temporal, and institutional conditions (communicative distance, **text function**). Because of the special **pragmatic** features of text sorts, they determine situations, e.g. writ of execution, joke, conversation.

References
Suter, H.-J. 1993. *The wedding report: a prototypical approach to the study of traditional text types.* Amsterdam.
Van Dijk, T.A. 1972. Foundations for typologies of texts. *Semiotica* 6.297–323.

text typology

The classification of texts in **text linguistics**. Within a hierarchical typology, classes of texts can be formed according to text-external and text-internal criteria. This can be done (a) according to the pragmatic criteria of the **text function**, directions, literary text, rhetorical text, informational text; (b) according to pragmatic criteria of communicative distance: written and spoken text, radio broadcasts, letters, conversations; (c) according to the **thematic development**: descriptive text, argumentative text, dissertations, narratives, description. A consistent, terminologically unified text typology does not yet exist. It presupposes a **text theory** with a differentiated concept of text, in which the text classes of different everyday language and the criteria for classification are systematically grounded.

References
⇒ **text linguistics**, **text types**

texteme

An analogue to the **phoneme** and **morpheme**, an artificial word for the abstract, theoretical unit 'text,' which represents the basis of the concretely realized text of the **parole** (⇒ **langue vs parole**) and its constitutive properties. (⇒ *also* **type-token relation**, **etic vs emic analysis**)

References
⇒ **text**

textology ⇒ **text theory**

textphoric [Grk *phóras* from *phérein* 'to carry']

A semantic–syntactic system of reference within a text. The phenomenon of textphoric is based semantically on co-referentiality and appears syntactically as pronominalization (⇒ **personal pronoun**), i.e. as **syntagmatic substitution** by a **pro-form**. In a broader sense, textphoric also includes other non-pronominal forms of resumption of elements in a text (⇒ *also* **contiguity**, **isotopy**, **recurrence**).

References
⇒ **discourse grammar**, **reference**, **text linguistics**

textual reference

Text-internal reference of a referring, 'phoric' element (e.g. pronouns) to a referentially identical expression that either precedes it in the text (= anaphorical reference, ⇒ **anaphora**) or follows it (= cataphorical reference, ⇒ **cataphora**); cf. the changing pronominalization in *When he entered the room, Philip saw that it was empty.* Textual reference is an important text-constitutive means for creating **cohesion**, and therefore it is a central theme in **discourse grammar**. (⇒ *also* **textphoric**)

TG ⇒ **transformational grammar**

Thai (*also* Siamese)

Official language of Thailand, with approx. 30 million speakers, the largest language of the Thai family, which is a part of the **Austro-Thai** language group.

Characteristics: **tonal language** (five tones, sometimes with glottalization). Morphologically **isolating**; word order SVO, complex pronominal system with politeness distinctions; **classifiers**. Numerous lexical borrowings from **Sanskrit** and Pali, also from **Chinese**. Writing system developed from Sanskrit.

References
Danvivathana, N. 1987. *The Thai writing system.* Hamburg.
Gainey, J.W. and T. Thongkham. 1977. *Language map of Thailand and Handbook.* Bangkok.
Noss, R.B. 1964. *Thai reference grammar.* Washington, DC.
Pankhuenkhat, R. 1988. *Thai language family.* Bangkok.
Pattamdilok, K. 1977. *The history of the Thai language.* Bangkok.

thematic development

A term from **text linguistics**: the specific structure in which the text theme is arranged into the content of the text. The thematic development is carried out by the connection of part of the content according to semantic relations like specification, ordering, or reasoning. The basic forms of thematic development are the descriptive, the narrative, the explicative and the argumentative. The kind of thematic development is an important structural criterion of **text typology**. (⇒ *also* **argumentation, narrative structures**)

thematic relation (*also* lexical relation, semantic role)

Case-like semantic relations postulated by Gruber (1967), used by C.J. Fillmore as 'deep cases' in **case grammar**, and later reworked by Jackendoff (1972). In the sentence *Caroline is checking a book out from the library* the NPs are assigned the following thematic relations: *Caroline* = agent, *from the library* = location and source, *a book* = theme. Since in many syntactic models each NP can have only one thematic relation assigned to it, thematic relations can clarify ambiguous constructions; they can also describe relations, e.g. between verb pairs such as *sell/buy, give/get*: in the sentences *Philip will give Caroline the dictionary* and *Caroline will get the dictionary from Philip* both the subject NPs *Caroline* and *Philip* are the agent, but in the sentence with *give* the subject is also the source whereas in the example with *get* it is also the goal.

By forming a hierarchy of the thematic relations in the order (a) agent, (b) location/source/goal, (c) theme, exceptions to syntactic processes can be simplified, for example, the distribution of the **reflexive pronouns** and the behavior of certain verbs when undergoing **passive** transformation. Jackendoff (1983) tries to show that the thematic structure is inherent in lexical relations; it is with their aid that we structure our experiences. The spatial field is given a predominant position, because it is more directly accessible through our sensory perceptions. (cf. *also* ⇒ **case grammar**)

References

Carlson, G. 1984. Thematic roles and their role in semantic interpretation. *Linguistics* 22.259–79.

Clark, R. 1989. *Thematic theory in syntax and interpretation*. London.

Gruber, J.S. 1967. *Studies in lexical relations*. Bloomington, IN.

Jackendoff, R.S. 1972. *Semantic interpretation in generative grammar*. Cambridge, MA.

——— 1983. *Semantics and cognition*. Cambridge, MA.

Palmer, F.R. 1994. *Grammatical roles and relations*. Cambridge.

Rauh, G. 1988. *Tiefenkasus, thematische Relationen und Thetarollen*. Tübingen.

Wilkins, W. (ed.). 1988. *Syntax and semantics*, vol.

21: *Thematic relations*. New York.
⇒ **case grammar**

thematic verb ⇒ stem vowel

thematic vowel ⇒ stem vowel

theme vs rheme (*also* focus vs background/presupposition)

1 Structure of utterances according to communicative criteria which can be tested by comparing question–answer pairs: *Who sang the song? Caroline (sang the song)*. The information formulated in the question (*sang the song*) is the theme of the answer and is usually omitted in the answer; the information sought in the question is the rheme of the answer (*Caroline*). Previous mention is only one of many ways of thematizing linguistic material. The theme can also be understood from the context without previous mention. There are also utterances, especially at the beginning of a discourse, which contain only rhematic material. In contrast, an utterance without a rheme is uninformative and violates **maxims of conversation**.

The terms theme and rheme have been defined according to various criteria: The theme is often understood as 'known,' 'given,' 'previously mentioned,' or 'presupposed' information present in the context, while the rheme is defined as the negation of these characteristics. Although each of these criteria is relevant to a certain extent, they nevertheless do not suffice for a proper definition. For one thing, the terms used in the definition are themselves imprecise and need clarification. Another problem is that there are numerous counter examples: in the question–answer pair *Who did you see? Your mother*, the mother is known to both of the speakers, but is nevertheless the rheme of the answer. Reis (1977) has demonstrated that theme–rheme cannot be equated with **presupposition–assertion**. Furthermore, the unclear concept given/new information cannot be clarified with the feature [+previously mentioned], e.g. *Numerous journalists managed to get into the courtroom. The judge pointed out to the journalists that …* In spite of the previous mention in the first utterance, *journalists* is a part of the rheme in the second utterance, because this NP is embedded in another predication in the second utterance, and a theme–rheme analysis can only be made when consideration is given to the syntactic and semantic relations of an utterance. The problem posed by relational expressions (especially verbs) has led to the controversial assumption that theme-–rheme structure should not be seen as binary but rather as scalar with degrees of communicative dynamism (see Firbas 1964): the theme has the smallest and the rheme the highest degree of communicative dynamism, because the rheme promotes the communicative process the most. The verb is usually in the transitional zone between these two poles.

Formally, **word order** and **stress** (Hammond 1988) indicate which elements are functioning as the theme or the rheme of an utterance. In many languages either the left or the right periphery of a sentence is the preferred place for the rheme, such as in **topicalization, left vs right dislocation**, and **cleft sentences**, in English. The nuclear (i.e. main) sentence stress is placed within the rheme (as a universal law, see Gundel 1988; Harlig and Bardovi-Harlig 1988).

More recently, research on theme vs rheme has focused on universal laws for marking theme vs rheme (see the contributions in Hammond 1988), on how theme-rheme can be applied to other sentence types such as interrogatives and imperatives (see von Stechow, 1980), as well as on the relationship between theme-rheme and focusing particles.

2 Structure of utterance with regard to sentence topic (what is being talked about) and comment (what is being said about it) (⇒ **topic vs comment**).

The usages in 1 and 2 are often not sufficiently distinguished from each other in the research, resulting in numerous cases of terminological confusion which are further enhanced by the various definitional criteria. Thus for 'theme' we find the terms 'topic,' 'background,' 'presupposition,' and for 'rheme,' 'comment,' 'focus,' 'predication' (in various combinations).

References

Abraham, W., and S. de Meij (eds) 1986. *Topic, focus, and configurationality*. Amsterdam.

Chafe, W. 1976. Givenness, contrastiveness, definiteness, subjects, topics and point of view. In C.N. Li (ed.), *Subject and topic*. New York. 25–56.

Dahl, Ö. (ed.) 1974. *Topic and comment, contextual boundness and focus*. Hamburg.

Daneš, F. 1974. Functional sentence perspective and the organization of the text. In F. Daneš and J. Firbas (eds), *Papers on functional sentence perspective*. The Hague. 106–28.

Daneš, F. and J. Firbas (eds) 1974. *Papers on functional sentence perspective*. The Hague.

Firbas, J. 1964. On defining the theme in functional sentence analysis. *TLP* 1.267–80.

Foley, W.A. and R.D. van Valin. 1985. Information packaging in the clause. In T. Shopen (ed.), *Language typology and syntactic description*. Cambridge. Vol. 1, 282–364.

Givón, T. 1988. The pragmatics of word order: predictability, importance and attention. In M. Hammond *et al.* (eds), *Studies in syntactic typology*. Amsterdam. 243–84.

Gundel, J.K. 1977. *The role of topic and comment in linguistic theory*. Bloomington, IN.

—— 1988. Universals of topic–comment structure. In M. Hammond *et al.* (eds), *Studies in syntactic typology*. Amsterdam. 209–42.

Hammond, M. *et al.* 1988. *Studies in syntactic typology*. Amsterdam.

Harlig, J. and K. Bardovi-Harlig. 1988. Accentuation typology, word order and theme–rheme structure. In M. Hammond *et al.* (eds), *Studies in syntactic typology*. Amsterdam. 125–46.

Kuno, S. 1972. Functional sentence perspective. *LingI* 3.269–320.

Primus, B. 1993. Word order and information structure. In J. Jacobs *et al.* (eds), *Syntax: an international handbook of contemporary research*. Berlin. 880–96.

Reis, M. 1977. *Präsuppositionen und Syntax*. Tübingen.

Rochemont, M.S. 1986. *Focus in generative grammar*. Amsterdam.

Sgall, P. *et al.* 1973. *Topic, focus and generative semantics*. Kronberg.

Von Stechow, A. 1980. *Notes on topic and focus of interrogatives and indicatives*. Constance.

Ward, G. 1988. *The semantics and pragmatics of preposing*. New York.

Weigand, E. 1979. Zum Zusammenhang von Thema/ Rhema und Subjekt/Prädikat. *ZGL* 7.167–89.

Bibliography

Tyl, Z. 1970. *A tentative bibliography of studies in functional sentence perspective (1900–1970)*. Prague.

thesaurus

1 Scholarly dictionary with the purpose of codifying the whole vocabulary of a language, e.g. *Thesaurus linguae Latinae*.

2 A thesaurus is, generally speaking, any dictionary that defines **lexemes** through a semantic **paraphrase** (*cock* = 'adult male fowl,' 'rooster'). More commonly, it is a special type of dictionary that provides lists of synonymous expressions for most words in a given language. Such dictionaries apply the concept of **synonymy** in its broadest sense. Modern thesauruses also frequently provide antonyms (⇒ **antonymy**) for the entries. (⇒ *also* **lexicography, semantics**)

References

Hayakawa, S.I. 1968. *Modern guide to synonyms and related words*. New York.

Laird, C.G. 1971. *Webster's New World thesaurus*. New York. (New rev. edn updated by W.D. Lutz, 1985.)

Roget, P.M. 1852. *Roget's thesaurus of synonyms and antonyms*. (New edn rev. by S.R. Roget. New York, 1972.)

Urdang, L. 1991. *Oxford thesaurus*. Oxford.

theta criterion [*abbrev.* θ-criterion]

A term from Chomsky's **Government and Binding theory** which refers to the components of **universal grammar** that mediate between thematic role and their syntactic realization as specific arguments of a predicate. The theta criterion says that one **argument** must correspond to each thematic role and vice versa, where arguments are particular referential NPs. According to the theta criterion, in a sentence like *three robbers are in the woods*, the *three robbers* must be part of the sentence: **Are in the woods* is ungrammatical because it does not contain enough arguments. Likewise, **Three robbers are in the woods the stolen beer* has one argument too many and is also ungrammatical. The precise formulation of the theta criterion is only possible by referring to the term **chain**. Various theories make reference to the distinction between the different thematic roles, cf. **control**, **binding**, **case theory**.

References
Chomsky, N. 1981. *Lectures on government and binding*. Dordrecht. Ch. 6.
Grimshaw, J. and A. Mester. 1988. Light verbs and θ-marking. *LingI* 19.205–32.
Jackendoff, R. 1972. *Semantic interpretation in generative grammar*. Cambridge, MA.
——— 1987. The status of thematic relations in linguistic theory. *LingI* 18.369–412.
Lasnik, H. 1988. Subjects and the theta-criterion. *NL&LT* 6.1–17.
Ostler, N. 1980. *A theory of case linking and agreement*. Bloomington, IN.
⇒ **valence**

theta role ⇒ thematic relation, theta criterion

Thurneysen's Law

A regularity of dissimilation in **Gothic** according to which the voicing of fricatives after an unaccented vowel is the opposite of the voicing of the preceding stem-final consonants; cf. *waldufni* 'force' – *fraistubni* 'temptation'; *gabaúrjoþus* 'lust' – *wratodus* 'journey'; *agis* : *agisis* 'fear, terror' (nom. : gen.) – *hatis* : *hatizis* 'hate' (nom. : gen.).

References
Collinge, N.E. 1985. *The laws of Indo-European*. Amsterdam and Philadelphia. 183–91.
Thuneysen, R. 1898. Spirantenwechsel im Gotischen. *IF* 8.204–14.

Tibetan ⇒ Tibeto-Burman

Tibeto-Burman

Branch of the **Sino-Tibetan** languages, largest languages are **Burmese** (about 22 million speakers) and Tibetan (about 4 million speakers).

Characteristics: case system and verb agreement; partially **ergative** but topic-prominent languages also exist. In some languages transitive verbs are marked for the relationship between subject and object according to the hierarchy first – second – third person, singular – plural. Number (sometimes with **dual** forms), distinction between **inclusive and exclusive** forms of the first person plural.

References
Beyer, S.V. 1992. *The Classical Tibetan language*. Albany, NY.
Hale, A. 1982. *Research on Tibeto-Burman languages*. The Hague.
Losang, T. 1986–91. *Modern Tibetan language*, 2 vols. Dharmasala.
Matisoff, J. 1973. *The grammar of Lahu*. Berkeley, CA.
Van Driem, G. 1987. *A grammar of Limbu*. Berlin.

Dictionaries
Buck, S.H. 1969. *Tibetan–English dictionary*. Washington, DC.
Chandra Das, S. 1902. *Tibetan–English dictionary*, rev. edn. Calcutta.
Jäschke, H.A. 1881. *Tibetan–English dictionary*. London. (Repr. 1990.)

Tigre ⇒ Semitic

Tigrinya ⇒ Ge'ez, Semitic

tilde [Lat. *titulus* 'title']

Diacritic mark in the shape of a small horizontal snake-like line above a Latin or Greek letter. In **Portuguese**, the tilde is used to designate nasal vowels: *São Paolo*, *naciões* ('nations'); in ancient **Greek**, and in **Lithuanian** dictionaries, the tilde marks a distinctive syllabic tone; in **Spanish** it denotes a palatal *n* ‹ñ›, in older printings it marked a double consonant or served as an *n*. In **Greenlandic** it marks vowel length as well as following-consonant length. It is used in non-Latin scripts, e.g. the Persian–Arabic script.

References
⇒ **writing**

timbre [Grk *týmpanon* 'drum']

Acoustic-physical characteristic of sounds that is represented on a spectrograph by varying forms and distributions of the sound intensity at particular frequencies. Every sound consists of several parts whose number, sequencing, and intensity determine the timbre. Comprising frequencies with a particular intensity are the **formants**. Corresponding to acoustic features are articulatory differences in the sizes and shape of the **resonance chamber**. (⇒ *also* **phonetics**, **quality**)

Tlingit ⇒ Na-Dené

tmesis

Rearrangement of compound words through separating the parts, usually with another word inserted between them: *that man – how dearly ever parted* (Shakespeare) for *however*. (⇒ **hyperbaton**)

Reference
Nespor, M. and I. Vogel. 1986. *Prosodic phonology*. Dordrecht.

Tocharian

Now extinct branch of **Indo-European** consisting of the languages Tocharian A and Tocharian B, handed down in a large number of written documents in the North Indian Brahmi script between the fifth and the tenth centuries; the first documents were found in Central Asia (Tarim valley, 1890). Although Tocharian is the easternmost Indo-European language branch, it has characteristics that are otherwise only found in the western branches (⇒ **centum vs satem languages**).

References
Adams, D.Q. 1988. *Tocharian historical phonology and morphology*. New Haven, CT.
Krause, W. 1952. *Westtocharische Grammatik*, vol. 1: *Das Verbum*. Heidelberg.
—— 1955. *Tocharisch*. (Handbuch der Orientalistik I, vol. 4,3.) Leiden. (Repr. 1971.)
Krause, W. and W. Thomas. 1960–4. *Tocharisches Elementarbuch*, 2 vols. Heidelberg.
Pinault, G. 1989. Introduction au tokharien. *LALIES* 7.1–224.
Schlerath, B. (ed.) 1994. *Tocharisch: Akten der Fachtagung der Indogermanischen Gesellschaft, Berlin 1990*. Reykjavík.
Schulze, W., E. Sieg, and W. Siegling. 1931. *Tocharische Grammatik*. Göttingen.
Van Windekens, A.J. 1976–82. *Le Tokharien confronté avec les autres langues indo-europénnes*, 2 vols. Louvain.

Bibliographies
Schwentner, E. 1959. *Tocharische Bibliographie, 1890–1958*. Berlin.
Thomas, W. 1985. *Die Erforschung des Tocharischen*. Stuttgart.
Zimmer, S. 1976. *Tocharische Bibliographie, 1959–1975*. Heidelberg.

Journal
Tocharian and Indo-European Studies.

Tok Pisin

Widely spoken **pidgin** and **creole** language in Papua New Guinea with English **superstratum**.

Characteristics: relatively simple phonology (no fricatives, prenasalization); small basic vocabulary and thus extremely productive compounding (e.g. *papamama* 'parents,' *bikbus* (< *big bush*) 'jungle,' *haus kuk* 'kitchen'). No nominal inflection; complex number system with pronouns (singular, dual, trio, plural, also **inclusive/exclusive** distinction). **Tense**, **mood**, and **aspect** are expressed periphrastically. Verb agreement in the third person marked with *i-* (< *he*); the suffix *-im* (< *him*) shows transitivity. The few prepositions have relatively broad meaning. Word order: SOV.

References
Romaine, S. 1992. *Language, education and development: urban and rural Tok Pisin in Papua New Guinea*. Oxford.
Wurm, S.A. and P. Mühlhäusler (eds) 1985. *Handbook of Tok Pisin*. Canberra.

token reflexive word ⇒ deictic expression

tonal accent ⇒ pitch accent

tonal language

Language in which tone contours have phonological relevance, that is, make a difference in meaning, cf. **Chinese** and **Vietnamese**. (⇒ *also* **tone**)

References
⇒ **tonology**

tonal pattern

Phonologically distinctive change in pitch. In **tonal languages** this distinctiveness is found on the lexical level, in intonational languages on the syntactic and pragmatic levels. (⇒ *also* **intonation**, **intonational phrase**, **pitch accent**, **stress**^{2})

tone

1 (*also* **sound**) In acoustic phonetics, term for occurrence of sounds with simple, period waves.

2 (*also* **intonation**^{2}) Phenomena of pitch that refer to morphologically defined segments (morphs, words) to the extent that different pitches in a language are distinctive. Such languages are known as **tonal languages**. In phonology, the term 'toneme' (in analogy to 'phoneme') is used to denote phonetically distinctive tones. A five-level notational system is used to indicate tones, with *1* for the lowest and *5* for the highest tones. These are written as subscripts following the syllable they affect. Punu, a **Miao-Yao** language, has eight distinctive tones: cu_{33} 'together,' cu_{22} 'the last of all,' cu_{12} 'bridge,' cu_{43} 'wine, alcohol,' cu_{42}

'order,' cu_{31} 'hook,' cu_{21} 'just,' cu_{231} 'drought.'

References
⇒ **phonetics, tonology**

toneme ⇒ **tone**

Tongan ⇒ **Malayo-Polynesian**

tonology

Study of the tonal structure of linguistic expressions which in some languages (e.g. **Vietnamese, Chinese**) has the same affect on meaning as phonological, syllabic, and accent features.

References
Fromkin, V.A. (ed.) 1978. *Tone: a linguistic survey.* New York.
Pike, K.L. 1988. *Tone languages.* Ann Arbor, MI.
Snider, K. and H. Van der Hulst (eds) 1993. *The phonology of tone: the representation of tonal register.* Berlin and New York.

top down ⇒ **bottom up vs top down**

topic [Grk *tópos* 'place']

1 A subdiscipline of **rhetoric**: the study of topoi. Also a general term for the topic structure of a text. (⇒ **topos**)

2 ⇒ **topic vs comment**

topic-prominent language ⇒ **topic vs comment**

topic vs comment (*also* topic vs predication)

1 Analysis of sentences according to communicative criteria into the topic (what is being talked about) and the comment (what is being said about the topic). Although there is no commonly accepted definition of topic and comment, a number of heuristic criteria have been established for identifying the topic of an utterance. For instance, a sentence in which an element X is the topic, answers the question *What about X?* (see Gundel, 1977). For example, the sentence *Caroline met Philip yesterday* is a better answer to the question *What about Caroline?* than to the question *What about Philip?* This shows *Caroline* to be the topic and *met Philip* the comment. However, the interpretation of *Philip* as the topic is also possible, if somewhat unnatural. Sgall (1974) proposes that the topic constituent X as opposed to the predication Y can be tested by embedding it in the performative formula *I tell you Y about X.* The topic and comment isolated by such tests is independent of **theme vs rheme** analysis, which is based on other criteria. Thus the topic cannot be defined as the old or known information. As an answer to the question *Who met Philip?*, *Caroline* is the topic although it is new,

previously unknown information.

Although topic and comment can be considered to be semantic or pragmatic relations, they are affected by various syntactic properties of sentences. There is a strong tendency to express the topic as the syntactic subject, especially in the **Indo-European** languages, which are considered to be 'subject-prominent.' But even in these languages there are constructions in which a non-subject is the topic, cf. the left-dislocation sentence construction. (⇒ **left vs right dislocation**) As for this guy, I'm not giving him a penny. In 'topic-prominent' languages such as **Korean**, **Japanese**, and **Tagalog**, any sentence element can be made the topic by using particles or affixes. On subject vs topic prominent languages, see Li and Thompson (1976) and Gundel (1988). In addition, initial position in the sentence is another criterion for the topic, according to Halliday (1967) and Li & Thompson (1976). Passivization can change the topic–comment structure of a sentence: *I helped the child* vs *The child was helped by me.*

The most important semantic property of the topic is its referential (specific) interpretation. In this regard, the topic and comment correspond to the basic semantic functions of **reference** and **predication**. In the expression *There's a fly in my soup*, there is no specific referential constituent which can function as the topic; such sentences are termed 'thetic' or 'presentational.' Expressions which have a topic–comment structure are termed 'categorial' (see Kuroda 1972; Sasse 1987). The topic relation is relevant for the description of many linguistic phenomena, not only in topic-prominent languages, but also in subject-prominent languages; see Givón (1983) on verb agreement and Kuno (1987) on pronouns.

2 Analysis of utterances according to the communicative criteria of given/known information vs new information (⇒ **theme vs rheme**).

Both of these definitions of 'topic' and 'comment' are frequently used in the literature without being adequately distinguished from each other, often resulting in terminological confusion and inaccuracy. Thus the term 'theme' is often used for topic in both definitions 1 and 2, and instead of 'comment' the terms 'predication' or 'focus' also occur, all in various combinations.

References
Abraham, W. and S. de Meij (eds) 1986. *Topic, focus and configurationality.* Amsterdam.
Bossong, G. 1989. Morphemic marking of topic and focus. In M. Kefer and J. van der Auwera (eds), *Universals of language.* Brussels.
Chafe, W. 1976. *Givenness, contractiveness, definiteness, subjects, topics and point of view.* In C.N. Li

(ed.), *Subject and topic*. New York. 25–56.

Davidson, A. 1984. *Syntactic markedness and the definition of sentence topic*. Lg 60.707–846.

Dittmar, N. (ed.) 1992. *Topic: from grammar to discourse*. Berlin and New York.

Givón, T. 1983. *Topic continuity in discourse: quantitative cross-language studies*. Amsterdam.

—— 1988. The pragmatics of word order: predictability, importance and attention. In M. Hammond *et al.* (eds), *Studies in syntactic typology*. Amsterdam. 243–84.

Gundel, J. 1977. *The role of topic and comment in linguistic theory*. Bloomington, IN.

—— 1988. Universals of topic–comment structure. In M. Hammond *et al.* (eds), *Studies in syntactic typology*. Amsterdam. 209–42.

Halliday, M.A.K. 1967. Notes on transitivity and theme in English. *JL* 3:1.37–81, 3:2: 199–244.

Hinds, J., S. Maynard, and S. Iwasaki (eds) 1987. *Perspectives on topicalization*. Amsterdam.

Kuno, S. 1972. Functional sentence perspective. *LingI* 3.269–320.

—— 1987. *Functional syntax: anaphora, discourse and empathy*. Chicago, IL.

Kuroda, S. 1972. The categorical and thetic judgement: evidence from Japanese syntax. *FoLi* 9.153–8.

Lambrecht, K. 1987. Sentence focus, information structure, and the thetic–categorial distinction. *BLS* 13.366–82

Li, C.N. (ed.) 1976. *Subject and topic*. New York.

Li, C.N. and S.A. Thompson. 1976. Subject and topic: a new typology of language. In C.N. Li (ed.), *Subject and topic*. New York. 457–90.

Primus, B. 1993. Word order and information structure. In J. Jacobs *et al.* (eds), *Syntax: an international handbook on contemporary research*. Berlin. 880–96.

Reinhart, T. 1981. Pragmatics and linguistics: an analysis of sentence topics. *Philosophica* 27.53–94.

Sasse, H.-J. 1987. The thetic/categorical distinction revisited. *Linguistics* 25.511–80.

Sgall, P. 1974. Zur Stellung des Thema vs Rhema in der Sprachbeschreibung. In F. Daneš and J. Firbas (eds), *Papers on functional sentence perspective*. Prague. 54–74.

Ulrich, M. 1985. *Thetisch und kategorisch*. Tübingen.

topic vs predication ⇒ topic vs comment

topicalization

Placement of a non-subject constituent at the beginning of the sentence: *He declared his candidacy yesterday* vs *Yesterday he declared his candidacy*. Topicalization is used for specific communicative purposes. A distinction is generally made between 'true' topicalization, where the topicalized element functions as the theme or topic (⇒ **theme vs rheme**, **topic vs comment**), and 'false' topicalization, which serves to emphasize or contrast the element in question. In general, all major sentence con-

stituents except the subject and the finite verb can be topicalized.

References

Gruber, J. 1967. Topicalization in child language. *FL* 3.37–88.

—— 1975. 'Topicalization' revisited. *FL* 13.57–72.

Gundel, J.K. 1977. *The role of topic and comment in linguistic theory*. Bloomington, IN.

Lipka, L. 1976. Topicalization, case grammar, and lexical decomposition in English. *ArchL* 7.118–41.

topological fields ⇒ positional fields

toponomastics ⇒ toponymy

topology

1 ⇒ **word order**

2 Spatial relations between objects whose specification is necessary for descriptions of space (especially for the use of **prepositions**). Such topological concepts (which are probably universal) include inner (*in, inside of*) vs outer (*outside of*), vertical (*over, above, on*) vs horizontal (*next to, to the side of, right/left*), proximity vs distance, directions, and others. (⇒ *also* **deixis**)

References

Cresswell, M.J. 1978. Prepositions and points of view. *Ling&P* 2.1–41.

Jarvella, R.J. and W. Klein (eds) 1982. *Speech, place and action*. Chichester.

Li, C.N. 1976. *Subject and topic*. New York.

Lutzeier, P. 1981. Words and worlds. In H.J. Eikmeyer and H. Rieser (eds), *Words, worlds and contexts*. Berlin. 75–106.

Miller, G.A. and P.N. Johnson-Laird. 1976. *Language and perception*. Cambridge, MA.

Svorou, S. 1994. *The grammar of space*. Amsterdam and Philadelphia, PA.

Wunderlich, D. 1982. Sprache und Raum. *StL* 12.1–19, 13.37–59.

⇒ **deixis**

toponymic [Grk *ónyma* 'name']

Term for geographic areas such as cities, villages, states, and countries. (⇒ *also* **onomastics**, **toponymy**)

toponymy (*also* toponomastics)

Subdiscipline of **onomastics** concerned with the development, origin, and distribution of geographical names.

topos

A term that originates in the study of **argumentation** in classical **rhetoric** for (a) a place for possible arguments for general argumentative points of view, like quantity or time (locus communis), and later expanded to a differentiated system of comprehension; (b) individual arguments originating from a specific place (e.g. topos of quantity: *the more, the better*; topos of quality: *the rarer, the better*).

References
Bagnall, N. 1985. *A defence of clichés*. London.
Hunter, L. 1991. *Towards a definition of topos: approaches to analogical reasoning*. Basingstoke.
Quasthoff, U. 1978. The uses of stereotype in everyday argument. *JPrag* 2.1–48.
Redfern, W.D. 1989. *Clichés and coinages*. Oxford.
Zijderveld, A. 1979. *On clichés*. London.

Tosk ⇒ Albanian

Totonac

Language family of Mexico with the two languages, Totonac (about 240,000 speakers) and Tepehua (about 18,000 speakers).

Characteristics: complex consonant system similar to the neighboring **Mayan languages**; richly developed morphology with a tendency towards **polysynthesis**; simple nominal morphology, numeral classification, and **classifying verbs**.

References
Bishop, R. *et al.* 1968. *Totonac from clause to discourse*. Norman, OK.
McQuown, N. 1940. *A grammar of the Totonac language*. New Haven, CT.
⇒ **North and Central American languages**

trace theory

A concept developed by Chomsky (1975) in the Revised Extended Standard Theory (REST; ⇒ **transformational grammar**) whereby every movement of an NP-constituent from a particular position in the sentence leaves a trace at **surface structure**. Traces are abstract empty nodes which have the same referential index as the moved NP. Certain traces are understood as analogous to visible, bound anaphors. On the one hand, traces are based on interesting parallels between transformations and certain anaphoric processes like pronominalization and reflexivization; on the other hand, they are based on the theoretical goals of the REST, to unify their semantic interpretation at deep structure to surface structure. The range of possible transformations is reduced to one general transformation called **move-α**. The resulting structures are constrained by equating the traces left by the movement transformation with existing types of bound anaphoras whose distribution is restricted by existing constraints.

References
Chomsky, N. 1973. Conditions on transformations. In S.R. Anderson and P. Kiparsky (eds), *Festschrift for Morris Halle*. New York. 232–86.
—— 1975. *Reflections on language*. New York.
—— 1976. Conditions on rules of grammar. *LingA* 2.303–51.
Chomsky, N. and H. Lasnik. 1977. Filters and control. *LingI* 8.425–504.
—— and —— 1978. A remark on contraction. *LingI* 9.268–74.
Fiengo, R.W. 1974. Semantic conditions on surface structure. Dissertation, MIT, Cambridge, MA.
Lightfoot, D. 1977. On traces and conditions on rules. In P.W. Culicover, T. Wasow, and A. Akmajian (eds), *Formal syntax*. New York. 207–47.
Postal, P.M. and G.K. Pullum. 1978. Traces and the description of English complementizer contraction. *LingI* 9.1–29.
Pullum, G.K. and R.D. Borsley. 1980. Comments on the two central claims of 'trace theory.' *Linguistics* 18.73–104.
⇒ **transformational grammar**

tractable

An **algorithm** is tractable if it provides a solution to a problem in time and space proportional to some polynomial function of the length of the problem (⇒ **complexity**). For example, context-free languages may be parsed in time proportional to n^3, where n is the length of the input string (⇒ **parsing**). Derivatively, a problem is tractable if there exists a tractable algorithm solving it. Intractable problems (those for which no polynomial time/space algorithm exists) are felt to be too costly – in general – for computation. For example, checking the satisfiability of a propositional formula requires checking an exponential number of combinations of the atoms which occur in it.

Reference
Garey, M. and D. Johnson. 1979. *Computers and intractability: a guide to the theory of NP completeness*. New York.

trade language

1 Spoken colloquial language of the late Middle Ages, in contrast to the written language of the bureaucracies.

2 Generally speaking, a language in which laws, public announcements, trade agreements, and political documents of international significance are composed, e.g. **English**, **French**, **German**, **Spanish**, **Russian**, and others. (⇒ *also* **interlingua**, **koiné**)

3 Term sometimes used synonymously with **pidgin**.

traditional grammar ⇒ school grammar

transcortical aphasia ⇒ aphasia

transcription

1 Process and result of rendering a text in one script (e.g. a logographic one such as **Chinese**)

Philip washes himself from *Philip*₁ *washes Philip*₁

SA: NP₁ – X –   NP₁   –Y

         1   2   3   4 = >

SC: 1 – 2 –   ⎡ +Pron   ⎤   – 4 (= obligatory)
                      ⎣ +Reflexive ⎦

into the form of an (alphabetic) text. In transcription, a one-to-one correspondence rarely exists. More than any other system, the IPA (see the chart on p. xix) can be used most successfully as a transcription language. **Chinese** is transcribed according to the Pīnyīn system, **Japanese** according either to the Hepburn or Kunrei-siki systems.

2 ⇒ **phonetic transcription**

transfer

Term from psychology for the intensifying or retardive influence of earlier behavioral patterns in learning new behavioral patterns. In linguistics, the transfer of linguistic features of the mother tongue onto the foreign language; a distinction is made between positive transfer (based on similiarities between the two languages) and negative transfer (⇒ **interference**).

transformation

1 A term coined by Z.S. Harris for the relationship between linguistic expressions at **surface structure** that paraphrase each other and have the same linguistic environment (⇒ **transformational analysis**).

Reference
Harris, Z.S. 1952. Discourse analysis. *Lg* 28.1–30.

2 In Chomsky's model of **transformational grammar**, formal operations which mediate between the **deep structure** and the **surface structure** of sentences. Transformations transfer the **tree diagrams** generated by **phrase structure rules** from deep structure to derived tree diagrams at surface structure. Stated in technical terms: transformations are operations of phrase markers on phrase markers. Transformational rules are different from phrase structure rules in that their operational domain is not restricted to individual nodes, but extends to the whole phrase structure tree, which they modify according to precise conditions. Formally, transformations consist of two components: the **structural analysis** (SA), which indicates which relevant structural properties phrase structure markers must have for the

transformations to apply, and the structural change (SC), which describes the effect of the transformation: see diagram above. (Note: *X* and *Y* are symbols for optional constituents; the corresponding indexing of the NPs denotes their referential identity; the double arrow indicates a transformation). All transformations are based on the **deletion** and insertion of constituents. Operations derived from these are **substitution** (the deletion and insertion of different elements in the same place) and **permutation** (the deletion of an element from one place and its insertion in another). In his 1957 model, Chomsky distinguished between the following two types of transformation. (a) Singular vs generalized transformations: singular transformations operate on individual constituents, whereas generalized transformations generate complex sentences by combining different tree diagrams into one complex tree diagram which guarantees the infinite capacity of the generative model (⇒ **recursiveness**). (b) Obligatory vs optional transformations: obligatory transformations regulate formal (morphological) processes like agreement, whereas all transformations that change meaning belong to the group of optional transformations. Transformations which change the meaning of a sentence must introduce new semantic information on the way from deep structure to surface structure. In his 1965 model, Chomsky makes all transformations obligatory and meaning-neutral. This hypothesis was subsequently maintained, but led (in **generative semantics**) to very abstract elements in deep structure, for example, the feature *Q* for questions directs the interpretation of the question and induces the corresponding syntactic transformations. The order in which transformations apply is not optional (⇒ **extrinsic vs intrinsic ordering of rules**). For individual examples of transformations, ⇒ **equi-NP deletion**, **extraposition**, **gapping**, **imperative transformation**, **nominalization**, **pronominalization** (⇒ **personal pronoun**), **reflexivation**, (⇒ **reflexive pronoun**), **topicalization**. In further revisions of transformational grammar, the number of transformations is reduced more and more and becomes restricted to **movement transforma- tions** and deletion. In Chomsky (1981), the movement transformations in core grammar are reduced to **move-α**, where α is a variable for all constituents, which can be moved to designated positions in the sentence. The collapse of all transformational processes to a single move- ment transformation corresponds to an increase in the use of constraints on the applications of these functions. (⇒ *also* **filter**, **trace theory**)

References
Chomsky, N. 1957. *Syntactic structures*. The Hague
—— 1965. *Aspects of the theory of syntax*. Cam- bridge, MA.
—— 1981. *Lectures on government and binding*. Dordrecht.
⇒ **transformational grammar**

transformational analysis

A technique for syntactic analysis developed by Harris (1952), which is based on the **surface structure** equivalence between linguistic expressions. In order to compare complex expressions, they are transformed to simple expressions. Nominalization and pronominal- ization are replaced by explicit forms. For example, *a rarely heard expression*: *an expres- sion which is rarely heard*. Certain restrictions apply to such rewritings: no lexical morphemes may be used which would change the meaning, and the transformed expression must be a good substitute for the original expression.

References
Bense, E. 1957. Co-occurrence and transformation in linguistic structure. *Lg* 33.283–340.
—— 1965. Transformational theory. *Lg* 41.363–401.
—— 1970. *Papers in structural and transforma- tional linguistics*. Dordrecht.
Harris, Z.S. 1952. Discourse analysis. *Lg* 28.1–30.

transformational cycle

A principle for the use of **transformational rules** in **transformational grammar**. Rules are first applied to the sentence at the lowest part of the **tree diagram** and then continue cyclically to the next highest level. (⇒ *also* **principle of cyclic rule application**)

transformational grammar

1 A generic term for any **generative grammar** which uses **transformations**.

2 In a narrower sense, the theory developed by N. Chomsky. The goal of this theory is to illustrate the implicit knowledge of language, based on current language use, by a system of explicit rules. Differing from the taxonomic **structuralism** of Harris, Bloomfield, and oth- ers, which is based on the segmentation and

classification of concrete language data, Chomsky's model refers to the ability of com- petent speakers and to the linguistic intuitions which a competent speaker can make explicit about his/her language. Historically, Chomsky belongs to the tradition of **rationalism** of Leibnitz and Descartes. By elaborating the concept of 'innate ideas,' Chomsky turns against the behaviorist approaches of the **American structuralists** and expands his theo- ry to a theory of language acquisition. The development of competence is explained by the innate **language acquisition device** on the basis of grammar **universals**. Therefore the formulation of the theory takes precedence over the analysis of data, and transformational gram- mar proceeds deductively by laying down hypotheses about the linguistic generation mechanism, taking the creative aspects of lin- guistic ability into account. This is true of Chomsky's first theory, which appeared in his 1957 book *Syntactic structures*: an infinite set of **kernel sentences**, produced by context-free **phrase structure rules**, forms the basis for the application of transformational rules, which ensure an infinite set of sentences by finite means. In the second phase of transformational grammar, documented in Chomsky's *Aspects of the theory of syntax* in 1965, the original syntactic theory is expanded to a general theory of grammar which includes **phonology** and **semantics**. The following revisions are charac- teristic of the so-called 'aspects model' (also known as the standard theory, ST): the gram- mar, in the sense of a comprehensive linguistic theory, consists of a generative, syntactic com- ponent as well as interpretive, semantic, and phonological components. The basis of the syntax is the **deep structure** which is formed by context-free phrase structure rules and lex- ical rules. The context-free phrase structure rules guarantee **recursiveness** by **self- embedded constructions**; recursiveness was achieved by generalizing transformations in the earlier model. The deep structure contains all semantically relevant information at an abstract basic level of structure and is the point of departure for the semantic interpretation of sentences. The works of Katz in the area of **interpretive semantics** are relevant here. The corresponding **surface structure** is derived from meaning-neutral transformations such as deletion. The surface structure forms the basis for the phonological–phonetic representation. Criticism of this conception was, above all, based on the role of semantics, since the semantic interpretation of a sentence is depend- ent on surface structure phenomena such as **intonation**, **word order**, and the **theme–**

rheme division. This led to the development of two competing approaches in the 1960s and 1970s: **generative semantics** and the extended standard theory. Revisions of the standard theory were instigated by Jackendoff (1972) and Chomsky (1972) and lie in a restriction on the range of transformations through universal **constraints** and in semantic interpretation, which refers to the deep structure and surface structure. Changes occurring since 1973 have led to the introduction of the term Revised Extended Standard theory (= REST), which differs from the extended standard theory in the following ways: (a) the exact delimiting and definition of the individual grammatical components, especially the strict division between syntax and semantics (as well as phonology, stylistics, and pragmatics); (b) the application of **markedness** theory, which was developed in phonology; (c) the reduction of transformations to structure-preserving transformations, especially **move-α**; (d) the universal formulation of constraints, which correspond to psychologically interpretable universals and which are specified by language-specific parameters; (e) the introduction of traces as abstract empty category nodes in the surface structure, which mark and make accessible the former position of transposed NP-constituents; (f) the semantic interpretation can only operate on a single level of the surface structure which encodes semantic information from deep structure. In Chomsky's GB theory (⇒ **Government and Binding Theory**), the term government takes on a central meaning; within **core grammar**, a strong modularization of the syntax is attempted; phenomena of individual languages are captured by suitable parameterization. (⇒ *also* **binding theory, empty category principle, logical form, governing category**)

References

Abraham, W. (ed.) 1983. *On the formal syntax of the Westgermania*. Amsterdam.
Akmajian, A. and F. Heny. 1965. *An introduction to the principles of transformational syntax*. Cambridge, MA.
Anderson, J. and G. Bower. 1974. *Human associative memory*. New York.
Aoun, J. 1986. *Generalized binding: the syntax and logical form of wh-interrogatives*. Dordrecht.
Bach, E. 1974. *Syntactic theory*. New York.
Bach, E. and R.T. Harms (eds) 1968. *Universals in linguistic theory*. New York.
Baker, C.L. 1978. *Introduction to generative transformational syntax*. Englewood Cliffs, NJ.
Belletti, A., L. Brandi, and L. Rizzi (eds) 1981. *Theory of markedness in generative grammar: proceedings of the 1979 GLOW conference*. Pisa.
Bennis, H. and A. Groos. 1980. The government-binding theory: an overview. *Lingua e Stile* 15:4.565–92.
Bierwisch, M. 1963. *Grammatik des deutschen Verbs*. Berlin.
Bierwisch, M. and K.E. Heidolph (eds) 1970. *Progress in linguistics*. The Hague.
Bouchard, D. 1984. *On the content of empty categories*. Dordrecht.
Burt, M.K. 1971. *From deep to surface structure*. New York.
Chomsky, N. 1955. *The logical structure of linguistic theory*. (Mimeo, MIT.) Cambridge, MA. (Repr. as *The logical structure of linguistic theory*. New York, 1975.)
——— 1957. *Syntactic structures*. The Hague.
——— 1964a. *Current issues in linguistic theory*. The Hague.
——— 1964b. The logical basis of linguistic theory. In H.C. Lunt (ed.), *Proceedings of the ninth international congress of linguistics*. The Hague. 914–78.
——— 1965. *Aspects of the theory of syntax*. Cambridge, MA.
——— 1971. Deep structure, surface structure, and semantic interpretation. In D.D. Steinberg and L.A. Jakobovits (eds), *Semantics*. London. 183–216.
——— 1972. *Studies on semantics in generative grammar*. The Hague.
——— 1973. Conditions on transformations. In S.R. Anderson and P. Kiparsky (eds), *A Festschrift for Morris Halle*. New York. 232–86.
——— 1975. *Reflections on language*. New York.
——— 1976. *The logical structure of linguistic theory*. New York.
——— 1977a. *Essays on form and interpretation*. New York.
——— 1977b. On wh-movement. In P.W. Culicover, T. Wasow, and A. Akmajian (eds), *Formal syntax*. New York. 71–132.
——— 1980a. On binding. *LingI*. 11.1–46.
——— 1980b. *Rules and representations*. New York.
——— 1981. *Lectures on government and binding*. Dordrecht.
——— 1982. *Some concepts and consequences of the theory of government and binding*. Cambridge, MA.
——— 1986a. *Barriers*. Cambridge, MA.
——— 1986b. *Knowledge of language: its nature, origin and use*. New York.
——— 1987. *Language and problems of knowledge*. Cambridge, MA.
Chomsky, N. and H. Lasnik. 1977. Filters and control. *LingI* 8.425–504.
——— and ——— 1978. A remark on contraction. *LingI* 9.268–74.
Culicover, P., T. Wasow, and A. Akmajian (eds) 1977. *Formal syntax*. New York.
Derwing, B.L. 1973. *Transformational grammar as a theory of language acquisition*. Cambridge.
Dittmann, J. 1981. Rezeption und Kritik der Sprachtheorie Noam Chomskys in der Bundesrepublik Deutschland. *DSp* 9.61–96, 147–80.
Edmonds, J.E. 1976. *A transformational approach to*

English syntax. New York.
—— 1985. *A unified theory of syntactic categories.* Dordrecht.

Edmondson, J.A. 1981. *Einführung in die Transformationssyntax des Deutschen.* Tübingen.

Fillmore, C.J. and T.D. Langendoen (eds) 1971. *Studies in linguistic semantics.* New York.

Fodor, J.A. and J.J. Katz (eds) 1964. *The structure of language: readings in the philosophy of language.* Englewood Cliffs, NJ.

Freidin, R. 1992. *Foundations of generative syntax.* Cambridge, MA.

Gazdar, G. 1981. Unbounded dependencies and coordinate structure. *LingI* 12.155–84.

Gazdar, G., E. Klein, and G.K. Pullum (eds) 1983. *Order, concord and constituency.* Dordrecht.

Geest, W. de and Y. Putseys (eds) 1984. *Proceedings of the international conference on sentential complementation.* Dordrecht.

Gross, M. 1968. *Grammaire transformationnelle du français: syntaxe du verbe.* Paris.

Guéron, J., H.G. Obenauer, and J.-Y. Pollock (eds) 1985. *Grammatical representation.* Dordrecht.

Haider, H. and K. Netter. 1991. *Representation and derivation in the theory of grammar.* Dordrecht.

Haider, H. and M. Prinzhorn (eds) 1986. *Verb second phenomena in Germanic languages.* Dordrecht.

Harman, G. (ed.) 1974. *On Noam Chomsky: critical essays.* Garden City, NY.

Heny, F. (ed.) 1981. *Binding and filtering.* London.

Horrocks, G. 1987. *Generative grammar.* London.

Huber, W. and W. Kummer. 1974. *Transformationelle Syntax des Deutschen,* vol. I. Munich.

Huddleston, R. 1976. *An introduction to English transformational syntax.* London.

Jackendoff, R.S. 1972. *Semantic interpretation in generative grammar.* Cambridge, MA.

Jacobs, R.A. and P.S. Rosenbaum. 1968. *English transformational grammar.* Waltham, MA.

—— (eds) 1970. *Readings in English transformational grammar.* Waltham, MA.

Kayne, R. 1975. *French syntax: the transformational cycle.* Cambridge, MA.

—— 1984. *Connectedness and binary branching.* Dordrecht.

Keyser, S.J. (ed.) 1978. *Recent transformational studies in European languages.* Cambridge, MA.

Kiefer, F. (ed.) 1969. *Studies in syntax and semantics.* Dordrecht.

Kiefer, F. and N. Ruwet (eds) 1973. *Generative grammar in Europe.* Dordrecht.

Kimball, J.P. (ed.) 1972. *Syntax and semantics,* vol. 1. New York.

Koster, J. 1978. *Locality principles in syntax.* Dordrecht.

—— 1987. *Domains and dynasties: the radical autonomy of syntax.* Dordrecht.

Koutsoudas, A. 1966. *Writing transformational grammars.* New York.

Lang, E. 1967. *Terminologie der generativen Grammatik.* Berlin.

Langendoen, T.D. 1969. *A study of syntax. the generative–transformational approach to the structure of American English.* New York.

—— 1970. *Essentials of English grammar.* New York.

Lasnik, H. 1990. *Essays on restrictiveness and learnability.* Dordrecht.

Lasnik, H. and M. Saito. 1992. *Move α – conditions on its application and output.* Cambridge, MA.

Manzini, R. 1992. *Locality: a theory and some of its empirical consequences.* Cambridge, MA.

Marantz, A. 1984. *On the nature of grammatical relations.* Cambridge, MA.

May, R. and J. Koster (eds) 1981. *Levels of syntactic representation.* Dordrecht.

Muysken, P. and H. van Riemskijk (eds) 1986. *Features and projections.* Dordrecht.

Newmeyer, F.J. 1980. *Linguistic theory in America: the first quarter-century of transformational generative grammar.* New York.

—— 1983. *Grammatical theory: its limits and its possibilities.* Chicago, IL.

—— 1995. *Generative linguistics. A historical perspective.* London.

Ouhalla, J. 1991. *Functional categories and parametric variation.* London.

—— 1994. *Introducing transformational grammar: from rules to principles and parameters.* London.

Palmatier, R.A. 1972. *A glossary for English transformational grammar.* New York.

Pesetsky, D.M. 1982. Paths and categories. Dissertation, MIT, Cambridge, MA.

Piattelli-Palmarini, M. (ed.) 1980. *Language and learning: the debate between Jean Piaget and Noam Chomsky.* London.

Putnam, H. 1975. The 'innateness hypothesis' and explanatory models in linguistics. In his *Mind, language and reality.* Cambridge. 107–16.

Radford, A. 1981. *Transformational syntax: a student's guide to Chomsky's Extended Standard Theory.* Cambridge.

—— 1988. *Transformational grammar: a first course.* Cambridge.

Reibel, D.A. and S.A. Schane (eds) 1969. *Modern studies in English: readings in transformational grammar.* Englewood Cliffs, NJ.

Reinhart, T. 1983. *Anaphora and semantic interpretation.* London.

Safir, K. 1985. *Syntactic chains.* Cambridge.

Soames, S. and D.M. Perlmutter. 1979. *Syntactic argumentation and the structure of English.* Berkeley, CA.

Stockwell, R.P., R. Schachter, and B. Hall Partee. 1968. *Integration of transformational theories on English syntax,* 2 vols. Los Angeles, CA.

—— 1973. *The major syntactic structures of English.* New York.

Stowell, T. 1981. Origins of phrase structure. Dissertation, MIT, Cambridge, MA.

Thiersch, C. 1978. Topics in German syntax. Dissertation, MIT, Cambridge, MA.

—— 1980. New developments in generative syntax. In H.H. Lieb (ed.), *Oberflächensyntax und Semantik.* Tübingen. 9–31.

Thomas, O. 1965. *Transformational grammar and the teacher of English.* New York.

Toman, J. (ed.) 1985. *Studies in German grammar*. Dordrecht.

Van Riemsdijk, H. (ed.) 1976. *Green ideas blown up*. Amsterdam.

Van Riemskijk, H. and E. Williams. 1986. *Introduction to the theory of grammar*. Cambridge, MA.

Wilks, Y. 1972. *Grammar, meaning and the machine analysis of language*. London.

Bibliographies

Dingwall, W.O. 1965. *Transformational generative grammar: a bibliography*. Washington, DC.

Koerner, K., M. Tajima, and C.P. Otero. 1986. *Noam Chomsky: a personal bibliography, 1951–1986*. Amsterdam.

Welte, W. 1974. *Moderne Linguistik: Terminologie/ Bibliographie. Ein Handbuch und Nachschlagewerk auf der Basis der generativ-transformationellen Sprachtheorie*, 2 vols. Munich.

Journal

The Linguistic Review.
⇒ **constraints**, **filter**, **Government and Binding theory**, **interpretive semantics**, **logical form**, **morphology**, **phrase structure**, **trace theory**, **universal grammar**

transformational history

The sequence of **transformations** which takes a sentence from **deep structure** to **surface structure**.

transformationalist hypothesis ⇒ lexicalist vs transformationalist hypothesis

transformational marker

In the early versions of **transformational grammar**, the formal representation of the **derivational history** of the **surface structure** of a sentence from its **deep structure**.

transformational rule ⇒ transformation

transformative (*also* verb of change)

Verbal **aspect** subsumed under the category of non-duratives. Transformative verbs indicate a transition from one state to another (e.g. *age*, *cool off*, *go blind*), where the new state is often a negation of the old state: *cool off* = *no longer be hot*. (⇒ *also* **durative vs non-durative**)

References
⇒ **aspect**

transition network grammar ⇒ augmented transition network grammar

transitional area [Lat. *transitio* 'going across, passage'] (*also* convergence area)

Term used in **dialectology** to denote the prevalence of varied linguistic traits in geographically neighboring areas; a convergence area arises when linguistic changes (in the sense of a **wave theory** of language change from the originating center of a difference to the periphery) appear to take place less and less generally or when the process of the wave-shaped dispersion gradually comes to an end.

References
⇒ **dialectology**

transitional competence ⇒ interlanguage

transitional sound ⇒ steady-state sound vs transitional sound

transitive relation

Two-place relation *R* for which, regarding any three objects *x*, *y*, *z*, it is the case that $R(x, y) \wedge R(y, z) \rightarrow R(x, z)$. This is the case, for example, for some kinship terms: if it is the case that *Philip is the brother of Jacob and Jacob is the brother of Caroline*, then it is also true that *Philip is the brother of Caroline*. On the other hand, the relation 'is a friend of' is not transitive: *x is a friend of z* may be false, if *x is a friend of y and y is a friend of z* is true. A relation is intransitive if there are no three objects *x*, *y*, *z*, for which it is true that $R(x, y) \wedge R(y, x) \wedge R(x, z)$; for example, it cannot be the case that *x is the father of y, y is the father of z and x is the father of z*.

References
⇒ **formal logic**, **set theory**

transitivity

1 **Valence** property of verbs which require a direct object, e.g. *read*, *see*, *hear*. Used more broadly, verbs which govern other objects (e.g. **dative**, **genitive**) can also be termed 'transitive'; while only verbs which have no object at all (e.g. *sleep*, *rain*) would be intransitive. Hopper and Thompson (1980) introduce other factors of transitivity in the framework of **universal grammar**, which result in a graduated concept of transitivity. In addition to the selection of a direct object, other semantic roles as well as the properties of **adverbials**, **mood**, affirmation vs **negation**, and aspect play a role. A maximally transitive sentence contains a non-negated **resultive** verb in the indicative which requires at least a subject and direct object; the verb complements function as **agent** and **affected object**, are **definite** and animate (⇒ **animate vs inanimate**). Using data from various languages, Hopper and Thompson demonstrate that each of the factors listed above as affecting transitivity is important for marking transitivity through **case**, **adpositions**, or verbal inflection. Thus in many languages (e.g. **Lithuanian**, **Polish**, Middle High **German**) affirmation vs negation correlates with the selection of case for objects in such

a way that in affirmative sentences the object is usually in the accusative, while in negated sentences the object of the same verb occurs in the genitive or in another oblique case.

References

Hoekstra, T. 1984. *Transitivity: grammatical relations in government–binding theory*. Dordrecht.

Hopper, P.J. and S.A. Thompson. 1980. Transitivity in grammar and discourse. *Lg* 56.251–300.

—— (eds) 1982. *Syntax and semantics*, vol. 15: *Studies in transitivity*. New York.

Moravcsik, E.A. 1978. Case marking of objects. In J.H. Greenberg (ed.), *Universals of human language*. Stanford, CA. Vol. 4. 250–89.

2 On transitivity in logic, ⇒ **transitive relation**.

translation

1 In the broad sense, 'translation' refers to the process and result of transferring a text from the **source language** into the **target language**.

2 In the narrow sense, it refers to rendering a written text into another language as opposed to simultaneously **interpreting** spoken language.

3 In foreign-language instruction, translation is considered, by some, to be a 'fifth skill' (next to the traditional '**four skills**' of speaking, listening, reading, and writing). Translation is a method used to practice and test competence and performance in a second language.

Translators are generally trained at private, government, or military institutes as well as at some colleges and universities. Studies in translation focus on linguistic, psychological, aesthetic, pedagogical, and professional aspects. Most such studies have been of greater use to the area of computer and **machine-aided translation** than to the practical concerns of human interpreters. Some important issues in translation include: (a) the typology of translation, which differentiates between the translation of literary vs scientific or professional texts, and between human vs machine-aided translation; philological translation, which is concerned with the process of communication in the source language and culture; and pragmatically based simultaneous translation; (b) the format of equivalent units (sounds, words, phrases, etc.). An equivalent communicative effect is all the more difficult to attain, the greater the cultural distance between the receivers of the source and target text (problem of translatability) (⇒ **linguistic determinism**, **Sapir–Whorf hypothesis**). In this area, recent discussions center on the intercultural implications of translation and have all but dispensed with the concept of 'equivalence.'

References

Bell, R.T. 1991. *Translation and translating: theory and practice*. London.

Brislin, R.W. (ed.) 1976. *Translation: applications and research*. New York.

Catford, J.C. 1965. *A linguistic theory of translation*. London.

Cummings, R. and S. Gillespie (eds) 1991. *Translation and literature*. Edinburgh.

Gentzler, E. 1993. *Contemporary translation theories*. London.

Grähs, L., G. Korlén, and B. Malmberg (eds) 1978. *Theory and practice of translation*. Bern.

Guenthner-Reutter, M. and F. Guenthner (eds) 1975. *Anthology on the theory of translation*. Cambridge.

Gutt, E.A. 1991. *Translation and relevance*. Oxford.

Hatim, B. and I. Mason. 1990. *Discourse and the translator*. London.

Hewson, L. and J. Martin. 1991. *Redefining translation: the variational approach*. London.

Holmes, J.S. 1988. *Translated! Essays and papers on translation and translation studies*. Amsterdam.

Holmes, J.S., J. Lambert, and R. van den Broeck (eds) 1976. *Literature and translation*. Louvain.

Kelly, L.G. 1979. *The true interpreter: a history of translation theory and practice in the west*. Oxford.

Larson, M. (ed.) 1991. *Translation: theory and practice, tension and interdependence*. Amsterdam and Philadelphia, PA.

Lörscher, W. 1990. *Translation performance, translation process, and translation strategies: a psycholinguistic investigation*. Tübingen.

Newmark, P. 1991. *About translation*. Clevedon.

Snell-Hornby, M. 1988. *Translation studies: an integrated approach*. Amsterdam.

Titford, C. and A.E. Hieke (eds) 1985. *Translation in foreign language teaching and testing*. Tübingen.

Venuti, L. 1992. *Rethinking translation*. London.

Zlateva, P. 1993. *Translation as social action: Russian and Bulgarian perspectives*. London.

Journals

International Journal of Translation Studies. *Target*.

4 Term used in L. Tesnière's **dependency grammar** in addition to **connection** and **junction** which expresses the third process for constructing sentences or complex expressions. With translation, a function word (translative), such as a preposition or conjunction, changes the syntactic category of an expression and makes its connection in the sentence possible. For example, the noun *time* can be made into an 'adjective' with the preposition *of*, which can be combined with *end*: *the end of time*.

References

⇒ **dependency grammar**

translative

1 Morphological locative case in some lan-

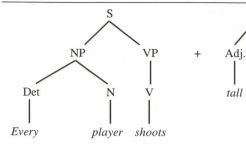

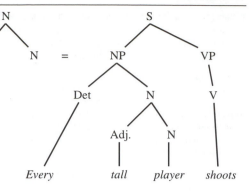

guages (e.g. **Finnish**). It expresses the fact that an object moves along a specific location.

2 ⇒ **translation**[4]

transliteration [Lat. *littera* 'letter (of the alphabet)']

The process and result of transcribing a text written in an alphabetic or syllabic writing system into an alphabetic text. In transliteration, characters are generally converted one-to-one, though the process often involves imparting characteristics (such as word breaks and capitalization) of the target script onto the source script.

Reference
Barry, R.K. (ed.) 1991. *ALA-LC romanization tables: transliteration schemes for non-Roman scripts.* Washington, DC.

transparent context ⇒ **opaque vs transparent context**

transphrastic analysis

Analysis of the grammatical relationships between sentences of a text (⇒ **discourse grammar**), such as the reference of an expression through pronominalization. (⇒ **personal pronoun**)

transposition [Lat. *transponere* 'to move across']

1 In **word formation**, a change in word class as new expressions are formed through **suffixation**: *read* (= verb), *readable* (= adjective), *reader* (= noun). (⇒ *also* **modification**)

2 ⇒ **metathesis**

tree-adjoining grammar (*abbrev.* TAG)

A mildly context-sensitive extension (⇒ **mildly context-sensitive language**, **context-sensitive grammar**) of **context-free** (CF) **grammar**, including operations which adjoin trees in a recursive way (⇒ **recursiveness**) (see diagram above).

TAG is distinguished among grammar models in being essentially tree-based, and has been explored both as a formalization of **transformational grammar** (Kroch and Joshi) and as an alternative grammar model (Abeille). There exist lexicalized unification-based (⇒ **unification grammar**) and stochastic (⇒ **stochastic grammar**) variants. TAG is especially popular in **computational linguistics**.

References
Abeille, A. 1991. Une grammaire lexicalisée d'arbres adjoints pour le français. Dissertation. Paris.
Joshi, A. 1987. An introduction to tree-adjoining grammars. In A. Manaster-Ramer (ed.), *Mathematics of language*. Amsterdam.
Kroch, A. and A. Joshi. 1987. Linguistic relevance of tree-adjoining grammars. *University of Pennsylvania Computer and Information Science MS-CIS 85–18.*
Shabes, Y. 1992. Stochastic lexicalized tree-adjoining grammars. *COLING 1992.*
⇒ **anaphora**, **discourse grammar**, **textphoric**

tree diagram (*also* branching diagram, graph, phrase structure diagram)

A special type of graphic representation used to depict linguistic structures (⇒ **graph**[2]). Borrowing from the concept of a tree, a tree diagram consists of a root and several branching nodes and branches. In such representations of the hierarchical relations and inner structures, nodes represent grammatical categories (e.g. *S*, *NP*, *VP*) and the branches represent the relationships of **domination**. Each pair of nodes has a twofold relationship, one of dominance and one of precedence. In a tree diagram, *S* immediately dominates *NP* and *VP*, and indirectly all other nodes in the tree, while each node which is to the left of another node precedes the one to the right, provided that none of the nodes dominates the other. Thus *VP* precedes *VP*, *Det* precedes *N*, and so on. Tree diagrams of natural languages are also subject to certain rules of wellformedness; thus, for

(a)

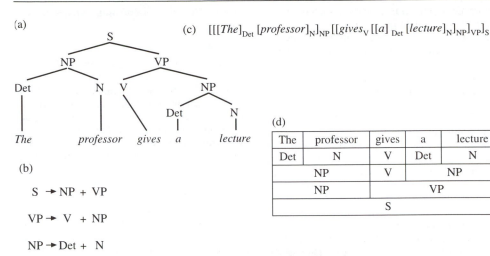

(c) $[[[The]_{Det} \; [professor]_N]_{NP} \; [[gives_V \; [[a] \;_{Det} \; [lecture]_N]_{NP}]_{VP}]_S$

(b)

$$S \rightarrow NP + VP$$

$$VP \rightarrow V + NP$$

$$NP \rightarrow Det + N$$

(d)

The	professor	gives	a	lecture
Det	N	V	Det	N
NP		V	NP	
NP		VP		
S				

example, crossing branches are not allowed, because the tree diagram (a) is equivalent to the **phrase structure rules** in (b), the **labeled bracketing** in (c), and the **box diagram** in (d), and the crossing of constituents cannot be represented. See the example *The professor gives a lecture.*

tree-pruning convention

In **transformational grammar**, a metatheoretical arrangement introduced by J.R. Ross which deletes an embedded sentence node which does not branch. These nodes can result from **deletion** or **movement transformations**. This happens in **generative semantics** when attributive adjectives are derived from relative clauses, where, according to the tree-pruning convention, the sentence constituent which formed the relative clause in the **tree diagram** is eliminated.

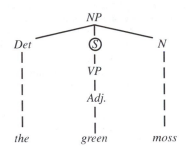

Reference

Ross, J.R. 1969. A proposed rule of tree-pruning. In D.A. Reibel and S.A. Schane (eds), *Modern studies in English: readings in transformational grammar.* Englewood Cliffs, NJ. 288–99.

trema $\Rightarrow$ **diaeresis**[2]

trill $\Rightarrow$ **vibrant**

trope [Grk *trópos* 'turn; manner']

A term in **rhetoric** for expressions with a transferable meaning (e.g. **metaphor**), which can be understood as a substitute for a denotatively suitable word. That is to say, trope is a semantic substitution. Tropes are classified according to their semantic relationships with the substituted word, e.g. as **antonomasia**, **synecdoche**, **emphasis**, **metonymy**, **litotes**, and **irony**, among others. Classical rhetorical theory distinguishes the **figure of speech** from the trope as a paradigmatic variation, based on syntagmatic variation.

References

Campbell, B. 1969. Metaphor, metonymy, and literalness. *General Linguistics* 9.149–66.

Ortony, A. (ed.) 1979. *Metaphor and thought.* Cambridge.

Ricoeur, P. 1978. *The rule of metaphor: multidisciplinary studies in the creation of meaning in language.* London.

Schoefer, P. and D. Rice. 1977. Metaphor, metonymy and synecdoche revis(it)ed. *Semiotica* 21.121–49.

Shapiro, M. and M.A. Shapiro. 1976. *Hierarchy and the structure of tropes.* Bloomington, IN.

White, H. 1978. *The tropics of discourse.* Baltimore, MD.

$\Rightarrow$ **figure of speech**

truncation rule

In Arnoff's (1976) **word formation**, proposed type of rule that deletes an **affix** occurring between a **root** and a second **suffix**. According to the model of *employee, presentee*, the suffixation of *-ee* would generate **nominat+ee, *evacuat+ee* instead of *nomin+ee, evacu+ee.*

According to the rule-governed formation of *nominate+ee* a deletion is applied that eliminates the morpheme *-ate* and places *-ee* immediately at the connection point of the verb root.

Reference
Aronoff, M. 1976. *Word formation in generative grammar*. Cambridge, MA.

truth condition

An assumption about situation(s) that must be given in order that certain sentences about the situation(s) can apply or be considered true. In the semantic description of natural languages, problems arise in regard to truth conditions in the following cases: (a) sentence types such as interrogatives or imperatives which, contrary to declaratives, are neither true nor false, (b) use of deictic expressions such as *I, now*, and *here*, whose contribution to determining **truth values** can only be analyzed depending on the given speech situation; (c) **reference** to different 'possible words' as they are created through verbs of believing or knowing ($\Rightarrow$ **intension, vagueness**). The explication of truth conditions of sentences is seen in more recent grammatical theories (such as **categorial grammar, Montague grammar**) as the basic principle of an adequate description of language. Thus, the **synonymy** between two propositions can be defined as similarity or concordance of their truth conditions or of the situations in which these sentences are true. See Dummet (1975) for a criticism of the formulation of truth conditions as part of linguistic description.

References
Dummett, M.A.E. 1975. What is a theory of meaning? In S. Guttenplan (ed.), *Mind and language*. Oxford. 97–138.
——— 1976. What is a theory of meaning (II)? In G. Evans and J. Mcdowell (eds), *Truth and meaning*. Oxford. 67–137.
$\Rightarrow$ **formal logic, possible world, truth value**

truth-functional

Property of **logical connectives**, whose invariant meaning guarantees that the whole meaning of complex sentences can be represented as a function of the **truth values** of the component clauses. ($\Rightarrow$ *also* **extension, propositional logic**)

truth table

Method developed independently by Post (1921) and Wittgenstein (1922) of defining **logical connectives** on the basis of **truth values**. Since the truth value of complex propositions connected by constants (such as *and, or*) is dependent on the truth values of the component propositions and on the meaning of their constants, these relations can be represented in a matrix. In the first vertical column the different possible combinations for the individual component propositions are entered: t = 'true,' f = 'false'; the number of the horizontal lines is 2^n, whereby *n* is the number of actual component propositions (= atomic sentences) in the propositional connection: two component propositions yield four, five component propositions yield thirty-two lines. The far-right line indicates the truth value applied to the distribution of the truth values by the constants (cf. the examples shown in **conjunction, disjunction, implication**, and others). The following table provides an overview of the most important two-place sentence **operators** and the distribution of their truth values.

References
Post, E. 1921. Introduction to a general theory of elementary propositions. *AJM* 43.163–85.
Wittgenstein, L. 1922. *Tractatus logico-philosophicus*. London.

truth value

In two-value **formal logic** the semantic evaluation of propositions with 'true' or 'false.' A proposition is 'true,' if the state of affairs designated by it is true, otherwise it is 'false.' The assertion *It's raining* is true only if it is raining. Some forms of logic use a three-value system which specifies not only true and false propositions, but also 'indefinite' propositions (see Blau 1978) ($\Rightarrow$ **truth table** for more information on the study of the truth values of complex propositions based on the truth values of their component propositions and their **logical connectives**). The concept of assigning

p q	Negation	Adjunction	Conjunction	Implication	Equivalence	Contravalence	Tautology	Contradiction
	$\neg p$	$p \vee q$	$p \wedge q$	$p \rightarrow q$	$p \leftrightarrow q$	$p \succ\!\!\prec q$	e. g. $p \rightarrow (q \rightarrow p)$	e. g. $p \wedge (q \wedge \neg q)$
t t	f	t	t	t	t	f	t	f
t f	f	t	f	f	f	t	t	f
f t	t	t	f	t	f	t	t	f
f f	t	f	f	t	t	f	t	f

extensional truth values in propositional logic is fundamental to the semantic description of natural languages (⇒ **Montague grammar**).

References
Bäuerle, R. *et al* (eds) 1979. *Semantics from different points of view*. Berlin.
Black, M. 1948. The semantic definition of truth. *Analysis* 8.49–62.
Blau, U. 1978. *Die dreiwertige Logik der Sprache*. Berlin.
Davidson, D. 1967. Truth and meaning. *Synthese* 17.304–33.
Evans, G. and J. McDowell (eds) 1976. *Meaning and truth*. Oxford.
Kripke, S. 1975. Outline of a theory of truth. *JP* 72.690–716.
Linsky, L. (ed.) 1952. *Semantics and the philosophy of language*. Chicago, IL.
Quine, W.V.O. 1970. *Philosophy of logic*. Englewood Cliffs, NJ. (2nd rev. edn 1973.)
Tarski, A. 1944. The semantic approach of truth and foundation of semantics. *PPR* 4.341–75.

Tsimshian ⇒ Penutian

Tuareg ⇒ Berber

Tungusic

Branch of the **Altaic** languages with approx. twelve languages and 80,000 speakers in northeast Asia. The best known language is Manchu, the language of the Manchu dynasty in China (1644–1911), today with about 20,000 speakers.

References
Benzing, J. 1956. *Die tungusischen Sprachen*. Wiesbaden.
Fuchs, W. *et al.* 1968. *Tungusologie*. (Handbuch der Orientalistik I, vol. 5,3). Leiden.
Hänisch, E. 1961. *Mandschu-Grammatik*. Leipzig.
Malchukov, A.L. 1994. *Ewen*. Munich.

Bibliography
Stary, G. 1990. *Manchu studies: an international bibliography*, 3 vols. Wiesbaden.

Tupi

Language family in the southern part of South America with approx. fifty languages; the most important is **Guaraní** (about 3 million speakers), which Greenberg (1987) assigns to the **Equatorial languages**. These languages have spread out southward from the Amazon basin in historical times.

Characteristics: relatively simple sound system; some languages have a **gender** system.

References
Greenberg, J.H. 1987. *Language in the Americas*. Stanford, CA.
Kakumasu, J. 1986. Urubu-Kaapor. In D.C. Derbyshire and G. Pullum (eds), *Handbook of Amazo-

nean languages. Berlin. 326–403.
⇒ **South American languages**

Turing machine

Designed by and named for A.M. Turing, a conceptual model of a universal computer with infinitely large storage capacity. Owing to the fact that they would be prohibitively inefficient, Turing machines cannot be directly realized (even allowing for memory limitations); however, they serve an important function in the exact definition of important basic concepts such as **algorithm** and recursive functions (⇒ **recursiveness**). Concerning the equivalence of **automata** and formal grammars, the Turing machine corresponds to a type of unrestricted rewriting system, since it can produce any recursively enumerable set of strings (sentences).

References
Chomsky, N. and G. Miller. 1958. Finite state languages. *Information and Control* 1.91–112.
Turing, A.M. 1936. On computable numbers with an application to the *Entscheidungsproblem*. *Proceedings of the London Mathematical Society* 27:2.230–65.

Turkana ⇒ Chari-Nile languages

Turkic

Branch of the **Altaic** languages with about thirty closely related languages and 80 million speakers in Central Asia and Asia Minor; a written tradition has existed for over 1,000 years. The largest languages are **Turkish** (about 45 million speakers), Uzbeki (about 10 million speakers), and Azerbaijani (about 8 million speakers).

References
Boeschoeten, H.E. and L. Verhoeven. 1991. *Turkish linguistics today*. Leiden.
Menges, K.H. 1968. *The Turkic languages and peoples*. Wiesbaden. (2nd corr. edn 1993.)
Rona-Tas, A. 1991. *An introduction to Turkology*. Szeged.
Spuler, B. (ed.) 1963. *Turkologie*. (Handbuch der Orientaliskik I, vol. 5,1.) Leiden. (Repr. with additions 1982.)

Bibliography
Hazai, G. and B. Kellner-Heinkele. 1986. *Bibliographisches Handbuch der Turkologie: eine Bibliographie der Bibliographien vom 18. Jahrhundert bis 1979*, vol. I. Wiesbaden. (Vol. 2, 3 in prep.)

Dictionary
Waterson, N. 1980. *Uzbek–English dictionary*. Oxford.

Turkish

Largest **Turkic** language with approx. 45 million speakers, the official language of Turkey.

Characteristics (many of which are typical of **Altaic** languages): **vowel harmony**, rich **agglutinating** morphology, rich case system, agreement, SOV word order which can be changed fairly freely, subordination of relative clauses by special participial verb forms (converbs); simple number system (where the plural is not expressed if a number is connected with the noun). Possessive constructions of the type *the man his donkey*. Turkish has a long literary tradition (until 1928 in Arabic script, now Latin alphabet). Numerous lexical borrowings from **Persian** and **Arabic**, which have been partially suppressed in language reforms.

References

Ergunvanli, E.E. 1984. *The function of word order in Turkish grammar*. Berkeley, CA.

Lees, R.B. 1961. *The phonology of Modern Standard Turkish*. Bloomington, IN.

Lewis, G.L. 1967. *Turkish grammar*. Oxford.

Slobin, D. and K. Zimmer (eds) 1986. *Studies in Turkish linguistics*. Amsterdam.

Underhill, R. 1976. *Turkish grammar*. Cambridge, MA.

Dictionary

Iz, F., H.C. Hony, and A.D. Alderson (eds) 1978/84. *The Oxford Turkish dictionary, Turkish–English*, 3rd edn, *English–Turkish*, 2nd edn, 2 vols. Oxford. (Reissued in 1 vol. 1991.)

turn

Engaging in talk implies that participants take turns. Various turn definitions exist. (a) A turn is determined by formal criteria, e.g. emphasizing the boundaries, i.e. a turn is delimited by pauses/silences, or it is identified as a syntactic unit, which allows for subsequent **turn-taking**. (b) A turn is determined by functional criteria, e.g. it coincides with at least one move (**interchange**); thus, **back channel** does not constitute a turn. (c) A turn is considered to be a turn-in-a-series, whose length and structure is determined interactively (**recipient design**, **sequential organization**, **turn-taking**); ideally, such a turn has a tripartite structure, as B's answer to A: its first part establishes some relationship to the prior turn, its third part some relation to the following turn (cf. *well* and the tag question *couldn't I*, respectively, in B's utterance):

A: *How can he get to the station?*
B: *Well, I could drive him, couldn't I?*
A: *Oh, yes, please do.*

References

Atkinson, J. and J. Heritage (eds) 1984. *Structures of social action: studies in conversational analysis*. Cambridge.

Boden, D. and D. Zimmermann (eds) 1991. *Talk and social structure*. Cambridge.

Edelsky, C. 1981. Who's got the floor? *LSoc* 10.383–421.

Goodwin, C. 1981. *Conversational organization: interaction between speakers and hearers*. New York.

Goodwin, C. and J. Heritage. 1990. Conversation analysis. *Annual Review of Anthropology* 19.283–307.

Goodwin, M.H. 1990. *He-said-she-said: talk as social organization among black children*. Bloomington, IN.

Grimshaw, A. 1990. *Conflict talk*. New York.

Jaffe, J. & S. Feldstein. 1970. *Rhythms of dialogue*. New York.

Maynard, D. (ed.) 1987. *Language and social interaction*. Special issue of *Social Psychology Quarterly* 50.101–226.

Maynard, D. and S. Clayman. 1991. The diversity of ethnomethodology. *Annual Review of Sociology* 17.385–418.

Owen, M. 1981. Conversational units and the use of 'well'. In P. Werth (ed.), *Conversation and discourse*. London. 99–116.

Sacks, H., E.A. Schegloff, and G. Jefferson. 1974. A simplest systematics for the organization of turn-taking for conversation. *Lg* 50.696–735.

Schegloff, E. 1979. The relevance of repair to syntax-for-conversation. In T. Givón (ed.), *Syntax and semantics*, vol. 12. *Discourse and syntax*. New York. 261–86.

turn-taking

Turn-taking is a basic characteristic in interactions, but its realizations are culturally bound, change with age (e.g. Philips 1976; Garvey and Berninger 1981) and vary from discourse type to discourse type. Turn-taking is discussed in various models (for an overview see Wiemann and Knapp 1975; Wilson *et al* 1984): (a) a turn-taking system as a stochastic model, a simulation of statistically frequent patterns; physical properties of acoustic signals are analyzed in sequence and during simultaneous speaking and patterns of silence. Turn transition is treated as a probabilistic process (e.g. Jaffe and Feldstein 1979); (b) turn-taking based on a set of discrete, conventional verbal and non-verbal signals to be defined independently (e.g. Duncan and Fiske 1977); (c) turn-taking as an interactive mechanism that guarantees a no-gap procedure since it is managed locally by the participants, i.e. who is talking to whom about what for how long is determined by the speaker and the listener at each place where transfer is possible ('transition relevance place') potentially, after a syntagm. In such a place, either the speaker designated by the prior speaker (via verbal or non-verbal means, e.g. **adjacency pair**) or the speaker who is first to start takes a turn, or the current speaker continues. Thus, this system of turn-taking is considered to

provide an intrinsic motivation for the participants to listen (**sequential organization,
turn**).

References
Duncan, S. and D.W. Fiske. 1977. *Face-to-face
interaction: research, methods and theory.* Hills-
dale, NJ.
Garvey, C. and G. Berninger. 1981. Timing and turn-
taking in children's conversations. *DPr* 4.27–57.
Goodwin, C. 1981. *Conversational organization:
interaction between speakers and hearers.* New
York.
Jaffe, J. and S. Feldstein. 1970. *Rhythms of dialogue.*
New York.
Philips, S.U. 1976. Some sources of cultural variability in the regulation of talk. *LSoc* 5.81–95.
Sacks, H., E. Schegloff, and G. Jefferson. 1974. A
simplest systematics for the organization of turn-
taking for conversation. *Lg* 50.696–735.
Wiemann, J.M. and M.L. Knapp. 1975. Turn-taking
in conversations. *JC* 25.75–92.
Wilson, T., J.M. Wiemann, and D.H. Zimmerman.
1984. Models of turn-taking. *JLSP* 3.159–83.
⇒ **conversation analysis**

Twi-Fante ⇒ Kwa

twin formula

A term from phraseology (⇒ **idiomatics**) to
indicate an unchanging word pair that is joined
by a conjunction or a preposition, often with
alliteration or assonance (e.g. tried and true).
The elements of a twin formula can be identical, synonymous, antonymous or complementary. (⇒ **formula**)

References
⇒ **idiomatics**

two-field theory

In K. Bühler's theory of language, principal
designation for the theory of the **index field of
language** (i.e. the situational context) and the
symbol field of language (i.e. the linguistic
context). (⇒ *also* **axiomatics of linguistics,
deixis, I–now–here origo**)

References
⇒ **axiomatics of linguistics**

type theory

Logical theory developed by B. Russell and
A.N. Whitehead based on a hierarchic gradation of logical objects (like **set, function,
relation**, and **predicate**). A set or a predicate
must always be on a higher level (or represent
a higher 'type') than the elements or objects
that are contained in the set or to which the
predicate can be applied. The purpose of this
conception is to avoid set-theoretical antinomies of Russell's type (the set of all sets that
themselves are not contained as an element
would simultaneously contain and not contain
themselves). Russell himself first proposed a
'bifurcated theory of types' which was modified in the second edition of the *Principia* to
the so-called 'simple theory of types.' In
Church's (1940) formulation, this became the
basis of R. Montague's 'intensional type logic,'
which entered theoretical linguistics as the
logical language of description called **Montague grammar**.

References
Church, A. 1940. A formulation of the simple theory
of types. *Symbolic Logic* 5.
Copi, I.M. 1971. *The theory of logical types.* Lon-
don.
Gallin, D. 1975. *Intensional and higher order modal
logic.* Amsterdam.
Montague, R. 1974. Universal grammar. In R.H.
Thomason (ed.), *Formal philosophy: selected
papers of R. Montague.* New Haven, CT. 222–46.
(Orig. 1970.)
Whitehead, A.N. and B. Russell. 1910/13. *Principia
mathematica.* Cambridge. (2nd edn 1925/27. Repr.
1950.)

type–token relation

Term from statistics used to distinguish
between individual linguistic expressions (=
tokens) and the abstract class of which these
tokens are members (= types). This type–token
relationship corresponds to the relationship
between **langue vs parole**, as well as the
distinction between **etic vs emic analysis**.

Tzeltal ⇒ Mayan languages

U

Ubangi ⇒ Adamawa-Ubangi

Ubykh ⇒ North-West Caucasian

Udmurt ⇒ Finno-Ugric

Ugaritic ⇒ Semitic

Ugric ⇒ Finno-Ugric

Ukrainian

East **Slavic** language with approx. 35 million speakers, primarily in the Ukraine, but also in other former Soviet republics, the eastern Balkans, and Canada. Ukrainian began to develop as a literary language at the end of the eighteenth century, before which the East Slavic recension of **Old Church Slavic** was used. The modern literary language has developed since 1918. Ukrainian is written in the **Cyrillic** alphabet with the additional characters ⟨„‚⟩ (only in emigrant publications), ⟨ï⟩. Ukrainian, **Russian**, and **Belorussian** have a high degree of mutual intelligibility.

References
Grammars
Bilodid, I. (ed.) 1969–1973. *Sučasna ukraïns'ka literaturna mova*, 5 vols. Kiev.
Danylenko, A. and S. Vakulenko. 1994. *Ukrainian*. Munich.
Humesky, A. 1980. *Modern Ukrainian*. Edmonton.
Medushevskyi, A.P. 1963. *Ukrainian grammar*. Kiev.
Shevelov, G.Y. 1963. *The syntax of modern literary Ukrainian: the simple sentence*. The Hague.
Stechischin, J.W. 1977. *Ukrainian grammar*, 6th edn. Winnipeg.

History and dialectology:
Atlas ukraïns'koï movy. 1984/8. 2 vols. Kiev.
Ilarion, Metropolitan of Winnipeg and All Canada. 1980. *Istorija ukranïs'koï literaturnoï movy*, 3rd edn. Winnipeg.
Istorija ukraïns'koï movy. 1978–83. 5 vols. Kiev.
Shevelov, G.Y. 1979. *A historical phonology of the Ukrainian language*. Heidelberg.

Dictionary
Slovnyk ukraïns'koï movy. 1970–80. 11 vols. Kiev.

Etymological dictionary
Mel'nyčuk, O. 1982– . *Etymolohičnyj slovnyk ukraïns'koï movy v semy tomax*. (Vols 1–3 by 1993.) Kiev.

Bibliography
Červinska, L.F. 1985. *Pokažčyk z ukraïns'koï movy. Charkiv 1929–1930: Materialien zu einer ukrai-*
nistischen sprachwissenschaftlichen Bibliographie. Kiev.
⇒ **Slavic**

ultimate [Lat. *ultimus* 'end; last']

The last **syllable** of a word.

umlaut (*also* vowel mutation)

1 German term for an (anticipated, partial) **assimilation** of the **vowel** of the syllable with main stress to the vowel of the following (secondary stressed or unstressed) syllable (⇒ **vowel harmony**). A distinction can be drawn between **palatalization** (or 'fronting'), velarization (or 'backing,' ⇒ **secondary articulation**), raising, and lowering (⇒ **raising vs lowering**). The most significant example is *i*-umlaut, found in all Germanic dialects (with the exception of **Gothic**), which brought about a palatalization of back vowels and a palatalization and raising of low vowels. English reflexes of *i*-umlaut can be found in various plural forms (e.g. *mouse > mice*) and in other cases (e.g. *drench < West Gmc. *drankjan*). When the conditioners for umlaut disappeared, umlaut became grammaticalized (⇒ **grammaticalization, morphologization**). This is especially clear in languages such as German, where umlaut plays a role in plural formation (*Haus : Häuser* 'house : houses') and in derivation (*Häuschen* 'little house'). *A*-umlaut, which occurred in various Germanic dialects, is also known as **breaking**.

References
Bach, E.R. and D. King. 1970. Umlaut in modern German. *Glossa* 4.3–21.
Hamans, C. 1985. Umlaut in a Dutch dialect. In H. van der Hulst and N. Smith (eds), *Advances in nonlinear phonology*, Dordrecht. 267–303.
King, R. 1969. *Historical linguistics and generative grammar*. Frankfurt.
Lieber, R. 1981. On the organization of the lexicon. Bloomington, IN.
Penzl, H. 1949. Umlaut and secondary umlaut in Old High German. *Language* 25.233–45. -
Robinson, O.W. 1975. Abstract phonology and the history of Umlaut. *Lingua* 37.1–29.
Twaddell, W.F. 1938. A note on Old High German umlaut. *Monatshefte* 30.177–81.
Wurzel, W.U. 1984. Was bezeichnet der Umlaut im Deutschen? *ZPSK* 37.647–63.

2 **Diacritic** used in **German** (*ä, ö, ü*), **Swedish**

(*ä*, *ö*), and **Icelandic** (*ö*) to mark vowel muta-tion (**umlaut**[1]). (⇒ *also* **diaeresis**)

unaccusative (*also* unaccusative or ergative hypothesis)

A certain class of intransitive verbs in **nom-inative** languages such as German, Dutch, Italian, or French that are often analyzed as syntactically unaccusative or ergative. The terms unaccusative or ergative have been justi-fied by a very broad definition of ergativity (⇒ **ergative language**): the subjects of the ergative intransitive verbs share some properties with the objects of transitive verbs. Cf. *Das Kind* (Subj.) *zerbrach den Stock* (Acc. Obj.) 'The child broke the stick' vs *Der Stock* (Subj.) *zerbrach* 'The stick broke.' This is quite obvi-ous in this pair of sentences, where a lexical derivation rule connects a transitive verb with its intransitive variant (described as ergativity by Lyons 1968 and Anderson 1971). Within **Relational Grammar** (Perlmutter 1978; Davies 1984) and generative grammar (van den Besten 1985; Burzio 1986; Grewendorf 1989) these facts were treated syntactically by analyz-ing the surface subjects of unaccusative (or ergative) verbs as underlying objects. Certain syntactic constructions are supposed to be sen-sitive to this distinction in that they either apply only to unaccusatives (e.g. *ne*-cliticization in Italian, perfect auxiliary selection in **Italian**, **German**, and **Dutch**, attributive use of past participles, topicalization of subject + past participle in German), or only to standard unergative verbs (e.g. impersonal passives, cre-ation of *-er* agent nouns). Cf. *Das Kind hat gelacht* 'The child has laughed' vs *Das Kind ist weggegangen* 'The child has gone away,' *Hier wurde gelacht* 'Somebody laughed here' vs **Hier wurde weggegangen* 'Somebody went away.' Linguists working with ergative lan-guages have criticized the use of the term ergative for the phenomena mentioned above, since they are different from the morphological and syntactic ergativity found in ergative lan-guages (cf. Comrie 1978; Dixon 1987; Primus 1994). Every genuine ergative language is morphologically ergative, i.e. uses the zero-marked case, the **absolutive**, for *den Stock/der Stock* in the examples above. Furthermore, in a genuine ergative language *den Stock/der Stock* are expected to behave syntactically like sub-jects in a nominative language. Contrary to what is expected, these noun phrases behave like surface or underlying objects in nominative languages.

There are also semantic analyses of the two types of intransitive verbs mentioned above and these are neutral with respect to the ergative hypothesis. The overviews in van Valin (1990), Dowty (1991), and Primus (1994) clarify the matters typologically: the two types of intrans-itive verbs characterize what is commonly called split intransitivity within more recent research. Split intransitivity is the defining property of the **active language** type.

References
Anderson, J.M. 1971. *The grammar of case*. Cam-bridge.
Burzio, L. 1981. *Intransitive verbs and Italian aux-iliaries*. Cambridge, MA.
——— 1986. *Italian Syntax: a Government–Binding approach*. Dordrecht.
Comrie, B. 1978. Ergativity. In W.P. Lehmann (ed.), *Syntactic typology: studies in the phenomenology of language*. Austin, TX. 329–94.
Davies, W.D. 1984. Antipassives: Choctaw evidence for universal characterization. In D.M. Perlmutter and C.G. Rosen (eds), *Studies in relational gram-mar*. Chicago, IL. 331–76.
Dixon, R.M.W. (ed.) 1987. *Studies in ergativity*. *Lingua* 71 (special issue).
Dowty, D. 1991. Thematic proto-roles, proto-roles, and argument selections. *Lg* 67.547–691.
Grewendorf, G. 1989. *Ergativity in German*. Dor-drecht.
Keyser, J. and T. Roeper. 1984. On the middle and ergative constructions in English. *LIn* 15.381–416.
Levin, B. and M. Rappaport Hovav. 1992. The lexical semantics of verbs of motion: the perspective from unaccusativity. In I. Roca (ed.), *Thematic struc-ture: its role in grammar*. Berlin and New York. 247–69.
Lyons, J. 1968. *Introduction to theoretical linguis-tics*. Cambridge.
Perlmutter, D.M. 1978. Impersonal passives and the unaccusative hypothesis. *PBLS* 4.157–89. Berke-ley, CA.
Primus, B. 1994. Relational typology. In J. Jacobs *et al.* (eds), *Syntax: an international handbook of contemporary research*. Berlin. Vol. 2, 1076–109.
Shannon, T. 1990. The unaccusative hypothesis and the history of the perfect auxiliary in Germanic and Romance. In H. Andernes and K. Koerner (eds), *Historical linguistics, 1987*. Amsterdam. 461–88.
Valin, R.D. van. 1990. Semantic parameters of split intransitivity. *Lg* 66.221–60.
van den Besten, H. 1985. Some remarks on the Ergative Hypothesis. In W. Abraham (eds), *Erklär-ende Syntax des Deutschen*. Tübingen. 53–74.

unaccusative hypothesis ⇒ unaccusative

unchecked ⇒ checked vs unchecked

uncial

A wide-spread Roman book script whose capi-tal letters are rounded off and have no broken lines.

References
⇒ writing

underlying form (*also* underlying representation)

In generative **phonology**, the hypothetical abstract base form described with binary **distinctive features** and transformed by **phonological rules** (such as **assimilation**, **palatalization**, and others) into their respective concrete (i.e. phonetic) forms. For example, in representing devoicing of voiced consonants, one proceeds from underlying voiced consonants (hence: /fɪʃd/ for *fished*, as opposed to /fɪʃt/) (⇒ **voiced vs voiceless**). The voiceless variants of the **surface structure** are given through a corresponding phonological rule. 'Room for play' between the underlying form and the realized form becomes more and more restricted with regard to requirements such as learnability (⇒ **abstractness controversy**).

References
⇒ phonology

underlying representation ⇒ underlying form

underlying structure ⇒ deep structure

unification ⇒ unification grammar

unification grammar

1 In its broadest sense, an umbrella term for all generative grammar models, especially those generative grammars that use a unification operation in their rule systems.

2 In a narrower sense, a member of a family of newer grammatical models in which feature unification is used (usually in conjunction with other feature operations) to capture the information flow in derivation. Various particular approaches belong to this group: grammatical models like **Generalized Phrase Structure Grammar** (GPSG) and **Lexical-Functional Grammar** (LFG), grammatical formalisms capable of producing expressions for implementation on the computer, like **Functional Unification Grammar** (FUG) and **PATR-II**; as well as a series of newer models that present forms mixed from existing approaches and theories like **Head-driven Phrase Structure Grammar** (HPSG) and **Categorial Unification Grammar** (CUG). Since all these models were developed at Stanford University and at neighboring institutions in the San Francisco Bay Area, they are known as Bay Area Grammars. Other terminology includes Unification-based Grammars, Constraint-based Grammars, and Information-based Grammars. Unification

grammar is based on the further development of linguistic **features**. Every linguistic unit (word or phrase) is characterized by a **feature structure**, that is, by a number of attribute–value pairs, whose values can be either atomic symbols or feature structures. Attributive values within a feature structure can be coreferential (also co-indexed), that is, they can describe the same linguistic unit. Feature structures for syntactic units are often termed 'complex categories.' They are usually represented as feature matrices (Figure 1) or feature graphics (Figure 2). In the following simplified feature structure of a verb, the coreference of the [AGR] features induces the **agreement** between the verb and the subject.

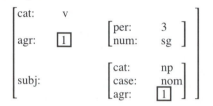

Figure 1 Feature matrix

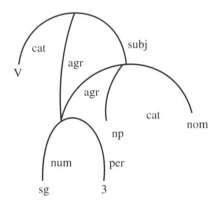

Figure 2 Equivalent feature graph

In a unification grammar, phrase structure rules indicate which parts of the feature structure of a syntactic unit are coreferent with which parts of the feature structure of their immediate constituents and which are co-referent (⇒ **coreferentiality**) with the feature structure of the immediately dominating constituent. These coreferences between the descriptions of the constituents in a syntactic tree take care of the information flow in syntactic derivation and are used to represent dependencies between constituents (agreement, **government**, **control**, and non-local dependencies). Coreference of two feature structures means that their contents are 'unified.' If the contents do not contradict each other (i.e. assign incompatible values to at least one feature), the result is unification by the addition of the information in the two unified structures. In the case of a contradiction, the unification does not succeed, and a special category is generated which signals the inconsistency. The unification is usually expressed by brackets, which include the feature structures to be unified. Equivalent notations for Figures 1 and 2 are:

$$\begin{bmatrix} \text{per:} & 3 \\ \text{num:} & \text{sg} \end{bmatrix} = \begin{bmatrix} \text{per: } 3 \end{bmatrix} \wedge \begin{bmatrix} \text{num: sg} \end{bmatrix}$$

$$= \begin{bmatrix} \text{per: } 3 \end{bmatrix} \cup \begin{bmatrix} \text{num: sg} \end{bmatrix}$$

A unification grammar was first suggested by Kay (1979). Independent representational formalisms with unification structures were developed in related work in the area of **knowledge representation** in **artificial intelligence** (Ait-Kaci 1984; Smolka and Ait-Kaci 1987). The semantics of unification formalisms was developed by Kaspar and Rounds (1986), Johnson (1988), and Smolka (1988). The result of this work is a feature logic with a bundle theory semantics. A special property of unification grammar is its declarativity. This results from the monotonicity of the unification operation. The order of the steps applied is unimportant for the result of a derivation. In this respect, unification grammar is particularly suited to **computational linguistics**, since the grammar allows for multiple strategies. It is also not bound to a particular direction of processing; so the same grammar can be used for **parsing** and generation. Models of unification grammar are differentiated by the role which the phrase structure plays in the syntactic description. In most models, a context-free phrase structure tree is constructed by syntactic rules. The feature structures are associated with the phrase structure nodes and bound together by co-references. In other models (like FUG or HPSG), the phrase structure itself is represented inside the feature structure, so the feature structure is adequate for description. The models also differ in the extensions they use. Frequently used extensions of the grammatical formalisms are generalization or **disjunction**, **templates** (feature macros, type-names), **functional uncertainty** and **value bundle features**. Significant differences are also found in the expansion of the types of description on the grammatical level: while, for example, GPSG describes only syntactic conformities with the help of feature structures, the feature-based descriptions of HPSG also extend to semantics

and phonology. While there are only a few investigations in phonology and phonetics, in semantics there are several attempts to integrate **situation semantics** and **discourse representation theory** into models of unification grammar (e.g. Johnson and Klein 1986; Fenstad *et al.* 1987; Pollard and Sag 1988). In addition to the models of Bay Area Grammar, in their broadest sense later developments like Tree Unification Grammar (TUG) are also unification grammars (Popowich 1989). It is also necessary to include the **logical grammars** from the tradition of logic programming, in which the feature structures are represented by logic terms and term unification plays the role of feature unification. Theoretically, every formal generative grammar model could probably be encoded as a unification grammar. Thus there are already suggestions that existing grammatical models like **dependency grammar** and Tree-Adjoining Grammar be supplemented by using the tools of unification grammar (Hellwig 1986; Vijay-Shanker and Joshi 1988).

References

Ait-Kaci, H. 1984. *A new model of computation based on a calculus of type subsumption*. Philadelphia, PA.

Bresnan, J. (ed.) 1982. *The mental representation of grammatical relations*. Cambridge, MA.

Calder, J., E. Klein, and H. Zeevat. 1988. Unification Categorial Grammar: a concise, extendible grammar for natural language processing. In *COLING 88*. Budapest. Vol. 1, 83–6.

Fenstad, J.E., P.K. Halvorsen, T. Langholm, and J. van Benthem. 1987. *Situations, language and logic*. Dordrecht.

Gazdar, G. *et al.* 1985. *Generalized Phrase Structure Grammar*. Cambridge, MA.

Hellwig, P. 1986. Dependency Unification Grammar. In *COLING 86*. Bonn. 195–8.

Johnson, M. 1988. *Attribute–value logic and the theory of grammar*. Stanford, CA.

Johnson, M. and E. Klein. 1986. Discourse, anaphora and parsing. In *COLING 86*. Bonn. 669–75.

Kasper, R. and W. Rounds. 1986. A logical semantics for feature structures. In *ACL proceedings 24*. New York. 257–66.

Kay, M. 1979. Functional Grammar. *PBLS* 5.142–58.

——— 1984. Functional Unification Grammar. In *COLING 84*. Stanford, CA. 75–8.

——— 1985. Parsing in Functional Unification Grammar. In D. Dowty, L. Karttunen, and A. Zwicky (eds), *Natural language parsing*. Cambridge. 251–78.

Pollard, C. and I.A. Sag. 1988. *An information-based syntax and semantics*, vol. 1: *Fundamentals*. (CSLI Lecture Notes 13.) Stanford, CA.

Popowich, F. 1989. Tree Unification Grammar. In *ACL proceedings 27*. Vancouver. 228–36.

Shieber, S.M. *et al.* 1983. The formalism and imple-

mentation of PATR-II. In *Research on interactive acquisition and use of knowledge. (SRI international.)* Menlo Park, CA. 39–79.
—— 1986. *An introduction to unification-based approaches to grammar.* (CSLI Lecture Notes 4.) Stanford, CA.
Shieber, S.M., L. Karttunen, and F. Pereira (eds) 1984. *Notes from the unification underground.* (SRI Technical Note 327.) Menlo Park, CA.
Smolka, G. 1988. A feature logic with subsorts. In *LILOG Report 33.* Stuttgart.
Smolka, G. and H. Ait-Kaci. 1987. Inheritance hierarchies: semantics and unification. *Journal of Symbolic Computation* 7.343–70.
Uszkoreit, H. 1986. Categorial Unification Grammars. In *COLING 86.* Bonn. 187–94.
—— 1988. From feature bundles to abstract data types: new directions in the representation and processing of linguistic knowledge. In A. Blaser (ed.), *Natural language at the computer.* Berlin. 31–64.
Vijay-Shanker, K. and A.K. Joshi. 1988. Feature structure based tree adjoining grammars. In *COLING 88.* Budapest. Vol. 2, 714–19.

unilateral implication ⇒ implication

union set ⇒ set

unique morpheme ⇒ pseudomorpheme, semi-morpheme

unitary base hypothesis

In Aronoff's (1976) theory of **word formation**, a presupposed condition that the syntactic-semantic specification of the **base** of every **word formation rule** is always unambiguous. According to the unitary base hypothesis, one and the same **affix** cannot be combined with two or more categories. Apparent counter-examples like N-*able* (*fashionable*) and V-*able* (*acceptable*) can be traced to homonymic affixes.

Reference
Aronoff, M. 1976. *Word formation in generative grammar.* Cambridge, MA.

universal [Lat. *universalis* 'having general application'] (*also* language universal)

Grammatical universals are properties (or hypotheses about such properties) which are common to all human languages. According to Greenberg (1966), the following formal and logical typology of universals can be postulated: (a) unrestricted universals (e.g. every language has vowels); (b) unidirectional implications between two properties (e.g. if a language has a **dual** in its number system, then it also has a **plural**, but not vice versa); (c) limited equivalence, which refers to bidirectional implications between non-universal properties (e.g. if a language has a lateral **click**, then it also

has a dental click and vice versa); (d) statistical universals, which have the character of quasi-universals (e.g. with very few exceptions, nasals occur in all the world's languages); (e) statistical correlations, which refer to the relations between properties (such as, if a certain property is present, e.g. a specification of the second person singular, then the probability of the third person being specified is greater than if the second person is not specified). Studies attempting to explain language universals generally assume one of the following three basic theoretical points of departure. (a) All languages have developed from one common language. Because all languages seem to be subject to constant change, this explanation is usually unsatisfactory. (b) Language fulfills the same functions in all language communities, and this has conditioned similar grammatical structures in all languages. (c) All languages have the same biological basis in humans with regard to their innate speech ability. Points (b) and (c) are not always mutually exclusive, but may actually complement each other. In the model going back to Noam Chomsky, universals are the basis of the innate **language acquisition device**, which enables children to learn the complex grammar of a natural language in a very short time (⇒ **universal grammar**). On universals of language change, see Kiparsky in Bach and Harms 1968, King 1969.

References
Bach, E. and R.T. Harms. 1968. *Universals in linguistic theory.* New York.
Butterworth, B., B. Comrie, and Ö. Dahl (eds) 1984. *Explanations for language universals.* Berlin.
Chomsky, N. 1965. *Aspects of the theory of syntax.* Cambridge, MA.
—— 1975. *Reflections on language.* New York.
Comrie, B. 1981. *Language universals and linguistic typology.* Oxford. (2nd edn 1989.)
Croft, W. 1990. *Typology and universals.* Cambridge.
Décsy, G. (ed.) 1988. *A select catalog of language universals.* Bloomington, IN.
Goddard, C. and A. Wierzbicka (eds) 1994. *Semantics and lexical universals.* Amsterdam and Philadelphia, PA.
Greenberg, J.H. (ed.) 1963. *Universals of language.* Cambridge, MA.
—— 1966. *Language universals, with special reference to feature hierarchies.* The Hague.
—— 1986. *The role of universals in linguistic explanation.* Stanford, CA.
Greenberg J.H. *et al* (eds) 1978. *Universals of human language,* 4 vols. Stanford, CA.
Hawkins, J.A. (ed.) 1988. *Explaining language universals.* Oxford.
Hawkins, J.A. and M. Grell-Mann (eds) 1992. *The evolution of human languages.* Reading, MA.

King, R. 1969. *Historical linguistics and generative grammar*. Englewood Cliffs, NJ.

Lehmann, W.P. 1978. *Syntactic typology: studies in the phenomenology of language*. Austin, TX.

Rutherford, W.E. 1987. *Language universals and second language acquisition*, 2nd edn. Amsterdam.

Seiler, H. *et al.* (eds) 1982–6. *Apprehension*, 3 vols. Tübingen.

Seiler, H. and W. Premper. 1989. *Partizipation*. Tübingen.

⇒ **language typology**, **semantics**

universal grammar

1 ⇒ **general grammar**

2 In N. Chomsky's Revised Extended Standard Theory (= REST) of **transformational grammar**, universal grammar corresponds to the genetically determined biological foundations of language acquisition. The goal of linguistic description is to postulate general traits and tendencies in all languages on the basis of studies on grammars of individual languages. These universal structures are seen in correlation with psychological phenomena of linguistic development. The concept of universal grammar is based on the assumption of an unmarked **core grammar** describing the 'natural case,' which is seen as part of competence (⇒ **competence vs performance**). Through maturation, i.e. actualization of the rules and constraints in individual languages, the specific individual grammar is developed on the basis of universal grammar. (⇒ *also* **markedness**)

References

Arnold, D. *et al.* (eds) 1989. *Essays on grammatical theory and universal grammar*. Oxford.

Chomsky, N. 1975. *Reflections on language*. New York.

Cook, V. 1988. *Chomsky's universal grammar*. Oxford.

Eubank, L. 1990. *Point counterpoint: universal grammar in the second language*. Amsterdam.

Halle, M., J. Bresnan, and G.A. Miller (eds) 1978. *Linguistic theory and psychological reality*. Cambridge, MA.

Hornstein, N. 1990. *As time goes by: tense and universal grammar*. Cambridge, MA.

Lightfoot, D. 1991. *How to set parameters: arguments from language change*. Cambridge, MA.

Saleemi, A.P. 1992. *Universal grammar and language learnability*. Cambridge.

Smith, C.S. 1991. *The parameter of aspect*. Dordrecht.

Speas, M.J. 1990. *Phrase structure in natural language*. Dordrecht.

White, L. 1989. *Universal grammar and second language acquisition*. Amsterdam and Philadelphia, PA.

⇒ **language acquisition**, **language acquisition device**, **logical form**, **sign language**, **transformational grammar**

universal language

1 **Artificial language** usually modeled after a mathematical system of signs and used as a formal language and a means of representing information in philosophy and science. G.W. Leibniz's idea of a 'characteristica universalis,' in which the logical relationship of simple ideas to complex thoughts was to be illustrated through corresponding combinations of signs, is particularly well known. In the modern notational system of mathematics, **formal logic**, physics, and chemistry, the ideal of a universal language has become partly realized.

2 ⇒ **interlingua**

universal operator ⇒ operator

universal proposition

Proposition about all elements (individuals, states of affairs, and the like) of a particular domain, in contrast to **existential propositions** which refer to at least one element of a certain domain. In **formal logic**, universal propositions are symbolized by means of the so-called universal **quantifier**: $\forall x\,[H(x) \rightarrow M(x)]$, read as: 'for every x it is the case that if x has the property H (e.g. "being human"), then it also has the property M (e.g. "being mortal").' As a rule, propositions about scientific laws take the form of universal propositions.

universal quantifier ⇒ operator

unmarked word order ⇒ word order

unmotivated ⇒ arbitrariness

unrounded ⇒ rounded vs unrounded

unrounding (*also* delabialization)

Articulatory change (usually caused, in turn, by other processes of change) of rounded front vowels to less marked, 'simpler' unrounded vowels, e.g. the unrounding of the front vowels [y, ø] brought about by **umlaut** to [i, e] in English and in some German dialects. (⇒ *also* **labialization**)

References

⇒ **language change**, **sound change**

upper case vs lower case ⇒ capital vs small

Uralic

Language family of northwestern Asia and eastern Europe consisting of two branches: the **Finno-Ugric** languages (about twenty languages, 22 million speakers, **Finnish** and **Hungarian** are the best known) and the Samoyedic languages in the Urals (about five languages,

30,000 speakers, largest language Nenets). Yukagiric in northern Siberia (a few hundred speakers) is probably related to the Uralic languages; both are generally combined into a Uralic-Yukagiric language group. A possible relationship to the **Altaic** languages has been suggested, as well as to Chukchi (⇒ **Paleo-Siberian**) and **Indo-European**.

The relatedness of the Uralic languages was already established before that of the Indo-European languages (the Finno-Ugric languages in the seventeenth century, the Uralic languages altogether at the end of the eighteenth century by the Hungarian S. Gyarmathi).

Characteristics: typologically quite diverse; most have rich morphology (**agglutinating**). Well-developed case systems, often with numerous adverbials, e.g. locative case. The verb often agrees with the subject and the object, which can sometimes show focusing. Word order: SOV, sometimes SVO or free word order. Negation expressed by an auxiliary. No true sentence conjunction; instead, numerous infinitive forms for subordinating clauses (converbs). In the smaller languages **dual** pronominal forms sometimes occur; number marking with nouns is not well developed. A large inventory of vowels; **vowel harmony** is widespread.

References
Abondolo, D. (ed.) 1996. *The Uralic languages*. London.
Bouda, K. 1952 *Die Verwandtschaftsverhältnisse der tschuktschischen Sprachgruppe (Tschuktschisch, Korjakisch, Kamtschatkisch)*. Salamanca.
Collinder, B. 1960. *Comparative grammar of the Uralic languages*, handbook 3. Stockholm.
——— 1965a. *Hat das Uralische Verwandte? Eine sprachvergleichende Untersuchung*. Uppsala.
——— 1965b. *An introduction to the Uralic languages*. Berkeley, CA.
——— 1969. *Survey of the Uralic languages*, handbook 2, 2nd edn. Hamburg.
Comrie, B. 1981. *The languages of the Soviet Union*. Cambridge.
Hajdú, P. and D. Hajdú. 1987. *Die uralischen Sprachen und Literaturen*. Hamburg.
Sinor, D. (ed.) 1988. *The Uralic languages. Description, history and foreign influences*. (Handbuch der Orientalistik 8, vol. I.) Leiden.

Etymological dictionaries
Collinder, B. 1977. *An etymological dictionary of the Uralic languages*, handbook 1, 2nd edn. Hamburg.
Reidei, K. 1988–91. *Uralisches etymologisches Wörterbuch*, 3 vols. Wiesbaden.

Journal
Mémoires de la Société Finno-Ougriénne. Ural-Altaische Jahrbücher.

Urdu ⇒ Hindi-Urdu

use ⇒ usage vs use

user modeling

In **dialogue systems**, a component which attempts to be sensitive to the various sorts of users a system may encounter. Such user modeling takes into account user aspects, such as the degree of domain expertise, the degree of system familiarity (knowing how to use the specific system), the various purposes a system may serve for users, and perhaps even past system use. The linguistic basis of user modeling is found in **speech act theory** and **conversation analysis**.

References
Computational Linguistics. 1988. Special issue in user modeling.
Wahlster, W. and A. Kobsa (eds) 1988. *User modeling in dialog systems*. Berlin.

Journal
User Modeling and User-Adapted Interaction.

Uto-Aztecan

Language family of North and Central America with approx. twenty-five languages divided into 8 different branches. Among the Uto-Aztecan languages are **Nahuatl**, the language of the Aztec empire (today approx. 1.2 million speakers in Mexico), Tarahumara in northern Mexico (about 35,000 speakers), Pima-Papago (about 25,000 speakers) and **Hopi** (about 7,000 speakers) in Arizona. The reconstruction of Uto-Aztecan is surprisingly advanced; it was proposed as a group in 1859 by J.K. Buschmann. Typologically the Uto-Aztecan languages are very diverse.

References
Bright, W. (ed.) 1992. *The collected works of Edward Sapir*, vol. X: *Southern Paiute and Ute linguistics and ethnography*. Berlin and New York.
Campbell, L. 1985. *The Pipil language of El Salvador*. Berlin.
Givón, T. 1981. *A grammar of Ute*. Ignaciao.
Hill, J.H. 1983. Language death in Uto-Aztecan. *IJAL* 49.258–76.
Langacker, R. 1977– . *Studies in Uto-Aztekan grammar*. Arlington, V A.
Miller, W.R. 1967. *Uto-Aztecan cognate sets*. Berkeley and Los Angeles, CA.
——— 1984. The classification of Uto-Aztekan languages based on lexical evidence. *IJAL* 50.1–24.
Steele, S. 1979. Uto-Aztecan: an assessment for historical and comparative linguistics. In L. Campbell and M. Mithun (eds), *The languages of native America: historical and comparative assessment*. Austin, TX. 444–544.
Voegelin, C.F., F.M. Voegelin, and K.L. Hale. 1962.

Typological and comparative grammar of Uto-Aztecan. Baltimore, MD.
⇒ **North and Central American languages**

utterance

1 The string of sounds or written symbols produced by a speaker between two pauses. An utterance can consist of a single word or several sentences. As opposed to the abstract term **sentence** which relates to the level of *langue* (⇒ **langue vs parole**), the utterance works on the level of the *parole* and refers to actual speech sequences in specific situations. (*also* **competence vs performance**

2 ⇒ **speech act theory**

utterance act

In J.R. Searle's **speech act theory**, a part of the performance of a speech act: the utterance of morphemes, words, sentences. An utterance act for Searle corresponds to Austin's **phonetic act** and **phatic act**. (⇒ *also* **locution**)

References
Austin, J.L. 1962. *How to do things with words.* Oxford.
Searle, J.R. 1969. *Speech acts: an essay in the philosophy of language.* Cambridge.

uvula

Protuberance at the back end of the **velum** used as a **place of articulation** in the formation of **uvular** sounds.

References
⇒ **phonetics**

uvular

Speech sound classified according to its **place of articulation** (**uvula**), e.g. the voiced fricative [ʁ] in Fr. [ʁuʒ] 'rouge,' the voiceless plosive [q] in Greenlandic [qaˈjaq] 'kayak' or [anoːʁaˈaq] 'anorak.'

References
⇒ **phonetics**

Uzbeki ⇒ **Turkic**

V

vagueness

Term that is complementary to **ambiguity**: whereas ambiguity refers to ambiguousness which in the framework of grammatical models is represented through multiple descriptions, vagueness in the sense of 'pragmatic indeterminacy' is predictable, but not the object of internal linguistic representation. An expression is pragmatically vague with respect to certain semantic features which it leaves unspecified; e.g. *person* is not specified with reference to the features [male] vs [female], [old] vs [young].

References
Channell, J. 1994. *Vague language*. Oxford.
⇒ **ambiguity**

valence [Lat. *valere* 'to be worth'] (*also* valency)

The term 'valence' comes from chemistry, where it is used to indicate the property of atoms to bind or replace a certain number of hydrogen atoms in a molecule. Its use in linguistics can be traced back to Tesnière (1959), although the concept of valence under different names can be found earlier in linguistics. Valence is the ability of a **lexeme** (e.g. verb, adjective, noun) to predetermine its syntactic environment in that it places certain requirements on the surrounding constituents in reference to their grammatical characteristics. Thus the verbs *greet* and *help* require a direct object (which cannot be omitted in the case of *greet*), *inhabit* requires a locative complement.

Closely related to valence is the concept of valence dependency (*also* valence binding). In a sentence, a constituent X is valence-dependent on a lexeme Y if at least one of the valence requirements of Y is present in X. In this case, X is a **complement** (Tesnière: *actant*) of the constituent containing Y.

In the older literature based on Tesnière's work, verbs are organized according to the number of complements they require: (a) zero-valence (*also* avalent) verbs, including **impersonal verbs** (although the *it* that is required can be considered to be a complement); (b) monovalent verbs: intransitive verbs such as *exist*, *sleep*; (c) bivalent verbs: transitive verbs with an object: *love*, *leave*, *hear*; (d) trivalent verbs such as *give*, *inform*, *characterize*. In newer works on valence, different classifications have been introduced which indicate not only the number, but also the type of complements that are required, especially in reference to semantic characteristics.

In order to distinguish between obligatory complements and free complements (= optional, **free adjunct**) which are not required by the verb, many different criteria and tests have been suggested: elimination test, replacement test, derivation of embedded sentences, ability to be added freely, association test. None of these tests (and no combination of them) is 100 percent reliable, however.

The concept of valence overlaps with traditional concepts such as **government** and **transitivity**, as well as with more recent concepts such as the relationship between **argument** and **predicate**, **complementation** and **modification** and **thematic relations** (⇒ **theta criterion**). These, as well as the number of suggested tests, point to the lack of a single unifying concept of valence. Such a theory of valence would need to handle the following problems. (a) What are reliable tests for valence-dependency? (b) At what level of the grammar (syntax, semantics, pragmatics, lexicon) must valence be handled, and what are the relationships between the manifestations of valence at these different levels? (c) What is the status of valence theory in individual languages, universal theory, and the study of language change? (d) What significance does valence have for the production of didactically oriented dictionaries or grammars? (⇒ *also* **dependency grammar**)

References
Abraham, W. (ed.) 1978. *Valence, semantic case and grammatical relations*. Amsterdam.
Allerton, D.J. 1982. *Valency and the English verb*. London.
Heringer, H.J. 1986. The verb and its semantic power: association as a basis for valence theory. *JoS* 4.79–99.
Lehmann, C. 1985. On grammatical relationality. *FoLi* 19.67–109.
Tesnière, L. 1959. *Eléments de syntaxe structurale*. Paris.

Bibliographies
Hays, D.G. 1965. *An annotated bibliography of publications on dependency theory*. Santa Monica, CA.
Schumacher, H. and N. Trautz. 1976. Bibliographie zur Valenz und Dependenz. In H. Schumacher

(ed.), *Untersuchungen zur Verbvalenz*. Tübingen. 317–43.

⇒ **dependency grammar**

Valencian ⇒ **Catalan**

valency ⇒ **valence**

value bundle feature

An extension of the descriptive apparatus of **unification grammar** by features that can have more than one value. Value bundle features are used in **Functional Unification Grammar**, **Lexical-Functional Grammar** and **Head-driven Phrase Structure Grammar**.

References
⇒ **unification grammar**

variability

Phonetic variability of a **vowel** during **articulation**. The difference between the features 'variable' vs 'constant' represents the difference between **diphthongs** and **monophthongs**.

References
⇒ **phonetics**

variable ⇒ **variability**

variable rule

Concept developed by Labov (1969) and Cedergren and Sankoff (1974) to describe linguistic variation using statistical methods. A speaker's choice between (at least) two linguistic (phonological, morphological, syntactic) alternatives and their dependency on linguistic and extralinguistic environmental conditions (phonological or syntactic context, discourse function of an utterance, situative context of a conversation, identity of the speaker with a particular social group, and so on) can be calculated using individual statistical models as an indication of the probability of use of a particular variable rule.

References
Cedergren, H. and D. Sankoff. 1974. Variable rules: performance as a statistical reflection of competence. *Lg* 50.333–55.
Labov, W. 1969. Contraction, deletion and inherent variability of the English copula. *Lg* 45.715–62.
Rousseau, P. and D. Sankoff. 1978. Advances in variable rule methodology. In D. Sankoff (ed.), *Linguistic variation: models and methods*. New York. 97–117.
Sankoff, D. 1988. Variable rules. In U. Ammon *et al.* (eds), *Soziolinguistik/Socolinguistics: an international handbook on the science of language and society*. Berlin. Vol. 3, 984–97.

variant

Distinctive realizations of abstract linguistic units on all levels of linguistic description, e.g.

the **allophones** [d] and [t], according to their distribution, form combinatory phonetic variants of the phoneme /d/, cf. [sɛd] vs [fɪʃt] in *said* vs *fished*. There are also 'free variants,' whose distribution is not environmentally conditioned, cf. the different realizations of *r* in English.

References
⇒ **phonology**

variational linguistics

In **sociolinguistics**, descriptive approaches that presume the systematically ordered heterogeneity of natural languages. Such linguistic variants result from (a) spatial differences (⇒ **dialect**), (b) class-specific linguistic behavior, (c) situative factors (e.g. formal vs informal conversational contexts), (d) stages of language acquisition, (e) language contact, and (f) the origin and development of **pidgin** and **creole** languages. In all cases phonological, morphological, syntactic, lexical, and pragmatic traits of linguistic behavior vary with regard to extralinguistic factors. Concerning the empirical investigation and the theoretical description of linguistic variations, two recent methodological positions can be differentiated: first, the concept of quantitatively determinable **variable rules** (see Labov, Cedergren and Sankoff); and second, the approach of **implicational analysis** (see DeCamp, Bailey, Bickerton). Besides the description of linguistic variety, variational linguistics is concerned with the problems of the origin and quantification of linguistic varieties in relation to extralinguistic factors, above all with certain aspects of **applied linguistics** such as **linguistic norms**, **language acquisition**, and **language contact**.

References
Bailey, C.-J.N. 1973. *Variation and linguistic theory*. Arlington, VA.
Biber, D. 1991. *Variation across speech and writing*. Cambridge.
Bickerton, D. 1971. Inherent variability and variable rules. *FL* 7.457–92.
Cedergren, N.J. and D. Sankoff. 1974. Variable rules: performance as a statistical reflection of competence. *Lg* 50.333–55.
Decamp, D. 1971. Implicational scales and sociolinguistic linearity. *Linguistics* 73.30–43.
Fasold, R.W. (ed.) 1983. *Variation in the form and use of language*. Washington, DC.
——— 1985. Perspectives on sociolinguistic variation. *LSoc* 14.515–25.
——— 1990. *The sociolinguistics of change*. Oxford.
Fasold, R.W. and D. Schiffrin (eds) 1989. *Language change and variation*. Amsterdam.
Fasold, R.W. and R.W. Shuy (eds) 1975. *Analyzing variation in language: papers from the second*

colloquium on New Ways of Analyzing Variation, 1973. Washington, DC.

—— 1977. *Studies in language variation: semantics, syntax, phonology, pragmatics, social situations, ethnographic approaches*. Washington, DC.

Labov, W. 1969. Contraction, deletion and inherent variability of the English copula. *Language* 45.715–62.

—— 1972. *Sociolinguistic patterns*. Philadelphia, PA.

Lieb, H.-H. 1993. *Linguistic variables: towards a unified theory of linguistic variation*. Amsterdam and Philadelphia, PA.

O'Donnell, W.R. and L. Todd. 1980. *Variety in contemporary English*. London.

Quirke, R. 1995. *Grammatical and lexical variance in English*. London.

Romaine, S. 1982. *Socio-historical linguistics: its status and methodology*. Cambridge.

Sankoff, D. (ed.) 1978. *Linguistic variation: models and methods*. New York.

—— (ed.) 1986. *Diversity and diachrony*. Amsterdam.

—— 1988a. Variable rules. In U. Ammon *et al.* (eds), *Sociolinguistics: an international handbook of the science of language and society*. Berlin and New York. Vol. 2, 984–97.

—— 1988b. Sociolinguistics and syntactic variation. In F. Newmeyer (ed.), *Linguistics: The Cambridge survey*. Cambridge. 140–61.

Sankoff, D. and H. Cedergren (eds) 1981. *Variation omnibus*. Edmonton.

Journals
Language Variation and Change.
⇒ **implicational analysis**, **variable rule**

variety

Generic term for a particular coherent form of language in which specific extralinguistic criteria can be used to define it as a variety. For example, a geographically defined variety is known as a **dialect**, a variety with a social basis as a **sociolect**, a functional variety as **jargon** or a **sublanguage**, a situative variety as a **register**.

Vedic ⇒ Indo-Aryan, Sanskrit

velar [Lat. *velum* 'sail']
Speech sound classified according to its **place of articulation** (velum), e.g. [kʰ] and [ŋ] in English [kʰiŋ] *king*. (⇒ *also* **articulatory phonetics**, **phonetics**)

References
⇒ **phonetics**

velaric

1 Of or referring to the **velum**.

2 Sounds formed with the velaric **airstream mechanism**.

velaric airstream mechanism ⇒ **airstream mechanism**

velarization ⇒ **secondary articulation**

velum

Soft, sail-shaped membrane attached to the hard palate that is used as a **place of articulation** in the formation of **velar** sounds.

References
⇒ **phonetics**

venetic ⇒ Indo-European

Venn diagram

Representational model for set-theoretical relations introduced in mathematical logic by the English logician J. Venn (1834–1923). With the aid of overlapping circles (or ellipses), relations between sets are illustrated. See the diagrams under **set**.

Veps ⇒ Finno-Ugric

verb [Lat. *verbum* 'word'; translation of Grk *rhēma* 'that which is said; predicate']

Type of word with a complex system of forms and functions. Verbs indicate phenomena which take place during time: activities, processes, and states. Morphologically, they are marked by **conjugation**, as well as the grammatical categories of **voice**, **mood**, **tense**, **person**, and **number** (the latter two in **agreement** with the subject), and in some languages, **aspect**. Because of its **valence**, the verb is the syntactic center of a sentence; it is related to the subject by agreement. Grammatically, finite forms (⇒ **finite verb form**) are distinguished from non-finite forms (⇒ **non-finite verb form**). **Main verbs** have different functions from **modal auxiliaries** in the formation of the predicate. The valence of the verb determines the number and kind of **complements**. The relationship between the subject and the verb is reflected in the distinction between **impersonal** and personal verbs; the object–verb relation is reflected in reciprocal (⇒ **reciprocity**) and **reflexive** use of verbs. The pattern of conjugation determines whether a verb is regular or irregular (⇒ **irregular verb**). Semantically, there exists a number of controversial classifications based both on semantics and syntax, such as the following: (a) action verbs (*read*, *buy*); (b) process verbs (*run*, *swim*, *climb*); (c) **stative verbs** (*sleep*, *live*, *stay*); (d) verbs of occurrence (*succeed*, *happen*); (e) **weather verbs** (*rain*, *snow*).

References
Aarts, B. and C.F. Meyer (eds). 1995. *The verb in*

contemporary English. A theory and description. Cambridge.

Bolinger, D. 1971. *The phrasal verb in English.* Cambridge, MA.

Kilby, D. 1984. *Descriptive syntax and the English verb.* London.

Lightfoot, D. and N. Hornstein (eds). 1994. *Verb movement.* Cambridge.

Palmer, F.R. 1987. *The English verb.* New York.

⇒ **complementation, conjugation, valence**

verb of action (*also* action-denoting verb)

Semantically defined class of verbs denoting activities: *learn, sing, write, swim.* (⇒ *also* **static vs dynamic, stative verb**)

verb of change ⇒ **transformative**

verb phrase (*abbrev.* VP)

Syntactic category of generative **transformational grammar** which functions as the immediate constituent of the sentence and which must contain a verb. According to the **valence** of the verb, the number and kind of the obligatory complements may vary; in addition, any number of free complements are possible. The border between obligatory and free complements is often difficult to draw.

References
⇒ **transformational grammar**

verba sentiendi

Semantically defined class of verbs that denote processes of sensual perception, belief, opinion, thought, feeling, etc. (e.g. *feel, believe, see, know,* etc.). In **Latin**, verba sentiendi are constructed with the **accusative** and an **infinitive** (*audio te ridere* 'I heard you laughing'). This type of construction is not possible in English, but is paralleled by constructions using the present participle or by *that-* or *how-*clauses: e.g. *I saw him working, I saw that he was working, I saw how he was working.* (⇒ **accusative plus infinitive construction**)

verbal adjective ⇒ **gerundive**

verbal agnosia ⇒ **agnosia**

verbal apraxia ⇒ **apraxia**

verbum substentium

Term in **Latin** grammar for the verb *esse* 'to be' when it is not used as a **auxiliary** verb, but rather as a main verb with the meaning 'presence,' 'existence,' 'behavior,' and the like.

verbal paraphasia ⇒ **paraphasia**

verbal repertoire

1 Seen individually, every set of linguistic varieties that a speaker commands and employs in specific contexts.

2 Seen collectively, the total set of all linguistic varieties that are at the disposal of the speakers of a **speech community**.

verbal vs root compound

In the **word formation** of Roeper and Siegel (1978), terms coined to denote two types of **composition**. Verbal compounds show, as their second element, a deverbal derivate; their first elements are understood as an argument of the base verb (*oven-cleaner, strange-sounding, expert-tested*). The relation that connects the first element with the second element of root compounds, on the other hand, is not grammatically given, but is basically open (*apron string*). (⇒ *also* **determinative compound, inheritance**)

References
Roeper, T. and M. Siegel, 1978. A lexical transformation for verbal compounds. *LingI* 9.199–259.

Selkirk, E. 1982. *The syntax of words.* Cambridge.

Verner's law

Discovered by the Dane Karl Verner in 1875 (published in 1877), an exception to the Germanic sound shift (⇒ **Grimm's law**) that was later designated as a 'law' by linguists. Based on comparative studies of **Sanskrit** and **Greek** with the **Germanic** dialects, Verner recognized that the placement of free word stress in **Indo-European** was the cause for apparent irregularities in the consonantism of etymologically related words which Grimm had dubbed '**grammatical alternation**.' According to Verner's observation, the Germanic voiceless **fricatives** [f, θ, χ, s] resulting from the Germanic sound shift became, in the proto-Germanic period, the corresponding voiced fricatives (β, ð, ɣ, z] in medial and final position when in a voiced environment, if the immediately preceding vowel did not carry the main stress; cf. IE *pətḗr, : Goth. *fadar* ('father') in contrast to OInd. *bhrā́tar* : Goth. *broþar* ('brother'). In the derivation of *father* the IE/Grk *t* developed into a voiced fricative (Goth. *d* = [ð]), since the stress lay behind the dental, while in *brother* the IE/OInd. *t*, according to the Germanic sound shift, was shifted to a voiceless fricative. Phonetically, this sound change can be plausibly explained by differences in air pressure according to the position of the stress; phonologically it is a matter of phoneme splitting (**sound change**), that takes place when the free stress in Germanic is fixed on the root syllable since, at that point in time, the original (allophonic) complementary distribution was suspended.

For synchronic reflexes of Verner's law, ⇒ **grammatical alternation**.

References
Collinge, N.E. 1985. *The laws of Indo-European.* Amsterdam and Philadelphia. 203–16.
Prokosch, E. 1938. *A comparative Germanic grammar.* Baltimore, MD.
Rooth, E. 1974. *Das Vernersche Gesetz in Forschung und Lehre.* Lund.
Verner, K. 1877. Eine Ausnahme der ersten Lautverschiebung. *ZVS* 23, new series 3.97–130.
⇒ **Germanic language change**, **sound change**

vibrant (*also* trill)

Speech sound classified according to its **manner of articulation**, namely intermittent articulation through the vibration of the lower lip, the tip of the tongue, or uvula against the upper lip (or upper teeth), alveolar ridge, hard palate (or back of the tongue), cf. [r] in **Italian** ['roːma] *Roma* 'Rome'; the fricative vibrant [r̝] in **Czech** ['dvoraːk] *Dvořák*. The trilled *r*-sounds in Spanish, French, and German are vibrants.

References
⇒ **phonetics**

Vietnamese

Largest **Mon-Khmer** language (approx. 50 million speakers), official language of Vietnam.
  Characteristics: **tonal language** (six tones); twelve vowels, also diphthongs and triphthongs. Morphologically **isolating**. Word order: SVO. Numerous lexical borrowings from **Chinese**; Chinese characters were previously used, but now a Latin alphabet with **diacritic** marks for marking tone is employed.

References
Emeneau, M.B. 1951. *Studies in Vietnamese (Annamese) grammar.* Berkeley, CA.
Khác Viên, N. *et al.* 1976. *Linguistic essays.* Hanoi.
Tompson, L.C. 1965. *A Vietnamese grammar.* Seattle, WA.
Van Chình, T. 1970. *Structure de la langue vietnamienne.* Paris.

visible speech

Process developed and so called by A.B. Bell as a way to make acoustic phenomena visible through corresponding graphic recording. Acoustic signals are measured with regard to **quantity** (= time co-ordinate), frequency (= **pitch**), and intensity (= amplitude) and made visible in **spectrograms**. Through such graphic representations of sound structures as they occur through time, **speech sounds** can be classified according to their acoustic characteristics. The binary phonological **oppositions** of Halle and Jakobson are based on the results of visible speech, which was developed originally as an aid for the instruction of deaf persons.

References
Bell, M. 1867. *Visible speech: universal alphabetics of self interpreting physiological letters for writing of all languages in one alphabet.* London.
Jakobson, R. and M. Halle. 1956. *Fundamentals of language.* The Hague. (2nd rev. edn 1975.)

visual agnosia ⇒ agnosia

vocabulary (*also* lexicon)

1 Total set of all the words in a language at a particular point in time. Quantitative data about the range of the vocabulary (e.g. over 1 million words for English) are problematic and depend on the particular estimate of the number of words (as 'word' is construed in each case) and whether vocabulary from **sublanguages** is counted as well. The average speaker has a vocabulary of approx. 6,000–10,000 words and exhibits great differences between his/her active and passive vocabularies. The vocabulary of a language can be categorized according to various criteria: (a) based on the **semantic relations** existing between words or groups of words, like **synonymy**, **antonymy**, etc.; (b) based on the formation of words (**morphology**); (c) based on the historical aspects of **loan words**, foreign words, or **word families**; (d) based on regional or social classes (⇒ **dialects**, **jargons**, **sublanguages**); (e) based on the statistical frequency and usage (⇒ **frequency dictionary**); and (g) based on pedagogic considerations (⇒ **basic vocabulary**) for a graded vocabulary.

References
Aitchison, J. 1987. *Words in the mind: an introduction to the mental lexicon.* Oxford.
Carter, R. 1987. *Vocabulary: applied linguistic perspectives.* London.
Jackson, H. 1988. *Words and their meaning.* London and New York.

2 ⇒ **alphabet**[2]

vocal cords [Lat. *vocalis* 'producing a sound']

Cord-like folds of mucus membrane in the interior larynx composed of connective tissue and muscles that are used for **phonation**. (⇒ *also* **articulatory phonetics**, **phonetics**)

vocal tract

The air passages above the **larynx**, in which **speech sounds** are produced: the laryngeal cavity, the **pharynx**, the nasal cavity, and the **oral cavity**. These four **resonance** chambers are connected on the inside to the **vocal cords** and on the outside to the openings in the nose and mouth. (⇒ *also* **articulatory phonetics**)

vocalic vs non-vocalic

Basic phonologic **opposition** in **distinctive feature** analysis, based on acoustically analyzed and spectrally defined criteria (⇒ **acoustic phonetics**, **spectral analysis**). Acoustic characteristic: in vocalic sounds, sharply defined **formants** appear on the **spectrogram**. Articulatory characteristic: unconstricted vs constricted airflow through the **vocal tract**. The distinctions between **vowels** and **consonants** are universal. **Liquids** have both consonantal and vocalic features.

References

Jakobson, R. *et al.* 1951. *Preliminaries to speech analysis*, vol. 18. Cambridge, MA. (6th edn 1965.)
⇒ **distinctive feature**, **phonetics**

vocative [Lat. *vocare* 'to call']

Morphological **case** in **Indo-European** languages which serves to mark the **person** addressed by the speaker, e.g. Rum. *Maria* (nom.) vs *Mario* (voc.). In most modern Indo-European languages, the **nominative** case has replaced the vocative case for this function.

References
⇒ **case**

vocative function of language ⇒ appellative function of language

vocoid ⇒ contoid vs vocoid

voice (*also* diathesis)

Grammatical category of verbs which in **nominative languages** includes **active**, **passive** and in a few languages middle (⇒ **middle voice**) forms. The choice of voice depends on the relationship between semantic roles (⇒ **agent**, **patient**) and syntactic functions (⇒ **subject**, **object**). In the active voice the performer of an action (agent) is designated by the subject, while in passive constructions the subject function is connected to other semantic roles (patient, benefactive, etc.) The middle expresses a process that originates from the subject and affects the subject (⇒ **reflexivity**). There is also a middle construction without an agent subject: *The vase broke*. The three voices are realized differently in various languages: the middle is expressed by verb inflection in **Sanskrit** and Classical **Greek**, and by reflexive constructions in modern Indo-European languages.

The use of active and passive depends primarily on stylistic and communicative functional considerations: because the active subject becomes an optional prepositional phrase in passive constructions and is usually no longer the first element in the sentence, passive constructions involve a change in the topic vs comment structure in that the original topic of the active sentence becomes part of the comment in the corresponding passive sentence (⇒ **topic vs comment**). Cf. *The thief was apprehended* vs *The police apprehended the thief*.

Older variants of **transformational grammar** as well as **relational grammar** treat active and passive sentences as synonymous paraphrases which can be derived from a common underlying structure. There are problems with this analysis in sentences with quantifiers, such as *all*, *somebody* and *every*, because the relative scope of the quantifiers changes, e.g. *Everybody loves somebody* (*somebody* in the **scope** of *everybody* vs *Somebody* (definite)) *is loved by everybody* (*somebody* outside the **scope** of *everybody*).

References

Andersen, P.K. 1991. *A new look at the passive*. Frankfurt.

Bach, E. 1979. In defense of passive. *LPh* 3.297–341.

Barber, E.J.W. 1975. Voice: beyond the passive. *BLS* 1.16–24.

Beedham, C. 1981. The passive in English, German and Russian. *JL* 17.319–27.

—— 1982. *The passive aspect in English, German and Russian*. Tübingen.

Bresnan, J. 1978. A realistic transformational grammar. In M. Halle *et al.* (eds), *Linguistic theory and psychological reality*. Cambridge, MA. 1–59.

—— 1982. The passive in lexical theory. In J. Bresnan (ed.), *The mental representation of grammatical relations*. Cambridge, MA. 3–86.

Davidson, A. 1980. Peculiar passives. *Lg* 56.42–66.

Fox, B. and P.J. Hopper (eds), 1994. *Voice: form and function*. Amsterdam and Philadelphia, PA.

Gazdar, G. and Sag, J. 1981. Passive and reflexive in phrase structure grammar. In J. Groenendijk *et al.* (eds), *Formal methods in the study of language*. Amsterdam.

Givón, T. 1982. Transitivity, topicality and the Ute impersonal passive. In J.P. Hopper and S.A. Thompson (eds), *Studies in transitivity*. New York. 143–60.

—— (ed.) 1994. *Voice and inversion*. Amsterdam and Philadelphia, PA.

Haspelmath, M. 1990. The grammaticalization of passive morphology. *Studies of language* 14.25–72.

Klaiman, M.H. 1991. *Grammatical voice*. Cambridge.

Keenan, E.I. 1975. Some universals of passive in Relational Grammar. *CLS* 11.340–52.

—— 1985. Passive in the world's languages. In T.

Shopen (ed.), *Language typology and syntactic description*. Cambridge. Vol. 1, 243–81.

Parker, P. 1976. Language change and the passive voice. *Lg* 52.449–60.

Siewierska, A. 1984. *The passive: a comparative linguistics analysis*. London.

Shibatani, M. 1985. Passives and related constructions: a prototype analysis. *Lg* 61.821–48.

—— (ed.) 1988. *Passive and voice*. Amsterdam.

Stein, G. 1979. *Studies in the function of the passive*. Tübingen.

voice disorder

A distinction is drawn between organic and functional disorders. Organically based voice disorders derive from primary impairments of an organ used in phonation, for example, the **larynx** (⇒ **dysphonia**) or the **velum** (⇒ **rhinophonia**). A functionally based disorder constitutes an interference in the ability of the vocal organs to adequately perform their speaking or singing functions due to social-emotional factors (e.g. hysteria or depression) or environmental factors (e.g. hoarseness due to vocal abuse in a noisy workplace). Functional disorders may entail physical symptoms (e.g. edema), but these are considered to be secondary causal agents.

voice mutation ⇒ breaking

voice onset time ⇒ glottalization

voiced vs voiceless

Binary phonological **opposition** in **distinctive feature** analysis, based on acoustically analyzed and spectrally defined criteria (⇒ **acoustic phonetics**, **spectral analysis**). Acoustic characteristics: presence or absence of a periodic component on the lower range of the **spectrogram**. Articulatory characteristics: periodic vibration or non-vibration of the **vocal cords**. In English, all **vowels**, the **liquids** [l, r], and the **nasals** [m, n, ŋ] are voiced. The voiced consonants [b, d, g, v, z, ð, ʒ] stand in opposition to the voiceless consonants [p, t, k, f, s, θ, ʃ]. Voiced and voiceless **laterals** are found in Greenlandic, cf [i'lʋ] ‹igdlo› ‘igloo’ vs [i'lʋ] ‹ilo› ‘innards.’ Voiceless vowels are found in the **Nilo-Saharan** language Ik, in the **Sino-Tibetan** language Dafla, in the **Altaic** language Baonang, and in **Japanese**, cf. [hɤkɯsai] ‘Hokusai.’ In the Pama-Nyungan language Bandjalnag as well as in all other indigenous languages of Australia all vowels and all consonants are said to be voiced. In some languages (among others English), the distinction of voiced vs voiceless coincides with the opposition of **tense vs lax**. For diacritics, see the IPA chart on p. xix.

References
Jakobson, R. *et al*. 1951. *Preliminaries to speech analysis*, vol. 26, Cambridge, MA. (6th edn 1965.)
⇒ **distinctive feature**, **phonetics**

voicing assimilation ⇒ assimilation

Volapük

Artificial language created by J.M. Schleyer in 1879 as an international language (⇒ **planned language**). Volapük has a simple phonetic-phonological sound system; its morphological structure is based on the **agglutinating** structure of Turkish; the vocabulary is primarily based on English roots, cf. the construction: *vol-* (from Eng. *world*) + *-a-* ‘genitive’ + *pük* (from Eng. *speak*), hence ‘language of the world.’ Because the grammar of Volapük was generally too complicated and the word formation too arbitrary, it soon disappeared in favor of **Esperanto**.

References
⇒ **interlinguistics**

Volgaic ⇒ Finno-Ugric

volitional [MLat. *volition-*, from Lat. *volo* ‘I wish’]

Characteristic of a verbal action that is carried out intentionally. This feature plays a role as a syntactic category in Hindi (⇒ **Hindi-Urdu**).

Voltaic ⇒ Gur

Vot ⇒ Finno-Ugric

vowel [Lat. *vocalis* (sc. *littera*)]

Phonetically, an **approximant** formed with pulmonic air (as a rule egressively, i.e. through exhaling), whereby the airstream encounters no obstruction (neither stopping or friction) in the **resonance chamber**. Ingressive vowels, in which the air flows into the initiating chamber, are only known as a paralinguistic phenomenon.

In general, vowels are voiced (⇒ **voiced vs voiceless**), or uttered in a **murmuring** or creaky voice. In English, all vowels are voiced. Murmured vowels are found in Gujarati (⇒ **Indo-Aryan**): [baɾ] ‘twelve’ vs [ba̤ɾ] ‘outside,’ while vowels pronounced in a creaky voice are found in Lango (of Nigeria): [leː] ‘animal’ vs [lḛ] ‘ax.’ Voiceless vowels are found in some languages as free or combinatory variants, e.g. in **Japanese** [hɤkɯsai] ‘Hokusai’ and **French** [ʁy] *rue* 'street' (with [y] as an optional vowel in °final position).

Oral and nasal vowels are distinguished, e.g. in French [ʃa] *chat* 'cat' vs [ʃã] *champ* 'field,' [mɔt] *motte* 'clump' vs [mɔ̃t] *monte* 'climbs,' [mɛ] *mais* 'but' vs [mɛ̃] *main* 'hand.'

(a) Regarding the **place of articulation**, a (rough) distinction is drawn between front (pre-dorso-palatal), middle (medio-dorso-velar), and back (post-dorso-velar) vowels. Occasionally, for simplification, front vowels are called palatals; all others are called velars. Front vowels of English are [i, ɪ, e, ɛ, æ], back vowels [u, ʊ, o, ɔ, ʌ, ɑ, ɐ], middle vowels [ə, ʌ, a]. (b) With regard to the degree of openness of the oral part of the resonance chamber, a (rough) distinction is drawn between closed, mid, and open vowels. This distinction corresponds to the relative position of the tongue as being placed high, middle, or low. In a broad transcription of English vowels, [i, ɪ, ʊ, v] are vowels with a high tongue position, [e, ɛ, ə, o, ɔ] are vowels with a middle tongue position, and [æ, ʌ, a, ɑ, ɐ] are vowels with a low tongue position. In a narrow transcription of English vowels, a greater number of degrees of openness must be taken into consideration; (⇒ **vowel chart**). (c) With regard to the **secondary articulation** of labialization, a distinction is drawn between rounded and unrounded vowels (⇒ **rounded vs unrounded**). In English, the rounded vowels are [u, ʊ, o, ɔ], the unrounded vowels [i, e, ə, ɛ, ʌ, æ, a, ɑ, ɐ]. If one gives the vowels in each of the groups (a)–(c) a single dimension, the vowels can be represented in a three-dimensional **vowel block**.

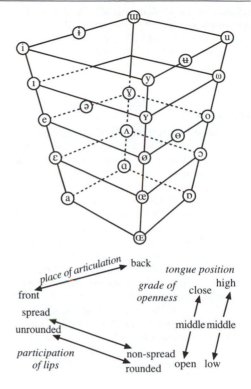

Reference
Rosner, B.S. and J.B. Pickering. *The perception of vowels*. Oxford.

vowel block

Schematic representation of the **vowels** according to the three dimensions (a) high (closed) vs low (open), (b) front vs back, (c) rounded (non-

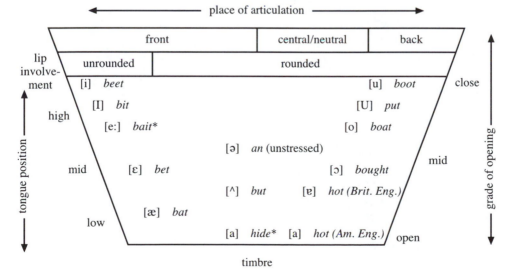

*Occurs as first element in a diphthong

spread) vs unrounded (spread). In the graphic representation of the IPA chart, these three dimensions are shrunk to a pseudo-two-dimensional trapezium (⇒ **vowel chart**).

References
⇒ **phonetics**

vowel chart

Schematized representation of the **vowels** in a geometric form. The classification rests on the physiological and articulatory actions of the tongue and lips in the production of the vowels. From the vowel chart originally developed by C.F. Hellwag (1754–1835), in which [i], [u], and [a] formed the corners of the geometric figure, the vowel 'square' (or trapezoid) was developed as the *a*-sound was differentiated into a front *æ* and a back *a*. The vowel chart has a three-dimensional basis: (a) vertical tongue or jaw height (high, middle, deep); (b) horizontal tongue placement (front, neutral/central, back); and (c) shape of lips (rounded, unrounded) (⇒ **vowel block**). The vowel chart is recommended by the International Phonetic Association (IPA) for use as a classificatory schema for all vowel systems. (⇒ *also* **phonetic transcription**)

References
Hellwag, C.F. 1781. *Dissertatio de formatione loque-lae.* Tübingen. (Repr. Heilbronn, 1886.)

Jones, D. 1950. *The phoneme, its nature and use.* Cambridge.
⇒ **phonetics**

vowel gradation ⇒ ablaut

vowel harmony

1 In the broad sense, every form of qualitative **assimilation** between vowels with regard to their **place of articulation**: e.g. all forms of **umlaut**. Vowel harmony is an assimilatory process that can be explained phonetically as a way to facilitate articulation.

2 In the narrow sense, qualitative dependence of the suffix vowel on the root vowel, cf. the distribution of the plural allomorph in **Turkish** {-ler, -lar} in *evler* 'the houses' and *atlar* 'the horses' and the **Finnish** case endings {-ssä, -ssa} in *Helsingissä* 'in Helsinki' and *Saksassa* 'in Germany.'

References
Hulst, H. van der and N. Smith (eds). 1988. *Features, segmental structure and harmony processes.* Part 2. Dordrecht.
Vago, R.M. (ed.). 1980. *Issues in vowel harmony.* Amsterdam.
⇒ **historical linguistics, phonology**

vowel mutation ⇒ umlaut

VP ⇒ verb phrase

Vulgar Latin ⇒ Latin

W

Wakashan

Language family spoken primarily in Canada, one member, Makah, in Washington, USA. The most important languages are Nootka (about 1,800 speakers) and Kwakiutl (about 1,000 speakers). Wakashan is typologically similar to the neighboring **Salishan** languages.

References
Grubb, D.M. 1977. *A practical writing system and short dictionary of Kwakw'ala (Kwakiutl)*. Ottawa.
Jacobsen, W.H. 1979. Wakashan comparative studies. In L. Campbell and M. Mithun (eds), *The languages of Native America: historical and comparative assessment*. Austin, TX. 766–91.
Liedtke, S. 1994. Wakashan, Salishan and Penutian: Cognate sets. *LDDS* 9.
Lincoln, N.J. and J.C. Rath. 1980. *North Wakashan comparative root list*. Ottawa.
Sapir, E. and M. Swadesh. 1939. *Nootka texts, tales and ethnological narratives, with grammatical notes and lexical materials*. Philadelphia, PA.

Wappo ⇒ Gulf languages

Warlpiri ⇒ Australian languages

Washo ⇒ Hokan

wave theory

Originally developed by Schuchardt (1868) and perhaps independently, though later, by Schmidt (1872), image used to explain the origin and development of individual languages through gradual linguistic differentiation and not – as in Schleicher's **genetic tree theory** – through abrupt branching. A nucleus of innovation is postulated which radiates outwards in the form of waves and spreads linguistic changes and developments, much like waves that are emitted and partly overlap when stones are dropped in water. Language varieties that are spatially and/or temporally neighboring accordingly usually display a language inventory with correspondences common in many areas.

A fundamentally new conception of this model has been developed in the recent approaches in the **language change** theories of **variational linguistics** and **sociolinguistics**. These are based on the assumption that a **sound change** first starts in restricted phonological contexts with minimal quantitative frequency and qualitative intensity within a certain social group in certain (usually informal) situations and then spreads successively, qualitatively intensified, to further phonological contexts, social groups, and situations, each with a larger probability of use, until finally it is categorically realized in all contexts with all speakers; the process of change is then completed.

References
Bailey, C.-J. 1973. *Variation and linguistic theory*. Arlington, VA.
Goebl, H. 1983. Stammbaum und Welle. *ZS* 2.3–44.
Pulgram, E. 1953. Family tree, wave theory, and dialectology. *Orbis* 2.67–72.
Schmidt, J. 1872. *Die Verwandtschaftsverhältnisse der indogermanischen Sprachen*. Weimar.
Schuchardt, H. 1868. *Der Vokalismus des Vulgärlateins*, vol. 3. Leipzig.

weakening

Phonetically motivated process of **sound change** that leads to the reduction of sounds and, in extreme cases, to loss of segments; typically this occurs in positions where assimilation is favored or in syllabically 'weak' positions (e.g. in final position, in unstressed syllables). Two types of weakening are distinguished. (a) Consonant weakening (also lenisization): this denotes a weakening of **consonant** strength (through a reduction in air pressure and muscle tension or an increase in **sonority**) to the complete loss of a segment; cf. the development of [p] > [b] > [β] in the comparison of Lat. *lupus* > OSpan. *lobo* [lobo] > Span. *lobo* [loβo] 'wolf' or the loss of [d] in comparison to Lat. *vidēre* with Span. *ver* 'see.' This process is also to be found in **Celtic** languages. (b) Vowel weakening: this is a term for all processes that lead to a weakening of the articulatory movement in the sense of an increasing centralization of vowels and finally a total loss of the vowel; cf. the loss of final vowels in English: OE *nama* [nama] > ME *name* [nɛmə], Mod. Eng. *name* [neim]. Reduction processes of these types occur more often in less 'carefully enunciated' speech styles in informal situations. (⇒ **rapid vs slow speech**)

References
⇒ **sound change**

weather verb

Verb belonging to the semantically and syntactically motivated subgroup of verbs which denote weather phenomena with no discernible agent (*rain*, *snow*). (⇒ *also* **impersonal verb, valence**)

weight principle (*also* principle of increasing constituents)

Principle of word order formulated by O. Behaghel ('Gesetz der wachsenden Glieder') for German, which states that shorter constituents precede longer ones. The weight principle is assumed to be a universal word order rule within **Functional Grammar** (see Siewierska 1988; Dik 1989). Hawkins (1990, 1994) has shown that the short-before-long principle holds only for certain types of languages, such as English and German. In other language types (e.g. Japanese, Korean) longer constituents preferably precede shorter ones. Hawkins assumes that the weight principle belongs to language performance (i.e. language parsing or processing).

References
Behaghel, O. 1932. *Deutsche Syntax*. Vol. 4. Heidelberg.
Dik, S. 1989. *The theory of Functional Grammar*. Dordrecht.
Hawkins, J.A. 1990. A parsing theory of word order universals. *LingI* 21.223–61.
—— 1994. *A performance theory of order and constituency*. Cambridge.
Primus, B. 1993. Word order and information structure: a performance-based account of topic positions and focus positions. In J. Jacobs *et al.* (eds), *Syntax: an international handbook of contemporary research*. Berlin. 880–96.
—— 1994. Grammatik und Performanz: Faktoren der Wortstellungsvariation im Mittelfeld. *S&P* 32.39–86.
Siewierska, A. 1988. *Word order rules*. London.

wellformedness ⇒ **constraints**

Welsh

Celtic language spoken in Wales by approx. 400,000 speakers, belongs to the Brythonic group and is thus p-Celtic. Attested since the eighth century with a fairly rich literary tradition. The language was heavily influenced first by **Latin**, then later by Norman **French** and **English**.

References
Morris Jones, J. 1913. *A Welsh grammar*. Oxford.
King, G. 1993. *Modern Welsh: a comprehensive grammar*. London.
Stephens, M. (ed.) 1973. *The Welsh language today*. Llandysul.
Thorne, D.A. 1993. *A comprehensive Welsh grammar*. Oxford.
Dictionary
Geiriadur Prifsgol Cymru. A dictionary of the Welsh language. 1950– . (Vol. 41 1990.) Cardiff.

Wernicke's aphasia

Language disorder (also known as 'fluent' or 'sensory aphasia') named after the German psychiatrist Carl Wernicke (1858–1905). Unlike other acquired language disorders, Wernicke's aphasia is associated with a great degree of fluency and unimpaired prosody. Other typical characteristics are: (a) frequent omissions, permutations, or additions of sounds (so-called 'phonemic **paraphasia**') (⇒ **jargon**); (b) choice of semantically related words of the same syntagmatic category as the target word (so-called 'semantic paraphasia') (⇒ **neologism**); (c) morphological errors; (d) problems with **selection restrictions**; and (e) in some languages, contamination of syntactic constructions (⇒ **paragrammatism**). Comprehension of words and sentences is often severely impaired, though reading and writing may be less so.

References
Caplan, D. 1987. *Neurolinguistics and linguistic aphasiology*. Cambridge.
Daffner, K.R. *et al.* 1991. Broca's aphasia following damage to Wernicke's area: for or against traditional aphasiology. *Archives of Neurology* 48.766–8.
Ellis, A.W., D. Miller, and G. Sin. 1983. Wernicke's aphasia and normal language processing: a case study in cognitive neuropsychology. *Cognition* 15.111–14.
Kolk, H. and C. Heeschen. 1992. Agrammatism, paragrammatism and the management of language. *Language and Cognitive Processes* 7.89–129.
Zurif, E. *et al.* 1993. An on-line analysis of syntactic processing in Broca's and Wernicke's aphasia. *B&L* 45 (special issue), 448–64.

Wernicke's area

A region in the brain named after its discoverer, the psychiatrist Carl Wernicke (1858–1905). It is located in the back part of the first temporal gyrus in the language dominant hemisphere, and is part of the supply area of the aorta temporalis posterior. Wernicke believed that this region was the center for sound images of words. A lesion in this area is said to lead to **Wernicke's aphasia**. (⇒ *also* **language and brain, language area**)

References
Caplan, D. 1987. *Neurolinguistics and linguistic aphasiology*. Cambridge.
⇒ **Wernicke's aphasia**

West Atlantic

Branch of the **Niger-Congo** languages with forty-three languages spoken in areas of West Africa extending, in the case of **Fula**, to Lake

Chad. Other large languages are Wolof and Serer (Senegal).

Characteristics: complex **noun class** systems are typical, with up to twenty-five classes; classes are marked by prefixes or suffixes, often connected to a change of the initial consonants of roots, agreement and a rich voice system (in Fula including middle voice).

Reference
Sapir, J.D. 1971. West Atlantic: an inventory of the languages, their noun class systems and consonant alternations. In T.A. Sebeok (ed.), *Current trends in linguistics*. The Hague. Vol. 7, 45–112.

West Germanic ⇒ Germanic

West Germanic consonant gemination ⇒ gemination

wh-island constraint

A hypothesis of **transformational grammar** by which indirect questions introduced by question pronouns are islands for **movement transformations**. (⇒ *also* **propositional island constraint**)

References
Reinhart, T. 1981. A second COMP position. In A. Belletti, L. Brandi, and L. Rizzi (eds), *Theory of markedness in generative grammar*. Pisa. 517–57.
Rudin, C. 1981. 'Who what to whom said': an argument from Bulgarian against cyclic wh-movement. *PCLS* 17.353–60.

wh-movement

In **transformational grammar**, the movement of a *wh*-**node** to initial position in a sentence (⇒ **COMP position**). In **Government and Binding theory**, movements to a non-argument position include *wh*-movement and are differentiated from NP movement. (⇒ *also* **movement transformation**, **move-α**)

References
⇒ **transformational grammar**

wh-node

The position in a sentence occupied by a question word or relative pronoun (e.g. *who*, *why*, *what*, *when*, *where*, *which*, and *how*). In **transformational grammar** it is assumed that question words and relative pronouns are positioned within the sentence at **deep structure** and are moved to the beginning of questions by *wh*-**movement** before **surface structure**. This sentence-initial position is the **COMP position**.

Reference
Rudin, Catherine. 1988. On multiple questions and multiple WH fronting. *NL & LT* 6(4).445–502.

wh-question

Interrogative sentence formed with an **interrogative pronoun** (*who?, whom?, what?*) or an interrogative adverb (*when?, where?*) which serves to make more precise a state of affairs which is already assumed to be known, for example, *Whom did you meet at the concert?*

wh-word ⇒ interrogative pronoun, *wh*-question

White Russian ⇒ Belorussian

Winutian ⇒ Penutian

Wiyot ⇒ Algonquian

Wolof ⇒ West Atlantic

word

Term used intuitively in everyday language for a basic element of language; numerous linguistic attempts at defining the concept are not uniform and remain controversial. A word is characterized by different, often contradictory traits depending on the theoretical background and descriptive context. Compare the following suggestions for defining words, listed according to their level of description: (a) phonetic-phonological level: words are the smallest segments of sound that can be theoretically isolated by word accent and **boundary markers** like **pauses**, clicks, and the like, and which are further isolated on a (b) orthographic-graphemic level by blank spaces in writing or print; (c) on the morphological level, words are characterized as the basic elements of grammatical paradigms like **inflection** and are distinguished from the morphologically characterized **word forms**, cf. *write* vs *writes*, *wrote*, *written*; they are structurally stable and cannot be divided, and can be described as well by specific rules of **word formation**; (d) on the lexical-semantic level, words are the smallest, relatively independent carriers of meaning that are codified in the lexicon, and (e) can be described syntactically as the smallest permutable and substitutable units of a sentence. Although the essence of all these definitions can be boiled down to the three components of acoustic and semantic identity, morphological stability, and syntactic mobility as the main criteria, the term 'word' has been subject to multifaceted terminological differentiation or given up in favor of concepts like **morpheme**, **lexeme**, and **formative**. In **X-bar theory**, the lexical category (notation: X^0) is equal to the concept of 'word.'

References
Di Sciullo, A.M. and E. Williams. 1987. *On the*

definition of word. Cambridge, MA.

Hyman, L.M. 1978. Word demarcation. In J.H. Greenberg *et al.* (eds), *Universals of human language.* Stanford, CA. 443–70.

Juilland, A. and A. Roceric. 1975. *The decline of the word.* Saratoga, CA.

Kramsky, J. 1969. *The word as a linguistic unit.* The Hague.

Lyons, J. 1968. *Introduction to theoretical linguistics.* Cambridge.

Zirmunsky, V.M. 1966. The word and its boundaries. *Linguistics* 27.65–91.

Bibliography
Juilland, A. and A. Roceric. 1972. *The linguistic concept of word: analytic bibliography.* The Hague.

word atlas

The dialect-geographical (⇒ **dialect geography**) codification of lexical characteristics, whose recording is based on neutral questions such as 'What do you call the paper receptacle used to carry groceries?' On the basis of the answers a word map for *bag/sack* arises that shows the distribution of the two expressions in the given speech area. The word atlas was originally designed in Germany as a compendium to the German **linguistic atlas** and the techniques used to develop it have been of lasting influence on other atlas projects.

References
⇒ **dialect geography, fieldwork, linguistic atlas**

word comparison

Compilation of etymologically related words or word **roots** from different languages undertaken in order to document the genetic relationships on the lexical, phonological, and morphological levels, e.g.: Eng. *mother*, Ger. *Mutter*, OInd. *mātár*, Grk *métēr*, Lat. māter.

word expert

Parsing with word experts is based on the assumption that the individual word is the linguistic unit relevant for the process of interpretation. In this way, parsing with word experts amounts to 'lexical syntax' in artificial intelligence. 'Word experts' are a basis for analytic processes; syntactic regularities are not explicitly represented, but are coded implicitly by the interaction of word experts. (⇒ *also* **artificial intelligence**)

Reference
Small, S.C. and J.J. Rieger. 1982. Parsing and comprehending with word experts. In W.G. Lehnert (ed.), *Strategies in natural language processing.* Hillsdale, NJ. 89–147.

word family

Set of words within a language whose similar stem morphemes can be traced to the same etymological **root**, e.g. *eat, edible, eatery,* among others. One of the principal sources of such word families are the strong verbs (⇒ **strong vs weak verb**) whose different vowel gradations (⇒ **ablaut**) form the basis for new words. The number of elements of a word family depends on the meaning of the stem morpheme and on the frequency of its use. Often the etymological connection between words is not synchronically transparent, cf. *borrow, bargain.*

Reference
Keller, H.H. 1987. *A German word family dictionary, together with English equivalents.* Berkeley, CA.
⇒ **etymology, semantic change**

word form

The concretely realized grammatical form of a word in the context of a sentence. The word in the surface structure that corresponds to the **lexeme** as the (unalterable) abstract base unit of the lexicon is realized according to grammatical categories (such as tense, number, case, person, and so on) in altered 'word forms,' cf. *picture, paint* in *Interesting pictures were painted.*

Reference
Matthews, P.H. 1974. *Morphology.* London. (2nd edn 1991.)

word formation

Investigation and description of processes and rule-governed formation of new complex words on the basis of already existing linguistic resources. Depending on the areas of interest, word formation looks at the structure of the vocabulary from a historical-genetic or synchronic-functional aspect. The following are the main tasks of word formation: (a) classification of the elements of word formation, such as simple or complex words, **base morphemes**, derivational elements (⇒ **affix, prefix, suffix**); (b) description of the types and models according to which the formations can be ordered structurally; (c) description of the semantic aspects of the processes involved in word formation.

Word formation deals with the description of the structure of both **nonce words** and **neologisms** (⇒ **occasional vs usual word formation**) as well as of set words (usual form, **lexicalization**). These must be viewed as two sides of the same phenomenon, for new words can arise only according to the already existing prototypes in the lexicalized vocabulary of the language. The greatest part of all word formations can be subsumed under **derivation** (the creation of new words through suffixes of a specific word class: *read* + *er*, *read* + *ing*, *read* + *able*), **prefixation** (attachment of a bound prefix to a free morpheme (*un* + *readable*, *mis* + *interpret*), **composition** (compounds of several free morphemes: *fire* + *man*, *bath* + *room*), and **conversion**[2] (the change of word class of a stem: *camp* (noun) > *camp* (verb). **Clippings**, **abbreviations**, and **blends** are seen as peripheral processes of word formation.

The decision about the role of word formation in the framework of a comprehensive grammar is dependent on the given presupposed language theory: since complex words on the one hand have typical lexical word characteristics (e.g. they are subject to lexicalization and demotivation), but on the other hand in part show similarities with regularities of sentence formation (relations of **paraphrase**, **recursiveness**), the issues of word formation touch upon **morphology** and **syntax**, on the formal side, and **semantics**, **lexicology**, and **pragmatics**, on the content side. Such different interpretations of word formation find their expression in the **lexicalist vs transformationalist hypothesis** particularly clearly, but also in more recent studies on **word syntax**.

References
Adams, V. 1973. *An introduction to modern English word formation*. London.
Anderson, S. 1992. *A-morphous morphology*. Cambridge:
Bauer, L. 1983. *English word-formation*. London.
Bybee, J. 1985. *Morphology*. Amsterdam.
Clark, E.V. and H.H. Clark. 1979. When nouns surface as verbs. *Language* 55.767–811.
Di Sciullo, A.M. and E. Williams. 1987. *On the definition of word*. Cambridge, MA.
Downing, P. 1977. On the creation and use of English compound nouns. *Language* 53.810–42.
Dowty, D. 1979. *Word meaning and Montague grammar*. Dordrecht.
Hammond, M. and M. Noonan (eds) *Theoretical morphology*. New York.
Jackendoff, R. 1975. Morphological and semantic regularities in the lexicon. *Lg* 51.639–71.
Kastovsky, D. 1978. *Wortbildung und Semantik*. Düsseldorf, Bern and Munich.
Krahe, H. and W. Meid. 1967. *Germanische Sprachwissenschaft*, vol. 3: *Wortbildungslehre*. Berlin.
Lieber, R. 1981. *On the organization of the lexicon*. Bloomington, IN.
—— 1983. Argument linking and compounds in English. *LingI* 14.251–85.
—— 1992. *Deconstructing morphology*. Chicago, IL.
Lipka, L. 1972. *Semantic structure and word formation: verb-particle constructions in contemporary English*. Munich.
Marchand, H. 1960. *The categories and types of present-day English word-formation*. Munich. (2nd edn 1966.)

Matthews, P. 1974. *Morphology*. Cambridge. (2nd edn 1991.)
Selkirk, E. 1982. *The syntax of words*. Cambridge, MA
Spencer, A. 1991. *Morphological theory*. Cambridge.
Stein, G. 1973. *English word-formation over two centuries*. Tübingen.

Generative views
Aronoff, M. 1976. *Word formation in generative grammar*. Cambridge, MA.
Scalise, S. 1984. *Generative morphology*. Dordrecht. (2nd edn 1986.)

Bibliography
Seymour, R.K. 1968. *A bibliography of word formation in the Germanic languages*. Durham, NC.

word formation rule

Within the lexicalist approach (⇒ **lexicalist vs transformationalist hypothesis**) of **word formation**, Aronoff (1976) was the first to work out the characteristics of the rules that generate new complex words in the **lexicon** on the basis of the words already present therein. The results of the word formation rules transfer directly into the lexicon as fully specified lexical units of the language. Later theories of **word syntax** are based on the assumption that the formation and interpretation of complex words represent the results of the modular interaction of different components of the grammar.

Reference
Aronoff, M. 1976. *Word formation in generative grammar*. Cambridge, MA.

word grammar ⇒ **dependency grammar**

word meaning ⇒ **lexical meaning vs grammatical meaning**

word order (*also* linear precedence, serialization, **topology**)

Word order refers to the linear relation of words and phrases within larger units. An important distinction in word order studies is that between rigid and variable, or free, word order. Rigid word order means that a change in the order of elements within a phrase changes the syntactic function and the semantic interpretation of these elements, e.g. *That man sleeps* vs *man that sleeps*; *Philip sees Caroline* vs *Caroline sees Philip*. Variable (or free) word order means that linear rearrangements do not trigger such grammatical changes, e.g. *Philip I saw* vs *I saw Philip*. Although many languages exhibit considerable word order variation, it is commonly acknowledged that no genuine free word order language exists. Therefore, word order studies are carried out in terms of linearization patterns that are commonly referred to as 'basic (or dominant, unmarked, natural) word order.' This term captures the fact that there are word order preferences, rather than strict word order rules in terms of the grammatical status of the elements involved. With regard to the major constituents of the clause (⇒ **syntactic function**) the term 'basic order' is typically identified with the order that occurs in stylistically neutral, independent, indicative clauses with full noun phrase (NP) participants, where the subject is a definite human **agent**, the object is a definite non-human **patient** and the verb represents an action, not a state or a process (⇒ **process vs action**). Since basic order refers to preferences pertaining to **markedness**, another criterion for basic order is its statistical dominance in texts (for problems with this criterion, see Siewierska 1988). The fact that basic order is stylistically (e.g. pragmatically) neutral can be tested by trying to use the relevant expression as an answer to different questions. By this heuristic criterion *Philip I saw* is established as a marked (or non-basic) order for English, because it cannot be an answer to a question such as *What's new?*, *Who saw Philip?*, or *What did you do?*

Word order studies have produced different rules for basic or rigid order, among which universals of basic order are of special interest. The characteristic of word order which is most often discussed is the relative order of S(ubject), O(bject), and V(erb). In most of the world's languages, S almost always precedes O, so that of the six possible orderings of S, O, and V, the most common patterns are SOV (e.g. **Turkish**, **Japanese**), SVO (e.g. **English**, **French**), and VSO (e.g. Irish, Maori) (see Greenberg 1963; Mallinson and Blake 1981; Hawkins 1983; Tomlin 1986). The basic order of the **major constituents** of the clause correlates with the basic order of minor elements, such as that of noun and attribute, adposition and its complement, complementizer and the rest of the embedded sentence. The universal principle underlying these correlations is that the head of a phrase tends to be placed at the same side of the phrase, preferably at its periphery (see Greenberg 1963; Vennemann 1974, 1976; Hawkins 1983, 1990). This principle explains the fact that in head-final languages the basic order is SOV, complement–postposition, sentence–complementizer, attribute–noun (e.g. Japanese, Turkish). In head-initial languages the order of these elements is reversed (e.g. Irish, Maori). The fact that rather few languages adhere to this principle consistently for all phrases is explained by **language change**, **language contact**, or other intervening factors (see Vennemann 1974). As to pragmatic word order rules, two competing universal preferences have been postulated: the theme of an utterance tends to precede the rheme (⇒ **functional sentence perspective**, ⇒ **theme vs rheme**); the reverse principle that most important and thus rhematic information precedes thematic information was put forward by Givón (1983, 1988); (for a critique of both assumptions, see Primus 1993: Hawkins 1994). It is generally agreed, that a sentence topic tends to precede the comment (⇒ **topic vs comment**; Gundel 1988; Primus 1993). A 'stylistic' universal ordering preference which is based on language performance (see Hawkins 1990, 1994) is the **weight principle**.

References

Abraham, W. and S. de Meij (eds) 1986. *Topic, focus, and configurationality*. Amsterdam.

Andersen, P.K. 1983. *Word order typology and comparative constructions*. Amsterdam.

Behaghel, O. 1932. *Deutsche Syntax*. Vol. 4. Heidelberg.

Bossong, G. 1989. Morphemic marking of topic and focus. In M. Kefer and J. van der Auwera (eds), *Universals of language*. Brussels.

Campbell, L., V. Bubenik, and L. Saxon. 1988. Word order universals. *CJL* 33.209–30.

Davidson, A. 1984. Syntactic markedness and the definition of sentence topic. *Language* 60.707–846.

Dik, S. 1989. *The theory of Functional Grammar*. Dordrecht.

Downing, P. and M. Noonan. 1995. *Word order in discourse*. Amsterdam and Philadelphia, PA.

Ebert, R.P. 1980. Variation study and word order change. *CLS* 16.52–61.

Givón, T. 1983. Topic continuity in discourse: quantitative cross-language studies. Amsterdam.

——— 1988. The pragmatics of word order: predictability, importance and attention. In M. Hammond *et al.* (eds), *Studies in syntactic typology*. Amsterdam. 243–84.

Greenberg, J.H. 1963. Some universals of grammar with particular reference to the order of meaningful elements. In J.H. Greenberg (ed.), *Universals of language*. Cambridge, MA. 73–113.

——— 1966. *Language universals, with special reference to feature hierarchies*. The Hague.

——— 1974. *Language typology: a historical and analytic overview*. The Hague.

Gundel, J.K. 1988. Universals of topic–comment structure. In M. Hammond *et al.* (eds), *Studies in syntactic typology*. Amsterdam. 209–42.

Hammond, M.T., E.A. Moravcsik, and J.R. Wirth (eds) 1988. *Studies in syntactic typology*, Part 2: *Word order*. Amsterdam.

Hawkins, J.A. 1983. *Word order universals*. New York.

——— 1990. A parsing theory of word order universals. *LJ* 21.223–61.

——— 1994. *A performance theory of order and constituency*. Cambridge.

Keenan, E.L. 1978. On surface form and logical

form. In B.B. Kachru (ed.), *Linguistics in the seventies: directions and prospects*. Urbana, IL.

Krifka, M. 1985. Harmony or consistency. *TL* 12.73–96.

Lambrecht, K. 1987. Sentence focus, information structure, and the thetic-categorial distinction. *BLS* 13.366–82.

Lehmann, W.P. 1978. *Syntactic typology: studies in the phenomenology of language*. Austin, TX.

Li, Ch.N. (ed.) 1976. *Subject and topic*. New York.

Mallinson, G. and B.J. Blake. 1981. *Language typology*. Amsterdam.

Meisel, J.M. and M.D. Dal. 1979. *Linear order and generative theory*. Amsterdam.

Nuyts, J. and G. de Schutter (eds) 1987. *Getting one's words into line: on the word order and functional grammar*. Dordrecht.

Pafel, J. 1993. Scope and word order. In J. Jacobs *et al.* (eds), *Syntax: an international handbook of contemporary research*. Berlin and New York. 867–80.

Payne, D.L. 1990. *The pragmatics of word order: typological dimensions of verb initial languages*. Berlin and New York.

—— (ed.) 1992. *Pragmatics of word order flexibility*. Amsterdam and Philadelphia, PA.

Primus, B. 1993. Word order and information structure: a performance-based account of topic positions and focus positions. In J. Jacobs *et al.* (eds), *Syntax: an international handbook of contemporary research*. Berlin and New York. 880–96.

Pullum, G.K. 1977. Word order universals and grammatical relations. In P. Cole and J.M. Saddock (eds) *Grammatical relations*. New York. 249–78.

Siewierska, A. 1988. *Word order rules*. London.

Tomlin, R.S. 1986. *Basic word order: functional principles*. London.

Uszkoreit, H. 1987. *Word order and constituent structure in German*. Stanford, CA.

Vennemann, T. 1974a. Theoretical word order studies: results and problems. *Papiere zur Linguistik* 7.5–25.

—— 1974b. Analogy in generative grammar: the origin of word order. *PICL* 11.2. 79–83.

—— 1975. *Word order and word order change*. Austin, TX.

—— 1976. Categorial grammar and the order of meaningful elements. In A. Juilland (ed.) *Linguistic studies offered to J. Greenberg*, 3 vols. Saratoga, CA. 615–34.

Vennemann, T. and R. Harlow. 1977. Categorial grammar and consistent basic VX serialization. *TL* 4.227–54.

word stress ⇒ stress²

word structure

Following a suggestion by Williams (1981), analogy of the structure of complex words (⇒ **word formation**) with the structural principles of phrases, especially with that of X-bar syntax (⇒ **X-bar theory**). As in phrasal syntax, the **head** constituent determines the features of the whole word over the **percolation** mechanism,

which is known from the syntax. In particular, the concept of 'head' is taken over in word structure in a variant that defines it according to its position, which constitutes a parameter determined by the individual languages. In English and German the head is on the right, in Hebrew and perhaps French on the left. In a relativized variant of the head concept, Di Sciullo and Williams (1987), unlike Selkirk (1982), assume that the inflectional **affixes** can function like the derivational **suffixes** as (relativized) heads with regard to the inflectional structure of the word. The set of categories in word structure is smaller than in the phrase syntax: the lexical categories *N*, *A*, *V*, and *P* (abbreviated: X°) alone appear to participate in word formation processes, together with bound affixes. Still, it is debated whether syntactic categories like *NP*, *VP*, and *S* can occur as non-head constituents. (⇒ *also* **syntactic affixation**)

References

Selkirk, E. 1982. *The syntax of words*. Cambridge.

Di Sciullo, A.M. and E. Williams 1987. *On the definition of word*. Cambridge, MA.

Williams, E. 1981. On the notions 'lexically related' and 'head of word.' *LingI* 12.245–74.

⇒ **word syntax**

word syntax

Application of more recent theories and knowledge of syntax to the structure of the word. (⇒ *also* **inheritance**, **theta criterion**, **word structure**, **X-bar theory**)

References

Boase, J. and J. Toman. 1986. On θ-role assignment in German compounds. *FoLi* 20.319–39.

Di Sciullo, A.M. and E. Williams. 1987. *On the definition of word*. Cambridge, MA.

Selkirk, E. 1982. *The syntax of words*. Cambridge, MA.

Toman, J. 1983. *Wortsyntax*. Tübingen.

—— 1986. Zu neueren Entwicklungen in der Theorie der Wortstruktur. *StL* 19.1–21.

Williams, E. 1981. Argument structure and morphology. *TLR* 1.81–114.

—— 1981. On the notions 'lexically related' and 'head of word.' *LingI* 12.245–74.

writing (*also* script)

Means of recording spoken language through a conventionalized system of graphic signs. The millennia-old history of writing is strongly characterized by magic, religion, and mysticism, but also by the culturally and historically conditioned change in materials (stone, leather, bone, parchment), writing utensils, and writing techniques over the centuries. The numerous (and various) attempts at developing a typology of writing systems are based on different principles of classification, though they all attempt to reflect the development of writing from the earliest signs that stood for objects, to the signs used in writing for words or meaningful units (⇒ **morpheme**), to the phonetically based alphabetic systems. (⇒ *also* **alphabetic writing system, cuneiform, graphemics, hieroglyphics, ideography, logography, pictography, rune**)

References
Cohen, M. 1958. *La grande invention de l'écriture et son volution*, 3 vols. Paris.
Coulmas, F. 1971. *Über Schrift*. Frankfurt.
—— 1989. *The writing systems of the world*. Oxford.
Coulmas, F. and K. Ehlich (eds) 1983. *Writing in focus*. Berlin, New York, and Amsterdam.
Daniels, P.T. and W. Bright (ed.). 1995. *The world's writing systems*. Oxford.
Diringer, D. 1948/9. *The alphabet: a key to the history of mankind*. London.
—— 1962. *Writing*. London.
Driver, G.R. 1976. *Semitic writing: from photograph to alphabet*. London.
Gelb, I.J. 1952. *A study of writing: the foundation of grammatology*. London.
Günther, H. and O. Ludwig (eds) 1994. *Writing and its use: an interdisciplinary handbook of international research*. Berlin and New York.
Haarmann, H. 1990. *Universalgeschichte der Schrift*. Frankfurt.
Hall, R.A., Jr. 1957. *A theory of graphemics*. Ithaca, NY.
Harris, R. 1995. *Signs in writing*. London.
Miller, D.G. 1994. *Ancient scripts and phonological knowledge*. Amsterdam and Philadelphia, PA.
Nakanishi, A. 1980. *Writing systems of the world: alphabets, syllabaries, pictograms*. Rutland, VT.
Olson, D.R. 1994. *The world on paper*. Cambridge.
Pöldes-Papp, K. 1966. *Vom Felsenbild zum Alphabet: die Geschichte der Schrift von ihren frühesten Vorstufen bis zur lateinischen Schreibschrift*. Stuttgart.
Sampson, G. 1985. *Writing systems*. London etc.
Trager, G.L. 1974. Writing and writing systems. In T.A. Sebeok (ed.), *Current trends in linguistics*. The Hague. Vol. 12, 373–496.
⇒ **alphabetical writing system**

written language

1 Generally speaking, the written counterpart of any variety of language.

2 More specifically, a particular type of a language that seeks to emulate a particular standard and is characterized by rules of usage. (⇒ *also* **standard language**)

References
Akinnaso, F.N. 1982. On the differences between spoken and written language. *L&S* 25.97–125.
—— 1986. On the similarities between spoken and written language. *L&S* 28.323–59.
Biber, D. 1988. *Variation across speech and writing*. Cambridge.
Chafe, W.L. and D. Tannen. 1987. The relation between written and spoken language. *Annual Review of Anthropology* 16.383–407.
Danes, F. *et al.* (eds) 1992. *Writing vs speaking*. Tübingen.
Redeker, G. 1984. On the differences between spoken and written language. *DPr* 7.43–55.
Stein, D. (ed.) 1992. *Co-operating with written texts: the pragmatics and comprehension of written texts*. Berlin and New York.
Vachek, J. 1989. *Written language revisited*. Amsterdam.
Wallace, C. 1988. Punctuation and the prosody of written language. *Written Communication* 5.395–426.

Wu ⇒ Chinese

X

X-bar theory (*also* X-bar syntax)

A theoretical concept in **transformational grammar** which restricts the form of context-free **phrase structure rules**. This theory was developed by Chomsky (1970) and Jackendoff (1977) on the following premises: (a) all syntactically complex categories of all natural languages (NP, VP, PP, etc.) are formed according to universal structural principles; (b) all lexical categories can be defined according to a limited inventory of syntactic features like [±N] and [±V], e.g. verb = [+V, –N], noun = [–V, +N], adjective = [+V, +N], preposition = [–V, –N]; (c) a distinction can be made between the levels of complexity within phrases, such that phrases themselves (NPs, VPs, PPs) are maximally complex categories of the type N, V, P. Lexical categories of the type N, V, P are minimally complex. There is another level of complexity which falls between these two. The phrase *the House of Commons* [det N PP] is maximally complex because it cannot be expanded further as an NP. *House* [N] is minimally complex, while *House of Commons* [N PP] belongs to an intermediate category. The whole phrase can be denoted using the notation N^2, N'', or $\bar{\bar{N}}$; this level of projection is also referred to as NP.

House	N^0	N	N
House of Commons	N^1	N′	$\bar{N}$
The House of Commons	N^2	N″	$\bar{\bar{N}}$

Every possible phrase structure rule is derived from X in the general form X^i [...X^j...], where (i) the dots stand for any number of categories of maximal complexity, and (ii) the indices ^{i} and ^{j} stand for the level of complexity of the category X and (iii) X^j cannot be more complex than X^i. Phrase structure rules like $VP \rightarrow A\ NP$ are ruled out by these **constraints**. The term 'X-bar' arises from the notation where one or more bars are placed above the constituent X to represent the levels of complexity. For that reason, the following notation may be used: X, X', X'', X^0, X^1, X^2, or X, $\bar{X}$, $\bar{\bar{X}}$, where the maximal projection can also be referred to as XP.

References

Bresnan, J. 1977. Transformations and categories in syntax. In R. Butts and J. Hintikka (eds), *Basic problems in methodology and linguistics*. Dordrecht. 261–82.

Chomsky, N. 1970. Remarks on nominalization. In R.A. Jacobs and P.S. Rosenbaum (eds), *Readings in English transformational grammar*. Waltham, MA. 170–221.

Edmonds, J.E. 1985. *A unified theory of syntactic categories*. Dordrecht.

Hornstein, N. and D. Lightfoot. 1981. *Explanation in linguistics*. London.

Jackendoff, R. 1977. Constraints on phrase structure rules. In P.W. Culicover, T. Wasow, and A. Akmajian (eds), *Formal syntax*. New York. 249–83.

——— 1977. *X-bar syntax: a study of phrase structure*. Cambridge, MA.

Kornai, A. and G. Pullum. 1990. The X-bar theory of phrase structure. *Language* 66.24–50.

Speas, M. 1990. *Phrase structure in natural language*. Dordrecht.

Stowell, T. 1981. Origins of phrase structure. Dissertation. Cambridge, MA.

Stuurman, F. 1985. *Phrase structure theory in generative grammar*. Dordrecht.

⇒ **transformational grammar**

Xhosa ⇒ **Bantu**

Y

Yao ⇒ Miao-Yao

yes–no question

Interrogative sentence marked grammatically in English by inverted word order or interrogative **intonation** and which requires *yes* or *no* as an answer: *Is Jacob coming?*

References
⇒ **interrogative**

Yiddish

Variant of **German** which arose during the Middle Ages as a trade language of Jews in important centers of commerce (countries along the Rhine and Danube). Today the East European branch of Yiddish (language of the Ashkenazic Jews) has approx. 5 million speakers as either a native or a second language in Israel, Poland, Lithuania, the United States, Latin America, Argentina, Russia, and other countries. Yiddish, based on German from the late Middle Ages, is mixed with influences from **Hebrew**, **Aramaic**, **Slavic**, and the **Romance languages**. Due to migrations in the late Middle Ages, two branches of Yiddish developed: West Yiddish (extinct) and East Yiddish, differing primarily in their lexicons and sound systems. The unity of Yiddish was preserved until the nineteenth century by the use of the Hebrew alphabet, which is written from right to left. Because it did not undergo the changes of standard German, Yiddish represents a conservative phonological stage, which in many ways is identical to the German of the Middle Ages. Yiddish influence on English can be seen primarily in loan-words: *meshuggene*, *shlock*, etc.

References
Fishman, J.A. 1965. *Yiddish in America: sociolinguistic description and analysis*. Bloomington, IN. (= *IJAL* 31:2, pub. 36.)
—— 1991. *Yiddish: turning to life*. Amsterdam and Philadelphia, PA.
Herzog, M. 1965. *The Yiddish language in northern Poland: its geography and history*. Bloomington, IN. (= *IJAL* 31:2, pub. 37.)
Katz, D. 1987. *Grammar of the Yiddish language*. London.
—— (ed) 1988. *Dialects of the Yiddish language: papers from the second annual Oxford Winter symposium in Yiddish language and literature*. Oxford.
Weber, M.H. 1987. Yiddish. *Cahiers de linguistique sociale* 10.6–129.
Weinreich, U. 1960. *College Yiddish: an introduction to the Yiddish language and to Jewish life and culture*, 3rd rev. edn. New York.
—— 1980. *History of the Yiddish language*. Chicago, IL.

Dictionaries
Harduf, D.M. 1985. *English–Yiddish, Yiddish–English dictionary*. Willowdale.
Weinreich, U. 1968. *Modern English–Yiddish, Yiddish–English dictionary*. New York.

Yokuts ⇒ Penutian

Yoruba

Largest **Kwa** language (about 19 million speakers, southwest Nigeria).
Characteristics: **tonal language** (three tones), nasal vowels, **vowel harmony**. Morphology: only derivation, no inflection. Word order: SVO. Logophoric pronouns (⇒ **logophoricity**), **serial verb construction**.

References
Bamgboṣe, A. 1966. *A grammar of Yoruba*. Cambridge.
Fagborun, J.G. 1994. *The Yoruba koiné: its history and linguistic innovations*. Munich.
Rowlands, E.C. 1969. *Teach yourself Yoruba*. London.

Bibliography
Adewole, L.O. 1987. *The Yoruba language: published works and doctoral dissertations 1843–1986*. Hamburg.

Yucatec ⇒ Mayan languages

Yue ⇒ Chinese

Yuit ⇒ Eskimo-Aleut

Yukagir ⇒ Paleo-Siberian, Uralic

Yuki ⇒ Gulf languages

Yukic-Gulf ⇒ Gulf languages

Yuman ⇒ Hokan

Yuorok ⇒ Algonquian

Yupik ⇒ Eskimo-Aleut

Z

Zapotec ⇒ Oto-Mangue

Zenaga ⇒ Berber

zero morpheme

1 Morphologically non-overt grammatical determiner that is posited in the form of zero (Ø) for the purpose of maintaining regularity in inflectional paradigms for forms otherwise marked by **affixes**, for example for the unmarked plural forms in *sheep*, *fish* vs *cats*, *fences* or as a marker of the tense distinction in the verbs *cut*, *hit* vs *sang* / (*has*) *sung*, *jumped* / (*has*) *jumped*. (⇒ *also* **morphology**)

2 In the **word formation** theory of Marchand (1960), postulated derivational suffix to account for the opposition of formations like *legal+ize* 'to make legal' : *clean+Ø* 'to make clean' and *atom+ize* 'to turn into atoms' : *cash+Ø* 'to turn into cash.' Since the semantic difference between *clean* (adjective), *cash* (noun) on the one hand and (*to*) *clean* and (*to*) *cash* (verbs) on the other hand is otherwise marked in the language systematically by a word **formative** like *-ize*, *-ify*, Marchand feels justified in assuming a non-overt correlate with the same content. The relevance of the zero morpheme for word formation is disputed by Lieber (1981).

References
Lieber, R. 1981. Morphological conversion within a restrictive theory of the lexicon. In M. Moortgat, H. van der Hulst, and T. Hoekstra (eds), *The scope of lexical rules*. Dordrecht. 161–200.
Marchand, H. 1960. *The categories and types of present–day English word-formation*. Munich. (2nd edn 1969.)
⇒ **morphology**, **word formation**

zeugma [Grk *zeûgma* 'bond']

A **figure of speech** and type of **abbreviation**. Originally, it was a general term of grammatical **ellipsis** (e.g. *He drank beer, she wine*), but is now used more specifically for certain co-ordinated structures whose common predicate connects two semantically or syntactically unequal parts of the sentence: (a) syntactically incongruous zeugma: *He's drinking beer, we wine*; (b) semantically incongruous zeugma: *He travelled with his wife and his umbrella*. **Apokoinou** is a special type of zeugma.

References
⇒ **figure of speech**

Zipf's law (*also* law of least effort)

Regular correlation established through empirical observation and statistical procedures by G.K. Zipf between the number of occurrences of words in specific texts and specific speakers or authors and their ranking in a list of their overall frequency. The logarithms of both of these variables are in a constant relation to each other, i.e. the product of the rank and frequency is constant. This formula is independent of text type, age of the text and language, and is thus universal in nature, which Zipf attributes, among other things, to the economical principle of least effort, which underlies all human behavior. In addition, a correlation exists between the length of a word and its frequency. Just as in morse code, the most frequently occurring letter, 'e,' is given the shortest symbol, a single dot, so one-syllable words occur most often in a language.

References
Billmeier, G. 1969. *Worthäufigkeitsverteilungen vom Zipfschen Typ, überprüft an deutschem Textmaterial*. Bonn.
Birkhan, H. 1979. *Das Zipf'sche Gesetz, das schwache Präteritum und die germanische Lautverschiebung*. Vienna.
Collinge, N.E. 1985. *The laws of Indo-European*. Amsterdam and Philadelphia, PA. 256–8.
Mandelbrot, B. 1954. Structure formelle des textes et communication. *Word* 10.1–27.
Zipf, G.K. 1935. *The psycho-biology of language*, 2nd edn. Boston, MA.

zoosemiotics [Grk *zõon* 'living being, animal']

Term introduced by Sebeok (1963) that delineates a direction of study treating the investigation of specific kinds of animal communication systems (ants, bees, chimpanzees) (⇒ **animal communication**) as well as the characteristics of communication in biological systems as a whole. Zoosemiotics, as the 'study of signs in animal language,' can yield important information about the origin and development of human language (⇒ **anthroposemiotics**).

References
Evans, W.F. 1968. *Communication in the animal world*. New York.

Frings, H. and M. Frings. 1964. *Animal communication*. New York.

Krampen, M. 1981. Phytosemiotics. *Semiotica* 36.187–209.

Thorpe, W.H. 1961. *Bird-song*. Cambridge.

Sebeok, T.A. (ed.) 1968. *Animal communication: techniques of study and results of research*. Bloomington, IN.

—— 1972. *Perspectives in zoosemiotics*. The Hague.

—— 1977. Zoosemiotic components of human communication. In T.A. Sebeok (ed.), *How animals communicate*. Bloomington, IN. 1055–77.

Smith, W.J. 1974. Zoosemiotics: ethology and the theory of signs. In T.A. Sebeok (ed.), *Current trends in linguistics*. The Hague. Vol. 12, 561–628.

⇒ **animal communication**

Zoque ⇒ **Mixe-Zoque**

Zulu ⇒ **Bantu**

Zuni ⇒ **Penutian**